THE DEVELOPER'S HANDBOOK TO DB2 FOR COMMON SERVERS

Other McGraw-Hill Books of Interest

ALLEN, BAMBARA, BAMBARA • *Informix: Client/Server Application Development*

ANDERSON • *Client/Server Database Design with SYBASE*

BIGUS • *Data Mining with Neural Networks: Solving Business Problems from Application Development to Decision Support*

FORTIER • *Database Systems Handbook*

INMON • *Data Stores, Data Warehousing, and the Zachman Framework*

JONES • *Developing Client/Server Applications with Microsoft Access*

LEACH • *Software Reuse: Methods, Models, and Costs*

MATTISON • *Data Warehousing: Strategies, Technologies, and Techniques*

NORTH • *The Complete Guide to Java Database Programming*

SHETH AND KLAS • *Multimedia Metadata Management Handbook*

To order or receive additional information on these or any other McGraw-Hill titles, please call 1-800-822-8158 in the United States. In other countries, contact your local McGraw-Hill representative.

THE DEVELOPER'S HANDBOOK TO DB2 FOR COMMON SERVERS

Roger E. Sanders

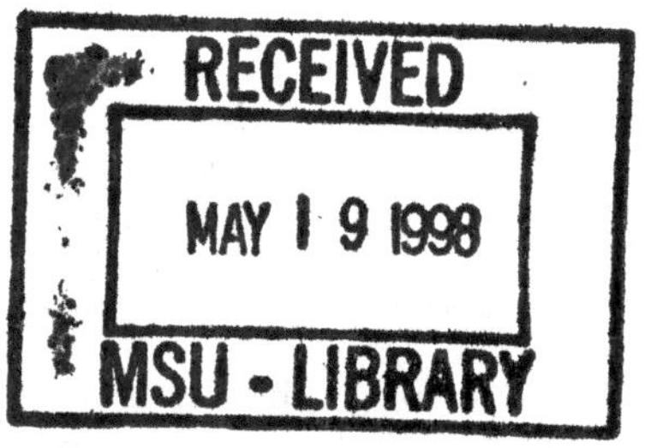

McGraw-Hill
New York San Francisco Washington, D.C. Auckland Bogotá
Caracas Lisbon London Madrid Mexico City Milan
Montreal New Delhi San Juan Singapore
Sydney Tokyo Toronto

Library of Congress Cataloging-in-Publication Data

Sanders, Roger E.
The developer's handbook to DB2 for common servers / Roger E. Sanders.
p. cm.
Includes index.
ISBN 0-07-057725-0
1. IBM Database 2. 2. Database management. 3. SQL (Computer program language) 4. Client/server computing. 5. Computer software—Development. I. Title.
QA76.9.D3S2537 1997
005.75'65—dc21 97-13125
CIP

McGraw-Hill

A Division of The **McGraw-Hill** *Companies*

1 2 3 4 5 6 7 8 9 0 DOC/DOC 9 0 2 1 0 9 8 7

ISBN 0-07-057725-0

The sponsoring editor for this book was John Wyzalek, the editing supervisor was Kellie Hagan, and the production supervisor was Suzanne W.B. Rapcavage. It was set in Times Roman by Jana Fisher through the services of Barry E. Brown (Broker—Editing, Design and Production).

Printed and bound by R.R. Donnelley & Sons Company.

McGraw-Hill books are available at special quantity discounts to use as premiums and sales promotions, or for use in corporate training programs. For more information, please write to the Director of Special Sales, McGraw-Hill, 11 West 19th Street, New York, NY 10011. Or contact your local bookstore.

Information contained in this work has been obtained by The McGraw-Hill Companies, Inc. ("McGraw-Hill") from sources believed to be reliable. However, neither McGraw-Hill nor its authors guarantees the accuracy or completeness of any information published herein and neither McGraw-Hill nor its authors shall be responsible for any errors, omissions, or damages arising out of use of this information. This work is published with the understanding that McGraw-Hill and its authors are supplying information but are not attempting to render engineering or other professional services. If such services are required, the assistance of an appropriate professional should be sought.

HB1B

To my loving wife and best friend, Beth, my daughter, Kristen, and my son, Tyler. Their support and encouragement were invaluable.

CONTENTS

PART 1

BASIC DATABASE CONCEPTS

PART 2

APPLICATION DEVELOPMENT FUNDAMENTALS

FOREWORD

The world of DB2 sure has expanded in these past few years. As few as three years ago there was only one DBMS, known as DB2, and it ran on a mainframe. But time marches on and computing needs shift and expand. Today, IBM manufactures and sells versions of DB2 that run not only on MVS-based mainframes, but also on OS/2, AIX, Windows NT, various "flavors" of UNIX, VSE, VM, and AS/400.

Although my primary background is with DB2 for MVS, I have had the opportunity to work with many DBMS products over the years. From Xbase to XDB to Microsoft Access to Oracle, Sybase, and DB2 for OS/2, the diversity within products called *database management systems* never ceases to amaze me. Although a sound knowledge of relational theory is unarguably essential, one quickly learns that it is never enough "to keep those production databases humming." Now, an in-depth knowledge of each specific DBMS product is required (in addition to relational theory) to create optimal application databases and systems.

This comprehensive book by Roger Sanders covers the version of DB2 that IBM calls DB2 for Common Servers, and it provides an in-depth look "under the hood" of that DB2. The complex client/server environment in which DB2 runs requires users to have an in-depth knowledge of all aspects of database development and administration. Roger has done an impeccable job of providing, in a single resource, just about everything you would want to know about DB2 for OS/2 and DB2 for AIX. Whether your primary job is that of DBA or application developer or system performance expert, this book will provide something of interest.

The speed at which today's technology is changing is phenomenal. Many of the features covered in this book were merely theory a few years ago. From compound queries to extensible data types to triggers and stored procedures to superexclusive locks to multiple optimization levels (via the Starburst optimizer), DB2 is pushing the technological envelope for what is considered a relational DBMS. No doubt this trend will continue. In the coming years, expect DB2 to adopt features and techniques of object-oriented technology, multidimensional databases, temporal and spatial processing, and fuzzy logic. How can we expect to keep pace with this change unless we attempt to understand the nuances of today's technology? Thankfully, this book is here to help us.

Truly, the only constant is change. Anyone who doubts this need only examine the independent software market. Ten years ago, the number-one vendor was Cullinet, a provider of network DBMS products. In 1996, the company no longer exists. I think it is a fair assumption that ten years from now a similar scenario will exist. As we progress toward our uncertain but undoubtedly exciting future, the best we can do to keep up with technology is invest in educational and enlightening books such as this . . . and continue learning.

Craig S. Mullins
PLATINUM Technology, Inc.
Oakbrook Terrace, IL
70410.237@compuserve.com

ACKNOWLEDGMENTS

A project of this magnitude requires both a great deal of time and the support of many different people. I would like to express my gratitude to the following people for their contributions:

Bob Koteen, IBM DB2 Developer Assistance Program Bob was my key contact at IBM; without his wonderful support, this book would never have been possible. Among other things, Bob made sure I received beta and general availability (GA) copies of the DB2 product and its documentation as soon as they were available. He also helped me track down the people and resources I needed to produce this book.

Bryan Blackwell Bryan helped me set up a work area on a RISC 6000 workstation that I could telnet to in order to test all my example programs with DB2 for AIX. He also installed new releases of DB2 for AIX as they became available, and provided me with the information I needed to compile and test my sample programs on the RISC 6000 platform.

Frank Pellow, Senior Development Analyst (DB2 for OS/2 and DB2 for AIX development) Frank technically reviewed a large portion of the manuscript, and pointed out where things were wrong or where improvements could be made.

Barbara Isa, IBM Author Program Coordinator Barbara worked with me and IBM's legal department to obtain the appropriate permissions to use selected tables and appendices from IBM Database 2 documentation in this book.

Debbie Landers Debbie helped me obtain access to a RISC 6000 workstation, and she provided me with the development tools I needed to create and test the example programs on both the OS/2 Warp and the AIX 4.0 operating systems.

Dianne Littwin Dianne taught me a little bit about the book publishing business and provided support while I searched for the right publisher.

Julia Fisher Julia helped me prepare the book proposal, reviewed and corrected my grammar in the first two sections of the manuscript, and provided encouragement throughout the project.

Richard Smith Richard helped me decide on the best format to use for each section, performed a technical review for various parts of the manuscript, and provided encouragement throughout this project.

Lewis Church Lewis reviewed and corrected many of my C++ example programs.

Thomas Cox Thomas helped me understand ODBC, reviewed and corrected many of my C++ call-level interface example programs, and helped me decide on the best format to use to present the CLI material. Best of luck to you, Thomas, as you begin your new job with ODBC development at Microsoft Corporation.

Dave Hock, President of HockWare Dave provided me with evaluation copies of VisPro/C and VisPro/Reports for OS/2, which I used to develop many of the C language embedded SQL examples. Dave also reviewed parts of the manuscript for technical accuracy.

I would also like to thank Brad Schepp, Stacey Spurlock, and the rest of the staff at McGraw-Hill for their help and particularly their patience as I discovered that a book of this magnitude takes a lot longer to write than I had anticipated.

Most of all, I would like to thank my wife, Beth, for all of her help in preparing this book, for her gentle prodding and encouragement, and for overlooking all the things that did not get done while I was writing this book.

INTRODUCTION

Database 2 (DB2) for Common Servers, version 2.1, has been available to relational database application programmers developing software for the OS/2 Warp and AIX 4.0 operating systems since August 1995. Recently, however, this product was made available to relational database application programmers developing software for Windows NT, HP-UX, SINIX, and the Solaris operating environment. DB2 for Common Servers has the following advantages over other relational databases:

- It provides a natural transition from Database 2 (DB2) for MVS, AS/400, VM, and VSE for users in the process of migrating to PC and workstation environments.
- It provides a direct link to legacy data residing on IBM mainframes through an add-on package called Distributed Database Connectivity Services (DDCS).
- It is a full 32-bit database, so it operates more efficiently than most other 16-bit databases.

DB2 for Common Servers is not a new product; it has existed in some form or another on OS/2 since 1989. The earliest version was called Database Manager, and it was bundled with OS/2 in a product called OS/2 Extended Edition. This was IBM's first attempt to put its popular Database 2 product (which had been available for MVS operating systems on IBM mainframes since 1983) on a PC. Through the years, IBM's PC version of DB2 has matured to the point where it is now one of the most powerful database products available for a wide variety of platforms. For example, DB2 was the backbone of the information delivery system that IBM provided for the 1996 Summer Olympics in Atlanta, which was used to store and process over 60 gigabytes of data!

WHY I WROTE THIS BOOK

Although DB2 for Common Servers has been available since 1989, very few books have been written about it. And as the DB2 product evolved, the books that were written were not revised to reflect the differences in the product, and eventually they went out of print. By 1993, when the DB2/2 GA product was released (with DB2/6000 following shortly after), no book existed that focused on DB2 application development. (Robert Orfali and Dan Harkey's *Client/Server Programming with OS/2 2.1* contained four chapters covering the Extended Services 1.0 database manager and later DB2/2, but since this book addressed client/server programming rather than DB2 application programming, its information about DB2 was limited.) This meant that IBM's product manuals and online help were the only resources available to application developers writing applications for DB2/2.

In the summer of 1992, while developing a specialized DB2 (then it was called the Extended Services 1.0 Database Manager) application that used many of DB2's application programming interface (API) calls, I discovered how lacking some of the IBM manuals for this product really were. Since there were no other reference books available, I had to spend a considerable amount of trial and error programming in order to complete my DB2 application. While talking to other DB2 application developers who were having similar experiences because of inadequate documentation, I saw the need for a good DB2 programming reference guide.

WHO IS THIS BOOK FOR?

This book is for anyone who is interested in creating DB2 for Common Server database applications. It is written primarily for database application programmers and analysts who are familiar with SQL and are designing and/or coding software applications that access one or more DB2 databases. Experienced C/C++ programmers with little experience developing DB2 database applications will benefit most from the material covered in this book. Experienced DB2 database application developers who are familiar with the version 1.0 DB2/2 product will also benefit from this book because it describes, in detail, the new features available only in the version 2.1 product. In either case, this book is meant to be a single resource that provides you with almost everything you need to know in order to design and develop DB2 database applications.

To get the most out of this book, you should have a working knowledge of the C or the C++ programming language. An understanding of relational database concepts and structured query language (SQL) will also be helpful, although not crucial, since more complex topics such as subqueries and recursive queries are not addressed even though a large portion of this book is devoted to SQL.

HOW THIS BOOK IS ORGANIZED

This book is divided into five major parts. Part 1 discusses basic relational database concepts. Before you can successfully develop a DB2 database application, you must first have a good understanding of DB2's underlying database architecture and data consistency mechanisms. Two chapters in this section are designed to provide you with that understanding:

Chapter 1 explains relational database concepts and describes the components of a DB2 for Common Servers database. This chapter also describes the internal file structures used by DB2 for data and database object storage. Chapter 2 discusses the mechanisms that DB2 provides for maintaining data integrity. These mechanisms include transactions, isolation levels, row- and table-level locking, and transaction logging. Together, these two chapters lay the groundwork for the rest of this book.

Part 2 discusses database application development fundamentals. Once you have a good understanding of DB2's underlying database architecture and consistency mechanisms, you also need to understand general database application development as it applies to DB2. The five chapters in this section describe the different types of applications that can be developed for DB2, and provide you with an understanding of the methods used to develop each type:

Chapter 3 discusses the application development process as it applies to DB2. This chapter describes basic DB2 application design and identifies the main elements of a DB2 application. It also explains how the database application development and testing environment are established before the application development process begins.

Chapter 4 explains how embedded structured query language (SQL) applications are written, and identifies the main components of an embedded SQL application. It also describes the steps you must take to convert embedded SQL application source-code files into executable programs.

Chapter 5 explains how to write call-level interface (CLI) applications, and identifies the main components of a CLI application. It also describes the steps you must take to convert CLI application source-code files into executable programs.

Chapter 6 explains how to write application programming interface (API) programs. The chapter identifies the types of available APIs and describes how and when they should be used in an application. It also describes the steps in converting API application source-code files into executable programs.

Chapter 7 discusses various optimization techniques you can use to improve embedded SQL, CLI, and API application performance.

Part 3 describes each structured query language (SQL) statement recognized by DB2 as it would be used in an embedded SQL application. This section is designed to be a detailed embedded SQL reference. The five chapters in this section group SQL statements according to their functionality:

Chapter 8 describes the embedded SQL statements for constructing an embedded SQL application. You must include one or more of these statements in every embedded SQL application you develop. The chapter explains, in detail, each SQL statement and provides a C (and often a C++) sample program that illustrates how to code the statement in an application program.

Chapter 9 describes the embedded SQL statements for connecting to and disconnecting from a DB2 database, as well as the SQL statements for granting and revoking user-data access privileges. It describes, in detail, each SQL statement and provides complementary C (and often C++) sample programs that illustrate how to code the statement in an application program.

Chapter 10 describes the embedded SQL statements for creating and destroying DB2 data objects (e.g., tables, table spaces, indexes, and views). It describes each SQL statement in detail and provides a C (and often a C++) sample program that illustrates how to code the statement in an application program.

Chapter 11 describes the embedded SQL statements for manipulating data stored in a DB2 database. The chapter also explains each SQL statement in detail and provides a C (and often a C++) sample program that illustrates how to code the statement in an application program.

Chapter 12 describes the embedded SQL statements for setting up event monitors, defining triggers, and invoking stored procedures. It explains each SQL statement in detail and provides C (and often a C++) sample programs that illustrate how to code the statement in an application program.

Part 4 describes each call-level interface (CLI) function provided with and recognized by DB2. CLI functions are IBM's version of ODBC. This section is designed to be a detailed CLI function reference, and the five chapters in this section group CLI functions according to their functionality:

Chapter 13 describes the CLI functions for connecting to a data source (database), as well as those for performing the initialization and cleanup required in every CLI application. The chapter explains each CLI function in detail, providing a C (and often a C++) sample program that illustrates how to code the function call in an application program.

Chapter 14 describes the CLI functions for retrieving and setting both CLI/ODBC driver control options and data source control options. It explains each CLI function in detail, providing a complementary C (and often a C++) sample program that illustrates how to code the function call in an application program.

Chapter 15 describes the CLI functions for defining, preparing, and executing dynamic SQL statements. It explains each CLI function in detail and provides a C (and often a C++) sample program that illustrates how to code the function call in an application program.

Chapter 16 describes the CLI functions for retrieving and processing the results returned by dynamic SQL statements that have been prepared and executed. It explains each CLI function in detail and provides a C (often a C++) sample program that illustrates how to code the function call in an application program.

Chapter 17 describes the CLI functions for retrieving information from a data source's system catalog (e.g., a DB2 database's system catalog table). Each of these CLI functions are explained in detail, and you're given a C (often a C++) sample program that illustrates how to code the function call in an application program.

Part 5 describes each application programming interface (API) function provided by DB2. API functions are designed to work directly with the DB2 database manager to perform environment, maintenance, and utility operations. This section is designed to be a detailed API function reference, and the eight chapters in this section group API functions according to their functionality:

Chapter 18 describes the API functions for preparing and binding embedded SQL applications to a DB2 database. It also describes the API functions for performing general tasks, such as retrieving messages for SQL return codes and SQL states, that can be used in almost any application. Each API function in this chapter is explained in detail and accompanied by a C sample program that illustrates how to code the function call in an application program.

Chapter 19 describes the API functions for starting, stopping, and controlling the DB2 database manager server background processes. This chapter also describes the API functions for creating, deleting, and controlling DB2 databases. Each API function is explained in detail and accompanied by a C sample program that illustrates how to code the function call in an application program.

Chapter 20 describes the API functions for configuring the DB2 database manager and a DB2 database. Each API function is explained in detail and accompanied by a C sample program that illustrates how to code the function call in an application program.

Chapter 21 describes the API functions for adding entries to, removing entries from, and displaying the contents of the special directories that DB2 uses to keep track of databases, workstation nodes, and database connectivity services (DCS) databases that can be accessed from a single workstation. This chapter also describes the API functions for registering and deregistering a DB2 server workstation with a Novell NetWare server. Each API function in this chapter is explained in detail and accompanied by a C sample program that illustrates how to code the function call in an application program.

Chapter 22 describes the API functions for obtaining information about table spaces and tablespace containers that have been created for a database. This chapter also describes the API functions for reorganizing data in and updating statistics for a database table. Each API function is explained in detail and accompanied by a C sample program that illustrates how to code the function call in an application program.

Chapter 23 describes the API functions for migrating, backing up, and restoring DB2 databases. It also describes the API functions used to manipulate recovery history files and apply roll-forward recovery to DB2 databases after they are restored. Each API function in this chapter is explained in detail and accompanied by a C sample program that illustrates how to code the function call in an application program.

Chapter 24 describes the API functions for copying data between DB2 databases and external data files. Each API function is explained in detail and accompanied by a C sample program that illustrates how to code the function call in an application program.

Chapter 25 describes the API functions for obtaining information about database activity at a specific point in time. It also describes the API functions for processing in-doubt transactions that might not exist after an application using two-phase commits fails. Each API function in this chapter is explained in detail and accompanied by a C sample program that illustrates how to code the function call in an application program.

A WORD ABOUT THE EXAMPLES

The example programs are an essential part of this book, and it is imperative that they are accurate. To make the use of each embedded SQL statement, CLI function, and API function clear, I have included only the required overhead and reduced error checking. I have also tailored the examples so they verify that the embedded SQL statement, CLI function, and API function being demonstrated actually executes as expected. For example, an example program might retrieve and display a record in a table before and after it is modified to verify that the SQL statement or function doing the modification worked. Also, I have tried to tailor the example programs so they work with the sample database provided with the DB2 for Common Servers product (refer to the installation documentation to see how to create this database).

When I started this book, DB2 for Common Servers version 2.1 existed only for the OS/2 Warp and AIX 4.0 operating systems. I have compiled and tested each example on OS/2 Warp, and I have compiled and tested most of the example programs on AIX 4.0. Each section overview shows the compiler scripts and compilers I used to produce executable programs from these examples on both platforms. Theoretically, the examples should compile and execute on the remaining DB2 for Common Servers platforms.

FEEDBACK AND SOURCE CODE ON THE WORLD WIDE WEB

I have tried to make sure the information and examples provided in this book are accurate, but I am not infallible. If you find a problem with some information or any of the examples, please send the correction to me so I can make the appropriate changes in future printings. Also, if you have comments about this book, I would like to hear them. The best way to communicate with me is via the World Wide Web home page I have established for this book, at http://www.ntwrks.com/~rsanders.

As mentioned earlier, all of the example programs were compiled and tested on at least one operating system. If you type them in exactly as they appear in the book, they should compile and execute successfully. Or you can obtain electronic copies of these programs directly from the World Wide Web home page described above. The examples are stored in the file DB2EXAMP.2IP. You will need to provide the password **N8433E** to PKZIP to extract the files.

LIMITS OF LIABILITY AND WARRANTY DISCLAIMER

Both the publisher and I have used our best efforts in preparing this book and the example programs it contains. These efforts include obtaining technical verification of portions of the manuscript from the DB2 development staff at IBM and developing, researching, and testing these programs on both OS/2 Warp and AIX 4.0 platforms to determine their effectiveness and accuracy. We make no warranty of any kind, expressed or implied, with regard to these programs or the documentation contained in this book. We shall not be liable in any event for incidental or consequential damages in connection with or arising out of the furnishing, performance, or use of either this documentation or these example programs.

REGISTERED TRADEMARKS

- AIX, APPN, AS/400, C Set++, Database 2, Database 2 OS/400, DataPropagator, DB2, DB2/2, DB2/400, DB2/6000, DB2 for AIX, DB2 for OS/2, Distributed Database Connection Services/2, DDCS/2, Distributed Relational Database Architecture, DRDA, Extended Services for OS/2, First Failure Support Technology/2, FFST/2, IBM, MVS, Operating System/2, OS/2, RISC System/6000, SAA, SQL/DS, VisualAge, VisualGen, VisualInfo, and VM/ESA are registered trademarks owned by International Business Machines Corporation.
- 1-2-3, Lotus, and Symphony are registered trademarks owned by Lotus Development Corporation.
- Microsoft, Windows, Windows NT, and ODBC are registered trademarks owned by Microsoft Corporation.
- IPX/SPX, NetWare, and Novell are registered trademarks owned by Novell, Inc.
- HP-UX is a registered trademark owned by Hewlett-Packard Company.
- SINIX is a registered trademark owned by Siemens Nixdorf.
- Solaris is a registered trademark owned by Sun Microsystems, Inc.
- UNIX is a registered trademark in the United States and other countries, exclusively leased through X/Open Company, Ltd.

All other products or service names mentioned in this book are trademarks of their respective owners.

Part 1

BASIC DATABASE CONCEPTS

CHAPTER 1

DB2 DATABASE ARCHITECTURE

Before you begin developing database applications, you need to understand the underlying architecture of DB2 for Common Servers, version 2.1. In the first part of this chapter, I will describe the relational database model and its data-handling operations. Then I will show you the data objects and support objects that make up a DB2 database. Finally, I will discuss the directory, subdirectory, and file-naming conventions used by DB2 for storing these data and system objects. Let's begin with a definition of *relational database management system.*

THE RELATIONAL DATABASE

DB2 for Common Servers, version 2.1, is a 32-bit relational database management systems. A *relational database management system* is a database management system designed around a set of powerful mathematical concepts known as *relational algebra*. The first relational database model was introduced in the early 1970s by Mr. E. F. Codd, at the IBM San Jose Research Center. This model is based on the following operations, identified in relational algebra:

SELECTION. This operation selects a record or records from a table based on a specified condition.

PROJECTION. This operation returns a column or columns from a table based on some condition.

JOIN. This operation allows you to paste two or more tables together. Each table must have a common column before a JOIN can work.

UNION. This operation combines two similar tables to produce a set of all records found in both tables. Each table must have compatible columns before a UNION can work. In other words, each field in the first table must match a field in the second table. Essentially, a UNION of two tables is the same as mathematically adding two tables.

DIFFERENCE. This operation tells you what records are unique to one table when two tables are compared. Again, each table must have identical columns before a DIFFERENCE can work. Essentially, a DIFFERENCE of two tables is the same as mathematically subtracting two tables.

INTERSECTION. This operation tells you what records are common to two or more tables when they are compared. This operation involves performing the UNION and DIFFERENCE operations twice.

PRODUCT. This operation combines two dissimilar tables to produce a set of all records found in both tables. Essentially, a PRODUCT of two tables is the same as mathematically multiplying two tables. A PRODUCT operation, however, can often produce unwanted side-effects, requiring you to use the PROJECTION operation to clean it up.

As you can see, data is perceived to exist in one or more two-dimensional tables in a relational database. These tables are made up of rows and columns, where each record (row) is divided into fields (columns) that contain individual pieces of information. Although the data is not actually stored this way, visualizing a collection of two-dimensional tables makes it easier to describe data needs in easy-to-understand terms.

RELATIONAL DATABASE OBJECTS

A relational database system is more than just a collection of two-dimensional tables. Additional objects exist that aid in data storage and retrieval, database structure control, and database disaster recovery. In general, objects are items about which DB2 retains information. These objects can be divided into two basic categories: data objects and support objects.

Data objects are the database objects used to store and manipulate data. Data objects also control how user data (and some system data) is organized. They include:

- Databases
- Table spaces
- Tables
- User-defined data types
- User-defined functions
- Check constraints
- Indexes
- Views
- Packages (access plans)
- Triggers
- Aliases
- Event monitors

Databases

A database object is simply a set of all DB2-related objects. When you create a DB2 database, you are establishing an administrative entity that provides an underlying structure for an eventual collection of tables, views, associated indexes, etc., as well as the table spaces in which they reside. Figure 1.1 illustrates a simple database object. The database structure also includes things such as system catalogs, transaction recovery logs, and disk storage directories. Data (or user) objects are always accessed from within the underlying structure of a database.

Table Spaces

A table space logically groups (or partitions) data objects such as tables, views, and indexes based on their data types. Up to three table spaces can be used per table; typically the first one is used for table data (by default), a second one is used for indexes, and the third one is used for large object (LOB) fields. Table spaces are designed to provide a level of indirection between user tables and the database in which they reside. There are two basic types of table spaces: database managed spaces (DMSs), which supports raw devices and files, and system managed spaces (SMSs), which supports directories. SMS table spaces are primarily used for compatibility with existing DB2/2 and

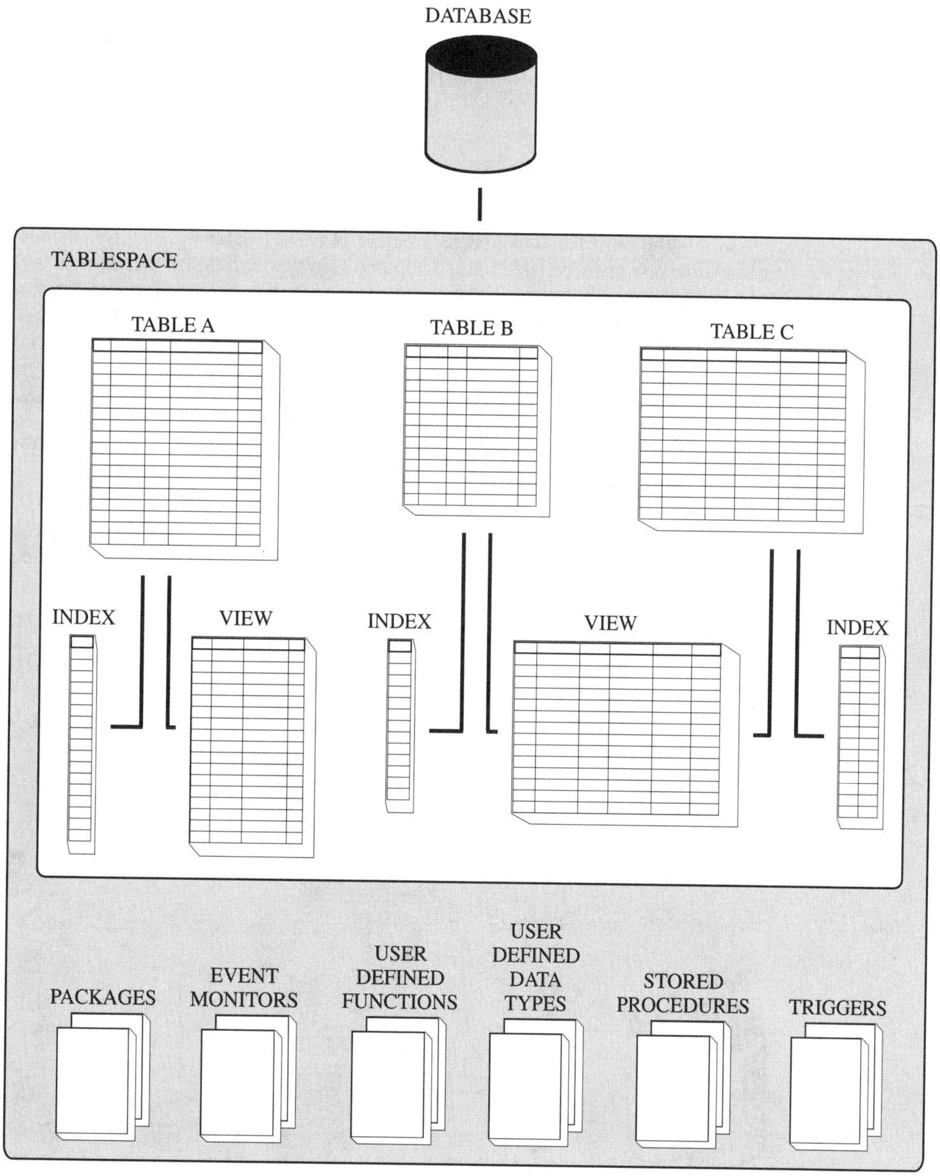

FIGURE 1.1 Database object and its related data objects.

DB2/6000 version 1.*x* databases. As mentioned earlier, table spaces can also allocate storage areas for large objects (LOBs), and control the device, file, or directory where both the LOBs and table data are to be stored. Table spaces can span multiple physical disk drives, and their size can be extended at any time (stopping and restarting the database is not necessary). Figure 1.2 illustrates how you can use table spaces to direct a database object to store its table data on one physical disk drive and the table's corresponding indexes on another physical disk drive.

Note: It is important to recognize that the table space concept implemented by DB2 for OS/2 and DB2 for AIX is very different from the table space concept used by DB2 for MVS.

Tables

The table is the most fundamental data object of a DB2 database. All user data is stored in and retrieved from one or more tables in a database. Two types of tables can exist in a DB2 database. Tables that are created by the user in order to store user data are referred to as *base tables*. Temporary tables that are created (and deleted) by DB2 from one or more base tables in order to satisfy the result of a query are known as *result tables*. Each table is an unordered collection of rows, and each table contains a fixed number of columns. The definition of the columns in the table makes up the table structure, and the rows contain the actual table data. The storage representation of a row is called a *record*, and the storage representation of a column is called a *field*. At each intersection of a row and column in a database table is a specific data item called a *value*. Figure 1.3 shows the structure of a simple database table.

Data Types. Each column in a table is assigned a DB2 data type during its creation. This ensures that only data of the correct type is stored in the table. The following data types are available in DB2:

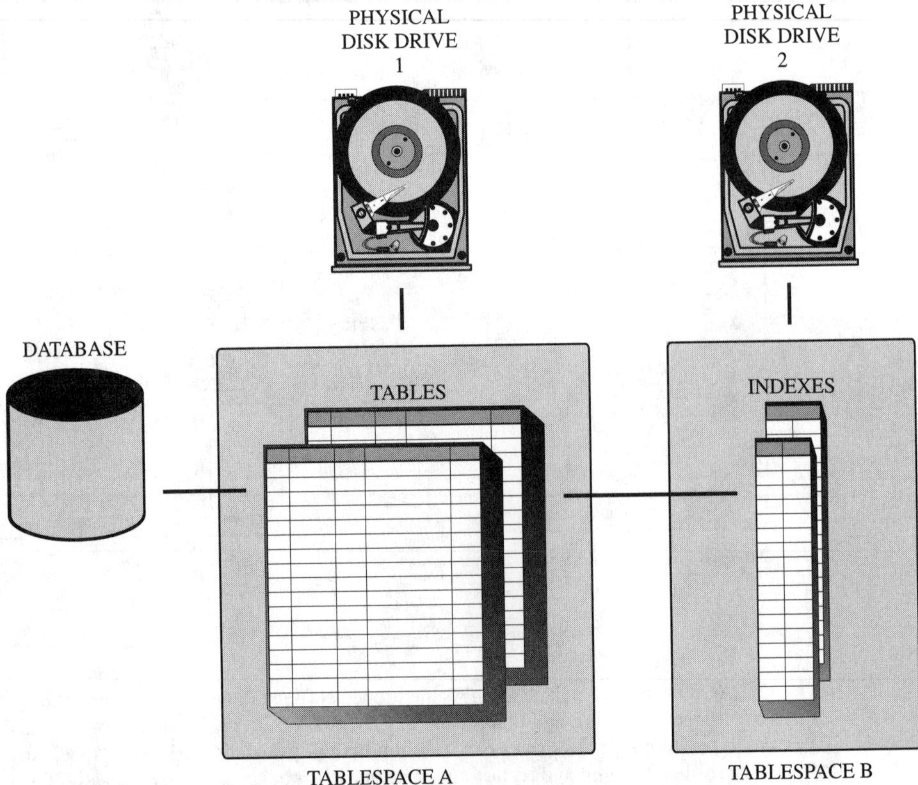

FIGURE 1.2 Using table spaces to separate the physical storage of tables and indexes.

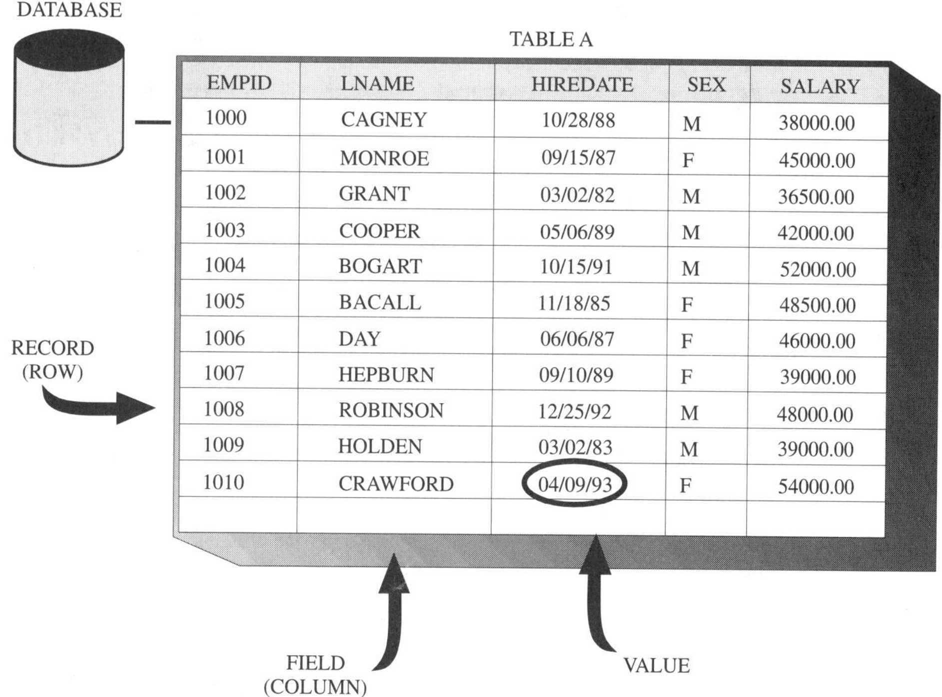

EMPID	LNAME	HIREDATE	SEX	SALARY
1000	CAGNEY	10/28/88	M	38000.00
1001	MONROE	09/15/87	F	45000.00
1002	GRANT	03/02/82	M	36500.00
1003	COOPER	05/06/89	M	42000.00
1004	BOGART	10/15/91	M	52000.00
1005	BACALL	11/18/85	F	48500.00
1006	DAY	06/06/87	F	46000.00
1007	HEPBURN	09/10/89	F	39000.00
1008	ROBINSON	12/25/92	M	48000.00
1009	HOLDEN	03/02/83	M	39000.00
1010	CRAWFORD	04/09/93	F	54000.00

FIGURE 1.3 Simple database table.

SMALLINT. A small integer is a binary integer with a precision of 15 bits. The range of a small integer is –32,768 to +32,767.

INTEGER. A large integer is a binary integer with a precision of 31 bits. The range of a large integer is –2,147,483,648 to +2,147,483,647.

DOUBLE. A double-precision floating-point number is a 64-bit approximation of a real number. The number can be zero or can range from –1.79769E+308 to –2.225E-307, and 2.225E–307 to 1.79769E+308.

DECIMAL. A decimal value is a packed decimal number with an implicit decimal point. The position of the decimal point is determined by the precision and the scale of the number. The range of a decimal variable or the numbers in a decimal column is $-n$ to $+n$, where the absolute value of n is the largest number that can be represented with the applicable precision and scale.

CHAR. A character string is a sequence of bytes. The length of the string is the number of bytes in the sequence and must be between 1 and 254.

VARCHAR. A varying-length character string is a sequence of bytes in varying lengths up to 4,000 bytes.

LONG VARCHAR. A long varying-length character string is a sequence of bytes in varying lengths up to 32,700 bytes.

GRAPHIC. A graphic string is a sequence of bytes that represents double-byte character data. The length of the string is the number of double-byte characters in the sequence and must be between 1 and 127.

VARGRAPHIC. A varying-length graphic string is a sequence of bytes in varying lengths up to 2,000 double-byte characters.

LONG VARGRAPHIC. A long varying-length graphic string is a sequence of bytes in varying lengths up to 16,350 double-byte characters.

CLOB. A character large-object string is a varying-length string measured in bytes that can be up to two gigabytes long. A CLOB can store large single-byte character strings or multibyte character-based data, such as documents written with a single character set.

DBCLOB. A double-byte character large-object string is a varying-length string of double-byte characters that can be up to 1,073,741,823 characters long. A DBCLOB can store large double-byte character-based data such as documents written with a single character set. A DBCLOB is considered to be a graphic string.

BLOB. A binary large-object string is a varying-length string measured in bytes that can be up to two gigabytes (2,147,483,647 bytes) long. A BLOB is primarily intended to hold nontraditional data, such as pictures, voice, and mixed media. BLOBs can also hold structured data for user-defined types and functions.

DATE. A date is a three-part value (year, month, and day) designating a calendar date. The range of the year part is 0001 to 9,999, the range of the month part is 1 to 12, and the range of the day part is 1 to *n* (28, 29, 30, or 31), where *n* depends on the month and whether or not the year value corresponds to a leap year.

TIME. A time is a three-part value (hour, minutes, and seconds) designating a time of day under a 24-hour clock. The range of the hour part is 0 to 24, the range of the minutes part is 0 to 59, and the range of the seconds part is also 0 to 59. If the hour part is set to 24, the minutes and seconds must be zero.

TIMESTAMP. A timestamp is a seven-part value (year, month, day, hour, minutes, seconds, and microseconds) that designates a calendar date and time of day under a 24-hour clock. The ranges for each part are the same as defined for the previous two data types; the range for the fractional specification of microseconds is 0 to 999,999.

Distinct type. A distinct type is a user-defined data type that shares its internal representation (source type) with one of the previous data types, but is considered to be a separate, incompatible type for most SQL operations. For example, a user can define an AUDIO data type for referencing external .WAV files that uses the BLOB data type for its internal source type. Distinct types do not automatically acquire the functions and operators of their source types, since these might no longer be meaningful. However, user-defined functions and operators can be created and applied to distinct types to replace this lost functionality.

For more information about DB2 data types, refer to the *IBM Database 2 SQL Reference, version 2* product manual.

Check Constraints

When you create or alter a table, you can also establish restrictions on data entry for one or more columns in the table. These restrictions, known as *check constraints*, are to ensure that none of the data entered (or changed) in a table violates predefined conditions. The conditions defined for a check constraint cannot contain any SQL queries, and they cannot refer to columns within another table. Tables can be defined with or without check constraints, and check constraints can define multiple restrictions on the data in a table. Check constraints are defined in the CREATE TABLE and ALTER TABLE SQL statements. If you define a check constraint in the ALTER TABLE SQL statement for a table that already contains data, the existing data will usually be checked against the new condition before the ALTER TABLE statement can be successfully completed. However, you can place the table in a check-pending state with the SET CONSTRAINTS SQL statement, which allows the ALTER TABLE SQL statement to execute without checking existing data. If you place a table in a check-pending state, you must execute the SET CONSTRAINTS SQL statement again in order to check the existing data and return the table to a normal state.

Indexes

An *index* is an ordered set of pointers to the rows of a base table. Each index is based on the values of data in one or more columns (refer to the definition of *key*, later in this section), and more than one index can be defined for a table. An index uses a balanced *binary tree* (a hierarchical data structure in which each element has at most one predecessor but can have many successors) to order the values of key columns in a table. When you index a table by one or more of its columns, DB2 can access data directly and more efficiently because the index is ordered by the columns to be retrieved. Also, since an index is stored separately from its associated table, it provides a way to define keys outside of the table definition. Once you create an index, the DB2 database manager automatically builds the appropriate binary tree structure and maintains it. Figure 1.4 shows a simple table and its corresponding index.

DB2 uses indexes to help you locate rows (records) in a table quickly. If you create an index of frequently used columns in a table, you will see improved performance on row access and updates. A unique index (refer to the following paragraph) helps maintain data integrity by ensuring that each row of data in a table is unique. Indexes also allow greater concurrency when more than one transaction accesses the same table. Since row retrieval is faster, locks do not last as long. However, these benefits are not without a price. Indexes increase actual disk-space requirements and cause a slight decrease in performance whenever an indexed table's data is updated (because all indexes defined for the table must also be updated).

A *key* is a column (or set of columns) in a table or index that can identify or access a particular row (or rows) of data. A key that is composed of more than one column is called a *composite key*. A column can be part of several composite keys. A key that is defined in such a way that it identifies a single row of data within a table is called a *unique key*. A unique key that is part of the definition of a table is called a *primary key*. A table can have only one primary key, and the columns of a primary key cannot contain null (missing) values. A key that references (or points to) a primary key in another table is called a *foreign key*. A foreign key establishes a referential link to a primary key, and the columns defined in each key must match. In Figure 1.4, the EMPID column is the primary key for Table A.

Views

A *view* is an alternative way of representing data that exists in one or more tables. Essentially, it is a named specification of a result table. The specification is a predefined data selection that occurs

INDEX A

KEY	ROW
1000	8
1001	2
1002	5
1003	7
1004	1
1005	6
1006	10
1007	3
1008	9
1009	11
1010	4

TABLE A

	EMPID	LNAME	HIREDATE
ROW 1 →	1004	CAGNEY	10/28/88
ROW 2 →	1001	MONROE	09/15/87
ROW 3 →	1007	GRANT	03/02/82
ROW 4 →	1010	COOPER	05/06/89
ROW 5 →	1002	BOGART	10/15/91
ROW 6 →	1005	BACALL	11/18/85
ROW 7 →	1003	DAY	06/06/87
ROW 8 →	1000	HEPBURN	09/10/89
ROW 9 →	1008	ROBINSON	12/25/92
ROW 10 →	1006	HOLDEN	03/02/83
ROW 11 →	1009	CRAWFORD	03/02/83

FIGURE 1.4 Simple database table and its corresponding index. The EMPID column is the primary key.

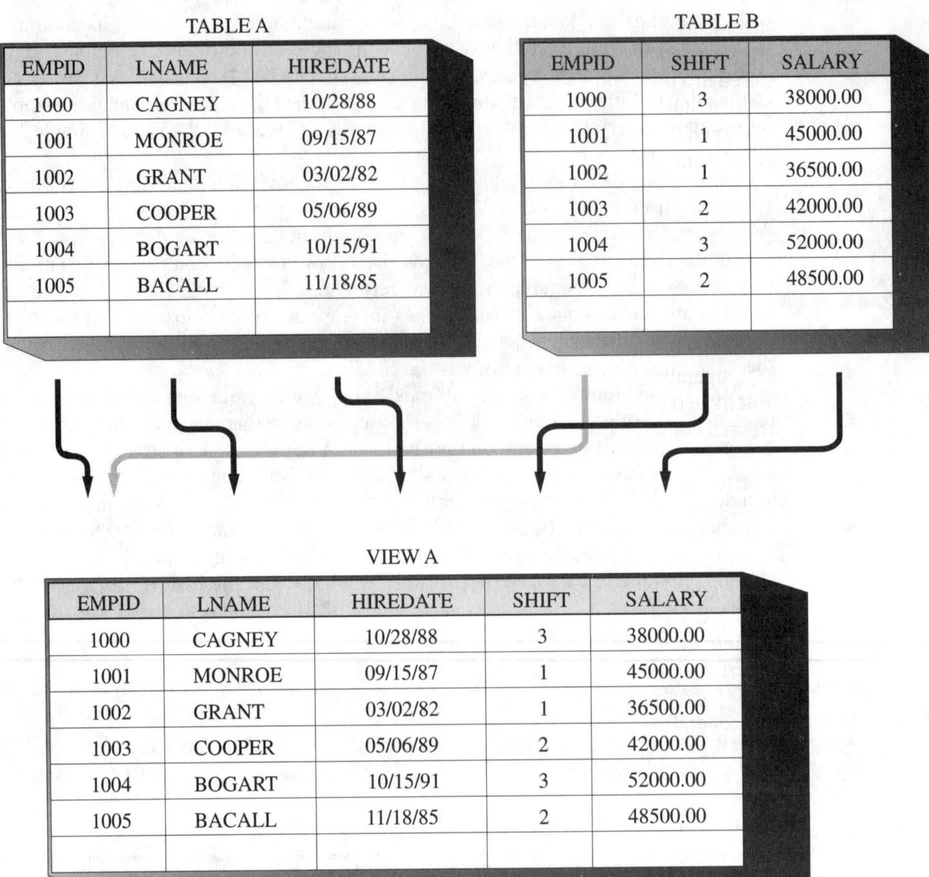

TABLE A

EMPID	LNAME	HIREDATE
1000	CAGNEY	10/28/88
1001	MONROE	09/15/87
1002	GRANT	03/02/82
1003	COOPER	05/06/89
1004	BOGART	10/15/91
1005	BACALL	11/18/85

TABLE B

EMPID	SHIFT	SALARY
1000	3	38000.00
1001	1	45000.00
1002	1	36500.00
1003	2	42000.00
1004	3	52000.00
1005	2	48500.00

VIEW A

EMPID	LNAME	HIREDATE	SHIFT	SALARY
1000	CAGNEY	10/28/88	3	38000.00
1001	MONROE	09/15/87	1	45000.00
1002	GRANT	03/02/82	1	36500.00
1003	COOPER	05/06/89	2	42000.00
1004	BOGART	10/15/91	3	52000.00
1005	BACALL	11/18/85	2	48500.00

FIGURE 1.5 View created from two separate tables. Since the EMPID column is common in both tables, it joins the tables to create a single view.

whenever the view is referenced in an SQL statement. For this reason, you can picture a view as having columns and rows, just like a base table. In fact, a view can be used just like a base table in most cases. Although a view looks like a base table, it does not exist as a table in physical storage, so it does not contain data. Instead, a view refers to data stored in other base tables (although a view might refer to another view, the reference is ultimately to data stored in one or more base tables). Figure 1.5 illustrates the relationship between base tables and views.

A view can include any number of columns from one or more base tables. It can also include any number of columns from other views, so a view can be a combination of columns from both views and tables. When the column of a view comes from a column of a base table, that column inherits any constraints that apply to the column of the base table. For example, if a view includes a column that is a unique key for its base table, operations using that view are subject to the same constraint as operations using the base table.

Packages (Access Plans)

A *package* (or *access plan*) is an object that contains control structures used to execute SQL statements. If an application program intends to access a database, it must embed the appropriate SQL statements in the program source code. When the program source code is converted to an executable object, (static SQL) or executed (dynamic SQL) the strategy for each embedded SQL statement is stored in a package. The control structures (called *sections*) are the bound or operational form of the embedded SQL statements, and they include information such as what indexes to use and how to use them.

When developing DB2 for Common Servers database applications, you should hide package creation from users whenever possible. An application can create a package for itself by binding to a database. Packages and binding are discussed in more detail in Chapter 4, WRITING EMBEDDED SQL APPLICATIONS.

Triggers

A *trigger* is a set of actions that are executed (or triggered) by an INSERT, UPDATE, or DELETE SQL operation on a specified table. Whenever the appropriate SQL operation is executed, the trigger is activated and the set of actions begins execution. You can use triggers along with foreign keys (referential constraints) and check constraints to enforce data integrity rules. You can also use triggers to apply updates to other tables in the database, to automatically generate and/or transform values for inserted or updated rows, and to invoke user-defined functions.

When creating a trigger, you must first define and then later use the following criteria to determine if the trigger should be activated:

Subject table. The table for which the trigger is defined.

Trigger event. A specific SQL operation that updates the subject table. The operation could be INSERT, UPDATE, or DELETE.

Activation time. Indicates whether the trigger should be activated before or after the trigger event is performed on the subject table.

Set of affected rows. The rows of the subject table on which the INSERT, UPDATE, or DELETE SQL operation is performed.

Trigger granularity. Defines whether the actions of the trigger will be performed once for the SQL operation or once for each of the rows in the set of affected rows.

Triggered action. An optional search condition and the set of SQL statements that are executed whenever the trigger is activated. The triggered action is executed only if the search condition evaluates to true.

At times, triggered actions might need to refer to the original values in the set of affected rows. This reference can be made with transition variables and/or transition tables. Transition variables are temporary storage variables that use the names of the columns in the subject table, qualified by a specified name that identifies whether the reference is to the old value (prior to the SQL operation) or the new value (after the SQL operation). Transition tables also use the names of the columns of the subject table, but they have a specified name that allows the complete set of affected rows to be treated as a single table. As with transition variables, transition tables can be defined for both the old values and the new values.

You can specify multiple triggers for a single table. The order in which the triggers are activated is based on the order in which they were created, so the most recently created trigger is the last trigger activated. Activating one trigger that executes SQL statements might cause other triggers to be activated (or even the the same trigger to be reactivated). This event is referred to as *trigger cascading*. When trigger cascading occurs, referential integrity delete rules can be activated, so a single SQL operation can significantly change a database. Whenever you create a trigger, therefore, make sure to thoroughly examine the effects it operation will have on all other triggers and on referential integrity.

Aliases

An *alias* is an alternate name for a table or view. Aliases can be referenced in the same way the original table or view is referenced. An alias can also be an alternate name for another alias. This process of aliases referring to each other is known as *alias chaining*. Since aliases are publicly referenced names, you require no special authority or privilege to use them (unlike tables and views).

Event Monitors

An *event monitor* observes each event that occurs to another specified object and records all selected events to either a named pipe or an external file. Essentially, event monitors are "tracking" devices that inform other applications (either via named pipes or files) whenever specified event conditions occur. Event monitors allow you to observe the events taking place in a database when database applications run. Once defined, event monitors can automatically be started each time a database is opened.

Schemas

All data objects are organized (by the database administrator) into schemas, which provide a logical classification of the objects in the database. Object names consist of two parts. The first (leftmost) part is called the *qualifier* or *schema*, and the second (rightmost) part is called the *simple* (or *unqualified*) *name*. Syntactically, these two parts are concatenated as a single string of characters separated by a period. When an object such as a table space, table, index, view, alias, user-defined data type, user-defined function, package, event monitor, or trigger is created, it is assigned to an appropriate schema through its name. Figure 1.6 illustrates how a table is assigned to a particular schema during the table creation process.

This completes the discussion of data objects; on to support objects. Support objects are database objects that contain descriptions of all objects in the database, provide transaction and failure support, and control system resource usage. Support objects include:

- System catalog views
- Recovery log file
- DB2 database manager configuration file
- Database configuration files

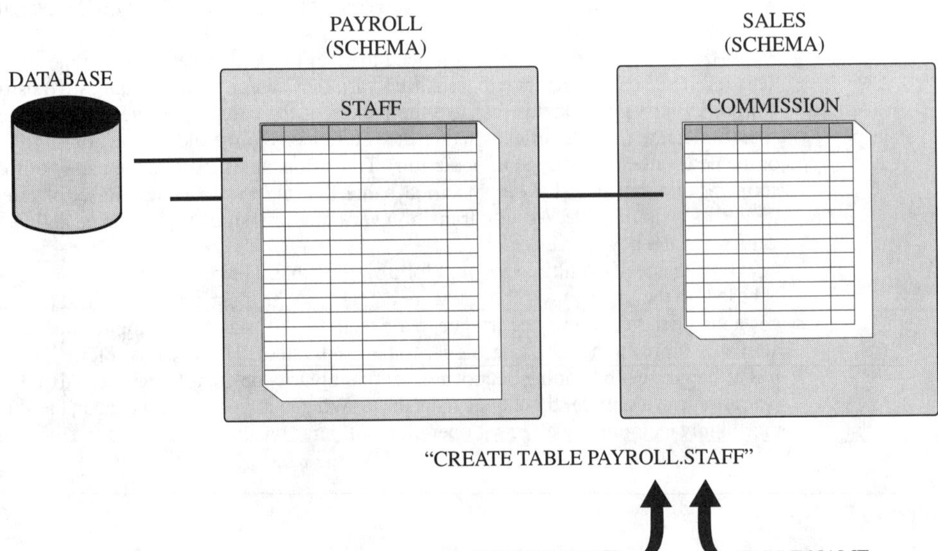

FIGURE 1.6 Implementing schemas with the CREATE SQL statement.

System Catalog Views

DB2 creates and maintains a set of views and base tables for each created database. These views and base tables are collectively known as the *system catalog*. The system catalog tables contain accurate descriptions of all objects in the database at all times. DB2 automatically updates the system catalog tables in response to SQL data definition statements, environment routines, and certain utility routines. The catalog views are like any other database views, with the exception that they cannot be explicitly created, updated (with the exception of some specific updateable views), or dropped. You can retrieve data in the catalog views the same way you retrieve data from any other view in the database. For a complete listing of the DB2 catalog views, refer to the *IBM Database 2 SQL Reference* product manual.

Recovery Log File

The database recovery log file keeps a running record of all changes made to tables in a database, and it serves two important purposes. First, the recovery log file provides necessary support for transaction processing. Since an independent record of all database changes is written to the recovery log, the sequence of changes making up a transaction can be removed from the database if the transaction is rolled back. Second, the recovery log file ensures that a system power outage or application error will not leave the database in an inconsistent state. In the event of a failure, the changes already made that have not been made permanent (committed) are rolled back and all committed transactions, which might not have been physically written to disk, are redone. Database recovery logging is always active and cannot be turned off. These actions ensure the integrity of the database.

You can also keep additional recovery log files to provide forward recovery in the event of disk (media) failure. The roll-forward database recovery utility uses these additional database recovery logs, called *archived logs*, to allow a database to be rebuilt to a specified point in time. In addition to using the information in the active database recovery log to rebuild a database, archived logs are used to reapply previous changes. In order for roll-forward database recovery to work correctly, you are required to have both a previous backup version of the database and a recovery log containing changes made to the database since that backup was made. The following is a list of the types of database recovery logs that pertain to roll-forward recovery:

Active log files. Active log files contain information for transactions whose changes have not yet been written to the database files. Active log files contain information necessary to roll back any active transaction not committed during normal processing. They also contain transactions that are committed but not yet physically written from memory (buffer pool) to disk (database files).

Online archived log files. There is an activity that is parallel with logging that automatically dumps the active transaction log file to an archive log file whenever transaction activity ceases, the active log file is closed, or the active log file gets full. An archived log is said to be online when it is stored in the database log path directory.

Offline archived log files. Archived log files can be stored in locations other than the database log path directory. An archived log file is said to be offline when it is not stored in the database log path directory.

> Note: If an online archived log file does not contain any active transactions, it will be overwritten the next time an archive log file is generated. On the other hand, if an archived log file contains active transactions, it will not be overwritten by other active transaction log dumps until all active transactions stored in it have been made permanent.

If you erase an active log file, the database becomes unusable and must be restored before it can be used again. If you erase an archived log file, either online or offline, roll-forward recovery will be possible only up to the erased log file.

Configuration Files

Like all computer software applications, DB2 uses system resources when it is installed and when it runs. In the OS/2 and AIX environment, runtime resource management (for example, RAM and shared control blocks) are managed by the operating system. If, however, an application is greedy for system resources, problems can occur for both it and other concurrently running applications.

DB2 provides two sets of configuration parameters for you to control its consumption of system resources. One set of parameters exist for the DB2 database manager system itself in a DB2 database manager configuration file. This file specifies parameters to be used when creating databases (for example, database code page, collating sequence, and DB2 release level). It also controls system resources used by all database applications (for example, as total shared RAM).

A second set of parameters exist for each database in a database configuration file. This file specifies parameters that indicate the current state of the database (for example, backup pending flag, database consistency flag, roll-forward pending flag). It also specifies parameters that define the amount of system resources the database can use (for example, buffer pool size, database logging, sort memory size). A database configuration file exists for each database, so a change to one database configuration file does not affect other databases. By fine-tuning these two configuration files, you can tailor DB2 for optimum performance in any number of operating system environments. For more information about DB2 configuration file parameters, refer to the *IBM Database 2 Planning Guide* product manual.

DB2 DATABASE DIRECTORIES

DB2 uses a set of directories for establishing an environment, storing data objects, and enabling data access to both local and other remote workstations and databases. The directories used by DB2 are as follows:

- Physical database directory
- Volume directory
- System directory
- Workstation directory
- Database connection services directory

These directories define the overall DB2 database manager operating environment. Figure 1.7 illustrates DB2's directory structure.

Physical Database Directory

When a database is created, DB2 creates a separate subdirectory to store control files (such as log header files) and to allocate containers for default table spaces. Objects associated with the database are usually stored in the database subdirectory, but they can be stored in other various locations, including system devices. All databases subdirectories are created within the path specified in the CREATE DATABASE command. The naming scheme for database subdirectories is SQLOOOO1 through SQL*nnnnn*; the number for *nnnnn* is incremented each time a new database is created. (For example, directory SQL00001 contains all objects associated with the first database created, SQLOOOO2 contains all objects for the second database created, and so on.) DB2 automatically creates and maintains these subdirectories.

Volume Directory

In addition to the physical database directory, a volume directory exists on every logical disk drive available on a workstation that contains one or more DB2 databases. This directory contains one en-

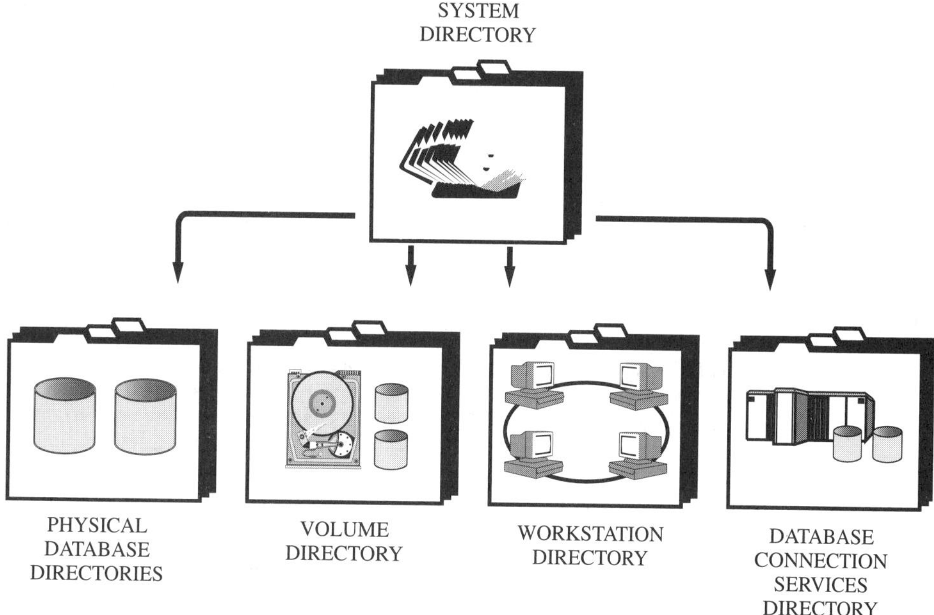

FIGURE 1.7 DB2's directory structure.

try for each database that is physically stored on that logical disk drive. The volume directory is automatically created when the first database is created on the logical disk drive, and DB2 updates its contents each time a database creation or deletion event occurs. Each entry in the volume directory contains the following information:

- The database name, provided with the CREATE DATABASE command
- The database alias name (which is the same as the database name)
- The database comment, provided with the CREATE DATABASE command
- The name of the root directory for the database
- The product name and release number associated with the database
- Other system information, including the code page the database was created under and entry type (which is always **Home**)
- The actual number of volume database directories that exist on a workstation, which is determined by the number of logical disk drives on that workstation that contain one or more DB2 databases

System Directory

The system database directory is the master directory for a DB2 workstation. It contains one entry for each local and remote cataloged database that can be accessed by DB2 from a particular workstation. Databases are implicitly cataloged when the CREATE DATABASE command is issued, and can also be explicitly cataloged with the CATALOG DATABASE command. The system directory resides on the logical disk drive where the DB2 product software is installed. Each entry in the system directory contains the following information:

- The database name provided with the CREATE DATABASE or CATALOG DATABASE command
- The database alias name (which is usually the same as the database name)

- The database comment, provided with the CREATE DATABASE or CATALOG DATABASE command
- The logical disk drive on which the database resides if it is local
- The node name on which the database resides if it is remote
- The database entry type, which tells whether or not the database is indirect (which means it resides on the same workstation as the system database directory file)
- The product name and release number associated with the database
- Other system information, including the code page under which the database was created

Workstation Directory

The workstation or node directory contains one entry for each remote database server workstation that can be accessed. The workstation directory also resides on the logical disk drive where the DB2 product software is installed. Entries in the workstation directory are used in conjunction with entries in the system directory to make connections to remote DB2 for Common Server database servers. Entries in the workstation directory are also used in conjunction with entries in the database connection services directory to make connections to host (MVS, AS/400, etc.) database servers. Each entry in the workstation directory contains the following information:

- The node name of the remote server workstation where a DB2 database resides
- The node name comment
- The local logical unit (LU) name that identifies the local LU alias and other system network architecture (SNA) information
- The partner LU name that identifies the partner LU alias and other SNA information
- The mode name that identifies the SNA transmission service profile
- The network ID that identifies the advanced peer-to-peer networking (APPN) if APPN is used
- The NETBIOS network server name if NETBIOS is used
- The NETBIOS adapter number if NETBIOS is used
- Other system information, including the code page under which the comment was created

Database Connection Services Directory

A database connection services directory exists only if the distributed database connection services (DDCS) product is installed on the workstation. This directory resides on the logical disk drive where the DDCS product software is installed. The database connection services directory contains one entry for each host (MVS, AS/400, etc.) database that DB2 can access via the DDCS distributed database relational architecture (DRDA) services. Each entry in the connection services directory contains the following information:

- The local database name
- The target database name
- The database comment
- The application requester .DLL file that executes the DRDA protocol to communicate with the host database
- LU 6.2 communication protocol parameters
- SQLCODE mapping requirements
- Other system information, including the code page under which the comment was created

> Note: To avoid potential problems, do not create directories that use the same naming scheme as the physical database directories, and do not manipulate the volume, system, workstation, and database connection services directories that have been created by DB2.

SUMMARY

The goal of this chapter was to provide you with an overview of the underlying architecture of a DB2 for Common Servers, version 2.1, database. You should now understand the relational database model and be familiar with the following data objects and support objects:

- Data objects
  - Databases
  - Table spaces
  - Tables
  - User-defined data types
  - User-defined functions
  - Check constraints
  - Indexes
  - Views
  - Packages (access plans)
  - Triggers
  - Aliases
  - Event monitors
- Support objects
  - System catalog views
  - Recovery log files
  - DB2 database manager configuration file
  - Database configuration files

Finally, you should be aware of how DB2 for Common Servers creates and uses the following directories and subdirectories on your storage media:

- Physical database directory
- Volume directory
- System directory
- Workstation directory
- Database connection services directory

It is important that you are comfortable with these DB2 database concepts before you begin your database application design work (and especially before you actually begin writing the source code for your application). The next chapter continues to present these concepts by discussing the database consistency mechanisms available in DB2 for Common Servers, version 2.1.

CHAPTER 2

DATABASE CONSISTENCY MECHANISMS

Once you understand the underlying architecture of DB2 for Common Servers, version 2.1, you should become familiar with the mechanisms DB2 uses to provide and maintain database consistency. This chapter will introduce you to the concepts of database consistency and the three mechanisms DB2 uses to enforce it: transactions, locking, and transaction logging. In the first part of this chapter I will define database consistency and examine the requirements a database management system must meet in order to provide and maintain it. Next, I will describe the heart of all data manipulation: the transaction. Then I will discuss the locking mechanism and examine how it is used by multiple transactions working concurrently to maintain data integrity. The chapter concludes with a discussion of transaction logging and the data recovery process used by DB2 in the event of application or system failure. Let's begin by defining database consistency.

WHAT IS DATABASE CONSISTENCY?

The best way to define database consistency is by example. Suppose your company owns a chain of restaurants and your database is designed to keep track of supplies in those restaurants. To facilitate the supply purchasing process, your database contains an inventory table for each restaurant in the chain; whenever supplies are received or used by a restaurant, the inventory table for that restaurant is updated. Now, suppose some bottles of ketchup are physically moved from one restaurant to another. The value for the number of ketchup bottles in the donating restaurant's table needs to be lowered and the value for the number of ketchup bottles in the receiving database's table needs to be raised in order to accurately represent this inventory move. If the person recording this transfer in your database lowers the number of ketchup bottles in the donating restaurant's inventory table but forgets to raise the number in the receiving restaurant's inventory table, your database will become inconsistent because the total ketchup bottle inventory is now incorrect.

A database can become inconsistent if a user forgets to make all necessary changes (as in the previous example), if the system crashes when the user is in the middle of making changes, or if a database application for some reason stops prematurely. Inconsistency can also occur when several users are accessing database tables at the same time. For example, one user might read another user's changes before all tables are properly updated and take some inappropriate action or make an incorrect change to the database based on the premature data. In order to properly maintain database consistency, you must answer the following questions:

- How can I maintain generic consistency of a database, since I do not know what each individual database owner/user wants?
- How can I keep a single application from accidentally destroying database consistency?
- How can I ensure that multiple applications accessing the same data at the same time will not destroy database consistency?
- If the system fails while a database is in use, how can I restore it to a consistent state?

DB2 provides the solutions to these questions with transactions, locking, and logging mechanisms.

TRANSACTIONS

A transaction or a unit of work is a recoverable sequence of one or more SQL operations within an application process that are grouped as a single unit. The initiation and termination of a transaction define the points of database consistency within an application process; either all SQL operations within a transaction are performed, or the effects of the SQL operations are completely undone.

A transaction is automatically initiated when the application process defining it is started. A transaction is terminated by either a COMMIT operation, a ROLLBACK operation, or the end of the application process that started it. A COMMIT or ROLLBACK operation affects only the database changes made within the transaction it ends. As long as these database changes remain uncommitted, other application processes are usually unable to see them (there are exceptions, which I will cover later) and they can be backed out with the ROLLBACK operation. Once the database changes are committed, however, they become accessible by other application processes and can no longer be backed out with a ROLLBACK operation.

A database application program can do all of its work in a single transaction, or divide its operations into several sequential transactions. Data used within a transaction is protected from being changed or seen by other transactions through various isolation levels.

Transactions provide generic database consistency by ensuring that changes become permanent only when you issue an SQL COMMIT command or via API calls defined within a transaction manager. It is up to you, however, to ensure that the sequence of SQL operations in each transaction results in a consistent database. DB2 then ensures that each transaction is either completed (committed) or removed (rolled back) as a single unit of work. If a failure occurs before the transaction is complete, DB2 will back out all uncommitted changes in order to restore the database consistency that it assumes existed when the transaction was initiated. Figure 2.1 shows the effects of both a successful transaction and a transaction that failed.

CONCURRENCY AND ISOLATION LEVELS

Maintaining database consistency and data integrity while allowing more than one application to access the same data at the same time is known as *concurrency*. DB2 enforces concurrency by using isolation levels. An isolation level determines how data is locked or isolated from other processes while it is being accessed. DB2 supports the following isolation levels:

- Repeatable Read
- Read Stability
- Cursor Stability
- Uncommitted Read

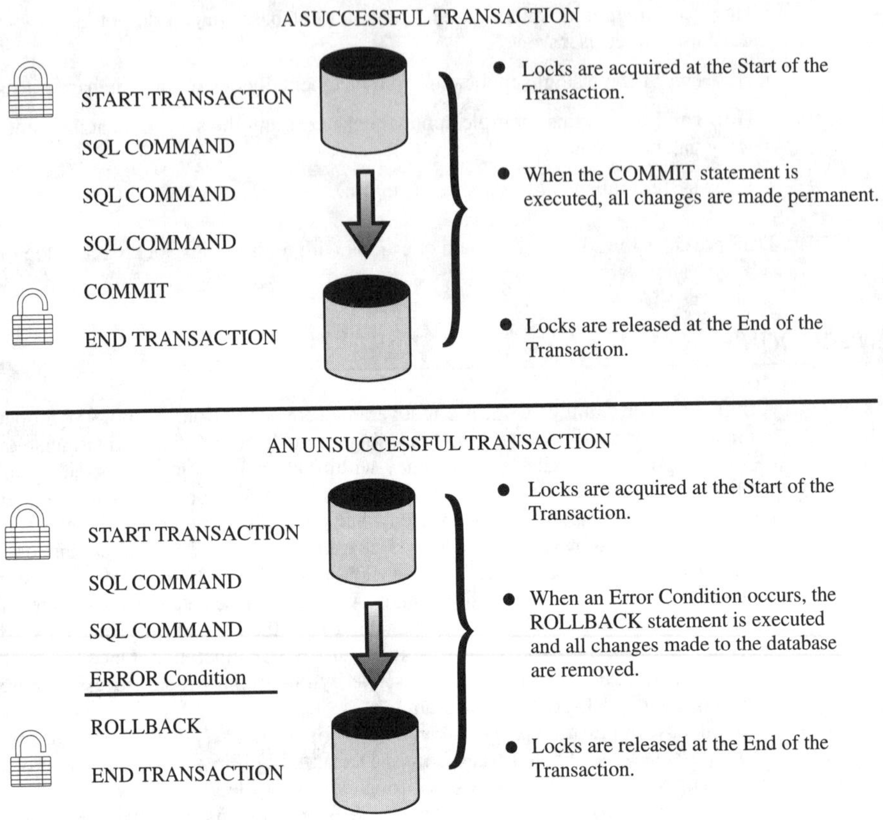

A SUCCESSFUL TRANSACTION

START TRANSACTION
SQL COMMAND
SQL COMMAND
SQL COMMAND
COMMIT
END TRANSACTION

- Locks are acquired at the Start of the Transaction.
- When the COMMIT statement is executed, all changes are made permanent.
- Locks are released at the End of the Transaction.

AN UNSUCCESSFUL TRANSACTION

START TRANSACTION
SQL COMMAND
SQL COMMAND
ERROR Condition
ROLLBACK
END TRANSACTION

- Locks are acquired at the Start of the Transaction.
- When an Error Condition occurs, the ROLLBACK statement is executed and all changes made to the database are removed.
- Locks are released at the End of the Transaction.

FIGURE 2.1 Events that take place during the execution of a successful and an unsuccessful transaction.

Repeatable Read

The repeatable read isolation level locks all the rows an application retrieves within a single transaction. If you use the repeatable read isolation level, SELECT SQL statements issued multiple times within the same transaction will yield the same result. A transaction under the repeatable read isolation level can retrieve and operate on the same rows as many times as needed until it completes. However, no other transactions can update, delete, or insert a row (which would affect the result table being accessed) until the isolating transaction is complete. Transactions under the repeatable read isolation level cannot see uncommitted changes of other transactions.

Read Stability

The read stability isolation level locks only those rows that an application retrieves within a transaction. This ensures that any row read by a transaction is not changed by other transactions until the transaction holding the lock is terminated. Unfortunately, if a transaction using the read stability isolation level issues the same query more than once, it can retrieve new rows that were entered by other transactions that now meet the search criteria. This is because the read stability isolation level ensures that all retrieved data remains unchanged until the time that the transaction sees the data, even when temporary tables or row blocking is used.

Cursor Stability

The cursor stability isolation level locks any row being accessed by a transaction, as long as the cursor is positioned on that row. This lock remains in effect until the next row is fetched or until the transaction is terminated. If a transaction under the cursor stability isolation level has retrieved a row from a table, no other transactions can update or delete that row as long as the cursor is positioned on it. Additionally, if a transaction under the cursor stability isolation level changes the row it retrieves, no other applications can update or delete that row until the isolating transaction is terminated. When a transaction has locked a row with the cursor stability isolation level, other transactions can insert, delete, or change rows on either side of that locked row, as long as the locked row is not accessed via an index. Therefore, the same SELECT SQL statement issued twice within a single transaction might not always yield the same results. Transactions under the cursor stability isolation level cannot see uncommitted changes made by other transactions.

Uncommitted Read

The uncommitted read isolation level allows a transaction to access uncommitted changes made by other transactions (in either this or other applications). A transaction made while the uncommitted read isolation level is in effect does not lock other applications out of the row it is reading unless another transaction attempts to drop or alter the table. If a transaction under the uncommitted read isolation level accesses a read-only cursor, it can access most uncommitted changes made by other transactions. However, the transaction cannot access tables, views, and indexes that are being created or dropped by other transactions until those transactions are complete. All other changes made by other transactions can be read before they are committed or rolled back. If a transaction made under the uncommitted read isolation level accesses an updateable cursor, it will behave as if the cursor stability isolation level is in effect.

Specifying the Isolation Level

You specify the isolation level for embedded SQL statements when precompiling the application or binding it to a database. The isolation level for a call-level interface (CLI) statement is set by the CLI statement handle. In most cases, you set the isolation level for embedded SQL applications written in a supported compiled language (such as C and C++) with the ISOLATION option of the command-line processor PREP or BIND commands. In other cases, you can set an embedded SQL application's isolation level by using the PREP or BIND API calls. The default for all applications is the cursor stability isolation level.

LOCKING

Along with isolation levels, DB2 provides locks for concurrency control and controlled data access. A lock allows you to associate a data resource with a single transaction to control how other transactions interact with that resource while it is associated with the transaction that acquired the lock. The transaction with which the resource is associated is said to "hold" or "own" the lock. When a data resource in the database is accessed by a transaction, that resource is locked according to the previously specified isolation level. This lock prevents other transactions from accessing the data resource in a way that would interfere with the owning transaction. Once the owning transaction is terminated (either committed or rolled back), any changes made to the data resource are either made permanent or removed and the data resource is unlocked so it can be used by other transactions. Figure 2.2 illustrates the principles of data resource locking.

If one transaction tries to access a data resource in a way that is incompatible with a lock held by another transaction, that transaction must wait until the owning transaction has ended. This is known

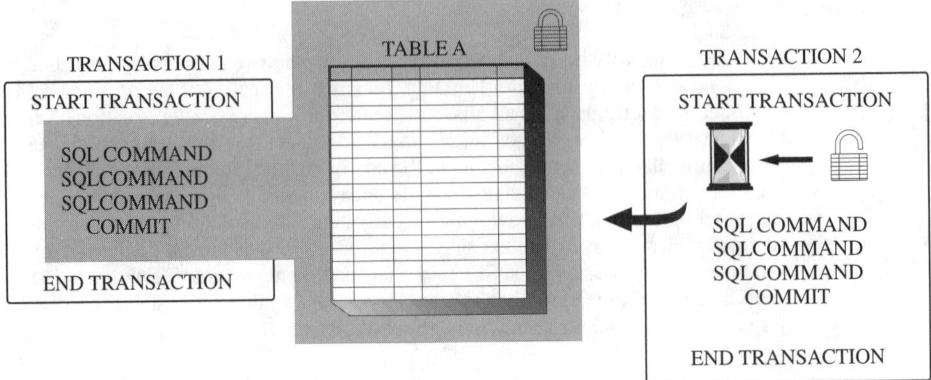

FIGURE 2.2 DB2 prevents uncontrolled concurrent table access by using locks. In this example, transaction 1 has locked table A and transaction 2 must wait until the lock is released before it can execute.

as a *lock wait*. When this event occurs, the transaction attempting to access the data resource simply stops execution until the owning transaction has terminated and the incompatible lock is released. Locks are automatically provided by DB2 for each transaction, so you do not need to explicitly request that a data resource be locked.

Lock Attributes

Locks used by DB2 have the following basic attributes:

Object. The object attribute identifies the data resource being locked. Tables are the only data resource objects that can be explicitly locked by an application. DB2 can set locks on other types of resources, such as indexes, but these locks are for internal purposes only.

Size. The size attribute specifies the physical size of the portion of the data resource that is being locked. A lock does not always have to control an entire data resource. For example, rather than giving an application exclusive control over an entire table, DB2 can give the lock exclusive control only over the row that needs to change.

Duration. The duration attribute specifies the length of time a lock is held. The three isolation levels previously described control the duration of a lock.

Mode. The mode attribute specifies the type of access allowed for the lock owner, as well as the type of access permitted for concurrent users of the locked data resource. It is sometimes referred to as the "state" of the lock.

Lock States

As a transaction performs its operations, DB2 automatically acquires locks on the data resources it references. These locks are placed on a table, a row (or multiple rows), or both a table and a row (or rows). The only object a transaction can explicitly lock is a table. A transaction can affect row locks only by issuing a COMMIT or a ROLLBACK statement. The locks that are explicitly placed on a data resource by a transaction can have one of the following states:

Exclusive (X). If a table or row lock is set with the Exclusive state, the lock owner can both read and change data in the locked table, but only uncommitted read applications can access the locked table or row(s). Exclusive locks are best used with data resources that are going to be manipulated with the INSERT, UPDATE, and/or DELETE SQL statements.

Share (S). If a lock is set with the Share state, the lock owner and any other concurrent applications can read but cannot change data in the locked table or row. As long as a table is not Share-locked, individual rows in that table can be Share-locked. If, however, a table is Share-locked, no row Share locks in that table can be set by the lock owner. If either a table or a row is Share-locked, other concurrent applications can read the data but cannot change it.

Update (U). If a lock is set in the Update state, the lock owner can update data in the locked data table and automatically acquires Exclusive locks on the rows it updates. Other concurrent applications can read but cannot update the data in the locked table.

Superexclusive (Z). If a lock is set in the Superexclusive state, the lock owner can alter a table, drop a table, create an index, or drop an index. This lock is automatically acquired on a table whenever an application attempts any one of these operations. No other concurrent applications can read or update the table until this lock is removed.

In addition to these four primary locks, there are special locks used only on tables. They are called intention locks and are used to signify that rows within the table can be locked. These locks are always placed on the table before any rows within the table are locked. Intention locks can have one of the following states:

Intent None (IN). If an intention lock is set with the Intent None state, the lock owner can read data in the locked data table, including uncommitted data, but it cannot change this data. In this mode, no row locks are acquired by the lock owner, so other concurrent applications can read and change data in the table.

Intent Share (IS). If an intention lock is set in the Intent Share state, the lock owner can read data in the locked data table, but cannot change the data. Again, since the lock owner acquires no row locks, other concurrent applications can both read and change data in the table. When a transaction owns an Intent Share lock on a table, it acquires a Share lock on each row it reads. This intention lock is acquired when a transaction does not convey the intent to update any rows in the table.

Intent Exclusive (IX). If an intention lock is set in the Intent Exclusive state, the lock owner and any other concurrent applications can read and change data in the locked data table. When the lock owner reads data from the data table, it acquires a Share lock on each row it reads and an Update and Exclusive lock on each row it updates. Other concurrent applications can both read and update the locked data table. This intent lock is acquired when a transaction conveys the intent to update rows in the table. The SQL SELECT FOR UPDATE, UPDATE WHERE, and INSERT statements convey the intent to update.

Share with Intent Exclusive (SIX). If an intention lock is set with the Share with Intent Exclusive state, the lock owner can both read and change data in the locked data table. The lock owner acquires Exclusive locks on the rows it updates but not on the rows it reads, so other concurrent applications can read but not update the data in the locked table.

As a transaction performs its operations, DB2 automatically acquires appropriate locks as data objects are referenced. Figure 2-3 illustrates the logic DB2 uses to determine the type of lock to acquire on a referenced data object.

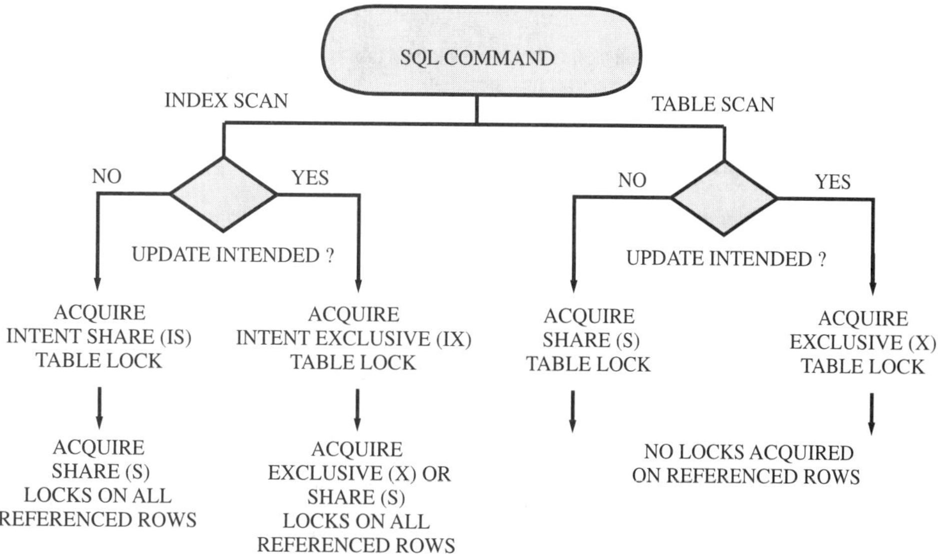

FIGURE 2-3 Logic used by DB2 to determine which type of lock(s) to acquire.

Locks and Application Performance

When developing DB2 applications, you must be aware of several factors concerning the uses of locks and the effect they have on the performance of an application. The following factors can affect application performance:

- Concurrency versus lock size
- Deadlocks
- Lock compatibility
- Lock conversion
- Lock escalation

Concurrency Versus Lock Size. As long as multiple transactions access tables for the purpose of reading data, concurrency should be only a minor concern. It becomes more of an issue, however, when at least one transaction writes to a table. Unless an appropriate index is defined on a table, there is almost no concurrent write access to that table. Concurrent updates are possible only with Intent Share or Intent Exclusive locks. If no index exists for the locked table, the entire table must be scanned for the appropriate data row (table scan). In this case, the owner transaction must hold a Share or an Exclusive lock on the table. Simply creating indexes on all tables does not guarantee concurrency. DB2's optimizer decides for you whether indexes are used in processing your SQL statement, so, even if you have defined indexes, the optimizer might choose to perform a table scan for any of several reasons:

- No index is defined for your search criteria (WHERE clause). The index key must match the columns used in the WHERE clause in order for the optimizer to use the index to help locate the desired rows. If you choose to optimize for high concurrency, make sure your table design includes a primary key for each table that will be updated. These primary keys should then be used whenever these tables are referenced with the UPDATE SQL statement.
- Direct access might be faster than via an index. The table must be large enough so the optimizer thinks it is worthwhile to take the extra step of going through the index, rather than just searching all the rows in the table. For example, the optimizer would probably not use any index defined on a table with only four rows of data.
- A large number of row locks will be acquired. If many rows in a table will be accessed by the transaction, the optimizer will probably acquire a table lock.

Any time one transaction holds a lock on a table or row, other transactions might be denied access until the owner transaction has terminated. To optimize for maximum concurrency, a small row-level lock is usually better than a large table lock. Since locks require storage space (to keep) and processing time (to manage), you can minimize both of these factors by using one large lock rather than many small ones.

Deadlocks. Two or more transactions contending for locks can result in a situation known as a *deadlock*. Consider the following example: Transaction 1 locks Table A with an Exclusive lock and Transaction 2 locks Table B with an Exclusive lock. Now, suppose Transaction 1 attempts to lock Table B with an Exclusive lock and Transaction 2 attempts to lock Table A with an Exclusive lock. Both transactions will be suspended until their second lock request is granted. Because neither lock request can be granted until one of the transactions performs a COMMIT or ROLLBACK and because neither transaction can perform a COMMIT or ROLLBACK because they are both suspended (waiting on locks), a deadlock situation has occurred. Figure 2.4 illustrates this scenario.

A deadlock is more precisely referred to as a "deadlock cycle" because the transactions involved in a deadlock form a circle of wait states. Each transaction in the circle is waiting for a lock held by one of the other transactions in the circle. When a deadlock cycle occurs, all the transactions involved in the deadlock will wait indefinitely, unless an outside agent takes action to end the deadlock. DB2 contains an asynchronous system background process associated with each active database, which is re-

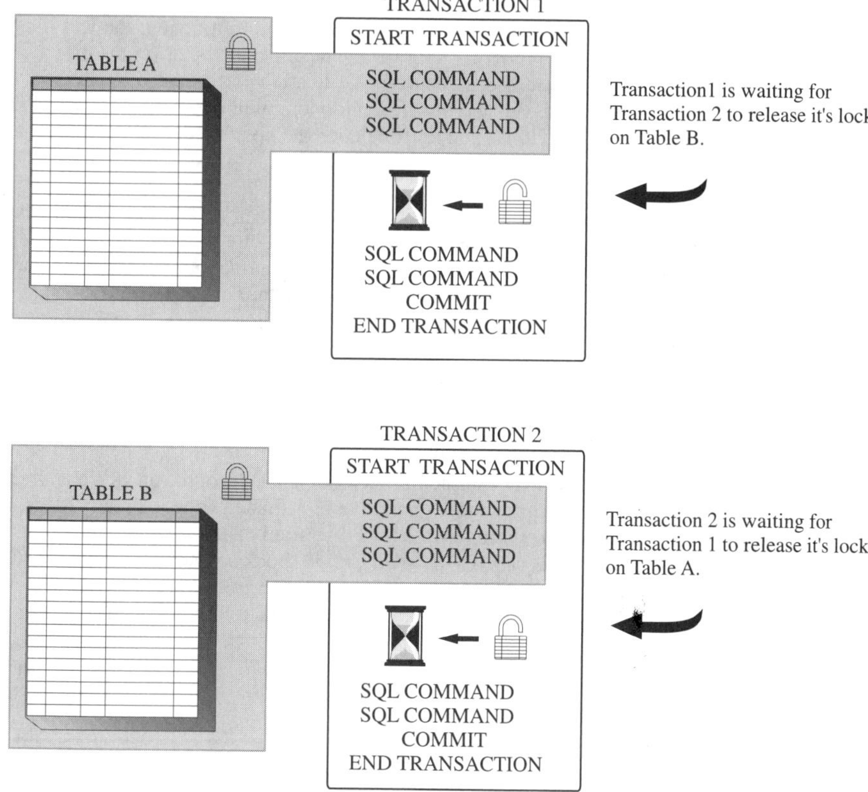

FIGURE 2.4 Deadlock cycle between two transactions.

sponsible for finding and resolving deadlocks in the locking subsystem. This process is called the *deadlock detector*. When a database becomes active, the deadlock detector is started as part of the process that initializes the database for use. The deadlock detector stays "asleep" most of the time, but "wakes up" at preset intervals to check whether or not deadlocks exist between transactions in the database. Normally, the deadlock detector sees that there are no deadlocks on the database and goes back to sleep. If the deadlock detector discovers a deadlock on the database, however, it selects one of the transactions in the cycle to roll back and terminate. The transaction that is rolled back receives an SQL error code and all of its locks are released. The remaining transaction can now proceed since the deadlock cycle is broken. It is possible, but very unlikely, that more than one deadlock cycle exists on a database. If more than one deadlock cycle exists, the detector will find each remaining cycle and terminate one of the offending transactions in the same manner, until all deadlock cycles are broken.

Since a deadlock cycle requires at least two transactions, you might assume that two data objects are always involved in the deadlock. This is not true. A certain type of deadlock, known as a *conversion deadlock*, can occur on a single data object. A conversion deadlock occurs when two or more transactions already hold compatible locks on an object, and then each requests new, incompatible lock modes on that same object. A conversion deadlock usually occurs between two transactions searching for rows via an index (index scan). Using an index scan, each transaction acquires Share and Exclusive locks on rows. When each transaction has read the same row and then attempts to update that row, a conversion deadlock situation occurs.

Application designers need to watch out for deadlock scenarios when designing high-concurrency applications that are to be run by multiple concurrent users. In situations where it is likely that the same set of rows will be read and then updated by multiple copies of the same application program, that program should be designed to roll back and retry any transactions that might be terminated as a result of a deadlock. As a general rule, the shorter the transaction, the less likely it is to get into a deadlock. Selecting the proper interval for the deadlock detector (in the database configuration file) is also necessary to ensure good concurrent application performance. An interval that is too short will cause unnecessary overhead, and one that is too long will allow a deadlock to delay a process for an unacceptable amount of time. You must balance the possible delays in resolving deadlocks with the overhead of detecting them.

Lock Compatibility. If the state of one lock placed on a data resource allows another lock to be placed on the same resource, the two locks (or states) are said to be *compatible*. Whenever a transaction holds a lock on a data resource and a second transaction requests a lock on the same resource, DB2 examines the two lock states to determine whether or not they are compatible. If the locks are compatible, the lock is granted to the second transaction (as long as no other transaction is waiting for the data resource). If the locks are incompatible, however, the second transaction must wait until the first transaction releases its lock (in fact, the second transaction must wait until all existing incompatible locks are released). Table 2-1 shows a lock-compatibility matrix that identifies which locks are compatible and which are not.

Lock Conversion. When a transaction accesses a data resource on which it already holds a lock and the mode of access requires a more restrictive lock than the one it already holds, the state of the lock is changed to the more restrictive state. The operation of changing the state of a lock already held to a more restrictive state is called a *lock conversion*. Lock conversion occurs because a transaction can hold only one lock on a data resource at a time. The conversion case for row locks is simple. A conversion occurs only if an Exclusive lock is needed and a Share or Update lock is held.

TABLE 2-1 Lock Compatibility Matrix

		Lock held by first transaction								
	Lock Type	none	IN	IS	S	IX	SIX	U	X	Z
Lock requested by second transaction	none	yes	yes	yes	yes	yes	yes	yes	yes	yes
	IN	yes	yes	yes	yes	yes	yes	yes	ye	no
	IS	yes	yes	yes	yes	yes	yes	yes	no	no
	S	yes	yes	yes	yes	no	no	yes	no	no
	IX	yes	yes	yes	no	yes	no	no	no	no
	SIX	yes	yes	yes	no	no	no	no	no	no
	U	yes	yes	yes	yes	no	no	no	no	no
	X	yes	yes	no	no	no	no	no	no	no
	Z	yes	no	no	no	no	no	no	no	no

IN Intent none
IS Intent share
S Share
IX Intent exclusive
SIX Share with intent exclusive
U Update
X Exclusive
Z Superexclusive
yes Locks are compatible, therefore the lock requested is granted
no Locks are not compatible, therefore the requesting transaction must wait for the held lock to be released or for a timeout to occur.

Source: IBM Database 2 Application Programming Guide, page 143.

There are more distinct lock conversions for tables than there are for rows. In most cases, conversions result in the requested lock state becoming the new state of the lock currently held whenever the requested state is the higher state. However, Intent Exclusive and Share locks are special cases, since neither is considered to be more restrictive than the other. If one of these locks is held and the other is requested, the resulting conversion is to a Share with Intent Exclusive lock. Lock conversion can cause locks only to increase restriction. Once a lock has been converted, it stays at the highest level obtained until the transaction is terminated.

Lock Escalation. All locks require space for storage and, since this space is finite, DB2 limits the amount of space the system can use for locks. Furthermore, a limit is placed on the space each transaction can use for its own locks. A process known as *lock escalation* occurs when too many record locks are issued in the database and one of these space limitations is exceeded. Lock escalation is the process of converting several locks on individual rows in a table into a single table-level lock. When a transaction requests a lock after the lock space is full, one of its tables is selected and lock escalation takes place to create space in the lock list data structure. If enough space is not freed up, another table is selected for escalation, and so on, until enough space has been freed for the transaction to continue. If there is still not enough space in the lock list after all the transaction's tables have been escalated, the transaction is asked to either commit or roll back all changes made since its initiation (i.e., it receives an SQL error code) and the transaction is terminated.

An important point to remember is that an attempted escalation occurs only to the transaction that encounters a limit. This is because, in most cases, the lock storage space will be filled when that transaction reaches its own transaction lock limit. If the system storage lock space limit is reached, however, a transaction that does not hold many locks might try to escalate, fail, and then be terminated. This means that offending transactions holding many locks over a long period of time can cause other transactions to terminate prematurely. If escalation becomes objectionable, there are two ways to solve the problem:

- Increase the number of locks in the database configuration file (with a corresponding increase in memory). This might be the best solution if concurrent access to the table by other processes is very important. There is a point of diminishing returns on index access and record locking, even when concurrency is the primary concern. The overhead of obtaining record-level locks can impose more delays to other processes, which negates the benefits of concurrent access to the table.
- Locate and adjust the offending transaction (or transactions), which might be the one terminating prematurely, and explicitly issue LOCK TABLE statements within it. This might be the best choice if memory size is crucial or if an extremely high percentage of the rows are being locked.

Transaction Logging

Transaction logging is simply a method of keeping track of what changes have been made to a database. Every change made to a row of data in a database table is recorded in the active log file as an individual log record. Each log record enables DB2 to either remove or apply the data change to the database. In order to fully understand transaction logging operations, it is important to know what the transaction log contains, how transaction logging works, how the transaction log gets synchronized, and how to manage log file space.

How Transaction Logging Works. Each time you change a row in a table, it is made with an UPDATE, INSERT, or DELETE SQL statement. If you use the INSERT SQL statement, a transaction record containing the new row is written to the log file. If you use the UPDATE SQL statement, transaction records containing the old row information and the new row information are written to the log file (two separate records are written). If you use the DELETE SQL statement, a transaction record containing the old row information is written to the log file. These types of transaction log records make up the majority of the records in the transaction log file. Other transaction records also exist, which indicate whether a ROLLBACK or a COMMIT has occurred. These log records end a sequence of data log records for a single transaction.

Whenever a ROLLBACK or a COMMIT log record is written, it is immediately forced out to the active log file. This ensures that all the log records of a completed transaction are in the log file and will not be lost due to a system failure. Because more than one transaction might be using a database at any given time, the active log file contains the changes made by multiple transactions. To keep everything straight in the log, each log record contains an identifier of the transaction that created it. In addition, all the log records for a single transaction are chained together.

If a COMMIT occurs, all log records for the committed transaction are no longer needed once all changes made by that transaction are physically written to the disk. If a ROLLBACK occurs, DB2 processes each log record written by the transaction in reverse order and backs out all changes made. This is why both "before" and "after" image UPDATE records are written to the log file.

Log File and Database Synchronization. DB2 can maintain consistency only by keeping the log file and database synchronized. This synchronization is achieved with a write-ahead logging technique. When a transaction changes a row in a table, that change is actually made in a memory buffer contained in the database buffer pool and written to the disk later. As a result, the most current data changes made to a working database are in the buffer pool, not on the disk. Write-ahead logging preserves consistency by writing the log record of a row change to the disk before the change itself is written from the memory buffer to the disk. Log records are written to disk whenever a transaction terminates (with a COMMIT or ROLLBACK) or whenever the buffer pool manager writes the memory buffer to the disk database.

If the system crashes, the log file and database will no longer be synchronized. Fortunately, the log file contains a record of every uncommitted change made to the database because the log record of the change is forced to disk before the actual change is written. This allows the recovery process to restore the database to a consistent state. The recovery process is discussed in more detail in the section *Database Recovery* later in this chapter.

Managing Log File Space. As you have seen, DB2 writes records to the log file sequentially to support transactions. Since the log file grows until it is reset, if no limits were imposed on the log file size, all free space on the system disk would eventually become full of log records. DB2's Log Manager controls the size of the log file and, whenever possible, resets the log to an empty state. The growth of the log is controlled by the initial size of the primary log files, the size limit for each secondary log file, and the number of primary and secondary log files. When the primary log file is filled, the Log Manager allocates space for a secondary log file, and the overflow is stored there.

Whenever the primary log file becomes empty due to transaction inactivity (i.e., no transactions have uncommitted records in the log), it is reset and any allocated secondary log files are released. If a transaction runs out of log space, either because the maximum primary log file size was reached and a secondary file was not used or because there was too little disk space to allocate the next secondary log file, a rollback occurs and the transaction is terminated. Regardless of cause, this continues until the log's inactive state is reached and the log is reset to its minimum size.

If two or more continuously overlapping transactions (e.g., high volume and high activity rate) are running, the primary log file might never be reset. Continuously overlapping transactions are not likely, but they can happen when two or more transactions starting at close intervals use the same database. When designing a database system in which the transaction arrival rate is high, you should increase the log file size in order to reduce the probability of transactions being rolled back due to insufficient log file space.

You can also prevent the primary log file from being reset if a lengthy transaction (one that causes many log records to be written before it commits them) is running. You must consider how these transactions are used, as well as the amount of log file space needed to support them, when designing the database system. If other transactions are running concurrently with a lengthy transaction, the log file space requirement will go up. A lengthy transaction should probably run by itself (no other transactions), and it should probably open the database for exclusive usage and fill up the log file before making its COMMIT. Any transaction that never ends execution (i.e., never performs a ROLLBACK or COMMIT) is a faulty application, since it will eventually cause itself and possibly other transactions to fail.

Database Recovery. *Database recovery* is the process of returning the data in a database to a consistent state in the event of a system failure (such as a power failure in the middle of a work session). If a DB2 database is active when a system failure occurs, that database is left in an inconsistent state until the next time it is accessed. At that time, a special recovery process is run that restores the database to a new consistent state. This new consistent state is defined by the transaction boundaries of any applications that were using the database when the system failure occurred. This recovery process is made possible by the database log file (see *Recovery Log File* in Chapter 1). Since the log file contains both a "before" and "after" image of every change made to a row, all transaction records stored in the log file can be either removed from or added to the database, as necessary.

DB2 determines whether or not database recovery is needed by examining the recovery log file the first time a database is opened after a system failure occurs. If the log file shows that the database was not shut down normally, the disk image of the database could be inconsistent since changes made by completed transactions (still in the memory buffers) might have been lost. To restore the database to a consistent state, DB2 does the following:

- Any change made by a transaction that was in flight (had not committed or rolled back) is removed from the database. DB2 works backward through the log file; if an uncommitted change is found in the database, the record is restored to the "before" image retrieved from the log file.
- Any change made by a committed transaction that is not found in the database is written to the database. As DB2 scans the log file, any committed log records found that are not in the database are written to the database.
- If a transaction was in the process of a ROLLBACK, the ROLLBACK is completed so all changes made to the database by that transaction are removed.

Since DB2 knows that changes are consistent only when they are explicitly committed, all the work done by the in-flight transactions are considered inconsistent and must be backed out of the database to preserve database consistency.

As described previously, during the recovery process, DB2 must scan the log file to restore the database to a consistent state. While scanning the log file, DB2 reads the database to determine whether it contains the committed or uncommitted changes. If the log file is large, it could take quite a while to scan the whole log and read associated rows from the database. Fortunately, it is usually unnecessary to scan the whole log since the actions recorded at the beginning of the log file have been in the log file longer than the other actions. The chance is therefore greater that their transactions are complete and that the data has already been written to the database, and no recovery actions are required for the log records generated by these transactions.

If there were some way to skip these log records during the recovery process, the length of time necessary to recover the entire database could be shortened. This is the purpose of the soft checkpoint, which establishes a pointer in the log at which to begin database recovery. All log file records recorded before this checkpoint are the result of completed transactions, and their changes have already been written to the database. A soft checkpoint is most useful when log files are large, since it can reduce the number of log records that are examined during database recovery. The more often the soft checkpoint is updated, the faster the database can be recovered from a system failure.

SUMMARY

It is extremely important to understand database consistency before designing your database application. It is also one of the more complicated aspects of database application design. This chapter provided you with an overview of the database consistency mechanisms in DB2 for Common Servers, version 2.1. You should now know what database consistency is and how to maintain it. You should also be familiar with transactions and how your application uses them to work with a database. You should be familiar with the following isolation levels:

- Repeatable read
- Read stability
- Cursor stability
- Uncommitted read

You should also understand the following lock attributes:

- Object
- Size
- Duration
- Mode

and lock states:

- Exclusive (X)
- Share (S)
- Update (U)
- Superexclusive (Z)
- Intent None (IN)
- Intent Share (IS)
- Intent Exclusive (IX)
- Share with Intent Exclusive (SIX)

You should be familiar with lock size, deadlocks, lock compatibility, lock conversion, and lock escalation. Finally, you should be aware of how transaction logging works and how transaction logs are used to restore database consistency in the event of a system failure.

As you build your database application, you will need to understand most of the information covered in this chapter. Incorporating this information in your application as you develop it will help you catch potential consistency problems in your application design. This chapter is the end of Part 1, BASIC DATABASE CONCEPTS. The next chapter begins Part 2, APPLICATION DEVELOPMENT FUNDAMENTALS.

Part 2

APPLICATION DEVELOPMENT FUNDAMENTALS

CHAPTER 3

THE APPLICATION DEVELOPMENT PROCESS

The DB2 database application development process begins with application design and continues with the actual source-code development. Before you can begin the application design, however, you need to understand just what a DB2 database application is. In the first part of this chapter I will define a simple application program and explain how a DB2 database application is different. Then I will explain DB2 application design and the four main elements associated with DB2 application development, as well as how to establish a DB2 database application development and testing environment. Finally, I will discuss transaction management and creating and preparing source-code files. Let's begin by answering the question "What is a DB2 database application?"

WHAT IS A DB2 DATABASE APPLICATION?

Before I can identify the elements of a DB2 database application, I need to start with a simple application. Most simple applications contain five essential parts:

- Input
- Logic (decision control)
- Memory (data storage and retrieval)
- Arithmetic (calculation)
- Output

Input is the way the application receives the information it needs to produce solutions for the problems it was designed to solve. Once input has been received, *logic* takes over and determines what information should be placed in or taken out of *memory* (data storage) and what *arithmetic* operations should be performed. Non-database applications use functions supplied by the operating system to store data in and retrieve data from simple byte-oriented files. Once the application has reached a solution to the problem it was designed to solve, it provides the appropriate *output* in the form of either an answer or a specific action.

A DB2 database application contains these same five elements. The difference between a simple application program and a DB2 application program is the method of data storage and retrieval, and decision control used. In DB2 applications, operating system file input/output (I/O) is replaced with

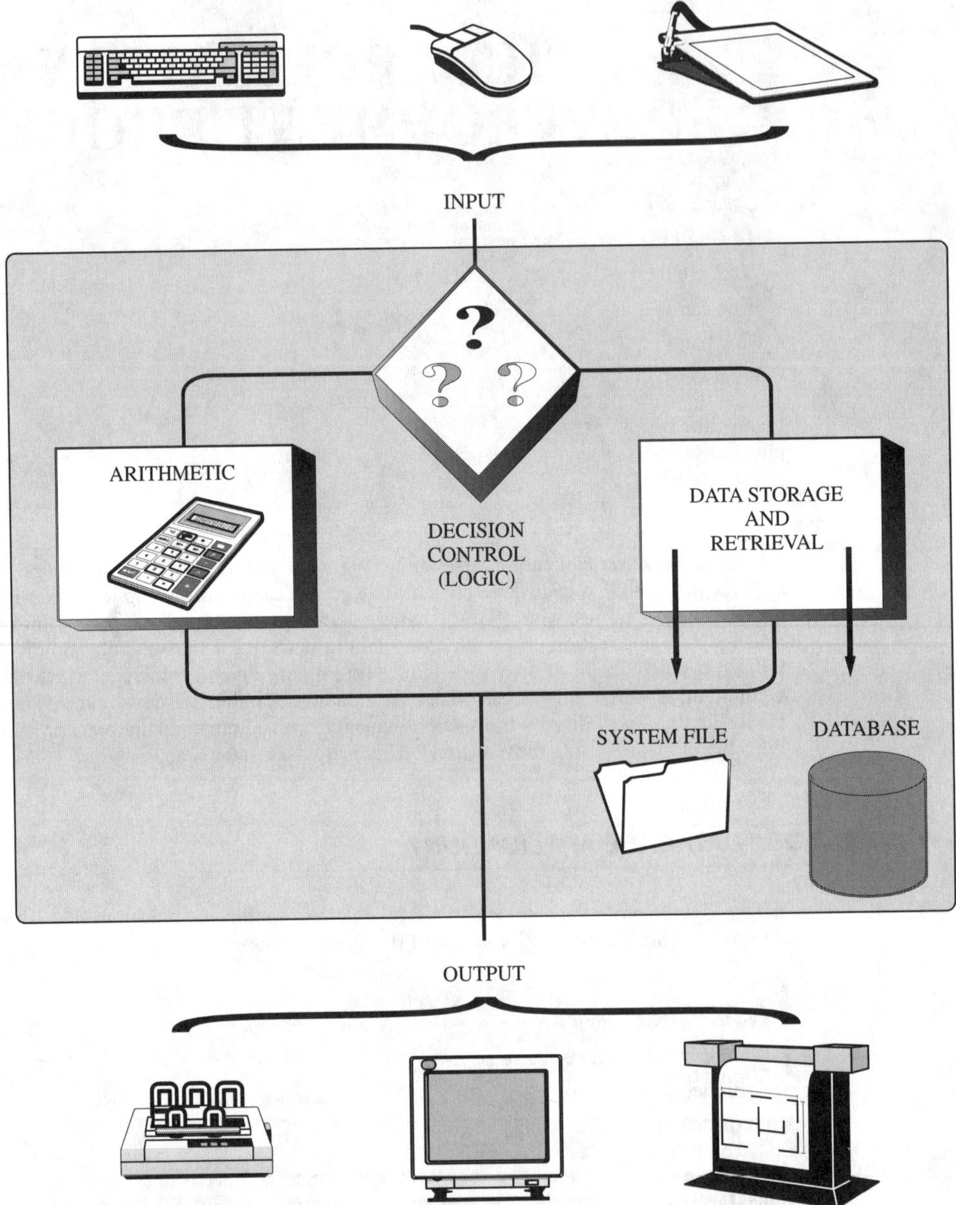

FIGURE 3.1 Elements of a simple application and a DB2 database application.

DB2 database I/O, which provides more than just data storage and retrieval. DB2 database applications also require less decision control (logic). Thanks to the nonprocedural nature of structured query language (SQL), you can have DB2 applications retrieve only the data they need by restricting SELECT SQL statements with WHERE, GROUP, and HAVING clauses. In addition, you can eliminate data sorting routines by using the SQL ORDER BY clause. Figure 3.1 illustrates the essential parts of both a simple application program and a DB2 database application program.

DESIGNING A DB2 DATABASE APPLICATION

Designing an efficient database application program requires a good understanding of how the production database is designed. If no written database design document exists, it is a good idea to produce one before you begin designing the actual database application. A good database design document should provide the answers to the following questions:

- What data will be stored in the database?
- How will the data be stored?
- What are the functional dependencies in the database?
- How can I isolate the functional dependencies in the database?
- How can I reduce or eliminate data redundancy?
- What keys do I need to create in order to establish referential data integrity?

Ideally, the best database design document will evolve based on the requirements of the database applications that will access the database. Once the database design document has been prepared, the application designing process can begin. Application design considerations should include the following:

- Transaction definitions
- Transaction management and logging
- Volatility and volume of data
- Security considerations
- Remote units of work (RUOW)
- Distributed units of work (DUOW)

ELEMENTS OF A DB2 DATABASE APPLICATION

Now that you know how a DB2 database application differs from a simple application, let's examine the specific elements of a DB2 database application. The following elements are the major building blocks of DB2 database applications:

- A high-level programming language
- Structured query language (SQL) statements
- Call-level interface (CLI) function calls (optional)
- Application programming interface (API) calls (optional)

Each of these elements accomplishes specific tasks in the overall design of a DB2 database application. You can accomplish almost any DB2 task by using a high-level programming language in conjunction with an SQL statement, a CLI function call, or an API call, although some tasks require several of these elements. This book will describe each of these elements in detail so you can decide which combination best suits your application needs.

High-Level Programming Language

A high-level programming language provides the framework within which all SQL statements, CLI function calls, and API calls are embedded. This framework allows you to control the sequence of your application's tasks (logic) and provides a way for your application to collect user input and provide appropriate output. A high-level programming language also allows you to use operating-system

API calls and DB2 application elements (SQL statements, CLI function calls, and API calls) within the same application program. In essence, the high-level programming language takes care of everything except data storage and retrieval.

By combining operating-system API calls and DB2 elements, you can develop DB2 database applications that incorporate operating system specific file I/O for referencing external data files. You can also use the high-level programming language to incorporate Presentation Manager functions and/or User Interface class library routines in the application for both collecting user input and displaying application output. Additionally, by building a DB2 database application with a high-level language, you can exploit the computer hardware to enhance application performance (e.g., optimizing for high-level processors such as the Pentium processor) and simplify user interaction (e.g., using special I/O devices like light pens and scanners). DB2 for Common Servers, version 2.0, provides support for the following high-level languages:

- C
- C++
- COBOL
- FORTRAN
- REXX
- Visual BASIC (through the DB2 Stored Procedure Builder)

All examples in this book were written in C and C++ and compiled with IBM's VisualAge C++ 32-bit compiler for OS/2 and IBM's CSET++ 2.1 for AIX.

Structured Query Language (SQL) Statements

Structured query language (SQL) is a standardized language used to create, store, manipulate, and retrieve data in a relational database. SQL statements are executed by DB2, not by the operating system. Since SQL is nonprocedural by design, it is not an actual programming language; therefore, most database applications are a combination of the decision and sequence control of a high-level programming language and the data storage, manipulation, and retrieval capabilities of SQL statements. There are two different ways to use SQL statements in an application program—static SQL and dynamic SQL—and each method has its advantages and disadvantages.

Static SQL. A *static SQL* statement is hardcoded in the application program when the source-code file is written. Since SQL statements are in the source code itself, all static SQL statement formats are known in advance by the application. Unfortunately, high-level programming language compilers cannot interpret SQL statements, so all source-code files containing static SQL statements must be processed by an SQL precompiler before they can be compiled. Likewise, DB2 cannot work directly with high-level programming language variables. Instead, DB2 works with host variables that are defined in a special place within an embedded SQL source-code file (so the SQL precompiler can recognize them). The SQL precompiler translates all SQL statements in a source-code file into their appropriate host-language function calls and converts the actual SQL statements into host-language comments. The SQL precompiler also evaluates declared data types of the host variables and determines which data conversion methods to use when moving data to and from the database. Additionally, the SQL precompiler performs error checking on each coded SQL statement and ensures that appropriate host-variable data types are used for their respective table column values.

Static SQL has the advantage of executing quickly, since its operational form already exists in a package (access plan) in the database. Unfortunately, all static SQL statements must be prepared before the application program can be executed and they cannot be modified at runtime. Because of this, if an application uses static SQL, its operational package(s) must be "bound" to each database the application will work with before the static SQL statements can be executed. (Refer to Chapter 4, WRITING EMBEDDED SQL APPLICATIONS, for more information.)

> Note: Since static SQL applications require prior knowledge of database, table, schema, and field names, changes made to these objects after the application is developed could produce undesirable results.

Dynamic SQL. Although static SQL statements are fairly easy to use, they are limited because their format must be known in advance by the precompiler and they can use only host variables. A *dynamic SQL* statement does not have a precoded fixed format, so the data objects it uses can change each time the statement is executed. This is useful for an application that has an SQL requirement where the format and the syntax of the SQL statement is not known at the time the source code is written. Dynamic SQL statements do not have to be precompiled (although the overhead for dynamic SQL statements must be precompiled) and bound to the database they will access. Instead, they are compiled to create an executable program, and all binding (explained in Chapter 4) takes place at execution rather than during compilation.

Since dynamic SQL statements are dynamically created based on the flow of application logic at execution time, they are more powerful than static SQL statements. Unfortunately, dynamic SQL statements are also more complicated to implement. Executing dynamic SQL statements requires that you prepare the statements at application runtime, so most dynamic SQL statements will execute more slowly than their equivalent static SQL counterparts. Since dynamic SQL statements use the most current database statistics during execution, however, there are some cases when a dynamic SQL statement will execute faster than its equivalent static SQL statement. Dynamic SQL statements also allow the optimizer to see the real values of arguments, so they are not confined to using host variables. Figure 3.2 shows how both static and dynamic SQL applications interact with a DB2 database.

Call-Level Interface (CLI) Function Calls

The call-level interface (CLI) is a collection of application programming interface (API) calls developed for database access that use function calls to invoke dynamic SQL statements. The important difference between embedded dynamic SQL statements and CLI function calls lies in how the actual SQL statements are invoked. With dynamic SQL, an application prepares and executes SQL for a single database management system (DBMS), in this case DB2. In order for a dynamic SQL application to work with a different DBMS, the application would have to be precompiled and recompiled for that DBMS. With CLI, an application uses procedure calls at execution time to perform SQL operations. Since CLI applications do not have to be precompiled, they can be executed on a variety of database systems without undergoing any alteration.

In order to understand the call-level interface, it is important to understand what DB2's CLI is based on and to compare it with existing callable SQL interfaces. The X/Open Company and SQL Access Group (SAG), now a part of X/Open, jointly developed a standard specification for a callable SQL interface, called X/Open call-level interface or X/Open CLI. The goal of the X/Open CLI is to increase the portability of database applications by allowing them to become independent of any one database management system's programming interface. Most of the X/Open CLI specification has been accepted as part of the new ISO call-level interface draft international standard (ISO CLI DIS). DB2's CLI is based on this ISO CLI DIS standard interface specification.

In 1991, Microsoft Corporation developed a callable SQL interface known as open database connectivity (ODBC) for the Microsoft Windows operating system. ODBC is based on a preliminary draft of the X/Open CLI, but provides extended functions that support additional capability. The ODBC specification also defines an operating environment where database-specific ODBC drivers are dynamically loaded (based on the database name provided with the connection request) at application runtime by an ODBC driver manager. This driver manager (for Microsoft Windows) provides a central point of control for each dynamic link library (DLL) that implements ODBC function calls and interacts with a specific DBMS. Each database-specific ODBC

STATIC SQL APPLICATIONS

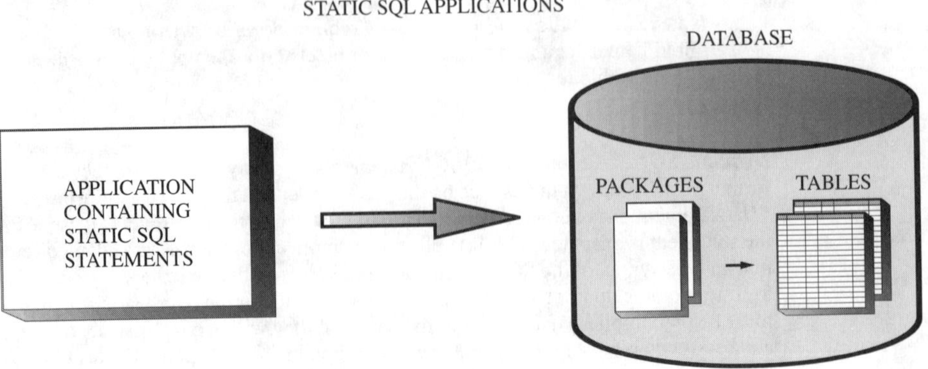

The operational form of static SQL statements are stored as packages in the database. Applications containing static SQL statements use these packages to access table data.

DYNAMIC SQL APPLICATIONS

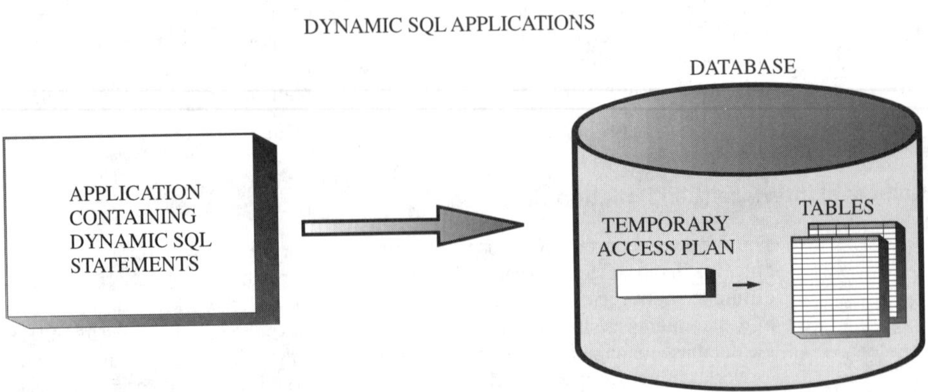

The operational form of dynamic SQL statements are automatically created at application run time. Temporary access plans, generated when dynamic SQL statements are prepared, are used to access table data.

FIGURE 3.2 How structured query language (SQL) applications interact with a DB2 database.

DLL is called an ODBC driver. With these drivers, an application can be linked directly to a single ODBC driver library rather than to each DBMS's library. When the application runs, the ODBC driver manager mediates its function calls and ensures that they are directed to the appropriate DBMS-specific ODBC driver. Figure 3.3 shows how CLI applications interact with a DB2 database via the driver manager.

Applications that incorporate DB2's CLI are linked directly to the DB2 CLI load library. The DB2 CLI load library can then be loaded as an ODBC driver by any ODBC driver manager. DB2's CLI provides support for all ODBC Level-1 functions and all but three ODBC Level-2 functions—SQLBrowseConnect(), SQLDescribeParm(), and SQLSetPos() are not supported; some X/Open CLI functions, and some DB2-specific functions are. The CLI specifications defined for ISO, X/Open, ODBC, and DB2 are continually evolving in a cooperative manner in order to produce new functions that provide additional capabilities.

Application Programming Interface (API) Function Calls

Application programming interface (API) calls are a collection of DB2 function calls that provide DB2 services other than the data storage, manipulation, and retrieval services provided by SQL statements and CLI function calls. API calls are embedded within a high-level programming language and operate in a fashion similar to other host-language function calls. Each API function has both a call and a return interface, and the calling program must wait until a requested API function completes before it can continue. The services provided by the API function calls can be divided into the following categories:

- Database manager control APIs
- Database manager configuration APIs
- Database control APIs
- Database configuration APIs
- Database directory management APIs
- DCS directory management APIs
- Node directory management APIs
- Netware support APIs
- Backup/recovery APIs
- Operational utility APIs
- Database monitoring APIs
- Data utility APIs
- General application programming APIs
- Application preparation APIs
- Remote server connection APIs
- Table space management APIs
- Transaction APIs
- Miscellaneous APIs

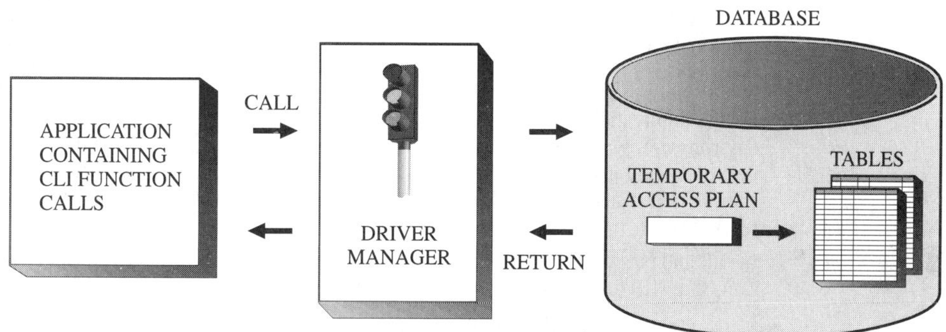

FIGURE 3.3 How call-level interface (CLI) applications interact with a DB2 database.

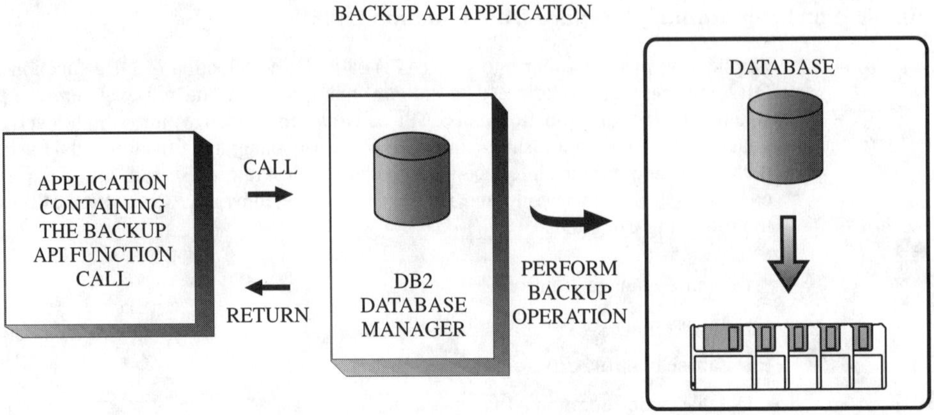

FIGURE 3.4 How the BACKUP application programming interface (API) call is processed by DB2.

An application can use APIs to access DB2 facilities that are not available via SQL statements or CLI function calls. In addition, you can write applications containing only APIs that will perform the following functions:

- Manipulate the DB2 environment by cataloging and uncataloging databases and workstations (nodes), by scanning system database and workstation directories, and by creating, deleting, and migrating databases.
- Perform routine database maintenance by backing up and restoring databases, and by importing and exporting data from other data files.
- Manipulate the DB2 database manager configuration file and other DB2 database configuration files.
- Perform specific client/server operations.
- Provide a runtime interface for precompiled SQL statements.
- Precompile embedded SQL applications.

Figure 3.4 illustrates how an application containing the BACKUP API interacts with the DB2 database manager to back up a DB2 database.

ESTABLISHING THE DB2 DATABASE APPLICATION DEVELOPMENT ENVIRONMENT

Before you can begin developing DB2 database applications, you must establish the appropriate application development/operating system environment by performing the following steps:

1. Install the appropriate DB2 for Common Servers software product on the workstation you will use for the application development. If the database application will be developed in a client-server environment, you must install the DB2 Server product software on the workstation that will act as the server, and install the appropriate DB2 Client Application Enabler software on all client workstations. You must also install a communication protocol that is common to both client and server workstations.
2. Install and properly configure the DB2 Software Developer's Kit (SDK) software on all workstations that will be used for application development.
3. Install and properly configure a high-level language compiler on all workstations that will be used for application development.
4. Make sure you can establish a connection to the appropriate database.

Note: If you will be incorporating dynamic and static SQL statements into the application program, the high-level language compiler being used must be supported by DB2.

For additional information on how to accomplish these tasks, refer to the installation documentation for DB2, DB2 SDK, the appropriate compiler, and the appropriate communications package.

You can develop DB2 database applications on any workstation that has the DB2 Software Developer's Kit (DB2 SDK) installed. You can run DB2 database applications either at a DB2 server workstation or on any client workstation that has the appropriate DB2 Client Application Enabler software installed. You can even develop applications so one part of the application runs on the client workstation and another part runs on the server workstation. When a DB2 database application is divided across workstations like this, the part that resides on the server workstation is known as a *stored procedure*. Stored procedures are covered in more detail in Chapter 8, APPLICATION PROGRAMMING LANGUAGE CONSTRUCT STATEMENTS.

In order to precompile, compile, and link DB2 database applications, your environment paths need to be properly set (OS/2's CONFIG.SYS file (DB2 for OS/2) or your default shell profile (DB2 for AIX)). Figure 3.5 illustrates how to set some key environment paths in an OS/2 CONFIG.SYS file and an AIX user profile.

```
                          O/S 2 CONFIG.SYS

REM ** Path Environment Variables **
SET PATH=C:\MUGLIB;C:\IBMCPP\BIN;C:\IBMCPP\HELP;
    C:\IBMCPP\SMARTS\SCRIPTS;C:\SQLLIB\BIN;C:\SQLLIB\ALT;
LIBPATH=C:\IBMCPP\DLL;C:\IBMCPP\SAMPLES\TOOLKIT\DLL;
    C:\MUGLIB\DLL;C:\SQLLIB\DLL;C:\SQLLIB\ALT;C:\SQLLIB\FUNCTION;

REM ** VisualAge C++ Environment Variables **
SET CPPLOCAL=C:\IBMCPP
SET CPPMAIN=C:\IBMCPP
SET CPPWORK=C:\IBMCPP
SET LOCPATH=C:\IBMCPP\LOCALE
SET INCLUDE=C:\MUGLIB;C:\IBMCPP\INCLUDE;C:\IBMCPP\INCLUDE\OS2;
    C:\IBMCPP\INC;C:\IBMCPP\INCLUDE\SOM;C:\SQLLIB\INCLUDE;
SET VBPATH=.;C:\IBMCPP\DDE4VB
SET TMPDIR=C:\IBMCPP\TMP
SET LPATH=C:\IBMCPP\MACROS
SET CODELPATH=C:\IBMCPP\CODE\MACROS;C:\IBMCPP\MACROS
SET LIB=C:\MUGLIB;C:\IBMCPP\LIB;C:\IBMCPP\DLL;C:\SQLLIB\LIB;
SET TMP=C:\IBMCPP\TMP

REM ** DB2 Environment Variables **
SET DB2INSTANCE=DB2
SET DB2PATH=C:\SQLLIB
SET COBCPY=C:\SQLLIB\INCLUDE\COBOL_MF
SET FINCLUDE=C:\SQLLIB\INCLUDE
SET DB2CHKPTR=ON
SET FTB1DIR=C:\FTW\WORK
SET FTB1PATH=C:\FTW
SETFTBBASE=C:\FTW
FTB1PRELOAD=30
SET DSSPATH=C:\FTW
```

```
                          AIX USER PROFILE
PATH=/usr/bin:/etc:/usr/sbin:/usr/ucb:$HOME/bin:/user/bin/X11:/sbin:.:
$HOME/sqllib/bin:$HOME/sqllib/admn:$HOME/sql/lib/misc
```

FIGURE 3.5 Environment settings defined in a CONFIG.SYS file (OS/2) and a .profile file (AIX). Note: This is only a partial listing that focuses on DB2 and compiler-specific settings.

If you follow the installation instructions that come with the DB2 SDK and the supported high-level language compiler, your environment should automatically support application development. If, however, after installing the DB2 SDK and your high-level language compiler you are unable to precompile, compile, and link your application, check the environment paths and make sure they point to the correct drives and directories.

ESTABLISHING THE DB2 DATABASE APPLICATION TESTING ENVIRONMENT

As with any other application, the best way to ensure that a database application performs as expected is to thoroughly test it. You must perform this testing both during the actual development of the application and after the application coding phase has been completed. In order to thoroughly test your application, establish an appropriate testing environment that includes the following:

- A testing database
- Appropriate testing tables
- Valid test data

Creating a Testing Database

If your application creates, alters, or drops tables, views, indexes, or any other data objects, you should create a temporary database for testing purposes. If your application updates, inserts, or deletes data from tables and views, you should also use a testing database in order to prevent your application from corrupting production-level data while it is being tested. You can create a testing database in any of the following ways:

- By writing a small application that calls the CREATE DATABASE API call, either with a high-level programming language (such as C) or as a command file with REXX.
- By issuing the CREATE DATABASE command from the DB2 command-line processor.
- By backing up the production database to diskette (or a network) and then restoring it on a dedicated application development and/or testing workstation.

Creating Testing Tables and Views

To determine which testing tables and views you will need in the test database, you must first analyze the data needs of the application (or part of the application) being tested. You can perform this analysis by preparing a list of all data the application accesses and then describing how each data item in the list is accessed. When the analysis is complete, you can construct the test tables and views that are necessary for testing the application in any of the following ways:

- By writing a small application in a high-level programming language that executes the CREATE TABLE or CREATE VIEW SQL statement and creates all necessary tables and views (it could be the same application that creates the testing database).
- By issuing the CREATE TABLE or CREATE VIEW command from the DB2 command-line processor.
- By backing up the production database to diskette (or a network) and restoring it on a dedicated application development and/or testing workstation.

If you are developing the database schema along with the application, you might want to refine the definitions of the test tables repeatedly throughout the development process. Tables and views cannot usually be created and accessed within the same database application because the DB2 database manager cannot bind SQL statements to tables and views that do not already exist. To make the process of creating and changing tables less time-consuming and to avoid this binding problem, you can create and modify a separate application that creates all necessary tables and views as you are developing the main application. When the main application development is complete, you can then use the application that creates tables and views to set up production databases, and incorporate it into an application installation program.

Generating Test Data

The data an application uses during testing should be valid data that represents all possible data input conditions. If the application is designed to check the validity of input data, the test data should include both valid and invalid data. This is necessary in order to verify that the valid data is processed appropriately and the invalid data is detected and handled correctly. You can insert test data into tables in any of the following ways:

- By writing a small application that executes the INSERT ... VALUES SQL statement. This statement will insert one or more rows into the specified table each time it is issued.
- By writing a small application that executes the INSERT ... SELECT SQL statement. This statement will obtain data from an existing table and insert it into the specified table each time it is issued.
- By writing a small application that calls the IMPORT API call. You can use this API call to load large amounts of new or existing data, and also use it in conjunction with the EXPORT API to duplicate one or more tables that have already been populated in a production database.
- By writing a small application that calls the LOAD API call. You can also use this API call to load large amounts of new or existing data.
- By backing up the production database to diskette (or a network) and restoring it on a dedicated application development and/or testing workstation.

MANAGING TRANSACTIONS

If you might recall, in Chapter 2 I identified *transactions* as the basic building block that DB2 uses to maintain database consistency. All data storage, manipulation, and retrieval must be performed within one or more transactions, and any application that successfully connects to a database automatically initiates a transaction. The application, therefore, must end the transaction by issuing either a COMMIT or a ROLLBACK SQL statement (or equivalent API calls) or by disconnecting from the database (which automatically performs a COMMIT in DB2 for Common Servers).

> Note: It is bad practice to disconnect from a database and allow it to automatically end the transaction since some database management systems behave differently than others (for example, DB2/400 will perform a ROLLBACK instead of a COMMIT).

The COMMIT SQL statement makes all changes in the transaction permanent, while the ROLLBACK SQL statement removes all these changes from the database. Once a transaction has ended, all locks held by the transaction are freed and another transaction can access the previously locked data. (Refer to Chapter 2 for more information).

Applications should be developed in such a way that they end transactions on a timely basis, so other applications (or other transactions within the same application) are not denied access to necessary data resources for long periods of time. Applications should also be developed so their transactions do not inadvertently cause deadlock situations to occur. During the execution of an application program, you can issue explicit COMMIT or ROLLBACK SQL statements to ensure that transactions are terminated on a timely basis. Keep in mind, however, that once a COMMIT or ROLLBACK SQL statement has been issued, it cannot be stopped and its effects cannot easily be reversed.

CREATING AND PREPARING SOURCE-CODE FILES

The high-level programming language statements in an application program are usually written to a standard ASCII text file, known as a *source-code file*, with any text or source-code editor. The source-code files must have the proper file extension for the host language in which the code is written (e.g., C source files have a .C extension and COBOL source files have a .COB extension) in order for the high-level language compiler to know what to do with them.

If your application is written in an interpreted language such as REXX, you can execute it from the operating-system command prompt directly by entering the program name after connecting to the required database. Applications written in interpreted host languages do not need to be precompiled, compiled, or linked. If your application was written in a compiled host language such as C, however, you must perform additional steps to build your application. Before you can compile your program, you must precompile it. Simply stated, *precompiling* is the process of converting embedded SQL statements into DB2 runtime API calls that a host compiler can process. The SQL calls are then stored in a package, in a bind file, or in both, depending on the precompiler options you specify. After the program is precompiled, compiled, and linked, it must then be bound to the test or the production database. *Binding* is the process of creating a package from the source code or bind file and storing it in the required database. If your application accesses more than one database, it must be bound to each database before it can be executed. Precompiling and binding are required only if the source files contain SQL statements; if they contain only CLI function calls and/or API calls, precompiling and binding are not necessary. The details of how to write code for a DB2 application program containing SQL statements, CLI function calls, and API calls are contained in Chapters 4, 5, and 6.

SUMMARY

The goal of this chapter was to provide you with an overview of the DB2 database application development process. You should now understand what a DB2 database application is and be familiar with the following elements of database application design:

- Defining transactions
- Transaction management and logging
- Volatility and volume of data
- Security considerations
- Remote units of work (RUOW)
- Distributed units of work (DUOW)

And you should be familiar with the following application development elements and the specific tasks they accomplish:

- A high-level programming language
- Structured query language (SQL) statements
- Call-level interface (CLI) function calls
- Application programming interface (API) calls

You should also be able to establish a DB2 database application development environment and create testing databases, testing tables, and test data. Finally, you should understand how to create source-code files and convert them into executable application programs. The next chapter (4) continues to present DB2 database application development fundamentals by focusing on the development of embedded SQL applications for DB2 for Common Servers, version 2.1.

CHAPTER 4

WRITING EMBEDDED SQL APPLICATIONS

4

DB2 for Common Servers embedded SQL applications must be written so they conform to a specific embedded SQL application program model. This model structures your embedded SQL source-code files so the SQL precompiler can process them. This chapter will introduce you to the embedded SQL application program model and the steps required to convert an embedded SQL source-code file into an executable DB2 database application. In the first part of the chapter I will describe the database program model's basic parts—the epilog, the body, and the prolog—and their functionality. Then I will take a look at designing and using common error-handling routines. I will examine exception, signal, and interrupt handlers and discuss the importance of including them in an embedded SQL application program. Finally, the chapter concludes with a discussion of how to use the precompiler, compiler, and linker to convert an embedded SQL source-code file into an executable application. Let's begin with a description of using DB2's command-line processor to prototype embedded SQL statements.

PROTOTYPING EMBEDDED SQL STATEMENTS

As you design and code your DB2 application program, you should take advantage of DB2's command-line processor tool to prototype portions of your embedded SQL source code. DB2's command-line processor allows you to test SQL statements that define and manipulate information stored in database tables, indexes, or views. Using the command-line processor, you can add, delete, or update database information, as well as execute queries that produce information about the columns and data types defined for specific tables. In some cases, you will need to change the syntax for the command-line processor before coding it, but in most cases the syntax will be the same. For more information about the DB2 command-line processor, refer to the *IBM Database 2 Command Reference* manual. Prototyping SQL statements before embedding them in a source-code file can help reduce the amount of errors, both during the precompilation process and when the final application is tested.

THE MAIN PARTS OF AN EMBEDDED SQL SOURCE-CODE FILE

Once an application's embedded SQL statements are prototyped, you can begin writing the application's source-code files. A DB2 embedded SQL application program source-code file framework can be divided into the following three main parts:

- Prolog
- Body
- Epilog

Certain SQL statements must come at the beginning of the source-code file in order to properly handle the transition from high-level language to embedded SQL statements. Likewise, certain SQL statements must come at the end of the source-code file in order to handle the transition from embedded SQL statements back to high-level language. The C source-code example shown in Figure 4.1 sum-

```
                    EMBEDDED SQL SOURCE CODE FRAME WORK
/* Include Appropriate Header Files */
#include <sql.h>
#include <sqlenv.h>
 ...
/* Declare Host Variables */
EXEC SQL BEGIN DECLARE SECTION;
 long lTaskID;                                          PROLOG
 long lProjectID;
 char szTaskTxt[41];
 ...
EXEC SQL END DECLARE SECTION;
/* Set Up Error Handling */
EXEC SQL INCLUDE SQLCA;
EXEC SQL WHENEVER SQL ERROR GO TO ERRORCHK;

/* Connect To The Database */
EXEC SQL CONNECT TO PROJECTS;
/* Retrieve Data From The Database */
EXEC SQL DECLARE TASK_DESC_CURSOR FOR
 SELECT WRK_PRJ_ID,
        TSK_DESC_TXT
FROM PROJECTS.TASKS                                     BODY
WHERE TASK_ID = :lTaskID;                               (SQL STATEMENTS)
EXEC SQL OPEN TASK_DESC_CURSOR;
while(sqlca.sqlcode==SQL_RC_OK)
 {
 EXEC SQL FETCH TASK_DESC_CURSOR
   INTO :lProjectID,
        szTaskTxt;
 printf("ProjectID = %ld, Task = %ld\n",
      lProjectID, szTaskTxt);
 }
EXEC SQL CLOSE TASK_DESC_CURSOR;

/* Terminate The Transaction */
EXEC SQL COMMIT RELEASE;
/* Disconnect From The Database */
EXEC SQL DISCONNECT CURRENT;
/* Error Handling Routine */                            EPILOG
ERRORCHK:
printf("Error Code = %d\n", sqlca.sqlcode);
 ...
```

FIGURE 4.1 Sample source-code framework for embedded SQL applications.

marizes the general framework of an embedded SQL source-code file. You must, of course, tailor this framework to suit your own application source-code file needs.

Creating the Prolog

The *prolog*, as the name implies, is located at the beginning of each embedded SQL source-code file. It contains the declarations of all host variables, null indicator variables, and SQL data structures that DB2 uses to interact with the application program. The prolog can also contain SQL statements that tell the precompiler to generate source code that evaluates SQL statement return codes and branches to other portions of the source-code file (the epilog) if an error, warning, or exception condition occurs.

Declaring Host Variables. All high-level programming language variables (host variables) that interact with DB2 must be defined within an SQL declare section. The start of an SQL declare section is defined by the BEGIN DECLARE SECTION SQL statement, and the end of an SQL declare section is defined by the END DECLARE SECTION SQL statement. An application program can contain multiple SQL declare sections.

Host variables declared within an SQL declare section can receive data from a DB2 database or transfer data to it via embedded SQL statements. Host variables that receive data from a DB2 database are known as *output host variables*, while those that transfer data to a DB2 database are known as *input host variables*. Host variables will work correctly in SQL statements only if their attributes are compatible with the data types and lengths of the database columns they will be associated with. In other words, you must define input and output host variables so their data types and length attributes are similar to the data type and width of the column they either retrieve data from or write data to. In order to determine the appropriate data type to assign to a host variable, you must know what its corresponding column's data type is (DB2 data types are explained in Chapter 1). After you have identified the column's data type, you can refer to the conversion chart in the *IBM Database 2 SQL Reference* product manual to code the appropriate declarations.

Declaring and Using Indicator Variables. You must prepare applications to receive null values if they access database table columns defined as "nullable." You retrieve null values by associating an indicator variable with any host variable that can receive a null. Because indicator variables must be accessible by both DB2 and a host language, they must be declared as host variables that correspond to the DB2 type SMALLINT. You can also use indicator variables to signal an application when data has been truncated. In most cases, if an indicator variable contains a positive value after data is retrieved into its corresponding host variable, that value represents the actual length of the data that was returned (the exception to this rule is when the accessed data is a TIME or LOB data type). The C source code in Figure 4.2 illustrates how to define host variables and indicator variables in an embedded SQL application.

Declaring SQL Data Structures. A DB2 database application uses several data structures when communicating with DB2. The three most commonly used data structures are the SQL communication area (SQLCA), SQL descriptor area (SQLDA), and SQL character (SQLCHAR) data structures. SQLCA is a data structure through which DB2 transmits return codes to an application program. DB2 updates the SQLCA data structure after most of the API calls are completed and each time an embedded executable SQL statement is processed. SQLDA is a data structure by which applications can transfer data to and from DB2. The SQLDA data structure consists of a header followed by an array of structures, each of which describes an element of data. The SQLCHAR data structure allows applications to transfer variable-length data to and from DB2. It is used by applications transferring data to and from DB2 database columns that are variable in length, such as columns created with the VARCHAR and LONG VARCHAR data types. Refer to Appendix A, SQL DATA STRUCTURES, for a complete description of the fields of these three data structures.

You can create each of these data structures by embedding the appropriate statement within the prolog (EXEC SQL INCLUDE SQLCA, EXEC SQL INCLUDE SQLDA, or EXEC SQL INCLUDE SQLCHAR) or by including the appropriate header file(s) to get the data structure definition and de-

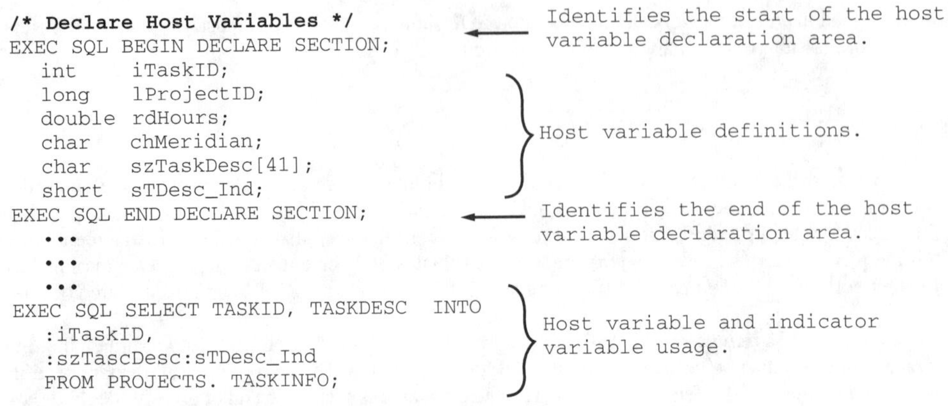

/* Declare Host Variables */
EXEC SQL BEGIN DECLARE SECTION;
int iTaskID;
long lProjectID;
double rdHours;
char chMeridian;
char szTaskDesc[41];
short sTDesc_Ind;
EXEC SQL END DECLARE SECTION;
...
...
...
EXEC SQL SELECT TASKID, TASKDESC INTO
:iTaskID,
:szTascDesc:sTDesc_Ind
FROM PROJECTS. TASKINFO;
Identifies the start of the host variable declaration area.
Host variable definitions.
Identifies the end of the host variable declaration area.
Host variable and indicator variable usage.

FIGURE 4.2 Declaring host variables.

claring structure variables within the SQL declare section. Because the size of the SQLDA and SQLCHAR data structures is not fixed, you must use pointers in conjunction with these structures and allocate the necessary storage for them. The actual size of the SQLDA and SQLCHAR data structures will depend on the number and size of the distinct data items being passed by these structures.

Of these three data structures, the one used most often by an embedded SQL application is the SQL communication area (SQLCA) data structure. This is because DB2 transmits return codes to an application program each time an SQL statement is processed through the SQLCA data structure. If the precompiler finds an EXEC SQL INCLUDE SQLCA statement in your source-code file, the host language definition of the SQLCA structure and one structure variable, named sqlca, will be inserted into the source-code file. DB2 then communicates with your application program by using elements within this sqlca data structure variable as storage for warning flags, error codes, and diagnostic information. After executing each SQL statement, DB2 places a return code value in both the SQLCODE and SQLSTATE members of the sqlca data structure. The SQLCODE member of the sqlca data structure contains an integer value that summarizes the results of the execution of the SQL statement. An SQLCODE value of zero means the SQL statement was successfully executed; a positive SQLCODE value means the SQL statement was successfully executed, but an exception condition occurred (such as the truncation of data); and a negative SQLCODE value means an error condition occurred and the SQL statement failed. The SQLSTATE member of the sqlca data structure contains a character field that provides a standard error code common across all of IBM's relational database products. Refer to the *IBM Database 2 Message Reference* for a complete listing of SQLCODE and SQLSTATE error conditions.

Using the WHENEVER SQL Statement. A good application will evaluate the SQLCODE value after every SQL statement is executed to determine whether or not the SQL operation was successful. This can become very lengthy and time-consuming, however, if the application contains many SQL statements. Fortunately, since every SQL statement in a source-code file must be processed by the precompiler, it is possible to have the precompiler generate the necessary code to check SQL statement return codes. You can tell the precompiler to add error checking after each SQL statement by including the WHENEVER SQL statement in the source-code file. The WHENEVER SQL statement causes the precompiler to generate source code that causes the application to go to a specified label if an error, warning, or exception condition occurs when an SQL statement is executed. There are three versions of the WHENEVER SQL statement, one for each of the following set of return codes:

Error codes. Any condition that results in a negative SQLCODE value

Warning codes. Any condition that results in a positive SQLCODE value (other than 100)

Not Found codes. Any condition that results in an SQLCODE value of 100 or an SQLSTATE of 02000

```
/* Set Up Error Handling */
EXEC SQL INCLUDE SQLCA;
EXEC SQL WHENEVER SQLERROR GOTO ERRCHK;
EXEC SQL WHENEVER SQLWARNING GOTO WARNCHK;
EXEC SQL WHENEVER NOT FOUND GOTO NOTFCHK;
...

/* Turn Off Error Handling */
EXEC SQL WHENEVER SQLERROR CONTINUE;
EXEC SQL WHENEVER SQLWARNING CONTINUE;
EXEC SQL WHENEVER NOT FOUND CONTINUE;
...
```
ERROR HANDLER ROUTINE IN INITIALIZATION AND TERMINATION

```
/* Terminate The Transaction */
EXEC SQL COMMIT RELEASE;
/* Disconnect From The Database */
EXEC SQL DISCONNECT CURRENT;
/*Error Handling Routine */
ERRCHK:
printf("Error Code = %d\n", sqlca.sqlcode);
...

/*Warning Handling Routine */
WARNCHK:
printf("ErrorCode=%d\n",sqlca.sqlcode);
...

/* Unresolved Error Handling Routine */
NOTFCHK:
printf("Error Code = %d\n", sqlca.sqlcode);
...
```
ERROR HANDLING ROUTINES

FIGURE 4.3 Using the WHENEVER statement to set up error-handling routines.

A source-code file can have any combination of these three versions of the WHENEVER SQL statement active at any time. The order in which the three versions are declared is insignificant.

The WHENEVER SQL statement affects all subsequent executable SQL statements, until another WHENEVER statement alters the situation. If the WHENEVER SQL statement is not used, the default action is to continue application processing even if an error, warning, or exception condition occurs. Each WHENEVER SQL statement can tell the precompiler either to continue without generating source code or to generate code that transfers program control to a specific label whenever the corresponding condition exists. The C source-code example in Figure 4.3 illustrates the various ways of coding the WHENEVER SQL statement.

The WHENEVER SQL statement must appear before the SQL statements you want to affect, otherwise the precompiler, by default, will not generate additional error-handling code. For this reason, the WHENEVER SQL statement is usually coded in the prolog portion of the source-code file.

Creating the Body

The *body* follows the prolog and makes up the bulk of the embedded SQL source-code file. It contains all the SQL statements that enable your application program to access and manipulate data stored in the database. The body usually begins with a CONNECT SQL statement, which establishes a connection to a database server. After the connection is established, the application program can issue SQL statements that manipulate data, define and maintain database objects, and initiate control operations such as granting user authority or committing changes to the database. All of these SQL statements comprise the remainder of the body.

Establishing a Database Server Connection. A DB2 application program must connect to the target database server before it can begin executing SQL statements. This connection identifies the authorization ID of the user running the application program and the name of the physical database on which the application program will be run. You can establish a connection between the application program and the database server by including the CONNECT SQL statement in the source-code file. You can also obtain a database server connection by implicitly issuing the CONNECT SQL statement to the appropriate database server via the DB2 command-line processor. It is good practice for the first SQL statement executed by an embedded SQL application program to be the CONNECT SQL statement. This ensures that all other SQL statements will be executed against the correct database (an application can implicitly connect to a default database).

There are two types of available database connections: Type 1 and Type 2. If a Type 1 connection is used, only one database connection is allowed for a single transaction. So once you establish a connection to a database and start a transaction, that transaction must be either committed or rolled back before you can connect to another database. On the other hand, if you're using a Type 2 connection, you can make multiple database connections in a single transaction.

> Note: If a DB2 application program needs only one CONNECT SQL statement and if that application program is made up of more than one source-code file, the CONNECT SQL statement needs to be only in the body of the source-code file that will be executed first.

Starting a Transaction. A *transaction*, also known as a *unit of work*, is a sequence of embedded SQL statements, possibly mixed with other host language code, that the database manager treats as a single process (refer to Chapters 1 and 2 for more information about transactions). A transaction is started implicitly when the first executable SQL statement begins, and it is ended by either a COMMIT or a ROLLBACK SQL statement or when the application program ends. The next executable SQL statement that follows a COMMIT or a ROLLBACK SQL statement automatically initiates a new transaction. Transactions are initiated in the body of an embedded SQL source-code file rather than the prolog because the SQL statements used in the prolog are not executable statements.

DB2 maintains the consistency of data (refer to Chapter 2) by ensuring that either all or none of the SQL operations within a transaction are completed. Suppose, for example, that money is to be deducted from one account and added to another. If both of these database table updates are placed in a single transaction and if a system failure occurs while they are in progress, when the system is restarted the data will automatically be restored to the state it was in before the transaction began. On the other hand, if a SQL statement error occurs, all changes made by the statement in error will be restored and any work done in the transaction prior to execution of the statement in error will not be undone unless you specifically roll it back. Therefore, do not rely on DB2 alone to maintain data integrity in your applications. It is a good idea to commit transactions as soon as application requirements permit. In particular, design transactions so uncommitted changes are not held over a terminal read request. Failing to observe this rule of thumb can result in locks (and consequently other resources) being held for long periods of time.

Creating the Epilog

The *epilog*, as the name implies, is located at the end of the embedded SQL source-code file. It contains SQL statements that terminate the current transaction and perform error processing if WHENEVER SQL statements were used in the prolog or the body. The epilog also contains an SQL statement that releases the program's connection to the database server if the source-code file is the last one to be executed.

Ending the Current Transaction. Each application program source-code file must explicitly end its current transaction before it terminates. You can ensure that this is done by placing either a COMMIT or a ROLLBACK SQL statement within the source-code file's epilog. When a transaction ends with the COMMIT SQL statement, all the database changes made during that transaction are permanently saved and all locks acquired by that transaction are released. When a transaction ends with the ROLLBACK SQL statement, all the database changes made during the transaction are removed and all locks acquired by that transaction are released. If the source-code file does not explicitly end the current transaction, DB2 will automatically issue a COMMIT SQL statement upon successful termination of the application program and all changes made to the database during the pending transaction will be saved, unless one of the following conditions occurs:

- A log full condition is encountered
- A system condition occurs that causes DB2 processing to end abnormally (such as a system power failure)

Although an implicit COMMIT SQL statement is automatically provided for any application that accesses a DB2 for OS/2 or AIX database, your application should still issue an explicit transaction termination statement to ensure that the desired action (either rollback or commit) is performed.

Disconnecting From the Database Server. You can make sure a DB2 application program releases its connection to the target database server before it returns control to the operating system by including the DISCONNECT SQL statement in the source-code file. You can also release the database server connection by implicitly issuing the DISCONNECT SQL statement on the appropriate database server via the DB2 command-line processor. Just as it is good practice for an application to issue the CONNECT SQL statement before any other SQL statements, it is good practice to make sure the DISCONNECT SQL statement is the last SQL statement issued. A DB2 application program needs one DISCONNECT SQL statement for each CONNECT SQL statement it contains. If you are using a Type 2 connection, such a connection will normally be initiated and terminated within a single transaction (within the body of the source-code file). If you are using a Type 1 connection, it will normally be terminated in the epilog of the source-code file.

> Note: If a DB2 application program needs only one CONNECT SQL statement and if that application program is made up of more than one source-code file, the DISCONNECT SQL statement needs to be only in the epilog of the source-code file that will be executed last.

Defining WHENEVER SQL Statement Error-Handling Routines. I have already discussed how the WHENEVER SQL statement tells the precompiler to generate source code that causes an application to go to a specified label if an error, warning, or exception condition occurs when an SQL statement is executed. Since many WHENEVER SQL statements can exist within a single source-code file, there can be many different labels and corresponding error-handling routines. These labels and the error-handling source code that follow them are normally the last items in the source-code file epilog. The source code following a specific label should contain logic that evaluates the error indicators in the SQL communication area (SQLCA) data structure. Then, depending on the values found in these error indicators, the program can perform any of the following actions:

- Execute the next sequential program instruction
- Perform some other special function(s)
- Roll back the current transaction and terminate the application program

Unfortunately, the WHENEVER SQL statement transfers program control with a GO TO statement rather than a function call/return interface. So your application has no way of knowing where the WHENEVER SQL statement was invoked, nor does it have any way of returning execution control back to that point. For this reason, most of these types of error-handling routines elect to roll back the current transaction and terminate the application program. The next section will show you how to get around this limitation by creating and using your own common error-handling routines rather than the WHENEVER SQL statements.

CREATING AND USING A COMMON ERROR-HANDLING ROUTINE

Because an application program has no way of knowing where a WHENEVER SQL statement was invoked and no way of returning execution control back to that point in the application, you should consider writing a common error-handling routine that evaluates the SQL return code (sqlca.sqlcode value) and performs the appropriate actions. You can then add statements in your source-code file to call this routine after every executable SQL statement instead of using the WHENEVER SQL statement. Here is a list of several other reasons for using a common error-handling routine:

Code reuse. Coding the same error-handling statements repeatedly is inefficient. By writing a single common error-handling routine once and using it multiple times, you can reduce your overall development effort. Also, if a common error-handling routine is designed correctly, it can link with and be used by other database application programs developed in the future.

Reduced testing. Once a common error-handling routine has been thoroughly tested, it is no longer necessary to test similar error-handling scenarios in different parts of an application.

Improved diagnostics. By using a common error-handling routine, you can get helpful debugging and error determination information in a common and consistent format.

Migration and portability. Since SQL error conditions and error messages often change with new DB2 product releases, it is easier to change a single error-handling routine than to change many SQL statement error-handling routines. Also, at some point you might decide to run your application against a different database product. Since various database products have their own product-specific SQL return codes, the application will most likely require error-handling routine changes.

As mentioned earlier, error information is returned in the SQLCODE, SQLSTATE, and SQLWARN fields of the SQL communication area (SQLCA) structure, and this information is updated after every executable SQL statement has completed. Therefore, source-code files that contain executable SQL statements must provide at least one SQLCA data structure variable (usually named sqlca). The SQLCODE member of the SQLCA data structure contains the return-code value of the last SQL statement that was executed. If an error condition occurs, the SQLSTATE member of the SQLCA data structure will contain a standardized error-code number that is consistent across other IBM database products (such as DB2 for MVS). The SQLWARN member of the SQLCA data structure might contain warning flags, even if the SQLCODE value is zero. The first element of the SQLWARN array will contain a blank if all other elements in the array are blank. If, on the other hand, at least one other element in the array contains a warning character, the first element in the array will contain a '**W**'.

A common error-handling routine should first determine whether or not an error or warning condition has occurred by checking the values of the SQLCODE and SQLWARN fields. If the common error-handling routine discovers that an error or warning has occurred (the SQLCODE value is nonzero or the first element of SQLWARN is '**W**'), it should process the error accordingly. At a minimum, the error-handling routine should notify users that an error or warning has occurred and provide enough information so the problem can be corrected. You could accomplish this by having the program test the SQLCODE value against all the possible error values, and display an error or warning message for each. Writing a routine to do this would be quite a large task, considering the number of possible SQLCODE error return values available. Fortunately, DB2 provides a special API routine that retrieves error message text for you. This API, known as the GET ERROR MESSAGE API, is covered in more detail in Chapter 21. The one drawback to using this API is that the messages it provides can be quite technical and not particularly meaningful to an end user of the application program. In some cases, therefore, it might be better for your error-handling routine to provide its own messages for a few specific error codes. Once the common error-handling routine has displayed appropriate error message text to the user, program control can return back to the point in the application program from which the common error-handling routine was called.

USING EXCEPTION, SIGNAL, AND INTERRUPT HANDLERS

A DB2 database application program must be able to shut down gracefully whenever an exception, signal, or interrupt occurs. This is usually done with an exception, signal, or interrupt handler routine. The actual type of handler routine is determined by the operating system on which the application program is run, as shown here:

DOS. Press Ctrl-C or Ctrl-Break to cause an interrupt.
OS/2. Press Ctrl-C or Ctrl-Break to initiate an operating system exception.
AIX. Press Ctrl-C to produce a signal.

DB2 provides an API call you can use to install a default exception, signal, or interrupt handler routine. If this API call is issued before any other API calls or SQL statements, any DB2 operations currently in progress will be ended gracefully whenever an exception, signal, or interrupt occurs (a ROLLBACK SQL statement is normally executed in order to avoid the risk of inconsistent data).

The default exception, signal, or interrupt handler is adequate for most simple, single-task applications. If however, your application program is a multithread or multiprocess application, you might need to provide a customized exception, signal, or interrupt handler. A typical exception, signal, or interrupt handler examines some state information about the executing process in order to determine whether or not the exception, signal, or interrupt should be ignored. If the exception, signal, or interrupt is honored and the current process terminated, the handler "cleans up" and then returns control to the operating system. A custom exception, signal, or interrupt handler routine should call the INTERRUPT API as part of this clean-up step. This API call notifies DB2 that a termination has been requested. DB2 then examines what, if any, database operation is in progress and takes the appropriate action to cleanly terminate that operation. Some database operations, such as the COMMIT and ROLLBACK SQL statements, cannot be terminated and are allowed to complete since their completion is necessary to maintain data consistency.

Note: SQL statements other than COMMIT and ROLLBACK should never be placed in exception, signal, and interrupt error-handling routines.

CREATING EXECUTABLES AND PACKAGES

Once your embedded SQL source-code files are written, the next step is to convert them into an executable DB2 database application program and to create the corresponding packages that will be used by DB2 at application runtime. This conversion and package creation process involves the following steps (illustrated in Figure 4.4):

1. Precompile the source-code files to convert embedded SQL source-code statements into DB2 runtime APIs and to create their corresponding packages. You can automatically store these packages in a database, or write them to a bind file and "bind" them to the database later.
2. Compile the precompiled source-code files to create object modules.
3. Link the object modules to create an executable program.
4. Bind the packages that were stored in bind files to the appropriate DB2 database(s).

Precompiling Source-Code Files

When SQL statements are embedded in a source-code file, they must be converted to DB2 runtime API calls (function calls) that the high-level language compiler can understand. This conversion

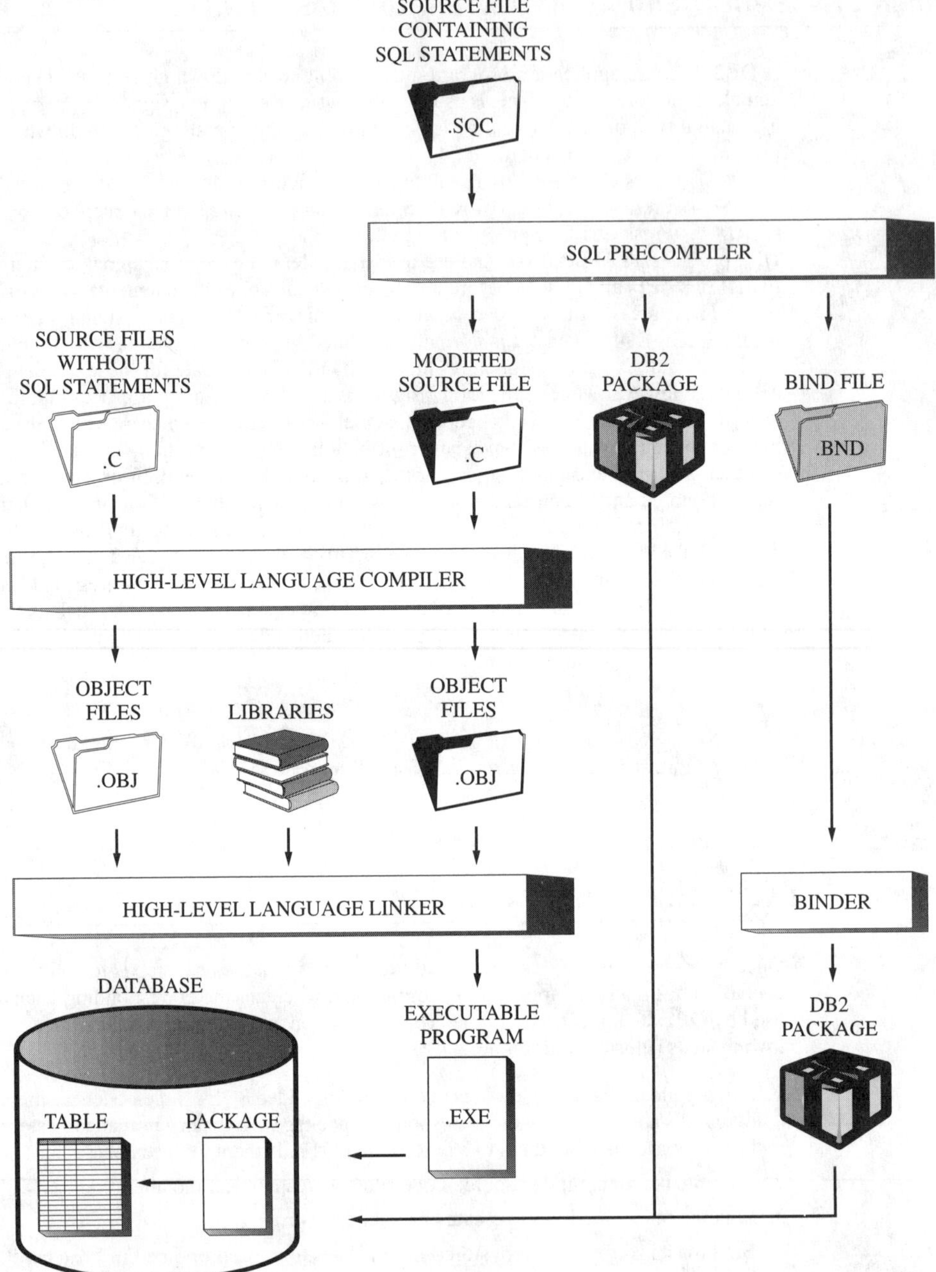

FIGURE 4.4 Process used to convert embedded SQL source-code files (containing static SQL statements) into executable DB2 application programs.

process is performed by the DB2 precompiler that is included in the DB2 software development kit. Precompilation converts a source-code file with embedded SQL statements into a high-level language source-code file made up entirely of high-level language statements. This is important, because the high-level language compiler cannot interpret SQL statements and thus cannot create the appropriate object code files used by the linker to produce an executable program.

Precompilation also creates a corresponding package that contains, among other things, one or more data access plans. Data access plans contain information on how the SQL statements in the source-code file are to be processed by DB2 at application runtime. For example, an access plan might contain instructions that specify an index to use when a certain SELECT SQL statement is executed. Access plans are subdivided into sections that contain individual plans for each SQL statement found in the source-code file. You must create a package for each source-code file that contains static SQL statements.

C and C++ source-code files containing embedded SQL statements must have the .SQC file extension. This file extension lets the precompiler know that the source code it will produce will be compiled by a C or C++ compiler. C and C++ source-code files that do not contain SQL statements should have the normal .C extension. You might be tempted to make your application development process easier by giving all your C and C++ source-code files the .SQC file extension. By using this approach, you do not need to distinguish between the source-code files that require precompilation and those that do not because they will all be precompiled. Unfortunately, it also has the following disadvantages:

- Application development time is increased since an additional step is required to convert .SQC source-code files into an executable program. Performing this step, even though it is not required, wastes valuable time.
- Locating compiler errors is more difficult. The .C file's line numbers don't match the original .SQC file's line numbers, so you must examine the .C file to determine which .SQC file statement caused the problem.
- Build dependencies are increasingly complex. Make files must ensure that the .C file is re-created each time the .SQC file is modified, and this complexity is unnecessarily increased if files that don't contain SQL statements are precompiled.
- Some C/C++ language statements might cause precompiler errors to occur. This can be avoided if the "offensive" statements do not have to be precompiled.

When a source-code file is precompiled, the precompiler verifies that all table names and columns referenced in the embedded SQL statements actually exist. Therefore, a database containing these data objects must be created before the source-code file can be successfully precompiled. Since a database must exist before the source-code files can be precompiled, complete your database design before you begin writing the database application program.

Compiling Source-Code Files

After the source-code file is successfully precompiled, it must be compiled by a high-level language compiler (such as VisualAge C++, Wactom C/C++, or Borland C/C++). The high-level language compiler takes the source-code file created by the precompiler and converts it into an object module that the linker will use to create the executable program. Locating errors reported during the compilation process can sometimes be difficult, since compiler error messages report statement line numbers from the precompiled source-code file (.C), not the original source-code file (.SQC). This means that you must first look in the generated source-code file (.C) to see what is wrong with your high-level language statement, and then go back to the original source-code file (.SQC) to correct the problem. Once the problem is corrected, the source-code file (.SQC) must be precompiled and compiled again.

> Note: Never make changes to the precompiler-generated source-code file (.C) because they will be lost the next time the original source-code file (.SQC) is precompiled.

Linking Object Modules

Once the source file is compiled without errors, the resulting object module can be input to the linker. The linker combines specified object modules, high-level language libraries, and DB2 libraries to produce an executable application (provided no errors or unresolved external references occur). For OS/2 systems, this executable application can be either an executable load module (.EXE) or a dynamic link library (.DLL). For AIX systems, it can be either an executable load module or a shared library.

Creating and Binding Packages

As mentioned earlier, when a source-code file is precompiled, the precompiler generates a corresponding package that contains, among other things, one or more data access plans. The process of storing this package in an appropriate database (a database containing data objects referenced in the source-code file) is known as *binding*. By default, packages are automatically bound to the database used for precompiling during the precompile process. However, by specifying the appropriate precompiler options, you can elect to store this package in a separate file, and then perform the binding process at a later time. Performing the binding process later as a separate step is more desirable if:

- You want to delay binding until you have a application program that compiles and links successfully. There is no need to waste time binding until you have a program that is ready to execute.
- You want to create the package under a different qualifier (schema) or under multiple qualifiers.
- You want to run your program against many different databases. By delaying the binding process, you can precompile your program once and bind it to multiple databases. Otherwise, you will have to precompile, compile, and link all embedded SQL source-code files whenever you want to run your program against a new database.
- You want to run your program against the same database on many different machines. If your program always runs against the same database, you might think you need to bind your program only once. This is true only if you plan to install that exact database on every machine that will run your application program (that database contains the access plan). By delaying the binding process, you can dynamically create your application database on each machine and then bind your program to the newly created database as part of your application installation process. If your application comes with or creates its own database, you can bind all your applications to that database immediately after the database is created.
- If your application is a general-purpose utility, you can issue the bind function call when the user first invokes it against a particular database.

Bind filenames, unless otherwise specified, are taken from the name of the source-code file being precompiled, and their file extension is .BND. For example, if you were to precompile the file EMPLOYEE.SQC without specifying a bind filename, the bind file EMPLOYEE.BND would automatically be generated.

A WORD ABOUT TIMESTAMPS

Whenever the precompiler generates a package or a bind file, it automatically places a timestamp inside the package or bind file, and it places a matching timestamp inside the modified source-code file. Each time the application is executed, these timestamps are automatically checked for equality. If, for some reason, the timestamps no longer match, an SQL error will occur and the application will not execute. By default, when you bind an application to a database, the first eight characters of the source-code file name are used as the package name (you can override this default by specifying a package name with the PACKAGE USING option of the precompiler). This means that if you precompile and bind two applications with the same name, the second application's package will overwrite the first application's package. Then the next time you try to execute the first application, you will get a timestamp error because the timestamp for the modified source-code file no longer matches that of the package in the database. This problem can also occur if you precompile and bind the same source-code file at two different time intervals while building a large application. In order to help cut down on timestamp errors, it is a good idea to always specify a package name during the precompile process. This is especially true if many developers are working on the same application and precompiling against a remote database.

Note: During application program development, if binding is not automatically performed by the precompiler, you might forget to rebind a particular source-code file's package after making corrections. In this case, when you attempt to run this program, a timestamp error will occur because the timestamp of the access plan in the database is not the same as the timestamp associated with the source-code file's object module. If this type of timestamp error occurs, simply rebind the appropriate bind file and try running your application program again.

RUNNING, TESTING, AND DEBUGGING EMBEDDED SQL APPLICATIONS

Once your application program is successfully precompiled, compiled, linked, and bound to a database, you can run the program and determine whether or not it performs as expected. You should be able to run your DB2 application program just like you would run any other application program on your particular operating system. If problems occur, you can do the following to help test and debug your code:

- When compiling and linking, specify the proper compiler and linker options so you can use the executable program with a symbolic debugger (usually provided with the high-level language compiler).
- Build and test your SQL statements with the DB2 command-line processor before you embed them in a source-code file. Remember that the precompilation process can complicate debugging because symbolic debuggers work with the high-level language statements generated by the precompiler instead of the actual SQL statements that were embedded.
- Make full use of DB2's error-handling APIs. Display all generated error message and return codes whenever an SQL statement fails.
- Use DB2's Explain facility to get an idea of the performance costs of the INSERT, SELECT, UPDATE, or DELETE SQL statements you are using in your application program. The Explain facility does not execute the SQL statement it is explaining; instead, it places the information about the structure and execution performance of the subject SQL statement into user-supplied database tables. You can use this information to isolate and correct "bottleneck" areas in you application. For information about the DB2 Explain facility and how to use it, refer to the *IBM Database 2 SQL Reference* and the *IBM Database 2 Administration Guide.*
- Make full use of the DB2 Bind File Dump (**db2bfd**) tool. With this tool, you can easily display the contents of a DB2 bind file to verify the SQL statements within it and display the precompile options used when the bind file was created. For information about the DB2 Bind File Dump tool and how to use it, refer to the *IBM Database 2 Application Programming Guide.*

SUMMARY

The goal of this chapter was to provide you with an overview of how embedded SQL source-code files are structured and to describe the processes involved in converting embedded SQL source-code files into executable database application programs. You should now understand how to use the DB2 command-line processor to prototype your SQL statements. You should also know that an embedded SQL source-code file is divided into the following three parts:

- Prolog
- Body
- Epilog

You should know how to declare and use host variables and SQL data structures, and you should understand how errors can be processed: either with the WHENEVER SQL statement or with a common error-handling routine. You should understand what causes exceptions, signals, and interrupts to occur, and you should know how to design routines to trap and process them. You should also be familiar with the following steps, used to convert embedded SQL source-code files into executable database applications:

- Precompiling
- Compiling
- Linking
- Binding

Finally, you should be aware of how to run, test, and debug your DB2 database application once it has been precompiled, compiled, linked, and bound to a database. The precompiler and binder will be discussed in more detail in Chapter 8 when I start describing DB2's SQL statements. The next chapter continues this examination of DB2's application development toolset by showing you the differences between embedded SQL and call-level interface (CLI) applications, and demonstrating how CLI database applications are developed.

CHAPTER 5

WRITING CLI APPLICATIONS

5

DB2 for Common Servers call-level interface (CLI) applications are similar to embedded SQL applications, except they use function calls to pass dynamic SQL statements to DB2 rather than executing the SQL statement themselves. This chapter will introduce you to CLI applications and the steps required to convert a CLI source-code file to an executable DB2 database application. In the first part of this chapter I will describe the differences between embedded SQL statements and CLI function calls. Then I will describe the three main parts of a CLI application: initialization, transaction processing, and termination. Next, I will discuss the design and implementation of common error-handling routines, focusing on the retrieval and analysis of return codes and SQLSTATE values. The chapter concludes with a discussion of how to use the compiler and linker to convert a CLI application source-code file to an executable program. Let's begin with an examination of the differences between embedded SQL statements and CLI function calls.

DIFFERENCES BETWEEN EMBEDDED SQL AND CLI FUNCTION CALLS

In the last chapter, you saw that DB2 database applications that use embedded SQL require a precompiler to convert the SQL statements into high-level language source code that is then compiled, bound to the database, and executed. In contrast, DB2 database applications that use CLI function calls do not require precompilation or binding. Instead, they use a standardized set of function calls to execute SQL statements (and related services) at application runtime. At first glance, this difference seems important only because it eliminates two steps in the conversion from source-code file to executable application (subsequently reducing application development time). You will soon see, however, that the difference between embedded SQL and CLI applications is larger than you might think.

Normally, SQL precompilers are designed specifically for the database product they are packaged with. This means that precompilers essentially tie embedded SQL applications to a single database product. If you want your embedded SQL application to work with other database products, therefore, you must rebuild it using the other database product's precompiler. Additionally, if the other database product uses access plans (packages), you will also have to bind your embedded SQL application to the new database(s). Because DB2 CLI applications do not require precompilation, they do not have to be recompiled or rebound in order to work with other database products. So once a DB2 CLI application is written and successfully compiled, it can immediately be run against other database products that support ODBC/CLI. CLI function calls and embedded SQL statements also differ in the following ways:

- CLI function calls do not require the explicit declaration of host variables. Instead, any variable defined in a CLI application source-code file can send or retrieve data to and from a DB2 database.
- CLI function calls do not require the explicit declaration of cursors. Instead, cursors are automatically generated by DB2 as needed for processing multiple-row SELECT SQL statements and positioned UPDATE and DELETE SQL statements.
- The OPEN SQL statement is unnecessary in CLI applications. Since cursors are automatically generated by DB2 for CLI function calls that need them, they are also automatically opened by DB2 whenever a multiple-row SELECT SQL statement is executed.
- Unlike embedded SQL, CLI function calls allow parameter markers to be used in their SQL statements.
- CLI function calls manage the information related to an SQL statement by using statement handles that treat the data as an abstract object. This statement handle means that the CLI application does not need to use database-specific data structures such as SQLCA, SQLDA, and SQLCHAR. An environment handle and a connection handle are also provided with CLI applications so they can reference global variables and connection specific information.
- Unlike embedded SQL, CLI can support two or more concurrent transactions on different database server connections. CLI can also support two or more connections to the same database server at the same time.

Despite these differences between CLI function calls and embedded SQL statements, there is an important common concept between the two. Applications that use CLI function calls can execute any SQL statement that can be dynamically prepared in embedded SQL. This is guaranteed because a CLI application passes all of its SQL statements directly to DB2 for dynamic execution instead of attempting to execute them itself.

> Note: CLI can also accept some SQL statements that cannot be dynamically prepared in embedded SQL, such as compound SQL statements. In addition, CLI will process any SQL statement that can be dynamically prepared by the DBMS product the CLI application is running against. This is because some DBMS products support SQL statements that other DBMS products do not.

By allowing the database product, in this case DB2, to execute all SQL statements, you guarantee the portability of CLI applications. This is not always the case with embedded SQL statements because their dynamic preparation can vary with each relational database product. Also, since COMMIT and ROLLBACK SQL statements can be dynamically prepared by some database products but not by others, they are not used in CLI applications. Instead, CLI applications use the SQLTransact() function call to perform ROLLBACKs and COMMITs. This ensures that CLI applications can successfully end their transactions, regardless of what database product is being used.

PROTOTYPING CLI FUNCTION CALLS

As you design and code your DB2 CLI application program, you should take advantage of DB2's Interactive CLI tool to prototype your CLI function calls. Interactive CLI allows you to test CLI function calls before you place them into a high-level language application program. Interactive CLI provides support for both CLI-related commands (commands that correspond to and have the same name as each CLI function call) and support commands (commands that do not have an equivalent CLI function call). Interactive CLI commands can be submitted either Interactively or via an input file. Likewise, the results of Interactive CLI commands can be either displayed on the terminal or written to an output file. In addition, the Interactive CLI command driver can capture all commands entered during a session and write them to a file, creating a "command script" input file that can be edited and rerun later. Prototyping CLI function calls before coding them in a source-code file can help reduce the amount of errors that are found, both during the precompilation process and when the final application is tested. For more information about the DB2 Interactive CLI application, refer to the *Interactive CLI (Applet) Documentation* manual.

> Note: Because Interactive CLI is a testing tool provided for application developers who want to use it, IBM makes no guarantees about its performance. Also, since Interactive CLI is not intended for end users, it does not have extensive error-checking built into it. This means that Interactive CLI can crash over something as simple as a closing delimiter at the end of a string parameter not being coded.

THE MAIN PARTS OF A CLI SOURCE-CODE FILE

Once an application's CLI function calls are prototyped, you can begin writing the application's source-code files (provided you already have a good understanding of SQL). The contents of a DB2 CLI application program source-code file are organized to perform the following three distinct tasks:

- Initialization
- Transaction processing
- Termination

The program performs each of these actions by calling one or more DB2 CLI functions, and the actions must be performed in the sequence shown or an error condition will occur. In addition, there are general tasks, such as error handling, that can occur throughout the CLI application source-code file(s).

The Initialization Task

The *initialization task* allocates and initializes the resources needed by the transaction processing task. These resources generally consist of data areas that are identified by unique handles. A *handle* is simply a pointer variable that refers to a data object controlled by DB2 CLI and referenced by CLI function calls. By using handles, the application is freed from the responsibility of having to allocate and manage global variables and/or data structures (such as the SQLCA, SQLDA, and SQLCHAR data structures that are used in embedded SQL applications). The three types of handles used by CLI function calls are as follows:

Environment handle. The *environment handle* refers to the data object that contains global information about the current state of the application. The program allocates this handle by calling the SQLAllocEnv() CLI function call. Only one environment handle can be allocated per application, and it must be allocated before connection handles can be allocated.

Connection handle. The *connection handle* refers to a data object that contains information associated with a database connection being managed by DB2. This data object includes general status information, transaction status information, and diagnostic information. The program allocates each connection handle by calling the SQLAllocConnect() CLI function call, and must allocate a connection handle for each connection it makes to a database server. These connection handles are then used to establish database connections and allocate SQL statement handles for use within those connections.

Statement handle. The *statement handle* refers to a data object that contains information about an SQL statement being managed by DB2. Statement handles are usually not allocated in the initialization task, but rather in the transaction processing task.

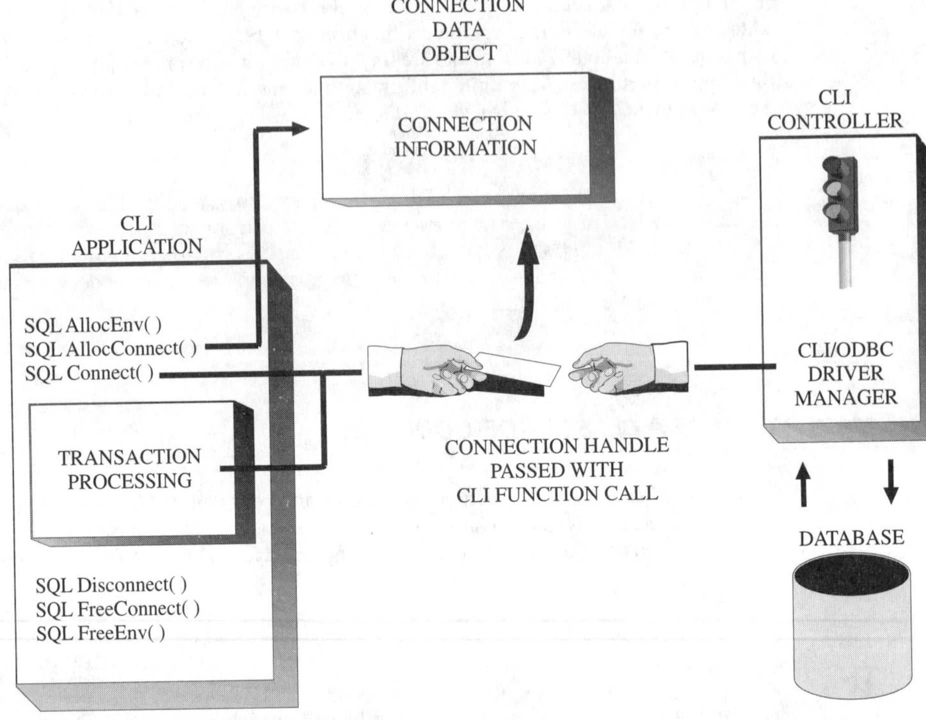

FIGURE 5.1 How connection handles are established and used.

Once the environment and connection data objects are allocated and their handles are initialized, they are passed to DB2 whenever a CLI function call is made. After the CLI function call is executed, DB2 stores the results of that call in the data areas to which the handles point and returns program control to the calling application. Once the calling application receives program control back from the CLI function call, it can then use these handles to retrieve and evaluate the results of the CLI function call.

In order to connect concurrently to more than one data source (or multiple times to the same data source), an application must call the SQLAllocConnect() CLI function call once for each connection it plans to establish. You can then use the handles returned from these calls with the SQLConnect() CLI function call to request the desired database connections. Using these connection handles ensures that multithreaded applications can use one connection per thread without encountering problems since DB2 CLI allocates and maintains separate data structures for each connection. Figure 5.1 illustrates how a connection data object is allocated by an application and how its handle is passed to the DB2 CLI controller with CLI function calls.

The Transaction Processing Task

The *transaction processing task* follows the initialization task and makes up the bulk of a CLI application source-code file. This is where the SQL statements that query and/or modify database data are passed to DB2 (or another database product) via CLI function calls. The transaction processing task essentially performs the following five steps:

1. Allocating statement handles
2. Preparing and executing SQL statements
3. Processing the results

4. Committing or rolling back the transaction
5. Freeing statement handles

Figure 5.2 illustrates these five steps and the CLI function calls that perform them.

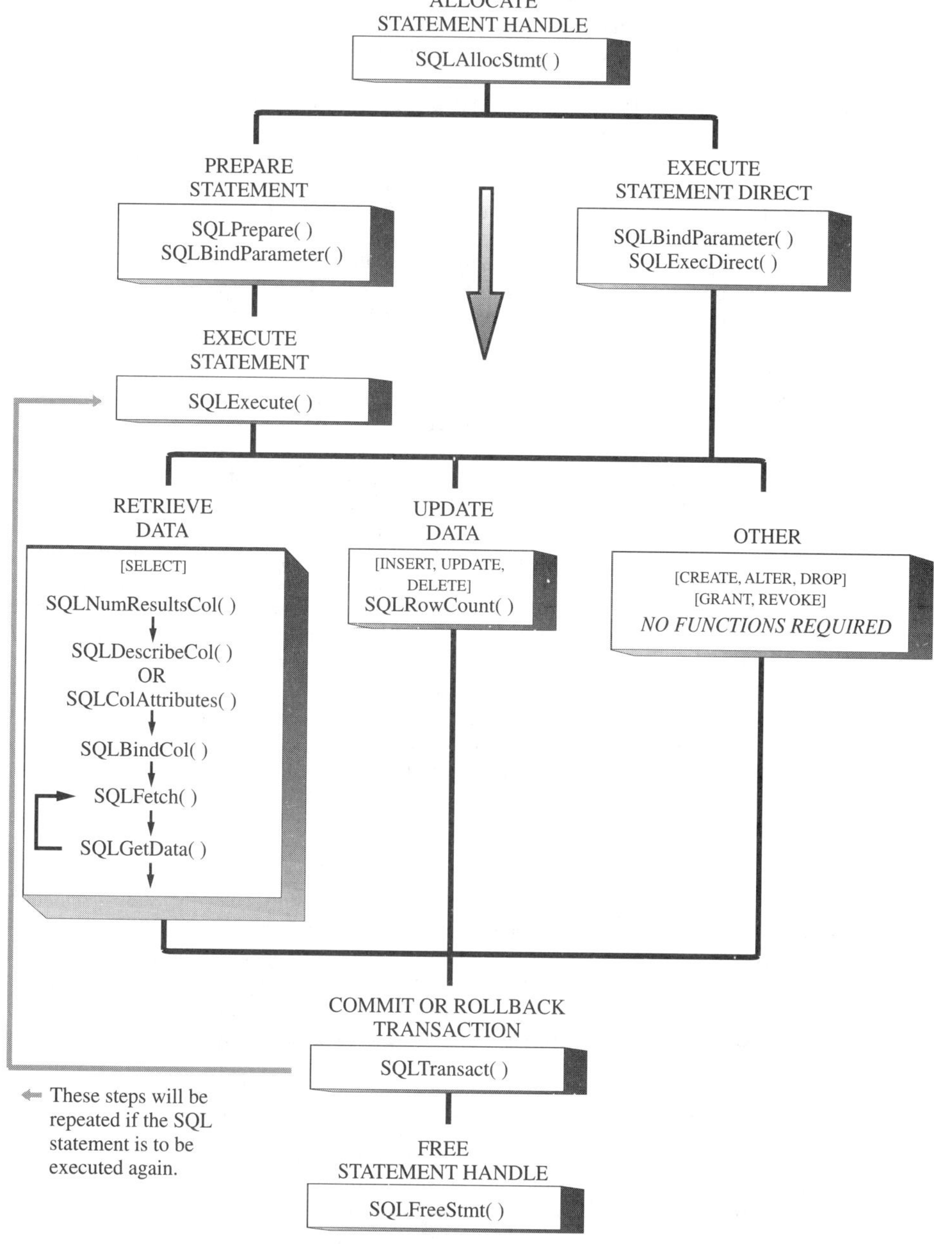

FIGURE 5.2 The typical order of CLI function calls in a DB2 CLI application. Note that not all CLI function calls or possible paths are shown.

Allocating Statement Handles. As mentioned earlier, a statement handle refers to a data object that contains information about a single SQL statement managed by DB2. This data object includes information such as the SQL statement text, any dynamic SQL statement arguments, cursor information, bindings for dynamic SQL statement arguments and columns, result values, and status information. A program allocates a statement handle by calling the SQLAllocStmt() CLI function call; a statement handle must be allocated for an SQL statement before that SQL statement can be executed. Also, each allocated statement handle must be associated with a specific database connection handle. The maximum number of statement handles that can be allocated at any one time is limited only by the amount of available system resources (usually stack space).

Preparing and Executing SQL Statements. Once an SQL statement handle is allocated, you can use two methods to specify and execute the actual SQL statement:

Prepare and then execute. This method separates the preparation of the SQL statement from the actual execution and is normally used when an SQL statement will be executed repeatedly (usually with different parameter values) or when the application needs information about the columns in the result data set before the SQL statement can be executed.

Execute directly. This method combines the preparation and execution into a single step; it is normally used when an SQL statement will be executed only once or when the application does not need additional information about the columns in the result set before the SQL statement can be executed.

Both of these preparation and execution methods allow parameter markers to be used in place of an expression (or host variables) in an SQL statement. Parameter markers are represented by the question mark (?) character and indicate the position in the SQL statement where the contents of application variables are to be substituted when the SQL statement is prepared and executed. Parameter markers are referenced sequentially, from left to right, starting at 1. When an application variable is associated with a parameter marker in an SQL statement, it is *bound* to that parameter marker (this is not the same as the binding operation in an embedded SQL application). Binding occurs when you call the SQLBindParameter() CLI function and specify the number of the parameter marker, a pointer to the application variable, the SQL data type of the parameter, and the data type and length of the variable as input parameters. Once you have bound a parameter marker to a variable, the information about that variable remains in effect until it is overridden or until the application unbinds it or frees its corresponding statement handle. The data type of the application variable should be the same as the data type required by the SQL statement, whenever possible. If you bind a variable of a data type that is different from the data type required by the SQL statement to a parameter marker, DB2 will automatically attempt to convert the contents of the bound variable to the required data type.

The application variables bound to parameter markers are known as *deferred arguments*, since only a pointer to them is passed when the SQLBindParameter () CLI function is called. No data is read from a deferred variable until the actual SQL statement is executed. By using deferred arguments in your application, you can execute the same SQL statement many times and receive different results simply by modifying the contents of the bound parameter variables.

Processing the Results After you have prepared and executed the SQL statement, you must retrieve and process the results of the statement execution. You can obtain result information from the data storage areas to which the connection and statement handles point. If the SQL statement was not a SELECT statement, then the only required processing is the normal check of the CLI function call return code to ensure that no errors occurred. If the SQL statement was a SELECT statement, however, you will need to perform the following steps to retrieve each row of the result data set produced:

1. Determine the structure (number of columns, column types, and data lengths) of the result data set.
2. Bind the application variables to the columns in the result data set (optional).
3. Repeatedly fetch the next row of data from the result data set into the bound application variables. You can retrieve columns not previously bound to application variables by calling the SQLGetData() CLI function after each successful fetch.

The first step analyzes the prepared or executed SQL statement to determine the structure of the result data set. If the SQL statement was hardcoded into the application, this step isn't necessary since the structure of the result data set is already known. If the SQL statement was generated at runtime (entered by a user), then the application will need to query the result data set in order to obtain this information. You can obtain the result data set's structure information by calling the SQLNumResultsCol(), SQLDescribeCol(), and/or SQLColAttributes() CLI functions after the SQL statement has been either prepared or executed.

The second step binds application variables to columns in the result data set so the application program can retrieve column data directly into them. Columns in a result data set are bound to deferred application variables similarly to how application variables are bound to parameter markers, but this time the variables are used as output arguments and data is written to them whenever the SQLFetch() CLI function call is used. Because you can also use the SQLGetData() CLI function call to retrieve data, application variable binding is optional.

The third step actually retrieves the data stored in the result data set by repeatedly calling the SQLFetch() CLI function call until no more data exists. If any columns have been bound, the corresponding application variables will automatically be updated. The SQLGetData() CLI function call must retrieve data from any columns not previously bound. This CLI function call is also useful for retrieving variable-length columns in smaller pieces, which cannot be done with bound application variables. You can retrieve all column data in the result data set by using any combination of these two methods. If any data conversion is necessary, it will occur automatically when the SQLFetch() CLI function is called (if bound variables are used), or it can be can be indicated when the SQLGetData() CLI function call is invoked. While performing these steps, the application should always check the return code each time a CLI function call is made to ensure that no errors have occurred.

If the SQL statement was a positioned UPDATE or DELETE statement, it will be necessary to use a cursor (a movable pointer to a row within a result data set). Unlike embedded SQL, where cursor names are used to retrieve, update, or delete rows, in CLI a cursor name is needed only for positioned UPDATE and DELETE SQL statements since they reference a cursor by name. Fortunately, this cursor name is automatically generated when the SQLAllocStmt() CLI function call is executed.

Ending the Transaction (ROLLBACK or COMMIT). I stated earlier that a transaction is a group of SQL statements that can be treated as a single operation. This means that all SQL statements within the operation are guaranteed to be completed (committed) or undone (rolled back), as if they were a single SQL statement. In CLI, an application can contain multiple database connections. When this happens, each database connection automatically has its own transaction. Figure 5.3 illustrates how this takes place by showing the transaction boundaries in a CLI application that contains multiple database connections.

You can configure CLI applications to run in either auto-commit or manual-commit mode. In auto-commit mode, each SQL statement is treated as a complete transaction and automatically committed if the SQL statement is successfully executed. For nonquery SQL statements, the commit takes place immediately after the statement is executed. For query SQL statements, the commit takes place immediately after the cursor being used is closed (remember that CLI function calls automatically declare and open a cursor if it is needed). In manual-commit mode, transactions are started implicitly the first time the application accesses the database (at the first occurrence of SQLPrepare(), SQLExecDirect(), SQLGetTypeInfo(), or any other CLI function call that returns a result data set in the source-code file). These transactions are then ended whenever the SQLTransact() CLI function call is invoked. This CLI function call will either roll back or commit the changes made to the database by the current transaction. Therefore, all SQL statements executed between the first database access and the SQLTransact() CLI function call are treated as a single transaction.

The auto-commit mode is the default commit mode and is normally sufficient for very simple CLI applications. However, larger applications, particularly applications that need to perform database updates, should switch to manual-commit mode as soon as the database connection is established. An application can switch between auto-commit mode and manual-commit mode by invoking the SQLSetConnectionOption() CLI function call.

The only rule about when to end a transaction is that all transactions must be ended before the connection to the database is terminated (before the SQLDisconnect() CLI function call is invoked). However, it is not a good idea to wait this long before you COMMIT or ROLLBACK a transaction because of the concurrency, locking, and logging problems that can arise (refer to TRANSACTIONS

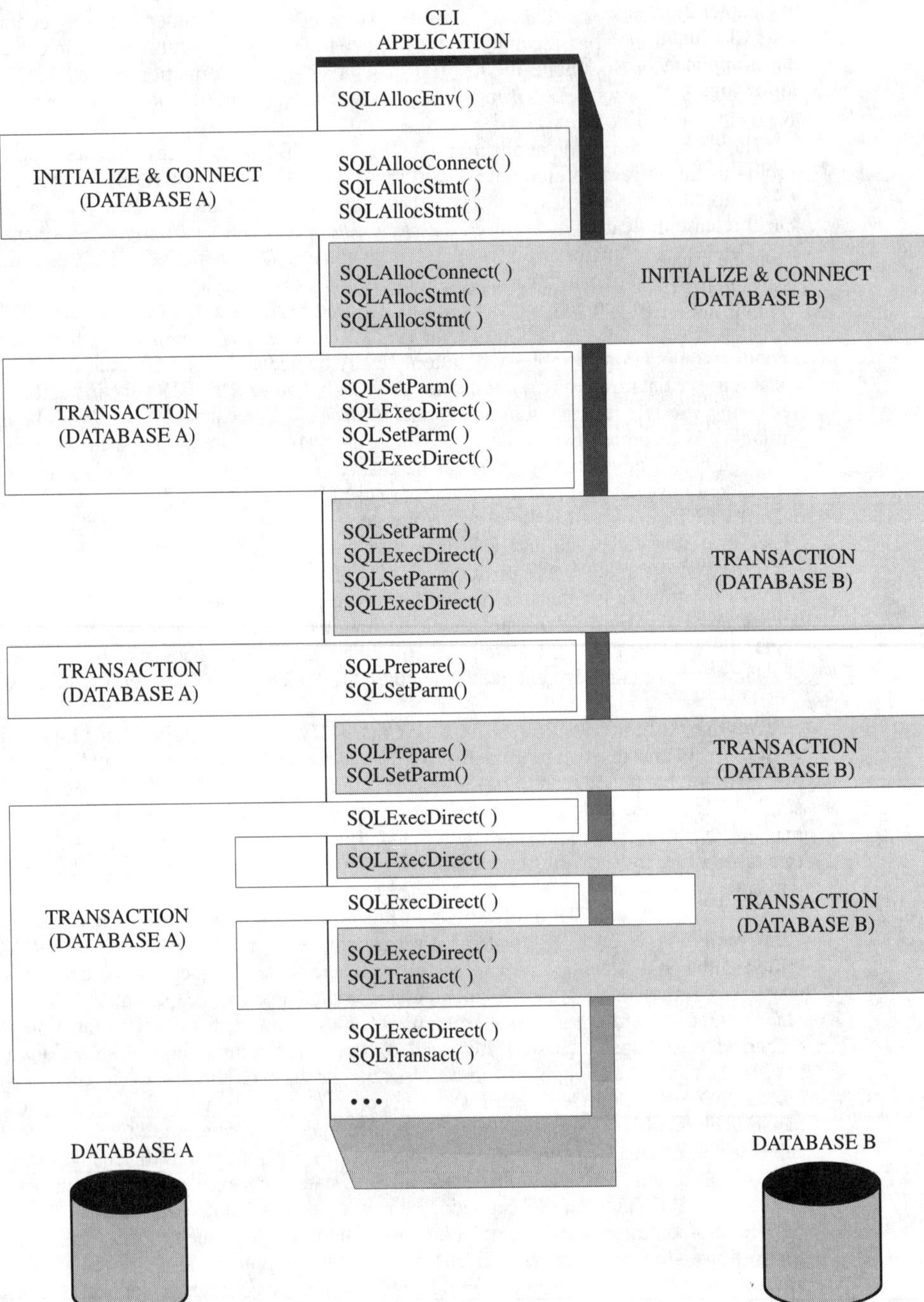

FIGURE 5.3 Transaction boundaries in a CLI application that uses multiple connects.

in Chapter 2). Likewise, it is not a good idea to use the auto-commit mode or to call the SQLTransact() CLI function call after each SQL statement is executed because this increases overhead and reduces application performance. When trying to decide the best time to end a transaction, consider the following:

- Only the current transaction can be committed or rolled back, so all dependent SQL statements should be kept within the same transaction.
- Various table and row locks can be held by the current transaction. Ending the current transaction will release these locks and allow other applications access to the data.
- Once a transaction has successfully been committed or rolled back, it is fully recoverable from the system log files. Any transaction that is open at the time of a system failure or application program trap is not recoverable, so end transactions as soon as is reasonably possible.

> Note: DB2 guarantees that successfully committed or rolled back transactions are fully recoverable from the system log files. This might not be true for other database products. When developing applications for multiple database packages, refer to their documentation to determine when transactions are recoverable.

When defining transaction boundaries, keep in mind that all resources associated with the transaction, except those associated with a held cursor, are released, but prepared SQL statements, cursor names, bound parameters, and column bindings are maintained from one transaction to the next. This means that once an SQL statement has been prepared, it does not need to be prepared again, even after a COMMIT or ROLLBACK occurs, as long as it remains associated with the same statement handle. By default, cursors are preserved after a transaction is committed and emptied after a transaction is rolled back.

Freeing SQL Statement Handles. After the results of an executed SQL statement are processed, the SQL statement handle's data object that was allocated when the transaction processing began needs to be freed. You can free SQL statement handles by invoking the SQLFreeStmt() CLI function call. This CLI function call can perform one or more of the following tasks:

- Unbind all previously bound column application variables
- Unbind all previously bound parameter application variables
- Close any open cursors and discard their results
- Drop the SQL statement handle and release all associated resources

> Note: Once an SQL statement handle is freed it can be reused, provided it has not been dropped. If an SQL statement handle is reused, however, any cached access plan for the SQL statement associated with that handle will be discarded.

The Termination Task

The *termination task* is located at the end of the CLI application source-code file. This is where all the resources allocated by the initialization task are freed and returned to the operating system. As you have already seen, these resources consist of an environment handle and one or more connection handles that point to data storage areas. You can free the environment data storage area by calling the SQLFreeEnv() CLI function, using the environment handle as a parameter. Then you can free all connection data storage areas by calling the SQLFreeConnect() CLI function, using a connection handle as a parameter. The SQLFreeConnect() CLI function call must be made for each connection handle that exists. After these data storage areas are freed, the unique handles that identified them can be used by other tasks in other source-code files.

ERROR HANDLING

In the last chapter, you saw that error handling is an important part of every DB2 embedded SQL database application program. The same holds true for CLI applications and, like embedded SQL applications, the best way to handle error conditions is with a common error-handling routine. Whenever a CLI function call is executed, a special value known as a *return code* is returned to the calling application. A common error-handling routine should first determine whether or not an error or warning condition has occurred by checking this return-code value. If the common error-handling routine discovers that an error or warning has occurred, it should examine the SQLCA data structure and/or SQLSTATE, and process the error accordingly. At a minimum, an error-handling routine should notify users that an error or warning has occurred and provide enough information so the problem can be corrected.

Evaluating Return Codes

As mentioned earlier, whenever a CLI function call is executed, a return-code value is returned to the calling application. The following is a list of all possible return codes that can be generated by a CLI function:

SQL_SUCCESS. The CLI function completed successfully. No additional SQLSTATE information is available.

SQL_SUCCESS_WITH_INFO. The CLI function completed successfully, with a warning or other information.

SQL_NO_DATA_FOUND. The function returned successfully, but no relevant data was found.

SQL_INVALID_HANDLE. The CLI function failed due to an invalid input handle (environment handle, connection handle, or statement handle).

SQL_NEED_DATA. The application tried to execute an SQL statement, but the CLI function call failed because parameter data was missing that the application had indicated would be available (passed) at execution time.

SQL_ERROR. The CLI function failed.

The program should always check the return-code value after a CLI function call is executed to determine whether or not the call was successful. In the event a CLI function was not successful, the SQLSTATE can be examined to provide additional information about what caused the CLI function call to fail.

Evaluating SQLSTATEs (Diagnostic Messages)

Although the CLI function return code notifies the application program if an error or warning condition prevented the CLI function call from executing properly, it does not provide the application (or the developer or the user) with specific information about what caused the error or warning condition to occur. Since information about an error or warning condition is usually necessary, DB2 (as well as other relational database products) has a set of diagnostic error message codes that are referred to as SQLSTATEs. Therefore, SQLSTATEs can help determine exactly what went wrong whenever a CLI function call fails. Since different database servers often have different diagnostic message codes, DB2 provides a standard set of SQLSTATEs that are defined by the X/Open CLI and the emerging ISO standard specification. This standardization of SQLSTATEs allows application developers to use consistent error and warning message routines across different relational database product platforms.

SQLSTATEs are alphanumeric strings, five characters (bytes) in length, with the format *ccsss*, where *cc* indicates the error message class and *sss* indicates the error message subclass. Any SQL-

STATE with a class of **01** is a warning, any SQLSTATE with a class of **S1** is an error that was generated by either the DB2 CLI or the ODBC driver, and any SQLSTATE with a class of **IM** is an error that was generated only by the ODBC driver manager.

> Note: The X/Open CLI and the emerging ISO standard specification has reserved class HY for CLI implementations, which are currently equivalent to the S1 class. IBM still uses the S1 class in order to line up with ODBC version 2. Take this into consideration if you are developing applications that will follow the X/Open standard in the future.

The SQLError() CLI function can be used to retrieve SQLSTATEs from the database server. This CLI function also returns a native error code if the actual error code was generated by the server. When connected to DB2, the native error code will always be the SQLCODE value. If the error code was generated by the DB2 CLI driver instead of the database server, then the native error code will be set to –99999. SQLSTATEs include both additional IBM-defined SQLSTATEs returned by the database server and DB2 CLI-defined SQLSTATEs for conditions not defined in the X/Open CLI standard specification. This is done so the maximum amount of diagnostic information is returned to the calling application. When executing CLI database application programs on the Windows operating system with ODBC, you can also receive ODBC-defined SQLSTATEs.

The following is a set of guidelines to be considered whenever you use SQLSTATEs in your application:

- Always check the CLI function return code before calling the SQLError() CLI function call to determine whether or not diagnostic information is available.
- Use the standard set of SQLSTATEs rather than the native error codes to increase application portability.
- Build dependencies only on the subset of DB2 CLI SQLSTATEs that are defined by the X/Open CLI and the emerging ISO standard specification, and return any additional ones as information only (*dependencies* is when the application makes logic-flow decisions based on specific SQLSTATEs).
- For maximum diagnostic information, return the text message along with the SQLSTATE value (if applicable, the text message will also include the IBM-defined SQLSTATE). It is also useful for the application to print out the name of the function that returned the error.

Evaluating SQLCA Return Codes

You saw in the last chapter that embedded SQL applications rely on the SQLCA data structure for information about the success or failure of an SQL statement's execution. Although CLI applications can retrieve much of the same information by evaluating the SQLSTATEs, they might still need to examine the SQLCA data structure. You can use the SQLGetSQLCA() CLI function call, if needed, to retrieve information about the last SQL statement executed. It is important to remember that the SQLCA structure will contain meaningful information only if the last executed SQL statement interacted with the database (i.e., a CONNECT, PREPARE, EXECUTE, FETCH, or DISCONNECT SQL statement).

CREATING EXECUTABLE APPLICATIONS

Once your CLI source-code files are written, the next step is to convert them into an executable DB2 database application program. This conversion process involves the following steps:

1. Compile the source-code files to create object modules.
2. Link the object modules to create an executable program.

After you have written a CLI source-code file, you must compile it with a high-level language compiler (such as VisualAge C++, Watcom C/C++, or Borland C/C++). The high-level language compiler converts the source-code file into an object module that the linker will use to create the executable program. Once the source file has been compiled without errors, the resulting object module is input to the linker. The linker combines specified object modules, high-level language libraries, and DB2 libraries to produce an executable application (provided no errors or unresolved external references occur). For OS/2 systems, this executable application can be either an executable load module (.EXE) or a dynamic link library (.DLL). For AIX systems, the executable application can be either an executable load module or a shared library. Figure 5.4 illustrates the conversion from source-code file to executable application.

RUNNING, TESTING, AND DEBUGGING CLI APPLICATIONS

Once your application program has been successfully compiled and linked, you can run the program and determine whether or not it performs as expected. You should be able to run your DB2 application program just like you would run any other application program on your particular operating system. If problems occur, you can use the following to help test and debug your code:

- When compiling and linking, specify the proper compiler and linker options so you can use the executable program with a symbolic debugger (usually provided with the high-level language compiler).
- Make full use of the SQLError() CLI function call. Display all generated error message and return codes whenever a CLI function call fails.

ADVANTAGES AND DISADVANTAGES OF USING CLI FUNCTION CALLS

DB2's call-level interface offers the following key advantages over embedded SQL:

- CLI provides a consistent interface for executing SQL statements, regardless of which database server the application is connected to.
- CLI increases the portability of applications by removing the dependence on database-specific precompilers. Applications can be distributed as ready-to-run executable programs or as runtime libraries, but not as source code, which must be precompiled and rebuilt for each database product.
- CLI applications do not have to be bound to each database they connect to. Instead, only the bind files shipped with DB2 CLI need to be bound to a database once in order for many CLI applications to run against it.
- CLI applications can connect to multiple databases and they can establish multiple connections to the same database within a single application. In order to connect concurrently to one or more database servers, the application must call the SQLAllocConnect() CLI function for each connection it needs. You can then use the resulting connection handles to request database connections via the SQLConnect() CLI function call.
- CLI is better suited for client-server environments in which the target database product is not known at the time the application is built.
- CLI eliminates the need for application-controlled global data storage areas, such as the SQLCA, SQLDA, and SQLCHAR data structures needed by embedded SQL. By replacing these global data storage areas with allocated storage areas that the application can reference via handles, CLI enables the development of multithreaded applications in which each thread can have its own connection and separate commit scope area.
- CLI provides enhanced parameter input and data fetching capability by allowing you to specify arrays of data on input by retrieving multiple rows of data directly into an array and executing an SQL statement multiple times to produce different result sets (through the use of parameter markers). CLI also allows you to retrieve multiple rows generated from a stored procedures call.

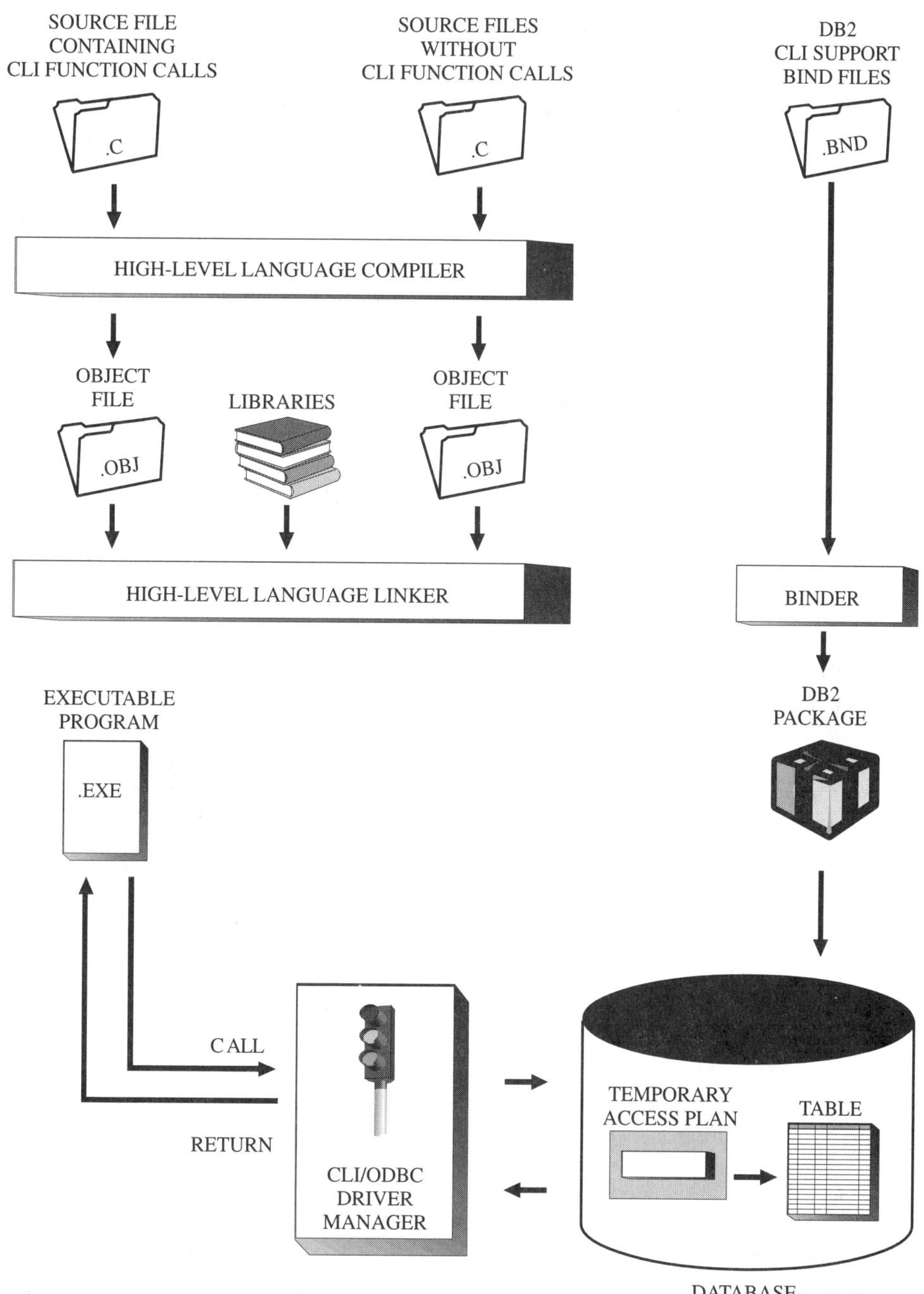

FIGURE 5.4 Process to convert CLI source-code files into executable DB2 application programs.

- CLI provides a consistent interface to query system catalog information contained in the catalog tables from various database products. This shields the application from catalog changes across different releases of database servers, as well as differences among different database products.
- CLI provides extended data conversion, resulting in less application code requirements when converting information between various SQL and high-level language data types.
- CLI incorporates both the ODBC and the X/Open CLI function calls, both of which are accepted industry-standard specifications. CLI is also aligned with the emerging ISO CLI standard. This means you can apply any time already spent learning these specifications to CLI application development.

CLI applications, however, cannot take advantage of the API calls offered by DB2 (e.g., Get Error Message, Backup, and Restore) and still remain portable. DB2's APIs can still be called from a CLI application, but the CLI application can no longer execute on other database platforms without first being modified, recompiled, or both. Another disadvantage of CLI is shown in a performance comparison between dynamic and static SQL. As described in the last chapter, dynamic SQL is prepared at runtime and static SQL is written directly into the source-code file and prepared when the source-code file is precompiled. Since preparing SQL statements requires additional processing time, static SQL is usually more efficient. If you feel your application should use static SQL in order to increase performance, then using DB2's call-level interface might not be an option.

You can take advantage of both CLI and embedded SQL by creating static SQL stored procedures and invoking them from within a CLI application. It is also possible to write key modules with embedded SQL and link them to CLI applications. This approach, however, complicates the application design and should be considered only if static SQL stored procedures, for some reason, cannot be used.

SUMMARY

The goal of this chapter is to provide you with an overview of how call-level interface (CLI) application source-code files are structured and to describe the processes involved in converting CLI application source-code files into executable database application programs. You should now understand how to use the IBM Interactive CLI application to prototype your CLI function call. You should also understand how applications using embedded SQL statements differ from applications using CLI function calls. You should know that a CLI application source-code file is divided into the following three tasks:

- Initialization
- Transaction processing
- Termination

You should also know that the transaction processing task is responsible for performing the following five steps:

1. Allocating statement handles
2. Preparing and executing SQL statements
3. Processing the results
4. Committing or rolling back the transaction
5. Freeing all allocated statement handles

You should understand how to process errors with a common error-handling routine by evaluating CLI function call return codes, SQLSTATE values, and SQLCA values. You should also be familiar with the following steps for converting embedded SQL source-code files to executable database applications:

- Compiling
- Linking

Finally, you should know the advantages and disadvantages of using CLI function calls and be aware of how to run, test, and debug your DB2 CLI database application once it has been compiled and linked. The next chapter completes this examination of DB2's application development toolset by looking at DB2's application programming interface (API) calls and demonstrating how API database applications are developed.

CHAPTER 6

WRITING API APPLICATIONS

6

DB2 application programming interface (API) calls are a set of functions that are not part of the standard SQL sublanguage or the call-level interface (CLI) routines. Where SQL and CLI are used to add, modify, and retrieve data from a database, API calls provide an interface to the DB2 Database Manager. API calls are often included in embedded SQL or CLI applications to provide additional functionality not covered by SQL or CLI (such as starting and stopping DB2's Database Manager). However, you can develop complete API applications that control database environments, modify database configurations, and perform administrative tasks. You can also use API applications to fine-tune database performance and perform routine database maintenance.

> Note: When API calls are added to a CLI application, its portability is reduced because other database products will not know what to do when they encounter DB2-specific API calls.

In the first part of this chapter I will describe the basic structure of an API database application source-code file. Then I will describe the types of API calls available with DB2, their naming conventions, and the special data structures some API calls use. Next I will discuss how to evaluate API return codes and display error messages. The chapter concludes with a discussion of using the compiler and linker to convert an API application source-code file to an executable program. Let's begin with the basic structure of an API application source-code file.

THE BASIC STRUCTURE OF AN API SOURCE-CODE FILE

An API application program source-code file written in C or C++ can be divided into two main parts: the header and the body. The header contains, among other things, the host-language compiler preprocessor statements that are used to merge the contents of the appropriate DB2 API header file(s) with the host-language source-code file. These header files contain the API function prototype definitions and the structure templates for the special data structures required by some of the APIs. The body contains the local variable declaration statements, the variable assignment statements, and the statements that invoke the desired API calls. The body also contains additional processing statements and error-handling statements required for the application to perform the desired task. The sample source code in Figure 6.1 illustrates these two parts, along with some of the C language statements that might be found in them.

API SOURCE CODE FRAMEWORK

```
/* Include Appropriate Header Files*/
#include <stdio.h>
#include <stdlib.h>
#include <string.h>
  ...
#include <sqljra.h>
#include <sqljacb.h>
#include <sqlenv.h>
/* Declare Function Prototypes */
int main(int argc, char *argv []);
  ...

/* Declare Procedure */
int main(int argc, char *argv[])
{
    /* Declare Local Variables */
    struct sqledinfo *pDB_DirInfo = NULL;
    unsigned short usHandle = 0;
    unsigned short usDBCount = 0;
    struct sqlca   sqlRetCode;
    ...
    /*Get The Database Directory Information */
    sqledosd(0, &usHandle, &usDBCount, &sqlRetCode);
    /*Scan The Directory Buffer And Print Info */
    for (; usDBCount !=0; usDBCount--)
        {
        sqledgne(usHandle, &pDB_DirInfo, &sqlRetCode)
        printf("%.8s\t", pDB_DirInfo->alias);
        printf("%.8s\t", pDB_DirInfo->alias);
        printf("%.30s\n", pDB_DirInfo->comment);
        }
    /* Free Resources (Directory Info Buffer) */
    sqledcls (usHandle, &sqlRetCode);
    ...
    /* Return To The Operating System */
    return((int) sqlRetCode.sqlcode);
}
```

HEADER (header files and function prototypes) — BODY (procedure)

FIGURE 6.1 Parts of an API source-code file.

TYPES OF API FUNCTION CALLS

DB2's rich set of API function calls are broken down into the following categories:

- Database manager control APIs
- Database manager configuration APIs
- Database control APIs
- Database configuration APIs
- Database directory management APIs
- DCS directory management APIs
- Node directory management APIs
- NetWare support APIs
- Backup/recovery APIs
- Operational utility APIs

- Database monitoring APIs
- Data utility APIs
- General application programming APIs
- Application preparation APIs
- Remote server connection APIs
- Table-space management APIs
- Transaction APIs
- Miscellaneous APIs

Each API function call falls into one of these categories according to its functionality. The following describes each of these categories in more detail.

Database manager control APIs. Database manager control APIs are a set of function calls that start and stop the DB2 database manager background process. This background process must be running before any application can gain access to a DB2 database, and you can start it either by embedding the START DATABASE MANAGER API in your application program or by issuing the START DATABASE MANAGER command from the operating system command prompt (or a shell script).

Database manager configuration APIs. The database manager configuration APIs are a set of function calls for retrieving, changing, or resetting the information stored in the DB2 database manager configuration file. The DB2 database manager configuration file contains configuration parameters that affect the overall performance of DB2's database manager and its global resources. These APIs are rarely used in embedded SQL or CLI application programs; only API application programs that provide some type of generalized database utilities have a use for these API calls.

Database control APIs. Database control APIs are a set of function calls that create new databases, drop (delete) or migrate existing databases, and restart DB2 databases that were not stopped correctly (this usually happens if a database was open when a system failure occurred).

Database configuration APIs. Every database has its own configuration file that is created automatically when the CREATE DATABASE API call (or command) is executed. Database configuration APIs are a set of function calls used to retrieve, change, or reset the information stored in these database configuration files. Each database configuration file contains configuration parameters that affect the performance of an individual database and its resource requirements. These APIs are rarely used in embedded SQL or CLI application programs; only API application programs that provide some type of generalized database utilities use them.

Database directory management APIs. Database directory management APIs are a set of function calls that catalog and uncatalog databases, change database comments (descriptions), and view the entries stored in the DB2 database directory.

DCS directory management APIs. DCS directory management APIs are a set of function calls used to catalog and uncatalog databases accessed via the distributed database connection services package. These APIs can also view the entries stored in the DB2 DDCS directory.

Node directory management APIs. Node directory management APIs are a set of function calls that catalog and uncatalog remote workstations, and view the entries stored in the DB2 workstation directory.

NetWare support APIs. NetWare support APIs are a set of function calls that register and deregister a DB2 database server workstation's address in the NetWare bindery (on the network server).

Backup/recovery APIs. Backup/recovery APIs are a set of function calls that back up and restore databases, perform roll-forward recoveries on databases, and view the entries stored in the DB2 recovery history files. Every database has its own recovery file, which is created automatically when the CREATE DATABASE API call (or command) is executed. Once created, this history file is automatically updated whenever the database or its table space(s) are backed up or restored. The recovery history file can reset the database to the state it was in at any specific point in time.

Operational utility APIs. Operational utility APIs are a set of function calls used to change lock states on table spaces, reorganize the data in database tables, update statistics on database tables, and force all users off a database (i.e., break all connections to a database).

Database monitoring APIs. Database monitoring APIs are a set of function calls used to collect information about the current state of a DB2 database.

Data utility APIs. Data utility APIs are a set of function calls that import data from and export data to various PC and RISC/6000 file formats.

General application programming APIs. General application programming APIs are a set of function calls used in conjunction with embedded SQL statements, CLI function calls, and/or other API function calls to develop robust database application programs. These APIs perform such tasks as retrieving SQL and API error messages, retrieving SQLSTATEs, installing signal and interrupt handlers, and copying and freeing memory buffers used by other APIs.

Application preparation APIs. Application preparation APIs are a set of function calls that precompile, bind, and rebind embedded SQL source-code files.

Remote server connection APIs. Remote server connection APIs are a set of function calls that attach to and detach from workstations (nodes) at which instance-level functions are executed. The functions essentially establish (and remove) a logical instance attachment to a specified workstation and start (or end) a physical communications connection to that workstation.

Table-space management APIs. Table-space management APIs are a set of function calls that set table spaces and retrieve information about existing table spaces.

Transaction APIs. Transaction APIs are a set of function calls that allow two-phase commit-compliant applications to execute problem-solving functions on transactions that are tying up system resources (otherwise known as *in-doubt transactions*). For DB2, these resources include locks on tables and indexes, log space, and transaction storage memory. Transaction APIs are used in applications that need to query, commit, roll back, or cancel in-doubt transactions. You can cancel in-doubt transactions by removing log records and releasing log pages associated with the transaction.

Miscellaneous APIs. Miscellaneous APIs are a set of function calls that do not fall into any of the categories previously listed. Some of these APIs retrieve user authorization information, to set and retrieve settings for connections made by application processes, and to provide accounting information to DRDA servers.

API NAMING CONVENTIONS

Although most embedded SQL statements and CLI routines are endowed with long and descriptive names, DB2's API calls do not follow this pattern. Instead, each API function name is creatively packed with as much information as possible in eight characters. The conventions used by DB2 for naming API function calls are as follows:

- Each API name has a maximum of eight characters.
- Each API name begins with the letters *sql*.
- The fourth character in each API name denotes the functional area to which the API call belongs:

  -e for C-specific environment services.
  -u for C-specific general utilities.
  -f for C-specific configuration services.
  -a for C-specific application services.
  -m for C-specific monitor services.
  -b for C-specific table and table-space query services.
  -o for C-specific SQLSTATE services.
  -g for a generic (language-independent) version of the above services.
- The last four characters describe the function. As you might imagine, this four-letter limitation results in some strange abbreviations.

There is a C-language version of API function calls that are optimized for the C programming language. There is also a language-independent generic API call that corresponds to almost every C-language API call available. If you are developing an API application program with C or C++, you should use the C-language specific version of the API calls. If, however, you are developing an API application program with another language, such as COBOL, REXX, or FORTRAN, you must use the generic API calls instead of their C-language counterparts.

API DATA STRUCTURES

Most API application source-code files must contain declaration statements that create special data structure variables. These special data structure variables are used to either provide input information to or store return information from specific API calls. Table 6.1 lists the names of the data structure templates stored in the DB2 API header files, along with brief descriptions of what each data structure is used for.

TABLE 6.1 Data Structures Used by DB2's API Calls

Data structure name	Function
SQLA_FLAGINFO	Holds flagger information
SQL-AUTHORIZATIONS	Returns authorizations information to an application program
SQLB_TBSCONTQRY_DATA	Returns container data to an application program
SQLB_TBSQRY_DATA	Returns table-space data to an application program
SQLB_TBS_STATS	Returns additional table-space statistics to an application program
SQLCA	Returns error and warning information to an application program
SQLCHAR	Transfers variable-length data between an application program and DB2
SQLDA	Transfers collections of data between an application program and DB2
SQLDCOL	Passes column information to the IMPORT and EXPORT APIs.
SQL_DIR_ENTRY	Transfers database connection services directory information between an application program and DB2
SQLE_CONN_SETTING	Specifies connection setting types and values
SQLEDBCOUNTRYINFO	Transfers country information between an application program and DB2
SQLEDBDESC	Passes creation parameters to the CREATE DATABASE API
SQLEDINFO	Returns database directory information about a single entry in the system or local database directory to an application program
SQLENINFO	Returns node directory information about a single entry in the node directory to an application program
SQLE_NODE_CPIC	Passes information for cataloging CPIC nodes to the CATALOG NODE API
SQLE_NODE_IPXSPX	Passes information for cataloging IPX/SPX nodes to the CATALOG NODE API
SQLE_NODE_LOCAL	Passes information for cataloging LOCAL nodes to the CATALOG NODE API
SQLE_NODE_NETB	Passes NetBIOS parameters for nodes cataloged using the NetBIOS protocol to the CATALOG NODE API
SQLE_NODE_STRUCT	Passes information for cataloging nodes to the CATALOG NODE API
SQLE_NODE_TCPIP	Passes information for cataloging TCP/IP nodes to the CATALOG NODE API

TABLE 6.1 Data Structures Used by DB2's API Calls *(Continued)*

Data structure name	Function
SQLE_REG_NWBINDERY	Passes information for registering or deregistering the DB2 server in/from the bindery on the NetWare file server
SQLUEXPT_OUT	Transfers EXPORT information between an application program and DB2
SQLFUPD	Passes configuration file information to DB2
SQLMA	Sends database system monitor requests from an application program to DB2
SQLM_COLLECTED	Transfers database system monitor collection count information between an application program and DB2
SQLM_RECORDING_GROUP	Transfers database system monitor monitor group information between an application program and DB2
SQLOPT	Passes bind options information to the BIND API and precompile options information to the PRECOMPILE PROGRAM API
SQLUHINFO	Passes information from the recovery history file to an application program
SQLUIMPT_IN	Transfers IMPORT information between an application program and DB2 (input)
SQLUIMPT_OUT	Transfers IMPORT information between an application program and DB2 (output)
SQLULOAD_IN	Transfers LOAD information between an application program and DB2 (input)
SQLULOAD_OUT	Transfers LOAD information between an application program and DB2 (output)
SQLU_MEDIA_LIST	Holds a list of target media (BACKUP) or source media (RESTORE) for a backup image
SQLU_TABLESPACE_BKRST_LIST	Passes a list of table-space names to an application program
SQLXA_RECOVER	Provides a list of in-doubt transactions to an application program
SQLXA_XID	Identifies an in-doubt transaction to an application program

API data structure templates are made available to C and C++ applications when the appropriate compiler preprocessor statements (#include <*xxxxxxxx*.h>) are placed in the header portion of the source-code file. Once the structure templates are made available to the source-code file, the corresponding structure variables must be declared and initialized before they can be used in an API function call. In addition to API-specific structure templates, every source-code file that contains one or more API calls must, at a minimum, declare a variable of the SQLCA data structure type. This variable is used by almost every API call to store status information when the API call completes execution.

ERROR HANDLING

You have already seen that error handling is an important part of every DB2 embedded SQL and CLI database application program. The same holds true for DB2 API applications. Whenever an API call is executed, status information is returned to the calling application by the following:

- The API function call return code
- The SQLCA data structure variable
- The SQLSTATE

Like embedded SQL and CLI applications, the best way to handle error conditions is with a common error-handling routine (refer to Chapter 4 for more information).

Evaluating Return Codes

Whenever an API function call is executed, a special value, known as a *return code*, is returned to the calling application. A common error-handling routine should first determine whether or not an error or warning condition has occurred by checking this return-code value. If the common error-handling routine discovers that an error or warning has occurred, it should process the error accordingly. At a minimum, an error-handling routine should notify users that an error or warning has occurred and provide enough information to correct the problem.

Evaluating SQLCA Return Codes

I noted earlier that each API application must declare a variable of the SQLCA data structure type. Whenever an API call is invoked from an application program, the address of this variable is almost always passed as the last parameter for the API call. This variable is then used by DB2 to store status information when the API call completes execution.

If an error or warning condition occurs during the execution of the API function call, an error return-code value is returned to the calling application and additional information about the warning or error is placed in the SQLCA data structure variable. To save space, this information is stored in the form of a coded number. You can invoke the GET ERROR MESSAGE API by using this data structure variable to translate the coded number into a more meaningful description, which can then be used to correct the problem. Incorporating the GET ERROR MESSAGE API call into your API application during the development phase will help you quickly determine when there is a problem in the way an API call was invoked.

Evaluating SQLSTATEs

If an error or warning condition occurs during the execution of an API function call, a standardized error-code value is also placed in the SQLCA data structure variable. Like the SQLCA return-code value, the SQLSTATE information is stored in the form of a coded number. You can use the GET SQLSTATE API to translate this coded number into a more meaningful error-message description, which can be used to correct the problem. Incorporating the GET SQLSTATE API call into your API application during the development phase can also help you quickly determine when there is a problem in the way an API call was invoked.

CREATING EXECUTABLE APPLICATIONS

Once you have written your API source-code files, you must convert them into an executable DB2 database application program. This is a two-step process:

1. Compile the source-code files to create object modules.
2. Link the object modules to create an executable program.

After you have written an API source-code file, you must compile it with a high-level language compiler (such as VisualAge C++, Watcom C/C++, and Borland C/C++). The high-level language compiler converts the source-code file into an object module used by the linker to create the executable program. Once the source file has been compiled without errors, the resulting object module is input to the linker. The linker combines specified object modules, high-level language libraries, and DB2

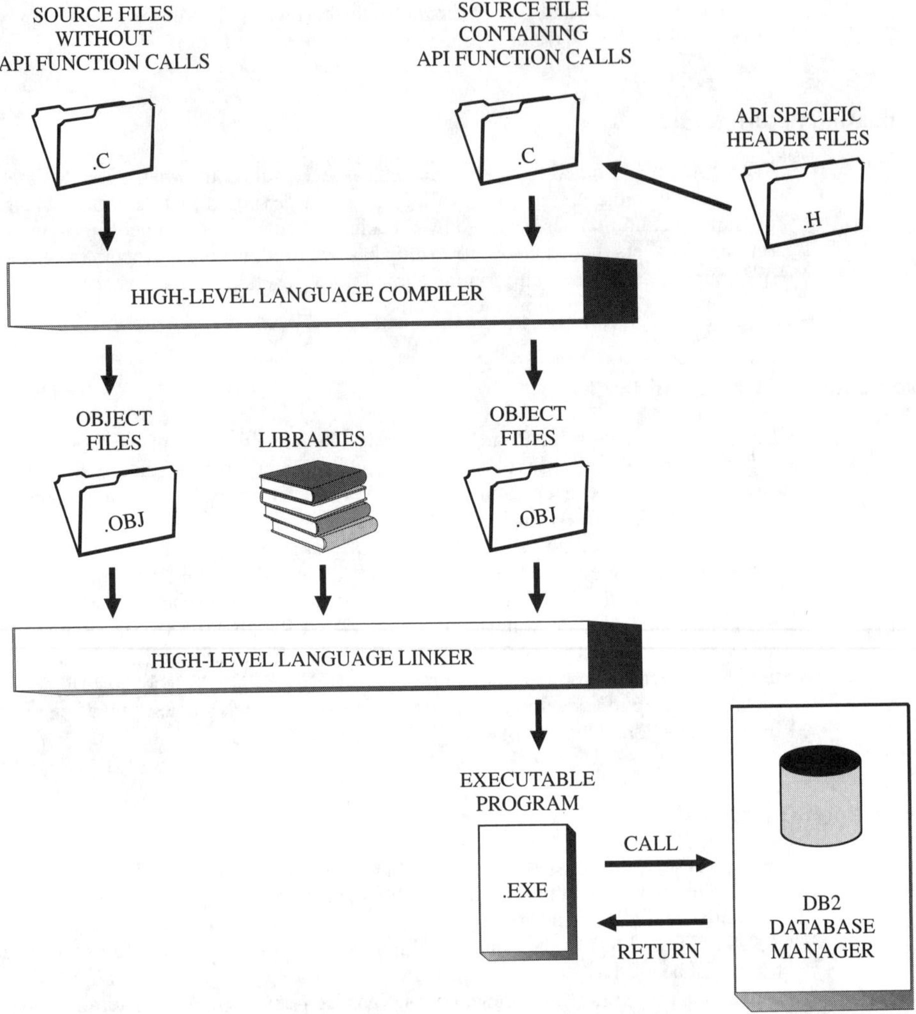

FIGURE 6.2 Process for converting API source-code files into executable DB2 application programs.

libraries to produce an executable application (provided no errors or unresolved external references occur). For OS/2 systems, the executable application can be either an executable load module (.EXE) or a dynamic link library (.DLL). For AIX systems, the executable application can be either an executable load module or a shared library. Figure 6.2 illustrates the process of converting a source-code file to an executable application.

RUNNING, TESTING, AND DEBUGGING API APPLICATIONS

Once your application program is successfully compiled and linked, you can run the program and determine whether or not it performs as expected. You should be able to run your DB2 application program as you would any other application program on your particular operating system. If problems occur, you can do the following to help test and debug your code:

- When compiling and linking, specify the proper compiler and linker options so the executable program can be used with a symbolic debugger (usually provided with the high-level language compiler).
- Make full use of the GET ERROR MESSAGE and GET SQLSTATE API function calls.
- Display all generated error message and return codes whenever an API function call fails.

Note: Because some APIs require a database connection before they can be executed, consider creating a temporary database to use while testing your API application to avoid inadvertently corrupting a production database.

SUMMARY

The goal of this chapter was to provide you with an overview of how application programming interface (API) application source-code files are structured and to describe the processes involved in converting API application source-code files into executable database application programs. You should know that API calls are divided according to their functionality, into the following groups:

- Database manager control APIs
- Database manager configuration APIs
- Database control APIs
- Database configuration APIs
- Database directory management APIs
- DCS directory management APIs
- Node directory management APIs
- NetWare support APIs
- Backup/recovery APIs
- Operational utility APIs
- Database monitoring APIs
- Data utility APIs
- General application programming APIs
- Application preparation APIs
- Remote server connection APIs
- Table-space management APIs
- Transaction APIs
- Miscellaneous APIs

You should also be familiar with the API routine naming conventions and the special data structures they require. You should know how to detect errors by evaluating the API return codes and how to translate SQLCA-coded values into useful error messages with the GET ERROR MESSAGE API function call. You should also be familiar with the two-step process of converting embedded SQL source-code files to executable database applications:

- Compiling
- Linking

Finally, you should know how to run, test, and debug your DB2 API database application once it has been compiled and linked. The next chapter will add to what you already know about developing embedded SQL, CLI, and API applications by describing some tips and techniques for optimizing your application's performance.

CHAPTER 7

IMPROVING APPLICATION PERFORMANCE

7

You can use a number of programming techniques to improve the runtime performance of DB2 database applications. In general, any technique that minimizes the use of system resources or reduces the amount of time to access data in very large tables will improve application performance. In the first part of this chapter, I will describe some of these techniques and show you how to construct SQL queries so they maintain data integrity while reducing execution time. Then I will examine indexes and establish useful guidelines for you to follow when deciding whether or not to create one. Next, I will discuss precompiler optimization classes and show you how to rewrite queries for optimum performance. Finally, I will show you how to use table-space management, row blocking, transaction locking, and code-page management to increase application performance. Let's begin by looking at how to structure SQL queries so they require the shortest execution time.

TUNING EMBEDDED SQL QUERIES

Structured query language (SQL) is an extremely flexible language, so you can use it to write many SQL queries in several different forms that produce the same results. However, the way you write your SQL queries can greatly affect the performance of an application since some forms execute much faster than others. The greatest performance variances occur in queries that contain SELECT SQL statements and those that access two or more tables.

Queries Containing SELECT SQL Statements

SELECT SQL statements can take a long time to execute if they are not properly coded and structured. Because they can vary greatly in structure, the following are a few things to keep in mind when writing these types of SQL statements:

- Specify only necessary columns when creating a select list. In other words, if you don't need the data, don't retrieve it. Although it might be simpler to specify all columns with an asterisk (SELECT *), doing so will add processing requirements to your query, cause it to retrieve data that might not be used, and negatively affect overall application performance.
- Limit the number of rows being selected by using predicates (=, <, >, BETWEEN, NOT, IN, LIKE, etc.) to restrict the answer set to only the rows you require. If you find that your application frequently

uses these predicates against a particular data column, consider creating an index for this column to improve performance.

- Avoid data-type conversions whenever possible. When comparing values, it is usually more efficient to use items of the same data type. Data-type conversions can result in inaccuracies due to limited precision. Performance will be also be reduced due to the additional overhead required by the conversion process. Whenever possible, use integer data types rather than float or decimal data types, and use date-time and numeric data types rather than character data types.
- Specify indexed columns when using DISTINCT, ORDER BY, and GROUP BY SQL clauses. By specifying indexed columns, you greatly reduce the time needed to process the statements. You should also create unique indexes for these columns whenever appropriate. Try to avoid using these clauses unless they are absolutely necessary.
- If the number of rows you need in your data set is significantly less than the possible number of rows that could be returned by your query, specify the OPTIMIZE FOR clause with your SELECT SQL statement.
- Specify the FOR UPDATE OF clause when creating cursors that will be used to update data. This will cause DB2 to initially choose more appropriate locking levels, thus possibly avoiding a lock escalation, lock conversion, or deadlock cycle.
- Avoid using the SELECT COUNT(*) SQL statement to check for the existence of rows in large tables. Counting all rows in large tables can greatly affect performance. When checking for the existence of rows in a table, it is more efficient to perform a single-row selection (SELECT INTO) and evaluate the SQLCODE value to determine whether or not data exists.
- Whenever possible, use dynamic SQL and parameter markers for long or complex queries. This allows the optimizer to select an access path based on the specific value of the parameter marker rather than the unknown value of a host variable. Access plans based on specific values can significantly increase performance.

Queries That Access Two or More Tables

Queries that access two or more tables can also take a long time to execute if they are not coded properly. When writing this type of query, consider using joins rather than subqueries (SELECT SQL statements that contain other SELECT SQL statements) whenever possible. Queries containing joins can usually be processed much more efficiently than queries with multiple SELECT SQL statements (as is the case with subqueries). The following are a few other things to keep in mind when writing queries that access two or more tables:

- If possible, avoid using expressions and OR clauses with join predicates. Some expressions and the OR clause might not always be usable by DB2; if so, the most efficient join method will not be selected.

- Use joins instead of correlated subqueries whenever possible. Joins usually require less time and resources to process than correlated subqueries, because a correlated subquery must be reevaluated for each row of the outer query.

- Use joins instead of noncorrelated subqueries preceded by the IN predicate whenever possible. Even though a noncorrelated subquery is evaluated only once, the column used with the IN predicate is compared against the subquery's output (a set of values) by every row of the table referenced in the outer SELECT statement. If large tables are used, this comparison can take a significant amount of time.

- Whenever possible, create an index on the column(s) in each table used by the join. A join can be processed more efficiently if related indexes are defined on each of the columns referenced in the join predicate.

Compound Queries

Compound queries group several SQL statements into a single executable block. Although each SQL statement in a compound query could be executed individually, grouping them together into one executable block reduces the amount of overhead DB2 needs to process them. When executing compound queries on remote servers, you also reduce the amount of requests that have to be transmitted across the network between your application and DB2.

INDEX MANAGEMENT

As you have just seen in the previous guidelines, indexes play an important part in application performance. Unfortunately, you have no control over whether or not your application will use an index. DB2 makes this decision for you by evaluating table and index information found in the system catalog views. Therefore, it is up to you to create indexes that can improve performance and to continually collect statistics about these indexes (using the RUNSTATS utility) to keep the system catalog views up to date. In order for you to do this effectively, you must understand how indexes reduce the time it takes to perform a database query.

If an index does not exist for any of the columns specified in a database query, a relation scan must be performed on each table referenced in that query. The larger the table, the longer the relation scan takes. On the other hand, if an index exists for one or more of the specified columns, an index scan can be performed. Index files are generally smaller and require less time to read than an entire database table, particularly if the table is large. Each index entry consists of a search-key value and a pointer to the row containing that value. Since indexes are arranged in ascending or descending order by search-key value, only the bracketed portions of the index file usually need to be scanned. This means that rows can usually be located much faster with an index scan than with a relation scan.

At first glance, it appears that indexes always reduce database access time. A closer look shows, however, that indexes can also adversely affect application performance. Before creating an index to improve application performance, you need to take the following into account:

- Every index requires a certain amount of disk space for storage. The exact amount of required disk space is determined by the size of the table and the size and number of columns in the index.
- Each time an INSERT or DELETE operation is performed on a database table, DB2 must update every index on that table. This is also true for all UPDATE operations that change an index-key value.
- Each time the LOAD utility is used to populate a database table, DB2 must rebuild every index on that table.
- Every index on a table potentially adds an alternative access path for the database query optimizer to consider. This could result in the selection of a less efficient path.

> Note: You can use the SQL Explain facility to determine which index, if any, is used to process your database query.

Guidelines for Creating Indexes

When creating indexes, you need to consider your application program's needs. Whether or not an index should be created depends on the actual data being stored and its intended uses. The following is a set of guidelines on when and how to create indexes:

- If you will perform frequent queries on tables that occupy several data pages (a *data page* is a unit of storage within a table or index, usually 4KB in size), create an index on one or more of the columns referenced by the query.

- If you will search for particular values in a table on a regular basis, create an index on one or more appropriate columns in that table.
- If you plan on joining tables, create an index on the columns used in the join.
- If you will perform frequent queries and transactions that contain a WHERE clause, create an index on the columns specified in the WHERE clause.
- If you will perform frequent queries and transactions that contain an ORDER BY, DISTINCT, or GROUP BY clause, create an index on the columns specified in these clauses.
- Define primary keys and unique keys whenever possible. Unique indexes can help the optimizer avoid performing certain operations, such as sorts.
- Avoid creating indexes that are partial keys of existing index keys. For example, if you created an index using columns A, B, C, and D, then creating a second index on columns A, B, and D is unnecessary.
- Create indexes on foreign keys to improve overall performance of delete and update operations on the parent table.
- When creating multiple-column indexes, specify the column most often used with the = predicate in your application as the primary-key column.

Optimizing Index Performance

You can often improve index performance by storing the index in a different table space than the one that stores other table data. This approach can allow a more efficient use of disk storage devices by reducing the actual movement of the read/write heads. Also, if the index table space resides on a faster device than the table data, the time required to perform an index scan will be much shorter than the time needed to perform a relation scan. If your application frequently uses SQL statements that require data ordering (in other words, the ORDER BY, DISTINCT, and GROUP BY clauses) and there is an appropriate index to satisfy this ordering, the DB2 optimizer might not use the index. This will occur when index clustering is poor or when the table is small enough that it is faster to scan the table and sort it in memory. After creating a new index and routinely thereafter, use the RUNSTATS utility to collect (or update) index statistics. Since the DB2 optimizer uses these statistics to determine whether or not to use an index, you can improve data access performance by keeping them up to date.

> Note: The performance of static SQL statements depends on the statistics of the database at the time the embedded SQL source-code file is precompiled or bound. In most cases, static SQL statements execute faster than the same dynamic SQL statement since the overhead of preparing an executable form of the equivalent dynamic SQL statement is done at runtime. However, if the statistics of the database change, the equivalent dynamic SQL statement will automatically see these changes (and possibly improve in performance) while the static SQL statements will not. For example, if an index is added to a database after a static SQL statement is precompiled, the SQL statement will not be able to take advantage of the new index until the source-code file is precompiled and bound to the database again.

TABLE-SPACE MANAGEMENT

You saw in Chapter 1 that by creating table spaces you can assign the location of a database and its table data to a directory, file, or device. You also saw how to store tables and their corresponding indexes on separate physical storage devices. Now let's take a look at how the characteristics of table spaces can affect the performance of DB2 database applications.

The physical characteristics of the disk media being used to store DB2 data can significantly affect the I/O cost of executing a query. During the precompile process, the SQL optimizer evaluates these I/O costs when it creates an access plan for an SQL statement. The optimizer primarily uses two items to help estimate the I/O costs of accessing data from a table space: overhead and transfer rate. Table-space *overhead* provides a estimate (in milliseconds) of the amount of time needed by the physical disk drive before any data can be read into memory. Overhead activity includes any overhead required by the disk drive's I/O controller, as well as the disk's rotational latency and average seek time. *Transfer rates* provide an estimate (in milliseconds) of the amount of time required to read one page of data into memory. Table space I/O costs can influence the SQL optimizer in a number of ways, including whether or not to use indexes and selecting tables for the inner and outer tables of a join.

When creating a table space, keep in mind that the overhead and transfer rate can increase or decrease overall query performance. For optimal performance, the overhead value for defining a table space should be the best average time needed for disk seeks and latency for all devices to which the table space is assigned. Likewise, the transfer rate value used for defining a table space should be the best average time needed for reading one 4KB page into memory for all devices to which the table space is assigned. Ideally, each device should have similar overhead and transfer-rate characteristics. You can obtain these media-specific values either from the hardware specifications provided with the disk drive or through experimentation.

When considering the I/O cost of accessing data in a table space, keep in mind that the SQL optimizer can also evaluate the potential impact of prefetching data from the disk on overall query performance. The PREFETCHSIZE and EXTENTSIZE values specified when you create a table space define how much data will be written to a data buffer pool before DB2 will use it. By prefetching data, you can significantly reduce the overhead and waiting time associated with reading data from a table space.

You can modify most table-space parameter values with the ALTER TABLESPACE SQL statement. After making changes to a table space, it is a good idea to rebind all applications that access data in that table space to ensure that the SQL optimizer has generated the most efficient data access plans for those applications.

USING THE PRECOMPILER OPTIMIZATION FEATURE

You saw earlier how query structure affects an application's performance. Because you might not always use the best query structures for your application, the SQL precompiler contains a query rewrite stage, which allows you to reorganize your SQL queries into structures that execute more quickly. This query rewrite stage is particularly important for precompiling queries that are very complex, such as those containing many subqueries or joins. When an embedded SQL source-code file is precompiled, you can specify the number of query rewrite rules to apply to SQL statements by providing an optimization class value as a precompiler option. There are five optimization class values to choose from:

0. This class directs the optimizer to use a minimal amount of optimization when precompiling an SQL query. Use this class only in special circumstances that require the lowest possible query compilation overhead, such as an application that contains only very simple dynamic SQL statements.

1. This class directs the optimizer to use a subset of query rewrite rules when precompiling an SQL query. This class is roughly equivalent to the set of query rewrite rules used in version 1.0 of DB2/2 and DB2/6000. Some additional low-cost optimization features not found in the version 1.0 product are also included in this class.

3. This class directs the optimizer to use most query rewrite rules when precompiling an SQL query. This class also incorporates a limited use of composite inner tables and a limited use of Cartesian products when performing optimization. This class is designed for most normal situations and is roughly equivalent to the optimization characteristics used by DB2 for MVS/ESA.

5. This class directs the optimizer to use a significant amount of optimization. This class is ideally suited for situations that have one or more large central tables that contain codes for certain record attributes and are joined with several smaller "look-up" tables to get the values of these codes. This class directs the optimizer to use most of the query rewrite rules when precompiling an SQL query. This class also incorporates dynamic programming join enumerations, including limited use of Cartesian products.

9. This class directs the optimizer to use all query rewrite rules when precompiling an SQL query. This class also incorporates join enumerations, including full use of composite inner tables and Cartesian products when performing optimization. This class should be used only in special circumstances, such as applications containing very complex and long-running queries that access large tables of data.

Specifying the Optimization Class

You can use any one of these optimization classes to create a more efficient access plan for the SQL statements contained in the source-code file being precompiled, but their use increases the precompile time and system resource usage. Therefore, you want to select a lower optimization class number if you have very small databases, very simple queries, or limited system resources on your database server, or if you want to reduce precompile time.

Although the optimization class is typically specified as a parameter for the SQL precompiler, you can specify it within an embedded SQL source-code file via the SET CURRENT QUERY OPTIMIZATION SQL statement. To ensure that a dynamic SQL statement always uses the same optimization class, you might want to include this SQL statement in your application program. Otherwise, the dynamic SQL statement will be bound to the database with the default query optimization class. If you specify an optimization class as a parameter for the SQL precompiler but later decide to change it rather than precompile the source-code file again, you can simply rebind the appropriate bind file (as long as deferred binding was used when the source-code file was originally precompiled).

Determining Which Optimization Class to Use

Most SQL statements are adequately optimized with the default query optimization class. Source-code precompilation time and resource consumption, at any optimization class level, is primarily determined by the complexity of the query being precompiled, especially if the query contains joins and subqueries. However, precompilation time and resource usage can also be affected by the amount of query rewrites being performed by the specified optimization class. No matter which optimization class you use, you can expect to see a longer precompile time and greater resource usage for a very complex query than for a simple one. When determining the best optimization class to use, consider the following:

- Does your embedded SQL source-code file contain complex queries (queries that join multiple tables or include subselects)? More complex queries often require large amounts of optimization to produce the best access plan.
- Does your embedded SQL source-code file contain efficient, well-written queries? Poorly written queries or queries produced by an SQL query generator might require more optimization to produce the best access plan.
- How important is query performance to your application? The greater the need for optimum performance, the greater the need for more optimization.
- Does your application use dynamic SQL? Dynamic SQL statements are bound and executed at application runtime, so you should consider whether or not the overhead of additional optimization for dynamic SQL statements improves your application's overall performance.

Once you have taken these factors into consideration, use the following "rules of thumb" to select the best query optimization class:

- Start by using the default query optimization class (3).
- If you feel you need an optimization class other than the default, try class 1 or 5.

- Use a lower optimization class (0 or 1) for queries that have a short runtime (less than 1 second).
- Use a higher optimization class (3 or 5) for queries that have a long runtime (greater than 10 seconds).
- Use optimization class 1 if your queries access many tables with join predicates on the same column.

ROW BLOCKING

Row blocking is another technique you can use to improve application performance. Row blocking returns a group of rows rather than a single row to an application in response to a FETCH SQL statement. When row blocking is used, DB2's overhead is reduced because multiple rows are retrieved in a single operation. These rows are stored in a cache and processed one row at a time for each FETCH SQL statement in the application. When all the rows in a block have been processed, another block of rows is retrieved for processing by DB2.

Memory for the cache is automatically allocated when the cursor is opened, and it is automatically freed when the cursor is closed. The size of the cache is determined by a database configuration parameter that is used to allocate memory for all I/O blocks. Row blocking can lead to results not entirely consistent with the database if it is used in conjunction with the cursor stability or the uncommitted read isolation level. When these isolation levels are used, the rows being retrieved by the application from the memory cache (block) are not locked at the database. This means that another application can update a row in the database while your application is reading a copy of that row from the block. Therefore, your application should acquire a repeatable read isolation level lock on all rows being accessed in the block until the transaction using this data is complete.

LOCKS AND APPLICATION PERFORMANCE

In multitasking environments like OS/2 and AIX, you can have several applications (or several copies of the same application) concurrently running and trying to access the same data resource. It is very important for DB2 to regulate these concurrent applications so data is not corrupted and performance is not impaired. You saw in Chapter 2 that DB2 provides concurrency control and prevents uncontrolled data access by means of locks. Essentially, a *lock* is a means of associating a DB2 data resource (row or table) with a transaction to control how other transactions access the same data resource. Locking guarantees that a transaction maintains control over a database row or table until all of its processing is complete. This principle protects the consistency and security of data while concurrent applications are running. In order to maintain data integrity, DB2 implicitly acquires all locks needed by a transaction.

Your application can override DB2's rules for acquiring row locks by explicitly locking an entire table with the LOCK TABLE SQL statement. This SQL statement can lock a specified table so that:

- Other applications can retrieve but not update, delete, or insert rows in the locked table.
- Other applications (except those with an Uncommitted Read isolation level) cannot access the rows in the locked table.

> Note: A table lock acquired with the LOCK TABLE SQL statement applies only to a single table. Any parent and/or dependent tables of the specified table are not locked. When developing your application, you must determine whether or not it is necessary to lock parent, dependent, or other accessible tables in order to achieve the desired result in terms of database concurrency and application performance.

Once a table lock is acquired, it is not released until the transaction is committed or rolled back. If a table is normally shared among several applications, you might want to lock it for the following reasons:

- You want to access data that is consistent in time (data current for a table at a specific point in time). If a table experiences frequent activity, the only way to ensure that the entire table remains stable is to lock it.
- You want to update a large part of the table. When updating several rows in a table, it is more efficient to lock the entire table than it is to lock each row as it is updated and then unlock the row later when the changes have been committed.

The way locks are acquired and released can greatly affect application performance, especially if the application is running concurrently with other applications. When designing and developing database applications, it is important to keep in mind the following points about locking:

- Small transactions promote concurrent access of data by many users. Include COMMIT SQL statements whenever your application is logically at a point of consistency (when the data you have changed is consistent). When a COMMIT SQL statement is issued, all locks are released, with the exception of table locks associated with cursors created with the WITH HOLD option.
- Locks are automatically acquired, even if a transaction only reads rows. Therefore, it is important to explicitly commit every transaction.
- By default, DB2 ensures that your transactions do not retrieve uncommitted data (rows that have been updated by other transactions not yet committed). If your application contains transactions that need to access uncommitted data, make sure to use the Uncommitted Read isolation level.

CODE-PAGE SELECTION

OS/2, AIX, and other operating systems store many different national character sets in what are known as *code pages*. The code-page value is automatically set in the database configuration file when a database is created. Likewise, a code-page value is assigned to an application when it is compiled. Whenever an application and a database are not using the same code page, data must be mapped from one code page to the other, which might require data conversion. This mapping and data conversion increases the overall processing time for applications running with code pages different from the code pages of the databases with which they interact. Application performance can always be improved if both the application and the database use the same code page.

SUMMARY

The goal of this chapter was to provide you with some tips for improving the performance of your DB2 for Common Servers application. You should now know how to write SQL queries so they execute quickly, and how and when to create indexes that improve SQL query performance. You should know that the precompiler uses five optimization classes to rewrite queries for increased performance, and you should know how and when to use those five classes. You should also know to use row blocking and table locks to increase transaction execution time and maintain data integrity. Finally, you should know that different code-page settings affect application performance. This chapter concludes Section 2, APPLICATION DEVELOPMENT FUNDAMENTALS. The next section will take a closer look at the coding syntax and purpose of each DB2 SQL statement.

Part 3

STRUCTURED QUERY LANGUAGE (SQL) STATEMENTS

The third part of this book describes the structured query language (SQL) statements you can use to develop embedded SQL applications for DB2. It is designed to be a reference, providing information about the syntax and semantics of each SQL statement that DB2 supports. It is also designed to show, by example, how each SQL statement is coded in an embedded SQL C and C++ application program. Each statement is presented as a main section, and the subsections under each statement contain the following information:

Purpose	*Short description telling what the SQL statement does.*
Syntax	*Full SQL statement syntax.*
Parameters	*Detailed description of all SQL statement parameters.*
Options	*Detailed description of any SQL statement options.*
Description	*Detailed information about the SQL statement.*
Comments	*Special notes or instructions about the SQL statement.*
Prerequisites	*Things that must occur before the SQL statement can be executed.*
Authorizations	*Authorization requirements for using the SQL statement.*
See Also	*Related SQL statements.*
Examples	*C and C++ examples demonstrating how to use the SQL statement in a source-code file.*

SYNTAX CONVENTIONS

The syntax section for each SQL statement shows the basic format to use when coding the statement. I have used the following conventions to present SQL statement syntax:

[parameter]	*Parameters shown inside brackets are required parameters and must be specified.*
<parameter>	*Parameters shown inside angle brackets are optional parameters and do not have to be specified.*
parameter | parameter	*Parameters or other items separated by vertical bars indicate that you must select one item from the list of presented items.*
parameter, . . .	*If a parameter is followed by a comma and three periods, multiple instances of that parameter can be included in the statement.*

The following examples illustrates these syntax conventions:

```
EXEC SQL CONNECT TO [server-name] <connection-mode> <USER
   [authorization-ID] USING [password]>;
```

In this example, both connection-mode and USER [authorization-ID] USING [password] are optional parameters, as indicated by the angle brackets. The server-name, authorization-ID, and password parameters are required, as indicated by the brackets. However, authorization ID and password are required parameters only if the USER [authorization-ID] USING [password] option is specified.

```
EXEC SQL RELEASE [server-name | CURRENT | ALL <SQL>];
```

In this example, server-name, CURRENT, or ALL <SQL> can be specified, as indicated by the vertical bar. One of these items must be specified, as indicated by the brackets. If ALL is selected, SQL can be added (ALL SQL), but it is not required, as indicated by the angle brackets.

```
EXEC SQL CREATE <UNIQUE> INDEX [index-name] ON [table-name]
   ([column-name <ASC | DESC>,...]);
```

In this example, index-name, table-name, and at least one column-name must be specified, as indicated by the brackets. UNIQUE, ASC, and DESC are options, as indicated by the angle brackets. Either ASC or DESC can be specified as an option, but not both (as indicated by the vertical bar). More than one column-name <ASC | DESC> option can be specified, as indicated by the , . . . that follows the option.

HOW THE EXAMPLES WERE DEVELOPED

All the sample programs shown in Part 3 of this book were compiled and executed on the OS/2 Warp operating system (compiled with IBM's VisualAge C++), and most were compiled and executed on the AIX 4.0 operating system (compiled with IBM's C Set++ for AIX, version 3.0).

The following command file (C_COMP.CMD) was used to compile the C sample programs on the OS/2 Warp operating system:

```
REM *** BUILD EMBEDDED SQL EXAMPLES COMMAND FILE      ***
echo off

REM *** CONNECT TO THE SAMPLE DATABASE                ***
db2 connect to sample user etpdd6z using sanders

REM *** PRECOMPILE THE EMBEDDED SQL SOURCE CODE FILE ***
db2 prep %1.sqc bindfile using %1.bnd > ERROR.DAT

REM *** COMPILE THE SOURCE CODE FILE                  ***
icc /W3 /Ti+ /G4 /Gs+ /Ss+ /DLINT_ARGS /c %1.c >> ERROR.DAT

REM *** LINK THE PROGRAM                              ***
ilink /NOFREE /NOI /DEBUG /ST:32000 %1.obj,,,OS2386 DB2API
   SQL_DYN,DB2_DEF.DEF >> ERROR.DAT

REM *** BIND THE APPLICATION TO THE SAMPLE DATABASE  ***
db2 bind %1.bnd > ERROR.DAT

REM *** DISCONNECT FROM THE SAMPLE DATABASE           ***
db2 connect reset

REM *** CLEAN UP                                      ***
del %1.c
del %1.obj
```

The following command file (CPP_COMP.CMD) was used to compile the C++ sample programs on the OS/2 Warp operating system:

```
REM *** BUILD EMBEDDED SQL EXAMPLES COMMAND FILE      ***
echo off

REM *** CONNECT TO THE SAMPLE DATABASE                ***
db2 connect to sample user etpdd6z using sanders

REM *** PRECOMPILE THE EMBEDDED SQL SOURCE CODE FILE ***
db2 prep %1.sqx bindfile using %1.bnd > ERROR.DAT

REM *** COMPILE THE SOURCE CODE FILE                  ***
icc /W3 /Ti+ /G4 /Gs+ /Ss+ /DLINT_ARGS /c /Td %1.cxx >> ERROR.DAT

REM *** LINK THE PROGRAM                              ***
ilink /NOFREE /NOI /DEBUG /ST:32000 %1.obj,,,OS2386 DB2API
   SQL_DYN,DB2_DEF.DEF >> ERROR.DAT

REM *** BIND THE APPLICATION TO THE SAMPLE DATABASE  ***
db2 bind %1.bnd >> ERROR.DAT

REM *** DISCONNECT FROM THE SAMPLE DATABASE           ***
db2 connect reset

REM *** CLEAN UP                                      ***
del %1.cxx
del %1.obj
```

Both of these command files reference the following link definitions file (DB2_DEF.DEF):

```
; This File Contains The Link Definitions That Are Used To Link
; Most Of The DB2 2.1 Embedded SQL Sample Programs

NAME          DBM     WINDOWCOMPAT

PROTMODE
```

The following command file (C_COMP) was used to compile the C sample programs on the AIX 4.0 operating system:

```
# BUILD EMBEDDED SQL EXAMPLES COMMAND FILE
#! /bin/ksh
#
# CONNECT TO THE SAMPLE DATABASE
db2 connect to sample user etpdd6z using sanders
#
# PRECOMPILE THE EMBEDDED SQL SOURCE CODE FILE
db2 prep ${1} .sqc bindfile
#
# COMPILE THE SOURCE CODE FILE
compstr='xlC -I/usr/lpp/db2_02_01/include -qcpluscmt -c '${1} .c
echo $compstr
$compstr
#
# LINK THE PROGRAM
linkstr='xlC -o '${1} ' '${1} '.o -ldb2 -L/usr/lpp/db2_02_01/lib'
echo $linkstr
```

```
$linkstr
#
# BIND THE APPLICATION TO THE SAMPLE DATABASE
db2 bind ${1} .bnd
#
# DISCONNECT FROM THE SAMPLE DATABASE
db2 connect reset
```

The following command file (C_COMP) was used to compile the C++ sample programs on the AIX 4.0 operating system:

```
# BUILD EMBEDDED SQL EXAMPLES COMMAND FILE
#! /bin/ksh
#
# CONNECT TO THE SAMPLE DATABASE
db2 connect to sample user etpdd6z using sanders
#
# PRECOMPILE THE EMBEDDED SQL SOURCE CODE FILE
db2 prep ${1} .sqC bindfile
#
# COMPILE THE SOURCE CODE FILE
compstr='xlC -I/usr/lpp/db2_02_01/include -c '${1} .C
echo $compstr
$compstr
#
# LINK THE PROGRAM
linkstr='xlC -o '${1} ' '${1} '.o -ldb2 -L/usr/lpp/db2_02_01/lib'
echo $linkstr
$linkstr
#
# BIND THE APPLICATION TO THE SAMPLE DATABASE
db2 bind ${1} .bnd
#
# DISCONNECT FROM THE SAMPLE DATABASE
db2 connect reset
```

It is important to remember that you must start the DB2 database manager by issuing either the startdbm command (OS/2) or the db2 start database manager command (AIX) at the command prompt before any embedded SQL applications can be compiled or executed. Also, keep in mind that the default qualifier USERID is valid only for OS/2. When DB2 is installed on AIX, the default qualifier for the SAMPLE database is determined by the authorization ID of the user installing the DB2 product.

SPECIAL CASES

The compile script files for Type 2 connection, user-defined function, and stored procedures examples had to be slightly modified. For Type 2 connects, I changed the line:

```
db2 prep %1.sqc bindfile using %1.bnd > ERROR.DAT
```

to:

```
db2 prep %1.sqc connect 2 bindfile using %1.bnd > ERROR.DAT
```

and added the following lines:

```
REM *** CONNECT TO THE BOOK SAMPLE DATABASE ***
db2 connect to booksamp user etpdd6z using sanders
REM *** BIND THE APPLICATION TO THE BOOK SAMPLE DATABASE ***
db2 bind %1.bnd >> ERROR.DAT
```

> *Note: I also created a database named BOOKSAMP and added the table TEMP_EMP to this database before these examples were tested (refer to the following section, SET-UP FILES). You can create the database BOOKSAMP by issuing the command "db2 create database booksamp" from both the OS/2 and the AIX command prompt.*

For user-defined functions, the following command file (UDF_COMP.CMD) was used to compile the C sample user-defined function on the OS/2 Warp operating system:

```
REM *** BUILD USER-DEFINED FUNCTION COMMAND FILE      ***
echo off

REM *** COMPILE THE SOURCE CODE FILE                  ***
icc /W3 /Ti+ /G4 /Ge- /Ss+ /DLINT_ARGS /c %1.c >> ERROR.DAT

REM *** LINK THE PROGRAM                              ***
ilink /NOFREE /NOI /DEBUG /ST:32000 %1.obj,%1.DLL,,OS2386 DB2API
   SQL_DYN,UDF_DEF.DEF >> ERROR.DAT

REM *** CLEAN UP                                      ***
del %1.obj
```

This command file references the following link definitions file (UDF_DEF.DEF):

```
; This File Contains The Link Definitions That Are Used To Link
; A User-Defined Function

LIBRARY       COUNTER INITINSTANCE TERMINSTANCE PROTMODE
DATA          MULTIPLE NONSHARED READWRITE LOADONCALL
CODE          LOADONCALL
EXPORTS       udfCounter
```

For stored procedures, the following command file (SP_COMP.CMD) was used to compile the C sample stored procedure on the OS/2 Warp operating system:

```
REM *** BUILD EMBEDDED SQL STORED PROCEDURE COMMAND FILE ***
echo off

REM *** CONNECT TO THE SAMPLE DATABASE                   ***
db2 connect to sample user etpdd6z using sanders

REM *** PRECOMPILE THE EMBEDDED SQL SOURCE CODE FILE     ***
db2 prep %1.sqc bindfile using %1.bnd >> ERROR.DAT
```

```
REM *** COMPILE THE SOURCE CODE FILE                            ***
icc /W3 /Ti+ /G4 /Ge- /Ss+ /DLINT_ARGS /c %1.c >>>> ERROR.DAT

REM *** LINK THE PROGRAM                                        ***
ilink /NOFREE /NOI /DEBUG /ST:32000 %1.obj,%1.DLL,,OS2386 DB2API
   SQL_DYN,SP_DEF.DEF >>>> ERROR.DAT

REM *** BIND THE APPLICATION TO THE SAMPLE DATABASE             ***
db2 bind %1.bnd >>>> ERROR.DAT

REM *** DISCONNECT FROM THE SAMPLE DATABASE                     ***
db2 connect reset

REM *** CLEAN UP                                                ***
del %1.c
del %1.obj
CR;LF
```

This command file references the following link definitions file (SP_DEF.DEF):

```
; This File Contains The Link Definitions That Are Used To Link
; A Stored Procedure

LIBRARY       ST_PROC INITINSTANCE TERMINSTANCE PROTMODE
DATA          MULTIPLE NONSHARED READWRITE LOADONCALL
CODE          LOADONCALL
EXPORTS       st_proc
```

SET-UP FILES

In addition to the compile script files and link definition files, I created two additional programs to create special tables that are used by some of the sample programs. The following file creates the table TEMP_EMP in the BOOKSAMP database for the Type 2 connection examples:

```
#include <stdio.h>
#include <stdlib.h>
#include <sql.h>

int main()
{
    /* Include The SQLCA Data Structure Variable */
    EXEC SQL INCLUDE SQLCA;

    /* Declare The Local Memory Variables */
    int  rc = EXIT_SUCCESS;

    /* Connect To The BOOKSAMP Database */
    EXEC SQL CONNECT TO BOOKSAMP USER etpdd6z USING sanders;

    /* Delete The TEMP_EMP Table */
    EXEC SQL DROP TABLE TEMP_EMP;
```

```
    /* Create The TEMP_EMP Table */
    EXEC SQL CREATE TABLE TEMP_EMP
        (EMPID          INTEGER         NOT NULL,
         LASTNAME       CHAR(18)        NOT NULL,
         FIRSTNAME      CHAR(18)        NOT NULL,
         DEPTNO         CHAR(3),
         PRIMARY KEY(EMPID));

    /* Print A MesSage Indicating The Table Has Been Created */
    printf("Table TEMP_EMP Has Been Created\n");

    /* Commit The Transaction */
    EXEC SQL COMMIT;

    /* Disconnect From The SAMPLE Database */
    EXEC SQL DISCONNECT CURRENT;

    /* Return To The Operating System */
    return(rc);
}
```

Note: This file must be compiled and bound against the BOOKSAMP database.

The following file was used to create the table MA_EMP_ACT and the index MA_EMPNO in the SAMPLE database for the INSERT, UPDATE, and DELETE examples:

```
#include <stdio.h>
#include <stdlib.h>
#include <sql.h>

int main()
{
    /* Include The SQLCA Data Structure Variable */
    EXEC SQL INCLUDE SQLCA;

    /* Declare The Local Memory Variables */
    int  rc = EXIT_SUCCESS;

    /* Connect To The SAMPLE Database */
    EXEC SQL CONNECT TO SAMPLE USER etpdd6z USING sanders;

    /* Delete The MA_EMP_ACT Table And Its Index */
    EXEC SQL DROP INDEX MA_EMPNO;
    EXEC SQL DROP TABLE MA_EMP_ACT;

    /* Create The MA_EMP_ACT Table */
    EXEC SQL CREATE TABLE MA_EMP_ACT
        (EMPNO          CHAR(6)         NOT NULL,
         PROJNO         CHAR(6)         NOT NULL,
         ACTNO          SMALLINT        NOT NULL,
         EMPTIME        DECIMAL(5,2),
         EMSTDATE       DATE,
         EMENDATE       DATE);

    /* Create An Index For The MA_EMP_ACT Table */
```

```
    EXEC SQL CREATE UNIQUE INDEX MA_EMPNO
         ON TEMP_PROJ (EMPNO);

    /* Print A MesSage Indicating The Table Has Been Created */
    printf("Table And Index Have Been Created\n");

    /* Commit The Transaction */
    EXEC SQL COMMIT;

    /* Disconnect From The SAMPLE Database */
    EXEC SQL DISCONNECT CURRENT;

    /* Return To The Operating System */
    return(rc);
}
```

CHAPTER 8

APPLICATION PROGRAMMING LANGUAGE CONSTRUCT STATEMENTS

8

The programming language construct SQL statements consist of commands and "set up" statements that allow you to embed other SQL statements within a high-level language source-code file. These statements include:

- SQL precompiler directives that identify the beginning and end of host and indicator variable sections.
- An SQL precompiler directive that incorporates SQL data structures and other high-level source-code files into a single source-code file.
- SQL precompiler directives that combine multiple SQL statements into a single SQL statement block.
- SQL precompiler directives that define how error and warning conditions are to be processed.
- Dynamic SQL support.

Table 8.1 lists the programming language construct SQL statements available with DB2.

SQL Precompiler Directives

The SQL precompiler directive statements relay special information to the SQL precompiler when the source-code file is being precompiled. These SQL statements are never executed at application runtime; they are a "no operation" when placed among other executable statements. Because these SQL statements are not executable, they do not generate SQL return codes. They should, therefore, not be followed by source code that checks the results of an SQL return code. If one of the SQL precompiler directive statements is coded incorrectly, the error will be reported when it is processed by the SQL precompiler.

Dynamic SQL Support

The programming language construct SQL statements that do not function as SQL precompiler directives allow you to prepare and execute dynamic SQL statements. Dynamic SQL provides maximum

TABLE 8.1 Programming Language Construct SQL Statements

Statement	Description
BEGIN DECLARE SECTION	Marks the beginning of a host variable declaration section.
END DECLARE SECTION	Marks the end of a host variable declaration section.
INCLUDE	Inserts code and/or structure declarations into a source-code file.
WHENEVER	Defines actions to be taken when error or warning conditions occur (based on SQL return code values).
BEGIN COMPOUND	Marks the beginning of a compound SQL statement block, which combines one or more SQL substatements into an executable block that is treated as a single SQL statement.
END COMPOUND	Marks the end of a compound SQL statement block.
PREPARE	Prepares an SQL statement (and optional parameter markers) for execution.
DESCRIBE	Describes the result columns of a prepared SELECT statement.
EXECUTE	Executes a prepared SQL statement.
EXECUTE IMMEDIATE	Prepares and executes an SQL statement.
SET CURRENT QUERY OPTIMIZATION	Specifies the amount of optimization techniques to use when preparing SQL statements.
SET CURRENT PACKAGESET	Specifies the schema name to use when selecting a package for processing subsequent SQL statements.
SET CURRENT EXPLAIN SNAPSHOT	Specifies whether or not Explain information should be captured for SQL statements.

flexibility by allowing you to construct SQL statements at runtime. Generally, you build dynamic SQL statements by combining static text (for example, SELECT ... FROM) with other data made available to the program during execution (for example, input from a terminal). In some cases, however, entire dynamic SQL statements can be made available to an application at runtime. Once you have constructed and stored a dynamic statement in a character-array host variable, you can prepare it for execution with the PREPARE statement and execute it either with the EXECUTE statement or the DECLARE CURSOR statement. Alternatively, you can use the EXECUTE IMMEDIATE statement to prepare and execute dynamic SQL statements (other than SELECT statements) in a single step.

Not all SQL statements can be dynamically prepared; some statements can be executed only as static SQL. The following is a list of all the SQL statements that can be dynamically created and prepared:

- CREATE
- ALTER
- DROP
- SELECT
- INSERT
- UPDATE
- DELETE
- GRANT
- REVOKE
- COMMIT
- ROLLBACK
- COMMENT ON

- SET CONSTRAINTS
- SET CURRENT EXPLAIN SNAPSHOT
- SET CURRENT FUNCTION PATH
- SET CURRENT QUERY OPTIMIZATION
- SET EVENT MONITOR STATE
- SIGNAL SQLSTATE
- LOCK TABLE

> Note: SELECT statements cannot contain INTO clauses

Dynamic SQL and Parameter Markers

An SQL statement that will be dynamically prepared cannot contain references to host variables. It can, however, contain parameter markers that are replaced by the values of host variables when the prepared SQL statement is executed. A parameter marker is simply a question mark (?) that is placed where a host variable would be referenced if the SQL statement string were a static SQL statement.

Two types of parameter markers are available: typed and untyped. A typed parameter marker is specified along with its target data type and has the general form:

```
CAST(? AS data-type)
```

This notation is not a function call, but rather a "promise" that the data type of the value replacing the parameter marker at runtime will either be the data type specified or a data type that can be converted to the data type specified. For example, in the following SQL statement:

```
UPDATE EMPLOYEE SET LASTNAME = CAST(? AS VARCHAR(12))
   WHERE EMPNO = '000050'
```

The value for the LASTNAME column is provided at runtime and the data type of that value will either be VARCHAR(12) or a data type that can be converted to VARCHAR(12). Typed parameter markers can be used in dynamic SQL statements whenever host variables are referenced by the parameter marker and the data type is known.

An untyped parameter marker is specified without its target data type and has the form of a single question mark. The data type of an untyped parameter marker is determined by the context in which it is used. For example, in the following SQL statement:

```
UPDATE EMPLOYEE SET LASTNAME = ?
   WHERE EMPNO = '000050'
```

The value for the LASTNAME column is provided at run time and the data type of that value will be the same data type as that assigned to the LASTNAME column. You can use untyped parameter markers in dynamic SQL statements in selected locations where host variables are supported. These locations and the resulting data types are shown in Table 8.2.

Caching

The executable sections generated for both dynamic and static SQL Data Manipulation Language (DML) statements (i.e. SELECT, INSERT, UPDATE, and DELETE statements) are placed in a special buffer, known as the agent package cache, the first time they are used and remain there until the either the database connection ends or the agent package cache space is required for another statement's executable section. This means that once a DML statement has been prepared, it can be executed multiple times without having to be re-prepared. Other SQL statements, such as Data Definition Language (DDL) statements, are not cached; therefore they must be prepared each time they are executed.

TABLE 8.2 Untyped Parameter Marker Usage

Untyped parameter marker location	Resulting data type
Expressions (including select list, CASE, and VALUES)	
Alone in a select list.	Error
Both operands of a single arithmetic operator, after considering operator precedence and order of operation rules. Includes cases such as ? + ? + 10.	Error
One operand of a single operator in an arithmetic expression (other than a datetime expression). Includes cases such as ? + ? * 10.	The data type of the other operand
Labeled duration within a datetime expression. (Note: The portion of a labeled duration that indicates the type of units cannot be a parameter marker.)	DECIMAL(15,0)
Any other operand of a datetime expression (for instance, timecol + ? or ? _ datecol).	Error
Both operands of a CONCAT operator.	Error
One operand of a CONCAT operator, where the other operand is a non-CLOB character data type.	If one operand is either CHAR(n) or VARCHAR(n) and n is less than 128, then the other is VARCHAR(254 – n). In all other cases the data type is VARCHAR(254).
One operand of a CONCAT operator, where the other operand is a non-DBCLOB graphic data type.	If one operand is either GRAPHIC(n) or VARGRAPHIC(n) and n is less than 64, then the other is VARCHAR(127 – n). In all other cases the data type is VARCHAR(127).
One operand of a CONCAT operator, where the other operand is large object string.	Same as that of the other operand.
A value on the right-hand side of a SET clause of an UPDATE statement.	The data type of the column. If the column is defined as a user-defined distinct type, then it is the source data type of the user-defined distinct type.
The expression following CASE in a simple CASE expression.	Error
At least one of the result expressions in a CASE expression (both simple and searched), with the rest of the result expressions either untyped parameter markers or NULLs.	Error
Any or all expressions following WHEN in a simple CASE expression.	Result of applying the "rules for result data types" to the expression following CASE and the expressions following WHEN that are not untyped parameter markers.
A result expression in a CASE expression (both simple and searched), where at least one result expression is not NULL and not an untyped parameter marker.	Result of applying the "rules for result data types" to all result expressions other than NULL or untyped parameter markers.
Alone as a column expression in a single-row VALUES clause that is not within an INSERT statement.	Error
Alone as a column expression in a multirow VALUES clause that is not within an INSERT statement, and for which the column expressions in the same position in all other row expressions are untyped parameter markers.	Error
Alone as a column expression in a multirow VALUES clause that is not within an INSERT statement, and for which the expression in the same position of at least one other row expression is not an untyped parameter marker or NULL.	Result of applying the "rules for result data types" on all operands other than untyped parameter markers.

TABLE 8.2 Untyped Parameter Marker Usage *(Continued)*

Untyped parameter marker location	Resulting data type
Alone as a column expression in a single-row VALUES clause within an INSERT statement.	The data type of the column. If the column is defined as a user-defined distinct type, then it is the source data type of the user-defined distinct type.
Alone as a column expression in a multirow VALUES clause within an INSERT statement.	The data type of the column. If the column is defined as a user-defined distinct type, then it is the source data type of the user-defined distinct type.
Predicates	
Both operands of a comparison operator.	Error
One operand of a comparison operator, where the other operand is anything other than an untyped parameter marker.	The data type of the other operand.
All operands of a BETWEEN predicate.	Error
Either the first and second, or first and third operands of a BETWEEN predicate.	Same as that of the only nonparameter marker.
Remaining BETWEEN situations (one untyped parameter marker only).	Result of applying the "rules for result data types" on all operands other than untyped parameter markers.
All operands of an IN predicate.	Error
Both the first and second operands of an IN predicate.	Result of applying the "rules for result data types" on all operands of the IN list (operands to the right of IN keyword) other than untyped parameter markers.
The first operand of an IN predicate, where the right-hand side is a full select.	Data type of the selected column.
Any or all operands of the IN list of the IN predicate.	Data type of the first operand (left-hand side).
The first operand and zero or more operands in the IN list, excluding the first operand of the IN list.	Result of applying the "rules for result data types" on all operands of the IN list (operands to the right of IN keyword) other than untyped parameter markers.
All three operands of the LIKE predicate.	Match expression (operand 1) and pattern expression (operand 2) are VARCHAR (4000). Escape expression (operand 3) is VARCHAR(2).
The match expression of the LIKE predicate when either the pattern expression or the escape expression is other than an untyped parameter marker.	Either VARCHAR(4000) or VARGRAPHIC (2000), depending on the data type of the first operand that is not an untyped parameter marker.
The pattern expression of the LIKE predicate when either the match expression or the escape expression is other than an untyped parameter marker.	Either VARCHAR(4000) or VARGRAPHIC (2000), depending on the data type of the first operand that is not an untyped parameter marker. If the data type of the match expression is BLOB, the data type of the pattern expression is assumed to be BLOB(4000).
The escape expression of the LIKE predicate when either the match expression or the pattern expression is other than an untyped parameter marker.	Either VARCHAR(2) or VARGRAPHIC(1), depending on the data type of the first operand that is not an untyped parameter marker. If the data type of the match expression or pattern expression is BLOB, the data type of the escape expression is assumed to be BLOB(1).

TABLE 8.2 Untyped Parameter Marker Usage *(Continued)*

Untyped parameter marker location	Resulting data type
Operand of the NULL predicate.	Error
Functions	
All operands of COALESCE (also called VALUE) or NULLIF.	Error
Any operand of COALESCE, where at least one operand is other than an untyped parameter marker.	Result of applying the "rules for result data types" on all operands other than untyped parameter markers.
An operand of NULLIF, where the other operand is not an untyped parameter marker.	The data type of the other operand.
POSSTR (both operands)	Both operands are VARCHAR(4000).
POSSTR (one operand, where the other operand is a character data type)	VARCHAR(4000)
POSSTR (one operand, where the other operand is a graphic data type)	VARGRAPHIC(2000)
POSSTR (the search-string operand, where the other operand is a BLOB)	BLOB(4000)
SUBSTR (1st operand)	VARCHAR(4000)
SUBSTR (second and third operands).	INTEGER
The first operand of the TRANSLATE scalar function.	Error
The second and third operands of the TRANSLATE scalar function.	VARCHAR(4000) if the first operand is a character type; VARGRAPHIC(2000) if the first operand is a graphic type.
The fourth operand of the TRANSLATE scalar function.	VARCHAR(2) if the first operand is a character type; VARGRAPHIC(1) if the first operand is a graphic type.
The second operand of the TIMESTAMP scalar function.	TIME
Unary minus	DOUBLE PRECISION
Unary plus	DOUBLE PRECISION
All other operands of all other scalar functions, including user-defined functions.	Error
Operand of a column function.	Error

Adapted from IBM Database 2 SQL Reference, pages 424–428.

When an untyped parameter marker is used in a function (including arithmetic operators, CONCAT, and datetime operators) with an unqualified function name, the qualifier is set to SYSIBM for function resolution.

Static SQL executable sections are created and stored in a system catalog table at precompile time, and are read into the agent package cache from the system catalog table at application runtime. Dynamic SQL executable sections are placed directly in the agent package cache after they are created by either the PREPARE or the EXECUTE IMMEDIATE statement. DB2 can also create dynamic SQL executable sections by implicitly recompiling executable sections. DB2 will recompile executable sections, as required, whenever environment changes occur. The following is a list of SQL statements and actions that can cause environment changes to occur, which in turn can cause cached executable sections to be recompiled:

- ALTER TABLE
- ALTER TABLESPACE
- CREATE INDEX

- CREATE TABLE
- CREATE TRIGGER
- CREATE FUNCTION
- DROP (all objects)
- REORG (reorganizing a system catalog table)
- RUNSTATS (regenerating statistics on any table or index)
- UPDATE (updating statistics in any system catalog table)

If an executable section needs to be recompiled because of environment changes, it will be recompiled when the next PREPARE, EXECUTE, EXECUTE IMMEDIATE, or OPEN statement is executed.

Each executable section is cached on a per-agent basis, and executable sections are not shared between agents. Each PREPARE statement in an application program places one executable section in the agent package cache; multiple executable sections can exist in the agent package cache. All EXECUTE IMMEDIATE statements, on the other hand, must share the same executable section cache space. Therefore, only one cached executable section (SQL statement) exists for all EXECUTE IMMEDIATE statements at a given time. This means that if the same PREPARE statement or any EXECUTE IMMEDIATE statement is issued multiple times (using a different SQL statement each time), only the last SQL statement used will remain in the agent package cache for reuse.

The optimal way to use the agent package cache is to issue several PREPARE statements at the start of the application and then to issue an EXECUTE statement for the relevant prepared SQL statement when it is required. This way, once the executable section for an SQL statement has been created, you can reuse it over multiple transactions without having to reprepare it. Table 8.3 identifies the behavior that can be expected from cached dynamic SQL statements.

TABLE 8.3 Expected Behavior From Cached Dynamic SQL Statements

Request	Behavior
PREPARE	Subsequent preparations of the same statement will not incur the cost of recompiling the statement if the executable section for the statement is still valid. The cost and cardinality estimates for the current cached executable section will be returned. These values might differ from the values returned from any previous PREPARE for the same SQL statement. There is no need to issue a PREPARE statement subsequent to a COMMIT or ROLLBACK statement.
EXECUTE	An EXECUTE statement might incur the cost of recompiling the statement if it has become invalid (due to environment changes) since it was originally prepared. If an executable section is recompiled, the current environment will be used, not the environment that existed when the statement was originally prepared.
EXECUTE IMMEDIATE	Subsequent EXECUTE IMMEDIATE statements for the same SQL statement will not incur the cost of recompiling the statement as long as the executable section is still valid.
OPEN	An OPEN request for dynamically defined cursors might incur the cost of recompiling the SQL statement if it has become invalid (due to environment changes) since it was originally prepared. If an executable section is recompiled, the current environment will be used, not the environment that existed when the statement was originally prepared.
FETCH	No behavior changes should be expected, but some applications might experience lock timeouts and deadlocks due to catalog locks being acquired for cursors declared as WITH HOLD after a commit operation.
ROLLBACK	Only dynamic sections compiled or recompiled during the transaction with the rollback operation are invalidated, and catalog locks are freed.
COMMIT	Dynamic sections are not invalidated, but catalog locks are freed. Cursors not defined as WITH HOLD cursors are closed and their locks are freed.

BEGIN DECLARE SECTION

Purpose The BEGIN DECLARE SECTION statement tells the SQL precompiler where the host variable and indicator variable declaration section begins in a high-level language source-code file.

Syntax

```
EXEC SQL BEGIN DECLARE SECTION;
```

Description The BEGIN DECLARE SECTION statement identifies the start of the host variable and indicator variable declaration section to the SQL precompiler. Host variables and indicator variables are high-level language (i.e., C or C++) variables that can be referenced by one or more SQL statements. Host variables allow an application using static embedded SQL statements to pass data to and receive data from a DB2 database. Likewise, indicator variables allow an application using static embedded SQL statements to pass null values to or receive null values from a DB2 database. Indicator variables also store data truncation information whenever character data must be truncated in order for it to be stored in a host variable whose size is smaller than the character data needs.

Comments

- A BEGIN DECLARE SECTION statement must be paired with an END DECLARE SECTION statement, and these statement pairs cannot be nested.
- Host variables and indicator variables must be defined in the declare section before they can be referenced by other SQL statements.
- Host variables that will be used in conjunction with large object (LOB) data types must have their data type and length preceded with the SQL TYPE IS keywords.
- You can define host variables and indicator variables in other files and incorporate them into the declare section by using the INCLUDE statement.
- No SQL statements, other than the INCLUDE statement, can be coded in the declare section.
- Program variables declared outside the host variable declaration section cannot have the same name as that of a host variable defined within the host variable declaration section.

Authorization No authorization is required to execute this statement.

See Also INCLUDE, END DECLARE SECTION

Examples The following C program illustrates how various types of host variables and indicator variables are defined and later used to retrieve data from the EMPLOYEE table in the SAMPLE database:

```
#include <stdio.h>
#include <stdlib.h>
#include <sql.h>

int main()
{
    /* Include The SQLCA Data Structure Variable */
    EXEC SQL INCLUDE SQLCA;

    /* Set Up A Simple SQL Error Handler */
    EXEC SQL WHENEVER SQLERROR GOTO EXIT;

    /* Declare The Local Memory Variables */
```

```
    int  rc = EXIT_SUCCESS;
    char *pszLastName;

    /* Declare The SQL Host Memory Variables */
    EXEC SQL BEGIN DECLARE SECTION;
        char           szEmpNo[7];          // Character String
        char           (*szLastName)[16];   // Pointer To 16-Byte String
        char           szHireDate[11];      // Date (Character String)
        short          sEdLevel;            // Short Integer
        double         rdSalary;            // Double
        short          rdSalaryNI;          // Null Indicator (Short)
        SQL TYPE IS CLOB(5K) clobResume;    // 5K CLOB
    EXEC SQL END DECLARE SECTION;

    /* Allocate Memory For The Pointer Variable */
    if ((pszLastName = (char *) malloc(16)) == NULL)
        {
        printf("ERROR : Memory Allocation Failed !\n");
        return(EXIT_FAILURE);
        }
    szLastName = (unsigned char (*)[16]) pszLastName;

    /* Connect To The SAMPLE Database */
    EXEC SQL CONNECT TO SAMPLE USER etpdd6z USING sanders;

    /* Retrieve A Record From The EMPLOYEE Table */
    EXEC SQL SELECT EMPNO,
                    LASTNAME,
                    HIREDATE,
                    EDLEVEL,
                    SALARY
        INTO :szEmpNo,
             :*szLastName,
             :szHireDate,
             :sEdLevel,
             :rdSalary INDICATOR :rdSalaryNI
        FROM USERID.EMPLOYEE
        WHERE EMPNO = '000150';

    /* Print The Information Retrieved */
    printf("Employee No. : %s\nName    : %s\nOf Hire : %s\n",
           szEmpNo, szLastName, szHireDate);
    if (rdSalaryNI << 0)
        printf("Salary       : Not Available");
    else
        printf("Salary       : $%.2lf\n", rdSalary);

    /* Normally We Would Commit The Updates Here - In This Case We */
    /* Do Not Want To Change The SAMPLE Database                   */
//  EXEC SQL COMMIT;

EXIT:
    /* If An Error Has Occurred, Display The SQL Return Code */
    if (sqlca.sqlcode != SQL_RC_OK)
        {
        printf("SQL ERROR : %ld\n", sqlca.sqlcode);
        rc = EXIT_FAILURE;
        }

    /* Issue A Rollback To Free All Locks */
    EXEC SQL ROLLBACK;
```

```
    /* Turn Off The SQL Error Handler */
    EXEC SQL WHENEVER SQLERROR CONTINUE;

    /* Disconnect From The SAMPLE Database */
    EXEC SQL DISCONNECT CURRENT;

    /* Free Memory Allocated For The Pointer Variable */
    if (pszLastName)
        free(pszLastName);

    /* Return To The Operating System */
    return(rc);
}
```

The following C++ program illustrates how various types of host variables and indicator variables are defined as private members of a class and later used to by class methods to retrieve data from the EMPLOYEE table in the SAMPLE database:

```
#include <iostream.h>
#include <stdlib.h>
#include <sql.h>

/* Define The Employee Class */
class Employee
{
    private:

        /* Include The SQLCA Data Structure Variable */
        EXEC SQL INCLUDE SQLCA;

        /* Declare The SQL Host Memory Variables */
        EXEC SQL BEGIN DECLARE SECTION;
            char      szEmpNo[7];            // Character String
            char      (*szLastName)[16];     // Pointer To 16-Byte String
            char      szHireDate[11];        // Date (Character String)
            short     sEdLevel;              // Short Integer
            double    rdSalary;              // Double
            short     rdSalaryNI;            // Null Indicator (Short)
        EXEC SQL END DECLARE SECTION;
        char *pszLastName;

    /* Declare The Member Function Prototypes */
    public:
        Employee();                                   // Constructor
        ~Employee() { delete []pszLastName; }         // Destructor
        short int getData();
        void      printData();
} ;
/* Define The Class Constructor */
Employee::Employee()
{
   pszLastName = new char[16];
   szLastName = (char (*)[16]) pszLastName;
}

/* Define The getData() Member Function */
short int Employee::getData(void)
{
    /* Retrieve A Record From The EMPLOYEE Table */
    EXEC SQL SELECT EMPNO,
        LASTNAME,
```

```
        HIREDATE,
        EDLEVEL,
        SALARY
    INTO :szEmpNo,
         :*szLastName,
         :szHireDate,
         :sEdLevel,
         :rdSalary INDICATOR :rdSalaryNI
    FROM USERID.EMPLOYEE
    WHERE EMPNO = '000260';

    /* Return The SQL Return Code */
    return(sqlca.sqlcode);
}

/* Define The printData() Member Function */
void Employee::printData(void)
{
    /* Print The Information Retrieved */
    cout << "Employee No. : " << szEmpNo << endl;
    cout << "Last Name    : " << *szLastName << endl;
    cout << "Date Of Hire : " << szHireDate << endl;
    if (rdSalaryNI < 0)
        cout << "Salary       : NULL" < endl;
    else
        {
        cout.setf(ios::showpoint);
        cout << "Salary       : $" < rdSalary < endl;
        }
}

int main()
{
    /* Declare The Local Memory Variables */
    short int rc = EXIT_SUCCESS;            // Must Be Declared Here
                                            // For The SQL Precompiler

    /* Include The SQLCA Data Structure Variable */
    EXEC SQL INCLUDE SQLCA;

    /* Set Up A Simple SQL Error Handler */
    EXEC SQL WHENEVER SQLERROR GOTO EXIT;

    /* Create An Instance Of The EMPLOYEE Class */
    Employee empInfo;

    /* Connect To The SAMPLE Database */
    EXEC SQL CONNECT TO SAMPLE USER etpdd6z USING sanders;
    /* Retrieve A Record From The EMPLOYEE Table */
    rc = empInfo.getData();

    /* Print The Information Retrieved */
    empInfo.printData();

EXIT:
    /* If An Error Has Occurred, Display The SQL Return Code */
    if (sqlca.sqlcode != SQL_RC_OK)
        {
        cout << "SQL ERROR : " << sqlca.sqlcode << endl;
        rc = EXIT_FAILURE;
        }
```

```
    /* Issue A Rollback To Free All Locks */
    EXEC SQL ROLLBACK;

    /* Turn Off The SQL Error Handler */
    EXEC SQL WHENEVER SQLERROR CONTINUE;

    /* Disconnect From The SAMPLE Database */
    EXEC SQL DISCONNECT CURRENT;

    /* Return To The Operating System */
    return(rc);
}
```

END DECLARE SECTION

Purpose The END DECLARE SECTION statement tells the SQL precompiler where the host variable and indicator variable declaration section ends in a high-level language source-code file.

Syntax `EXEC SQL END DECLARE SECTION;`

Description The END DECLARE SECTION statement identifies the end of the host variable and indicator variable declaration section to the SQL precompiler.

Comment An END DECLARE SECTION statement must be paired with a BEGIN DECLARE SECTION statement, and these statement pairs cannot be nested.

Prerequisite The BEGIN DECLARE SECTION statement must appear in an embedded SQL source-code file before the END DECLARE SECTION statement.

Authorization No authorization is required to execute this statement.

See Also BEGIN DECLARE SECTION

Examples See the examples provided for the previous statement, BEGIN DECLARE SECTION.

INCLUDE

Purpose The INCLUDE statement allows you to add an SQLCA data structure variable or a SQLDA data structure declaration to a high-level language source-code file. You can also use the INCLUDE statement to incorporate the text contained in other external files into a single high-level language source-code file.

Syntax `EXEC SQL INCLUDE [SQLCA | SQLDA | filemane];`

Parameters

SQLCA Identifies the high-level language header file that defines an SQL communication area (SQLCA) data structure variable (for C and C++, this file is sqlca.h). This SQLDA data structure variable contains other variables that DB2 uses to provide success, warning, or error information about SQL statements and API calls to DB2 applications. For a complete description of the SQLCA data structure, refer to Appendix A, SQL DATA STRUCTURES.

SQLDA Identifies the high-level language header file that defines the SQL descriptor area (SQLDA) data structure (for C and C++, this file is sqlda.h). This data structure defines a SQLDA variable that contains other variables that pass data between embedded SQL applications and DB2. For a complete description of the SQLDA data structure, refer to Appendix A.

filename Identifies any external file that contains text to be added to (included in) the source-code file being precompiled. For C and C++ applications, the external file must have one of the following extensions:

.h	C and C++ source code header files (either OS/2 or AIX)
.sqc	C source-code files (either OS/2 or AIX)
.sqx	C++ source-code files (OS/2)
.sqC	C++ source-code files (AIX)

Description The INCLUDE statement incorporates the text contained in external files into the declaration section of a high-level language source-code file. These external files can be either user-defined source-code files or high-level language header files supplied with the compiler. Because the header files containing the SQL communications area (SQLCA) data structure variable and the SQL descriptor area (SQLDA) structure description are used the most, special versions of the INCLUDE statement are provided that automatically map to these header files. When a program is precompiled, the INCLUDE statement is replaced by the source-code statements in these files. Therefore, make sure to specify the INCLUDE statement at a point in your application program so the resulting source-code statements will not generate precompiler or compiler errors.

Comments

- You must write any external source-code file to be incorporated into a application via the INCLUDE statement in the high-level language implied by the filename extension.
- If the filename specified with the INCLUDE statement is greater than 18 characters or if it contains characters not allowed in an SQL identifier, then it must be placed within single quotation marks (i.e., EXEC SQL INCLUDE 'LongFileName.SQC').
- INCLUDE statements can be nested, but they cannot be used in cyclical conditions. For example, if the file FILE_A.SQC contains an INCLUDE statement that incorporates file FILE_B.SQC, then it is not valid for FILE_B.SQC to INCLUDE FILE_A.SQC).

Authorization No authorization is required to execute this statement.

See Also BEGIN DECLARE SECTION

Examples The following C program illustrates how the INCLUDE statement defines an SQL communication area (SQLCA) data structure variable, which is then used throughout the program to determine whether or not SQL statements were executed successfully:

```
#include <stdio.h>
#include <stdlib.h>
#include <sql.h>

int main()
{
    /* Include The SQLCA Data Structure Variable */
    EXEC SQL INCLUDE SQLCA;

    /* Declare The Local Memory Variables */
    int  rc = EXIT_SUCCESS;

    /* Declare The SQL Host Memory Variables */
    EXEC SQL BEGIN DECLARE SECTION;
        long   lNumRecs;
    EXEC SQL END DECLARE SECTION;
```

```
    /* Connect To The Sample Database */
    EXEC SQL CONNECT TO SAMPLE USER etpdd6z USING sanders;
    if (sqlca.sqlcode != SQL_RC_OK)
        {
        printf("SQL ERROR : %ld\n", sqlca.sqlcode);
        return(EXIT_FAILURE);
        }

    /* Count The Number Of Records In The PROJECT Table */
    EXEC SQL SELECT COUNT(*)
        INTO :lNumRecs
        FROM USERID.PROJECT;

    if (sqlca.sqlcode != SQL_RC_OK)
        {
        printf("SQL ERROR : %ld\n", sqlca.sqlcode);
        rc = EXIT_FAILURE;
        goto EXIT;
        }

    /* Print The Information Retrieved */
    printf("There are %ld records in the PROJECT table", lNumRecs);

EXIT:
    /* Issue A Rollback To Free All Locks */
    EXEC SQL ROLLBACK;
    if (sqlca.sqlcode != SQL_RC_OK)
        {
        printf("SQL ERROR : %ld\n", sqlca.sqlcode);
        rc = EXIT_FAILURE;
        }

    /* Disconnect From The SAMPLE Database */
    EXEC SQL DISCONNECT CURRENT;
    if (sqlca.sqlcode != SQL_RC_OK)
        {
        printf("SQL ERROR : %ld\n", sqlca.sqlcode);
        rc = EXIT_FAILURE;
        }

    /* Return To The Operating System */
    return(rc);
}
```

The following C++ program illustrates how the INCLUDE statement is used to define an SQLCA structure variable as a private member of a class. This SQLCA data structure variable is then used by class methods to provide return codes that indicate whether or not the SQL statements contained in the methods were successfully executed.

```
#include <iostream.h>
#include <stdlib.h>
#include <sql.h>

/* Define The Project Class */
class Project
{
    private:

        /* Include The SQLCA Data Structure Variable */
        EXEC SQL INCLUDE SQLCA;
```

```
        /* Declare The SQL Host Memory Variables */
        EXEC SQL BEGIN DECLARE SECTION;
            long   lNumRecs;
        EXEC SQL END DECLARE SECTION;

     /* Declare The Member Function Prototypes */
     public:
        short int countRecs();
        void      printCount();
} ;

/* Define The countRecs() Member Function */
short int Project::countRecs(void)
{
    /* Count The Number Of Records In The PROJECT Table */
    EXEC SQL SELECT COUNT(*)
        INTO :lNumRecs
        FROM USERID.PROJECT;

    /* Return The SQL Return Code */
    return(sqlca.sqlcode);
}

/* Define The printCount() Member Function */
void Project::printCount(void)
{
    /* Print The Information Retrieved */
    cout <<, "There are " << lNumRecs;
    cout << " Records In The PROJECT Table" << endl;
}

int main()
{
    /* Declare The Local Memory Variables */
    short int rc = EXIT_SUCCESS;          // Must Be Declared Here
                                          // For The SQL Precompiler

    /* Include The SQLCA Data Structure Variable */
    EXEC SQL INCLUDE SQLCA;               // Local To The Main Function

    /* Create An Instance Of The PROJECT Class */
    Project projectInfo;

    /* Connect To The SAMPLE Database */
    EXEC SQL CONNECT TO SAMPLE USER etpdd6z USING sanders;

    /* Count The Number Of Records Stored In The PROJECT Table */
    rc = projectInfo.countRecs();

    /* Print The Information Retrieved */
    projectInfo.printCount();
EXIT:
    /* If An Error Has Occurred, Display The SQL Return Code */
    if (sqlca.sqlcode != SQL_RC_OK)
        {
        cout << "SQL ERROR : " << sqlca.sqlcode << endl;
        rc = EXIT_FAILURE;
        }

    /* Issue A Rollback To Free All Locks */
    EXEC SQL ROLLBACK;
```

```
    /* Turn Off The SQL Error Handler */
    EXEC SQL WHENEVER SQLERROR CONTINUE;

    /* Disconnect From The SAMPLE Database */
    EXEC SQL DISCONNECT CURRENT;

    /* Return To The Operating System */
    return(rc);
}
```

WHENEVER

Purpose The WHENEVER statement specifies an action to be taken when a specified exception condition occurs.

Syntax

```
EXEC SQL WHENEVER [exception-condition] [action];
```

Parameters

exception-condition Identifies the type of exception condition that must occur before the specified action can be performed. The exception condition can be any of the following predefined types:

SQLERROR Any condition that produces a negative SQL return code (*sqlca.sqlcode*) when an SQL statement is executed.

SQLWARNING Any condition that produces a positive SQL return code other than +100 or a warning condition (*sqlca.sqlwarn[0]* = **'W'**) when an SQL statement is executed.

NOT FOUND Any condition that produces an SQL return code of +100 or an SQLSTATE of **02**000 when an SQL statement is executed. This return code is typically generated whenever a SELECT statement or a CURSOR cannot find any records that match the specified search criteria.

action Identifies what is supposed to happen (the action to be taken) when the specified exception condition occurs. The action can be any of the following:

CONTINUE	Ignores the exception condition and allows the next sequential instruction in the source-code file to be executed.
GOTO or GO TO [<:>*host-label*]	Traps the exception condition and passes control to the first instruction in the source-code file that follows the host label. The form of the host label can vary, depending on the high-level (host) language being used. In some cases, the host label can be a single token, optionally preceded by a colon.

Description The WHENEVER statement specifies the action to be taken by a DB2 application whenever a specified exception condition occurs. Three types of exception conditions can occur; so three forms of the WHENEVER can exist in a source-code file. Also, because the action an application takes when one of these exception condition occurs might vary throughout the life of the application, multiple WHENEVER statements can be placed throughout a source-code file. When the SQL precompiler encounters a WHENEVER statement, it generates the additional source code necessary for evaluating return-code values and performing the specified action.

Comments

- Every executable SQL statement used in a source-code file falls within the scope of the last WHENEVER statement specified prior to its execution. By default, an implicit WHENEVER [exception-condition] CONTINUE statement exists for each exception condition until an explicit WHENEVER statement is specified.

- The scope of a WHENEVER statement is defined by its location in the sequential listing of the statements in a source-code file. This sequential listing might not always be the same as the actual program execution sequence.
- Once program control is passed to the statements following a host label, it cannot be returned to the next instruction following the SQL statement that caused the exception condition to occur. Therefore, the exception condition handling instructions associated with a host label should contain some method for gracefully exiting the application (or source-code file).

Authorization No authorization is required to execute this statement.

Example The following C program illustrates how the various types of WHENEVER statements can control the way exception conditions are processed throughout execution of a DB2 application:

```
#include <stdio.h>
#include <stdlib.h>
#include <string.h>
#include <sql.h>

int main(int argc, char *argv[])
{
    /* Include The SQLCA Data Structure Variable */
    EXEC SQL INCLUDE SQLCA;

    /* Set Up SQL Error, Warning, And "Not Found" Handlers */
    EXEC SQL WHENEVER SQLERROR GOTO ERROR;
    EXEC SQL WHENEVER SQLWARNING GOTO WARNING;
    EXEC SQL WHENEVER NOT FOUND GOTO NOT_FOUND;

    /* Declare The Local Memory Variables */
    int   rc = EXIT_SUCCESS;

    /* Declare The SQL Host Memory Variables */
    EXEC SQL BEGIN DECLARE SECTION;
        char    szEmpMatch[7];
        char    szEmpNo[7];
        char    szLastName[16];           // Change Size (16) To 8 To
                                          // Generate A WARNING
    EXEC SQL END DECLARE SECTION;

    /* Store The User-Supplied Employee Number In The Host Variable */
    strcpy(szEmpMatch, "000010");               // Default Employee ID
    if (argc >= 2)
        strncpy(szEmpMatch, argv[1], sizeof(szEmpMatch));
    else
        {
        printf("No Employee Number Specified - Using 000010\n");
        strncpy(szEmpMatch, "000010", sizeof(szEmpMatch));
        }

    /* Connect To The SAMPLE Database */
    EXEC SQL CONNECT TO SAMPLE USER etpdd6z USING sanders;

    /* Retrieve A Matching Record From The EMPLOYEE Table */
    EXEC SQL SELECT EMPNO,
```

```
                       LASTNAME
              INTO :szEmpNo,
                   :szLastName
              FROM USERID.EMPLOYEE
              WHERE EMPNO = :szEmpMatch;

          /* Print The Information Retrieved */
          printf("Employee No. : %s\nName      : %s\n",
                 szEmpNo, szLastName);

          /* Turn Off The SQL Warning And "Not Found" Handlers */
          EXEC SQL WHENEVER SQLWARNING CONTINUE;
          EXEC SQL WHENEVER SQLERROR CONTINUE;

          /* Issue A Rollback To Free All Locks */
          EXEC SQL ROLLBACK;

          /* Disconnect From The SAMPLE Database */
          EXEC SQL DISCONNECT CURRENT;

          /* Return To The Operating System */
          return(rc);

          /* Error Handler */
      ERROR:
          /* If An Error Has Occurred, Display The SQL Return Code */
          if (sqlca.sqlcode != SQL_RC_OK)
              printf("SQL ERROR : %ld\n", sqlca.sqlcode);

          /* Issue A Rollback To Free All Locks */
          EXEC SQL ROLLBACK;

          /* Turn Off The SQL Error Handler */
          EXEC SQL WHENEVER SQLERROR CONTINUE;

          /* Disconnect From The SAMPLE Database */
          EXEC SQL DISCONNECT CURRENT;

          /* Return To The Operating System */
          return(EXIT_FAILURE);

          /* Warning Handler */
      WARNING:
          printf("SQL WARNING : %5s\n", sqlca.sqlstate);

          /* Issue A Rollback To Free All Locks */
          EXEC SQL ROLLBACK;

          /* Turn Off The SQL Error Handler */
          EXEC SQL WHENEVER SQLERROR CONTINUE;
          /* Disconnect From The SAMPLE Database */
          EXEC SQL DISCONNECT CURRENT;

          /* Return To The Operating System */
          return(EXIT_FAILURE);

          /* "Not Found" Handler */
      NOT_FOUND:
          printf("REQUESTED DATA NOT FOUND\n");

          /* Issue A Rollback To Free All Locks */
          EXEC SQL ROLLBACK;
```

```
        /* Turn Off The SQL Error Handler */
        EXEC SQL WHENEVER SQLERROR CONTINUE;

        /* Disconnect From The SAMPLE Database */
        EXEC SQL DISCONNECT CURRENT;

        /* Return To The Operating System */
        return(EXIT_FAILURE);
    }
```

> Note: The WHENEVER statement is used in a C++ program in a similar manner.

BEGIN COMPOUND

Purpose The BEGIN COMPOUND statement tells the SQL precompiler where a compound SQL statement block begins and how to process the SQL substatements contained within it.

Syntax

```
EXEC SQL BEGIN COMPOUND [compound-type] STATIC <STOP AFTER FIRST number
STATEMENTS>
```

Parameters

compound-type Identifies the type of compound SQL statement to be created when all SQL substatements are grouped together to form a single SQL statement. The compound type can be one of the following predefined types:

- ATOMIC — The compound SQL statement is processed so if one SQL substatement fails, all changes made to the database by any SQL substatements within the compound SQL statement block will be rolled back (undone).
- NOT ATOMIC — The compound SQL statement is processed so if one SQL substatement fails, changes made to the database by other SQL substatements within the compound SQL statement block will be committed and only changes made to the database by the SQL substatement(s) that failed will be rolled back.

number Identifies the number of SQL substatements to be executed in a compound SQL statement block. The STOP AFTER FIRST number STATEMENTS option controls the number of SQL substatements that are actually executed. For example, if 50 SQL substatements exist in a compound SQL statement block and the STOP AFTER FIRST 25 STATEMENTS option is specified, only the first 25 SQL substatements will be executed).

Description The BEGIN COMPOUND statement identifies the start of a compound SQL statement block to the SQL precompiler. This statement also defines how database changes made by SQL substatements within the compound SQL statement block are to be processed if an error occurs. Input variables for all SQL substatements within a compound SQL statement retain their original value throughout the compound SQL statement block. This means that the SQL substatements should be treated as if they are executed nonsequentially; therefore, there should be no interdependencies with other SQL substatements within the same compound SQL statement block. All executable SQL statements can be used in a compound SQL statement block, except for these:

- SET CONNECTION
- CONNECT

- DISCONNECT
- OPEN
- FETCH
- CLOSE
- PREPARE
- DESCRIBE
- EXECUTE IMMEDIATE
- RELEASE
- ROLLBACK
- CALL
- BEGIN COMPOUND
- END COMPOUND

Comments

- A BEGIN COMPOUND statement must be paired with an END COMPOUND statement and these statement pairs cannot be nested. All SQL statements within the BEGIN COMPOUND statement and the END COMPOUND statement are treated as a single SQL statement by DB2.
- No SQL substatements in a compound SQL statement block can be preceded by "EXEC SQL."
- If a COMMIT statement is one of the SQL substatements, it must be the last substatement in the list. Placing COMMIT in this position ensures that it will be issued even if the STOP AFTER FIRST number STATEMENT option is used.
- An error will occur (SQLSTATE **25**000) if a COMMIT statement is used along with a Type 2 CONNECT or in an application running in an XA distributed transaction processing environment.
- No high-level language code (except for comments) is allowed within the SQL substatements of a compound SQL statement, so no host language code is allowed between the BEGIN COMPOUND statement and the END COMPOUND statement.
- When developing applications that will work with the distributed database connectivity service (DDCS) product, you must use the NOT ATOMIC compound SQL statement compound type.
- Only one SQLCA data structure variable records the results of a compound SQL statement. Most of the information in that SQLCA data structure variable is associated with the last SQL substatement executed in the compound SQL statement block. If an error or warning condition occurs, this SQLCA data structure variable will contain the following information:

  –The *sqlcode* and *sqlstate* values are normally the return codes associated with the last substatement executed. The only exception to this is when data is not found (described next).

  –If a "No Data Found" warning (SQLSTATE **02**000) is returned, then that warning is given precedence over any other warning condition so any previously defined WHENEVER NOT FOUND exception condition can be processed.

  –The *sqlwarn* indicators represent an accumulation of the indicators set by all SQL substatements within the compound SQL statement block.

  –If one or more errors occurred during the execution of a compound SQL statement are defined as being NOT ATOMIC, and if none of these errors are of a serious nature, the *sqlerrmc* will contain information on up to a maximum of seven of these errors. The first token of the *sqlerrmc* indicates the total number of errors that occurred and the remaining tokens contain the ordinal position and the

SQLSTATE of the failing SQL substatement within the compound SQL statement. The format of the *sqlerrmc* character string is as follows:

```
nnnXsssccccc<Xsssccccc><Xsssccccc>...<Xsssccccc>
```

where the substring *Xsssccccc* can be repeated up to six more times. The elements in the *sqlerrmc* character string are as follows:

nnn The total number of SQL substatements that produced errors. This field is left-justified and padded with blanks. Note that if the value of this field exceeds 999, counting starts over at 0.

X The token separator X ‘FF’.

sss The ordinal position of the SQL substatement that caused the error. For example, if the third SQL substatement failed, this field would contain a left-justified 3 (‘3’). Note that if the value of this field exceeds 999, counting starts over at 0.

ccccc The SQLSTATE error value.

–The second *sqlerrd* field in the SQLCA data structure variable contains the number that corresponds to the number of SQL substatements that failed (returned negative SQLCODEs).

–The third *sqlerrd* field in the SQLCA data structure variable contains an accumulation of the number of rows affected by all SQL substatements in the compound SQL statement block.

–The fourth *sqlerrd* field in the SQLCA data structure variable contains the number corresponding to the number of SQL substatements that were successful (*sqlcode* equal to 0). For example, if the fifth SQL substatement in a compound SQL statement block failed, the fourth *sqlerrd* field would be set to 4, indicating that four SQL substatements were successfully processed before the error occurred.

–The fifth *sqlerrd* field in the SQLCA data structure variable contains an accumulation of the number of rows updated or deleted because of enforcing referential integrity constraints for all SQL substatements in the compound SQL statement block that triggered such constraint activity.

Authorization No authorization is required to use the BEGIN COMPOUND statement, but the privileges held by the authorization ID must include those required to execute each individual SQL substatement contained within the compound SQL statement block.

Example The following C program illustrates how the BEGIN COMPOUND and END COMPOUND statements can group several UPDATE statements together as a single compound SQL statement:

```
#include <stdio.h>
#include <stdlib.h>
#include <sql.h>
int main()
{
    /* Include The SQLCA Data Structure Variable */
    EXEC SQL INCLUDE SQLCA;

    /* Set Up A Simple SQL Error Handler */
    EXEC SQL WHENEVER SQLERROR GOTO EXIT;

    /* Declare The Local Memory Variables */
    int  rc = EXIT_SUCCESS;

    /* Declare The SQL Host Memory Variables */
    EXEC SQL BEGIN DECLARE SECTION;
        char    szEmpNo[7];
        double  rdSalary;
```

```
    EXEC SQL END DECLARE SECTION;

    /* Connect To The SAMPLE Database */
    EXEC SQL CONNECT TO SAMPLE USER etpdd6z USING sanders;

    /* Retrieve A Record From The EMPLOYEE Table */
    EXEC SQL SELECT EMPNO,
                    SALARY
        INTO :szEmpNo,
             :rdSalary
        FROM USERID.EMPLOYEE
        WHERE EMPNO = '000050';

    /* Print The Information Retrieved - This Will Show A Record */
    /* Before It Is Changed By The Compound SQL Statement        */
    printf("Employee No. : %7s Original Salary : $%.2lf\n",
           szEmpNo, rdSalary);

    /* Begin The Compound SQL Statement Block                        */
    /* This Block Contains SQL Substatements That Will Give Each     */
    /* Employee A Cost-Of-Living Salary Increase (Increase Amount    */
    /* Is Based On Their Job Type )                                  */
    EXEC SQL BEGIN COMPOUND ATOMIC STATIC

        UPDATE USERID.EMPLOYEE SET SALARY = SALARY * 1.15
            WHERE JOB = 'PRES';
        UPDATE USERID.EMPLOYEE SET SALARY = SALARY * 1.12
            WHERE JOB = 'MANAGER';
        UPDATE USERID.EMPLOYEE SET SALARY = SALARY * 1.10
            WHERE JOB = 'SALESREP';
        UPDATE USERID.EMPLOYEE SET SALARY = SALARY * 1.10
            WHERE JOB = 'FIELDREP';
        UPDATE USERID.EMPLOYEE SET SALARY = SALARY * 1.10
            WHERE JOB = 'ANALYST';
        UPDATE USERID.EMPLOYEE SET SALARY = SALARY * 1.08
            WHERE JOB = 'DESIGNER';
        UPDATE USERID.EMPLOYEE SET SALARY = SALARY * 1.06
            WHERE JOB = 'OPERATOR';
        UPDATE USERID.EMPLOYEE SET SALARY = SALARY * 1.04
            WHERE JOB = 'CLERK';
      /* COMMIT;                          Normally You Would Commit  */
      /*                                  The Updates Here - In This */
      /*                                  Case We Do Not Want To     */
      /*                                  Modify The SAMPLE Database */

    /* End The Compound SQL Statement Block */
    END COMPOUND;

    /* Retrieve The Same Record From The EMPLOYEE Table */
    EXEC SQL SELECT EMPNO,
                    SALARY
        INTO :szEmpNo,
             :rdSalary
        FROM USERID.EMPLOYEE
        WHERE EMPNO = '000050';

    /* Print The Information Retrieved - This Will Show The Record */
    /* After It Has Been Changed By The Compound SQL Statement     */
    printf("Employee No. : %7s New Salary      : $%.2lf\n",
           szEmpNo, rdSalary);

EXIT:
    /* If An Error Has Occurred, Display The SQL Return Code */
```

```
        if (sqlca.sqlcode != SQL_RC_OK)
            {
            printf("SQL ERROR : %ld\n", sqlca.sqlcode);
            rc = EXIT_FAILURE;
            }

        /* Issue A Rollback To Free All Locks And Restore The Data */
        EXEC SQL ROLLBACK;

        /* Turn Off The SQL Error Handler */
        EXEC SQL WHENEVER SQLERROR CONTINUE;

        /* Disconnect From The SAMPLE Database */
        EXEC SQL DISCONNECT CURRENT;

        /* Return To The Operating System */
        return(rc);
}
```

Note: The BEGIN COMPOUND and END COMPOUND statements are used in a C++ program in a similar manner.

END COMPOUND

Purpose The END COMPOUND statement tells the SQL precompiler where a compound SQL statement block ends.

Syntax

```
END COMPOUND;
```

Description The END COMPOUND statement identifies the end of a compound SQL statement block to the SQL precompiler.

Comment An END COMPOUND statement must be paired with a BEGIN COMPOUND statement and these statement pairs cannot be nested. All SQL statements within the BEGIN COMPOUND statement and the END COMPOUND statement are treated as a single SQL statement by DB2.

Prerequisite The BEGIN COMPOUND statement must appear in an embedded SQL source-code file before the END COMPOUND statement.

Authorization No authorization is required to execute this statement.

See Also BEGIN COMPOUND

Example See the example provided for previous statement, BEGIN COMPOUND.

PREPARE

Purpose The PREPARE statement converts a dynamic SQL statement string into a prepared SQL statement that can be executed by DB2.

Syntax

```
EXEC SQL PREPARE [statement-name] <Options> FROM [statement-string];
```

Parameters

statement-name Identifies the prepared SQL statement to be executed by DB2. If the statement name identifies an SQL statement that has already been prepared, that previously prepared SQL statement is destroyed. For this reason, the statement name must not identify a previously prepared SELECT statement that is part of an open cursor.

statement-string Identifies the SQL statement character string to be prepared for execution. The statement string is stored in a character string host variable (either a fixed-length or a variable-length string) whose size must not exceed 32,765 bytes. Only the SQL statements shown earlier in the chapter can be used in the statement string and they must not contain comments or references to other host variables. Also, the SQL statement string must not begin with "EXEC SQL" and it must not contain a statement terminator (a semicolon, ;), with the exception of the CREATE TRIGGER statement, which can include semicolons to separate multiple triggered SQL statements. In addition, SELECT statement strings cannot contain an INTO clause.

Option

INTO [descriptor-name] Identifies an output SQL descriptor area (SQLDA) data structure variable that will contain information about the prepared SQL statement after the PREPARE statement is successfully executed. You can execute the DESCRIBE statement as an alternative to this option.

Description

The PREPARE statement dynamically prepares an SQL statement for execution by creating an executable SQL statement, known as a prepared statement, from a character string form of the SQL statement, known as a statement string.

Comments

- When the PREPARE statement is executed, the statement string is automatically parsed and checked for errors. If the statement string contains errors or is invalid, a prepared statement is not created and information about the error condition that prevented its creation is stored in the specified SQLCA data structure variable. Likewise, any subsequent EXECUTE or OPEN statements that reference the unprepared statement will generate the same error since an implicit prepare is performed by the system for these statements.
- DECLARE CURSOR statements can reference only prepared SELECT statements; any other prepared SQL statement will generate an error. On the other hand, EXECUTE statements can reference any prepared SQL statements other than SELECT statements.
- Once an SQL statement has been prepared, it can be executed (by either the EXECUTE or by the DECLARE CURSOR statement) many times. In fact, if a prepared statement will be executed only once, and if it does not contain parameter markers, it is more efficient to use the EXECUTE IMMEDIATE statement rather than the PREPARE and EXECUTE statements.
- Caching the executable sections of SQL data manipulation language (DML) statements can affect the behavior of an EXECUTE IMMEDIATE statement. Refer to the beginning of the chapter for more information about statement caching.
- All prepared statements created within a transaction are destroyed when that transaction is terminated, except for prepared statements referenced by open cursors declared with the WITH HOLD option. These prepared statements are not destroyed until the cursor is closed.

Authorization

The authorization needed to use the PREPARE statement is determined by the actual SQL statement being prepared. For SQL statements where authorization checking is performed at statement preparation time, e.g., data manipulation language (DML) statements, the privileges held by the authorization ID of the statement must include those required to execute the prepared SQL statement. For SQL statements in which authorization checking is performed at statement execution time, e.g., data definition language (DDL), GRANT, and REVOKE statements, no authorization is required to use this statement. However, authorization will be checked when the prepared SQL statement is executed.

See Also EXECUTE, EXECUTE IMMEDIATE, DECLARE CURSOR, BEGIN DECLARE SECTION, END DECLARE SECTION

Example The following C program illustrates how the PREPARE statement prepares and executes various types of dynamic SQL statements:

```
#include <stdio.h>
#include <stdlib.h>
#include <string.h>
#include <sql.h>
#include <sqlda.h>

/* Define The Local Function Prototypes */
void ltrim(char *szString);

int main(int argc, char* argv[])
{
    /* Include The SQLCA Data Structure Variable */
    EXEC SQL INCLUDE SQLCA;

    /* Set Up A Simple SQL Error Handler */
    EXEC SQL WHENEVER SQLERROR GOTO EXIT;

    /* Declare The Local Memory Variables */
    int             rc = EXIT_SUCCESS;
    struct sqlda    *out_sqlda;          // SQLDA Data Structure Pointer
    char            szEmpNo[7];          // Employee Number
    short           sEmpNoInd;           // Employee No. Indicator
    char            szSalary[10];        // Salary
    short           sSalaryInd;          // Salary Indicator

    /* Declare The SQL Host Memory Variables */
    EXEC SQL BEGIN DECLARE SECTION;
        char    szSelectString[80];
        char    szUpdateString[80];
    EXEC SQL END DECLARE SECTION;
    /* Make Sure The Percent Increase Was Entered */
    if (argc < 2)
        {
        printf("ERROR - Percentage Increase Must Be Specified\n");
        sqlca.sqlcode = SQL_RC_OK;
        return(EXIT_FAILURE);
        }

    /* Build The Select SQL Statement String */
    strcpy(szSelectString, "SELECT EMPNO, CHAR(SALARY, '.') FROM ");
    strcat(szSelectString, "USERID.EMPLOYEE WHERE JOB = 'MANAGER'");

    /* Build The Update SQL Statement String */
    strcpy(szUpdateString, "UPDATE USERID.EMPLOYEE SET SALARY = ");
    strcat(szUpdateString, "SALARY * 1.");
    strcat(szUpdateString, argv[1]);
    strcat(szUpdateString, " WHERE JOB = 'MANAGER'");

    /* Allocate And Initialize An SQLDA Data Structure Variable */
```

```
if ((out_sqlda = (struct sqlda *) malloc(SQLDASIZE(2))) == NULL)
    {
    printf("ERROR : Unable To Allocate Memory For SQLDA !\n");
    return(EXIT_FAILURE);
    }
out_sqlda->sqln = 2;

/* Connect To The SAMPLE Database */
EXEC SQL CONNECT TO SAMPLE USER etpdd6z USING sanders;

/* Prepare The Select SQL Statement */
EXEC SQL PREPARE SQL_STMNT1 INTO :*out_sqlda FROM :szSelectString;

/* Store The Address Of Local Memory Variables In The    */
/* Appropriate SQLDA->SQLVAR Data And Indicator Pointers */
out_sqlda->sqlvar[0].sqldata = (unsigned char *) &szEmpNo;
out_sqlda->sqlvar[0].sqlind = (short *) &sEmpNoInd;
out_sqlda->sqlvar[1].sqldata = (unsigned char *) &szSalary;
out_sqlda->sqlvar[1].sqlind = (short *) &sSalaryInd;

/* Declare The Dynamic Cursor */
EXEC SQL DECLARE DYN_CURSOR CURSOR FOR SQL_STMNT1;

/* Open The Dynamic Cursor */
EXEC SQL OPEN DYN_CURSOR;

/* If The Cursor Was Successfully Opened, Fetch The Records */
/* Into Local Memory Variables                              */
printf("Original Employee Salary Information\n");
while (sqlca.sqlcode == SQL_RC_OK)
    {
    EXEC SQL FETCH DYN_CURSOR USING DESCRIPTOR :*out_sqlda;

    /* Print The Information Retrieved - This Will Show The */
    /* Records Before They Are Modified                     */
    if (sqlca.sqlcode == SQL_RC_OK)
        {
        ltrim(szSalary);
        printf("Employee ID : %s\t Salary : $%s\n",
            szEmpNo, szSalary);
        }
    }                                       /* End Of WHILE   */
/* Close The Cursor */
EXEC SQL CLOSE DYN_CURSOR;

/* Prepare The Update SQL Statement */
EXEC SQL PREPARE SQL_STMNT2 FROM :szUpdateString;

/* Execute The Prepared SQL Statement */
EXEC SQL EXECUTE SQL_STMNT2;

/* Open The Dynamic Cursor */
EXEC SQL OPEN DYN_CURSOR;

/* If The Cursor Was Successfully Opened, Fetch The Records */
/* Into Local Memory Variables                              */
printf("Employee Salary Information\n");
while (sqlca.sqlcode == SQL_RC_OK)
    {
    EXEC SQL FETCH DYN_CURSOR USING DESCRIPTOR :*out_sqlda;

    /* Print The Information Retrieved - This Will Show The */
```

```
        /* Records After They Have Been Modified                    */
        if (sqlca.sqlcode == SQL_RC_OK)
            {
            ltrim(szSalary);
            printf("Employee ID : %s\t Salary : $%s\n",
                szEmpNo, szSalary);
            }
        }                                         /* End Of WHILE    */

    /* Close The Cursor */
    EXEC SQL CLOSE DYN_CURSOR;

    /* Normally You Would Commit The Updates Here - In This Case We */
    /* Do Not Want To Change The SAMPLE Database                    */
//  EXEC SQL COMMIT;

EXIT:
    /* If An Error Has Occurred, Display The SQL Return Code */
    if (sqlca.sqlcode != SQL_RC_OK)
        {
        printf("SQL ERROR : %ld\n", sqlca.sqlcode);
        rc = EXIT_FAILURE;
        }

    /* Issue A Rollback To Free All Locks */
    EXEC SQL ROLLBACK;

    /* Turn Off The SQL Error Handler */
    EXEC SQL WHENEVER SQLERROR CONTINUE;

    /* Disconnect From The SAMPLE Database */
    EXEC SQL DISCONNECT CURRENT;

    /* Free Memory Allocated For The SQLDA Data Structure Variable */
    if (out_sqlda)
        free(out_sqlda);

    /* Return To The Operating System */
    return(rc);
}
/* Function To Remove Leading Zeros From Number Strings */
void ltrim(char *szString)
{

    /* Declare The Local Memory Variables */
    short   i, j;

    /* Find The Position Of The First Character That Is Not "0" */
    for (j = 0; j < strlen(szString); j++)
        if (szString[j] != '0')
            break;

    /* Move All Characters In The String Forward */
    for (i = 0; i < strlen(szString) - j; i++, j++)
        szString[i] = szString[j];

    /* Terminate The New String */
    szString[i] = '';
    return;
}
```

The following C++ program illustrates how the PREPARE statement prepares and executes various types of dynamic SQL statements within class methods:

```
#include <iostream.h>
#include <stdlib.h>
#include <string.h>
#include <sql.h>
#include <sqlda.h>

/* Define The Employee Class */
class Employee
{
    private:

        /* Include The SQLCA Data Structure Variable */
        EXEC SQL INCLUDE SQLCA;

        /* Declare The SQL Host Memory Variables */
        EXEC SQL BEGIN DECLARE SECTION;
            char    szSelectString[80];
            char    szUpdateString[80];
        EXEC SQL END DECLARE SECTION;

        /* Declare All Other Private Memory Variables */
        struct sqlda    *out_sqlda;      // SQLDA Data Structure Pointer
        char            szEmpNo[7];      // Employee Number
        short           sEmpNoInd;       // Employee No. Indicator
        char            szSalary[12];    // Salary
        short           sSalaryInd;      // Salary Indicator

        /* Declare The Private Member Function Prototype */
        void      ltrim(char *szString);

    /* Declare The Public Member Function Prototypes */
    public:
        Employee(const char *szString);           // Constructor
        ~Employee() { delete []out_sqlda; }       // Destructor
        short int getData();
        short int updateData();
} ;
/* Define The Class Constructor */
Employee::Employee(const char *szPercent)
{
    /* Build The Select SQL Statement String */
    strcpy(szSelectString, "SELECT EMPNO, CHAR(SALARY) FROM ");
    strcat(szSelectString, "USERID.EMPLOYEE WHERE JOB = 'MANAGER'");

    /* Build The Update SQL Statement String */
    strcpy(szUpdateString, "UPDATE USERID.EMPLOYEE ");
    strcat(szUpdateString, "SET SALARY = SALARY * 1.");
    strcat(szUpdateString, szPercent);
    strcat(szUpdateString, " WHERE JOB = 'MANAGER'");
}

/* Define The getData() Member Function */
short int Employee::getData()
{
    /* Allocate And Initialize An SQLDA Data Structure Variable */
    out_sqlda = (struct sqlda *) new char [SQLDASIZE(2)];
    if (out_sqlda != NULL)
        out_sqlda->sqln = 2;
```

```
    /* Prepare The Insert SQL Statement */
    EXEC SQL PREPARE SQL_STMNT1 INTO :*out_sqlda FROM :szSelectString;

    /* Store The Address Of Local Memory Variables In The   */
    /* Appropriate SQLDA SQLVAR Data And Indicator Pointers */
    out_sqlda->sqlvar[0].sqldata = (char *) &szEmpNo;
    out_sqlda->sqlvar[0].sqlind = (short *) &sEmpNoInd;
    out_sqlda->sqlvar[1].sqldata = (char *) &szSalary;
    out_sqlda->sqlvar[1].sqlind = (short *) &sSalaryInd;

    /* Declare The Dynamic Cursor */
    EXEC SQL DECLARE DYN_CURSOR CURSOR FOR SQL_STMNT1;

    /* Open The Dynamic Cursor */
    EXEC SQL OPEN DYN_CURSOR;

    /* If The Cursor Was Successfully Opened, Fetch The Records */
    /* Into Local Memory Variables                              */
    cout << endl << "Employee Salary Information" << endl;
    while (sqlca.sqlcode == SQL_RC_OK)
        {
        strcpy(szEmpNo, "      ");

        EXEC SQL FETCH DYN_CURSOR USING DESCRIPTOR :*out_sqlda;

        /* Print The Information Retrieved - This Will Show The */
        /* Records Before They Are Modified                     */
        if (sqlca.sqlcode == SQL_RC_OK)
            {
            ltrim(szSalary);
            cout << "Employee ID : " << szEmpNo << "   Salary : $";
            cout << szSalary << ".00" << endl;
            }
        }                                        /* End Of WHILE   */

    /* Close The Cursor */
    EXEC SQL CLOSE DYN_CURSOR;

    /* Return The SQL Return Code */
    return(sqlca.sqlcode);
}
/* Define The updateData() Member Function */
short int Employee::updateData()
{
    /* Prepare The Update SQL Statement */
    EXEC SQL PREPARE SQL_STMNT2 FROM :szUpdateString;

    /* Execute The Prepared SQL Statement */
    EXEC SQL EXECUTE SQL_STMNT2;

    /* Return The SQL Return Code */
    return(sqlca.sqlcode);
}

/* Define The ltrim() Member Function */
void Employee::ltrim(char *szString)
{
    /* Declare The Local Memory Variables */
    short   i, j;

    /* Find The Position Of The First Character That Is Not "0" */
    for (j = 0; j < strlen(szString); j++)
        if (szString[j] != '0')
```

```
            break;

    /* Move All Characters In The String Forward */
    for (i = 0; i < strlen(szString) - j; i++, j++)
        szString[i] = szString[j];

    /* Terminate The New String */
    szString[i] = '';
    return;
}

int main(int argc, char* argv[])
{
    /* Declare The Local Memory Variables */
    short int rc = EXIT_SUCCESS;           // Must Be Declared Here
                                           // For The SQL Precompiler

    /* Include The SQLCA Data Structure Variable */
    EXEC SQL INCLUDE SQLCA;                // Local To The Main Function

    /* Set Up A Simple SQL Error Handler */
    EXEC SQL WHENEVER SQLERROR GOTO EXIT;

    /* Make Sure The Percent Increase Was Entered */
    if (argc < 2)
        {
        cout << "ERROR - Percentage Increase Must Be Specified";
        cout << endl;
        return(EXIT_FAILURE);
        }

    /* Create An Instance Of The Employee Class */
    Employee EmpInfo(argv[1]);

    /* Connect To The SAMPLE Database */
    EXEC SQL CONNECT TO SAMPLE USER etpdd6z USING sanders;

    /* Print The Data Records In The EMPLOYEE Table That Will Be */
    /* Modified                                                  */
    rc = EmpInfo.getData();
    /* Update The Data Records In The EMPLOYEE Table */
    rc = EmpInfo.updateData();

    /* Print The Data Records Again - This Will Show That The */
    /* Records Have Been Modified                             */
    rc = EmpInfo.getData();

    /* Normally You Would Commit The Updates Here - In This Case We */
    /* Do Not Want To Change The SAMPLE Database                    */
//  EXEC SQL COMMIT;

EXIT:
    /* If An Error Has Occurred, Display The SQL Return Code */
    if (sqlca.sqlcode != SQL_RC_OK)
        {
        cout << "SQL ERROR : " << sqlca.sqlcode << endl;
        rc = EXIT_FAILURE;
        }

    /* Issue A Rollback To Free All Locks */
    EXEC SQL ROLLBACK;
```

```
    /* Turn Off The SQL Error Handler */
    EXEC SQL WHENEVER SQLERROR CONTINUE;

    /* Disconnect From The SAMPLE Database */
    EXEC SQL DISCONNECT CURRENT;

    /* Return To The Operating System */
    return(rc);
}
```

DESCRIBE

Purpose The DESCRIBE statement allows you to obtain information about a dynamically prepared SQL statement.

Syntax

```
EXEC SQL DESCRIBE [statement-name] INTO [descriptor-name];
```

Parameters

statement-name Identifies the SQL statement for which information is to be obtained. The statement name must identify an SQL statement that has already been prepared with the PREPARE statement.

descriptor-name Identifies an SQL descriptor area (SQLDA) structure variable. DB2's database manager stores information about the SQL statement being described in this data structure variable.

Description The DESCRIBE statement obtains information about a prepared SQL statement and stores it in an SQL descriptor area (SQLDA) data structure variable. Before the DESCRIBE statement is executed, the SQLDA data structure variable must be appropriately allocated and the *sqln* field in this SQLDA data structure variable must be set to a value greater than or equal to zero. After the DESCRIBE statement is executed, DB2 assigns values to the fields in this SQLDA data structure as follows:

sqldaid The first five bytes of this character string field are set to "SQLDA," and the sixth and eighth bytes are set to the space character. The seventh byte, known as the SQLDOUBLED byte, is set to 2 if the SQLDA contains two *sqlvar* entries for every column found in the result table (if the result table contains LOB and/or distinct type columns). If the SQLDA contains one *sqlvar* entry for every column found in the result table or if there is not enough room in the SQLDA data structure to store all the information returned by the DESCRIBE statement, this byte is set to the space character.

sqldabc This field contains the size of the SQLDA data structure.

sqld If the prepared SQL statement is a SELECT statement, this field contains the number of columns in the SELECT result table; otherwise, this field contains 0.

sqlvar If the value of *sqld* is 0 or greater than the value of *sqln*, no values are assigned to occurrences of *sqlvar*. If the value of *sqld* is greater than 0 but less than or equal to the value of *sqln*, values are assigned to occurrences of *sqlvar* so the first occurrence of *sqlvar* contains a description of the first column of the result table, the second occurrence of *sqlvar* contain a description of the second column of the result table, and so on. The description of a column consists of the values assigned to the following *sqlvar* fields:

sqltype A code that identifies the data type of the result table column and indicates whether or not the column can contain null values.

sqllen A value that indicates the length of the result table column, dependent on the data type of the column. *sqllen* is always 0 if the column contains a LOB data type.

sqlname If the derived result table column is not a simple column reference, then this field contains an ASCII numeric literal value that represents the derived column's original position within the SELECT statement's select list. Otherwise, this field contains the name of the result table column.

sqllonglen The length attribute of a BLOB, CLOB, or DBCLOB column.

sqldatatype_name If the result table column contains a distinct type, this field will contain the fully qualified distinct type name. Otherwise, the high-order portion of this field will contain the schema name "SYSIBM," and the low-order portion of this field will contain the corresponding name in the TYPENAME column of the SYSCAT.DATATYPES catalog view.

Note: The values for the *sqllonglen* and *sqldatatype_name* fields are set only if the number of *sqlvar* entries are doubled to accommodate LOB or distinct type columns (i.e., the SQL-DOUBLED byte of the *sqldaid* character string value is set to 2).

Comments

- There are three possible ways to allocate memory storage for the SQLDA data structure variable:

Technique 1 Allocate an SQLDA data structure variable with enough occurrences of *sqlvar* to accommodate the largest select list the application will have to process (the *sqln* field value will equal the maximum number of columns expected in a result data set). If the select list will contain LOB or distinct type columns, the number of SQLVARs should be twice the maximum number of columns expected in a result data set; otherwise, the number should be the same as the maximum number of columns. Once the memory is allocated for the SQLDA structure data variable, the application can use it many times. Unfortunately, this technique uses a large amount of memory storage that is not deallocated (and therefore cannot be reused) until the application ends.

Technique 2 Execute a DESCRIBE statement with an SQLDA that has no occurrences of *sqlvar* (i.e., the *sqln* field value is 0). After the DESCRIBE statement is executed, the value found in the *sqld* field will be the number of columns found in the result data set. Because the *sqln* field was set to 0, a warning with SQLSTATE **01**005 will be returned. If the SQLCODE accompanying that warning is equal to either +237, +238, or +239, the number of SQLVAR entries needed will be double the value returned in *sqld* field. Otherwise, the number of SQLVAR entries needed will be the value returned in the *sqld* field. Now that you know the number of occurrences of *sqlvar* that will be needed, allocate an SQLDA data structure variable with enough occurrences of *sqlvar* and set the *sqln* field value accordingly. Then execute the DESCRIBE statement again using the new SQLDA data structure variable. This technique allows for better storage management than the first technique, but it doubles the number of DESCRIBE statements needed and adds more processing overhead.

Technique 3 Allocate an SQLDA data structure variable that is large enough to handle most (perhaps all) select lists, but that is also reasonably small. Execute the DESCRIBE statement and check the SQLSTATE and SQLCODE values. If an error or warning occurs because the SQLDA data structure variable is too small, use the *sqld* value returned to allocate a larger SQLDA data structure variable and execute the DESCRIBE statement again using the new SQLDA data structure variable. This technique is a nice compromise between the first two techniques, but its effectiveness depends on choosing a good size for the original SQLDA data structure variable.

- In order to obtain an accurate description of the result table columns of a prepared SELECT SQL statement, the number of occurrences of *sqlvar* (*sqln* field value) must not be less than the number of columns that will be returned to the result data set.

- All prepared statements created by a transaction are destroyed when the transaction terminates, so an SQL statement cannot be described if either a COMMIT or a ROLLBACK statement is executed after it is prepared.
- If an LOB value larger than 1 megabyte will be returned in the result data set, keep in mind that all manipulations of this LOB will affect memory. In these cases, it is better to allocate memory storage for the SQLDA data structure variable by using the second technique, by setting the *sqltype* field value to SQL_TYP_xLOB_LOCATOR or SQL_TYP_xLOB_FILE, and by setting the *sqllen* field value accordingly before allocating memory for the second SQLDA data structure variable. This way, you can use LOB locators or file reference variables and avoid having to retrieve large amounts of data into the SQLDA data structure variable.

Prerequisites Before the DESCRIBE statement is executed, the SQL statement must be prepared with the PREPARE statement. Also, the SQLDA data structure variable must have the appropriate amount of memory storage allocated and the *sqln* field of this SQLDA data structure variable must be set to indicate how many occurrences of SQLVAR will be needed to describe the SQL statement.

Authorization No authorization is required to execute this statement.

See Also PREPARE, EXECUTE

Example The following C program illustrates how the DESCRIBE statement populates an SQLDA data structure variable, which then retrieves data from the STAFF table in the SAMPLE database:

```
#include <stdio.h>
#include <stdlib.h>
#include <string.h>
#include <sql.h>
#include <sqlda.h>

int main(int argc, char* argv[])
{
    /* Include The SQLCA Data Structure Variable */
    EXEC SQL INCLUDE SQLCA;

    /* Set Up A Simple SQL Error Handler */
    EXEC SQL WHENEVER SQLERROR GOTO EXIT;

    /* Declare The Local Memory Variables */
    int            rc = EXIT_SUCCESS;
    struct sqlda   *out_sqlda;          // SQLDA Data Structure Pointer
    struct VARCHAR {                    // VARCHAR Data Structure
        short size;
        char  string[10];
        } stEmpName;                    // Employee Name
    short          sEmpNameInd;         // Employee Name Indicator
    short          sEmpID;              // Employee ID
    short          sEmpIDInd;           // Employee ID Indicator
    short          sYears;              // Years Of Service
    short          sYearsInd;           // Years Of Service Indicator
    char           szEmpName[11];       // Employee Name String

    /* Declare The SQL Host Memory Variables */
```

```
EXEC SQL BEGIN DECLARE SECTION;
    char     szPrepString[80];
EXEC SQL END DECLARE SECTION;

/* Make Sure The Job Type Was Entered */
if (argc < 2)
    {
    printf("ERROR - Job Type Must Be Specified\n");
    return(EXIT_FAILURE);
    }

/* Build The SQL Statement String */
strcpy(szPrepString, "SELECT NAME, ID, YEARS FROM USERID.STAFF ");
strcat(szPrepString, "WHERE JOB = '");
strcat(szPrepString, argv[1]);
strcat(szPrepString, "'");

/* Connect To The Sample Database */
EXEC SQL CONNECT TO SAMPLE USER etpdd6z USING sanders;

/* Prepare The SQL Statement */
EXEC SQL PREPARE SQL_STATEMENT FROM :szPrepString;

/* Allocate And Initialize An SQLDA Data Structure Variable */
if ((out_sqlda = (struct sqlda *) malloc(SQLDASIZE(3))) == NULL)
    {
    printf("ERROR : Unable To Allocate Memory For SQLDA !\n");
    goto EXIT;
    }
out_sqlda->sqln = 3;

/* Describe The Prepared SQL Statement */
EXEC SQL DESCRIBE SQL_STATEMENT INTO :*out_sqlda;
/* Store The Address Of Local Memory Variables In The      */
/* Appropriate SQLDA->SQLVAR Data And Indicator Pointers */
out_sqlda->sqlvar[0].sqldata = (unsigned char *) &stEmpName;
out_sqlda->sqlvar[0].sqlind = (short *) &sEmpNameInd;
out_sqlda->sqlvar[1].sqldata = (unsigned char *) &sEmpID;
out_sqlda->sqlvar[1].sqlind = (short *) &sEmpIDInd;
out_sqlda->sqlvar[2].sqldata = (unsigned char *) &sYears;
out_sqlda->sqlvar[2].sqlind = (short *) &sYearsInd;

/* Declare The Dynamic Cursor */
EXEC SQL DECLARE DYN_CURSOR CURSOR FOR SQL_STATEMENT;

/* Open The Dynamic Cursor */
EXEC SQL OPEN DYN_CURSOR;

/* If The Cursor Was Successfully Opened, Fetch The Records */
/* Into Local Memory Variables                               */
printf("    Name        ID   Years\n");
printf("-------------------------\n");
while (sqlca.sqlcode == SQL_RC_OK)
    {
    EXEC SQL FETCH DYN_CURSOR USING DESCRIPTOR :*out_sqlda;

    /* Print The Record */
    if (sqlca.sqlcode == SQL_RC_OK)
        {
```

```
            strncpy(szEmpName, " ", 10);
            strncpy(szEmpName, stEmpName.string, stEmpName.size);
            printf("%10s %5d %5d\n", szEmpName, sEmpID, sYears);
            }
        }                                           /* End Of WHILE     */

    /* Close The Cursor */
    EXEC SQL CLOSE DYN_CURSOR;

EXIT:
    /* If An Error Has Occurred, Display The SQL Return Code */
    if (sqlca.sqlcode != SQL_RC_OK)
        {
        printf("SQL ERROR : %ld\n", sqlca.sqlcode);
        rc = EXIT_FAILURE;
        }

    /* Issue A Rollback To Free All Locks */
    EXEC SQL ROLLBACK;

    /* Turn Off The SQL Error Handler */
    EXEC SQL WHENEVER SQLERROR CONTINUE;

    /* Disconnect From The SAMPLE Database */
    EXEC SQL DISCONNECT CURRENT;

    /* Free Memory Allocated For The SQLDA Data Structure Variable */
    if (out_sqlda)
        free(out_sqlda);

    /* Return To The Operating System */
    return(rc);
}
```

The following C++ program illustrates how the DESCRIBE statement populates an SQLDA data structure variable, which is then used by member functions to retrieve data from the STAFF table in the SAMPLE database:

```
#include <iostream.h>
#include <stdlib.h>
#include <string.h>
#include <sql.h>
#include <sqlda.h>

/* Define The Staff Class */
class Staff
{
    private:

        /* Include The SQLCA Data Structure Variable */
        EXEC SQL INCLUDE SQLCA;

        /* Declare The SQL Host Memory Variables */
        EXEC SQL BEGIN DECLARE SECTION;
            char    szPrepString[80];
        EXEC SQL END DECLARE SECTION;

        /* Declare All Other Private Memory Variables */
        struct sqlda   *out_sqlda;       // SQLDA Data Structure Pointer
        struct VARCHAR {                 // VARCHAR Data Structure
            short size;
```

```
            char  string[10];
            }  stEmpName;               // Employee Name
        short           sEmpNameInd;    // Employee Name Indicator
        short           sEmpID;         // Employee ID
        short           sEmpIDInd;      // Employee ID Indicator
        short           sYears;         // Years Of Service
        short           sYearsInd;      // Years Of Service Indicator
        char            szEmpName[11];  // Employee Name String

    /* Declare The Public Member Function Prototypes */
    public:
        Staff(const char *szString);          // Constructor
        ~Staff() { delete []out_sqlda; }      // Destructor
        short int getData();
} ;

/* Define The Class Constructor */
Staff::Staff(const char *szJobCode)
{
    /* Build The Select SQL Statement String */
    strcpy(szPrepString, "SELECT NAME, ID, YEARS FROM USERID.STAFF ");
    strcat(szPrepString, "WHERE JOB = '");
    strcat(szPrepString, szJobCode);
    strcat(szPrepString, "'");
}

/* Define The GetData() Member Function */
short int Staff::getData()
{
    /* Prepare The Select SQL Statement */
    EXEC SQL PREPARE SQL_STATEMENT FROM :szPrepString;

    /* Allocate And Initialize An SQLDA Data Structure Variable */
    out_sqlda = (struct sqlda *) new char [SQLDASIZE(3)];
    if (out_sqlda != NULL)
        out_sqlda->sqln = 3;

    /* Describe The Select SQL Statement */
    EXEC SQL DESCRIBE SQL_STATEMENT INTO :*out_sqlda;

    /* Store The Address Of Local Memory Variables In The   */
    /* Appropriate SQLDA SQLVAR Data And Indicator Pointers */
    out_sqlda->sqlvar[0].sqldata = (char *) &stEmpName;
    out_sqlda->sqlvar[0].sqlind = (short *) &sEmpNameInd;
    out_sqlda->sqlvar[1].sqldata = (char *) &sEmpID;
    out_sqlda->sqlvar[1].sqlind = (short *) &sEmpIDInd;
    out_sqlda->sqlvar[2].sqldata = (char *) &sYears;
    out_sqlda->sqlvar[2].sqlind = (short *) &sYearsInd;

    /* Declare The Dynamic Cursor */
    EXEC SQL DECLARE DYN_CURSOR CURSOR FOR SQL_STATEMENT;

    /* Open The Dynamic Cursor */
    EXEC SQL OPEN DYN_CURSOR;

    /* If The Cursor Was Successfully Opened, Fetch The Records */
    /* Into Local Memory Variables                              */
    cout << "    Name       ID   Years" << endl;
    cout << "-------------------------" << endl;
    while (sqlca.sqlcode == SQL_RC_OK)
        {
```

```
            EXEC SQL FETCH DYN_CURSOR USING DESCRIPTOR :*out_sqlda;

            /* Print The Record */
            if (sqlca.sqlcode == SQL_RC_OK)
                {
                strncpy(szEmpName, " ", 10);
                strncpy(szEmpName, stEmpName.string, stEmpName.size);
                cout.width(10);
                cout << szEmpName;
                cout.width(6);
                cout << sEmpID;
                cout.width(6);
                cout << sYears << endl;
                }
            }                                           /* End Of WHILE   */

        /* Close The Cursor */
        EXEC SQL CLOSE DYN_CURSOR;

        /* Return The SQL Return Code */
        return(sqlca.sqlcode);
}

int main(int argc, char* argv[])
{
    /* Declare The Local Memory Variables */
    short int rc = EXIT_SUCCESS;            // Must Be Declared Here
                                            // For The SQL Precompiler

    /* Include The SQLCA Data Structure Variable */
    EXEC SQL INCLUDE SQLCA;                 // Local To The Main Function

    /* Set Up A Simple SQL Error Handler */
    EXEC SQL WHENEVER SQLERROR GOTO EXIT;
    /* Make Sure The Job Type Was Entered */
    if (argc < 2)
        {
        cout << "ERROR - Job Type Must Be Specified" << endl;
        return(EXIT_FAILURE);
        }

    /* Create An Instance Of The Staff Class */
    Staff StaffInfo(argv[1]);

    /* Connect To The SAMPLE Database */
    EXEC SQL CONNECT TO SAMPLE USER etpdd6z USING sanders;

    /* Print The Data Records In The STAFF Table */
    rc = StaffInfo.getData();

EXIT:
    /* If An Error Has Occurred, Display The SQL Return Code */
    if (sqlca.sqlcode != SQL_RC_OK)
        {
        cout << "SQL ERROR : " << sqlca.sqlcode << endl;
        rc = EXIT_FAILURE;
        }

    /* Issue A Rollback To Free All Locks */
    EXEC SQL ROLLBACK;

    /* Turn Off The SQL Error Handler */
```

```
    EXEC SQL WHENEVER SQLERROR CONTINUE;

    /* Disconnect From The SAMPLE Database */
    EXEC SQL DISCONNECT CURRENT;

    /* Return To The Operating System */
    return(rc);
}
```

EXECUTE

Purpose The EXECUTE statement submits a prepared dynamic SQL statement to DB2 for execution.

Syntax `EXEC SQL EXECUTE [statement-name] <Options>;`

Parameter

statement-name Identifies the SQL statement to be executed by DB2. The statement name must identify an SQL statement that has already been prepared, and the prepared SQL statement must not be a SELECT statement.

Options

USING[host-variable,...] Identifies one or more host variables for which values are substituted for parameter markers (question marks) in a prepared SQL statement. If the prepared SQL statement includes parameter markers, you must use the USING option and the number of host variables identified must be the same as the number of parameter markers in the prepared SQL statement.

USING DESCRIPTOR [descriptor-name] Identifies an input SQL descriptor area (SQLDA) data structure variable that contains a valid description of the host variables that will be used by the SQL statement when it is executed. Before the EXECUTE statement is processed with the USING DESCRIPTOR option, you must set the following fields in the SQLDA data structure variable:

sqln This field indicates the number of *sqlvar* occurrences that will occur in the SQLDA data structure variable.

sqldabc This field specifies the total number of bytes of memory storage allocated for the SQLDA data structure variable. Since the SQLDA data structure variable must have enough storage allocated for it to contain all *sqlvar* occurrences, the value in the *sqldabc* field must be greater than or equal to 16 + *sqln* * (*n*), where *n* is the length of a single *sqlvar* occurrence.

sqld This field indicates the number of occurrences of *sqlvar* variables that are to be used when the statement is processed. The value in this field must be set to a value greater than or equal to zero and less than or equal to the value in the *sqln* field.

sqlvar field(s) Each occurrence of this field specifies the attributes of a single variable. If you need to accommodate LOB or distinct type result columns, two *sqlvar* entries must exist for every select-list item (or column of the result table).

Description The EXECUTE statement submits a dynamic SQL statement to DB2 for execution after it has been prepared by the PREPARE statement. When a dynamic SQL statement is prepared, an executable statement known as a prepared statement is created from the original character statement string.

Comments

- Before a prepared SQL statement is executed, each parameter marker it contains is replaced by the value of the parameter marker's corresponding host variable. For typed parameter markers, the attributes of the target host variable are those specified by the CAST specification. For untyped parameter markers, the attributes of the target host variable are determined by the context in which the parameter marker is used (refer to the beginning of the chapter for more information). For example, the host variable V corresponds to parameter marker P. When the SQL statement containing parameter marker P is executed, the value of V is assigned to the target variable for P in accordance with the rules for assigning a value to a column:
  –V must be compatible with the target column.
  –If V is a string, its length must not be greater than the length attribute of the target column.
  –If V is a number, the absolute value of its integral part must not be greater than the maximum absolute value of the integral part of the target column.
  –If the attributes of V are not identical to the attributes of the target column, the value is converted to conform to the attributes of the target column.
- When the prepared statement is executed, the value used in place of P is the value of the target variable for P. For example, if V is defined as char V[6] (C and C++) and the target column is defined as CHAR(8), the value used in place of P is the value of V padded with two blanks.
- Caching the executable sections of SQL data manipulation language (DML) statements can affect the behavior of an EXECUTE statement. Refer to the beginning of the chapter for more information about statement caching.

Prerequisites

Before you can use the EXECUTE statement, the SQL statement to be executed must be prepared with the PREPARE statement.

Authorization

Authorization needed to use the EXECUTE statement is determined by the actual SQL statement being submitted to DB2 for execution. For SQL statements in which authorization checking is performed at statement execution time, i.e., data definition language (DDL), GRANT, and REVOKE statements, the privileges held by the authorization ID of the statement must include those required to execute the prepared SQL statement. For SQL statements where authorization checking is performed at statement preparation time, i.e., data manipulation language (DML) statements, no authorization is required to use this statement.

See Also

PREPARE, DESCRIBE, EXECUTE IMMEDIATE

Examples

The following C program illustrates the various ways to use the EXECUTE statement to execute dynamically prepared SQL statements:

```
#include <stdio.h>
#include <stdlib.h>
#include <string.h>
#include <ctype.h>
#include <sql.h>

/* Define The Local Function Prototypes */
void uppercase(char *szString);

int main(int argc, char* argv[])
{
    /* Include The SQLCA Data Structure Variable */
    EXEC SQL INCLUDE SQLCA;
```

```
/* Set Up A Simple SQL Error Handler */
EXEC SQL WHENEVER SQLERROR GOTO EXIT;

/* Declare The Local Memory Variables */
int  rc = EXIT_SUCCESS;

/* Declare The SQL Host Memory Variables */
EXEC SQL BEGIN DECLARE SECTION;
    char    szInsertString[80];
    char    szDeleteString[140];
    char    szDeptNo[4];              // Department Number
    struct VARCHAR {                  // VARCHAR Data Structure
            short size;
            char  string[30];
            }  stDeptName;            // Department Name
    char    szManagerNo[7];           // Manager Number
    char    szMgrDept[4];             // Managing Department Number
    char    szNull[16];               // Null String
EXEC SQL END DECLARE SECTION;

/* Make Sure All Information Was Entered */
if (argc < 4)
    {
    printf("ERROR - Department Number, Department Name, ");
    printf("Manager Number,\n         and Managing Department ");
    printf("Number Must Be Specified\n");
    return(EXIT_FAILURE);
    }
/* Convert The User-Supplied Values To Uppercase */
uppercase(argv[1]);
uppercase(argv[2]);
uppercase(argv[3]);
uppercase(argv[4]);

/* Store The User-Supplied Values In The Appropriate Variables */
strcpy(szDeptNo, argv[1]);
strcpy(stDeptName.string, argv[2]);
stDeptName.size = strlen(stDeptName.string);
strcpy(szManagerNo, argv[3]);
strcpy(szMgrDept, argv[4]);

/* Build The Insert SQL Statement String (Using Parameter */
/* Markers)                                               */
strcpy(szInsertString, "INSERT INTO USERID.DEPARTMENT ");
strcat(szInsertString, "VALUES(?,?,?,?,?)");

/* Connect To The Sample Database */
EXEC SQL CONNECT TO SAMPLE USER etpdd6z USING sanders;

/* Prepare The Insert SQL Statement */
EXEC SQL PREPARE SQL_STMNT1 FROM :szInsertString;

/* Execute The Prepared Insert SQL Statement (Using Parameter */
/* Markers)                                                   */
EXEC SQL EXECUTE SQL_STMNT1 USING :szDeptNo, :stDeptName,
                                  :szManagerNo, :szMgrDept,
                                  :szNull;

/* Clear The Local Memory Variables */
stDeptName.string[0] = '';
stDeptName.size = 0;
szManagerNo[0] = '';
```

```
    szMgrDept[0] = '';

    /* Retrieve The New Record From The DEPARTMENT Table */
    EXEC SQL SELECT DEPTNO,
                    DEPTNAME,
                    MGRNO,
                    ADMRDEPT
             INTO :szDeptNo,
                  :stDeptName,
                  :szManagerNo,
                  :szMgrDept
             FROM USERID.DEPARTMENT
             WHERE DEPTNO = :szDeptNo;

    /* Print The Data Retrieved By The Select SQL Statement */
    printf("DEPTNO = %s\n", szDeptNo);
    printf("DEPTNAME = %s\n", stDeptName.string);
    printf("MGRNO = %s\n", szManagerNo);
    printf("ADMRDEPT = %s\n\n", szMgrDept);

    /* Build The Delete SQL Statement String */
    strcpy(szDeleteString, "DELETE FROM USERID.DEPARTMENT WHERE ");
    strcat(szDeleteString, "DEPTNO = '");
    strcat(szDeleteString, argv[1]);
    strcat(szDeleteString, "'");

    /* Prepare The Delete SQL Statement */
    EXEC SQL PREPARE SQL_STMNT2 FROM :szDeleteString;
    /* Execute The Prepared Delete SQL Statement */
    EXEC SQL EXECUTE SQL_STMNT2;

    /* Attempt To Retrieve The New Record From The DEPARTMENT */
    /* Table Again The Record Should Now Be Deleted           */
    EXEC SQL SELECT DEPTNO,
                    DEPTNAME,
                    MGRNO,
                    ADMRDEPT
             INTO :szDeptNo,
                  :stDeptName,
                  :szManagerNo,
                  :szMgrDept
             FROM USERID.DEPARTMENT
             WHERE DEPTNO = :szDeptNo;

    /* If The Record Could Not Be Found, It Was Deleted Successfully */
    if (sqlca.sqlcode == 100)
        printf("Requested record has been deleted.\n");

    /* Normally You Would Commit The Updates Here - In This Case We */
    /* Do Not Want To Change The SAMPLE Database                    */
//  EXEC SQL COMMIT;

EXIT:
    /* If An Error Has Occurred, Display The SQL Return Code */
    if (sqlca.sqlcode != SQL_RC_OK)
        {
        printf("SQL ERROR : %ld\n", sqlca.sqlcode);
        rc = EXIT_FAILURE;
        }
```

```
    /* Issue A Rollback To Free All Locks */
    EXEC SQL ROLLBACK;

    /* Turn Off The SQL Error Handler */
    EXEC SQL WHENEVER SQLERROR CONTINUE;

    /* Disconnect From The SAMPLE Database */
    EXEC SQL DISCONNECT CURRENT;

    /* Return To The Operating System */
    return(rc);
}

/* Function To Convert Strings To Uppercase */
void uppercase(char *szString)
{

    /* Declare The Local Memory Variables */
    short   i;

    /* Convert Each Character To Uppercase */
    for (i = 0; i < strlen(szString); i++)
        szString[i] = toupper(szString[i]);
    return;
}
```

The following C++ program illustrates the various ways to use the EXECUTE statement to execute dynamically prepared SQL statements within methods:

```
#include <iostream.h>
#include <stdlib.h>
#include <ctype.h>
#include <sql.h>

#define NOT_FOUND   100

/* Define The Local Function Prototypes */
void uppercase(char *szString);

/* Define The Employee Class */
class Department
{
    private:

        /* Include The SQLCA Data Structure Variable */
        EXEC SQL INCLUDE SQLCA;

        /* Declare The SQL Host Memory Variables */
        EXEC SQL BEGIN DECLARE SECTION;
         char     szInsertString[80];
         char     szDeleteString[140];
         char     szDeptNo[4];             // Department Number
         struct VARCHAR {                  // VARCHAR Data Structure
                  short size;
                  char  string[30];
                  }  stDeptName;           // Department Name
         char     szManagerNo[7];          // Manager Number
         char     szMgrDept[4];            // Managing Department Number
         char     szNull[16];              // Null String
        EXEC SQL END DECLARE SECTION;
```

```
    /* Declare The Member Function Prototypes */
    public:
       Department::Department(char *szArg1, char *szArg2,
                              char *szArg3, char *szArg4);
       short int insertRecord();
       short int deleteRecord(char *szDeptNo);
       short int getData();
       void      printData();
} ;

/* Define The Class Constructor */
Department::Department(char *szArg1, char *szArg2,
                       char *szArg3, char *szArg4)
{
    /* Store The User-Supplied Values In The Appropriate Variables */
    strcpy(szDeptNo, szArg1);
    strcpy(stDeptName.string, szArg2);
    stDeptName.size = strlen(szArg2);
    strcpy(szManagerNo, szArg3);
    strcpy(szMgrDept, szArg4);
}

/* Define The insertRecord() Member Function */
short int Department::insertRecord(void)
{
    /* Build The Insert SQL Statement String (Using Parameter */
    /* Markers)                                                */
    strcpy(szInsertString, "INSERT INTO USERID.DEPARTMENT ");
    strcat(szInsertString, "VALUES(?,?,?,?,?)");

    /* Prepare The Insert SQL Statement */
    EXEC SQL PREPARE SQL_STMNT1 FROM :szInsertString;

    /* Execute The Prepared Insert SQL Statement */
    EXEC SQL EXECUTE SQL_STMNT1 USING :szDeptNo, :stDeptName,
                                      :szManagerNo, :szMgrDept,
                                      :szNull;

    /* Return The SQL Return Code */
    return(sqlca.sqlcode);
}

/* Define The deleteRecord() Member Function */
short int Department::deleteRecord(char *szDeptNo)
{
    /* Build The Delete SQL Statement String */
    strcpy(szDeleteString, "DELETE FROM USERID.DEPARTMENT WHERE ");
    strcat(szDeleteString, "DEPTNO = '");
    strcat(szDeleteString, szDeptNo);
    strcat(szDeleteString, "'");

    /* Prepare The Delete SQL Statement */
    EXEC SQL PREPARE SQL_STMNT2 FROM :szDeleteString;

    /* Execute The Prepared Delete SQL Statement */
    EXEC SQL EXECUTE SQL_STMNT2;

    /* Return The SQL Return Code */
    return(sqlca.sqlcode);
}
```

```
/* Define The getData() Member Function */
short int Department::getData(void)
{
    /* Clear The Private Memory Variables */
    stDeptName.string[0] = '';
    stDeptName.size = 0;
    szManagerNo[0] = '';
    szMgrDept[0] = '';

    /* Retrieve The New Record From The DEPARTMENT Table */
    EXEC SQL SELECT DEPTNO,
                    DEPTNAME,
                    MGRNO,
                    ADMRDEPT
             INTO :szDeptNo,
                  :stDeptName,
                  :szManagerNo,
                  :szMgrDept
             FROM USERID.DEPARTMENT
             WHERE DEPTNO = :szDeptNo;

    /* Return The SQL Return Code */
    return(sqlca.sqlcode);
}

/* Define The printData() Member Function */
void Department::printData(void)
{
    /* Print The Information Retrieved */
    cout << "Department Number : " << szDeptNo << endl;
    cout << "Department Name   : ";
    cout.width(10);
    cout << stDeptName.string << endl;
    cout << "Manager Number    : " << szManagerNo << endl;
    cout << "Managing Dept.    : " << szMgrDept << endl << endl;
}

int main(int argc, char *argv[])
{
    /* Declare The Local Memory Variables */
    short int rc = EXIT_SUCCESS;           // Must Be Declared Here
                                           // For The SQL Precompiler

    /* Include The SQLCA Data Structure Variable */
    EXEC SQL INCLUDE SQLCA;

    /* Set Up A Simple SQL Error Handler */
    EXEC SQL WHENEVER SQLERROR GOTO EXIT;

    /* Make Sure All Information Was Entered */
    if (argc < 4)
        {
        cout << "ERROR - Department Number, Department Name, ";
        cout << "Manager Number, " << endl;
        cout << "        and Managing Department Number Must Be ";
        cout << "Specified" << endl;
        return(EXIT_FAILURE);
        }

    /* Convert The User-Supplied Values To Uppercase */
    uppercase(argv[1]);
    uppercase(argv[2]);
```

```
    uppercase(argv[3]);
    uppercase(argv[4]);

    /* Create An Instance Of The EMPLOYEE Class */
    Department DeptInfo(argv[1], argv[2], argv[3], argv[4]);

    /* Connect To The SAMPLE Database */
    EXEC SQL CONNECT TO SAMPLE USER etpdd6z USING sanders;

    /* Insert The New Record Into The DEPARTMENT Table */
    DeptInfo.insertRecord();

    /* Retrieve The New Record From The DEPARTMENT Table */
    rc = DeptInfo.getData();

    /* Print The Information Retrieved */
    DeptInfo.printData();

    /* Delete The New Record From The DEPARTMENT Table */
    DeptInfo.deleteRecord(argv[1]);

    /* Attempt To Retrieve The New Record Again */
    if ((rc = DeptInfo.getData()) == NOT_FOUND)
        cout << "Requested Record Has Been Deleted" << endl;

    /* Normally You Would Commit The Updates Here - In This Case We */
    /* Do Not Want To Change The SAMPLE Database                    */
//  EXEC SQL COMMIT;

EXIT:
    /* If An Error Has Occurred, Display The SQL Return Code */
    if (sqlca.sqlcode != SQL_RC_OK)
        {
        cout << "SQL ERROR : " << sqlca.sqlcode << endl;
        rc = EXIT_FAILURE;
        }

    /* Issue A Rollback To Free All Locks */
    EXEC SQL ROLLBACK;

    /* Turn Off The SQL Error Handler */
    EXEC SQL WHENEVER SQLERROR CONTINUE;

    /* Disconnect From The SAMPLE Database */
    EXEC SQL DISCONNECT CURRENT;

    /* Return To The Operating System */
    return(rc);
}

/* Function To Convert Strings To Uppercase */
void uppercase(char *szString)
{

    /* Declare The Local Memory Variables */
    short   i;

    /* Convert Each Character To Uppercase */
    for (i = 0; i < strlen(szString); i++)
        szString[i] = toupper(szString[i]);
    return;
}
```

EXECUTE IMMEDIATE

Purpose The EXECUTE IMMEDIATE statement allows you to dynamically prepare an SQL statement and submit it to DB2 for execution.

Syntax

```
EXEC SQL EXECUTE IMMEDIATE [statement-string];
```

Parameter *statement-string* Identifies the SQL statement character string to be prepared and executed by DB2. The statement string is stored in a character string host variable (either a fixed-length or a variable-length string) whose size must not exceed 32,765 bytes. Only the SQL statements listed back in the section Dynamic SQL Support can be used in the statement string, and they must not contain parameter markers or references to host variables. Also, the SQL statement string must not begin with "EXEC SQL" and it must not contain a statement terminator (a semicolon, ;), unless it is the CREATE TRIGGER statement, which can include semicolons to separate multiple triggered SQL statements.

Description The EXECUTE IMMEDIATE statement dynamically prepares a character string form of an SQL statement and submits it to DB2 for execution. When a dynamic SQL statement is prepared, an executable statement known as a prepared statement is created from the original character statement string. This prepared statement is then submitted to DB2 for execution.

You can also perform the SQL statement preparation process by executing the PREPARE statement. Once the statement is prepared, you can submit it to DB2 for execution by invoking the EXECUTE statement. The EXECUTE IMMEDIATE statement combines the functionality of these two statements into a single-step process. However, this process does not allow the dynamic SQL statement being prepared to contain parameter markers and the EXECUTE and PREPARE process does.

Comments

- When the EXECUTE IMMEDIATE statement is executed, the specified statement string is parsed, checked for errors, and executed. If for some reason the statement string cannot be executed, the error condition that prevented its execution is stored in the SQLCA data structure variable. By examining the SQLDA data structure variable, you should be able to determine and correct any problems encountered when using the EXECUTE IMMEDIATE statement.
- Caching the executable sections of SQL data manipulation language (DML) statements can affect the behavior of an EXECUTE IMMEDIATE statement. Refer to the beginning of the chapter for more information about statement caching.

Authorization The authorization rules associated with the SQL statement being prepared and executed apply to the EXECUTE IMMEDIATE statement.

See Also PREPARE, EXECUTE, BEGIN DECLARE SECTION, END DECLARE SECTION

Example The following C program illustrates how the EXECUTE IMMEDIATE statement dynamically prepares and executes SQL statements:

```
#include <stdio.h>
#include <stdlib.h>
#include <string.h>
#include <sql.h>

int main(int argc, char* argv[])
{
```

```
/* Include The SQLCA Data Structure Variable */
EXEC SQL INCLUDE SQLCA;

/* Set Up A Simple SQL Error Handler */
EXEC SQL WHENEVER SQLERROR GOTO EXIT;

/* Declare The Local Memory Variables */
int  rc = EXIT_SUCCESS;

/* Declare The SQL Host Memory Variables */
EXEC SQL BEGIN DECLARE SECTION;
    char    szEmpNo[7];
    double  rdSalary;
    char    szPrepString[80];
EXEC SQL END DECLARE SECTION;

/* Make Sure The Job And Percent Increase Were Entered */
if (argc < 2)
    {
    printf("ERROR - Percentage Increase Must Be Specified.\n");
    return(EXIT_FAILURE);
    }
/* Connect To The SAMPLE Database */
EXEC SQL CONNECT TO SAMPLE USER etpdd6z USING sanders;

/* Retrieve A Record From The EMPLOYEE Table */
EXEC SQL SELECT EMPNO,
                SALARY
    INTO :szEmpNo,
         :rdSalary
    FROM USERID.EMPLOYEE
    WHERE EMPNO = '000050';

/* Print The Information Retrieved */
printf("Employee No. : %7s Original Salary : $%.2lf\n",
        szEmpNo, rdSalary);

/* Build The SQL Statement String */
strcpy(szPrepString, "UPDATE USERID.EMPLOYEE SET SALARY = ");
strcat(szPrepString, "SALARY * 1.");
strcat(szPrepString, argv[1]);
strcat(szPrepString, " WHERE JOB = 'MANAGER'");

/* Execute The Prepared SQL Statement Immediately */
EXEC SQL EXECUTE IMMEDIATE :szPrepString;

/* Retrieve The Updated Record From The EMPLOYEE Table */
EXEC SQL SELECT EMPNO,
                SALARY
    INTO :szEmpNo,
         :rdSalary
    FROM USERID.EMPLOYEE
    WHERE EMPNO = '000050';

/* Print The Information Retrieved - Verify The Changes Were Made */
printf("Employee No. : %7s New Salary      : $%.2lf\n",
        szEmpNo, rdSalary);

/* Issue A Rollback To Free All Locks And Restore The Data         */
/* Normally We Would Commit The Changes Before The EXIT Label -   */
/* In This Case We Do Not Want To Change The SAMPLE Database       */
EXEC SQL ROLLBACK;
```

```
EXIT:
    /* If An Error Has Occurred, Display The SQL Return Code
    if (sqlca.sqlcode != SQL_RC_OK)
        {
        printf("SQL ERROR : %ld\n", sqlca.sqlcode);
        rc = EXIT_FAILURE;
        }

    /* Issue A Rollback To Free All Locks */
    EXEC SQL ROLLBACK;

    /* Turn Off The SQL Error Handler */
    EXEC SQL WHENEVER SQLERROR CONTINUE;

    /* Disconnect From The SAMPLE Database */
    EXEC SQL DISCONNECT CURRENT;

    /* Return To The Operating System */
    return(rc);
}
```

Note: The EXECUTE IMMEDIATE statement is used in a C++ program in a similar manner.

SET CURRENT QUERY OPTIMIZATION

Purpose The SET CURRENT QUERY OPTIMIZATION statement specifies a class of optimization techniques to use when preparing dynamic SQL statements for execution.

Syntax

```
EXEC SQL SET CURRENT QUERY OPTIMIZATION <=> [optimization-level];
```

Parameter *optimization-level* Identifies the optimization class level to use when preparing one or more dynamic SQL statements. The optimization class level can be either the name of a host variable that contains the optimization class level number or any of the following values:

- 0 Indicates that a minimal amount of optimization techniques are to be used when the optimizer generates an access plan. This optimization class level is most suitable for simple dynamic SQL statements that access well-indexed tables.
- 1 Indicates that the amount of optimization techniques to be used when the optimizer generates an access plan. This optimization class level should be roughly equal to that provided by DB2 version 1.
- 3 Indicates that a moderate amount of optimization techniques are to be used when the optimizer generates an access plan.
- 5 Indicates that a significant amount of optimization techniques are to be used when the optimizer generates an access plan. This is the default optimization class used by DB2 when the SET CURRENT QUERY OPTIMIZATION statement or SQL precompiler option is not used.
- 9 Indicates that the maximum amount of optimization techniques are to be used when the optimizer generates an access plan. This optimization class can greatly expand the number of possible access paths that are evaluated before an access plan is created. For this reason, this class is typically used with SQL statements that contain very complex and long-running queries that access very large tables.

Description

The SET CURRENT QUERY OPTIMIZATION statement specifies a predefined class of optimization techniques to be used by DB2 when preparing dynamic SQL statements for execution. When the CURRENT QUERY OPTIMIZATION special register is set to a particular value by the SET CURRENT QUERY OPTIMIZATION statement, a class of query rewrite rules are enabled and certain optimization variables are assigned appropriate values for the class. These query rewrite rules and optimization variables are then used to prepare dynamic SQL statements to specify the optimum access plan for the statement.

Comments

- If you use a host variable to specify the optimization class type, it must be defined as an integer data type. Also, if you use a corresponding indicator variable, the value of that indicator variable must not be a null value.
- In general, changing the optimization class affects the execution time of the application, the compilation time, and the amount of resources required. Most SQL statements will be adequately optimized with the default query optimization class. Lower query optimization classes might be appropriate in cases where a significant amount of resources are consumed by simple SQL queries. Choose higher optimization classes only after carefully considering the amount of additional resources that might be required and verifying that this class level will actually generate a better access plan.
- Each optimization class is a numerically identified set of optimization techniques. Any number outside the range of 0 to 9 will return an SQL error. Any unsupported number within this range will return an SQL warning and will be replaced by the next lowest optimization class level number.
- It is important to note that there is no direct relationship between optimization class levels. Each class of optimization is developed to handle particular types of SQL statements or for particular database or operating system environments.
- Dynamically prepared SQL statements use the optimization class set by the most recently executed SET CURRENT QUERY OPTIMIZATION statement. In cases where a SET CURRENT QUERY OPTIMIZATION statement is not yet executed, the query optimization class is 5, the same class used by default for statically bound SQL statements within the application.
- Statically bound statements do not use the CURRENT QUERY OPTIMIZATION special register, so this statement does not affect them. Instead, you can use the QUERYOPT SQL precompiler option during preprocessing or binding to specify the optimization class to use when preparing statically bound SQL statements.
- The value of the CURRENT QUERY OPTIMIZATION special register is not affected by how the transaction containing the SET CURRENT QUERY OPTIMIZATION statement is terminated. In other words, if a transaction that contains the SET CURRENT QUERY OPTIMIZATION class is rolled back, the CURRENT QUERY OPTIMIZATION special register will not be changed to its original state.

Authorization

No authorization is required to execute this statement.

Example

The following C program illustrates how the SET CURRENT QUERY OPTIMIZATION statement can set the optimization class before a dynamic SQL statement is prepared:

```
#include <stdio.h>
#include <stdlib.h>
#include <string.h>
#include <sql.h>
#include <sqlda.h>
```

```
int main()
{
    /* Include The SQLCA Data Structure Variable */
    EXEC SQL INCLUDE SQLCA;

    /* Set Up A Simple SQL Error Handler */
    EXEC SQL WHENEVER SQLERROR GOTO EXIT;

    /* Declare The Local Memory Variables */
    int  rc = EXIT_SUCCESS;

    /* Declare The SQL Host Memory Variables */
    EXEC SQL BEGIN DECLARE SECTION;
        char    szUpdateString[80];
        char    szDeleteString[80];
        short   sQueryOptLevel;
        long    lSalary;
    EXEC SQL END DECLARE SECTION;
    /* Build The Update SQL Statement String */
    strcpy(szUpdateString, "UPDATE USERID.EMPLOYEE ");
    strcat(szUpdateString, "SET SALARY = SALARY * 1.12 ");
    strcat(szUpdateString, "WHERE JOB = 'MANAGER'");

    /* Build The Delete SQL Statement String */
    strcpy(szDeleteString, "DELETE FROM USERID.EMPLOYEE ");
    strcat(szDeleteString, "WHERE EMPNO = '000020'");

    /* Connect To The Sample Database */
    EXEC SQL CONNECT TO SAMPLE USER etpdd6z USING sanders;

    /* Set The Current Query Optimization To 3 */
    EXEC SQL SET CURRENT QUERY OPTIMIZATION 3;

    /* Prepare The Insert SQL Statement */
    EXEC SQL PREPARE SQL_STMNT1 FROM :szUpdateString;

    /* Set The Current Query Optimization To 5 (Using A Host-Variable) */
    sQueryOptLevel = 5;
    EXEC SQL SET CURRENT QUERY OPTIMIZATION :sQueryOptLevel;

    /* Prepare The Update SQL Statement */
    EXEC SQL PREPARE SQL_STMNT2 FROM :szDeleteString;

    /* Get The Largest Salary In The EMPLOYEE Table */
    EXEC SQL SELECT MAX(SALARY)
        INTO :lSalary
        FROM USERID.EMPLOYEE
        WHERE JOB = 'MANAGER';

    /* Print The Information Retrieved */
    printf("The Highest Salary Before The Update : $%ld\n", lSalary);

    /* Execute The Prepared UPDATE Statement */
    EXEC SQL EXECUTE SQL_STMNT1;

    /* Get The Largest Salary In The EMPLOYEE Table After The Update */
    EXEC SQL SELECT MAX(SALARY)
        INTO :lSalary
        FROM USERID.EMPLOYEE
        WHERE JOB = 'MANAGER';

    /* Print The Information Retrieved */
```

```
    printf("The Highest Salary After The Update   : $%ld\n", lSalary);

    /* Execute The Prepared DELETE Statement */
    EXEC SQL EXECUTE SQL_STMNT2;

    /* Get The Largest Salary In The EMPLOYEE Table After The Delete */
    EXEC SQL SELECT MAX(SALARY)
        INTO :lSalary
        FROM USERID.EMPLOYEE
        WHERE JOB = 'MANAGER';

    /* Print The Information Retrieved */
    printf("The Highest Salary After The Delete   : $%ld\n", lSalary);

    /* Normally You Would Commit The Changes Here - In This Case We  */
    /* Do Not Want To Change The SAMPLE Database                     */
//  EXEC SQL COMMIT;
EXIT:
    /* If An Error Has Occurred, Display The SQL Return Code */
    if (sqlca.sqlcode != SQL_RC_OK)
        {
        printf("SQL ERROR : %ld\n", sqlca.sqlcode);
        rc = EXIT_FAILURE;
        }

    /* Issue A Rollback To Free All Locks */
    EXEC SQL ROLLBACK;

    /* Turn Off The SQL Error Handler */
    EXEC SQL WHENEVER SQLERROR CONTINUE;

    /* Disconnect From The SAMPLE Database */
    EXEC SQL DISCONNECT CURRENT;

    /* Return To The Operating System */
    return(rc);
}
```

Note: The SET CURRENT QUERY OPTIMIZATION statement is used in a C++ program in a similar manner.

SET CURRENT PACKAGESET

Purpose The SET CURRENT PACKAGESET statement is used to specify the schema name that will be used when selecting package(s) needed for executing subsequent SQL statements.

Syntax

```
EXEC SQL SET CURRENT PACKAGESET <=> [schema-name];
```

Parameters

schema-name Identifies the schema name to use when selecting one or more packages. The schema name can either be a character string constant, or it can be the name of a host-variable that contains a character string that refers to the schema name.

Description The SET CURRENT PACKAGESET statement is used to specify the schema name that an application will use when selecting a package for an executable SQL statement. Unlike most of the other SET . . . statements, the SET CURRENT PACKAGESET statement does not require a special register in order to be implemented.

Comments

- If a host variable is used to specify the package schema name type, it must be defined as a character string variable with a length attribute no larger than 8 characters (bytes). Also, if a corresponding indicator variable is used, the value of that indicator variable must not be a null value.
- The COLLECTION bind option is used to create a package with a specified schema name. This schema name can then be set as the default schema name to use with the SET CURRENT PACKAGESET statement.
- The SET CURRENT PACKAGESET statement does not interact with a CURRENT PACKAGESET special register like DB2 for MVS/ESA does.

Authorization No authorization is required to execute this statement.

Example The following C program illustrates how the SET CURRENT PACKAGESET statement can be used to change the way date values are displayed by changing the schema name used to select the package for processing an SQL statement.

```
#include <stdio.h>
#include <stdlib.h>
#include <string.h>
#include <sql.h>

int main()
{
    /* Include The SQLCA Data Structure Variable */
    EXEC SQL INCLUDE SQLCA;

    /* Set Up A Simple SQL Error Handler */
    EXEC SQL WHENEVER SQLERROR GOTO EXIT;

    /* Declare The Local Memory Variables */
    int   rc = EXIT_SUCCESS;
    char  szEmpID[7];
    char  szBirthDate[11];

    /* Declare The SQL Host Memory Variables */
    EXEC SQL BEGIN DECLARE SECTION;
        char      szEmpNo[7];
        char      szBDate[11];
    EXEC SQL END DECLARE SECTION;

    /* Connect To The SAMPLE Database */
    EXEC SQL CONNECT TO SAMPLE USER etpdd6z USING sanders;

    /* Declare The EMP_BDATE Table Cursor */
    EXEC SQL DECLARE EMP_BDATE CURSOR FOR
        SELECT EMPNO,
               BIRTHDATE
        FROM USERID.EMPLOYEE
        WHERE JOB = 'CLERK';

    /* Open The Cursor */
    EXEC SQL OPEN EMP_BDATE;

    /* If The Cursor Was Successfully Opened, Fetch The Records Into Host  */
    /* Variables                                                            */
```

```
    printf("PACKAGESET = CH8EX10A\n");
    while (sqlca.sqlcode == SQL_RC_OK)
        {
        EXEC SQL FETCH EMP_BDATE
            INTO :szEmpNo,
                 :szBDate;

        /* If The FETCH Was Successful, Print The Data */
        if (sqlca.sqlcode == SQL_RC_OK)
            {
            strncpy(szEmpID, " ", 6);
            strncpy(szBirthDate, " ", 6);
            strncpy(szEmpID, szEmpNo, 6);
            strncpy(szBirthDate, szBDate, 10);
            szEmpID[6] = 0;
            szBirthDate[10] = 0;
            printf("Employee No. : %6s\tBirthdate : %10s\n",
                   szEmpID, szBirthDate);
            }
        }                                           /* End Of WHILE   */

    /* Close The Cursor */
    EXEC SQL CLOSE EMP_BDATE;

    /* Change The Package */
    EXEC SQL SET CURRENT PACKAGESET 'CH8EX10B';

    /* Open The Cursor */
    EXEC SQL OPEN EMP_BDATE;

    /* If The Cursor Was Successfully Opened, Fetch The Records Into Host */
    /* Variables                                                          */
    printf("\nPACKAGESET = CH8EX10B\n");
    while (sqlca.sqlcode == SQL_RC_OK)
        {
        EXEC SQL FETCH EMP_BDATE
            INTO :szEmpNo,
                 :szBDate;

        /* If The FETCH Was Successful, Print The Data */
        if (sqlca.sqlcode == SQL_RC_OK)
            {
            strncpy(szEmpID, " ", 6);
            strncpy(szBirthDate, " ", 6);
            strncpy(szEmpID, szEmpNo, 6);
            strncpy(szBirthDate, szBDate, 10);
            szEmpID[6] = 0;
            szBirthDate[10] = 0;
            printf("Employee No. : %6s\tBirthdate : %10s\n",
                   szEmpID, szBirthDate);
            }
        }                                           /* End Of WHILE   */

    /* Close The Cursor */
    EXEC SQL CLOSE EMP_BDATE;

EXIT:
    /* If An Error Has Occured, Display The SQL Return Code */
    if (sqlca.sqlcode != SQL_RC_OK)
        {
        printf("SQL ERROR : %ld\n", sqlca.sqlcode);
```

```
            rc = EXIT_FAILURE;
            }

        /* Issue A Rollback To Free All Locks */
        EXEC SQL ROLLBACK;

        /* Turn Off The SQL Error Handler */
        EXEC SQL WHENEVER SQLERROR CONTINUE;

        /* Disconnect From The SAMPLE Database */
        EXEC SQL DISCONNECT CURRENT;

        /* Return To The Operating System */
        return(rc);
}
```

NOTE: The SET CURRENT PACKAGESET statement is used in a C++ program in a similar manner.

After this sample program is precompiled and compiled, it must be bound to the SAMPLE database by issuing the following commands:

1. DB2 CONNECT TO SAMPLE USER <username> USING <password>
2. DB2 BIND CH8EX10A.BND DATETIME USA
3. DB2 BIND CH8EX10A BND DATETIME EUR COLLECTION 'CH8EX10B'

When compiled, bound as described above, and executed this sample program will produce the following output:

```
PACKAGESET = CH8EX10A

        Employee No.: 000120        Birthdate: 10/18/1942
        Employee No.: 000230        Birthdate: 05/30/1935
        Employee No : 000240        Birthdate: 03/31/1954
        Employee No.: 000250        Birthdate: 11/12/1939
        Employee No.: 000260        Birthdate: 10/05/1936
        Employee No.: 000270        Birthdate: 05/26/1953

PACKAGESET = CH8EX10B

        Employee No.: 000120        Birthdate: 18.10.1942
        Employee No.: 000230        Birthdate: 30.05.1935
        Employee No.: 000240        Birthdate: 31.03.1954
        Employee No.: 000250        Birthdate: 12.11.1939
        Employee No.: 000260        Birthdate: 05.10.1936
        Employee No.: 000270        Birthdate: 26.05.1953
```

SET CURRENT EXPLAIN SNAPSHOT

Purpose The SET CURRENT EXPLAIN SNAPSHOT statement is used enable or disable the Explain Snapshot Facility or to cause Explain information to be captured for dynamic SQL statements.

Syntax

```
EXEC SQL SET CURRENT EXPLAIN SNAPSHOT <=> [facility-state];
```

Parameters

facility-state Identifies the state to place the Explain Snapshot Facility in. The facility state can either be the name of a host-variable that contains the facility state, or it can be any of the following values:

NO Indicates that the Explain Snapshot Facility should be disabled.

YES Indicates that the Explain Snapshot Facility should be enabled and that Explain information is to be captured for all eligible static SQL statements within the application as they are executed.

EXPLAIN Indicates that the Explain Snapshot Facility should be enabled and that Explain information is to be captured for all eligible static SQL statements within the application but the statements themselves are not to be executed.

Description

The SET CURRENT EXPLAIN SNAPSHOT statement is used enable or disable the Explain Snapshot Facility, or to cause Explain information to be captured for dynamic SQL statements (instead of executing them). The Explain Snapshot Facility is designed to capture the access plans that are generated for SQL statements. By examining this access plan information, "bottle necks" can be found, and changes can be made to either the database or to the SQL statement to improve overall application performance.

Before the Explain Snapshot Facility can be used, appropriate Explain tables must first be created. A DB2 command line processor script that creates these tables is provided (**EXPLAIN.DDL**) in the **misc** sub-directory of the **sqllib** directory where DB2 was installed. Refer to the header portion of this file for information on how to use it.

Once the Explain Snapshot Facility is enabled, a snapshot of the internal representation of each eligible dynamically prepared SQL statement is inserted into the SNAPSHOT column of the EXPLAIN_STATEMENT table. This information can then be examined using DB2 Visual Explain.

Comments

- If a host variable is used to specify the facility state, it must be defined as a character string variable with a length attribute no larger than 8 characters (bytes). Also, if a corresponding indicator variable is used, the value of that indicator variable must not be a null value.
- If a host variable is used to specify the facility state, the value it contains must be either "NO", "YES", or "EXPLAIN" (any leading or trailing blanks should be removed).
- When Explain information is captured for dynamically prepared SQL statements, the statements themselves are not executed.
- Explain information can also be captured for statically prepared SQL statements by using the EXPLSNAP precompiler option while precompiling the static embedded SQL source code file or while binding the static embedded SQL application to a database. If the ALL value of the EXPLSNAP option is specified and the CURRENT EXPLAIN SNAPSHOT special register value is "NO," Explain information will be captured for static SQL statements at application run-time. If, however, the ALL value of the EXPILSNAP option is specified and the CURRENT EXPLAIN SNAPSHOT special register value is "YES" or "EXPLAIN," the EXPLSNAP option will be ignored.
- The value of the CURRENT EXPLAIN SNAPSHOT special register is not affected by how the transaction in which the SET CURRENT EXPLAIN SNAPSHOT statement was used is terminated (i.e. if a transaction that contains the SET CURRENT EXPLAIN SNAPSHOT statement class is rolled back, the CURRENT EXPLAIN SNAPSHOT special register will not bc changed to its original state).

Authorization

No authorization is required to use this statement to disable the Explain Snapshot Facility.

Only users with either system administrator (SYSADM) authority, database administrator (DBADM) authority, or INSERT authority for the Explain tables are allowed to enable the Explain Snapshot Facility.

Example The following C program illustrates how the SET CURRENT EXPLAIN SNAPSHOT statement can be used to write information about an SQL statement to the Explain tables.

```
#include <stdio.h>
#include <stdlib.h>
#include <string.h>
#include <sql.h>

int main()
{
    /* Include The SQLCA Data Structure Variable */
    EXEC SQL INCLUDE SQLCA;

    /* Set Up A Simple SQL Error Handler */
    EXEC SQL WHENEVER SQLERROR GOTO EXIT;

    /* Declare The Local Memory Variables */
    int  rc = EXIT_SUCCESS;

    /* Declare The SQL Host Memory Variables */
    EXEC SQL BEGIN DECLARE SECTION;
        char    szEmpNo[7];
        double  rdSalary;
        char    szPrepString[80];
    EXEC SQL END DECLARE SECTION;

    /* Connect To The SAMPLE Database */
    EXEC SQL CONNECT TO SAMPLE USER etpdd6z USING sanders;

    /* Turn On The Explain Facility - Do Not Execute The SQL Statements */
    EXEC SQL SET CURRENT EXPLAIN SNAPSHOT = EXPLAIN;

    /* Retrieve A Record From The EMPLOYEE Table */
    EXEC SQL SELECT EMPNO,
                    SALARY
        INTO :szEmpNo,
             :rdSalary
        FROM USERID.EMPLOYEE
        WHERE EMPNO = '000050';

    /* Print The Information Retrieved */
    printf("Employee No. : %7s Salary : $%.2lf\n",
           szEmpNo, rdSalary);

    /* Turn Off The Explain Facility */
    EXEC SQL SET CURRENT EXPLAIN SNAPSHOT = NO;

 EXIT:
    /* If An Error Has Occured, Display The SQL Return Code */
    if (sqlca.sqlcode != SQL_RC_OK)
        {
        printf("SQL ERROR : %ld\n", sqlca.sqlcode);
        rc = EXIT_FAILURE;
        }

    /* Issue A Rollback To Free All Locks */
```

```
        EXEC SQL ROLLBACK;

        /* Turn Off The SQL Error Handler */
        EXEC SQL WHENEVER SQLERROR CONTINUE;

        /* Disconnect From The SAMPLE Database */
        EXEC SQL DISCONNECT CURRENT;

        /* Return To The Operating System */
        return(rc);
    }
```

> NOTE: The SET CURRENT EXPLAIN SNAPSHOT statement is used in a C++ program in a similar manner.

When compiled and executed this sample program will produce the following output:

```
Employee No : 000050 Salary: $40175.00
```

When the Explain facility is used to view the Explain information produced, it will display the following information:

```
DB2 for OS/2 Version 2.1.0, 5622-044 (c) Copyright IBM Corp. 1991, 1995
Licensed Material - Program Property of IBM
IBM DATABASE 2 SQL Explain Tool

******************** PACKAGE ***************************************

Package Name = ETPDD6Z.CH8EX11A
        Prep Date = 1996/03/08
        Prep Time = 21:28:56:007

        Bind Timestamp = 1996-03-08-21.29.24.070000

        Isolation Level          = Cursor Stability
        Blocking                 = Block Unambiguous Cursors
        Query Optimization Class = 5

-------------------- SECTION ---------------------------------------
Section = 1


SQL Statement:
  SET CURRENT EXPLAIN SNAPSHOT = EXPLAIN


Table Constructor
|  1-Row(s)
Set Statement
End of Section


-------------------- SECTION ---------------------------------------
Section = 2


SQL Statement:
```

```
  SELECT EMPNO, SALARY INTO :szEmpNo , :rdSalary
  FROM USERID.EMPLOYEE
  WHERE EMPNO = '000050'


Access Table Name = USERID.EMPLOYEE  ID = 5
|  #Columns = 2
|  Relation Scan
|  |  Prefetch Eligible
|  Lock Intents
|  |  Table: Intent Share
|  |  Row   : Share
|  Sargable Predicate(s)
|  |  #Predicates = 1
End of Section


-------------------- SECTION ----------------------------------------
Section = 3


SQL Statement:
  SET CURRENT EXPLAIN SNAPSHOT = NO


Table Constructor
|  1-Row(s)
Set Statement
End of Section
```

NOTE: The preceeding output was produced by running the program **DB2EXPLN.EXE** (OS/2) that is found in the **misc** sub-directory of the **sqllib** directory where DB2 was installed. The database name provided to this application was SAMPLE and the package name provided was CH8EX11A.

CHAPTER 9

DATA CONTROL STATEMENTS

9

SQL data control statements consist of commands that control the execution of other SQL statements to ensure that a database remains consistent and secure in multiuser environments. These statements include:

- SQL statements that manage database server connections.
- SQL statements that process and terminate transactions.
- SQL statements that obtain table locks thereby restricting concurrent access during the life of a transaction.
- SQL statements that authorize or restrict access to database, table, index, and view data objects.

Table 9.1 lists the SQL data control statements available with DB2.

Connection Management

A database application process must be connected to a database server before any SQL statements that reference data objects can be executed. DB2 provides support for two types of database connections. These two types, known simply as Type 1 and Type 2, support two different types of transaction semantics. Type 1 connections support a single database connection per transaction (remote unit of work), while Type 2 connections support multiple database connections per transaction (application-directed distributed unit of work).

With a Type 1 connection, an application process can be connected to only one database server (the current server) at a time. Therefore, all SQL statements using a Type 1 connection must reference data objects that are managed by the same database server, and all transactions must be executed by the same database server. With a Type 2 connection, an application process can be connected to several database servers at any given time. This means that each SQL statement can reference data objects managed by many different database servers. Type 1 and Type 2 connection semantics are outlined in Table 9.2.

States of an Application

At any given time, an embedded SQL application can be in any of the following states:

- Connectable and unconnected
- Connectable and connected
- Unconnectable and connected
- Implicitly connectable (provided implicit connect is available)

TABLE 9.1 Data Control SQL Statements

Statement	Description
CONNECT	Establishes a connection to a database server according to the Rules for Remote Unit of Work (Type 1) or Application-Directed Distributed Unit of Work (Type 2).
SET CONNECTION	Changes the state of a database server connection from "dormant" to "current", thereby making the specified connection the current database server.
RELEASE	Places one or more database server connections in the release-pending state.
DISCONNECT	Terminates one or more database server connections when there is no active transaction.
COMMIT	Terminates a transaction and makes all database changes made by that transaction permanent.
ROLLBACK	Terminates a transaction and backs out all database changes made by that transaction.
LOCK TABLE	Prevents concurrent processes from either changing or accessing a database table.
GRANT (Database Authorities)	Gives a user authorizations that apply to an entire database.
GRANT (Index Privileges)	Gives a user the CONTROL privilege on indexes in a database.
GRANT (Package Privileges)	Gives a user authorizations that apply to packages in a database.
GRANT (Table or View Privileges)	Gives a user authorizations that apply to tables and views.
REVOKE (Database Authorities)	Removes authorizations that apply to an entire database from a user.
REVOKE (Index Privileges)	Removes the CONTROL privilege on indexes in a database from a user.
REVOKE (Package Privileges)	Removes authorizations that apply to packages in a database from a user .
REVOKE (Table or View Privileges)	Removes authorizations that apply to tables and views from a user .

TABLE 9.2 Type 1 and Type 2 Connection Semantics

Type 1 connections	Type 2 connections
Each transaction can connect to only a single database server.	Each transaction can connect to multiple database servers.
The current transaction must be committed or rolled back before a connection to another database server can be established.	The current transaction does not have to be committed or rolled back before connecting to another database server.
The CONNECT statement establishes the current connection. Subsequent SQL requests are forwarded to this connection until it is changed by another CONNECT statement.	The CONNECT statement establishes the current connection if this is the first database connection. If you are switching to a dormant connection and the SQLRULES precompiler option is set to STD, then you must use the SET CONNECTION statement instead of CONNECT.
Connecting to the current connection is valid and does not change the current connection.	Connecting to the current connection is valid and does not change the current connection if the SQLRULES precompiler option is set to DB2. If the SQLRULES precompiler option is set to STD, then you must use the SET CONNECTION statement instead of the CONNECT statement.

TABLE 9.2 Type 1 and Type 2 Connection Semantics *(Continued)*

Type 1 connections	Type 2 connections
Connecting to another database server automatically disconnects the current connection and the new connection becomes the current connection. Only one connection is maintained within a transaction.	Connecting to another database server places the current connection into the dormant state, and the new connection becomes the current connection. Multiple connections can be maintained within a transaction. If the CONNECT statement specifies a database server on a dormant connection, it becomes the current connection. Connecting to a dormant connection with the CONNECT statement is allowed only if the SQLRULES precompiler option is set to DB2; otherwise, you must use the SET CONNECTION statement.
The SET CONNECTION statement is supported for Type 1 connections, but the only valid target is the current connection.	The SET CONNECTION statement is supported for Type 2 connections to change the state of a connection from dormant to current.
Connecting with the USER/USING option disconnects the current connection and establishes a new connection with the given authorization name and password.	Connecting with the USER/USING option is accepted only when there is no current or dormant connection to the specified database server.
The CONNECT RESET statement can terminate (disconnect) the current connection.	The CONNECT RESET statement can explicitly connect you to the default application server if you have defined a default database. You can use the DISCONNECT statement to terminate a specified connection. You can also use the COMMIT statement to terminate a connection, provided the connection is placed in the release-pending state by the RELEASE statement before the current transaction is terminated. Note: All connections in the release-pending state will be disconnected at the next COMMIT. An alternative method for terminating connections is to use the precompiler options DISCONNECT(EXPLICIT), DISCONNECT(CONDITIONAL), or DISCONNECT(AUTOMATIC).
After the CONNECT RESET statement is used to disconnect the current connection, if the next SQL statement is not a CONNECT statement, then implicit connect to the default database server (if one has been defined) will be performed.	The CONNECT RESET statement is equivalent to an explicit connect to the default database server (if one has been defined).
If consecutive CONNECT RESET statements are issued, an error will occur.	If consecutive CONNECT RESET statements are issued, an error will occur only if the SQLRULES(STD) precompiler option was specified. This option disallows the use of the CONNECT statement to existing connections.
The CONNECT RESET statement implicitly commits the current transaction.	The CONNECT RESET statement does not commit the current transaction.
If an existing connection is terminated by the system for whatever reason, then subsequent non-CONNECT SQL statements made to this database server will result in an error (SQLSTATE of **08**003).	If an existing connection is terminated by the system, COMMIT, ROLLBACK, and SET CONNECTION statements are still permitted.

TABLE 9.2 Type 1 and Type 2 Connection Semantics *(Continued)*

Type 1 connections	Type 2 connections
The current transaction is implicitly committed when the application process terminates successfully.	The current transaction is implicitly committed when the application process terminates successfully.
The current connection is disconnected when the application process terminates.	All connections (current, dormant, and release-pending) are disconnected when the application process terminates.
Regardless of whether there is a current connection when a CONNECT statement fails (with an error other than "server name not defined in the local directory"), the application process is placed in the unconnected state. Subsequent non-CONNECT statements will receive an error (SQLSTATE of **08**003).	If a current connection exists when a CONNECT statement fails, the current connection is unaffected. If no current connection exists when a CONNECT statement fails, the program is placed in an unconnected state. Subsequent non-CONNECT statements will receive an error (SQLSTATE of **08**003).

If an application process does not have a current connection, then it is in an unconnected state. When an application process is unconnected, only the CONNECT, DISCONNECT, SET CONNECTION, RELEASE, COMMIT, and ROLLBACK statements can be executed, unless implicit connect (specified by an SQL precompiler option) and a default database server (specified via the DB2DBDFT environment variable) are available.

Whenever an application process has a current connection, then it is in a connected state. When connected, it can execute SQL statements that refer to data objects managed by the current database server. An application process in the unconnected state enters the connected state when it successfully executes the CONNECT or the SET CONNECTION statement. If an unconnected application process attempts to execute SQL statements, an implicit connect will be made, provided implicit connect is available and a default database server has been specified.

A connected application process enters the unconnected state when its current connection is intentionally ended or when an unsuccessfully executed SQL statement causes the application server to roll back and the database connection to be severed. You can intentionally end a connection by executing either a DISCONNECT statement or a COMMIT statement after a RELEASE statement has placed the current connection in the release-pending state. How connections are ended when the DISCONNECT statement executes is determined by the value specified in the DISCONNECT SQL precompiler option at application precompile time. If the AUTOMATIC value is specified, then all open connections are ended; if the CONDITIONAL value is used, then all connections that do not have open WITH HOLD cursors are ended.

States of a Connection

When an application process successfully executes a CONNECT statement, the connection that existed prior to the execution of the CONNECT statement (if one existed) is placed in a dormant state, the new database server name is added to the set of connections, and the new connection is placed into both the current state and the held state. When an application process successfully executes a RELEASE statement, a connection is removed from the held state and placed in a release-pending state, which means that the connection will be terminated at the next successful COMMIT operation (a ROLLBACK operation has no effect on connections). A held state means that a connection will not be disconnected at the next COMMIT operation.

All connections are initially placed in the held state and can be moved into the release-pending state when the RELEASE statement is successfully executed. Once a connection is placed in the release-pending state, it cannot be returned to the held state. A connection remains in a release-pending state across transaction boundaries whenever a ROLLBACK statement is issued or whenever a unsuccessful COMMIT statement results in a rollback. Even if a connection is not explicitly placed in the release-pending state, it can still be terminated by a COMMIT operation if the right conditions exist for the specified DISCONNECT precompiler option.

Regardless of whether a connection is in the held or release-pending state, a connection can also be in the current state or in the dormant state. When a connection is in the current state, SQL statements executed by the application process refer to data objects managed by that database server. When a connection is in the dormant state, that connection is no longer current and no SQL statement can reference its data objects. The COMMIT, ROLLBACK, DISCONNECT ALL, and RELEASE ALL statements can still reference dormant connections since they do not refer to actual data objects. The SET CONNECTION and CONNECT RESET statements change the state of the connection for the named database server, from the held state to the current state, and place any other existing connections in the dormant state. At any point in time, only one connection can be in the current state. When a dormant connection becomes current within the same transaction, the state of all locks, cursors, and prepared statements are restored to the condition they were in the last time the connection was current.

A connection is terminated when the DISCONNECT statement is executed or when the COMMIT statement is executed while the connection is in the release-pending state. A connection can also be ended because of a communication failure. When a connection is terminated, all resources acquired by the application process through the connection and all resources used to create and maintain the connection are deallocated and released. Whenever the current connection is terminated, the application process is placed in the unconnected state. All connections of an application process are automatically terminated whenever the process is terminated. Figure 9.1 illustrates these application process state and connection state transitions.

SQL Precompiler Options That Affect Connection Management

The processing of some DB2 connection management statements is determined by the following set of precompiler options:

CONNECT(1 | 2). Specifies whether CONNECT statements are to be processed with Type 1 or Type 2 semantics. CONNECT(1) is the default, so Type 1 semantics are supported if this option is not specified.

SQLRULES(DB2 | STD). Specifies whether Type 2 CONNECT statements should be processed according to DB2 or SQL92 standard (STD) rules. DB2 rules allow connections to switch between the current and dormant state; the SQL92 standard does not. SQLRULES(DB2) is the default.

DISCONNECT (EXPLICIT | CONDITIONAL | AUTOMATIC). Specifies what database connections are to be disconnected when a commit occurs. If the EXPLICIT flag is used, only those connections explicitly marked for release by the SQL RELEASE statement are disconnected. If the CONDITIONAL flag is used, connections with no open cursors that were declared with the WITH HOLD option, as well as connections explicitly marked for release by the SQL RELEASE statement, are disconnected. If the AUTOMATIC flag is used, all connections will be disconnected. DISCONNECT(EXPLICIT) is the default.

SYNCPOINT (ONEPHASE | TWOPHASE | NONE). Specifies how commits or rollbacks are to be coordinated among multiple database connections. If the ONEPHASE flag is used, updates can occur only on one database connection within a transaction; all other databases connections are treated as read-only. If the TWOPHASE flag is used, a transaction manager (TM) will be used at runtime to coordinate two-phase commits among databases supporting this protocol. If the NONE flag is used, a transaction manager is not available to perform two-phase commits and single updates, so multiple reader rules are not enforced. In this case, when a COMMIT or ROLLBACK statement is executed, individual commits or rollbacks are posted to all database connections. If one or more of these commits or rollbacks fail an error occurs. SYNCPOINT(ONEPHASE) is the default.

Each of these connection options governs the way DB2 manages database connections. Since an application can consist of multiple source-code files, each of these files can be precompiled with

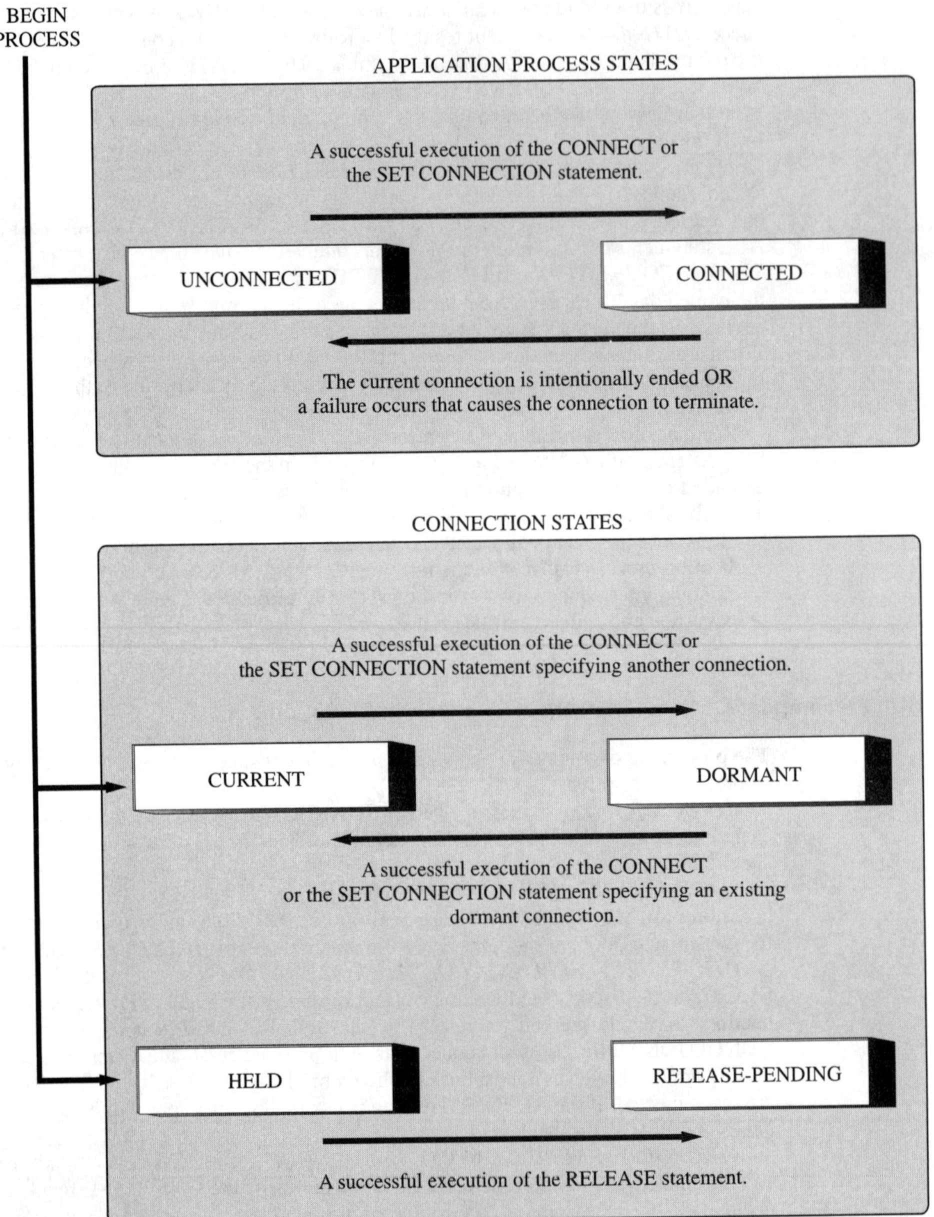
BEGIN
PROCESS
APPLICATION PROCESS STATES
A successful execution of the CONNECT or
the SET CONNECTION statement.
UNCONNECTED
CONNECTED
The current connection is intentionally ended OR
a failure occurs that causes the connection to terminate.
CONNECTION STATES
A successful execution of the CONNECT or
the SET CONNECTION statement specifying another connection.
CURRENT
DORMANT
A successful execution of the CONNECT
or the SET CONNECTION statement specifying an existing
dormant connection.
HELD
RELEASE-PENDING
A successful execution of the RELEASE statement.

FIGURE 9.1 Application process state and connection state transitions.

different connection options. Unless a SET CLIENT application programming interface (API) has been executed, the connection options used when the source-code file containing the first CONNECT statement was precompiled will define the connection options that will be used at application runtime. If a CONNECT statement from a source-code file preprocessed with different connection options is subsequently executed, you must execute the SET CLIENT API first to set the runtime connection options equal to the precompiler options used to precompile the source-code file, or an error will occur.

Note: Once the SET CLIENT API has been executed, the connection options used when the source-code file was precompiled are ignored.

DB2's SQL Authorization Facility

DB2 provides the SQL authorization subsystem to ensure that multiple users can share a database and still maintain control over the data objects they create. This subsystem controls which data objects and resources a user can access or create, based on each user's authorization ID. Before users can perform any SQL operation, they must have the appropriate authority required for that operation. SQL authorization privileges are given to users via the GRANT statement, and they are taken away from users with the REVOKE statement. The SQL authorization subsystem maintains a system of privilege hierarchies that provides the following three broad levels of authorization control:

SYSADMN (system administrator). This is the highest level of authority that DB2 provides. Only users with this authority level can:

- Create or drop a database.
- Catalog or uncatalog remote workstations and databases.
- Migrate a database or reinstall DB2.
- Change the database configuration file.
- Restore a database from backup.
- Grant or revoke the next highest level of authority.

A user with system administrator authorization is also automatically granted all lower-level privileges.

DBADM (database administrator). This is the second highest level of authority that DB2 provides. A user with this level of authority has unlimited privileges on any data object within a specific database. Only users with this (or SYSADM) authority can:

- Back up a database.
- Grant and revoke lower-level privileges, including all database privileges other than the DBADM privilege.

Whenever a database is created, the creator is automatically given unlimited privileges to any object in that database. Also, the CONNECT, CREATETAB, and BINDADD privileges are automatically granted to the PUBLIC for new databases when they are created.

CONTROL. This level of authority provides a user with full control over a specific database object, such as a table, package, or index. The creator of a database object, with the exception of a view object, automatically receives CONTROL privilege for that object. The creator of a view object does not automatically receive CONTROL privileges, but rather privileges equal to those held for each of the tables referenced by the view. If a user has the CONTROL authorization for table objects, he or she is allowed to reorganize the table and run statistics against it. In addition, the CONTROL authorization provides a full set of privileges on any of the table operations. These privileges can, in turn, be granted to other users of the table. Users with either SYSADM or DBADM authorization automatically have CONTROL privileges and all table privileges on any database object.

CONNECT

Purpose

The CONNECT statement allows you to establish a connection to one or more database servers, collect information about the current database server connection, or terminate a connection to one or more database servers.

Syntax

```
EXEC SQL CONNECT;

EXEC SQL CONNECT TO [server-name] <connection-mode> <USER [authorization-ID]
   USING [password]>;

EXEC SQL CONNECT USER [authorization-ID] USING [password];

EXEC SQL CONNECT RESET;
```

> Note: This statement can be executed in any of the preceding formats; each format will produce a different result.

Parameters

server-name Identifies the application database server name to which the connection is made. The server name can be either the actual database server name or the name of a host variable that contains the database server name. The server name is actually a database alias that identifies the actual database server.

connection-mode Identifies the mode to use when establishing the connection. The connection mode can be one of the following:

IN SHARE MODE	This mode allows concurrent applications to execute at the database server.
IN EXCLUSIVE MODE	This mode prevents concurrent applications from executing at the database server unless they have the same authorization ID as the user holding the exclusive lock.

authorization-ID Identifies the user attempting to connect to the application database server.

password Identifies the password of the user attempting to connect to the application database server.

Description

The CONNECT statement allows you to collect information about the current database server connection, establish a new connection to one or more database servers, or terminate a connection to one or more database servers. There are two types of available database connections: Type 1 and Type 2. A Type 1 CONNECT statement supports a single database connection per transaction (remote unit of work). A Type 2 CONNECT statement supports multiple database connections per transaction (application-directed distributed unit of work).

The syntax of the CONNECT statement is the same for both of these types of connections, but in most cases their functionality is very different. The type of connections an application will support (either Type 1 or Type 2) is determined by an SQL precompiler option specified when the application is precompiled.

If Type 1 connections are being used and if implicit connect is available (specified by an SQL precompiler option), you can automatically establish a default database server connection when the application requester is initialized. If you execute the CONNECT statement without any options (as shown in the first syntax example) under these conditions, DB2 will attempt to establish a connection to the default database server. If Type 2 connections are being used or if implicit connect is not available, however, information about the current database server connection (if one exists) will be returned to various fields of the SQLCA data structure variable. This form of the CONNECT statement does not require the application process to be in the connectable state, nor does it change the state of the current connection if a connection exists.

If you execute the CONNECT statement and specify a database server name (as shown in the second syntax example), DB2 will attempt to establish a connection to the specified database server. If Type 1 connections are supported and implicit connect is available, you can execute the CONNECT statement with only the user name and password information (as shown in the third syntax example). This will attempt to establish a connection to the default database server. On the other hand, if Type 2 connections are supported and the CONNECT statement is executed with only user name and password information, DB2 will process it like a Type 2 CONNECT RESET statement. Before either of these two forms of the CONNECT statement can be successfully executed, the application attempting to establish the database server connection must be in a connectable state (refer to the beginning of the chapter for more information).

If the CONNECT RESET form of the CONNECT statement is executed (as shown in the last syntax example) and Type 1 connections are supported, the current transaction will be committed and the current database server connection will be terminated. If this form of the CONNECT statement is executed and Type 2 connections are supported, the application will attempt to connect to the default database server if one exists; otherwise, this form of the CONNECT statement will be ignored.

Comments

- If a host variable is used to specify the server name, it must be defined as a character string variable with a length attribute no larger than eight, and it must not have a corresponding indicator variable. The actual server name stored within the host variable must be left-justified and it must not contain quotation marks.

Note: DB2 for MVS supports a 16-byte server name, and both SQL/DS and DB2/400 support an 18-byte database server name. Only DB2 for OS/2 and DB2 for AIX, version 2.1, support the use of an 8-byte database alias name with the CONNECT statement. However, you can map the database alias name to a 16 or 18-byte database name with the database connection service directory listings.

- If the SQLRULES(STD) SQL precompiler option is used along with Type 2 connections, the server name must not identify an existing database server connection or an SQL error will occur.
- Because the specified server name is actually a database alias, it must be listed in the application requester's local database directory.
- If a host variable specifies the authorization ID, it must be defined as a character string variable with a length attribute no larger than eight, and it must not have a corresponding indicator variable. The actual user name stored within the host variable must be left-justified and it must not contain quotation marks.
- If a host variable specifies the password, it must be defined as a character string variable with a length attribute no larger than 18, and it must not have a corresponding indicator variable. The actual password stored within the host variable must be left-justified and it must not contain quotation marks.
- Whenever the CONNECT statement is successfully executed, the actual name of the database server (not its alias) is placed in the CURRENT SERVER special

register, and information about the current server connection is stored in the SQLCA data structure variable as follows:

-The *sqlerrp* field contains information about the database server. If the database server is an IBM product, the value in the SQLERRP field will have the form *pppvvrrm*, where *ppp* identifies the IBM product ("DSN"-DB2 for MVS; "ARI"-SQL/DS; "QSQ"-DB2/400; and "SQL"-DB2 for OS/2 and AIX), *vv* is the IBM product version number, *rr* is the IBM product release number, and *m* is the IBM product modification number.

-The *sqlerrmc* field contains the following information, with each value separated by 0xFF: the country code of the application server (blanks for DDCS), the code page of the application server (CCSID for DDCS), the authorization ID associated with the connection, the database alias, the type of platform on which the application server is running ("QAS"-DB2/400; "QDB2"-DB2 for MVS; "QDB2/2"-DB2 common server for OS/2; "QDB2/6000"-DB2 common server for AIX; "QDB2/HPUX"-DB2 common server for HP-UX; "QDB2/NT"-DB2 common server for NT; "QDB2/SNI"-DB2 common server for Siemens Nixdorf; "QDB2/SUN"-DB2 common server for Solaris; "QOS/2 DBM"-Extended Services 1.0 Database Manager; "QSQLDS/VM"-SQL/DS for VM; "QSQLDS/VSE"-SQL/DS for VSE), the agent ID that identifies the agent executing within DB2 on behalf of the application (the same as the agent ID element returned by the DB2 database monitor), the agent index (which identifies the index of the agent ID and is used for service), and the connection node number (for version 2.1-always zero).

-The *sqlerrd[3]* field indicates whether or not the database associated with the connection is updatable. A database is usually updatable and this value is set to 1. If the authorizations associated with the user indicate that the user cannot perform updates, however, the database is changed to read-only and this value is set to 2.

-The *sqlerrd[4]* field contains information about the connection's characteristics. The value of this field will be one of the following:

0 N/A

1 One-phase commit

2 One-phase commit and read-only (applicable only for connections to DRDA1 databases in a transaction processing monitor environment, which is used whenever the SYNCPOINT(TWOPHASE) SQL precompiler option is specified)

3 Two-phase commit

- Whenever the CONNECT statement fails, the name of the module at the application requester that detected the error is placed in the SQLERRP field of the SQLCA data structure variable. The first three characters of this module name identify the database server if it is an IBM product (see earlier in this section for a list of the available IBM product codes).
- If the CONNECT TO form of a Type 1 CONNECT statement is successful, the application is disconnected from the current database server, all open cursors are closed, all prepared SQL statements are destroyed, and all locks are released before the connection to the new database server is established.
- If the SQLRULES(DB2) SQL precompiler option is used and the CONNECT TO form of a Type 2 CONNECT statement is successful, a connection to the specified database server is either established (if it does not already exist) or changed from the dormant to the current state.
- If the CONNECT TO form of the CONNECT statement is unsuccessful because the application process is not in a connectable state or because the server name specified is not listed in the local database directory, the connection states of all database server connections remain unchanged. This means that the application

remains connected to the current server and all other servers (if any) remain in the dormant state. If the CONNECT TO statement is unsuccessful for any other reason and Type 1 connections are being used, the application is placed in the unconnected state.

- It is good practice to make the CONNECT statement the first executable SQL statement submitted by an application process.
- If a CONNECT statement is issued to the current database server with a different authorization ID and password, the connection is terminated and reestablished. When this scenario occurs, all open cursors are closed by DB2, even if they were created with the WITH HOLD option. On the other hand, if a CONNECT statement is issued to the current application server with the same authorization ID and password, the connection is not terminated and DB2 acts as if this statement was never submitted. In this case, open cursors are not closed.
- Although you can use the CONNECT statement to establish or switch database server connections, the CONNECT TO [server-name] <USER/USING> version of the statement will be successful only when no current or dormant connection to the specified database server exist. All existing connections to a database server must be released before a connection to the same server can be established with this form of the CONNECT statement. Release all connections to the specified server by issuing a DISCONNECT or RELEASE statement followed by a COMMIT statement.
- Implicit connects are supported for both Type 1 and Type 2 connections. However, in order to execute SQL statements on the default database, you must first use the CONNECT RESET or CONNECT [server-name] <USER/USING> version of the statement to establish the database connection. If you issue the CONNECT statement with no operands, information about the current connection will be displayed if a current server connection exists. If Type 1 connections are supported, DB2 will attempt to connect to the default database if no current connection exists. If Type 2 connections are supported, DB2 will not attempt to connect to the default database server.
- SQL statements that reference data objects must be dynamically prepared when you are using Type 2 connections.

Authorization Only users with system administrator (SYSADM), database administrator (DBADM), or CONNECT authority for the specified database server are allowed to execute this statement.

See also DISCONNECT, RELEASE, SET CONNECTION, COMMIT

Examples The following C program illustrates how to establish a Type 1 database connection with the CONNECT statement:

```
#include <stdio.h>
#include <stdlib.h>
#include <sql.h>
int main()
{
    /* Include The SQLCA Data Structure Variable */
    EXEC SQL INCLUDE SQLCA;

    /* Set Up A Simple SQL Error Handler */
    EXEC SQL WHENEVER SQLERROR GOTO EXIT;
```

```
    /* Declare The Local Memory Variables */
    int  rc = EXIT_SUCCESS;

    /* Declare The SQL Host Memory Variables */
    EXEC SQL BEGIN DECLARE SECTION;
        long    lTotalComm;
    EXEC SQL END DECLARE SECTION;

    /* Connect To The SAMPLE Database (Type 1 Connection) */
    EXEC SQL CONNECT TO SAMPLE USER etpdd6z USING sanders;

    /* Retrieve The Total Amount Of Commissions Paid From The */
    /* EMPLOYEE Table                                          */
    EXEC SQL SELECT SUM(COMM)
        INTO :lTotalComm
        FROM USERID.EMPLOYEE;

    /* Print The Information Retrieved */
    printf("The company paid $ %.2ld.00 in commissions.\n",
          lTotalComm);

EXIT:
    /* If An Error Has Occurred, Display The SQL Return Code */
    if (sqlca.sqlcode != SQL_RC_OK)
        {
        printf("SQL ERROR : %ld\n", sqlca.sqlcode);
        rc = EXIT_FAILURE;
        }

    /* Issue A Rollback To Free All Locks */
    EXEC SQL ROLLBACK;

    /* Turn Off The SQL Error Handler */
    EXEC SQL WHENEVER SQLERROR CONTINUE;

    /* Disconnect From The SAMPLE Database */
    EXEC SQL DISCONNECT CURRENT;

    /* Return To The Operating System */
    return(rc);
}
```

Note: The CONNECT Statement is used in a C++ program to establish a Type 1 connection in a similar manner.

The following C program illustrates how to use the CONNECT statement to establish two separate Type 2 database connections:

```
#include <stdio.h>
#include <stdlib.h>
#include <string.h>
#include <sql.h>
#include <sqlda.h>

int main()
{
```

```
/* Include The SQLCA Data Structure Variable */
EXEC SQL INCLUDE SQLCA;

/* Set Up A Simple SQL Error Handler */
EXEC SQL WHENEVER SQLERROR GOTO EXIT;

/* Declare The Local Memory Variables */
int            rc = EXIT_SUCCESS;
struct sqlda   *out_sqlda1;         // SQLDA Data Structure Pointer
struct sqlda   *out_sqlda2;         // SQLDA Data Structure Pointer
char           szEmpNo[7];          // Employee Number
short          sEmpNoInd;           // Employee No. Indicator
short          sEmpID;              // Employee ID
short          sEmpIDInd;           // Employee ID Indicator
char           szDeptNo[3];         // Department Number
short          sDeptNoInd;          // Department No. Indicator

/* Declare The SQL Host Memory Variables */
EXEC SQL BEGIN DECLARE SECTION;
    char    szSelectString1[80];
    char    szSelectString2[80];
EXEC SQL END DECLARE SECTION;

/* Build The First Select SQL Statement String */
strcpy(szSelectString1, "SELECT EMPNO, WORKDEPT FROM ");
strcat(szSelectString1, "USERID.EMPLOYEE WHERE EMPNO = '000100'");

/* Build The Second Select SQL Statement String */
strcpy(szSelectString2, "SELECT EMPID, DEPTNO FROM ");
strcat(szSelectString2, "ETPDD6Z.TEMP_EMP WHERE EMPID = 100");

/* Allocate And Initialize An SQLDA Data Structure Variable */
if ((out_sqlda1 = (struct sqlda *) malloc(SQLDASIZE(2))) == NULL)
    {
    printf("ERROR : Unable To Allocate Memory For SQLDA !\n");
    return(EXIT_FAILURE);
    }
out_sqlda1->sqln = 2;

/* Allocate And Initialize Another SQLDA Data Structure Variable */
if ((out_sqlda2 = (struct sqlda *) malloc(SQLDASIZE(2))) == NULL)
    {
    printf("ERROR : Unable To Allocate Memory For SQLDA !\n");
    return(EXIT_FAILURE);
    }
out_sqlda2->sqln = 2;

/* Connect To The BOOKSAMP Database (Type 2 Connection) */
EXEC SQL CONNECT TO BOOKSAMP USER etpdd6z USING sanders;

/* Connect To The SAMPLE Database (Type 2 Connection) */
EXEC SQL CONNECT TO SAMPLE USER etpdd6z USING sanders;

/* Prepare The First Select SQL Statement */
EXEC SQL PREPARE SQL_STMNT1 INTO :*out_sqlda1
         FROM :szSelectString1;

/* Store The Address Of Local Memory Variables In The    */
```

```
/* Appropriate SQLDA->SQLVAR Data And Indicator Pointers */
out_sqlda1->sqlvar[0].sqldata = (unsigned char *) &szEmpNo;
out_sqlda1->sqlvar[0].sqlind = (short *) &sEmpNoInd;
out_sqlda1->sqlvar[1].sqldata = (unsigned char *) &szDeptNo;
out_sqlda1->sqlvar[1].sqlind = (short *) &sDeptNoInd;

/* Declare The First Dynamic Cursor */
EXEC SQL DECLARE DYN_CURSOR1 CURSOR FOR SQL_STMNT1;

/* Open The First Dynamic Cursor */
EXEC SQL OPEN DYN_CURSOR1;

/* If The Cursor Was Successfully Opened, Fetch The Records */
/* Into Local Memory Variables                               */
printf("Record retrieved from SAMPLE database :\n");
while (sqlca.sqlcode == SQL_RC_OK)
    {
    EXEC SQL FETCH DYN_CURSOR1 USING DESCRIPTOR :*out_sqlda1;

    /* Print The Information Retrieved */
    if (sqlca.sqlcode == SQL_RC_OK)
        {
        printf("Employee ID : %sDepartment : %s\n",
            szEmpNo, szDeptNo);
        }
    }                                      /* End Of WHILE    */

/* Close The First Cursor */
EXEC SQL CLOSE DYN_CURSOR1;

/* Make The BOOKSAMP Database The Current Database Server */
EXEC SQL SET CONNECTION BOOKSAMP;

/* Prepare The Second Select SQL Statement */
EXEC SQL PREPARE SQL_STMNT2 INTO :*out_sqlda2
         FROM :szSelectString2;

/* Store The Address Of Local Memory Variables In The     */
/* Appropriate SQLDA->SQLVAR Data And Indicator Pointers */
out_sqlda2->sqlvar[0].sqldata = (unsigned char *) &sEmpID;
out_sqlda2->sqlvar[0].sqlind = (short *) &sEmpIDInd;
out_sqlda2->sqlvar[1].sqldata = (unsigned char *) &szDeptNo;
out_sqlda2->sqlvar[1].sqlind = (short *) &sDeptNoInd;

/* Declare The Second Dynamic Cursor */
EXEC SQL DECLARE DYN_CURSOR2 CURSOR FOR SQL_STMNT2;

/* Open The Second Dynamic Cursor */
EXEC SQL OPEN DYN_CURSOR2;

/* If The Cursor Was Successfully Opened, Fetch The Records */
/* Into Local Memory Variables                               */
printf("\nRecord retrieved from BOOKSAMP database :\n");
while (sqlca.sqlcode == SQL_RC_OK)
    {
    EXEC SQL FETCH DYN_CURSOR2 USING DESCRIPTOR :*out_sqlda2;
    /* Print The Information Retrieved */
    if (sqlca.sqlcode == SQL_RC_OK)
        {
        printf("Employee ID : %d\t Department : %s\n",
            sEmpID, szDeptNo);
```

```
            }
        }                                               /* End Of WHILE     */

    /* Close The Second Cursor */
    EXEC SQL CLOSE DYN_CURSOR2;

EXIT:
    /* If An Error Has Occurred, Display The SQL Return Code */
    if (sqlca.sqlcode != SQL_RC_OK)
        {
        printf("SQL ERROR : %ld\n", sqlca.sqlcode);
        rc = EXIT_FAILURE;
        }

    /* Issue A Rollback To Free All Locks */
    EXEC SQL ROLLBACK;

    /* Turn Off The SQL Error Handler */
    EXEC SQL WHENEVER SQLERROR CONTINUE;

    /* Disconnect From Both Databases */
    EXEC SQL DISCONNECT ALL;

    /* Free Memory Allocated For The SQLDA Data Structure Variables */
    if (out_sqlda1)
        free(out_sqlda1);

    if (out_sqlda2)
        free(out_sqlda2);

    /* Return To The Operating System */
    return(rc);
}
```

The following C++ program illustrates how to use the CONNECT statement to establish two separate Type-2 database connections:

```
#include <iostream.h>
#include <stdlib.h>
#include <string.h>
#include <sql.h>
#include <sqlda.h>

/* Define The Employee Class */
class Employee
{
    private:

       /* Include The SQLCA Data Structure Variable */
       EXEC SQL INCLUDE SQLCA;

       /* Declare The SQL Host Memory Variables */
       EXEC SQL BEGIN DECLARE SECTION;
           char    szSelectString1[80];
           char    szSelectString2[80];
       EXEC SQL END DECLARE SECTION;
       /* Declare All Other Private Memory Variables */
       struct sqlda   *out_sqlda1;      // SQLDA Data Structure Pointer
       struct sqlda   *out_sqlda2;      // SQLDA Data Structure Pointer
       char           szEmpNo[6];       // Employee Number
       short          sEmpNoInd;        // Employee No. Indicator
```

```
        short         sEmpID;            // Employee ID
        short         sEmpIDInd;         // Employee ID Indicator
        char          szDeptNo[3];       // Department Number
        short         sDeptNoInd;        // Department No. Indicator

    /* Declare The Public Member Function Prototypes */
    public:
        Employee();                      // Constructor
        ~Employee();                     // Destructor
        short int getSAMPLEData();
        short int getBOOKSAMPData();
} ;

/* Define The Class Constructor */
Employee::Employee(void)
{
    /* Build The First Select SQL Statement String */
    strcpy(szSelectString1, "SELECT EMPNO, WORKDEPT FROM ");
    strcat(szSelectString1, "USERID.EMPLOYEE WHERE EMPNO = '000100'");

    /* Build The Second Select SQL Statement String */
    strcpy(szSelectString2, "SELECT EMPID, DEPTNO FROM ");
    strcat(szSelectString2, "ETPDD6Z.TEMP_EMP WHERE EMPID = 100");
}

/* Define The Class Destructor */
Employee::~Employee(void)
{
    delete []out_sqlda1;
    delete []out_sqlda2;
}

/* Define The getSAMPLEData() Member Function */
short int Employee::getSAMPLEData()
{
    /* Allocate And Initialize An SQLDA Data Structure Variable */
    out_sqlda1 = (struct sqlda *) new char [SQLDASIZE(2)];
    if (out_sqlda1 != NULL)
        out_sqlda1->sqln = 2;

    /* Prepare The First Select SQL Statement */
    EXEC SQL PREPARE SQL_STMNT1 INTO :*out_sqlda1
             FROM :szSelectString1;

    /* Store The Address Of Local Memory Variables In The     */
    /* Appropriate SQLDA->SQLVAR Data And Indicator Pointers */
    out_sqlda1->sqlvar[0].sqldata = (char *) &szEmpNo;
    out_sqlda1->sqlvar[0].sqlind = (short *) &sEmpNoInd;
    out_sqlda1->sqlvar[1].sqldata = (char *) &szDeptNo;
    out_sqlda1->sqlvar[1].sqlind = (short *) &sDeptNoInd;

    /* Declare The First Dynamic Cursor */
    EXEC SQL DECLARE DYN_CURSOR1 CURSOR FOR SQL_STMNT1;

    /* Open The First Dynamic Cursor */
    EXEC SQL OPEN DYN_CURSOR1;
    /* If The Cursor Was Successfully Opened, Fetch The Records */
    /* Into Local Memory Variables                               */
    cout << "Record retrieved from SAMPLE database :" << endl;
    while (sqlca.sqlcode == SQL_RC_OK)
        {
```

```
        EXEC SQL FETCH DYN_CURSOR1 USING DESCRIPTOR :*out_sqlda1;

        /* Print The Information Retrieved */
        if (sqlca.sqlcode == SQL_RC_OK)
            {
            cout << "Employee ID : " << szEmpNo << "   Department : ";
            cout << szDeptNo << endl;
            }
        }                       /* End Of WHILE    */

    /* Close The First Cursor */
    EXEC SQL CLOSE DYN_CURSOR1;

    /* Return The SQL Return Code */
    return(sqlca.sqlcode);
}

/* Define The getBOOKSAMPData() Member Function */
short int Employee::getBOOKSAMPData()
{
    /* Allocate And Initialize An SQLDA Data Structure Variable */
    out_sqlda2 = (struct sqlda *) new char [SQLDASIZE(2)];
    if (out_sqlda2 != NULL)
        out_sqlda2->sqln = 2;

    /* Prepare The Second Select SQL Statement */
    EXEC SQL PREPARE SQL_STMNT2 INTO :*out_sqlda2
             FROM :szSelectString2;

    /* Store The Address Of Local Memory Variables In The    */
    /* Appropriate SQLDA->SQLVAR Data And Indicator Pointers */
    out_sqlda2->sqlvar[0].sqldata = (char *) &sEmpID;
    out_sqlda2->sqlvar[0].sqlind = (short *) &sEmpIDInd;
    out_sqlda2->sqlvar[1].sqldata = (char *) &szDeptNo;
    out_sqlda2->sqlvar[1].sqlind = (short *) &sDeptNoInd;

    /* Declare The Second Dynamic Cursor */
    EXEC SQL DECLARE DYN_CURSOR2 CURSOR FOR SQL_STMNT2;

    /* Open The Second Dynamic Cursor */
    EXEC SQL OPEN DYN_CURSOR2;

    /* If The Cursor Was Successfully Opened, Fetch The Records */
    /* Into Local Memory Variables                              */
    cout << endl << "Record retrieved from BOOKSAMP database :" << endl;
    while (sqlca.sqlcode == SQL_RC_OK)
        {
        EXEC SQL FETCH DYN_CURSOR2 USING DESCRIPTOR :*out_sqlda2;

        /* Print The Information Retrieved */
        if (sqlca.sqlcode == SQL_RC_OK)
            {
            cout << "Employee ID : " << sEmpID << "     Department : ";
            cout << szDeptNo << endl;
            }
        }                                       /* End Of WHILE    */
    /* Close The Second Cursor */
    EXEC SQL CLOSE DYN_CURSOR2;

    /* Return The SQL Return Code */
    return(sqlca.sqlcode);
```

```
}

int main()
{
    /* Declare The Local Memory Variables */
    short int rc = EXIT_SUCCESS;              // Must Be Declared Here
                                              // For The SQL Precompiler

    /* Include The SQLCA Data Structure Variable */
    EXEC SQL INCLUDE SQLCA;

    /* Set Up A Simple SQL Error Handler */
    EXEC SQL WHENEVER SQLERROR GOTO EXIT;

    /* Create An Instance Of The Employee Class */
    Employee EmpInfo;

    /* Connect To The BOOKSAMP Database (Type 2 Connection) */
    EXEC SQL CONNECT TO BOOKSAMP USER etpdd6z USING sanders;

    /* Connect To The SAMPLE Database (Type 2 Connection) */
    EXEC SQL CONNECT TO SAMPLE USER etpdd6z USING sanders;

    /* Retrieve And Display A Record In The SAMPLE Database */
    rc = EmpInfo.getSAMPLEData();

    /* Make The BOOKSAMP Database The Current Database Server */
    EXEC SQL SET CONNECTION BOOKSAMP;

    /* Retrieve And Display A Record In The BOOKSAMP Database */
    rc = EmpInfo.getBOOKSAMPData();

EXIT:
    /* If An Error Has Occurred, Display The SQL Return Code */
    if (sqlca.sqlcode != SQL_RC_OK)
        {
        cout << "SQL ERROR : " << sqlca.sqlcode << endl;
        rc = EXIT_FAILURE;
        }

    /* Issue A Rollback To Free All Locks */
    EXEC SQL ROLLBACK;

    /* Turn Off The SQL Error Handler */
    EXEC SQL WHENEVER SQLERROR CONTINUE;

    /* Disconnect From Both Databases */
    EXEC SQL DISCONNECT ALL;

    /* Return To The Operating System */
    return(rc);
}
```

SET CONNECTION

Purpose The SET CONNECTION statement allows you to make a specified database server the current database server by changing the state of a database connection from dormant to current.

Syntax

```
EXEC SQL SET CONNECTION [server-name];
```

Parameters

server-name Identifies the application database server name. The server name can be either the actual database server name or the name of a host variable that contains the database server name. The server name is actually a database alias that identifies the actual database server.

Description

The SET CONNECTION statement changes the state of a database connection from dormant to current. When the SET CONNECTION statement is executed, the specified database server becomes the current database server, and the database server that was the current server before the SET CONNECTION statement was executed is placed in the dormant state.

Comments

- If a host variable specifies the server name, it must be defined as a character string variable with a length attribute no larger than eight, and it must not have a corresponding indicator variable. The actual server name stored within the host variable must be left-justified and it must not contain quotation marks.
- Because the specified server name is actually a database alias, it must be listed in the application requester's local database directory.
- If the SET CONNECTION statement is executed with the current database server specified as the server name, the states of all database connections will remain unchanged.
- After the SET CONNECTION statement executes, the current server special register is updated with the current server name and the SQLCA data structure variable is updated accordingly. Refer to the CONNECT statement for more information about how connection information is stored in the SQLCA data structure variable.
- Using the SET CONNECTION statement in conjunction with Type 1 CONNECT statements will cause an error to occur since dormant connections are not supported by Type 1 connections.
- If the SQLRULES(DB2) SQL precompiler option is used (refer to the beginning of the chapter), you can use the CONNECT statement in place of the SET CONNECTION statement since Type 2 CONNECT statements are the only Type of supported CONNECT statements.
- When a connection is placed in the current state, made dormant, and then made current again within the same transaction, the connection will reflect its last use with regard to the status of locks, cursors, and prepared SQL statements.

Prerequisites

Before the SET CONNECTION statement can be executed, a connection to the specified database server must first exist. This means that a CONNECT statement for the database server must appear in an embedded SQL source-code file before the SET CONNECTION statement, otherwise an error will occur.

Authorization

No authorization is required to execute this statement.

See Also

CONNECT, DISCONNECT, RELEASE

Examples

See the examples provided for the last statement, CONNECT.

RELEASE

Purpose

The RELEASE statement places one or more database connections in the release-pending state.

Syntax

```
EXEC SQL RELEASE [server-name | CURRENT | ALL <SQL>];
```

Parameters

server-name Identifies the application database server name to be placed in the release-pending state. The server name can be either the actual database server name or the name of a host variable that contains the database server name. The server name is actually a database alias that identifies the actual database server.

CURRENT Indicates that the current database connection is to be placed in the release-pending state.

ALL <SQL> Indicates that all existing connections are to be placed in the release-pending state.

Description

The RELEASE statement places one or more database connections in the release-pending state. Once a connection is placed in this state, it will be terminated during the next execution of the COMMIT statement. If the current server connection is in the release-pending state, when the next COMMIT operation is performed the application process will be placed in the unconnected state until a new connection is established (by the successful execution of either the CONNECT or the SET CONNECTION statement).

Comments

- If you use a host variable to specify the server name, it must be defined as a character string variable with a length attribute no larger than eight, and it must not have a corresponding indicator variable. The actual server name stored within the host variable must be left-justified and it must not contain quotation marks.
- If the database server name is "CURRENT" or "ALL," it will have to be specified via a host variable.
- Whenever the COMMIT statement terminates the current connection (that was placed in a release-pending state), the next SQL statement to be executed should be either CONNECT or SET CONNECTION.
- When using Type 1 connections, there is no need to use the RELEASE statement since the CONNECT RESET statement performs the same function.
- The RELEASE statement does not close open cursors, nor does it release resources.
- Once a connection is placed in the release-pending state, the ROLLBACK statement will not change the state of the connection back to the held state.
- The RELEASE statement does not prevent the further use of the connection.
- You can terminate database server connections by issuing the COMMIT statement if either the DISCONNECT(AUTOMATIC) or the DISCONNECT(CONDITIONAL) SQL precompiler option is in effect.
- If the DISCONNECT statement is unsuccessful, the connection state of the application process and the states of its connections will remain unchanged.
- The DISCONNECT statement cannot be executed from within the transaction processing monitor environment, which is used whenever the SYNCPOINT (TWOPHASE) SQL precompiler option is specified.

Prerequisites

Before the RELEASE statement can be executed, a connection to the specified database server must first exist. This means that a CONNECT statement for the database server must appear in an embedded SQL source-code file before the RELEASE statement, otherwise an error will occur.

Authorization

No authorization is required to execute this statement.

See Also

CONNECT, DISCONNECT, SET CONNECTION, COMMIT

Example The following C program illustrates how to use the RELEASE statement to place a connection in the release-pending state so it is terminated at the next successful execution of a COMMIT statement:

```
#include <stdio.h>
#include <stdlib.h>
#include <sql.h>

#define NOT_FOUND         100
#define NO_CONNECTION   -1024

int main()
{
    /* Include The SQLCA Data Structure Variable */
    EXEC SQL INCLUDE SQLCA;

    /* Set Up A Simple SQL Error Handler */
    EXEC SQL WHENEVER SQLERROR GOTO EXIT;

    /* Declare The Local Memory Variables */
    int  rc = EXIT_SUCCESS;

    /* Declare The SQL Host Memory Variables */
    EXEC SQL BEGIN DECLARE SECTION;
        char      szDeptNo[4];
        struct VARCHAR {                        // VARCHAR Data Structure
                short size;
                char  string[30];
                }  stDeptName;
    EXEC SQL END DECLARE SECTION;

    /* Connect To The SAMPLE Database */
    EXEC SQL CONNECT TO SAMPLE USER etpdd6z USING sanders;

    /* Put The Connection To The Sample Database In */
    /* Release-Pending State                       */
    EXEC SQL RELEASE CURRENT;

    /* Add A Record To The DEPARTMENT Table */
    EXEC SQL INSERT INTO USERID.DEPARTMENT
        VALUES ('E22', 'SYSTEMS SUPPORT', '000100', 'E01', ' ');
    /* Commit The Transaction - This Will Release The Connection */
    EXEC SQL COMMIT;

    /* Turn Off The Simple SQL Error Handler */
    EXEC SQL WHENEVER SQLERROR CONTINUE;

    /* Try To Issue A Rollback - Should Get "Not Connected" Error */
    EXEC SQL ROLLBACK;
    if (sqlca.sqlcode == NO_CONNECTION)
        {
        printf("Connection to database has been terminated - ");
        printf("Reconnecting ...\n\n");
        }
    else
        goto EXIT;

    /* Turn The Simple SQL Error Handler Back On */
    EXEC SQL WHENEVER SQLERROR GOTO EXIT;
```

```
    /* Reconnect To The Sample Database */
    EXEC SQL CONNECT TO SAMPLE USER etpdd6z USING sanders;

    /* Retrieve The New Record (Verifies That Record Was Added) */
    EXEC SQL SELECT DEPTNO, DEPTNAME
        INTO :szDeptNo,
             :stDeptName
        FROM USERID.DEPARTMENT
        WHERE DEPTNO = 'E22';

    /* Print The Information Retrieved */
    printf("New Record Added\n");
    printf("Dept. No. : %s \tDept. Name : %s\n",
           szDeptNo, stDeptName.string);

    /* Delete The New Record From The DEPARTMENT Table */
    EXEC SQL DELETE FROM USERID.DEPARTMENT
        WHERE DEPTNO = 'E22';

    /* Commit The Transaction */
    EXEC SQL COMMIT;

    /* Verify That The Record Is Gone */
    EXEC SQL SELECT DEPTNO, DEPTNAME
        INTO :szDeptNo,
             :stDeptName
        FROM USERID.DEPARTMENT
        WHERE DEPTNO = 'E22';

    /* Print The Information Retrieved */
    if (sqlca.sqlcode == NOT_FOUND)
        {
        sqlca.sqlcode = SQL_RC_OK;
        printf("\nRecord has been deleted.\n");
        }

EXIT:
    /* If An Error Has Occurred, Display The SQL Return Code */
    if (sqlca.sqlcode != SQL_RC_OK)
        {
        printf("SQL ERROR : %ld\n", sqlca.sqlcode);
        rc = EXIT_FAILURE;
        }
    /* Issue A Rollback To Free All Locks */
    EXEC SQL ROLLBACK;

    /* Turn Off The SQL Error Handler */
    EXEC SQL WHENEVER SQLERROR CONTINUE;

    /* Disconnect From The SAMPLE Database */
    EXEC SQL DISCONNECT CURRENT;

    /* Return To The Operating System */
    return(rc);
}
```

Note: The RELEASE statement is used in a C++ program in a similar manner.

DISCONNECT

Purpose The DISCONNECT statement terminates one or more database connections.

Syntax

```
EXEC SQL DISCONNECT [server-name | CURRENT | ALL <SQL>];
```

Parameters

server-name Identifies the application database server name to be terminated. The server name can be either the actual database server name or the name of a host variable that contains the database server name. The server name is actually a database alias that identifies the actual database server.

CURRENT Indicates that the current database connection is to be terminated.

ALL <SQL> Indicates that all existing connections are to be terminated.

Description The DISCONNECT statement terminates the connection to each specified database server. When the current database server connection is terminated, the application process is placed in the unconnected state until a new connection is established by the successful execution of either the CONNECT or the SET CONNECTION statement. Transactions must usually be terminated before the DISCONNECT statement can be executed. The one exception to this rule is when a single database connection is specified to be disconnected and no database transactions occurred after the connection was established.

Comments

- If a host variable specifies the server name, it must be defined as a character string variable with a length attribute no larger than eight, and it must not have a corresponding indicator variable. The actual server name stored within the host variable must be left-justified and it must not contain quotation marks.
- If the database server name is "CURRENT" or "ALL," it must be specified via a host variable.
- Whenever the DISCONNECT statement destroys the current connection, the next SQL statement to be executed should be either the CONNECT or the SET CONNECTION statement.
- When using Type 1 connections, the DISCONNECT CURRENT and DISCONNECT ALL <SQL> statements act the same as the CONNECT RESET statement, with one exception: they will not automatically perform a COMMIT operation.
- If you specify a server name with the DISCONNECT statement while using a Type 1 connection, the server name must identify the current connection since Type 1 connections can support only one connection at a time.
- You can terminate database server connections by issuing the COMMIT statement when either the DISCONNECT(AUTOMATIC) or DISCONNECT(CONDITIONAL) SQL precompiler option is in effect.
- If the DISCONNECT statement is unsuccessful, the connection state of the application process and the states of its connections will remain unchanged.
- The DISCONNECT statement cannot be executed from within the transaction processing monitor environment, which is used whenever the SYNCPOINT (TWOPHASE) SQL precompiler option is specified.

Prerequisites Before the DISCONNECT statement can be executed, a connection to the specified database server must exist. This means that a CONNECT statement for the database server must appear in an embedded SQL source-code file before the DISCONNECT statement, otherwise an error will occur. Also, all active transactions must be terminated before the database connection they are using is terminated.

Authorization No authorization is required to execute this statement.

See Also CONNECT, RELEASE, SET CONNECTION, COMMIT

Examples See the examples provided for the CONNECT statement, earlier in the chapter.

COMMIT

Purpose The COMMIT statement terminates a transaction and makes all database changes made by that transaction permanent.

Syntax

```
EXEC SQL COMMIT <WORK>;
```

Description The COMMIT statement terminates the current transaction and make all database changes made by that transaction permanent, but only changes made by the following statements will be made permanent with a COMMIT:

- ALTER TABLESPACE
- ALTER TABLE
- COMMENT ON
- CREATE
- DROP
- INSERT
- UPDATE
- DELETE
- GRANT
- REVOKE

Not all SQL statements fall under the control of a transaction. Changes made to the database by any of the following statements are made permanent, independent of the COMMIT statement:

- SET CONNECTION
- SET CURRENT EXPLAIN SNAPSHOT
- SET CURRENT FUNCTION PATH
- SET CURRENT PACKAGESET
- SET CURRENT QUERY OPTIMIZATION
- SET EVENT MONITOR STATE

All locks acquired by the transaction after its initiation are released when the COMMIT statement is executed, with the exception of table locks acquired for open cursors declared with the WITH HOLD option. When the current transaction terminates, all open cursors not declared with the WITH HOLD option are closed, all prepared statements not associated with open cursors that were declared with the WITH HOLD option are destroyed, and all LOB locators are freed (even if they are associated with LOB values retrieved via a cursor that was declared with the WITH HOLD clause). Open cursors that were declared with the WITH HOLD option remain open, and the cursor pointer is positioned before the next logical row of the cursor result table. Likewise, all prepared statements that reference these open cursors are retained.

Comments

- If the database application ends normally or if a RESET statement is executed without first executing a COMMIT or a ROLLBACK statement, DB2 will attempt to commit all changes made to the database. However, forcing DB2 to implicitly commit changes is not good programming practice. Each application should terminate all its transactions by explicitly executing either the COMMIT or the ROLLBACK statement.
- Caching the executable sections of SQL data manipulation language (DML) statements can affect the behavior of a COMMIT statement. Refer to the beginning of Chapter 8 for more information about statement caching.

Authorization No authorization is required to execute this statement.

See Also ROLLBACK

Examples The following C program illustrates how the COMMIT statement terminates a transaction:

```
#include <stdio.h>
#include <stdlib.h>
#include <sql.h>

#define NOT_FOUND   100

int main()
{
    /* Include The SQLCA Data Structure Variable */
    EXEC SQL INCLUDE SQLCA;

    /* Set Up A Simple SQL Error Handler */
    EXEC SQL WHENEVER SQLERROR GOTO EXIT;

    /* Declare The Local Memory Variables */
    int  rc = EXIT_SUCCESS;

    /* Declare The SQL Host Memory Variables */
    EXEC SQL BEGIN DECLARE SECTION;
        char      szDeptNo[4];
        struct VARCHAR {                         // VARCHAR Data Structure
                short size;
                char  string[30];
                }  stDeptName;
    EXEC SQL END DECLARE SECTION;

    /* Connect To The SAMPLE Database */
    EXEC SQL CONNECT TO SAMPLE USER etpdd6z USING sanders;

    /* Add A Record To The DEPARTMENT Table */
    EXEC SQL INSERT INTO USERID.DEPARTMENT
        VALUES ('E22', 'SYSTEMS SUPPORT', '000100', 'E01', ' ');

    /* Commit The Transaction */
    EXEC SQL COMMIT;

    /* Retrieve The New Record (Verifies That Record Was Added) */
    EXEC SQL SELECT DEPTNO, DEPTNAME
        INTO :szDeptNo,
             :stDeptName
        FROM USERID.DEPARTMENT
        WHERE DEPTNO = 'E22';
```

```
    /* Print The Information Retrieved */
    printf("New Record Added\n");
    printf("Dept. No. : %s \tDept. Name : %s\n\n",
          szDeptNo, stDeptName.string);

    /* Delete The Record Table */
    EXEC SQL DELETE FROM USERID.DEPARTMENT
        WHERE DEPTNO = 'E22';

    /* Commit The Transaction */
    EXEC SQL COMMIT;

    /* Verify That The Record Is Gone */
    EXEC SQL SELECT DEPTNO, DEPTNAME
        INTO :szDeptNo,
             :stDeptName
        FROM USERID.DEPARTMENT
        WHERE DEPTNO = 'E22';

    /* Print A Message If The Record No Longer Exists */
    if (sqlca.sqlcode == NOT_FOUND)
        {
        sqlca.sqlcode = SQL_RC_OK;
        printf("\nRecord has been deleted.\n");
        }

EXIT:
    /* If An Error Has Occurred, Display The SQL Return Code */
    if (sqlca.sqlcode != SQL_RC_OK)
        {
        printf("SQL ERROR : %ld\n", sqlca.sqlcode);
        rc = EXIT_FAILURE;
        }

    /* Issue A Rollback To Free All Locks */
    EXEC SQL ROLLBACK;

    /* Turn Off The SQL Error Handler */
    EXEC SQL WHENEVER SQLERROR CONTINUE;
    /* Disconnect From The SAMPLE Database */
    EXEC SQL DISCONNECT CURRENT;

    /* Return To The Operating System */
    return(rc);
}
```

Note: The COMMIT statement is used in a C++ program in a similar manner.

ROLLBACK

Purpose The ROLLBACK statement terminates a transaction and backs out (removes) all database changes made by that transaction.

Syntax

```
EXEC SQL ROLLBACK <WORK>;
```

Description

The ROLLBACK statement terminates a transaction and backs out (removes) all database changes made by that transaction, but only changes made by the following statements can be removed with ROLLBACK:

- ALTER TABLESPACE
- ALTER TABLE
- COMMENT ON
- CREATE
- DROP
- INSERT
- UPDATE
- DELETE
- GRANT
- REVOKE

Not all SQL statements fall under the control of a transaction. Changes made to the database by any of the following statements are made permanent independent of the ROLLBACK statement:

- SET CONNECTION
- SET CURRENT EXPLAIN SNAPSHOT
- SET CURRENT FUNCTION PATH
- SET CURRENT PACKAGESET
- SET CURRENT QUERY OPTIMIZATION
- SET EVENT MONITOR STATE
- RELEASE

When the ROLLBACK statement is executed, all locks acquired by the transaction after its initiation are released, all open cursors are closed, all prepared statements are destroyed, and all LOB locators are freed.

Comments

- If the database application ends abnormally, DB2 will attempt to back out all changes made to the database. However, forcing DB2 to implicitly roll back changes is not good programming practice. Each application should terminate all its transactions by explicitly executing either the ROLLBACK or the COMMIT statement.
- Any time data is retrieved from a database table, locks are automatically acquired by the retrieving SQL statements. Therefore, you should use a ROLLBACK statement to terminate read-only transactions so all acquired locks are correctly released and the database remains undisturbed.
- Caching the executable sections of SQL data manipulation language (DML) statements can affect the behavior of a ROLLBACK statement. Refer to the beginning of Chapter 8 for more information about statement caching.

Authorization No authorization is required to execute this statement.

See Also COMMIT

Example The following C program illustrates how the ROLLBACK statement terminates a transaction:

```
#include <stdio.h>
#include <stdlib.h>
#include <sql.h>

#define NOT_FOUND   100

int main()
{
    /* Include The SQLCA Data Structure Variable */
    EXEC SQL INCLUDE SQLCA;

    /* Set Up A Simple SQL Error Handler */
    EXEC SQL WHENEVER SQLERROR GOTO EXIT;

    /* Declare The Local Memory Variables */
    int  rc = EXIT_SUCCESS;

    /* Declare The SQL Host Memory Variables */
    EXEC SQL BEGIN DECLARE SECTION;
        char      szDeptNo[4];
        struct VARCHAR {                          // VARCHAR Data Structure
                short size;
                char  string[30];
                }  stDeptName;
    EXEC SQL END DECLARE SECTION;

    /* Connect To The SAMPLE Database */
    EXEC SQL CONNECT TO SAMPLE USER etpdd6z USING sanders;

    /* Add A Record To The DEPARTMENT Table */
    EXEC SQL INSERT INTO USERID.DEPARTMENT
        VALUES ('E22', 'SYSTEMS SUPPORT', '000100', 'E01', ' ');

    /* Roll Back The Transaction */
    EXEC SQL ROLLBACK;

    /* Attempt To Retrieve The New Record           */
    /* (Verifies That ROLLBACK Deleted The Record) */
    EXEC SQL SELECT DEPTNO, DEPTNAME
        INTO :szDeptNo,
             :stDeptName
        FROM USERID.DEPARTMENT
        WHERE DEPTNO = 'E22';

    /* Print A Message If The Record No Longer Exists */
    if (sqlca.sqlcode == NOT_FOUND)
        {
        sqlca.sqlcode = SQL_RC_OK;
        printf("\nRecord has been deleted by the ROLLBACK ");
        printf("statement.\n");
        }

 EXIT:
    /* If An Error Has Occurred, Display The SQL Return Code */
    if (sqlca.sqlcode != SQL_RC_OK)
        {
        printf("SQL ERROR : %ld\n", sqlca.sqlcode);
        rc = EXIT_FAILURE;
```

```
        }

    /* Issue A Rollback To Free All Locks */
    EXEC SQL ROLLBACK;

    /* Turn Off The SQL Error Handler */
    EXEC SQL WHENEVER SQLERROR CONTINUE;

    /* Disconnect From The SAMPLE Database */
    EXEC SQL DISCONNECT CURRENT;

    /* Return To The Operating System */
    return(rc);
}
```

Note: The ROLLBACK statement is used in a C++ program in a similar manner.

LOCK TABLE

Purpose The LOCK TABLE statement prevents concurrent application transactions from changing or using a database table.

Syntax

```
EXEC SQL LOCK TABLE [table-name] IN [SHARE | EXCLUSIVE] MODE;
```

Parameters

table-name Identifies the table for which the lock is being requested.

SHARE This mode prevents concurrent application transactions from executing anything other than read-only operations against the specified table.

EXCLUSIVE This mode prevents concurrent application transactions from executing any type of operation, including read-only operations, against the specified table.

Description The LOCK TABLE statement prevents concurrent application transactions from modifying or viewing a specific database table. A table lock is acquired by the current transaction as soon as the LOCK TABLE statement is executed, as long as that transaction does not already have a similar lock on the specified table. Once the table lock is acquired, it is held until the acquiring transaction terminates.

Comments

- The table being locked must be a base table that exists on the application server; it cannot be a system catalog table.
- When a table lock is acquired in EXCLUSIVE mode, concurrent application transactions running at the uncommitted read isolation level will still be able to execute read-only transactions against the locked table.

Authorization Only users with system administrator (SYSADM) authority, database administrator (DBADM) authority, CONTROL authority on the specified table, or SELECT authority on the specified table are allowed to execute this statement.

Example The following C program illustrates how the LOCK TABLE statement locks a table for the life of a transaction:

```
#include <stdio.h>
#include <stdlib.h>
```

```
#include <sql.h>

int main()
{
    /* Include The SQLCA Data Structure Variable */
    EXEC SQL INCLUDE SQLCA;

    /* Set Up A Simple SQL Error Handler */
    EXEC SQL WHENEVER SQLERROR GOTO EXIT;

    /* Declare The Local Memory Variables */
    int  rc = EXIT_SUCCESS;

    /* Declare The SQL Host Memory Variables */
    EXEC SQL BEGIN DECLARE SECTION;
        long   lNumRecs;
    EXEC SQL END DECLARE SECTION;

    /* Connect To The SAMPLE Database */
    EXEC SQL CONNECT TO SAMPLE USER etpdd6z USING sanders;

    /* Lock The STAFF Table So No One Can Edit It While You  */
    /* Count The Records In It                                */
    EXEC SQL LOCK TABLE USERID.STAFF IN SHARE MODE;
    printf("The STAFF table has been locked.\n\n");

    /* Count The Number Of Records In The STAFF Table */
    EXEC SQL SELECT COUNT(*)
        INTO :lNumRecs
        FROM USERID.STAFF;

    /* Print The Information Retrieved */
    printf("There are %ld records in the STAFF table.\n\n", lNumRecs);

EXIT:
    /* If An Error Has Occurred, Display The SQL Return Code */
    if (sqlca.sqlcode != SQL_RC_OK)
        {
        printf("SQL ERROR : %ld\n", sqlca.sqlcode);
        rc = EXIT_FAILURE;
        }

    /* Issue A Rollback To Free All Locks */
    EXEC SQL ROLLBACK;
    printf("The STAFF table is no longer locked.\n\n");

    /* Turn Off The SQL Error Handler */
    EXEC SQL WHENEVER SQLERROR CONTINUE;

    /* Disconnect From The SAMPLE Database */
    EXEC SQL DISCONNECT CURRENT;

    /* Return To The Operating System */
    return(rc);
}
```

Note: The LOCK TABLE statement is used in a C++ program in a similar manner.

GRANT (DATABASE AUTHORITIES)

Purpose This form of the GRANT statement gives database authorities to a specific user, a specific group of users, or all users.

Syntax

```
EXEC SQL GRANT [authority-type,...] ON DATABASE TO [authorization-ID,...];
```

Parameters *authority-type* Identifies the type of authority to be given to a specific user, a specific group of users, or all users. The type of authority can be any of the following:

BINDADD Allows the user to create packages.

CONNECT Allows the user to access the database.

CREATETAB Allows the user to create base tables.

CREATE_NOT_FENCED Allows the user to register user-defined functions with application servers.

DBADM Gives the user database administrator authority. Users who have this authority are automatically given BINDADD, CONNECT, CREATETAB, and CREATE_NOT_FENCED authority.

authorization-ID Identifies the user(s) to receive the specified authority. The authorization-ID can be any of the following:

USER [*user-name*]	Identifies a specific user.
GROUP [*group-name*]	Identifies a specific group of users.
PUBLIC	Indicates all users.

Description This form of the GRANT statement gives authorities that apply to an entire database, rather than privileges that apply to specific objects within the database, to a specific user, a specific group of users, or all users. These authorities control what the database users can and cannot do while working with DB2 databases.

Comments

- When users have BINDADD or CREATETAB authority, they are automatically given CONTROL authority on all packages and tables they create. The creator of a package or table retains the CONTROL authority on that package or table as long as it exists in the database, even if the BINDADD or CREATETAB authority is later revoked.
- No explicit authority is necessary to create a view. You can create views at any time if you have either the CONTROL or the SELECT authority on each base table referenced by the view.
- When registering user-defined functions, take care not to create adverse side effects.
- Once a user-defined function is registered as NOT FENCED, it will continue to run in this manner, even if the CREATE_NOT_FENCED authority is later revoked from the user who registered it.
- If users have database administrator authority (DBADM), they can grant any or all database privileges to other users.
- Database administrator authority (DBADM) cannot be granted to PUBLIC.
- The authorization ID of the user receiving the authority cannot be the same as the authorization ID of the user issuing the statement.
- If the keyword USER or GROUP is not specified along with the user or group name, DB2 will do the following:
  -If the name is defined in the user profile management system as a user name or if the name does not exist, DB2 will assume the name is a group name.

-If the name is defined in the user profile management system as a group name, DB2 will assume the name is a group name.

-If the name is defined in the user profile management system as both a user name and a group name, DB2 will return an error.

Authorization Only users with system administrator (SYSADM) authority are allowed to grant database administrator (DBADM) authority. Users with either SYSADM or DBADM authority are allowed to grant all other authority types.

See Also REVOKE (database authorities), GRANT (index privileges), GRANT (package privileges), GRANT (table or view privileges), CREATE FUNCTION

Examples See the examples provided for the REVOKE (database authorities) statement, later in the chapter.

GRANT (INDEX PRIVILEGES)

Purpose This form of the GRANT statement gives a specific user, a specific group of users, or all users the ability to drop an index (index CONTROL authority).

Syntax

```
EXEC SQL GRANT CONTROL ON INDEX [index-name] TO [authorization-ID,...];
```

Parameters

index-name Identifies the index for which the index CONTROL authority is being given.

authorization-ID Identifies the user(s) receiving index CONTROL authority. The authorization-ID can be any of the following:

USER [*user-name*]	Identifies a specific user.
GROUP [*group-name*]	Identifies a specific group of users.
PUBLIC	Indicates all users.

Description This form of the GRANT statement gives the CONTROL authority for a specified index to a specific user, a specific group of users, or all users. This authority controls whether or not the user(s) can drop the specified index.

Comments

- The CONTROL authority is automatically given to the user who creates an index.
- The authorization ID of the user receiving the authority cannot be the same as the authorization ID of the user issuing the statement.
- If the keyword USER or GROUP is not specified along with the user or group name, DB2 will do the following:

  -If the name is defined in the user profile management system as a user name or if the name does not exist, DB2 will assume the name is a group name.
  -If the name is defined in the user profile management system as a group name, DB2 will assume the name is a group name.
  -If the name is defined in the user profile management system as both a user name and a group name, DB2 will return an error.

Authorization Only users with either system administrator (SYSADM) authority or database administrator (DBADM) authority are allowed to execute this statement.

See Also REVOKE (index privileges), GRANT (database authorities), GRANT (package privileges), GRANT (table or view privileges)

Examples See the examples provided for the REVOKE (index privileges) statement, later in the chapter.

GRANT (PACKAGE PRIVILEGES)

Purpose This form of the GRANT statement gives package authorities to a specific user, a specific group of users, or all users.

Syntax

```
EXEC SQL GRANT [authority-type,...] ON PACKAGE [package-name]
   TO [authorization-ID,...];
```

Parameters

authority-type Identifies the type of authority given to a specific user, a specific group of users, or all users. The type of authority can be any of the following:

BIND	Allows the user to bind the specified package.
CONTROL	Allows the user to drop the specified package and to grant package privileges to other users.
EXECUTE	Allows the user to execute the specified package.

package-name Identifies the package for which the specified authorities are being given.

authorization-ID Identifies the user(s) receiving the specified authorities. The authorization-ID can be any of the following:

USER [*user-name*]	Identifies a specific user.
GROUP [*group-name*]	Identifies a specific group of users.
PUBLIC	Indicates all users.

Description This form of the GRANT statement gives package authorities to a specific user, a specific group of users, or all users. These authorities control what the users can and cannot do while working with DB2 packages.

Comments

- The BIND authority is really the authority to rebind a package because the package must first be bound by a user with BINDADD authority before it even exists.
- Users must hold the necessary privileges on each table referenced by static SQL statements referenced by the package, along with the BIND authority, before they can actually rebind a package. This is because authorizations for static SQL statements are verified at package bind time.
- The CONTROL authority is automatically given to the user who creates a package.
- The BIND and EXECUTE authorizations are automatically granted to users who receive the CONTROL authority.
- The authorization ID of the user receiving the authority cannot be the same as the authorization ID of the user issuing the statement.
- If the keyword USER or GROUP is not specified along with the user or group name, DB2 will do the following:
  -If the name is defined in the user profile management system as a user name or if the name does not exist, DB2 will assume the name is a group name.
  -If the name is defined in the user profile management system as a group name, DB2 will assume the name is a group name.
  -If the name is defined in the user profile management system as both a user name and a group name, DB2 will return an error.

Authorization Only users with either system administrator (SYSADM) authority or database administrator (DBADM) authority are allowed to grant CONTROL authority. Users with SYSADM authority, DBADM authority, or CONTROL authority on the specified package are allowed to grant all other authority types.

See Also REVOKE (package privileges), GRANT (database authorities), GRANT (index privileges), GRANT (table or view privileges)

Examples See the examples provided for the REVOKE (package privileges) statement, later in this chapter.

GRANT (TABLE/VIEW PRIVILEGES)

Purpose This form of the GRANT statement gives table and view authorities to a specific user, a specific group of users, or all users.

Syntax

```
EXEC SQL GRANT [authority-type,...] ON [<TABLE> table-name | view-name]
   TO [authorization-ID,...];
```

Parameters

authority-type Identifies the type of authority given to a specific user, a specific group of users, or all users. The type of authority can be any of the following:

ALTER	Allows the user to add columns to the base table or view, create or drop primary and foreign keys on the base table, add or change the comment associated with the base table, and create or drop a check constraint on the table.
CONTROL	Allows the user to drop the base table or view, grant table or view privileges to other users, and run the RUNSTATS utility against the table and its indexes.
DELETE	Allows the user to delete rows from the specified table or updatable view.
INDEX	Allows the user to create indexes on the specified table.
INSERT	Allows the user to insert rows into the specified table or updatable view, and to run the IMPORT facility.
REFERENCES	Allows the user to create or drop foreign keys that reference the specified table as a parent.
SELECT	Allows the user to retrieve rows from the specified table or view, create a view on the specified table, and run the EXPORT utility.
UPDATE	Allows the user to update rows in the specified table or updatable view.
ALL <PRIVILEGES>	Gives the user all the previously listed privileges.

table-name	Identifies the table for which the specified authorities are being given.
view-name	Identifies the view for which the specified authorities are being given.
authorization-ID	Identifies the user(s) receiving the specified authorities. The authorization-ID can be any of the following:
USER [*user-name*]	Identifies a specific user.

GROUP [*group-name*]	Identifies a specific group of users.
PUBLIC	Indicates all users.

Description This form of the GRANT statement gives table and view authorities to a specific user, a specific group of users, or all users. These authorities control what the users can and cannot do while working with DB2 tables and views.

Comments

- Users must have both the ALTER and REFERENCES authority in order to create or drop foreign keys on a table.
- The ALTER, DELETE, INSERT, INDEX, REFERENCES, SELECT, and UPDATE authorizations for both tables and views are automatically granted to users who receive the CONTROL authority.
- The CONTROL authority is automatically given to the user who creates a base table.
- The CONTROL authority is automatically given to the user who creates a view if that user holds the CONTROL authority on all tables and views referenced by that view.
- When users have INDEX authority, they are automatically given CONTROL authority on all indexes they create. The creator of an index retains the CONTROL authority on that index as long as it exists in the database, even if the INDEX authority is later revoked.
- No privileges can be granted on an inoperable view.
- Privileges granted to PUBLIC or to user groups are not used for authorization checking performed when packages containing references to static SQL statements are bound to a database. Nor are they used when CREATE VIEW statements are processed. With DB2, table privileges granted to PUBLIC or user groups apply only to dynamically prepared SQL statements.
- The authorization ID of the user receiving the authority cannot be the same as the authorization ID of the user issuing the statement.
- If the keyword USER or GROUP is not specified along with the user or group name, DB2 will do the following:
  -If the name is defined in the user profile management system as a user name or if the name does not exist, DB2 will assume the name is a group name.
  -If the name is defined in the user profile management system as a group name, DB2 will assume the name is a group name.
  -If the name is defined in the user profile management system as both a user name and a group name, DB2 will return an error.

Authorization Only users with either system administrator (SYSADM) authority or database administrator (DBADM) authority are allowed to grant CONTROL authority. Users with SYSADM authority, DBADM authority, or CONTROL authority on the specified table or view are allowed to grant all other authority types.

See Also REVOKE (table or view privileges), GRANT (database authorities), GRANT (index privileges), GRANT (package privileges)

Examples See the examples provided for the REVOKE (table/view privileges) statement, later in this chapter.

REVOKE (DATABASE AUTHORITIES)

Purpose This form of the REVOKE statement takes database authorities away from a specific user, a specific group of users, or all users.

Syntax

```
EXEC SQL REVOKE [authority-type,...] ON DATABASE FROM [authorization-ID,...];
```

Parameters

authority-type Identifies the type of authority to be taken away from a specific user, a specific group of users, or all users. The type of authority can be any of the following:

BINDADD	Takes away the user's ability to create packages.
CONNECT	Takes away the user's ability to access the database.
CREATETAB	Takes away the user's ability to create base tables.
CREATE_NOT_FENCED	Takes away the user's ability to register user-defined functions with application servers.
DBADM	Takes away the user's database administrator authority.

authorization-ID Identifies from whom the specified authorities are being taken. The authorization-ID can be any of the following:

USER [*user-name*]	Identifies a specific user.
GROUP [*group-name*]	Identifies a specific group of users.
PUBLIC	Indicates all users.

Description This form of the REVOKE statement removes authorities that apply to an entire database, rather than privileges that apply to specific objects within the database, from a specific user, a specific group of users, or all users. These authorities control what the database users can and cannot do while working with DB2 databases.

Comments

- Users retain CONTROL authority on all packages and base tables they have created, even if the BINDADD authority or the CREATETAB authority is revoked.
- If a user holds DBADM authority, that authority must first be revoked before the BINDADD authority, CREATETAB authority, or CREATE_NOT_FENCED authority can be revoked.
- Once a user-defined function has been registered as NOT FENCED, it will continue to run in this manner, even if the CREATE_NOT_FENCED authority is later revoked from the user who registered it.
- Revoking DBADM authority does not automatically revoke privileges the user has on objects in the database, nor does it revoke the BINDADD, CONNECT, CREATETAB, and CREATE_NOT_FENCED authorities, which were automatically given to the user when the DBADM authority was granted.
- The authorization ID of the user receiving the authority cannot be the same as the authorization ID of the user issuing the statement.
- If the keyword USER or GROUP is not specified along with the user or group name, DB2 will do the following:
  -If the name is defined in the user profile management system as a user name or if the name does not exist, DB2 will assume the name is a group name.
  -If the name is defined in the user profile management system as a group name, DB2 will assume the name is a group name.
  -If the name is defined in the user profile management system as both a user name and a group name, DB2 will return an error.

Authorization Only users with system administrator (SYSADM) authority can revoke database administrator (DBADM) authority. Users with either SYSADM or DBADM authority can revoke all other authority types.

See Also GRANT (database authorities), REVOKE (index privileges), REVOKE (package privileges), REVOKE (table or view privileges)

Examples The following C program illustrates how the REVOKE statement can take database authorizations away from all PUBLIC users and from specified users:

```
#include <stdio.h>
#include <stdlib.h>
#include <string.h>
#include <sql.h>

int main()
{
    /* Include The SQLCA Data Structure Variable */
    EXEC SQL INCLUDE SQLCA;

    /* Set Up A Simple SQL Error Handler */
    EXEC SQL WHENEVER SQLERROR GOTO EXIT;

    /* Declare The Local Memory Variables */
    int  rc = EXIT_SUCCESS;

    /* Connect To The SAMPLE Database */
    EXEC SQL CONNECT TO SAMPLE USER etpdd6z USING sanders;

    /* Grant The CONNECT Authority To All PUBLIC Users */
    EXEC SQL GRANT CONNECT ON DATABASE TO PUBLIC;
    printf("CONNECT Authority has been given to PUBLIC.\n");

    /* Grant The CREATETAB And The BINDADD Authority To */
    /* Two Specified Users                               */
    EXEC SQL GRANT CREATETAB, BINDADD ON DATABASE
             TO USER kristen, USER tyler;
    printf("CREATETAB And BINDADD Authority has been given to ");
    printf("kristen and tyler.\n\n");

    /* Revoke The CONNECT Authority From All PUBLIC Users */
    EXEC SQL REVOKE CONNECT ON DATABASE FROM PUBLIC;
    printf("CONNECT Authority has been taken away from PUBLIC.\n");

    /* Revoke The CREATETAB (Create Tables) Authority From */
    /* Specified Users                                      */
    EXEC SQL REVOKE CREATETAB, BINDADD ON DATABASE
             FROM USER kristen, USER tyler;
    printf("CREATETAB And BINDADD Authority has been taken away ");
    printf("from kristen and tyler.\n");

EXIT:
    /* If An Error Has Occurred, Display The SQL Return Code */
    if (sqlca.sqlcode != SQL_RC_OK)
        {
        printf("SQL ERROR : %ld\n", sqlca.sqlcode);
        rc = EXIT_FAILURE;
        }

    /* Turn Off The SQL Error Handler */
    EXEC SQL WHENEVER SQLERROR CONTINUE;

    /* Issue A Rollback To Free All Locks */
```

```
    EXEC SQL ROLLBACK;

    /* Disconnect From The SAMPLE Database */
    EXEC SQL DISCONNECT CURRENT;

    /* Return To The Operating System */
    return(rc);
}
```

The following C++ program illustrates how the REVOKE statement can take database authorizations away from all PUBLIC users and from a specified user:

```
#include <iostream.h>
#include <stdlib.h>
#include <string.h>
#include <sql.h>

/* Define The Authorization Class */
class Authorization
{
    private:

        /* Include The SQLCA Data Structure Variable */
        EXEC SQL INCLUDE SQLCA;

        /* Declare The SQL Host Memory Variables */
        EXEC SQL BEGIN DECLARE SECTION;
            char    szGrantString[80];
            char    szRevokeString[80];
        EXEC SQL END DECLARE SECTION;

    /* Declare The Public Member Function Prototypes */
    public:
        short int grantPublic();
        short int grantUser(const char *szAuthID);
        short int revokePublic();
        short int revokeUser(const char *szAuthID);
} ;

/* Define The grantPublic() Member Function */
short int Authorization::grantPublic(void)
{
    /* Grant The CONNECT, BINDADD, And CREATETAB Authority To All */
    /* PUBLIC Users                                               */
    EXEC SQL GRANT CONNECT, BINDADD, CREATETAB ON DATABASE TO PUBLIC;

    if (sqlca.sqlcode == SQL_RC_OK)
        {
        cout << "The following Authority has been given to PUBLIC :";
        cout << endl << "CONNECT" << endl;
        cout << "BINDADD" << endl;
        cout << "CREATETAB" << endl << endl;
        }

    /* Return The SQL Return Code */
    return(sqlca.sqlcode);
}

/* Define The grantUser() Member Function */
short int Authorization::grantUser(const char *szAuthID)
```

```
{
    /* Build The Grant SQL Statement String */
    strcpy(szGrantString, "GRANT CONNECT, BINDADD, CREATETAB ");
    strcat(szGrantString, "ON DATABASE TO USER ");
    strcat(szGrantString, szAuthID);

    /* Grant The CONNECT, BINDADD, And CREATETAB Authority To A */
    /* Specified User                                           */
    EXEC SQL EXECUTE IMMEDIATE :szGrantString;

    if (sqlca.sqlcode == SQL_RC_OK)
        {
        cout << "The following Authority has been given to ";
        cout << szAuthID << " :" << endl;
        cout << "CONNECT" << endl;
        cout << "BINDADD" << endl;
        cout << "CREATETAB" << endl << endl;
        }

    /* Return The SQL Return Code */
    return(sqlca.sqlcode);
}

/* Define The revokePublic() Member Function */
short int Authorization::revokePublic(void)
{
    /* Revoke The CONNECT, BINDADD, And CREATETAB Authority From All */
    /* PUBLIC Users                                                  */
    EXEC SQL REVOKE CONNECT, BINDADD, CREATETAB ON DATABASE
             FROM PUBLIC;

    if (sqlca.sqlcode == SQL_RC_OK)
        {
        cout << "The following Authority has been taken away from PUBLIC :";
        cout << endl << "CONNECT" << endl;
        cout << "BINDADD" << endl;
        cout << "CREATETAB" << endl << endl;
        }

    /* Return The SQL Return Code */
    return(sqlca.sqlcode);
}

/* Define The revokeUser() Member Function */
short int Authorization::revokeUser(const char *szAuthID)
{
    /* Build The Revoke SQL Statement String */
    strcpy(szRevokeString, "REVOKE CONNECT, BINDADD, CREATETAB ");
    strcat(szRevokeString, "ON DATABASE FROM USER ");
    strcat(szRevokeString, szAuthID);

    /* Revoke The CONNECT, BINDADD, And CREATETAB Authority From A */
    /* Specified User                                              */
    EXEC SQL EXECUTE IMMEDIATE :szRevokeString;

    if (sqlca.sqlcode == SQL_RC_OK)
        {
        cout << "The following Authority has been taken away from ";
        cout << szAuthID << " :" << endl;
```

```
            cout << "CONNECT" << endl;
            cout << "BINDADD" << endl;
            cout << "CREATETAB" << endl;
            }

        /* Return The SQL Return Code */
        return(sqlca.sqlcode);
}

int main()
{
        /* Declare The Local Memory Variables */
        short int rc = EXIT_SUCCESS;            // Must Be Declared Here
                                                // For The SQL Precompiler

        /* Include The SQLCA Data Structure Variable */
        EXEC SQL INCLUDE SQLCA;

        /* Set Up A Simple SQL Error Handler */
        EXEC SQL WHENEVER SQLERROR GOTO EXIT;

        /* Create An Instance Of The Authorization Class */
        Authorization Privilege;

        /* Connect To The SAMPLE Database */
        EXEC SQL CONNECT TO SAMPLE USER etpdd6z USING sanders;

        /* Grant The PUBLIC Authorizations */
        rc = Privilege.grantPublic();

        /* Grant Authorizations For User beth */
        rc = Privilege.grantUser("beth");

        /* Revoke The PUBLIC Authorizations */
        rc = Privilege.revokePublic();
        /* Revoke Authorizations For User beth */
        rc = Privilege.revokeUser("beth");

EXIT:
        /* If An Error Has Occurred, Display The SQL Return Code */
        if (sqlca.sqlcode != SQL_RC_OK)
            {
            cout << "SQL ERROR : " << sqlca.sqlcode << endl;
            rc = EXIT_FAILURE;
            }

        /* Issue A Rollback To Free All Locks */
        EXEC SQL ROLLBACK;

        /* Turn Off The SQL Error Handler */
        EXEC SQL WHENEVER SQLERROR CONTINUE;

        /* Disconnect From The SAMPLE Database */
        EXEC SQL DISCONNECT CURRENT;

        /* Return To The Operating System */
        return(rc);
}
```

REVOKE (INDEX PRIVILEGES)

Purpose This form of the REVOKE statement takes the ability to drop an index (CONTROL authority) away from a specific user, a specific group of users, or all users.

Syntax

```
EXEC SQL REVOKE CONTROL ON INDEX [index-name] FROM [authorization-ID,...];
```

Parameters

index-name Identifies the index for which the CONTROL authority is being removed.

authorization-ID Identifies from whom the index CONTROL authority is being taken. The authorization-ID can be any of the following:

USER [*user-name*]	Identifies a specific user.
GROUP [*group-name*]	Identifies a specific group of users.
PUBLIC	Indicates all users.

Description This form of the REVOKE statement takes CONTROL authority for a specified index away from a specific user, a specific group of users, or all users. This authority controls whether or not the specified users can drop the specified index. CONTROL authority is automatically granted to users when they create an index.

Comments

- The authorization ID of the user receiving the authority cannot be the same as the authorization ID of the user issuing the statement.
- If the keyword USER or GROUP is not specified along with the user or group name, DB2 will do the following:
  -If the name is defined in the user profile management system as a user name or if the name does not exist, DB2 will assume the name is a group name.
  -If the name is defined in the user profile management system as a group name, DB2 will assume the name is a group name.
  -If the name is defined in the user profile management system as both a user name and a group name, DB2 will return an error.

Authorization Only users with system administrator (SYSADM) authority or database administrator (DBADM) authority can execute this statement.

See Also GRANT (index privileges), REVOKE (database authorities), REVOKE (package privileges), REVOKE (table or view privileges)

Examples The following C program illustrates how the REVOKE statement can take index CONTROL authority away from all PUBLIC users and from specified users:

```
#include <stdio.h>
#include <stdlib.h>
#include <string.h>
#include <sql.h>

int main()
{
    /* Include The SQLCA Data Structure Variable */
    EXEC SQL INCLUDE SQLCA;

    /* Set Up A Simple SQL Error Handler */
    EXEC SQL WHENEVER SQLERROR GOTO EXIT;
```

```
    /* Declare The Local Memory Variables */
    int  rc = EXIT_SUCCESS;

    /* Connect To The SAMPLE Database */
    EXEC SQL CONNECT TO SAMPLE USER etpdd6z USING sanders;

    /* Create An Index On The EMPLOYEE Table */
    EXEC SQL CREATE INDEX EMP_NUM ON USERID.EMPLOYEE(EMPNO);
    printf("Index EMP_NUM has been created for the EMPLOYEE table.\n");

    /* Grant The Index CONTROL Authority To All PUBLIC Users */
    EXEC SQL GRANT CONTROL ON INDEX EMP_NUM TO PUBLIC;
    printf("Index CONTROL Authority has been given to PUBLIC.\n");

    /* Grant The Index CONTROL Authority To Two Specified Users */
    EXEC SQL GRANT CONTROL ON INDEX EMP_NUM TO USER kristen, USER tyler;
    printf("Index CONTROL Authority has been given to ");
    printf("kristen and tyler.\n\n");

    /* Revoke The Index CONTROL Authority From All PUBLIC Users */
    EXEC SQL REVOKE CONTROL ON INDEX EMP_NUM FROM PUBLIC;
    printf("Index CONTROL Authority has been taken away ");
    printf("from PUBLIC.\n");

    /* Revoke The Index CONTROL Authority From Two Specified Users */
    EXEC SQL REVOKE CONTROL ON INDEX EMP_NUM
            FROM USER kristen, USER tyler;
    printf("Index CONTROL Authority has been taken away from ");
    printf("kristen and tyler.\n");

    /* Delete The Index On The EMPLOYEE Table */
    EXEC SQL DROP INDEX EMP_NUM;
    printf("Index EMP_NUM has been deleted.\n");

EXIT:
    /* If An Error Has Occurred, Display The SQL Return Code */
    if (sqlca.sqlcode != SQL_RC_OK)
        {
        printf("SQL ERROR : %ld\n", sqlca.sqlcode);
        rc = EXIT_FAILURE;
        }

    /* Issue A Rollback To Free All Locks */
    EXEC SQL ROLLBACK;

    /* Turn Off The SQL Error Handler */
    EXEC SQL WHENEVER SQLERROR CONTINUE;

    /* Disconnect From The SAMPLE Database */
    EXEC SQL DISCONNECT CURRENT;

    /* Return To The Operating System */
    return(rc);
}
```

The following C++ program illustrates how the REVOKE statement can take index CONTROL authority away from all PUBLIC users and from a specified user:

```
#include <iostream.h>
#include <stdlib.h>
#include <string.h>
```

```
#include <sql.h>

/* Define The Authorization Class */
class Authorization
{
    private:

        /* Include The SQLCA Data Structure Variable */
        EXEC SQL INCLUDE SQLCA;

        /* Declare The SQL Host Memory Variables */
        EXEC SQL BEGIN DECLARE SECTION;
            char    szGrantString[80];
            char    szRevokeString[80];
        EXEC SQL END DECLARE SECTION;

    /* Declare The Public Member Function Prototypes */
    public:
        short int grantPublic();
        short int grantUser(const char *szAuthID);
        short int revokePublic();
        short int revokeUser(const char *szAuthID);
} ;

/* Define The grantPublic() Member Function */
short int Authorization::grantPublic(void)
{
    /* Grant The Index CONTROL Authority To All PUBLIC Users */
    EXEC SQL GRANT CONTROL ON INDEX EMP_NUM TO PUBLIC;

    if (sqlca.sqlcode == SQL_RC_OK)
        {
        cout << "Index CONTROL Authority has been given to PUBLIC.";
        cout << endl;
        }
    /* Return The SQL Return Code */
    return(sqlca.sqlcode);
}

/* Define The grantUser() Member Function */
short int Authorization::grantUser(const char *szAuthID)
{
    /* Build The Grant SQL Statement String */
    strcpy(szGrantString, "GRANT CONTROL ON INDEX EMP_NUM ");
    strcat(szGrantString, "TO USER ");
    strcat(szGrantString, szAuthID);

    /* Grant The Index CONTROL Authority To The Specified User */
    EXEC SQL EXECUTE IMMEDIATE :szGrantString;

    if (sqlca.sqlcode == SQL_RC_OK)
        {
        cout << "Index CONTROL Authority has been given to ";
        cout << szAuthID << "." << endl << endl;
        }

    /* Return The SQL Return Code */
    return(sqlca.sqlcode);
}

/* Define The revokePublic() Member Function */
```

```
short int Authorization::revokePublic(void)
{
    /* Revoke The Index CONTROL Authority From All PUBLIC Users */
    EXEC SQL REVOKE CONTROL ON INDEX EMP_NUM FROM PUBLIC;

    if (sqlca.sqlcode == SQL_RC_OK)
        {
        cout << "Index CONTROL Authority has been taken away ";
        cout << "from PUBLIC." << endl;
        }

    /* Return The SQL Return Code */
    return(sqlca.sqlcode);
}

/* Define The revokeUser() Member Function */
short int Authorization::revokeUser(const char *szAuthID)
{
    /* Build The Revoke SQL Statement String */
    strcpy(szRevokeString, "REVOKE CONTROL ON INDEX EMP_NUM ");
    strcat(szRevokeString, "FROM USER ");
    strcat(szRevokeString, szAuthID);

    /* Revoke The Index CONTROL Authority From The Specified User */
    EXEC SQL EXECUTE IMMEDIATE :szRevokeString;

    if (sqlca.sqlcode == SQL_RC_OK)
        {
        cout << "Index CONTROL Authority has been taken away from ";
        cout << szAuthID << "." << endl;
        }

    /* Return The SQL Return Code */
    return(sqlca.sqlcode);
}
int main()
{
    /* Declare The Local Memory Variables */
    short int rc = EXIT_SUCCESS;            // Must Be Declared Here
                                            // For The SQL Precompiler

    /* Include The SQLCA Data Structure Variable */
    EXEC SQL INCLUDE SQLCA;

    /* Set Up A Simple SQL Error Handler */
    EXEC SQL WHENEVER SQLERROR GOTO EXIT;

    /* Create An Instance Of The Authorization Class */
    Authorization Privilege;

    /* Connect To The SAMPLE Database */
    EXEC SQL CONNECT TO SAMPLE USER etpdd6z USING sanders;

    /* Create An Index On The EMPLOYEE Table */
    EXEC SQL CREATE INDEX EMP_NUM ON USERID.EMPLOYEE(EMPNO);
    cout << "Index EMP_NUM has been created for the EMPLOYEE table.";
    cout << endl;

    /* Grant The PUBLIC Authorizations */
    rc = Privilege.grantPublic();

    /* Grant Authorizations For User beth */
```

```
    rc = Privilege.grantUser("beth");

    /* Revoke The PUBLIC Authorizations */
    rc = Privilege.revokePublic();

    /* Revoke Authorizations For User beth */
    rc = Privilege.revokeUser("beth");

    /* Delete The Index On The EMPLOYEE Table */
    EXEC SQL DROP INDEX EMP_NUM;
    cout << "Index EMP_NUM has been deleted." << endl;

EXIT:
    /* If An Error Has Occurred, Display The SQL Return Code */
    if (sqlca.sqlcode != SQL_RC_OK)
        {
        cout << "SQL ERROR : " << sqlca.sqlcode << endl;
        rc = EXIT_FAILURE;
        }

    /* Issue A Rollback To Free All Locks */
    EXEC SQL ROLLBACK;

    /* Turn Off The SQL Error Handler */
    EXEC SQL WHENEVER SQLERROR CONTINUE;

    /* Disconnect From The SAMPLE Database */
    EXEC SQL DISCONNECT CURRENT;

    /* Return To The Operating System */
    return(rc);
}
```

REVOKE (PACKAGE PRIVILEGES)

Purpose This form of the REVOKE statement takes package authorities away from a specific user, a specific group of users, or all users.

Syntax

```
EXEC SQL REVOKE [authority-type,...] ON PACKAGE [package-name]
   FROM [authorization-ID,...];
```

Parameters

authority-type Identifies the type of authority to be taken away from a specific user, a specific group of users, or all users. The type of authority can be any of the following:

- BIND — Takes away the user's ability to bind the specified package. If a user holds CONTROL authority on the package, that authority must first be revoked before the BIND authority can be revoked.
- CONTROL — Takes away the user's ability to drop the specified package and to grant package privileges to other users.
- EXECUTE — Takes away the user's ability to execute the specified package. If the user holds CONTROL authority on the package, that authority must first be revoked before the EXECUTE authority can be revoked.

package-name Identifies the package for which the specified authorities are being taken.

authorization-ID Identifies from whom the specified authorities are being taken. The authorization-ID can be any of the following:

USER [*user-name*]	Identifies a specific user.
GROUP [*group-name*]	Identifies a specific group of users.
PUBLIC	Indicates all users.

Description This form of the REVOKE statement takes package authorities away from a specific user, a specific group of users, or all users. These authorities control what the user(s) can and cannot do while working with DB2 packages.

Comments

- The authorization ID of the user receiving the authority cannot be the same as the authorization ID of the user issuing the statement.
- If the keyword USER or GROUP is not specified along with the user or group name, DB2 will do the following:
  -If the name is defined in the user profile management system as a user name or if the name does not exist, DB2 will assume the name is a group name.
  -If the name is defined in the user profile management system as a group name, DB2 will assume the name is a group name.
  -If the name is defined in the user profile management system as both a user name and a group name, DB2 will return an error.

Authorization Only users with system administrator (SYSADM) authority or database administrator (DBADM) authority can revoke CONTROL authority. Users with SYSADM authority, DBADM authority, or CONTROL authority on the specified package can revoke all other authority types.

See Also GRANT (package privileges), REVOKE (database authorities), REVOKE (index privileges), REVOKE (table or view privileges)

Examples The following C program illustrates how the REVOKE statement can take package authorizations away from all PUBLIC users and from specified users:

```
#include <stdio.h>
#include <stdlib.h>
#include <string.h>
#include <sql.h>

int main()
{
    /* Include The SQLCA Data Structure Variable */
    EXEC SQL INCLUDE SQLCA;

    /* Set Up A Simple SQL Error Handler */
    EXEC SQL WHENEVER SQLERROR GOTO EXIT;

    /* Declare The Local Memory Variables */
    int  rc = EXIT_SUCCESS;

    /* Connect To The SAMPLE Database */
    EXEC SQL CONNECT TO SAMPLE USER etpdd6z USING sanders;

    /* Grant The Package CONTROL Authority To All PUBLIC Users */
    EXEC SQL GRANT CONTROL ON PACKAGE CH8EX1A TO PUBLIC;
    printf("Package CONTROL Authority has been given to PUBLIC.\n");

    /* Grant The Package CONTROL And EXECUTE Authority To */
```

```
    /* Two Specified Users                                   */
    EXEC SQL GRANT CONTROL, EXECUTE ON PACKAGE CH8EX1A
             TO USER kristen, USER tyler;
    printf("Package CONTROL and EXECUTE Authority has been given to ");
    printf("kristen and tyler.\n\n");

    /* Revoke The Package CONTROL Authority From All PUBLIC Users */
    EXEC SQL REVOKE CONTROL ON PACKAGE CH8EX1A FROM PUBLIC;
    printf("Package CONTROL Authority has been taken away from ");
    printf("PUBLIC.\n");

    /* Revoke The Package CONTROL And EXECUTE Authority From */
    /* Two Specified Users                                   */
    EXEC SQL REVOKE CONTROL, EXECUTE ON PACKAGE CH8EX1A
             FROM USER kristen, USER tyler;
    printf("Package CONTROL and EXECUTE Authority has been taken ");
    printf("away from kristen and tyler.\n");

EXIT:
    /* If An Error Has Occurred, Display The SQL Return Code */
    if (sqlca.sqlcode != SQL_RC_OK)
        {
        printf("SQL ERROR : %ld\n", sqlca.sqlcode);
        rc = EXIT_FAILURE;
        }

    /* Issue A Rollback To Free All Locks */
    EXEC SQL ROLLBACK;

    /* Turn Off The SQL Error Handler */
    EXEC SQL WHENEVER SQLERROR CONTINUE;

    /* Disconnect From The SAMPLE Database */
    EXEC SQL DISCONNECT CURRENT;
    /* Return To The Operating System */
    return(rc);
}
```

The following C++ program illustrates how the REVOKE statement can take package authorizations away from all PUBLIC users and from a specified user:

```
#include <iostream.h>
#include <stdlib.h>
#include <string.h>
#include <sql.h>

/* Define The Authorization Class */
class Authorization
{
    private:

       /* Include The SQLCA Data Structure Variable */
       EXEC SQL INCLUDE SQLCA;

       /* Declare The SQL Host Memory Variables */
       EXEC SQL BEGIN DECLARE SECTION;
           char    szGrantString[80];
           char    szRevokeString[80];
       EXEC SQL END DECLARE SECTION;

    /* Declare The Public Member Function Prototypes */
```

```
    public:
       short int grantPublic();
       short int grantUser(const char *szAuthID);
       short int revokePublic();
       short int revokeUser(const char *szAuthID);
} ;

/* Define The grantPublic() Member Function */
short int Authorization::grantPublic(void)
{
    /* Grant The BIND, CONTROL, And EXECUTE Authority To All */
    /* PUBLIC Users                                           */
    EXEC SQL GRANT BIND, CONTROL, EXECUTE ON PACKAGE CH8EX1A TO PUBLIC;

    if (sqlca.sqlcode == SQL_RC_OK)
        {
        cout << "The following Authority has been given to PUBLIC :";
        cout << endl << "BIND" << endl;
        cout << "CONTROL" << endl;
        cout << "EXECUTE" << endl << endl;
        }

    /* Return The SQL Return Code */
    return(sqlca.sqlcode);
}

/* Define The grantUser() Member Function */
short int Authorization::grantUser(const char *szAuthID)
{
    /* Build The Grant SQL Statement String */
    strcpy(szGrantString, "GRANT BIND, CONTROL, EXECUTE ");
    strcat(szGrantString, "ON PACKAGE CH8EX1A TO USER ");
    strcat(szGrantString, szAuthID);
    /* Grant The BIND, CONTROL, And EXECUTE Authority To */
    /* A Specified User                                   */
    EXEC SQL EXECUTE IMMEDIATE :szGrantString;

    if (sqlca.sqlcode == SQL_RC_OK)
        {
        cout << "The following Authority has been given to ";
        cout << szAuthID << " :" << endl;
        cout << "BIND" << endl;
        cout << "CONTROL" << endl;
        cout << "EXECUTE" << endl << endl;
        }

    /* Return The SQL Return Code */
    return(sqlca.sqlcode);
}

/* Define The revokePublic() Member Function */
short int Authorization::revokePublic(void)
{
    /* Revoke The BIND, CONTROL, And EXECUTE Authority */
    /* From All PUBLIC Users                            */
    EXEC SQL REVOKE BIND, CONTROL, EXECUTE ON PACKAGE CH8EX1A
    FROM PUBLIC;

    if (sqlca.sqlcode == SQL_RC_OK)
        {
```

```
            cout << "The following Authority has been taken away from ";
            cout << "PUBLIC :" << endl << "BIND" << endl;
            cout << "CONTROL" << endl;
            cout << "EXECUTE" << endl << endl;
            }

        /* Return The SQL Return Code */
        return(sqlca.sqlcode);
}

/* Define The revokeUser() Member Function */
short int Authorization::revokeUser(const char *szAuthID)
{
        /* Build The Revoke SQL Statement String */
        strcpy(szRevokeString, "REVOKE BIND, CONTROL, EXECUTE ");
        strcat(szRevokeString, "ON PACKAGE CH8EX1A FROM USER ");
        strcat(szRevokeString, szAuthID);

        /* Revoke The BIND, CONTROL, And EXECUTE Authority From A */
        /* Specified User                                          */
        EXEC SQL EXECUTE IMMEDIATE :szRevokeString;

        if (sqlca.sqlcode == SQL_RC_OK)
            {
            cout << "The following Authority has been taken away from ";
            cout << szAuthID << " :" << endl;
            cout << "BIND" << endl;
            cout << "CONTROL" << endl;
            cout << "EXECUTE" << endl;
            }

        /* Return The SQL Return Code */
        return(sqlca.sqlcode);
}
int main()
{
        /* Declare The Local Memory Variables */
        short int rc = EXIT_SUCCESS;            // Must Be Declared Here
                                                // For The SQL Precompiler

        /* Include The SQLCA Data Structure Variable */
        EXEC SQL INCLUDE SQLCA;

        /* Set Up A Simple SQL Error Handler */
        EXEC SQL WHENEVER SQLERROR GOTO EXIT;

        /* Create An Instance Of The Authorization Class */
        Authorization Privilege;

        /* Connect To The SAMPLE Database */
        EXEC SQL CONNECT TO SAMPLE USER etpdd6z USING sanders;

        /* Grant The PUBLIC Authorizations */
        rc = Privilege.grantPublic();

        /* Grant Authorizations For User beth */
        rc = Privilege.grantUser("beth");

        /* Revoke The PUBLIC Authorizations */
        rc = Privilege.revokePublic();
```

```
    /* Revoke Authorizations For User beth */
    rc = Privilege.revokeUser("beth");

EXIT:
    /* If An Error Has Occurred, Display The SQL Return Code */
    if (sqlca.sqlcode != SQL_RC_OK)
        {
        cout << "SQL ERROR : " << sqlca.sqlcode << endl;
        rc = EXIT_FAILURE;
        }

    /* Issue A Rollback To Free All Locks */
    EXEC SQL ROLLBACK;

    /* Turn Off The SQL Error Handler */
    EXEC SQL WHENEVER SQLERROR CONTINUE;

    /* Disconnect From The SAMPLE Database */
    EXEC SQL DISCONNECT CURRENT;

    /* Return To The Operating System */
    return(rc);
}
```

REVOKE (TABLE/VIEW PRIVILEGES)

Purpose This form of the REVOKE statement takes table and view authorities away from a specific user, a specific group of users, or all users.

Syntax

```
EXEC SQL REVOKE [authority-type,...] ON [<TABLE> table-name | view-name]
   FROM [authorization-ID,...];
```

Parameters *authority-type* Identifies the type of authority to be taken away from a specific user, a specific group of users, or all users. The type of authority can be any of the following:

ALTER	Takes away the user's ability to add columns to the base table or view, create or drop primary and foreign keys on the base table, add or change the comment associated with the base table, and create or drop a check constraint on the table.
CONTROL	Takes away the user's ability to drop the base table or view, grant table or view privileges to other users, and run the RUNSTATS utility against the table and its indexes.
DELETE	Takes away the user's ability to delete rows from the specified table or updatable view.
INDEX	Takes away the user's ability to create indexes on the specified table.
INSERT	Takes away the user's ability to insert rows into the specified table or updatable view.
REFERENCES	Takes away the user's ability to create or drop foreign keys that reference the specified table as a parent.
SELECT	Takes away the user's ability to retrieve rows from the specified table or view, create a view on the specified table, and run the EXPORT utility.
UPDATE	Takes away the user's ability to update rows in the specified table or updatable view.

ALL <PRIVILEGES> Takes away all the previously listed privileges.

table-name Identifies the table for which the specified authorities are being taken.

view-name Identifies the view for which the specified authorities are being taken.

authorization-ID Identifies from whom the specified authorities are being taken. The authorization-ID can be any of the following:

USER [*user-name*] Identifies a specific user.
GROUP [*group-name*] Identifies a specific group of users.
PUBLIC Indicates all users.

Description This form of the REVOKE statement takes table and view authorities away from a specific user, a specific group of users, or all users. These authorities control what the user(s) can and cannot do while working with DB2 tables and views.

Comments

- The users retain CONTROL authority on all indexes they have created, even if the INDEX authority is revoked.
- When the CONTROL authority is taken away from a user, other table and view authorities are not automatically revoked.
- If an authorization to create a view is revoked from a user, that authorization is also revoked from any dependent views.
- The authorization name associated with the user who creates a view is stored as the view's DEFINER in the SYSCAT.VIEWS catalog table. If the DEFINER of the view loses a SELECT privilege for some object on which the view definition depends (or if an object on which the view definition depends is dropped or made inoperative), then the view will be made inoperative. If, however, a database administrator (DBADM) or a system administrator (SYSADM) explicitly revokes all privileges on the view from the DEFINER, the record in the SYSTABAUTH catalog table for the DEFINER will be deleted and the view will remain operative.
- Privileges on inoperative views cannot be revoked.
- All packages that depend on a database object for which a privilege has been revoked are marked invalid. A package remains invalid until either the application is successfully rebound or the application is executed and the database manager successfully rebinds the application using information stored in the system catalogs. You can successfully rebind packages marked invalid because a privilege is revoked without having to make additional grants. For example, if a package owned by USER_A contains a SELECT from table TABLE_1 and the SELECT privilege for table TABLE_1 is revoked from USER_A, then the package will be marked invalid. If the SELECT authority is later regranted or if the user holds DBADM authority, the package will be successfully rebound the next time the application is executed.
- Table or view authorizations cannot be taken away from a user who has CONTROL authorization on the object unless the CONTROL authorization is also revoked.
- The authorization ID of the user receiving the authority cannot be the same as the authorization ID of the user issuing the statement.
- If the keyword USER or GROUP is not specified along with the user or group name, DB2 will do the following:
  –If the name is defined in the user profile management system as a user name or if the name does not exist, DB2 will assume the name is a group name.
  –If the name is defined in the user profile management system as a group name, DB2 will assume the name is a group name.
  –If the name is defined in the user profile management system as both a user name and a group name, DB2 will return an error.

Authorization Only users with either system administrator (SYSADM) authority or database administrator (DBADM) authority can revoke CONTROL authority. Users with SYSADM authority, DBADM authority, or CONTROL authority on the specified table or view can revoke all other authority types.

See Also GRANT (table or view privileges), REVOKE (database authorities), REVOKE (index privileges), REVOKE (package privileges)

Examples The following C program illustrates how to use the REVOKE statement to take table authorizations away from all PUBLIC users and from specified users:

```
#include <stdio.h>
#include <stdlib.h>
#include <string.h>
#include <sql.h>

int main()
{
    /* Include The SQLCA Data Structure Variable */
    EXEC SQL INCLUDE SQLCA;

    /* Set Up A Simple SQL Error Handler */
    EXEC SQL WHENEVER SQLERROR GOTO EXIT;
    /* Declare The Local Memory Variables */
    int  rc = EXIT_SUCCESS;

    /* Connect To The SAMPLE Database */
    EXEC SQL CONNECT TO SAMPLE USER etpdd6z USING sanders;

    /* Grant The Table CONTROL Authority To All PUBLIC Users */
    EXEC SQL GRANT CONTROL ON TABLE USERID.EMP_ACT TO PUBLIC;
    printf("Table CONTROL Authority has been given to PUBLIC.\n");

    /* Grant The Table INSERT And DELETE Authority To */
    /* Two Specified Users                            */
    EXEC SQL GRANT INSERT, DELETE ON TABLE USERID.EMP_ACT
             TO USER kristen, USER tyler;
    printf("Table INSERT and DELETE Authority has been given to ");
    printf("kristen and tyler.\n\n");

    /* Revoke The Table CONTROL Authority From All PUBLIC Users */
    EXEC SQL REVOKE CONTROL ON TABLE USERID.EMP_ACT FROM PUBLIC;
    printf("Table CONTROL Authority has been taken away from PUBLIC.\n");

    /* Revoke The Table INSERT And DELETE Authority From */
    /* Two Specified Users                               */
    EXEC SQL REVOKE INSERT, DELETE ON TABLE USERID.EMP_ACT
             FROM USER kristen, USER tyler;
    printf("Table INSERT and DELETE Authority has been taken away ");
    printf("from kristen and tyler.\n");

EXIT:
    /* If An Error Has Occurred, Display The SQL Return Code */
    if (sqlca.sqlcode != SQL_RC_OK)
        {
        printf("SQL ERROR : %ld\n", sqlca.sqlcode);
        rc = EXIT_FAILURE;
        }
```

```
    /* Issue A Rollback To Free All Locks */
    EXEC SQL ROLLBACK;

    /* Turn Off The SQL Error Handler */
    EXEC SQL WHENEVER SQLERROR CONTINUE;

    /* Disconnect From The SAMPLE Database */
    EXEC SQL DISCONNECT CURRENT;

    /* Return To The Operating System */
    return(rc);
}
```

The following C++ program illustrates how to use the REVOKE statement to take table authorizations away from all PUBLIC users and from a specified user:

```
#include <iostream.h>
#include <stdlib.h>
#include <string.h>
#include <sql.h>

/* Define The Authorization Class */
class Authorization
{
    private:
       /* Include The SQLCA Data Structure Variable */
       EXEC SQL INCLUDE SQLCA;

       /* Declare The SQL Host Memory Variables */
       EXEC SQL BEGIN DECLARE SECTION;
           char    szGrantString[80];
           char    szRevokeString[80];
       EXEC SQL END DECLARE SECTION;

    /* Declare The Public Member Function Prototypes */
    public:
       short int grantPublic();
       short int grantUser(const char *szAuthID);
       short int revokePublic();
       short int revokeUser(const char *szAuthID);
} ;

/* Define The grantPublic() Member Function */
short int Authorization::grantPublic(void)
{
    /* Grant The CONTROL, INSERT And DELETE Authority To All */
    /* PUBLIC Users                                           */
    EXEC SQL GRANT CONTROL, INSERT, DELETE
             ON TABLE USERID.EMP_ACT TO PUBLIC;

    if (sqlca.sqlcode == SQL_RC_OK)
        {
        cout << "The following Authority has been given to PUBLIC :";
        cout << endl << "CONTROL" << endl;
        cout << "INSERT" << endl;
        cout << "DELETE" << endl << endl;
        }

    /* Return The SQL Return Code */
    return(sqlca.sqlcode);
}
```

```
/* Define The grantUser() Member Function */
short int Authorization::grantUser(const char *szAuthID)
{
    /* Build The Grant SQL Statement String */
    strcpy(szGrantString, "GRANT CONTROL, INSERT, DELETE ");
    strcat(szGrantString, "ON TABLE USERID.EMP_ACT TO USER ");
    strcat(szGrantString, szAuthID);

    /* Grant The CONTROL, INSERT And DELETE Authority To */
    /* A Specified User                                  */
    EXEC SQL EXECUTE IMMEDIATE :szGrantString;

    if (sqlca.sqlcode == SQL_RC_OK)
        {
        cout << "The following Authority has been given to ";
        cout << szAuthID << " :" << endl;
        cout << "CONTROL" << endl;
        cout << "INSERT" << endl;
        cout << "DELETE" << endl << endl;
        }

    /* Return The SQL Return Code */
    return(sqlca.sqlcode);
}
/* Define The revokePublic() Member Function */
short int Authorization::revokePublic(void)
{
    /* Revoke The CONTROL, INSERT, And DELETE Authority */
    /* From All PUBLIC Users                            */
    EXEC SQL REVOKE CONTROL, INSERT, DELETE
            ON TABLE USERID.EMP_ACT FROM PUBLIC;

    if (sqlca.sqlcode == SQL_RC_OK)
        {
        cout << "The following Authority has been taken away from ';
        cout << "PUBLIC :" << endl;
        cout << "CONTROL" << endl;
        cout << "INSERT" << endl;
        cout << "DELETE" << endl << endl;
        }

    /* Return The SQL Return Code */
    return(sqlca.sqlcode);
}

/* Define The revokeUser() Member Function */
short int Authorization::revokeUser(const char *szAuthID)
{
    /* Build The Revoke SQL Statement String */
    strcpy(szRevokeString, "REVOKE CONTROL, INSERT, DELETE ");
    strcat(szRevokeString, "ON TABLE USERID.EMP_ACT FROM USER ");
    strcat(szRevokeString, szAuthID);

    /* Revoke The CONTROL, INSERT, And DELETE Authority From A */
    /* Specified User                                          */
    EXEC SQL EXECUTE IMMEDIATE :szRevokeString;

    if (sqlca.sqlcode == SQL_RC_OK)
        {
        cout << "The following Authority has been taken away from ";
        cout << szAuthID << " :" << endl;
        cout << "CONTROL" << endl;
```

```
            cout << "INSERT" << endl;
            cout << "DELETE" << endl;
            }

        /* Return The SQL Return Code */
        return(sqlca.sqlcode);
}

int main()
{
        /* Declare The Local Memory Variables */
        short int rc = EXIT_SUCCESS;            // Must Be Declared Here
                                                // For The SQL Precompiler

        /* Include The SQLCA Data Structure Variable */
        EXEC SQL INCLUDE SQLCA;

        /* Set Up A Simple SQL Error Handler */
        EXEC SQL WHENEVER SQLERROR GOTO EXIT;

        /* Create An Instance Of The Authorization Class */
        Authorization Privilege;

        /* Connect To The SAMPLE Database */
        EXEC SQL CONNECT TO SAMPLE USER etpdd6z USING sanders;

        /* Grant The PUBLIC Authorizations */
        rc = Privilege.grantPublic();

        /* Grant Authorizations For User beth */
        rc = Privilege.grantUser("beth");

        /* Revoke The PUBLIC Authorizations */
        rc = Privilege.revokePublic();

        /* Revoke Authorizations For User beth */
        rc = Privilege.revokeUser("beth");

EXIT:
        /* If An Error Has Occurred, Display The SQL Return Code */
        if (sqlca.sqlcode != SQL_RC_OK)
            {
            cout << "SQL ERROR : " << sqlca.sqlcode << endl;
            rc = EXIT_FAILURE;
            }

        /* Issue A Rollback To Free All Locks */
        EXEC SQL ROLLBACK;

        /* Turn Off The SQL Error Handler */
        EXEC SQL WHENEVER SQLERROR CONTINUE;

        /* Disconnect From The SAMPLE Database */
        EXEC SQL DISCONNECT CURRENT;

        /* Return To The Operating System */
        return(rc);
}
```

CHAPTER 10

DATA DEFINITION STATEMENTS

SQL data definition statements consist of commands used to define the data objects that make up a database. This group includes:

- SQL statements that create various data objects such as table spaces, tables, indexes, and views.
- SQL statements that alter table space and table data objects.
- An SQL statement that obtains information about defined primary key, foreign key, and check constraints.
- An SQL statement that deletes various data objects.
- An SQL statement that sets or modifies the description associated with each data object in the database.

Table 10.1 lists the SQL data definition statements available with DB2.

TABLE 10.1 SQL Data Definition Statements

Statement	Description
CREATE TABLESPACE	Defines and creates a table space.
ALTER TABLESPACE	Changes the definition of an existing DMS table space.
CREATE TABLE	Defines and creates a table.
ALTER TABLE	Changes the definition of an existing table.
CREATE INDEX	Defines and creates an index on a table.
CREATE VIEW	Defines and creates a view on one or more tables or views.
CREATE ALIAS	Defines an alias for a table, view, or another alias.
CREATE DISTINCT TYPE	Defines and creates distinct data types.
SET CONSTRAINTS	Toggles the check-pending state on and off and checks entered data for constraint violations.
COMMENT ON	Adds or replaces the comment (in the system catalog tables) that describes an object.
DROP	Deletes an object and removes its definition from the database.
CREATE FUNCTION	Registers a user-defined function in the system catalog.
SET CURRENT FUNCTION PATH	Changes the value of the CURRENT FUNCTION PATH special register, which is used to locate the definitions of both internal and user-defined functions.

Creating Table Spaces

A table space is a storage model that provides a level of indirection between a database and the tables and indexes stored within that database. By using table spaces, you can assign the location of database data directly to a specific directory, device, or file. Table spaces can improve database and application performance, provide a more flexible database configuration, and provide better data integrity.

When you create a table space within a database with the CREATE TABLESPACE statement, the designated container (directory, device, or file) is assigned to it and its definitions and attributes are stored in the database system catalog. If the specified directory name does not exist, DB2 will automatically create it. Once a table space is created, you can modify it, if necessary, with the ALTER TABLESPACE statement.

Creating Tables

Tables allow you to organize and store data. They are created with the CREATE TABLE statement. When this statement is executed, the table is given a name and a definition is provided for each of its columns. You can store tables together in a single table space or in separate table spaces. If a table will be dropped and created often, it is more efficient to store it in its own table space; then the table space can be dropped instead of the table.

You can define up to 255 columns for a table. Each column in a table represents the attributes of an entity. The column name should describe the information that will be stored in the column and it should be easily recognizable. Also, each column name must be unique within a table. The data type associated with a column dictates the type of data the column will contain, its size, and its precision (in some cases). DB2 uses various character string, numeric, date, time, graphic, and large object (LOB) data types for data storage. In addition to these built-in data types, DB2 supports the use of user-defined data types, as long as they can be mapped back to one of the built-in data types.

You can impose referential integrity by adding referential constraints to table and column definitions when creating the table. Just include the PRIMARY KEY clause, the FOREIGN KEY clause, or the REFERENCES clause in the table definition provided for the CREATE TABLE or ALTER TABLE statement. Once referential constraints are established, DB2 will automatically check them each time data is entered into the database and maintain them accordingly. The primary goal of referential constraints is to maintain data integrity wherever one database object references another.

Referential integrity requires that table definitions contain full descriptions of both primary and foreign keys. A primary index (key) forces the values of the columns specified in the primary key to be unique. A foreign key references the primary key in the same or another table. The number of columns in the foreign key must be equal to the number of columns in the primary key being referenced. Also, the column definitions must have the same data types and lengths. Foreign keys are assigned constraint names (either explicitly or implicitly), and you can use this name to turn the constraint checking on or off.

You can also define check constraints for a table. Check constraints specify a search condition that is enforced for each row of the table for which the check constraint is defined. Check constraint definitions are also specified as part of the table definition when the table is created or changed. Once defined, a check constraint is automatically activated whenever an INSERT or UPDATE statement modifies the data stored in a table. Like foreign keys, check constraints are assigned constraint names (either explicitly or implicitly), which you can use to turn the constraint checking on or off.

Creating Indexes

An index is a list of the locations of rows (pointers), sorted by the contents of one or more specified columns in either ascending or descending order. Indexes typically speed up access to a table. They also enforce logical designs and referential constraints. For example, you could create a unique index to ensure that the data entered in one or more specified columns does not contain duplicate values.

You can define any number of indexes on a particular base table via the CREATE INDEX statement, and they can help the performance of queries. There are some tradeoffs, however; the more indexes there are for a table, the more maintenance DB2 must perform during insert, update, and delete operations. In fact, creating a large number of indexes for a table that receives many updates can slow down rather than improve performance. So you want to create indexes only when there is a clear advantage to having them. If the table for which an index is being created is empty, the index will be created but no index entries will be made until the table is populated. If the table for which an index is being created already contains data, the index will be created and index entries will be made for the existing data. Once created, indexes are automatically maintained by DB2.

Whenever an application program processes rows in a table based on a key value (specified in a WHERE clause), you can use an index based on that key value to access rows directly. This is important because the rows in a base table are not ordered. When you insert rows into a base table, they are placed in the first available storage location that can accommodate them. When searching for specific rows in a table that is not indexed, the entire table must be scanned. An index eliminates the need to perform a lengthy sequential search.

Note: An index is never directly used by an application program. Instead, the decision of whether or not to use an index and which index to use is made by the DB2 optimizer as SQL data manipulation statements are processed.

Creating Views

Views are derived from one or more base tables or views, and you can use them interchangeably with base tables and aliases when retrieving data. When you make changes to the data shown in an updatable view, that data is actually changed in the base table itself. You can use views to make a subset of table data available to an application program. A view can have column names that are different from the actual names of the corresponding column names in the tables on which the view is based. Columns in a view inherit the NOT NULL and NOT NULL WITH DEFAULT attributes from the base table or view from which the view is derived, except when the columns are derived from an expression.

A view can be classified as deletable, updatable, insertable, or read-only, depending on how it is created:

Deletable A view is considered deletable if all the following conditions are true:

- Each FROM clause of the outer fullselect identifies only one base table, deletable view, deletable nested table expression, or deletable common table expression.
- The outer fullselect does not include a VALUES clause, a GROUP BY clause, or a HAVING clause.
- The outer fullselect does not include column functions, such as MIN() and MAX(), in the select list.
- The outer fullselect does not include SET operations (UNION, EXCEPT, or INTERSECT), with the exception of the UNION ALL operation.
- The base tables specified in the operands of a UNION ALL operation must not be the same table and each operand must be deletable.
- The select list of the outer fullselect does not include the DISTINCT keyword.

Updatable A view is considered updatable if any column of the view is updatable. A column of a view is considered updatable if all the following conditions are true:

- The view is considered deletable.
- The column resolves to a column of the base table.

- All the corresponding columns of the operands of a UNION ALL operation have exactly matching data types (including length and precision) if the fullselect of the view includes a UNION ALL operation.

Insertable A view is considered insertable if all columns of the view are updatable and if the fullselect of the view does not include a UNION ALL operation.

Read-only A view is considered read-only if it is not deletable. The READONLY column in the SYSCAT.VIEWS system catalog table indicates whether or not a view is read-only.

If a view is no longer available for SQL statements that reference it, it is classified as an "inoperative" view. A view becomes inoperative if any of the following conditions occur:

- An authorization on which the view definition is dependent is revoked.
- An object, such as a table, alias, or function, on which the view definition is dependent is dropped.
- A view on which the view definition is dependent becomes inoperative.

In practical terms, an inoperative view is one in which the view definition has been unintentionally dropped. For example, when an alias is dropped, any view defined with that alias is made inoperative. All dependent views also become inoperative and packages dependent on the view are no longer valid. Until an inoperative view is explicitly recreated or dropped, all SQL statements using that inoperative view cannot be precompiled (with the exception of the CREATE ALIAS, CREATE VIEW, DROP VIEW, and COMMENT ON TABLE statements). Until an inoperative view has been explicitly dropped, its qualified name cannot be used by another view, table, or alias. You can re-create an inoperative view by issuing a CREATE VIEW statement, with the definition text stored in the TEXT column of the SYSCAT.VIEWS system catalog of the inoperative view. When re-creating an inoperative view, it is necessary to explicitly grant any authorizations required on that view to others, since all authorization records on a view are deleted if the view is marked inoperative. It is not necessary to explicitly drop an inoperative view before re-creating it. Issuing a CREATE VIEW statement with the same view name as an inoperative view will cause the inoperative view to be replaced. Inoperative views are indicated by an "X" in the VALID column of the SYSCAT.VIEWS catalog view and an "X" in the STATUS column of the SYSCAT.TABLES catalog view. A new view cannot be created if it uses an inoperative view in its definition.

Creating Aliases

An alias is an indirect method for referencing a table or view. Aliases allow SQL statements to be independent of the fully qualified names of base tables and views. Once you create an alias with the CREATE ALIAS statement, its definition does not have to be changed unless the referenced table or view name changes.

You can use aliases in views, trigger definitions, and any SQL statement (except for table check constraint definitions) that can reference a table or view. The alias is replaced by the actual table or view name it refers to when the application is precompiled.

Each alias name must be unique and can refer only to a table or view within the same database. You can define an alias for a table, view, or alias that does not yet exist, but the referenced table, view, or alias must exist before any SQL statements containing the alias can be precompiled.

Creating Distinct Types

Distinct types are user-defined data types derived from an existing built-in data type (integer, decimal, character, date, time, etc.) and are created with the CREATE DISTINCT TYPE statement. Distinct types share the same representations as the data type they are derived from, but by definition the distinct type and its source data type are incompatible. Therefore, they cannot be compared to each other. Instances of the same distinct type can be compared against each other, but only if the WITH COMPARISONS option is specified in the CREATE DISTINCT TYPE statement. Instances of distinct types cannot be used as arguments for most system-provided or built-in functions, or operands of operations that are defined in their source data type. Similarly, the source data type cannot be used in arguments or operands that expect a distinct data type.

Creating User-Defined Functions

User-defined functions extend and add to the support provided by built-in SQL functions. User-defined functions can also add function support for distinct data types that is comparable to the built-in functions provided for their source data types. Two types of user-defined functions can be created with the CREATE FUNCTION statement:

- A sourced function, whose implementation is inherited from some other existing function.
- An external function, which references an external function written in a high-level programming language, such as C or C++.

User-defined functions that are registered with the database can be used anywhere an expression is allowed. If a user-defined function is dropped, packages dependent on it are marked inoperative. A user-defined function cannot be dropped if a view, trigger, table check constraint, or another user-defined function is dependent on it.

CREATE TABLESPACE

Purpose The CREATE TABLESPACE statement allows you to create a new table space within a database, assign containers to a table space, and record table space definitions and attributes in the system catalog tables.

Syntax

```
EXEC SQL CREATE <tablespace-type> TABLESPACE [tablespace-name] MANAGED BY
     [tablespace-manager] USING ('[container-string,...]') <Options>;
```

Parameters

tablespace-type Identifies the type of data that will be stored in the table space. The tablespace type can be any of the following:

REGULAR Indicates that the table space will be used to store all data except temporary tables. If no table space type is specified, this is the default.

LONG Indicates that the table space will be used to store LONG VARCHAR, LONG VARGRAPHIC, BLOB, CLOB, and/or DBCLOB table column data. In this case, the created table space must be database managed.

TEMPORARY Indicates that the table space will be used to store temporary tables. Temporary tables are work areas created and used by DB2 to perform operations such as sorts or joins.

tablespace-name Identifies the name of the table space.

tablespace-manager Identifies how the table space will be managed. The tablespace-manager can be any of the following:

SYSTEM Indicates that the table space is to be a system-managed space (SMS).

DATABASE Indicates that the table space is to be a database-managed space (DMS).

container-string Identifies one or more containers that will belong to the table space and be used to store the table space's data. For SMS table spaces, each container string must identify either an absolute or a relative directory name. For DMS table spaces, the type of the container (either FILE or DEVICE) and its size (in 4KB pages) must be specified (for example: FILE, 'temp/tspace.tsp', 5000). If the container is a FILE container, each container string must identify either an absolute or a relative directory name. If the container is a DEVICE container, each container string must identify the name of a device that already exists. With DMS table spaces, a mixture of both FILE and DEVICE containers can be specified.

Options

EXTENTSIZE [number-of-pages] Specifies the number of 4KB pages that will be written to a container before advancing to the next container. DB2 cycles repeatedly through the specified containers as data is stored. The *number-of-pages* value can be any number between 2 and 256.

PREFETCHSIZE [number-of-pages] Specifies the number of pages that will be read from the table space when data prefetching is performed. Prefetching reads in data needed by a query before it is referenced by the query, so the query does not wait for I/O to be performed. If the *number-of-pages* value is 0, no prefetching will be done.

OVERHEAD [24.1 | number-of-milliseconds] Specifies the I/O controller overhead and disk seek and latency time, in milliseconds. The *number-of-milliseconds* value should be an average number for all containers that belong to the table space, if that value is not the same for all containers. If the OVERHEAD option is not specified, a default value of 24.1 milliseconds will be used. The OVERHEAD value is used to determine the cost of I/O during query optimization.

TRANSFERRATE [0.9 | number-of-milliseconds] Specifies the amount of time, in milliseconds, needed to read one 4KB page into memory. The *number-of-milliseconds* value should be an average number for all containers that belong to the table space, if that value is not the same for all containers. If the TRANSFERRATE option is not specified, a default value of 0.9 milliseconds will be used. The TRANSFERRATE value is used to determine the cost of I/O during query optimization.

Description

The CREATE TABLESPACE statement allows you to create a new table space within a database, assign containers to a table space, and record a table space definition and attributes in the system catalog tables. A table space can be either a system-managed space (SMS) or a database-managed space (DMS). All SMS table spaces are managed by the operating system's file manager, while all DMS table spaces are managed by DB2. Table spaces allow you to assign the location of database and table data directly to a directory name, a device name, or a specified file.

Comments

- The table space name cannot begin with the characters "SYS," and it cannot be a name already being used by another table space.
- The device string cannot exceed 240 bytes in length.
- If a directory name specified in the container string is not an absolute directory name, it will be treated as a directory relative to the database directory. If the last component of the directory name does not exist, it will be created by DB2. When the table space is dropped, all corresponding components created by DB2 are deleted.
- The CREATE TABLESPACE statement will fail if any component of a specified directory name does not exist.
- The format of the container string is dependent on the operating system and is specified in the normal manner for the operating system. For example, an OS/2 directory path is a drive letter followed by a colon, and has a backslash (\) character between each subdirectory. An AIX directory path begins with a forward slash (/) character and has a forward slash between each subdirectory.
- Remote resources (such as LAN-redirected drives on OS/2 or NFS-mounted file systems on AIX) can produce unpredictable results, so they are not supported.

- When specifying a FILE container, the container string must be an absolute or relative filename. If the filename is not absolute, it is relative to the database directory. If any component of the container string (path and filename) does not exist, it will be created and initialized to the specified size by DB2. When the table space is dropped, the file is deleted. If the file already exists, it will be overwritten; if it is smaller than the specified size, it will be extended. Existing files that are larger than the specified size are not truncated.
- DEVICE containers are not supported on OS/2.
- All containers must be unique across all databases; the size of each container can differ, but optimal performance is achieved only when all containers are the same size.
- When more than one TEMPORARY table space exists in the database, they are used in a round-robin fashion in order to balance their usage.

Authority Only users with either system control (SYSCTRL) authority or system administrator (SYSADM) authority are allowed to execute this statement.

See Also ALTER TABLESPACE, CREATE TABLE, DROP

Examples The following C program illustrates how the CREATE TABLESPACE statement is used to create a SMS and DMS table space:

```
#include <stdio.h>
#include <stdlib.h>
#include <string.h>
#include <sql.h>

int main()
{
    /* Include The SQLCA Data Structure Variable */
    EXEC SQL INCLUDE SQLCA;

    /* Set Up A Simple SQL Error Handler */
    EXEC SQL WHENEVER SQLERROR GOTO EXIT;

    /* Declare The Local Memory Variables */
    int   rc = EXIT_SUCCESS;
    char  szDefinerID[9];

    /* Declare The SQL Host Memory Variables */
    EXEC SQL BEGIN DECLARE SECTION;
        char      szTBSpace[18];
        char      szDefiner[8];
    EXEC SQL END DECLARE SECTION;

    /* Connect To The SAMPLE Database */
    EXEC SQL CONNECT TO SAMPLE USER etpdd6z USING sanders;

    /* Create A Regular SMS Table Space */
    EXEC SQL CREATE TABLESPACE SMS_SPACE
        MANAGED BY SYSTEM
        USING ('G:_TBSP.TSP')
        EXTENTSIZE 64
        PREFETCHSIZE 32;

    /* Print A Message Telling That The Table Space Was Created */
    printf("The SMS Table Space SMS_SPACE has been created.\n");
```

```
    /* Create A Temporary DMS Table Space */
    EXEC SQL CREATE TEMPORARY TABLESPACE TEMPSPACE2
        MANAGED BY DATABASE
        USING (FILE 'G:.TSP' 4000)
        EXTENTSIZE 256;

    /* Print A Message Telling That The Table Space Was Created */
    printf("The DMS Table Space TEMPSPACE2 has been created.\n");

    /* Commit The Transaction */
    EXEC SQL COMMIT;

    /* Now Retrieve The Records From The SYSCAT.TABLESPACES Table */
    /* To Verify That The Table Spaces Were Created               */

    /* Declare The SYS_TABLESPACES Table Cursor */
    EXEC SQL DECLARE SYS_TABLESPACES CURSOR FOR
        SELECT TBSPACE,
               DEFINER
        FROM SYSCAT.TABLESPACES;

    /* Open The Cursor */
    EXEC SQL OPEN SYS_TABLESPACES;

    /* If The Cursor Was Successfully Opened, Fetch The Records Into */
    /* Host Variables                                                 */
    printf("\nContents of SYSCAT.TABLESPACES\n\n");
    while (sqlca.sqlcode == SQL_RC_OK)
        {
        EXEC SQL FETCH SYS_TABLESPACES
            INTO :szTBSpace,
                 :szDefiner;

        /* If The FETCH Was Successful, Print The Data */
        if (sqlca.sqlcode == SQL_RC_OK)
            {
            strncpy(szDefinerID, " ", 8);
            strncpy(szDefinerID, szDefiner, 8);
            szDefinerID[8] = 0;
            printf("Table Space : %18s\t Definer: %8s\n",
                   szTBSpace, szDefinerID);
            }
        }                                          /* End Of WHILE    */

    /* Close The Cursor */
    EXEC SQL CLOSE SYS_TABLESPACES;

    /* Delete The Table Spaces */
    EXEC SQL DROP TABLESPACE SMS_SPACE;
    EXEC SQL DROP TABLESPACE TEMPSPACE2;

    /* Commit The Transaction */
    EXEC SQL COMMIT;

EXIT:
    /* If An Error Has Occurred, Display The SQL Return Code */
    if (sqlca.sqlcode != SQL_RC_OK)
        {
        printf("SQL ERROR : %ld\n", sqlca.sqlcode);
        rc = EXIT_FAILURE;
        }
```

```
    /* Turn Off The SQL Error Handler */
    EXEC SQL WHENEVER SQLERROR CONTINUE;

    /* Disconnect From The SAMPLE Database */
    EXEC SQL DISCONNECT CURRENT;

    /* Return To The Operating System */
    return(rc);
}
```

The following C++ program illustrates how the CREATE TABLESPACE statement is used by class methods to create a SMS and DMS table space:

```
#include <iostream.h>
#include <stdlib.h>
#include <string.h>
#include <sql.h>

/* Define The TableSpace Class */
class TableSpace
{
    private:

        /* Include The SQLCA Data Structure Variable */
        EXEC SQL INCLUDE SQLCA;

        /* Declare The Local Memory Variables */
        char  szDefinerID[9];

        /* Declare The SQL Host Memory Variables */
        EXEC SQL BEGIN DECLARE SECTION;
            char      szCreateString[255];
            char      szTBSpace[18];
            char      szDefiner[8];
        EXEC SQL END DECLARE SECTION;

    /* Declare The Public Member Function Prototypes */
    public:
        short int createSMS_Space();
        short int createDMS_Space(const char *szFileName);
        short int getSysInfo();
} ;

/* Define The createSMS_Space() Member Function */
short int TableSpace::createSMS_Space(void)
{
    /* Create A Regular SMS Table Space */
    EXEC SQL CREATE TABLESPACE SMS_SPACE
        MANAGED BY SYSTEM
        USING ('G:_TBSP.TSP')
        EXTENTSIZE 64
        PREFETCHSIZE 32;

    /* Print A Message Telling That The Table Space Was Created */
    if (sqlca.sqlcode == SQL_RC_OK)
        {
        cout << "The SMS Table Space SMS_SPACE has been created.";
        cout << endl;
        }
```

```
    /* Return The SQL Return Code */
    return(sqlca.sqlcode);
}

/* Define The createDMS_Space() Member Function */
short int TableSpace::createDMS_Space(const char *szFileName)
{
    /* Build The Create Tablespace SQL Statement String */
    strcpy(szCreateString, "CREATE TEMPORARY TABLESPACE TEMPSPACE2 ");
    strcat(szCreateString, "MANAGED BY DATABASE USING (FILE '");
    strcat(szCreateString, szFileName);
    strcat(szCreateString, "' 4000) EXTENTSIZE 256");

    /* Create The DMS Table Space */
    EXEC SQL EXECUTE IMMEDIATE :szCreateString;

    /* Print A Message Telling That The Table Space Was Created */
    if (sqlca.sqlcode == SQL_RC_OK)
        {
        cout << "The DMS Table Space TEMPSPACE2 has been created.";
        cout << endl;
        }

    /* Return The SQL Return Code */
    return(sqlca.sqlcode);
}

/* Define The getSysInfo() Member Function */
short int TableSpace::getSysInfo(void)
{
    /* Declare The SYS_TABLESPACES Table Cursor */
    EXEC SQL DECLARE SYS_TABLESPACES CURSOR FOR
        SELECT TBSPACE,
               DEFINER
        FROM SYSCAT.TABLESPACES;

    /* Open The Cursor */
    EXEC SQL OPEN SYS_TABLESPACES;

    /* If The Cursor Was Successfully Opened, Fetch The Records Into */
    /* Host Variables                                                */
    cout << endl << "Contents of SYSCAT.TABLESPACES" << endl << endl;
    while (sqlca.sqlcode == SQL_RC_OK)
        {
        EXEC SQL FETCH SYS_TABLESPACES
            INTO :szTBSpace,
                 :szDefiner;

        /* If The FETCH Was Successful, Print The Data */
        if (sqlca.sqlcode == SQL_RC_OK)
            {
            strncpy(szDefinerID, " ", 8);
            strncpy(szDefinerID, szDefiner, 8);
            szDefinerID[8] = 0;
            cout << "Table Space : ";
            cout.width(18);
            cout << szTBSpace;
            cout << ": " << szDefinerID << endl;
            }
        }                                          /* End Of WHILE    */
```

```
        /* Close The Cursor */
        EXEC SQL CLOSE SYS_TABLESPACES;

        /* Return The SQL Return Code */
        return(sqlca.sqlcode);
    }

    int main()
    {
        /* Declare The Local Memory Variables */
        short int rc = EXIT_SUCCESS;            // Must Be Declared Here
                                                // For The SQL Precompiler

        /* Include The SQLCA Data Structure Variable */
        EXEC SQL INCLUDE SQLCA;

        /* Set Up A Simple SQL Error Handler */
        EXEC SQL WHENEVER SQLERROR GOTO EXIT;

        /* Create An Instance Of The TableSpace Class */
        TableSpace tablespace;

        /* Connect To The SAMPLE Database */
        EXEC SQL CONNECT TO SAMPLE USER etpdd6z USING sanders;

        /* Create A Regular SMS Table Space */
        rc = tablespace.createSMS_Space();

        /* Create A Temporary DMS Table Space */
        rc = tablespace.createDMS_Space("G:\TEMPTBSP.TSP");

        /* Commit The Transaction */
        EXEC SQL COMMIT;

        /* Now Retrieve The Records From The SYSCAT.TABLESPACES Table */
        /* To Verify That The Table Spaces Were Created                */
        rc = tablespace.getSysInfo();

        /* Delete The Table Spaces */
        EXEC SQL DROP TABLESPACE SMS_SPACE;
        EXEC SQL DROP TABLESPACE TEMPSPACE2;

        /* Commit The Transaction */
        EXEC SQL COMMIT;

    EXIT:
        /* If An Error Has Occurred, Display The SQL Return Code */
        if (sqlca.sqlcode != SQL_RC_OK)
            {
            cout << "SQL ERROR : " << sqlca.sqlcode << endl;
            rc = EXIT_FAILURE;
            }

        /* Issue A Rollback To Free All Locks */
        EXEC SQL ROLLBACK;

        /* Turn Off The SQL Error Handler */
        EXEC SQL WHENEVER SQLERROR CONTINUE;

        /* Disconnect From The SAMPLE Database */
        EXEC SQL DISCONNECT CURRENT;
        /* Return To The Operating System */
        return(rc);
    }
```

ALTER TABLESPACE

Purpose The ALTER TABLESPACE statement allows you to modify an existing table space.

Syntax

```
EXEC SQL ALTER TABLESPACE [tablespace-name] <Options>;
```

Parameters *tablespace-name* Identifies the name of the table space to be created.

Options

ADD (FILE | DEVICE ' [container-string] ' [number-of-pages], . . .) Specifies that one or more new containers are to be added to the table space. This option specifies the type of the container (either FILE or DEVICE), the file or device name, and the container size in 4KB pages. If the container is a FILE container, each container string must identify either an absolute or a relative directory name. If the container is a DEVICE container, each *container-string* must identify the name of a device that already exists.

PREFETCHSIZE [number-of-pages] Specifies the number of pages that will be read from the table space when data prefetching is performed. Prefetching reads in data needed by a query before it is referenced by the query, so the query does not wait for I/O to be performed. If the *number-of-pages* value is set to 0, no prefetching will be done.

OVERHEAD [number-of-milliseconds] Specifies the I/O controller overhead and disk seek and latency time, in milliseconds. The *number-of-milliseconds* value should be an average number for all containers that belong to the table space, if that value is not the same for all containers. The OVERHEAD value allows you to determine the cost of I/O during query optimization.

TRANSFERRATE [number-of-milliseconds] Specifies the amount of time, in milliseconds, needed to read one 4KB page into memory. The *number-of-milliseconds* value should be an average number for all containers that belong to the table space, if that value is not the same for all containers. The TRANSFERRATE value can determine the cost of I/O during query optimization.

Description The ALTER TABLESPACE statement allows you to modify an existing table space by doing any of the following:

- Adding one or more containers to a DMS table space (a table space created with the MANAGED BY DATABASE option).
- Modifying the PREFETCHSIZE setting for a table space.
- Modifying the OVERHEAD setting for a table space.
- Modifying the TRANSFERRATE setting for a table space.

Whenever new containers are added to a table space, the contents of the table space are automatically redistributed across all containers in order to balance their usage. When the PREFETCHSIZE, OVERHEAD, and TRANSFERRATE settings are changed, their values are automatically used to determine the cost of I/O during query optimization.

Comments

- The format of the container string is dependent on the operating system and is specified in the normal manner for the operating system. For example, an OS/2 directory path begins with a drive letter followed by a colon, and has a backslash character between each subdirectory. An AIX directory path begins with a forward slash character and has a forward slash character between each subdirectory.
- Remote resources (such as LAN-redirected drives on OS/2 or NFS-mounted file systems on AIX) can produce unpredictable results, so they are not supported.

- If you are specifying a FILE container, the container string must be an absolute or relative filename. If the filename is not absolute, it is relative to the database directory. If any component of the container string (path and filename) does not exist, it will be created and initialized to the specified size by DB2. When the table space is dropped, the file is deleted. If the file already exists, it will be overwritten; if it is smaller than the specified size, it will be extended. Existing files larger than the specified size are not truncated.
- DEVICE containers are not supported on OS/2.
- All containers must be unique across all databases; the size of each container can differ, but optimal performance is achieved only when all containers are the same size.
- When adding more than one container to a table space, you should add all the containers either in one ALTER TABLESPACE statement or in one transaction, so the cost of rebalancing is incurred only once.

Authority Only users with either system control (SYSCTRL) authority or system administrator (SYSADM) authority are allowed to execute this statement.

See Also CREATE TABLESPACE, DROP

Examples The following C program illustrates how the ALTER TABLESPACE statement can be used to change the PREFETCHSIZE value for an existing table space:

```
#include <stdio.h>
#include <stdlib.h>
#include <sql.h>

int main()
{
    /* Include The SQLCA Data Structure Variable */
    EXEC SQL INCLUDE SQLCA;

    /* Set Up A Simple SQL Error Handler */
    EXEC SQL WHENEVER SQLERROR GOTO EXIT;

    /* Declare The Local Memory Variables */
    int   rc = EXIT_SUCCESS;

    /* Declare The SQL Host Memory Variables */
    EXEC SQL BEGIN DECLARE SECTION;
        char       szTBSpace[18];
        short      sPrefetchSize;
    EXEC SQL END DECLARE SECTION;

    /* Connect To The SAMPLE Database */
    EXEC SQL CONNECT TO SAMPLE USER etpdd6z USING sanders;

    /* Create A DMS Table Space */
    EXEC SQL CREATE TABLESPACE DMS_SPACE
        MANAGED BY DATABASE
        USING (FILE 'G:_TBSP.TSP' 4000)
        EXTENTSIZE 256;

    /* Print A Message Telling That The Table Space Was Created */
    printf("The DMS Table Space DMS_SPACE has been created.\n");
```

```
    /* Commit The Transaction */
    EXEC SQL COMMIT;

    /* Now Retrieve The Record From The SYSCAT.TABLESPACES */
    /* Table To Verify That The Table Space Was Created    */
    EXEC SQL SELECT TBSPACE,
                    PREFETCHSIZE
        INTO :szTBSpace,
             :sPrefetchSize
        FROM SYSCAT.TABLESPACES
        WHERE TBSPACE = 'DMS_SPACE';

    printf("\nContents of SYSCAT.TABLESPACES\n");
    printf("Table Space : %s\t Prefetch Size : %d\n",
            szTBSpace, sPrefetchSize);

    /* Change The Prefetch Size For The DMS Table Space */
    EXEC SQL ALTER TABLESPACE DMS_SPACE
        PREFETCHSIZE 64;

    /* Now Retrieve The Record From The SYSCAT.TABLESPACES Table */
    /* Again To Verify That The Table Space Was Created          */
    EXEC SQL SELECT TBSPACE,
                    PREFETCHSIZE
        INTO :szTBSpace,
             :sPrefetchSize
        FROM SYSCAT.TABLESPACES
        WHERE TBSPACE = 'DMS_SPACE';

    printf("\nContents of SYSCAT.TABLESPACES after ALTER statement.\n");
    printf("Table Space : %s\t Prefetch Size : %d\n",
            szTBSpace, sPrefetchSize);

    /* Delete The Table Space */
    EXEC SQL DROP TABLESPACE DMS_SPACE;

    /* Commit The Transaction */
    EXEC SQL COMMIT;

EXIT:
    /* If An Error Has Occurred, Display The SQL Return Code */
    if (sqlca.sqlcode != SQL_RC_OK)
        {
        printf("SQL ERROR : %ld\n", sqlca.sqlcode);
        rc = EXIT_FAILURE;
        }

    /* Turn Off The SQL Error Handler */
    EXEC SQL WHENEVER SQLERROR CONTINUE;

    /* Disconnect From The SAMPLE Database */
    EXEC SQL DISCONNECT CURRENT;

    /* Return To The Operating System */
    return(rc);
}
```

The following C++ program illustrates how the ALTER TABLESPACE statement is used by class methods to change the PREFETCHSIZE value for an existing table space:

```
#include <iostream.h>
#include <stdlib.h>
#include <string.h>
#include <sql.h>

/* Define The TableSpace Class */
class TableSpace
{
    private:

        /* Include The SQLCA Data Structure Variable */
        EXEC SQL INCLUDE SQLCA;

        /* Declare The Local Memory Variables */
        char  szDefinerID[9];

        /* Declare The SQL Host Memory Variables */
        EXEC SQL BEGIN DECLARE SECTION;
            char      szCreateString[255];
            char      szTBSpace[18];
            short     sPrefetchSize;
        EXEC SQL END DECLARE SECTION;

    /* Declare The Public Member Function Prototypes */
    public:
        short int createDMS_Space(const char *szFileName);
        short int alterDMS_Space();
        short int getSysInfo();
} ;

/* Define The createDMS_Space() Member Function */
short int TableSpace::createDMS_Space(const char *szFileName)
{
    /* Build The Create Tablespace SQL Statement String */
    strcpy(szCreateString, "CREATE TABLESPACE DMS_SPACE ");
    strcat(szCreateString, "MANAGED BY DATABASE USING (FILE '");
    strcat(szCreateString, szFileName);
    strcat(szCreateString, "' 4000) EXTENTSIZE 256");

    /* Create The DMS Table Space */
    EXEC SQL EXECUTE IMMEDIATE :szCreateString;

    /* Print A Message Telling That The Table Space Was Created */
    if (sqlca.sqlcode == SQL_RC_OK)
        {
        cout << "The DMS Table Space DMS_SPACE has been created.";
        cout << endl;
        }

    /* Return The SQL Return Code */
    return(sqlca.sqlcode);
}

/* Define The alterDMS_Space() Member Function */
short int TableSpace::alterDMS_Space(void)
{
    /* Change The Prefetch Size For The DMS Table Space */
    EXEC SQL ALTER TABLESPACE DMS_SPACE
        PREFETCHSIZE 64;
```

```
    /* Return The SQL Return Code */
    return(sqlca.sqlcode);
}

/* Define The getSysInfo() Member Function */
short int TableSpace::getSysInfo(void)
{
    /* Retrieve The Record From The SYSCAT.TABLESPACES Table */
    EXEC SQL SELECT TBSPACE,
                    PREFETCHSIZE
        INTO :szTBSpace,
             :sPrefetchSize
        FROM SYSCAT.TABLESPACES
        WHERE TBSPACE = 'DMS_SPACE';

    /* Print The Record */
    cout << endl << "Contents of SYSCAT.TABLESPACES" << endl;
    cout << "Table Space : " << szTBSpace << "Size : ";
    cout << sPrefetchSize << endl;

    /* Return The SQL Return Code */
    return(sqlca.sqlcode);
}

int main()
{
    /* Declare The Local Memory Variables */
    short int rc = EXIT_SUCCESS;              // Must Be Declared Here
                                              // For The SQL Precompiler

    /* Include The SQLCA Data Structure Variable */
    EXEC SQL INCLUDE SQLCA;

    /* Set Up A Simple SQL Error Handler */
    EXEC SQL WHENEVER SQLERROR GOTO EXIT;

    /* Create An Instance Of The TableSpace Class */
    TableSpace tablespace;

    /* Connect To The SAMPLE Database */
    EXEC SQL CONNECT TO SAMPLE USER etpdd6z USING sanders;

    /* Create A Regular DMS Table Space */
    rc = tablespace.createDMS_Space("G:\DMS_TBSP.TSP");

    /* Commit The Transaction */
    EXEC SQL COMMIT;

    /* Now Retrieve The Record From The SYSCAT.TABLESPACES Table */
    /* To Verify That The Table Space Was Created                */
    rc = tablespace.getSysInfo();

    /* Change The Prefetch Size For The DMS Table Space */
    rc = tablespace.alterDMS_Space();

    /* Now Retrieve The Record From The SYSCAT.TABLESPACES Table */
    /* Again To Verify That The Prefetch Size Was Changed        */
    rc = tablespace.getSysInfo();

    /* Delete The Table Space */
    EXEC SQL DROP TABLESPACE DMS_SPACE;
```

```
        /* Commit The Transaction */
        EXEC SQL COMMIT;

    EXIT:
        /* If An Error Has Occurred, Display The SQL Return Code */
        if (sqlca.sqlcode != SQL_RC_OK)
            {
            cout << "SQL ERROR : " << sqlca.sqlcode << endl;
            rc = EXIT_FAILURE;
            }

        /* Issue A Rollback To Free All Locks */
        EXEC SQL ROLLBACK;

        /* Turn Off The SQL Error Handler */
        EXEC SQL WHENEVER SQLERROR CONTINUE;

        /* Disconnect From The SAMPLE Database */
        EXEC SQL DISCONNECT CURRENT;

        /* Return To The Operating System */
        return(rc);
    }
```

CREATE TABLE

Purpose The CREATE TABLE statement allows you to create a database table.

Syntax

```
EXEC SQL CREATE TABLE [table-name] ([column-definition,...] |
   [constraint-definition]) <DATA CAPTURE [data-capture-type]>
   <IN [tablespace-name] <tablespace-options>>;
```

Parameters

table-name Identifies the name of the table to be created.

column-definition Identifies the column or columns to be part of the table. The syntax for a column definition is as follows:

```
[column-name] [data-type] <options | LOB-options>
```

where:

column-name Specifies the name of the column.

data-type Specifies the built-in data type to be used for data storage. The data type can be any of the following:

INTEGER	Large integer. INT is a synonym for INTEGER.
SMALLINT	Small integer
DOUBLE	Floating-point number. DOUBLE PRECISION and FLOAT can be used as synonyms for DOUBLE.
DECIMAL(*width, precision*)	Decimal number. The width integer specifies the total number of digits in the number (1 to 31). The precision integer specifies the number of digits to the right of the decimal place (0 to width). If width and precision values are not specified, the default values 5, 0 are used. DEC, NUMERIC, and NUM are synonyms for DECIMAL.

CHARACTER(*size*) <FOR BIT DATA>	A fixed-length character string, 1 to 254 characters long (specified in size). If the size value is not specified, the default value 1 is used. If the FOR BIT DATA option is specified, the contents of the character string will be treated as binary data and code page conversions will not be performed. CHAR can be used as a synonym for CHARACTER.
VARCHAR(*size*) <FOR BIT DATA>	A varying-length character string with a maximum size from 1 to 4000 characters. The FOR BIT DATA option has the same meaning as it does in CHARACTER. CHARACTER VARYING or CHAR VARYING are synonyms for VARCHAR.
LONG VARCHAR <FOR BIT DATA>	A varying-length character string with a maximum size of 32,700 characters. The FOR BIT DATA option has the same meaning as it does in the CHARACTER data type.
GRAPHIC(*size*)	A fixed-length graphic string from 1 to 127 bytes (specified in the size value). If a size is not specified, the default value 1 is used.
VARGRAPHIC(*size*)	A varying-length graphic string with a maximum size from 1 to 2000 bytes.
LONG VARGRAPHIC	A varying-length graphic string with a maximum size of 16,350 bytes.
DATE	A date.
TIME	A time.
TIMESTAMP	A timestamp.
BLOB (*size* <K I M I G>)	A binary large object string of a specified number (size) of bytes. If the K option is used, the size is in kilobytes; if the M option is used, the size indicates megabytes; and if the G option is used, the size is in gigabytes. Any number of spaces (or no spaces) are allowed between the size value and the letter K, M, or G.
CLOB (*size* <K I M I G>)	A character large object string of a specified number (size) of bytes. The K, M, and G option have the same meaning as described for the BLOB data type.
DBCLOB (*size* <K I M I G>)	A double-byte character large object string of a specified number (size) of double-byte characters. The K, M, and G option have the same meaning as described for the BLOB data type.

distinct-type-name Specifies the name of a distinct data type. If a distinct data type name is specified without a schema name, the schema name specified in the FUNCPATH option at the time the application was bound to the database will be used for static SQL statements. The schema name specified in the CURRENT FUNCTION PATH is used to determine the schema name for the distinct data type name of dynamic SQL statements.

options Specifies additional options for a data column. The options value can be either of the following:

NOT NULL Prevents the column from containing null values. If this options clause is not specified, the column can contain null values and its default value is either the null value or the value provided by the WITH DEFAULT option clause.

WITH DEFAULT Stores a default value other than the null value in the column if a data value is not supplied. The default value is dependent on the data type of the column. Table 10.2 lists the default values used by DB2 for each column type.

TABLE 10.2 Data Type Default Values

Data type	Default value
INTEGER	0
SMALLINT	0
DOUBLE	0
DECIMAL	0
CHARACTER *	Blanks
VARCHAR *	A string length of 0
LONG VARCHAR *	A string length of 0
GRAPHIC	Double-byte blanks
VARGRAPHIC	A string length of 0
LONG VARGRAPHIC	A string length of 0
DATE	A date value corresponding to January 1, 0001 for existing rows. The current date value for new rows.
TIME	A time value corresponding to 0 hours, 0 minutes, and 0 seconds for existing rows. The current time value for new rows.
TIMESTAMP	A timestamp value corresponding to January 1, 0001, 0 hours, 0 minutes, and 0 seconds for existing rows. The current timestamp value for new rows.
BLOB	No default value available.
CLOB	No default value available.
DBCLOB	No default value available.

* If this data type is specified with the FOR BIT DATA option, the data will be treated as binary data and the default value is a string length of 0.

LOB-options Specifies additional options for an LOB data column. The LOB option value can be any of the following:

LOGGED Specifies that changes made to a BLOB, CLOB, or DBCLOB column are written to the active log file. The data in these columns is then recoverable with database utilities (such as RESTORE DATABASE). This option is the default, but keep in mind that the total size of the log file for an entire database in DB2 version 2 is 1 gigabyte. Therefore, you should not log large BLOB, CLOB, and/or DBCLOB columns.

NOT LOGGED Specifies that changes made to a BLOB, CLOB, or DBCLOB column are not written to the active log file. This option has no effect on a commit or rollback operation.

COMPACT Specifies that the values in a BLOB, CLOB, or DBCLOB column take up minimal disk space (free any extra disk pages in the last group used by the LOB value), rather than leave left-over space at the end of the LOB storage area that might facilitate subsequent append operations. Keep in mind that storing data this way might affect performance in a length-increasing operation (such as append) on the column.

NOT COMPACT Specifies that the values in a BLOB, CLOB, or DBCLOB column are not compressed. This is the default option.

constraint-definition Specifies the type of constraint to which every row inserted or updated in the table must conform. The syntax for a constraint definition is determined by the constraint type being defined and can be any of the following:

```
CONSTRAINT [constraint-name] PRIMARY KEY [column-name,...]

CONSTRAINT [constraint-name] FOREIGN KEY (column-name,...) REFERENCES
   [table-name] <(column-name,...)> ON DELETE [delete-option]
   ON UPDATE [update-action]

CONSTRAINT [constraint-name] CHECK (check-condition)
```

where:

constraint-name Specifies the name of the constraint being created.

column-name Specifies one or more columns to be part of the primary key, foreign key, or check constraint. Each specified column name must be a valid column in the table.

table-name Specifies the base table that contains a primary key with the same number of comparable columns as the foreign key being created.

delete-option Specifies what action is to be taken on the dependent tables when a row in the parent table is deleted. The following delete options are available:

NO ACTION Indicates that no action is taken on dependent tables when a row is deleted. This option is the default and is enforced after all other referential constraints are validated.

RESTRICT Indicates that no action is taken on dependent tables when a row is deleted. If this option is specified, it is enforced before all other constraints, including constraints with modifying rules such as CASCADE or SET NULL.

CASCADE Indicates that the delete operation is copied to all dependent tables.

SET NULL Indicates that each nullable column of the foreign key of each dependent value is set to NULL. This delete option must not be specified unless some column of the foreign key allows null values.

update-option Specifies what action is taken on the dependent tables when a row in the parent table is updated. The following update options are available:

NO ACTION Indicates that no action is taken on dependent tables when a row is updated. This option is specified by default and is enforced after all other referential constraints are validated.

RESTRICT Indicates that no action is taken on dependent tables when a row is updated. If this option is specified, it is enforced before all other constraints, including constraints with modifying rules such as CASCADE or SET NULL.

check-condition Specifies a search condition that must evaluate to TRUE before data can be added to the table. This search condition is enforced when rows are inserted into the table, when rows in the table are updated, or whenever the SET CONSTRAINTS statement is executed with the IMMEDIATE CHECKED option.

data-capture-type Indicates whether extra information for data propagation (copying) is written to the active log file. The data capture type can be one of the following:

NONE Indicates that no extra information is written to the log file. This option is the default.

CHANGES Indicates that extra information about SQL changes to this table is written to the log file. This option is required if this table is copied with a propagation manager such as the Data Propagator Relational (DPropR) program, an IBM application that copies data between DB2 databases on platforms that support distributed relational database architecture (DRDA) connectivity when predefined criteria is met.

tablespace-name Identifies the name of the table space in which the table is created. The specified table space specified must be REGULAR.

tablespace-options Specifies the table space in which indexes and/or long column values are stored. The table space options can be either or both of the following:

INDEX IN [*tablespace-name*] Specifies the table space in which all indexes created for the table reside. This option is allowed only if the specified primary table space is a DMS table space (refer to the CREATE TABLESPACE statement for more information).

LONG IN [*tablespace-name*] Specifies the table space in which the values for all long values (LONG VARCHAR, LONG VARGRAPHIC, BLOB, CLOB, DBCLOB data types, or distinct data types with any of these as the source data type) is stored. This option is allowed only if the specified primary table space is a DMS table space and if the table space name refers to a LONG table space (refer to the CREATE TABLESPACE statement for more information).

Description The CREATE TABLE statement allows you to create a database table by specifying the names and attributes of each column in the table as the table definition. The table definition can also include other table attributes, such as primary key definitions and check constraints.

Comments

- If no qualifier (schema) is provided with the table name, the authorization ID of the current user will be used as the qualifier when the table is created. If a qualifier is provided with the table name, it cannot be "SYSIBM", "SYSCAT", or "SYSSTAT."

- The table name cannot be a name that is already being used by another table, alias, or view.
- Do not qualify column names and do not use the same name for more than one column in the same table.
- A table can contain up to 255 columns, but the sum of the byte counts of all columns in a table must not be greater than 4005.
- If a column in the table is defined as a user-defined distinct data type, then the data type of the column is the distinct data type and the size and precision of the column are the size and precision of the source type referenced by the user-defined distinct data type.
- If a column defined as a distinct data type is also a foreign key of a referential constraint, then the data type of the corresponding column of the primary key must be the same distinct data type.
- The table name specified in the REFERENCES clause of a foreign key must identify a base table described in the system catalog. This table name must not identify a system catalog table.
- The specified foreign key must have the same number of columns as the primary key of the referenced table. Also, the data type of each column of the foreign key must be comparable to its corresponding column in the primary key it references. (In this situation, datetime columns are not considered to be compatible with string columns.)
- The referential constraint specified by a FOREIGN KEY clause defines a relationship in which the table being referenced is the parent and the table for which the foreign key is defined is the dependent. A description of this referential constraint relationship is recorded in the system catalog.
- The PRIMARY KEY clause must not be specified more than once, and the specified columns in the key must be defined as NOT NULL. Also, each column name specified must identify a column of the table, and the same column can be identified only once.
- The number of identified columns in a primary or a foreign key must not exceed 16, and the sum of their length attributes must not exceed 255 bytes. No BLOB, CLOB, DBCLOB, LONG VARCHAR, or LONG VARGRAPHIC column can be used as part of a primary key (even if the length attribute of the column is small enough to fit within the 255-byte limit).
- A unique primary index is automatically created for the columns (ascending order for each column) specified in the table definition when a new table is created. The name of this index is "SYSIBM.SQL," followed by a character timestamp (*yymmddhhmmssxxx*) that corresponds to when the index was created.
- If a foreign key is specified, all packages with a delete dependency on the parent table or an update dependency on at least one column in the primary key are marked invalid.
- The description of a table is recorded in the system catalog tables along with its primary key and default index.
- A check constraint must not contain any of the following:
  –Subqueries
  –Column functions
  –Variant user-defined functions
  –User-defined functions using the EXTERNAL ACTION option
  –User-defined functions using the SCRATCHPAD option

–Host variables
–Parameter markers
–Special registers
–An alias

- If a check constraint is specified as part of a column definition, then each referenced column must refer to a column previously defined in the CREATE TABLE statement.
- Check constraints are not checked for inconsistencies, duplicate conditions, or equivalent conditions. Therefore, you can define contradictory or redundant check constraints that will produce errors at application runtime.
- You can specify a check constraint condition of IS NOT NULL for a column, but it is recommended to directly enforce nullability by using the NOT NULL attribute of a column instead of a check constraint.
- If the TABLESPACE clause is not specified, the table will be created in the first table space created by the current user. If no table space for the user can be found, the table will be placed into the default table space USERSPACE1. If the table space USERSPACE1 has been dropped, the table will not be created and the CREATE TABLE statement will fail.

Authorization Only users with either system administrator (SYSADM) authority, database administrator (DBADM) authority, or CREATETAB authority for the current database are allowed to execute this statement.

See Also ALTER TABLE, DROP

Examples The following C program illustrates how the CREATE TABLE statement allows you to create a database table within a specific table space:

```
#include <stdio.h>
#include <stdlib.h>
#include <string.h>
#include <sql.h>

int main()
{
    /* Include The SQLCA Data Structure Variable */
    EXEC SQL INCLUDE SQLCA;

    /* Set Up A Simple SQL Error Handler */
    EXEC SQL WHENEVER SQLERROR GOTO EXIT;

    /* Declare The Local Memory Variables */
    int   rc = EXIT_SUCCESS;
    char  szTable[19];
    char  szDefinerID[9];

    /* Declare The SQL Host Memory Variables */
    EXEC SQL BEGIN DECLARE SECTION;
        char      szTableName[18];
        char      szTBSpace[18];
        char      szDefiner[8];
    EXEC SQL END DECLARE SECTION;

    /* Connect To The SAMPLE Database */
    EXEC SQL CONNECT TO SAMPLE USER etpdd6z USING sanders;

    /* Create A DMS Table Space */
    EXEC SQL CREATE TABLESPACE EMP_SPACE
```

```
    MANAGED BY DATABASE
    USING (FILE 'G:_TBSP.TSP' 4000)
    EXTENTSIZE 256;

/* Print A Message Telling That The Table Space Was Created */
printf("The DMS Table Space EMP_SPACE has been created.\n");

/* Create A Temporary Table */
EXEC SQL CREATE TABLE TEMP_EMP
        (EMPID       INTEGER      NOT NULL,
         LASTNAME    CHAR(18)     NOT NULL,
         FIRSTNAME   CHAR(18)     NOT NULL,
         DEPTNO      CHAR(3),
    PRIMARY KEY(EMPID))
    IN EMP_SPACE;

/* Print A Message Telling That The Table Was Created */
printf("The Table TEMP_EMP has been created.\n");

/* Commit The Transaction */
EXEC SQL COMMIT;

/* Now Retrieve The Records From The SYSCAT.TABLESPACES And */
/* SYSCAT.TABLES Tables To Verify That The Table Space And  */
/* Table Were Created                                        */

/* Retrieve The Record From The SYSCAT.TABLESPACES Table */
EXEC SQL SELECT TBSPACE,
                DEFINER
    INTO :szTBSpace,
         :szDefiner
    FROM SYSCAT.TABLESPACES
    WHERE TBSPACE = 'EMP_SPACE';

printf("\nContents of SYSCAT.TABLESPACES\n\n");
strncpy(szDefinerID, " ", 8);
strncpy(szDefinerID, szDefiner, 8);
szDefinerID[8] = 0;
printf("Table Space : %s\t Definer: %s\n",
        szTBSpace, szDefinerID);

/* Retrieve The Record From The SYSCAT.TABLES Table */
EXEC SQL SELECT TABNAME,
                TBSPACE,
                DEFINER
    INTO :szTableName,
         :szTBSpace,
         :szDefiner
    FROM SYSCAT.TABLES
    WHERE TABNAME = 'TEMP_EMP';

printf("\nContents of SYSCAT.TABLES\n\n");
strncpy(szDefinerID, " ", 8);
strncpy(szDefinerID, szDefiner, 8);
szDefinerID[8] = 0;
printf("Table Name : %sTable Space : %s\t Definer: %s\n",
        szTableName, szTBSpace, szDefinerID);

/* Delete The Table Space And Table (Deleting The Table Space */
/* Automatically Deletes The Table Defined In It)              */
EXEC SQL DROP TABLESPACE EMP_SPACE;
```

```
    /* Commit The Transaction */
    EXEC SQL COMMIT;

EXIT:
    /* If An Error Has Occurred, Display The SQL Return Code */
    if (sqlca.sqlcode != SQL_RC_OK)
        {
        printf("SQL ERROR : %ld\n", sqlca.sqlcode);
        rc = EXIT_FAILURE;
        }

    /* Turn Off The SQL Error Handler */
    EXEC SQL WHENEVER SQLERROR CONTINUE;

    /* Disconnect From The SAMPLE Database */
    EXEC SQL DISCONNECT CURRENT;

    /* Return To The Operating System */
    return(rc);
}
```

The following C++ program illustrates how the CREATE TABLE statement is used by class methods to create a database table within a specific table space:

```
#include <iostream.h>
#include <stdlib.h>
#include <string.h>
#include <sql.h>

/* Define The Table Class */
class Table
{
    private:

        /* Include The SQLCA Data Structure Variable */
        EXEC SQL INCLUDE SQLCA;

        /* Declare The Local Memory Variables */
        char  szTable[19];
        char  szDefinerID[9];

        /* Declare The SQL Host Memory Variables */
        EXEC SQL BEGIN DECLARE SECTION;
            char      szCreateString[255];
            char      szTableName[18];
            char      szTBSpace[18];
            char      szDefiner[8];
        EXEC SQL END DECLARE SECTION;

    /* Declare The Public Member Function Prototypes */
    public:
        short int createDMS_Space();
        short int createTable();
        short int createDMS_Space(const char *szFileName);
        short int getSysInfo();
} ;

/* Define The createDMS_Space() Member Function */
short int Table::createDMS_Space(void)
{
```

```
    /* Create A Regular SMS Table Space */
    EXEC SQL CREATE TABLESPACE EMP_SPACE
        MANAGED BY DATABASE
        USING (FILE 'G:_TBSP.TSP' 4000)
        EXTENTSIZE 256;

    /* Print A Message Telling That The Table Space Was Created */
    if (sqlca.sqlcode == SQL_RC_OK)
        {
        cout << "The DMS Table Space EMP_SPACE has been created.";
        cout << endl;
        }

    /* Return The SQL Return Code */
    return(sqlca.sqlcode);
}

/* Define The createTable() Member Function */
short int Table::createTable(void)
{
    /* Create A Temporary Table */
    EXEC SQL CREATE TABLE TEMP_EMP
            (EMPID       INTEGER      NOT NULL,
             LASTNAME    CHAR(18)     NOT NULL,
             FIRSTNAME   CHAR(18)     NOT NULL,
             DEPTNO      CHAR(3),
        PRIMARY KEY(EMPID))
        IN EMP_SPACE;

    /* Print A Message Telling That The Table Was Created */
    if (sqlca.sqlcode == SQL_RC_OK)
        cout << "The Table TEMP_EMP has been created." << endl;

    /* Return The SQL Return Code */
    return(sqlca.sqlcode);
}

/* Define The getSysInfo() Member Function */
short int Table::getSysInfo(void)
{
    /* Retrieve The Record From The SYSCAT.TABLESPACES Table */
    EXEC SQL SELECT TBSPACE,
                    DEFINER
        INTO :szTBSpace,
             :szDefiner
        FROM SYSCAT.TABLESPACES
        WHERE TBSPACE = 'EMP_SPACE';

    cout << endl << "Contents of SYSCAT.TABLESPACES" << endl << endl;
    strncpy(szDefinerID, " ", 8);
    strncpy(szDefinerID, szDefiner, 8);
    szDefinerID[8] = 0;
    cout << "Table Space : " << szTBSpace;
    cout << " Definer : " << szDefinerID << endl;

    /* Retrieve The Record From The SYSCAT.TABLES Table */
    EXEC SQL SELECT TABNAME,
                    TBSPACE,
                    DEFINER
        INTO :szTableName,
             :szTBSpace,
```

```
            :szDefiner
        FROM SYSCAT.TABLES
        WHERE TABNAME = 'TEMP_EMP';

    cout << endl << "Contents of SYSCAT.TABLES" << endl << endl;
    strncpy(szDefinerID, " ", 8);
    strncpy(szDefinerID, szDefiner, 8);
    szDefinerID[8] = 0;
    cout << "Table Name : " << szTableName;
    cout << " Table Space : " << szTBSpace;
    cout << " Definer : " << szDefinerID << endl;

    /* Return The SQL Return Code */
    return(sqlca.sqlcode);
}

int main()
{
    /* Declare The Local Memory Variables */
    short int rc = EXIT_SUCCESS;            // Must Be Declared Here
                                            // For The SQL Precompiler

    /* Include The SQLCA Data Structure Variable */
    EXEC SQL INCLUDE SQLCA;

    /* Set Up A Simple SQL Error Handler */
    EXEC SQL WHENEVER SQLERROR GOTO EXIT;

    /* Create An Instance Of The Table Class */
    Table table;

    /* Connect To The SAMPLE Database */
    EXEC SQL CONNECT TO SAMPLE USER etpdd6z USING sanders;

    /* Create A Regular DMS Table Space */
    rc = table.createDMS_Space();

    /* Create A Temporary Table */
    rc = table.createTable();

    /* Commit The Transaction */
    EXEC SQL COMMIT;

    /* Now Retrieve The Records From The SYSCAT.TABLES Table */
    /* To Verify That The Table Was Created                  */
    rc = table.getSysInfo();

    /* Delete The Table Space And Table (Deleting The Table Space */
    /* Automatically Deletes The Table Defined In It)             */
    EXEC SQL DROP TABLESPACE EMP_SPACE;

    /* Commit The Transaction */
    EXEC SQL COMMIT;

 EXIT:
    /* If An Error Has Occurred, Display The SQL Return Code */
    if (sqlca.sqlcode != SQL_RC_OK)
        {
        cout << "SQL ERROR : " << sqlca.sqlcode << endl;
        rc = EXIT_FAILURE;
        }
```

```
    /* Issue A Rollback To Free All Locks */
    EXEC SQL ROLLBACK;

    /* Turn Off The SQL Error Handler */
    EXEC SQL WHENEVER SQLERROR CONTINUE;

    /* Disconnect From The SAMPLE Database */
    EXEC SQL DISCONNECT CURRENT;

    /* Return To The Operating System */
    return(rc);
}
```

ALTER TABLE

Purpose You can use the ALTER TABLE statement to modify existing database tables.

Syntax

```
EXEC SQL ALTER TABLE [table-name] ADD COLUMN [column-definition,...]
   <DATA CAPTURE [data-capture-type]>;

EXEC SQL ALTER TABLE [table-name] ADD [constraint-definition]
   <DATA CAPTURE [data-capture-type]>;

EXEC SQL ALTER TABLE [table-name] DROP PRIMARY KEY <DATA CAPTURE
   [data-capture-type]>;

EXEC SQL ALTER TABLE [table-name] DROP FOREIGN KEY [constraint-name]
   <DATA CAPTURE [data-capture-type]>;

EXEC SQL ALTER TABLE [table-name] DROP CONSTRAINT [constraint-name]
   <DATA CAPTURE [data-capture-type]>;

EXEC SQL ALTER TABLE [table-name] DROP CHECK [constraint-name]
   <DATA CAPTURE [data-capture-type]>;
```

Parameters

table-name Identifies the name of the table to be modified.

column-definition Identifies the column or columns to be part of the table. The syntax for a column definition is as follows:

```
[column-name] [data-type] <options | LOB-options>
```

where:

column-name Specifies the name of the column.

data-type Specifies the built-in data type to be used for data storage. The data type can be any of the following:

INTEGER	Large integer. INT is a synonym for INTEGER.
SMALLINT	Small integer.
DOUBLE	Floating-point number. DOUBLE PRECISION and FLOAT can be used as a synonyms for DOUBLE.
DECIMAL(*width, precision*)	Decimal number. The width integer specifies the total number of digits in the number (1 to 31). The precision integer specifies the number of digits to the right of the decimal place (0 to width). If width and pre-

	cision values are not specified, the default values 5, 0 are used. DEC, NUMERIC and NUM can be used as synonyms for DECIMAL.
CHARACTER(*size*) <FOR BIT DATA>	A fixed-length character string from 1 to 254 characters. If the size value is not specified, the default value 1 is used. If the FOR BIT DATA option is specified, the contents of the character string will be treated as binary data and code page conversions will not be performed. CHAR can be used as a synonym for CHARACTER.
VARCHAR(*size*) <FOR BIT DATA>	A varying-length character string of a maximum of 1 to 4000 characters. The FOR BIT DATA option has the same meaning as it does in the CHARACTER data type. CHARACTER VARYING or CHAR VARYING are synonyms for VARCHAR.
LONG VARCHAR <FOR BIT DATA>	A varying-length character string with a maximum size of 32,700 characters. The FOR BIT DATA option has the same meaning as it does in the CHARACTER data type.
GRAPHIC(*size*)	A fixed-length graphic string from 1 to 127 bytes. If the size value is not specified, the default value 1 is used.
VARGRAPHIC(*size*)	A varying-length graphic string of a maximum of 1 to 2000 bytes.
LONG VARGRAPHIC	A varying-length graphic string with a maximum size of 16,350 bytes.
DATE	A date.
TIME	A time.
TIMESTAMP	A time stamp.
BLOB (*size* <K | M | G>)	A binary large object string of a specified number of bytes. If the K option is used, the size is in kilobytes; if the M option is used, the size indicates megabytes; and if the G option is used, the size is in gigabytes. Any number of spaces (including no spaces) are allowed between the size value and the letter K, M, or G.
CLOB (*size* <K | M | G>)	A character large object string of a specified number of bytes. The K, M, and G option have the same meaning as described for the BLOB data type.

DBCLOB (*size* <K | M | G>) — A double-byte character large object string of a specified number of double-byte characters. The K, M, and G option have the same meaning as described for the BLOB data type.

distinct-type-name — Specifies the name of a distinct data type. If a distinct data type name is specified without a schema name, the schema name specified in the FUNCPATH option at the time the application was bound to the database will be used for static SQL statements. The schema name specified in the CURRENT FUNCTION PATH determines the schema name for the distinct data type name for dynamic SQL statements.

options Specifies additional options for a data column. The options value can be any of the following:

NOT NULL — Prevents the column from containing null values. If this option clause is not specified, the column can contain null values and its default value is either the null value or the value provided by the WITH DEFAULT option clause.

WITH DEFAULT — Stores a default value other than the null value in the column if a data value is not supplied. The default value is dependent on the data type of the column. Table 10-2 (refer to the CREATE TABLE statement) lists the default values used by DB2 for each column type.

LOB-options Specifies additional options for an LOB data column. The LOB options value can be any of the following:

LOGGED — Specifies that changes made to a BLOB, CLOB, or DBCLOB column are to be written to the active log file. The data in these columns will then be recoverable with database utilities (such as RESTORE DATABASE). This option is the default, but keep in mind that the total size of the log file for an entire database in DB2 version 2 is 1 gigabyte. Therefore, do not log large BLOB, CLOB, and/or DBCLOB columns.

NOT LOGGED — Specifies that changes made to a BLOB, CLOB, or DBCLOB column are not written to the active log file. This option has no effect on a commit or rollback operation.

COMPACT — Specifies that the values in a BLOB, CLOB, or DBCLOB column take up minimal disk space (free any extra disk pages in the last group used by the LOB value), rather than leave any left-over space at the end of the LOB storage area, which might facilitate subsequent append operations. Keep in mind that storing data this way might affect the performance of length-increasing operations (such as append) on the column.

NOT COMPACT — Specifies that the values in a BLOB, CLOB, or DBCLOB column are not compressed. This is the default option.

constraint-definition Specifies the type of constraint that every row inserted or updated in the table must conform to. The syntax for a constraint definition is determined by the constraint type being defined and can be any of the following:

```
CONSTRAINT [constraint-name] PRIMARY KEY [column-name,...]

CONSTRAINT [constraint-name] FOREIGN KEY (column-name,...) REFERENCES
   [table-name] <(column-name,...)> ON DELETE [delete-option]
   ON UPDATE [update-action]

CONSTRAINT [constraint-name] CHECK (check-condition)
```

where:

constraint-name Specifies the name of the constraint being created.

column-name Specifies one or more columns to be part of the primary key, foreign key, or check constraint. Each specified column name must be a valid column in the table.

table-name Specifies the base table that contains a primary key with the same number of comparable columns as the foreign key being created.

delete-option Specifies the action to be taken on the dependent tables when a row in the parent table is deleted. The following delete options are available:

- NO ACTION Indicates that no action is taken on dependent tables when a row is deleted. This is the default action.
- RESTRICT Indicates that no action is taken on dependent tables when a row is deleted.
- CASCADE Indicates that the delete operation is copied to all dependent tables.
- SET NULL Indicates that each nullable column of the foreign key of each dependent value is set to NULL. Do not specify this delete option unless some column of the foreign key allows null values.

update-option Specifies the action to be taken on the dependent tables when a row in the parent table is updated. The following update options are available:

- NO ACTION Indicates that no action is taken on dependent tables when a row is updated. This option is specified by default and is enforced after all other referential constraints are validated.
- RESTRICT Indicates that no action is taken on dependent tables when a row is updated. If this option is specified, it is enforced before all other constraints, including constraints with modifying rules such as CASCADE or SET NULL.

check-condition Specifies a search condition that must evaluate to TRUE before data can be added to the table.

data-capture-type Indicates whether extra information for data propagation (copying) is written to the active log file. The data capture type can be one of the following:

- NONE Indicates that no extra information is written to the log file. This is the default.
- CHANGES Indicates that extra information about SQL changes to the table are written to the log file. This option is required if this table is copied with a propagation manager such as the Data Propagator Relational (DPropR) program, an IBM application that copies data between DB2 databases on platforms that support distributed relational database architecture (DRDA) connectivity when predefined criteria is met.

constraint-name Specifies the name of the FOREIGN KEY, CONSTRAINT, or CHECK CONSTRAINT being removed from the table (in the DROP versions of the ALTER TABLE statement).

Description The ALTER TABLE statement modifies existing database tables. You can use it to:

- Add one or more columns to the table.
- Add or drop a primary key definition
- Add or drop a foreign key definition
- Add or drop a check constraint definition
- Change the data capture option

Comments

- The specified table name must refer to a table that has a description in the system catalog tables. The specified table name cannot be the name of a system catalog table or an existing view.
- Do not qualify column names nor use the same name for more than one column in the same table.
- A table can contain up to 255 columns, but the sum of the byte counts of all columns in a table must not be greater than 4005 bytes.
- If a column in the table is defined as a user-defined distinct data type, then the data type of the column is the distinct data type and the size and precision of the column are the size and precision of the source type referenced by the user-defined distinct data type.
- If a column defined as a distinct data type is also a foreign key of a referential constraint, then the data type of the corresponding column of the primary key must be the same distinct data type.
- The table name specified in the REFERENCES clause of a foreign key must identify a base table described in the system catalog. The table name must not identify a system catalog table.
- The specified foreign key must have the same number of columns as the primary key of the referenced table. Also, the data type of each column of the foreign key must be comparable to its corresponding column in the primary key it references. (In this situation, datetime columns are not compatible with string columns.)
- The referential constraint specified by a FOREIGN KEY clause defines a relationship in which the table being referenced is the parent and the table for which the foreign key is defined is the dependent. Refer to the system catalog for a description of this referential constraint relationship.
- The PRIMARY KEY clause must not be specified more than once, and the specified columns in the key must be defined as NOT NULL. Also, each column name specified must identify a column of the table, and the same column can be identified only once.
- The number of identified columns in a primary or a foreign key must not exceed 16, and the sum of their length attributes must not exceed 255 bytes. No BLOB, CLOB, DBCLOB, LONG VARCHAR, or LONG VARGRAPHIC column can be used as part of a primary key (even if the length attribute of the column is small enough to fit within the 255-byte limit).
- A unique primary index is automatically created for the columns (ascending order for each column) specified in the table definition when a new table is created. The name of this index is "SYSIBM.SQL," followed by a character timestamp (*yymmddhhmmssxxx*) corresponding to the time the index is created.
- If a foreign key is specified, all packages with a delete dependency on the parent table or an update dependency on at least one column in the primary key are marked invalid.
- The description of a table is recorded in the system catalog tables along with its primary key and default index.
- A check constraint must not contain any of the following:
  –Subqueries
  –Column functions

–Variant user-defined functions
–User-defined functions using the EXTERNAL ACTION option
–User-defined functions using the SCRATCHPAD option
–Host variables
–Parameter markers
–Special registers
–An alias

- If a check constraint is specified as part of a column definition, then each column referenced must refer to a column previously defined in the CREATE TABLE statement.
- Check constraints are not checked for inconsistencies, duplicate conditions, or equivalent conditions. Therefore, you can define contradictory or redundant check constraints that produce errors at application runtime.
- A check-constraint condition of IS NOT NULL can be specified for a column, but it is best to enforce nullability by using the NOT NULL attribute of a column instead of a check constraint.
- ADD column clauses are processed before any other clause. All other clauses are processed in the order they are specified.
- Columns added to a table with the ALTER TABLE statement are not automatically added to existing views that reference the table.
- Changes made to primary or foreign keys can have several different effects on packages and other foreign keys. If a primary key is added, there is no effect on packages, foreign keys, or existing primary keys. If a primary key is dropped, all dependent foreign keys will be dropped and further action will be taken for each dependent foreign key as specified in the next item. If a foreign key is added or dropped, all packages with an insert or update dependency on the object table and all packages with a delete or update dependency on at least one column in the foreign key will be invalidated.
- Adding a check constraint or a referential constraint to a table that already exists that is not in check-pending state (refer to the SET CONSTRAINTS statement for more information) will cause the constraint to be immediately evaluated against the existing rows to enforce the constraint. However, if a table is in the check-pending state, adding a check or referential constraint will not immediately enforce the constraint. Instead, the corresponding constraint type flags used by the check-pending operation will be updated accordingly. The SET CONSTRAINTS statement needs to be issued to enforce the new constraint.
- Adding or dropping a check constraint results in invalidation of all packages with an insert dependency on the specified table or update dependency on at least one of the columns specified in the constraint.

Authorization Only users with either system administrator (SYSADM) authority, database administrator (DBADM) authority, ALTERTAB authority for the specified table, or CONTROL authority for the specified table are allowed to execute the ADD version of this statement.

Only users with either SYSADM authority, DBADM authority, REFERENCES authority for the specified table, or CONTROL authority for the specified table are allowed to execute the DROP version of this statement.

See Also CREATE TABLE, DROP

Examples The following C program illustrates how the ALTER TABLE statement can be used to add a column to an existing table:

```
#include <stdio.h>
#include <stdlib.h>
```

```
#include <sql.h>
int main()
{
    /* Include The SQLCA Data Structure Variable */
    EXEC SQL INCLUDE SQLCA;

    /* Set Up A Simple SQL Error Handler */
    EXEC SQL WHENEVER SQLERROR GOTO EXIT;

    /* Declare The Local Memory Variables */
    int   rc = EXIT_SUCCESS;

    /* Declare The SQL Host Memory Variables */
    EXEC SQL BEGIN DECLARE SECTION;
        char      szColName[18];
    EXEC SQL END DECLARE SECTION;

    /* Connect To The SAMPLE Database */
    EXEC SQL CONNECT TO SAMPLE USER etpdd6z USING sanders;

    /* Create A Temporary Employee Table */
    EXEC SQL CREATE TABLE TEMP_EMP
            (EMPID       INTEGER       NOT NULL,
             LASTNAME    CHAR(18)      NOT NULL,
             FIRSTNAME   CHAR(18)      NOT NULL,
             DEPTNO      CHAR(3),
        PRIMARY KEY(EMPID));

    /* Print A Message Telling That The Table Was Created */
    printf("The Table TEMP_EMP has been created.\n");

    /* Commit The Transaction */
    EXEC SQL COMMIT;

    /* Now Retrieve The Records From The SYSCAT.COLUMNS Table */
    /* To Verify That The Table Was Created                   */

    /* Declare The SYS_COLUMNS Table Cursor */
    EXEC SQL DECLARE SYS_COLUMNS CURSOR FOR
        SELECT COLNAME
        FROM SYSCAT.COLUMNS
        WHERE TABNAME = 'TEMP_EMP';

    /* Open The Cursor */
    EXEC SQL OPEN SYS_COLUMNS;

    /* If The Cursor Was Successfully Opened, Fetch The Records Into */
    /* Host Variables                                                */
    printf("\nContents of SYSCAT.COLUMNS\n\n");
    while (sqlca.sqlcode == SQL_RC_OK)
        {
        EXEC SQL FETCH SYS_COLUMNS
            INTO :szColName;

        /* If The FETCH Was Successful, Print The Data */
        if (sqlca.sqlcode == SQL_RC_OK)
            printf("Column Name : %18s\n", szColName);
        }

    /* Close The Cursor */
    EXEC SQL CLOSE SYS_COLUMNS;
```

```
    /* Add A Column To The Temporary Employee Table */
    EXEC SQL ALTER TABLE TEMP_EMP
        ADD SALARY    DECIMAL(9,2);

    /* Open The Cursor */
    EXEC SQL OPEN SYS_COLUMNS;

    /* Now Retrieve The Records From The SYSCAT.COLUMNS Table */
    /* Again To Verify That The Table Was Modified            */

    /* If The Cursor Was Successfully Opened, Fetch The Records Into */
    /* Host Variables                                                */
    printf("\nContents of SYSCAT.COLUMNS after ALTER statement.\n\n");
    while (sqlca.sqlcode == SQL_RC_OK)
        {
        EXEC SQL FETCH SYS_COLUMNS
            INTO :szColName;

        /* If The FETCH Was Successful, Print The Data */
        if (sqlca.sqlcode == SQL_RC_OK)
            printf("Column Name : %18s\n", szColName);
        }

    /* Close The Cursor */
    EXEC SQL CLOSE SYS_COLUMNS;

    /* Delete The Table Table */
    EXEC SQL DROP TABLE TEMP_EMP;

    /* Commit The Transaction */
    EXEC SQL COMMIT;

EXIT:
    /* If An Error Has Occurred, Display The SQL Return Code */
    if (sqlca.sqlcode != SQL_RC_OK)
        {
        printf("SQL ERROR : %ld\n", sqlca.sqlcode);
        rc = EXIT_FAILURE;
        }

    /* Turn Off The SQL Error Handler */
    EXEC SQL WHENEVER SQLERROR CONTINUE;

    /* Disconnect From The SAMPLE Database */
    EXEC SQL DISCONNECT CURRENT;

    /* Return To The Operating System */
    return(rc);
}
```

The following C++ program illustrates how the ALTER TABLE statement is used by class methods to add a column to an existing table:

```
#include <iostream.h>
#include <stdlib.h>
#include <string.h>
#include <sql.h>

/* Define The Table Class */
class Table
{
    private:
```

```
        /* Include The SQLCA Data Structure Variable */
        EXEC SQL INCLUDE SQLCA;

        /* Declare The Local Memory Variables */
        char  szDefinerID[9];

        /* Declare The SQL Host Memory Variables */
        EXEC SQL BEGIN DECLARE SECTION;
            char      szColName[18];
        EXEC SQL END DECLARE SECTION;

    /* Declare The Public Member Function Prototypes */
    public:
        short int createTable();
        short int alterTable();
        short int getSysInfo();
} ;

/* Define The createTable() Member Function */
short int Table::createTable(void)
{
    /* Create A Temporary Table */
    EXEC SQL CREATE TABLE TEMP_EMP
            (EMPID       INTEGER      NOT NULL,
             LASTNAME    CHAR(18)     NOT NULL,
             FIRSTNAME   CHAR(18)     NOT NULL,
             DEPTNO      CHAR(3),
        PRIMARY KEY(EMPID));

    /* Print A Message Telling That The Table Was Created */
    if (sqlca.sqlcode == SQL_RC_OK)
        cout << "The Table TEMP_EMP has been created." << endl;

    /* Return The SQL Return Code */
    return(sqlca.sqlcode);
}

/* Define The alterTable() Member Function */
short int Table::alterTable(void)
{
    /* Add A Column To The Temporary Employee Table */
    EXEC SQL ALTER TABLE TEMP_EMP
        ADD SALARY    DECIMAL(9,2);

    /* Return The SQL Return Code */
    return(sqlca.sqlcode);
}

/* Define The getSysInfo() Member Function */
short int Table::getSysInfo(void)
{
    /* Declare The SYS_COLUMNS Table Cursor */
    EXEC SQL DECLARE SYS_COLUMNS CURSOR FOR
        SELECT COLNAME
        FROM SYSCAT.COLUMNS
        WHERE TABNAME = 'TEMP_EMP';

    /* Open The Cursor */
    EXEC SQL OPEN SYS_COLUMNS;
    /* If The Cursor Was Successfully Opened, Fetch The Records Into */
    /* Host Variables                                                */
    cout << endl << "Contents of SYSCAT.COLUMNS" << endl << endl;
```

```
    while (sqlca.sqlcode == SQL_RC_OK)
        {
        EXEC SQL FETCH SYS_COLUMNS
            INTO :szColName;

        /* If The FETCH Was Successful, Print The Data */
        if (sqlca.sqlcode == SQL_RC_OK)
            {
            cout << "Column Name : " ;
            cout.width(18);
            cout << szColName << endl;
            }
        }

    /* Close The Cursor */
    EXEC SQL CLOSE SYS_COLUMNS;

    /* Return The SQL Return Code */
    return(sqlca.sqlcode);
}

int main()
{
    /* Declare The Local Memory Variables */
    short int rc = EXIT_SUCCESS;            // Must Be Declared Here
                                            // For The SQL Precompiler

    /* Include The SQLCA Data Structure Variable */
    EXEC SQL INCLUDE SQLCA;

    /* Set Up A Simple SQL Error Handler */
    EXEC SQL WHENEVER SQLERROR GOTO EXIT;

    /* Create An Instance Of The Table Class */
    Table table;

    /* Connect To The SAMPLE Database */
    EXEC SQL CONNECT TO SAMPLE USER etpdd6z USING sanders;

    /* Create A Temporary Table */
    rc = table.createTable();

    /* Commit The Transaction */
    EXEC SQL COMMIT;

    /* Now Retrieve The Records From The SYSCAT.TABLES Table */
    /* To Verify That The Table Was Created                  */
    rc = table.getSysInfo();

    /* Add A Column To The Table */
    rc = table.alterTable();

    /* Now Retrieve The Records From The SYSCAT.TABLES Table */
    /* Again To Verify That The Column Was Added             */
    rc = table.getSysInfo();

    /* Delete The Table */
    EXEC SQL DROP TABLE TEMP_EMP;
    /* Commit The Transaction */
    EXEC SQL COMMIT;
```

```
EXIT:
    /* If An Error Has Occurred, Display The SQL Return Code */
    if (sqlca.sqlcode != SQL_RC_OK)
        {
        cout << "SQL ERROR : " << sqlca.sqlcode << endl;
        rc = EXIT_FAILURE;
        }

    /* Issue A Rollback To Free All Locks */
    EXEC SQL ROLLBACK;

    /* Turn Off The SQL Error Handler */
    EXEC SQL WHENEVER SQLERROR CONTINUE;

    /* Disconnect From The SAMPLE Database */
    EXEC SQL DISCONNECT CURRENT;

    /* Return To The Operating System */
    return(rc);
}
```

CREATE INDEX

Purpose The CREATE INDEX statement creates an index for a database table.

Syntax

```
EXEC SQL CREATE <UNIQUE> INDEX [index-name] ON [table-name] (column-name
   <ASC | DESC>,...);
```

Parameters

index-name Identifies the name of the index to be created.

table-name Identifies the name of the table for which the index is to be created.

column-name Identifies one or more columns to be part of the index key. The order in which the index entries appear for each column is determined by one of the following options:

- ASC This indicates that the column's index entries are placed in ascending order.
- DESC This indicates that the column's index entries are placed in descending order.

If no order option is specified, the column's index entries are placed in ascending order.

Description The CREATE INDEX statement allows you to create one or more indexes for an existing database table. Indexes can be created only for base tables (not views) described in the SYSCAT.TABLES system catalog table. If the specified table does not contain data, a description of the index will be created and index entries will be created as data is inserted into the table. If the specified table already contains data, appropriate index entries will automatically be generated for the data when the index is created, and new index entries will be created each time data is inserted into the table.

When a unique index is created for a table (the UNIQUE option is specified with the CREATE INDEX statement), the specified table cannot have two or more rows with the same value in the index key (columns). This unique constraint is enforced each time new rows are added to the specified table and each time an existing row in the specified table is updated. The definitions for all indexes are stored in the SYSCAT.INDEXES system catalog table.

Comments

- If no qualifier (schema) is provided with the index name, the authorization ID of the current user will be used as the qualifier when the index is created. If a qualifier is provided with the index name, it cannot be SYSIBM, SYSCAT, or SYSSTAT. In other words, indexes cannot be created for system catalog tables.
- The index name cannot be a name already used by another index.
- The CREATE INDEX statement will fail if the specified index matches an existing unique index that references the same columns, in the same column order, with the same ascending and descending specifications.
- Whenever the CREATE INDEX statement is executed with the UNIQUE option, constraints are checked to ensure that the specified table specified does not contain rows with duplicate key values. If duplicate key values exist in the table, the index will not be created.
- Each specified column name must be an unqualified name that identifies a column of the specified base table. Up to 16 columns can be specified in an index, but no column name can be repeated.
- The sum of the length attributes of the specified columns must not exceed 255 bytes. This number can be reduced by system overhead, which varies according to the data type of the column and whether or not it can contain null values. No LONG VARCHAR, LONG VARGRAPHIC, BLOB, CLOB, or DBCLOB column can be used as part of an index (even if its length attribute is small enough to fit within the 255-byte limit).
- Once an index is created for a table, you should run the RUNSTATS utility on that table. The RUNSTATS utility will update the statistics that exist for all database tables, columns, and indexes. These statistics determine the optimal access path to use when a package is created for embedded SQL statements. By updating these statistics, embedded SQL statements that refer to the table can take advantage of the new index.

Authorization

Only users with either system administrator (SYSADM) authority, database administrator (DBADM) authority, CONTROL authority for the specified table, or INDEX authority for the specified table are allowed to execute this statement.

See Also

CREATE TABLE, DROP

Examples

The following C program illustrates how the CREATE INDEX statement can be used to create an index for a table:

```
#include <stdio.h>
#include <stdlib.h>
#include <string.h>
#include <sql.h>

int main()
{
    /* Include The SQLCA Data Structure Variable */
    EXEC SQL INCLUDE SQLCA;

    /* Set Up A Simple SQL Error Handler */
    EXEC SQL WHENEVER SQLERROR GOTO EXIT;

    /* Declare The Local Memory Variables */
    int   rc = EXIT_SUCCESS;
    char  szDefinerID[9];
```

```
    /* Declare The SQL Host Memory Variables */
    EXEC SQL BEGIN DECLARE SECTION;
        char        szIndexName[18];
        char        szTableName[18];
        char        szDefiner[8];
    EXEC SQL END DECLARE SECTION;

    /* Connect To The SAMPLE Database */
    EXEC SQL CONNECT TO SAMPLE USER etpdd6z USING sanders;

    /* Create A Temporary Project Table */
    EXEC SQL CREATE TABLE TEMP_PROJ
        (PROJNO        INTEGER       NOT NULL,
         PROJNAME      VARCHAR(24)   NOT NULL,
         DEPTNO        CHAR(3),
         STARTDATE     DATE,
         ENDDATE       DATE);

    /* Print A Message Telling That The Table Was Created */
    printf("The Table TEMP_PROJ has been created.\n");

    /* Create An Index For The Temporary Project Table */
    EXEC SQL CREATE INDEX PROJ_BY_DEPT
         ON TEMP_PROJ (PROJNO, DEPTNO);

    /* Print A Message Telling That The Index Was Created */
    printf("Index PROJ_BY_DEPT has been created for the TEMP_PROJ table.\n");

    /* Commit The Transaction */
    EXEC SQL COMMIT;

    /* Now Retrieve The Records From The SYSCAT.INDEXES */
    /* Table To Verify That The Index Was Created       */
    EXEC SQL SELECT INDNAME,
                    TABNAME,
                    DEFINER
        INTO :szIndexName,
             :szTableName,
             :szDefiner
        FROM SYSCAT.INDEXES
        WHERE TABNAME = 'TEMP_PROJ';

    printf("\nContents of SYSCAT.INDEXES\n\n");
    strncpy(szDefinerID, " ", 8);
    strncpy(szDefinerID, szDefiner, 8);
    szDefinerID[8] = 0;
    printf("Index Name : %s\t Table Name : %s\t Definer: %s\n",
           szIndexName, szTableName, szDefinerID);

    /* Delete The Table And The Index */
    EXEC SQL DROP INDEX PROJ_BY_DEPT;
    EXEC SQL DROP TABLE TEMP_PROJ;

    /* Commit The Transaction */
    EXEC SQL COMMIT;

EXIT:
    /* If An Error Has Occurred, Display The SQL Return Code */
    if (sqlca.sqlcode != SQL_RC_OK)
        {
        printf("SQL ERROR : %ld\n", sqlca.sqlcode);
```

```
        rc = EXIT_FAILURE;
        }

    /* Turn Off The SQL Error Handler */
    EXEC SQL WHENEVER SQLERROR CONTINUE;

    /* Disconnect From The SAMPLE Database */
    EXEC SQL DISCONNECT CURRENT;

    /* Return To The Operating System */
    return(rc);
}
```

The following C++ program illustrates how the CREATE INDEX statement is used by class methods to create an index for a table:

```
#include <iostream.h>
#include <stdlib.h>
#include <string.h>
#include <sql.h>

/* Define The Table Class */
class Table
{
    private:

        /* Include The SQLCA Data Structure Variable */
        EXEC SQL INCLUDE SQLCA;

        /* Declare The Local Memory Variables */
        char  szDefinerID[9];

        /* Declare The SQL Host Memory Variables */
        EXEC SQL BEGIN DECLARE SECTION;
            char      szIndexName[18];
            char      szTableName[18];
            char      szDefiner[8];
        EXEC SQL END DECLARE SECTION;

    /* Declare The Public Member Function Prototypes */
    public:
        short int createTable();
        short int createIndex();
        short int getSysInfo();
} ;

/* Define The createTable() Member Function */
short int Table::createTable(void)
{
    /* Create A Temporary Project Table */
    EXEC SQL CREATE TABLE TEMP_PROJ
        (PROJNO       INTEGER       NOT NULL,
         PROJNAME     VARCHAR(24)   NOT NULL,
         DEPTNO       CHAR(3),
         STARTDATE    DATE,
         ENDDATE      DATE);

    /* Print A Message Telling That The Table Was Created */
    if (sqlca.sqlcode == SQL_RC_OK)
        cout << "The Table TEMP_PROJ has been created." << endl;
```

```
    /* Return The SQL Return Code */
    return(sqlca.sqlcode);
}

/* Define The createIndex() Member Function */
short int Table::createIndex(void)
{
    /* Create An Index For The Temporary Project Table */
    EXEC SQL CREATE INDEX PROJ_BY_DEPT
         ON TEMP_PROJ (PROJNO, DEPTNO);

    /* Print A Message Telling That The Index Was Created */
    if (sqlca.sqlcode == SQL_RC_OK)
        {
        cout << "Index PROJ_BY_DEPT has been created for the ";
        cout << "TEMP_PROJ table." << endl;
        }

    /* Return The SQL Return Code */
    return(sqlca.sqlcode);
}

/* Define The getSysInfo() Member Function */
short int Table::getSysInfo(void)
{
    /* Retrieve The Record From The SYSCAT.INDEXES */
    /* Table To Verify That The Index Was Created  */
    EXEC SQL SELECT INDNAME,
                    TABNAME,
                    DEFINER
        INTO :szIndexName,
             :szTableName,
             :szDefiner
        FROM SYSCAT.INDEXES
        WHERE TABNAME = 'TEMP_PROJ';

    cout << endl << "Contents of SYSCAT.INDEXES" << endl << endl;
    strncpy(szDefinerID, " ", 8);
    strncpy(szDefinerID, szDefiner, 8);
    szDefinerID[8] = 0;
    cout << "Index Name : " << szIndexName << " Table Name : ";
    cout << szTableName << " Definer : " << szDefinerID << endl;

    /* Return The SQL Return Code */
    return(sqlca.sqlcode);
}

int main()
{
    /* Declare The Local Memory Variables */
    short int rc = EXIT_SUCCESS;            // Must Be Declared Here
                                            // For The SQL Precompiler

    /* Include The SQLCA Data Structure Variable */
    EXEC SQL INCLUDE SQLCA;

    /* Set Up A Simple SQL Error Handler */
    EXEC SQL WHENEVER SQLERROR GOTO EXIT;

    /* Create An Instance Of The Table Class */
    Table table;
```

```
    /* Connect To The SAMPLE Database */
    EXEC SQL CONNECT TO SAMPLE USER etpdd6z USING sanders;

    /* Create A Temporary Table */
    rc = table.createTable();

    /* Create An Index For The Table */
    rc = table.createIndex();

    /* Commit The Transaction */
    EXEC SQL COMMIT;

    /* Now Retrieve The Records From The SYSCAT.INDEXES Table */
    /* To Verify That The Index Was Created                   */
    rc = table.getSysInfo();

    /* Delete The Table And The Index */
    EXEC SQL DROP INDEX PROJ_BY_DEPT;
    EXEC SQL DROP TABLE TEMP_PROJ;

    /* Commit The Transaction */
    EXEC SQL COMMIT;

EXIT:
    /* If An Error Has Occurred, Display The SQL Return Code */
    if (sqlca.sqlcode != SQL_RC_OK)
        {
        cout << "SQL ERROR : " << sqlca.sqlcode << endl;
        rc = EXIT_FAILURE;
        }

    /* Issue A Rollback To Free All Locks */
    EXEC SQL ROLLBACK;

    /* Turn Off The SQL Error Handler */
    EXEC SQL WHENEVER SQLERROR CONTINUE;

    /* Disconnect From The SAMPLE Database */
    EXEC SQL DISCONNECT CURRENT;

    /* Return To The Operating System */
    return(rc);
}
```

CREATE VIEW

Purpose The CREATE VIEW statement allows you to create a view for one or more database tables and/or views.

Syntax

```
EXEC SQL CREATE VIEW [view-name] <(column-name,...)> AS
   <WITH common-table-expression,...> [fullselect] <WITH [constraint-type]
   CHECK OPTION>;
```

Parameters

view-name Identifies the name of the view to be created.

column-name Identifies the column or columns to be part of the view.

common-table-expression Defines a common table expression that can be referenced by name in the FROM clause of the fullselect statement following it.

fullselect Defines the full form of the SELECT statement used to construct the view. This SELECT statement cannot contain references to host variables or parameter markers.

constraint-type Specifies the type of constraint to which every row inserted or updated through the view must conform. The constraint type can be any of the following:

CASCADED This indicates that the view will inherit the search conditions as constraints from any updatable view on which it is dependent. Likewise, any views that reference the view are dependent on the view's constraints.

LOCAL This indicates that any views that reference the view are dependent on the view's search condition as a constraint for an update or insert.

If no option is specified, the cascaded constraint type will be used.

Description

The CREATE VIEW statement can create a view for one or more database tables and/or views. A view provides an alternate way of looking at the data in one or more base tables. You create views by specifying a SELECT statement that is executed each time the view is referenced in an SQL statement. Therefore, views have columns and rows, and can be processed just like base tables. Whether a view can be used in an insert, update, or delete operation depends on its definition (as described in the beginning of the chapter).

Comments

- If no qualifier (schema) is provided with the view name, the authorization ID of the current user will be used as the qualifier when the view is created. If a qualifier is provided with the view name, it cannot be "SYSIBM", "SYSCAT", or "SYSSTAT." In other words, views cannot be created for system catalog tables.
- The view name cannot be a name already being used by another table, alias, or view.
- If the name of an inoperative view is specified with the CREATE VIEW statement, the new view will replace the inoperative view.
- If a list of column names is specified, it must contain one name for each column in the result table of the SELECT statement. Each column-name must be unique and unqualified. If a list of column names is not specified, the columns of the view inherit the names of the columns of the result table of the SELECT statement.
- If the result table of the SELECT statement will contain duplicate column names (which can occur in a JOIN) or an unnamed column (a column derived from a constant, function, expression, or set operation not named with the AS clause of the select list), you must specify a list of column names.
- You must not specify WITH CHECK OPTION if the view being created is read-only.
- Columns in a view inherit the NOT NULL WITH DEFAULT attribute from the base table or view they reference, except when the columns are derived from an expression.
- When a row is inserted or updated into the updatable view, it is checked against the constraints (primary key, referential integrity, and check) if any are defined on the base table.
- If the WITH CHECK OPTION is specified for an updatable view that does not allow inserts, then only rows being updated will be checked for constraints.
- If the WITH CHECK OPTION is omitted, some constraint checking might still occur during insert or update operations if the view is directly or indirectly dependent on another view created with WITH CHECK OPTION. Likewise, be-

cause the definition of the original view is not used as a constraint, rows might be inserted or updated through the new view that do not conform to the definition of the original view.

- Columns in a view inherit the NOT NULL WITH DEFAULT attribute from its base table or view columns whenever these columns are not derived from an expression.
- When a row is inserted into or updated in an updatable view, the data in that row is checked against any primary key constraints, referential integrity constraints, and check constraints that exist for the view's base table.

Authorization Only users with either system administrator (SYSADM) authority, database administrator (DBADM) authority, CONTROL authority for the specified table or view, or SELECT authority for the specified table or view are allowed to execute this statement.

See Also CREATE TABLE, DROP

Examples The following C program illustrates how to use the CREATE VIEW statement to create a view that references one base table:

```
#include <stdio.h>
#include <stdlib.h>
#include <string.h>
#include <sql.h>

int main()
{
    /* Include The SQLCA Data Structure Variable */
    EXEC SQL INCLUDE SQLCA;

    /* Set Up A Simple SQL Error Handler */
    EXEC SQL WHENEVER SQLERROR GOTO EXIT;

    /* Declare The Local Memory Variables */
    int    rc = EXIT_SUCCESS;
    char   szDefinerID[9];

    /* Declare The SQL Host Memory Variables */
    EXEC SQL BEGIN DECLARE SECTION;
        char        szViewName[18];
        char        szDefiner[8];
    EXEC SQL END DECLARE SECTION;

    /* Connect To The SAMPLE Database */
    EXEC SQL CONNECT TO SAMPLE USER etpdd6z USING sanders;

    /* Create A Temporary Project Table */
    EXEC SQL CREATE TABLE TEMP_PROJ
        (PROJNO       INTEGER       NOT NULL,
         PROJNAME     VARCHAR(24)   NOT NULL,
         DEPTNO       CHAR(3),
         STARTDATE    DATE,
         ENDDATE      DATE);

    /* Print A Message Telling That The Table Was Created */
    printf("The Table TEMP_PROJ has been created.\n");

    /* Create A View For The Temporary Project Table */
    EXEC SQL CREATE VIEW PROJECT_ID AS
```

```
          SELECT PROJNO,
                 PROJNAME
          FROM TEMP_PROJ;

     /* Print A Message Telling That The View Was Created */
     printf("View PROJECT_ID has been created for the TEMP_PROJ table.\n");

     /* Commit The Transaction */
     EXEC SQL COMMIT;

     /* Now Retrieve The Records From The SYSCAT.VIEWS */
     /* Table To Verify That The View Was Created      */
     EXEC SQL SELECT VIEWNAME,
                     DEFINER
         INTO :szViewName,
              :szDefiner
         FROM SYSCAT.VIEWS
         WHERE VIEWNAME = 'PROJECT_ID';

     printf("\nContents of SYSCAT.VIEWS\n\n");
     strncpy(szDefinerID, " ", 8);
     strncpy(szDefinerID, szDefiner, 8);
     szDefinerID[8] = 0;
     printf("View Name : %s\t Definer: %s\n",
             szViewName, szDefinerID);

     /* Delete The Table And The View */
     EXEC SQL DROP VIEW PROJECT_ID;
     EXEC SQL DROP TABLE TEMP_PROJ;

     /* Commit The Transaction */
     EXEC SQL COMMIT;

EXIT:
     /* If An Error Has Occurred, Display The SQL Return Code */
     if (sqlca.sqlcode != SQL_RC_OK)
         {
         printf("SQL ERROR : %ld\n", sqlca.sqlcode);
         rc = EXIT_FAILURE;
         }

     /* Turn Off The SQL Error Handler */
     EXEC SQL WHENEVER SQLERROR CONTINUE;

     /* Disconnect From The SAMPLE Database */
     EXEC SQL DISCONNECT CURRENT;

     /* Return To The Operating System */
     return(rc);
}
```

The following C++ program illustrates how the CREATE VIEW statement is used by class methods to create a view that references one base table:

```
#include <iostream.h>
#include <stdlib.h>
#include <string.h>
#include <sql.h>

/* Define The Table Class */
class Table
```

```
{
    private:

       /* Include The SQLCA Data Structure Variable */
       EXEC SQL INCLUDE SQLCA;

       /* Declare The Local Memory Variables */
       char  szDefinerID[9];

       /* Declare The SQL Host Memory Variables */
       EXEC SQL BEGIN DECLARE SECTION;
          char       szViewName[18];
          char       szDefiner[8];
       EXEC SQL END DECLARE SECTION;

    /* Declare The Public Member Function Prototypes */
    public:
       short int createTable();
       short int createView();
       short int getSysInfo();
} ;

/* Define The createTable() Member Function */
short int Table::createTable(void)
{
    /* Create A Temporary Project Table */
    EXEC SQL CREATE TABLE TEMP_PROJ
        (PROJNO       INTEGER       NOT NULL,
         PROJNAME     VARCHAR(24)   NOT NULL,
         DEPTNO       CHAR(3),
         STARTDATE    DATE,
         ENDDATE      DATE);

    /* Print A Message Telling That The Table Was Created */
    if (sqlca.sqlcode == SQL_RC_OK)
        cout << "The Table TEMP_PROJ has been created." << endl;

    /* Return The SQL Return Code */
    return(sqlca.sqlcode);
}

/* Define The createView() Member Function */
short int Table::createView(void)
{
    /* Create A View For The Temporary Project Table */
    EXEC SQL CREATE VIEW PROJECT_ID AS
         SELECT PROJNO,
                PROJNAME
         FROM TEMP_PROJ;

    /* Print A Message Telling That The View Was Created */
    if (sqlca.sqlcode == SQL_RC_OK)
        {
        cout << "View PROJECT_ID has been created for the ";
        cout << "TEMP_PROJ table." << endl;
        }

    /* Return The SQL Return Code */
    return(sqlca.sqlcode);
}
```

```
/* Define The getSysInfo() Member Function */
short int Table::getSysInfo(void)
{
    /* Retrieve The Records From The SYSCAT.VIEWS */
    /* Table To Verify That The View Was Created  */
    EXEC SQL SELECT VIEWNAME,
                    DEFINER
        INTO :szViewName,
             :szDefiner
        FROM SYSCAT.VIEWS
        WHERE VIEWNAME = 'PROJECT_ID';

    cout << endl << "Contents of SYSCAT.VIEWS" << endl << endl;
    strncpy(szDefinerID, " ", 8);
    strncpy(szDefinerID, szDefiner, 8);
    szDefinerID[8] = 0;

    cout << "View Name : " << szViewName << " Definer : ";
    cout << szDefinerID << endl;

    /* Return The SQL Return Code */
    return(sqlca.sqlcode);
}

int main()
{
    /* Declare The Local Memory Variables */
    short int rc = EXIT_SUCCESS;             // Must Be Declared Here
                                             // For The SQL Precompiler

    /* Include The SQLCA Data Structure Variable */
    EXEC SQL INCLUDE SQLCA;

    /* Set Up A Simple SQL Error Handler */
    EXEC SQL WHENEVER SQLERROR GOTO EXIT;

    /* Create An Instance Of The Table Class */
    Table table;

    /* Connect To The SAMPLE Database */
    EXEC SQL CONNECT TO SAMPLE USER etpdd6z USING sanders;

    /* Create A Temporary Table */
    rc = table.createTable();

    /* Create A View */
    rc = table.createView();

    /* Commit The Transaction */
    EXEC SQL COMMIT;

    /* Now Retrieve The Records From The SYSCAT.VIEWS Table */
    /* To Verify That The View Was Created                  */
    rc = table.getSysInfo();

    /* Delete The Table And The View */
    EXEC SQL DROP VIEW PROJECT_ID;
    EXEC SQL DROP TABLE TEMP_PROJ;

    /* Commit The Transaction */
    EXEC SQL COMMIT;
```

```
EXIT:
    /* If An Error Has Occurred, Display The SQL Return Code */
    if (sqlca.sqlcode != SQL_RC_OK)
        {
        cout << "SQL ERROR : " << sqlca.sqlcode << endl;
        rc = EXIT_FAILURE;
        }

    /* Issue A Rollback To Free All Locks */
    EXEC SQL ROLLBACK;

    /* Turn Off The SQL Error Handler */
    EXEC SQL WHENEVER SQLERROR CONTINUE;

    /* Disconnect From The SAMPLE Database */
    EXEC SQL DISCONNECT CURRENT;

    /* Return To The Operating System */
    return(rc);
}
```

CREATE ALIAS

Purpose The CREATE ALIAS statement defines an alias (additional name) for a table, view, or another alias.

Syntax

```
EXEC SQL CREATE ALIAS [alias-name] FOR [data-object-name];
```

Parameters

alias-name Identifies the name of the alias to be created.

data-object-name Identifies the name of the database table, view, or existing alias for which the new alias is to be created.

Description The CREATE ALIAS statement defines an alias for a database table, a view, or another alias. An alias is simply another name to use when referencing a particular table or view in an embedded SQL statement. Aliases can also be defined for other aliases, thereby creating an alias chain. The definitions of all aliases are stored in the SYSCAT.TABLES system catalog table.

Comments

- If no qualifier (schema) is provided with the alias name, the authorization ID of the current user will be used as the qualifier when the alias is created.
- The alias name cannot be a name already being used by another database table, view, or existing alias.
- An alias can be defined for a data object that does not exist at the time of the alias creation (in this case, the warning SQLSTATE 01522 will be issued). However, the referenced data object must exist before embedded SQL statements containing the alias can be successfully precompiled.
- An alias chain is resolved the same way a single alias is, and is subject to the same restrictions as a single alias when it is used in an embedded SQL statement. If an alias used in a view definition or an SQL statement used in a package points to an alias chain, then a dependency is recorded for the view or package on each alias in the chain.
- Alias chains are searched for repetitive cycles each time a new alias is created. If a new alias would cause a repetitive cycle to occur, it will not be created.

- The term SYNONYM can be used in place of ALIAS in the statement EXEC SQL CREATE SYNONYM [*alias-name*] FOR [*data-object-name*] so existing DB2 for MVS/ESA CREATE SYNONYM statements do not have to be modified.

Authorization No authorization is required to execute this statement if the schema name of the new alias matches the current authorization ID. Only users with either system administrator (SYSADM) authority or database administrator (DBADM) authority can create aliases that have different schema names. The authorizations required to reference a particular table or view are also required to reference an alias for that particular table or view.

See Also DROP

Examples The following C program illustrates how to use the CREATE ALIAS statement to create an alias for an existing base table:

```
#include <stdio.h>
#include <stdlib.h>
#include <string.h>
#include <sql.h>

int main()
{
    /* Include The SQLCA Data Structure Variable */
    EXEC SQL INCLUDE SQLCA;

    /* Set Up A Simple SQL Error Handler */
    EXEC SQL WHENEVER SQLERROR GOTO EXIT;

    /* Declare The Local Memory Variables */
    int   rc = EXIT_SUCCESS;
    char  szDefinerID[9];

    /* Declare The SQL Host Memory Variables */
    EXEC SQL BEGIN DECLARE SECTION;
        char      szTableName[18];
        char      szDefiner[8];
    EXEC SQL END DECLARE SECTION;

    /* Connect To The SAMPLE Database */
    EXEC SQL CONNECT TO SAMPLE USER etpdd6z USING sanders;

    /* Create A Temporary Department Table */
    EXEC SQL CREATE TABLE TEMP_DEPT
        (DEPTNO      CHAR(3)       NOT NULL,
         DEPTNAME    VARCHAR(24)   NOT NULL,
         DEPTMGR     CHAR(6),
         EMPCOUNT    INTEGER);

    /* Print A Message Telling That The Table Was Created */
    printf("The Table TEMP_DEPT has been created.\n");

    /* Create An Alias For The Temporary Department Table */
    EXEC SQL CREATE ALIAS DEPARTMENTS
         FOR TEMP_DEPT;

    /* Print A Message Telling That The Alias Was Created */
    printf("Alias DEPTARTMENTS has been created for the TEMP_DEPT table.\n");
```

```
    /* Commit The Transaction */
    EXEC SQL COMMIT;

    /* Now Retrieve The Records From The SYSCAT.TABLES */
    /* Table To Verify That The Alias Was Created      */
    EXEC SQL SELECT TABNAME,
                    DEFINER
        INTO :szTableName,
             :szDefiner
        FROM SYSCAT.TABLES
        WHERE TABNAME = 'DEPARTMENTS';

    printf("\nContents of SYSCAT.TABLES\n\n");
    strncpy(szDefinerID, " ", 8);
    strncpy(szDefinerID, szDefiner, 8);
    szDefinerID[8] = 0;
    printf("Alias Name : %s\t Definer: %s\n",
            szTableName, szDefinerID);

    /* Delete The Table And The Alias */
    EXEC SQL DROP ALIAS DEPARTMENTS;
    EXEC SQL DROP TABLE TEMP_DEPT;

    /* Commit The Transaction */
    EXEC SQL COMMIT;

EXIT:
    /* If An Error Has Occurred, Display The SQL Return Code */
    if (sqlca.sqlcode != SQL_RC_OK)
        {
        printf("SQL ERROR : %ld\n", sqlca.sqlcode);
        rc = EXIT_FAILURE;
        }

    /* Turn Off The SQL Error Handler */
    EXEC SQL WHENEVER SQLERROR CONTINUE;

    /* Disconnect From The SAMPLE Database */
    EXEC SQL DISCONNECT CURRENT;

    /* Return To The Operating System */
    return(rc);
}
```

The following C++ program illustrates how the CREATE ALIAS statement is used by class methods to create an alias for an existing base table:

```
#include <iostream.h>
#include <stdlib.h>
#include <string.h>
#include <sql.h>

/* Define The Table Class */
class Table
{
    private:

        /* Include The SQLCA Data Structure Variable */
        EXEC SQL INCLUDE SQLCA;
```

```
        /* Declare The Local Memory Variables */
        char  szDefinerID[9];

        /* Declare The SQL Host Memory Variables */
        EXEC SQL BEGIN DECLARE SECTION;
            char      szTableName[18];
            char      szDefiner[8];
        EXEC SQL END DECLARE SECTION;

    /* Declare The Public Member Function Prototypes */
    public:
        short int createTable();
        short int createAlias();
        short int getSysInfo();
} ;

/* Define The createTable() Member Function */
short int Table::createTable(void)
{
    /* Create A Temporary Department Table */
    EXEC SQL CREATE TABLE TEMP_DEPT
        (DEPTNO       CHAR(3)       NOT NULL,
         DEPTNAME     VARCHAR(24)   NOT NULL,
         DEPTMGR      CHAR(6),
         EMPCOUNT     INTEGER);

    /* Print A Message Telling That The Table Was Created */
    if (sqlca.sqlcode == SQL_RC_OK)
        cout << "The Table TEMP_DEPT has been created." << endl;

    /* Return The SQL Return Code */
    return(sqlca.sqlcode);
}

/* Define The createAlias() Member Function */
short int Table::createAlias(void)
{
    /* Create An Alias For The Temporary Department Table */
    EXEC SQL CREATE ALIAS DEPARTMENTS
         FOR TEMP_DEPT;

    /* Print A Message Telling That The Alias Was Created */
    if (sqlca.sqlcode == SQL_RC_OK)
        {
        cout << "Alias DEPARTMENTS has been created for the ";
        cout << "TEMP_DEPT table." << endl;
        }

    /* Return The SQL Return Code */
    return(sqlca.sqlcode);
}

/* Define The getSysInfo() Member Function */
short int Table::getSysInfo(void)
{
    /* Now Retrieve The Records From The SYSCAT.TABLES */
    /* Table To Verify That The Alias Was Created      */
    EXEC SQL SELECT TABNAME,
                    DEFINER
```

```
        INTO :szTableName,
             :szDefiner
        FROM SYSCAT.TABLES
        WHERE TABNAME = 'DEPARTMENTS';

    cout << endl << "Contents of SYSCAT.TABLES" << endl << endl;
    strncpy(szDefinerID, " ", 8);
    strncpy(szDefinerID, szDefiner, 8);
    szDefinerID[8] = 0;
    cout << "Alias Name : " << szTableName << ": ";
    cout << szDefinerID << endl;

    /* Return The SQL Return Code */
    return(sqlca.sqlcode);
}

int main()
{
    /* Declare The Local Memory Variables */
    short int rc = EXIT_SUCCESS;              // Must Be Declared Here
                                              // For The SQL Precompiler

    /* Include The SQLCA Data Structure Variable */
    EXEC SQL INCLUDE SQLCA;

    /* Set Up A Simple SQL Error Handler */
    EXEC SQL WHENEVER SQLERROR GOTO EXIT;

    /* Create An Instance Of The Table Class */
    Table table;

    /* Connect To The SAMPLE Database */
    EXEC SQL CONNECT TO SAMPLE USER etpdd6z USING sanders;

    /* Create A Regular SMS Table Space */
    rc = table.createTable();

    /* Create A Temporary DMS Table Space */
    rc = table.createAlias();

    /* Commit The Transaction */
    EXEC SQL COMMIT;

    /* Now Retrieve The Records From The SYSCAT.TABLESPACES Table */
    /* To Verify That The Table Spaces Were Created                */
    rc = table.getSysInfo();

    /* Delete The Table And The Index */
    EXEC SQL DROP ALIAS DEPARTMENTS;
    EXEC SQL DROP TABLE TEMP_DEPT;

    /* Commit The Transaction */
    EXEC SQL COMMIT;

EXIT:
    /* If An Error Has Occurred, Display The SQL Return Code */
    if (sqlca.sqlcode != SQL_RC_OK)
        {
        cout << "SQL ERROR : " << sqlca.sqlcode << endl;
        rc = EXIT_FAILURE;
        }
```

```
    /* Issue A Rollback To Free All Locks */
    EXEC SQL ROLLBACK;

    /* Turn Off The SQL Error Handler */
    EXEC SQL WHENEVER SQLERROR CONTINUE;

    /* Disconnect From The SAMPLE Database */
    EXEC SQL DISCONNECT CURRENT;

    /* Return To The Operating System */
    return(rc);
}
```

CREATE DISTINCT TYPE

Purpose The CREATE DISTINCT TYPE statement defines a distinct, user-defined data type.

Syntax

```
EXEC SQL CREATE DISTINCT TYPE [distinct-type-name] AS [source-data-type]
   WITH COMPARISONS;
```

Parameters

distinct-type-name Identifies the name of the distinct data type to be created.

source-data-type Identifies the built-in data type to be used as the internal representation of the distinct data type. The type of source data type can be any of the following:

INTEGER	This indicates that the distinct data type is internally represented by the built-in INTEGER data type. INT can be used as a synonym for INTEGER.
SMALLINT	This indicates that the distinct data type is internally represented by the built-in SMALLINT data type.
DOUBLE	This indicates that the distinct data type is internally represented by the built-in DOUBLE data type. DOUBLE PRECISION and FLOAT are synonyms for DOUBLE.
DECIMAL (*width, precision*)	This indicates that the distinct data type is internally represented by the built-in DECIMAL data type. DEC, NUMERIC, and NUM are synonyms for DECIMAL.
CHARACTER (*size*) <FOR BIT DATA>	This indicates that the distinct data type is internally represented by the built-in CHARACTER data type. If the FOR BIT DATA option is specified, the contents of the internal data type will be treated as binary data and code page conversions will not be performed. CHAR is a synonym for CHARACTER.
VARCHAR (*size*) <FOR BIT DATA>	This indicates that the distinct data type is internally represented by the

	built-in VARCHAR data type. The FOR BIT DATA option has the same meaning as the one for the CHARACTER data type.
LONG VARCHAR <FOR BIT DATA>	This indicates that the distinct data type is internally represented by the built-in LONG VARCHAR data type. The FOR BIT DATA option has the same meaning as the one for the CHARACTER data type.
GRAPHIC (*size*)	This indicates that the distinct data type is internally represented by the built-in GRAPHIC data type.
VARGRAPHIC (*size*)	This indicates that the distinct data type is internally represented by the built-in VARGRAPHIC data type.
LONG VARGRAPHIC	This indicates that the distinct data type is internally represented by the built-in LONG VARGRAPHIC data type.
DATE	This indicates that the distinct data type is internally represented by the built-in DATE data type.
TIME	This indicates that the distinct data type is internally represented by the built-in TIME data type.
TIMESTAMP	This indicates that the distinct data type is internally represented by the built-in TIMESTAMP data type.
BLOB (*size* <K I M I G>)	This indicates that the distinct data type is internally represented by the built-in BLOB data type. If the K option is used, the size is in kilobytes; if the M option is used, the size is in megabytes; and if the G option is used, the size is in gigabytes.
CLOB (*size* <K I M I G>)	This indicates that the distinct data type is internally represented by the built-in CLOB data type. The K, M, and G options have the same meaning as those for the BLOB data type.
DBCLOB (*size* <K I M I G>)	This indicates that the distinct data type is internally represented by the built-in VARGRAPHIC data type. The K, M, and G options are the same as described for the BLOB data type.

Description The CREATE DISTINCT TYPE statement defines a distinct data type. All distinct data types must use a built-in data type for their internal representation in order for DB2 to store and process its data appropriately. When a distinct data type is created, the following functions are generated to convert data between the new distinct data type and its internal source data type:

- Converting data from the distinct data type to its source data type.
- Converting data from the source data type to the distinct data type.
- Converting data from the built-in INTEGER data type to the distinct data type if its source data type is SMALLINT.
- Converting data from the built-in VARCHAR data type to the distinct data type if its source data type is CHAR.
- Converting data from the built-in VARGRAPHIC data type to the distinct data type if its source data type is GRAPHIC.

In general, these functions have the following format:

```
CREATE FUNCTION [source-type-name][distinct-type-name]
RETURNS [source-type-name]

CREATE FUNCTION [distinct-type-name] [source-type-name]
RETURNS [distinct-type-name]
```

In cases where the source data type is a parameterized type, like DECIMAL(width, precision) or CHAR(size), the function that converts data from the distinct data type to its source type has the same name as the source data type (DECIMAL, CHAR, etc.) and returns the parameter values provided when the distinct data type was created. Likewise, the function that converts data from the source data type to the distinct data type has function input parameter values that match the parameter values provided when the distinct data type was created. For example, if a distinct data type is created with the following statement:

```
EXEC SQL CREATE DISTINCT TYPE SHIRTSIZE AS CHAR(3) WITH COMPARISONS;
```

and is executed, the following SQL statements would be executed in order to create the appropriate data conversion functions:

```
FUNCTION CHAR (SHIRTSIZE) RETURNS CHAR (3)
FUNCTION SHIRTSIZE (CHAR (3)) RETURNS SHIRTSIZE
```

The schema used for the generated cast functions is the same as the schema provided for the distinct data type name. Functions that support comparison operators like =, < >, <, < =, >, and > = for the distinct data type are also generated if the source data type for the distinct data type is not one of the following:

- LONG VARCHAR
- LONG VARGRAPHIC
- BLOB
- CLOB
- DBCLOB

Consequently, none of the built-in functions, such as AVG, MAX, and MIN, are supported for distinct data types unless the CREATE FUNCTION statement is used to register user-defined functions for the distinct data type that references the built-in function.

The definitions for distinct data types are stored in the SYSCAT.DATATYPES system catalog table, and the definitions of all corresponding conversion functions are stored in the SYSCAT.FUNCTIONS system catalog table.

Comments

- If no qualifier (schema) is provided with the distinct data type name, the authorization ID of the current user will be used as the qualifier when the distinct data type is created.
- The distinct data type name cannot be a name already being used by another distinct data type. If conversion functions are generated for this distinct data type, functions with this name and same signature must not already exist in the database.
- If the source data type for a distinct data type is LONG VARCHAR, LONG VARGRAPHIC, BLOB, CLOB, or DBCLOB, the WITH COMPARISONS keywords must be removed from the SQL statement.
- Use DECIMAL and DOUBLE instead of NUMERIC and FLOAT when creating distinct data types for portable applications.

Authorization No authorization is required to execute this statement if the schema name of the new distinct data type matches the current authorization ID. Only users with either system administrator (SYSADM) authority or database administrator (DBADM) authority are allowed to create distinct data types with other schema names.

See Also CREATE FUNCTION, DROP

Examples The following C program illustrates how to use the CREATE DISTINCT TYPE statement to create a distinct data type that references an integer source data type:

```
#include <stdio.h>
#include <stdlib.h>
#include <string.h>
#include <sql.h>

int main()
{
    /* Include The SQLCA Data Structure Variable */
    EXEC SQL INCLUDE SQLCA;

    /* Set Up A Simple SQL Error Handler */
    EXEC SQL WHENEVER SQLERROR GOTO EXIT;

    /* Declare The Local Memory Variables */
    int    rc = EXIT_SUCCESS;

    /* Declare The SQL Host Memory Variables */
    EXEC SQL BEGIN DECLARE SECTION;
        char      szTypeName[18];
        char      szSourceName[18];
    EXEC SQL END DECLARE SECTION;

    /* Connect To The SAMPLE Database */
    EXEC SQL CONNECT TO SAMPLE USER etpdd6z USING sanders;

    /* Create A Distinct Data Type */
    EXEC SQL CREATE DISTINCT TYPE EMP_NUMBER
        AS INTEGER WITH COMPARISONS;

    /* Print A Message Telling That The Distinct Type Was Created */
    printf("The Distinct Type EMP_NUMBER has been created.\n");

    /* Create A Temporary Employee Table Using The Distinct Type */
    EXEC SQL CREATE TABLE TEMP_EMP
```

```
        (EMPID       EMP_NUMBER   NOT NULL,
         LASTNAME    CHAR(18)     NOT NULL,
         FIRSTNAME   CHAR(18)     NOT NULL,
         DEPTNO      CHAR(3),
        PRIMARY KEY(EMPID));

    /* Print A Message Telling That The Table Was Created */
    printf("The Table TEMP_EMP has been created.\n");

    /* Commit The Transaction */
    EXEC SQL COMMIT;

    /* Now Retrieve The Records From The SYSCAT.DATATYPES */
    /* Table To Verify That The Distinct Type Was Created */
    EXEC SQL SELECT TYPENAME,
                    SOURCENAME
        INTO :szTypeName,
             :szSourceName
        FROM SYSCAT.DATATYPES
        WHERE TYPENAME = 'EMP_NUMBER';

    printf("\nContents of SYSCAT.DATATYPES\n\n");
    printf("Distinct Type Name : %s\t Source Type Name : %s\n",
            szTypeName, szSourceName);

    /* Delete The Table And The Distinct Type */
    EXEC SQL DROP TABLE TEMP_EMP;
    EXEC SQL DROP DISTINCT TYPE EMP_NUMBER;

    /* Commit The Transaction */
    EXEC SQL COMMIT;

EXIT:
    /* If An Error Has Occurred, Display The SQL Return Code */
    if (sqlca.sqlcode != SQL_RC_OK)
        {
        printf("SQL ERROR : %ld\n", sqlca.sqlcode);
        rc = EXIT_FAILURE;
        }

    /* Turn Off The SQL Error Handler */
    EXEC SQL WHENEVER SQLERROR CONTINUE;

    /* Disconnect From The SAMPLE Database */
    EXEC SQL DISCONNECT CURRENT;

    /* Return To The Operating System */
    return(rc);
}
```

The following C++ program illustrates how the CREATE DISTINCT TYPE statement is used by class methods to create a distinct data type to reference an integer source data type:

```
#include <iostream.h>
#include <stdlib.h>
#include <string.h>
#include <sql.h>

/* Define The DistinctType Class */
class DistinctType
```

```
{
   private:

      /* Include The SQLCA Data Structure Variable */
      EXEC SQL INCLUDE SQLCA;

      /* Declare The SQL Host Memory Variables */
      EXEC SQL BEGIN DECLARE SECTION;
          char       szTypeName[18];
          char       szSourceName[18];
      EXEC SQL END DECLARE SECTION;

   /* Declare The Public Member Function Prototypes */
   public:
      short int createType();
      short int createTable();
      short int getSysInfo();
} ;

/* Define The createType() Member Function */
short int DistinctType::createType(void)
{
    /* Create A Distinct Data Type */
    EXEC SQL CREATE DISTINCT TYPE EMP_NUMBER
        AS INTEGER WITH COMPARISONS;

    /* Print A Message Telling That The Distinct Type Was Created */
    if (sqlca.sqlcode == SQL_RC_OK)
        {
        cout << "The Distinct Type EMP_NUMBER has been created.";
        cout << endl;
        }

    /* Return The SQL Return Code */
    return(sqlca.sqlcode);
}

/* Define The createTable() Member Function */
short int DistinctType::createTable(void)
{
    /* Create A Temporary Employee Table Using The Distinct Type */
    EXEC SQL CREATE TABLE TEMP_EMP
        (EMPID        EMP_NUMBER    NOT NULL,
         LASTNAME     CHAR(18)      NOT NULL,
         FIRSTNAME    CHAR(18)      NOT NULL,
         DEPTNO       CHAR(3),
        PRIMARY KEY(EMPID));

    /* Print A Message Telling That The Table Was Created */
    if (sqlca.sqlcode == SQL_RC_OK)
        cout << "The Table TEMP_EMP has been created." << endl;

    /* Return The SQL Return Code */
    return(sqlca.sqlcode);
}

/* Define The getSysInfo() Member Function */
short int DistinctType::getSysInfo(void)
{
    /* Retrieve The Records From The SYSCAT.DATATYPES Table */
    /* To Verify That The Distinct Type Was Created */
```

```
    EXEC SQL SELECT TYPENAME,
                    SOURCENAME
        INTO :szTypeName,
             :szSourceName
        FROM SYSCAT.DATATYPES
        WHERE TYPENAME = 'EMP_NUMBER';

    cout << endl << "Contents of SYSCAT.DATATYPES" << endl << endl;
    cout << "Distinct Type Name : " << szTypeName;
    cout << " Source Type Name : " << szSourceName << endl;

    /* Return The SQL Return Code */
    return(sqlca.sqlcode);
}

int main()
{
    /* Declare The Local Memory Variables */
    short int rc = EXIT_SUCCESS;           // Must Be Declared Here
                                           // For The SQL Precompiler

    /* Include The SQLCA Data Structure Variable */
    EXEC SQL INCLUDE SQLCA;

    /* Set Up A Simple SQL Error Handler */
    EXEC SQL WHENEVER SQLERROR GOTO EXIT;

    /* Create An Instance Of The DistinctType Class */
    DistinctType distinct;

    /* Connect To The SAMPLE Database */
    EXEC SQL CONNECT TO SAMPLE USER etpdd6z USING sanders;

    /* Create A Distinct Data Type */
    rc = distinct.createType();

    /* Create A Table Using The Distinct Data Type */
    rc = distinct.createTable();

    /* Commit The Transaction */
    EXEC SQL COMMIT;

    /* Now Retrieve The Records From The SYSCAT.DATATYPES Table */
    /* To Verify That The Distinct Type Was Created             */
    rc = distinct.getSysInfo();

    /* Delete The Table And The Distinct Type */
    EXEC SQL DROP TABLE TEMP_EMP;
    EXEC SQL DROP DISTINCT TYPE EMP_NUMBER;

    /* Commit The Transaction */
    EXEC SQL COMMIT;

EXIT:
    /* If An Error Has Occurred, Display The SQL Return Code */
    if (sqlca.sqlcode != SQL_RC_OK)
        {
        cout << "SQL ERROR : " << sqlca.sqlcode << endl;
        rc = EXIT_FAILURE;
        }
```

```
        /* Issue A Rollback To Free All Locks */
        EXEC SQL ROLLBACK;

        /* Turn Off The SQL Error Handler */
        EXEC SQL WHENEVER SQLERROR CONTINUE;

        /* Disconnect From The SAMPLE Database */
        EXEC SQL DISCONNECT CURRENT;

        /* Return To The Operating System */
        return(rc);
}
```

SET CONSTRAINTS

Purpose The SET CONSTRAINTS statement allows you to turn check constraint and referential constraint checking off and on.

Syntax

```
EXEC SQL SET CONSTRAINTS FOR [table-name,...] [check-state]
   <FOR EXCEPTION IN [table-name] USE [exception-table-name]>];

EXEC SQL SET CONSTRAINTS FOR [table-name,...] [constraint-type,...]
   IMMEDIATE UNCHECKED;
```

Parameters

table-name Identifies the name of the table for which constraint checking is turned either off or on.

check-state Specifies the state of the specified table's constraint checking. The check state can be one of the following values:

OFF	Indicates that the specified tables' foreign key constraints and check constraints are turned off. With this option, the table is placed into the check-pending state.
IMMEDIATE CHECKED	Indicates that the specified tables' constraints are turned on and any constraint checking that was deferred is enforced.

exception-table-name Identifies the name of the exception table to which the row's failing constraint enforcement is written when constraint checking is turned on.

constraint-type Identifies the type of constraints checking to be turned on. The constraint type can be any of the following:

ALL	Indicates both foreign key constraint checking and check constraint checking.
FOREIGN KEY	Indicates foreign key constraint checking only.
CHECK	Indicates check constraint checking only.

Options

FOR EXCEPTION IN Indicates that any row in violation of a foreign key constraint or a check constraint is copied to an exception table and deleted from the specified table. When this option is specified along with the IMMEDIATE CHECKED check state, constraint checking is turned on and the specified tables are taken out of the check-pending state, even if an error occurs during constraint enforcement.

Description The SET CONSTRAINTS statement can perform any of the following functions:

- Turn off referential constraint and check constraint checking for one or more tables.

- Turn referential constraint and check constraint checking back on for one or more tables and enforce all deferred checking that accumulated after constraint checking was turned off.
- Turn referential constraint and check constraint checking back on for one or more tables and ignore all deferred checking that accumulated after constraint checking was turned off.

When referential constraint and/or check constraint checking is turned off for a table, the table is placed into a check-pending state, which allows only limited access by a restricted set of statements and commands. If the table is already in the check-pending state because one type of constraint checking is turned off, the other type of constraint checking will also be turned off. When referential constraint and/or check constraint checking is turned back on for a table, the table is taken out of check-pending state and the table is either checked for constraint violations or all constraint violations are ignored. The check constraint state change is not extended to any tables not explicitly specified in the SET CONSTRAINTS statement. Therefore, if the parent of a dependent table is placed in the check-pending state, the foreign key constraint checking of the dependent table cannot be bypassed (whereas the check constraints checking can).

When new constraints are added to a table (via the ALTER TABLE statement) they are normally enforced immediately. However, if the table is in the check-pending state when a new constraint is added, the enforcement of these new constraints is deferred until the table is taken out of the check-pending state.

Comments

- If the specified table is a parent table, the check-pending state for foreign key constraints is extended to all dependent and descendent tables.
- When deferred constraint checking is enforced (IMMEDIATE CHECKED), if one or more errors are detected and if the FOR EXCEPTION option is not specified, only the first error detected will be returned to the application. When an error occurs, all constraint checking is turned back off and the specified tables are left in the check-pending state.
- Using the SELECT, INSERT, UPDATE, or DELETE statements is disallowed on a table either in the check-pending state itself or requiring access to another table in the check-pending state. (For example, the DELETE statement cannot be executed against a row in a parent table that cascades to a dependent table in the check-pending state.) Also, packages, views, and any other data objects that depend on a table in the check-pending state will return an error if they attempt to access the table at runtime.
- The CREATE INDEX statement cannot reference any tables in the check-pending state.
- The EXPORT, IMPORT, REORG, and REORGCHK utilities cannot be executed against a table in the check-pending state. Note that the IMPORT utility differs from the LOAD utility in that it always checks the constraints immediately.
- The LOAD, BACKUP, RESTORE, ROLLFORWARD, UPDATE SATISTICS, RUNSTATS, and LIST HISTORY utilities can be executed against a table, even if the table is in the check-pending state. Also, the ALTER TABLE, COMMENT ON, DROP TABLE, CREATE ALIAS, CREATE TRIGGER, CREATE VIEW, GRANT, REVOKE, and SET CONSTRAINTS statements can reference a table in the check-pending state.
- The IMMEDIATE UNCHECKED version of this statement is intended to be used only by utility programs, not application programs. This version of the SET CONSTRAINTS statement is used only if the specified table's constraints are turned on with no checking for constraint integrity, or if the specified table has one type of

constraint checking turned on but is left in the check-pending state. The first scenario occurs when you execute the IMMEDIATE UNCHECKED version of this statement by specifying either ALL, FOREIGN KEY, or CHECK when only a foreign key or check constraints are off for that table. The second scenario occurs when both types of constraint checking are turned off for a table and the IMMEDIATE UNCHECKED version of this statement is executed with only the FOREIGN KEY or the CHECK constraint type specified. In either case, the user must assume responsibility for data integrity with respect to the specific constraints.

- If the IMMEDIATE UNCHECKED version of this statement is used, the fact that constraints were turned on with no deferred checking will be recorded in the system catalog tables (the value in the CONST CHECKED column in the SYSCAT.TABLES view will be set to "U"). This value remains until either the specified table is put back into the check-pending state or all unchecked constraints for the table are dropped.
- While constraints are being checked, the following locks are held:
  - –An exclusive lock on each table specified in the SET CONSTRAINTS invocation.
  - –A shared lock on each table that is not listed in the SET CONSTRAINTS invocation but is a parent table of one of the dependent tables being checked.
- If a ROLLBACK statement is issued during constraint checking, all the effects of the checking, including deleting from the original and inserting into the exception tables, will be rolled back.

Authorization Only users with either system administrator (SYSADM) authority, database administrator (DBADM) authority, or CONTROL authority for the specified table are allowed to execute this statement.

If the FOR EXCEPTION option is being used to place exception records in one or more exception tables and the user does not have either SYSADM authority or DBADM authority, they must also have INSERT authority on each exception table being referenced.

Examples The following C program illustrates how to use the SET CONSTRAINTS statement to turn check constraint checking off and on:

```
#include <stdio.h>
#include <stdlib.h>
#include <string.h>
#include <sql.h>

int main()
{
    /* Include The SQLCA Data Structure Variable */
    EXEC SQL INCLUDE SQLCA;

    /* Set Up A Simple SQL Error Handler */
    EXEC SQL WHENEVER SQLERROR GOTO EXIT;

    /* Declare The Local Memory Variables */
    int   rc = EXIT_SUCCESS;
    char  szDefinerID[9];

    /* Declare The SQL Host Memory Variables */
    EXEC SQL BEGIN DECLARE SECTION;
        char      szConstName[18];
        char      szTableName[18];
        char      szDefiner[8];
    EXEC SQL END DECLARE SECTION;
```

```
    /* Connect To The SAMPLE Database */
    EXEC SQL CONNECT TO SAMPLE USER etpdd6z USING sanders;

    /* Create A Temporary Project Table */
    EXEC SQL CREATE TABLE TEMP_PROJ
        (PROJNO      INTEGER       NOT NULL,
         PROJNAME    VARCHAR(24)   NOT NULL,
         DEPTNO      CHAR(3),
         STARTDATE   DATE,
         ENDDATE     DATE,
        PRIMARY KEY (PROJNO),
        CONSTRAINT VALDATE CHECK(ENDDATE > STARTDATE));

    /* Print A Message Telling That The Table And Check Constraint */
    /* Were Created                                                */
    printf("The Table TEMP_PROJ has been created.\n");
    printf("The Check Constraint VALDATE has been created for the ");
    printf("TEMP_PROJ table.\n");

    /* Commit The Transaction */
    EXEC SQL COMMIT;

    /* Turn Constraint Checking Off */
    EXEC SQL SET CONSTRAINTS FOR TEMP_PROJ OFF;

    /* Now Retrieve The Records From The SYSCAT.CHECKS Table */
    /* To Verify That The Check Constraint Was Created       */
    EXEC SQL SELECT CONSTNAME,
                    TABNAME,
                    DEFINER
        INTO :szConstName,
             :szTableName,
             :szDefiner
        FROM SYSCAT.CHECKS
        WHERE TABNAME = 'TEMP_PROJ';

    printf("\nContents of SYSCAT.CHECKS\n\n");
    strncpy(szDefinerID, " ", 8);
    strncpy(szDefinerID, szDefiner, 8);
    szDefinerID[8] = 0;
    printf("Check Constraint : %s\t Table Name : %s\t Definer: %s\n",
            szConstName, szTableName, szDefinerID);

    /* Turn Constraint Checking Back On */
    EXEC SQL SET CONSTRAINTS FOR TEMP_PROJ IMMEDIATE CHECKED;

    /* Delete The Table And The Check Constraint */
    EXEC SQL DROP TABLE TEMP_PROJ;

    /* Commit The Transaction */
    EXEC SQL COMMIT;

EXIT:
    /* If An Error Has Occurred, Display The SQL Return Code */
    if (sqlca.sqlcode != SQL_RC_OK)
        {
        printf("SQL ERROR : %ld\n", sqlca.sqlcode);
        rc = EXIT_FAILURE;
        }
```

```
    /* Turn Off The SQL Error Handler */
    EXEC SQL WHENEVER SQLERROR CONTINUE;

    /* Disconnect From The SAMPLE Database */
    EXEC SQL DISCONNECT CURRENT;

    /* Return To The Operating System */
    return(rc);
}
```

The following C++ program illustrates how to use the SET CONSTRAINTS statement to turn check constraint checking off and on:

```
#include <iostream.h>
#include <stdlib.h>
#include <string.h>
#include <sql.h>

/* Define The Table Class */
class Table
{
    private:

      /* Include The SQLCA Data Structure Variable */
      EXEC SQL INCLUDE SQLCA;

      /* Declare The Local Memory Variables */
      char  szDefinerID[9];

      /* Declare The SQL Host Memory Variables */
      EXEC SQL BEGIN DECLARE SECTION;
          char      szConstName[18];
          char      szTableName[18];
          char      szDefiner[8];
      EXEC SQL END DECLARE SECTION;

    /* Declare The Public Member Function Prototypes */
    public:
      short int createTable();
      short int getSysInfo();
} ;

/* Define The createTable() Member Function */
short int Table::createTable(void)
{
    /* Create A Temporary Project Table */
    EXEC SQL CREATE TABLE TEMP_PROJ
        (PROJNO       INTEGER       NOT NULL,
         PROJNAME     VARCHAR(24)   NOT NULL,
         DEPTNO       CHAR(3),
         STARTDATE    DATE,
         ENDDATE      DATE,
        PRIMARY KEY (PROJNO),
        CONSTRAINT VALDATE CHECK(ENDDATE > STARTDATE));

    /* Print A Message Telling That The Table And Check Constraint */
    /* Were Created                                                */
    if (sqlca.sqlcode == SQL_RC_OK)
        {
        cout << "The Table TEMP_PROJ has been created." << endl;
        cout << "The Check Constraint VALDATE has been created for ";
```

```
            cout << "the TEMP_PROJ table." << endl;
            }

        /* Return The SQL Return Code */
        return(sqlca.sqlcode);
    }

    /* Define The getSysInfo() Member Function */
    short int Table::getSysInfo(void)
    {
        /* Now Retrieve The Records From The SYSCAT.CHECKS Table */
        /* To Verify That The Check Constraint Was Created       */
        EXEC SQL SELECT CONSTNAME,
                        TABNAME,
                        DEFINER
            INTO :szConstName,
                 :szTableName,
                 :szDefiner
            FROM SYSCAT.CHECKS
            WHERE TABNAME = 'TEMP_PROJ';

        cout << endl << "Contents of SYSCAT.CHECKS" << endl << endl;
        strncpy(szDefinerID, " ", 8);
        strncpy(szDefinerID, szDefiner, 8);
        szDefinerID[8] = 0;
        cout << "Check Constraint : ";
        cout << szConstName << "Name : ";
        cout << szTableName << " Definer : " << szDefinerID << endl;

        /* Return The SQL Return Code */
        return(sqlca.sqlcode);
    }

    int main()
    {
        /* Declare The Local Memory Variables */
        short int rc = EXIT_SUCCESS;            // Must Be Declared Here
                                                // For The SQL Precompiler

        /* Include The SQLCA Data Structure Variable */
        EXEC SQL INCLUDE SQLCA;

        /* Set Up A Simple SQL Error Handler */
        EXEC SQL WHENEVER SQLERROR GOTO EXIT;

        /* Create An Instance Of The Table Class */
        Table table;

        /* Connect To The SAMPLE Database */
        EXEC SQL CONNECT TO SAMPLE USER etpdd6z USING sanders;

        /* Create A Temporary Table */
        rc = table.createTable();

        /* Commit The Transaction */
        EXEC SQL COMMIT;

        /* Turn Constraint Checking Off */
        EXEC SQL SET CONSTRAINTS FOR TEMP_PROJ OFF;

        /* Now Retrieve The Records From The SYSCAT.TABLESPACES Table */
        /* To Verify That The Table Spaces Were Created               */
        rc = table.getSysInfo();
```

```
    /* Turn Constraint Checking Back On */
    EXEC SQL SET CONSTRAINTS FOR TEMP_PROJ IMMEDIATE CHECKED;

    /* Delete The Table And The Check Constraint */
    EXEC SQL DROP TABLE TEMP_PROJ;

    /* Commit The Transaction */
    EXEC SQL COMMIT;

EXIT:
    /* If An Error Has Occurred, Display The SQL Return Code */
    if (sqlca.sqlcode != SQL_RC_OK)
        {
        cout << "SQL ERROR : " << sqlca.sqlcode << endl;
        rc = EXIT_FAILURE;
        }

    /* Issue A Rollback To Free All Locks */
    EXEC SQL ROLLBACK;

    /* Turn Off The SQL Error Handler */
    EXEC SQL WHENEVER SQLERROR CONTINUE;

    /* Disconnect From The SAMPLE Database */
    EXEC SQL DISCONNECT CURRENT;

    /* Return To The Operating System */
    return(rc);
}
```

COMMENT ON

Purpose The COMMENT ON statement allows you to add or replace comments in the description column (REMARKS) of the system catalog tables for a specified data object.

Syntax

```
EXEC SQL COMMENT ON [object-type] [object-name] IS [comment-string];

EXEC SQL COMMENT ON [table-name | view-name] ([column-name] IS
   [comment-string],...);
```

> Note: This statement can be executed in any of the preceding formats; each will produce a different result.

Parameters

object-type Identifies the type of database object for which the description is to be changed. The object type can be any of the following:

ALIAS	Indicates the comment is associated with an alias.
COLUMN	Indicates the comment is associated with a specific table or view column.
CONSTRAINT	Indicates the comment is associated with a constraint.
DISTINCT TYPE	Indicates the comment is associated with a user-defined data type. DATA TYPE is a synonym for DISTINCT TYPE.
FUNCTION <(data-type, . . .)>	Indicates the comment is associated with an instance of a user-defined function. ROUTINE is a synonym for FUNCTION. You can

use the data types specified with the CREATE FUNCTION statement to identify the specific function instance to drop.

SPECIFIC FUNCTION	Indicates the comment is associated with a particular user-defined function.
INDEX	Indicates the comment is associated with an index.
PACKAGE	Indicates the comment is associated with a package.
TABLE	Indicates the comment is associated with a database table or view.
TABLESPACE	Indicates the comment is associated with a table space.
TRIGGER	Indicates the comment is associated with a trigger.

object-name Identifies the name of the database object as it is described in the database system catalog. If the TABLE data object is specified, the object name can be either the name of a table or a view.

comment-string Specifies the comment text to be added or replaced.

table-name Identifies the name of the table for which a column description is to be changed.

view-name Identifies the name of the view for which a column description is to be changed.

column-name Identifies the column or columns for which the description is to be changed.

Description The COMMENT ON statement adds or replaces comments in the description (REMARKS) column of the system catalog tables for a specified data object. Normally, a description of an object is provided when the object is created. However, if a description was not provided when the object was created or if the provided description is no longer accurate, you can use the COMMENT ON statement to add to or modify that description.

Comments

- If no qualifier (schema) is provided with the object name, the authorization ID of the current user will be used as the qualifier when this statement is executed.
- The description for a column in an inoperative view cannot be added to or changed.
- If the description for a column or constraint is to be modified, you must specify the object name as *table-name.column-name*, *view-name.column-name*, or *table-name.constraint-name*.
- You can specify a user-defined function name by providing the function signature along with the function name. The function signature is simply a listing of each data type passed to the function as a parameter.
- When specifying data types for a function, you can use an empty set of parentheses in place of size and precision values, i.e., DECIMAL() instead of DECIMAL(9,3), if these values are not meant to be part of the function specification criteria.
- The comment string cannot exceed 254 characters (bytes) in length. (A carriage return/line feed counts as one character.)

Authorization The authorizations required to execute this statement are determined by the specified object data type. Table 10.3 lists each data type and the authorizations needed to change the description associated with them.

See Also CREATE ALIAS, CREATE DISTINCT TYPE, CREATE FUNCTION, CREATE INDEX, CREATE TABLE, CREATE TABLESPACE, CREATE TRIGGER, CREATE VIEW

TABLE 10.3 Authorizations for Executing the COMMENT ON Statement for a Specific Object

Data object	Authorization required
ALIAS	SYSADM authority, DBADM authority, or the alias owner authorization ID as recorded in the TABSCHEMA column of the SYSCAT.TABLES system catalog table.
COLUMN	Authorization required to comment on the base table or view (see TABLE and VIEW).
CONSTRAINT	Authorization required to comment on the base table the constraint is for (see TABLE).
DISTINCT TYPE	SYSADM authority, DBADM authority, or the distinct type owner authorization ID as recorded in the TYPESCHEMA column of the SYSCAT.DATATYPES system catalog table.
FUNCTION	SYSADM authority, DBADM authority, or the distinct type owner authorization ID as recorded in the FUNCSCHEMA column of the SYSCAT.FUNCTIONS system catalog table.
INDEX	SYSADM authority, DBADM authority, CONTROL authorization for the index, or CONTROL authorization for the table that the index references.
PACKAGE	SYSADM authority, DBADM authority, or CONTROL authorization for the package.
TABLE	SYSADM authority, DBADM authority, or CONTROL authorization for the base table.
TABLESPACE	SYSADM or SYSCTRL authority.
TRIGGER	SYSADM authority, DBADM authority, or the trigger owner authorization ID as recorded in the TRIGSCHEMA column of the SYSCAT.TRIGGERS system catalog table.
VIEW	SYSADM authority, DBADM authority, CONTROL authority for the view, or the view owner authorization ID as recorded in the DEFINER column of the SYSCAT.VIEWS system catalog table.

SYSADM - system administrator
DBADM - database administrator
SYSCTRL - system control

Examples The following C program illustrates how to use the COMMENT ON statement to set the description associated with a table, the table's columns, and an index:

```
#include <stdio.h>
#include <stdlib.h>
#include <string.h>
#include <sql.h>

int main()
{
    /* Include The SQLCA Data Structure Variable */
    EXEC SQL INCLUDE SQLCA;

    /* Set Up A Simple SQL Error Handler */
    EXEC SQL WHENEVER SQLERROR GOTO EXIT;

    /* Declare The Local Memory Variables */
    int    rc = EXIT_SUCCESS;

    /* Declare The SQL Host Memory Variables */
    EXEC SQL BEGIN DECLARE SECTION;
        char       szTableName[18];
        char       szIndexName[18];
        char       szComment[256];
    EXEC SQL END DECLARE SECTION;

    /* Connect To The SAMPLE Database */
    EXEC SQL CONNECT TO SAMPLE USER etpdd6z USING sanders;
```

```
/* Create A Temporary Project Table */
EXEC SQL CREATE TABLE TEMP_PROJ
    (PROJNO      INTEGER      NOT NULL,
     PROJNAME    VARCHAR(24)  NOT NULL,
     DEPTNO      CHAR(3),
     STARTDATE   DATE,
     ENDDATE     DATE);

/* Print A Message Telling That The Table Was Created */
printf("The Table TEMP_PROJ has been created.\n");

/* Create An Index For The Temporary Project Table */
EXEC SQL CREATE INDEX PROJ_BY_DEPT
     ON TEMP_PROJ (PROJNO, DEPTNO);

/* Print A Message Telling That The Index Was Created */
printf("Index PROJ_BY_DEPT has been created for the TEMP_PROJ ");
printf("table.\n");

/* Commit The Transaction */
EXEC SQL COMMIT;

/* Set The Comment For The Temporary Project Table */
EXEC SQL COMMENT ON TABLE TEMP_PROJ
     IS 'Temporary Project Table';

/* Set The Comment For Each Column In The Temporary Project */
/* Table                                                    */
EXEC SQL COMMENT ON TEMP_PROJ
     (PROJNO IS 'Project Number',
      PROJNAME IS 'Project Name',
      DEPTNO IS 'Department Number',
      STARTDATE IS 'Starting Date Of Project',
      ENDDATE IS 'Ending Date Of Project');

/* Set The Comment For The Temporary Project Table Index */
EXEC SQL COMMENT ON INDEX PROJ_BY_DEPT
     IS 'Projects By Departments';

/* Now Retrieve The Records From The SYSCAT.TABLES */
/* Table To Verify That The Comment Was Entered     */
EXEC SQL SELECT TABNAME,
                REMARKS
    INTO :szTableName,
         :szComment
    FROM SYSCAT.TABLES
    WHERE TABNAME = 'TEMP_PROJ';

printf("\nContent of SYSCAT.TABLES\n\n");
printf("Table Name : %s\n Comment: %s\n",
       szTableName, szComment);

/* Now Retrieve The Records From The SYSCAT.INDEXES */
/* Table To Verify That The Comment Was Entered      */
EXEC SQL SELECT INDNAME,
                TABNAME,
                REMARKS
    INTO :szIndexName,
         :szTableName,
         :szComment
```

```
        FROM SYSCAT.INDEXES
        WHERE TABNAME = 'TEMP_PROJ';

    printf("\nContents of SYSCAT.INDEXES\n\n");
    printf("Index Name : %s\t Table Name : %s\nComment: %s\n",
           szIndexName, szTableName, szComment);

    /* Delete The Table And The Index */
    EXEC SQL DROP INDEX PROJ_BY_DEPT;
    EXEC SQL DROP TABLE TEMP_PROJ;

    /* Commit The Transaction */
    EXEC SQL COMMIT;

EXIT:
    /* If An Error Has Occurred, Display The SQL Return Code */
    if (sqlca.sqlcode != SQL_RC_OK)
        {
        printf("SQL ERROR : %ld\n", sqlca.sqlcode);
        rc = EXIT_FAILURE;
        }

    /* Turn Off The SQL Error Handler */
    EXEC SQL WHENEVER SQLERROR CONTINUE;

    /* Disconnect From The SAMPLE Database */
    EXEC SQL DISCONNECT CURRENT;

    /* Return To The Operating System */
    return(rc);
}
```

The following C++ program illustrates how the COMMENT ON statement is used by class methods to set the description associated with a table, the table's columns, and an index:

```
#include <iostream.h>
#include <stdlib.h>
#include <string.h>
#include <sql.h>

/* Define The Table Class */
class Table
{
    private:

        /* Include The SQLCA Data Structure Variable */
        EXEC SQL INCLUDE SQLCA;

        /* Declare The Local Memory Variables */
        char  szDefinerID[9];

        /* Declare The SQL Host Memory Variables */
        EXEC SQL BEGIN DECLARE SECTION;
            char      szTableName[18];
            char      szIndexName[18];
            char      szComment[256];
        EXEC SQL END DECLARE SECTION;

    /* Declare The Public Member Function Prototypes */
    public:
```

```
        short int createTable();
        short int createIndex();
        short int setTableComment();
        short int setIndexComment();
        short int getSysInfo();
} ;

/* Define The createTable() Member Function */
short int Table::createTable(void)
{
    /* Create A Temporary Project Table */
    EXEC SQL CREATE TABLE TEMP_PROJ
        (PROJNO       INTEGER       NOT NULL,
         PROJNAME     VARCHAR(24)   NOT NULL,
         DEPTNO       CHAR(3),
         STARTDATE    DATE,
         ENDDATE      DATE);

    /* Print A Message Telling That The Table Was Created */
    if (sqlca.sqlcode == SQL_RC_OK)
        cout << "The Table TEMP_PROJ has been created." << endl;

    /* Return The SQL Return Code */
    return(sqlca.sqlcode);
}

/* Define The createIndex() Member Function */
short int Table::createIndex(void)
{
    /* Create An Index For The Temporary Project Table */
    EXEC SQL CREATE INDEX PROJ_BY_DEPT
         ON TEMP_PROJ (PROJNO, DEPTNO);

    /* Print A Message Telling That The Index Was Created */
    if (sqlca.sqlcode == SQL_RC_OK)
        {
        cout << "Index PROJ_BY_DEPT has been created for the ";
        cout << "TEMP_PROJ table." << endl;
        }

    /* Return The SQL Return Code */
    return(sqlca.sqlcode);
}

/* Define The setTableComment() Member Function */
short int Table::setTableComment(void)
{
    /* Set The Comment For The Temporary Project Table */
    EXEC SQL COMMENT ON TABLE TEMP_PROJ
         IS 'Temporary Project Table';

    if (sqlca.sqlcode != SQL_RC_OK)
        return(sqlca.sqlcode);

    /* Set The Comment For Each Column In The Temporary Project */
    /* Table                                                     */
    EXEC SQL COMMENT ON TEMP_PROJ
         (PROJNO IS 'Project Number',
          PROJNAME IS 'Project Name',
          DEPTNO IS 'Department Number',
          STARTDATE IS 'Starting Date Of Project',
          ENDDATE IS 'Ending Date Of Project');
```

```
    /* Return The SQL Return Code */
    return(sqlca.sqlcode);
}

/* Define The setIndexComment() Member Function */
short int Table::setIndexComment(void)
{
    /* Set The Comment For The Temporary Project Table Index */
    EXEC SQL COMMENT ON INDEX PROJ_BY_DEPT
         IS 'Projects By Departments';

    /* Return The SQL Return Code */
    return(sqlca.sqlcode);
}

/* Define The getSysInfo() Member Function */
short int Table::getSysInfo(void)
{
    /* Retrieve The Records From The SYSCAT.TABLES Table */
    /* To Verify That The Comment Was Entered            */
    EXEC SQL SELECT TABNAME,
                    REMARKS
        INTO :szTableName,
             :szComment
        FROM SYSCAT.TABLES
        WHERE TABNAME = 'TEMP_PROJ';

    cout << endl << "Contents of SYSCAT.TABLES" << endl << endl;
    cout << "Table Name : " << szTableName << endl;
    cout << "Comment : " << szComment << endl;

    /* Retrieve The Records From The SYSCAT.INDEXES Table */
    /* To Verify That The Comment Was Entered             */
    EXEC SQL SELECT INDNAME,
                    TABNAME,
                    REMARKS
        INTO :szIndexName,
             :szTableName,
             :szComment
        FROM SYSCAT.INDEXES
        WHERE TABNAME = 'TEMP_PROJ';

    cout << endl << "Contents of SYSCAT.INDEXES" << endl << endl;
    cout << "Index Name : " << szIndexName;
    cout << "Name : " << szTableName << endl;
    cout << "Comment : " << szComment << endl;

    /* Return The SQL Return Code */
    return(sqlca.sqlcode);
}

int main()
{
    /* Declare The Local Memory Variables */
    short int rc = EXIT_SUCCESS;            // Must Be Declared Here
                                            // For The SQL Precompiler

    /* Include The SQLCA Data Structure Variable */
    EXEC SQL INCLUDE SQLCA;

    /* Set Up A Simple SQL Error Handler */
    EXEC SQL WHENEVER SQLERROR GOTO EXIT;
```

```
    /* Create An Instance Of The Table Class */
    Table table;

    /* Connect To The SAMPLE Database */
    EXEC SQL CONNECT TO SAMPLE USER etpdd6z USING sanders;

    /* Create A Temporary Table */
    rc = table.createTable();

    /* Create An Index For The Table */
    rc = table.createIndex();

    /* Commit The Transaction */
    EXEC SQL COMMIT;

    /* Create A Comment For The Temporary Table */
    rc = table.setTableComment();

    /* Create A Comment For The Index */
    rc = table.setIndexComment();

    /* Now Retrieve The Records From The SYSCAT.TABLES And The */
    /* SYSCAT.INDEXES Table To Verify That The Comments Were   */
    /* Entered                                                 */
    rc = table.getSysInfo();

    /* Delete The Table And The Index */
    EXEC SQL DROP INDEX PROJ_BY_DEPT;
    EXEC SQL DROP TABLE TEMP_PROJ;

    /* Commit The Transaction */
    EXEC SQL COMMIT;

EXIT:
    /* If An Error Has Occurred, Display The SQL Return Code */
    if (sqlca.sqlcode != SQL_RC_OK)
        {
        cout << "SQL ERROR : " << sqlca.sqlcode << endl;
        rc = EXIT_FAILURE;
        }

    /* Issue A Rollback To Free All Locks */
    EXEC SQL ROLLBACK;

    /* Turn Off The SQL Error Handler */
    EXEC SQL WHENEVER SQLERROR CONTINUE;

    /* Disconnect From The SAMPLE Database */
    EXEC SQL DISCONNECT CURRENT;

    /* Return To The Operating System */
    return(rc);
}
```

DROP

Purpose The DROP statement deletes an existing database object.

Syntax

```
EXEC SQL DROP [object-type] [object-name];
```

Parameters

object-type Identifies the type of database object to be deleted, which can be any of the following:

ALIAS	Indicates an alias. SYNONYM is a synonym for ALIAS.
DISTINCT TYPE	Indicates a user-defined data type. DATA TYPE is a synonym for DISTINCT TYPE.
EVENT MONITOR	Indicates an event monitor.
FUNCTION <(*data-type*, . . .)>	Indicates an instance of a user-defined function. ROUTINE is a synonym for FUNCTION. You can use the data types specified with the CREATE FUNCTION statement to identify the specific function instance to drop.
SPECIFIC FUNCTION	Indicates a particular user-defined function.
INDEX	Indicates an index.
PACKAGE	Indicates a package. PROGRAM is a synonym for PACKAGE.
TABLE	Indicates a database table.
TABLESPACE	Indicates a table space.
TRIGGER	Indicates a trigger.
VIEW	Indicates a view.

object-name Identifies the name of the database object, as it is described in the database system catalog.

Description

The DROP statement deletes an existing data object from a database. When an object is deleted from a database, its description is removed from the appropriate system catalog table and any packages in the database that reference that object are made invalid.

Each data object can have one or more different data objects that are directly or indirectly dependent upon it. How those dependent data objects are processed when a data object is deleted is determined by the dependency relationship that exists between the objects. Four different types of dependency relationships can exist:

Restrict A data object cannot be dropped as long as its dependent objects exist.

Cascade When a data object is dropped, all dependent objects are dropped unless the dependent data object has a restrict dependency on some other data object.

Inoperative When a data object is dropped, all dependent objects become inoperative and remain so until a user takes some explicit action to make the operative again.

Automatic Invalidation/Revalidation When a data object is dropped, all dependent objects become invalid. DB2 automatically attempts to revalidate any invalid data objects.

Table 10.4 shows some common dependencies between data objects in DB2.

Comments

- If no qualifier (schema) is provided with the object name, the authorization ID of the current user will be used as the qualifier when this statement is executed.
- If an alias is deleted, all tables, views, and triggers that referenced the alias are made inoperative.
- If a distinct type is used in the column definition of a table or if a distinct type is used as a parameter or a return value for a function that cannot be dropped, that distinct type cannot be deleted.
- If a distinct type is deleted, then every function with parameters or return values of that distinct type will also be deleted. If for some reason one of these functions cannot be deleted, the statement will fail.
- If an event monitor is on, it cannot be deleted.

TABLE 10.4 Data Object Dependencies

Data object	Dependency objects	Dependency type
Table	Table space	Cascade or restrict
	Distinct data type	Restrict
	User-defined function instance	Restrict
Index	Base Table	Cascade
View	Base Table	Inoperative
	Alias	Inoperative
	View	Inoperative
	User-defined function instance	Restrict
	Authorization	Inoperative
User-defined function instance	Distinct data type	Cascade
	User-defined function instance	Restrict
Constraint	Base Table	Cascade
	Index	Restrict
	User-defined function instance	Restrict
	Constraint	Cascade
Trigger	base table	Inoperative
	Alias	Inoperative
	View	Inoperative
	User-defined function instance	Restrict
	Privilege	Inoperative
Package	Base Table	Automatic invalidation/revalidation
	Referential constraints	Automatic invalidation/revalidation
	Check constraints	Automatic invalidation/revalidation
	Alias	Automatic invalidation/revalidation
	Index	Automatic invalidation/revalidation
	View	Automatic invalidation/revalidation
	User-defined function instance	Inoperative
	Trigger	Automatic invalidation/revalidation
	Authorization	Automatic invalidation/revalidation

Dependency types	Description
Restrict	The underlying object cannot be dropped as long as the object depending on it exists.
Cascade	Dropping the underlying object causes the object that depends on it to be dropped as well. If one underlying object cannot be dropped because it has a restrict dependency on some other object, it will not be dropped.
Inoperative	Dropping an underlying object causes the object that depends on it to become inoperative and remain inoperative until the user takes some explicit action.
Automatic invalidation/revalidation	Dropping an underlying object causes the object that depends on it to become invalid. DB2 must perform some implicit action to revalidate the invalid object.

- If event files exist in an event monitor's target path when an event monitor is deleted, they will not be deleted. If a new event monitor using the target path where the event files are stored is later created, however, the event files will be deleted.
- You can delete functions implicitly generated by the CREATE DISTINCT TYPE statement only by deleting the distinct type with which they are associated.
- You can specify a user-defined function name by providing the function signature along with the function name. The function signature simply lists each data type passed to the function as a parameter.
- When specifying data types for a function, you can use an empty set of parentheses in place of size and precision values, i.e., DECIMAL( ) instead of DECIMAL(9,3), if these values are not meant to be part of the function specification criteria.
- You cannot drop a function that has the schema "SYSIBM" or "SYSFUN."
- All dependencies on a function by other data objects (except for packages) must be removed before the function itself can be removed.
- A user-defined function can be deleted while it is in use. If an open cursor contains a reference to a user-defined function that is deleted before the cursor is closed, subsequent fetches will continue to work correctly.
- If a package that depends on a user-defined function is executing, it is impossible for another user to delete the function before the package completes its current transaction. Once the current transaction has completed, the user-defined function will be deleted and the package marked inoperative. All other requests for this package will then generate errors until the package is explicitly rebound to the database.
- If the body of a function is deleted (not the same as deleting the function) while an application that needs the function's body is executing, the statement that refers to the function might fail, depending on whether or not DB2 has already loaded the function's body into memory.
- If a table is deleted, all indexes, primary keys, foreign keys, and check constraints that reference the table will be dropped and all views and triggers that reference the table will be made inoperative.
- If a table space is deleted, all data objects defined in the table space will also be deleted. Likewise, all data objects with dependencies on the table space will either be deleted or invalidated and all dependent views and triggers will be made inoperative.
- A table space cannot be deleted if one or more existing tables store one or more of its parts in it.
- A system table space cannot be deleted and a temporary table space cannot be deleted if it is the only temporary table space in the database.
- When a table space is deleted, all directories and subdirectories created by DB2 when the table space was created are also deleted.
- When a view is deleted, any view or trigger directly or indirectly dependent on that view is marked inoperative and all packages dependent on either the view that was dropped or a view made inoperative when the view was dropped are invalidated.
- Packages with dependencies on a table, index, or function are marked inoperative when the data object is deleted. Once a package is marked inoperative, it must either be rebound to the database by the BIND or REBIND statement or be re-prepared by the PREP command.

Authorization The authorizations required to execute this statement are determined by the object type specified. Table 10.5 lists each data type and the authorizations needed to delete them.

TABLE 10.5 Authorizations for Executing the DROP Statement for a Specific Object

Data object	Authorization required
ALIAS	SYSADM authority, DBADM authority, or the alias owner authorization ID as recorded in the TABSCHEMA column of the SYSCAT.TABLES system catalog table.
DISTINCT TYPE	SYSADM authority, DBADM authority, or the distinct type owner authorization ID as recorded in the TYPESCHEMA column of the SYSCAT.DATATYPES system catalog table.
EVENT MONITOR	SYSADM or DBADM authority.
FUNCTION	SYSADM authority, DBADM authority, or the distinct type owner authorization ID as recorded in the FUNCSCHEMA column of the SYSCAT.FUNCTIONS system catalog table.
INDEX	SYSADM authority, DBADM authority, CONTROL authorization for the index, or CONTROL authorization for the table that the index references.
PACKAGE	SYSADM authority, DBADM authority, or CONTROL authorization for the package.
TABLE	SYSADM authority, DBADM authority, or CONTROL authorization for the base table.
TABLESPACE	SYSADM or SYSCTRL authority.
TRIGGER	SYSADM authority, DBADM authority, or the trigger owner authorization ID as recorded in the TRIGSCHEMA column of the SYSCAT.TRIGGERS system catalog table.
VIEW	SYSADM authority, DBADM authority, CONTROL authority for the view, or the view owner authorization ID as recorded in the DEFINER column of the SYSCAT.VIEWS system catalog table.

SYSADM - system administrator
DBADM - database administrator
SYSCTRL - system control

See Also CREATE ALIAS, CREATE DISTINCT TYPE, CREATE EVENT MONITOR , CREATE FUNCTION, CREATE INDEX, CREATE TABLE, CREATE TABLESPACE, CREATE TRIGGER, CREATE VIEW

Examples Refer to the previous CREATE statements for examples that illustrate how to use the DROP statement to delete an existing data object.

CREATE FUNCTION

Purpose The CREATE FUNCTION statement registers a user-defined function with a database server.

Syntax

```
EXEC SQL CREATE FUNCTION [function-name] ([input-data-type,...])
   RETURNS [output-data-type] <CAST FROM [alternative-data-type]>
   <SPECIFIC [specific-name]> EXTERNAL NAME '[function-source]'
   <external-function-options>;

EXEC SQL CREATE FUNCTION [function-name] ([input-data-type,...])
   RETURNS [output-data-type] <CAST FROM [alternative-data-type]>
   <SPECIFIC [specific-name]> <internal-function-options>;
```

Parameters

function-name Identifies the name of the function being defined.

input-data-type Identifies one or more input parameters needed by the function, and specifies the data type of each parameter. One data type entry must be specified for each input parameter the function expects to receive.

output-data-type Specifies the output data type returned by the function.

alternative-data-type Specifies an alternate data type the function is to return to the calling statement (instead of the output data type normally returned by the function).

specific-name Specifies a unique name for the instance of the function being defined. This is the name used to invoke, drop (remove), and comment on the function.

function-source Specifies the library name or full path name of a file containing the actual implementation code that DB2 will invoke when attempting to execute the function being defined. The function-source string is specified as follows:

```
'[library-ID | absolute-path-name] <! function-ID>'
```

where:

library-ID Identifies the library name of the file containing the function implementation code.

absolute-path-ID Identifies the full path name of the file containing the function implementation code.

function-ID Identifies the entry point name of the function implementation code to be invoked.

External Function Options

LANGUAGE C. Specifies the language or language interface convention in which the user-defined function body is written. At this time, only C programming language conventions (LANGUAGE C) are supported, so DB2 will call the user-defined function as if it were a C function. The user-defined function must conform to the C language calling and linkage convention as defined by the ANSI C standard. User-defined functions can be written in either C or C++, since both of these languages conform to the required interface conventions. This option is mandatory.

PARAMETER STYLE DB2SQL. Specifies the conventions for passing parameters to and returning the value from user-defined external functions. The DB2SQL value reflects the conventions defined in DBL:YOW-006 (ISO working draft) SQL persistent stored modules (SQL/PSM), the ISO/ANSI draft standard as of March 1995. This option is mandatory.

<NOT> VARIANT. Specifies whether or not the function always returns the same results for given argument values. If the function can return different results for given argument values depending on some state value(s) that affect the final output, that function is considered to be a VARIANT function. An example of a VARIANT function would be a random-number generator. One of these options (either VARIANT or NOT VARIANT) must be specified.

<NOT> FENCED. Specifies whether or not the function is considered "safe" to run in DB2's database manager operating environment's process or address space. If this option is not specified, the FENCED option is used by default for all functions created without the SOURCE option. All other functions (those created with the SOURCE option) inherit this attribute from the SOURCE function.

<NOT> NULL CALL. Specifies whether or not calls to the user-defined function should be made if any of the arguments is null. If this option is not specified, the NOT NULL CALL option is used by default for all external functions. When the NOT NULL CALL option is specified, if any one of the function's arguments is null, the user-defined function will not be called and the null value will be returned as the result. When the NULL CALL option is specified, the user-defined function is called regardless of whether any of the function's arguments are null, and either the null value or a normal (non-null) value is returned as the result.

NO SQL. Specifies that the function cannot issue any SQL statements. If the function contains SQL statements, an error will be generated at application run-time. This option is mandatory.

<NO> EXTERNAL ACTION. Specifies whether or not the function performs some action that changes the state of an object not managed by DB2. Examples of an external action might be sending a message, ringing the bell, or writing a record to a file. One of these options (either EXTERNAL ACTION or NO EXTERNAL ACTION) must be specified.

<NO> SCRATCHPAD. Specifies whether or not a scratch pad is provided for an external function. If a user-defined function is re-entrant (which is strongly recommended), a scratch pad allows that function to save its current state from one call to the next. If the SCRATCHPAD option is specified, the first time the function is invoked, memory is allocated for a scratch pad and each subsequent invocation receives the memory address of the scratch pad as an additional argument.

<NO> FINAL CALL. Specifies whether or not a final call is made to an external function. The purpose of this option is to notify the external function to free any system resources it has acquired. This is extremely useful when used with the SCRATCHPAD option in situations where the external function acquires system resources (such as memory) and places them in the scratch pad memory buffer. If this option is not specified, the NO FINAL CALL option will be used by default.

Internal Function Options

SOURCE [source-function-name]. Specifies that the function being created is to be implemented by another function (the source function) already known by DB2. The source function name identifies the particular function to be used as the source function and is valid only if there is exactly one specific function in the specified schema with this function name.

SPECIFIC [specific-function-name]. Specifies that the function being created is to be implemented by a specific user-defined function (the source function), identified as specific-function-name. The specific function name can be either specified or defaulted to at function creation time. This option is not valid if the source function is built-in.

[function-name] ([data-type, . . .]). Specifies that the function being created is to be implemented by a function whose signature uniquely identifies the source function. This option is the only valid method for indicating that the source function is built-in, such as MIN() or MAX(). Each specified data type must match the data type specified with the CREATE FUNCTION statement in the corresponding comma-delimited position. It is not necessary to specify the length and/or precision values for the parameterized data types. Instead, you can code an empty set of parentheses to indicate that these attributes are to be ignored when looking for a data type match. However, if a length and/or precision value is specified, those values must exactly match the ones specified with the CREATE FUNCTION statement.

Description

The CREATE FUNCTION statement allows you to register a user-defined function with a database server. A user-defined function is simply a set of high-level programming language instructions that processes one or more specified input values to produce some resultant output value. User-defined functions can be defined as either external or sourced functions. External functions are defined to the database with a reference to function within an object code library that is executed when the function is invoked. Sourced functions are defined to the database with a reference to another built-in or user-defined function already known to DB2.

Database functions are divided into two different categories: scalar and column. Scalar functions produce a single value from one or more different values. Column functions are designed to work on several database rows together to produce a single value. External functions can be only scalar functions, whereas sourced functions can be both scalar and column functions. Either type can be very useful in providing additional flexibility for user-defined data types.

A user-defined function is generally identified by its schema, function name, and the number and data types of its input parameters (also known as the function parameter list). This combination is referred to as the function signature and it must be unique within the database system catalog tables. There can be more than one function with the same name in the same schema, provided the parameters list is different. If two or more functions have the same name within the same schema, that function is referred to being overloaded. The overloaded function concept is not unlike that used by C++ and other object-oriented programming languages. A function name is also considered to be overloaded if more than one function with the same name exists in a function path. In this case, the functions might also have the same parameter list.

You can invoke a function by including its qualified name (schema.function), followed by its list of arguments enclosed in parentheses. You can also invoke a function without specifying its schema name. In this case, the function path and the parameter list help you to determine the correct function to invoke (function resolution). For dynamic SQL applications, the function path to search is stored in the CURRENT FUNCTION PATH special register (refer to the SET CURRENT FUNCTION PATH statement for more information).

Comments

- The function name, including its implicit or explicit qualifiers and parameter list, must not identify a function that already exists at the application server. The unqualified function name and its parameter list does not have to be unique across schemas.
- If no qualifier (schema) is provided with the function name, the authorization ID of the current user will be used as the qualifier when the function is created. If a qualifier is provided with the function name, it cannot be "SYSIBM", "SYSCAT", or "SYSSTAT."
- A number of names used as keywords in predicates are reserved for system use, and therefore cannot be used as a function name. These reserved names are =, <, >, > =, < =, < >, SOME, ANY, ALL, NOT, AND, OR, BETWEEN, NULL, LIKE, EXISTS, IN, UNIQUE, OVERLAPS, SIMILAR, and MATCH.
- Do not give a user-defined function the same name as a built-in function, unless it is an intentional override. Giving a user-defined function the same name as a built-in function (with consistent arguments) is inviting trouble; the application might fail, or, perhaps worse, the application might appear to run successfully while providing an incorrect result.
- You can register a function that does not require input parameters. In this case, code only the parentheses with no intervening data types specified.
- No two identically named functions within the same schema are permitted to have the exact same parameter list. Sizes and precisions are not considered in this parameter list comparison. Therefore, CHAR(8) and CHAR(35) are considered to be the same data type, as are DECIMAL(11,2) and DECIMAL (4,3). Some further bundling of data types causes them to be treated as the same data type for this purpose, such as DECIMAL and NUMERIC. For example, given these statements:

  ```
  CREATE FUNCTION PART (INT, CHAR(15))
  CREATE FUNCTION PART (INT, CHAR(40))
  CREATE FUNCTION ANGLE (DECIMAL(12,2))
  CREATE FUNCTION ANGLE (DECIMAL(10,7))
  ```

  The second and fourth statements would fail because they are considered to be a duplicate functions.
- For external functions, SQL data types specified in the function parameter list must have a corresponding data type in the language with which the function body is written (C or C++). Refer to the language-specific sections of the application programming guide for more information about mapping the SQL data types and host language data types with respect to user-defined functions. Also, consider the following:

–The FOR BIT DATA option affects the format of VARCHAR and LONG VARCHAR arguments.
–The body of the user-defined function should handle datetime data types as character values.
–The body of the user-defined function should handle distinct data types as their base types.
–The body of the user-defined function can handle BLOB, CLOB, and DBCLOB data types.
–The body of the user-defined function cannot handle DECIMAL (or NUMERIC) data types if that body is written in C or C++.

- For sourced functions, you can use any valid SQL input or output data type, provided it can be cast to the data type of the corresponding parameter of the SOURCE function. Also, with sourced functions it is not necessary to specify size or precision values for parameterized data types; instead, empty parentheses can be used.
- The function return value cannot be cast as a distinct data type.
- The CAST FROM option cannot be used with sourced functions.
- The unqualified form of a function's specific name is an SQL identifier (with a maximum length of 18). The qualified form is a schema name followed by a period and an SQL identifier. The specific name, including the implicit or explicit qualifier, must not be the same as the specific name of another function.
- If no schema is specified with the specific function name, the schema name that was used for the function name is also used for the specific name. If a schema name is specified, it must be the same as the explicit or implicit schema name supplied for the function name.
- If a specific name is not provided, a unique specific name will be generated by DB2, in the form SQL*yymmddhhmmsshhn*, where:
  –*yy* is the current year
  –*mm* is the current month
  –*dd* is the current day
  –*hh* is the current hour
  –*mm* is the current minutes
  –*ss* is the current seconds
  –*hh* is the current hundredths of a second
  –*n* is a uniqueness digit that is almost always 0
- The function source string must be enclosed in single quotes, and any leading or trailing blanks must be removed.
- DB2 will look for the library specified in the function source string in either the . . . /sqllib/function directory (AIX) or the . . . directory (OS/2), where . . . represents the controlling drive or directory being used to run DB2.
- If a library name or absolute path name is specified in the function source string but no function entry point name is provided, DB2 will use the main entry point of the library.
- Sourced functions inherit the function source information from the source function, so an error will occur if you specify this option when defining sourced functions.
- If a function is registered as FENCED, DB2 will prevent its internal resources (e.g., data buffers) from being accessed by the function.
- Most user-defined functions should be able to run either as FENCED or NOT FENCED. Generally, a FENCED function does not perform as well as a NOT FENCED function.
- You must reregister a function (by dropping and then re-creating it) in order to change it from FENCED to NOT FENCED. Special authority is required to register a user-defined function as NOT FENCED (see the next section, Authorization).

- Using NOT FENCED functions that were not adequately tested can result in compromised integrity. DB2 protects against many of the common types of inadvertent failures that can occur, but it cannot guarantee complete integrity when NOT FENCED user-defined functions are used.
- If a scratch pad is used by a user-defined function, it will have the following characteristics:
  - –A size of 100 bytes.
  - –Each byte initialized to null (0x00).
  - –A scope limited to the SQL statement that referenced the function. One scratch pad exists for each reference to the user-defined function. In the following SQL statement, for example, three scratch pads are created:

```
EXEC SQL SELECT A, MyFunction(A) FROM TABLEB
WHERE MyFunction(A) > 20 OR MyFunction(A) < 10
```

  - –Persistence (its content is preserved from one function call to the next, so changes made to the scratch pad by the user-defined function on one call are there on the next call).
  - –Being used as a central storage point for system resources acquired by the external function. For example, the user-defined function could acquire a block of memory on its first call, store its address in the scratch pad, and refer to it in subsequent calls.
- If the FINAL CALL option is specified, at execution time an additional argument is passed to the user-defined function that specifies the type of call being made. The following types of calls are available:

First call. The first call made to the external function that is associated with the user-defined function referenced in an SQL statement. All system resources needed by the function are acquired at this time. The first call is treated as a normal call.

Normal call. SQL arguments are passed to the external function and a result is returned. The normal call is the first call made to the external function that is associated with the user-defined function referenced in an SQL statement.

Final call. The last call made to the external function that is associated with the user-defined function referenced in an SQL statement. The final call allows the external function to free up resources acquired during the first call. The final call is not a normal call, and can occur at the following times:

End-of-statement	This is when the current cursor is closed (for cursor-oriented statements) or when the current SQL statement is through executing.
End-of-transaction	This occurs when the normal end-of-statement does not occur; for example, the logic of an application might for some reason bypass the close of the cursor. If a commit or rollback operation occurs while a cursor defined as WITH HOLD referencing a user-defined function is open, a final call will be made when the cursor is closed or when the application terminates rather than at the end of the transaction.

- If the NO FINAL CALL option is specified (default option), then no call-type argument will be passed to the external function and no final call will be made.
- If no qualifier (schema) is provided with the source or specific function name, the values in the CURRENT FUNCTION PATH special register will be used to locate the function. In this case, the first schema in the function path that has a function with the source function name defined is selected as the source function name schema.
- If a specified source or specific function name cannot be found or if more than one instance of the specified source or specific function name is found (i.e., the

function is overloaded), an error condition will be returned and the CREATE FUNCTION statement will fail.

- The unqualified name of a user-defined function and the unqualified name of its source function can (and usually will) be different.
- A function named as the source function of another function can itself use another function as its source. Use extreme care when using this facility because it could be very difficult to debug an application if an indirectly invoked function produces an error.
- The EXTERNAL NAME '[*function-source*]' clause, along with the external function options, are invalid if specified in conjunction with source functions (because user-defined source functions automatically inherit these attributes from their source function).
- No warning is given in situations where the size or precision of the user-defined function's return data type is longer than that of the value returned by its source function or if a pad/zero-fill operation is performed by the chosen cast function.
- The term castable means that one data type can be cast to another data type with the cast specification. Neither size nor precision values are considered for parameterized data types such as CHAR and DECIMAL when determining whether or not one data type is castable to another data type, so errors might occur with a user-defined function that results from an attempt to cast a value of the one data type to another data type.
- When choosing data types for user-defined function input parameters, consider how the rules of promotion shown in Table 10.6 will affect their input values. Based on the rules of promotion, you should use the following data types for input parameters:

  INTEGER instead of SMALLINT, VARCHAR instead of CHAR, VARGRAPHIC instead of GRAPHIC

TABLE 10.6 Data Type Precedence Rules

Data type	Data type promotion list (best-to-worst order)
CHAR	CHAR, VARCHAR, LONG VARCHAR, CLOB
VARCHAR	VARCHAR, LONG VARCHAR, CLOB
LONG VARCHAR	LONG VARCHAR, CLOB
GRAPHIC	GRAPHIC, VARGRAPHIC, LONG VARGRAPHIC, DBCLOB
VARGRAPHIC	VARGRAPHIC, LONG VARGRAPHIC, DBCLOB
LONG VARGRAPHIC	LONG VARGRAPHIC, DBCLOB
BLOB	BLOB
CLOB	CLOB
DBCLOB	DBCLOB
SMALLINT	SMALLINT, INTEGER, DECIMAL, DOUBLE
INTEGER	INTEGER, DECIMAL, DOUBLE
DECIMAL	DECIMAL, DOUBLE
DOUBLE	DOUBLE
DATE	DATE
TIME	TIME
TIMESTAMP	TIMESTAMP
Distinct type	Distinct type (same name)

Each data type on the left can be promoted to the data type on the right. The best choice for data type promotion is always to the same data type.

Adapted from the Data Type Precedence Table on pages 61 and 62 of the IBM Database 2 SQL Reference for Common Servers manual.

Authorization No authorization is required to create a function under the same schema name that matches the authorization ID of the current user. Only users with either system administrator (SYSADM) authority or database administrator (DBADM) authority are allowed to create functions in another schema.

In addition to the authorization rules described above, users without either SYSADM authority or DBADM authority must have CREATE_NOT_FENCED authorization in order to create a function that is NOT FENCED.

See Also SET CURRENT FUNCTION PATH, CREATE DISTINCT TYPE, DROP

Examples The following C program illustrates how the CREATE FUNCTION statement can be used to register a user-defined function in DB2 for OS/2:

```
#include <stdio.h>
#include <stdlib.h>
#include <string.h>
#include <sql.h>

int main()
{
    /* Include The SQLCA Data Structure Variable */
    EXEC SQL INCLUDE SQLCA;

    /* Set Up A Simple SQL Error Handler */
    EXEC SQL WHENEVER SQLERROR GOTO EXIT;

    /* Declare The Local Memory Variables */
    int   rc = EXIT_SUCCESS;
    char  szDefinerID[9];

    /* Declare The SQL Host Memory Variables */
    EXEC SQL BEGIN DECLARE SECTION;
        char      szFuncName[18];
        char      szDefiner[8];
    EXEC SQL END DECLARE SECTION;

    /* Connect To The SAMPLE Database */
    EXEC SQL CONNECT TO SAMPLE USER etpdd6z USING sanders;

    /* Create A User Defined Function */
    EXEC SQL CREATE FUNCTION COUNTER()
        RETURNS INTEGER
        EXTERNAL NAME 'G:!udfCounter'
        LANGUAGE C
        PARAMETER STYLE DB2SQL
        VARIANT
        NOT FENCED
        NOT NULL CALL
        NO SQL
        NO EXTERNAL ACTION
        SCRATCHPAD
        NO FINAL CALL;

    /* Print A Message Telling That The User Defined Function Was */
    /* Created                                                    */
    printf("The User Defined Function COUNTER() has been created.\n");

    /* Commit The Transaction */
    EXEC SQL COMMIT;

    /* Now Retrieve The Records From The SYSCAT.FUNCTIONS Table */
    /* To Verify That The User Defined Function Was Created     */
```

```
    EXEC SQL SELECT FUNCNAME,
                    DEFINER
        INTO :szFuncName,
             :szDefiner
        FROM SYSCAT.FUNCTIONS
        WHERE FUNCSCHEMA = 'ETPDD6Z';

    printf("\nContents of SYSCAT.FUNCTIONS\n\n");
    strncpy(szDefinerID, " ", 8);
    strncpy(szDefinerID, szDefiner, 8);
    szDefinerID[8] = 0;
    printf("User Defined Function Name : %s\t Definer: %s\n",
            szFuncName, szDefinerID);

    /* Delete The User Defined Function */
    EXEC SQL DROP FUNCTION COUNTER();

    /* Commit The Transaction */
    EXEC SQL COMMIT;

EXIT:
    /* If An Error Has Occurred, Display The SQL Return Code */
    if (sqlca.sqlcode != SQL_RC_OK)
        {
        printf("SQL ERROR : %ld\n", sqlca.sqlcode);
        rc = EXIT_FAILURE;
        }

    /* Turn Off The SQL Error Handler */
    EXEC SQL WHENEVER SQLERROR CONTINUE;

    /* Disconnect From The SAMPLE Database */
    EXEC SQL DISCONNECT CURRENT;

    /* Return To The Operating System */
    return(rc);
}
```

The following C++ program illustrates how the CREATE FUNCTION statement is used by class methods to register a user-defined function in DB2 for OS/2:

```
#include <iostream.h>
#include <stdlib.h>
#include <string.h>
#include <sql.h>

/* Define The UDFunction Class */
class UDFunction
{
    private:

        /* Include The SQLCA Data Structure Variable */
        EXEC SQL INCLUDE SQLCA;

        /* Declare The Local Memory Variables */
        char  szDefinerID[9];

        /* Declare The SQL Host Memory Variables */
        EXEC SQL BEGIN DECLARE SECTION;
            char      szFuncName[18];
            char      szDefiner[8];
        EXEC SQL END DECLARE SECTION;
```

```
    /* Declare The Public Member Function Prototypes */
    public:
       short int createFunction();
       short int getSysInfo();
} ;

/* Define The createFunction() Member Function */
short int UDFunction::createFunction(void)
{
    /* Create A User Defined Function */
    EXEC SQL CREATE FUNCTION COUNTER()
        RETURNS INTEGER
        EXTERNAL NAME 'G:!udfCounter'
        LANGUAGE C
        PARAMETER STYLE DB2SQL
        VARIANT
        NOT FENCED
        NOT NULL CALL
        NO SQL
        NO EXTERNAL ACTION
        SCRATCHPAD
        NO FINAL CALL;

    /* Print A Message Telling That The User Defined Function Was */
    /* Created                                                     */
    if (sqlca.sqlcode == SQL_RC_OK)
        {
        cout << "The User Defined Function COUNTER() has been created.";
        cout << endl;
        }

    /* Return The SQL Return Code */
    return(sqlca.sqlcode);
}

/* Define The getSysInfo() Member Function */
short int UDFunction::getSysInfo(void)
{
    /* Retrieve The Records From The SYSCAT.FUNCTIONS Table */
    /* To Verify That The User Defined Function Was Created */
    EXEC SQL SELECT FUNCNAME,
                    DEFINER
        INTO :szFuncName,
             :szDefiner
        FROM SYSCAT.FUNCTIONS
        WHERE FUNCSCHEMA = 'ETPDD6Z';

    cout << endl << "Contents of SYSCAT.FUNCTIONS" << endl << endl;
    strncpy(szDefinerID, " ", 8);
    strncpy(szDefinerID, szDefiner, 8);
    szDefinerID[8] = 0;
    cout << "User Defined Function Name : " << szFuncName;
    cout << ": " << szDefinerID << endl;

    /* Return The SQL Return Code */
    return(sqlca.sqlcode);
}

int main()
{
```

```
    /* Declare The Local Memory Variables */
    short int rc = EXIT_SUCCESS;            // Must Be Declared Here
                                            // For The SQL Precompiler

    /* Include The SQLCA Data Structure Variable */
    EXEC SQL INCLUDE SQLCA;

    /* Set Up A Simple SQL Error Handler */
    EXEC SQL WHENEVER SQLERROR GOTO EXIT;

    /* Create An Instance Of The UDFunction Class */
    UDFunction function;

    /* Connect To The SAMPLE Database */
    EXEC SQL CONNECT TO SAMPLE USER etpdd6z USING sanders;

    /* Create A User Defined Function */
    rc = function.createFunction();

    /* Commit The Transaction */
    EXEC SQL COMMIT;

    /* Now Retrieve The Records From The SYSCAT.FUNCTIONS Table */
    /* To Verify That The User Defined Function Was Created     */
    rc = function.getSysInfo();

    /* Delete The User Defined Function */
    EXEC SQL DROP FUNCTION COUNTER();

    /* Commit The Transaction */
    EXEC SQL COMMIT;

EXIT:
    /* If An Error Has Occurred, Display The SQL Return Code */
    if (sqlca.sqlcode != SQL_RC_OK)
        {
        cout << "SQL ERROR : " << sqlca.sqlcode << endl;
        rc = EXIT_FAILURE;
        }

    /* Issue A Rollback To Free All Locks */
    EXEC SQL ROLLBACK;

    /* Turn Off The SQL Error Handler */
    EXEC SQL WHENEVER SQLERROR CONTINUE;

    /* Disconnect From The SAMPLE Database */
    EXEC SQL DISCONNECT CURRENT;

    /* Return To The Operating System */
    return(rc);
}
```

This C program contains the actual source code for the Counter function. This program must be compiled and linked to produce the dynamic link library (.DLL) file referenced by the CREATE FUNCTION statement in the previous sample programs before they will work.

```
#include <sqlsystm.h>
```

```
struct scratchpad {
   long  lLength;
   long  lCounter;
   char  szNotUsed[96];
   } ;

void SQL_API_FN udfCounter (long                   *plOutput,
                            short                  *psOutNI,
                            char                   *pszSQLSTATE,
                            char                   *pszFuncName,
                            char                   *pszSpecName,
                            char                   *pszMsgText,
                            struct scratchpad  *ptrScratchPad)

{
   *plOutput = ++ptrScratchPad->lCounter;
   *psOutNI = 0;

   return;
}
```

SET CURRENT FUNCTION PATH

Purpose The SET CURRENT FUNCTION PATH statement allows you to replace or modify the list of schema names that specify the location of user-defined functions.

Syntax

```
EXEC SQL SET CURRENT FUNCTION PATH <=> [schema-name,...];
```

Parameters

schema-name Identifies a schema that exists at the database server. The schema name can be either a user-defined schema name or one or more of the following values:

SYSTEM PATH	Identifies the SYSIBM and SYSFUN schema names.
USER	Identifies the authorization ID of the user that invoked the DB2 application (the value in the USER special register).
CURRENT FUNCTION PATH	Identifies the list of schema names stored in the CURRENT FUNCTION PATH special register before this statement is executed.

Description The SET CURRENT FUNCTION PATH statement allows you to replace or modify the list of schema names stored in the CURRENT FUNCTION PATH special register. This list of schema names tells DB2 where to look when trying to resolve user-defined function references and user-defined data type references in SQL statements.

Comments

- If a host variable specifies the schema name, it must be defined as an CHAR or VARCHAR data type, its length must not exceed 8, and its value must not be set to null. Also, if a corresponding indicator variable is used, the value of that indicator variable must not be null.
- If a host variable specifies the schema name, all characters in the text string must be left-justified and specified in the same case; no case conversion will take place.
- A schema name cannot appear more than once in the CURRENT FUNCTION PATH list.

- The number of schema names that can be specified in this statement is limited by the total length of the specification string. You can build the CURRENT FUNCTION PATH special register string by removing trailing blanks from each specified schema name, bracketing each schema name with double quotations (doubling quotations as necessary), and delimiting each schema name with a comma. The length of this final string cannot exceed 254 characters (bytes).
- The schema name "SYSIBM" is always assumed to be the first schema name in the list, so it does not need to be specified.
- When this statement is executed, no validation checking is performed to ensure that the specified schema actually exists. This means that if a specified schema name does not exist, subsequent SQL statements might either operate incorrectly or fail to execute.
- The CURRENT FUNCTION PATH special register resolves user-defined functions and data types in dynamic SQL statements. You must use the FUNCPATH bind option when specifying a schema name list to use while processing static SQL statements.

Authorization No authorization is required to execute this statement.

Example The following C program illustrates how to use the SET CURRENT FUNCTION PATH statement to specify a list of schema names to use when trying to locate user-defined functions:

```
#include <stdio.h>
#include <stdlib.h>
#include <string.h>
#include <sql.h>

int main()
{
    /* Include The SQLCA Data Structure Variable */
    EXEC SQL INCLUDE SQLCA;

    /* Set Up A Simple SQL Error Handler */
    EXEC SQL WHENEVER SQLERROR GOTO EXIT;

    /* Declare The Local Memory Variables */
    int    rc = EXIT_SUCCESS;

    /* Declare The SQL Host Memory Variables */
    EXEC SQL BEGIN DECLARE SECTION;
        short          sCounter;
        struct VARCHAR {
            short size;
            char  string[15];
            }  stLastName;
        char           szLastName[15];
    EXEC SQL END DECLARE SECTION;

    /* Connect To The SAMPLE Database */
    EXEC SQL CONNECT TO SAMPLE USER etpdd6z USING sanders;

    /* Set The Current Function Path */
    EXEC SQL SET CURRENT FUNCTION PATH = SYSTEM PATH, "ETPDD6Z";

    /* Declare The EMPLOYEE Salary Cursor */
    /* NOTE: The Function Counter() Must Be Created In Another */
```

```
    /* Application - Otherwise Binding Cannot Occur */
    EXEC SQL DECLARE EMP_CURSOR CURSOR FOR
        SELECT COUNTER(),
               LASTNAME
        FROM USERID.EMPLOYEE
        WHERE JOB = 'DESIGNER';

    /* Open The Cursor */
    EXEC SQL OPEN EMP_CURSOR;

    /* If The Cursor Was Successfully Opened, Fetch The Records Into */
    /* Host Variables                                                 */
    while (sqlca.sqlcode == SQL_RC_OK)
        {
        EXEC SQL FETCH EMP_CURSOR
            INTO :sCounter,
                 :stLastName;

        /* If The FETCH Was Successful, Print The Data */
        if (sqlca.sqlcode == SQL_RC_OK)
            {
            strncpy(szLastName, " ", 15);
            strncpy(szLastName, stLastName.string, stLastName.size);
            printf("Row : %02d - Last Name : %s\n ",
                   sCounter, szLastName);
            }
        }                                           /* End Of WHILE   */

    /* Close The Cursor */
    EXEC SQL CLOSE EMP_CURSOR;

    /* Commit The Transaction */
    EXEC SQL COMMIT;

EXIT:
    /* If An Error Has Occurred, Display The SQL Return Code */
    if (sqlca.sqlcode != SQL_RC_OK)
        {
        printf("SQL ERROR : %ld\n", sqlca.sqlcode);
        rc = EXIT_FAILURE;
        }

    /* Turn Off The SQL Error Handler */
    EXEC SQL WHENEVER SQLERROR CONTINUE;

    /* Disconnect From The SAMPLE Database */
    EXEC SQL DISCONNECT CURRENT;

    /* Return To The Operating System */
    return(rc);
}
```

Note: The SET CURRENT FUNCTION PATH statement is used in a C++ program in a similar manner.

CHAPTER 11

DATA MANIPULATION STATEMENTS

11

Data manipulation SQL statements consist of commands that allow you to add data to and manipulate data stored in a database. This group includes:

- An SQL statement to insert data into base tables.
- An SQL statement to change data already been inserted into base tables.
- An SQL statement to remove data from base tables.
- SQL statements to retrieve data from the database.
- An SQL statement to free resources for retrieving BLOB, CLOB, and DBCLOB data from the database.

Table 11.1 lists the data manipulation SQL statements available with DB2.

TABLE 11.1 SQL Data Manipulation Statements

Statement	Description
INSERT	Inserts one or more rows of data into a table.
UPDATE	Updates the values of one or more columns in one or more rows of data in a table.
DELETE	Deletes (removes) one or more rows of data from a table.
DECLARE CURSOR	Defines a SQL cursor.
OPEN	Prepares a SQL cursor so it can be used to retrieve values from the database when the FETCH statement is executed.
FETCH	Retrieves rows of data from an open SQL cursor and assigns the values retrieved to host variables.
CLOSE	Closes a SQL cursor.
SELECT INTO	Retrieves a single row of data from the database and assigns the values retrieved to host variables.
VALUES INTO	Retrieves a single row of data from either the database or from special register variables and assigns the values to host variables.
FREE LOCATOR	Removes the association between a LOB locator variable and its value.

Adding Data

When you first create a database table, it does not contain data. You need to use the INSERT statement to add rows of data to a table. The INSERT statement has two general forms. One uses a VALUES clause to specify individual values for the columns of one or more rows, and the second uses a SELECT statement for copying values contained in another table or view. No matter which form is used, you must supply a value for each table column defined with the NOT NULL option, for every row inserted. Any other columns in the table not explicitly assigned a value will be implicitly assigned the NULL value unless the column was defined with the WITH DEFAULT option, in which case the default value will be implicitly assigned to the column.

If you use the VALUES form of this statement, you must first specify a list of column names, and the values provided must match the columns in that list. If the list of column names is omitted, the list of data values must be in the same order as the columns in the table into which they are inserted, and the number of values must equal the number of columns in the table. Also, each value must be compatible with the data type of the column into which it is inserted.

The second form of the INSERT statement is very handy for populating a table with values from rows in another table. With this form of the INSERT statement, you must specify a fullselect that identifies the columns contained in other tables and/or views.

Changing Data

Once you have added rows of data to a table, you can modify them with the UPDATE statement. You can provide a WHERE clause with the UPDATE statement to specify the row or rows to be deleted. Then when the UPDATE statement is executed, one or more column values in one or more rows of a table will be modified, depending on how many rows satisfy the search condition specified in the WHERE clause. If the WHERE clause is omitted, DB2 will update each row in the table or view with the values supplied. You can also use the UPDATE statement to delete a value from a nullable column without removing the row, by changing the column value to NULL.

Deleting Data

You can use the DELETE statement to remove one or more rows from a table. As with UPDATE, you can provide a WHERE clause with the DELETE statement to specify the row or rows to be deleted. Then one or more rows of the table will be removed when the DELETE statement is executed, depending on how many rows satisfy the search condition specified in the WHERE clause. If a WHERE clause is not specified, all rows in the table will be deleted. The DELETE statement does not remove specific columns from a row; when a row is deleted, the entire row (all columns of data) is removed.

Retrieving Data

SELECT is the very heart of SQL data manipulation statements, and is used specifically to retrieve information. The power of SELECT lies in its ability to construct complex queries with an infinite number of variations, using a finite set of rules. SELECT is recursive, meaning that the input of a SQL statement can be the output of a successive number of nested SELECTs. For example, nested SELECT subqueries can be embedded within the INSERT, UPDATE, DELETE, and CREATE VIEW statements.

The Basic SELECT

The SELECT command in its most basic form consists of the SELECT-FROM-WHERE statement, which has the following structure:

```
SELECT <selection-list>
FROM <table-list>
WHERE <search_condition>
```

The selection list is the comma-separated list of columns to be retrieved. You can use an asterisk (*) to obtain all the columns in a table without listing each column name. By default, the basic form of SELECT returns all the rows that match the query conditions, including duplicate rows. You can use the DISTINCT qualifier to retrieve only the unique rows that match the query. You can also use the selection list to perform arithmetic operations on selected data and compute values for a group of rows, based on SQL functions such as AVG( ) and SUM( ).

The table list is the comma-separated list of tables or views from which the selection-list columns are retrieved. The table list can also define correlation names, which are shorthand alternate names for tables or views, used to join a table to itself or with subqueries that use the same table name.

The search condition describes the rows in which you are interested and consists of one or more predicates. Each predicate specifies a test that DB2 applies to each row of a table and evaluates to true, false, or unknown. You can combine predicates in a search by using parentheses or Boolean operators such as AND, OR, and NOT. Whenever a predicate results in true, it means that the SQL statement is to be applied to that row; if the predicate results in false, no operation is performed for that row. Predicates can compare a column with a value, a column with another column from the same table, or a column with another column from a different table. A basic predicate compares two values; a quantified predicate compares a value with a collection of values. The following is a list of the comparison operators that can be used with predicates:

Logic operators These are the familiar relational operators =, < >, <, >, < =, > =, and NOT. You can use these operators to compare two expressions or an expression with the result of a subquery (a predicate that contains embedded SELECT statements). You can use NOT to form the negative of any of the other operators.

IS NULL Tests for NULL expressions.

BETWEEN . . . AND Compares a value with a range of values. The search condition is satisfied by any value that falls between the two specified values.

IN Tests group membership. A group can be specified through a subquery or through lists of values in a statement.

LIKE Searches for strings that match certain patterns. The percent character (%) is a special matching character that can be used in place of an unknown string of characters. The underscore character (_) is also a special matching character that stands for any single character.

EXISTS Tests for the existence of certain rows. This predicate evaluates to true if the subquery returns one or more rows.

ALL Used in predicates that involve subqueries. A predicate is true when the specified relationship is true for all rows returned by a subquery. It is also true if no rows are returned by a subquery.

SOME or ANY Used in predicates that involve subqueries. The result of this predicate is true when the specified relationship is true for at least one row returned by a subquery. All values specified in predicates must be of compatible data types.

UNION Combines or merges the result tables of two SELECTs and eliminates duplicate rows.

EXCEPT Generates a result table consisting of all unique rows from the first SELECT statement that are not generated by the second SELECT statement.

INTERSECT Generates a result table consisting of unique rows that are common in the results of two SELECT statements.

Ordering Output Rows. Data stored in relational database tables have no explicit order, but you can sort the output of a SELECT query by applying the ORDER BY clause on the columns returned by the query. If the ORDER BY clause is used, the output will be returned in ascending order by default. You can override this default, however, by specifying the DESC keyword on any column that needs to be returned in descending order.

Grouping and Summarizing Output Rows. You can obtain summary rows with the GROUP BY and HAVING clauses. When these clauses are used, the characteristics of groups of rows are returned, as opposed to those of individual rows. The GROUP BY clause groups all rows that have the same value for a given column into a single row. DB2 then processes each group to produce a single-row result for the entire group. When the SELECT clause is applied to groups, it is used in conjunction with functions that return a single value for a given column within a group. Think of the HAVING clause as a WHERE clause for groups that is used as a search condition for eliminating groups, just as the WHERE clause is used as a search condition for eliminating rows. This means that the HAVING clause can be used only if the GROUP BY clause is specified.

Joins. The ability to join one or more tables with a single SELECT statement is one the more powerful features of relational databases. Joins allows you to retrieve data from two or more tables. The SELECT statement retrieves the requested information based on matching column values in the specified tables. DB2 allows you to join up to 15 tables with a single SELECT statement.

Subqueries. A subquery is a query within a query. These nested queries appear within the search condition of a WHERE or a HAVING clause. A subquery can be used within a search condition for the INSERT, DELETE, and UPDATE statements. It can include search conditions of its own, and these search conditions can in turn include more subqueries. When subqueries are processed, DB2 performs the innermost query first and then uses the results to execute the next outer query, and so on until all queries are resolved. A subquery can return either a single value or a set of values. If a set of values are to be returned, you must specify one of the following keywords: IN, ALL, ANY, SOME, EXIST, or NOT EXIST. In special cases, the innermost query can execute once for each result row in the outer query. These type of queries are known as correlated subqueries, and are used to search for one or more values that can be different for each row. The SELECT statement can have several forms in an embedded SQL application:

- With a DECLARE CURSOR statement if the SELECT statement will return multiple rows of data.
- As a SELECT INTO statement if the SELECT statement will return only one row of data.
- Along with the PREPARE statement to execute dynamic SQL statements.
- As a subquery that is part of the search condition (fullselect) of another SQL statement, such as INSERT, UPDATE, or DELETE.

Retrieving Multiple Rows Using a Cursor

DB2 uses a mechanism called a cursor to retrieve multiple rows of data from a database. A cursor is a temporary result table that holds all rows retrieved by a SELECT statement. The set of rows in a cursor is determined by the number of rows that satisfy the search condition provided with the SELECT statement. A cursor makes the rows from its result table available to an application by identifying or pointing to a current row of the table (a cursor position pointer). You can sequentially retrieve each row from the result table by using the FETCH statement until an end-of-data condition (the NOT FOUND condition, SQLCA.SQLCODE = 100) is reached. The steps involved in using a cursor in an application program are as follows:

1. Specify (define) the cursor using the DECLARE CURSOR statement.
2. Execute the query and build the result table by using the OPEN statement.
3. Retrieve the rows in the result table, one at a time, using the FETCH statement.
4. Modify or delete the current row (if appropriate) with either the UPDATE or the DELETE statement.
5. Terminate the cursor and delete the result table using the CLOSE statement.

An application can use several cursors concurrently, but each cursor requires its own set of DECLARE CURSOR, OPEN, CLOSE, and FETCH statements.

Types of Cursors

Cursors fall into one of the following categories:

Read-only The rows in the cursor's result table can only be read. Read-only cursors are used when an application needs to just read data. A cursor is considered read-only if it is based on a read-only SELECT statement. If a cursor is determined to be read only, repeatable read locks are still gathered and maintained on system tables needed by the transaction that contains the cursor. Therefore, it is important for applications to periodically issue COMMIT statements, even for read-only cursors.

Updatable The rows in the cursor's result table can be updated. Updatable cursors are used when an application intends to modify data as rows in the cursor are fetched. In order for a cursor to be updatable, the SELECT statement specified for the DECLARE CURSOR statement can refer to only one table or view and it must include the FOR UPDATE clause, naming each column that will be updated (unless the LANGLEVEL MIA precompile option is used).

Ambiguous The category of this type of cursor cannot be determined (updatable or read-only) from its definition or context. This can happen when a dynamic SQL statement is encountered that could be used to change a cursor that would otherwise be considered read-only. Ambiguous cursors are treated as read-only cursors if the BLOCKING ALL option is specified during precompiling or binding. Otherwise, it is considered updatable. Cursors that are processed dynamically are always considered ambiguous.

INSERT

Purpose The INSERT statement allows you to add data to (insert rows into) a database table or updatable view.

Syntax

```
EXEC SQL INSERT INTO [table-name | view-name] <([column-name,...])>
   [data-statement];
```

Parameters

table-name Identifies the name of the table to which data is to be added.

view-name Identifies the name of the updatable view to which data is to be added.

column-name Identifies one or more columns in which the data is to be stored.

data-statement Identifies the data values or a SELECT statement that will generate the data values to be inserted into the table or updatable view. The data statement can be any of the following:

VALUES <(> [*expression*, . . .] <)> Identifies the actual data values to be inserted into the table or updatable view. The expression can be an actual value, equation, NULL, or DEFAULT.

<WITH [*common-table-expression*, . . .]> [*fullselect*] Identifies a SELECT statement that will generate the appropriate data values by retrieving them from other tables and/or views. If this data statement is used, the following information must be provided:

common-table-expression Defines one or more common table expressions that can be referenced by name in the FROM clause of the fullselect statement that follows it.

fullselect Defines the full form of the SELECT statement to copy data from one table to another. This SELECT statement cannot contain references to host variables or parameter markers.

Description The INSERT statement adds data to (inserts rows into) a database table or updatable view.

Comments

- The table name or view name must identify a table or view that exists at the application server, but it must not identify a system catalog table, a view of a system catalog table, or a read-only view.
- A value cannot be inserted into a view column that was derived from a constant, expression, or scalar function.
- A value cannot be inserted into a column in a view if that column refers to the same base table column as the other column of the view. If the object of the insert operation is a view with such columns, you must specify a list of column names and the list must not contain these columns.
- You must specify the columns for which insert values are provided. Each name must be an unqualified name that identifies a column of the table or view. The same column must not be identified more than once. A view column that cannot accept insert values cannot be used.
- Omission of the column list is an implicit specification in which every column of the table or view is identified in a left-to-right order. This list is established when the statement is prepared and therefore does not include columns added to a table after the statement preparation.
- The implicit column list is established at prepare time, so an INSERT statement embedded in an application program does not use any columns that might have been added to the table or view after prepare time.
- You must introduce one or more rows of values to be inserted.
- Each host variable named must be described in the program in accordance with the rules for declaring host variables.
- The number of values provided for each row must equal the number of names in the column list. The first value is inserted in the first column in the list, the second value in the second column, and so on.
- The NULL value should be specified only for nullable columns.
- If the DEFAULT value is specified, the value inserted into the column will depend on how the column was defined, as follows:
  –If the WITH DEFAULT option was specified for the column when the table was created (or altered), the default value is based on the data type of the column.
  –If the WITH DEFAULT or NOT NULL option was not specified for the column when the table was created (or altered), the default value inserted into the column is NULL.
  –If the NOT NULL option was specified and the WITH DEFAULT option was not specified for the column when the table was created, the DEFAULT value cannot be used for that column.
- When the base tables of both the INSERT statement and the fullselect or any subquery of the fullselect are the same table, the fullselect is completely evaluated before any rows are inserted.
- If a SELECT statement is used, the number of columns in the result table produced by the SELECT statement must equal the number of names specified in the column list. The value of the first column of the result table is inserted into the first column in the list, the second value into the second column, and so on.
- If the base table referred to in a SELECT statement is self-referencing, then the subselect must not return more than one row, unless the foreign key of the inserted row is null because one of its columns was omitted from the column list.
- The value inserted in any column not in the column list is either the default value of the column or NULL. Columns that do not allow null values and that are not defined as NOT NULL WITH DEFAULT must be included in the column list. If data is added to an updatable view, all columns of the base table to which the

view refers that are not in the view must have either have a default value specified or allow null values.

- If the value to be inserted in a column is a number, the column must be a numeric column with the capacity to represent the integral part of the number. If the value to be inserted in a column is a string, the column must be either a string column with a length attribute at least as large as the length of the string or a datetime column if the string represents a date, time, or timestamp value.
- If the table or base table of the specified updatable view has one or more unique indexes, each row inserted into the table must conform to the constraints imposed by those indexes.
- If a view whose definition includes WITH CHECK OPTION is specified, each row inserted into the view must conform to the definition of the view (refer to the CREATE VIEW statement for more information).
- For each referential constraint defined on a table, each non-null value inserted into a column of the foreign key must be equal to value of a primary key of the parent table.
- Values inserted into a table or updatable view must satisfy the check conditions of all check constraints defined for the specified table.
- Insert statements might cause triggers to be executed. A trigger in turn might cause other statements to be executed, which will or will not be successful depending on the values inserted.
- After the INSERT statement is successfully executed, the third variable of the SQLERRD(3) field (*sqlca.errd[2]*) of the SQLCA data structure variable will indicate the number of rows actually inserted.
- Unless appropriate locks already exist, one or more exclusive locks are acquired when the INSERT statement executes. Until the locks are released, an inserted row can be accessed only by the following:
  –The application process that performed the insert.
  -Another application process using the uncommitted read (UR) isolation level with a read-only cursor, SELECT INTO statement, or a subselect used in a subquery.

Authorization Only users with system administrator (SYSADM) authority, database administrator (DBADM) authority, INSERT authority for the specified table or updatable view, or CONTROL authority for the specified table or updatable view are allowed to execute the VALUES( ) form of this statement. Users who want to use the fullselect form of this statement and who who do not have SYSADM or DBADM authority must have SELECT authority for the tables and/or views referenced in the fullselect statement.

See Also CREATE TABLE, UPDATE, DELETE

Examples The following C program illustrates how to use the INSERT statement to add one or more rows of data to a database table:

```
#include <stdio.h>
#include <stdlib.h>
#include <string.h>
#include <sql.h>

int main()
{
    /* Include The SQLCA Data Structure Variable */
    EXEC SQL INCLUDE SQLCA;
```

```
/* Set Up A Simple SQL Error Handler */
EXEC SQL WHENEVER SQLERROR GOTO EXIT;

/* Declare The Local Memory Variables */
int  rc = EXIT_SUCCESS;
char  szEmpNum[7];
char  szProjNum[7];

/* Declare The SQL Host Memory Variables */
EXEC SQL BEGIN DECLARE SECTION;
    char      szEmpNo[6];
    char      szProjNo[6];
    short     sActNo;
EXEC SQL END DECLARE SECTION;

/* Connect To The SAMPLE Database */
EXEC SQL CONNECT TO SAMPLE USER etpdd6z USING sanders;

/* Insert Records Into The MA_EMP_ACT Table Using A FullSelect */
EXEC SQL INSERT INTO MA_EMP_ACT
    SELECT * FROM USERID.EMP_ACT
    WHERE SUBSTR(PROJNO, 1, 2) = 'MA' AND ACTNO < 100;

/* Print A Message Telling That The Data Was Inserted */
printf("Multiple rows have been added to the MA_EMP_ACT table.\n");

/* Insert A Single Record Into The MA_EMP_ACT Table */
EXEC SQL INSERT INTO MA_EMP_ACT
    VALUES ('001000',
            'AD5200',
                 200,
                1.00,
          '1995-01-01',
           '1996-02-01');

/* Print A Message Telling That The Data Was Inserted */
printf("One row has been added to the MA_EMP_ACT table.\n");

/* Commit The Transaction */
EXEC SQL COMMIT;

/* Now Retrieve The Records From The MA_EMP_ACT Table */
/* To Verify That The Data Was Inserted                */

/* Declare The SELECT_CURSOR Table Cursor */
EXEC SQL DECLARE SELECT_CURSOR CURSOR FOR
    SELECT EMPNO,
           PROJNO,
           ACTNO
    FROM ETPDD6Z.MA_EMP_ACT;

/* Open The Cursor */
EXEC SQL OPEN SELECT_CURSOR;

/* If The Cursor Was Successfully Opened, Fetch The Records Into */
/* Host Variables                                                 */
printf("\nContents of ETPDD6Z.MA_EMP_ACT\n\n");
while (sqlca.sqlcode == SQL_RC_OK)
    {
    EXEC SQL FETCH SELECT_CURSOR
```

```
            INTO :szEmpNo,
                 :szProjNo,
                 :sActNo;

        /* If The FETCH Was Successful, Print The Data */
        if (sqlca.sqlcode == SQL_RC_OK)
            {
            strncpy(szEmpNum, " ", 6);
            strncpy(szProjNum, " ", 6);
            strncpy(szEmpNum, szEmpNo, 6);
            strncpy(szProjNum, szProjNo, 6);
            szEmpNum[6] = 0;
            szProjNum[6] = 0;
            printf("%6s %6s %d\n",
                   szEmpNum, szProjNum, sActNo);
            }
        }                                       /* End Of WHILE    */

    /* Close The Cursor */
    EXEC SQL CLOSE SELECT_CURSOR;

EXIT:
    /* If An Error Has Occurred, Display The SQL Return Code */
    if (sqlca.sqlcode != SQL_RC_OK)
        {
        printf("SQL ERROR : %ld\n", sqlca.sqlcode);
        rc = EXIT_FAILURE;
        }

    /* Issue A Rollback To Free All Locks */
    EXEC SQL ROLLBACK;

    /* Turn Off The SQL Error Handler */
    EXEC SQL WHENEVER SQLERROR CONTINUE;

    /* Disconnect From The SAMPLE Database */
    EXEC SQL DISCONNECT CURRENT;

    /* Return To The Operating System */
    return(rc);
}
```

The following C++ program illustrates how the INSERT statement is used by class methods to add one or more rows of data to a database table:

```
#include <iostream.h>
#include <stdlib.h>
#include <string.h>
#include <sql.h>

/* Define The Table Class */
class Table
{
    private:

        /* Include The SQLCA Data Structure Variable */
        EXEC SQL INCLUDE SQLCA;

        /* Declare The Local Memory Variables */
        char   szEmpNum[7];
        char   szProjNum[7];
```

```
        /* Declare The SQL Host Memory Variables */
        EXEC SQL BEGIN DECLARE SECTION;
            char      szEmpNo[6];
            char      szProjNo[6];
            short     sActNo;
        EXEC SQL END DECLARE SECTION;

    /* Declare The Public Member Function Prototypes */
    public:
        short int insertSingleRow();
        short int insertMultipleRows();
        short int showRecords();
} ;

/* Define The insertSingleRow() Member Function */
short int Table::insertSingleRow(void)
{
    /* Insert A Single Record Into The MA_EMP_ACT Table */
    EXEC SQL INSERT INTO MA_EMP_ACT
        VALUES ('001000',
                'AD5200',
                     200,
                    1.00,
            '1995-01-01',
             '1996-02-01');

    /* Print A Message Telling That The Data Was Inserted */
    if (sqlca.sqlcode == SQL_RC_OK)
        {
        cout << "One row has been added to the MA_EMP_ACT table.";
        cout << endl;
        }

    /* Return The SQL Return Code */
    return(sqlca.sqlcode);
}

/* Define The insertMultipleRows() Member Function */
short int Table::insertMultipleRows()
{
    /* Insert Records Into The MA_EMP_ACT Table Using A FullSelect */
    EXEC SQL INSERT INTO MA_EMP_ACT
        SELECT * FROM USERID.EMP_ACT
        WHERE SUBSTR(PROJNO, 1, 2) = 'MA' AND ACTNO < 100;

    /* Print A Message Telling That The Data Was Inserted */
    if (sqlca.sqlcode == SQL_RC_OK)
        {
        cout << "Multiple rows have been added to the MA_EMP_ACT ";
        cout << "table." << endl;
        }

    /* Return The SQL Return Code */
    return(sqlca.sqlcode);
}

/* Define The showRecords() Member Function */
short int Table::showRecords(void)
{
    /* Declare The SELECT_CURSOR Table Cursor */
    EXEC SQL DECLARE SELECT_CURSOR CURSOR FOR
```

```
        SELECT EMPNO,
               PROJNO,
               ACTNO
        FROM ETPDD6Z.MA_EMP_ACT;

    /* Open The Cursor */
    EXEC SQL OPEN SELECT_CURSOR;

    /* If The Cursor Was Successfully Opened, Fetch The Records Into */
    /* Host Variables                                                */
    cout << endl << "Contents of ETPDD6Z.MA_EMP_ACT" << endl << endl;
    while (sqlca.sqlcode == SQL_RC_OK)
        {
        EXEC SQL FETCH SELECT_CURSOR
            INTO :szEmpNo,
                 :szProjNo,
                 :sActNo;

        /* If The FETCH Was Successful, Print The Data */
        if (sqlca.sqlcode == SQL_RC_OK)
            {
            strncpy(szEmpNum, " ", 6);
            strncpy(szProjNum, " ", 6);
            strncpy(szEmpNum, szEmpNo, 6);
            strncpy(szProjNum, szProjNo, 6);
            szEmpNum[6] = 0;
            szProjNum[6] = 0;
            cout << szEmpNum << " " << szProjNum << " " << sActNo;
            cout << endl;
            }
        }                                          /* End Of WHILE   */

    /* Close The Cursor */
    EXEC SQL CLOSE SELECT_CURSOR;

    /* Return The SQL Return Code */
    return(sqlca.sqlcode);
}

int main()
{
    /* Declare The Local Memory Variables */
    short int rc = EXIT_SUCCESS;             // Must Be Declared Here
                                             // For The SQL Precompiler

    /* Include The SQLCA Data Structure Variable */
    EXEC SQL INCLUDE SQLCA;

    /* Set Up A Simple SQL Error Handler */
    EXEC SQL WHENEVER SQLERROR GOTO EXIT;

    /* Create An Instance Of The Table Class */
    Table table;

    /* Connect To The SAMPLE Database */
    EXEC SQL CONNECT TO SAMPLE USER etpdd6z USING sanders;

    /* Insert Records Into The MA_EMP_ACT Table Using A FullSelect */
    rc = table.insertMultipleRows();

    /* Insert A Single Record Into The MA_EMP_ACT Table */
    rc = table.insertSingleRow();
```

```
    /* Commit The Transaction */
    EXEC SQL COMMIT;

    /* Now Retrieve The Records From The ETPDD6Z.MA_EMP_ACT Table */
    /* To Verify That The Data Rows Were Added                     */
    rc = table.showRecords();

EXIT:
    /* If An Error Has Occurred, Display The SQL Return Code */
    if (sqlca.sqlcode != SQL_RC_OK)
        {
        cout << "SQL ERROR : " << sqlca.sqlcode << endl;
        rc = EXIT_FAILURE;
        }

    /* Issue A Rollback To Free All Locks */
    EXEC SQL ROLLBACK;

    /* Turn Off The SQL Error Handler */
    EXEC SQL WHENEVER SQLERROR CONTINUE;

    /* Disconnect From The SAMPLE Database */
    EXEC SQL DISCONNECT CURRENT;

    /* Return To The Operating System */
    return(rc);
}
```

UPDATE

Purpose The UPDATE statement allows you to change data in a database table or updatable view.

Syntax

```
EXEC SQL UPDATE [table-name | view-name] <<AS> [correlation-name]>
SET [assignment-statement] <WHERE [where-clause]>;

EXEC SQL UPDATE [table-name | view-name] SET [assignment-statement]
WHERE CURRENT OF [cursor-name];
```

Parameters

table-name Identifies the name of the table that contains the data to be changed.

view-name Identifies the name of the updatable view that references the data to be changed.

correlation-name Identifies a shorthand name that can be used within the search condition to refer to the table or view. For example, if the table EMPLOYEES has the correlation name EMP, then the search condition WHERE EMP.EMPID = '000100' would be the same as WHERE EMPLOYEES.EMPID = '000100'.

assignment-statement Identifies how the specified data rows in the specified table or updatable view are to be assigned new values. The syntax for an assignment statement can be either of the following:

```
[column-name,...] = [expression,...]
([column-name,...]) = ([expression,...] | [row-fullselect])
```

where:

column-name Identifies the column or columns in which the new data values are to be stored.

expression Identifies the actual data values to be nserted into the table or updatable view. The expression can be an actual value, equation, NULL, or DEFAULT, but the expression cannot include a column function except when it occurs within a scalar fullselect.

row-fullselect Defines the full form of a SELECT statement used to generate the appropriate data values by retrieving a single row with the same number of columns as the number of columns specified in the first portion of the assignment statement from other tables and/or views. This SELECT statement cannot contain references to host variables or parameter markers.

where-clause Identifies the search criteria to use when selecting one or more rows for retrieving a single row of data into the result table.

cursor-name Identifies the name of the opened cursor to be used in the update operation. The cursor name must identify a cursor that has already been described with the DECLARE CURSOR statement and opened with the OPEN statement.

Description The UPDATE statement changes data in a database table or updatable view. Updating a row of an updatable view actually updates a row in the base table to which the view refers. There are two ways to update data in a table, by either a searched or a positioned update. A searched update updates one or more rows from a table, depending on a specific search condition. A positioned update updates exactly one row in a base table, as determined by the current location of the cursor position pointer of an open cursor.

In order to perform a positioned update, you must include the FOR UPDATE clause in the DECLARE CURSOR statement to tell the system that you want to update some columns of the cursor result table. You can specify a column in the FOR UPDATE clause without specifying it in the fullselect, so you can update columns not explicitly retrieved by the cursor. If the FOR UPDATE clause is specified without column names, all columns of the table or view identified in the first FROM clause of the outer fullselect are considered to be updatable.

Comments

- Each specified column name must identify a column of the specified table or view. Column names must not be qualified, and a column cannot be specified more than once. Also, column names for specified views must not identify a view column that is derived from a scalar function, constant, expression, or special register.
- When performing positioned updates, if the UPDATE clause was specified in the select statement of the cursor, each column name in the assignment clause must also appear in the UPDATE clause. If the UPDATE clause was not specified in the select statement of the cursor and the LANGLEVEL MIA precompiler option was used when the application was precompiled, the name of any updatable column can be specified. If the LANGLEVEL SAA1 option was used when the application was precompiled, however, either explicitly or by default, no columns can be updated.
- An expression can contain references to columns of the target table of the UPDATE statement. For each updated row, the value of such a column in an expression is the value of the column in the row before the row was updated.
- The NULL value should be specified only for nullable columns.
- If the DEFAULT value is specified, the default value inserted into the column depends on how the column was defined, as follows:
  –If the WITH DEFAULT option was specified for the column when the table was created (or altered), the default value inserted is based on the data type of the column.

–If the WITH DEFAULT option or the NOT NULL option was not specified for the column when the table was created (or altered), the default value inserted into the column is NULL.

–If the NOT NULL option was specified and the WITH DEFAULT option was not specified for the column when the table was created, the DEFAULT value cannot be used for that column.

- A row fullselect can contain references to columns of the target table of the UPDATE statement. In this case, for each updated row, the value of such a column in an expression is the value of the column in the row before the row was updated.
- If the result of the row fullselect is NOT FOUND (no rows), then null values will be assigned to the specified columns. If the row fullselect returns multiple rows, an error will occur.
- If the WHERE [where-clause] option is omitted, all rows of the table or view will be updated.
- Each column name used in the search condition, other than in a subquery, must name a column that exists in the table or view. When the search condition includes a subquery in which the same table is the base object of both the UPDATE and the subquery, the subquery is completely evaluated before any rows are updated.
- The search condition is applied to each row of the table or view, and the rows that are updated are those for which the result of the search-condition is true. If the search condition contains a subquery, you can think of it as executing each time the search condition is applied to a row and using the results to apply the search condition. In actuality, a subquery with no correlated references is executed only once, and a subquery with a correlated reference might have to be executed once for each row found in the table or view.
- If you specify the WHERE CURRENT OF CURSOR search condition, the specified table or updatable view name must also be named in the FROM clause of the SELECT statement of the cursor, and the result table of the cursor must not be read-only.
- If the table or the base table of the specified updatable view has one or more unique indexes, each updated row must conform to the constraints imposed by those indexes.
- If a view was not defined with the WITH CHECK OPTION, rows can be changed so they no longer conform to the definition of the view. Such rows are updated in the base table of the view and will no longer appear in the view.
- If you specify a view whose definition includes WITH CHECK OPTION, each updated row must conform to the definition of the view (refer to the CREATE VIEW statement for more information).
- The value of a column that is part of the primary key of a parent table must not be changed.
- If a column to be updated is part of a primary key (the table is not a parent table) or part of a unique index, the number of rows selected for update must not be greater than 1.
- For each referential constraint defined for a table, each non-null value updated for a column of the foreign key must be equal to the value of a primary key of the parent table.
- Updated values in a table or updatable view must satisfy the check conditions of all check constraints defined for the specified table. When processing an UPDATE statement, only the check constraints that refer to the updated columns are checked.

- If an update value violates any constraints or if any type of error occurs during the execution of the UPDATE statement, no rows will be updated.
- After the UPDATE statement is successfully executed, the third variable of the SQLERRD(3) field (*sqlca.errd[2]*) of the SQLCA data structure variable will indicate the number of rows actually updated.
- The SQLERRD(5) field (*sqlca.errd[4]*) of the SQLCA data structure variable contains a value corresponding to the number of rows that were affected by referential constraints and triggered statements.
- Unless appropriate locks already exist, one or more exclusive locks are acquired when the UPDATE statement executes. Until the locks are released, an updated row can be accessed only with the following:
  –The application process that performed the update.
  –Another application process using the uncommitted read (UR) isolation level with a read-only cursor, SELECT INTO statement, or subselect used in a subquery.

Prerequisites If the WHERE CURRENT OF CURSOR search condition is specified, a DECLARE CURSOR statement and OPEN statement for the named cursor must precede the UPDATE statement in the program. Also, the cursor position pointer must be positioned on the row being updated in the cursor result table.

Authorization Only users with either system administrator (SYSADM) authority, database administrator (DBADM) authority, UPDATE authority for the specified table or updateable view, or CONTROL authority for the specified table or updateable view are allowed to execute this statement as long as no row-fullselect statement is specified.

Users that wish to use the row-fullselect form of this statement that do not have system administrator authority or database administrator authority must also have SELECT authority for the tables and/or views that are referenced in the fullselect statement.

See Also INSERT, DELETE, DECLARE CURSOR, OPEN CURSOR, FETCH

Examples The following C program illustrates how the UPDATE statement can be used to modify existing data in a database table:

```
#include <stdio.h>
#include <stdlib.h>
#include <string.h>
#include <sql.h>

int main()
{
    /* Include The SQLCA Data Structure Variable */
    EXEC SQL INCLUDE SQLCA;

    /* Set Up A Simple SQL Error Handler */
    EXEC SQL WHENEVER SQLERROR GOTO EXIT;

    /* Declare The Local Memory Variables */
    int   rc = EXIT_SUCCESS;
    char  szEmpNum[7];
    char  szProjNum[7];

    /* Declare The SQL Host Memory Variables */
    EXEC SQL BEGIN DECLARE SECTION;
        char      szEmpNo[6];
        char      szProjNo[6];
        short     sActNo;
    EXEC SQL END DECLARE SECTION;
```

```
    /* Connect To The SAMPLE Database */
    EXEC SQL CONNECT TO SAMPLE USER etpdd6z USING sanders;

    /* Update A Record In The MA_EMP_ACT Table */
    EXEC SQL UPDATE MA_EMP_ACT
        SET PROJNO = 'MA5200'
        WHERE PROJNO = 'AD5200';

    /* Print A Message Telling That A Record Was Updated */
    printf("One record was updated in the MA_EMP_ACT table.\n");

    /* Commit The Transaction */
    EXEC SQL COMMIT;

    /* Now Retrieve The Records From The MA_EMP_ACT Table */
    /* To Verify That The Record Was Updated               */

    /* Declare The SELECT_CURSOR Table Cursor */
    EXEC SQL DECLARE SELECT_CURSOR CURSOR FOR
        SELECT EMPNO,
               PROJNO,
               ACTNO
        FROM ETPDD6Z.MA_EMP_ACT;

    /* Open The Cursor */
    EXEC SQL OPEN SELECT_CURSOR;

    /* If The Cursor Was Successfully Opened, Fetch The Records Into */
    /* Host Variables                                                */
    printf("\nContents of ETPDD6Z.MA_EMP_ACT\n\n");
    while (sqlca.sqlcode == SQL_RC_OK)
        {
        EXEC SQL FETCH SELECT_CURSOR
            INTO :szEmpNo,
                 :szProjNo,
                 :sActNo;

        /* If The FETCH Was Successful, Print The Data */
        if (sqlca.sqlcode == SQL_RC_OK)
            {
            strncpy(szEmpNum, " ", 6);
            strncpy(szProjNum, " ", 6);
            strncpy(szEmpNum, szEmpNo, 6);
            strncpy(szProjNum, szProjNo, 6);
            szEmpNum[6] = 0;
            szProjNum[6] = 0;
            printf("%6s %6s %d\n",
                   szEmpNum, szProjNum, sActNo);
            }
        }                                         /* End Of WHILE   */

    /* Close The Cursor */
    EXEC SQL CLOSE SELECT_CURSOR;

EXIT:
    /* If An Error Has Occurred, Display The SQL Return Code */
    if (sqlca.sqlcode != SQL_RC_OK)
        {
        printf("SQL ERROR : %ld\n", sqlca.sqlcode);
        rc = EXIT_FAILURE;
        }

    /* Issue A Rollback To Free All Locks */
    EXEC SQL ROLLBACK;
```

```
    /* Turn Off The SQL Error Handler */
    EXEC SQL WHENEVER SQLERROR CONTINUE;

    /* Disconnect From The SAMPLE Database */
    EXEC SQL DISCONNECT CURRENT;

    /* Return To The Operating System */
    return(rc);
}
```

The following C++ program illustrates how the UPDATE statement is used by class methods to modify existing data in a database table:

```
#include <iostream.h>
#include <stdlib.h>
#include <string.h>
#include <sql.h>

/* Define The Table Class */
class Table
{
    private:

        /* Include The SQLCA Data Structure Variable */
        EXEC SQL INCLUDE SQLCA;

        /* Declare The Local Memory Variables */
        char  szEmpNum[7];
        char  szProjNum[7];

        /* Declare The SQL Host Memory Variables */
        EXEC SQL BEGIN DECLARE SECTION;
            char      szEmpNo[6];
            char      szProjNo[6];
            short     sActNo;
        EXEC SQL END DECLARE SECTION;

    /* Declare The Public Member Function Prototypes */
    public:
        short int updateRows();
        short int showRecords();
} ;

/* Define The updateRows() Member Function */
short int Table::updateRows(void)
{
    /* Update A Record Into The MA_EMP_ACT Table */
    EXEC SQL UPDATE MA_EMP_ACT
        SET PROJNO = 'MA5200'
        WHERE PROJNO = 'AD5200';

    /* Print A Message Telling That A Record Was Updated */
    if (sqlca.sqlcode == SQL_RC_OK)
        {
        cout << "One record was updated in the MA_EMP_ACT table.";
        cout << endl;
        }

    /* Return The SQL Return Code */
    return(sqlca.sqlcode);
}
```

```
/* Define The showRecords() Member Function */
short int Table::showRecords(void)
{
    /* Declare The SELECT_CURSOR Table Cursor */
    EXEC SQL DECLARE SELECT_CURSOR CURSOR FOR
        SELECT EMPNO,
               PROJNO,
               ACTNO
        FROM ETPDD6Z.MA_EMP_ACT;

    /* Open The Cursor */
    EXEC SQL OPEN SELECT_CURSOR;

    /* If The Cursor Was Successfully Opened, Fetch The Records Into*/
    /* Host Variables                                                */
    cout << endl << "Contents of ETPDD6Z.MA_EMP_ACT" << endl << endl;
    while (sqlca.sqlcode == SQL_RC_OK)
        {
        EXEC SQL FETCH SELECT_CURSOR
            INTO :szEmpNo,
                 :szProjNo,
                 :sActNo;

        /* If The FETCH Was Successful, Print The Data */
        if (sqlca.sqlcode == SQL_RC_OK)
            {
            strncpy(szEmpNum, " ", 6);
            strncpy(szProjNum, " ", 6);
            strncpy(szEmpNum, szEmpNo, 6);
            strncpy(szProjNum, szProjNo, 6);
            szEmpNum[6] = 0;
            szProjNum[6] = 0;
            cout << szEmpNum << " " << szProjNum << " " << sActNo;
            cout << endl;
            }
        }                                           /* End Of WHILE    */

    /* Close The Cursor */
    EXEC SQL CLOSE SELECT_CURSOR;

    /* Return The SQL Return Code */
    return(sqlca.sqlcode);
}

int main()
{
    /* Declare The Local Memory Variables */
    short int rc = EXIT_SUCCESS;            // Must Be Declared Here
                                            // For The SQL Precompiler

    /* Include The SQLCA Data Structure Variable */
    EXEC SQL INCLUDE SQLCA;

    /* Set Up A Simple SQL Error Handler */
    EXEC SQL WHENEVER SQLERROR GOTO EXIT;

    /* Create An Instance Of The Table Class */
    Table table;

    /* Connect To The SAMPLE Database */
    EXEC SQL CONNECT TO SAMPLE USER etpdd6z USING sanders;
```

```
    /* Update A Record In The MA_EMP_ACT Table */
    rc = table.updateRows();

    /* Commit The Transaction */
    EXEC SQL COMMIT;

    /* Now Retrieve The Records From The ETPDD6Z.MA_EMP_ACT Table */
    /* To Verify That The Record Was Updated                      */
    rc = table.showRecords();

EXIT:
    /* If An Error Has Occurred, Display The SQL Return Code */
    if (sqlca.sqlcode != SQL_RC_OK)
        {
        cout << "SQL ERROR : " << sqlca.sqlcode << endl;
        rc = EXIT_FAILURE;
        }

    /* Issue A Rollback To Free All Locks */
    EXEC SQL ROLLBACK;

    /* Turn Off The SQL Error Handler */
    EXEC SQL WHENEVER SQLERROR CONTINUE;

    /* Disconnect From The SAMPLE Database */
    EXEC SQL DISCONNECT CURRENT;

    /* Return To The Operating System */
    return(rc);
}
```

DELETE

Purpose The DELETE statement removes data from a database table or updatable view.

Syntax

```
EXEC SQL DELETE FROM [table-name | view-name] <<AS> [correlation-name]>
   <WHERE [search-condition]>;
```

Parameters

table-name Identifies the name of the table that contains the data to be deleted.

view-name Identifies the name of the updatable view that references the data to be deleted.

correlation-name Identifies an alternate name for the specified table or view. You can use correlation names in place of the actual table or view name in the WHERE search condition.

search-condition Specifies a condition for selecting the rows to be deleted. Each column name in the search condition must identify a column that exists in the specified table or view. The search condition is applied to each row of the specified table or view, and rows that meet the search condition criteria are deleted. If the specified search condition is CURRENT OF cursor-name, the current row of the specified cursor will be deleted. If no search condition is specified, the entire contents of the specified table or view will be deleted.

Description The DELETE statement allows you to remove data from a database table or updatable view. If a row is deleted from a view, it is actually deleted from the table on which the view is based. There are two ways to remove data from a table, with either a searched delete or a positioned delete. A searched delete will delete one or more rows from a table, depending on a specific search condition; a positioned delete will delete exactly one row from a table, as determined by the current location of the cursor position pointer of an open cursor.

Normally, the FOR UPDATE clause is not required as part of the DECLARE CURSOR statement in order for the cursor to allow positioned deletes. The only exception to this occurs when dynamic SQL is used for either the SELECT statement portion of the DECLARE CURSOR statement or the DELETE statement in an application previously precompiled with LANGLEVEL set to SAA1 and bound with the BLOCKING ALL option. In this case, the FOR UPDATE clause must be included in the SELECT statement.

Positioned deletes cause the row being referenced by the cursor to be deleted. This leaves the cursor positioned before the next row, and a FETCH statement must be issued before any additional WHERE CURRENT OF operations can be performed against the cursor.

Comments

- If the specified search condition contains a subquery with no correlated references, the subquery will be executed once and the results used when the search condition for each row are evaluated. If the specified search condition contains a subquery with one or more correlated references, however, the subquery might have to be executed once for each row. If a subquery refers to the object table of a DELETE statement or a dependent table with a delete rule of CASCADE or SET NULL, the subquery will be completely evaluated before any rows are deleted.
- If the object table of a DELETE statement is self-referencing with a delete rule of NO ACTION, RESTRICT, or SET NULL, the number of rows for which the search condition is true must not be greater than one.
- If the CURRENT OF cursor name search condition is used with the DETETE statement, the specified table or view name must also be specified in the FROM clause of the SELECT statement used to define the cursor, the result table of the cursor must not be read-only, and the cursor position pointer must be positioned on a row since that row is the one to be deleted. When the record is deleted, the cursor position pointer is moved to the next row of the result table if one exists, or past the last row if there is no next row.
- If either the specified table or the base table of the specified view is a parent table, the rows selected for deletion must not have any dependents in a relationship with a delete rule of RESTRICT or NO ACTION, and the delete operation must not cascade to descendent rows that have dependents in a relationship with a delete rule of RESTRICT or NO ACTION. (Refer to the CREATE TABLE statement for more information.) If the delete operation is not prevented by a RESTRICT or NO ACTION delete rule, all selected rows will be deleted. Also, the nullable columns of the foreign keys of any rows that are their dependents in a relationship with a delete rule of SET NULL are set to the null value, and any rows that are their dependents in a relationship with a delete rule of CASCADE are also deleted (the same rules apply to those rows).
- If an error occurs during the execution of a multiple-row DELETE, no changes will be made to the database.
- Unless appropriate locks already exist, one or more exclusive locks are acquired during the execution of the DELETE statement in order to prevent other application processes from performing operations on the table. Issuing a COMMIT or ROLLBACK statement will release these acquired locks. Until the locks are released, the effect of the delete operation will be seen only by the application process that performed the deletion and any other applications using the uncommitted read (UR) isolation level.

- If an application deletes a row on which any of its open cursors are currently positioned, the cursor position pointers of those cursors will be placed on the next row of their result table.
- The SQLERRD(3) field (*sqlca.errd[2]*) of the SQLCA data structure variable contains a value that corresponds to the number of rows that were actually deleted from the specified table (or view) after the DELETE statement executes. This value does not include rows that were deleted as a result of a CASCADE delete rule.
- The SQLERRD(5) field (*sqlca.errd[4]*) of the SQLCA data structure variable contains a value corresponding to the number of rows that were affected by referential constraints and triggered statements. This value includes rows deleted as a result of a CASCADE delete rule and rows in which foreign keys were set to NULL as the result of a SET NULL delete rule. This value also includes the number of rows that were inserted, updated, and/or deleted as the result of a triggered action.
- If an error occurs that prevents the DELETE statement from deleting all rows matching the search condition and/or performing all operations required by existing referential constraints, no changes will be made to the specified table.

Prerequisites If you use the CURRENT OF cursor-name search condition, the cursor name must identify a cursor defined by a DECLARE CURSOR statement and opened by an OPEN statement. Therefore, a DECLARE CURSOR statement and an OPEN statement must be executed before the DELETE statement if a positioned delete is to be performed.

Authorization Users with either system administrator (SYSADM) authority or database administrator (DBADM) authority are allowed to execute this statement regardless of what table is specified. All other users must have either DELETE authority or CONTROL authority for the table (or base table(s) referenced by the view) specified. If a searched DELETE is to be performed, users must also have SELECT authority for the specified table (or base tables referenced by the specified view).

See Also INSERT, UPDATE, DECLARE CURSOR, OPEN, FETCH

Examples The following C program illustrates how the DELETE statement is used to remove a row of data from a database table:

```
#include <stdio.h>
#include <stdlib.h>
#include <string.h>
#include <sql.h>

int main()
{
    /* Include The SQLCA Data Structure Variable */
    EXEC SQL INCLUDE SQLCA;

    /* Set Up A Simple SQL Error Handler */
    EXEC SQL WHENEVER SQLERROR GOTO EXIT;

    /* Declare The Local Memory Variables */
    int   rc = EXIT_SUCCESS;
    char  szEmpNum[7];
    char  szProjNum[7];

    /* Declare The SQL Host Memory Variables */
    EXEC SQL BEGIN DECLARE SECTION;
```

```
        char        szEmpNo[6];
        char        szProjNo[6];
        short       sActNo;
    EXEC SQL END DECLARE SECTION;

    /* Connect To The SAMPLE Database */
    EXEC SQL CONNECT TO SAMPLE USER etpdd6z USING sanders;

    /* Delete A Record From The MA_EMP_ACT Table */
    EXEC SQL DELETE FROM MA_EMP_ACT
        WHERE EMPNO = '001000';

    /* Print A Message Telling That A Record Was Deleted */
    printf("One record was deleted from the MA_EMP_ACT table.\n");

    /* Commit The Transaction */
    EXEC SQL COMMIT;

    /* Now Retrieve The Records From The MA_EMP_ACT Table */
    /* To Verify That The Record Was Deleted              */

    /* Declare The SELECT_CURSOR Table Cursor */
    EXEC SQL DECLARE SELECT_CURSOR CURSOR FOR
        SELECT EMPNO,
               PROJNO,
               ACTNO
        FROM ETPDD6Z.MA_EMP_ACT;

    /* Open The Cursor */
    EXEC SQL OPEN SELECT_CURSOR;

    /* If The Cursor Was Successfully Opened, Fetch The Records Into */
    /* Host Variables                                                */
    printf("\nContents of ETPDD6Z.MA_EMP_ACT\n\n");
    while (sqlca.sqlcode == SQL_RC_OK)
        {
        EXEC SQL FETCH SELECT_CURSOR
            INTO :szEmpNo,
                 :szProjNo,
                 :sActNo;

        /* If The FETCH Was Successful, Print The Data */
        if (sqlca.sqlcode == SQL_RC_OK)
            {
            strncpy(szEmpNum, " ", 6);
            strncpy(szProjNum, " ", 6);
            strncpy(szEmpNum, szEmpNo, 6);
            strncpy(szProjNum, szProjNo, 6);
            szEmpNum[6] = 0;
            szProjNum[6] = 0;
            printf("%6s %6s %d\n",
                   szEmpNum, szProjNum, sActNo);
            }
        }                                       /* End Of WHILE    */

    /* Close The Cursor */
    EXEC SQL CLOSE SELECT_CURSOR;

EXIT:
    /* If An Error Has Occurred, Display The SQL Return Code */
    if (sqlca.sqlcode != SQL_RC_OK)
```

```
        {
        printf("SQL ERROR : %ld\n", sqlca.sqlcode);
        rc = EXIT_FAILURE;
        }

    /* Issue A Rollback To Free All Locks */
    EXEC SQL ROLLBACK;

    /* Turn Off The SQL Error Handler */
    EXEC SQL WHENEVER SQLERROR CONTINUE;

    /* Disconnect From The SAMPLE Database */
    EXEC SQL DISCONNECT CURRENT;

    /* Return To The Operating System */
    return(rc);
}
```

The following C++ program illustrates how the DELETE statement is used by class methods to remove a row of data from a database table:

```
#include <iostream.h>
#include <stdlib.h>
#include <string.h>
#include <sql.h>

/* Define The Table Class */
class Table
{
    private:

        /* Include The SQLCA Data Structure Variable */
        EXEC SQL INCLUDE SQLCA;

        /* Declare The Local Memory Variables */
        char  szEmpNum[7];
        char  szProjNum[7];

        /* Declare The SQL Host Memory Variables */
        EXEC SQL BEGIN DECLARE SECTION;
            char      szEmpNo[6];
            char      szProjNo[6];
            short     sActNo;
        EXEC SQL END DECLARE SECTION;

    /* Declare The Public Member Function Prototypes */
    public:
        short int deleteRow();
        short int showRecords();
} ;

/* Define The deleteRow() Member Function */
short int Table::deleteRow(void)
{
    /* Delete A Record From The MA_EMP_ACT Table */
    EXEC SQL DELETE FROM MA_EMP_ACT
        WHERE EMPNO = '001000';

    /* Print A Message Telling That A Record Was Deleted */
    if (sqlca.sqlcode == SQL_RC_OK)
```

```
        {
        cout << "One record was deleted from the MA_EMP_ACT table.";
        cout << endl;
        }

    /* Return The SQL Return Code */
    return(sqlca.sqlcode);
}

/* Define The showRecords() Member Function */
short int Table::showRecords(void)
{
    /* Declare The SELECT_CURSOR Table Cursor */
    EXEC SQL DECLARE SELECT_CURSOR CURSOR FOR
        SELECT EMPNO,
               PROJNO,
               ACTNO
        FROM ETPDD6Z.MA_EMP_ACT;

    /* Open The Cursor */
    EXEC SQL OPEN SELECT_CURSOR;

    /* If The Cursor Was Successfully Opened, Fetch The Records Into */
    /* Host Variables                                                 */
    cout << endl << "Contents of ETPDD6Z.MA_EMP_ACT" << endl << endl;
    while (sqlca.sqlcode == SQL_RC_OK)
        {
        EXEC SQL FETCH SELECT_CURSOR
            INTO :szEmpNo,
                 :szProjNo,
                 :sActNo;

        /* If The FETCH Was Successful, Print The Data */
        if (sqlca.sqlcode == SQL_RC_OK)
            {
            strncpy(szEmpNum, " ", 6);
            strncpy(szProjNum, " ", 6);
            strncpy(szEmpNum, szEmpNo, 6);
            strncpy(szProjNum, szProjNo, 6);
            szEmpNum[6] = 0;
            szProjNum[6] = 0;
            cout << szEmpNum << " " << szProjNum << " " << sActNo;
            cout << endl;
            }
        }                                        /* End Of WHILE   */

    /* Close The Cursor */
    EXEC SQL CLOSE SELECT_CURSOR;

    /* Return The SQL Return Code */
    return(sqlca.sqlcode);
}

int main()
{
    /* Declare The Local Memory Variables */
    short int rc = EXIT_SUCCESS;            // Must Be Declared Here
                                            // For The SQL Precompiler

    /* Include The SQLCA Data Structure Variable */
    EXEC SQL INCLUDE SQLCA;
```

```
    /* Set Up A Simple SQL Error Handler */
    EXEC SQL WHENEVER SQLERROR GOTO EXIT;

    /* Create An Instance Of The Table Class */
    Table table;

    /* Connect To The SAMPLE Database */
    EXEC SQL CONNECT TO SAMPLE USER etpdd6z USING sanders;

    /* Delete A Record From The MA_EMP_ACT Table */
    rc = table.deleteRow();

    /* Commit The Transaction */
    EXEC SQL COMMIT;

    /* Now Retrieve The Records From The ETPDD6Z.MA_EMP_ACT Table */
    /* To Verify That The Record Was Deleted                      */
    rc = table.showRecords();

EXIT:
    /* If An Error Has Occurred, Display The SQL Return Code */
    if (sqlca.sqlcode != SQL_RC_OK)
        {
        cout << "SQL ERROR : " << sqlca.sqlcode << endl;
        rc = EXIT_FAILURE;
        }

    /* Issue A Rollback To Free All Locks */
    EXEC SQL ROLLBACK;

    /* Turn Off The SQL Error Handler */
    EXEC SQL WHENEVER SQLERROR CONTINUE;

    /* Disconnect From The SAMPLE Database */
    EXEC SQL DISCONNECT CURRENT;

    /* Return To The Operating System */
    return(rc);
}
```

DECLARE CURSOR

Purpose The DECLARE CURSOR statement defines a cursor.

Syntax

```
EXEC SQL DECLARE [cursor-name] CURSOR <WITH HOLD> FOR [select-statement |
   statement-name];
```

Parameters

cursor-name Identifies the name of the cursor to be created. The cursor name cannot be used by another cursor.

select-statement Identifies a SELECT statement that will be used to produce a result data set for the cursor. This SELECT statement cannot include parameter markers, but it can include references to host variables.

statement-name Identifies a prepared SELECT statement that will be used to produce a result data set for the cursor. The statement name cannot be the name of a prepared statement used by another cursor.

Description The DECLARE CURSOR statement defines a cursor. A cursor is a named control structure that allows you to manipulate two or more rows of data in a database. The actual data stored in a cursor is determined by a SELECT statement. When a declared cursor is opened, the SELECT statement associated with the cursor is executed, the appropriate data is retrieved and stored in a temporary result table, and the cursor pointer is positioned so it points to the first record in the result table. Data is then retrieved from the result table each time you execute the FETCH statement.

Normally, all resources used by a cursor are maintained by the transaction that declared and opened the cursor. If a transaction is terminated with the COMMIT statement, the following actions take place:

- All open cursors defined with the WITH HOLD option remain open and the cursor position pointer is positioned before the next logical row of data in the results table.
- All prepared SQL statements that reference open cursors defined with the WITH HOLD option are retained.
- All acquired locks are released, except for table locks acquired for open cursors defined with the WITH HOLD option.
- Only FETCH and CLOSE statements can be executed against cursors defined with the WITH HOLD option once the transaction is terminated by a COMMIT statement. The UPDATE and DELETE CURRENT OF CURSOR statements are valid only while the transaction is active.
- LOB locators are freed.
- In some cases, packages might be re-created either explicitly (by binding the package) or implicitly (because the package is invalidated and then dynamically re-created the first time it is referenced) within a transaction. When the transaction is terminated with the COMMIT statement, all held cursors are closed in a re-created package and all prepared statements that referenced held cursors are dropped. This action could result in errors during subsequent execution.

If a transaction is terminated by the ROLLBACK statement, the following takes place:

- All open cursors are closed.
- All prepared SQL statements are dropped.
- All acquired locks are released.
- LOB locators are freed.

Comments

- Cursors can be referenced only within the source-code file that defines and opens them. Therefore, a program called from another program or a different source-code file within the same program cannot use a cursor that was opened by the calling program.
- If the SELECT statement of a cursor contains references to the CURRENT DATE, CURRENT TIME, or CURRENT TIMESTAMP special registers, the value for the special registers will be the same for each record in the cursor result table. This is because the value is determined once, when the cursor is opened.
- If the name of a prepared SELECT statement is used to define a cursor, the SELECT statement must first be prepared by the PREPARE statement before the cursor can be opened.
- For more efficient processing, DB2 can block data for read-only cursors when the data is retrieved from a remote database server. Using the UPDATE clause in the SELECT statement helps DB2 determine whether or not a cursor is updatable. Using the UPDATE clause also helps determine the appropriate data access path to use.

- An open cursor designates a cursor result table and a position pointer relative to the rows of that result table. The actual data in the result table is determined by the SELECT statement associated with the cursor.
- You can use cursors that reside in stored procedures invoked by a CLI function call rather than the CALL statement to define result data sets that are returned directly to the client application (the application invoking the stored procedure).

Authorization The SELECT statement used to define the result data set of a cursor determines which authorizations are required to execute this statement. Users with either system administrator (SYSADM) authority or database administrator (DBADM) authority are allowed to execute this statement regardless of what tables or views are referenced by the SELECT statement. All other users must have either SELECT authority or CONTROL authority for each table or view referenced by the SELECT statement.

If the SELECT statement is a prepared statement, the authorization ID is determined at application run-time and the authority check is performed when the SELECT statement is prepared. If the SELECT statement is not a prepared statement, the authorization ID is determined when the application is precompiled.

See Also PREPARE, SELECT, OPEN, FETCH, CLOSE

Examples Refer to the FETCH statement for an example that illustrates how to use the DECLARE CURSOR statement to define an SQL cursor.

OPEN

Purpose The OPEN statement opens a previously declared cursor.

Syntax

```
EXEC SQL OPEN [cursor-name] <Options>;
```

Parameters *cursor-name* Identifies the name of a cursor that was defined in a previous DECLARE CURSOR statement.

Options

USING [host-variable, . . .] Identifies one or more host variables for which values are substituted for parameter markers (question marks) in the SELECT statement that was used to define the cursor. (Refer to the beginning of Chapter 8 for more information about parameter markers.) If the SELECT statement includes parameter markers, the USING option must be specified and the number of identified host variables must be the same as the number of parameter markers used in the SELECT statement.

USING DESCRIPTOR [descriptor-name] Identifies an input SQL descriptor area (SQLDA) data structure variable containing a valid description of the host variables that will be used by the SELECT statement when it is executed. Before the OPEN statement is processed with the USING DESCRIPTOR option, the following fields must be set in the SQLDA data structure variable:

sqln This field indicates the number of *sqlvar* occurrences in the SQLDA data structure variable.

sqldabc This field specifies the total number of bytes of memory storage allocated for the SQLDA data structure variable. Since the SQLDA data structure variable must have enough allocated storage to contain all *sqlvar* occurrences, the value in the *sqldabc* field must be greater than or equal to 16 + *sqln* * (*n*), where *n* is the length of a single *sqlvar* occurrence.

sqld	This field indicates the number of occurrences of *sqlvar* variables to be used when processing the statement. The value in this field must be set to a value greater than or equal to zero and less than or equal to the value in the *sqln* field.
sqlvar field(s)	Each occurrence of this field specifies the attributes of a single variable. If LOB or distinct type result columns need to be accommodated, two *sqlvar* entries must exist for every select-list item (or column of the result table).

Description

The OPEN statement allows you to open a previously declared cursor. When a cursor is opened, all rows meeting the specifications of the cursor definition are retrieved into a cursor result table. The data in the cursor result table is derived by evaluating the SELECT statement that defines the cursor and using the current values of any host variables specified in either the statement or the USING option of the OPEN statement. The rows of the result table can be derived either during the execution of the OPEN statement (and a temporary table will be created to hold them) or during the execution of each subsequent FETCH statement. In either case, the cursor is placed in the open state and the cursor position pointer is positioned before the first row of data in the cursor result table. If the cursor result table is empty, the state of the cursor is effectively "after the last row" and any subsequent FETCH statements will generate a NOT FOUND condition.

Comments

- Before a cursor's SELECT statement is executed, each parameter marker it contains is replaced by the value of the parameter marker's corresponding host variable. For typed parameter markers, the attributes of the target host variable are specified by the CAST specification. For untyped parameter markers, the attributes of the target host variable are determined by the context in which the parameter marker is used (refer to the beginning of Chapter 8 for more information). For example, suppose the host variable V corresponds to parameter marker P. When the SELECT statement containing parameter marker P is executed, the value of V is assigned to the target variable for P, in accordance with the following rules for assigning a value to a column:
  –V must be compatible with the target column.
  –If V is a string, its length must not be greater than the length attribute of the target column.
  –If V is a number, the absolute value of its integral part must not be greater than the maximum absolute value of the integral part of the target column.
  –If the attributes of V are not identical to the attributes of the target column, the value will be converted to conform to the attributes of the target column.
  –When the SELECT statement is executed, the value used in place of P is the value of the target variable for P. For example, if V is defined as char V[6] (C and C++) and the target column is defined as CHAR(8), then the value used in place of P will be the value of V padded with two blanks.
- The USING [*host-variable*, . . .] option is intended to be used with a prepared SELECT statement that contains parameter markers. However, it can also be used when the SELECT statement of the cursor is part of the DECLARE CURSOR statement. In this case, the OPEN statement is executed as if each host variable in the SELECT statement were a parameter marker, except that the attributes of the target variables are the same as the attributes of the host variables in the SELECT statement. The effect is to override the values of the host variables in the SELECT statement of the cursor with the values of the host variables specified in the USING clause.

- All cursors in a program are in the closed state when the program is initiated. All cursors, except open cursors declared with the WITH HOLD option, are returned to the closed state when a program issues a COMMIT statement. All cursors, regardless of how they were defined, are placed in the closed state whenever the program issues a ROLLBACK statement. A cursor will also be returned to the closed state, regardless of how it was defined, if the CLOSE statement is executed (with the appropriate cursor name specified) or if an error is detected that makes the position of the cursor unpredictable. The only way to change the state of a cursor from closed to open is to execute an OPEN statement.
- To retrieve rows from the cursor result table of a cursor, you must execute one or more FETCH statements when the cursor is open.
- In some cases, the result table of a cursor is derived during the execution of FETCH statements. In other cases, the entire result table is transferred to a temporary table during the execution of the OPEN statement. When temporary tables are used, the results of an application program can differ in these two ways:
  -An error can occur during OPEN that would otherwise not occur until some later FETCH statement.
  -INSERT, UPDATE, and DELETE statements executed in the transaction while the cursor is open will not affect the result table.
- Conversely, if temporary tables are not used, INSERT, UPDATE, and DELETE statements executed while the cursor is open can affect the result table if they are issued either by concurrent transactions or by the same transaction that opened the cursor. Chapter 2 describes how locking can control the effect of INSERT, UPDATE, and DELETE operations executed by concurrent transactions. The cursor result table can also be affected by operations executed by your own transaction, and the effect of such operations is not always predictable.

Authorization The SELECT statement used to define the result data set of a cursor determines which authorizations are required to execute this statement. Users with either system administrator (SYSADM) authority or database administrator (DBADM) authority are allowed to execute this statement regardless of what tables or views are referenced by the SELECT statement. All other users must have either SELECT authority or CONTROL authority for each table or view referenced by the SELECT statement.

If the SELECT statement is a prepared statement, authorization ID is determined at application run-time and the authority check is performed when the SELECT statement is prepared. If the SELECT statement is not a prepared statement, the authorization ID is determined when the application is precompiled.

See Also DECLARE CURSOR, FETCH, CLOSE

Examples Refer to the next statement, FETCH, for examples that illustrate how to use the OPEN statement to open an SQL cursor.

FETCH

Purpose The FETCH statement allows you to retrieve a record from a cursor result table.

Syntax

```
EXEC SQL FETCH [cursor-name] [storage-area];
```

Parameters

cursor-name Identifies the name of the opened cursor to be used in the fetch operation. The cursor name must identify a cursor already described with the DECLARE CURSOR statement and opened with the OPEN statement.

storage-area Identifies where the data being retrieved from the cursor is to be stored. The storage area location is specified with one of the following:

INTO [*host-variable*, . . .] Identifies one or more host variables in which the values from the cursor result table are to be stored. Each host variables must be described in accordance with the rules for declaring host variables (refer to the BEGIN DECLARE SECTION statement for more information). For BLOB, CLOB, or DBCLOB values, the host variable can be either a regular host variable a locator variable, or a file-reference variable.

USING DESCRIPTOR [*descriptor-name*] Identifies an output SQL descriptor area (SQLDA) data structure variable that contains descriptions of each column in the cursor result table. If the FETCH statement retrieves a row into an SQLDA data structure variable, that variable must first be appropriately allocated and the *sqln* field of this SQLDA data structure variable must be set to a value equal to the number of columns in the cursor result table. After the FETCH statement is executed, DB2 assigns values to the fields in this SQLDA data structure as follows:

sqldaid The first five bytes of this character string field are set to "SQLDA," and the sixth and eighth bytes are set to the space character. The seventh byte, known as the SQLDOUBLED byte, is set to 2 if the SQLDA contains two *sqlvar* entries for every column found in the result table (e.g., if the result table contains LOB and/or distinct type columns). If the SQLDA contains one *sqlvar* entry for every column found in the result table or if there is not enough room in the SQLDA data structure to store all information returned by the FETCH statement, this byte will be set to the space character.

sqldabc This field contains the size of the *sqlda* data structure.

sqld This field contains a value that corresponds to the number of columns in the cursor result table.

sqlvar field(s) Values are assigned to occurrences of *sqlvar* so the first occurrence of *sqlvar* contains a description of the first column of the result table, the second occurrence of *sqlvar* contains a description of the second column of the result table, and so on. The description of a column consists of the values assigned to the following *sqlvar* fields:

sqltype A code that identifies the data type of the result table column, which indicates whether or not the column can contain null values.

sqllen A value that indicates the length of the result table column, dependent on the data type of that column. *sqllen* is always 0 if the column contains a LOB data type.

sqlname	If the derived result table column is not a simple column reference, then this field will contain an ASCII numeric literal value, which represents the derived column's original position within the SELECT statement's select list; otherwise, this field contains the name of the result table column.
sqllonglen	The length attribute of a BLOB, CLOB, or DBCLOB column.
sqldatatype_name	If the result table column contains a distinct type, this field will contain the fully qualified distinct type name. Otherwise, the high-order portion of this field will contain the schema name "SYSIBM" and the low-order portion will contain the corresponding name in the TYPENAME column of the SYSCAT.DATATYPES catalog view.

> Note: The values for the SQLLONGLEN and SQLDATATYPE_NAME fields are set only if the number of SQLVAR entries are doubled to accommodate LOB or distinct type columns (e.g., if the SQLDOUBLED byte of the SQLDAID character string value is set to 2).

Description The FETCH statement retrieves a record from a cursor result table into either host variables or into a SQLDA data structure variable. An open cursor has three possible positions: before a row of data, on a row of data, or after the last row of data. If the cursor position pointer is positioned before a row, it will be positioned on that row and the values of that row will be assigned to host variables when the FETCH statement is executed. If the cursor position pointer is on a row, that row is the current row of the cursor. When a record is retrieved from a cursor, the cursor position pointer is moved to the next record in the cursor result table.

If you use the FETCH statement to retrieve a row into host variables, the first value in the result row is assigned to the first host variable in the list, the second value is assigned to the second host variable, and so on.

Comments

- If a cursor is referenced in an UPDATE or DELETE statement, the cursor position pointer must first be placed on a row in the cursor via a FETCH statement.
- When retrieving values into LOB locators, if it is not necessary to retain the locator across multiple FETCH statements, then it is good practice to issue a FREE LOCATOR statement before issuing the next FETCH statement.
- It is possible for an error to occur that leaves the cursor in an unpredictable state.
- Caching the executable sections of SQL data manipulation language (DML) statements can affect the behavior of a FETCH statement. Refer to the beginning of Chapter 8 for more information on statement caching.

Authorization The SELECT statement used to define the result data set of a cursor determines which authorizations are required to execute this statement. Users with either system administrator (SYSADM) authority or database administrator (DBADM) authority are allowed to execute this statement regardless of what tables or views are referenced by the SELECT statement. All other users must have either SELECT authority or CONTROL authority for each table or view referenced by the SELECT statement.

If the SELECT statement is a prepared statement, the authorization ID is determined at application run-time and the authority check is performed when the SELECT statement is prepared. If the SELECT statement is not a prepared statement, the authorization ID is determined when the application is precompiled.

See Also DECLARE CURSOR, OPEN, CLOSE, FREE LOCATOR

Examples The following C program illustrates how to retrieve data from a database table using a cursor:

```
#include <stdio.h>
#include <stdlib.h>
#include <string.h>
#include <sql.h>
#include <sqlda.h>

int main()
{
    /* Include The SQLCA Data Structure Variable */
    EXEC SQL INCLUDE SQLCA;

    /* Set Up A Simple SQL Error Handler */
    EXEC SQL WHENEVER SQLERROR GOTO EXIT;

    /* Declare The Local Memory Variables */
    int             rc = EXIT_SUCCESS;
    char            szEmpNum[7];
    char            szProjNum[7];
    struct sqlda    *out_sqlda;          // SQLDA Data Structure Pointer
    struct VARCHAR {                     // VARCHAR Data Structure
        short size;
        char  string[10];
        }  stEmpName;                    // Employee Name
    short           sEmpNameInd;         // Employee Name Indicator
    short           sEmpID;              // Employee ID
    short           sEmpIDInd;           // Employee ID Indicator
    short           sYears;              // Years Of Service
    short           sYearsInd;           // Years Of Service Indicator
    char            szEmpName[11];       // Employee Name String

    /* Declare The SQL Host Memory Variables */
    EXEC SQL BEGIN DECLARE SECTION;
        char      szEmpNo[6];
        char      szProjNo[6];
        short     sActNo;
        char      szPrepString[80];
    EXEC SQL END DECLARE SECTION;

    /* Connect To The SAMPLE Database */
    EXEC SQL CONNECT TO SAMPLE USER etpdd6z USING sanders;

    /* Declare The SELECT_CURSOR Table Cursor */
    EXEC SQL DECLARE SELECT_CURSOR CURSOR FOR
        SELECT EMPNO,
               PROJNO,
               ACTNO
        FROM ETPDD6Z.MA_EMP_ACT;

    /* Open The Cursor */
    EXEC SQL OPEN SELECT_CURSOR;

    /* If The Cursor Was Successfully Opened, Fetch The Records Into */
    /* Host Variables                                                 */
```

```
printf("\n");
printf("   ID    Project No.   Account\n");
printf("-----------------------------\n");
while (sqlca.sqlcode == SQL_RC_OK)
    {
    EXEC SQL FETCH SELECT_CURSOR
        INTO :szEmpNo,
             :szProjNo,
             :sActNo;

    /* If The FETCH Was Successful, Print The Data */
    if (sqlca.sqlcode == SQL_RC_OK)
        {
        strncpy(szEmpNum, " ", 6);
        strncpy(szProjNum, " ", 6);
        strncpy(szEmpNum, szEmpNo, 6);
        strncpy(szProjNum, szProjNo, 6);
        szEmpNum[6] = 0;
        szProjNum[6] = 0;
        printf(" %6s  %8s         %d\n",
               szEmpNum, szProjNum, sActNo);
        }
    }                                        /* End Of WHILE   */

/* Close The Cursor */
EXEC SQL CLOSE SELECT_CURSOR;

/* Build The SQL Statement String */
strcpy(szPrepString, "SELECT NAME, ID, YEARS FROM USERID.STAFF ");
strcat(szPrepString, "WHERE JOB = 'Mgr'");

/* Prepare The SQL Statement */
EXEC SQL PREPARE SQL_STATEMENT FROM :szPrepString;

/* Allocate And Initialize An SQLDA Data Structure Variable */
out_sqlda = (struct sqlda *) malloc(SQLDASIZE(3));
out_sqlda->sqln = 3;

/* Describe The Prepared SQL Statement */
EXEC SQL DESCRIBE SQL_STATEMENT INTO :*out_sqlda;

/* Store The Address Of Local Memory Variables In The    */
/* Appropriate SQLDA->SQLVAR Data And Indicator Pointers */
out_sqlda->sqlvar[0].sqldata = (unsigned char *) &stEmpName;
out_sqlda->sqlvar[0].sqlind = (short *) &sEmpNameInd;
out_sqlda->sqlvar[1].sqldata = (unsigned char *) &sEmpID;
out_sqlda->sqlvar[1].sqlind = (short *) &sEmpIDInd;
out_sqlda->sqlvar[2].sqldata = (unsigned char *) &sYears;
out_sqlda->sqlvar[2].sqlind = (short *) &sYearsInd;

/* Declare The Dynamic Cursor */
EXEC SQL DECLARE DYN_CURSOR CURSOR FOR SQL_STATEMENT;

/* Open The Dynamic Cursor */
EXEC SQL OPEN DYN_CURSOR;

/* If The Cursor Was Successfully Opened, Fetch The Records */
/* Into Local Memory Variables                              */
printf("\n");
printf("    Name      ID   Years\n");
printf("------------------------\n");
```

```
    while (sqlca.sqlcode == SQL_RC_OK)
        {
        EXEC SQL FETCH DYN_CURSOR USING DESCRIPTOR :*out_sqlda;

        /* Print The Record */
        if (sqlca.sqlcode == SQL_RC_OK)
            {
            strncpy(szEmpName, " ", 10);
            strncpy(szEmpName, stEmpName.string, stEmpName.size);
            printf("%10s %5d %5d\n", szEmpName, sEmpID, sYears);
            }
        }                                           /* End Of WHILE   */

    /* Close The Cursor */
    EXEC SQL CLOSE DYN_CURSOR;

EXIT:
    /* If An Error Has Occurred, Display The SQL Return Code */
    if (sqlca.sqlcode != SQL_RC_OK)
        {
        printf("SQL ERROR : %ld\n", sqlca.sqlcode);
        rc = EXIT_FAILURE;
        }

    /* Issue A Rollback To Free All Locks */
    EXEC SQL ROLLBACK;

    /* Turn Off The SQL Error Handler */
    EXEC SQL WHENEVER SQLERROR CONTINUE;

    /* Disconnect From The SAMPLE Database */
    EXEC SQL DISCONNECT CURRENT;

    /* Return To The Operating System */
    return(rc);
}
```

The following C++ program illustrates how to retrieve data from a database table, using a cursor:

```
#include <iostream.h>
#include <stdlib.h>
#include <string.h>
#include <sql.h>
#include <sqlda.h>

/* Define The Table Class */
class Table
{
    private:

        /* Include The SQLCA Data Structure Variable */
        EXEC SQL INCLUDE SQLCA;

        /* Declare All Other Private Memory Variables */
        struct sqlda   *out_sqlda;       // SQLDA Data Structure Pointer
        char           szEmpNum[7];
        char           szProjNum[7];
        struct VARCHAR {                 // VARCHAR Data Structure
```

```
            short size;
            char  string[10];
            }  stEmpName;                   // Employee Name
        short          sEmpNameInd;         // Employee Name Indicator
        short          sEmpID;              // Employee ID
        short          sEmpIDInd;           // Employee ID Indicator
        short          sYears;              // Years Of Service
        short          sYearsInd;           // Years Of Service Indicator
        char           szEmpName[11];       // Employee Name String

        /* Declare The SQL Host Memory Variables */
        EXEC SQL BEGIN DECLARE SECTION;
            char      szEmpNo[6];
            char      szProjNo[6];
            short     sActNo;
            char      szPrepString[80];
        EXEC SQL END DECLARE SECTION;

    /* Declare The Public Member Function Prototypes */
    public:
        short int showRecords();
        short int dynamicShowRecords();
} ;

/* Define The showRecords() Member Function */
short int Table::showRecords(void)
{
    /* Declare The SELECT_CURSOR Table Cursor */
    EXEC SQL DECLARE SELECT_CURSOR CURSOR FOR
        SELECT EMPNO,
               PROJNO,
               ACTNO
        FROM ETPDD6Z.MA_EMP_ACT;

    /* Open The Cursor */
    EXEC SQL OPEN SELECT_CURSOR;

    /* If The Cursor Was Successfully Opened, Fetch The Records Into */
    /* Host Variables                                                */
    cout << endl << "   ID    Project No. Account" << endl;
    cout << "-----------------------------" << endl;
    while (sqlca.sqlcode == SQL_RC_OK)
        {
        EXEC SQL FETCH SELECT_CURSOR
            INTO :szEmpNo,
                 :szProjNo,
                 :sActNo;

        /* If The FETCH Was Successful, Print The Data */
        if (sqlca.sqlcode == SQL_RC_OK)
            {
            strncpy(szEmpNum, " ", 6);
            strncpy(szProjNum, " ", 6);
            strncpy(szEmpNum, szEmpNo, 6);
            strncpy(szProjNum, szProjNo, 6);
            szEmpNum[6] = 0;
            szProjNum[6] = 0;
            cout << " ";
            cout.width(6);
```

```
            cout << szEmpNum << "  ";
            cout.width(8);
            cout << szProjNum << "          " << sActNo;
            cout << endl;
            }
        }                                         /* End Of WHILE   */

    /* Close The Cursor */
    EXEC SQL CLOSE SELECT_CURSOR;

    /* Return The SQL Return Code */
    return(sqlca.sqlcode);
}

/* Define The dynamicShowRecords() Member Function */
short int Table::dynamicShowRecords(void)
{
    /* Build The SQL Statement String */
    strcpy(szPrepString, "SELECT NAME, ID, YEARS FROM USERID.STAFF ");
    strcat(szPrepString, "WHERE JOB = 'Mgr'");

    /* Prepare The Select SQL Statement */
    EXEC SQL PREPARE SQL_STATEMENT FROM :szPrepString;

    /* Allocate And Initialize An SQLDA Data Structure Variable */
    out_sqlda = (struct sqlda *) new char [SQLDASIZE(3)];
    if (out_sqlda != NULL)
        out_sqlda->sqln = 3;

    /* Describe The Select SQL Statement */
    EXEC SQL DESCRIBE SQL_STATEMENT INTO :*out_sqlda;

    /* Store The Address Of Local Memory Variables In The   */
    /* Appropriate SQLDA SQLVAR Data And Indicator Pointers */
    out_sqlda->sqlvar[0].sqldata = (char *) &stEmpName;
    out_sqlda->sqlvar[0].sqlind = (short *) &sEmpNameInd;
    out_sqlda->sqlvar[1].sqldata = (char *) &sEmpID;
    out_sqlda->sqlvar[1].sqlind = (short *) &sEmpIDInd;
    out_sqlda->sqlvar[2].sqldata = (char *) &sYears;
    out_sqlda->sqlvar[2].sqlind = (short *) &sYearsInd;

    /* Declare The Dynamic Cursor */
    EXEC SQL DECLARE DYN_CURSOR CURSOR FOR SQL_STATEMENT;

    /* Open The Dynamic Cursor */
    EXEC SQL OPEN DYN_CURSOR;

    /* If The Cursor Was Successfully Opened, Fetch The Records */
    /* Into Local Memory Variables                              */
    cout << endl << "    Name      ID   Years" << endl;
    cout << "------------------------" << endl;
    while (sqlca.sqlcode == SQL_RC_OK)
        {
        EXEC SQL FETCH DYN_CURSOR USING DESCRIPTOR :*out_sqlda;

        /* Print The Record */
        if (sqlca.sqlcode == SQL_RC_OK)
            {
            strncpy(szEmpName, " ", 10);
            strncpy(szEmpName, stEmpName.string, stEmpName.size);
            cout.width(10);
```

```
            cout << szEmpName;
            cout.width(6);
            cout << sEmpID;
            cout.width(6);
            cout << sYears << endl;
            }
        }                                          /* End Of WHILE   */

    /* Close The Cursor */
    EXEC SQL CLOSE DYN_CURSOR;

    /* Return The SQL Return Code */
    return(sqlca.sqlcode);
}

int main()
{
    /* Declare The Local Memory Variables */
    short int rc = EXIT_SUCCESS;              // Must Be Declared Here
                                              // For The SQL Precompiler

    /* Include The SQLCA Data Structure Variable */
    EXEC SQL INCLUDE SQLCA;

    /* Set Up A Simple SQL Error Handler */
    EXEC SQL WHENEVER SQLERROR GOTO EXIT;

    /* Create An Instance Of The Table Class */
    Table table;

    /* Connect To The SAMPLE Database */
    EXEC SQL CONNECT TO SAMPLE USER etpdd6z USING sanders;

    /* Retrieve The Records From The ETPDD6Z.MA_EMP_ACT Table */
    rc = table.showRecords();

    /* Retrieve The Records From The USERID.STAFF Table */
    rc = table.dynamicShowRecords();

EXIT:
    /* If An Error Has Occurred, Display The SQL Return Code */
    if (sqlca.sqlcode != SQL_RC_OK)
        {
        cout << "SQL ERROR : " << sqlca.sqlcode << endl;
        rc = EXIT_FAILURE;
        }

    /* Issue A Rollback To Free All Locks */
    EXEC SQL ROLLBACK;

    /* Turn Off The SQL Error Handler */
    EXEC SQL WHENEVER SQLERROR CONTINUE;

    /* Disconnect From The SAMPLE Database */
    EXEC SQL DISCONNECT CURRENT;

    /* Return To The Operating System */
    return(rc);
}
```

CLOSE

Purpose The CLOSE statement closes a previously opened cursor.

Syntax

```
EXEC SQL CLOSE [cursor-name];
```

Parameters *cursor-name* Identifies the name of the cursor to be closed.

Description The CLOSE statement allows you to close a cursor that is currently open. If a result table was created when the cursor was opened, it is destroyed when the cursor is closed.

Comments

- When a transaction is terminated, all cursors belonging to an application that were not declared with the WITH HOLD option are implicitly closed.
- Closing an open cursor does not cause a rollback or commit operation to occur.
- Special rules apply when you use cursors within stored procedures. Refer to the CALL statement for more information.

Prerequisites The cursor must have been declared by the DECLARE CURSOR statement and opened by the OPEN statement before you can execute the CLOSE statement.

Authorization No authorization is required to execute this statement.

See Also DECLARE CURSOR, OPEN, FETCH , CALL

Examples Refer to the FETCH statement for an example that illustrates how to use the CLOSE statement to close an open SQL cursor.

SELECT INTO

Purpose The SELECT INTO statement allows you to retrieve a single row of data from one or more tables and/or views into a temporary result data set and store it into host memory variables.

Syntax

```
EXEC SQL SELECT [column-name,...] INTO [host-variable,...] FROM [from-clause]
   <WHERE [where-clause]> <GROUP BY [group-by-clause]> <HAVING
   [having-clause]>;
```

Parameters

column-name Identifies one or more column names that will make up the result data set. These column names can be either the same name as a column in the referenced table/view or a temporary name provided by DB2. For example, SELECT EMPNO would specify an actual column name and SELECT MAX(SALARY) would specify a temporary name for a calculated value.

host-variable Identifies one or more host variables in which the values from the result table are to be stored. Each host variables must be described in accordance with the rules for declaring host variables (refer to the BEGIN DECLARE SECTION statement for more information).

from-clause Identifies the tables and/or views from which the single row of data is to be retrieved.

where-clause Identifies the search criteria to use when retrieving the single row of data into the result data set.

group-by-clause Identifies how the single row of data is to be organized in the result data set.

having-clause Identifies the search criteria to use when retrieving the single row of data into the result data set.

Description The SELECT INTO statement retrieves a single row of data from one or more tables and/or views into a temporary result data set and stores it into host memory variables. When the SELECT INTO statement is executed, the data row is first loaded into the result data set; then the first value in the result data set row is assigned to the first variable in the host variable list, the second value is assigned to the second variable, and so on.

Comments

- If the number of provided host variables is less than the number of column values in the result data set, a warning will be returned ('**W**' is assigned to the SQLWARN3 field (*sqlca.sqlwarn[2]*) of the SQLCA data structure variable).
- The data types for each host variable must be compatible with the data types of the corresponding columns result data set.
- After the SELECT INTO statement is executed, if the result data set is empty (because no data rows were found that matched the specified where clause, group by clause, or having clause), then the NOT FOUND value (+100) will be stored in the SQLCA data structure variable and no values will be assigned to the host variables.
- After the SELECT INTO statement is executed, if the result data set contains more than one data row (because multiple data rows were found that matched the specified where clause, group by clause, or having clause), an error condition will be returned and no values will be assigned to the host variables. When this condition occurs, either provide a more specific where clause, group by clause, or having clause for the SELECT INTO statement or consider using a cursor.

Authorization Only users with either system administrator (SYSADM) authority, database administrator (DBADM) authority, SELECT authority for the specified tables and/or views, or CONTROL authority for the specified tables and/or views are allowed to execute this statement.

See Also *VALUES INTO, DECLARE CURSOR, OPEN, FETCH, CLOSE*

Example The following C program illustrates how the SELECT INTO statement can be used to retrieve data from a database table:

```
#include <stdio.h>
#include <stdlib.h>
#include <sql.h>

int main()
{
    /* Include The SQLCA Data Structure Variable */
    EXEC SQL INCLUDE SQLCA;

    /* Set Up A Simple SQL Error Handler */
    EXEC SQL WHENEVER SQLERROR GOTO EXIT;

    /* Declare The Local Memory Variables */
    int  rc = EXIT_SUCCESS;
```

```
        /* Declare The SQL Host Memory Variables */
        EXEC SQL BEGIN DECLARE SECTION;
           double     rdMaxSalary;
        EXEC SQL END DECLARE SECTION;

        /* Connect To The SAMPLE Database */
        EXEC SQL CONNECT TO SAMPLE USER etpdd6z USING sanders;

        /* Retrieve The Largest Salary In The EMPLOYEE Table Into A */
        /* Host Variable                                            */
        EXEC SQL SELECT DOUBLE(MAX(SALARY))
            INTO :rdMaxSalary
            FROM USERID.EMPLOYEE;

        /* Print The Largest Salary Value Retrieved */
        printf("Largest Salary : %lf\n", rdMaxSalary);

    EXIT:
        /* If An Error Has Occurred, Display The SQL Return Code */
        if (sqlca.sqlcode != SQL_RC_OK)
            {
            printf("SQL ERROR : %ld\n", sqlca.sqlcode);
            rc = EXIT_FAILURE;
            }

        /* Issue A Rollback To Free All Locks */
        EXEC SQL ROLLBACK;

        /* Turn Off The SQL Error Handler */
        EXEC SQL WHENEVER SQLERROR CONTINUE;

        /* Disconnect From The SAMPLE Database */
        EXEC SQL DISCONNECT CURRENT;

        /* Return To The Operating System */
        return(rc);
    }
```

Note: The SELECT INTO statement is used in a C++ program in a similar manner.

VALUES INTO

Purpose The VALUES INTO statement produces a result data set with a single row of data and stores the values in that row into host memory variables.

Syntax

```
EXEC SQL VALUES <(> [expression,...] <)> INTO [host-variable,...];
```

Parameters

expression Identifies one or more expressions that will define the values for one or more columns of the result data set.

host-variable Identifies one or more host variables in which the values from the result data set are to be stored. Each host variable must be described in accordance with the rules for declaring host variables (refer to the BEGIN DECLARE SECTION statement for more information).

Description

The VALUES INTO statement allows you to produce a result data set with a single row of data and store the values in that row into host memory variables. When the VALUES INTO statement is executed, the data is loaded into the result data set. Then the first value in the result data set row is assigned to the first variable in the host variable list, the second value is assigned to the second variable, and so on.

This statement retrieves information from special registers and functions, whereas the SELECT INTO statement retrieves data from database tables and views.

Comments

- If the number of provided host variables is less than the number of column values in the result table, a warning will be returned ('**W**' is assigned to the SQLWARN3 field (*sqlca.sqlwarn[2]*) of the SQLCA data structure variable).
- The data types for each host variable must be compatible with the data types of their corresponding columns in the result data set.
- If any error occurs during the execution of the VALUES INTO statement, no values will be assigned to the host variables.

Authorization

No authorization is required to execute this statement.

See Also

SELECT INTO

Example

The following C program illustrates how the VALUES INTO statement can be used to retrieve data from the CURRENT FUNCTION PATH special register:

```
#include <stdio.h>
#include <stdlib.h>
#include <sql.h>

int main()
{
    /* Include The SQLCA Data Structure Variable */
    EXEC SQL INCLUDE SQLCA;

    /* Set Up A Simple SQL Error Handler */
    EXEC SQL WHENEVER SQLERROR GOTO EXIT;

    /* Declare The Local Memory Variables */
    int  rc = EXIT_SUCCESS;

    /* Declare The SQL Host Memory Variables */
    EXEC SQL BEGIN DECLARE SECTION;
        char    szFunctionPath[256];
    EXEC SQL END DECLARE SECTION;

    /* Connect To The SAMPLE Database */
    EXEC SQL CONNECT TO SAMPLE USER etpdd6z USING sanders;

    /* Retrieve The Value Of The CURRENT FUNCTION PATH Special */
    /* Register Into A Host Variable                           */
    EXEC SQL VALUES (CURRENT FUNCTION PATH)
        INTO :szFunctionPath;

    /* Print The Value Of The CURRENT FUNCTION PATH Special */
    /* Register                                             */
    printf("CURRENT FUNCTION PATH = %s\n", szFunctionPath);
```

```
EXIT:
    /* If An Error Has Occurred, Display The SQL Return Code */
    if (sqlca.sqlcode != SQL_RC_OK)
       {
       printf("SQL ERROR : %ld\n", sqlca.sqlcode);
       rc = EXIT_FAILURE;
       }

    /* Issue A Rollback To Free All Locks */
    EXEC SQL ROLLBACK;

    /* Turn Off The SQL Error Handler */
    EXEC SQL WHENEVER SQLERROR CONTINUE;

    /* Disconnect From The SAMPLE Database */
    EXEC SQL DISCONNECT CURRENT;

    /* Return To The Operating System */
    return(rc);
}
```

Note: The VALUES INTO statement is used in a C++ program in a similar manner.

FREE LOCATOR

Purpose The FREE LOCATOR statement removes the association between a locator variable and its current value.

Syntax

```
EXEC SQL FREE LOCATOR [variable-name];
```

Parameters

variable-name Identifies the name of the locator variable that currently has a locator value assigned to it. The locator variable must be defined as a host variable.

Description The FREE LOCATOR statement allows you to remove the association between a locator variable and its current value. A locator variable is simply a host variable containing a locator that represents a large object (LOB) value on the database server. Since LOB values can be very large, transferring these values from a database server to application host variables can be very time-consuming, and the amount of memory needed to store the retrieved LOB values can be very large. However, since most application programs process LOB values in pieces rather than as a whole, an entire LOB value does not need to be retrieved at one time. A locator (also known as an LOB locator) allows an application program to manipulate a LOB value in the database system without having to load the entire LOB value into application memory. Once an application program retrieves a LOB locator into a host variable, it can then apply SQL functions to the associated LOB value by using the locator.

It is important to understand that a LOB locator represents a value, not a location or row in the database, so LOB locators do not store extra copies of the data. Instead, they store a description of the base LOB value; the actual data to which a locator refers materializes only when it is assigned to some location (e.g., a host variable or another table record). Once a value is selected into a locator, no operation performed on the original row or table will affect the value referenced by the locator. The value associated with a LOB locator remains valid until the transaction using the locator ends or until the locator is explicitly freed with the FREE LOCATOR statement.

Comments

- The LOB locator is not a database type, so it is never stored in the database and cannot be referenced in views and check constraints. However, since a locator is a representation of a BLOB, CLOB, or DBCLOB data type, there are SQLTYPEs for LOB locators so that they can be described within an SQLDA data structure variable used by a OPEN, FETCH, or EXECUTE statement.
- Like other host variables, when an indicator variable associated with a LOB locator variable is NULL, the value of the LOB that the locator variable references is NULL.

Prerequisites

The locator variable must have a valid locator assigned to it before it can be freed. This means that the current transaction must have issued an OPEN or a SELECT INTO statement that referenced the locator variable, and the locator variable must not have already been freed by an earlier FREE LOCATOR statement.

Authorization

No authorization is required to execute this statement.

See Also

BEGIN DECLARE SECTION, END DECLARE SECTION, OPEN, FETCH, EXECUTE, SELECT INTO

Example

The following C program illustrates how the FREE LOCATOR statement can be used to free a LOB locator variable:

```
#include <stdio.h>
#include <stdlib.h>
#include <sql.h>

int main()
{
    /* Include The SQLCA Data Structure Variable */
    EXEC SQL INCLUDE SQLCA;

    /* Set Up A Simple SQL Error Handler */
    EXEC SQL WHENEVER SQLERROR GOTO EXIT;

    /* Declare The Local Memory Variables */
    int  rc = EXIT_SUCCESS;

    /* Declare The SQL Host Memory Variables */
    EXEC SQL BEGIN DECLARE SECTION;
        SQL TYPE IS CLOB_LOCATOR   clobResume;
        long                       lDeptInfoBegin;
        long                       lDeptInfoEnd;
        long                       lDeptInfoSize;
        char                       szDeptInfo[1000];
    EXEC SQL END DECLARE SECTION;

    /* Connect To The SAMPLE Database */
    EXEC SQL CONNECT TO SAMPLE USER etpdd6z USING sanders;

    /* Retrieve A CLOB Data Value From The EMP_RESUME Table, Using */
    /* A LOB Locator                                                */
    EXEC SQL SELECT RESUME
```

```
        INTO :clobResume
        FROM USERID.EMP_RESUME
        WHERE EMPNO = '000130' AND RESUME_FORMAT = 'ascii';

    /* Get The Starting Position Of The Department Information */
    EXEC SQL VALUES (POSSTR(:clobResume, 'Department Information'))
        INTO :lDeptInfoBegin;

    /* Get The Ending Position Of The Department Information */
    EXEC SQL VALUES (POSSTR(:clobResume, 'Education'))
        INTO :lDeptInfoEnd;

    /* Retrieve The Department Information From The Resume CLOB */
    lDeptInfoSize = lDeptInfoEnd - lDeptInfoBegin;
    EXEC SQL VALUES (SUBSTR(:clobResume, :lDeptInfoBegin, :lDeptInfoSize))
        INTO :szDeptInfo;

    /* Print The Information Retrieved */
    printf("%s\n", szDeptInfo);

    /* Free The LOB Locator */
    EXEC SQL FREE LOCATOR :clobResume;

    /* Print A Message Telling That The LOB Locator Was Freed */
    printf("The LOB Locator has been freed.\n");

    /* Rollback The Transaction To Free Acquired Locks */
    EXEC SQL ROLLBACK;

EXIT:
    /* If An Error Has Occurred, Display The SQL Return Code */
    if (sqlca.sqlcode != SQL_RC_OK)
        {
        printf("SQL ERROR : %ld\n", sqlca.sqlcode);
        rc = EXIT_FAILURE;
        }

    /* Turn Off The SQL Error Handler */
    EXEC SQL WHENEVER SQLERROR CONTINUE;

    /* Disconnect From The SAMPLE Database */
    EXEC SQL DISCONNECT CURRENT;

    /* Return To The Operating System */
    return(rc);
}
```

Note: The FREE LOCATOR statement is used in a C++ program in a similar manner.

CHAPTER 12

EVENT MONITOR, TRIGGER, AND STORED PROCEDURE PROCESSING STATEMENTS

12

SQL event monitor, trigger, and stored procedure processing statements consist of commands for creating event monitors and triggers, and invoking stored procedures. This group includes:

- SQL statements that define event monitors and turn event monitors on and off.
- SQL statements that define triggers and perform special trigger event actions.
- An SQL statement that invokes stored procedures.

Table 12.1 lists the event monitor, trigger, and stored procedure processing statements available with DB2.

TABLE 12.1 SQL Event Monitor, Trigger, and Stored Procedure Processing Statements

Statement	Description
CREATE EVENT MONITOR	Defines and creates an event monitor (specifies the events in the database to monitor).
SET EVENT MONITOR STATE	Activates or deactivates an event monitor.
CREATE TRIGGER	Defines and creates an SQL trigger.
SET	Assigns values to NEW transition variables within a trigger.
SIGNAL SQLSTATE	Signals an error condition from within a trigger.
CALL	Invokes a stored procedure.

Using Event Monitors

Event monitors are designed to provide information about specific database events as they take place. If there are a series of events to be monitored, such as executing a sequence of SQL statements, an event monitor can record information as each event occurs, in this case as each SQL statement is executed. You can create event monitors either by issuing SQL event monitor statements interactively through the DB2 command-line processor or by embedding SQL event monitor statements in an application program. Using event monitors allows you to better manage your databases and the applications that use them. For example:

- You can detect and correct situations that cause deadlock cycles to occur by collecting deadlock information.
- You can gather and analyze database usage information by collecting information at the connection (application) level.
- You can improve capacity planning by collecting statistical data for database objects and applications and examining this data for trends to help predict future data storage needs.
- You can tune applications, either by analyzing connection and transaction data or by collecting SQL statement event data and analyzing all "heavy" SQL statement data.
- You can also tune databases by analyzing data collected on database objects (buffer pools, table spaces, tables, etc.). Close analysis of this data can help you to identify database configuration parameter values that need to be changed.

Table 12.2 lists both the type of events that can be monitored when information is captured by the event monitor and the type of information collected for each event.

TABLE 12.2 Events That Can be Monitored with an Event Monitor, When the Information is Captured, and What Information is Collected

Event type	When information is captured	Information captured
Deadlock	Whenever a deadlock cycle occurs.	Information on the resources and applications involved in the deadlock cycle.
Connection	When an application disconnects from the database.	Information about the database connections established and dropped, along with the total number of SQL statements and sorts executed within the connection.
Transaction	When a transaction terminates (either ROLLBACK or COMMIT).	Transaction start and stop (CPU) times.
Statement	When a SQL statement completes execution.	Identification information about each SQL statement executed.
Database	When the last application connected to a database drops its connection.	Statistical information about database operation, tables, and table spaces.
Tablespace	When the last application connected to a database drops its connection.	Information on buffer pool usage.
Table	When the last application connected to a database drops its connection.	Overflow information.

Adapted from information provided on page 35 and page 36 of the *Database 2 Database System Monitor Guide and Reference for Common Servers* product reference manual.

Before creating an event monitor, you must be connected to the database you will be monitoring (event monitor data can be collected for only a single database). When an event monitor is defined via the CREATE EVENT MONITOR statement, its definition is stored in the system catalog tables. Once an event monitor is defined, it can either be automatically started at database startup or it can be explicitly started with the SET EVENT MONITOR STATE statement. You can create any number of event monitors for a database, and turn them ON and OFF as needed. This allows you to maintain a collection of various event monitors and allows you to turn on an appropriate number of these event monitors (up to 32 can be active, or ON, for a database at any given time) in order to achieve your desired level of monitoring. When a database is stopped, all active event monitors are automatically terminated. When the database is brought back on line, only event monitors defined as auto-start are restarted.

Event Counting

Event monitor counting starts at zero and represents a count of events that have occurred since one of the following starting points, depending on the monitor event for which the event monitor is defined:

- Event monitor startup for database, table space, and tables.
- Event monitor startup for existing connections.
- Application connection for connections made after the connection event monitor was started.
- Start of the next transaction or SQL statement after the event monitor was started.
- Occurrence of a deadlock after the event monitor was started.

If a statement event monitor starts after an SQL statement starts, the database system monitor will collect information when the next SQL statement begins execution. This means that a statement event monitor will not return information about SQL statements DB2 is in the process of executing when the event monitor was started. This is also true for transaction event monitors. When an event monitor is activated, its counters are automatically initialized to zero. You can reset an event monitor's counters to zero by turning the event monitor OFF and then back ON again.

The amount of information produced by an event monitor can be quite extensive. The definition options available with the CREATE EVENT MONITOR statement can help you control the quantity of information gathered by an event monitor. First, you can use the special WHERE clause to filter the data recorded for connections, transactions, and SQL statements. Second, you can use the WRITE TO option to control where the data generated by an event monitor is written. If you plan to analyze the data sometime after it has been recorded, you can direct the output to file. On the other hand, if you have an application that needs to deal with the information immediately, you can direct the output to a named pipe. In addition to the WRITE TO option, you can specify additional options (if the output of an event monitor is to be written to one or more files) that can affect the overall performance of the event monitor and DB2.

If an event monitor's output will be written to a file, you must specify a path (directory name) where the event monitor creates its event data files. A path is required because each event monitor writes its event data to a set of sequenced files, similar to the method used for writing transaction log files. The specified path can be absolute or relative; relative paths are relative to the db2event subdirectory found in the database directory. Each event monitor has its own path, so multiple event monitors do not write their data to the same directory.

If an event monitor's output will be written to a named pipe, you must specify the named pipe where the data is logged. When event monitor output is directed to a pipe, I/O is always blocked and buffering is performed by the pipe. When an event monitor that writes to a named pipe is activated, the named pipe must already have been opened for reading by a monitoring application and there must be enough space in the named pipe. If the monitoring application does not read the data fast enough from the named pipe, the pipe will fill up and overflow. Pipe overflows can also occur on platforms (such as OS/2) where the creator of the pipe can define the size of the named pipe buffer; the smaller the named pipe buffer, the greater the chance an overflow will occur. When a pipe overflow occurs, the monitor creates overflow event records indicating that an overflow has occurred. Since the event monitor is not turned off when an overflow occurs, monitor data is lost. If there are outstanding overflow event records when the event monitor is deactivated, a diagnostic message will be logged. Otherwise, the overflow event records will be written to the pipe as soon as possible.

File overflows are also possible if the event monitor is created in nonblocking mode.

> Note: If your operating system allows you to define the size of the pipe buffer (such as OS/2), use a pipe buffer of at least 32KB. For high-volume event monitors, set the monitoring application's process priority equal to or higher than the agent process priority.

Event Monitor Data Stream Format. The data stream of event monitor data has the same format whether it is written to a named pipe or to a file. The event monitor stream is prefixed by a header record that defines the source of the event monitor data. For an event monitor that generates multiple event data files, the header record is written only to the first file (00000000.evt). For an event monitor that writes to a pipe, the event header is written each time the event monitor is activated. The remainder of the data stream data consists of a series of event records. The first four bytes of each of these records is an unsigned integer that represents the length of the record. The next four bytes identify the record type. This record type is designed to help an application determine which data structure to use when reading the event monitor data.

IBM's Event Monitor Productivity Tool. IBM's Event Monitor Productivity Tool (db2evmon) is a utility that allows you to easily display the data collected by an event monitor. It is located in the **misc** subdirectory of the **sqllib** directory wherever DB2 is installed. Its syntax is:

```
db2evmon [database-alias] [event-monitor-name]
```

where:

database-alias. Specifies the database name or alias for which the event monitor was defined.

event-monitor-name. Identifies the name of the event monitor. This is a one-part SQL identifier name that can be either ordinary or delimited.

If the specified event monitor writes its output data to a pipe, db2evmon will display a formatted form of this output, using **stdout**, as the designated events occur. If db2evmon is used in this manner, it must be turned on before the event monitor is activated. If the specified event monitor writes its output data to one or more files, db2evmon will format the files for display and display their contents to **stdout**. In this case, the event monitor is activated before the db2evmon application is started. If additional data is written to the file after the db2evmon tool runs, you must run it again in order to see the new data.

> Note: The Event Monitor Productivity Tool is provided "as is" without any warranty of any kind, including the warranties of merchantability and fitness for a particular purpose, which are expressly disclaimed.

Defining and Using Triggers

A passive database processing system can become a more active one if you use triggers. Triggers are a set of actions that are activated (or triggered) by an INSERT, UPDATE, or DELETE operation on a specified base table. With triggers, you can:

- Validate input data by using the SIGNAL SQLSTATE statement, the built-in RAISE_ERROR function, or one or more user-defined functions to return an SQLSTATE that indicates an error has occurred whenever invalid data is discovered. Triggers are appropriate for performing validations on transitional data, that is, validations that compare data values before and after an update operation takes place. Validation of nontransitional data is usually better handled by check and referential constraints.
- Automatically generate values for newly inserted rows (often referred to as "performing a surrogate function"), that is, implement user-defined default values that might be based on other values in the row or on values in other tables.
- Read from other tables for cross-referencing purposes.
- Write to other tables for audit-trail purposes.
- Support alerts (for example, by sending electronic mail messages).

Triggers are defined and created by the CREATE TRIGGER statement. Every trigger is associated with an event, and a trigger is activated whenever an event occurs in the database. Trigger events occur when a change is made to the base table (initiated by an INSERT, UPDATE, or DELETE statement or by the action of a referential constraint) referenced by the trigger (the subject table). Once activated, the set of rows in the subject table that are affected by the trigger event are determined and the SQL statements defined as the trigger action are executed. Triggered actions can take place only once for the trigger event or for each row affected by the trigger event.

Trigger Activation Time. The trigger activation time specifies whether the triggered action is to be performed before or after the trigger event completes its operation. If the activation time is specified as BEFORE, the triggered actions are activated for each row in the set of affected rows before the triggering SQL operation is performed. BEFORE triggers must be executed for each row that will be affected by the trigger event. If the activation time is specified as AFTER, the triggered actions are activated for each row in the set of affected rows or for the statement, depending on the trigger granularity, after the triggering SQL operation is performed.

The different activation times of triggers reflect their different purposes. Basically, BEFORE triggers are an extension to the constraint subsystem of the database management system. Therefore, they are generally used to:

- Perform validation of input data.
- Automatically generate values for newly inserted rows.
- Read from other tables for cross-referencing purposes.

BEFORE triggers are not used to further modify the database because they are activated before the triggering SQL operation is applied to the database.

AFTER triggers are like a module of application logic that resides in the database and executes every time a specific event occurs. As part of an application, AFTER triggers always see the database in a consistent state. Because AFTER triggers are executed after the integrity constraints that might be violated by the triggering event are checked, they can perform operations that an application program could also perform. Therefore, they are generally used to:

- Perform follow-up actions on trigger events against other columns within the same table.
- Perform follow-up actions on trigger events against other tables within the database.
- Perform actions outside the database (for example, to support alerts).

Note: Actions performed outside the database are not rolled back if the transaction that activated the trigger is rolled back.

Because of the different nature of BEFORE and AFTER triggers, a different set of SQL operations define the triggered actions of BEFORE and AFTER triggers. Likewise, different trigger granularities are supported in BEFORE and AFTER triggers.

Transition Variables. When a triggered action is executed FOR EACH ROW, it might be necessary to refer to the value of the columns in the row, in the set of affected rows, for which the trigger is currently executing. In this case, the triggered action can refer to the columns of the row for which it is currently executing by using two transition variables, provided they were defined in the REFERENCING clause of the CREATE TRIGGER statement when the trigger was created. There are two kinds of transition available variables, specified as OLD and NEW, together with a correlation name. They are defined as follows:

OLD correlation-name Specifies a correlation name that captures the original state of the row before the triggering SQL operation is applied.

NEW correlation-name Specifies a correlation name that captures the value for updating the row in the database when the triggering SQL operation was/is applied.

Not every transition variable can be defined for every trigger. Transition variables can be defined depending on the kind of trigger event:

INSERT A trigger that is activated by an INSERT event can refer to only a NEW transition variable because, before an INSERT trigger event is executed, the affected row does not exist in the database. In other words, there is no original state of the row being added.

UPDATE A trigger that is activated by an UPDATE event can refer to both OLD and NEW transition variables.

DELETE A trigger that is activated by a DELETE event can refer to only an OLD transition variable because there are no new values specified in the delete operation.

Transition variables can be specified only for triggers whose granularity is FOR EACH ROW.

Transition Tables. In some triggers, it might be necessary to refer to the whole set of affected rows rather than a single affected row, e.g., if the trigger body needs to apply aggregations such as MIN(), MAX(), or AVG() over the set of affected rows. In this case, the triggered action can refer to the set of affected rows for which it is currently executing by using two transition tables, provided they were defined in the REFERENCING clause of the CREATE TRIGGER statement when the trigger was created. Just like transition variables, there are two kinds of transition variables available, specified as OLD_TABLE and NEW_TABLE, together with a table-name. They are as follows:

OLD_TABLE table-name Specifies the name of the table that captures the original state of the set of affected rows before the triggering SQL operation is applied.

NEW_TABLE table-name Specifies the name of the table that captures the values used to update the rows in the database when the triggering SQL operation is applied.

Transition tables are read-only, and the same rules that define the types of transition variables for a trigger event (INSERT, UPDATE, or DELETE) also apply for transition tables.

The scope of both the OLD_TABLE and the NEW_TABLE transition table-name is the trigger body. Within the trigger body, these table names take precedence over the name of any other table with the same unqualified table-name within the schema. In order to reference another table with the same table name, that table name must first be qualified.

Triggered Actions. When you activate a trigger, its associated triggered action runs. Every created trigger has exactly one triggered action, which, in turn, can have two components:

- An optional triggered action condition or WHEN clause.
- One or more triggered SQL statements.

The triggered action condition defines whether or not the set of triggered statements perform for the row or for the statement for which the triggered action is executing. The set of triggered SQL statements defines the actions to be performed by the trigger when its event occurs. These triggered SQL statements carry out the real actions caused when you activate a trigger. In most cases, if any triggered SQL statement returns a negative return code, the triggering SQL statement together with all trigger and referential constraint actions will be rolled back and an error will be generated.

Using Functions Within Triggered Events. Both built-in and user-defined functions can be invoked within a triggered event. When a triggered SQL statement contains a function invocation with an unqualified function name, the function invocation is resolved based on the function path at the time of creation of the trigger. User-defined functions are written in either the C or C++ programming language and are capable of controlling logic flow, performing error handling and recovery, and accessing system and library functions. This capability allows a triggered action to perform non-SQL types of operations when a trigger is activated by executing a user-defined function. For example, a user-defined function could send an electronic mail message and thereby act as an alert mechanism. External actions performed by user-defined functions are not under transaction control and are run regardless of the success or failure of any other triggered SQL statements within the triggered action.

Trigger Cascading. When a triggered SQL statement is executed, it might cause an event to occur, which in turn might cause another (or a second instance of the same) trigger to be activated. Therefore, activating one trigger can cascade the activation of one or more other triggers. The supported runtime depth level of trigger cascading is 16. If a trigger at level 17 is activated, an error condition will be returned and the triggering statement will be rolled back.

Ordering Multiple Triggers. As triggers are defined (with the CREATE TRIGGER statement), their creation time is registered in the database in the form of a timestamp. The value of this timestamp subsequently orders the activation of triggers when there is more than one trigger defined on the same subject table with the same trigger event and the same activation time. The timestamp is also used when one or more AFTER triggers are activated by the triggering SQL operation and referential constraint actions are caused directly or indirectly (that is, recursively by other referential constraints) by the triggering SQL operation.

Older triggers are activated before newer triggers to ensure that new triggers can be used as incremental additions to the changes that affect the database. By activating triggers in ascending order of creation, you can ensure that the actions of new triggers run on a database that reflects the result of the activation of all old triggers.

Using Stored Procedures

Stored procedures are DB2's way of developing database applications that can run in a client/server environment. This technique allows an application running on a client workstation to invoke another procedure that is stored on a database server workstation. This procedure executes and accesses the database locally and returns information back to the client application that invoked it. In order to use this technique, you must write an application in two separate parts: the calling part, which resides and executes on the client workstation, and the stored procedure part, which resides and executes on the database server workstation.

In a client/server environment, all database access must go across the network, which, in some cases, can result in poor application performance. By using stored procedures, most of the database processing can be performed by the database server, without transmitting unnecessary data across the network. For this reason, stored procedures provide the following advantages:

Reduced network traffic In applications that process large amounts of data but require only a subset of the data to be returned to the user, only the records actually required at the client workstation need to be transmitted across the network.

Improved performance of server-intensive work Applications executing multiple SQL statements without user intervention can improve their performance by executing their SQL statements directly on the server workstation. A typical application requires two trips across the network for each SQL statement it executes, whereas an application using stored procedures requires two trips across the network for each group of SQL statements processed by the stored procedure. This can greatly reduce the number of trips an application must make across the network, resulting in a savings in the overhead associated with each trip.

Access to features that exist only on the database server Stored procedures that execute on the database server can take advantage of the following features:

- Commands to list directories on the server (such as LIST DATABASE DIRECTORY and LIST NODE DIRECTORY), which can run only on the server.
- Access to large amounts of memory and disk space if the server computer is so equipped.
- Direct access to additional software installed only on the database server workstation.

Writing Stored Procedures. As mentioned earlier, in order for an application to use stored procedures, it must be written in two separate sections. The first section, the calling procedure, is contained in a client application and executes on the client workstation. This part can be written in any of the supported host languages. The second section, the stored procedure, executes at the location of the database on the database server and must be written in one of the supported languages for that database server. The client application is responsible for performing the following steps:

1. Declaring, allocating, and initializing storage for the optional data structures and host variables.
2. Connecting to the database server.
3. Invoking the stored procedure with the CALL statement.
4. Performing a COMMIT or ROLLBACK to terminate the transaction(s).
5. Disconnecting from the database server.

When invoked, the stored procedure does the following:

1. Accepts the SQLDA data structure from the client application (host variables are passed through an SQLDA data structure variable generated by DB2 when the CALL statement is executed).
2. Executes on the database server under the same transaction as the client application.
3. Returns SQLCA information and optional output data to the client application.

These two sections must be built in separate steps, so applications using stored procedures have special compile and link requirements. The precompile, compile, and link requirements of the client application are identical to those of a normal DB2 application. The stored procedure section must be precompiled, compiled, and linked to produce a library. Special compile options are required for this, and the application must be bound to the database server before it can be executed.

When testing stored procedure applications, it is helpful to execute the procedures locally on the same workstation (which must be configured as a both a client and a server). After the application executes locally without error, you can move the stored procedure section to the database server workstation, for further testing or implementation.

Invoking Stored Procedures. As noted previously, you invoke a stored procedure by executing the CALL statement. Although version 1.1 of DB2/2 uses an API to invoke a stored procedure, the CALL statement is the recommended method of invoking stored procedures for version 2.1. The stored procedure executes when it is called by the client application, and control is returned to the client application when the stored procedure finishes processing.

The return value of a stored procedure is never returned to the client application. Instead, it is used by DB2 to determine if the server procedure should be released from memory upon exit. Therefore, a stored procedure should return one of the following values:

SQLZ_DISCONNECT_PROC Tells DB2 to release (unload) the library that contains the stored procedure.

SQLZ_HOLD_PROC Tells DB2 to keep the library containing the stored procedure in main memory so it will be ready for the next invocation of the stored procedure.

If the stored procedure is invoked only once, the SQLZ_DISCONNECT_PROC value should be returned. If the client application invokes the same stored procedure multiple times, the SQLZ_HOLD_PROC value should be returned. If you use this return value, the last invocation of the stored procedure should return the value SQLZ_DISCONNECT_PROC to remove the library from main memory. Otherwise, the library will remain in main memory until the DB2 database manager is stopped.

CREATE EVENT MONITOR

Purpose The CREATE EVENT MONITOR statement allows you to create a monitor to record certain events that occur during database operation.

Syntax

```
EXEC SQL CREATE EVENT MONITOR [event-monitor-name] FOR [event,...]
   WRITE TO [target] [start-mode];
```

Parameters

event-monitor-name Identifies the name of the event monitor to be created.

event Specifies the type of event to record. The event can be any of the following:

DATABASE	Specifies that the event monitor is to record a database event when the last connection to the database is terminated.
TABLES	Specifies that the event monitor is to record a table event for each table that is active when the last connection to the database is terminated. An active table is a table that has changed since the first connection to the database was established.
DEADLOCKS	Specifies that the event monitor is to record a deadlock event whenever a deadlock cycle occurs.
TABLESPACES	Specifies that the event monitor is to record a table space event for each table space when the last connection to the database is terminated.
CONNECTIONS <*event-options*>	Specifies that the event monitor is to record a connection event whenever an application disconnects from the database.
STATEMENTS <*event-options*>	Specifies that the event monitor is to record a statement event whenever an SQL statement successfully executes.
TRANSACTIONS <*event-options*>	Specifies that the event monitor is to record a transaction event whenever a transaction is terminated (i.e., whenever there is a commit or rollback operation).

target Specifies where the type of event data is to be written. The target can be either of the following:

PIPE [*pipe-name*]	Specifies that the event monitor data is to be written to the specified pipe name.
FILE [*filename*] <*file-options*>	358 358

Specifies that the event monitor data is to be written to the specified filename.

start-mode Specifies how and when the event monitor is started. The start mode can be either of the following:

MANUALSTART	Specifies that the event monitor is to be manually started with the SET EVENT MONITOR STATE statement. By default, all event monitors are created with the MANUALSTART start mode.
AUTOSTART	Specifies that the event monitor is to be automatically started each time the database is started.

Event option

This option identifies a filter that determines which applications cause a CONNECTION, STATEMENT, or TRANSACTION event to occur. It has the following syntax:

```
WHERE <NOT> [comparison_string1] [comparison-operator] [comparison-string2]
   <AND | OR >,...
```

If the result of comparing the event condition to this filter is TRUE, then the application will generate the requested event. To determine if an application will generate events for a particular event monitor, you must evaluate the WHERE option for each active connection when an event monitor is first turned on and for each new connection to the database at connect time. The WHERE option is not evaluated for each event. If no WHERE option is specified, then all CONNECTION, STATEMENT, and/or TRANSACTION events of the specified event type will be monitored. The WHERE option requires the following parameters:

comparison-string1 Specifies the information about a connection to be compared to comparison string 2 in order to determine whether or not the connection should generate a CONNECTION, STATEMENT, or TRANSACTION event (whichever was specified before the WHERE option). The value for comparison string 1 can be any of the following:

APPL_ID Specifies that the application ID of each connection should be compared with comparison-string2.

AUTH_ID Specifies that the authorization ID of each connection should be compared with comparison-string2.

APPL_NAME Specifies that the application program name of each connection should be compared with comparison-string2. The application program name is the first 20 bytes of the application program filename, following the last path separator.

comparison-operator Specifies how the specified APPL_ID, AUTH_ID, or APPL_NAME of each application that connects to the database is to be compared to comparison-string2. The comparison operator can be =, < >, >, > =, <, < =, LIKE, or NOT LIKE.

comparison-string2 Specifies a string to be compared with the specified APPL_ID, AUTH_ID, or APPL_NAME of each application that connects to the database. The value of comparison-string2 must be a string constant, so host variables and other string expressions are not allowed.

You can specify multiple event conditions by placing the keyword AND or OR between each <NOT> [*comparison_string1*] [*comparison-operator*] [*comparison-string2*] option.

File options

MAXFILES [number-of-files] Specifies the maximum number of event files that the event monitor will create. If the value specified for the number of files is NONE, there will be no limit to the number of event files created by the event monitor. Otherwise, the number-of-files value specifies the limit for the number of event monitor files that will exist for a particular event monitor at any time. MAXFILES NONE is the default value if no number-of-files value is specified. Whenever an event monitor has to create another file, it checks to make sure that the number of event files in the directory is less than the number-of-files value. If the maximum limit has already been reached, the event monitor will turn itself off. If an application removes the event files from the directory after they are written, then the total number of files an event monitor can produce can exceed the number-of-files value. This option allows a user to guarantee that the event data will consume only a specified amount of disk space.

MAXFILESIZE [number-of-pages] Specifies the maximum size for an event file. If the value specified for the number of pages is NONE, there will be no limit on an event file's size. Otherwise, the number-of-pages value specifies the maximum size, in 4KB page units, for each event monitor file. Whenever an event monitor writes a new event record to a file, it checks the current file size to ensure that the file will not exceed the specified size limit when the new record is added. If the resulting file would be too large, then the event monitor switches to the next file. The default number-of-pages values for this option are:

OS/2 200 4KB pages
AIX 1000 4KB pages

BUFFERSIZE [number-of-pages] Specifies the size of the event monitor buffers (in units of 4KB pages). All event monitor file I/O is buffered to improve the performance of the event monitors. As buffer size is increased, the amount of I/O performed by the event monitor is decreased. When an event monitor is started, two buffers of the specified size are allocated. Event monitors use double buffering to permit asynchronous I/O.

BLOCKED Specifies that each agent generating an event should wait for an event buffer to be written out to disk if both event buffers are full. You should specify the BLOCKED option to guarantee that no event data is lost. This option is specified by default.

NONBLOCKED Specifies that each agent generating an event should not wait for the event buffer to be written out to disk if both event buffers are full. NONBLOCKED event monitors do not slow down database operations to the extent of BLOCKED event monitors, but NONBLOCKED event monitors are subject to data loss on highly active systems.

APPEND Specifies that, if event data files already exist when the event monitor is turned on, then the event monitor will append the new event data to the existing data files. When the event monitor is reactivated, it resumes writing to the event files as if it had never been turned off. APPEND is the default option. The APPEND option does not apply at CREATE EVENT MONITOR time if there is existing event data in the directory where the newly created event monitor is to write its event data. At CREATE EVENT MONITOR time, all event files (*.evt) are erased from the target directory.

REPLACE Specifies that, if event data files already exist when the event monitor is turned on, then the event monitor will erase all the event files and start writing data to file 00000000.evt.

Description

The CREATE EVENT MONITOR statement creates a monitor to records certain events that occur when you use the database. By recording and examining this information, you can:

- Improve database and application performance.
- Fine-tune database and database manager configuration parameters.
- Pinpoint the source and cause of various problems.
- Gain a better understanding about how DB2 operates.
- Closely examine user and application activity.

The amount of information collected by an event monitor can be quite large. You can control how much information is collected by using the special WHERE event option to filter the data collected by the monitor. You can also control where the data is written. If you want to analyze the information immediately, you can send it via a named pipe to another application that is waiting to process it. If you want to analyze the data sometime after it has been recorded, you can send it to one or more files. For more detailed information about using event monitors and interpreting data from named pipes and files, refer to the *IBM Database System Monitor Guide and Reference* product manual.

Event monitor definitions are recorded in the SYSCAT.EVENTMONITORS catalog view while the events themselves are recorded in the SYSCAT.EVENTS catalog view.

Comments

- If the target for the event monitor is a named pipe, the event monitor will write its data to the pipe in a single stream (as if it were a single, infinitely long file). When writing data to a pipe, an event monitor does not perform blocked writes.

This means that whenever the pipe buffer is full, the event monitor discards the data. It is the monitoring application's responsibility to read all data promptly from a named pipe in order to prevent data loss.

- The naming rules for pipes are platform-specific. On the AIX operating system, pipe names are treated like filenames. As a result, relative pipe names are permitted and are treated like relative path filenames. On OS/2, however, a special syntax is used to name pipes, so absolute pipe names are required.
- The existence of a named pipe is not checked when an event monitor is created. It is the responsibility of the monitoring application to create and open the pipe for reading before the event monitor is activated. If the named pipe is not available, the event monitor will turn itself off and either log an error in the system error log file (if the event monitor was activated at database start time as a result of the AUTOSTART option) or return an error condition (if the event monitor is activated via the SET EVENT MONITOR STATE statement).
- If the target for the event monitor is a file (or a set of files), the event monitor will write out its stream of data as a series of eight-character numbered files with the extension "evt." (00000000.evt, 00000001.evt, 0000002.evt, etc.). The data should be treated as one logical file even though it is actually broken up into smaller pieces.
- An event monitor will never split a single event record across two files, but it might write related records in two different flies. It is the responsibility of the application that uses this data to keep track of such related information when processing the event files.
- The path portion of an event monitor filename must be known at the server, but the path itself could reside on another node (in an AIX-based system, for example, this might be an NFS mounted file).
- The specified path for the event monitor files is not checked when an event monitor is created, but DB2 checks the target path when the event monitor is activated. At that time, if the target path does not exist, the event monitor will turn itself off and either log an error in the system error log file (if the event monitor was activated at database start time as a result of the AUTOSTART option) or return an error condition (if the event monitor is activated via the SET EVENT MONITOR STATE statement).
- If an absolute path (a path that starts with the root directory on AIX or a disk identifier on OS/2) is specified, then the specified path will be used. If a relative path (a path that does not start with the root) is specified, then the path relative to the DB2EVENT directory in the database directory will be used. When a relative path is specified, the DB2EVENT directory converts it into an absolute path. This absolute path is then stored in the SYSCAT.EVENTMONITORS catalog table, and thereafter no distinction is made between absolute and relative paths.
- It is possible to create two or more event monitors that have the same target path. However, once one of these event monitors is activated for the first time and as long as the target path directory is not empty, it will be impossible to activate any of the other event monitors that reference the target path.
- If the BUFFERSIZE option is not specified, the minimum and default size of each buffer is one 4KB page. The maximum size of the buffer is limited by the size of the database heap (DBHEAP) since event monitor buffers are allocated from this heap. When using many event monitors simultaneously, increase the size of the database heap (DBHEAP database configuration parameter).
- Event monitors that write their data to a pipe also have two internal (nonconfigurable) buffers that are one 4KB page in size. These buffers are also allocated from the database heap (DBHEAP). For each active event monitor that has a pipe target, increase the size of the database heap by two pages.

- The number of specified MAXFILESIZE pages must be greater than the number of BUFFERSIZE pages or an error will occur.
- If MAXFILESIZE NONE is specified, then MAXFILES 1 must also be specified. This option means that one file (named "00000000.evt") will contain all the event data for the specified event monitor.
- Highly active event monitors should have larger buffers than relatively inactive event monitors.
- Each event type (DATABASE, TABLES, DEADLOCKS, etc.) can be specified only once in a particular event monitor definition.

Authorization Only users with either system administrator (SYSADM) authority or database administrator (DBADM) authority are allowed to execute this statement.

See Also SET EVENT MONITOR STATE

Examples The following C program illustrates how to use the CREATE EVENT MONITOR statement to create an event monitor that monitors connection events and an event monitor that monitors deadlock cycle events:

```
#include <stdio.h>
#include <stdlib.h>
#include <string.h>
#include <sql.h>

int main()
{
    /* Include The SQLCA Data Structure Variable */
    EXEC SQL INCLUDE SQLCA;

    /* Set Up A Simple SQL Error Handler */
    EXEC SQL WHENEVER SQLERROR GOTO EXIT;

    /* Declare The Local Memory Variables */
    int    rc = EXIT_SUCCESS;
    char   szDefinerID[9];

    /* Declare The SQL Host Memory Variables */
    EXEC SQL BEGIN DECLARE SECTION;
        char       szEMonName[18];
        char       szDefiner[8];
    EXEC SQL END DECLARE SECTION;

    /* Connect To The SAMPLE Database */
    EXEC SQL CONNECT TO SAMPLE USER etpdd6z USING sanders;

    /* Create An Connection Detector Event Monitor */
    EXEC SQL CREATE EVENT MONITOR CONNECTION_EVENTS
        FOR CONNECTIONS
        WRITE TO FILE 'G:'
        MAXFILES 10
        MAXFILESIZE 1024
        NONBLOCKED
        APPEND
        AUTOSTART;

    /* Print A Message Telling That The Event Monitor Was Created */
    printf("The Event Monitor CONNECTION_EVENTS has been created.\n");
```

```
    /* Create A Deadlock Detector Event Monitor */
    EXEC SQL CREATE EVENT MONITOR DEADLOCK_EVENTS
        FOR DEADLOCKS
        WRITE TO FILE 'G:'
        MAXFILES 1
        MAXFILESIZE NONE
        AUTOSTART;

    /* Print A Message Telling That The Event Monitor Was Created */
    printf("The Event Monitor DEADLOCK_EVENTS has been created.\n");

    /* Commit The Transaction */
    EXEC SQL COMMIT;

    /* Now Retrieve The Records From The SYSCAT.EVENTMONITORS Table */
    /* To Verify That The Event Monitors Were Created               */

    /* Declare The SYS_EVENTMONITORS Table Cursor */
    EXEC SQL DECLARE SYS_EVENTMONITORS CURSOR FOR
        SELECT EVMONNAME,
               DEFINER
        FROM SYSCAT.EVENTMONITORS;

    /* Open The Cursor */
    EXEC SQL OPEN SYS_EVENTMONITORS;

    /* If The Cursor Was Successfully Opened, Fetch The Records Into */
    /* Host Variables                                                */
    printf("\nContents of SYSCAT.EVENTMONITORS\n\n");
    while (sqlca.sqlcode == SQL_RC_OK)
        {
        EXEC SQL FETCH SYS_EVENTMONITORS
            INTO :szEMonName,
                 :szDefiner;

        /* If The FETCH Was Successful, Print The Data */
        if (sqlca.sqlcode == SQL_RC_OK)
            {
            strncpy(szDefinerID, " ", 8);
            strncpy(szDefinerID, szDefiner, 8);
            szDefinerID[8] = 0;
            printf("Event Monitor : %18s\tDefiner: %8s\n",
                   szEMonName, szDefinerID);
            }
        }                                        /* End Of WHILE    */

    /* Close The Cursor */
    EXEC SQL CLOSE SYS_EVENTMONITORS;

    /* Delete The Event Monitors */
    EXEC SQL DROP EVENT MONITOR CONNECTION_EVENTS;
    EXEC SQL DROP EVENT MONITOR DEADLOCK_EVENTS;

    /* Commit The Transaction */
    EXEC SQL COMMIT;

EXIT:
    /* If An Error Has Occurred, Display The SQL Return Code */
    if (sqlca.sqlcode != SQL_RC_OK)
        {
```

```
        printf('SQL ERROR : %ld\n', sqlca.sqlcode);
        rc = EXIT_FAILURE;
        }

    /* Issue A Rollback To Free All Locks */
    EXEC SQL ROLLBACK;

    /* Turn Off The SQL Error Handler */
    EXEC SQL WHENEVER SQLERROR CONTINUE;

    /* Disconnect From The SAMPLE Database */
    EXEC SQL DISCONNECT CURRENT;

    /* Return To The Operating System */
    return(rc);
}
```

The following C++ program illustrates how the CREATE EVENT MONITOR statement is used by class methods to create an event monitor that monitors connection events and an event monitor that monitors deadlock cycle events:

```
#include <iostream.h>
#include <stdlib.h>
#include <string.h>
#include <sql.h>

/* Define The EventMonitor Class */
class EventMonitor
{
    private:

       /* Include The SQLCA Data Structure Variable */
       EXEC SQL INCLUDE SQLCA;

       /* Declare The Local Memory Variables */
       char  szDefinerID[9];

       /* Declare The SQL Host Memory Variables */
       EXEC SQL BEGIN DECLARE SECTION;
           char      szCreateString[255];
           char      szEMonName[18];
           char      szDefiner[8];
       EXEC SQL END DECLARE SECTION;

    /* Declare The Public Member Function Prototypes */
    public:
       short int createConnectMonitor();
       short int createDeadlockMonitor(const char *szFileName);
       short int getSysInfo();
} ;

/* Define The createConnectMonitor() Member Function */
short int EventMonitor::createConnectMonitor(void)
{
    /* Create An Connection Detector Event Monitor */
    EXEC SQL CREATE EVENT MONITOR CONNECTION_EVENTS
        FOR CONNECTIONS
        WRITE TO FILE 'G:'
        MAXFILES 10
        MAXFILESIZE 1024
```

```
        NONBLOCKED
        APPEND
        AUTOSTART;

    /* Print A Message Telling That The Event Monitor Was Created */
    if (sqlca.sqlcode == SQL_RC_OK)
        {
        cout << "The Event Monitor CONNECTION_EVENTS has been";
                "created.";
        cout << endl;
        }

    /* Return The SQL Return Code */
    return(sqlca.sqlcode);
}

/* Define The createDeadlockMonitor() Member Function */
short int EventMonitor::createDeadlockMonitor(const char *szFileName)
{
    /* Build The Create Event Monitor SQL Statement String */
    strcpy(szCreateString, "CREATE EVENT MONITOR DEADLOCK_EVENTS ");
    strcat(szCreateString, "FOR DEADLOCKS WRITE TO FILE '");
    strcat(szCreateString, szFileName);
    strcat(szCreateString, "' MAXFILES 1 MAXFILESIZE NONE AUTOSTART");

    /* Create A Deadlock Detector Event Monitor */
    EXEC SQL EXECUTE IMMEDIATE :szCreateString;

    /* Print A Message Telling That The Event Monitor Was Created */
    if (sqlca.sqlcode == SQL_RC_OK)
        {
        cout << "The Event Monitor DEADLOCK_EVENTS has been created.";
        cout << endl;
        }

    /* Return The SQL Return Code */
    return(sqlca.sqlcode);
}

/* Define The getSysInfo() Member Function */
short int EventMonitor::getSysInfo(void)
{
    /* Declare The SYS_EVENTMONITORS Table Cursor */
    EXEC SQL DECLARE SYS_EVENTMONITORS CURSOR FOR
        SELECT EVMONNAME,
               DEFINER
        FROM SYSCAT.EVENTMONITORS;

    /* Open The Cursor */
    EXEC SQL OPEN SYS_EVENTMONITORS;

    /* If The Cursor Was Successfully Opened, Fetch The Records Into */
    /* Host Variables                                                */
    cout << endl << "Contents of SYSCAT.EVENTMONITORS" << endl <<
endl;
    while (sqlca.sqlcode == SQL_RC_OK)
        {
        EXEC SQL FETCH SYS_EVENTMONITORS
            INTO :szEMonName,
                 :szDefiner;
```

```
        /* If The FETCH Was Successful, Print The Data */
        if (sqlca.sqlcode == SQL_RC_OK)
            {
            strncpy(szDefinerID, " ", 8);
            strncpy(szDefinerID, szDefiner, 8);
            szDefinerID[8] = 0;
            cout << "Event Monitor : ";
            cout.width(18);
            cout << szEMonName;
            cout << ": " << szDefinerID << endl;
            }
        }                                           /* End Of WHILE    */

    /* Close The Cursor */
    EXEC SQL CLOSE SYS_EVENTMONITORS;

    /* Return The SQL Return Code */
    return(sqlca.sqlcode);
}

int main()
{
    /* Declare The Local Memory Variables */
    short int rc = EXIT_SUCCESS;            // Must Be Declared Here
                                            // For The SQL Precompiler

    /* Include The SQLCA Data Structure Variable */
    EXEC SQL INCLUDE SQLCA;

    /* Set Up A Simple SQL Error Handler */
    EXEC SQL WHENEVER SQLERROR GOTO EXIT;

    /* Create An Instance Of The EventMonitor Class */
    EventMonitor event;

    /* Connect To The SAMPLE Database */
    EXEC SQL CONNECT TO SAMPLE USER etpdd6z USING sanders;

    /* Create An Connection Detector Event Monitor */
    rc = event.createConnectMonitor();

    /* Create A Deadlock Detector Event Monitor */
    rc = event.createDeadlockMonitor("G:\DLOCKS");

    /* Commit The Transaction */
    EXEC SQL COMMIT;

    /* Now Retrieve The Records From The SYSCAT.EVENTMONITORS Table */
    /* To Verify That The Event Monitors Were Created               */
    rc = event.getSysInfo();

    /* Delete The Event Monitors */
    EXEC SQL DROP EVENT MONITOR CONNECTION_EVENTS;
    EXEC SQL DROP EVENT MONITOR DEADLOCK_EVENTS;

    /* Commit The Transaction */
    EXEC SQL COMMIT;

EXIT:
    /* If An Error Has Occurred, Display The SQL Return Code */
    if (sqlca.sqlcode != SQL_RC_OK)
```

```
        {
        cout << "SQL ERROR : " << sqlca.sqlcode << endl;
        rc = EXIT_FAILURE;
        }

    /* Issue A Rollback To Free All Locks */
    EXEC SQL ROLLBACK;

    /* Turn Off The SQL Error Handler */
    EXEC SQL WHENEVER SQLERROR CONTINUE;

    /* Disconnect From The SAMPLE Database */
    EXEC SQL DISCONNECT CURRENT;

    /* Return To The Operating System */
    return(rc);
}
```

SET EVENT MONITOR STATE

Purpose The SET EVENT MONITOR STATE statement activates or deactivates an event monitor.

Syntax

```
EXEC SQL SET EVENT MONITOR [event-monitor-name] STATE <=>
    [event-monitor-state];
```

Parameters

event-monitor-name Identifies the name of the event monitor to activate or deactivate.

event-monitor-state Identifies the state in which to place the event monitor. The event monitor state can be the name of a host variable that contains the event monitor state or either of the following values:

0 Indicates that the specified event monitor should be deactivated.

1 Indicates that the specified event monitor should be activated.

Description The SET EVENT MONITOR STATE statement allows you to activate or deactivate an event monitor. When an event monitor is active, specific data is tracked whenever the event being monitored takes place.

Comments

- If a host variable specifies the event monitor state, it must be defined as an integer data type and it must contain the value 0 or 1. Also, if a corresponding indicator variable is used, the value of that indicator variable must not be null.
- If an event monitor is already active, attempting to activate it will result in a warning. You can determine the current state of an event monitor (active or inactive) by executing the built-in EVENT_MON_STATE function.
- Although an unlimited number of event monitors can be defined, no more than 32 event monitors can be active at the same time.
- In order to activate an event monitor, the transaction in which the event monitor was created must be committed. This prevents an application from creating an event monitor, activating the monitor, and then rolling back the transaction. Such an action would leave an event monitor active even though it was no longer defined in the system catalog.
- If the number or size of the event monitor files exceeds the value specified for the MAXFILES or MAXFILESIZE options that were provided with the CREATE EVENT MONITOR statement, an error will occur.

- If the target path of the event monitor that was specified with the CREATE EVENT MONITOR statement is already in use by another event monitor, an error will occur.
- When an event monitor is activated, any counters associated with it are reset.

Authorization Only users with either system administrator (SYSADM) authority or database administrator (DBADM) authority are allowed to execute this statement.

See Also CREATE EVENT MONITOR

Examples The following C program illustrates how to use the SET EVENT MONITOR STATE statement to turn an event monitor that monitors connection events ON and OFF:

```
#include <stdio.h>
#include <stdlib.h>
#include <sql.h>

int main()
{
    /* Include The SQLCA Data Structure Variable */
    EXEC SQL INCLUDE SQLCA;

    /* Set Up A Simple SQL Error Handler */
    EXEC SQL WHENEVER SQLERROR GOTO EXIT;

    /* Declare The Local Memory Variables */
    int  rc = EXIT_SUCCESS;

    /* Connect To The SAMPLE Database */
    EXEC SQL CONNECT TO SAMPLE USER etpdd6z USING sanders;

    /* Create An Connection Detector Event Monitor */
    EXEC SQL CREATE EVENT MONITOR CONNECTION_EVENTS
        FOR CONNECTIONS
        WRITE TO FILE 'G:'
        MAXFILES 1
        MAXFILESIZE NONE
        NONBLOCKED
        APPEND
        MANUALSTART;

    /* Print A Message Telling That The Event Monitor Was Created */
    printf("The Event Monitor CONNECTION_EVENTS has been created.\n");

    /* Commit The Transaction - The Event Monitor Creation Transaction */
    /* Must Be Committed Before The SET EVENT MONITOR Statement Can    */
    /* Be Executed                                                     */
    EXEC SQL COMMIT;

    /* Activate The Connection Event Monitor */
    EXEC SQL SET EVENT MONITOR CONNECTION_EVENTS STATE = 1;

    /* Print A Message Telling That The Event Monitor Is Active */
    printf("The Event Monitor CONNECTION_EVENTS is now active.\n");

    /* Commit The Transaction */
    EXEC SQL COMMIT;

    /* Disconnect From The SAMPLE Database */
    EXEC SQL DISCONNECT CURRENT;
```

```
    /* Re-Connect To The SAMPLE Database - Should Write Event To File */
    EXEC SQL CONNECT TO SAMPLE USER etpdd6z USING sanders;

    /* De-activate The Connection Event Monitor */
    EXEC SQL SET EVENT MONITOR CONNECTION_EVENTS STATE = 0;

    /* Print A Message Telling That The Event Monitor Is No Longer */
    /* Active                                                      */
    printf("The Event Monitor CONNECTION_EVENTS is no longer active.\n");

    /* Delete The Event Monitor */
//  EXEC SQL DROP EVENT MONITOR CONNECTION_EVENTS;

    /* When The Connection Monitor Is Deleted, The File Associated   */
    /* With The Monitor Will Be Deleted. By Commenting This Line Out, */
    /* You Can Examine The Event Monitor File After This Program Is  */
    /* Executed                                                      */

EXIT:
    /* If An Error Has Occurred, Display The SQL Return Code */
    if (sqlca.sqlcode != SQL_RC_OK)
        {
        printf("SQL ERROR : %ld\n", sqlca.sqlcode);
        rc = EXIT_FAILURE;
        }

    /* Issue A Rollback To Free All Locks */
    EXEC SQL ROLLBACK;

    /* Turn Off The SQL Error Handler */
    EXEC SQL WHENEVER SQLERROR CONTINUE;

    /* Disconnect From The SAMPLE Database */
    EXEC SQL DISCONNECT CURRENT;

    /* Return To The Operating System */
    return(rc);
}
```

> Note: The SET EVENT MONITOR STATE statement is used in a C++ program in a similar manner.

CREATE TRIGGER

Purpose The CREATE TRIGGER statement defines a trigger in the database.

Syntax

```
EXEC SQL CREATE TRIGGER [trigger-name] [activation-time] [activation-event]
   ON [table-name] <reference-options> [granularity] MODE DB2SQL
   <WHEN ([search-condition])> [triggered-action];
```

Parameters

trigger-name Identifies the name of the trigger to be created.

activation-time Identifies when the associated triggered action is to be applied to the database. The activation time can be any of the following:

NO CASCADE BEFORE — Specifies that the associated triggered action is to be applied before any changes to the subject table, caused by the activation event, are applied to the database. It also specifies that this triggered action will not cause other triggered actions to be activated.

AFTER — Specifies that the associated triggered action is to be applied after any changes caused to the subject table, by the activation event, are applied to the database. It also specifies that this triggered action can cause other triggered actions to be activated.

activation-event Identifies the type of event that must be applied to the subject table in order to cause the triggered action to occur. The activation event can be any of the following:

INSERT — Specifies that the triggered action associated with the trigger is executed whenever an INSERT operation is applied to the subject table.

DELETE — Specifies that the triggered action associated with the trigger is executed whenever a DELETE operation is applied to the subject table.

UPDATE < OF *column-name*, . . . > Specifies that the triggered action associated with the trigger is executed whenever an UPDATE operation is applied to either all columns of the subject table or a specified list of columns of the subject table. If the OF column-name,... option is specified:

column-name Identifies one or more columns that exist in the specified table.

table-name Identifies the name of the subject table for the trigger. The table name must specify either a base table or an alias that refers to a base table.

granularity Identifies how the triggered action is to be applied. The trigger granularity event can be any of the following:

FOR EACH ROW — Specifies that the triggered action associated with the trigger is to be executed once for each row of the subject table affected by the activation event.

FOR EACH STATEMENT — Specifies that the triggered action associated with the trigger is to be executed only once for the whole statement that generates the activation event. This type of granularity can be specified only if the AFTER activation time is used.

search-condition Specifies a condition that can be evaluated to either TRUE, FALSE, or unknown. The search condition allows you to determine whether or not the triggered action should be executed.

triggered-action Specifies the action to be performed when a trigger is activated. The triggered action is composed of one or more SQL statements. If multiple SQL statements are defined as the triggered action, they must be preceded by the BEGIN ATOMIC keywords, followed by the END keyword, and separated by semicolons (;). Each statement is executed in the order it is specified.

Reference Options

REFERENCING [reference-type] Specifies the correlation names for the transition variables and/or the table names (identifiers) of the transition tables that can be used by the triggering action. You can make each row affected by an activation event (INSERT, DELETE, or UPDATE) available to the triggered action by qualifying the column names with the appropriate correlation name or identifier. The following reference types are available:

OLD <AS> [correlation-name] Specifies a name for the row state of a specific row in the subject table prior to the activation event.

NEW <AS> [correlation-name] Specifies a name for the row state of a specific row in the subject table after it is modified by the activation event or by a SET statement in a NO CASCADING BEFORE trigger that has already been executed.

OLD_TABLE <AS> [identifier] Specifies a temporary table name for the state of a set of rows in the subject table prior to the activation event.

REFERENCING NEW_TABLE <AS> [identifier] Specifies a temporary table name for the row state of a set of rows in the subject table after it is modified by the activation event or by a SET statement in a NO CASCADING BEFORE trigger that has already been executed.

The following rules apply when using the REFERENCING [reference-type] option:

- Each specified correlation name and table name must be unique for the trigger being defined.
- Only one OLD and/or one NEW correlation name can be specified for the same trigger.
- Only one OLD_TABLE and/or one NEW_TABLE identifier can be specified for the same trigger.
- The OLD correlation name and the OLD_TABLE identifier can be used only if the trigger event is either a DELETE operation or an UPDATE operation. If the operation is a DELETE, then the OLD correlation name will capture the state of the deleted row. If the operation is an UPDATE, then the OLD correlation name will capture the state of the row before the UPDATE operation is executed. The same rules apply to the OLD_TABLE identifier and the set of affected rows it references.
- The NEW correlation name and the NEW_TABLE identifier can be used only if the trigger event is either an INSERT operation or an UPDATE operation. In both operations, the NEW correlation name captures the state of the row as provided by the original operation and as modified by any NO CASCADE BEFORE trigger that has executed to this point. The same rules applies to the NEW_TABLE identifier and the set of affected rows it references.
- OLD_TABLE and NEW_TABLE identifiers cannot be defined for a NO CASCADE BEFORE trigger.
- OLD and NEW correlation names cannot be defined in a FOR EACH STATEMENT trigger.
- Transition tables cannot be modified.
- The total number of specified references cannot exceed the limit for the number of columns in a table, and the sum of their lengths cannot exceed the maximum length of a row in a table.
- The scope of each defined correlation name and identifier is the entire trigger definition.

Description

The CREATE TRIGGER statement allows you to define a trigger in a database. A trigger is a schema object associated with a base table that defines a set of actions to be executed either before or after an insert, update, or delete operation is performed against that base table. When such an operation (denoted as the triggering operation) takes place, the trigger is said to be activated. Once activated, the set of rows in the corresponding base (subject) table that are affected by the operation are selected and the action of the trigger is executed. During trigger execution, the trigger action condition is tested and, if satisfied, the triggered SQL statements are executed. Such execution can take place either only once for the operation or once for each row affected by the operation, depending on how the trigger is defined. Trigger definitions are stored in the SYSCAT.TRIGGERS system catalog table.

Comments

- If no qualifier (schema) is provided with the trigger name, the authorization ID of the current user will be used as the qualifier when the trigger is created. If a qualifier is provided with the trigger name, it cannot be "SYSIBM", "SYSCAT", or "SYSSTAT." In other words, triggers cannot be created for system catalog tables.
- The view name cannot be a name that is already being used by another table, alias, or view.
- If a trigger is created for an UPDATE or DELETE operation, the trigger will be activated, even if the UPDATE or DELETE statement does not affect rows in the subject table of the trigger.
- If the WHEN option is specified with a trigger, the associated triggered action will be performed only if the specified search condition evaluates as TRUE. Otherwise, the associated triggered action is always performed.
- If the trigger is defined as a NO CASCADE BEFORE trigger, then the SQL statement must be one or more of the following:
  –A fullselect (SELECT) statement
  –A SET transition variable statement
  –A SIGNAL SQLSTATE statement
- If the trigger is defined as an AFTER trigger, then the SQL statement must be one (or more) of the following:
  –An INSERT statement
  –A searched UPDATE statement
  –A searched DELETE statement
  –A fullselect (SELECT) statement
  –A SIGNAL SQLSTATE statement
- The results of a fullselect statement are visible only within the triggered action.
- The triggered action cannot reference undefined transition variables.
- Adding a trigger to a table that already contains rows will not cause any triggered actions to be activated. Therefore, if the trigger is designed to enforce constraints on the data in the table, those constraints cannot be satisfied by existing rows.
- If the activation events for two triggers occur simultaneously (i.e., if two triggers have the same activation event for the same specified table), then the triggers will be executed in the same order in which they were created: the newer trigger executing after the older one.
- If a column is added to the subject table after a trigger is defined, the following rules apply:
  –If the trigger is an UPDATE trigger specified without an explicit column list, then an update to the new column will activate the trigger.

–The column will not be visible in the body of the trigger.
–The OLD_TABLE and NEW_TABLE transition tables will not contain this column.

- If a column is added to any table referenced by a triggered action, the new column will not be visible to the triggered action.
- Creating a trigger causes certain packages to be marked invalid, as follows:
  –If an update trigger is created without an explicit column list, packages that have an update dependency on the target table will be invalidated.
  –If an update trigger is created with an explicit column list, then packages that have an update dependency on at least one of the columns in the column list for the target table will be invalidated.
  –If an insert trigger is created, packages that have an insert dependency on the target table will be invalidated.
  –If a delete trigger is created, packages that have a delete dependency on the target table will be invalidated.
- Invalidated packages remain invalid until the application program is explicitly bound or rebound, or until it is executed and DB2 automatically rebinds it.
- If a trigger is no longer available and therefore can never be activated, it is considered to be inoperative. A trigger becomes inoperative if:
  –An authorization that the creator of the trigger was required to have for the trigger to execute is revoked.
  –An object on which the trigger action is dependent, such as a table, view, or alias, is deleted (dropped).
  –A view on which the trigger action is dependent becomes inoperative.
  –An alias used by the trigger to refer to the subject table is deleted (dropped).
- In practical terms, the definition of an inoperative trigger has been dropped as a result of cascading rules for DROP or REVOKE statements. When a view is dropped, for example, any trigger with a SQL statement in its triggered action that was using that view is made inoperative. When a trigger is made inoperative, all packages containing statements for performing operations that were activating the trigger are marked invalid. When the package is rebound (automatically or implicitly), the inoperative trigger is completely ignored. Similarly, applications with dynamic SQL statements that perform operations that activate the trigger will also ignore all inoperative triggers. Inoperative triggers are indicated by an "X" in the VALID column of the SYSCAT.TRIGGERS system catalog table. The text of the inoperative trigger definition is stored in the TEXT column of this system catalog table.
- An inoperative trigger name can still be specified in the DROP TRIGGER and COMMENT ON TRIGGER statements.
- You can re-create an inoperative trigger by issuing a new CREATE TRIGGER statement without explicitly dropping the inoperative trigger.
- Errors that occur during the execution of SQL statements in the triggered action are returned via the SQLSTATE **09000** ("An error occurred in a triggered SQL statement in trigger [trigger-name] . . .") error, unless the error is considered severe. The *sqlerrmc* field of the SQLCA data structure variable (for nonsevere errors) includes the trigger name, SQLCODE, SQLSTATE, and as many tokens of the failure as will fit. The SQL statement in a triggered action can be the SIGNAL SQLSTATE statement or it can contain the RAISE_ERROR function. In both of these cases, the SQLSTATE **09000** is

returned and the actual SQLSTATE specified when generating the error is included in the *sqlerrmc* field of the SQLCA data structure.

- Warning conditions generated by the SQL statements in a triggered action are not returned during trigger execution.

Authorization

Only users with either system administrator (SYSADM) authority, database administrator (DBADM) authority, or ALTER and SELECT authority for the table on which the trigger is defined are allowed to execute this statement.

In addition, the user must have the appropriate authorizations to execute the SQL statements specified within the triggered action.

See Also

SET, SIGNAL SQLSTATE

Examples

The following C program illustrates how to use the CREATE TRIGGER statement to create a trigger that is designed to raise employees' bonuses by 2 percent and their commissions by 5 percent whenever they receive a salary increase greater than 10 percent:

```
#include <stdio.h>
#include <stdlib.h>
#include <sql.h>

int main()
{
    /* Include The SQLCA Data Structure Variable */
    EXEC SQL INCLUDE SQLCA;

    /* Set Up A Simple SQL Error Handler */
    EXEC SQL WHENEVER SQLERROR GOTO EXIT;

    /* Declare The Local Memory Variables */
    int  rc = EXIT_SUCCESS;

    /* Declare The SQL Host Memory Variables */
    EXEC SQL BEGIN DECLARE SECTION;
        char    szEmpNo[7];
        double  rdSalary;
        double  rdBonus;
        double  rdComm;
    EXEC SQL END DECLARE SECTION;

    /* Connect To The SAMPLE Database */
    EXEC SQL CONNECT TO SAMPLE USER etpdd6z USING sanders;

    /* Create A Trigger - Whenever Salary Is Increased > 10%,   */
    /* Increase The Bonus By 2% And Increase The Commission By 5% */
    EXEC SQL CREATE TRIGGER RAISE_MONEY
        AFTER
        UPDATE OF SALARY ON USERID.EMPLOYEE
        REFERENCING NEW AS N OLD AS O
        FOR EACH ROW
        MODE DB2SQL
        WHEN (N.SALARY > 1.1 * O.SALARY)
        BEGIN ATOMIC
            UPDATE USERID.EMPLOYEE SET BONUS = BONUS * 1.02;
            UPDATE USERID.EMPLOYEE SET COMM = COMM * 1.05;
        END;

    /* Print A Message Telling That The Trigger Was Created */
    printf("The Trigger RAISE_MONEY has been created.\n");
```

```
        /* Commit The Transaction */
        EXEC SQL COMMIT;

        /* Now Retrieve A Record From The USERID.EMPLOYEE Table, Update   */
        /* The Record So That The Trigger Is Activated, Then Retrieve The */
        /* Record Again To Verify That The Trigger Worked Correctly       */

        /* Retrieve A Record From The EMPLOYEE Table */
        EXEC SQL SELECT EMPNO,
                        SALARY,
                        BONUS,
                        COMM
            INTO :szEmpNo,
                 :rdSalary,
                 :rdBonus,
                 :rdComm
            FROM USERID.EMPLOYEE
            WHERE EMPNO = '000010';

        /* Print The Information Retrieved - This Will Show The Record */
        /* Before It Is Changed By The Trigger                         */
        printf("\nEmployee No. : %7s Salary     : $%.2lf\n",
               szEmpNo, rdSalary);
        printf("                        Bonus      : $%.2lf\n", rdBonus);
        printf("                        Commission : $%.2lf\n", rdComm);

        /* Update The Record - Activate The Trigger */
        EXEC SQL UPDATE USERID.EMPLOYEE
            SET (SALARY) = (SALARY * 1.11)
            WHERE EMPNO = '000010';

        /* Retrieve The Updated Record From The EMPLOYEE Table */
        EXEC SQL SELECT EMPNO,
                        SALARY,
                        BONUS,
                        COMM
            INTO :szEmpNo,
                 :rdSalary,
                 :rdBonus,
                 :rdComm
            FROM USERID.EMPLOYEE
            WHERE EMPNO = '000010';

        /* Print The Information Retrieved - This Will Show The Record */
        /* After It Is Changed By The Trigger                          */
        printf("\nEmployee No. : %7s Salary     : $%.2lf\n",
               szEmpNo, rdSalary);
        printf("                        Bonus      : $%.2lf\n", rdBonus);
        printf("                        Commission : $%.2lf\n", rdComm);

        /* Issue A Rollback Ignore All Changes */
        EXEC SQL ROLLBACK;

        /* Delete The Trigger */
        EXEC SQL DROP TRIGGER RAISE_MONEY;

        /* Commit The Transaction */
        EXEC SQL COMMIT;

    EXIT:
        /* If An Error Has Occurred, Display The SQL Return Code */
```

```
    if (sqlca.sqlcode != SQL_RC_OK)
        {
        printf("SQL ERROR : %ld\n", sqlca.sqlcode);
        rc = EXIT_FAILURE;
        }

    /* Issue A Rollback To Free All Locks */
    EXEC SQL ROLLBACK;

    /* Turn Off The SQL Error Handler */
    EXEC SQL WHENEVER SQLERROR CONTINUE;

    /* Disconnect From The SAMPLE Database */
    EXEC SQL DISCONNECT CURRENT;

    /* Return To The Operating System */
    return(rc);
}
```

The following C++ program illustrates how the CREATE TRIGGER statement is used by a class method to create a trigger that is designed to raise employees' bonuses by 2 percent and their commissions by 5 percent whenever they receive a salary increase greater than 10 percent:

```
#include <iostream.h>
#include <stdlib.h>
#include <string.h>
#include <sql.h>

/* Define The Trigger Class */
class Trigger
{
    private:

       /* Include The SQLCA Data Structure Variable */
       EXEC SQL INCLUDE SQLCA;

       /* Declare The SQL Host Memory Variables */
       EXEC SQL BEGIN DECLARE SECTION;
           char     szEmpNo[7];
           double   rdSalary;
           double   rdBonus;
           double   rdComm;
       EXEC SQL END DECLARE SECTION;

    /* Declare The Public Member Function Prototypes */
    public:
       short int createTrigger();
       short int printRecord();
} ;

/* Define The createTrigger() Member Function */
short int Trigger::createTrigger(void)
{
    /* Create A Trigger - Whenever Salary Is Increased > 10%,    */
    /* Increase The Bonus By 2% And Increase The Commission By 5% */
    EXEC SQL CREATE TRIGGER RAISE_MONEY
        AFTER
        UPDATE OF SALARY ON USERID.EMPLOYEE
        REFERENCING NEW AS N OLD AS O
```

```
            FOR EACH ROW
            MODE DB2SQL
            WHEN (N.SALARY > 1.1 * O.SALARY)
            BEGIN ATOMIC
                UPDATE USERID.EMPLOYEE SET BONUS = BONUS * 1.02;
                UPDATE USERID.EMPLOYEE SET COMM = COMM * 1.05;
            END;

    /* Print A Message Telling That The Trigger Was Created */
    if (sqlca.sqlcode == SQL_RC_OK)
        {
        cout << "The Trigger RAISE_MONEY has been created." << endl;
        }

    /* Return The SQL Return Code */
    return(sqlca.sqlcode);
}

/* Define The printRecord() Member Function */
short int Trigger::printRecord(void)
{
    /* Retrieve A Record From The EMPLOYEE Table */
    EXEC SQL SELECT EMPNO,
                    SALARY,
                    BONUS,
                    COMM
        INTO :szEmpNo,
             :rdSalary,
             :rdBonus,
             :rdComm
        FROM USERID.EMPLOYEE
        WHERE EMPNO = '000010';

    /* Print The Information Retrieved */
    cout << endl << "Employee No. : ";
    cout.width(7);
    cout << szEmpNo;
    cout << " Salary     : $";
    cout << rdSalary << endl;
    cout << "                          Bonus      : $";
    cout << rdBonus << endl;
    cout << "                          Commission : $";
    cout << rdComm << endl;

    /* Return The SQL Return Code */
    return(sqlca.sqlcode);
}

int main()
{
    /* Declare The Local Memory Variables */
    short int rc = EXIT_SUCCESS;        // Must Be Declared Here
                                        // For The SQL Precompiler

    /* Include The SQLCA Data Structure Variable */
    EXEC SQL INCLUDE SQLCA;

    /* Set Up A Simple SQL Error Handler */
    EXEC SQL WHENEVER SQLERROR GOTO EXIT;
    /* Create An Instance Of The Trigger Class */
```

```
    Trigger table;

    /* Connect To The SAMPLE Database */
    EXEC SQL CONNECT TO SAMPLE USER etpdd6z USING sanders;

    /* Create A Trigger - Whenever Salary Is Increased > 10%,    */
    /* Increase The Bonus By 2% And Increase The Commission By 5% */
    rc = table.createTrigger();

    /* Commit The Transaction */
    EXEC SQL COMMIT;

    /* Now Retrieve A Record From The USERID.EMPLOYEE Table, Update   */
    /* The Record So That The Trigger Is Activated, Then Retrieve The */
    /* Record Again To Verify That The Trigger Worked Correctly       */

    /* Retrieve A Record From The EMPLOYEE Table And Print The    */
    /* Information Retrieved - This Will Show The Record Before It Is */
    /* Changed By The Trigger                                     */
    rc = table.printRecord();

    /* Update The Record - Activate The Trigger */
    EXEC SQL UPDATE USERID.EMPLOYEE
        SET (SALARY) = (SALARY * 1.11)
        WHERE EMPNO = '000010';

    /* Retrieve The Updated Record From The EMPLOYEE Table And Print */
    /* The Information Retrieved - This Will Show The Record After  */
    /* Is Changed By The Trigger                                    */
    rc = table.printRecord();

    /* Issue A Rollback Ignore All Changes */
    EXEC SQL ROLLBACK;

    /* Delete The Trigger */
    EXEC SQL DROP TRIGGER RAISE_MONEY;

    /* Commit The Transaction */
    EXEC SQL COMMIT;

EXIT:
    /* If An Error Has Occurred, Display The SQL Return Code */
    if (sqlca.sqlcode != SQL_RC_OK)
        {
        cout << "SQL ERROR : " << sqlca.sqlcode << endl;
        rc = EXIT_FAILURE;
        }

    /* Issue A Rollback To Free All Locks */
    EXEC SQL ROLLBACK;

    /* Turn Off The SQL Error Handler */
    EXEC SQL WHENEVER SQLERROR CONTINUE;

    /* Disconnect From The SAMPLE Database */
    EXEC SQL DISCONNECT CURRENT;

    /* Return To The Operating System */
    return(rc);
}
```

SET

Purpose The SET statement assigns values to NEW transition variables from within a trigger.

Syntax

```
SET <(> <correlation-name> [column-name] ,...] <)> = <(>
   [expression,... | row-fullselect] <)>;
```

Parameters

correlation-name Identifies the name provided for referencing NEW transition variables when the trigger was created (refer to the CREATE TRIGGER statement for more information).

column-name Identifies the column to be updated.

expression Identifies the new value to be inserted into the specified column. The expression can be an actual value, equation, NULL, or DEFAULT, but the expression cannot include a column function except when it occurs within a scalar fullselect.

row-fullselect Defines the full form of a SELECT statement for generating the appropriate data values by retrieving a single row with the same number of columns as the number of columns specified before the assignment statement (=) from other tables and/or views.

Description The SET statement allows you to assign values to NEW transition variables from within a trigger. This statement can be used only in the triggered action of a BEFORE trigger whose granularity is defined as FOR EACH ROW (refer to the CREATE TRIGGER statement for more information).

Comments

- Each specified column name must identify a column of the subject table of the trigger. A column cannot be specified more than once.
- An expression can contain references to OLD and NEW transition variables, provided they are qualified by the appropriate correlation name.
- The NULL value should be specified for only nullable columns.
- If the DEFAULT value is specified, which default value is inserted into the column depends on how the column was defined, as follows:
  –If the WITH DEFAULT option was specified for the column when the table was created (or altered), the default value will be based on the data type of the column.
  –If neither the WITH DEFAULT option nor the NOT NULL option were specified for the column when the table was created (or altered), the default value inserted into the column will be NULL.
  –If the NOT NULL option was specified and the WITH DEFAULT option was not specified for the column when the table was created, the DEFAULT value is not used.
- A row fullselect can contain references to both OLD and NEW transition variables, provided they are qualified by the appropriate correlation name.
- If the row fullselect returns multiple rows, an error will occur.
- If more than one assignment is specified, all expressions and row fullselects will be evaluated before the assignments are performed. Thus, references to columns in an expression or row fullselect are always the value of the transition variable prior to any assignment in the single SET transition variable statement.

Prerequisites A trigger must be defined with the CREATE TRIGGER statement before the SET transition variable statement can be executed.

Authorization Only users with either system administrator (SYSADM) authority, database administrator (DBADM) authority, UPDATE authority for the subject table of the trigger, or CONTROL authority for the subject table of the trigger are allowed to execute this statement as long as no row-fullselect statement is specified.

Users that wish to use the row-fullselect form of this statement that do not have SYSADM authority or DBADM authority must also have SELECT authority for the tables and/or views that are referenced in the fullselect statement.

See Also CREATE TRIGGER, SIGNAL SQLSTATE

Examples The following C program illustrates how the SET statement is used by a triggered action to raise employees' bonuses by 2 percent and their commissions by 5 percent whenever they receive a salary increase greater than 10 percent:

```
#include <stdio.h>
#include <stdlib.h>
#include <sql.h>

int main()
{
    /* Include The SQLCA Data Structure Variable */
    EXEC SQL INCLUDE SQLCA;

    /* Set Up A Simple SQL Error Handler */
    EXEC SQL WHENEVER SQLERROR GOTO EXIT;

    /* Declare The Local Memory Variables */
    int  rc = EXIT_SUCCESS;

    /* Declare The SQL Host Memory Variables */
    EXEC SQL BEGIN DECLARE SECTION;
        char    szEmpNo[7];
        double  rdSalary;
        double  rdBonus;
        double  rdComm;
    EXEC SQL END DECLARE SECTION;

    /* Connect To The SAMPLE Database */
    EXEC SQL CONNECT TO SAMPLE USER etpdd6z USING sanders;

    /* Create A Trigger - Whenever Salary Is Increased > 10%,     */
    /* Increase The Bonus By 2% And Increase The Commission By 5% */
    EXEC SQL CREATE TRIGGER RAISE_MONEY
        NO CASCADE BEFORE
        UPDATE OF SALARY ON USERID.EMPLOYEE
        REFERENCING NEW AS N OLD AS O
        FOR EACH ROW
        MODE DB2SQL
        WHEN (N.SALARY > 1.1 * O.SALARY)
        BEGIN ATOMIC
            SET (N.SALARY, N.BONUS, N.COMM) =
                (O.SALARY * 1.1, O.BONUS * 1.02, O.COMM * 1.05);
        END;

    /* Print A Message Telling That The Trigger Was Created */
    printf("The Trigger RAISE_MONEY has been created.\n");

    /* Commit The Transaction */
    EXEC SQL COMMIT;
```

```
/* Now Retrieve A Record From The USERID.EMPLOYEE Table, Update  */
/* The Record So That The Trigger Is Activated, Then Retrieve The */
/* Record Again To Verify That The Trigger Worked Correctly       */

/* Retrieve A Record From The EMPLOYEE Table */
EXEC SQL SELECT EMPNO,
                SALARY,
                BONUS,
                COMM
    INTO :szEmpNo,
         :rdSalary,
         :rdBonus,
         :rdComm
    FROM USERID.EMPLOYEE
    WHERE EMPNO = '000010';

/* Print The Information Retrieved - This Will Show The Record */
/* Before It Is Changed By The Trigger                         */
printf("\nEmployee No. : %7s Salary     : $%.2lf\n",
      szEmpNo, rdSalary);
printf("                              Bonus      : $%.2lf\n", rdBonus);
printf("                              Commission : $%.2lf\n", rdComm);

/* Update The Record - Activate The Trigger */
EXEC SQL UPDATE USERID.EMPLOYEE
    SET (SALARY) = (SALARY * 1.11)
    WHERE EMPNO = '000010';

/* Retrieve The Updated Record From The EMPLOYEE Table */
EXEC SQL SELECT EMPNO,
                SALARY,
                BONUS,
                COMM
    INTO :szEmpNo,
         :rdSalary,
         :rdBonus,
         :rdComm
    FROM USERID.EMPLOYEE
    WHERE EMPNO = '000010';

/* Print The Information Retrieved - This Will Show The Record */
/* After It Is Changed By The Trigger                          */
printf("\nEmployee No. : %7s Salary     : $%.2lf\n",
      szEmpNo, rdSalary);
printf("                              Bonus      : $%.2lf\n", rdBonus);
printf("                              Commission : $%.2lf\n", rdComm);

/* Issue A Rollback Ignore All Changes */
EXEC SQL ROLLBACK;

/* Delete The Trigger */
EXEC SQL DROP TRIGGER RAISE_MONEY;

/* Commit The Transaction */
EXEC SQL COMMIT;

EXIT:
    /* If An Error Has Occurred, Display The SQL Return Code */
    if (sqlca.sqlcode != SQL_RC_OK)
        {
        printf("SQL ERROR : %ld\n", sqlca.sqlcode);
```

```
        rc = EXIT_FAILURE;
        }

    /* Issue A Rollback To Free All Locks */
    EXEC SQL ROLLBACK;

    /* Turn Off The SQL Error Handler */
    EXEC SQL WHENEVER SQLERROR CONTINUE;

    /* Disconnect From The SAMPLE Database */
    EXEC SQL DISCONNECT CURRENT;

    /* Return To The Operating System */
    return(rc);
}
```

Note: The SET statement is used in a C++ program in a similar manner.

SIGNAL SQLSTATE

Purpose The SIGNAL SQLSTATE statement signals a user-defined error from within a trigger.

Syntax

```
SIGNAL SQLSTATE [SQL-state] ([diagnostic-string]);
```

Parameters

SQL-state Identifies a character string constant value that represents an SQLSTATE.

diagnostic-string Identifies a character string that describes the error condition.

Description The SIGNAL SQLSTATE statement signals an error from within a trigger. When the SIGNAL SQLSTATE statement is executed, a user-defined SQLSTATE value and a diagnostic string are returned to the application. Since the SIGNAL SQLSTATE statement can be used only in a trigger, the SQLSTATE and diagnostic string are returned in the *sqlerrmc* field of the SQLCA data structure variable as part of an SQLSTATE **09**000 and SQLCODE -723 error ("An error occurred in a triggered SQL statement in trigger [trigger-name] . . .").

Comments

- The specified SQLSTATE must be a character string that contains exactly five characters, and it must adhere to the following rules for application-defined SQLSTATEs:
  –Each character must be either a numerical digit (0 through 9) or a nonaccented uppercase letter (A through Z).
  –The first two characters of the string identify the SQLSTATE class, and the last three characters identify the SQLSTATE subclass. If the SQLSTATE class begins with characters that fall in the range of 0 through 6 or A through H, then the subclass characters must fall in the range of I through Z. If the SQLSTATE class begins with characters that fall in the range of 7 through 9 or I though Z, then the subclass characters must fall in the range of 0 through 9 or A through Z.
  –If the SQLSTATE string constant does not conform to these rules, an error will occur.

- The diagnostic string should be defined as either a CHAR or VARCHAR data type, up to 70 characters (bytes) long. If the diagnostic string is longer than 70 bytes, it will be truncated.

Prerequisites You must define a trigger with the CREATE TRIGGER statement before the SIGNAL SQLSTATE statement can be executed.

Authorization No authorization is required to execute this statement.

See Also CREATE TRIGGER, SET

Examples The following C program illustrates how the SIGNAL SQLSTATE statement can used by a triggered action to signal an error condition whenever an employee receives a salary increase greater than 10 percent:

```
#include <stdio.h>
#include <stdlib.h>
#include <sql.h>

int main()
{
    /* Include The SQLCA Data Structure Variable */
    EXEC SQL INCLUDE SQLCA;

    /* Set Up A Simple SQL Error Handler */
    EXEC SQL WHENEVER SQLERROR GOTO EXIT;

    /* Declare The Local Memory Variables */
    int  rc = EXIT_SUCCESS;

    /* Declare The SQL Host Memory Variables */
    EXEC SQL BEGIN DECLARE SECTION;
        char    szEmpNo[7];
        double  rdSalary;
        double  rdBonus;
        double  rdComm;
    EXEC SQL END DECLARE SECTION;

    /* Connect To The SAMPLE Database */
    EXEC SQL CONNECT TO SAMPLE USER etpdd6z USING sanders;

    /* Create A Trigger - Whenever Salary Is Increased > 10%, Signal */
    /* An Error Condition                                             */
    EXEC SQL CREATE TRIGGER RAISE_LIMIT
        AFTER
        UPDATE OF SALARY ON USERID.EMPLOYEE
        REFERENCING NEW AS N OLD AS O
        FOR EACH ROW
        MODE DB2SQL
        WHEN (N.SALARY > 1.1 * O.SALARY)
        BEGIN ATOMIC
            SIGNAL SQLSTATE '75000' ('Salary Increase > 10%');
        END;

    /* Print A Message Telling That The Trigger Was Created */
    printf("The Trigger RAISE_LIMIT has been created.\n");

    /* Commit The Transaction */
    EXEC SQL COMMIT;
```

```
    /* Now Retrieve A Record From The USERID.EMPLOYEE Table, Update  */
    /* The Record So That The Trigger Is Activated, Then Retrieve The */
    /* Record Again To Verify That The Trigger Worked Correctly      */

    /* Retrieve A Record From The EMPLOYEE Table */
    EXEC SQL SELECT EMPNO,
                    SALARY,
                    BONUS,
                    COMM
        INTO :szEmpNo,
             :rdSalary,
             :rdBonus,
             :rdComm
        FROM USERID.EMPLOYEE
        WHERE EMPNO = '000010';

    /* Print The Information Retrieved - This Will Show The Record */
    /* Before It Is Changed By The Trigger                         */
    printf("\nEmployee No. : %7s Salary     : $%.2lf\n",
           szEmpNo, rdSalary);
    printf("                          Bonus      : $%.2lf\n", rdBonus);
    printf("                          Commission : $%.2lf\n", rdComm);

    /* Attempt To Update The Record - The Trigger Will Display An */
    /* Error Message                                              */
    EXEC SQL UPDATE USERID.EMPLOYEE
        SET SALARY = SALARY * 1.11
        WHERE EMPNO = '000010';

    /* Issue A Rollback Ignore All Changes */
    EXEC SQL ROLLBACK;

    /* Delete The Trigger */
    EXEC SQL DROP TRIGGER RAISE_LIMIT;

    /* Commit The Transaction */
    EXEC SQL COMMIT;

EXIT:
    /* If An Error Has Occurred, Display The SQL Return Code */
    if (sqlca.sqlcode != SQL_RC_OK)
        {
        printf("SQL ERROR : %ld\n", sqlca.sqlcode);
        rc = EXIT_FAILURE;
        }

    /* Issue A Rollback To Free All Locks */
    EXEC SQL ROLLBACK;

    /* Turn Off The SQL Error Handler */
    EXEC SQL WHENEVER SQLERROR CONTINUE;

    /* Disconnect From The SAMPLE Database */
    EXEC SQL DISCONNECT CURRENT;

    /* Return To The Operating System */
    return(rc);
}
```

Note: The SIGNAL SQLSTATE statement is used in a C++ program in a similar manner.

CALL

Purpose The CALL statement invokes a stored procedure.

Syntax

```
EXEC SQL CALL [<procedure-location!> procedure-name] <Options>;
```

Parameters

procedure-location Identifies the library or absolute path where the specified stored procedure can be found. The absolute path is the complete path to the stored procedure library.

procedure-name Identifies the name of the stored procedure to be invoked.

> Note: The procedure location and procedure name are treated as a single parameter, and the exclamation character (!) acts as a delimiter between the two. This allows multiple stored procedures to be stored in the same location. The procedure location/procedure name combination can be either a character string constant or the name of a host variable that contains a character string referring to the procedure location and procedure name.

Options

([host-variable, . . .]) Identifies one or more host variables that will be used to pass data to and receive data from the stored procedure. The number of identified host variables must be the same as the number of parameter values expected by the stored procedure, and their data types must also be the same.

USING DESCRIPTOR [descriptor-name] Identifies an input SQL descriptor area (SQLDA) data structure variable that contains a valid description of the host variables to be used to pass data to and receive data from the stored procedure. Before the CALL statement can be processed with the USING DESCRIPTOR option, you must set the following fields in the SQLDA data structure variable:

sqln This field indicates the number of *sqlvar* occurrences in the SQLDA data structure variable.

sqldabc This field specifies the total number of bytes of memory storage allocated for the SQLDA data structure variable. Since the SQLDA data structure variable must have enough allocated storage to contain all *sqlvar* occurrences, the value in the *sqldabc* field must be greater than or equal to 16 + *sqln* * (*n*), where *n* is the length of a single *sqlvar* occurrence.

sqld This field indicates the number of occurrences of *sqlvar* variables to be used when the statement is processed. The value in this field must be set to a value greater than or equal to zero and less than or equal to the value in the *sqln* field.

sqlvar field(s) Each occurrence of this field specifies the attributes of a single variable. If LOB or distinct-type result columns need to be accommodated, two *sqlvar* entries must exist for every select-list item (or column of the result table). Each specified *sqlvar* field must initialize the following *sqlvar* fields:

sqltype A code that identifies the data type of the variable and indicates whether or not the variable can contain null values.

sqllen	A value that indicates the length of the data stored in the variable, dependent on the data type of that column. *sqllen* is always 0 if the *sqltype* specifies a LOB data type.
sqldata	The address of the memory location that stores the actual data value of the variable.
sqlind	The address of the memory location that stores the data value of any indicator variable associated with the variable.
len.sqllonglen	The length attribute of a BLOB, CLOB, or DBCLOB variable.
sqldatalen	The address of the memory location containing the actual length, in bytes, of the data in the buffer to which the *sqldata* field points.
sqldatatype_name	If the variable was defined as a distinct type, this field will contain the fully qualified distinct-type name.

Note: The values for the *sqllonglen* and *sqldatatype_name* fields are set only if the number of *sqlvar* entries are doubled to accommodate LOB or distinct-type columns (e.g., the SQLDOUBLED byte of the *sqldaid* character string value is set to 2). Also, if your application works with character strings defined as FOR BIT DATA, you need to initialize the *sqldaid* field and the *sqlname* field of each *sqlvar* that defines a FOR BIT DATA element in order to indicate that the SQLDA includes FOR BIT DATA definitions.

Description

The CALL statement invokes a stored procedure that is physically located at the database server workstation in a client/server environment. Applications that use the CALL statement must be designed to run in two parts; one part resides and executes on the client workstation, and the other part resides and executes on the database server workstation (where the database itself resides). The part of the application residing on the server workstation is referred to as a stored procedure. A stored procedure queries data from the database (at the same workstation where the database resides) and returns the retrieved information to the calling application, which is usually located at a different, remote server workstation.

Before a client application calls (invokes) a stored procedure, it must first establish a connection to a database and it must declare, allocate, and initialize the SQLDA data structure variable or any host variables to be passed to the stored procedure. DB2 automatically allocates duplicate storage within the stored procedure for these variables based on the storage allocated by the client application.

Comments

- If a host variable specifies the procedure location/procedure name, it must be defined as a CHAR data type with a maximum length of 254 characters (bytes), and it cannot include a reference to an indicator variable.
- If a host variable is not used to specify the procedure-location/procedure-name, the procedure-location/procedure-name specified cannot contain blanks or special characters. Also, the procedure-location/procedure-name specified will be converted to uppercase before the CALL statement is executed. If it is necessary to use lower case characters, blanks, or special characters in the procedure-location/procedure-name, a host variable should be used.
- Indicator variables should be assigned to each host variable or each variable defined in the SQLDA data structure variable in order to avoid sending unnecessary data back and forth between an application and a stored procedure. The

associated indicator variable can then be set to –1 whenever the host variable does intend to transmit data to the stored procedure. Likewise, the indicator variable can be set to –128 whenever the host variable does not intend to return data to the calling application.

- By default, stored procedure libraries are placed in either the **dll** subdirectory of the **sqllib** directory (OS/2) or the function subdirectory of the **sqllib** directory (AIX), which contains the DB2 product files. Unfenced stored procedures are placed in the unfenced subdirectory of either the **dll** (OS/2) or the function (AIX) subdirectory. You can change the default stored procedure library directories by modifying the LIBPATH variable in the operating system environment settings file (config.sys in OS/2 and .profile in AIX).
- If no procedure location is specified, the procedure name is used as the name of both the stored procedure library and the stored procedure function name within that library.
- The procedure name can take one of several forms, depending on the server where the procedure is stored. For DB2 for OS/400 (version 3.1 and later), the procedure name is assumed to be an external program name. For DB2 for MVS (version 4.1 and later), the procedure name is treated as a three-part name:

High order The location name of the server containing the stored procedure.
Middle "SYSPROC".
Low order Some value in the PROCEDURE column of the SYSIBM.SYSPROCEDURES system catalog table that specifies a stored procedure.

- The CALL statement will not work with existing database application remote interface (DARI) procedures.
- Stored procedures located on DB2 for MVS or DB2 for OS/400 servers support additional sources for procedure arguments (for example, constant values), but if they are invoked from a DB2 for Common Servers client, all procedure arguments must be provided via host variables.
- Both DB2 for MVS and DB2 for OS/400 servers support conversion between compatible data types when their stored procedures are invoked.
- The SQLDA structure is not passed to the stored procedure if the *sqld* (number of elements) field is set to 0. In this case, the stored procedure will receive a NULL pointer.
- Connection-related statements or commands such as CONNECT, CONNECT TO, CONNECT RESET, CREATE DATABASE, DROP DATABASE, BACKUP, RESTORE, or FORWARD RECOVERY cannot be executed by a stored procedure.
- Stored procedures run in the background, so they cannot write to the screen. They can, however, write to named pipes, message queues, and files.
- Stored procedures cannot contain commands to terminate the application. A stored procedure should always return control to the client application without terminating the current process.
- The values of all environment variables beginning with "DB2," with the exception of the "DB2CKPTR" environment variable, are captured and are available in all stored procedures whether or not they are fenced. Changes made to the environment variables after DB2 is started are not recognized by stored procedures.
- On AIX-based systems, stored procedures run under the UID of the DB2 agent process (NOT FENCED) or the UID that owns the db2dari executable (FENCED). This UID controls the system resources available to the stored procedure.
- DB2 automatically allocates a duplicate SQLDA structure at the database server for the stored procedure, if one was allocated by the client application. To reduce network traffic, it is important to indicate which host variables are input-only and

which ones are output-only. The client procedure should set the indicator of output-only SQLVARs to –1, and the stored procedure should set the indicator for input-only SQLVARs to –128. This allows DB2 to effectively choose which SQLVARs are passed. Note that an indicator variable is not reset if the client or server application sets it to a negative value (indicating that the SQLVAR should not be passed). If the host variable to which the SQLVAR refers is given a value in the stored procedure or the client code, its indicator variable should be set to either zero or a positive value so the value will be passed.

- Do not change the value of the *sqld*, *sqltype*, and *sqllen* fields of the SQLDA within a stored procedure, as these fields are compared to the original values set by the client application before data is returned. If they are different, one of the following SQLCODEs will be returned:
  SQLCODE-1113 (SQLSTATE 39502) The data type of a variable (that is, the value in *sqltype*) has changed.
  SQLCODE-1114 (SQLSTATE 39502) The length of a variable (that is, the value in *sqllen*) has changed.
  SQLCODE-1115 (SQLSTATE 39502) The *sqld* field has changed.
- In addition, do not change the pointers for the *sqldata* and *sqlind* fields, although you can change the value pointed to by these fields.
- Before a stored procedure returns control to the client procedure, make sure to copy its SQLCA information to the SQLCA parameter of the stored procedure, so it will be received for evaluation by the client application.

Authorization Only users with either system administrator (SYSADM) authority, database administrator (DBADM) authority, EXECUTE authority for the package associated with the stored procedure, or CONTROL authority for the package associated with the stored procedure are allowed to execute this statement on a DB2 for common servers.

The authorization required to execute this statement against other servers can vary, depending upon the server at which the stored procedure is located. For more information about authorizations required to execute stored procedures on other servers, consult the appropriate manuals for the DB2 product on that system.

Examples The following C programs illustrates how to use the CALL statement to invoke a stored procedure and pass data to it, using both host variables and a SQLDA data structure variable:

```
#include <stdio.h>
#include <stdlib.h>
#include <string.h>
#include <sqlenv.h>
#include <sqlca.h>
#include <sqlda.h>
#include <sqlutil.h>

int main()
{

    /* Include The SQLCA Data Structure Variable */
    EXEC SQL INCLUDE SQLCA;

    /* Set Up A Simple SQL Error Handler */
    EXEC SQL WHENEVER SQLERROR GOTO EXIT;

    /* Declare The Local Memory Variables */
    int             rc = EXIT_SUCCESS;
    struct sqlda    *inout_sqlda = NULL;
```

```
/* Declare The SQL Host Memory Variables */
EXEC SQL BEGIN DECLARE SECTION;
    char     procname[255]  = "st_proc";
    char     table_name[11] = "PRESIDENTS";
    char     data_item0[21] = "Washington";
    char     data_item1[21] = "Jefferson";
    char     data_item2[21] = "Lincoln";
    char     data_item4[21] = "Kennedy";
    char     data_item5[21] = "Johnson";
    char     data_item6[21] = "Nixon";
    short    tableind = 0;
    short    dataind0 = 0;
    short    dataind1 = 0;
    short    dataind2 = 0;
    char     szName[21];
EXEC SQL END DECLARE SECTION;

/* Connect To The SAMPLE Database */
EXEC SQL CONNECT TO SAMPLE USER etpdd6z USING sanders;

/* Print A Message Telling That The Database Connection Is */
/* Established And That The Application Is Attempting To   */
/* Invoke The Stored Procedure                             */
printf("Connected to the SAMPLES database.\n");
printf("Invoking the Stored Procedure ST_PROC.DLL with host ");
printf("variables.\n");

/* Invoke The Stored Procedure With The CALL Statement */
EXEC SQL CALL :procname (:table_name:tableind,
                         :data_item0:dataind0,
                         :data_item1:dataind1,
                         :data_item2:dataind2);

/* Print A Message Telling That The Stored Procedure Has   */
/* Completed Execution                                     */
printf("The Stored Procedure Is Complete.\n\n");

/* Allocate And Initialize An Input SQLDA Data Structure Variable */
inout_sqlda = (struct sqlda *) malloc(SQLDASIZE(4));
inout_sqlda->sqln = 4;
inout_sqlda->sqld = 4;

inout_sqlda->sqlvar[0].sqltype = SQL_TYP_NCSTR;
inout_sqlda->sqlvar[0].sqldata = table_name;
inout_sqlda->sqlvar[0].sqllen  = strlen(table_name) + 1;
inout_sqlda->sqlvar[0].sqlind  = &tableind;

inout_sqlda->sqlvar[1].sqltype = SQL_TYP_NCSTR;
inout_sqlda->sqlvar[1].sqldata = data_item4;
inout_sqlda->sqlvar[1].sqllen  = strlen(data_item4) + 1;
inout_sqlda->sqlvar[1].sqlind  = &dataind0;

inout_sqlda->sqlvar[2].sqltype = SQL_TYP_NCSTR;
inout_sqlda->sqlvar[2].sqldata = data_item5;
inout_sqlda->sqlvar[2].sqllen  = strlen(data_item5) + 1;
inout_sqlda->sqlvar[2].sqlind  = &dataind0;

inout_sqlda->sqlvar[3].sqltype = SQL_TYP_NCSTR;
inout_sqlda->sqlvar[3].sqldata = data_item6;
inout_sqlda->sqlvar[3].sqllen  = strlen(data_item6) + 1;
inout_sqlda->sqlvar[3].sqlind  = &dataind0;
```

```
    /* Print A Message Telling That The Application Is Attempting */
    /* To Invoke The Stored Procedure With An SQLDA Structure     */
    printf("Invoking the Stored Procedure ST_PROC.DLL with an ");
    printf("SQLDA data structure.\n");

    /* Invoke The Stored Procedure With The CALL Statement */
    tableind = dataind0 = dataind1 = dataind2 = 0;
    EXEC SQL CALL :procname USING DESCRIPTOR :*inout_sqlda;

    /* Print A Message Telling That The Stored Procedure Has   */
    /* Completed Execution                                     */
    printf("The Stored Procedure Is Complete.\n\n");

    /* Free Allocated Memory */
    free(inout_sqlda);

    /* Now Retrieve The Records From The ETPDD6Z.PRESIDENTS Table */
    /* To Verify That The Stored Procedure Worked Correctly       */

    /* Declare The SELECT_CURSOR Table Cursor */
    EXEC SQL DECLARE SELECT_CURSOR CURSOR FOR
        SELECT NAME
        FROM ETPDD6Z.PRESIDENTS;

    /* Open The Cursor */
    EXEC SQL OPEN SELECT_CURSOR;

    /* If The Cursor Was Successfully Opened, Fetch The Records Into Host */
    /* Variables                                                          */
    printf("\nContents of ETPDD6Z.PRESIDENT\n\n");
    while (sqlca.sqlcode == SQL_RC_OK)
        {
        EXEC SQL FETCH SELECT_CURSOR
            INTO :szName;

        /* If The FETCH Was Successful, Print The Data */
        if (sqlca.sqlcode == SQL_RC_OK)
            printf("Name : %s\n", szName);
        }                                           /* End Of WHILE   */

    /* Close The Cursor */
    EXEC SQL CLOSE SELECT_CURSOR;

EXIT:
    /* If An Error Has Occurred, Display The SQL Return Code */
    if (sqlca.sqlcode != SQL_RC_OK)
        {
        printf("SQL ERROR : %ld\n", sqlca.sqlcode);
        rc = EXIT_FAILURE;
        }

    /* Issue A Rollback To Free All Locks */
    EXEC SQL ROLLBACK;

    /* Turn Off The SQL Error Handler */
    EXEC SQL WHENEVER SQLERROR CONTINUE;

    /* Disconnect From The SAMPLE Database */
    EXEC SQL DISCONNECT CURRENT;

    /* Return To The Operating System */
    return(rc);
}
```

Note: The CALL statement is used in a C++ program in a similar manner.

The following C program illustrates how to write a stored procedure to create a table and insert data passed by the client application that invoked it into the new table:

```
#include <stdio.h>
#include <stdlib.h>
#include <string.h>
#include <memory.h>
#include <sql.h>
#include <sqlenv.h>
#include <sqlutil.h>

SQL_API_RC SQL_API_FN st_proc(void            *reserved1,
                              void            *reserved2,
                              struct sqlda    *inout_sqlda,
                              struct sqlca    *ca)
{

    /* Include The SQLCA Data Structure Variable */
    EXEC SQL INCLUDE SQLCA;

    /* Set Up A Simple SQL Error Handler */
    EXEC SQL WHENEVER SQLERROR GOTO EXIT;

    /* Declare The Local Memory Variables */
    int     rc = EXIT_SUCCESS;
    int     cntr = 0;
    char    *table_name;
    char    *data_items[3];
    short   data_items_length[3];
    int     num_of_data = 0;

    /* Declare The SQL Host Memory Variables */
    EXEC SQL BEGIN DECLARE SECTION;
        char    table_stmt[80]  = "CREATE TABLE ";
        char    insert_stmt[80] = "INSERT INTO ";
        char    insert_data[21];
    EXEC SQL END DECLARE SECTION;

    /* Assign The Data From The SQLDA Structure To Local Variables So */
    /* That We Don't Have To Refer To The SQLDA Structure Any More.   */
    /* This Will Provide Better Portability To Other Platforms Where  */
    /* The Parameter List Is Received Differently                     */

    table_name  = inout_sqlda->sqlvar[0].sqldata;
    num_of_data = inout_sqlda->sqld - 1;
    for (cntr = 0; cntr < num_of_data; cntr++)
        {
        data_items[cntr] = inout_sqlda->sqlvar[cntr+1].sqldata;
        data_items_length[cntr] = inout_sqlda->sqlvar[cntr+1].sqllen;
        }

    /* Turn The SQL Error Handler Off */
    EXEC SQL WHENEVER SQLERROR CONTINUE;
```

```
    /* Create The PRESIDENTS Table */
    strcat(table_stmt, table_name);
    strcat(table_stmt, " (name CHAR(20))");
    EXEC SQL EXECUTE IMMEDIATE :table_stmt;

    /* Turn The SQL Error Handler Back On */
    EXEC SQL WHENEVER SQLERROR GOTO EXIT;

    /* Generate An INSERT Statement */
    strcat(insert_stmt, table_name);
    strcat(insert_stmt, "  VALUES (?)");

    /* PREPARE The INSERT Statement, Then Insert The Data */
    EXEC SQL PREPARE S1 FROM :insert_stmt;

    for (cntr = 0; cntr < num_of_data; cntr++)
        {
        strncpy(insert_data, data_items[cntr],
data_items_length[cntr]);
        insert_data[data_items_length[cntr]] = '';
        EXEC SQL EXECUTE S1 USING :insert_data;
        }

EXIT:

    /* Update The SQLCA Return Code */
    memcpy(ca, &sqlca, sizeof(struct sqlca));

    /* Update The Output SQLDA. Since There's No Output To Return, */
    /* Set The Indicator Values To -128 (Return Only A Null Value  */
    if (inout_sqlda != NULL)
        {
        for (cntr = 0; cntr < inout_sqlda->sqld; cntr++)
            *(inout_sqlda->sqlvar[cntr].sqlind) = -128;
        }

    /* Turn The SQL Error Handler Off */
    EXEC SQL WHENEVER SQLERROR CONTINUE;

    /* Check The SQLCA For Errors - Commit or Rollback The Transaction */
    /* Based Upon The SQLCA Value                                      */
    if (sqlca.sqlcode == 0)
        EXEC SQL COMMIT;
    else
        EXEC SQL ROLLBACK;

    /* Return To The Calling Program System */
    return(SQLZ_DISCONNECT_PROC);
}
```

Part 4

CALL LEVEL INTERFACE (CLI) FUNCTIONS

This section describes the call-level interface (CLI) functions you can use to develop CLI/ODBC applications for DB2. It is designed as a reference that provides information about the syntax and semantics of each CLI function supported by DB2. It is also designed to show, by example, how each CLI function is coded in a C and C++ application program. Each function is presented as a main section, and the subsections under each function contain the following information:

Purpose	*Short description telling what the CLI function does.*
Syntax	*Full CLI function syntax.*
Parameters	*Detailed description of all CLI function parameters.*
Includes	*Header files that must be included by the application calling the CLI function.*
Description	*Detailed information about the CLI function.*
Return Codes	*Return code values that can be returned by the CLI function.*
SQLSTATEs	*SQLSTATE values that can be returned by the CLI function.*
Comments	*Special notes or instructions about the CLI function.*
Prerequisites	*Things that must occur before the CLI function can be executed.*
Restrictions	*Restrictions imposed when using the CLI function.*
See Also	*Related CLI functions.*
Examples	*C and C++ examples demonstrating how the CLI function is used in a source-code file.*

HOW THE EXAMPLES WERE DEVELOPED

All the sample programs shown in Part 4 of this book were compiled and executed on the OS/2 Warp operating system (compiled with IBM's VisualAge C++), and most were compiled and executed on the AIX 4.0 operating system (compiled with IBM's C Set++ for AIX, version 3.0).

The following command file (C_COMP.CMD) was used to compile the C sample programs on the OS/2 Warp operating system:

```
REM *** BUILD CLI EXAMPLES COMMAND FILE                ***
echo off

REM *** COMPILE THE SOURCE CODE FILE                   ***
icc /W3 /Ti+ /G4 /Gs+ /Ss+ /DLINT_ARGS /c %1.c > ERROR.DAT

REM *** LINK THE PROGRAM                               ***
ilink /NOFREE /NOI /DEBUG /ST:128000 %1.obj,,,OS2386 DB2API DB2CLI
   SQL_DYN,DB2_DEF.DEF >> ERROR.DAT

REM *** CLEAN UP                                       ***
del %1.obj
```

The following command file (CPP_COMP.CMD) was used to compile the C++ sample programs on the OS/2 Warp operating system:

```
REM *** BUILD CLI EXAMPLES COMMAND FILE                  ***
echo off

REM *** COMPILE THE SOURCE CODE FILE                     ***
icc -C+ /W3 /Ti+ /G4 /Gs+ /Ss+ /DLINT_ARGS /c /Td %1.cxx > ERROR.DAT

REM *** LINK THE PROGRAM                                 ***
ilink /NOFREE /NOI /DEBUG /ST:128000 %1.obj,,,OS2386 DB2API DB2CLI
   SQL_DYN,DB2_DEF.DEF >> ERROR.DAT

REM *** CLEAN UP                                         ***
del %1.obj
```

Both of these command files reference the following link definitions file (DB2_DEF.DEF):

```
; This File Contains The Link Definitions That Are Used To Link
; Most Of The DB2 2.1 CLI Sample Programs

NAME           DBM     WINDOWCOMPAT

PROTMODE
```

The following command file (CLI_COMP) was used to compile the C sample programs on the AIX 4.0 operating system:

```
# BUILD CLI EXAMPLES COMMAND FILE
#! /bin/ksh
#
# COMPILE THE SOURCE CODE FILE
compstr='xlC -I/usr/lpp/db2_02_01/include -qcpluscmt -c '${1} .c
echo $compstr
$compstr
#
# LINK THE PROGRAM
linkstr='xlC -o '${1} ' '${1} '.o -ldb2 -L/usr/lpp/db2_02_01/lib'
echo $linkstr
$linkstr
#
```

The following command file (CLIPCOMP) was used to compile the C++ sample programs on the AIX 4.0 operating system:

```
# BUILD CLI EXAMPLES COMMAND FILE
#! /bin/ksh
#
# COMPILE THE SOURCE CODE FILE
compstr='xlC -I/usr/lpp/db2_02_01/include -c '${1} .C
echo $compstr
$compstr
#
# LINK THE PROGRAM
linkstr='xlC -o '${1} ' '${1} '.o -ldb2 -L/usr/lpp/db2_02_01/lib'
echo $linkstr
$linkstr
#
```

You must start the DB2 database manager by issuing either the startdbm command (OS/2) or the db2 start database manager command (AIX) at the command prompt before CLI applications can be executed. Also, keep in mind that the default qualifier USERID is valid only for OS/2. When DB2 is installed on AIX, the default qualifier for the SAMPLE database is determined by the authorization ID of the user installing the DB2 product.

SPECIAL CASES

The following command file (CS_COMP.CMD) was used to compile the C sample program on the OS/2 Warp operating system for the SQLSetConnection( ) sample program:

```
REM *** BUILD EMBEDDED SQL EXAMPLES COMMAND FILE          ***
echo off

REM *** CONNECT TO THE SAMPLE DATABASE                    ***
db2 connect to sample user etpdd6z using sanders

REM *** PRECOMPILE THE EMBEDDED SQL SOURCE CODE FILE      ***
db2 prep ctable.sqc bindfile using ctable.bnd > ERROR.DAT

REM *** COMPILE THE PRECOMPILE GENERATED SOURCE CODE FILE ***
icc /W3 /Ti+ /G4 /Gs+ /Ss+ /DLINT_ARGS /c ctable.c >> ERROR.DAT

REM *** COMPILE THE SOURCE CODE FILE                      ***
icc /W3 /Ti+ /G4 /Gs+ /Ss+ /DLINT_ARGS /c ch13ex3a.c >> ERROR.DAT

REM *** LINK THE PROGRAM                                  ***
ilink /NOFREE /NOI /DEBUG /ST:128000 ch13ex3a.obj+ctable.obj,,,OS2386
   DB2API DB2CLI SQL_DYN,DB2_DEF.DEF >> ERROR.DAT

REM *** BIND THE APPLICATION TO THE SAMPLE DATABASE       ***
db2 bind ctable.bnd >> ERROR.DAT

REM *** DISCONNECT FROM THE SAMPLE DATABASE               ***
db2 connect reset

REM *** CONNECT TO THE BOOKSAMP DATABASE                  ***
db2 connect to booksamp user etpdd6z using sanders

REM *** BIND THE APPLICATION TO THE BOOKSAMP DATABASE     ***
db2 bind ctable.bnd >> ERROR.DAT

REM *** DISCONNECT FROM THE SAMPLE DATABASE               ***
db2 connect reset

REM *** CLEAN UP                                          ***
del ctable.c
del ctable.obj
del ch13ex3a.obj
```

Note: I created the database BOOKSAMP before testing this example by issuing the command "db2 create database booksamp" from both the OS/2 and the AIX command prompt.

CHAPTER 13

CLI/ODBC DATA SOURCE CONNECTION CONTROL FUNCTIONS

The CLI/ODBC data source connection control functions are a group of DB2 CLI function calls that are used to allocate resources and establish connections to specified data sources. This group includes:

13

- CLI functions that allocate memory storage areas for holding environment and connection information.
- CLI functions that establish connections to data sources.
- A CLI function that switches data source connections in a multiple-connection environment.
- A CLI function that terminates connection to data sources.
- CLI functions that free allocated memory storage areas for holding environment and connection information.

Table 13.1 lists the CLI/ODBC data source connection control functions available with DB2 CLI.

TABLE 13.1 CLI/ODBC Data Source Connection Control Functions

Function name	Description
SQLAllocEnv( )	Allocates an environment handle and its associated resources.
SQLAllocConnect( )	Allocates a data source connection handle and its associated resources.
SQLConnect( )	Establishes a connection to a specified data source using a specified user ID and password.
SQLDriverConnect( )	Establishes a connection to a specified data source using a connection string, or optionally displays the DB2 CLI graphical user interface so the end user can provide appropriate connection information.
SQLSetConnection( )	Switches connections in an application that supports multiple connections.
SQLDisconnect( )	Closes a data source connection.
SQLFreeConnect( )	Releases a data source connection handle.
SQLFreeEnv( )	Releases an environment handle.

Adapted from IBM's DATABASE 2 Call Level Interface Guide and Reference, Table 11, pages 103 to 106.

Data Sources

A data source consists of a database management system (DBMS), along with the platform on which the DBMS resides and the network (if any) used to access that platform. In order for a data source to be accessible to a DB2 CLI application, some type of CLI load library or ODBC driver must be available for the data source in order to provide special information to the application when it attempts to establish a connection.

Environment and Connection Handles

When requested, the DB2 CLI load library or ODBC driver manager allocates a memory storage area and returns an appropriate handle back to the requesting application. The returned handle is a pointer variable that refers to the allocated data object (memory buffer) controlled by DB2 CLI. These handles are used by an application to pass a block of information to each DB2 CLI function. By using handles, an application is freed from the responsibility of allocating and managing global variables and other data structures, such as the SQLDA or SQLCA data structures used in embedded SQL.

The CLI/ODBC interface defines and uses the following types of handles within a CLI application:

- One environment handle.
- One or more connection handles.
- One or more statement handles.

The environment handle identifies a memory storage area for storing (and passing) information about the global state of the application. This includes environment attributes, a list of valid connection handles, and the current connection handle used when the application supports multiple connections.

The connection handle(s) identify one or more memory storage areas for storing (and passing) information about a connection to a particular data source (database). This includes connection options, general status information, transaction status, and diagnostic information (SQLSTATEs). An application can be connected to several data sources at the same time, and can establish several distinct connections to the same data source. By using connection handles, multithreaded applications that use one connection per thread are thread-safe since separate data structures are allocated and maintained by DB2 CLI for each established connection.

Connecting to a Data Source

Most applications can connect to a data source by calling the SQLConnect( ) function and providing the data source name, user ID (or account name), and authentication string (or password) as input values. When an application calls the SQLConnect( ) function, the CLI load library uses the data source name to determine which bind files are needed to connect to a DB2 data source (the ODBC driver manager uses the data source to determine which driver DLL to load). If more information is needed to connect to a data source, the SQLDriverConnect( ) function can be called.

An application might pass all the necessary connection information to the data source, or it might ask the data source to prompt the user for required connection information (such as user ID or account name and authentication string or password). A data source can also read connection information from the appropriate section of the **db2cli.ini** or **odbc.ini** configuration file.

SQLAllocEnv

Purpose The SQLAllocEnv( ) function allocates memory for an environment handle, and initializes the CLI call level interface so it can be used by an application.

Syntax

```
SQLRETURN SQLAllocEnv (SQLHENV FAR *EnvHandle);
```

Parameters *EnvHandle* A pointer to a location in memory where this function is to store the starting address of the allocated environment information buffer.

Includes

```
#include <sqlcli1.h>
```

Description The SQLAllocEnv( ) function allocates an environment handle and its associated resources. A CLI application must execute this function before it attempts to call any other DB2 CLI function. The environment handle returned by this function is passed to all subsequent DB2 CLI function calls that require an environment handle as an input parameter. Once an environment buffer is allocated, subsequent calls to the SQLAllocEnv( ) function will return the existing environment buffer handle. The SQLFreeEnv( ) function must be executed before a CLI application terminates to guarantee that all resources associated with the environment handle are released.

Specifications DB2 CLI 1.1, ODBC 1.0, X/OPEN CLI, ISO CLI

Return Codes SQL_SUCCESS, SQL_ERROR

SQLSTATEs **58**004

Comments

- A CLI application can have only one active environment handle at any given time.
- If the SQL_ERROR return code is returned and the pointer to the environment handle is not equal to SQL_NULL_HENV, then the environment handle is a restricted handle and can be used only as a parameter for either the SQLError( ) function (to obtain additional diagnostic information) or the SQLFreeEnv( ) function (to free the restricted environment handle).
- If the SQL_ERROR return code is returned and the pointer to the environment handle is equal to SQL_NULL_HENV, then the SQLError( ) function cannot be executed since there is no environment handle with which to associate additional diagnostic information.

Restrictions There are no restrictions associated with this function call.

See Also SQLFreeEnv( ), SQLAllocConnect( )

Examples The following C program illustrates how to allocate an environment and connection handle and how to establish a connection to a data source:

```
#include <stdio.h>
#include <stdlib.h>
#include <sqlcli1.h>

int main()
{
    /* Declare The Local Memory Variables */
```

```
    SQLRETURN  rc = SQL_SUCCESS;
    SQLHENV    EnvHandle;
    SQLHDBC    DSCHandle;

    /* Allocate An Environment Handle */
    rc = SQLAllocEnv(&EnvHandle);

    /* Allocate A Connection Handle */
    rc = SQLAllocConnect(EnvHandle, &DSCHandle);

    /* Connect To The SAMPLE Database */
    rc = SQLConnect(DSCHandle, "SAMPLE", SQL_NTS, "etpdd6z", SQL_NTS,
                    "sanders", SQL_NTS);

    /* Display A Success Message */
    printf("Connected to SAMPLE database.\n");

    /* Disconnect From The SAMPLE Database */
    SQLDisconnect(DSCHandle);

    /* Free The Connection Handle */
    if (DSCHandle != NULL)
        SQLFreeConnect(DSCHandle);

    /* Free The Environment Handle */
    if (EnvHandle != NULL)
        SQLFreeEnv(EnvHandle);

    /* Return To The Operating System */
    return(rc);
}
```

The following C++ program illustrates how to allocate an environment and connection handle in a class constructor and how to create class methods that connect to and disconnect from a data source:

```
#include <iostream.h>
#include <string.h>
#include <sqlcli1.h>

/* Define The CLI Class */
class CLI
{
    /* Declare The Private Attribute Variables */
    private:
       SQLHENV    EnvHandle;
       SQLHDBC    DSCHandle;

    /* Declare The Public Attribute Variables */
    public:
       SQLRETURN  rc;

    /* Declare The Member Function Prototypes */
    CLI();                                   // Constructor
    ~CLI();                                  // Destructor
    SQLRETURN Connect(SQLCHAR* DBName,
                      SQLCHAR* UserID,
                      SQLCHAR* Password);
    SQLRETURN Disconnect();
```

```
} ;

/* Define The Class Constructor */
CLI::CLI()
{
    /* Initialize The Return Code Variable */
    rc = SQL_SUCCESS;

    /* Allocate An Environment Handle */
    rc = SQLAllocEnv(&EnvHandle);
    /* Allocate A Connection Handle */
    rc = SQLAllocConnect(EnvHandle, &DSCHandle);
}

/* Define The Class Destructor */
CLI::~CLI()
{
    /* Free The Connection Handle */
    if (DSCHandle != NULL)
        SQLFreeConnect(DSCHandle);

    /* Free The Environment Handle */
    if (EnvHandle != NULL)
        SQLFreeEnv(EnvHandle);
}

/* Define The Connect() Member Function */
SQLRETURN CLI::Connect(SQLCHAR* DBName,
                       SQLCHAR* UserID,
                       SQLCHAR* Password)
{
    /* Connect To The Specified Database */
    rc = SQLConnect(DSCHandle, DBName, SQL_NTS, UserID, SQL_NTS,
                    Password, SQL_NTS);

    /* Return The CLI Function Return Code */
    return(rc);
}

/* Define The Disconnect() Member Function */
SQLRETURN CLI::Disconnect(void)
{
    /* Disconnect From The Database */
    rc = SQLDisconnect(DSCHandle);

    /* Return The CLI Function Return Code */
    return(rc);
}

int main()
{
    /* Declare The Local Memory Variables */
    SQLRETURN  rc = SQL_SUCCESS;

    /* Create An Instance Of The CLI Class */
    CLI Sample;

    /* Connect To The SAMPLE Database - If Successful, Display */
    /* An Appropriate Message                                  */
    rc = Sample.Connect((SQLCHAR *) "SAMPLE", (SQLCHAR *) "etpdd6z",
```

```
                                   (SQLCHAR *) "sanders");
    if (rc == SQL_SUCCESS)
        cout << "Connected to SAMPLE database." << endl;

    /* Disconnect From The SAMPLE Database */
    Sample.Disconnect();

    /* Return To The Operating System */
    return(rc);
}
```

SQLAllocConnect

Purpose The SQLAllocConnect( ) function allocates memory for a connection handle within a specified environment.

Syntax

```
SQLRETURN SQLAllocConnect (SQLHENV      EnvHandle,
                           SQLHDBC FAR *DSCHandle);
```

Parameters

EnvHandle The environment handle where the address of the environment information buffer is stored.

DSCHandle A pointer to a location in memory where this function is to store the starting address of the allocated data source connection information buffer.

Includes

```
#include <sqlcli1.h>
```

Description The SQLAllocConnect( ) function allocates a connection handle and its associated resources within a specified environment. The data source connection handle is used by other DB2 CLI function calls to reference information related to the data source connection, including general status information, transaction state, and error information.

Specifications DB2 CLI 1.1, ODBC 1.0, X/OPEN CLI, ISO CLI

Return Codes SQL_SUCCESS, SQL_INVALID_HANDLE, SQL_ERROR

SQLSTATEs **S1**001, **S1**009, **S1**013, **S1**014

Comments

- If the value in the DSCHandle parameter points to a valid connection information buffer (allocated by a previous call to this function) when this function is executed, it will be overwritten and the memory buffer to which the original value pointed can no longer be freed. This type of programming error cannot be detected by DB2 CLI, so no associated return code or SQLSTATE is generated.
- You can determine the maximum number of connection handles that can be allocated at any one time by calling the SQLGetInfo( ) function with the *InfoType* parameter set to SQL_ACTIVE_CONNECTIONS.
- This function must be executed before SQLConnect( ) or SQLDriverConnect( ) are called.
- If the SQL_ERROR return code is returned by this function, the value SQL_NULL_HDBC will be stored in the DSCHandle parameter. When this occurs, call the SQLError( ) function using the current environment handle, with

the data source connection handle set to SQL_NULL_HDBC and the SQL statement handle set to SQL_NULL_HSTMT.

Prerequisites The SQLAllocEnv( ) function must be executed before this function is called.

Restrictions There are no restrictions associated with this function call.

See Also SQLAllocEnv( ), SQLFreeConnect( ), SQLConnect( ), SQLDriverConnect( ), SQLDisconnect( ), SQLGetConnectOption( ), SQLSetConnectOption( )

Examples See the examples provided for the SQLAllocEnv( ) function.

SQLConnect

Purpose The SQLConnect( ) function establishes a connection to a specified data source (database).

Syntax

```
SQLRETURN SQLConnect (SQLHDBC       DSCHandle,
                      SQLCHAR FAR   *DSName,
                      SQLSMALLINT   DSNameSize,
                      SQLCHAR FAR   *UserID,
                      SQLSMALLINT   UserIDSize,
                      SQLCHAR FAR   *Password,
                      SQLSMALLINT   PasswordSize);
```

Parameters

DSCHandle The data source connection handle where the address of the connection information buffer is stored.

DSName A pointer to a location in memory where the name or alias name of the data source is stored.

DSNameSize The length of the data source name value stored in the *DSName* parameter.

UserID A pointer to a location in memory where the authorization name (user identifier) of the user is stored.

UserIDSize The length of the user authorization name value stored in the *UserID* parameter.

Password A pointer to a location in memory where the password for the specified user authorization name is stored.

PasswordSize The length of the password value stored in the *Password* parameter.

Includes

```
#include <sqlcli1.h>
```

Description The SQLConnect( ) function establishes a connection to a specified data source (database). When using this function, an application must supply the name of a target data source and optionally a user name (authorization ID) and corresponding password (authorization string). The target data source name for an IBM relational database management system (RDBMS) database is the database alias. When a connection to the target data source is established, you can use the connection handle passed in the function call to reference all information about the connection, including status, transaction state, and error information.

Specifications DB2 CLI 1.1, ODBC 1.0, X/OPEN CLI, ISO CLI

Return Codes SQL_SUCCESS, SQL_SUCCESS_WITH_INFO, SQL_ERROR, SQL_INVALID _HANDLE

SQLSTATEs **08**001, **08**002, **08**004, **28**000, **58**004, **S1**001, **S1**009, **S1**013, **S1**090, **S1**501

Comments

- You can obtain a list of available data sources to which an application can connect by calling the SQLDataSources( ) function. However, before an IBM database alias can be returned by the SQLDataSources( ) function, its corresponding database must first be cataloged. Under the Windows operating system (using the ODBC driver manager), the user must catalog the database twice: once to the IBM RDBMS and once to the ODBC driver manager. You can accomplish this in a single step by using the DB2 Client Setup program included with IBM's DB2 Client Application Enabler products. Although the methods of cataloging a database are different between the ODBC driver manager and an IBM RDBMS, DB2 CLI applications are shielded from this. (One of the strengths of call-level interface is that the application does not have to know about the target data source until the SQLConnect( ) function is invoked at application runtime.) Mapping the data source name to an actual DBMS is outside the scope and responsibility of the CLI application.
- Input length parameters (e.g., *DSNameSize*, *UserIDSize*, and *PasswordSize*) can be set to either the actual length of their associated data values (not including a null-terminating character) or the value SQL_NTS to indicate that the associated data is a null-terminated string.
- The *DBName* and *UserID* parameter values must not contain blanks.
- Either this function or the SQLDriverConnect( ) function must be executed before the SQLAllocStmt( ) function can be called and before any SQL statements can be executed.
- Do not use the SQLDriverConnect( ) function to establish a data source connection whenever an application needs to:
  –Require the end user to specify more than just the data source name, user ID, and password arguments in order to establish the connection.
  –Display a graphical dialog box to prompt the user for connection information.
- The end user can specify various connection options in the **db2cli.ini** or **odbc.ini** configuration files. You can also set connection options by calling the SQLSetConnectOption( ) function after a connection has been established, or passing them to the data source as part of the connection string supplied to the SQLDriverConnect( ) function (when that function is used instead of this one to establish the data source connection).
- Stored procedures that contain DB2 CLI functions must make a null SQL-Connect( ) function call during their initialization. A null SQLConnect( ) function call is a SQLConnect( ) function call in which the data source name, user ID, and password are set to NULL and their corresponding length arguments are set to 0. The SQLAllocEnv( ) and SQLAllocConnect( ) functions must still be called before a null SQLConnect( ) function call, but the SQL-Transact( ) function does not have to be called before the SQLDisconnect( ) function can be called.

Prerequisites The SQLAllocConnect( ) function must be executed before this function can be called.

Restrictions The implicit connection (or default database) option available for IBM relational database management systems is not supported by DB2 CLI.

See Also SQLAllocConnect( ), SQLDriverConnect( ), SQLDisconnect( ), SQLGetConnect-Option( ), SQLSetConnectOption( ), SQLDataSources( ), SQLAllocStmt( )

Examples See the examples provided for the SQLAllocEnv( ) function.

SQLDriverConnect

Purpose The SQLDriverConnect( ) function establishes a connection to a specified data source when that data source requires additional information not provided by the SQLConnect( ) function or when you want your application to use the DB2 CLI graphical user interface to prompt the end user for required connection information.

Syntax

```
SQLRETURN SQLDriverConnect (SQLHDBC          DSCHandle,
                            SQLHWND          WindowHandle,
                            SQLCHAR FAR      *ConnectIn,
                            SQLSMALLINT      ConnectInSize,
                            SQLCHAR FAR      *ConnectOut,
                            SQLSMALLINT      ConnectOutMaxSize,
                            SQLSMALLINT FAR  *ConnectOutSize,
                            SQLUSMALLINT     DriverCompletion);
```

Parameters

DSCHandle The data source connection handle where the address of the connection information buffer is stored.

WindowHandle The platform-dependent window handle used to display the DB2 CLI graphical user interface if additional prompting is necessary in order to obtain all mandatory connection information. On Windows, this is the parent Windows handle; on OS/2, it is the parent Presentation Manager (PM) window handle; and on AIX, it is the parent MOTIF Widget window handle. If this parameter contains the NULL value, no dialog will be presented.

ConnectIn A pointer to a location in memory where a full, partial, or empty (null pointer) connection string is stored. This connection string passes one or more values needed to complete a data source connection to the specified data source.

ConnectInSize The length of the connection string value stored in the *ConnectIn* parameter.

ConnectOut A pointer to a location in memory where this function is to store the completed connection string, provided the connection was established successfully.

ConnectOutMaxSize The maximum size of the memory storage buffer where this function is to store the completed connection string.

ConnectOutSize A pointer to a location in memory where this function is to store the actual number of bytes written to the completed connection string memory storage buffer (*ConnectOut*). If the completed connection string's actual length is greater than or equal to the maximum string size value specified in the *ConnectOutMaxSize* parameter, the completed connection string will be truncated to *ConnectOutMaxSize* -1 characters.

DriverCompletion Indicates when DB2 displays the DB2 CLI graphical user interface that prompts the end user for more information. The *DriverCompletion* parameter must contain one of the following values:

SQL_DRIVER_PROMPT The DB2 CLI graphical user interface dialog is always opened. Information from both the connection string and the **db2cli.ini** or **odbc.ini** configuration file are used as initial values, which can be overridden or supplemented by data input via the opened dialog.

SQL_DRIVER_COMPLETE The DB2 CLI graphical user interface dialog is opened only if there is not enough information in the connection string to establish a connection to the specified data source. Information from the connection string is used as initial values, which can be overridden or supplemented by data input via the opened dialog.

SQL_DRIVER_COMPLETE_REQUIRED The DB2 CLI graphical user interface dialog is opened only if there is not enough mandatory information in the connection string to establish a connection to the specified data source. Information from the connection string is used as initial values, which can be overridden or supplemented by data input via the opened dialog. The end user is prompted only for mandatory information.

SQL_DRIVER_NOPROMPT The DB2 CLI graphical user interface dialog is not opened and the user is not prompted for any connection information. An attempt to establish a connection is made using the information provided in the connection string. If there is not enough information in the connection string to establish a connection to the specified data source, the value SQL_ERROR will be returned.

Includes

```
#include <sqlcli1.h>
```

Description

The SQLDriverConnect( ) function is an alternative to the SQLConnect( ) function. Both functions establish a connection to a specified data source, but SQLDriverConnect( ) function supports additional connection parameters and allows an application to prompt the user for connection information at application runtime. Use this function whenever the specified data source requires parameter values other than those supported by the SQLConnect( ) function to establish a connection. Use this function also whenever you want your application to use the DB2 CLI graphical user interface to prompt the user for mandatory connection information.

Once the SQLDriverConnect( ) function establishes a connection, the completed connection string used by the data source is returned to the calling application. Applications that need to set up multiple connections to the same data source for a given user ID should store this returned connection string for later use.

Specifications DB2 CLI 2.1, ODBC 1.0

Return Codes SQL_SUCCESS, SQL_SUCCESS_WITH_INFO, SQL_NO_DATA_FOUND, SQL_INVALID_HANDLE, SQL_ERROR

SQLSTATEs **01**004, **01**S00, **08**001, **08**002, **08**004, **28**000, **58**004, **S1**000, **S1**001, **S1**009, **S1**013, **S1**090, **S1**501

Comments

- The connection string stored in the *ConnectIn* parameter must have the following format:

```
[keyword] = [attribute]; ...
```

This keyword = attribute combination can be any of the following:

DSN = data source name This keyword specifies the name or alias name of the data source.

UID = user ID This keyword specifies the authorization name (user identifier) of the user.

PWD = password This keyword specifies the password for the specified authorization name. If there is no required password for the specified user ID, an empty password can be specified as PWD =.

AUTOCOMMIT = 1 | 0 This keyword specifies whether or not each SQL statement is treated as a single complete transaction. To be consistent with ODBC, DB2 CLI defaults with AUTOCOMMIT turned on (AUTOCOMMIT = 1).

This keyword also allows you to specify whether AUTOCOMMIT is enabled in a distributed unit of work (DUOW) environment. If a connection is part of a coordinated DUOW and AUTOCOMMIT is not set, the default does not apply and implicit commits arising from autocommit processing are suppressed.

BITDATA = 1 | 0 This keyword specifies whether or not ODBC binary data types (e.g., SQL_BINARY, SQL_VARBINARY, and SQL_LONGVARBINARY) are reported as binary-type data. IBM DBMSs support columns with binary data types by defining those columns as either BLOB or CHAR, VARCHAR, and LONG VARCHAR data types with the FOR BIT DATA attribute. By default, FOR BIT DATA and BLOB data types are treated as binary data types (BITDATA = 1). Specify BITDATA = 0 if you are sure that all columns defined as FOR BIT DATA or BLOB contain only character data and that the application is incapable of displaying binary data columns.

CONNECTTYPE = 1 | 2 This keyword specifies the default connect type to use, and accepts the following values:

1 Multiple concurrent connections, each with its own commit scope. The concurrent transactions are not coordinated (the default value).

2 Coordinated connections where multiple databases participate under the same DUOW. This setting works in conjunction with the SYNCPOINT setting to determine if a transaction manager should be used.

CURRENTSQLID = current_sqlid This keyword allows the end user and the application to name SQL objects without having to qualify them by schema name. This keyword is valid only for DB2 DBMSs that support the SET CURRENT SQLID SQL statement (such as DB2 for MVS/ESA). If this keyword is present when a connection is established, a SET CURRENT SQLID SQL statement will be sent to the DBMS.

CURSORHOLD = 1 | 0 This keyword controls how the completion of a transaction affects open cursors. This keyword accepts the following values:

1 Open cursors are preserved from one transaction to the next (the default value).

0 Open cursors are destroyed from one transaction to the next.

DB2ESTIMATE = 0 | large_positive_number This keyword determines whether DB2 CLI will pop up a graphic display window to report estimates returned by the DB2 version 2.1 optimizer at the end of SQL query statement preparation. By default, estimate values are not returned (DB2ESTIMATE = 0). If a large positive number is specified, that number will be used as the threshold value above which DB2 CLI displays the window to report estimates. The recommended value for DB2ESTIMATE is 60,000. This keyword is ignored for all non-DB2 version 2.x databases.

DB2EXPLAIN = 0 | 1 This keyword determines whether or not Explain output is generated by DB2. By default, Explain information is not generated (DB2EXPLAIN = 0). Before Explain information can be generated, the Explain tables must be created.

DB2OPTIMIZATION = positive_number (0 to 9) This keyword applies only to a DB2 version 2.x server. If this keyword is specified, DB2 CLI will issue the following SQL statement after a successful connection is established:

```
SET CURRENT QUERY OPTIMIZATION positive_number
```

This specifies the query optimization level at which the optimizer should process SQL queries. Refer to the SET CURRENT QUERY OPTIMIZATION SQL statement in Chapter 8 for additional information.

DBALIAS = database_alias This keyword allows you to specify data source name that contains more than eight characters.

DBNAME = dbname This keyword is used only when connecting to DB2 for MVS/ESA, and only if (base) table catalog information is requested by the application.

GRAPHIC = 0 | 1 This keyword controls whether or not DB2 CLI reports the IBM GRAPHIC (double-byte character support) as one of the supported data types when the SQLGetTypeInfo( ) function is called. By default, DB2 CLI does not report GRAPHIC data types (GRAPHIC = 0).

LOBMAXCOLUMNSIZE = lob_size This keyword allows you to override the 2GB (1GB for DBCLOB) value returned by the SQLGetTypeInfo( ) function for the COLUMN_SIZE column in SQL_CLOB, SQL_BLOB, and SQL_DBCLOB data types.

LONGDATACOMPAT = 0 | 1 This keyword indicates to DB2 CLI whether the application expects CLOB, BLOB, and DBCLOB data types to be reported as SQL_LONGVARCHAR, SQL_LONGVARBINARY, and SQL_LONGVARGRAPHIC data types, respectively, or as their native data type. By default, LOB data types are reported as SQL_CLOB, SQL_BLOB, and SQL_DBCLOB (LONGDATACOMPAT = 0).

MAXCONN = 0 | positive_number This keyword specifies the maximum number of connections allowed for each CLI application program. By default, an application can open as many connections as permitted by the system resources (MAXCONN = 0).

MODE = SHARE | EXCLUSIVE This keyword sets the CONNECT mode to either SHARE or EXCLUSIVE. By default, the CONNECT mode is set to SHARE (MODE = SHARE). If a mode is set by the application at connect time, this value is ignored.

PATCH1 = { 0 | 1 | 2 | 4 | 8 | 16 | . . . } This keyword specifies work-around patches for known ODBC applications. If you want the work-arounds to be additive, add the values together to form the keyword value. For example, if you want patches 1, 4, and 8, then specify PATCH1 = 13. By default, no work-around patches are used (PATCH1 = 0). For an up-to-date list of available patch values, refer to the DB20DBC.TXT file shipped with the DB2 SDK product.

SCHEMALIST = "'schema1', 'schema2', . . . " This keyword specifies a list of schemas in the database. If a large number of tables are defined in the database, you can specify a schema list to reduce the time it takes the application to query table information and to reduce the number of tables listed by the application. Each schema name must be delimited with single quotes, separated by commas, and in uppercase. The entire string must also be enclosed in double quotes. Note: This keyword replaces the OWNERLIST keyword used in previous releases. The OWNERLIST keyword is still supported, but SCHEMALIST is preferred.

SYNCPOINT = 1 | 2 This keyword allows you to specify how commits and rollbacks are coordinated among multiple database (DUOW) connections. This keyword accepts the following values:

1 A transaction manager is not used to perform two-phase commits; instead, a one-phase commit commits the work done by each database in a multiple database transaction (the default value).

2 A transaction manager is required to coordinate two-phase commits among databases supporting this.

SYSSCHEMA = sysschema This keyword indicates an alternative schema to be searched in place of the SYSCAT (or SYSIBM, SYSTEM) schemas when DB2 CLI and ODBC catalog function calls are issued to obtain system catalog information. If no value is specified, the default system schemas are:

–SYSCAT or SYSIBM on DB2 for Common Servers, version 2.1

–SYSIBM on DB2/2, version 1.x; DB2/6000, version 1.x; DB2 for MVS/ESA; and DB2 for OS/400

–SYSTEM on DB2 for VSE and DB2 for VM
–QSYS2 on DB2 for OS/400

Note: This keyword replaces the SYSOWNER keyword used in previous releases. The SYSOWNER keyword is still supported, but SYSSCHEMA is the preferred keyword to use.

TABLETYPE = "'TABLE' | ,'ALIAS' | ,'VIEW' | ,'INOPERATIVE VIEW' | ,'SYSTEM TABLE' | ,'SYNONYM' " This keyword specifies one or more table types to access. If a large number of tables are defined in the database, you can specify a table type string to reduce the time it takes the application to query table information, and reduce the number of tables listed by the application. Any number of the values can be specified, but each type must be delimited with single quotes, separated by commas, and in uppercase. The entire string must also be enclosed in double quotes.

TRANSLATEDLL = X:.DLL This keyword is used in Windows when connecting to DB2/2, version 1, or when using a version of DDCS for OS/2 prior to version 2.3 to provide proper mapping of NLS SBCS characters (such as the umlaut characters in German) to the corresponding characters in the Windows code page 1004. X:is the directory where the DB2 Client Application Enabler for Windows or the DB2 SDK for Windows product has been installed. DB2TRANS.DLL contains the code page mapping tables.

TRANSLATEOPTION = database_codepage_number This keyword specifies which code page number to use when translating characters to the Windows 1004 code page. Only two code page values are currently supported, number 437 and number 850. If any other value is specified, a warning will be returned on the connect request, indicating that translation is not possible.

TXNISOLATION = 1 | 2 | 8 | 16 | 32 This keyword sets the isolation level to one of the following values (the DB2 equivalents for SQL92 isolation levels are shown in brackets):

- 1 Read uncommitted [uncommitted read]
- 2 Read committed [cursor stability] (the default value)
- 8 Serializable [repeatable read]
- 16 Repeatable read [read stability]
- 32 No commit (DB2 for OS/400 only)

UNDERSCORE = 1 | 0 This keyword specifies whether the underscore character (_) is a wildcard character (to match any one character, including no character) or whether it is used as is. This parameter affects only catalog function calls that accept search pattern strings. By default, the underscore is treated as a wildcard for pattern matching (UNDERSCORE = 1).

POPUPMESSAGE = 0 | 1 This keyword specifies that a message box pops up every time DB2 CLI generates an error, which you can retrieve by calling the SQLError( ) function. This keyword is useful for debugging applications that don't report messages to users. By default, no message box is displayed (POPUPMESSAGE = 0).

SQLSTATEFILTER = "'S1COO','XXXXX', . . ." This keyword is used in conjunction with the POPUPMESSAGE = 1 keyword to prevent DB2 CLI from displaying errors associated with specified SQLSTATES states.

APPENDAPINAME = 0 | 1 This keyword specifies whether or not the DB2 CLI function (API) name that generated an error is appended to the error message information retrieved by the SQLError( ) function. By default, DB2 CLI function names are not displayed as part of the error message information returned by the SQLError( ) function (APPENDAPINAME = 0). If the function name is appended to the error message, it will be enclosed in curly braces, { } .

- If any *keyword* = *attribute* combination appears more than one time in the connection string, only the value associated with the first occurrence of the keyword is used; all others are ignored.
- If any keywords exist in either the **db2cli.ini** or the **odbc.ini** configuration file, their respective attributes (values) will augment the information passed to DB2 CLI in the connection string. If a keyword's attribute in either of these configuration files is different from the keyword attribute specified in the connection string, the attribute supplied in the connection string will take precedence.
- If the value of the *DriverCompletion* parameter is set to SQL_DRIVER_NOPROMPT, the DSN = data source name *keyword* = *attribute* combination must be specified in the connection string.
- If the user exits the DB2 CLI graphical user interface dialog without entering the required connection information, the SQL_NO_DATA_FOUND return code will be returned.
- Applications should allocate at least SQL_MAX_OPTION_STRING_LENGTH bytes for the *ConnectIn* connection string buffer.

Restrictions There are no restrictions associated with this function call.

See Also SQLAllocConnect( ), SQLConnect( ), SQLDisconnect( )

Examples The following C program illustrates how to establish a connection to a data source using the SQLDriverConnect( ) function:

```
#include <stdio.h>
#include <stdlib.h>
#include <sqlcli1.h>

int main()
{
    /* Declare The Local Memory Variables */
    SQLRETURN  rc = SQL_SUCCESS;
    SQLHENV    EnvHandle;
    SQLHDBC    DSCHandle;
    SQLCHAR    ConnectIn[50];
    SQLCHAR    ConnectOut[50];

    /* Allocate An Environment Handle */
    rc = SQLAllocEnv(&EnvHandle);

    /* Allocate A Connection Handle */
    rc = SQLAllocConnect(EnvHandle, &DSCHandle);

    /* Initialize A Connection String */
    sprintf(ConnectIn, "DSN=SAMPLE; UID=etpdd6z; PWD=sanders;");

    /* Connect To The SAMPLE Database */
    rc = SQLDriverConnect(DSCHandle, NULL, ConnectIn, SQL_NTS, NULL,
                          0, NULL, SQL_DRIVER_NOPROMPT);

    /* Display A Success Message */
    printf("Connected to SAMPLE database.\n");

    /* Disconnect From The SAMPLE Database */
```

```
    SQLDisconnect(DSCHandle);

    /* Free The Connection Handle */
    if (DSCHandle != NULL)
        SQLFreeConnect(DSCHandle);

    /* Free The Environment Handle */
    if (EnvHandle != NULL)
        SQLFreeEnv(EnvHandle);

    /* Return To The Operating System */
    return(rc);
}
```

The following C++ program illustrates how to create a class method that establishes a connection to a data source using the SQLDriverConnect( ) function:

```
#include <iostream.h>
#include <string.h>
#include <sqlcli1.h>

/* Define The CLI Class */
class CLI
{
    /* Declare The Private Attribute Variables */
    private:
       SQLHENV     EnvHandle;
       SQLHDBC     DSCHandle;
       SQLCHAR     ConnectIn[50];
       SQLCHAR     ConnectOut[50];

    /* Declare The Public Attribute Variables */
    public:
       SQLRETURN  rc;

    /* Declare The Member Function Prototypes */
    CLI();                                      // Constructor
    ~CLI();                                     // Destructor
    SQLRETURN Connect();
    SQLRETURN Disconnect();
} ;

/* Define The Class Constructor */
CLI::CLI()
{
    /* Initialize The Return Code Variable */
    rc = SQL_SUCCESS;

    /* Allocate An Environment Handle */
    rc = SQLAllocEnv(&EnvHandle);

    /* Allocate A Connection Handle */
    rc = SQLAllocConnect(EnvHandle, &DSCHandle);
}

/* Define The Class Destructor */
CLI::~CLI()
{
    /* Free The Connection Handle */
    if (DSCHandle != NULL)
```

```
            SQLFreeConnect(DSCHandle);

        /* Free The Environment Handle */
        if (EnvHandle != NULL)
            SQLFreeEnv(EnvHandle);
}

/* Define The Connect() Member Function */
SQLRETURN CLI::Connect()
{
    /* Initialize A Connection String */
    memcpy(ConnectIn, "DSN=SAMPLE; UID=etpdd6z; PWD=sanders;", 37);

    /* Connect To The SAMPLE Database */
    rc = SQLDriverConnect(DSCHandle, NULL, ConnectIn, SQL_NTS, NULL,
                          0, NULL, SQL_DRIVER_NOPROMPT);

    /* Return The CLI Function Return Code */
    return(rc);
}

/* Define The Disconnect() Member Function */
SQLRETURN CLI::Disconnect(void)
{
    /* Disconnect From The Database */
    rc = SQLDisconnect(DSCHandle);
    /* Return The CLI Function Return Code */
    return(rc);
}

int main()
{
    /* Declare The Local Memory Variables */
    SQLRETURN  rc = SQL_SUCCESS;

    /* Create An Instance Of The CLI Class */
    CLI Sample;

    /* Connect To The SAMPLE Database - If Successful, Display */
    /* An Appropriate Message                                  */
    rc = Sample.Connect();
    if (rc == SQL_SUCCESS)
        cout << "Connected to SAMPLE database." << endl;

    /* Disconnect From The SAMPLE Database */
    Sample.Disconnect();

    /* Return To The Operating System */
    return(rc);
}
```

SQLSetConnection

Purpose The SQLSetConnection( ) function switches from one data source connection to another in an application that supports multiple connections.

Syntax

```
SQLRETURN SQLSetConnection (SQLHDBC DSCHandle);
```

Parameters

DSCHandle The data source connection handle that contains the address of the connection information buffer associated with the connection to which the application wants to switch.

Includes

```
#include <sqlcli1.h>
```

Description

In DB2 CLI version 1.x, you can mix DB2 CLI calls with calls to routines containing embedded SQL as long as the data source connect requests are issued via the DB2 CLI connect function (and not through the CONNECT SQL statement). Therefore, the embedded SQL routines would use the existing DB2 CLI data source connection. Although this scenario still holds true with DB2 CLI version 2.x, a new complication exists because multiple concurrent data source connections are now supported. This means that it is no longer clear which data source connection an embedded SQL routine should use when it is invoked. In practice, the embedded SQL routine should use the data source connection associated with the most recent network activity. From the application's perspective, however, this connection cannot always be determined and it is difficult to keep track of the information.

The SQLSetConnection( ) function is used whenever an application needs to switch from one data source connection to another before an embedded SQL routine is envoked. This function should only be used when the application mixes DB2 CLI function calls with embedded SQL routines in situations where multiple data source connections are involved.

Specifications

DB2 CLI 2.1

Return Codes

SQL_SUCCESS, SQL_INVALID_HANDLE, SQL_ERROR

SQLSTATEs

08003, **S1**000

Comments

The SQLSetConnection( ) function is not needed at all if the application only uses DB2 CLI function calls. With DB2 CLI, each statement handle is implicitly associated with a data source connection handle, so there is never any confusion as to which data source connection a particular DB2 CLI function is applied.

Restrictions

There are no restrictions associated with this function call.

See Also

SQLConnect( ), SQLDriverConnect( )

Examples

The following C program illustrates how you can use the SQLSetConnection() function to switch between two active data source connections before executing an embedded SQL function:

```
#include <stdio.h>
#include <stdlib.h>
#include <sqlcli1.h>

int main()
{
    /* Declare The Local Memory Variables */
    SQLRETURN  rc = SQL_SUCCESS;
    SQLHENV    EnvHandle;
    SQLHDBC    DSCHandle[2];
    int        CreateTable();
```

```
/* Allocate An Environment Handle */
rc = SQLAllocEnv(&EnvHandle);

/* Allocate A Connection Handle */
rc = SQLAllocConnect(EnvHandle, &DSCHandle[0]);

/* Allocate A Second Connection Handle */
rc = SQLAllocConnect(EnvHandle, &DSCHandle[1]);

/* Connect To The SAMPLE Database */
rc = SQLConnect(DSCHandle[0], "SAMPLE", SQL_NTS, "etpdd6z",
                SQL_NTS, "sanders", SQL_NTS);

/* Display A Success Message */
printf("Connected to SAMPLE database.\n");

/* Connect To The BOOKSAMP Database */
rc = SQLConnect(DSCHandle[1], "BOOKSAMP", SQL_NTS, "etpdd6z",
                SQL_NTS, "sanders", SQL_NTS);

/* Display A Success Message */
printf("Connected to BOOKSAMP database.\n");

/* At This Point There Are Two Active Database Connections */
/* Make The Connection To The SAMPLE Database The Current  */
/* Connection                                              */
rc = SQLSetConnection(DSCHandle[0]);

/* Call The CreateTable() Function That Contains Embedded SQL */
if (CreateTable() != 0)
    {
    printf("ERROR : Unable to create table in SAMPLE ");
    printf("database.\n");
    }

else
    {
    printf("Table TEMP_EMP has been created in the SAMPLE ");
    printf("database.\n");
    }

SQLTransact(EnvHandle, DSCHandle[0], SQL_ROLLBACK);

/* Make The Connection To The BOOKSAMP Database The Current  */
/* Connection                                                */
rc = SQLSetConnection(DSCHandle[1]);

/* Call The CreateTable() Function That Contains Embedded SQL */
if (CreateTable() != 0)
    {
    printf("ERROR : Unable to create table in BOOKSAMP ");
    printf("database.\n");
    }

else
    {
    printf("Table TEMP_EMP has been created in the BOOKSAMP ");
    printf("database.\n");
    }

SQLTransact(EnvHandle, DSCHandle[1], SQL_ROLLBACK);
```

```
    /* At This Point A New Table Has Been Created On Both Databases */
    /* Disconnect From The SAMPLE Database */
    SQLDisconnect(DSCHandle[0]);

    /* Disconnect From The BOOKSAMP Database */
    SQLDisconnect(DSCHandle[1]);

    /* Free The First Connection Handle */
    if (DSCHandle[0] != NULL)
        SQLFreeConnect(DSCHandle[0]);

    /* Free The Second Connection Handle */
    if (DSCHandle[1] != NULL)
        SQLFreeConnect(DSCHandle[1]);

    /* Free The Environment Handle */
    if (EnvHandle != NULL)
        SQLFreeEnv(EnvHandle);

    /* Return To The Operating System */
    return(rc);
}
```

Note: The SQLSetConnection() function statement is used in a C++ program in a similar manner.

The embedded SQL function that creates a table in the database:

```
#include <sql.h>
#include <sqlenv.h>

/* Include The SQLCA Data Structure Variable */
EXEC SQL INCLUDE SQLCA;

/* Declare The Function Prototype */
int CreateTable();

/* Create The CreateTable() Embedded SQL Function */
int CreateTable()
{
    /* Create The TEMP_EMP Table */
    EXEC SQL CREATE TABLE TEMP_EMP
        (EMPID        INTEGER      NOT NULL,
         LASTNAME     CHAR(18)     NOT NULL,
         FIRSTNAME    CHAR(18)     NOT NULL,
         DEPTNO       CHAR(3),
         PRIMARY KEY(EMPID));

    /* Return To The Calling Function */
    return(sqlca.sqlcode);
}
```

This function is created in a separate file so only the embedded SQL portion of the application has to be precompiled.

SQLDisconnect

Purpose The SQLDisconnect( ) function closes the data source connection associated with a specified data source connection handle.

Syntax

```
SQLRETURN SQLDisconnect (SQLHDBC DSCHandle);
```

Parameters *DSCHandle* The data source connection handle where the address of the connection information buffer is stored.

Includes

```
#include <sqlcli1.h>
```

Description The SQLDisconnect( ) function closes the connection associated with a specified data source connection handle. If an application calls the SQLDisconnect( ) function before it has freed all the SQL statement handles associated with the specified connection, DB2 CLI will free them after it successfully disconnects from the data source. Once this function is called, either the SQLConnect( ) function must be called again to establish a connection to another data source or the SQLFreeConnect( ) function must be called to release the memory buffer associated with the data source connection handle.

Specifications DB2 CLI 1.1, ODBC 1.0, X/OPEN CLI, ISO CLI

Return Codes SQL_SUCCESS, SQL_SUCCESS_WITH_INFO, SQL_INVALID_HANDLE, SQL_ERROR

SQLSTATEs **01**002, **08**003, **25**000, **25**501, **58**004, **S1**001, **S1**010, **S1**013

Comments

- If the SQL_SUCCESS_WITH_INFO return code is returned, it implies that, even though the disconnect from the data source was successful, additional error or implementation specific diagnostic information is available.
- The SQLSTATE **25**501 does not apply to stored procedures that contain DB2 CLI functions.
- After the SQLDisconnect( ) function is called, the application can reuse the data source connection handle to establish a connection to another data source.

Prerequisites If an outstanding transaction exists for the specified data source connection, the SQLTransact( ) function must be executed before this function can be called.

Restrictions There are no restrictions associated with this function call.

See Also SQLAllocConnect( ), SQLConnect( ), SQLDriverConnect( ), SQLTransact( )

Examples See the examples provided for the SQLAllocEnv( ) function.

SQLFreeConnect

Purpose The SQLFreeConnect( ) function releases a data source connection handle and frees all memory associated with it.

Syntax

```
SQLRETURN SQLFreeConnect (SQLHDBC DSCHandle);
```

Parameters *DSCHandle* The data source connection handle where the address of the connection information buffer is stored.

Includes

```
#include <sqlcli1.h>
```

Description The SQLFreeConnect( ) function invalidates and frees a specified data source connection handle. Whenever a data source connection handle is freed, all DB2 CLI resources associated with that connection handle are also freed. Once this function is called, only the SQLFreeEnv( ) or SQLAllocConnect( ) functions can be called.

Specifications DB2 CLI 1.1, ODBC 1.0, X/OPEN CLI, ISO CLI

Return Codes SQL_SUCCESS, SQL_INVALID_HANDLE, SQL_ERROR

SQLSTATEs **58**004, **S1**001, **S1**010, **S1**013

Comments If this function is called while a data source connection still exists, the SQL_ERROR return code will be returned and the connection handle will remain valid.

Prerequisites The SQLDisconnect( ) function must be executed before this function can be called.

Restrictions There are no restrictions associated with this function call.

See Also SQLDisconnect( ), SQLFreeEnv( )

Examples See the examples provided for the SQLAllocEnv( ) function.

SQLFreeEnv

Purpose The SQLFreeEnv( ) function releases an environment handle and frees all memory associated with it.

Syntax

```
SQLRETURN SQLFreeEnv (SQLHENV EnvHandle);
```

Parameters *EnvHandle* The environment handle where the starting address of the environment buffer is stored.

Includes

```
#include <sqlcli1.h>
```

Description The SQLFreeEnv( ) function invalidates and frees an environment handle. Whenever an environment handle is freed, all resources associated with that environment handle are also freed. This function call is the last call a DB2 CLI application should make before it terminates.

Specifications DB2 CLI 1.1, ODBC 1.0, X/OPEN CLI, ISO CLI

Return Codes SQL_SUCCESS, SQL_INVALID, HANDLE, SQL_ERROR

SQLSTATEs **58**004, **S1**001, **S1**010, **S1**013

Comments

- If this function is called while a data source connection still exists, the SQL_ERROR return code will be returned and the environment handle will remain valid.

Prerequisites The SQLFreeConnect( ) function must be executed before this function can be called.

Restrictions There are no restrictions associated with this function call.

See Also SQLFreeConnect( )

Examples See the examples provided for the SQLAllocEnv( ) function.

CHAPTER 14

CLI/ODBC DRIVER AND DATA SOURCE OPTION CONTROL FUNCTIONS

The CLI/ODBC driver and data source option control functions are a group of DB2 CLI function calls you can use to obtain information about available data sources and/or set environment, connection, and SQL statement processing options. This group includes:

- A CLI function that generates a list of all data sources found to which an application can connect.
- CLI functions that return various types of information about the driver/data source, including information about supported CLI/ODBC functions and data types.
- CLI functions that retrieve the current values of environment, connection, and SQL statement options.
- CLI functions that specify values for environment, connection, and SQL statement options.

14

Table 14.1 lists the CLI/ODBC driver and data source option control functions available with DB2 CLI.

TABLE 14.1 CLI/ODBC Driver and Data Source Option Control Functions

Function name	Description
SQLDataSources( )	Generates a list of data sources to which an application can connect.
SQLGetInfo( )	Retrieves information about a specific driver or data source connection.
SQLGetFunctions( )	Retrieves information about the DB2 CLI function calls supported by a specific data source.
SQLGetTypeInfo( )	Retrieves information about the data types supported by a specific data source.
SQLGetEnvAttr( )	Retrieves the current value of an environment attribute option.
SQLSetEnvAttr( )	Changes the value of an environment attribute option.
SQLGetConnectOption( )	Retrieves the current value of a data source connection option.
SQLSetConnectOption( )	Changes the value of a data source connection option.
SQLGetStmtOption( )	Retrieves the current value of a SQL statement option.
SQLSetStmtOption( )	Changes the value of a SQL statement option.

Adapted from IBM's Database 2 Call Level Interface Guide and Reference, Table 11, pages 103 to 106.

Obtaining Information About a Data Source

Because a DB2 CLI application can connect to data sources other than DB2 databases, it needs to be able to obtain information about the data source to which it is connected. DB2 CLI provides the SQL-GetInfo( ) function for this purpose. It also allows an application to determine which CLI functions and data types are supported by calling the SQLGetFunctions( ) function and the SQLGetTypeInfo( ) function, respectively.

Environment, Connection, and SQL Statement Options

Environment, connection, and SQL statement handles each have a predefined set of options (or attributes) that can affect the behavior of DB2 CLI functions when they are executed. An application can retrieve the values associated with each option, but the number of options an application can change is limited. By changing the value of one or more of these predefined options, an application can change the overall behavior of DB2 CLI.

The environment attributes (or options) affect the behavior of DB2 CLI functions that operate under the specified environment. An application can retrieve the value of an environment attribute at any time by calling the SQLGetEnvAttr( ) function, and it can set an environment attribute by calling the SQLSetEnvAttr( ) function. However, the SQLSetEnvAttr( ) function can be called only as long as no connection handles are allocated within a specified environment; once a connection handle is allocated within an environment, that environment's attributes can no longer be altered.

The connection options affect the behavior of DB2 CLI functions that are executed against a specified connection. An application can retrieve the value of a connection option at any time by calling the SQLGetConnectOption( ) function, and it can set a connection option by calling the SQLSet-ConnectOption( ) function. Timing is very important when setting connection options, because:

- Some connection options can be set any time after the connection handle is allocated.
- Some connection options can be set only after the connection handle is allocated and before the actual connection to the data source is established.
- Some connection options can be set only after the connection handle is allocated and the connection to the data source is established.
- Some connection options can be set only after the connection handle is allocated and the connection to the data source is established, when there are no outstanding transactions or open cursors for the connection.

You can also use the SQLSetConnectOption( ) function to set statement options for all statement handles currently associated with a data source connection, as well as for all future statement handles to be allocated under the data source connection handle.

The SQL statement options affect the behavior of DB2 CLI functions that are executed for the specified SQL statement handle. An application can retrieve the value of an SQL statement option at any time by calling the SQLGetStmtOption( ) function, and can set a statement option by calling the SQLSetStmtOption( ) function. As with connection options, timing is very important when setting SQL statement options because some statement options can be set any time after the statement handle is allocated, while other statement options can be set only if there is no open cursor on the specified statement handle.

> Note: At this time, some statement options can be set to only one specific value.

Many applications can use the default option settings without incurring any problems; however, in certain situations, some of these default values are not appropriate for a particular end user of the application. Two methods are available with DB2 CLI that allow end users to change one or more of these default option settings at application runtime. The first method allows users to specify the new option value(s) in the connection string used by the SQLDriverConnect( ) function. The second method lets users specify the new option value(s) in the DB2 CLI configuration file **db2cli.ini.** If the application does not provide attribute values in the connection string passed to the SQLDriverConnect( ) function (the first method), the DB2 CLI configuration file might be the end user's only means of changing environment, connection, and SQL statement option values.

These two mechanisms for changing environment, connection, and SQL statement option values are primarily intended for end-user tuning; application developers should use the appropriate set option functions. If an application does call a set option or set attribute function with a value different from that found in the DB2 CLI configuration file or SQLDriverConnect( ) connection string, then the initial option value is overridden and the new value takes effect.

SQLDataSources

Purpose

The SQLDataSources( ) function produces a list of data source (database) names to which an application can connect.

Syntax

```
SQLRETURN SQLDataSources (SQLHENV           EnvHandle,
                          SQLUSMALLINT      Selection,
                          SQLCHAR FAR       *DSName,
                          SQLSMALLINT       DSNameMaxSize,
                          SQLSMALLINT FAR   *DSNameSize,
                          SQLCHAR FAR       *Description,
                          SQLSMALLINT       DescriptionMaxSize,
                          SQLSMALLINT FAR   *DescriptionSize);
```

Parameters

EnvHandle The environment handle where the address of the environment buffer is stored.

Selection Specifies which data source, in a list of data sources, for which this function is to retrieve information. This parameter can contain any of the following values:

SQL_FETCH_FIRST Retrieves information for the first data source name in the list.

SQL_FETCH_NEXT Retrieves information for the next data source name in the list.

DSName A pointer to a location in memory where this function is to store the retrieved data source name.

DSNameMaxSize The maximum size of the memory storage buffer where this function is to store the retrieved data source name.

DSNameSize A pointer to a location in memory where this function will return the actual number of bytes written to the *DSName* memory storage buffer.

Description A pointer to a location in memory where this function is to store the description of the retrieved data source name. For DB2 databases, this function will return the value stored in the Comment field associated with the retrieved database name.

DescriptionMaxSize The maximum size of the memory storage buffer where this function is to store the retrieved data source description.

DescriptionSize A pointer to a location in memory where this function will return the actual number of bytes written to the *Description* memory storage buffer.

Includes

```
#include <sqlcli1.h>
```

Description

The SQLDataSources( ) function produces a list of data source (database) names to which a connection can be made. A DB2 database (and its corresponding node, if the database physically resides on a remote server workstation) must be cataloged in order to be included in this list of data source names. This function is usually called before a connection to a data source is established.

Specifications DB2 CLI 1.1, ODBC 1.0, X/OPEN CLI, ISO CLI

Return Codes SQL_SUCCESS, SQL_SUCCESS_WITH_INFO, SQL_INVALID_HANDLE, SQL_NO_DATA_FOUND, SQL_ERROR

SQLSTATEs **01**004, **58**004, **S1**000, **S1**001, **S1**013, **S1**090, **S1**103

Comments

- The value stored in the *DSNMaxSize* parameter should always be less than or equal to SQL_MAX_DSN_LENGTH + 1.
- If this function is called with the *Selection* parameter set to SQL_FETCH_FIRST, information about the first data source in the list will always be returned. With the *Selection* parameter set to SQL_FETCH_NEXT, if the function is called:
  –directly following a SQLDataSources( ) function call where SQL_FETCH_FIRST is specified, information about the second data source in the list will be returned.
  –before any other SQLDataSources( ) function call, information about the first data source in the list will be returned.
  –when there are no more data source names in the list, the SQL_NO_DATA_FOUND return code will be returned. If the SQLDataSources( ) function is then called again, information about the first data source in the list will be returned.
  –at any other time, information about the next data source in the list will be returned.
- In an ODBC environment, the ODBC driver manager executes this function automatically.
- Since IBM relational database management systems always return the description of a database as a blank, padded, 30-byte string, this function will do the same.

Restrictions There are no restrictions associated with this function call.

Examples The following C program illustrates how the SQLDataSources( ) function produces a list of available data sources to which an application can connect:

```
#include <stdio.h>
#include <stdlib.h>
#include <sqlcli1.h>

int main()
{
    /* Declare The Local Memory Variables */
    SQLRETURN    rc = SQL_SUCCESS;
    SQLHENV      EnvHandle;
    SQLCHAR      DataSource[31];
    SQLCHAR      Description[255];
    SQLSMALLINT  BuffSize;
    SQLSMALLINT  DescSize;

    /* Allocate An Environment Handle */
    rc = SQLAllocEnv(&EnvHandle);

    /* Print The Information Header */
    printf("The Following Data Sources Are Available:\n\n");
```

```
    printf("ALIAS           Description (Comment)\n");
    printf("---------------------------------------\n");

    /* List The Data Sources That Are Available To The Application */
    while (rc != SQL_NO_DATA_FOUND)
        {

        /* Retrieve A Data Source Name */
        rc = SQLDataSources(EnvHandle, SQL_FETCH_NEXT, DataSource,
                            sizeof(DataSource), &BuffSize,
                            Description, sizeof(Description),
                            &DescSize);

        /* Print The Data Source Name */
        if (rc != SQL_NO_DATA_FOUND)
           printf("%-15s %s\n", DataSource, Description);
        }

    /* Free The Environment Handle */
    if (EnvHandle != NULL)
        SQLFreeEnv(EnvHandle);

    /* Return To The Operating System */
    return(rc);
}
```

The following C++ program illustrates how the SQLDataSources( ) function is used by class methods to produce a list of available data sources to which an application can connect:

```
#include <iostream.h>
#include <string.h>
#include <sqlcli1.h>

/* Define The CLI Class */
class CLI
{
    /* Declare The Private Attribute Variables */
    private:
       SQLHENV      EnvHandle;
       SQLCHAR      DataSource[31];
       SQLCHAR      Description[255];
       SQLSMALLINT  BuffSize;
       SQLSMALLINT  DescSize;

    /* Declare The Public Attribute Variables */
    public:
       SQLRETURN    rc;

    /* Declare The Member Function Prototypes */
    CLI();                                    // Constructor
    ~CLI();                                   // Destructor
    SQLRETURN ShowDataSources();
} ;

/* Define The Class Constructor */
CLI::CLI()
{
    /* Initialize The Return Code Variable */
    rc = SQL_SUCCESS;
```

```
    /* Allocate An Environment Handle */
    rc = SQLAllocEnv(&EnvHandle);
}

/* Define The Class Destructor */
CLI::~CLI()
{
    /* Free The Environment Handle */
    if (EnvHandle != NULL)
        SQLFreeEnv(EnvHandle);
}

/* Define The ShowDataSources() Member Function */
SQLRETURN CLI::ShowDataSources()
{
    /* Print The Information Header */
    cout << "The Following Data Sources Are Available: "<< endl;
    cout << endl < "ALIAS           Description (Comment)" << endl;
    cout << "----------------------------------------" << endl;

    /* List The Data Sources That Are Available To The Application */
    while (rc != SQL_NO_DATA_FOUND)
        {

        /* Retrieve A Data Source Name */
        rc = SQLDataSources(EnvHandle, SQL_FETCH_NEXT, DataSource,
                            sizeof(DataSource), &BuffSize,
                            Description, sizeof(Description),
                            &DescSize);

        /* Print The Data Source Name */
        if (rc != SQL_NO_DATA_FOUND)
            {
            cout.setf(ios::left);
            cout.width(16);
            cout << DataSource << Description << endl;
            }
        }

    /* Return The CLI Function Return Code */
    if (rc == SQL_NO_DATA_FOUND)
        rc = SQL_SUCCESS;
    return(rc);
}

int main()
{
    /* Declare The Local Memory Variables */
    SQLRETURN  rc = SQL_SUCCESS;

    /* Create An Instance Of The CLI Class */
    CLI Sample;

    /* List The Data Sources That Are Available To The Application */
    rc = Sample.ShowDataSources();

    /* Return To The Operating System */
    return(rc);
}
```

SQLGetInfo

Purpose The SQLGetInfo( ) function retrieves general information about the data source (database) to which the application is currently connected.

Syntax

```
SQLRETURN  SQLGetInfo (SQLHDBC          DSCHandle,
                       SQLUSMALLINT     InfoType,
                       SQLPOINTER       InfoValue,
                       SQLSMALLINT      InfoValueMaxSize,
                       SQLSMALLINT FAR *InfoValueSize);
```

Parameters

DSCHandle The data source connection handle where the address of the data source connection information buffer is stored.

InfoType A value that identifies the type of data source information to be retrieved. This parameter can contain any of the values shown in Table 14.2.

InfoValue A pointer to a location in memory where this function is to store the information retrieved from the data source. Depending on the type of information being retrieved, the following data types can be returned:

- 16-bit integer value
- 32-bit integer value
- 32-bit binary value
- 32-bit mask
- Null-terminated character string

InfoValueMaxSize The maximum size of the memory storage buffer where this function is to store the retrieved information.

InfoValueSize A pointer to a location in memory where this function is to store the actual number of bytes written to the *InfoValue* memory storage buffer.

Includes

```
#include <sqlcli1.h>
```

Description The SQLGetInfo( ) function retrieves general information about the data source (database) to which the application is currently connected. Table 14.2 alphabetically lists each value that can be specified for the *InfoType* parameter, along with a description of the information that will be returned for that value when the function is executed.

Specifications DB2 CLI 1.1, ODBC 1.0, X/OPEN CLI, ISO CLI

Return Codes SQL_SUCCESS, SQL_SUCCESS_WITH_INFO, SQL_INVALID_HANDLE, SQL_ERROR

SQLSTATEs **01**004, **08**003, **40**003, **08**S01, **58**004, **S1**001, **S1**009, **S1**090, **S1**096, **S1**C00

Comments

- If the value stored in the location pointed to by the *InfoValue* parameter is larger than the maximum buffer size (as specified in the *InfoValueMaxSize* parameter), the information will be truncated to *InfoValueMaxSize*
- 1 bytes, and the SQL_SUCCESS_WITH_INFO return code will be returned.
- If the value stored in the location pointed to by the *InfoValue* parameter is a null-terminated string, the number of characters in the string, minus the null terminating character, will be stored in the *InfoValueSize* parameter.

TABLE 14.2 Information Returned by the SQLGetInfo( ) Function

InfoType code	Data type returned	Description
SQL_ACCESSIBLE_PROCEDURES	Character string	Indicates whether or not all procedures returned by the SQL Procedures( ) function can be executed by the user. The following values can be returned for this *InfoType* code: Y: The user can execute all procedures returned by the SQL Procedures( ) function. N: Some of the procedures returned by the SQL Procedures( ) function cannot be executed by the user.
SQL_ACCESSIBLE_TABLES	Character string	Indicates whether or not the current user is guaranteed SELECT authorization to all tables returned by the SQLTables( ) function. The following values can be returned for this *InfoType* code: Y: The user is guaranteed SELECT authorization to all tables returned by the SQLTables( ) function. N: The user is not guaranteed SELECT authorization to all tables returned by the SQLTables( ) function.
SQL_ACTIVE_CONNECTIONS	16-bit integer	Specifies the maximum number of active connection handles the data source driver can have open at one time. If the value returned is 0, the maximum number of active connections allowed is dependent on the amount of system resources available. The MAXCONN keyword in the **db2cli.ini** configuration file or the SQL_MAX_CONNECTIONS environment and connection option can limit the number of active connections a data source can support.
SQL_ACTIVE_STATEMENTS	16-bit integer	Specifies the maximum number of active SQL statement handles the data source driver can support for a single connection. If the value returned is 0, the maximum number of active SQL statements allowed is dependent on the amount of data source system and DB2 CLI resources available.
SQL_ALTER_TABLE	32-bit mask	Indicates which clauses in the ALTER TABLE SQL statement are supported by the data source. The values SQL_AT_ADD_COLUMN and SQL_AT_DROP_COLUMN can be returned for this *InfoType* code.
SQL_BOOKMARK_PERSISTENCE	32-bit mask	Values returned for this *InfoType* code are recognized only by ODBC 2.0; the value 0 is returned by DB2 CLI.
SQL_COLUMN_ALIAS	Character string	Indicates whether or not the data source supports column aliases. The following values can be returned for this *InfoType* code: Y: The data source supports column aliases. N: The data source does not support column aliases.
SQL_CONCAT_NULL_BEHAVIOR	16-bit integer	Indicates how the data source handles the concatenation of NULL valued character data type columns with non-NULL valued character data type columns. The following values can be returned for this *InfoType* code: SQL_CB_NULL: The result is a NULL value (this is the case for all IBM relational database management system databases).

TABLE 14.2 Information Returned by the SQLGetInfo( ) Function *(Continued)*

InfoType code	Data type returned	Description
		SQL_CB_NON_NULL: The result is a concatenation of non-NULL valued value(s).
SQL_CONVERT_FUNCTIONS	32-bit mask	Identifies the scalar conversion functions supported by the data source. Values returned for this *InfoType* code are recognized only by ODBC; the value 0 is returned by DB2 CLI.
SQL_CORRELATION_NAME	16-bit integer	The degree of support for table correlation names that is provided by the data source. The following values can be returned for this *InfoType* code: SQL_CN_NONE: Table correlation names are not supported. SQL_CN_DIFFERENT: Table correlation names are supported, but they must be different from the name of the tables they represent. SQL_CN_ANY: Table correlation names are supported and can be any valid user-defined name.
SQL_CURSOR_COMMIT_BEHAVIOR	16-bit integer	Indicates how a COMMIT operation will affect cursors and prepared SQL statements within the data source. The following values can be returned for this *InfoType* code: SQL_CC_DELETE: Cursors are destroyed and access plans for prepared SQL statements are dropped. SQL_CC_CLOSE: Cursors are destroyed, but access plans for prepared SQL statements (including nonquery statements) are retained. SQL_CC_PRESERVE: Both cursors and access plans for prepared SQL statements (including nonquery statements) are retained. Applications can continue to fetch data or they can close their cursors and reexecute queries without having to reprepare the SQL statements. Note: After a COMMIT operation, a FETCH operation must take place to reposition the cursor before actions such as positioned UPDATEs and positioned DELETEs can be performed.
SQL_CURSOR_ROLLBACK_BEHAVIOR	16-bit integer	Indicates how a ROLLBACK operation will affect cursors and prepared SQL statements within the data source. The following values can be returned for this *InfoType* code: SQL_CC_DELETE: Cursors are destroyed and access plans for prepared SQL statements are dropped. SQL_CC_CLOSE: Cursors are destroyed, but access plans for prepared SQL statements (including nonquery statements) are retained. SQL_CC_PRESERVE: Both cursors and access plans for prepared SQL statements (including nonquery statements) are retained. Applications can continue to fetch data or they can close the cursors and reexecute queries without having to reprepare the SQL statements. Note: Only the value SQL_CC_DELETE or SQL_CC_CLOSE will be returned by a DB2 databases; SQL_CC_PRESERVE is not supported.

TABLE 14.2 Information Returned by the SQLGetInfo( ) Function *(Continued)*

InfoType code	Data type returned	Description
SQL_DATA_SOURCE_NAME	Character string	Identifies the name to be used in the *DSName* parameter of the SQLConnect( ) function, or the name to be provided as the DSN keyword value in the SQLDriverConnect( ) function connection string.
SQL_DATA_SOURCE_READ_ONLY	Character string	Indicates whether or not the data source is set to READ ONLY mode. The following values can be returned for this *InfoType* code: Y: The data source is set to READ ONLY mode. N: The data source is not set to READ ONLY mode.
SQL_DATABASE_NAME	Character string	Identifies the name of the current data source in use, provided the data source is a database. Note: The name of the current data source in use can also be returned if you execute the SELECT CURRENT SERVER query on any IBM RDBMS.
SQL_DBMS_NAME	Character string	Identifies the name of the RDBMS product being accessed by the data source driver (DB2/6000, DB2/2, etc.).
SQL_DBMS_VER	Character string	Identifies the version number of the RDBMS product being accessed. This information is returned in a string that has the format *mm.vv.rrrr*, where *mm* is the major version number, *vv* is the minor version number, and *rrrr* is the release number (e.g., 02.01.0000 would translate to major version 2, minor version 1, release 0). The database might also append a product-specific version number to this string (for example, 02.01.0000 DB2/2 2.1).
SQL_DEFAULT_TXN_ISOLATION	32-bit mask	The default transaction isolation level supported by the driver or data source. The following scenarios illustrate the terms that describe transaction isolation levels: Dirty read: Transaction 1 changes a row, and transaction 2 reads the changed row before transaction 1 commits the change. If transaction 1 rolls back the change, transaction 2 will have read a row considered to have never existed. Nonrepeatable read: Transaction 1 reads a row, and transaction 2 updates or deletes that row and commits the change. If transaction 1 attempts to reread the row, it will retrieve different row values (if the row was updated) or discover that the row no longer exists (if the row was deleted). Phantom: Transaction 1 reads a set of rows that satisfies some search criteria, and transaction 2 inserts a row that matches the search criteria. If transaction 1 reexecutes the query statement that read the rows, it will receive a different set of rows. If the data source supports transaction processing, one of the following values will be returned for this *InfoType* code: SQL_TXN_READ_UNCOMMITTED: Changes are immediately perceived by all transactions (dirty reads,

TABLE 14.2 Information Returned by the SQLGetInfo( ) Function *(Continued)*

InfoType code	Data type returned	Description
		nonrepeatable reads, and phantoms are possible). This is equivalent to IBM's uncommitted read (UR) isolation level.
		SQL_TXN_READ_COMMITTED: The row read by transaction 1 can be altered and committed by transaction 2 (dirty reads are not possible; nonrepeatable reads and phantoms are possible). This is equivalent to IBM's cursor stability (CS) isolation level.
		SQL_TXN_REPEATABLE_READ: A transaction can add or remove rows matching the search condition of a pending transaction (dirty reads and non-repeatable reads are not possible; phantoms are possible). This is equivalent to IBM's read stability (RS) isolation level.
		SQL_TXN_SERIALIZABLE: Data affected by a pending transaction is not available to other transactions (dirty reads, nonrepeatable reads, and phantoms are not possible). This is equivalent to IBM's repeatable read (RR) isolation level.
		SQL_TXN_VERSIONING: Not applicable to IBM RDBMS databases.
		SQL_TXN_NOCOMMIT: Any changes are effectively committed at the end of a successful operation; no explicit commit or rollback is allowed. This is a DB2 for OS/400 isolation level.
SQL_DRIVER_HDBC	32-bit binary	Identifies DB2 CLI's data source connection handle.
SQL_DRIVER_HENV	32-bit binary	Identifies DB2 CLI's environment handle.
SQL_DRIVER_HLIB	32-bit binary	Values returned for this *InfoType* code are recognized only by ODBC 2.0; the value 0 is returned by DB2 CLI.
SQL_DRIVER_HSTMT	32-bit binary	Identifies DB2 CLI's SQL statement handle. In an ODBC environment with an ODBC driver manager, if this *InfoType* code is specified, the driver manager SQL statement handle (the one returned from the SQLAllocStmt( ) function) must be passed as input in the *InfoValue* parameter of the SQLGetInfo( ) function. In this case, the *InfoValue* parameter acts as both an input and an output argument. The ODBC driver manager is responsible for returning the appropriate mapped value. ODBC applications that want to call DB2 CLI-specific functions (such as the LOB functions) can access them by passing these handle values to the functions after loading the DB2 CLI library and issuing an operating system call to invoke the desired functions.
SQL_DRIVER_NAME	Character string	Identifies the filename of the DB2 CLI implementation DLL.
SQL_DRIVER_ODBC_VER	Character string	Identifies the version number of ODBC that the CLI/ODBC Driver supports. The DB2 CLI driver will return the value 2.1.
SQL_DRIVER_VER	Character string	Identifies the version number of the DB2 CLI driver being accessed. This information is returned in a string that has the format *mm.vv.rrrr*, where *mm* is the major

TABLE 14.2 Information Returned by the SQLGetInfo( ) Function *(Continued)*

InfoType code	Data type returned	Description
		version number, *vv* is the minor version number, and *rrrr* is the release number (e.g., 02.01.0000 would translate to major version 2, minor version 1, release 0).
SQL_EXPRESSIONS_IN_ORDERBY	Character string	Indicates whether or not the data source supports the direct specification of expressions in the ORDER BY clause list. The following values can be returned for this *InfoType* code: Y: The database server supports the direct specification of expressions in the ORDER BY clause list. N: The database server does not support the direct specification of expressions in the ORDER BY clause list.
SQL_FETCH_DIRECTION	32-bit mask	Identifies the cursor fetch directions supported by the data source. The following values can be returned by for this *InfoType* code: SQL_FD_FETCH_FIRST SQL_FD_FETCH_NEXT SQL_FD_FETCH_LAST SQL_FD_FETCH_PREV SQL_FD_FETCH_RESUME SQL_FD_FETCH SQL_FD_FETCH_ABSOLUTE_RELATIVE Note: The value SQL_FD_FETCH_BOOKMARK is also valid for ODBC, but this value is not recognized by DB2 CLI.
SQL_FILE_USAGE	16-bit integer	Values returned for this *InfoType* code are recognized only by ODBC; the value 0 is returned by DB2 CLI.
SQL_GETDATA_EXTENSIONS	32-bit mask	Indicates what extensions (if any) to the SQLGetData( ) function are supported. The following extensions are currently identified and supported by DB2 CLI: SQL_GD_ANY_COLUMN: The SQLGetData( ) function can be called for unbound columns that precede the last bound column. SQL_GD_ANY_ORDER: The SQLGetData( ) function can be called for columns in any order. Note: The values SQL_GD_BLOCK and SQL_GD_BOUND are also valid for ODBC; however, these values are not recognized by DB2 CLI.
SQL_GROUP_BY	16-bit integer	Indicates the degree of support for the GROUP BY clause that is provided by the data source. The following values can be returned for this *InfoType* code: SQL_GB_NOT_SUPPORTED: The GROUP BY clause is not supported. SQL_GB_GROUP_BY_EQUALS_SELECT: The GROUP BY clause must contain all nonaggregated columns in the SELECT list; it cannot contain columns that are not in the select list. SQL_GB_GROUP_BY_CONTAINS_SELECT: The GROUP BY clause must contain all nonaggregated columns in the SELECT list. It can also contain columns not in the select list. SQL_GB_NO_RELATION: There is no relationship between the columns in the GROUP BY clause and columns in the SELECT list.

TABLE 14.2 Information Returned by the SQLGetInfo( ) Function *(Continued)*

InfoType code	Data type returned	Description
SQL_IDENTIFIER_CASE	16-bit integer	Indicates the type of case sensitivity used in object identifier names (such as table names). The following values can be returned for this *InfoType* code: SQL_IC_UPPER: Identifier names are stored in uppercase in the system catalog. SQL_IC_LOWER: Identifier names are stored in lowercase in the system catalog. SQL_IC_SENSITIVE: Identifier names are case-sensitive and are stored in mixed case in the system catalog. SQL_IC_MIXED: Identifier names are not case-sensitive and are stored in mixed case in the system catalog. Note: Identifier names in IBM RDBMS databases are not case-sensitive.
SQL_IDENTIFIER_QUOTE_CHAR	Character string	Indicates the character to be used as the starting and ending delimiter of quoted identifiers in an SQL statement.
SQL_KEYWORDS	Character string	A comma-separated list of all keywords recognized by the data source and not in the ODBC list of reserved words.
SQL_LIKE_ESCAPE_CLAUSE	Character string	Identifies whether or not an escape character is supported by the data source for the metacharacters percent (%) and underscore (_) in a LIKE predicate. The following values can be returned for this *InfoType* code: Y: The data source supports an escape character for the percent and underscore metacharacters in a LIKE predicate. N: The data source does not support an escape character for the percent and underscore metacharacters in a LIKE predicate.
SQL_LOCK_TYPES	32-bit mask	Values returned for this *InfoType* code are recognized only by ODBC; the value 0 is returned by DB2 CLI.
SQL_MAX_BINARY_LITERAL_LEN	32-bit integer	Specifies the maximum length (number of hexadecimal characters, excluding the literal prefix and suffix returned by the SQLGetTypeInfo( ) function) that a binary literal in a SQL statement can be. If the value returned is 0, either there is no limit or the limit is unknown.
SQL_MAX_CHAR_LITERAL_LEN	32-bit integer	Specifies the maximum length (number of characters, excluding the literal prefix and suffix returned by the SQLGetTypeInfo( ) function) that a character literal in an SQL statement can be. If the value returned is 0, either there is no limit or the limit is unknown.
SQL_MAX_COLUMN_NAME_LEN	16-bit integer	Specifies the maximum length (in bytes) that a column name in the data source can be. If the value returned is 0, either there is no limit or the limit is unknown.
SQL_MAX_COLUMNS_IN_GROUP_BY	16-bit integer	Specifies the maximum number of columns that the data source supports in a GROUP BY clause. If the value returned is 0, either there is no limit or the limit is unknown.

TABLE 14.2 Information Returned by the SQLGetInfo( ) Function *(Continued)*

InfoType code	Data type returned	Description
SQL_MAX_COLUMNS_IN_INDEX	16-bit integer	Specifies the maximum number of columns that the data source supports in an index. If the value returned is 0, either there is no limit or the limit is unknown.
SQL_MAX_COLUMNS_IN_ORDER_BY	16-bit integer	Specifies the maximum number of columns that the data source supports in an ORDER BY clause. If the value returned is 0, either there is no limit or the limit is unknown.
SQL_MAX_COLUMNS_IN_SELECT	16-bit integer	Specifies the maximum number of columns that the data source supports in a select list. If the value returned is 0, either there is no limit or the limit is unknown.
SQL_MAX_COLUMNS_IN_TABLE	16-bit integer	Specifies the maximum number of columns that the data source supports in a base table. If the value returned is 0, either there is no limit or the limit is unknown.
SQL_MAX_CURSOR_NAME_LEN	16-bit integer	Specifies the maximum length (in bytes) that a cursor name in the data source can be. If the value returned is 0, either there is no limit or the limit is unknown.
SQL_MAX_INDEX_SIZE	32-bit integer	Specifies the maximum number of bytes that the data source allows for the combined columns of an index. If the value returned is 0, either there is no limit or the limit is unknown.
SQL_MAX_OWNER_NAME_LEN or SQL_MAX_SCHEMA_NAME_LEN	16-bit integer	Specifies the maximum length (in bytes) that a schema qualifier name in the data source can be. If the value returned is 0, either there is no limit or the limit is unknown.
SQL_MAX_PROCEDURE_NAME_LEN	16-bit integer	Specifies the maximum length (in bytes) that a procedure name in the data source can be. If the value returned is 0, either there is no limit or the limit is unknown.
SQL_MAX_QUALIFIER_NAME_LEN or SQL_MAX_CATALOG_NAME_LEN	16-bit integer	Specifies the maximum length (in bytes) that a catalog qualifier name (the first part of a three-part table name) in the data source can be. If the value returned is 0, either there is no limit or the limit is unknown.
SQL_MAX_ROW_SIZE	32-bit integer	Specifies the maximum length (in bytes) that a single row of data in a table, in the data source can be. If the value returned is 0, either there is no limit or the limit is unknown.
SQL_MAX_ROW_SIZE_INCLUDES_LONG	Character string	Indicates whether or not the maximum row size value returned for the SQL_MAX_ROW_SIZE *InfoType* code includes the length of all product-specific long string data types (SQL_LONGVARCHAR, SQL_LONGBINARY, etc.). The following values can be returned for this *InfoType* code: Y: The value returned by the SQL_MAX_ROW_SIZE *InfoType* code includes the length of product-specific long string data types. N: The value returned by the SQL_MAX_ROW_SIZE *InfoType* code does not includes the length of product-specific long string data types.
SQL_MAX_STATEMENT_LEN	32-bit integer	Specifies the maximum length (in bytes) an SQL statement string can be, including the number of white spaces in the statement. If the value returned is 0, either there is no limit or the limit is unknown.

TABLE 14.2 Information Returned by the SQLGetInfo( ) Function *(Continued)*

InfoType code	Data type returned	Description
SQL_MAX_TABLE_NAME_LEN	16-bit integer	Specifies the maximum length (in bytes) a table name in the data source can be. If the value returned is 0, either there is no limit or the limit is unknown.
SQL_MAX_TABLES_IN_SELECT	16-bit integer	Specifies the maximum number of table names that are allowed in a FROM clause of a SELECT statement by the data source. If the value returned is 0, either there is no limit or the limit is unknown.
SQL_MAX_USER_NAME_LEN	16-bit integer	Specifies the maximum size (in bytes) that a user name or identifier in the data source can be. If the value returned is 0, either there is no limit or the limit is unknown.
SQL_MULT_RESULT_SETS	Character string	Indicates whether or not the data source supports multiple result sets. The following values can be returned for this *InfoType* code: Y: The data source supports multiple result sets. N: The data source does not support multiple result sets.
SQL_MULTIPLE_ACTIVE_TXN	Character string	Indicates whether or not active transactions on multiple connections are allowed by the data source. The following values can be returned for this *InfoType* code: Y: Active transactions on multiple connections are allowed. N: Only one connection at a time can have an active transaction; active transactions on multiple connections are not allowed. DB2 CLI returns N for all coordinated distributed unit of work (CONNECT TYPE 2) connections (since the transaction or unit of work spans all connections), and returns Y for all other connections.
SQL_NEED_LONG_DATA_LEN	Character string	Values returned for this *InfoType* code are recognized only by ODBC 2.0; the value N is returned by DB2 CLI.
SQL_NON_NULLABLE_COLUMNS	16-bit integer	Indicates whether or not nonnullable columns are supported by the data source. The following values can be returned for this *InfoType* code: SQL_NNC_NON_NULL: Columns can be defined as NOT NULL. SQL_NNC_NULL: All columns must be nullable.
SQL_NULL_COLLATION	16-bit integer	Indicates where NULL values will be placed in a sorted list. The following values can be returned for this *InfoType* code: SQL_NC_HIGH: NULL values are sorted at the high end of the list. SQL_NC_LOW: NULL values are sorted at the low end of the list.
SQL_NUMERIC_FUNCTIONS	32-bit mask	Identifies the ODBC scalar numeric functions supported by the data source. These functions are intended to be used with the ODBC vendor escape sequence. The following values can be returned for this *InfoType* code:

TABLE 14.2 Information Returned by the SQLGetInfo( ) Function *(Continued)*

InfoType code	Data type returned	Description
		SQL_FN_NUM_ABS SQL_FN_NUM_ACOS SQL_FN_NUM_ASIN SQL_FN_NUM_ATAN SQL_FN_NUM_ATAN2 SQL_FN_NUM_CEILING SQL_FN_NUM_COS SQL_FN_NUM_COT SQL_FN_NUM_DEGREES SQL_FN_NUM_EXP SQL_FN_NUM_FLOOR SQL_FN_NUM_LOG SQL_FN_NUM_LOG10 SQL_FN_NUM_MOD SQL_FN_NUM_PI SQL_FN_NUM_POWER SQL_FN_NUM_RADIANS SQL_FN_NUM_RAND SQL_FN_NUM_ROUND SQL_FN_NUM_SIGN SQL_FN_NUM_SIN SQL_FN_NUM_SQRT SQL_FN_NUM_TAN SQL_FN_NUM_TRUNCATE
SQL_ODBC_API_CONFORMANCE	16-bit integer	Identifies the level of ODBC conformance provided by the data source. The following values can be returned for this *InfoType* code: SQL_OAC_NONE: No level is supported. SQL_OAC_LEVEL1: Level 1 is supported. SQL_OAC_LEVEL2: Level 2 is supported.
SQL_ODBC_SAG_CLI_CONFORMANCE	16-bit integer	Identifies the level of compliance to the functions of the SQL access group (SAG) CLI specification that is provided by the data source. The following values can be returned for this *InfoType* code: SQL_OSCC_NOT_COMPLIANT: The data source driver is not SAG-compliant. SQL_OSCC_COMPLIANT: The data source driver is SAG-compliant.
SQL_ODBC_SQL_CONFORMANCE	16-bit integer	Identifies the level of compliance to ODBC SQL grammar that is supported by the data source. The following values can be returned for this *InfoType* code: SQL_OSC_MINIMUM: Minimum ODBC SQL grammar support is provided. SQL_OSC_CORE: Core ODBC SQL grammar is support is provided. SQL_OSC_EXTENDED: Extended ODBC SQL grammar support is provided. For more information about these three types of ODBC SQL grammar, refer to the ODBC 2.0 Programmer's Reference and SDK Guide.
SQL_ODBC_SQL_OPT_IEF	Character string	Indicates whether or not the data source supports the integrity-enhanced facility (IEF) defined in the SQL89 and the X/Open XPG4 embedded SQL specifications. The following values can be returned for this *InfoType* code: Y: IEF is supported by the data source. N: IEF is not supported by the data source.
SQL_ODBC_VER	Character string	Identifies the version number of ODBC that the data source driver supports. Since DB2 CLI will supports ODBC 2.1, it will return the string 02.10.

TABLE 14.2 Information Returned by the SQLGetInfo( ) Function *(Continued)*

InfoType code	Data type returned	Description
SQL_OJ_CAPABILITIES	32-bit mask	Identifies the types of outer joins supported by the data source. The following values can be returned for this *InfoType* code: SQL_OJ_LEFT: Left outer join is supported. SQL_OJ_RIGHT: Right outer join is supported. SQL_OJ_FULL: Full outer join is supported. SQL_OJ_NESTED: Nested outer join is supported. SQL_OJ_ORDERED: The tables underlying the columns in an outer join ON clause do not need to be in the same order as the tables in the JOIN clause. SQL_OJ_INNER: The inner table of an outer join can also be an inner join. SQL_OJ_ALL_COMPARISONS: Any predicate can be used in the outer join ON clause. If this bit is not set, the equality (=) operator is the only valid comparison operator in the ON clause.
SQL_ORDER_BY_COLUMNS_IN_SELECT	Character string	Indicates whether or not columns in ORDER BY clauses must be in the select list of the query. Valid values for this *InfoType* code are: Y: Columns in ORDER BY clauses must be in the select list. N: Columns in ORDER BY clauses do not have to be in the select list. If this *InfoType* code is not supported by the connected data source, N will be returned.
SQL_OUTER_JOINS	Character string	Identifies how outer joins are supported by the data source. The following values can be returned for this *InfoType* code: N: Outer joins are not supported. Y: The data source supports two-table outer joins (except for nested outer joins), and the driver supports the ODBC outer join request syntax. P: The data source supports two-table outer joins (except for nested outer joins), and the driver supports the ODBC outer join request syntax. However, columns on the left-hand side of the comparison operator in the ON clause must come from the left-hand table in the outer join and columns on the right side of the comparison operator must come from the right-hand table. Also, the right-hand table of an outer join cannot be included in an inner join. F: The data source supports two-table outer joins (including nested outer joins), and the driver supports the ODBC outer join request syntax. If this *InfoType* code is not supported by the connected data source, an empty string will be returned.
SQL_OWNER_TERM or SQL_SCHEMA_TERM	Character string	Specifies the data source (database) vendor's name for a schema (owner name).

TABLE 14.2 Information Returned by the SQLGetInfo( ) Function *(Continued)*

InfoType code	Data type returned	Description
SQL_OWNER_USAGE	32-bit mask	Identifies the type of SQL statements that have schema (owner names) associated with them when they are executed. The following values can be returned for this *InfoType* code: SQL_OU_DML_STATEMENTS: Schemas are supported in all data manipulation language (DML) statements. SQL_OU_PROCEDURE_INVOCATION: Schemas are supported in procedure invocation statements. SQL_OU_TABLE_DEFINITION: Schemas are supported in all table definition statements. SQL_OU_INDEX_DEFINITION: Schemas are supported in all index definition statements. SQL_OU_PRIVILEGE_DEFINITION: Schemas are supported in all privilege definition statements (e.g., grant and revoke SQL statements).
SQL_POS_OPERATIONS	32-bit mask	Values returned for this *InfoType* code are recognized only by ODBC; the value 0 is returned by DB2 CLI.
SQL_POSITIONED_STATEMENTS	32-bit mask	Identifies the degree of support provided by the data source for positioned UPDATE and positioned DELETE statements. The following values can be returned for this *InfoType* code: SQL_PS_POSITIONED_UPDATE: Positioned UPDATE support is provided. SQL_PS_POSITIONED_DELETE: Positioned DELETE support is provided. SQL_PS_SELECT_FOR_UPDATE: Indicates that the data source requires the FOR UPDATE clause to be specified with a query expression in order for a column to be updateable via the cursor.
SQL_PROCEDURE_TERM	Character string	Identifies the term or name a data source (database) vendor uses for a stored procedure. DB2 CLI will return the value of stored procedure.
SQL_PROCEDURES	Character string	Indicates whether or not the data source supports stored procedures. The following values can be returned for this *InfoType* code: Y: The data source supports stored procedures. N: The data source does not support stored procedures. Note: DB2 CLI supports the ODBC procedure invocation syntax.
SQL_QUALIFIER_LOCATION	16-bit integer	Indicates the position of the qualifier in a qualified table name as it is stored in the data source. DB2 CLI will return the value SQL_QL_START.
SQL_QUALIFIER_NAME_SEPARATOR or SQL_CATALOG_NAME_SEPARATOR	Character string	Identifies the character or characters used as a separator between a catalog name and the qualified name element that follows it.
SQL_QUALIFIER_TERM or SQL_CATALOG_TERM	Character string	Identifies the data source (database) vendor's terminology for a qualifier (the name that the vendor

TABLE 14.2 Information Returned by the SQLGetInfo( ) Function *(Continued)*

InfoType code	Data type returned	Description
		uses for the high-order part of a three-part name). Since DB2 CLI does not support three-part names, a zero-length string is returned. Note: For non-ODBC applications, use the SQL_CATALOG_TERM *InfoType* code instead of SQL_QUALIFIER_NAME.
SQL_QUALIFIER_USAGE	32-bit mask	Identifies the type of SQL statements that have qualifiers associated with them when they are executed. The following values can be returned for this *InfoType* code: SQL_QU_DML_STATEMENTS: Schemas are supported in all data manipulation language (DML) statements. SQL_QU_PROCEDURE_INVOCATION: Schemas are supported in procedure invocation statements. SQL_QU_TABLE_DEFINITION: Schemas are supported in all table definition statements. SQL_QU_INDEX_DEFINITION: Schemas are supported in all index definition statements. SQL_QU_PRIVILEGE_DEFINITION: Schemas are supported in all privilege definition statements (e.g., grant and revoke SQL statements).
SQL_QUOTED_IDENTIFIER_CASE	16-bit integer	Indicates the type of case sensitivity used in quoted identifier names (such as table names). The following values can be returned for this *InfoType* code: SQL_IC_UPPER: Quoted identifiers in SQL are case-insensitive and stored in uppercase in the system catalog. SQL_IC_LOWER: Quoted identifiers in SQL are case-insensitive and are stored in lowercase in the system catalog. SQL_IC_SENSITIVE: Quoted identifiers (delimited identifiers) in SQL are case-sensitive and are stored in mixed case in the system catalog. SQL_IC_MIXED: Quoted identifiers in SQL are case-insensitive and are stored in mixed case in the system catalog. Contrast this with the SQL_IDENTIFIER_CASE *InfoType* code, which determines how unquoted identifiers are stored in the system catalog.
SQL_ROW_UPDATES	Character string	Indicates whether or not changes are detected in rows between multiple fetches of the same rows by the data source. The following values can be returned for this *InfoType* code: Y: Changes are detected in rows between multiple fetches of the same rows. N: Changes are not detected in rows between multiple fetches of the same rows.
SQL_SCROLL_CONCURRENCY	32-bit mask	Identifies the concurrency options supported for a cursor by the data source. The following values can be returned for this *InfoType* code:

TABLE 14.2 Information Returned by the SQLGetInfo( ) Function *(Continued)*

InfoType code	Data type returned	Description
		SQL_SCCO_READ_ONLY: Cursors are read-only. No updates are allowed. SQL_SCCO_LOCK: Cursors use the lowest level of locking sufficient to ensure that a row can be updated. SQL_SCCO_TIMESTAMP: Cursors use optimistic concurrency control by comparing timestamp values. SQL_SCCO_VALUES: Cursors use optimistic concurrency control by comparing values. DB2 CLI returns the value SQL_SCCO_LOCK, indicating that the lowest level of locking sufficient to ensure the row can be updated is used.
SQL_SCROLL_OPTIONS	32-bit mask	Identifies the scroll options supported for scrollable cursors. The following values can be returned for this *InfoType* code: SQL_SO_FORWARD_ONLY: The cursor scrolls only forward. SQL_SO_KEYSET_DRIVEN: The driver saves and uses the keys for every row in the result data set. SQL_SO_STATIC: The data in the result data set is static. SQL_SO_DYNAMIC: The driver keeps the keys for every row in the rowset (the keyset size is the same as the rowset size). SQL_SO_MIXED: The driver keeps the keys for every row in the rowset (the keyset size is greater than the rowset size). DB2 CLI returns the value SQL_SO_FORWARD _ONLY, indicating that the cursor can be scrolled only forward.
SQL_SEARCH_PATTERN_ESCAPE	Character string	Identifies what the data source supports as an escape character, which permits the use of the pattern match metacharacters percent (%) and underscore (_) as valid characters in search patterns. If this value is a NULL string, the data source does not support search-pattern characters.
SQL_SERVER_NAME	Character string	Identifies the actual name of the data source specific server name, not an alias. (Some RDBMSs provide a different name with a CONNECT statement than the real server name of the database.)
SQL_SPECIAL_CHARACTERS	Character string	Identifies all characters that the data source allows in nondelimited identifiers, in addition to a-z, A-Z, 0-9, and _.
SQL_STATIC_SENSITIVITY	32-bit mask	Indicates whether or not changes made by an application with a positioned UPDATE or a positioned DELETE statement can be detected by that application. The following values can be returned for this *InfoType* code: SQL_SS_ADDITIONS: Added rows are visible to the cursor; the cursor can scroll to these rows. All DB2 databases see added rows.

TABLE 14.2 Information Returned by the SQLGetInfo( ) Function *(Continued)*

InfoType code	Data type returned	Description
		SQL_SS_DELETIONS: Deleted rows are no longer available to the cursor and do not leave a hole in the result data set; after the cursor scrolls from a deleted row, it cannot return to that row. SQL_SS_UPDATES: Updates to rows are visible to the cursor; if the cursor scrolls from and returns to an updated row, the data returned by the cursor is the updated data, not the original data.
SQL_STRING_FUNCTIONS	32-bit mask	Identifies the string handling functions supported by the data source. The following values can be returned for this *InfoType* code: SQL_FN_STR_ASCII SQL_FN_STR_CHAR SQL_FN_STR_CONCAT SQL_FN_STR_DIFFERENCE SQL_FN_STR_NSERT SQL_FN_STR_LCASE SQL_FN_STR_LEFT SQL_FN_STR_LENGTH SQL_FN_STR_LOCATE SQL_FN_STR_LOCATE_2 SQL_FN_STR_LTRIM SQL_FN_STR_REPEAT SQL_FN_STR_REPLACE SQL_FN_STR_RIGHT SQL_FN_STR_RTRIM SQL_FN_STR_SOUNDEX SQL_FN_STR_SPACE SQL_FN_STR_SUBSTRING SQL_FN_STR_UCASE If an application can call the LOCATE scalar function with the string1, string2, and start arguments, the SQL_FN_STR_LOCATE bitmask is returned. If an application can call the LOCATE scalar function with only the string1 and string2 arguments, the SQL_FN _STR_LOCATE_2 bitmask is returned. If the LOCATE scalar function is fully supported, both bitmasks are returned.
SQL_SUBQUERIES	32-bit mask	Identifies the predicates used by the data source to support subqueries. The following values can be returned for this *InfoType* code: SQL_SQ_COMPARISION: The comparison predicate is supported. SQL_SQ_EXISTS: The EXISTS predicate is supported. SQL_SQ_IN: The IN predicate is supported. SQL_SCL_QUANTIFIED: Predicates containing a quantification scalar function is supported. SQL_SQ_CORRELATE_SUBQUERIES: All predicates are supported.
SQL_SYSTEM_FUNCTIONS	32-bit mask	Identifies the scalar system functions supported by the data source. The following values can be returned for this *InfoType* code: SQL_FN_SYS_DBNAME, SQL_FN_SYS_IFNULL, and SQL_FN_SYS_USERNAME. Note: These functions are intended to be used with the escape sequence in ODBC.
SQL_TABLE_TERM	Character string	Identifies the data source vendors terminology for a table name.

TABLE 14.2 Information Returned by the SQLGetInfo( ) Function *(Continued)*

InfoType code	Data type returned	Description
SQL_TIMEDATE_ADD_INTERVALS	32-bit mask	Indicates whether or not the special ODBC system function TIMESTAMPADD is supported by the data source and, if it is, which time intervals are supported. The following values can be returned for this *InfoType* code: SQL_FN_TSI_FRAC_SECOND SQL_FN_TSI_SECOND SQL_FN_TSI_MINUTE SQL_FN_TSI_HOUR SQL_FN_TSI_DAY SQL_FN_TSI_WEEK SQL_FN_TSI_MONTH SQL_FN_TSI_QUARTER SQL_FN_TSI_YEAR
SQL_TIMEDATE_DIFF_INTERVALS	32-bit mask	Indicates whether or not the special ODBC system function TIMESTAMPDIFF is supported by the data source and, if it is, which time intervals are supported. The following values can be returned for this *InfoType* code: SQL_FN_TSI_FRAC_SECOND SQL_FN_TSI_SECOND SQL_FN_TSI_MINUTE SQL_FN_TSI_HOUR SQL_FN_TSI_DAY SQL_FN_TSI_WEEK SQL_FN_TSI_MONTH SQL_FN_TSI_QUARTER SQL_FN_TSI_YEAR
SQL_TIMEDATE_FUNCTIONS	32-bit mask	Identifies the date and time functions that are supported by the data source. The following values can be returned for this *InfoType* code: SQL_FN_TD_CURDATE SQL_FN_TD_CURTIME SQL_FN_TD_DAYNAME SQL_FN_TD_DAYOFMONTH SQL_FN_TD_DAYOFWEEK SQL_FN_TD_DAYOFYEAR SQL_FN_TD_HOUR SQL_FN_TD_MINUTE SQL_FN_TD_MONTH SQL_FN_TD_MONTHNAME SQL_FN_TD_NOW SQL_FN_TD_QUARTER SQL_FN_TD_SECOND SQL_FN_TD_TIMESTAMPADD SQL_FN_TD_TIMESTAMPDIFF SQL_FN_TD_WEEK SQL_FN_TD_YEAR Note: These functions are intended to be used with the escape sequence in ODBC.
SQL_TXN_CAPABLE	16-bit integer	Identifies the transaction support levels that are supported by the data source. The following values can be returned for this *InfoType* code: SQL_TC_NONE: Transactions not supported. SQL_TC_DML: Transactions can contain only DML statements (SELECT, INSERT, UPDATE, DELETE, etc.). Any DDL statement (CREATE TABLE, DROP INDEX, etc.) encountered in the transaction will cause an error to occur. SQL_TC_DDL_COMMIT: Transactions can contain only DML statements. Any DDL statement encountered in the transaction will cause the transaction to be committed. SQL_TC_DDL_IGNORE: Transactions can contain only DML statements. All DDL statements encountered in the transaction are ignored.

TABLE 14.2 Information Returned by the SQLGetInfo( ) Function *(Continued)*

InfoType code	Data type returned	Description
		SQL_TC_ALL: Transactions can contain both DDL and DML statements, in any order.
SQL_TXN_ISOLATION_OPTION	32-bit mask	Identifies the transaction isolation levels supported by the data source. The following scenarios illustrate the terms used to describe transaction isolation levels:
		Dirty read: Transaction 1 changes a row, and transaction 2 reads the changed row before transaction 1 commits the change. If transaction 1 rolls back the change, transaction 2 will have read a row considered to have never existed.
		Nonrepeatable read: Transaction 1 reads a row, and transaction 2 updates or deletes that row and commits the change. If transaction 1 attempts to reread the row, it will retrieve different row values (if the row was updated) or it will discover that the row no longer exists (if the row was deleted).
		Phantom: Transaction 1 reads a set of rows that satisfy some search criteria, and transaction 2 inserts a row that matches the search criteria. If transaction 1 reexecutes the query statement that read the rows, it will receive a different set of rows.
		If the data source supports transaction processing, one of the following values will be returned for this *InfoType* code:
		SQL_TXN_READ_UNCOMMITTED: Changes are immediately perceived by all transactions (dirty reads, nonrepeatable reads, and phantoms are possible). This is equivalent to IBM's uncommitted read (UR) isolation level.
		SQL_TXN_READ_COMMITTED: The row read by transaction 1 can be altered and committed by transaction 2 (dirty reads are not possible; nonrepeatable reads and phantoms are possible). This is equivalent to IBM's cursor stability (CS) isolation level.
		SQL_TXN_REPEATABLE_READ: A transaction can add or remove rows matching the search condition of a pending transaction (dirty reads and nonrepeatable reads are not possible; phantoms are possible). This is equivalent to IBM's read stability (RS) isolation level.
		SQL_TXN_SERIALIZABLE: Data affected by a pending transaction is not available to other transactions (dirty reads, nonrepeatable reads, and phantoms are not possible). This is equivalent to IBM's repeatable read (RR) isolation level.
		SQL_TXN_VERSIONING: Not applicable to IBM RDBMS databases.
		SQL_TXN_NOCOMMIT: Any changes are effectively committed at the end of a successful operation; no explicit commit or rollback is allowed. This is a DB2 for OS/400 isolation level.

TABLE 14.2 Information Returned by the SQLGetInfo( ) Function *(Continued)*

InfoType code	Data type returned	Description
SQL_UNION	32-bit mask	Indicates if and how the data source supports the UNION operator. The following values can be returned for this *InfoType* code: SQL_U_UNION: Supports the UNION clause SQL_U_UNION_ALL: Supports the ALL keyword in the UNION clause. If SQL_UNION_ALL is set, so is SQL_U_UNION.
SQL_USER_NAME	Character string	Specifies the user name used in a particular data source. This identifier should be specified with the SQLConnect( ) function call.

Adapted from IBM's Database 2 Call Level Interface Guide and Reference, Table 77, pages 248 to 260.

Restrictions There are no restrictions associated with this function call.

See Also SQLGetTypeInfo( )

Examples The following C program illustrates how the SQLGetInfo( ) function obtains information about a specific data source:

```
#include <stdio.h>
#include <stdlib.h>
#include <sqlcli1.h>

int main()
{
    /* Declare The Local Memory Variables */
    SQLRETURN     rc = SQL_SUCCESS;
    SQLHENV       EnvHandle;
    SQLHDBC       DSCHandle;
    SQLCHAR       Buffer[255];
    SQLSMALLINT   InfoSize;

    /* Allocate An Environment Handle */
    rc = SQLAllocEnv(&EnvHandle);

    /* Allocate A Connection Handle */
    rc = SQLAllocConnect(EnvHandle, &DSCHandle);

    /* Connect To The SAMPLE Database */
    rc = SQLConnect(DSCHandle, "SAMPLE", SQL_NTS, "etpdd6z", SQL_NTS,
                    "sanders", SQL_NTS);

    /* Obtain And Display Information About The Current Connection */
    rc = SQLGetInfo(DSCHandle, SQL_DATABASE_NAME, (SQLPOINTER)
                    &Buffer, sizeof(Buffer), &InfoSize);
    if (rc == SQL_SUCCESS)
        printf("Database Name : %s\n", Buffer);

    rc = SQLGetInfo(DSCHandle, SQL_DBMS_NAME, (SQLPOINTER) &Buffer,
                    sizeof(Buffer), &InfoSize);
    if (rc == SQL_SUCCESS)
```

```
        printf("DBMS Name     : %s\n", Buffer);

    rc = SQLGetInfo(DSCHandle, SQL_DRIVER_NAME, (SQLPOINTER) &Buffer,
                    sizeof(Buffer), &InfoSize);
    if (rc == SQL_SUCCESS)
        printf("Driver Name   : %s\n", Buffer);

    /* Disconnect From The SAMPLE Database */
    SQLDisconnect(DSCHandle);

    /* Free The Connection Handle */
    if (DSCHandle != NULL)
        SQLFreeConnect(DSCHandle);

    /* Free The Environment Handle */
    if (EnvHandle != NULL)
        SQLFreeEnv(EnvHandle);

    /* Return To The Operating System */
    return(rc);
}
```

The following C++ program illustrates how the SQLGetInfo( ) function can be used by class methods to obtain information about a specific data source:

```
#include <iostream.h>
#include <string.h>
#include <sqlcli1.h>

/* Define The CLI Class */
class CLI
{
    /* Declare The Private Attribute Variables */
    private:
       SQLHENV      EnvHandle;
       SQLHDBC      DSCHandle;
       SQLCHAR      Buffer[255];
       SQLSMALLINT  InfoSize;

    /* Declare The Public Attribute Variables */
    public:
       SQLRETURN  rc;

    /* Declare The Member Function Prototypes */
    CLI();                                  // Constructor
    ~CLI();                                 // Destructor
    SQLRETURN Connect();
    void      ShowConnectionInfo();
    SQLRETURN Disconnect();
} ;

/* Define The Class Constructor */
CLI::CLI()
{
    /* Initialize The Return Code Variable */
    rc = SQL_SUCCESS;

    /* Allocate An Environment Handle */
    rc = SQLAllocEnv(&EnvHandle);
```

```
    /* Allocate A Connection Handle */
    rc = SQLAllocConnect(EnvHandle, &DSCHandle);
}

/* Define The Class Destructor */
CLI::~CLI()
{
    /* Free The Connection Handle */
    if (DSCHandle != NULL)
        SQLFreeConnect(DSCHandle);

    /* Free The Environment Handle */
    if (EnvHandle != NULL)
        SQLFreeEnv(EnvHandle);
}

/* Define The Connect() Member Function */
SQLRETURN CLI::Connect()
{
    /* Connect To The SAMPLE Database */
    rc = SQLConnect(DSCHandle, (SQLCHAR *) "SAMPLE", SQL_NTS,
                    (SQLCHAR *) "etpdd6z", SQL_NTS,
                    (SQLCHAR *) "sanders", SQL_NTS);

    /* Return The CLI Function Return Code */
    return(rc);
}

/* Define The Disconnect() Member Function */
SQLRETURN CLI::Disconnect(void)
{
    /* Disconnect From The Database */
    rc = SQLDisconnect(DSCHandle);

    /* Return The CLI Function Return Code */
    return(rc);
}

/* Define The ShowConnectionInfo() Member Function */
void CLI::ShowConnectionInfo(void)
{
    /* Obtain And Display Information About The Current Connection */
    rc = SQLGetInfo(DSCHandle, SQL_DATABASE_NAME, (SQLPOINTER)
                    &Buffer, sizeof(Buffer), &InfoSize);
    if (rc == SQL_SUCCESS)
        cout << "Database Name : " << Buffer << endl;
    rc = SQLGetInfo(DSCHandle, SQL_DBMS_NAME, (SQLPOINTER) &Buffer,
                    sizeof(Buffer), &InfoSize);
    if (rc == SQL_SUCCESS)
        cout << "DBMS Name     : " << Buffer << endl;

    rc = SQLGetInfo(DSCHandle, SQL_DRIVER_NAME, (SQLPOINTER) &Buffer,
                    sizeof(Buffer), &InfoSize);
    if (rc == SQL_SUCCESS)
        cout << "Driver Name   : " << Buffer << endl;

    return;
}

int main()
```

```
{
    /* Declare The Local Memory Variables */
    SQLRETURN  rc = SQL_SUCCESS;

    /* Create An Instance Of The CLI Class */
    CLI Sample;

    /* Connect To The SAMPLE Database */
    if ((rc = Sample.Connect()) != SQL_SUCCESS)
        return(rc);

    /* Obtain And Display Information About The Current Connection */
    Sample.ShowConnectionInfo();

    /* Disconnect From The SAMPLE Database */
    Sample.Disconnect();

    /* Return To The Operating System */
    return(rc):
}
```

SQLGetFunctions

Purpose The SQLGetFunctions( ) function allows you to determine whether or not a specific CLI/ODBC function is supported by the data source to which the application is currently connected.

Syntax

```
SQLRETURN  SQLGetFunctions (SQLHDBC            DSCHandle,
                            SQLUSMALLINT       Function,
                            SQLUSMALLINT FAR   *Supported);
```

Parameters

DSCHandle The data source connection handle where the address of the data source connection information buffer is stored.

Function A value that identifies the CLI/ODBC function of interest. This parameter can contain any of the following values:

- SQL_API_SQLALLOCCONNECT
- SQL_API_SQLALLOCENV
- SQL_API_SQLALLOCSTMT
- SQL_API_SQLBINDCOL
- SQL_API_SQLBINDFILETOCOL
- SQL_API_SQLBINDFILETOPARAM
- SQL_API_SQLBINDPARAMETER
- SQL_API_SQLBROWSECONNECT
- SQL_API_SQLCANCEL
- SQL_API_SQLCOLATTRIBUTES
- SQL_API_SQLCOLUMNPRIVILEGES
- SQL_API_SQLCOLUMNS
- SQL_API_SQLCONNECT
- SQL_API_SQLDATASOURCES
- SQL_API_SQLBESCRIBECOL

- SQL_API_SQLDESCRIBEPARAM
- SQL_API_SQLDISCONNECT
- SQL_API_SQLDRIVERCONNECT
- SQL_API_SQLERROR
- SQL_API_SQLEXECDIRECT
- SQL_API_SQLEXECUTE
- SQL_API_SQLEXTENDEDFETCH
- SQL_API_SQLFETCH
- SQL_API_SQLFOREIGNKEYS
- SQL_API_SQLFREECONNECT
- SQL_API_SQLFREEENV
- SQL_API_SQLFREESTMT
- SQL_API_SQLGETCONNECTOPTION
- SQL_API_SQLGETCURSORNAME
- SQL_API_SQLGETDATA
- SQL_API_SQLGETENVATTR
- SQL_API_SQLGETFUNCTIONS
- SQL_API_SQLGETINFO
- SQL_API_SQLGETLENGTH
- SQL_API_SQLGETPOSITION
- SQL_API_SQLSQLGETSQLCA
- SQL_API_SQLGETSTMTOPTION
- SQL_API_SQLGETSUBSTRING
- SQL_API_SQLGETTYPEINFO
- SQL_API_SQLMORERESULTS
- SQL_API_SQLNATIVESQL
- SQL_API_SQLNUMPARAMS
- SQL_API_SQLNUMRESULTCOLS
- SQL_API_SQLPARAMDATA
- SQL_API_SQLPARAMOPTIONS
- SQL_API_SQLPREPARE
- SQL_API_SQLPRIMARYKEYS
- SQL_API_SQLPROCEDURECOLUMNS
- SQL_API_SQLPROCEDURES
- SQL_API_SQLPUTDATA
- SQL_API_SQLROWCOUNT
- SQL_API_SQLSETCOLATTRIBUTES
- SQL_API_SQLSETCONNECTION
- SQL_API_SQLSETCONNECTOPTION
- SQL_API_SQLSETCURSORNAME
- SQL_API_SQLSETENVATTR
- SQL_API_SQLSETPARAM
- SQL_API_SQLSETPOS

- SQL_API_SQLSETSCROLLOPTIONS
- SQL_API_SQLSETSTMTOPTION
- SQL_API_SQLSPECIALCOLUMNS
- SQL_API_SQLSTATISTICS
- SQL_API_SQLTABLEPRIVILEGES
- SQL_API_SQLTABLES
- SQL_API_TRANSACT
- SQL_API_ALL_FUNCTIONS

Supported A pointer to a location in memory where this function is to store the value SQL_TRUE or SQL_FALSE, depending on whether or not the specified function is supported by the connected data source.

Includes

```
#include <sqlcli1.h>
```

Description

The SQLGetFunctions( ) function determines whether or not a specific CLI/ODBC function is supported by the data source to which the application is currently connected. This information allows an application to adapt to varying levels of CLI/ODBC function support as it connects to and executes against various data sources.

Specifications

DB2 CLI 2.1, ODBC 1.0, X/OPEN CLI, ISO CLI

Return Codes

SQL_SUCCESS, SQL_INVALID_HANDLE, SQL_ERROR

SQLSTATEs

40003, **08**S01, **58**004, **S1**001, **S1**009, **S1**010, **S1**013

Comments

- If the *Function* parameter is set to SQL_API_ALL_FUNCTIONS, then the *Supported* parameter must point to a SQLSMALLINT array of 100 elements. This array, once populated, can be indexed by the *Function* values that are used to identify many of the functions. Some elements of this array will be unused and other elements are reserved. Because some *Function* values are greater than 100, you cannot use this method to obtain a list of all available functions because functions whose value is greater than 100 will not be included in the list. Therefore, the SQLGetFunction( ) function must be explicitly called for all *Function* values greater than or equal to 100. The complete set of *Function* values are defined in **sqlcli1.h**.
- The large object (LOB) support functions—SQLGetLength( ), SQLGetPosition( ), SQLGetSubString( ), SQLBindFileToCol( ), and SQLBindFileToParam( )—are not supported when you are connected to DB2/2 or DB2/6000 version 1.1, or other IBM RDBMSs that do not support LOB data types.

Prerequisites

A connection to a data source (database) must exist before this function is called.

Restrictions

There are no restrictions associated with this function call.

Examples

The following C program illustrates how to use the SQLGetFunctions( ) function to determine whether or not a specific CLI function is supported by the current data source:

```
#include <stdio.h>
#include <stdlib.h>
#include <sqlcli1.h>

int main()
```

```
{
    /* Declare The Local Memory Variables */
    SQLRETURN     rc = SQL_SUCCESS;
    SQLHENV       EnvHandle;
    SQLHDBC       DSCHandle;
    SQLUSMALLINT  Supported;

    /* Allocate An Environment Handle */
    rc = SQLAllocEnv(&EnvHandle);

    /* Allocate A Connection Handle */
    rc = SQLAllocConnect(EnvHandle, &DSCHandle);

    /* Connect To The SAMPLE Database */
    rc = SQLConnect(DSCHandle, "SAMPLE", SQL_NTS, "etpdd6z", SQL_NTS,
                    "sanders", SQL_NTS);

    /* Determine Whether Or Not The Current Data Source Supports */
    /* The SQLGetTypeInfo() Function                             */
    rc = SQLGetFunctions(DSCHandle, SQL_API_SQLGETTYPEINFO,
                         &Supported);
    if (rc == SQL_SUCCESS)
        {
        printf("The CLI function SQLGetTypeInfo() is ");
        if (Supported == TRUE)
            printf("supported by the current data source.\n");
        else
            printf("not supported by the current data source.\n");
        }

    /* Disconnect From The SAMPLE Database */
    SQLDisconnect(DSCHandle);

    /* Free The Connection Handle */
    if (DSCHandle != NULL)
        SQLFreeConnect(DSCHandle);

    /* Free The Environment Handle */
    if (EnvHandle != NULL)
        SQLFreeEnv(EnvHandle);

    /* Return To The Operating System */
    return(rc);
}
```

The following C++ program illustrates how the SQLGetFunctions( ) function can be used by class methods to determine whether or not a specific CLI function is supported by the current data source:

```
#include <iostream.h>
#include <string.h>
#include <sqlcli1.h>

/* Define The CLI Class */
class CLI
{
    /* Declare The Private Attribute Variables */
    private:
       SQLHENV       EnvHandle;
       SQLHDBC       DSCHandle;
       SQLUSMALLINT  Supported;
```

```
    /* Declare The Public Attribute Variables */
    public:
       SQLRETURN  rc;

    /* Declare The Member Function Prototypes */
    CLI();                                  // Constructor
    ~CLI();                                 // Destructor
    SQLRETURN Connect();
    SQLRETURN CheckFunction();
    SQLRETURN Disconnect();
} ;

/* Define The Class Constructor */
CLI::CLI()
{
    /* Initialize The Return Code Variable */
    rc = SQL_SUCCESS;

    /* Allocate An Environment Handle */
    rc = SQLAllocEnv(&EnvHandle);

    /* Allocate A Connection Handle */
    rc = SQLAllocConnect(EnvHandle, &DSCHandle);
}

/* Define The Class Destructor */
CLI::~CLI()
{
    /* Free The Connection Handle */
    if (DSCHandle != NULL)
        SQLFreeConnect(DSCHandle);

    /* Free The Environment Handle */
    if (EnvHandle != NULL)
        SQLFreeEnv(EnvHandle);
}

/* Define The Connect() Member Function */
SQLRETURN CLI::Connect()
{
    /* Connect To The SAMPLE Database */
    rc = SQLConnect(DSCHandle, (SQLCHAR *) "SAMPLE", SQL_NTS,
                    (SQLCHAR *) "etpdd6z", SQL_NTS,
                    (SQLCHAR *) "sanders", SQL_NTS);

    /* Return The CLI Function Return Code */
    return(rc);
}

/* Define The Disconnect() Member Function */
SQLRETURN CLI::Disconnect(void)
{
    /* Disconnect From The Database */
    rc = SQLDisconnect(DSCHandle);

    /* Return The CLI Function Return Code */
    return(rc);
}

/* Define The CheckFunction() Member Function */
SQLRETURN CLI::CheckFunction(void)
```

```
{
    /* Determine Whether Or Not The Current Data Source Supports */
    /* The SQLGetTypeInfo() Function                              */
    rc = SQLGetFunctions(DSCHandle, SQL_API_SQLGETTYPEINFO,
                         &Supported);
    if (rc == SQL_SUCCESS)
        {
        cout << "The CLI function SQLGetTypeInfo() is ";
        if (Supported == TRUE)
            cout << "supported by the current data source.";
        else
            cout << "not supported by the current data source.";
        cout << endl;
        }

    /* Return The CLI Function Return Code */
    return(rc);
}

int main()
{
    /* Declare The Local Memory Variables */
    SQLRETURN  rc = SQL_SUCCESS;

    /* Create An Instance Of The CLI Class */
    CLI Sample;

    /* Connect To The SAMPLE Database */
    if ((rc = Sample.Connect()) != SQL_SUCCESS)
        return(rc);

    /* Determine Whether Or Not The Current Data Source Supports */
    /* The SQLGetTypeInfo() Function                              */
    Sample.CheckFunction();

    /* Disconnect From The SAMPLE Database */
    Sample.Disconnect();

    /* Return To The Operating System */
    return(rc);
}
```

SQLGetTypeInfo

Purpose The SQLGetTypeInfo( ) function retrieves information about the data types supported by the data source (database) to which the application is currently connected.

Syntax

```
SQLRETURN  SQLGetTypeInfo (SQLHSTMT    StmtHandle,
                           SQLSMALLINT SQLDataType);
```

Parameters

StmtHandle The statement handle where the address of the SQL statement buffer is stored.

SQLDataType The SQL data type for which information is to be retrieved. This parameter can contain any of the following values:

- SQL_ALL_TYPES
- SQL_SMALLINT

- SQL_INTEGER
- SQL_NUMERIC
- SQL_DECIMAL
- SQL_REAL
- SQL_FLOAT
- SQL_DOUBLE
- SQL_CHAR
- SQL_VARCHAR
- SQL_LONGVARCHAR
- SQL_BLOB
- SQL_CLOB
- SQL_DBCLOB
- SQL_BINARY
- SQL_VARBINARY
- SQL_LONGVARBINARY
- SQL_GRAPHIC
- SQL_VARGRAPHIC
- SQL_LONGVARGRAPHIC
- SQL_DATE
- SQL_TIME
- SQL_TIMESTAMP

Includes

```
#include <sqlcli1.h>
```

Description The SQLGetTypeInfo( ) function retrieves information about the data types supported by the data source to which the application is currently connected. The information returned by this function is placed in a SQL result data set, and can be processed with the same functions used to process a result data set generated by a query. Table 14.3 describes this result data set.

TABLE 14.3 Result Data Set Returned by SQLGetTypeInfo( )

Column number	Column name	Data type	Description
1	TYPE_NAME	VARCHAR(128) NOT NULL	Character representation of the SQL data type name (for example, INTEGER, CHAR, VARCHAR, BLOB, and DATE).
2	DATA_TYPE	SMALLINT NOT NULL	SQL data type define values (for example, SQL_INTEGER, SQL_CHAR, SQL_VARCHAR, SQL_BLOB, and SQL_DATE).
3	COLUMN_SIZE	INTEGER	For numeric data types, this is the total number of digits. For character or binary string data types, this is the size of the string (string length) in bytes. For date, time, and timestamp data types, this is the total number of characters required to

TABLE 14.3 Result Data Set Returned by SQLGetTypeInfo( ) *(Continued)*

Column number	Column name	Data type	Description
			display the value when it is converted to a character string. For graphic (DBCS) data types, this is the size of the graphic string (string length) in double-byte characters.
4	LITERAL_PREFIX	VARCHAR(128)	One or more characters that DB2 recognizes as a prefix for a literal of this data type. This column is set to NULL for data types where a literal prefix is not applicable.
6	LITERAL_SUFFIX	VARCHAR(128)	One or more characters that DB2 recognizes as a suffix for a literal of this data type (FOR BIT DATA, NOT NULL, etc.). This column is set to NULL for data types where a literal suffix is not applicable.
7	CREATE_PARAMS	VARCHAR(128)	A list of keywords, separated by commas, corresponding to each parameter an application can specify in parentheses when using the name in the TYPE_NAME column as a data type in SQL (LENGTH, PRECISION, SCALE, etc.). The keywords appear in the list in the order required by the SQL syntax. This column is set to NULL for data types where one or more keywords are not applicable (such as INTEGER). Note: The intent of CREATE_PARAMS is to enable an application to customize the interface for a data definition language (DDL) builder. An application using this column should expect to to be able to determine only the number of arguments required to define the data type.
8	NULLABLE	SMALLINT NOT NULL	Indicates whether or not the data type accepts a NULL value. Valid values for this column are: SQL_NO_NULLS: The data type does not accept NULL values. SQL_NULLABLE: The data type accepts NULL values.
9	CASE_SENSITIVE	SMALLINT NOT NULL	Indicates whether or not the data type can be treated as case-sensitive for collation purposes. Valid values for this column are SQL_TRUE and SQL_FALSE.
10	SEARCHABLE	SMALLINT NOT NULL	Indicates how the data type is used in a WHERE clause. Valid values for this column are: SQL_SEARCHABLE: The data type can be used with any comparison operators in a WHERE clause. SQL_LIKE_ONLY: The data type can be used only in a WHERE clause LIKE predicate.

TABLE 14.3 Result Data Set Returned by SQLGetTypeInfo( ) *(Continued)*

Column number	Column name	Data type	Description
			SQL_ALL_EXCEPT_LIKE: The data type can be used with all comparison operators in a WHERE clause except a LIKE predicate. SQL_UNSEARCHABLE: The data type cannot be used in a WHERE clause.
11	UNSIGNED_ATTRIBUTE	SMALLINT	Indicates whether or not the data type is unsigned. Valid values for this column are SQL_TRUE, SQL_FALSE, and NULL (for data types where the attribute is not applicable).
12	FIXED_PREC_SCALE	SMALLINT NOT NULL	Indicates whether or not the data type is exact numeric and always has the same precision and scale (the same width and number of decimal places). Valid values for this column are SQL_TRUE and SQL_FALSE.
13	AUTO_INCREMENT	SMALLINT	Indicates whether or not a column of this data type is automatically set to a unique value whenever a row is inserted. Valid values for this column are SQL_TRUE and SQL_FALSE.
14	LOCAL_TYPE_NAME	VARCHAR(128)	Character representation of any localized (native language) name for the data type that is different from the regular data type name stored in the TYPE_NAME column. This column is set to NULL for data types where there is no localized name. This column is intended to be used for display purposes only. The character set of the string is locale-dependent and normally defaults to the character set of the database.
15	MINIMUM_SCALE	INTEGER	The minimum scale value of the SQL data type. If the data type has a fixed scale, both the MINIMUM_SCALE column and the MAXIMUM_SCALE column contain the same value. This column is set to NULL for data types where scale is not applicable.
16	MAXIMUM_SCALE	INTEGER	The maximum scale value of the SQL data type. If the maximum scale is not defined separately in the DBMS, but rather to be the same as the maximum length of the column, then this column contains the same value as the COLUMN_SIZE column. This column is set to NULL for data types where scale is not applicable.

Adapted from IBM's Database 2 Call Level Interface Guide and Reference, Table 89, pages 282 to 283.

Specifications DB2 CLI 1.1, ODBC 1.0, X/OPEN CLI, ISO CLI

Return Codes SQL_SUCCESS, SQL_INVALID_HANDLE, SQL_ERROR

SQLSTATEs **24**000, **40**003, **08**S01, **S1**001, **S1**004, **S1**010, **S1**T00

Comments

- If SQL_ALL_TYPES is specified for the *SQLType* parameter, information about all supported data types will be returned, in ascending order, by TYPE _NAME. All unsupported data types will be absent from this result data set.
- Since this function generates a result data set and is equivalent to executing a query, it will generate a cursor and begin a transaction. Before another SQL statement can be prepared and executed against the same SQL statement handle, the cursor created by this function must first be closed.
- If this function is called with an invalid SQLType parameter value, an empty result data set will be returned.
- If either the LONGDATACOMPAT keyword or the SQL_LONGDATA_COMPAT connection option is set, then SQL_LONGVARBINARY, SQL_LONGVARCHAR, and SQL_LONGVARGRAPHIC values will be returned in the DATA_TYPE column of the result data set in place of SQL_BLOB, SQL_CLOB, and SQL_DBCLOB values. (Refer to the SQLDriverConnect( ) and SQLSetConnectOption( ) functions for more information about connection options.)
- Persistent data type values returned in the DATA_TYPE column of the result data set can be used in a CREATE TABLE and an ALTER TABLE SQL statement. Nonpersistent data type values, such as locator and user-defined data types, are not returned as part of the result data set.
- Although new columns can be added and the names of the existing columns in the result data set might be changed in future releases of DB2 CLI, the position of the current columns in this data set will not change.

Restrictions The following ODBC-specified SQL data types (and their corresponding SQLType values) are not supported by any IBM RDBMS:

TINY INT SQL_TINYINT
BIG INT SQL_BIGINT
BIT SQL_BIT

See Also SQLBindCol( ), SQLColAttributes( ), SQLExtendedFetch( ), SQLGetInfo( )

Examples The following C program illustrates how to use the SQLGetTypeInfo( ) function to obtain information about a specific data type:

```
#include <stdio.h>
#include <stdlib.h>
#include <sqlcli1.h>

int main()
{
    /* Declare The Local Memory Variables */
    SQLRETURN       rc = SQL_SUCCESS;
    SQLHENV         EnvHandle;
```

```
    SQLHDBC       DSCHandle;
    SQLHSTMT      StmtHandle;
    SQLCHAR       TypeName[129];
    SQLSMALLINT   Nullable;
    SQLSMALLINT   Case;

    /* Allocate An Environment Handle */
    rc = SQLAllocEnv(&EnvHandle);

    /* Allocate A Connection Handle */
    rc = SQLAllocConnect(EnvHandle, &DSCHandle);

    /* Connect To The SAMPLE Database */
    rc = SQLConnect(DSCHandle, "SAMPLE", SQL_NTS, "etpdd6z", SQL_NTS,
                    "sanders", SQL_NTS);

    /* Allocate An SQL Statement Handle */
    rc = SQLAllocStmt(DSCHandle, &StmtHandle);

    /* Obtain And Display Information About The SQL_CHAR Data Type */
    rc = SQLGetTypeInfo(StmtHandle, SQL_CHAR);
    if (rc != SQL_ERROR)
        {

        /* Bind The Columns In The Result Data Set To Local */
        /* Storage Variables                                 */
        SQLBindCol(StmtHandle, 1, SQL_C_CHAR, (SQLPOINTER) &TypeName,
                   sizeof(TypeName), NULL);

        SQLBindCol(StmtHandle, 8, SQL_C_DEFAULT,
                   (SQLPOINTER) &Nullable, sizeof(Nullable), NULL);

        SQLBindCol(StmtHandle, 9, SQL_C_DEFAULT, (SQLPOINTER) &Case,
                   sizeof(Case), NULL);

        /* Retrieve And Display The Results */
        rc = SQLFetch(StmtHandle);
        printf("Data Type Name : %s\n", TypeName);

        printf("Case Sensitive : ");
        if (Case == TRUE)
            printf("Yes\n");
        else
            printf("No\n");

        printf("Nullable       : ");
        if (Case == TRUE)
            printf("Yes\n");
        else
            printf("No\n");
        }

    /* Disconnect From The SAMPLE Database */
    SQLDisconnect(DSCHandle);

EXIT:

    /* Free The SQL Statement Handle */
```

```
    if (StmtHandle != NULL)
        SQLFreeStmt(StmtHandle, SQL_DROP);

    /* Free The Connection Handle */
    if (DSCHandle != NULL)
        SQLFreeConnect(DSCHandle);

    /* Free The Environment Handle */
    if (EnvHandle != NULL)
        SQLFreeEnv(EnvHandle);

    /* Return To The Operating System */
    return(rc);
}
```

The following C++ program illustrates how the SQLGetTypeInfo( ) function can be used by class methods to obtain information about a specific data type:

```
#include <iostream.h>
#include <string.h>
#include <sqlcli1.h>

/* Define The CLI Class */
class CLI
{
    /* Declare The Private Attribute Variables */
    private:
       SQLHENV      EnvHandle;
       SQLHDBC      DSCHandle;
       SQLHSTMT     StmtHandle;
       SQLCHAR      TypeName[129];
       SQLSMALLINT  Nullable;
       SQLSMALLINT  Case;

    /* Declare The Public Attribute Variables */
    public:
       SQLRETURN  rc;

    /* Declare The Member Function Prototypes */
    CLI();                                      // Constructor
    ~CLI();                                     // Destructor
    SQLRETURN Connect();
    SQLRETURN ShowTypeInfo();
    SQLRETURN Disconnect();
} ;

/* Define The Class Constructor */
CLI::CLI()
{
    /* Initialize The Return Code Variable */
    rc = SQL_SUCCESS;

    /* Allocate An Environment Handle */
    rc = SQLAllocEnv(&EnvHandle);

    /* Allocate A Connection Handle */
```

```
    rc = SQLAllocConnect(EnvHandle, &DSCHandle);
}

/* Define The Class Destructor */
CLI::~CLI()
{
    /* Free The Connection Handle */
    if (DSCHandle != NULL)
        SQLFreeConnect(DSCHandle);

    /* Free The Environment Handle */
    if (EnvHandle != NULL)
        SQLFreeEnv(EnvHandle);
}

/* Define The Connect() Member Function */
SQLRETURN CLI::Connect()
{
    /* Connect To The SAMPLE Database */
    rc = SQLConnect(DSCHandle, (SQLCHAR *) "SAMPLE", SQL_NTS,
                    (SQLCHAR *) "etpdd6z", SQL_NTS,
                    (SQLCHAR *) "sanders", SQL_NTS);

    /* Allocate An SQL Statement Handle */
    rc = SQLAllocStmt(DSCHandle, &StmtHandle);

    /* Return The CLI Function Return Code */
    return(rc);
}

/* Define The Disconnect() Member Function */
SQLRETURN CLI::Disconnect(void)
{
    /* Disconnect From The Database */
    rc = SQLDisconnect(DSCHandle);

    /* Free The SQL Statement Handle */
    if (StmtHandle != NULL)
        SQLFreeStmt(StmtHandle, SQL_DROP);

    /* Return The CLI Function Return Code */
    return(rc);
}

/* Define The ShowTypeInfo() Member Function */
SQLRETURN CLI::ShowTypeInfo(void)
{
    /* Retrieve Information About The SQL_CHAR Data Type */
    rc = SQLGetTypeInfo(StmtHandle, SQL_CHAR);
    if (rc == SQL_SUCCESS)
        {

        /* Bind The Columns In The Result Data Set To Local Variables */
        SQLBindCol(StmtHandle, 1, SQL_C_CHAR, (SQLPOINTER) &TypeName,
                   sizeof(TypeName), NULL);

        SQLBindCol(StmtHandle, 8, SQL_C_DEFAULT,
```

```
                    (SQLPOINTER) &Nullable, sizeof(Nullable), NULL);

        SQLBindCol(StmtHandle, 9, SQL_C_DEFAULT, (SQLPOINTER) &Case,
                   sizeof(Case), NULL);

        /* Retrieve And Display The Results */
        rc = SQLFetch(StmtHandle);
        cout << "Data Type Name : " << TypeName << endl;

        cout << "Case Sensitive : ";
        if (Case == TRUE)
            cout << "Yes" << endl;
        else
            cout << "No" << endl;

        cout << "Nullable       : ";
        if (Case == TRUE)
            cout << "Yes" << endl;
        else
            cout << "No" << endl;
        }

    /* Return The CLI Function Return Code */
    return(rc);
}

int main()
{
    /* Declare The Local Memory Variables */
    SQLRETURN  rc = SQL_SUCCESS;

    /* Create An Instance Of The CLI Class */
    CLI Sample;

    /* Connect To The SAMPLE Database */
    if ((rc = Sample.Connect()) != SQL_SUCCESS)
        return(rc);

    /* Obtain And Display Information About The SQL_CHAR Data Type */
    Sample.ShowTypeInfo();

    /* Disconnect From The SAMPLE Database */
    Sample.Disconnect();

    /* Return To The Operating System */
    return(rc);
}
```

SQLGetEnvAttr

Purpose The SQLGetEnvAttr( ) function retrieves the current setting for a specified environment attribute.

Syntax

```
SQLRETURN  SQLGetEnvAttr (SQLHENV       EnvHandle,
                          SQLINTEGER    Attribute,
```

```
SQLPOINTER       Value,
SQLINTEGER       BufferLength,
SQLINTEGER FAR   *StringLength);
```

Parameters

EnvHandle The environment handle where the address of the environment buffer is stored.

Attribute The environment attribute for which information is to be retrieved. This parameter can contain any of the following values:

- SQL_ATTR_OUTPUT_NTS
- SQL_CONNECTTYPE
- SQL_MAXCONN
- SQL_SYNC_POINT

Value A pointer to a location in memory where this function is to store the current value of the specified environment attribute.

BufferLength The maximum size of the memory storage buffer where this function is to store the current value of the specified attribute. If the retrieved attribute value is not a character string value, this parameter will be ignored.

StringLength A pointer to a location in memory where this function will return the actual number of bytes written to the *Value* memory storage buffer if the attribute value retrieved is a character string; otherwise, the parameter is ignored.

Includes

```
#include <sqlcli1.h>
```

Description

The SQLGetEnvAttr( ) function retrieves the current setting for a specified environment attribute. This function can be called at any time after an environment handle is allocated, as long as that environment handle has not been freed. Table 14.4 alphabetically lists each value that can be specified for the *Attribute* parameter, along with a description of the information that will be returned for the value when this function is executed.

TABLE 14.4 Environment Attributes

Attribute	Data type	Description
SQL_ATTR_OUTPUT_NTS	32-bit integer	Controls the use of null termination in output parameter values. Valid values for this attribute are: SQL_TRUE: DB2 CLI uses null terminators to indicate the length of output character strings. This is the default value for this attribute. SQL_FALSE: DB2 CLI does not append null terminators to output character strings. This attribute can be changed only when there are no connection handles allocated under this environment. All CLI functions called for the specified environment and for connections and statements allocated under the specified environment that use character string parameters are affected by this attribute value.
SQL_CONNECTTYPE	32-bit integer	Specifies whether this application is to operate in a coordinated or uncoordinated distributed environment. If processing needs to be coordinated, then this attribute must be taken into consideration, along with the SQL_SYNC_POINT environment attribute. Valid values for this attribute are: SQL_CONCURRENT_TRANS: The application can have concurrent multiple connections to any one data source or to multiple data sources at any given time. Each data source connection has its own commit scope. No effort is made to enforce coordination of transactions. If an application issues a commit

TABLE 14.4 Environment Attributes *(Continued)*

Attribute	Data type	Description
		using the environment handle with the SQLTransact( ) function and not all of the connections are successfully committed, the application handles the recovery. When this value is specified, the current setting of the SQL_SYNC_POINT attribute is ignored. This is the default value for the attribute. SQL_COORDINATED_TRANS: The application wants to coordinate commits and rollbacks among multiple data source connections. This value corresponds to the specification of the Type 2 CONNECT in embedded SQL and must be considered in conjunction with the SQL_SYNC_POINT environment attribute. In contrast to the previous SQL_CONCURRENT_TRANS value, the application is permitted only one open connection per data source. This attribute can be changed only when there are no connection handles allocated under the environment. All data source connections within an application must have the same SQL_CONNECTTYPE and SQL_SYNCPOINT values. You can also change this attribute by calling the SQLSetConnect Option( ) function. However, it is recommended that an application set the SQL_CONNECTTYPE attribute at the environment level (with the SQLSetEnvAttr( ) function) rather than on a per-connection basis (with the SQLSetConnectionOption( ) function). ODBC applications designed to take advantage of coordinated DB2 transaction processing must set this attribute at the connection level for each connection with the SQLSetConnectOption( ) function, since the SQLSetEnvAttr( ) function is not supported by ODBC. Note: The SQL_CONNECTTYPE attribute is an IBM-defined attribute.
SQL_MAX_CONN	32-bit integer	Specifies the maximum number of concurrent data source connections an application can have open at one time. You can use this attribute to control the maximum number of connections allowed on a per-application basis. The value specified for this attribute must be 0 or a positive number. The default value for the attribute is 0, which means that an application can establish as many data source connections as system resources permit. On OS/2, if the NetBIOS protocol is in use, the value corresponds to the number of NetBIOS sessions concurrently reserved for use by the application. The range of values for OS/2 NetBIOS sessions is 1 to 254. If the value 0 (the default value for this attribute) is specified, five OS/2 NetBIOS sessions will be reserved. Reserved NetBIOS sessions cannot be used by other applications. The number of NetBIOS sessions (connections) specified by this attribute will be applied to any adapter number used by the DB2 NetBIOS protocol to connect to the remote data source. Note: The adapter number is specified in the node directory whenever a NetBIOS node is cataloged. The value in effect when the first connection to a data source is established is the value that will be used throughout the life of the application; once the first connection has been established, all attempts to change the value will be rejected. You can also change the attribute by calling the SQLSetConnectOption( ) function, but it is recommended that an application set the SQL_MAXCONN attribute at the environment level (with the SQLSetEnvAttr( ) function) rather than on a per-connection basis (with the SQLSetConnectionOption( ) function). ODBC applications must set this attribute at the connection level for each connection with using the SQLSetConnectOption( ) function, since the SQLSetEnvAttr( ) function is not supported by ODBC. Note: The SQL_MAXCONN attribute is an IBM-defined attribute.
SQL_SYNC_POINT	32-bit integer	Allows the application to choose between one-phase coordinated transactions and two-phase coordinated transactions. Valid values for this attribute are: SQL_ONEPHASE: Use the one-phase commit to commit the work done by each data source in a multiple-source transaction. To ensure data integrity,

TABLE 14.4 Environment Attributes *(Continued)*

Attribute	Data type	Description
		each transaction must ensure that only one data source, if any, gets updated. The first data source that has updates performed on it within a transaction becomes the only updatable data source in that transaction; all other accessed data sources are treated as read-only. All attempts to update a read-only data source within this transaction will be rejected. SQL_TWOPHASE: Use the two-phase commit to commit the work done by each data source in a multiple-source transaction. This value requires that you use a transaction manager to coordinate two-phase commits among the connected data sources supporting this protocol. Multiple read/write and multiple updatable data sources are allowed within a single transaction. All data source connections within an application must have the same SQL_CONNECTTYPE and SQL_SYNCPOINT values. You can change this attribute by calling the SQLSetConnectOption( ) function, but it is recommended that an application set the SQL_CONNECTTYPE attribute at the environment level (with the SQLSetEnvAttr( ) function) rather than on a per-connection basis (with the SQLSetConnectionOption( ) function). ODBC applications designed to take advantage of coordinated DB2 transaction processing must set these attributes at the connection level for each connection with the SQLSetConnectOption( ) function, since the SQLSetEnvAttr( ) function is not supported by ODBC. Note: The SQL_SYNC_POINT attribute is an IBM-defined attribute. In embedded SQL, there is an additional sync point value (SYNCPOINT_NONE) that is more restrictive than the SQL_CONCURRENT_TRANS value for the SQL_CONNECTTYPE attribute. Because the SYNCPOINT_NONE value does not allow multiple connections to the same data source, DB2 CLI does not support it.

Adapted from IBM's Database 2 Call Level Interface Guide and Reference, Table 128, pages 351 to 353.

Specifications DB2 CLI 2.1, X/OPEN CLI, ISO CLI

Return Codes SQL_SUCCESS, SQL_INVALID_HANDLE, SQL_ERROR

SQLSTATEs **S1**001, **S1**092

Comments If the *Attribute* parameter does not refer to an environment attribute that contains a string value, both the *BufferLength* and *StringLength* parameters are ignored.

Restrictions There are no restrictions associated with this function call.

See Also SQLSetEnvAttr( )

Examples The following C program illustrates how the SQLGetEnvAttr( ) function determines whether or not the null termination of output parameters is supported:

```
#include <stdio.h>
#include <stdlib.h>
#include <sqlcli1.h>

int main()
{
    /* Declare The Local Memory Variables */
```

```
    SQLRETURN    rc = SQL_SUCCESS;
    SQLHENV      EnvHandle;
    SQLINTEGER   OutputNTS;

    /* Allocate An Environment Handle */
    rc = SQLAllocEnv(&EnvHandle);

    /* Determine Whether Or Not Null-Termination Is Supported In */
    /* CLI Function Output Parameters                           */
    rc = SQLGetEnvAttr(EnvHandle, SQL_ATTR_OUTPUT_NTS,
                       (SQLPOINTER) &OutputNTS, 0, 0);

    /* Display The Information Retrieved */
    if (rc == SQL_SUCCESS)
        {
        printf("Null-termination of output parameters is ");
        if (OutputNTS == SQL_TRUE)
            printf("supported.\n");
        else
            printf("not supported.\n");
        }

    /* Free The Environment Handle */
    if (EnvHandle != NULL)
        SQLFreeEnv(EnvHandle);

    /* Return To The Operating System */
    return(rc);
}
```

The following C++ program illustrates how the SQLGetEnvAttr( ) function can be used by class methods to determine whether or not the null termination of output parameters is supported:

```
#include <iostream.h>
#include <string.h>
#include <sqlcli1.h>

/* Define The CLI Class */
class CLI
{
    /* Declare The Private Attribute Variables */
    private:
       SQLHENV      EnvHandle;
       SQLINTEGER   OutputNTS;

    /* Declare The Public Attribute Variables */
    public:
       SQLRETURN  rc;

    /* Declare The Member Function Prototypes */
    CLI();                                    // Constructor
    ~CLI();                                   // Destructor
    SQLRETURN ShowNTSInfo();
} ;

/* Define The Class Constructor */
CLI::CLI()
{
    /* Initialize The Return Code Variable */
    rc = SQL_SUCCESS;
```

```
    /* Allocate An Environment Handle */
    rc = SQLAllocEnv(&EnvHandle);
}

/* Define The Class Destructor */
CLI::~CLI()
{
    /* Free The Environment Handle */
    if (EnvHandle != NULL)
        SQLFreeEnv(EnvHandle);
}

/* Define The ShowNTSInfo() Member Function */
SQLRETURN CLI::ShowNTSInfo(void)
{
    /* Determine Whether Or Not Null-Termination Is Supported In */
    /* CLI Function Output Parameters                            */
    rc = SQLGetEnvAttr(EnvHandle, SQL_ATTR_OUTPUT_NTS,
                       (SQLPOINTER) &OutputNTS, 0, 0);

    /* Display The Information Retrieved */
    if (rc == SQL_SUCCESS)
        {
        cout << "Null-termination of output parameters is ";
        if (OutputNTS == SQL_TRUE)
            cout << "supported." << endl;
        else
            cout << "not supported." << endl;
        }

    /* Return The CLI Function Return Code */
    return(rc);
}

int main()
{
    /* Declare The Local Memory Variables */
    SQLRETURN  rc = SQL_SUCCESS;

    /* Create An Instance Of The CLI Class */
    CLI Sample;

    /* Determine Whether Or Not Null-Termination Is Supported In */
    /* CLI Function Output Parameters                            */
    rc = Sample.ShowNTSInfo();

    /* Return To The Operating System */
    return(rc);
}
```

SQLSetEnvAttr

Purpose The SQLSetEnvAttr( ) function sets an environment attribute associated with the current environment handle.

Syntax

```
SQLRETURN  SQLSetEnvAttr (SQLHENV     EnvHandle,
                          SQLINTEGER Attribute,
                          SQLPOINTER Value,
                          SQLINTEGER StringLength);
```

Parameters

EnvHandle A pointer to an environment handle where the starting address of the environment buffer is to be stored.

Attribute The environment attribute to be set. This parameter can contain any of the following values:

- SQL_ATTR_OUTPUT_NTS
- SQL_CONNECTTYPE
- SQL_MAXCONN
- SQL_SYNC_POINT

Value A pointer to a location in memory where the new value for the environment attribute is stored. Depending on the environment attribute being set, this pointer can reference either a 32-bit integer value or a null-terminated character string.

StringLength The length of the environment attribute value stored in the *Value* parameter if the attribute value is a character string; otherwise, this parameter is ignored.

Includes

```
#include <sqlcli1.h>
```

Description

The SQLSetEnvAttr( ) function sets an environment attribute associated with the current environment handle. Once an environment attribute is set, that attribute's value affects all data source connections that exist under the specified environment. Refer to the SQLGetEnvAttr( ) function for more information about each environment attribute available.

Specifications

DB2 CLI 2.1, X/OPEN CLI, ISO CLI

Return Codes

SQL_SUCCESS, SQL_SUCCESS_WITH_INFO, SQL_INVALID_HANDLE, SQL_ERROR

SQLSTATEs

S1009, **S1**011, **S1**092, **S1**C00

Comments

You can obtain the current value for an environment attribute by calling the SQLGetEnvAttr( ) function.

Restrictions

There are no restrictions associated with this function call.

See Also

SQLGetEnvAttr( )

Examples

The following C program illustrates how to use the SQLSetEnvAttr( ) function to restrict the number of connections that can be open at one time to five:

```
#include <stdio.h>
#include <stdlib.h>
#include <sqlcli1.h>

int main()
{
    /* Declare The Local Memory Variables */
    SQLRETURN     rc = SQL_SUCCESS;
    SQLHENV       EnvHandle;
    SQLINTEGER    NumConnections;

    /* Allocate An Environment Handle */
    rc = SQLAllocEnv(&EnvHandle);
```

```
    /* Determine The Maximum Number Of Concurrent Connections That */
    /* This Application Can Have Open At One Time                  */
    rc = SQLGetEnvAttr(EnvHandle, SQL_MAXCONN,
                       (SQLPOINTER) &NumConnections, 0, 0);

    /* Display The Information Obtained */
    if (rc == SQL_SUCCESS)
        {
        printf("This application can have ");
        if (NumConnections == 0)
            printf("any number of ");
        else
            printf("up to %d ", NumConnections);
        printf("connections open at one time.\n");
        }

    /* Set The Maximum Number Of Concurrent Connections That This */
    /* Application Can Have Open At One Time To 5                 */
    NumConnections = 5;
    rc = SQLSetEnvAttr(EnvHandle, SQL_MAXCONN,
                       (SQLPOINTER) NumConnections, 0);

    /* Determine Whether Or Not The Maximum Number Of Concurrent   */
    /* Connections That This Application Can Have Open At One Time */
    /* Has Been Set To 5                                           */
    rc = SQLGetEnvAttr(EnvHandle, SQL_MAXCONN,
                       (SQLPOINTER) &NumConnections, 0, 0);

    /* Display The Information Obtained */
    if (rc == SQL_SUCCESS)
        {
        printf("This application can have ");
        if (NumConnections == 0)
            printf("any number of ");
        else
            printf("up to %d ", NumConnections);
        printf("connections open at one time.\n");
        }

    /* Free The Environment Handle */
    if (EnvHandle != NULL)
        SQLFreeEnv(EnvHandle);

    /* Return To The Operating System */
    return(rc);
}
```

The following C++ program illustrates how the SQLSetEnvAttr( ) function can be used by class methods to restrict the number of connections that can be open at one time to five:

```
#include <iostream.h>
#include <string.h>
#include <sqlcli1.h>

/* Define The CLI Class */
class CLI
{
    /* Declare The Private Attribute Variables */
    private:
```

```
        SQLHENV       EnvHandle;
        SQLINTEGER    OutputNTS;
        SQLINTEGER    NumConnections;

    /* Declare The Public Attribute Variables */
    public:
        SQLRETURN  rc;

    /* Declare The Member Function Prototypes */
    CLI();                                      // Constructor
    ~CLI();                                     // Destructor
    SQLRETURN GetNumConnections();
    SQLRETURN SetNumConnections(SQLINTEGER NumConnections);
} ;

/* Define The Class Constructor */
CLI::CLI()
{
    /* Initialize The Return Code Variable */
    rc = SQL_SUCCESS;

    /* Allocate An Environment Handle */
    rc = SQLAllocEnv(&EnvHandle);
}

/* Define The Class Destructor */
CLI::~CLI()
{
    /* Free The Environment Handle */
    if (EnvHandle != NULL)
        SQLFreeEnv(EnvHandle);
}

/* Define The GetNumConnections() Member Function */
SQLRETURN CLI::GetNumConnections(void)
{
    /* Determine The Maximum Number Of Concurrent Connections That */
    /* This Application Can Have Open At One Time                  */
    rc = SQLGetEnvAttr(EnvHandle, SQL_MAXCONN,
                  (SQLPOINTER) &NumConnections, 0, 0);

    /* Display The Information Obtained */
    if (rc == SQL_SUCCESS)
        {
        cout << "This application can have ";
        if (NumConnections == 0)
            cout << "any number of ";
        else
            cout << "up to " << NumConnections << " ";
        cout << "connections open at one time." << endl;
        }

    /* Return The CLI Function Return Code */
    return(rc);
}

/* Define The SetNumConnections() Member Function */
SQLRETURN CLI::SetNumConnections(SQLINTEGER NumConnections)
{
    /* Set The Maximum Number Of Concurrent Connections That This */
    /* Application Can Have Open At One Time                      */
```

```
    rc = SQLSetEnvAttr(EnvHandle, SQL_MAXCONN,
                       (SQLPOINTER) NumConnections, 0);

    /* Return The CLI Function Return Code */
    return(rc);
}

int main()
{
    /* Declare The Local Memory Variables */
    SQLRETURN  rc = SQL_SUCCESS;

    /* Create An Instance Of The CLI Class */
    CLI Sample;

    /* Determine The Maximum Number Of Concurrent Connections That */
    /* This Application Can Have Open At One Time                  */
    Sample.GetNumConnections();
    /* Set The Maximum Number Of Concurrent Connections That This */
    /* Application Can Have Open At One Time To 5                 */
    Sample.SetNumConnections(5);

    /* Verify That The Maximum Number Of Concurrent Connections */
    /* That This Application Can Have Open At One Time Has Been */
    /* Set To 5                                                 */
    Sample.GetNumConnections();

    /* Return To The Operating System */
    return(rc);
}
```

SQLGetConnectOption

Purpose The SQLGetConnectOption( ) function retrieves the current setting for a specified connection option.

Syntax

```
SQLRETURN  SQLGetConnectOption (SQLHDBC       DSCHandle,
                                SQLUSMALLINT  Option,
                                SQLPOINTER    Value);
```

Parameters

DSCHandle The data source connection handle where the address of the data source connection information buffer is stored.

Option The connection option for which information is to be retrieved. This parameter can contain any of the following values:

- SQL_ACCESS_MODE
- SQL_AUTOCOMMIT
- SQL_CONNECTTYPE
- SQL_CURRENT_SCHEMA
- SQL_DB2ESTIMATE
- SQL_DB2EXPLAIN
- SQL_LOGIN_TIMEOUT
- SQL_LONGDATA_COMPAT
- SQL_MAXCONN

- SQL_QUIET_MODE
- SQL_SYNC_POINT
- SQL_TXN_ISOLATION
- SQL_WCHARTYPE

Value A pointer to a location in memory where this function is to store the current value of the specified connection option. Depending on the connection option value being retrieved, this pointer can reference either a 32-bit integer value or a null-terminated character string.

Includes

```
#include <sqlcli1.h>
```

Description The SQLGetConnectOption( ) function retrieves the current setting for a specified connection option. Table 14.5 alphabetically lists each value that can be specified for the *Option* parameter, along with a description of the information that will be returned for the value when this function is executed.

TABLE 14.5 Connect Options

Option	Data type	Description
SQL_ACCESS_MODE	32-bit integer	Specifies the type of requests that will be made to the connected data source. Valid values for this option are: SQL_MODE_READ_ONLY: Indicates that the application will not perform any updates on data from this point on, so less restrictive isolation levels and locking can be used (e.g., SQL_TXN_READ_UNCOMMITTED). Note: When the SQL_ACCESS_MODE option is set to SQL_MODE_READ_ONLY, DB2 CLI does not ensure that all requests made to the data source are read-only. If an update request is issued, DB2 CLI will process it using the transaction isolation level it has selected as a result of the SQL_MODE_READ_ONLY setting. SQL_MODE_READ_WRITE: Indicates that the application will update data from this point on; DB2 CLI will use the default transaction isolation level that was established for this connection. This is the default value. This option cannot be changed if there is an outstanding transaction on the associated connection handle.
SQL_AUTOCOMMIT	32-bit integer	Specifies whether to use auto-commit or manual-commit mode for terminating transactions. Valid values for this option are: SQL_AUTOCOMMIT_OFF: The application must manually commit or roll back all transactions by explicitly calling the SQLTransact( ) function. SQL_AUTOCOMMIT_ON: All SQL statements are implicitly committed. Each SQL statement that is not a query statement is committed immediately after it has been executed. Each SQL statement that is a query statement is committed immediately after the associated cursor is closed. By default, DB2 CLI operates in auto-commit mode (SQL_AUTOCOMMIT_ON). Note: For coordinated distributed unit of work connections, the default value for this option is SQL_AUTOCOMMIT_OFF. Since DB2 CLI applications written prior to version 2.1 assume that AUTOCOMMIT is turned off, you can override the default by using the AUTOCOMMIT keyword in the DB2 CLI initialization file (**db2cli.ini**). You can change this option as long as there is only one outstanding statement per connection. If there are two or more open cursors for a connection when this option is changed, unpredictable results might occur. An open cursor must be closed before another query is executed. Since, in many DB2 environments, the execution of an SQL statement and its commit might

TABLE 14.5 Connect Options *(Continued)*

Option	Data type	Description
		flow separately to the data source, auto-commit can be expensive. Take this into consideration when selecting the auto-commit mode. Also note that changing from manual-commit to auto-commit mode automatically commits any open transactions on the specified connection handle.
SQL_CONNECTTYPE	32-bit integer	Specifies whether this application is to operate in a coordinated or uncoordinated distributed environment. If processing needs to be coordinated, then you must take this option into consideration, along with the SQL_SYNC_POINT connection option. Valid values for this option are: SQL_CONCURRENT_TRANS: The application can have concurrent multiple connections to any one data source or to multiple data sources at any given time. Each data source connection has its own commit scope. No effort is made to enforce coordination of transactions. If an application issues a commit using the environment handle with the SQLTransact( ) function and not all the connections are successfully committed, the application will handle recovery. When this value is specified, the current setting of the SQL_SYNC_POINT option is ignored. This is the default value. SQL_COORDINATED_TRANS: The application wants to coordinate commit and rollbacks among multiple data source connections. This value corresponds to the specification of the Type-2 CONNECT in embedded SQL and must be considered in conjunction with the SQL_SYNC_POINT connection option. In contrast to the SQL_CONCURRENT_TRANS value, the application is permitted only one open connection per data source. This connection type causes the default value for the SQL_AUTOCOMMIT connection option to be set to SQL_AUTOCOMMIT_OFF. Changes to this option must take place before a connection request is made. All data source connections within an application must have the same SQL_CONNECTTYPE and SQL_SYNCPOINT values. The first established connection determines the SQL_CONNECTTYPE option value to use for all subsequent connections. When using DB2 CLI, it is recommended that an application set the SQL_CONNECTTYPE attribute at the environment level (with the SQLSetEnvAttr( ) function) rather than on a per-connection basis (with the SQLSetConnectionOption( ) function). ODBC applications designed to take advantage of coordinated DB2 transaction processing must set these attributes at the connection level for each connection with the SQLSetConnectOption( ) function, since the SQLSetEnvAttr( ) function is not supported by ODBC. Note: The SQL_CONNECTTYPE option is an IBM-defined option.
SQL_CURRENT_SCHEMA	Character string	Specifies the name of the schema to be used by DB2 CLI for the SQLColumns( ) function call whenever the SchemaName parameter is set to NULL. This option is useful when an application developer has coded a generic call to the SQLColumns( ) function that normally does not restrict the result set by schema name, but needs to constrain the result data set at isolated places in the code. This option can be set at any time and will become effective on the next call to the SQLColumns( ) function where the *SchemaName* parameter is set to NULL. To disable this option, assign it a 0-length string or a NULL pointer value. Note: The SQL_CURRENT_SCHEMA option is an IBM extension to the set of options defined in ODBC.
SQL_DB2ESTIMATE	32-bit integer	Specifies whether DB2 CLI will display a dialog box to report estimates returned by the optimizer at the end of SQL query preparation. The value specified for this option must be 0 or a very large positive number. The

TABLE 14.5 Connect Options *(Continued)*

Option	Data type	Description
		default value is 0, which means that DB2 CLI will not report estimates. If a large positive number is specified (recommended value is 60000), it is compared against the SQLERRD(4) field in the SQLCA associated with the PREPARE operation. If the SQL_DB2ESTIMATE value is larger, the estimates dialog box will be displayed. The graphical dialog box displays optimizer estimates and prompts the user to either continue with the execution of this query or cancel processing. This option is used in conjunction with the SQL_QUIET_MODE option and is applicable only to applications that use graphical user interfaces. An application can implement this feature directly, without using this option, by calling the SQLGetSQLCA( ) function immediately after calling the SQLPrepare( ) function for a query and then displaying the appropriate information in a dialog box, thus allowing a more integrated overall interface. This option can be set at any time and will become effective on the next time an SQL statement is prepared for the specified connection. Note: The SQL_DB2ESTIMATE option is an IBM defined option and applies only to DB2 for Common Servers, version 2.1 or higher.
SQL_DB2EXPLAIN	32-bit integer	Specifies whether or not Explain information should be generated. Valid values for this option are: SQL_DB2EXPLAIN ON: The SQL statement SET CURRENT EXPLAIN SNAPSHOT=YES will be sent to the DB2 data source to enable the Explain Snapshot facility. A snapshot of the internal representation of the SQL statement will then be created for each eligible dynamic SQL statement. This Explain information is inserted in the SNAPSHOT column of the EXPLAIN_STATEMENT table. SQL_DB2EXPLAIN_OFF: The SQL statement SET CURRENT EXPLAIN SNAPSHOT=NO will be sent to the DB2 data source to disable the Explain Snapshot facility and no Explain snapshot is taken. This is the default value for this option. Before Explain information can be generated, the Explain tables must be created and the current user authorization ID must have INSERT privileges for these tables. Refer to the SET CURRENT EXPLAIN SNAPSHOT SQL statement in Part 3 for more information. The SET CURRENT EXPLAIN SNAPSHOT statement is not under transaction control and is not affected by a ROLLBACK operation. This option can be set at any time and will become effective the next time an SQL statement is prepared for the specified connection. Note: SQL_DB2EXPLAIN is an IBM-defined option and applies only to DB2 for Common Servers, version 2.1 or higher.
SQL_LOGIN_TIMEOUT	32-bit integer	Specifies the number of seconds to wait for a login request to complete before returning control to the application. Since DB2 CLI does not support asynchronous execution of login functions, the only value recognized for this option at this time is 0, which means the connection attempt will wait until either a connection is established or until the underlying communication layer times out.
SQL_LONGDATA_COMPAT	32-bit integer	Specifies whether or not binary, character, and double-byte character large object data types (BLOB, CLOB, and DBCLOB) should be reported respectively as SQL_LONGBINARY, SQL_LONGVARCHAR, and SQL_LONGVARGRAPHIC, thereby enabling existing applications to access large object data types seamlessly. Valid values for this option are: SQL_LD_COMPAT_NO: Large object data types are reported as themselves (SQL_BLOB, SQL_CLOB, and SQL_DBCLOB). This is the default value for this option.

TABLE 14.5 Connect Options *(Continued)*

Option	Data type	Description
		SQL_LD_COMPAT_YES: Large object data types (BLOB, CLOB and DBCLOB) are reported as SQL_LONGVARBINARY, SQL_LONGVARCHAR and SQL_LONVARGRAPHIC data types.
		Note: SQL_LONGDATA_COMPAT is an IBM-defined option.
SQL_MAX_CONN	32-bit integer	Specifies the maximum number of concurrent data source connections that an application can have open at one time. This option can be used to control the maximum number of connections allowed on a per application basis. The value specified for this option must be 0 or a positive number. The default value for this option is 0, which means that an application can establish as many data source connections as system resources permit. On OS/2, if the NetBIOS protocol is in use, this value corresponds to the number of NetBIOS sessions that will be concurrently reserved for use by the application. The range of values for OS/2 NetBIOS sessions is 1 to 254. If the value 0 (the default value for this option) is specified, five OS/2 NetBIOS sessions will be reserved. Reserved NetBIOS sessions cannot be used by other applications. The number of NetBIOS sessions (connections) specified by this option will be applied to any adapter number that DB2 NetBIOS protocol uses to connect to the remote data source. Note: The adapter number is specified in the node directory whenever a NetBIOS node is cataloged. The value that is in effect when the first connection to a data source is established is the value that will be used throughout the life of the application; once the first connection has been established, all attempts to change this value will be rejected. When using DB2 CLI, it is recommended that an application set the SQL_MAXCONN attribute at the environment level (with the SQLSetEnvAttr( ) function) rather than on a per connection basis (with the SQLSetConnectionOption( ) function). ODBC applications must set this option at the connection level for each connection, using the SQLSetConnectOption( ) function, since the SQLSetEnvAttr( ) function is not supported by ODBC. Note: SQL_MAXCONN is an IBM-defined option.
SQL_QUIET_MODE	32-bit integer	Specifies the platform specific parent window handle to use when displaying child dialog boxes. If an application has never assigned a value to this option (using the SQLSetConnectOption( ) function), then DB2 CLI will return a null parent window handle to the SQLGetConnectOption( ) function for this option and a null parent window handle will be used to display all child dialog boxes. For example, if the SQL_DB2ESTIMATE option is set to a large integer value, DB2 CLI would display the dialog box containing optimizer information using a null window handle. (For some platforms, this means the dialog box would be centered in the middle of the screen.) If this option is set to a null pointer value, DB2 CLI will not display any child dialog boxes. In this case, if the SQL_DB2ESTIMATE option is set to a large integer value, DB2 CLI would not display the dialog box containing optimizer information because the application has indicated that it explicitly wants to suppress all such dialog boxes. If the value for this option is not a null pointer, then it should contain the address of the parent window handle of the application. Note: This option cannot be used to suppress the displaying of the connection information retrieval dialog box that can be displayed by the SQLDriverConnect( ) function (instead, this dialog box is suppressed by setting the *DriverCompletion* parameter to SQL_DRIVER_NOPROMPT).
SQL_SYNC_POINT	32-bit integer	Allows the application to choose between one-phase coordinated transactions and two-phase coordinated transactions. Valid values for this option are:
		SQL_ONEPHASE: One-phase commit is used to commit the work done by each data source in a multiple data source transaction. To ensure data

TABLE 14.5 Connect Options *(Continued)*

Option	Data type	Description
		integrity, each transaction must ensure that only one data source, if any, gets updated. The first data source that has updates performed on it within a transaction becomes the only updateable data source in that transaction; all other data sources accessed are treated as read-only. All attempts to update a read-only data source within this transaction are rejected. This is the default value for this option. SQL_TWOPHASE: Two-phase commit is used to commit the work done by each data source in a multiple data source transaction. This value requires the use of a transaction manager to coordinate two phase commits amongst the connected data sources that support this protocol. Multiple read-writeable and multiple updateable data sources are allowed within a single transaction. All data source connections within an application must have the same SQL_CONNECTTYPE and SQL_SYNCPOINT values. When using DB2 CLI, it is recommended that an application set the SQL_CONNECTTYPE attribute at the environment level (with the SQLSetEnvAttr( ) function) rather than on a per connection basis (with the SQLSetConnectionOption( ) function). ODBC applications that are designed to take advantage of coordinated DB2 transaction processing must set these attributes at the connection level for each connection, using the SQLSetConnectOption( ) function, since the SQLSetEnvAttr( ) function is not supported by ODBC. Note: The SQL_SYNC_POINT option is an IBM defined option. In embedded SQL, there is an additional sync point value (SYNCPOINT_NONE) that is more restrictive than the SQL_CONCURRENT_TRANS value for the SQL_CONNECTTYPE option. Because the SYNCPOINT_NONE value does not allow multiple connections to the same data source, DB2 CLI does not support it.
SQL_TXN_ISOLATION	32-bit integer	Sets the transaction isolation level for the current SQL statement handle. The following scenarios illustrate the terms that are used to describe transaction isolation levels: Dirty read: Transaction 1 changes a row, and transaction 2 reads the changed row before transaction 1 commits the change. If transaction 1 rolls back the change, transaction 2 will have read a row considered to have never existed. Nonrepeatable read: Transaction 1 reads a row, and transaction 2 updates or deletes that row and commits the change. If transaction 1 attempts to re-read the row, it will retrieve different row values (if the row was updated) or it will discover that the row no longer exists (if the row was deleted). Phantom: Transaction 1 reads a set of rows that satisfy some search criteria, and transaction 2 inserts a row that matches the search criteria. If transaction 1 reexecutes the query statement that read the rows it will receive a different set of rows. If the data source supports transaction processing, any of the following values will be accepted by DB2 CLI for this option, but each data source might support only a subset of these isolation levels (you can get a list of supported isolation levels at application runtime by calling the SQLGetInfo( ) function with the *InfoType* parameter set to SQL_TXN_ISOLATION _OPTIONS): SQL_TXN_READ_UNCOMMITTED: Dirty reads, reads that cannot be repeated, and phantoms are possible. SQL_TXN_READ_COMMITTED: Dirty reads are not possible. Reads that cannot be repeated and phantoms are possible. This is the default value for this option.

TABLE 14.5 Connect Options *(Continued)*

Option	Data type	Description
		SQL_TXN_REPEATABLE_READ: Dirty reads and reads that cannot be repeated are not possible. Phantoms are possible.
		SQL_TXN_SERIALIZABLE: Transactions can be serialized. Dirty reads, nonrepeatable reads, and phantoms are not possible.
		SQL_TXN_NOCOMMIT: Changes are effectively committed at the end of a successful operation; no explicit commit or rollback is allowed. This is analogous to autocommit. This is not an SQL92 isolation level, but an IBM defined extension that is supported only by DB2 for OS/400.
		In IBM terminology, SQL_TXN_READ_UNCOMMITTED is an uncommitted read, SQL_TXN_READ_COMMITTED is cursor stability, SQL_TXN_REPEATABLE_READ is read stability, and SQL_TXN _SERIALIZABLE is a repeatable read. This option cannot be changed if there is an open cursor on any associated SQL statement handle or if there is an outstanding transaction for the specified connection. Note: There is an IBM-defined statement option that allows you to set transaction isolation levels on a per-statement handle basis. Refer to the SQL_STMTTXN _ISOLATION option in Table 14-6 for more information.
SQL_WCHARTYPE	32-bit integer	Specifies, in a double-byte environment, which wchar_t (SQLDBCHAR) character format is to be used by an application. This option provides an application with the flexibility to choose between having wchar-t data in multi-byte format or in wide-character format. Valid values for this option are:
		SQL_WCHARTYPE_CONVERT: Implicit character code conversion occurs between graphic SQL data in the database and application variables. This allows an application to fully exploit the ANSI C mechanisms for dealing with wide character strings (L-literals, wc string functions, etc.) without having to explicitly convert the data to multibyte format before communicating with the data source. The disadvantage of using this option is that the implicit conversions provided may have an impact on the runtime performance of the application, and may increase overall memory requirements.
		SQL_WCHARTYPE_NOCONVERT: No implicit character code conversion occurs between graphic SQL data in the database and application variables. Data in the application variable is sent to and received from the database as unaltered DBCS characters. This option improves overall application performance, but the application must either retrain from using wide-character data in wchar_t (SQLDBCHAR) application variables, or it must explicitly call the wcstombs( ) and the mbstowcs( ) ANSI C functions to convert the data to and from multibyte format when it is passed to or received from the database. This is the default value for this option.
		For additional information on the use of multibyte application variables, refer to the *IBM Database 2 Application Programming Guide*. Note: SQL_WCHARTYPE is an IBM-defined option.

Adapted from IBM Database 2 Call Level Interface Guide and Reference, Table 123, pages 337 to 344.

Specifications DB2 CLI 2.1, ODBC 1.0, X/OPEN CLI

Return Codes SQL_SUCCESS, SQL_SUCCESS_WITH_INFO, SQL_INVALID_HANDLE, SQL_ERROR

SQLSTATEs **08**003, **40**003, **08**S01, **S1**001, **S1**009, **S1**092, **S1**C00

Comments

- Although the SQLSetConnectOption( ) function can set both connection and SQL statement options, the SQLGetConnectOption( ) function can only retrieve connection options. You must use SQLGetStmtOption( ) to retrieve SQL statement options.
- If this function is called, and the specified option has not been set (via the SQLSetConnectOption( ) function) and does not have a default value, the return code SQL_NO_DATA_FOUND will be returned.
- The maximum length of any character string returned by this function (excluding the null terminator) cannot exceed SQL_MAX_OPTION_STRING _LENGTH bytes.

Restrictions There are no restrictions associated with this function call.

See Also SQLSetConnectOption( ), SQLGetStmtOption( ), SQLSetStmtOption( )

Examples The following C program illustrates how to use the SQLGetConnectOption( ) function to determine whether or not transactions are automatically committed when they end:

```
#include <stdio.h>
#include <stdlib.h>
#include <sqlcli1.h>

int main()
{
    /* Declare The Local Memory Variables */
    SQLRETURN      rc = SQL_SUCCESS;
    SQLHENV        EnvHandle;
    SQLHDBC        DSCHandle;
    SQLUSMALLINT   AutoCommit;

    /* Allocate An Environment Handle */
    rc = SQLAllocEnv(&EnvHandle);

    /* Allocate A Connection Handle */
    rc = SQLAllocConnect(EnvHandle, &DSCHandle);

    /* Determine Whether Or Not AUTO COMMIT Is Turned ON */
    rc = SQLGetConnectOption(DSCHandle, SQL_AUTOCOMMIT,
                             (SQLPOINTER) &AutoCommit);

    if (rc == SQL_SUCCESS)
        if (AutoCommit == SQL_TRUE)
            printf("Transactions will automatically be committed.\n");
        else
            printf("Transactions must be committed manually.\n");

    /* Free The Connection Handle */
    if (DSCHandle != NULL)
        SQLFreeConnect(DSCHandle);

    /* Free The Environment Handle */
    if (EnvHandle != NULL)
        SQLFreeEnv(EnvHandle);
```

```
    /* Return To The Operating System */
    return(rc);
}
```

The following C++ program illustrates how the SQLGetConnectOption( ) function can be used by class methods to determine whether or not transactions are automatically committed when they end:

```
#include <iostream.h>
#include <string.h>
#include <sqlcli1.h>

/* Define The CLI Class */
class CLI
{
    /* Declare The Private Attribute Variables */
    private:
       SQLHENV        EnvHandle;
       SQLHDBC        DSCHandle;
       SQLUSMALLINT  AutoCommit;

    /* Declare The Public Attribute Variables */
    public:
       SQLRETURN  rc;

    /* Declare The Member Function Prototypes */
    CLI();                                // Constructor
    ~CLI();                               // Destructor
    SQLRETURN GetCommitState();
} ;

/* Define The Class Constructor */
CLI::CLI()
{
    /* Initialize The Return Code Variable */
    rc = SQL_SUCCESS;

    /* Allocate An Environment Handle */
    rc = SQLAllocEnv(&EnvHandle);

    /* Allocate A Connection Handle */
    rc = SQLAllocConnect(EnvHandle, &DSCHandle);
}

/* Define The Class Destructor */
CLI::~CLI()
{
    /* Free The Connection Handle */
    if (DSCHandle != NULL)
        SQLFreeConnect(DSCHandle);

    /* Free The Environment Handle */
    if (EnvHandle != NULL)
        SQLFreeEnv(EnvHandle);
}

/* Define The GetCommitState() Member Function */
SQLRETURN CLI::GetCommitState(void)
{
```

```
    /* Determine Whether Or Not AUTO COMMIT Is Turned ON */
    rc = SQLGetConnectOption(DSCHandle, SQL_AUTOCOMMIT,
                             (SQLPOINTER) &AutoCommit);

    if (rc == SQL_SUCCESS)
        {
        if (AutoCommit == SQL_TRUE)
            cout << "Transactions will automatically be committed.";
        else
            cout << "Transactions must be committed manually.';
        cout << endl;
        }

    /* Return The CLI Function Return Code */
    return(rc);
}

int main()
{
    /* Declare The Local Memory Variables */
    SQLRETURN  rc = SQL_SUCCESS;

    /* Create An Instance Of The CLI Class */
    CLI Sample;

    /* Determine Whether Or Not AUTO COMMIT Is Turned ON */
    Sample.GetCommitState();

    /* Return To The Operating System */
    return(rc);
}
```

SQLSetConnectOption

Purpose The SQLSetConnectOption( ) function sets a connection option associated with a specific data source connection handle.

Syntax

```
SQLRETURN  SQLSetConnectOption (SQLHDBC       DSCHandle,
                                SQLUSMALLINT Option,
                                SQLPOINTER   Value);
```

Parameters

DSCHandle The data source connection handle where the address of the data source connection information buffer is stored.

Option The connection option that is to be set. This parameter can contain any of the following values:

- SQL_ACCESS_MODE
- SQL_AUTOCOMMIT
- SQL_CONNECTTYPE
- SQL_CURRENT_SCHEMA
- SQL_DB2ESTIMATE
- SQL_DB2EXPLAIN
- SQL_LOGIN_TIMEOUT
- SQL_LONGDATA_COMPAT

- SQL_MAXCONN
- SQL_QUIET_MODE
- SQL_SYNC_POINT
- SQL_TXN_ISOLATION
- SQL_WCHARTYPE

Value A pointer to a location in memory where the new value for the connection option is stored. Depending on the connection option being set, this pointer can reference either a 32-bit integer value or a null-terminated character string.

Includes

```
#include <sqlcli1.h>
```

Description

The SQLSetConnectOption( ) function sets a connection option associated with a specific data source connection handle. You can also use this function to specify SQL statement options for all statement handles that exist for the current connection, as well as for all future SQL statement handles allocated for this connection. Refer to the SQLGetConnectOption( ) function for more information about each available connection option.

Specifications DB2 CLI 2.1, ODBC 1.0, X/OPEN CLI

Return Codes SQL_SUCCESS, SQL_SUCCESS_WITH_INFO, SQL_INVALID_HANDLE, SQL_ERROR

SQLSTATEs **01**000, **08**003, **08**S01, **40**003, **S1**001, **S1**009, **S1**010, **S1**011, **S1**092, **S1**C00

Comments

- All connection and statement options set by the SQLSetConnectOption( ) function remain in effect until the SQLFreeConnect( ) function is called or until they are modified by another SQLSetConnectOption( ) function call.
- If this function is called while any of the statement handles associated with the current connection are in a need-data state (in the middle of a SQLParamData( ) SQLPutData( ) sequence to process parameters that contain the SQL_DATA_AT_EXEC value), the return code SQL_ERROR will be returned.
- The maximum length of any character string supplied by this function (excluding the null terminator) must not exceed SQL_MAX_OPTION_STRING_LENGTH bytes.

Restrictions

To maintain compatibility with ODBC applications, the connection options SQL_CURRENT_QUALIFIER and SQL_PACKET_SIZE are recognized, but not supported. If either of these options are specified in a DB2 CLI application, the return code SQL_ERROR will be returned. The ODBC connection options SQL_TRANSLATE_DLL and SQL_TRANSLATE_OPTION are not supported since DB2 CLI handles code page conversion at the server workstation instead of at the client workstation.

See Also SQLGetConnectOption( ), SQLGetStmtOption( ), SQLSetStmtOption( )

Examples

The following C program illustrates how to use the SQLSetConnectOption( ) function to specify a default schema to use when table names are not qualified:

```
#include <stdio.h>
#include <stdlib.h>
#include <string.h>
```

```
#include <sqlcli1.h>

int main()
{
    /* Declare The Local Memory Variables */
    SQLRETURN      rc = SQL_SUCCESS;
    SQLHENV        EnvHandle;
    SQLHDBC        DSCHandle;
    SQLCHAR        Schema[31];
    SQLUSMALLINT   Supported;

    /* Allocate An Environment Handle */
    rc = SQLAllocEnv(&EnvHandle);
    /* Allocate A Connection Handle */
    rc = SQLAllocConnect(EnvHandle, &DSCHandle);

    /* Obtain The Current SCHEMA Being Used */
    rc = SQLGetConnectOption(DSCHandle, SQL_CURRENT_SCHEMA,
                             (SQLPOINTER) Schema);
    if (rc == SQL_SUCCESS)
        if (Schema[0] == '')
            printf("Currently, there is no default schema.\n");
        else
            printf("The current schema is : %s\n", Schema);

    /* Set The Current SCHEMA To "etpdd6z" */
    strcpy(Schema, "etpdd6z");
    rc = SQLSetConnectOption(DSCHandle, SQL_CURRENT_SCHEMA,
                             (SQLINTEGER) Schema);

    /* Verify That The SCHEMA Has Been Set To "etpdd6z" */
    rc = SQLGetConnectOption(DSCHandle, SQL_CURRENT_SCHEMA,
                             (SQLPOINTER) Schema);
    if (rc == SQL_SUCCESS)
        if (Schema[0] == '')
            printf("Currently, there is no default schema.\n");
        else
            printf("The current schema is : %s\n", Schema);

    /* Free The Connection Handle */
    if (DSCHandle != NULL)
        SQLFreeConnect(DSCHandle);

    /* Free The Environment Handle */
    if (EnvHandle != NULL)
        SQLFreeEnv(EnvHandle);

    /* Return To The Operating System */
    return(rc);
}
```

The following C++ program illustrates how the SQLSetConnectOption( ) function can be used by class methods to specify a default schema to use when table names are not qualified:

```
#include <iostream.h>
#include <string.h>
#include <sqlcli1.h>

/* Define The CLI Class */
class CLI
```

```
{
    /* Declare The Private Attribute Variables */
    private:
       SQLHENV       EnvHandle;
       SQLHDBC       DSCHandle;
       SQLCHAR       Schema[31];

    /* Declare The Public Attribute Variables */
    public:
       SQLRETURN  rc;

    /* Declare The Member Function Prototypes */
    CLI();                                   // Constructor
    ~CLI();                                  // Destructor
    SQLRETURN GetSCHEMA();
    SQLRETURN SetSCHEMA();
} ;

/* Define The Class Constructor */
CLI::CLI()
{
    /* Initialize The Return Code Variable */
    rc = SQL_SUCCESS;

    /* Allocate An Environment Handle */
    rc = SQLAllocEnv(&EnvHandle);

    /* Allocate A Connection Handle */
    rc = SQLAllocConnect(EnvHandle, &DSCHandle);
}

/* Define The Class Destructor */
CLI::~CLI()
{
    /* Free The Connection Handle */
    if (DSCHandle != NULL)
        SQLFreeConnect(DSCHandle);

    /* Free The Environment Handle */
    if (EnvHandle != NULL)
        SQLFreeEnv(EnvHandle);
}

/* Define The GetSCHEMA() Member Function */
SQLRETURN CLI::GetSCHEMA(void)
{
    /* Obtain The Current SCHEMA Being Used */
    rc = SQLGetConnectOption(DSCHandle, SQL_CURRENT_SCHEMA,
                             (SQLPOINTER) Schema);

    if (rc == SQL_SUCCESS)

    if (Schema[0] == '')
            cout << "Currently, there is no default schema.";
        else
            cout << "The current schema is : " << Schema;
        cout << endl;
        }

    /* Return The CLI Function Return Code */
    return(rc);
```

```
}

/* Define The SetSCHEMA() Member Function */
SQLRETURN CLI::SetSCHEMA(void)
{
    /* Set The Current SCHEMA To "etpdd6z" */
    strcpy((char *) Schema, "etpdd6z");
    rc = SQLSetConnectOption(DSCHandle, SQL_CURRENT_SCHEMA,
                             (SQLINTEGER) Schema);

    /* Return The CLI Function Return Code */
    return(rc);
}
int main()
{
    /* Declare The Local Memory Variables */
    SQLRETURN  rc = SQL_SUCCESS;

    /* Create An Instance Of The CLI Class */
    CLI Sample;

    /* Obtain The Current SCHEMA Being Used */
    Sample.GetSCHEMA();

    /* Set The Current SCHEMA To "etpdd6z" */
    Sample.SetSCHEMA();

    /* Verify That The SCHEMA Has Been Set To "etpdd6z" */
    Sample.GetSCHEMA();

    /* Return To The Operating System */
    return(rc);
}
```

SQLGetStmtOption

Purpose The SQLGetStmtOption( ) function retrieves the current setting for a specified SQL statement option.

Syntax

```
SQLRETURN  SQLGetStmtOption (SQLHSTMT      StmtHandle,
                             SQLUSMALLINT  Option,
                             SQLPOINTER    Value);
```

Parameters *StmtHandle* The statement handle where the address of the SQL statement buffer is stored.

Option The SQL statement option for which information is to be retrieved. This parameter can contain any of the following values:

- SQL_ASYNC_ENABLE
- SQL_BIND_TYPE
- SQL_CONCURRENCY
- SQL_CURSOR_HOLD
- SQL_CURSOR_TYPE
- SQL_MAX_LENGTH
- SQL_MAX_ROWS

- SQL_NODESCRIBE
- SQL_NOSCAN
- SQL_PARAMOPT_ATOMIC
- SQL_QUERY_TIMEOUT
- SQL_RETRIEVE_DATA
- SQL_ROWSET_SIZE
- SQL_STMTTXN_ISOLATION
- SQL_TXN_ISOLATION
- SQL_ROW_NUMBER

Value A pointer to a location in memory where this function is to store the current value of the specified SQL statement option. Depending on the SQL statement option value being retrieved, this pointer can reference either a 32-bit integer value or a null-terminated character string.

Includes

```
#include <sqlcli1.h>
```

Description

The SQLGetStmtOption( ) function retrieves the current setting for a specified SQL statement option. Table 14.6 alphabetically lists each value that can be specified for the *Option* parameter, along with a description of the information that will be returned for that value when the function is executed.

TABLE 14.6 SQL Statement Options

Option	Data type	Description
SQL_ASYNC_ENABLE	32-bit integer	Specifies whether or not a CLI function call is to be executed asynchronously. Valid values for this option are: SQL_ASYNC_ENABLE_OFF: DB2 CLI functions are to be executed synchronously. This is the default value for this option; it is also the only value supported by DB2 CLI since DB2 database servers do not currently support asynchronous capability. SQL_ASYNC-ENABLE_ON: DB2 CLI functions are to be executed asynchronously. This value is not currently supported by DB2 CLI and is therefore rejected.
SQL_BIND_TYPE	32-bit integer	Specifies the binding orientation to be used when the SQLExtendedFetch( ) function is called with the specified statement handle. Valid values for this option are: SQL_BIND_BY_COLUMN: Column-wise binding is to be used. This is the default value for this option. Or you can specify the length of the structure or an instance of a buffer into which result columns will be bound for row-wise binding. For row-wise binding, the length specified as the *Option* value must include space for all of the bound columns and any padding of the structure or buffer necessary to ensure that, when the address of a bound column is incremented with the specified length, it will point to the beginning of the same column in the next row. (By using the sizeof( ) operator with structures or unions in ANSI C, this behavior is guaranteed.)
SQL_CONCURRENCY	32-bit integer	Defines the concurrency level of a cursor. Valid values for this option are: SQL_CONCUR_READ_ONLY: The cursor is read-only; no updates are allowed. This is the default value for this option. SQL_CONCUR_LOCK: The cursor uses the lowest level of locking that is sufficient to ensure that a row can be updated.

TABLE 14.6 SQL Statement Options *(Continued)*

Option	Data type	Description
		This option cannot be changed if there is an open cursor on the associated SQL statement handle. Note: The ODBC values SQL_CONCUR_ROWVER and SQL_CONCUR_VALUES are not supported by DB2 CLI. If an application attempts to set the value of the SQL_CONCURRENCY option to either of these values, an error will occur and the value of this option will remain unchanged.
SQL_CURSOR_HOLD	32-bit integer	Specifies whether the cursor associated with the specified SQL statement handle is preserved (with the cursor pointer positioned in the same position) after a COMMIT operation, and whether the application that opened the cursor can continue retrieving data from it (fetch) without having to open the cursor again. Valid values for this option are SQL_CURSOR_HOLD_ON and SQL_CURSOR_HOLD_OFF. The default value supplied when an SQL statement handle is first allocated is SQL_CURSOR_HOLD_ON. This option cannot be changed if there is an open cursor on the associated SQL statement handle. The default value for this option in DB2 CLI version 1.x was SQL_CURSOR_HOLD_OFF. To support existing DB2 CLI applications, a migration step is used in conjunction with a CURSORHOLD keyword value that must exist in the DB2 CLI configuration file. Note: SQL_CURSOR_HOLD is an IBM-defined option.
SQL_CURSOR_TYPE	32-bit integer	Specifies the cursor type. Currently only the SQL_CURSOR_FORWARD _ONLY value is supported (and is therefore the default value for this option). This value causes the cursor to behave as a forward-only scrolling cursor. This option cannot be changed if there is an open cursor on the associated SQL statement handle. Note: The ODBC values SQL_CURSOR_STATIC, SQL_CURSOR_KEYSET_DRIVEN, and SQL_CURSOR_DYNAMIC are not supported by DB2 CLI. If an application attempts to set the value of the SQL_CURSOR_TYPE option to any of these values, an error will occur and the value of this option will remain unchanged.
SQL_MAX_LENGTH	32-bit integer	Specifies the maximum amount of data that can be retrieved from a single character or binary column. The value specified for this attribute must be 0 or a positive number. The default value for this option is 0, which means that DB2 CLI will attempt to return all available data for character or binary type data. If data is truncated because the value specified for the SQL_MAX_LENGTH option is less than the amount of data available, a SQLGetData( ), SQLFetch( ), or SQLExtendedFetch( ) function call will return SQL_SUCCESS instead of returning SQL_SUCCESS_WITH_INFO and SQLSTATE 01004 (data truncated).
SQL_MAX_ROWS	32-bit integer	Specifies the maximum number of rows to return to the application as the result of a query. The value specified for this attribute must be 0 or a positive number. The default value for this option is 0, which means that all rows are to be returned to an application.
SQL_NODESCRIBE	32-bit integer	Specifies whether DB2 CLI should automatically describe the column attributes of a result data set or wait for the application to specify the column attributes with the SQLSetColAttributes( ) function. Valid values for this option are SQL_NODESCRIBE_OFF and SQL_NODESCRIBE_ON. The default value supplied when an SQL statement handle is first allocated is SQL_NODESCRIBE_OFF. This option cannot be changed if there is an open cursor on the associated SQL statement handle. This option is used in conjunction with the SQLSetColAttributes( ) function by an application which has prior knowledge of the exact nature of the result data set that will be returned as the result of a query and which does not wish to incur the extra network traffic associated with obtaining the descriptor information

TABLE 14.6 SQL Statement Options *(Continued)*

Option	Data type	Description
		needed by DB2 CLI in order to provide client side processing. Note: SQL_NODESCRIBE is an IBM-defined option.
SQL_NOSCAN	32-bit integer	Specifies whether or not DB2 CLI will scan SQL strings for vendor escape clauses. Valid values for this option are: SQL_NOSCAN_OFF: SQL strings are always scanned for vendor escape clause sequences. This is the default value for this option. SQL_NOSCAN_ON: SQL strings are not scanned for vendor escape clauses; everything is sent directly to the data source for processing. An application can choose to turn off scanning if it never uses vendor escape sequences in the SQL strings that it sends to the data source. Doing so will eliminate the overhead processing associated with scanning and improve application performance.
SQL_PARAMOPT_ATOMIC	32-bit integer	If the SQLParamOptions( ) function has been used by an application to specify multiple values for parameter markers, this option determines whether the underlying processing should be done via ATOMIC or NOT_ATOMIC compound SQL. Valid values for this attribute are: SQL_ATOMIC_YES: The underlying processing makes use of ATOMIC Compound SQL. This is the default value for this option. SQL_ATOMIC_NO: The underlying processing makes use of NON_ATOMIC Compound SQL. ATOMIC Compound SQL is not supported by DB2/2, version 1.x, DB2/6000, version 1.x, or DRDA servers. If an application attempts to set the value of the SQL_PARAMOPT_ATOMIC option to SQL_ATOMIC_YES while attached to any of these servers, an error will occur.
SQL_QUERY_TIMEOUT	32-bit integer	Specifies the number of seconds to wait for an SQL statement to execute before returning control to the application. The value specified for this attribute must be 0 or a positive number. DB2 CLI only supports the value 0, except when the application is running on Windows, which means that DB2 CLI will wait indefinitely for an SQL statement to execute. On Windows, this option can be set and used to terminate long running queries. If a time out value is specified, the underlying Windows connectivity code will display a dialog box that informs the user that the specified number of seconds have elapsed and prompts the user to either continue processing or interrupt the query.
SQL_RETRIEVE_DATA	32-bit integer	Indicates whether DB2 CLI should actually retrieve data from the database when SQLExtendedFetch( ) function is called. Valid values for this option are: SQL_RD_ON: The SQLExtendedFetch( ) function does retrieve data when called. This is the default value for this option. SQL_RD_ON: The SQLExtendedFetch( ) function does not retrieve data when called. This value is useful for verifying whether or not rows exist in a result data set without incurring the overhead of sending long data from the connected data source. DB2 CLI will still internally retrieve data for all fixed length columns, such as INTEGER and SMALLINT, so overhead associated with the SQLExtendedFetch( ) function is not completely eliminated. This option cannot be changed if there is an open cursor on the associated SQL statement handle.
SQL_ROW_NUMBER	32-bit integer	Specifies the number of the current row in the entire result data set. If the number of the current row cannot be determined, or if there is no current

TABLE 14.6 SQL Statement Options *(Continued)*

Option	Data type	Description
		row, the value 0 is returned. Note: This is a read-only option, so it cannot be changed by the SQLSetStmtOption( ) function.
SQL_ROWSET_SIZE	32-bit integer	Specifies the number of rows that can be retrieved into a rowset. A rowset is the array of rows that is returned by each call to the SQLExtendedFetch( ) function. The value specified for this attribute must be 1 or a positive number. The default value for this option is 1, which means that one row will be retrieved. In this case making a SQLExtendedFetch( ) function call is equivalent to making a single SQLFetch( ) function call. This option can be changed even if there is an open cursor on the associated SQL statement handle. The change becomes effective the next time the SQLExtendedFetch( ) function is called.
SQL_STMTTXN_ISOLATION or SQL_TXN_ISOLATION	32-bit integer	Sets the transaction isolation level for the current SQL statement handle. The following scenarios illustrate the terms that are used to describe transaction isolation levels: Dirty Read: Transaction 1 changes a row, and transaction 2 reads the changed row before transaction 1 commits the change. If transaction 1 rolls back the change, transaction 2 will have read a row considered to have never existed. Nonrepeatable read: Transaction 1 reads a row, and transaction 2 updates or deletes that row and commits the change. If transaction 1 attempts to reread the row, it will retrieve different row values (if the row was updated) or it will discover that the row no longer exists (if the row was deleted). Phantom: Transaction 1 reads a set of rows that satisfy some search criteria, and transaction 2 inserts a row that matches the search criteria. If transaction 1 reexecutes the query statement that read the rows, it will receive a different set of rows. If the data source supports transaction processing, any of the following values are accepted by DB2 CLI for this option, but each data source can support only a subset of the isolation levels (you can get a list of supported isolation levels at application runtime by calling the SQLGetInfo( ) function with the *InfoType* parameter set to SQL_TXN_ISOLATION_OPTIONS): SQL_TXN_READ_UNCOMMITTED: Dirty reads, reads that cannot be repeated, and phantoms are possible. SQL_TXN_READ_COMMITTED: Dirty reads are not possible. Reads that cannot be repeated and phantoms are possible. This is the default value for this option. SQL_TXN_REPEATABLE_READ: Dirty reads and reads that cannot be repeated are not possible. Phantoms are possible. SQL_TXN_SERIALIZABLE: Transactions ran be serialized. Dirty reads, nonrepeatable reads, and phantoms are not possible. SQL_TXN_NOCOMMIT: Changes are effectively committed at the end of a successful operation; no explicit commit or rollback is allowed. This is analogous to autocommit. This is not an SQL92 isolation level, rather an IBM defined extension that is supported only by DB2 for OS/400. In IBM terminology, SQL_TXN_READ_UNCOMMITTED is an uncommitted read, SQL_TXN_READ_COMMITTED is cursor stability, SQL_TXN_REPEATABLE_READ is read stability, and SQL_TXN _SERIALIZABLE is a repeatable read. This option cannot be changed if there is an open cursor on the associated SQL statement handle. Changing this option causes the default value set at the connection level to be overridden (refer to the SQLGetConnectOption( ) and the SQLSetConnectOption( )

TABLE 14.6 SQL Statement Options *(Continued)*

Option	Data type	Description
		functions for more information). Note: The value SQL_STMTTXN_ISOLATION is synonymous with the value SQL_TXN_ISOLATION. However, since the ODBC driver manager does not recognize SQL_TXN_ISOLATION as an SQL statement option, ODBC applications that need to set translation isolation levels on a per statement basis must use the option SQL_STMTTXN_ISOLATION with the SQLSetStmtOption( ) function call. Also note that SQL_STMTTXN_ISOLATION/SQL_TXN_ISOLATION is an IBM-defined option at the SQL statement level.

Adapted from IBM Database 2 Call Level Interface Guide and Reference, Table 133, pages 363 to 366.

Specifications DB2 CLI 2.1, ODBC 1.0, X/OPEN CLI

Return Codes SQL_SUCCESS, SQL_INVALID_HANDLE, SQL_ERROR

SQLSTATEs **24**000, **40**003, **08**S01, **S1**001, **S1**009, **S1**010, **S1**092, **S1**C00

Comments

- This function can retrieve the value of any statement option that can be set by the SQLSetStmtOption( ) function, and the value of the SQL_ROW_NUMBER option, which is a read-only option that cannot be set by the SQLSetStmtOption( ) function. If the SQL_ROW_NUMBER statement option is specified as the *Option* parameter value, a 32-bit integer value that identifies the current row number in the result data set will be returned. If the current row number cannot be determined or if there is no current row, 0 will be returned.
- The ODBC read-only statement option SQL_GET_BOOKMARK is neither recognized nor supported by DB2 CLI. If this SQL statement option is specified in the *Option* parameter, the return code SQL_ERROR will be returned.
- The maximum length of any character string returned by this function (excluding the null-terminator) cannot exceed SQL_MAX_OPTION_STRING_LENGTH bytes.

Restrictions There are no restrictions associated with this function call.

See Also SQLSetConnectOption( ), SQLSetStmtOption( )

Examples The following C program illustrates how to use the SQLGetStmtOption( ) function to determine whether or not SQL statements are scanned for vendor escape clause sequences when they are submitted to the data source for processing:

```
#include <stdio.h>
#include <stdlib.h>
#include <sqlcli1.h>

int main()
{
    /* Declare The Local Memory Variables */
    SQLRETURN      rc = SQL_SUCCESS;
    SQLHENV        EnvHandle;
    SQLHDBC        DSCHandle;
    SQLHSTMT       StmtHandle;
```

```
    SQLUSMALLINT  ScanFlag;

    /* Allocate An Environment Handle */
    rc = SQLAllocEnv(&EnvHandle);

    /* Allocate A Connection Handle */
    rc = SQLAllocConnect(EnvHandle, &DSCHandle);

    /* Connect To The SAMPLE Database */
    rc = SQLConnect(DSCHandle, "SAMPLE", SQL_NTS, "etpdd6z", SQL_NTS,
                    "sanders", SQL_NTS);

    /* Allocate An SQL Statement Handle */
    rc = SQLAllocStmt(DSCHandle, &StmtHandle);

    /* Determine The Whether Or Not SQL Statement Strings Will Be */
    /* Scanned For Vendor Escape Clause Sequences                 */
    rc = SQLGetStmtOption(StmtHandle, SQL_NOSCAN,
                          (SQLPOINTER) &ScanFlag);

    if (rc == SQL_SUCCESS)
        {
        if (ScanFlag == SQL_NOSCAN_OFF)
            printf("SQL statements will be ");
        else
            printf("SQL statements will not be ");
        printf("scanned for vendor escape clause sequences.\n");
        }

    /* Disconnect From The SAMPLE Database */
    SQLDisconnect(DSCHandle);

    /* Free The SQL Statement Handle */
    if (StmtHandle != NULL)
        SQLFreeStmt(StmtHandle, SQL_DROP);

    /* Free The Connection Handle */
    if (DSCHandle != NULL)
        SQLFreeConnect(DSCHandle);

    /* Free The Environment Handle */
    if (EnvHandle != NULL)
        SQLFreeEnv(EnvHandle);

    /* Return To The Operating System */
    return(rc);
}
```

The following C++ program illustrates how the SQLGetStmtOption( ) function can be used by class methods to determine whether or not SQL statements are scanned for vendor escape clause sequences when they are submitted to the data source for processing:

```
#include <iostream.h>
#include <string.h>
#include <sqlcli1.h>

/* Define The CLI Class */
```

```
class CLI
{
    /* Declare The Private Attribute Variables */
    private:
       SQLHENV       EnvHandle;
       SQLHDBC       DSCHandle;
       SQLHSTMT      StmtHandle;
       SQLUSMALLINT  ScanFlag;

    /* Declare The Public Attribute Variables */
    public:
       SQLRETURN  rc;

    /* Declare The Member Function Prototypes */
    CLI();                                   // Constructor
    ~CLI();                                  // Destructor
    SQLRETURN Connect();
    SQLRETURN ShowECInfo();
    SQLRETURN Disconnect();
} ;

/* Define The Class Constructor */
CLI::CLI()
{
    /* Initialize The Return Code Variable */
    rc = SQL_SUCCESS;

    /* Allocate An Environment Handle */
    rc = SQLAllocEnv(&EnvHandle);

    /* Allocate A Connection Handle */
    rc = SQLAllocConnect(EnvHandle, &DSCHandle);
}

/* Define The Class Destructor */
CLI::~CLI()
{
    /* Free The Connection Handle */
    if (DSCHandle != NULL)
        SQLFreeConnect(DSCHandle);

    /* Free The Environment Handle */
    if (EnvHandle != NULL)
        SQLFreeEnv(EnvHandle);
}

/* Define The Connect() Member Function */
SQLRETURN CLI::Connect()
{
    /* Connect To The SAMPLE Database */
    rc = SQLConnect(DSCHandle, (SQLCHAR *) "SAMPLE", SQL_NTS,
                    (SQLCHAR *) "etpdd6z", SQL_NTS,
                    (SQLCHAR *) "sanders", SQL_NTS);

    /* Allocate An SQL Statement Handle */
    rc = SQLAllocStmt(DSCHandle, &StmtHandle);

    /* Return The CLI Function Return Code */
    return(rc);
```

```
}

/* Define The Disconnect() Member Function */
SQLRETURN CLI::Disconnect(void)
{
    /* Disconnect From The Database */
    rc = SQLDisconnect(DSCHandle);

    /* Free The SQL Statement Handle */
    if (StmtHandle != NULL)
        SQLFreeStmt(StmtHandle, SQL_DROP);

    /* Return The CLI Function Return Code */
    return(rc);
}

/* Define The ShowECInfo() Member Function */
SQLRETURN CLI::ShowECInfo(void)
{
    /* Determine The Whether Or Not SQL Statement Strings Will Be */
    /* Scanned For Vendor Escape Clause Sequences                 */
    rc = SQLGetStmtOption(StmtHandle, SQL_NOSCAN,
                          (SQLPOINTER) &ScanFlag);

    if (rc == SQL_SUCCESS)
        {
        if (ScanFlag == SQL_NOSCAN_OFF)
            cout << "SQL statements will be ";
        else
            cout << "SQL statements will not be ";
        cout << "scanned for vendor escape clause sequences.";
        cout << endl;
        }

    /* Return The CLI Function Return Code */
    return(rc);
}

int main()
{
    /* Declare The Local Memory Variables */
    SQLRETURN  rc = SQL_SUCCESS;

    /* Create An Instance Of The CLI Class */
    CLI Sample;

    /* Connect To The SAMPLE Database */
    if ((rc = Sample.Connect()) != SQL_SUCCESS)
        return(rc);

    /* Determine The Whether Or Not SQL Statement Strings Will Be */
    /* Scanned For Vendor Escape Clause Sequences                 */
    Sample.ShowECInfo();

    /* Disconnect From The SAMPLE Database */
    Sample.Disconnect();

    /* Return To The Operating System */
    return(rc);
}
```

SQLSetStmtOption

Purpose The SQLSetStmtOption( ) function sets a connection option associated with a specific SQL statement handle.

Syntax

```
SQLRETURN  SQLSetStmtOption (SQLHSTMT     StmtHandle,
                             SQLUSMALLINT Option,
                             SQLPOINTER   Value);
```

Parameters

StmtHandle The statement handle where the address of the SQL statement buffer is stored.

Option The SQL statement option to be set. This parameter can contain any of the following values:

- SQL_ASYNC_ENABLE
- SQL_BIND_TYPE
- SQL_CONCURRENCY
- SQL_CURSOR_HOLD
- SQL_CURSOR_TYPE
- SQL_MAX_LENGTH
- SQL_MAX_ROWS
- SQL_NODESCRIBE
- SQL_NOSCAN
- SQL_PARAMOPT_ATOMIC
- SQL_QUERY_TIMEOUT
- SQL_RETRIEVE_DATA
- SQL_ROWSET_SIZE
- SQL_STMTTXN_ISOLATION
- SQL_TXN_ISOLATION

Value A pointer to a location in memory where the new value for the SQL statement option is stored. Depending on the SQL statement option being set, this pointer can reference either a 32-bit integer value or a null-terminated character string.

Includes

```
#include <sqlcli1.h>
```

Description The SQLSetStmtOption( ) function sets an SQL statement option associated with a specific SQL statement handle. Refer to the SQLGetStmtOption( ) function for more information about the different SQL statement options available.

Specifications DB2 CLI 2.1, ODBC 1.0, X/OPEN CLI

Return Codes SQL_SUCCESS, SQL_SUCCESS_WITH_INFO, SQL_INVALID_HANDLE, SQL_ERROR

SQLSTATEs **01**S02, **24**000, **40**003, **08**S01, **S1**000, **S1**001, **S1**009, **S1**010, **S1**011, **S1**092, **S1**C00

Comments

- The SQLSetStmtOption( ) function can set only a connection option associated with a specific SQL statement handle. In order to set a connection option for all SQL statement handles associated with a connection handle, call the SQLSetConnectOption( ) function.

- All statement options set by the SQLSetStmtOption( ) function remain in effect until they are modified by either a SQLSetStmtOption( ) or a SQLSetConnectOption( ) function call.
- If you free a SQL statement handle by executing the SQLFreeStmt( ) function with the SQL_DROP option, all SQL statement options for that statement handle will be reset. If you free a SQL statement handle by executing the SQLFreeStmt( ) function with the SQL_CLOSE, SQL_UNBIND, or SQL_RESET_PARAMS option, all SQL statement options for that SQL statement handle will remain intact.
- The maximum length of any character string supplied by this function (excluding the null terminator) must not exceed SQL_MAX_OPTION_STRING_LENGTH bytes. No SQL statement option currently requires a string value.

Restrictions The SQL statement options SQL_KEYSET_SIZE, SQL_BOOKMARKS, and SQL_SIMULATE_CURSOR are neither recognized nor supported by DB2 CLI. If any of these options are specified in a DB2 CLI application, the SQL_ERROR return code will be returned.

See Also SQLColAttributes( ), SQLFetch( ), SQLExtendedFetch( ), SQLGetConnectOption( ), SQLGetData( ), SQLGetStmtOption( ), SQLParamOptions( ), SQLSetConnectOption( )

Examples The following C program illustrates how the SQLSetStmtOption( ) function can limit the size of a result data set produced by an SQL query to 100 rows:

```
#include <stdio.h>
#include <stdlib.h>
#include <sqlcli1.h>

int main()
{
    /* Declare The Local Memory Variables */
    SQLRETURN       rc = SQL_SUCCESS;
    SQLHENV         EnvHandle;
    SQLHDBC         DSCHandle;
    SQLHSTMT        StmtHandle;
    SQLUINTEGER     MaxRows;

    /* Allocate An Environment Handle */
    rc = SQLAllocEnv(&EnvHandle);

    /* Allocate A Connection Handle */
    rc = SQLAllocConnect(EnvHandle, &DSCHandle);

    /* Connect To The SAMPLE Database */
    rc = SQLConnect(DSCHandle, "SAMPLE", SQL_NTS, "etpdd6z", SQL_NTS,
                 "sanders", SQL_NTS);

    /* Allocate An SQL Statement Handle */
    rc = SQLAllocStmt(DSCHandle, &StmtHandle);

    /* Determine The Maximum Number Of Rows That Can Be Returned  */
    /* From An SQL Query                                          */
    rc = SQLGetStmtOption(StmtHandle, SQL_MAX_ROWS,
                          (SQLPOINTER) &MaxRows);

    if (rc == SQL_SUCCESS)
        {
        if (MaxRows == 0)
```

```
            printf("Any number of ");
        else
            printf("Up to %d ", MaxRows);
        printf("rows can be returned by an SQL query.\n");
        }

    /* Set The Maximum Number Of Rows That Can Be Returned From */
    /* An SQL Query To 100                                      */
    rc = SQLSetStmtOption(StmtHandle, SQL_MAX_ROWS, 100);

    /* Verify That The Maximum Number Of Rows That Can Be Returned */
    /* From An SQL Query Has Been Set To 100                       */
    rc = SQLGetStmtOption(StmtHandle, SQL_MAX_ROWS,
                          (SQLPOINTER) &MaxRows);

    if (rc == SQL_SUCCESS)
        {
        if (MaxRows == 0)
            printf("Any number of ");
        else
            printf("Up to %d ", MaxRows);
        printf("rows can be returned by an SQL query.\n");
        }
    /* Disconnect From The SAMPLE Database */
    SQLDisconnect(DSCHandle);

    /* Free The SQL Statement Handle */
    if (StmtHandle != NULL)
        SQLFreeStmt(StmtHandle, SQL_DROP);

    /* Free The Connection Handle */
    if (DSCHandle != NULL)
        SQLFreeConnect(DSCHandle);

    /* Free The Environment Handle */
    if (EnvHandle != NULL)
        SQLFreeEnv(EnvHandle);

    /* Return To The Operating System */
    return(rc);
}
```

The following C++ program illustrates how the SQLSetStmtOption( ) function can be used by class methods to limit the size of a result data set produced by an SQL query to 100 rows:

```
#include <iostream.h>
#include <string.h>
#include <sqlcli1.h>

/* Define The CLI Class */
class CLI
{
    /* Declare The Private Attribute Variables */
    private:
       SQLHENV        EnvHandle;
       SQLHDBC        DSCHandle;
       SQLHSTMT       StmtHandle;
       SQLINTEGER     MaxRows;

    /* Declare The Public Attribute Variables */
    public:
```

```
        SQLRETURN  rc;

    /* Declare The Member Function Prototypes */
    CLI();                                  // Constructor
    ~CLI();                                 // Destructor
    SQLRETURN Connect();
    SQLRETURN GetMaxRows();
    SQLRETURN SetMaxRows(SQLINTEGER MaxRows);
    SQLRETURN Disconnect();
} ;

/* Define The Class Constructor */
CLI::CLI()
{
    /* Initialize The Return Code Variable */
    rc = SQL_SUCCESS;

    /* Allocate An Environment Handle */
    rc = SQLAllocEnv(&EnvHandle);

    /* Allocate A Connection Handle */
    rc = SQLAllocConnect(EnvHandle, &DSCHandle);
}

/* Define The Class Destructor */
CLI::~CLI()
{
    /* Free The Connection Handle */
    if (DSCHandle != NULL)
        SQLFreeConnect(DSCHandle);

    /* Free The Environment Handle */
    if (EnvHandle != NULL)
        SQLFreeEnv(EnvHandle);
}

/* Define The Connect() Member Function */
SQLRETURN CLI::Connect()
{
    /* Connect To The SAMPLE Database */
    rc = SQLConnect(DSCHandle, (SQLCHAR *) "SAMPLE", SQL_NTS,
                    (SQLCHAR *) "etpdd6z", SQL_NTS,
                    (SQLCHAR *) "sanders", SQL_NTS);

    /* Allocate An SQL Statement Handle */
    rc = SQLAllocStmt(DSCHandle, &StmtHandle);

    /* Return The CLI Function Return Code */
    return(rc);
}

/* Define The Disconnect() Member Function */
SQLRETURN CLI::Disconnect(void)
{
    /* Disconnect From The Database */
    rc = SQLDisconnect(DSCHandle);

    /* Free The SQL Statement Handle */
    if (StmtHandle != NULL)
        SQLFreeStmt(StmtHandle, SQL_DROP);

    /* Return The CLI Function Return Code */
    return(rc);
```

```
}

/* Define The GetMaxRows() Member Function */
SQLRETURN CLI::GetMaxRows(void)
{
    /* Determine The Maximum Number Of Rows That Can Be Returned  */
    /* From An SQL Query                                          */
    rc = SQLGetStmtOption(StmtHandle, SQL_MAX_ROWS,
                      (SQLPOINTER) &MaxRows);

    if (rc == SQL_SUCCESS)
        {
        if (MaxRows == 0)
            cout << "Any number of ";
        else
            cout << "Up to " << MaxRows << " ";
        cout << "rows can be returned by an SQL query." << endl;
        }

    /* Return The CLI Function Return Code */
    return(rc);
}
/* Define The SetMaxRows() Member Function */
SQLRETURN CLI::SetMaxRows(SQLINTEGER MaxRows)
{
    /* Set The Maximum Number Of Rows That Can Be Returned From */
    /* An SQL Query To 100                                      */
    rc = SQLSetStmtOption(StmtHandle, SQL_MAX_ROWS, MaxRows);

    /* Return The CLI Function Return Code */
    return(rc);
}

int main()
{
    /* Declare The Local Memory Variables */
    SQLRETURN  rc = SQL_SUCCESS;

    /* Create An Instance Of The CLI Class */
    CLI Sample;

    /* Connect To The SAMPLE Database */
    if ((rc = Sample.Connect()) != SQL_SUCCESS)
        return(rc);

    /* Determine The Maximum Number Of Rows That Can Be Returned  */
    /* From An SQL Query                                          */
    Sample.GetMaxRows();

    /* Set The Maximum Number Of Rows That Can Be Returned From */
    /* An SQL Query To 100                                      */
    Sample.SetMaxRows(100);

    /* Verify That The Maximum Number Of Rows That Can Be Returned */
    /* From An SQL Query Has Been Set To 100                       */
    Sample.GetMaxRows();

    /* Disconnect From The SAMPLE Database */
    Sample.Disconnect();

    /* Return To The Operating System */
    return(rc);
}
```

CHAPTER 15

SQL STATEMENT PROCESSING FUNCTIONS

SQL statement processing functions are a group of DB2 CLI function calls that can prepare and execute SQL statements recognized by the connected data source. This group includes:

- A CLI function that allocates memory storage areas to SQL statement information.
- CLI functions that assign storage areas to parameter markers in a SQL statement.
- A CLI function that prepares a SQL statement for execution.
- CLI functions that execute SQL statements.
- A CLI function that retrieves information about how a SQL statement is translated for a data source.
- A CLI function that terminates the current transaction.
- A CLI functions that frees allocated memory storage areas that hold SQL statement information.

Table 15.1 lists the SQL statement processing functions available with DB2 CLI.

Allocating a SQL Statement Handle

Before a DB2 CLI application can submit a SQL statement to a data source for processing, it must first allocate a SQL statement handle by calling the SQLAllocStmt( ) function. When this call is executed, the DB2 CLI load library (or the ODBC driver manager) allocates a memory storage area and returns an appropriate handle back to the calling application. The returned handle is a pointer variable that refers to the allocated data object (memory buffer), which is controlled by DB2 CLI. The application can then use the handle to pass a block of information about the SQL statement to each DB2 CLI function that takes a SQL statement handle as an input parameter. By using SQL statement handles, the application is freed from the responsibility of allocating data structures, such as SQLDA and SQLCA, which are required for processing embedded SQL statements.

Setting Parameter Values

In embedded SQL applications, host variables can provide values to SQL statements at application runtime. Since host variables are not supported by DB2 CLI, however, you must use another method to provide runtime values to SQL statements in CLI applications. This is where parameter markers

TABLE 15.1 SQL Statement Processing Functions

Function name	Description
SQLAllocStmt( )	Allocates a SQL statement handle and its associated resources.
SQLPrepare( )	Prepares a SQL statement for execution.
SQLBindParameter( )	Assigns data storage for a parameter marker in a SQL statement (ODBC 2.0).
SQLBindFileToParm( )	Assigns a LOB file reference to a parameter marker in a SQL statement.
SQLSetParm( )	Assigns data storage for a parameter marker in a SQL statement (ODBC 1.0). Note: In ODBC 2.0, this function has been replaced by the SQLBindParameter( ) function.
SQLParamOptions( )	Specifies an array of multiple values for parameter markers.
SQLGetCursorName( )	Retrieves the cursor name for a cursor that is associated with a SQL statement handle.
SQLSetCursorName( )	Specifies a cursor name for a cursor that is associated with a SQL statement handle.
SQLExecute( )	Executes a prepared SQL statement.
SQLExecDirect( )	Prepares and executes a SQL statement immediately.
SQLNativeSql( )	Retrieves the text of a SQL statement after it has been translated by the data source driver.
SQLNumParams( )	Retrieves the number of parameter markers used in a SQL statement.
SQLParamData( )	Used in conjunction with the SQLPutData( ) function to process data-at-execution parameters (to support long data processing).
SQLPutData( )	Used in conjunction with the SQLParamData( ) function to send part or all of a data value associated with a parameter marker from the data source to the application (useful for processing long data values).
SQLCancel( )	Cancels an SQL statement.
SQLTransact( )	Rolls back or commits the current transaction.
SQLFreeStmt( )	Ends SQL statement processing, closes the associated cursor, discards pending result data, and optionally frees all resources associated with a statement handle.

Adapted from IBM's Database 2 Call Level Interface Guide and Reference, Table 11, pages 103 to 106.

15

come into play. A parameter marker is simply a question mark (?) placed anywhere in a SQL statement that a host variable would be referenced if the SQL statement were used in an embedded SQL application. For example, you could use the following SQL statement in a CLI application to insert a row of data into the EMPLOYEE table:

```
INSERT INTO EMPLOYEE (NAME, AGE, HIREDATE) VALUES (?, ?, ?)
```

An application can use parameter markers in a SQL statement whenever:

- It needs to execute the same prepared SQL statement several times with different parameter values.
- The parameter values are not known at the time the SQL statement is prepared.
- The parameter values need to be converted from one data type to another.

Before a parameter marker can actually be used, it must first be bound to a storage location, and the data types (along with the precision and scale) of both the storage location and the data source column associated with the parameter marker must be specified. You can perform this binding operation by calling either the SQLBindParameter( ) function or the SQLBindFileToParam( ) function for each parameter marker coded in the SQL statement. This binding process can take place before or after the SQL statement is prepared, but the actual value for each parameter must be placed in the appropriate storage location before the SQL statement is executed.

You can also bind arrays containing several values to a parameter marker. In this case, you must call the SQLParamOptions( ) function to specify that the storage area will contain an array instead of a single value. With this method, a CLI function that submits the SQL statement for execution has to be called only once, and the data source will execute it as many times as necessary to process each value in the array.

An application can change the value (or values) in a bound storage area at any time. When the SQL statement is sent to the data source for execution, the CLI/ODBC driver retrieves the current values in the bound storage areas and uses them to replace the parameter markers in the SQL statement.

Executing SQL Statements

DB2 CLI applications can submit a SQL statement to the data source for execution in two ways: prepared execution and direct execution. These methods are similar but not identical to the prepared and immediate methods of execution used by embedded SQL applications.

Prepared execution is a two-step process. In the first step, you create an executable SQL statement known as the prepared statement from the character form of the SQL statement by calling the SQLPrepare( ) function. In the second step, you send the prepared statement to the data source to be executed by calling the SQLExecute( ) function.

Direct execution combines these two steps into a single action. In this case, the character form of the SQL statement is sent directly to the data source to be both prepared and executed when the SQLExecDirect( ) function is called.

A prepared statement executes faster than an unprepared statement because the data source does not have to produce an access plan each time it executes the statement. When a SQL statement is prepared, the data source compiles the statement, produces an access plan, and returns an access plan identifier to the CLI/ODBC driver. Network traffic is reduced because the driver sends the access plan identifier to the data source instead of the entire statement.

An application should prepare a statement before executing it if either of the following conditions is true: if the application will execute the SQL statement more than once, possibly with intermediate changes to parameter values, or if the application needs to obtain information about the result data set prior to execution.

An application should execute a statement directly if both of the following are true: if the application will execute the statement only once, and if the application does not need information about the result data set prior to execution.

Data-at-Execution Values

An application can pass the value for a parameter marker to the data source when a SQL statement is executed. This can be particularly useful when the data value is so large that it needs to be sent in pieces. The SQLParamData( ) function can be used in conjunction with the SQLPutData( ) function to send data to a specified data source at SQL statement execution time in what is known as a data-at-execution sequence.

When the CLI/ODBC driver processes a call to either the SQLExecute( ) or SQLExecDirect( ) function and the SQL statement being executed contains one or more data-at-execution parameters, the driver returns the SQL_NEED_DATA return code to the calling application. To send parameter data to the data source, the application must do the following:

1. Call the SQLParamData( ) function to retrieve the address of the data storage area that was bound to the parameter marker.
2. Call the SQLPutData( ) function one or more times to send data for the parameter marker to the data source. (More than one call is necessary if the data value is larger than the buffer; multiple calls are allowed only if the C data type is character or binary and the SQL data type is character, binary, or data source-specific.)

3. Call the SQLParamData( ) function again to indicate that all data has been sent for the parameter. If there is another data-at-execution parameter in the SQL statement, the driver will return the address of the data storage area that was bound to the next data-at-execution parameter marker and the SQL_NEED_DATA for the function return code. Otherwise, the driver will return the SQL_SUCCESS return code.
4. Repeat steps 2 and 3 for all remaining data-at-execution parameters.

Completing Transactions

DB2 CLI applications can operate in two different modes: auto commit or manual commit. In auto-commit mode, every SQL statement is treated as a complete transaction, which is automatically committed. In manual-commit mode, a transaction consists of one or more statements. In manual-commit mode, when an application submits a SQL statement and no transaction is open, the driver implicitly starts a transaction. The transaction remains open until the application either commits or rolls back the transaction with the SQLTransact( ) function.

If a CLI/ODBC driver supports the SQL_AUTOCOMMIT connection option, the default transaction mode is auto commit; otherwise, it is manual commit. An application can call the SQLSetConnectOption( ) function at any time to switch between manual-commit and auto-commit mode. Committing or rolling back a transaction, either by calling the SQLTransact( ) function or by using the SQL_AUTOCOMMIT connection option, can cause the data source to delete the access plans for all SQL statement handles that exist for the connection handle.

SQLAllocStmt

Purpose

The SQLAllocStmt( ) function allocates memory for a SQL statement handle and associates the SQL statement handle with a specific data source connection.

Syntax

```
SQLRETURN  SQLAllocStmt (SQLHDBC      DSCHandle,
                         SQLHSTMT FAR *StmtHandle);
```

Parameters

DSCHandle The data source connection handle where the address of the data source connection information buffer is stored.

StmtHandle A pointer to a location in memory where this function is to store the starting address of the allocated SQL statement information buffer.

Includes

```
#include <sqlcli1.h>
```

Description

The SQLAllocStmt( ) function allocates memory for a SQL statement handle, and associates the SQL statement handle with a specific data source connection. DB2 CLI uses SQL statement handles to reference information associated with a SQL statement. This information includes descriptor information, attribute values, result data set values, cursor information, and status information for the SQL statement being processed. Each SQL statement must have its own statement handle, but statement handles can be reused by different SQL statements.

Specifications

DB2 CLI 1.1, ODBC 1.0, X/OPEN CLI, ISO CLI

Return Codes SQL_SUCCESS, SQL_INVALID, HANDLE, SQL_ERROR

SQLSTATEs **08**003, **08**S01, **40**003, **58**004, **S1**001, **S1**009, **S1**013, **S1**014

Comments

- There is no limit to the number of SQL statement handles that can be allocated at any one time.
- A SQL statement handle must exist before any of the following functions can be called:
  –SQLPrepare( )
  –SQLBindParameter( )
  –SQLExecute( )
  –SQLExecDirect( )
  –any other CLI function that requires a valid SQL statement handle as one of its input parameters.
- In order to execute a positioned UPDATE or DELETE operation, an application must use, at a minimum, two different SQL statement handles: one for the SELECT statement that retrieves the cursor result data set and one for the positioned UPDATE or DELETE statement.
- If the *StmtHandle* parameter already contains a valid address for a SQL statement buffer (that was allocated by a previous call to this function) when this function is called, the original statement handle address will be overwritten and the memory associated with the original statement handle address can no longer be freed. Since this type of "memory leak" situation is caused by a programming error, it cannot be detected by DB2 CLI.
- If the SQL_ERROR return code is returned by this function, the *StmtHandle* parameter will contain the value SQL_NULL_HSTMT. To find out why the SQL_ERROR return code was generated, call the SQLError( ) function using the same data source handle (DSCHandle), with the *StmtHandle* parameter set to SQL_NULL_HSTMT.

Prerequisites Either the SQLConnect( ) or the SQLDriverConnect( ) function must be executed before this function is called.

Restrictions There are no restrictions associated with this function call.

See Also SQLFreeStmt( ), SQLConnect( ), SQLDriverConnect( ), SQLGetStmtOption( ), SQLSetStmtOption( )

Examples The following C program illustrates how to allocate a SQL statement handle and how to prepare and execute an SQL statement:

```
#include <stdio.h>
#include <stdlib.h>
#include <string.h>
#include <sqlcli1.h>

int main()
{
    /* Declare The Local Memory Variables */
    SQLRETURN     rc = SQL_SUCCESS;
    SQLHENV       EnvHandle;
    SQLHDBC       DSCHandle;
    SQLHSTMT      StmtHandle;
    SQLCHAR       SQLStmt[80];
```

```
SQLCHAR      DeptNo[4];
SQLCHAR      DeptName[30];

/* Allocate An Environment Handle */
rc = SQLAllocEnv(&EnvHandle);

/* Allocate A Connection Handle */
rc = SQLAllocConnect(EnvHandle, &DSCHandle);

/* Connect To The SAMPLE Database */
rc = SQLConnect(DSCHandle, "SAMPLE", SQL_NTS, "etpdd6z", SQL_NTS,
                "sanders", SQL_NTS);

/* Allocate A SQL Statement Handle */
rc = SQLAllocStmt(DSCHandle, &StmtHandle);

/* Define And Prepare A SELECT SQL Statement */
strcpy(SQLStmt, "SELECT DEPTNO, DEPTNAME FROM USERID.DEPARTMENT");
SQLPrepare(StmtHandle, SQLStmt, SQL_NTS);

/* Execute The SQL Statement */
rc = SQLExecute(StmtHandle);

if (rc != SQL_ERROR)
    {
    /* Bind The Columns In The Result Data Set To Local */
    /* Storage Variables                                 */
    SQLBindCol(StmtHandle, 1, SQL_C_CHAR, (SQLPOINTER) DeptNo,
               sizeof(DeptNo), NULL);

    SQLBindCol(StmtHandle, 2, SQL_C_CHAR, (SQLPOINTER) DeptName,
               sizeof(DeptName), NULL);

    /* Retrieve And Display The Results */
    printf("Department     Department\n");
    printf("Number         Name\n");
    printf("--------------------------------------\n");
    while (rc != SQL_NO_DATA_FOUND)
        {

        /* Retrieve A Record From The Result Data Set */
        rc = SQLFetch(StmtHandle);

        /* Print The Information Retrieved */
        if (rc != SQL_NO_DATA_FOUND)
            printf("%-14s %s\n", DeptNo, DeptName);
        }
    }

/* Disconnect From The SAMPLE Database */
SQLDisconnect(DSCHandle);

/* Free The SQL Statement Handle */
if (StmtHandle != NULL)
    SQLFreeStmt(StmtHandle, SQL_DROP);

/* Free The Connection Handle */
if (DSCHandle != NULL)
    SQLFreeConnect(DSCHandle);

/* Free The Environment Handle */
```

```
    if (EnvHandle != NULL)
        SQLFreeEnv(EnvHandle);

    /* Return To The Operating System */
    return(rc);
}
```

The following C++ program illustrates how to allocate a SQL statement handle and how to prepare and execute an SQL statement:

```
#include <iostream.h>
#include <string.h>
#include <sqlcli1.h>

/* Define The CLI Class */
class CLI
{
    /* Declare The Private Attribute Variables */
    private:
       SQLHENV      EnvHandle;
       SQLHDBC      DSCHandle;
       SQLCHAR      Name[10];
       SQLCHAR      DeptNo[4];
       SQLCHAR      DeptName[30];

    /* Declare The Public Attribute Variables */
    public:
       SQLRETURN    rc;
       SQLHSTMT     StmtHandle;

    /* Declare The Member Function Prototypes */
    CLI();                                      // Constructor
    ~CLI();                                     // Destructor
    SQLRETURN Connect();
    SQLRETURN ShowResults();
    SQLRETURN Disconnect();
} ;

/* Define The Class Constructor */
CLI::CLI()
{
    /* Initialize The Return Code Variable */
    rc = SQL_SUCCESS;

    /* Allocate An Environment Handle */
    rc = SQLAllocEnv(&EnvHandle);

    /* Allocate A Connection Handle */
    rc = SQLAllocConnect(EnvHandle, &DSCHandle);
}

/* Define The Class Destructor */
CLI::~CLI()
{
    /* Free The Connection Handle */
    if (DSCHandle != NULL)
        SQLFreeConnect(DSCHandle);

    /* Free The Environment Handle */
    if (EnvHandle != NULL)
```

```
        SQLFreeEnv(EnvHandle);
}

/* Define The Connect() Member Function */
SQLRETURN CLI::Connect()
{
    /* Connect To The SAMPLE Database */
    rc = SQLConnect(DSCHandle, (SQLCHAR *) "SAMPLE", SQL_NTS,
                    (SQLCHAR *) "etpdd6z", SQL_NTS,
                    (SQLCHAR *) "sanders", SQL_NTS);

    /* Allocate A SQL Statement Handle */
    rc = SQLAllocStmt(DSCHandle, &StmtHandle);

    /* Return The CLI Function Return Code */
    return(rc);
}

/* Define The Disconnect() Member Function */
SQLRETURN CLI::Disconnect(void)
{
    /* Disconnect From The Database */
    rc = SQLDisconnect(DSCHandle);

    /* Free The SQL Statement Handle */
    if (StmtHandle != NULL)
        SQLFreeStmt(StmtHandle, SQL_DROP);

    /* Return The CLI Function Return Code */
    return(rc);
}

/* Define The ShowResults() Member Function */
SQLRETURN CLI::ShowResults(void)
{
    /* Bind The Columns In The Result Data Set To Local */
    /* Storage Variables                                */
    SQLBindCol(StmtHandle, 1, SQL_C_CHAR, (SQLPOINTER) DeptNo,
               sizeof(DeptNo), NULL);

    SQLBindCol(StmtHandle, 2, SQL_C_CHAR, (SQLPOINTER) DeptName,
               sizeof(DeptName), NULL);

    /* Retrieve And Display The Results */
    cout << "Department     Department" << endl;
    cout << "Number         Name" << endl;
    cout << "---------------------------------------------" << endl;
    while (rc != SQL_NO_DATA_FOUND)
        {

        /* Retrieve A Record From The Result Data Set */
        rc = SQLFetch(StmtHandle);

        /* Print The Information Retrieved */
        if (rc != SQL_NO_DATA_FOUND)
            {
            cout.setf(ios::left);
            cout.width(15);
            cout << DeptNo << DeptName << endl;
            }
        }
```

```
    /* Return The CLI Function Return Code */
    return(rc);
}

int main()
{
    /* Declare The Local Memory Variables */
    SQLRETURN  rc = SQL_SUCCESS;
    SQLCHAR    SQLStmt[80];

    /* Create An Instance Of The CLI Class */
    CLI Sample;

    /* Connect To The SAMPLE Database */
    if ((rc = Sample.Connect()) != SQL_SUCCESS)
        return(rc);

    /* Define A SELECT SQL Statement */
    strcpy((char *) SQLStmt, "SELECT DEPTNO, DEPTNAME FROM ");
    strcat((char *) SQLStmt, "USERID.DEPARTMENT");

    /* Prepare The SQL Statement */
    SQLPrepare(Sample.StmtHandle, SQLStmt, SQL_NTS);

    /* Execute The SQL Statement */
    rc = SQLExecute(Sample.StmtHandle);

    /* Display The Results Of The SQL Query */
    if (rc == SQL_SUCCESS)
        Sample.ShowResults();

    /* Disconnect From The SAMPLE Database */
    Sample.Disconnect();

    /* Return To The Operating System */
    return(rc);
}
```

SQLPrepare

Purpose The SQLPrepare( ) function sends a SQL statement (associated with a SQL statement handle) to the appropriate data source to be prepared for execution.

Syntax

```
SQLRETURN  SQLPrepare (SQLHSTMT     StmtHandle,
                       SQLCHAR FAR *SQLString,
                       SQLINTEGER   SQLStringSize);
```

Parameters

StmtHandle The SQL statement handle where the address of the SQL statement buffer is stored.

SQLString A pointer to a location in memory where the SQL statement string is stored.

SQLStringSize The length of the SQL statement string stored in the *SQLString* parameter.

Includes

```
#include <sqlcli1.h>
```

Description The SQLPrepare( ) function sends a SQL statement (associated with a SQL statement handle) to the appropriate data source to be prepared for execution. Once a SQL statement has been prepared, it can be either executed by the SQLExecute( ) function or referenced by other DB2 CLI functions (such as SQLNumParams( ) and SQLGetCursorName( )) via its associated SQL statement handle. SQL statements that have been prepared can be executed multiple times without having to be reprepared.

Specifications DB2 CLI 1.1, ODBC 1.0, X/OPEN CLI, ISO CLI

Return Codes SQL_SUCCESS, SQL_SUCCESS_WITH_INFO, SQL_INVALID_HANDLE, SQL_ERROR

SQLSTATEs **01**504, **01**508, **08**S01, **21**S01, **21**S02, **24**000, **34**000, **37***xxx*, **40**000, **40**003, **42***xxx*, **58**004, **S0**001, **S0**002, **S0**011, **S0**012, **S0**021, **S0**022, **S1**001, **S1**009, **S1**010, **S1**013, **S1**090, **S1**T00

Note: *xxx* means that any SQLSTATE subclass value with the class code 37 or 42 can be returned. Not all data sources are capable of reporting all these SQLSTATEs at SQL statement prepare time, so an application must be able to handle these conditions when calling both the SQLPrepare( ) function and the SQLExecute( ) function.

Comments

- The length of the SQL statement stored in the *SQLStringSize* parameter must be the exact length of the SQL statement if the statement is not null-terminated (the length is determined by the number of characters in the string). You can use the value SQL_NTS if the SQL statement is null-terminated.
- If there is an open cursor associated with the specified SQL statement handle, you must close it before using the SQL statement handle with this function.
- Once a SQL statement is prepared by this function, you can obtain information about the format of the result data that will be produced when the statement is executed (if the SQL statement was a query statement) by calling any of the following functions:
  –SQLNumResultCols( )
  –SQLDescribeCol( )
  –SQLColAttributes( )
- The SQL statement string being prepared might contain parameter markers; if so, call the SQLNumParams( ) function to determine the number of parameter markers in the statement. A parameter marker is represented by a question mark character (?) in a SQL statement, and indicates a position in the statement where an application-supplied value is substituted when the SQLExecute( ) function is called. The bind parameter functions—SQLBindParameter( ), SQLSetParam( ), and SQLBindFileToParam( )—bind (associate) application values with each parameter marker and indicate if any data conversion should be performed at the time the data is transferred to the data source. Once a SQL statement is prepared, all parameter markers in that statement must be bound before it can be executed.
- The SQL statement cannot be a COMMIT or a ROLLBACK statement. Only the SQLTransact( ) function can be used to issue COMMIT or ROLLBACK statements.

- If the SQL statement is a positioned UPDATE or DELETE statement, the cursor referenced by the SQL statement must be defined on a separate SQL statement handle, under the same connection handle and with the same isolation level.
- If the SQL statement contains vendor escape clause sequences, DB2 CLI will first modify the SQL statement text to the appropriate data-source-specific format before submitting it to the data source for preparation. If an application does not use vendor escape clause sequences, set the SQL_NOSCAN statement option to SQL_NOSCAN at the connection level so DB2 CLI will not perform this scan and conversion. Refer to the SQLSetStmtOption( ) function for more information.
- Since the SQL language has been substantially enhanced in DB2 for Common Servers, version 2.1, refer to Part 3 of this book, STRUCTURED QUERY LANGUAGE (SQL) STATEMENTS, for more information about DB2 SQL statements.

Restrictions There are no restrictions associated with this function call.

See Also SQLBindParameter( ), SQLBindFileToParam( ), SQLColAttributes( ), SQLDescribeCol( ), SQLExecute( ), SQLExecDirect( ), SQLNumParams( ), SQLNum ResultCols( ), SQLSetParam( )

Examples See the examples provided for the SQLAllocStmt( ) function in this chapter.

SQLBindParameter

Purpose The SQLBindParameter( ) function associates (binds) parameter markers in a SQL statement to application variables and/or large object (LOB) locators.

Syntax

```
SQLRETURN  SQLBindParameter (SQLHSTMT         StmtHandle,
                             SQLUSMALLINT     PMarkerNum,
                             SQLSMALLINT      ParameterType,
                             SQLSMALLINT      CDataType,
                             SQLSMALLINT      SQLDataType,
                             SQLUINTEGER      Precision,
                             SQLSMALLINT      Scale,
                             SQLPOINTER       Value,
                             SQLINTEGER       MaxValueSize,
                             SQLINTEGER FAR   *ValueSize);
```

Parameters

StmtHandle The SQL statement handle where the address of the SQL statement buffer is stored.

PMarkerNum The appropriate parameter marker number. Parameter markers are numbered sequentially from left to right, starting with 1, as they appear in the SQL statement.

ParameterType The appropriate parameter type. This parameter can contain any of the following values:

SQL_PARAM_INPUT	Indicates that the parameter marker is associated with an input parameter of a called stored procedure, or with a SQL statement that is not a stored-procedure CALL.
SQL_PARAM_INPUT_OUTPUT	Indicates that the parameter marker is associated with an input/output parameter of a called, stored procedure.

SQL_PARAM_OUTPUT — Indicates that the parameter marker is associated with an output parameter of a called, stored procedure, or with the return value of a stored procedure.

CDataType The C language data type of the parameter. The following C data types are supported:

- SQL_C_BIT
- SQL_C_BINARY
- SQL_C_TINYINT
- SQL_C_SHORT
- SQL_C_LONG
- SQL_C_FLOAT
- SQL_C_DOUBLE
- SQL_C_CHAR
- SQL_C_DBCHAR
- SQL_C_BLOB_LOCATOR
- SQL_C_CLOB_LOCATOR
- SQL_C_DBCLOB_LOCATOR
- SQL_C_DATE
- SQL_C_TIME
- SQL_C_TIMESTAMP
- SQL_C_DEFAULT

Note: The SQL_C_DEFAULT value causes data to be transferred from its default C data type to the specified SQL data type.

SQLDataType The SQL data type of the parameter. The following SQL data types are supported:

- SQL_BINARY
- SQL_VARBINARY
- SQL_LONGVARBINARY
- SQL_SMALLINT
- SQL_INTEGER
- SQL_DECIMAL
- SQL_NUMERIC
- SQL_REAL
- SQL_FLOAT
- SQL_DOUBLE
- SQL_CHAR
- SQL_VARCHAR
- SQL_LONGVARCHAR
- SQL_BLOB

- SQL_BLOB_LOCATOR
- SQL_CLOB
- SQL_CLOB_LOCATOR
- SQL_DBCLOB
- SQL_DBCLOB_LOCATOR
- SQL_DATE
- SQL_TIME
- SQL_TIMESTAMP
- SQL_GRAPHIC
- SQL_VARGRAPHIC
- SQL_LONGVARGRAPHIC

> Note: SQL_BLOB_LOCATOR, SQL_CLOB_LOCATOR, and SQL_DBCLOB_LOCATOR are application-related concepts, so they do not map to a specific data type.

Precision The total number of bytes of data that will be sent to the data source for the specified parameter marker or the maximum decimal precision of the number (if the *SQLDataType* parameter value is SQL_DECIMAL or SQL_NUMERIC).

Value A pointer to a location in memory where the value associated with the parameter marker is stored.

ValueMaxSize The maximum size of the memory storage buffer that stores the value associated with the parameter marker.

ValueSize A pointer to a location in memory where the size of the data value associated with the parameter marker is stored.

Includes

```
#include <sqlcli1.h>
```

Description

The SQLBindParameter( ) function associates (binds) parameter markers in a SQL statement to application variables and/or large object (LOB) locators. A parameter marker is represented by a question mark character in a SQL statement, and indicates a position in the statement where an application-supplied value is substituted when the statement is executed. Parameter markers can be bound to either application variables (for all data types) or large object (LOB) locator variables (for BLOB, CLOB, and DBCLOB data types). When parameter markers are bound to application variables, data is transferred from the application to the connected data source when either the SQLExecute( ) or the SQLExecDirect( ) function is called. If necessary, data conversion occurs as the data is transferred.

The SQLBindParameter( ) function essentially extends the capability of the SQLSetParam( ) function by providing a method for:

- Specifying whether a parameter marker is an input, an input/output, or an output parameter marker necessary for the proper handling of stored procedure parameters.
- Specifying an array of input parameter marker values when the SQLParamOptions( ) function is used in conjunction with the SQLBindParameter( ) function.

You can still use the SQLSetParam( ) function to bind single-element application variables to parameter markers that are not part of a stored procedure, but this function is no longer supported by ODBC.

Specifications DB2 CLI 2.1, ODBC 2.0

Return Codes SQL_SUCCESS, SQL_INVALID_HANDLE, SQL_ERROR

SQLSTATEs **07**006, **08**S01, **40**003, **58**004, **S1**001, **S1**003, **S1**004, **S1**009, **S1**010, **S1**013, **S1**090, **S1**093, **S1**094, **S1**104, **S1**105, **S1**C00

Comments

- If the *ParameterType* parameter contains the value SQL_PARAM_INPUT or SQL_PARAM_INPUT_OUTPUT, the memory buffer referenced by the *Value* parameter must contain valid input data value(s) and the memory buffer referenced by the *ValueSize* parameter must contain one of the following values before the SQL statement can be executed:
  –The corresponding length (size) of the data value
  –SQL_NTS if the data value is a null-terminated string
  –SQL_NULL_DATA if the data value is a NULL value
  –SQL_DATA_AT_EXEC if the value should be sent via SQLParamData( ) and SQLPutData( ) function calls at SQL statement execution time
- When the SQL statement is executed, the actual data value(s) for the parameter marker(s) are sent to the data source.
- If the *ParameterType* parameter contains the value SQL_PARAM_OUTPUT, data for the output stored procedure parameter is returned to the *Value* and the *ValueSize* parameter buffers (unless both parameters contain NULL pointers) after the CALL SQL statement is executed. In this case, the *ValueSize* parameter will contain one of the following values:
  –the actual number of bytes written to the *Value* memory storage buffer (excluding the null-termination character)
  –SQL_NULL_DATA if a null value was returned
  –SQL_NO_TOTAL if the number of bytes written to the *Value* memory storage buffer cannot be determined
- If the *Value* and the *ValueSize* parameters contain NULL pointers, any output data returned by the stored procedure will be discarded.
- If the SQL data type is a binary or single-byte character string, the value in the *Precision* parameter must specify the length, in bytes, of the string. If the SQL data type is a double-byte (graphic) character string, the value in the *Precision* parameter must specify the length, in double-byte characters, of the string.
- If the *SQLDataType* parameter value is SQL_TIMESTAMP, the *Scale* parameter represents the number of digits to the right of the decimal point in the character representation of the timestamp value. (For example, the *Scale* parameter value for 1996-05-15 12:35:18.002 would be 3.)
- The value in the *ValueMaxSize* parameter is used by DB2 CLI to determine whether or not to truncate character or binary output data for stored procedure output parameters. This data truncation is performed as follows:
  –For character data, if the number of bytes to be returned is greater than or equal to the *ValueMaxSize* parameter value, the data will be truncated to *ValueMaxSize* –1 byte and is null-terminated (unless null-termination has been turned off).
  –For binary data, if the number of bytes to be returned is greater than or equal to the *ValueMaxSize* parameter value, the data will be truncated to *ValueMaxSize* bytes.
- To specify a NULL value for a parameter marker, assign the value SQL_NULL _DATA to the *ValueSize* parameter.
- If the *CDataType* parameter is set to SQL_C_CHAR, the value stored in the *ValueSize* parameter must be the exact length of the data string to be passed to the data source if the data string is not null-terminated (the length is determined by the

number of characters in the string). The *ValueSize* parameter can contain either a NULL pointer or the value SQL_NTS if the actual data string is null-terminated.

- If the *CDataType* parameter is set to SQL_C_CHAR and the *SQLDataType* parameter is set to SQL_GRAPHIC, the value stored in the *ValueSize* parameter must never be SQL_NTS and the data string passed to the data source must never be a NULL string.
- The value specified in the *ValueSize* parameter for SQL_GRAPHIC data types should identify the number of octets occupied by the double-byte data, so this value should always be a multiple of 2.
- When parameter markers are bound to LOB locator variables, the LOB locator values themselves are supplied by the connected data source; therefore, only the LOB locator, not the LOB data itself, is transferred from the application to the data source when the SQL statement is executed.
- A LOB locator can be used in conjunction with the SQLGetSubString( ), SQLGetPosition( ), or SQLGetLength( ) functions.
- You can bind a LOB parameter marker directly to a file by using the SQLBindFileToParam( ) function. In this case, when the SQL statement is executed, DB2 CLI transfers the contents of the specified file directly to the connected data source.
- A variable must be bound to each parameter marker specified in a SQL statement before the statement can be executed. When this function is executed, both the *Value* and the *ValueSize* parameter are treated as deferred arguments. If the *ParameterType* parameter value is SQL_PARAM_INPUT or SQL_PARAM_INPUT_OUTPUT, their storage locations must be valid and they must contain input data values when the SQL statement is executed. Similarly, if the *ParameterType* parameter value is set to SQL_PARAM_OUTPUT or SQL_PARAM_INPUT_OUTPUT, the parameter marker storage locations must remain valid until the CALL SQL statement has been executed. This means that the SQLExecDirect( ) or SQLExecute( ) function call must be made in the same procedure scope as the SQLBindParameter( ) function call, or these storage locations must be dynamically allocated or declared statically or globally.
- All parameters bound by this function remain in effect until you call the SQLFreeStmt( ) function with either the SQL_DROP or the SQL_RESET_PARAMS option specified, or until this function is called again for the same parameter marker number. All LOB locators remain in effect until the transaction in which they were created is ended or until they are freed by the FREE LOCATOR SQL statement.
- Once the SQL statement is executed and the results are processed, an application might want to reuse the SQL statement handle to execute a different SQL statement. If the parameter marker specifications are different (e.g., the number of parameters or the data type has changed), call the SQLFreeStmt( ) function with the SQL_RESET_PARAMS option specified to reset or clear the current parameter bindings.
- The C buffer data type specified in the *CDataType* parameter must be compatible with the SQL data type specified in the *SQLDataType* parameter, or an error will occur.
- An application can pass the value for a parameter to the data source either by placing the value in the *Value* buffer or by making one or more calls to the SQLPutData( ) function. With the second option, the associated parameters are treated as data-at-execution parameters, which is specified when the SQL_DATA_AT_EXEC value is placed in the *ValueSize* buffer. This sets the *Value* parameter to a 32-bit value that will be returned on a subsequent SQL-

ParamData( ) function call and can be used to identify the parameter position. For more information about data-at-execution parameters, refer to the SQLParm Data( ) and the SQLPutData( ) functions.

- If the SQLParamOptions( ) function specifies multiple values for each parameter marker, the *ValueSize* parameter points to an array of SQLINTEGER values where each of elements can be one of the following values:
  –The corresponding length (size) of the data value
  –SQL_NTS if the data value is a null-terminated string
  –SQL_NULL_DATA if the data value is a NULL value
  –SQL_DATA_AT_EXEC if the value should be sent via SQLParamData( ) and SQLPutData( ) function calls at SQL statement execution time
- All parameter markers in SQL statements that do not call stored procedures are treated as input parameters. Parameter markers in SQL statements that call stored procedures can be input, output, or both input and output parameters. Even though the DB2 stored procedure argument convention typically implies that all procedure arguments are both input and output parameters, application programmers might still choose to specify the input or output nature of the parameter to follow a more rigorous coding style.
- If you cannot determine the parameter type for a parameter in a stored procedure, set the *ParameterType* parameter to SQL_PARAM_INPUT; if the data source returns a value for the parameter (because the parameter type is SQL_PARAM_OUTPUT), DB2 CLI will discard it.
- If the parameter type for a parameter in a stored procedure is treated as a SQL_PARAM_INPUT_OUTPUT or SQL_PARAM_OUTPUT parameter and the data source does not return a value, DB2 CLI will store the value SQL_NULL_DATA in the *Value* buffer. If the *Value* and the *ValueSize* parameters contain NULL pointers, DB2 CLI will discard the output value.
- If an application sets the parameter type for a parameter as SQL_PARAM _OUTPUT, data for the parameter will be returned to the application after the CALL SQL statement is processed.
- By default, the *ValueMaxSize* parameter specifies the size of the *Value* buffer if it contains a single value. If you call the SQLParamOptions( ) function to specify multiple values, provided for each parameter marker, the *ValueMaxSize* parameter will specify the size (including the null terminator for string values) of each element in the *Value* array. In this case, the value in the *ValueMaxSize* parameter also determines the location of values in the *Value* array.
- When SQLBindParameter( ) function binds an application variable to an output parameter for a stored procedure, DB2 CLI can provide some performance enhancement if the *Value* buffer is placed consecutively in memory after the *ValueSize* buffer, for example:

```
struct { SQLINTEGER ValueSize;
         SQLCHAR    Value[MAX_BUFFER];
       } column;
```

- A parameter marker can be bound to either a file or a storage location, but not to both. The most recent bind parameter function call used determines which type of binding is in effect when the SQL statement is executed.

Prerequisites

Call the SQLPrepare( ) function to prepare the SQL statement for execution before calling this function, unless you already know the attributes for the columns in the result data set.

Restrictions In ODBC 2.0, this function has replaced the SQLSetParam( ) function. The value SQL_DEFAULT_PARAM (a *Value* parameter value) was introduced in ODBC 2.0 to indicate that a stored procedure uses the default value of a parameter rather than a data value sent from the calling application. Because DB2 stored-procedure arguments do not have default values, specifying SQL_DEFAULT_PARAM for a *Value* parameter value will result in an error when the CALL statement is executed.

ODBC 2.0 also introduced the SQL_LEN_DATA_AT_EXEC(length) macro to calculate data lengths in the *Value* argument. This macro specifies the sum total length of all the data sent to the data source or stored procedure for character or binary C data via the subsequent SQLPutData( ) calls. Since the DB2 ODBC driver does not need this information, this macro is not provided and cannot be used. An ODBC application can determine whether or not the data source or driver needs this information by calling the SQLGetInfo( ) function with the SQL_NEED_LONG_DATA_LEN option specified. The DB2 ODBC driver will return the value N to indicate that this information is not needed by the SQLPutData( ) function.

See Also SQLExecute( ), SQLExecDirect( ), SQLParamData( ), SQLParamOptions( ), SQLPutData( )

Examples The following C program illustrates how to use the SQLBindParameter( ) function to bind local memory storage variables to parameter markers in an SQL statement:

```
#include <stdio.h>
#include <stdlib.h>
#include <string.h>
#include <sqlcli1.h>

int main(int argc, char *argv[])
{
    /* Declare The Local Memory Variables */
    SQLRETURN     rc = SQL_SUCCESS;
    SQLHENV       EnvHandle;
    SQLHDBC       DSCHandle;
    SQLHSTMT      StmtHandle;
    SQLCHAR       SQLStmt[80];
    SQLCHAR       EmpNo[7];
    SQLCHAR       FirstName[13];
    SQLCHAR       LastName[16];
    SQLSMALLINT   EdLevel;

    /* Make Sure An Education Level Was Entered */
    if (argc < 2)
        {
        printf("ERROR - Education Level Must Be Specified");
        return(EXIT_FAILURE);
        }
    EdLevel = atoi(argv[1]);

    /* Allocate An Environment Handle */
    rc = SQLAllocEnv(&EnvHandle);

    /* Allocate A Connection Handle */
    rc = SQLAllocConnect(EnvHandle, &DSCHandle);

    /* Connect To The SAMPLE Database */
    rc = SQLConnect(DSCHandle, "SAMPLE", SQL_NTS, "etpdd6z", SQL_NTS,
                    "sanders", SQL_NTS);

    /* Allocate A SQL Statement Handle */
    rc = SQLAllocStmt(DSCHandle, &StmtHandle);
```

```
    /* Define And Prepare A SELECT SQL Statement */
    strcpy(SQLStmt, "SELECT EMPNO, FIRSTNME, LASTNAME FROM ");
    strcat(SQLStmt, "USERID.EMPLOYEE WHERE EDLEVEL = ?");
    SQLPrepare(StmtHandle, SQLStmt, SQL_NTS);

    /* Bind The Parameter Marker To A Local Variable */
    SQLBindParameter(StmtHandle, 1, SQL_PARAM_INPUT, SQL_C_SHORT,
                     SQL_SMALLINT, 0, 0, (SQLPOINTER) &EdLevel, 0,
                     NULL);

    /* Execute The SQL Statement */
    rc = SQLExecute(StmtHandle);

    if (rc != SQL_ERROR)
        {
        /* Bind The Columns In The Result Data Set To Local */
        /* Storage Variables                                */
        SQLBindCol(StmtHandle, 1, SQL_C_CHAR, (SQLPOINTER) EmpNo,
                   sizeof(EmpNo), NULL);

        SQLBindCol(StmtHandle, 2, SQL_C_CHAR, (SQLPOINTER) FirstName,
                   sizeof(FirstName), NULL);

        SQLBindCol(StmtHandle, 3, SQL_C_CHAR, (SQLPOINTER) LastName,
                   sizeof(LastName), NULL);

        /* Retrieve And Display The Results */
        printf("Employee     Last         First\n");
        printf("Number       Name         Name\n");
        printf("----------------------------------\n");
        while (rc != SQL_NO_DATA_FOUND)
            {

            /* Retrieve A Record From The Result Data Set */
            rc = SQLFetch(StmtHandle);

            /* Print The Information Retrieved */
            if (rc != SQL_NO_DATA_FOUND)
                printf("%-12s %-12s %s\n", EmpNo, FirstName, LastName);
            }
        }

    /* Disconnect From The SAMPLE Database */
    SQLDisconnect(DSCHandle);

    /* Free The SQL Statement Handle */
    if (StmtHandle != NULL)
        SQLFreeStmt(StmtHandle, SQL_DROP);

    /* Free The Connection Handle */
    if (DSCHandle != NULL)
        SQLFreeConnect(DSCHandle);

    /* Free The Environment Handle */
    if (EnvHandle != NULL)
        SQLFreeEnv(EnvHandle);

    /* Return To The Operating System */
    return(rc);
}
```

The following C++ program illustrates how the SQLBindParameter( ) function is used to bind class private memory storage variables to parameter markers in an SQL statement:

```
#include <iostream.h>
#include <string.h>
#include <sqlcli1.h>

/* Define The CLI Class */
class CLI
{
    /* Declare The Private Attribute Variables */
    private:
       SQLHENV       EnvHandle;
       SQLHDBC       DSCHandle;
       SQLCHAR       EmpNo[7];
       SQLCHAR       FirstName[13];
       SQLCHAR       LastName[16];

    /* Declare The Public Attribute Variables */
    public:
       SQLRETURN     rc;
       SQLHSTMT      StmtHandle;

    /* Declare The Member Function Prototypes */
    CLI();                                      // Constructor
    ~CLI();                                     // Destructor
    SQLRETURN Connect();
    SQLRETURN ShowResults();
    SQLRETURN Disconnect();
} ;

/* Define The Class Constructor */
CLI::CLI()
{
    /* Initialize The Return Code Variable */
    rc = SQL_SUCCESS;

    /* Allocate An Environment Handle */
    rc = SQLAllocEnv(&EnvHandle);

    /* Allocate A Connection Handle */
    rc = SQLAllocConnect(EnvHandle, &DSCHandle);
}

/* Define The Class Destructor */
CLI::~CLI()
{
    /* Free The Connection Handle */
    if (DSCHandle != NULL)
        SQLFreeConnect(DSCHandle);

    /* Free The Environment Handle */
    if (EnvHandle != NULL)
        SQLFreeEnv(EnvHandle);
}

/* Define The Connect() Member Function */
SQLRETURN CLI::Connect()
{
```

```
    /* Connect To The SAMPLE Database */
    rc = SQLConnect(DSCHandle, (SQLCHAR *) "SAMPLE", SQL_NTS,
                  (SQLCHAR *) "etpdd6z", SQL_NTS,
                  (SQLCHAR *) "sanders", SQL_NTS);

    /* Allocate A SQL Statement Handle */
    rc = SQLAllocStmt(DSCHandle, &StmtHandle);

    /* Return The CLI Function Return Code */
    return(rc);
}

/* Define The Disconnect() Member Function */
SQLRETURN CLI::Disconnect(void)
{
    /* Disconnect From The Database */
    rc = SQLDisconnect(DSCHandle);

    /* Free The SQL Statement Handle */
    if (StmtHandle != NULL)
        SQLFreeStmt(StmtHandle, SQL_DROP);

    /* Return The CLI Function Return Code */
    return(rc);
}

/* Define The ShowResults() Member Function */
SQLRETURN CLI::ShowResults(void)
{
    /* Bind The Columns In The Result Data Set To Local */
    /* Storage Variables                                */
    SQLBindCol(StmtHandle, 1, SQL_C_CHAR, (SQLPOINTER) EmpNo,
               sizeof(EmpNo), NULL);

    SQLBindCol(StmtHandle, 2, SQL_C_CHAR, (SQLPOINTER) FirstName,
               sizeof(FirstName), NULL);

    SQLBindCol(StmtHandle, 3, SQL_C_CHAR, (SQLPOINTER) LastName,
               sizeof(LastName), NULL);

    /* Retrieve And Display The Results */
    cout << "Employee     Last         First" << endl;
    cout << "Number       Name         Name" << endl;
    cout << "------------------------------------" << endl;
    while (rc != SQL_NO_DATA_FOUND)
        {

        /* Retrieve A Record From The Result Data Set */
        rc = SQLFetch(StmtHandle);

        /* Print The Information Retrieved */
        if (rc != SQL_NO_DATA_FOUND)
            {
            cout.setf(ios::left);
            cout.width(13);
            cout << EmpNo;
            cout.setf(ios::left);
            cout.width(13);
            cout << FirstName << LastName << endl;
            }
        }
```

```
    /* Return The CLI Function Return Code */
    return(rc);
}

int main(int argc, char *argv[])
{
    /* Declare The Local Memory Variables */
    SQLRETURN    rc = SQL_SUCCESS;
    SQLCHAR      SQLStmt[80];
    SQLSMALLINT  EdLevel;

    /* Create An Instance Of The CLI Class */
    CLI Sample;

    /* Make Sure An Education Level Was Entered */
    if (argc < 2)
        {
        cout << "ERROR - Education Level Must Be Specified" << endl;
        return(EXIT_FAILURE);
        }
    EdLevel = atoi(argv[1]);

    /* Connect To The SAMPLE Database */
    if ((rc = Sample.Connect()) != SQL_SUCCESS)
        return(rc);

    /* Define And Prepare A SELECT SQL Statement */
    strcpy((char *) SQLStmt, "SELECT EMPNO, FIRSTNME, LASTNAME FROM ");
    strcat((char *) SQLStmt, "USERID.EMPLOYEE WHERE EDLEVEL = ?");
    SQLPrepare(Sample.StmtHandle, SQLStmt, SQL_NTS);

    /* Bind The Parameter Marker To A Local Variable */
    SQLBindParameter(Sample.StmtHandle, 1, SQL_PARAM_INPUT,
                     SQL_C_SHORT, SQL_SMALLINT, 0, 0,
                     (SQLPOINTER) &EdLevel, 0, NULL);

    /* Execute The SQL Statement */
    rc = SQLExecute(Sample.StmtHandle);

    /* Display The Results Of The SQL Query */
    if (rc == SQL_SUCCESS)
        Sample.ShowResults();

    /* Disconnect From The SAMPLE Database */
    Sample.Disconnect();

    /* Return To The Operating System */
    return(rc);
}
```

SQLBindFileToParam

Purpose The SQLBindFileToParam( ) function associates (binds) a parameter marker in a SQL statement to one or more file references.

Syntax

```
SQLRETURN  SQLBindFileToParm (SQLHSTMT         StmtHandle,
                              SQLUSMALLINT     PMarkerNum,
                              SQLSMALLINT      SQLDataType,
```

```
SQLCHAR FAR        *FileName,
SQLSMALLINT FAR *FileNameSize,
SQLUINTEGER FAR *FileOptions,
SQLSMALLINT      MaxFileNameSize,
SQLINTEGER FAR   *IndicatorValue);
```

Parameters

StmtHandle The SQL statement handle where the address of the SQL statement buffer is stored.

PMarkerIndex The appropriate parameter marker number. Parameter markers are numbered sequentially from left to right, starting with 1, as they appear in the SQL statement.

SQLDataType The SQL data type of the column referenced by the parameter marker. The following SQL data types are supported:

- SQL_BLOB
- SQL_CLOB
- SQL_DBCLOB

FileName A pointer to a location in memory where a filename or an array of filenames are stored. Filenames can be specified as complete, with both path names and filenames, or as relative (filename only). This parameter cannot contain a NULL value.

FileNameSize A pointer to a location in memory where the length of the filename or an array of filename lengths referenced by the *FileName* parameter are stored. If this parameter is set to NULL, the length SQL_NTS will be used and the *FileName* value will be a null-terminated string.

FileOptions A pointer to a location in memory where the file option or an array of file options to be used when writing to the file are stored. At this time, only the SQL_FILE_READ option is recognized. This option indicates that the file can be opened, read, and closed.

FileNameMaxSize The maximum size of the *FileName* memory storage buffer or the maximum size of each element in the *FileName* array.

IndicatorValue A pointer to a location in memory where this function stores an indicator value (or an array of indicator values). This indicator value should be set to SQL_NULL_DATA if the data value of the column referenced by the parameter marker is to be set to NULL; otherwise, set the value to 0.

Includes

```
#include <sqlcli1.h>
```

Description

The SQLBindFileToParam( ) function associates (binds) a parameter marker in a SQL statement to a file reference or an array of file references. This allows large object data in an external file to be transferred directly into a LOB column in the data source when the SQL statement containing the parameter marker is executed.

The LOB file reference parameters (*FileName*, *FileNameSize*, *FileOptions*) refer to a file within the application program's environment, on the client workstation. The application must ensure that these variables contain the name of a file, the length of the filename, and the appropriate file option (in this case, Read) before the SQLExecute( ) or SQLExecDirect( ) function is called. The values of these parameters can be changed (if necessary) between each SQLExecute( ) or SQLExecDirect( ) function call.

Specifications

DB2 CLI 2.1

Return Codes

SQL_SUCCESS, SQL_SUCCESS_WITH_INFO, SQL_INVALID_HANDLE, SQL_ERROR

SQLSTATEs **08**S01, **40**003, **58**004, **S1**001, **S1**004, **S1**009, **S1**010, **S1**013, **S1**090, **S1**093, **S1**C00

Comments

- If relative filename(s) are used, DB2 CLI will attempt to locate the file in the current directory path of the running DB2 CLI application.
- The maximum value the *FileNameSize* parameter can contain is 255, so filename strings should not exceed 255 characters.
- The SQLBindFileToParam( ) function must be called once for each parameter marker in the SQL statement whose value is obtained directly from a file when the SQL statement is executed.
- Values must be supplied for the *FileName*, *FileNameSize*, and *FileOptions* parameters before the SQL statement is executed. When the SQL statement is executed, the data for any parameter bound by the SQLBindFileToParam( ) function is read from the referenced file and passed to the data source.
- If the SQLParamOptions( ) function specifies multiple values for each parameter, the *FileName*, *FileNameSize*, and *FileOptions* parameters must point to arrays of LOB file reference variables, and the *MaxFileNameSize* parameter must point to an array of maximum lengths for each element in the *FileName* array. The *MaxFileNameSize* array allows DB2 CLI to determine the location of each element in the *FileName* array.
- LOB parameter markers can be bound to an input file with the SQLBindFileToParam( ) function, or to a stored buffer with the SQLBindParameter( ) function. The most recent bind parameter function call determines which type of binding is in effect when the SQL statement is executed.

Restrictions This function is not available when you are connected to data sources that do not support large object (LOB) data types. To determine whether or not this function is supported for the current data source connection, call the SQLGetFunctions( ) function with the *FunctionType* parameter set to SQL_API_SQLBINDFILETOPARAM and check the value of the *Exists* output parameter.

See Also SQLBindParameter( ), SQLExecute( ), SQLExecDirect( ), SQLParamOptions( )

Example The following C program illustrates how to use the SQLBindFileToParam( ) function to bind external files containing LOB data to a parameter marker in a SQL statement:

```
#include <stdio.h>
#include <stdlib.h>
#include <string.h>
#include <sqlcli1.h>

int main()
{
    /* Declare The Local Memory Variables */
    SQLRETURN     rc = SQL_SUCCESS;
    SQLHENV       EnvHandle;
    SQLHDBC       DSCHandle;
    SQLHSTMT      StmtHandle;
    SQLCHAR       SQLStmt[100];
    SQLCHAR       FileName[40];
    SQLSMALLINT   FNameSize;
    SQLUINTEGER   FOption;
    SQLINTEGER    FIndicator;
```

```
    /* Allocate An Environment Handle */
    rc = SQLAllocEnv(&EnvHandle);

    /* Allocate A Connection Handle */
    rc = SQLAllocConnect(EnvHandle, &DSCHandle);

    /* Connect To The SAMPLE Database */
    rc = SQLConnect(DSCHandle, "SAMPLE", SQL_NTS, "etpdd6z", SQL_NTS,
                    "sanders", SQL_NTS);

    /* Allocate A SQL Statement Handle */
    rc = SQLAllocStmt(DSCHandle, &StmtHandle);

    /* Define An INSERT SQL Statement */
    strcpy(SQLStmt, "INSERT INTO USERID.EMP_RESUME (EMPNO, ");
    strcat(SQLStmt, "RESUME_FORMAT, RESUME) VALUES ('000200', ");
    strcat(SQLStmt, "'ascii', ?)");
    SQLPrepare(StmtHandle, SQLStmt, SQL_NTS);

    /* Bind The Parameter Marker To An External File */
    SQLBindFileToParam(StmtHandle, 1, SQL_CLOB, FileName, &FNameSize,
                       &FOption, 255, &FIndicator);

    /* Initialize The SQLBindColToFile() Function's Parameters */
    strcpy(FileName, "RESUME.TXT");
    FNameSize = strlen(FileName);
    FOption = SQL_FILE_READ;
    FIndicator = 0;

    /* Execute The SQL Statement */
    rc = SQLExecute(StmtHandle);

    /* If The Record Was Successfully Added To The Database, Display */
    /* A Message Saying So                                           */
    if (rc == SQL_SUCCESS)
        {
        printf("Data from the file %s has been added to the ",
                FileName);
        printf("SAMPLE database.\n");
        }

    /* Disconnect From The SAMPLE Database */
    SQLDisconnect(DSCHandle);

    /* Free The SQL Statement Handle */
    if (StmtHandle != NULL)
        SQLFreeStmt(StmtHandle, SQL_DROP);

    /* Free The Connection Handle */
    if (DSCHandle != NULL)
        SQLFreeConnect(DSCHandle);

    /* Free The Environment Handle */
    if (EnvHandle != NULL)
        SQLFreeEnv(EnvHandle);

    /* Return To The Operating System */
    return(rc);
}
```

Note: The SQLBindFileToParam( ) function is used in a C++ program in a similar manner.

SQLSetParam

Purpose The SQLSetParam( ) function associates (binds) parameter markers in a SQL statement to application variables and/or LOB locators.

Syntax

```
SQLRETURN  SQLSetParam
                         (SQLHSTMT          StmtHandle,
                          SQLUSMALLINT      PMarkerNum,
                          SQLSMALLINT       CDataType,
                          SQLSMALLINT       SQLDataType,
                          SQLUINTEGER       Precision,
                          SQLSMALLINT       Scale,
                          SQLPOINTER        Value,
                          SQLINTEGER FAR    *ValueSize);
```

Parameters

StmtHandle The SQL statement handle where the address of the SQL statement buffer is stored.

PMarkerNum The appropriate parameter marker number. Parameter markers are numbered sequentially from left to right, starting with 1, as they appear in the SQL statement.

CDataType The C language data type of the parameter. The following C data types are supported:

- SQL_C_BIT
- SQL_C_BINARY
- SQL_C_TINYINT
- SQL_C_SHORT
- SQL_C_LONG
- SQL_C_FLOAT
- SQL_C_DOUBLE
- SQL_C_CHAR
- SQL_C_DBCHAR
- SQL_C_BLOB_LOCATOR
- SQL_C_CLOB_LOCATOR
- SQL_C_DBCLOB_LOCATOR
- SQL_C_DATE
- SQL_C_TIME
- SQL_C_TIMESTAMP
- SQL_C_DEFAULT

Note: The SQL_C_DEFAULT value causes data to be transferred from its default C data type to the specified SQL data type.

SQLDataType The SQL data type of the parameter. The following SQL data types are supported:

- SQL_BINARY
- SQL_VARBINARY
- SQL_LONGVARBINARY
- SQL_SMALLINT
- SQL_INTEGER
- SQL_DECIMAL
- SQL_NUMERIC
- SQL_REAL
- SQL_FLOAT
- SQL_DOUBLE
- SQL_CHAR
- SQL_VARCHAR
- SQL_LONGVARCHAR
- SQL_BLOB
- SQL_BLOB_LOCATOR
- SQL_CLOB
- SQL_CLOB_LOCATOR
- SQL_DBCLOB
- SQL_DBCLOB_LOCATOR
- SQL_DATE
- SQL_TIME
- SQL_TIMESTAMP
- SQL_GRAPHIC
- SQL_VARGRAPHIC
- SQL_LONGVARGRAPHIC

> Note: SQL_BLOB_LOCATOR, SQL_CLOB_LOCATOR, and SQL_DBCLOB_LOCATOR are application-related concepts, so they do not map to a specific data type.

Precision The total number of bytes of data sent to the data source for the specified parameter marker or the maximum decimal precision of the number (if the *SQLDataType* parameter value is SQL_DECIMAL or SQL_NUMERIC).

Scale The number of digits to the right of the decimal point if the *SQLDataType* parameter value is SQL_DECIMAL, SQL_NUMERIC, or SQL_TIMESTAMP.

Value A pointer to a location in memory where the value associated with the parameter marker is stored.

ValueSize A pointer to a location in memory where the size of the data value associated with the parameter marker is stored.

Includes

```
#include <sqlcli1.h>
```

Description

The SQLSetParam( ) function associates (binds) parameter markers in a SQL statement to application variables and/or LOB locators. A parameter marker is represented by a question mark character (?) in a SQL statement and indicates a position in the statement where an application-supplied value is substituted when the statement is executed. Parameter markers can be bound to either application variables (for all data types) or LOB locator variables (for BLOB, CLOB, and DBCLOB data types). When parameter markers are bound to application variables, data is transferred from the application to the connected data source when either the SQLExecute( ) or the SQLExecDirect( ) function is called. If necessary, data conversion occurs as the data is transferred.

Note: In ODBC 2.0, this function has been replaced by SQLBindParameter( ).

Specifications DB2 CLI 1.1, ODBC 1.0, X/OPEN CLI

Return Codes SQL_SUCCESS, SQL_INVALID, HANDLE, SQL_ERROR

SQLSTATEs **07**006, **08**S01, **40**003, **58**004, **S1**001, **S1**003, **S1**004, **S1**009, **S1**010, **S1**013, **S1**093, **S1**094, **S1**104, **S1**C00

Comments

- If the SQL data type is a binary or single-byte character string, the value in the *Precision* parameter must specify the length, in bytes, of the string. If the SQL data type is a double-byte (graphic) character string, the value in the *Precision* parameter must specify the length, in double-byte characters, of the string.
- If the *SQLDataType* parameter value is SQL_TIMESTAMP, the *Scale* parameter represents the number of digits to the right of the decimal point in the character representation of the timestamp value. (For example, the *Scale* parameter value for 1996-05-15 12:35:18.002 would be 3.)
- To specify a NULL value for a parameter marker, assign the value SQL_NULL _DATA to the *ValueSize* parameter.
- If the *CDataType* parameter is set to SQL_C_CHAR, the value stored in the *ValueSize* parameter must be the exact length of the data string to be passed to the data source if the data string is not null-terminated (the length is determined by the number of characters in the string). The *ValueSize* parameter can contain either a NULL pointer or the value SQL_NTS if the actual data string is null-terminated.
- If the *CDataType* parameter is set to SQL_C_CHAR and the *SQLDataType* parameter is set to SQL_GRAPHIC, the value stored in the *ValueSize* parameter must never be SQL_NTS and the data string passed to the data source must never be a NULL string.
- The value specified in the *ValueSize* parameter for SQL_GRAPHIC data types should identify the number of octets occupied by the double-byte data, so the value should always be a multiple of 2.
- When parameter markers are bound to LOB locator variables, the LOB locator values themselves are supplied by the connected data source. Only the LOB locator, not the LOB data itself, therefore, is transferred from the application to the data source when the SQL statement is executed.
- A LOB locator can be used in conjunction with the SQLGetSubString( ), SQLGetPosition( ), or SQLGetLength( ) function.
- You can bind a LOB parameter marker directly to a file with the SQLBindFileToParam( ) function. In this case, when the SQL statement is executed, DB2 CLI will transfer the contents of the specified file directly to the connected data source.

- A variable must be bound to each parameter marker specified in a SQL statement before that statement can be executed. When this function is executed, both the *Value* and the *ValueSize* parameters are treated as deferred arguments. Their storage locations, however, must be valid and they must contain data values when the SQL statement they are bound to is executed. This means that the SQLExecDirect( ) or SQLExecute( ) function call must be made in the same procedure scope as the SQLBindParameter( ) function call, or these storage locations must be dynamically allocated or declared statically or globally.
- All parameters bound by this function remain in effect until the SQLFreeStmt( ) function is called with either the SQL_DROP or the SQL_RESET_PARAMS option specified, or until this function is called again for the same parameter marker number. All LOB locators remain in effect until the transaction in which they were created is ended or until they are freed by the FREE LOCATOR SQL statement.
- Once the SQL statement is executed and the results are processed, an application might want to reuse the SQL statement handle to execute a different SQL statement. If the parameter marker specifications are different (e.g., the number of parameters or the length has changed), call the SQLFreeStmt( ) function with the SQL_RESET_PARAMS option specified to reset or clear the current parameter bindings.
- The C buffer data type specified in the *CDataType* parameter must be compatible with the SQL data type specified in the *SQLDataType* parameter, or an error will occur.
- An application can pass the value for a parameter to the data source either by placing the value in the *Value* buffer or by making one or more calls to the SQLPutData( ) function. With the second option, the associated parameters are treated as data-at-execution parameters, which is specified by the SQL_DATA_AT_EXEC value placed in the *ValueSize* buffer. This sets the *Value* parameter to a 32-bit value, which is returned on a subsequent SQLParamData( ) function call and can be used to identify the parameter position. For more information about data-at-execution parameters, refer to the SQLParmData( ) and SQLPutData( ) functions.
- Since the values stored in the variables referenced by *Value* and *ValueSize* parameters are not verified until the SQL statement is executed, data content or format errors are not detected or reported until either the SQLExecute( ) or the SQLExecDirect( ) function is called.

Prerequisites Call the SQLPrepare( ) function to prepare the SQL statement for execution before calling this function, unless you already know the attributes for the columns in the result data set.

Restrictions You cannot use this function to bind application variables to parameter markers in a stored procedure CALL statement, nor to bind an array of application variables to a parameter marker when the SQLParamOptions( ) function has specified multiple-input parameter values. In ODBC 2.0, this function has been replaced by SQLBindParameter( ), which does not have these restrictions and can therefore be used to perform these two tasks.

See Also SQLBindParameter( ), SQLBindFileToParam( ), SQLPrepare( ), SQLExecute( ), SQLExecDirect( )

Examples The following C program illustrates how to use the SQLSetParam( ) function to bind local memory storage variables to parameter markers in an SQL statement:

```
#include <stdio.h>
#include <stdlib.h>
#include <string.h>
#include <sqlcli1.h>
```

```
int main(int argc, char *argv[])
{
    /* Declare The Local Memory Variables */
    SQLRETURN     rc = SQL_SUCCESS;
    SQLHENV       EnvHandle;
    SQLHDBC       DSCHandle;
    SQLHSTMT      StmtHandle;
    SQLCHAR       SQLStmt[80];
    SQLCHAR       EmpNo[7];
    SQLCHAR       FirstName[13];
    SQLCHAR       LastName[16];
    SQLSMALLINT   EdLevel;

    /* Make Sure An Education Level Was Entered */
    if (argc < 2)
        {
        printf("ERROR - Education Level Must Be Specified");
        return(EXIT_FAILURE);
        }
    EdLevel = atoi(argv[1]);

    /* Allocate An Environment Handle */
    rc = SQLAllocEnv(&EnvHandle);

    /* Allocate A Connection Handle */
    rc = SQLAllocConnect(EnvHandle, &DSCHandle);

    /* Connect To The SAMPLE Database */
    rc = SQLConnect(DSCHandle, "SAMPLE", SQL_NTS, "etpdd6z", SQL_NTS,
                    "sanders", SQL_NTS);

    /* Allocate A SQL Statement Handle */
    rc = SQLAllocStmt(DSCHandle, &StmtHandle);

    /* Define And Prepare A SELECT SQL Statement */
    strcpy(SQLStmt, "SELECT EMPNO, FIRSTNME, LASTNAME FROM ");
    strcat(SQLStmt, "USERID.EMPLOYEE WHERE EDLEVEL = ?");
    SQLPrepare(StmtHandle, SQLStmt, SQL_NTS);

    /* Bind The Parameter Marker To A Local Variable */
    SQLSetParam(StmtHandle, 1, SQL_C_SHORT, SQL_SMALLINT, 0, 0,
            (SQLPOINTER) &EdLevel, NULL);

    /* Execute The SQL Statement */
    rc = SQLExecute(StmtHandle);

    if (rc != SQL_ERROR)
        {
        /* Bind The Columns In The Result Data Set To Local */
        /* Storage Variables                                */
        SQLBindCol(StmtHandle, 1, SQL_C_CHAR, (SQLPOINTER) EmpNo,
                   sizeof(EmpNo), NULL);

        SQLBindCol(StmtHandle, 2, SQL_C_CHAR, (SQLPOINTER) FirstName,
                   sizeof(FirstName), NULL);

        SQLBindCol(StmtHandle, 3, SQL_C_CHAR, (SQLPOINTER) LastName,
                   sizeof(LastName), NULL);

        /* Retrieve And Display The Results */
        printf("Employee    Last        First\n");
```

```
        printf("Number       Name         Name\n");
        printf("-----------------------------------\n");
        while (rc != SQL_NO_DATA_FOUND)
            {

            /* Retrieve A Record From The Result Data Set */
            rc = SQLFetch(StmtHandle);

            /* Print The Information Retrieved */
            if (rc != SQL_NO_DATA_FOUND)
                printf("%-12s %-12s %s\n", EmpNo, FirstName, LastName);
            }
        }

    /* Disconnect From The SAMPLE Database */
    SQLDisconnect(DSCHandle);

    /* Free The SQL Statement Handle */
    if (StmtHandle != NULL)
        SQLFreeStmt(StmtHandle, SQL_DROP);

    /* Free The Connection Handle */
    if (DSCHandle != NULL)
        SQLFreeConnect(DSCHandle);

    /* Free The Environment Handle */
    if (EnvHandle != NULL)
        SQLFreeEnv(EnvHandle);

    /* Return To The Operating System */
    return(rc);
}
```

The following C++ program illustrates how the SQLSetParam( ) function is used to bind class private memory storage variables to parameter markers in a SQL statement:

```
#include <iostream.h>
#include <string.h>
#include <sqlcli1.h>

/* Define The CLI Class */
class CLI
{
    /* Declare The Private Attribute Variables */
    private:
       SQLHENV       EnvHandle;
       SQLHDBC       DSCHandle;
       SQLCHAR       EmpNo[7];
       SQLCHAR       FirstName[13];
       SQLCHAR       LastName[16];

    /* Declare The Public Attribute Variables */
    public:
       SQLRETURN     rc;
       SQLHSTMT      StmtHandle;

    /* Declare The Member Function Prototypes */
    CLI();                                  // Constructor
    ~CLI();                                 // Destructor
```

```
    SQLRETURN Connect();
    SQLRETURN ShowResults();
    SQLRETURN Disconnect();
} ;

/* Define The Class Constructor */
CLI::CLI()
{
    /* Initialize The Return Code Variable */
    rc = SQL_SUCCESS;

    /* Allocate An Environment Handle */
    rc = SQLAllocEnv(&EnvHandle);

    /* Allocate A Connection Handle */
    rc = SQLAllocConnect(EnvHandle, &DSCHandle);
}

/* Define The Class Destructor */
CLI::~CLI()
{
    /* Free The Connection Handle */
    if (DSCHandle != NULL)
        SQLFreeConnect(DSCHandle);

    /* Free The Environment Handle */
    if (EnvHandle != NULL)
        SQLFreeEnv(EnvHandle);
}

/* Define The Connect() Member Function */
SQLRETURN CLI::Connect()
{
    /* Connect To The SAMPLE Database */
    rc = SQLConnect(DSCHandle, (SQLCHAR *) "SAMPLE", SQL_NTS,
                    (SQLCHAR *) "etpdd6z", SQL_NTS,
                    (SQLCHAR *) "sanders", SQL_NTS);

    /* Allocate A SQL Statement Handle */
    rc = SQLAllocStmt(DSCHandle, &StmtHandle);

    /* Return The CLI Function Return Code */
    return(rc);
}

/* Define The Disconnect() Member Function */
SQLRETURN CLI::Disconnect(void)
{
    /* Disconnect From The Database */
    rc = SQLDisconnect(DSCHandle);

    /* Free The SQL Statement Handle */
    if (StmtHandle != NULL)
        SQLFreeStmt(StmtHandle, SQL_DROP);

    /* Return The CLI Function Return Code */
    return(rc);
}

/* Define The ShowResults() Member Function */
SQLRETURN CLI::ShowResults(void)
```

```
{
    /* Bind The Columns In The Result Data Set To Local */
    /* Storage Variables                                 */
    SQLBindCol(StmtHandle, 1, SQL_C_CHAR, (SQLPOINTER) EmpNo,
               sizeof(EmpNo), NULL);

    SQLBindCol(StmtHandle, 2, SQL_C_CHAR, (SQLPOINTER) FirstName,
               sizeof(FirstName), NULL);

    SQLBindCol(StmtHandle, 3, SQL_C_CHAR, (SQLPOINTER) LastName,
               sizeof(LastName), NULL);

    /* Retrieve And Display The Results */
    cout << "Employee     Last         First" << endl;
    cout << "Number       Name         Name" << endl;
    cout << "-----------------------------------" << endl;
    while (rc != SQL_NO_DATA_FOUND)
        {

        /* Retrieve A Record From The Result Data Set */
        rc = SQLFetch(StmtHandle);

        /* Print The Information Retrieved */
        if (rc != SQL_NO_DATA_FOUND)
            {
            cout.setf(ios::left);
            cout.width(13);
            cout << EmpNo;
            cout.setf(ios::left);
            cout.width(13);
            cout << FirstName << LastName << endl;
            }
        }

    /* Return The CLI Function Return Code */
    return(rc);
}

int main(int argc, char *argv[])
{
    /* Declare The Local Memory Variables */
    SQLRETURN    rc = SQL_SUCCESS;
    SQLCHAR      SQLStmt[80];
    SQLSMALLINT  EdLevel;

    /* Create An Instance Of The CLI Class */
    CLI Sample;

    /* Make Sure An Education Level Was Entered */
    if (argc < 2)
        {
        cout << "ERROR - Education Level Must Be Specified" << endl;
        return(EXIT_FAILURE);
        }
    EdLevel = atoi(argv[1]);

    /* Connect To The SAMPLE Database */
    if ((rc = Sample.Connect()) != SQL_SUCCESS)
        return(rc);

    /* Define And Prepare A SELECT SQL Statement */
    strcpy((char *) SQLStmt, "SELECT EMPNO, FIRSTNME, LASTNAME FROM ");
```

```
    strcat((char *) SQLStmt, "USERID.EMPLOYEE WHERE EDLEVEL = ?");
    SQLPrepare(Sample.StmtHandle, SQLStmt, SQL_NTS);

    /* Bind The Parameter Marker To A Local Variable */
    SQLSetParam(Sample.StmtHandle, 1, SQL_C_SHORT, SQL_SMALLINT, 0, 0,
                (SQLPOINTER) &EdLevel, NULL);

    /* Execute The SQL Statement */
    rc = SQLExecute(Sample.StmtHandle);

    /* Display The Results Of The SQL Query */
    if (rc == SQL_SUCCESS)
        Sample.ShowResults();

    /* Disconnect From The SAMPLE Database */
    Sample.Disconnect();

    /* Return To The Operating System */
    return(rc);
}
```

SQLParamOptions

Purpose The SQLParamOptions( ) function specifies multiple values for each parameter marker assigned to a storage buffer by the SQLBindParameter( ) function.

Syntax

```
SQLRETURN SQLParamOptions (SQLHSTMT          StmtHandle,
                           SQLUINTEGER       NumRows,
                           SQLUINTEGER FAR   *RowIndex);
```

Parameters

StmtHandle The SQL statement handle where the address of the SQL statement buffer is stored.

NumRows The number of values (rows) provided for each parameter.

RowIndex A pointer to a location in memory where the value for the parameter array index (current row number) is stored.

Includes

```
#include <sqlcli1.h>
```

Description The SQLParamOptions( ) function specifies multiple values for each parameter marker in a SQL statement that has been assigned to a storage buffer by the SQL-BindParameter( ) function. Each time the SQL statement is executed, the RowIndex parameter specifies which set of values in the array of values to use. This allows an application to perform batched processing of the same SQL statement using a single set of SQLPrepare( ), SQLExecute(), and SQLBindParameter ( ) function calls.

Specifications DB2 CLI 2.1, ODBC 1.0

Return Codes SQL_SUCCESS, SQL_SUCCESS_WITH_INFO, SQL_INVALID_HANDLE, SQL_ERROR

SQLSTATEs **08**S01, **40**003, **S1**001, **S1**010, **S1**107

Comments

- If the *NumRows* parameter contains a value greater than 1, then the *Value* parameter in the SQLBindParameter( ) function points to an array of parameter marker values, and the *ValueSize* parameter points to an array of parameter marker value lengths.

- As each value in the array of parameter marker values is processed, the *Row Index* parameter is set to the array index number for that value. If an SQL statement failure occurs during the execution of a particular element in the set of values, execution will halt and the function that initiated the execution—SQLExecute( ), SQLExecDirect( ), or SQLParamData( )—will return the SQL _ERROR return code. When this happens, you can use the *RowIndex* parameter to determine which element in the array of parameter values failed, and how many elements of the array of parameter values were successfully processed.
- When the SQLParamData( ) function returns the SQL_NEED_DATA value, you can use the value in the *RowIndex* parameter to determine which element in the array of values is being used to supply data to the data source.
- If the SQL statement being processed is a query, the *RowIndex* parameter will contain the array index associated with the current result set returned by the SQLMoreResults( ) function, and it will be incremented each time the SQL-MoreResults( ) function is called.
- In environments where the connected data source supports compound SQL (DB2 for Common Servers, or DRDA environments with DDCS V2.3), all the data values in the array are packaged together with the execute request and treated as a single network flow.
- When connected to a DB2 for Common Servers, version 2.1 data source, an application can specify that either ATOMIC or NOT ATOMIC compound SQL be used. With ATOMIC compound SQL (the default), either all the elements of the array are processed successfully or none are processed at all. With NOT ATOMIC compound SQL, execution will continue even if an error is detected with one of the intermediate array elements. An application can select the type of compound SQL to use by setting the SQL_PARAMOPT_ATOMIC attribute with the SQLSetStmtOption( ) function call. For DRDA environments, compound SQL support is always NOT ATOMIC.
- You can determine the current value of the SQL_PARAMOPT_ATOMIC attribute by calling the SQLGetStmtOption( ) function.
- When connected to data sources that do not support compound SQL, DB2 CLI prepares the SQL statement and executes it once for each value in the array of parameter marker values.

Restrictions There are no restrictions associated with this function call.

See Also SQLBindParameter( ), SQLMoreResults( ), SQLSetStmtOption( )

Examples The following C program illustrates how to use the SQLParamOptions( ) function to tell CLI that three values will be provided for each parameter marker in a SQL statement:

```
#include <stdio.h>
#include <stdlib.h>
#include <string.h>
#include <sqlcli1.h>

int main()
{
    /* Declare The Local Memory Variables */
    SQLRETURN    rc = SQL_SUCCESS;
```

```
SQLHENV      EnvHandle;
SQLHDBC      DSCHandle;
SQLHSTMT     StmtHandle;
SQLCHAR      SQLStmt[255];
SQLSMALLINT  DeptNo[3]        = { 97, 98, 99};
SQLCHAR      DeptName[3][15]  = { "England", "North East", "Japan" };
SQLSMALLINT  Manager[3]       = { 70, 90, 100 } ;
SQLCHAR      Division[3][11] = { "Europe", "Canada", "Asia" };
SQLCHAR      Location[3][14] = { "London", "Toronto", "Tokyo" };

/* Allocate An Environment Handle */
rc = SQLAllocEnv(&EnvHandle);

/* Allocate A Connection Handle */
rc = SQLAllocConnect(EnvHandle, &DSCHandle);

/* Connect To The SAMPLE Database */
rc = SQLConnect(DSCHandle, "SAMPLE", SQL_NTS, "etpdd6z", SQL_NTS,
                "sanders", SQL_NTS);

/* Allocate A SQL Statement Handle */
rc = SQLAllocStmt(DSCHandle, &StmtHandle);

/* Define And Prepare An INSERT SQL Statement */
strcpy(SQLStmt, "INSERT INTO USERID.ORG (DEPTNUMB, DEPTNAME, ");
strcat(SQLStmt, "MANAGER, DIVISION, LOCATION) VALUES ");
strcat(SQLStmt, "( ?, ?, ?, ?, ?)");
SQLPrepare(StmtHandle, SQLStmt, SQL_NTS);

/* Tell CLI That Three Values Will Be Provided For Each */
/* Parameter Marker In The SQL Statement                */
SQLParamOptions(StmtHandle, 3, NULL);

/* Bind The Parameter Markers To Local Variables */
SQLBindParameter(StmtHandle, 1, SQL_PARAM_INPUT, SQL_C_SHORT,
                 SQL_SMALLINT, 0, 0, DeptNo, 0, NULL);

SQLBindParameter(StmtHandle, 2, SQL_PARAM_INPUT, SQL_C_CHAR,
                 SQL_VARCHAR, 15, 0, DeptName, 15, NULL);

SQLBindParameter(StmtHandle, 3, SQL_PARAM_INPUT, SQL_C_SHORT,
                 SQL_SMALLINT, 0, 0, Manager, 0, NULL);

SQLBindParameter(StmtHandle, 4, SQL_PARAM_INPUT, SQL_C_CHAR,
                 SQL_VARCHAR, 11, 0, Division, 11, NULL);

SQLBindParameter(StmtHandle, 5, SQL_PARAM_INPUT, SQL_C_CHAR,
                 SQL_VARCHAR, 14, 0, Location, 14, NULL);

/* Execute The SQL Statement */
rc = SQLExecute(StmtHandle);

/* Determine The Number Of Rows Affected By The INSERT Statement */
if (rc == SQL_SUCCESS)
    printf("3 rows have been added to the USERID.ORG table.\n");

/* Commit The Transaction */
SQLTransact(EnvHandle, DSCHandle, SQL_COMMIT);

/* Disconnect From The SAMPLE Database */
SQLDisconnect(DSCHandle);
```

```
    /* Free The SQL Statement Handle */
    if (StmtHandle != NULL)
        SQLFreeStmt(StmtHandle, SQL_DROP);

    /* Free The Connection Handle */
    if (DSCHandle != NULL)
        SQLFreeConnect(DSCHandle);

    /* Free The Environment Handle */
    if (EnvHandle != NULL)
        SQLFreeEnv(EnvHandle);

    /* Return To The Operating System */
    return(rc);
}
```

The following C++ program illustrates how the SQLSetParam( ) function is used by class methods to tell CLI that three values will be provided for each parameter marker in a SQL statement:

```
#include <iostream.h>
#include <string.h>
#include <sqlcli1.h>

/* Define The CLI Class */
class CLI
{
    /* Declare The Private Attribute Variables */
    private:
       SQLHENV      EnvHandle;
       SQLHDBC      DSCHandle;
       SQLHSTMT     StmtHandle;
       SQLCHAR      SQLStmt[255];
       SQLSMALLINT  DeptNo[3];
       SQLCHAR      DeptName[3][15];
       SQLSMALLINT  Manager[3];
       SQLCHAR      Division[3][11];
       SQLCHAR      Location[3][14];

    /* Declare The Public Attribute Variables */
    public:
       SQLRETURN  rc;

    /* Declare The Member Function Prototypes */
    CLI();                                  // Constructor
    ~CLI();                                 // Destructor
    SQLRETURN Connect();
    SQLRETURN InsertRows();
    SQLRETURN Disconnect();
} ;

/* Define The Class Constructor */
CLI::CLI()
{
    /* Initialize The Return Code Variable */
    rc = SQL_SUCCESS;

    /* Allocate An Environment Handle */
    rc = SQLAllocEnv(&EnvHandle);
```

```
    /* Allocate A Connection Handle */
    rc = SQLAllocConnect(EnvHandle, &DSCHandle);
}

/* Define The Class Destructor */
CLI::~CLI()
{
    /* Free The Connection Handle */
    if (DSCHandle != NULL)
        SQLFreeConnect(DSCHandle);

    /* Free The Environment Handle */
    if (EnvHandle != NULL)
        SQLFreeEnv(EnvHandle);
}

/* Define The Connect() Member Function */
SQLRETURN CLI::Connect()
{
    /* Connect To The SAMPLE Database */
    rc = SQLConnect(DSCHandle, (SQLCHAR *) "SAMPLE", SQL_NTS,
                    (SQLCHAR *) "etpdd6z", SQL_NTS,
                    (SQLCHAR *) "sanders", SQL_NTS);

    /* Allocate A SQL Statement Handle */
    rc = SQLAllocStmt(DSCHandle, &StmtHandle);

    /* Return The CLI Function Return Code */
    return(rc);
}

/* Define The Disconnect() Member Function */
SQLRETURN CLI::Disconnect(void)
{
    /* Disconnect From The Database */
    rc = SQLDisconnect(DSCHandle);

    /* Free The SQL Statement Handle */
    if (StmtHandle != NULL)
        SQLFreeStmt(StmtHandle, SQL_DROP);

    /* Return The CLI Function Return Code */
    return(rc);
}

/* Define The InsertRows() Member Function */
SQLRETURN CLI::InsertRows(void)
{
    /* Initialize The Input Array Variables */
    DeptNo[0] = 97;
    DeptNo[1] = 98;
    DeptNo[2] = 99;

    strcpy((char *) DeptName[0], "England");
    strcpy((char *) DeptName[1], "North East");
    strcpy((char *) DeptName[2], "Japan");

    Manager[0] = 70;
    Manager[1] = 90;
    Manager[2] = 100;

    strcpy((char *) Division[0], "Europe");
    strcpy((char *) Division[1], "Canada");
```

```
    strcpy((char *) Division[2], "Asia");
    strcpy((char *) Location[0], "London");
    strcpy((char *) Location[1], "Toronto");
    strcpy((char *) Location[2], "Tokyo");

    /* Define And Prepare An INSERT SQL Statement */
    strcpy((char *) SQLStmt, "INSERT INTO USERID.ORG (DEPTNUMB, ");
    strcat((char *) SQLStmt, "DEPTNAME, MANAGER, DIVISION, LOCATION) ");
    strcat((char *) SQLStmt, "VALUES ( ?, ?, ?, ?, ?)");
    SQLPrepare(StmtHandle, SQLStmt, SQL_NTS);

    /* Tell CLI That Three Values Will Be Provided For Each */
    /* Parameter Marker In The SQL Statement                */
    SQLParamOptions(StmtHandle, 3, NULL);

    /* Bind The Parameter Markers To Local Variables */
    SQLBindParameter(StmtHandle, 1, SQL_PARAM_INPUT, SQL_C_SHORT,
                     SQL_SMALLINT, 0, 0, DeptNo, 0, NULL);

    SQLBindParameter(StmtHandle, 2, SQL_PARAM_INPUT, SQL_C_CHAR,
                     SQL_VARCHAR, 15, 0, DeptName, 15, NULL);

    SQLBindParameter(StmtHandle, 3, SQL_PARAM_INPUT, SQL_C_SHORT,
                     SQL_SMALLINT, 0, 0, Manager, 0, NULL);

    SQLBindParameter(StmtHandle, 4, SQL_PARAM_INPUT, SQL_C_CHAR,
                     SQL_VARCHAR, 11, 0, Division, 11, NULL);

    SQLBindParameter(StmtHandle, 5, SQL_PARAM_INPUT, SQL_C_CHAR,
                     SQL_VARCHAR, 14, 0, Location, 14, NULL);

    /* Execute The SQL Statement */
    rc = SQLExecute(StmtHandle);

    /* Commit The Transaction */
    if (rc == SQL_SUCCESS)
        SQLTransact(EnvHandle, DSCHandle, SQL_COMMIT);

    /* Return The CLI Function Return Code */
    return(rc);
}

int main()
{
    /* Declare The Local Memory Variables */
    SQLRETURN  rc = SQL_SUCCESS;

    /* Create An Instance Of The CLI Class */
    CLI Sample;

    /* Connect To The SAMPLE Database */
    if ((rc = Sample.Connect()) != SQL_SUCCESS)
        return(rc);

    /* Insert 3 Row Of Data Into The USERID.ORG Table In The SAMPLE */
    /* Database                                                     */
    rc = Sample.InsertRows();

    /* If The Rows Were Added, Print A Message Saying So */
    if (rc == SQL_SUCCESS)
        {
```

```
        cout << "3 rows have been added to the USERID.ORG table.";
        cout << endl;
        }

    /* Disconnect From The SAMPLE Database */
    Sample.Disconnect();

    /* Return To The Operating System */
    return(rc);
}
```

SQLGetCursorName

Purpose The SQLGetCursorName( ) function retrieves the cursor name associated with a specific SQL statement handle.

Syntax

```
SQLRETURN SQLGetCursorName (SQLHSTMT          StmtHandle,
                            SQLCHAR FAR       *CursorName,
                            SQLSMALLINT       CursorNameMaxSize,
                            SQLSMALLINT FAR   *CursorNameSize);
```

Parameters

StmtHandle The SQL statement handle where the address of the SQL statement buffer is stored.

CursorName A pointer to a location in memory where this function is to store the retrieved cursor name.

CursorNameMaxSize The maximum size of the memory storage buffer where this function is to store the retrieved cursor name.

ConnectOutSize A pointer to a location in memory where this function is to store the actual number of bytes written to the *CursorName* memory storage buffer.

Includes

```
#include <sqlcli1.h>
```

Description The SQLGetCursorName( ) function retrieves the cursor name associated with a specific SQL statement handle. When this function is executed, the cursor name that was internally generated by DB2 CLI is returned, unless that cursor name was explicitly renamed by the SQLSetCursorName( ) function. In that case, the new cursor name will be returned.

Specifications DB2 CLI 1.1, ODBC 1.0, X/OPEN CLI, ISO CLI

Return Codes SQL_SUCCESS, SQL_SUCCESS_WITH_INFO, SQL_INVALID_HANDLE, SQL_ERROR

SQLSTATEs **01**004, **08**S01, **40**003, **58**004, **S1**001, **S1**010, **S1**013, **S1**090

Comments

- Internally generated cursor names always begin with the characters "SQLCUR" or "SQL_CUR."
- If a cursor name is explicitly set with SQLSetCursorName( ), this name will be returned until the SQL statement using the cursor is dropped or until another cursor name is explicitly set.
- Cursor names are always 18 characters or less in length, and are always unique within a data source connection.

Restrictions ODBC-generated cursor names begin with the characters "SQL_CUR," DB2-generated cursor names begin with the characters "SQLCUR," and X/Open-generated cursor names begin with either set of characters ("SQLCUR" or "SQL_CUR").

See Also SQLSetCursorName( ), SQLPrepare( ), SQLExecute( ), SQLExecDirect( )

Example The following C program illustrates how to use the SQLGetCursorName( ) function to obtain the system-generated name of a result data set cursor:

```
#include <stdio.h>
#include <stdlib.h>
#include <string.h>
#include <sqlcli1.h>

int main()
{
    /* Declare The Local Memory Variables */
    SQLRETURN    rc = SQL_SUCCESS;
    SQLHENV      EnvHandle;
    SQLHDBC      DSCHandle;
    SQLHSTMT     StmtHandle;
    SQLCHAR      SQLStmt[80];
    SQLCHAR      CursorName[19];
    SQLSMALLINT  CNameSize;

    /* Allocate An Environment Handle */
    rc = SQLAllocEnv(&EnvHandle);

    /* Allocate A Connection Handle */
    rc = SQLAllocConnect(EnvHandle, &DSCHandle);

    /* Connect To The SAMPLE Database */
    rc = SQLConnect(DSCHandle, "SAMPLE", SQL_NTS, "etpdd6z", SQL_NTS,
                "sanders", SQL_NTS);

    /* Allocate A SQL Statement Handle */
    rc = SQLAllocStmt(DSCHandle, &StmtHandle);

    /* Define A SELECT SQL Statement */
    strcpy(SQLStmt, "SELECT DEPTNO, DEPTNAME FROM USERID.DEPARTMENT ");
    strcat(SQLStmt, "WHERE ADMRDEPT = 'A00'");

    /* Execute The SQL Statement */
    rc = SQLExecDirect(StmtHandle, SQLStmt, SQL_NTS);

    /* Retrieve And Display The Cursor Name Assigned To The Result */
    /* Data Set                                                    */
    if (rc != SQL_ERROR)
        {
        if (SQLGetCursorName(StmtHandle, CursorName, sizeof(CursorName),
                         &CNameSize) == SQL_SUCCESS)
        printf("Cursor %s has been created.\n", CursorName);
        }

    /* Disconnect From The SAMPLE Database */
    SQLDisconnect(DSCHandle);

    /* Free The SQL Statement Handle */
```

```
    if (StmtHandle != NULL)
        SQLFreeStmt(StmtHandle, SQL_DROP);

    /* Free The Connection Handle */
    if (DSCHandle != NULL)
        SQLFreeConnect(DSCHandle);

    /* Free The Environment Handle */
    if (EnvHandle != NULL)
        SQLFreeEnv(EnvHandle);

    /* Return To The Operating System */
    return(rc);
}
```

> Note: The SQLGetCursorName( ) function is used in a C++ program in a similar manner.

SQLSetCursorName

Purpose The SQLSetCursorName( ) function associates a user-defined cursor name with an active SQL statement handle.

Syntax

```
SQLRETURN SQLSetCursorName (SQLHSTMT    StmtHandle,
                            SQLCHAR FAR *CursorName,
                            SQLSMALLINT CursorNameSize);
```

Parameters

StmtHandle The SQL statement handle where the address of the SQL statement buffer is stored.

CursorName A pointer to a location in memory where the cursor name is stored.

CursorNameSize The length of the cursor name specified in the *CursorName* parameter.

Includes

```
#include <sqlcli1.h>
```

Description The SQLSetCursorName( ) function associates a user-defined cursor name with an active SQL statement handle. DB2 CLI always generates and uses an internally generated cursor name when a query SQL statement is prepared or executed directly. This function allows an application to associate a user-defined cursor name with the internally generated cursor name. This user-defined cursor name can then be used in place of the internally generated cursor name in other SQL statements (such as positioned UPDATE or DELETE statements). Once assigned, the user-defined cursor name remains associated with the SQL statement handle until the SQL statement handle is deleted or until another SQLSetCursorName( ) function call changes it.

Specifications DB2 CLI 1.1, ODBC 1.0, X/OPEN CLI, ISO CLI

Return Codes SQL_SUCCESS, SQL_INVALID, HANDLE, SQL_ERROR

SQLSTATEs **34**000, **08**S01, **40**003, **58**004, **S1**001, **S1**009, **S1**010, **S1**013, **S1**090

Comments

- This function is optional since DB2 CLI automatically generates a cursor name whenever a SQL statement handle is allocated.
- Although the SQLGetCursorName( ) function returns the user-defined cursor name if one has been set, error messages associated with positioned UPDATE and DELETE SQL statements will reference only internally generated cursor names. For this reason, it is recommended that you not use user-defined cursor names in place of internal names.
- You must adhere to the following rules when creating user-defined cursor names:
  –Each cursor name must be less than or equal to 18 characters (bytes) in length. Any attempt to set a cursor name longer than 18 bytes will result in truncation of that cursor name to 18 bytes. No error or warning message generated when a cursor name is truncated.
  –Since internally generated names begin with the characters "SQLCUR" or "SQL_CUR," user-defined cursor names cannot begin with either of these strings. This avoids conflicts with internal names.
  –Since a cursor name is considered an identifier in SQL, cursor names must begin with an English letter (a to z, A to Z) followed by any combination of digits (0 to 9), English letters, or the underscore character. If a cursor name needs to contain characters other than those listed (such as National Language Set or Double-Byte Character Set characters), the cursor name must be enclosed in double quotation marks.
  –All cursor names within a single connection must be unique.
  –Unless the cursor name is enclosed in double quotes, all leading and trailing blanks from the user-defined cursor name string will be removed. Therefore, for more efficient processing, user-defined cursor names should not include leading or trailing spaces. If the cursor name is enclosed in double quotes, the first and last character in the *CursorName* string must be a double quotation mark.

Restrictions

There are no restrictions associated with this function call.

See Also

SQLGetCursorName( )

Example

The following C program illustrates how to use the SQLSetCursorName( ) function to assign a user-defined name (alias) to a result data set cursor:

```
#include <stdio.h>
#include <stdlib.h>
#include <string.h>
#include <sqlcli1.h>

int main()
{
    /* Declare The Local Memory Variables */
    SQLRETURN    rc = SQL_SUCCESS;
    SQLHENV      EnvHandle;
    SQLHDBC      DSCHandle;
    SQLHSTMT     StmtHandle;
    SQLCHAR      SQLStmt[80];
    SQLCHAR      DeptNo[4];
    SQLCHAR      DeptName[30];
    SQLCHAR      CursorName[19];
    SQLSMALLINT  CNameSize;
```

```
    /* Allocate An Environment Handle */
    rc = SQLAllocEnv(&EnvHandle);

    /* Allocate A Connection Handle */
    rc = SQLAllocConnect(EnvHandle, &DSCHandle);

    /* Connect To The SAMPLE Database */
    rc = SQLConnect(DSCHandle, "SAMPLE", SQL_NTS, "etpdd6z", SQL_NTS,
                    "sanders", SQL_NTS);

    /* Allocate A SQL Statement Handle */
    rc = SQLAllocStmt(DSCHandle, &StmtHandle);

    /* Define And Prepare A SELECT SQL Statement */
    strcpy(SQLStmt, "SELECT DEPTNO, DEPTNAME FROM USERID.DEPARTMENT ");
    strcat(SQLStmt, "WHERE ADMRDEPT = 'A00'");
    rc = SQLPrepare(StmtHandle, SQLStmt, SQL_NTS);

    /* Assign A Cursor Name To The Result Data Set */
    rc = SQLSetCursorName(StmtHandle, "DEPT_CURSOR", SQL_NTS);

    /* Execute The SQL Statement */
    SQLExecute(StmtHandle);

    /* Retrieve And Display The Cursor Name Assigned To The Result */
    /* Data Set                                                    */
    if (rc != SQL_ERROR)
        {
        if (SQLGetCursorName(StmtHandle, CursorName, sizeof(CursorName),
                             &CNameSize) == SQL_SUCCESS)
        printf("Cursor %s has been created.\n", CursorName);
        }

    /* Disconnect From The SAMPLE Database */
    SQLDisconnect(DSCHandle);

    /* Free The SQL Statement Handle */
    if (StmtHandle != NULL)
        SQLFreeStmt(StmtHandle, SQL_DROP);

    /* Free The Connection Handle */
    if (DSCHandle != NULL)
        SQLFreeConnect(DSCHandle);

    /* Free The Environment Handle */
    if (EnvHandle != NULL)
        SQLFreeEnv(EnvHandle);

    /* Return To The Operating System */
    return(rc);
}
```

Note: The SQLSetCursorName( ) function is used in a C++ program in a similar manner.

SQLExecute

Purpose The SQLExecute( ) function executes a specified SQL statement that the SQLPrepare( ) function successfully prepared, using the current values of any parameter marker variables bound to the SQL statement.

Syntax

```
SQLRETURN SQLExecute (SQLHSTMT StmtHandle);
```

Parameters *StmtHandle* The SQL statement handle where the address of the SQL statement buffer is stored.

Includes

```
#include <sqlcli1.h>
```

Description The SQLExecute( ) function executes a specified SQL statement that was successfully prepared by the SQLPrepare( ) function. The prepared SQL statement string can contain one or more parameter markers. These parameter markers are represented by question marks (?) in a SQL statement, which indicate a position in the statement where an application-supplied value is substituted when this function is called. When the prepared SQL statement executes, the current values of the application variables that are bound to the parameter markers coded in the SQL statement replace the parameter markers themselves.

Once the results from a SQLExecute( ) function call are processed, the prepared SQL statement can be executed again, with new (or the same) parameter marker values specified.

Specifications DB2 CLI 1.1, ODBC 1.0, X/OPEN CLI, ISO CLI

Return Codes SQL_SUCCESS, SQL_SUCCESS_WITH_INFO, SQL_INVALID_HANDLE, SQL_NEED_DATA, SQL_NO_DATA_FOUND, SQL_ERROR

SQLSTATEs **01**504, **01**508, **08**501, **07**001, **07**006, **21**S01, **21**S02, **22**001, **22**003, **22**005, **22**007, **22**008, **22**012, **23**000, **24**000, **24**504, **34**000, **37***xxx*, **40**000, **40**003, **08**S01, **42***xxx*, **42**8A1, **42**895, **44**000, **56**084, **58**004, **S0**001, **S0**002, **S0**011, **S0**012, **S0**021, **S0**022, **S1**001, **S1**010, **S1**013, **S1**090, **S1**503, **S1**T00

Note: *xxx* means that any SQLSTATE subclass value with the class code 37 or 42 can be returned.

Comments

- A SQL statement that has been executed by the SQLExecDirect( ) function cannot be reexecuted by this function unless it is first prepared with the SQLPrepare( ) function.
- If a prepared SQL statement being executed is a query statement that will produce a result data set containing multiple rows, this function will automatically generate a named cursor for the result data set and open it. If the SQLSetCursorName( ) function has associated a user-defined cursor name with the SQL statement handle associated with the prepared SQL statement, DB2 CLI will associate the user-defined cursor name with the internally generated one immediately after this function executes.
- If a result data set is generated by the executed SQL statement, you can use the SQLFetch( ) or SQLExtendedFetch( ) function to retrieve the next row (or rows) of data into bound variables, LOB locators, or LOB file references. You can also

retrieve data by calling the SQLGetData( ) function for any variables/columns that were not bound.

- In order to execute a SQL query statement that produces a result data set (cursor) more than once, you must first close any open cursors associated with the SQL statement handle by calling the SQLFreeStmt( ) function with the SQL_CLOSE option. The specified SQL statement handle must not contain an open cursor when this function is called.
- If the SQL statement is a positioned UPDATE or DELETE statement, the cursor referenced by the SQL statement must be defined on a separate SQL statement handle, under the same connection handle with the same isolation level. Also, the position pointer of the cursor referenced by the SQL statement must be positioned on a row in the result data set at the time this function is called.
- Do not use this function to execute SQL statements that contain parameter markers bound to arrays of input values. If the SQLParamOptions( ) function has specified that an array of input parameter values is bound to each parameter marker coded in the SQL statement, then you need to call the SQLExecDirect( ) function in order to process the entire array of input parameter values. This is because the SQLExecDirect( ) function can submit the entire array of values in a single call. If the executed SQL statement returns multiple result data sets (one for each set of input parameter values), then you can use the SQLMoreResults( ) function to advance to the next result data set once processing on the current result data set is complete.
- If the application has requested to input data-at-execution parameter values by calling the SQLParamData( ) function and the SQLPutData( ) function, the return code SQL_NEED_DATA will be returned when this function is executed.
- If the prepared SQL statement is a searched UPDATE or DELETE statement and no rows satisfy the search condition, the return code SQL_NO_DATA_FOUND will be returned when this function is executed.
- If the SQL statement contains vendor escape clause sequences, DB2 CLI will first modify the SQL statement text to the appropriate data-source-specific format before submitting it to the data source for preparation. If an application does not use vendor escape clause sequences, set the SQL_NOSCAN statement option to SQL_NOSCAN at the connection level so DB2 CLI does not perform this scan and conversion. Refer to the SQLSetStmtOption( ) function for more information.

Prerequisites You must call the SQLPrepare( ) function to prepare the SQL statement for execution and bind all parameter markers coded in the SQL statement to application variables or external files before calling this function.

Restrictions There are no restrictions associated with this function call.

See Also SQLPrepare( ), SQLExecDirect( ), SQLFetch( ), SQLExtendedFetch( ), SQL SetParam( ), SQLParamOptions( ), SQLBindParameter( ), SQLBindFileTo Param( ), SQLBindCol( ), SQLBindFileToCol( )

Examples See the examples provided for the SQLAllocStmt( ) function in this chapter.

SQLExecDirect

Purpose The SQLExecDirect( ) function directly prepares and executes a specified SQL statement.

Syntax

```
SQLRETURN SQLExecDirect (SQLHSTMT      StmtHandle,
                         SQLCHAR FAR   *SQLString,
                         SQLINTEGER    SQLStringSize);
```

Parameters

StmtHandle The SQL statement handle where the address of the SQL statement buffer is stored.

SQLString A pointer to a location in memory where the SQL statement to be executed is stored.

SQLStringSize The length of the SQL statement stored in the *SQLString* parameter.

Includes

```
#include <sqlcli1.h>
```

Description

The SQLExecDirect( ) function directly executes a specified SQL statement. Since the SQL statement is both prepared and executed in the same step, the specified SQL statement can be executed only once. Also, the connected data source to which the SQL statement is passed must be able to dynamically prepare and execute SQL statements.

Specifications

DB2 CLI 1.1, ODBC 1.0, X/OPEN CLI, ISO CLI

Return Codes

SQL_SUCCESS, SQL_SUCCESS_WITH_INFO, SQL_INVALID_HANDLE, SQL_NEED_DATA, SQL_NO_DATA_FOUND, SQL_ERROR

SQLSTATEs

01504, **01**508, **07**001, **07**006, **08**S01, **21**S01,**21**S02, **22**001, **22**003, **22**005, **22**007, **22**008, **22**012, **23**000, **24**000, **24**504, **34**000, **37***xxx*, **40**000, **40**003, **42***xxx*, **42**8A1, **42**895, **44**000, **56**084, **58**004, **S0**001, **S0**002, **S0**011, **S0**012, **S0**022, **S0**022, **S1**001, **S1**009, **S1**013, **S1**090, **S1**503, **S1**T00

> Note: *xxx* means that any SQLSTATE subclass value with the class code 37 or 42 can be returned.

Comments

- The length of the SQL statement stored in the *SQLStringSize* parameter must be the exact length of the SQL statement if the statement is not null-terminated (the length is determined by the number of characters in the string). The value SQL_NTS can be used if the SQL statement is null-terminated.
- If an open cursor is associated with the specified SQL statement handle, it must be closed before the SQL statement handle can be used with this function.
- The SQL statement string being prepared might contain parameter markers; if so, you can call the SQLNumParams( ) function to determine the number of parameter markers in the statement. A parameter marker is represented by a question mark character (?) in a SQL statement, and indicates a position in the statement where an application-supplied value is substituted when the function is called. The bind parameter functions—SQLBindParameter( ), SQLSetParam( ), and SQLBindFileToParam( )—bind (associate) application values with each parameter marker, and indicate if any data conversion should be performed at the time the data is transferred to the data source. Once a SQL statement has been prepared, all parameter markers in that statement must be bound before the statement can be executed.
- The SQL statement cannot be a COMMIT or a ROLLBACK statement. Only the SQLTransact( ) function can be used to issue COMMIT or ROLLBACK statements.

- If the SQL statement being executed is a query statement that will produce a result data set containing multiple rows, this function will automatically generate a named cursor for the result data set and open it. If the SQLSetCursorName( ) function associates a user-defined cursor name with the SQL statement handle associated with the SQL statement, DB2 CLI will associate the user-defined cursor name with the internally generated one immediately after this function executes.
- If a result data set is generated by the executed SQL statement, the SQLFetch( ) function or the SQLExtendedFetch( ) function can retrieve the next row (or rows) of data into bound variables, LOB locators, or LOB file references. You can also retrieve data by calling the SQLGetData( ) function for any variables/columns that were not bound.
- If the SQL statement is a positioned UPDATE or DELETE statement, the cursor referenced by the SQL statement must be defined on a separate SQL statement handle, under the same connection handle with the same isolation level. Also, the position pointer of the cursor referenced by the SQL statement must be positioned on a row in the result data set at the time this function is called.
- If the SQLParamOptions( ) function specifies that an array of input parameter values are bound to each parameter marker coded in the SQL statement, then call this function once to process the entire array of input parameter values. If the executed SQL statement returns multiple-result data sets (one for each set of input parameter values), then use the SQLMoreResults( ) function to advance to the next result data set once processing on the current result data set is complete.
- If the application has requested to input data-at-execution parameter values by calling the SQLParamData( ) and SQLPutData( ) functions, the return code SQL_NEED_DATA will be returned when this function is executed.
- If the SQL statement is a searched UPDATE or DELETE statement and no rows satisfy the search condition, the return code SQL_NO_DATA_FOUND will be returned when this function is executed.
- If the SQL statement contains vendor escape clause sequences, DB2 CLI will first modify the SQL statement text to the appropriate data-source-specific format before submitting it to the data source for preparation. If an application does not use vendor escape clause sequences, set the SQL_NOSCAN statement option to SQL_NOSCAN at the connection level so DB2 CLI does not perform this scan and conversion. Refer to the SQLSetStmtOption( ) function for more information.
- Since the SQL language has been substantially enhanced in DB2 for Common Servers, version 2.1, refer to Part 3 of this book, STRUCTURED QUERY LANGUAGE (SQL) STATEMENTS, for more information.

Restrictions There are no restrictions associated with this function call.

See Also SQLExecute( ), SQLBindParameter( ), SQLBindFileToParam( ), SQLBindCol( ), SQLBindFileToCol( ), SQLFetch( ), SQLExtendedFetch( ), SQLParamData( ), SQLPutData( ), SQLSetParam( )

Examples See the examples provided for the SQLGetCursorName( ) function in this chapter.

SQLNativeSql

Purpose The SQLNativeSql( ) function displays a specified SQL statement string as it would be seen (transformed) by the data source (database).

Syntax

```
SQLRETURN SQLNativeSql (SQLHDBC          DSCHandle,
                        SQLCHAR FAR      SQLStringIn,
                        SQLINTEGER       SQLStringInSize,
                        SQLCHAR FAR      *SQLStringOut,
                        SQLINTEGER       SQLStringOutMaxSize,
                        SQLINTEGER FAR   *SQLStringOutSize);
```

Parameters

DSCHandle The data source connection handle where the address of the data source connection information buffer is stored.

SQLStringIn A pointer to a location in memory where a SQL statement string to be translated is stored.

SQLStringInSize The length of the SQL statement string stored in the *SQLStringIn* parameter.

SQLStringOut A pointer to a location in memory where this function is to store the translated SQL statement string.

SQLStringOutMaxSize The maximum size of the memory storage buffer where this function is to store the translated SQL statement string.

SQLStringOutSize A pointer to a location in memory where this function is to store the actual number of bytes written to the translated SQL statement string memory storage buffer (*SQLStringOut*).

Includes

```
#include <sqlcli1.h>
```

Description

The SQLNativeSql( ) function displays a specified SQL statement string as it will be seen (transformed) by the data source. This function is used primarily to show how DB2 CLI interprets vendor escape clauses. The X/Open SQL CAE specification defines an escape clause as "a syntactic mechanism for vendor-specific SQL extensions to be implemented within the framework of standardized SQL." Both DB2 CLI and ODBC support vendor escape clauses, and escape clauses are currently used extensively by ODBC to define various SQL extensions. DB2 CLI translates these ODBC extensions into the correct DB2 syntax.

If an application accesses only DB2 data sources, there is no reason to use escape clauses. However, if an application accesses other data sources that offer the same SQL support but use different syntax, then using escape clauses will increase the portability of that application. Call this function whenever an application wants to examine or display the transformed SQL string that would be passed to the data source by DB2 CLI.

Specifications DB2 CLI 2.1, ODBC 1.0

Return Codes SQL_SUCCESS, SQL_SUCCESS_WITH_INFO, SQL_INVALID_HANDLE, SQL_ERROR

SQLSTATEs **01**004, **08**003, **37**000, **S1**001, **S1**009, **S1**090

Comments

- Translation (mapping) occurs only if the input SQL statement string *(SQLStringIn)* contains vendor escape clause sequences.
- DB2 CLI can detect only vendor escape clause syntax errors; since the transformed SQL string is not passed to the data source for preparation, syntax errors that might be detected by the data source are not displayed. (The statement is not passed to the data source for preparation because the preparation might inadvertently initiate a transaction.)

Restrictions There are no restrictions associated with this function call.

Example The following C program illustrates how to use the SQLNativeSql( ) function to show how a SQL statement will look after it has been translated into its corresponding native syntax (which will be used when the SQL statement is sent to the connected data source for processing):

```
#include <stdio.h>
#include <stdlib.h>
#include <string.h>
#include <sqlcli1.h>

int main()
{
    /* Declare The Local Memory Variables */
    SQLRETURN    rc = SQL_SUCCESS;
    SQLHENV      EnvHandle;
    SQLHDBC      DSCHandle;
    SQLHSTMT     StmtHandle;
    SQLCHAR      SQLStmt[255];
    SQLCHAR      OutStmt[255];
    SQLINTEGER   StmtSize;

    /* Allocate An Environment Handle */
    rc = SQLAllocEnv(&EnvHandle);

    /* Allocate A Connection Handle */
    rc = SQLAllocConnect(EnvHandle, &DSCHandle);

    /* Connect To The SAMPLE Database */
    rc = SQLConnect(DSCHandle, "SAMPLE", SQL_NTS, "etpdd6z", SQL_NTS,
                    "sanders", SQL_NTS);

    /* Allocate A SQL Statement Handle */
    rc = SQLAllocStmt(DSCHandle, &StmtHandle);

    /* Define And Prepare A SELECT SQL Statement */
    strcpy(SQLStmt, "SELECT PROJNO, PRSTDATE, PRENDATE FROM ");
    strcat(SQLStmt, "USERID.PROJECT FOR UPDATE OF PRENDATE");
    SQLPrepare(StmtHandle, SQLStmt, SQL_NTS);

    /* Retrieve The Transformed SQL Statement */
    SQLNativeSql(StmtHandle, SQLStmt, SQL_NTS, OutStmt,
                 sizeof(OutStmt), &StmtSize);

    if (StmtSize == SQL_NULL_DATA)
        printf("The SQL statement could not be transformed.\n");
    else
        {
        printf("Original SQL Statement :\n%s\n\n", SQLStmt);
        printf("Native SQL Statement   :\n%s\n", OutStmt);
        }

    /* Disconnect From The SAMPLE Database */
    SQLDisconnect(DSCHandle);

    /* Free The SQL Statement Handle */
    if (StmtHandle != NULL)
        SQLFreeStmt(StmtHandle, SQL_DROP);

    /* Free The Connection Handle */
    if (DSCHandle != NULL)
        SQLFreeConnect(DSCHandle);
```

```
    /* Free The Environment Handle */
    if (EnvHandle != NULL)
        SQLFreeEnv(EnvHandle);

    /* Return To The Operating System */
    return(rc);
}
```

Note: The SQLNativeSql( ) function is used in a C++ program in a similar manner.

SQLNumParams

Purpose The SQLNumParams( ) function retrieves the number of parameter markers used in a SQL statement.

Syntax

```
SQLRETURN SQLNumParams (SQLHSTMT        StmtHandle,
                        SQLSMALLINT FAR *PMarkerNum);
```

Parameters

StmtHandle The SQL statement handle where the address of the SQL statement buffer is stored.

PMarkerNum A pointer to a location in memory where this function is to store the number of parameter markers found in the SQL statement.

Includes `#include <sqlcli1.h>`

Description The SQLNumParams( ) function retrieves the number of parameter markers used in a SQL statement. You can use this function to determine how many SQLBind-Parameter( ) function calls and/or SQLBindFileToParam( ) function calls are needed to associate (bind) application variables and/or external data files to the SQL statement associated with the SQL statement handle.

Specifications DB2 CLI 2.1, ODBC 1.0

Return Codes SQL_SUCCESS, SQL_INVALID_HANDLE, SQL_ERROR

SQLSTATEs **08**S01, **40**003, **S1**001, **S1**009, **S1**010, **S1**013, **S1**T00

Comments If the statement does not contain any parameter markers, the *PMarkerNum* parameter value is set to 0.

Prerequisites You must call the SQLPrepare( ) function to prepare the SQL statement associated with the SQL statement handle (StmtHandle) before calling this function.

Restrictions There are no restrictions associated with this function call.

See Also SQLPrepare( ), SQLBindParameter( ), SQLBindFileToParam( )

Example The following C program illustrates how to use the SQLNumParams( ) function to obtain the number of parameter markers used in a SQL statement:

```
#include <stdio.h>
#include <stdlib.h>
```

```
#include <string.h>
#include <sqlcli1.h>

int main()
{
    /* Declare The Local Memory Variables */
    SQLRETURN    rc = SQL_SUCCESS;
    SQLHENV      EnvHandle;
    SQLHDBC      DSCHandle;
    SQLHSTMT     StmtHandle;
    SQLCHAR      SQLStmt[100];
    SQLSMALLINT  NumPMarkers;

    /* Allocate An Environment Handle */
    rc = SQLAllocEnv(&EnvHandle);

    /* Allocate A Connection Handle */
    rc = SQLAllocConnect(EnvHandle, &DSCHandle);

    /* Connect To The SAMPLE Database */
    rc = SQLConnect(DSCHandle, "SAMPLE", SQL_NTS, "etpdd6z", SQL_NTS,
                    "sanders", SQL_NTS);

    /* Allocate A SQL Statement Handle */
    rc = SQLAllocStmt(DSCHandle, &StmtHandle);

    /* Define And Prepare A SELECT SQL Statement */
    strcpy(SQLStmt, "INSERT INTO USERID.ORG (DEPTNUMB, DEPTNAME, ");
    strcat(SQLStmt, "MANAGER, DIVISION, LOCATION) VALUES ");
    strcat(SQLStmt, "( ?, ?, ?, ?, ?)");
    SQLPrepare(StmtHandle, SQLStmt, SQL_NTS);

    /* Obtain And Print The Number Of Parameter Markers Found In The */
    /* SQL Statement                                                  */
    rc = SQLNumParams(StmtHandle, &NumPMarkers);
    printf("Number of parameter markers in the SQL statement : %d\n",
           NumPMarkers);

    /* Disconnect From The SAMPLE Database */
    SQLDisconnect(DSCHandle);

    /* Free The SQL Statement Handle */
    if (StmtHandle != NULL)
        SQLFreeStmt(StmtHandle, SQL_DROP);

    /* Free The Connection Handle */
    if (DSCHandle != NULL)
        SQLFreeConnect(DSCHandle);

    /* Free The Environment Handle */
    if (EnvHandle != NULL)
        SQLFreeEnv(EnvHandle);

    /* Return To The Operating System */
    return(rc);
}
```

Note: The SQLNumParams( ) function is used in a C++ program in a similar manner.

SQLParamData

Purpose The SQLParamData( ) function works in conjunction with the SQLPutData( ) function to send parameter data values to a specified data source at SQL statement execution time.

Syntax

```
SQLRETURN SQLParamData (SQLHSTMT        StmtHandle,
                        SQLPOINTER FAR *Value);
```

Parameters

StmtHandle The SQL statement handle where the address of the SQL statement buffer is stored.

Value A pointer to a location in memory where the actual value associated with the parameter marker is stored. This should be the same location in memory that was specified in either the SQLBindParameter( ) or the SQLSetParam( ) function.

Includes

```
#include <sqlcli1.h>
```

Description An application can pass the value for a parameter marker to the data source when a SQL statement is executed. This can be particularly useful when the data value is so large that it needs to be sent in pieces. The SQLParamData( ) works in conjunction with the SQLPutData( ) function to send data to a specified data source at SQL statement execution time in what is known as a data-at-execution sequence.

Data-at-execution parameter markers are bound to application variables at the same time other parameter markers in the SQL statement are bound to application variables and/or external files. With data-at-execution parameters, however, the value SQL_DATA_AT_EXEC is specified during the binding process instead of the data value size. Before the SQL statement is executed, all data values are placed in the appropriate application variables that were bound to the SQL statement. When the SQL statement is executed and a SQL_DATA_AT_EXEC value is found, this function performs the data retrieval portion of the necessary data-at-execution sequence.

After this function executes, the SQLParamData( ) function is called one or more times to send the actual parameter data to the appropriate data source. This function is then called again to signal that all the data was sent for the current parameter and to advance to the next SQL_DATA_AT_EXEC parameter marker. If no more SQL_DATA_AT_EXEC parameters exist, this function will return the SQL_SUCCESS return code when all parameter markers are assigned data values and the associated SQL statement executes successfully (provided no errors occur during processing).

Specifications DB2 CLI 2.1, ODBC 1.0, X/OPEN CLI, ISO CLI

Return Codes SQL_SUCCESS, SQL_SUCCESS_WITH_INFO, SQL_INVALID_HANDLE, SQL_ERROR

SQLSTATEs **01**504, **01**508, **07**001, **07**006, **08**S01, **21**S01, **21**S02, **22**001, **22**003, **22**005, **22**007, **22**008, **22**012, **23**000, **24**000, **24**504, **34**000, **37***xxx*, **40**000, **40**003, **42***xxx*, **42**8A1, **42**895, **44**000, **56**084, **58**004, **S0**001, **S0**002, **S0**011, **S0**012, **S0**022, **S0**022, **S1**001, **S1**009, **S1**010, **S1**013, **S1**090, **S1**503, **S1**506, **S1**509, **S1**T00

> Note: *xxx* means that any SQLSTATE subclass value with the class code 37 or 42 can be returned.

Comments

- This function returns the SQL_NEED_DATA return code if there is at least one data-at-execution (SQL_DATA_AT_EXEC) parameter marker for which data is still not assigned.
- When this function returns the SQL_NEED_DATA return code, only SQLPutData( ) or SQLCancel( ) can be called. All other CLI functions that attempt to reference the same SQL statement handle will fail. In addition, all CLI function calls that reference the parent data source connection handle of the SQL statement handle will fail if they attempt to change any attribute or state of the connection associated with that connection handle. In other words, the following CLI functions cannot be executed on the parent data source connection handle:
  –SQLAllocConnect( )
  –SQLAllocStmt( )
  –SQLSetConnectOption( )
  –SQLNativeSql( )
  –SQLTransact( )

  If any of these functions are invoked during a data-at-execution sequence, they will return the SQL_ERROR return code with a SQLSTATE of **S1**010. The processing of the data-at-execution (SQL_DATA_AT_EXEC) parameters will not be affected.

Restrictions

There are no restrictions associated with this function call.

See Also

SQLBindParameter( ), SQLCancel( ), SQLExecute( ), SQLExecDirect( ), SQLPutData( ), SQLSetParm( )

Example

The following C program illustrates how to use SQLParamData( ), SQLPutData ( ), and SQLCancel( ) to insert a LOB data item into a data source table using the data-at-execution sequence:

```
#include <stdio.h>
#include <stdlib.h>
#include <string.h>
#include <sqlcli1.h>

int main()
{
    /* Declare The Local Memory Variables */
    SQLRETURN     rc = SQL_SUCCESS;
    SQLHENV       EnvHandle;
    SQLHDBC       DSCHandle;
    SQLHSTMT      StmtHandle;
    SQLCHAR       SQLStmt[100];
    SQLCHAR       InputParam[] = "Resume Data";
    SQLINTEGER    Length = SQL_DATA_AT_EXEC;
    SQLCHAR       FileName[] = "RESUME.TXT";
    FILE          *InFile;
    SQLINTEGER    Value = 0;
    SQLCHAR       Buffer[255];
    size_t        NumBytes = 0;
    size_t        FileSize = 0;

    /* Allocate An Environment Handle */
    rc = SQLAllocEnv(&EnvHandle);

    /* Allocate A Connection Handle */
    rc = SQLAllocConnect(EnvHandle, &DSCHandle);

    /* Connect To The SAMPLE Database */
    rc = SQLConnect(DSCHandle, "SAMPLE", SQL_NTS, "etpdd6z", SQL_NTS,
                    "sanders", SQL_NTS);
```

```
/* Allocate A SQL Statement Handle */
rc = SQLAllocStmt(DSCHandle, &StmtHandle);

/* Define And Prepare An INSERT SQL Statement */
strcpy(SQLStmt, "INSERT INTO USERID.EMP_RESUME (EMPNO, ");
strcat(SQLStmt, "RESUME_FORMAT, RESUME) VALUES ('000200', ");
strcat(SQLStmt, "'ascii', ?)");
SQLPrepare(StmtHandle, SQLStmt, SQL_NTS);

/* Bind The Parameter Marker To A Local Variable - This   */
/* Parameter Will Use SQLPutData() To Send Data In Pieces */
SQLBindParameter(StmtHandle, 1, SQL_PARAM_INPUT, SQL_C_DEFAULT,
                 SQL_CLOB, 0, 0, (SQLPOINTER) InputParam, 255,
                 &Length);

/* Execute The SQL Statement */
rc = SQLExecute(StmtHandle);

/* The Return Code SQL_NEED_DATA Should Be Returned, Indicating */
/* That SQLPutData() Needs To Be Called                         */
if (rc == SQL_NEED_DATA)
    {

    /* Open The External Data File - If An Error Occurs, Call      */
    /* The SQLCancel() Function To Terminate The Data-At-Execution */
    /* Sequence, Then Exit                                         */
    InFile = fopen((char *) FileName, "rb");
    if (InFile == NULL)
        {
        printf("ERROR : Unable to open file %s\n", FileName);
        SQLCancel(StmtHandle);
        goto EXIT;
        }

    /* As Long As There Is A Data-At-Execution Parameter */
    /* Marker That Needs Data ...                        */
    while (SQLParamData(StmtHandle, (SQLPOINTER *) &Value) ==
           SQL_NEED_DATA)
        {

        /* Note: If there were two or more data-at-execution  */
        /* parameters, Value would be used to determine which */
        /* parameter currently needed data.                   */

        /* As Long As There Is Data Available For The Parameter */
        /* Marker - Retrieve It From The File And Send It       */
        do
            {
            NumBytes = fread(Buffer, sizeof(char), 255, InFile);
            SQLPutData(StmtHandle, Buffer, NumBytes);
            FileSize = FileSize + NumBytes;

            /* Make Sure The Amount Of Data Written Does Not */
            /* Exceed The Column Size (Which Is 5K)          */
            if (FileSize > 5120)
                {
                printf("ERROR : Data exceeds column size !\n");
                SQLCancel(StmtHandle);
                goto EXIT;
                }
```

```
            } while (feof(InFile) == 0);

            /* Display A Message Telling How Many Bytes Were Sent */
            printf("Successfully inserted %u bytes from %s ",
                   FileSize, FileName);
            printf("into the database.\n");
            }

        /* Close The External Data File */
        fclose(InFile);
        }

    /* Disconnect From The SAMPLE Database */
    SQLDisconnect(DSCHandle);

EXIT:
    /* Free The SQL Statement Handle */
    if (StmtHandle != NULL)
        SQLFreeStmt(StmtHandle, SQL_DROP);

    /* Free The Connection Handle */
    if (DSCHandle != NULL)
        SQLFreeConnect(DSCHandle);

    /* Free The Environment Handle */
    if (EnvHandle != NULL)
        SQLFreeEnv(EnvHandle);

    /* Return To The Operating System */
    return(rc);
}
```

The following C++ program illustrates how SQLParamData( ), SQLPutData( ), and SQLCancel( ) can be used in a class method to insert a LOB data item into a data source table using the data-at-execution sequence:

```
#include <iostream.h>
#include <fstream.h>
#include <string.h>
#include <sqlcli1.h>

/* Define The CLI Class */
class CLI
{
    /* Declare The Private Attribute Variables */
    private:
       SQLHENV        EnvHandle;
       SQLHDBC        DSCHandle;

    /* Declare The Public Attribute Variables */
    public:
       SQLRETURN      rc;
       SQLHSTMT       StmtHandle;

    /* Declare The Member Function Prototypes */
    CLI();                                      // Constructor
    ~CLI();                                     // Destructor
    SQLRETURN Connect();
    SQLRETURN SendData();
    SQLRETURN Disconnect();
} ;
```

```
/* Define The Class Constructor */
CLI::CLI()
{
    /* Initialize The Return Code Variable */
    rc = SQL_SUCCESS;

    /* Allocate An Environment Handle */
    rc = SQLAllocEnv(&EnvHandle);

    /* Allocate A Connection Handle */
    rc = SQLAllocConnect(EnvHandle, &DSCHandle);
}

/* Define The Class Destructor */
CLI::~CLI()
{
    /* Free The Connection Handle */
    if (DSCHandle != NULL)
        SQLFreeConnect(DSCHandle);

    /* Free The Environment Handle */
    if (EnvHandle != NULL)
        SQLFreeEnv(EnvHandle);
}

/* Define The Connect() Member Function */
SQLRETURN CLI::Connect()
{
    /* Connect To The SAMPLE Database */
    rc = SQLConnect(DSCHandle, (SQLCHAR *) "SAMPLE", SQL_NTS,
                    (SQLCHAR *) "etpdd6z", SQL_NTS,
                    (SQLCHAR *) "sanders", SQL_NTS);

    /* Allocate A SQL Statement Handle */
    rc = SQLAllocStmt(DSCHandle, &StmtHandle);

    /* Return The CLI Function Return Code */
    return(rc);
}

/* Define The Disconnect() Member Function */
SQLRETURN CLI::Disconnect(void)
{
    /* Disconnect From The Database */
    rc = SQLDisconnect(DSCHandle);

    /* Free The SQL Statement Handle */
    if (StmtHandle != NULL)
        SQLFreeStmt(StmtHandle, SQL_DROP);

    /* Return The CLI Function Return Code */
    return(rc);
}

/* Define The SendData() Member Function */
SQLRETURN CLI::SendData(void)
{
    /* Declare The Local Memory Variables */
    ifstream      InFile;
    SQLINTEGER    Value = 0;
    SQLCHAR       Buffer[255];
```

```
    size_t       NumBytes = 0;
    size_t       FileSize = 0;

    /* Open The External Data File - If An Error Occurs, Call      */
    /* The SQLCancel() Function To Terminate The Data-At-Execution */
    /* Sequence, Then Exit                                         */
    InFile.open("RESUME.TXT", ios::in | ios::binary);
    if (InFile.fail())
        {
        cout << "ERROR : Unable to open file RESUME.TXT" << endl;
        SQLCancel(StmtHandle);
        return(SQL_ERROR);
        }

    /* As Long As There Is A Data-At-Execution Parameter Marker */
    /* That Needs Data ...                                      */
    while (SQLParamData(StmtHandle, (SQLPOINTER *) &Value) ==
           SQL_NEED_DATA)
        {

        /* Note: If there were two or more data-at-execution  */
        /* parameters, Value would be used to determine which */
        /* parameter currently needed data.                   */

        /* As Long As There Is Data Available For The Parameter */
        /* Marker - Retrieve It From The File And Send It       */
        while (InFile.read(Buffer, sizeof(Buffer)))
            {
            SQLPutData(StmtHandle, Buffer, sizeof(Buffer));
            FileSize = FileSize + sizeof(Buffer);

            /* Make Sure The Amount Of Data Written Does Not */
            /* Exceed The Column Size (Which Is 5K)          */
            if (FileSize > 5120)
                {
                cout << "ERROR : Data exceeds column size !" << endl;
                SQLCancel(StmtHandle);
                return(SQL_ERROR);
                }
            }

        /* Display A Message Telling How Many Bytes Were Sent */
        cout << "Successfully inserted " << FileSize ;
        cout << " bytes from RESUME.TXT into the database.";
        cout << endl;
        }

    /* Close The External Data File */
    InFile.close();

    /* Return The CLI Function Return Code */
    return(rc);
}

int main()
{
    /* Declare The Local Memory Variables */
    SQLRETURN    rc = SQL_SUCCESS;
    SQLCHAR      SQLStmt[100];
    SQLCHAR      InputParam[] = "Resume Data";
    SQLINTEGER   Length = SQL_DATA_AT_EXEC;
```

```
    /* Create An Instance Of The CLI Class */
    CLI Sample;

    /* Connect To The SAMPLE Database */
    if ((rc = Sample.Connect()) != SQL_SUCCESS)
        return(rc);

    /* Define And Prepare An INSERT SQL Statement */
    strcpy((char *) SQLStmt, "INSERT INTO USERID.EMP_RESUME (EMPNO, ");
    strcat((char *) SQLStmt, "RESUME_FORMAT, RESUME) VALUES ");
    strcat((char *) SQLStmt, ""('000200', 'ascii', ?)");
    SQLPrepare(Sample.StmtHandle, SQLStmt, SQL_NTS);

    /* Bind The Parameter Marker To A Local Variable - This   */
    /* Parameter Will Use SQLPutData() To Send Data In Pieces */
    SQLBindParameter(Sample.StmtHandle, 1, SQL_PARAM_INPUT,
                     SQL_C_DEFAULT, SQL_CLOB, 0, 0, (SQLPOINTER)
                     InputParam, 255, &Length);

    /* Execute The SQL Statement */
    rc = SQLExecute(Sample.StmtHandle);

    /* The Return Code SQL_NEED_DATA Should Be Returned, Indicating */
    /* That SQLPutData() Needs To Be Called                         */
    if (rc == SQL_NEED_DATA)
        Sample.SendData();

    /* Disconnect From The SAMPLE Database */
    Sample.Disconnect();

    /* Return To The Operating System */
    return(rc);
}
```

SQLPutData

Purpose The SQLPutData( ) function sends data for data-at-execution parameters to the appropriate data source at SQL statement execution time.

Syntax

```
SQLRETURN SQLPutData (SQLHSTMT    StmtHandle,
                      SQLPOINTER  Value,
                      SQLINTEGER  ValueSize);
```

Parameters

StmtHandle The SQL statement handle where the address of the SQL statement buffer is stored.

Value A pointer to a location in memory where the data value (or a portion of the data value) for the parameter marker specified in SQLBindParameter( ) or SQLSetParam( ) is stored.

ValueSize The length (number of bytes) of the data value stored in the *Value* parameter. This value specifies the amount of data that will be sent by this function call.

Includes

```
#include <sqlcli1.h>
```

Description The SQLPutData( ) function sends data for a parameter marker to the data source at SQL statement execution time. This function works in conjunction with the SQLParamData( ) function to send data to a specified data source in a data-at-execution sequence.

Data-at-execution parameter markers are bound to application variables at the same time other parameter markers in the SQL statement are bound to application variables and/or external files. With data-at-execution parameters, however, the value SQL_DATA_AT_EXEC is specified during the binding process instead of the data value size. Before the SQL statement is executed, all data values are placed in the appropriate application variables that were bound to the SQL statement. When the SQL statement is executed and a SQL_DATA_AT_EXEC value is found, the SQLParamData( ) function performs the necessary data retrieval portion of the data-at-execution sequence. This function then sends the appropriate data value (if necessary, in two or more pieces) to the data source, following a SQLParamData( ) function call that returns the value SQL_NEED_DATA. After all the pieces of data for the parameter marker are sent to the data source, you must call the SQLParamData( ) function again to signal that all the data has been sent for the current parameter and to advance to the next SQL_DATA_AT_EXEC parameter marker (if there are any more SQL_DATA_AT_EXEC parameters to be processed).

Specifications DB2 CLI 2.1, ODBC 1.0, X/OPEN CLI, ISO CLI

Return Codes SQL_SUCCESS, SQL_SUCCESS_WITH_INFO, SQL_INVALID_HANDLE, SQL_ERROR

SQLSTATEs **01**004, **22**001, **22**003, **22**005, **22**007, **40**003, **08**S01, **S1**001, **S1**009, **S1**010, **S1**090, **S1**T00

Note: Some of these SQLSTATEs might be reported on the final SQLParamData( ) function call rather than at the time the SQLPutData( ) function is called.

Comments

- The data to be sent to the data source must be in the form that was specified when the application variable containing the data was bound to the parameter marker in the SQL statement.
- If the data value to be sent to the data source is a null-terminated string, the value SQL_NTS can be specified in the *ValueSize* parameter. If the data value is a NULL value, the value SQL_NULL_DATA can be used.
- This function cannot be called more than once for a fixed-length C data type, such as SQL_C_INTEGER and SQL_C_LONG.
- The *ValueSize* parameter value is ignored for all fixed-length C data types.
- After a SQLPutData( ) function call is made, if the input data is character or binary data, the only legal CLI statement processing functions available for use are SQLParamData( ), SQLCancel( ), or another SQLPutData( ) function call. All other function calls using this SQL statement handle (*StmtHandle*) will fail. In addition, all function calls that reference the parent data source connection handle (*DSCHandle*) of the SQL statement handle will fail if they attempt to change any attribute or state of that connection. In other words, the following data source connection functions cannot be used:
  –SQLAllocConnect( )
  –SQLAllocStmt( )
  –SQLSetConnectOption( )

–SQLNativeSql( )
–SQLTransact( )

If any of these functions are invoked during a data-at-execution sequence, the return code SQL_ERROR with SQLSTATE **S1**010 will be returned and the processing of the data-at-execution sequence will not be affected.

- If one or more calls to this function for a single parameter marker results in SQL_SUCCESS, attempting to call this function with the *Value* parameter set to SQL_NULL_DATA for the same parameter marker will cause an error with the SQLSTATE of **22**005 to be generated. This error does not result in a change of state, so the SQL statement handle will still be in a SQL_NEED_DATA state and the application can continue sending parameter data.

Prerequisites The SQLFreeConnect( ) function must be executed before this function is called.

Authorization No authorization is required to execute this function call.

Restrictions A new value, SQL_DEFAULT_PARAM, was introduced in ODBC 2.0 to indicate that the procedure is to use the default value of a parameter rather than a value sent from the application. Since DB2 stored procedure arguments do not have the concept of default values, specifying this value for the *Value* parameter will result in an error when the CALL statement is executed since the SQL_DEFAULT_PARAM value is considered an invalid length.

ODBC 2.0 also introduced the SQL_LEN_DATA_AT_EXEC(*length*) macro to be used with the *Value* parameter to calculate data size. This macro is designed to specify the sum total length of the entire data sent for character or binary C data types via subsequent SQLPutData( ) calls. Since the DB2 ODBC driver does not need this information, the macro is not needed. An application can call the SQLGetInfo( ) function with the SQL_NEED_LONG_DATA_LEN option value to determine whether or not the data source driver needs this information. The DB2 ODBC driver will always return N to indicate that this information is not needed by the SQLPutData( ) function.

See Also SQLBindParameter( ), SQLExecute( ), SQLExecDirect( ), SQLParamData( ), SQLCancel( )

Examples See the examples provided for the SQLParamData( ) function in this chapter.

SQLCancel

Purpose The SQLCancel( ) function prematurely terminates a data-at-execution sequence associated with a specified SQL statement handle.

Syntax

```
SQLRETURN SQLCancel (SQLHSTMT StmtHandle);
```

Parameters *StmtHandle* The SQL statement handle where the address of the SQL statement buffer is stored.

Includes

```
#include <sqlcli1.h>
```

Description The SQLCancel( ) function prematurely terminates a data-at-execution sequence (and the subsequent execution of the SQL statement containing data-at-execution parameter markers) that is associated with a specified SQL statement handle. The data-at-execution sequence is a mechanism that passes data values to the data source at execution time. Refer to the SQLParamData( ) function for more information about this mechanism and the data-at-execution sequence.

Specifications DB2 CLI 1.1, ODBC 1.0, X/OPEN CLI, ISO CLI

Return Codes SQL_SUCCESS, SQL_INVALID_HANDLE, SQL_ERROR

SQLSTATEs **08**S01, **40**003, **S1**001, **S1**013, **S1**506

Comments

- In a multithreaded application, the SQLCancel( ) function cancels the original SQL statement request, which generates the SQLSTATE **S1**008.
- This function can be called any time after the SQLExecDirect( ) function or the SQLExecute( ) function returns the SQL_NEED_DATA return code to request values for any data-at-execution parameters that are defined, as long as the final SQLParamData( ) function call in the sequence has not been executed.
- Once the data-at-execution sequence processing has been canceled, you can call the SQLExecute( ) or SQLExecDirect( ) function again to reinitiate it.
- If the SQLCancel( ) function is executed on a SQL statement handle not associated with a data-at-execution sequence, the call will have the same effect as a call to the SQLFreeStmt( ) function with the SQL_CLOSE option specified. However, applications should never use this function to replace the SQLFreeStmt( ) function.

Restrictions DB2 CLI does not support asynchronous statement execution.

See Also SQLPutData( ), SQLParamData( )

Examples See the examples provided for the SQLParamData( ) function in this chapter.

SQLTransact

Purpose The SQLTransact( ) function requests a commit or a rollback operation for all active transactions associated with a specific connection or environment handle.

Syntax

```
SQLRETURN SQLTransact (SQLHENV       EnvHandle,
                       SQLHDBC       DSCHandle,
                       SQLUSMALLINT  Action);
```

Parameters

EnvHandle The environment handle where the address of the environment buffer is stored.

DSCHandle The data source connection handle where the address of the data source connection information buffer is stored.

Action The action to use to terminate the current transaction. This parameter can contain any of the following values:

SQL_COMMIT	Terminate the current transaction and make all data source changes made by that transaction permanent.
SQL_ROLLBACK	Terminate the current transaction and back out (remove) all data source changes made by that transaction.

Includes

```
#include <sqlcli1.h>
```

Description

The SQLTransact( ) function requests a commit or a rollback operation for all active transactions associated with a specific connection handle. This function can also request that a commit or rollback operation be performed for all active transactions found on all connections associated with a specific environment handle. When this function is called, all changes made to the data source (via the specified connection or environment handle) since the connection was established or since the last call to the SQLTransact( ) function was made (whichever is the most recent) are either committed to the data source or rolled back.

In DB2 CLI, a transaction begins implicitly when an application that does not already have an active transaction calls one of the following functions:

- SQLPrepare( )
- SQLExecute( )
- SQLExecDirect( )
- SQLGetTypeInfo( )
- one of the catalog functions.

A transaction ends when the application calls this function. All active transactions associated with a data source connection must be ended before the connection to the data source can be terminated.

Specifications

DB2 CLI 1.1, ODBC 1.0, X/OPEN CLI, ISO CLI

Return Codes

SQL_SUCCESS, SQL_INVALID_HANDLE, SQL_ERROR

SQLSTATEs

08003, **08**007, **58**004, **S1**001, **S1**012, **S1**013

Comments

- If the *DSCHandle* parameter contains a valid data source connection handle, the environment handle in *EnvHandle* will be ignored.
- If the *DSCHandle* parameter contains the value SQL_NULL_HDBC, the *Env Handle* parameter must contain the environment handle with which the connection is associated.
- If the *DSCHandle* parameter contains the value SQL_NULL_HDBC and the *EnvHandle* parameter contains a valid environment handle, then a commit or rollback will be issued on each active transaction found on each open connection in the environment. In this case, the SQL_SUCCESS return code value is returned only if success is reported from all affected connections. If the commit or rollback fails for one or more of the open connections, the SQL_ERROR return code value will be returned. You then need to call the SQLError( ) function for each connection handle in the environment to determine which connection(s) failed during the commit or rollback operation.
- If the SQL_CONNECTTYPE connection option is set to SQL_CONCURRENT_TRANS (the default setting), the application can have concurrent multiple connections to any one data source or to multiple data sources at any given time. Each data source connection has its own commit scope, and DB2 CLI

makes no effort to enforce coordination between transactions. Therefore, when the application attempts to commit transactions on all connections associated with an environment handle and not all the connection transactions get committed successfully, the application is responsible for handling data recovery.

- SQL statements prepared by the SQLPrepare( ) function are not destroyed when a transaction ends, so they can be executed in subsequent transactions without having to be reprepared.
- Cursor pointer positions are maintained after a transaction is committed unless one or more of the following conditions is true:
  –The server is a SQL/DS server.
  –The SQL_CURSOR_HOLD statement option for this connection handle is set to SQL_CURSOR_HOLD_OFF.
  –The CURSORHOLD keyword in the DB2 CLI initialization file is set so "cursor with hold" is not in effect and has not been overridden by a reset SQL_CURSOR_HOLD statement option.
  –The CURSORHOLD keyword is present in the connection string passed to the SQLDriverConnect( ) function call that set up this connection (which indicates that "cursor with hold" is not in effect), and it has not been overridden with a reset SQL_CURSOR_HOLD statement option.

  If the cursor pointer position is not maintained because one or more one of these conditions were met, the cursor will be closed and all pending results discarded. If the cursor position pointer is maintained after a commit, the application must issue a fetch to reposition the pointer to the next row in the result data set before it can continue processing the remaining data.

- To determine whether or not the cursor pointer position is maintained after a transaction is committed, call the SQLGetInfo( ) function with the value SQL_CURSOR_COMMIT_BEHAVIOR specified in the *InfoType* parameter.
- Open cursors are automatically closed after a rollback and all pending results are discarded.
- Statement handles are still valid after a transaction ends. They can be reused by subsequent SQL statements or you can deallocate them by calling the SQLFreeStmt( ) function.
- Cursor names, bound parameters, and column bindings remain in effect after a transaction ends.
- If no active transactions exist for the specified connection(s), the SQLTransact ( ) function will not affect the connected data sources and the return code SQL_SUCCESS will be returned.
- This function might fail during the execution of a COMMIT or ROLLBACK due to a loss of connection to the data source. If this situation occurs, the application might not be able to determine whether or not the COMMIT or ROLLBACK was successfully processed. If this occurs, a data source administrator's help may be required.

Restrictions There are no restrictions associated with this function call.

See Also SQLSetStmtOption( ), SQLGetInfo( ), SQLFreeStmt( )

Example The following C program illustrates how to use the SQLTransact( ) function to manually roll back a transaction:

```
#include <stdio.h>
#include <stdlib.h>
#include <string.h>
#include <sqlcli1.h>

int main()
{
    /* Declare The Local Memory Variables */
    SQLRETURN    rc = SQL_SUCCESS;
    SQLHENV      EnvHandle;
    SQLHDBC      DSCHandle;
    SQLHSTMT     StmtHandle;
    SQLCHAR      SQLStmt[255];

    /* Allocate An Environment Handle */
    rc = SQLAllocEnv(&EnvHandle);
    /* Allocate A Connection Handle */
    rc = SQLAllocConnect(EnvHandle, &DSCHandle);

    /* Connect To The SAMPLE Database */
    rc = SQLConnect(DSCHandle, "SAMPLE", SQL_NTS, "etpdd6z", SQL_NTS,
                    "sanders", SQL_NTS);

    /* Allocate A SQL Statement Handle */
    rc = SQLAllocStmt(DSCHandle, &StmtHandle);

    /* Turn The Automatic Commit Connection Option Off */
    SQLSetConnectOption(DSCHandle, SQL_AUTOCOMMIT, SQL_AUTOCOMMIT_OFF);

    /* Define An INSERT SQL Statement */
    strcpy(SQLStmt, "INSERT INTO USERID.ORG (DEPTNUMB, DEPTNAME, ");
    strcat(SQLStmt, "MANAGER, DIVISION, LOCATION) VALUES ");
    strcat(SQLStmt, "( 95, 'Japan', 70, 'Asia', 'Tokyo')");

    /* Execute The SQL Statement */
    rc = SQLExecDirect(StmtHandle, SQLStmt, SQL_NTS);
    if (rc == SQL_SUCCESS)
        printf("1 row has been added to the USERID.ORG table.\n");

    /* Rollback The Transaction */
    rc = SQLTransact(EnvHandle, DSCHandle, SQL_ROLLBACK);
    if (rc == SQL_SUCCESS)
        {
        printf("The current transaction has been rolled back - all ");
        printf("rows added have been removed.\n");
        }

    /* Disconnect From The SAMPLE Database */
    SQLDisconnect(DSCHandle);

    /* Free The SQL Statement Handle */
    if (StmtHandle != NULL)
        SQLFreeStmt(StmtHandle, SQL_DROP);

    /* Free The Connection Handle */
    if (DSCHandle != NULL)
        SQLFreeConnect(DSCHandle);

    /* Free The Environment Handle */
    if (EnvHandle != NULL)
```

```
        SQLFreeEnv(EnvHandle);

    /* Return To The Operating System */
    return(rc);
}
```

> Note: The SQLTransact( ) function is used in a C++ program in a similar manner.

SQLFreeStmt

Purpose The SQLFreeStmt( ) function stops all processing associated with a specific SQL statement handle, discards all pending results, closes any open cursors, and frees all memory associated with the handle.

Syntax

```
SQLRETURN SQLFreeStmt (SQLHSTMT     StmtHandle,
                       SQLUSMALLINT Option);
```

Parameters

StmtHandle The SQL statement handle where the address of the SQL statement buffer is stored.

Option The method to use when freeing the SQL statement handle. This parameter can contain any of the following values:

SQL_CLOSE	Close all cursors associated with the SQL statement handle and discard any pending results. In this case, the SQL statement handle itself is not destroyed.
SQL_DROP	Close all cursors associated with the SQL statement handle, discard any pending results, and free all resources associated with the SQL statement handle. In this case, the SQL statement handle is destroyed and must be reallocated before it can be used again.
SQL_UNBIND	Unbind (release) all column buffers currently bound to the SQL statement handle.
SQL_RESET_PARAMS	Release all parameter marker buffers bound to the SQL statement handle.

Includes

```
#include <sqlcli1.h>
```

Description The SQLFreeStmt( ) function invalidates and frees or reinitializes a SQL statement handle. When this function is invoked, one or more of the following actions take place:

- All processing being done by the SQL statement associated with the SQL statement handle is stopped.
- All open cursors associated with the SQL statement handle are closed.
- All parameters associated with application variables and LOB file references are reset.

- All result data set columns bound to application variables and LOB file references are unbound.
- All DB2 CLI resources associated with the SQL statement handle are freed and the SQL statement handle is deleted (dropped).

This function should be called for each SQL statement handle created with the SQLAllocStmt( ) function when all processing associated with that SQL statement handle is completed.

Specifications DB2 CLI 1.1, ODBC 1.0, X/OPEN CLI, ISO CLI

Return Codes SQL_SUCCESS, SQL_SUCCESS_WITH_INFO, SQL_INVALID_HANDLE, SQL_ERROR

SQLSTATEs **08**S01, **40**003, **58**004, **S1**001, **S1**010, **S1**092, **S1**506

Comments

- If this statement is called with the SQL_CLOSE option specified, all cursors associated with the SQL statement handle will be closed and all pending results discarded. You can reopen cursors by calling the SQLExecute( ) function (the same or different values can be supplied in application variables that were bound to the SQL statement handle before this function was called). The cursor name is retained until the SQL statement handle is dropped or until the next successful SQLSetCursorName( ) function call is executed.
- If this statement is called with the SQL_UNBIND option specified, all associations between application variables and/or file references and the columns of the result data set are destroyed. If this statement is called with the SQL_UNBIND option specified, all associations between application variables and/or file references and the parameter markers in the SQL statement referenced by the SQL statement handle are destroyed.
- This statement has no effect on LOB locators; the SQLExecDirect( ) function must be called with a FREE LOCATOR SQL statement in order to free a LOB locator.
- Before a SQL statement handle associated with a query, catalog function, or SQLGetTypeInfo( ) function can be reused, all open cursors associated with the SQL statement referenced by the SQL statement handle must be closed.
- In order for an SQL statement handle bound to application variables and/or file references to be reused, all parameters for the statement handle must be reset if the number or data type of the parameter markers in the SQL statement change.
- If a SQL statement handle is associated with a result data set that has columns bound to application variables and/or file references, and if the number or data type of the bound variables and/or file references changes, all bound columns must be unbound before the SQL statement handle can be reused.
- The SQL_SUCCESS_WITH_INFO return code cannot be returned if this function is called with the SQL_DROP option specified, since there would be no SQL statement handle to pass to the SQLError( ) function.

Restrictions There are no restrictions associated with this function call.

See Also SQLAllocStmt( ), SQLBindParameter( ), SQLBindFileToParam( ), SQLBindCol( ), SQLBindFileToCol( ), SQLFetch( ), SQLExtendedFetch( ), SQLSetParam( )

Examples See the examples provided for the SQLAllocStmt( ) function in this chapter.

CHAPTER 16

SQL STATEMENT RESULTS RETRIEVAL FUNCTIONS

The SQL statement results retrieval functions are a group of DB2 CLI function calls that are used for retrieving information from result data sets that are created when SQL statements are executed. This group includes:

- CLI functions that retrieve information about a result data set.
- A CLI function that defines the attributes for one or more columns in a result data set.
- CLI functions that assign storage areas to the columns in a result data set.
- CLI functions that retrieve one or more rows of data from a result data set.
- CLI functions that use LOB locators to locate and retrieve pieces of information from large object (LOB) data.
- CLI functions that retrieve diagnostic information about the most recently executed SQL statement.

Table 16.1 lists the SQL statement results retrieval functions available with DB2 CLI.

Result Data Sets

The SELECT SQL statement retrieves blocks of data that meet a specified set of criteria from embedded SQL applications. In DB2 CLI, you can send the SELECT statement to the connected data source to be processed in a similar manner. When a block of data is retrieved with a SELECT statement, it is placed into a buffer storage area and arranged into rows and columns. This buffer area, referred to as a result data set, can contain zero or more rows of data, depending on the selection criteria specified in the SELECT statement. Once a result data set is created, embedded SQL applications call the FETCH statement to retrieve the data into local application storage areas (host variables). The steps a DB2 CLI application must take to process a result data set depends on how much it knows about the result data set's format at the time the application is compiled. If an application knows the exact form of a SQL query it will execute, it can predict the format of the result data set at application compile time. If, however, the application does not know the exact form of a SQL query, it might not know the format of the result data set that will be produced until the SQL query statement is executed.

TABLE 16.1 SQL Statement Results Retrieval Functions

Function name	Description
SQLRowCount( )	Counts the number of rows affected by the execution of an INSERT, UPDATE, or DELETE SQL statement and returns the result.
SQLNumResultCols( )	Counts the number of columns that exist in a result data set created by a query and returns the result.
SQLDescribeCol( )	Describes the attributes of a column in a result data set.
SQLColAttributes( )	Retrieves information about one attribute of a column in a result data set.
SQLSetColAttributes( )	Defines the attributes of a column in a result data set.
SQLBindCol( )	Assigns data storage and specifies the data type for a column in a result data set.
SQLBindFileToCol( )	Assigns a LOB file reference to a column in a result data set.
SQLFetch( )	Retrieves a single row of data from a result data set.
SQLExtendedFetch( )	Retrieves multiple rows of data from a result data set.
SQLGetData( )	Retrieves data for a single column in the current row of a result data set.
SQLMoreResults( )	Determines whether or not there are more result data sets available; if there are, this function initializes processing for the next result data set.
SQLError( )	Retrieves diagnostic information associated with the most recently executed DB2 CLI function or SQL statement.
SQLGetSQLCA( )	Retrieves the SQLCA data structure values associated with the most recently executed SQL statement.
SQLGetLength( )	Retrieves the length of a string referenced by a LOB locator.
SQLGetPosition( )	Determines the starting position of a substring within a source string referenced by a LOB locator.
SQLGetSubString( )	Creates a new LOB locator that references a substring within a source string that is referenced by a LOB locator.

Adapted from IBM's Database 2 Call Level Interface Guide and Reference, Table 11, pages 103 to 106.

Assigning Application Storage Areas to Result Data Set Columns (Binding)

You saw in the last chapter how you must bind parameter markers in SQL statements to application variables and/or external file references before the values in using those variables and/or files with the SQL statement. In a similar fashion, you need to bind the columns in a result data set to application variables and/or external file references to facilitate retrieving the actual data in the result data set. This binding operation is performed with either the SQLBindCol( ) or the SQLBindFileToCol( ) function for each column in the result data set.

An application can bind the columns in a result data set to application variables and/or external file references either before or after a SQL query statement is prepared or executed. However, if the SQL statement is prepared or executed first, the application can retrieve information about the format of the result data set before binding occurs. If information about the result data set is unknown, the application needs to find out at least how many columns are in the result data set (and the data type for each) before it can assign (bind) storage areas to them.

Determining the Characteristics of a Result Data Set

An application can determine the characteristics of a result data set by calling the SQLNumResultCols( ), SQLColAttributes( ), and/or SQLDescribeCol( ) functions. SQLColAttributes( ) can determine how many columns exist in the result data set, while either SQLColAttributes( ) or

SQLDescribeCol( ) can describe the format of a column. If the format of the result data set is unknown, an application can use the information returned by these functions to bind the columns to application variables. You can call these functions any time after a SQL statement is prepared or executed.

You can sometimes use the SQLRowCount( ) function to determine how many rows exist in a result data set. Because it is not recommended and because few data sources support this functionality, however, applications designed to work with multiple data sources should not rely on it.

> Note: For optimal performance, an application should call the SQLColAttributes( ), SQLDescribeCol( ), and SQLNumResultCols( ) functions after a SQL statement is executed. In data sources that emulate SQL statement preparation, these functions sometimes execute more slowly before the SQL statement is executed because the information they retrieve is not readily available until after execution has occurred.

Assigning Application Storage Areas for Rowsets (Binding)

In addition to binding individual rows of data in a result data set to application variables, an application can bind multiple rows of data (known as a rowset) to application arrays. Before a rowset of data can be retrieved, you must call the SQLSetStmtOption( ) function with the SQL_ROWSET_SIZE option specified to set the rowset's size (the number of rows in the rowset). After the rowset's size is set, you must bind the columns in the rowset to arrays of the same size with the SQLBindCol( ) function. By default, rowsets are bound in column-wise fashion, but they can also be bound in row-wise fashion.

Column-Wise Binding. To assign storage for column-wise bound results, an application must perform the following steps for each column in the result data set to be bound:

1. Allocate an array of data storage buffers. This array should have as many elements in it as there are rows in the rowset.
2. Allocate an array of data size storage buffers to hold the number of bytes written to each element of the data storage array. This array should also have as many elements in it as there are rows in the rowset.
3. Call the SQLBindCol( ) function for each column to be bound. With each call, specify the address of the data storage array, the size of one element of the data storage array, the address of the number-of-bytes array, and the data type to which the data is to be converted.
4. Retrieve the data. As data is retrieved, the DB2 CLI driver will use the array element size to determine where to store successive rows of data in the array.

Row-Wise Binding. To assign storage for row-wise bound results, an application must perform the following steps:

1. Declare a structure that can hold a single row of retrieved data and the associated data lengths (number of bytes). This structure should contain one field to store data and one field to store the size (number of bytes) of the data value stored.
2. Allocate an array of these structures. The array should have as many elements in it as there are rows in the rowset.
3. Call the SQLBindCol( ) function for each column to be bound. With each call, specify the address of the column's data field in the first array element, the size of the data field, the address of the column's number-of-bytes field in the first array element, and the type to which the data will be converted.

4. Call the SQLSetStmtOption( ) function with the SQL_BIND_TYPE option and the size of the structure specified.
5. Retrieve the data. As the data is retrieved, the DB2 CLI driver will use the structure size to determine where to store successive rows of data in the array.

Fetching Result Data Set Data

A result data set is essentially a cursor. An application can retrieve data from the result data set by calling the SQLFetch( ) function after all binding is completed. Each time the SQLFetch( ) function is called, the DB2 CLI driver moves the cursor position pointer to the next row in the result data set and retrieves data for all bound columns. You can retrieve rowsets from the result data set by calling the SQLExtendedFetch( ) function after all column-wise or all row-wise binding is completed. Each time the SQLExtendedFetch( ) function is called, the DB2 CLI driver moves the cursor position pointer to the next unfetched row in the result data set and retrieves data for all bound columns, for each row in the rowset.

Although some ODBC-compatible data sources support different types of cursors, the cursor supported by DB2 CLI functions scrolls only forward, one row at a time. This means that in order to reretrieve a row of data that was already fetched from the result data set, an application must close the cursor by calling the SQLFreeStmt( ) function with the SQL_CLOSE option specified, reexecute the SQL statement, and refetch rows with the SQLFetch( ) function until the target row is retrieved.

Retrieving Data From Unbound Columns

To retrieve data from unbound columns (columns in the result data set that are not bound to application variables and/or external files), an application can call the SQLGetData( ) function. In this case, the application must first call the SQLFetch( ) or SQLExtendedFetch( ) function to position the cursor position pointer on the next row. It then calls the SQLGetData( ) function one or more times to retrieve data from specific unbound columns. If the data type of a column is character, binary, or data-source-specific and the column contains more data than can be retrieved in a single call, you can call the SQLGetData( ) function multiple times for that column, as long as the data is being transferred to a buffer of type SQL_C_CHAR or SQL_C_BINARY. In this manner, you can transfer LOB data from a result data set directly to an application variable or an external file, in several small pieces. In addition, the DB2 CLI LOB functions SQLGetSubString( ), SQLGetLength( ), and SQLGetPosition( ) can be used together with the SQLGetData( ) function to transfer only a specified portion of LOB data from the result data set to application variables and/or external files.

For maximum interoperability, an application should call only the SQLGetData( ) function for columns to the right of the rightmost bound column, and then only in left-to-right order. Also, do not use the SQLGetData( ) function to retrieve data from unbound columns in a rowset of data that has been retrieved by the SQLExtendedFetch( ) function.

An application can retrieve data from both bound and unbound columns in the same row, by binding the appropriate columns to application variables before calling the SQLFetch( ) or SQLExtendedFetch( ) function and the SQLGetData( ) function.

Retrieving Status, Warning, and Error Information

Each time a DB2 CLI function is called, the DB2 CLI driver executes the function and returns a predefined return code. These return codes indicate either that the CLI function was executed successfully or that it failed. An application is responsible for processing CLI function return codes. If a DB2 CLI function returns anything other than SQL_SUCCESS, you can call the SQLError( ) function (or, in some cases, the SQLGetSQLCA( ) function) to obtain additional information. Additional error or status information can come from one of two sources:

DB2 CLI function Indicates that a programming error was detected.

Data source Indicates that an error occurred during SQL statement processing.

Information returned by the SQLError( ) function is in the same format as the information provided by SQLSTATEs in the X/Open and SQL access group SQL CAE specification (1992).

Sometimes, a CLI function returns more than one error message. In this case, you can call the SQLError( ) function multiple times to retrieve all the error messages. Each time a CLI function other than SQLError( ) and SQLGetSQLCA( ) function is called, the error messages returned by the previous function are deleted.

SQLRowCount

Purpose The SQLRowCount( ) function retrieves a count of the number of rows in a table that were affected by an INSERT, UPDATE, or DELETE SQL statement.

Syntax

```
SQLRETURN SQLRowCount (SQLHSTMT   StmtHandle,
                       SQLINTEGER *RowCount);
```

Parameters

StmtHandle The statement handle where the address of the SQL statement buffer is stored.

RowCount A pointer to a location in memory where this function is to store the number that corresponds to the actual number of rows in the table that were affected by an INSERT, UPDATE, or DELETE SQL statement.

Includes

```
#include <sqlcli1.h>
```

Description The SQLRowCount( ) function retrieves the number of rows in a table or a view based on the table that were affected by an INSERT, UPDATE, or DELETE SQL statement. Rows in other tables that might have been affected by the SQL statement (for example, if cascaded deletes occurred) are not included in the row count returned by this function.

Specifications DB2 CLI 1.1, ODBC 1.0, X/OPEN CLI, ISO CLI

Return Codes SQL_SUCCESS, SQL_INVALID_HANDLE, SQL_ERROR

SQLSTATEs **08**S01, **40**003, **58**004, **S1**001, **S1**010, **S1**013

Comments This function will set the RowCount parameter value to –1 if the last SQL statement executed (using the specified SQL statement handle) was not an UPDATE, INSERT, or DELETE statement or if the last SQL statement submitted for execution failed.

Prerequisites Either the SQLExecute( ) or SQLExecDirect( ) function must be called before this function is called.

Restrictions There are no restrictions associated with this function call.

See Also SQLExecute( ), SQLExecDirect( ), SQLNumResultCols( )

Examples The following C program illustrates how to use the SQLRowCount( ) function to determine how many rows were affected by an INSERT operation:

```
#include <stdio.h>
#include <stdlib.h>
#include <string.h>
#include <sqlcli1.h>
```

```
int main()
{
    /* Declare The Local Memory Variables */
    SQLRETURN     rc = SQL_SUCCESS;
    SQLHENV       EnvHandle;
    SQLHDBC       DSCHandle;
    SQLHSTMT      StmtHandle;
    SQLCHAR       SQLStmt[255];
    SQLSMALLINT   DeptNo[3]       = { 97, 98, 99 } ;
    SQLCHAR       DeptName[3][15] = { "England", "North East", "Japan" } ;
    SQLSMALLINT   Manager[3]      = { 70, 90, 100 } ;
    SQLCHAR       Division[3][11] = { "Europe", "Canada", "Asia" } ;
    SQLCHAR       Location[3][14] = { "London", "Toronto", "Tokyo" } ;
    SQLINTEGER    RowNum;

    /* Allocate An Environment Handle */
    rc = SQLAllocEnv(&EnvHandle);

    /* Allocate A Connection Handle */
    rc = SQLAllocConnect(EnvHandle, &DSCHandle);

    /* Connect To The SAMPLE Database */
    rc = SQLConnect(DSCHandle, "SAMPLE", SQL_NTS, "etpdd6z", SQL_NTS,
                    "sanders", SQL_NTS);

    /* Allocate An SQL Statement Handle */
    rc = SQLAllocStmt(DSCHandle, &StmtHandle);

    /* Define And Prepare An INSERT SQL Statement */
    strcpy(SQLStmt, "INSERT INTO USERID.ORG (DEPTNUMB, DEPTNAME, ");
    strcat(SQLStmt, "MANAGER, DIVISION, LOCATION) VALUES ");
    strcat(SQLStmt, "( ?, ?, ?, ?, ?)");
    SQLPrepare(StmtHandle, SQLStmt, SQL_NTS);

    /* Tell CLI That Three Values Will Be Provided For Each */
    /* Parameter Marker In The SQL Statement                */
    SQLParamOptions(StmtHandle, 3, NULL);

    /* Bind The Parameter Markers To Local Variables */
    SQLBindParameter(StmtHandle, 1, SQL_PARAM_INPUT, SQL_C_SHORT,
                     SQL_SMALLINT, 0, 0, DeptNo, 0, NULL);

    SQLBindParameter(StmtHandle, 2, SQL_PARAM_INPUT, SQL_C_CHAR,
                     SQL_VARCHAR, 15, 0, DeptName, 15, NULL);

    SQLBindParameter(StmtHandle, 3, SQL_PARAM_INPUT, SQL_C_SHORT,
                     SQL_SMALLINT, 0, 0, Manager, 0, NULL);

    SQLBindParameter(StmtHandle, 4, SQL_PARAM_INPUT, SQL_C_CHAR,
                     SQL_VARCHAR, 11, 0, Division, 11, NULL);

    SQLBindParameter(StmtHandle, 5, SQL_PARAM_INPUT, SQL_C_CHAR,
                     SQL_VARCHAR, 14, 0, Location, 14, NULL);

    /* Execute The SQL Statement */
    rc = SQLExecute(StmtHandle);

    /* Determine The Number Of Rows Affected By The INSERT Statement */
    if (rc == SQL_SUCCESS)
        {
        SQLRowCount(StmtHandle, &RowNum);
```

```
        printf("%ld rows were affected by the INSERT statement.\n",
               RowNum);
        }

    /* Commit The Transaction */
    SQLTransact(EnvHandle, DSCHandle, SQL_COMMIT);

    /* Disconnect From The SAMPLE Database */
    SQLDisconnect(DSCHandle);

    /* Free The SQL Statement Handle */
    if (StmtHandle != NULL)
        SQLFreeStmt(StmtHandle, SQL_DROP);

    /* Free The Connection Handle */
    if (DSCHandle != NULL)
        SQLFreeConnect(DSCHandle);

    /* Free The Environment Handle */
    if (EnvHandle != NULL)
        SQLFreeEnv(EnvHandle);

    /* Return To The Operating System */
    return(rc);
}
```

The following C++ program illustrates how the SQLRowCount( ) function is used by class methods to determine how many rows were affected by an INSERT operation:

```
#include <iostream.h>
#include <string.h>
#include <sqlcli1.h>

/* Define The CLI Class */
class CLI
{
    /* Declare The Private Attribute Variables */
    private:
       SQLHENV       EnvHandle;
       SQLHDBC       DSCHandle;
       SQLHSTMT      StmtHandle;
       SQLCHAR       SQLStmt[255];
       SQLSMALLINT   DeptNo[3];
       SQLCHAR       DeptName[3][15];
       SQLSMALLINT   Manager[3];
       SQLCHAR       Division[3][11];
       SQLCHAR       Location[3][14];
       SQLINTEGER    RowNum;

    /* Declare The Public Attribute Variables */
    public:
       SQLRETURN  rc;

    /* Declare The Member Function Prototypes */
    CLI();                                      // Constructor
    ~CLI();                                     // Destructor
    SQLRETURN Connect();
    SQLRETURN InsertRows();
    SQLRETURN CountRows();
    SQLRETURN Disconnect();
} ;
```

```
/* Define The Class Constructor */
CLI::CLI()
{
    /* Initialize The Return Code Variable */
    rc = SQL_SUCCESS;

    /* Allocate An Environment Handle */
    rc = SQLAllocEnv(&EnvHandle);

    /* Allocate A Connection Handle */
    rc = SQLAllocConnect(EnvHandle, &DSCHandle);
}

/* Define The Class Destructor */
CLI::~CLI()
{
    /* Free The Connection Handle */
    if (DSCHandle != NULL)
        SQLFreeConnect(DSCHandle);

    /* Free The Environment Handle */
    if (EnvHandle != NULL)
        SQLFreeEnv(EnvHandle);
}

/* Define The Connect() Member Function */
SQLRETURN CLI::Connect()
{
    /* Connect To The SAMPLE Database */
    rc = SQLConnect(DSCHandle, (SQLCHAR *) "SAMPLE", SQL_NTS,
                    (SQLCHAR *) "etpdd6z", SQL_NTS,
                    (SQLCHAR *) "sanders", SQL_NTS);

    /* Allocate An SQL Statement Handle */
    rc = SQLAllocStmt(DSCHandle, &StmtHandle);

    /* Return The CLI Function Return Code */
    return(rc);
}

/* Define The Disconnect() Member Function */
SQLRETURN CLI::Disconnect(void)
{
    /* Disconnect From The Database */
    rc = SQLDisconnect(DSCHandle);

    /* Free The SQL Statement Handle */
    if (StmtHandle != NULL)
        SQLFreeStmt(StmtHandle, SQL_DROP);

    /* Return The CLI Function Return Code */
    return(rc);
}

/* Define The InsertRows() Member Function */
SQLRETURN CLI::InsertRows(void)
{
    /* Initialize The Input Array Variables */
    DeptNo[0] = 97;
    DeptNo[1] = 98;
    DeptNo[2] = 99;
```

```
    strcpy((char *) DeptName[0], "England");
    strcpy((char *) DeptName[1], "North East");
    strcpy((char *) DeptName[2], "Japan");

    Manager[0] = 70;
    Manager[1] = 90;
    Manager[2] = 100;

    strcpy((char *) Division[0], "Europe");
    strcpy((char *) Division[1], "Canada");
    strcpy((char *) Division[2], "Asia");

    strcpy((char *) Location[0], "London");
    strcpy((char *) Location[1], "Toronto");
    strcpy((char *) Location[2], "Tokyo");

    /* Define And Prepare An INSERT SQL Statement */
    strcpy((char *) SQLStmt, "INSERT INTO USERID.ORG (DEPTNUMB, ");
    strcat((char *) SQLStmt, "DEPTNAME, MANAGER, DIVISION, LOCATION) ");
    strcat((char *) SQLStmt, "VALUES ( ?, ?, ?, ?, ?)");
    SQLPrepare(StmtHandle, SQLStmt, SQL_NTS);

    /* Tell CLI That Three Values Will Be Provided For Each */
    /* Parameter Marker In The SQL Statement                */
    SQLParamOptions(StmtHandle, 3, NULL);

    /* Bind The Parameter Markers To Local Variables */
    SQLBindParameter(StmtHandle, 1, SQL_PARAM_INPUT, SQL_C_SHORT,
                     SQL_SMALLINT, 0, 0, DeptNo, 0, NULL);

    SQLBindParameter(StmtHandle, 2, SQL_PARAM_INPUT, SQL_C_CHAR,
                     SQL_VARCHAR, 15, 0, DeptName, 15, NULL);

    SQLBindParameter(StmtHandle, 3, SQL_PARAM_INPUT, SQL_C_SHORT,
                     SQL_SMALLINT, 0, 0, Manager, 0, NULL);

    SQLBindParameter(StmtHandle, 4, SQL_PARAM_INPUT, SQL_C_CHAR,
                     SQL_VARCHAR, 11, 0, Division, 11, NULL);

    SQLBindParameter(StmtHandle, 5, SQL_PARAM_INPUT, SQL_C_CHAR,
                     SQL_VARCHAR, 14, 0, Location, 14, NULL);

    /* Execute The SQL Statement */
    rc = SQLExecute(StmtHandle);

    /* Commit The Transaction */
    if (rc == SQL_SUCCESS)
        SQLTransact(EnvHandle, DSCHandle, SQL_COMMIT);

    /* Return The CLI Function Return Code */
    return(rc);
}

/* Define The CountRows() Member Function */
SQLRETURN CLI::CountRows(void)
{
    /* Determine The Number Of Rows Affected By The INSERT Statement */
    rc = SQLRowCount(StmtHandle, &RowNum);
    if (rc == SQL_SUCCESS)
        {
        cout << RowNum << " rows were affected by the INSERT ";
```

```
            cout << "statement." << endl;
            }

        /* Return The CLI Function Return Code */
        return(rc);
}

int main()
{
    /* Declare The Local Memory Variables */
    SQLRETURN  rc = SQL_SUCCESS;

    /* Create An Instance Of The CLI Class */
    CLI Sample;

    /* Connect To The SAMPLE Database */
    if ((rc = Sample.Connect()) != SQL_SUCCESS)
        return(rc);

    /* Insert 3 Row Of Data Into The USERID.ORG Table In The SAMPLE */
    /* Database                                                     */
    rc = Sample.InsertRows();

    /* Verify Whether Or Not 3 Rows Of Data Were Inserted */
    if (rc == SQL_SUCCESS)
       Sample.CountRows();

    /* Disconnect From The SAMPLE Database */
    Sample.Disconnect();

    /* Return To The Operating System */
    return(rc);
}
```

SQLNumResultCols

Purpose The SQLNumResultCols( ) function retrieves the number of columns that exist in a result data set that is associated with a SQL statement handle.

Syntax

```
SQLRETURN SQLNumResultCols (SQLHSTMT         StmtHandle,
                            SQLSMALLINT FAR *NumCols);
```

Parameters

StmtHandle The statement handle where the address of the SQL statement buffer is stored.

NumCols A pointer to a location in memory where this function is to store the number of columns in the result data set.

Includes

```
#include <sqlcli1.h>
```

Description The SQLNumResultCols( ) function retrieves the number of columns that exist in a result data set that is associated with a SQL statement handle. If the last SQL statement or CLI function executed (using the specified SQL statement handle) did not produce a result data set, the value 0 will be stored in the *NumCols* parameter (to indicate there are no columns) when this function is executed.

Specifications DB2 CLI 1.1, ODBC 1.0, X/OPEN CLI, ISO CLI

Return Codes SQL_SUCCESS, SQL_INVALID_HANDLE, SQL_ERROR

SQLSTATEs **08**S01, **40**003, **58**004, **S1**001, **S1**009, **S1**010, **S1**013, **S1**T00

Comments After this function has been called, one or more bind column function calls—SQL-BindCol( ) or SQLBindFileToCol( )—can bind the columns of the result data set to application variables and/or external files. The value returned in the *NumCols* parameter indicates the maximum number of bind column function calls needed.

Prerequisites Either the SQLPrepare( ) or SQLExecDirect( ) function must be called before this function is called.

Restrictions There are no restrictions associated with this function call.

See Also SQLBindCol( ), SQLBindFileToCol( ), SQLColAttributes( ), SQLDescribeCol ( ), SQLPrepare( ), SQLExecDirect( ), SQLGetData( )

Examples The following C program illustrates how to use the SQLNumResultCols( ) function to obtain the number of columns returned in a result data set:

```
#include <stdio.h>
#include <stdlib.h>
#include <string.h>
#include <sqlcli1.h>

int main()
{
    /* Declare The Local Memory Variables */
    SQLRETURN    rc = SQL_SUCCESS;
    SQLHENV      EnvHandle;
    SQLHDBC      DSCHandle;
    SQLHSTMT     StmtHandle;
    SQLCHAR      SQLStmt[80];
    SQLSMALLINT  NumCols;

    /* Allocate An Environment Handle */
    rc = SQLAllocEnv(&EnvHandle);

    /* Allocate A Connection Handle */
    rc = SQLAllocConnect(EnvHandle, &DSCHandle);

    /* Connect To The SAMPLE Database */
    rc = SQLConnect(DSCHandle, "SAMPLE", SQL_NTS, "etpdd6z", SQL_NTS,
                    "sanders", SQL_NTS);

    /* Allocate An SQL Statement Handle */
    rc = SQLAllocStmt(DSCHandle, &StmtHandle);

    /* Define And Prepare A SELECT SQL Statement */
    strcpy(SQLStmt, "SELECT * FROM USERID.EMPLOYEE");
    SQLPrepare(StmtHandle, SQLStmt, SQL_NTS);

    /* Determine The Number Of Columns In The Result Data Set */
    rc = SQLNumResultCols(StmtHandle, &NumCols);
    if (rc == SQL_SUCCESS)
        {
        printf("The result data set produced by the SQL query ");
        printf("contains %d columns.\n", NumCols);
        }
```

```
    /* Disconnect From The SAMPLE Database */
    SQLDisconnect(DSCHandle);

    /* Free The SQL Statement Handle */
    if (StmtHandle != NULL)
        SQLFreeStmt(StmtHandle, SQL_DROP);

    /* Free The Connection Handle */
    if (DSCHandle != NULL)
        SQLFreeConnect(DSCHandle);

    /* Free The Environment Handle */
    if (EnvHandle != NULL)
        SQLFreeEnv(EnvHandle);

    /* Return To The Operating System */
    return(rc);
}
```

Note: The SQLNumResultCols( ) function is used in a C++ program in a similar manner.

SQLDescribeCol

Purpose The SQLDescribeCol( ) function retrieves descriptor information (column name, data type, precision, scale, and nullability) for a specified column in a result data set.

Syntax

```
SQLRETURN SQLDescribeCol (SQLHSTMT          StmtHandle,
                          SQLUSMALLINT      ColNumber,
                          SQLCHAR FAR       *ColName,
                          SQLSMALLINT       ColNameMaxSize,
                          SQLSMALLINT FAR   *ColNameSize,
                          SQLSMALLINT FAR   *SQLDataType,
                          SQLUINTEGER FAR   *Precision,
                          SQLSMALLINT FAR   *Scale,
                          SQLSMALLINT FAR   *Nullable);
```

Parameters

StmtHandle The statement handle where the address of the SQL statement buffer is stored.

ColNumber The appropriate column number. Columns are numbered sequentially from left to right, starting with 1, as they appear in the result data set.

ColName A pointer to a location in memory where this function is to store the retrieved column name.

ColNameMaxSize The maximum size of the memory storage buffer that stores the retrieved column name.

ColNameSize A pointer to a location in memory where this function is to store the actual number of bytes written to the column name (*ColName*) memory storage buffer.

SQLDataType A pointer to a location in memory where this function is to store the SQL data type of the column. The following SQL data types are supported:

- SQL_BINARY
- SQL_VARBINARY
- SQL_LONGVARBINARY

- SQL_SMALLINT
- SQL_INTEGER
- SQL_DECIMAL
- SQL_NUMERIC
- SQL_REAL
- SQL_FLOAT
- SQL_DOUBLE
- SQL_CHAR
- SQL_VARCHAR
- SQL_LONGVARCHAR
- SQL_BLOB
- SQL_CLOB
- SQL_DBCLOB
- SQL_DATE
- SQL_TIME
- SQL_TIMESTAMP
- SQL_GRAPHIC
- SQL_VARGRAPHIC
- SQL_LONGVARGRAPHIC

Precision A pointer to a location in memory where this function is to store the maximum length, in bytes, for the column as it is defined in the data source.

Scale A pointer to a location in memory where this function is to store the number of digits to the right of the decimal point in columns that have SQL_DECIMAL, SQL_NUMERIC, or SQL_TIMESTAMP SQLDataTypes.

Nullable A pointer to a location in memory where this function is to store information about whether or not the column can contain NULL values. This parameter can contain one of two values:

SQL_NO_NULLS	Indicates that the column cannot contain NULL values
SQL_NULLABLE	Indicates that the column can contain NULL values.

Includes

```
#include <sqlcli1.h>
```

Description

The SQLDescribeCol( ) function retrieves descriptor information (column name, data type, precision, scale, and nullability) for a specified column in a result data set. If the various attributes about a result data set column (such as data type and length) are not known, you can call either this or the SQLColAttributes( ) function after a SQL query statement is prepared or executed to determine the attributes of a column before binding it to an application variable.

Specifications

DB2 CLI 1.1, ODBC 1.0, X/OPEN CLI, ISO CLI

Return Codes

SQL_SUCCESS, SQL_SUCCESS_WITH_INFO, SQL_INVALID_HANDLE, SQL_ERROR

SQLSTATEs

01004, **07**005, **08**S01, **40**003, **58**004, **S1**001, **S1**002, **S1**090, **S1**010, **S1**013, **S1**C00, **S1**T00

Comments

- If only one attribute of the descriptor information is needed, or if attribute information not returned by the SQLDescribeCol( ) function is needed, you can use

SQLColAttributes( ) in place of this function. Refer to the SQLColAttributes( ) function for more information.

- Columns in a result data set can be described in any order.
- If a null pointer value is specified for any of the pointer parameters, DB2 CLI will assume that the information is not needed and nothing will be returned.
- If a column's data type is user-defined, the built-in data type associated with the user-defined data type will be stored in the *SQLDataType* parameter when this function is executed. The SQLColAttributes( ) function must be called with the *DescriptionType* parameter set to SQL_COLUMN_DISTINCT_TYPE in order to obtain the actual user-defined data type.

Prerequisites You must call either the SQLPrepare( ) or SQLExecDirect( ) function before this function.

Restrictions The following ODBC-defined column data types are not supported by DB2 CLI:

- SQL_BIGINT
- SQL_BIT
- SQL_TINYINT

See Also SQLColAttributes( ), SQLPrepare( ), SQLExecDirect( ), SQLNumResultCols( )

Examples The following C program illustrates how to use the SQLDescribeCol( ) function to obtain information about a column in a result data set:

```
#include <stdio.h>
#include <stdlib.h>
#include <string.h>
#include <sqlcli1.h>

int main()
{
    /* Declare The Local Memory Variables */
    SQLRETURN      rc = SQL_SUCCESS;
    SQLHENV        EnvHandle;
    SQLHDBC        DSCHandle;
    SQLHSTMT       StmtHandle;
    SQLCHAR        SQLStmt[80];
    SQLSMALLINT    NumCols;

    SQLCHAR        ColName[32];
    SQLSMALLINT    ColNameLen;
    SQLSMALLINT    ColType;
    SQLUINTEGER    Precision;
    SQLSMALLINT    Scale;
    SQLSMALLINT    Nullable;

    /* Allocate An Environment Handle */
    rc = SQLAllocEnv(&EnvHandle);

    /* Allocate A Connection Handle */
    rc = SQLAllocConnect(EnvHandle, &DSCHandle);

    /* Connect To The SAMPLE Database */
    rc = SQLConnect(DSCHandle, "SAMPLE", SQL_NTS, "etpdd6z", SQL_NTS,
                    "sanders", SQL_NTS);
```

```
    /* Allocate An SQL Statement Handle */
    rc = SQLAllocStmt(DSCHandle, &StmtHandle);

    /* Define And Prepare A SELECT SQL Statement */
    strcpy(SQLStmt, "SELECT SALARY FROM USERID.STAFF WHERE ID = 10");
    SQLPrepare(StmtHandle, SQLStmt, SQL_NTS);

    /* Retrieve Information About The First Column In The Result Data */
    /* Set                                                             */
    rc = SQLDescribeCol(StmtHandle, 1, ColName, sizeof(ColName),
                        &ColNameLen, &ColType, &Precision, &Scale,
                        &Nullable);

    /* Display The Information Retrieved */
    if (rc == SQL_SUCCESS)
        {
        printf("Column Name : %s\n", ColName);
        printf("Data Type   : %d\n", ColType);
        printf("Precision   : %d\n", Precision);
        printf("Scale       : %d\n", Scale);
        printf("Nullable    : ");
        if (Nullable == TRUE)
            printf("Yes\n");
        else
            printf("No\n");
        }

    /* Disconnect From The SAMPLE Database */
    SQLDisconnect(DSCHandle);

    /* Free The SQL Statement Handle */
    if (StmtHandle != NULL)
        SQLFreeStmt(StmtHandle, SQL_DROP);

    /* Free The Connection Handle */
    if (DSCHandle != NULL)
        SQLFreeConnect(DSCHandle);

    /* Free The Environment Handle */
    if (EnvHandle != NULL)
        SQLFreeEnv(EnvHandle);

    /* Return To The Operating System */
    return(rc);
}
```

Note: The SQLDescribeCol( ) function is used in a C++ program in a similar manner.

SQLColAttributes

Purpose The SQLColAttributes( ) function retrieves descriptor information (column name, data type, precision, scale, and nullability) for a specified column in a result data set. You can also use this function to determine the number of columns in a result data set.

Syntax

```
SQLRETURN SQLColAttributes (SQLHSTMT          StmtHandle,
                            SQLUSMALLINT      ColNumber,
                            SQLUSMALLINT      Attribute,
                            SQLPOINTER        Description,
                            SQLSMALLINT       DescriptionMaxSize,
                            SQLSMALLINT FAR  *DescriptionSize,
                            SQLINTEGER FAR   *NumAttributes);
```

Parameters

StmtHandle The statement handle where the address of the SQL statement buffer is stored.

ColNumber The appropriate column number. Columns are numbered sequentially from left to right, starting with 1, as they appear in the result data set.

Attribute The column attribute for which information is to be retrieved. This parameter can contain any of the following values:

- SQL_COLUMN_AUTO_INCREMENT
- SQL_COLUMN_CASE_SENSITIVE
- SQL_COLUMN_CATALOG_NAME
- SQL_COLUMN_QUALIFIER_NAME
- SQL_COLUMN_COUNT
- SQL_COLUMN_DISPLAY_SIZE
- SQL_COLUMN_DISTINCT_TYPE
- SQL_COLUMN_LABEL
- SQL_COLUMN_LENGTH
- SQL_COLUMN_MONEY
- SQL_COLUMN_NAME
- SQL_COLUMN_NULLABLE
- SQL_COLUMN_PRECISION
- SQL_COLUMN_SCALE
- SQL_COLUMN_SCHEMA_NAME
- SQL_COLUMN_OWNER_NAME
- SQL_COLUMN_SEARCHABLE
- SQL_COLUMN_TABLE_NAME
- SQL_COLUMN_TYPE
- SQL_COLUMN_TYPE_NAME
- SQL_COLUMN_UNSIGNED
- SQL_COLUMN_UPDATABLE

Description A pointer to a location in memory where this function is to store the description of the column attributes.

DescriptionMaxSize The maximum size of the memory storage buffer where this function is to store the retrieved column attributes.

DescriptionSize A pointer to a location in memory where this function is to store the actual number of bytes written to the *Description* memory storage buffer.

NumAttributes A pointer to a location in memory where this function is to store the actual number of column attributes retrieved.

Includes

```
#include <sqlcli1.h>
```

Description The SQLColAttributes( ) function retrieves descriptor information (column name, data type, precision, scale, and nullability) for a specified column in a result data set.

This function can also determine the number of columns in a result data set. The SQLColAttributes( ) function is a more extensible alternative to the SQLDescribeCol( ) function, but it can only return information about a single attribute (multiple calls are required to retrieve information about multiple attributes). Table 16.2 alphabetically lists each value that can be specified for the *Attribute* parameter, along with a description of the information that will be returned for that value when the function is executed.

TABLE 16.2 Column Attributes

Attribute	Data type	Description
SQL_COLUMN_AUTO_INCREMENT	32-bit integer	Indicates whether or not the column data type is an auto increment data type. Valid values for this attribute are TRUE and FALSE; FALSE is returned for all DB2 SQL data types.
SQL_COLUMN_CASE_SENSITIVE	32-bit integer	Indicates whether or not the column data type is a case-sensitive data type. Valid values for this attribute are TRUE and FALSE. Case sensitivity does not apply to graphic and noncharacter data types, so FALSE is always returned for these data types.
SQL_COLUMN_CATALOG_NAME or SQL_COLUMN_QUALIFIER_NAME	Character string	Identifies the name of the catalog of the table that contains the column. An empty string is returned for this attribute since DB2 CLI supports only two-part naming conventions for table names. SQL_COLUMN_QUALIFIER_NAME is defined for compatibility with ODBC. DB2 CLI applications should use SQL_COLUMN_CATALOG_NAME.
SQL_COLUMN_COUNT	32-bit integer	Specifies the number of columns in the result data set.
SQL_COLUMN_DISPLAY_SIZE	32-bit integer	Specifies the maximum number of bytes needed to display the column data in character form. The following lists the display sizes used for each DB2 SQL data type: SQL_SMALLINT: 6 (a sign and 5 digits) SQL_INTEGER: 11 (a sign and 10 digits) SQL_DECIMAL: The precision of the column plus 2 (a sign, precision digits, and a decimal point) SQL_NUMERIC: The precision of the column plus 2 (a sign, precision digits, and a decimal point) SQL_REAL: 13 (a sign, 7 digits, a decimal point, the letter E, a sign, and 2 digits) SQL_FLOAT: 22 (a sign, 15 digits, a decimal point, the letter E, a sign, and 3 digits) SQL_DOUBLE: 22 (a sign, 15 digits, a decimal point, the letter E, a sign, and 3 digits) SQL_CHAR: The defined length of the column. SQL_VARCHAR: The defined length of the column. SQL_LONGVARCHAR: The maximum length of the column. SQL_BINARY: The defined length of the column times 2 (each binary byte is represented by a two-digit hexadecimal number).

TABLE 16.2 Column Attributes *(Continued)*

Attribute	Data type	Description
		SQL_VARBINARY: The defined length of the column times 2 (each binary byte is represented by a two-digit hexadecimal number). SQL_LONGVARBINARY: The maximum length of the column times 2. SQL_GRAPHIC: The defined length of the column times 2. SQL_VARGRAPHIC: The defined length of the column times 2. SQL_LONGVARGRAPHIC: The maximum length of the column times 2. SQL_BLOB: The defined length of the column times 2 (each binary byte is represented by a two-digit hexadecimal number). SQL_CLOB: The defined length of the column. SQL_DBCLOB: The defined length of the column times 2. SQL_DATE: 10 (a date in the format *yyyy-mm-dd*). SQL_TIME: 8 (a time in the format *hh:mm:ss*). SQL_TIMESTAMP: 19 (if the scale of the timestamp is 0) or 20 plus the scale of the timestamp (if the scale is greater than 0). This is the number of characters in the format *yyyy-mm-dd hh:mm:ss.fff*.
SQL_COLUMN_DISTINCT_TYPE	Character string	Specifies the name of the user defined data type assigned to the column. If a built-in SQL data type and not a user-defined data type is assigned to the column, an empty string will be returned. Note: The SQL_COLUMN_DISTINCT_TYPE attribute is an IBM-defined extension to the list of descriptor attributes defined by ODBC.
SQL_COLUMN_LABEL	Character string	Specifies the column label assigned to the column. If the column does not have a label, the column name or the column expression will be returned. If the column is unlabeled and unnamed, an empty string will be returned.
SQL_COLUMN_LENGTH	32-bit integer	Specifies the number of bytes of data associated with the column. This is the length, in bytes, of data that will be transferred with a fetch or a call to the SQLGetData( ) function for this column if SQL_C_DEFAULT is specified as the C data type. The following list shows the default length used for each DB2 SQL data type: SQL_SMALLINT: Two bytes. SQL_INTEGER: Four bytes. SQL_DECIMAL: The maximum number of digits plus 2 (a sign, digits, a decimal point, and digits). SQL_NUMERIC: The maximum number of digits plus 2 (a sign, digits, a decimal point, and digits). SQL_REAL: Four bytes. SQL_FLOAT: Eight bytes. SQL_DOUBLE: Eight bytes. SQL_CHAR: The defined length of the column. SQL_VARCHAR: The defined length of the column.

TABLE 16.2 Column Attributes *(Continued)*

Attribute	Data type	Description
		SQL_LONGVARCHAR: The maximum length of the column. SQL_BINARY: The defined length of the column. SQL_VARBINARY: The defined length of the column. SQL_LONGVARBINARY: The maximum length of the column. SQL_GRAPHIC: The defined length of the column times 2. SQL_VARGRAPHIC: The defined length of the column times 2. SQL_LONGVARGRAPHIC: The maximum length of the column times 2. SQL_BLOB: The defined length of the column. SQL_DBCLOB: The defined length of the column times 2. SQL_CLOB: The defined length of the column. SQL_DATE: 6 (the size of the DATE_STRUCT structure). SQL_TIME: 6 (the size of the TIME_STRUCT structure). SQL_TIMESTAMP: 16 (the size of the TIMESTAMP_STRUCT structure). If the specified column contains fixed-length character or binary string data, the actual length will be returned. If the specified column contains variable-length character or binary string data, the maximum length will be returned.
SQL_COLUMN_MONEY	32-bit integer	Indicates whether or not the column data type is a money data type. Valid values for this attribute are: TRUE and FALSE. FALSE is returned for all DB2 SQL data types.
SQL_COLUMN_NAME	character string	Specifies the column name assigned to the column. If the column was derived from an expression, the returned column name is data source product specific.
SQL_COLUMN_NULLABLE	32-bit integer	Indicates whether or not the column can contain null values. Valid values for this attribute are: SQL_NO_NULLS: The column cannot contain NULL values. SQL_NULLABLE: The column can contain null values.
SQL_COLUMN_PRECISION	32-bit integer	Specifies the precision of the data in the column, in units of digits. The following lists the default precision value used for each DB2 SQL data type: SQL_SMALLINT: 5 SQL_INTEGER: 10 SQL_DECIMAL: The defined maximum number of digits. SQL_NUMERIC: The defined maximum number of digits. SQL_REAL: 7 SQL_FLOAT: 15 SQL_DOUBLE: 15 SQL_CHAR: The defined length of the column. SQL_VARCHAR: The defined length of the column. SQL_LONGVARCHAR: The maximum length of the column. SQL_BINARY: The defined length of the column.

TABLE 16.2 Column Attributes *(Continued)*

Attribute	Data type	Description
		SQL_VARBINARY: The defined length of the column. SQL_LONGVARBINARY: The maximum length of the column. SQL_GRAPHIC: The defined length of the column. SQL_VARGRAPHIC: The defined length of the column. SQL_LONGVARGRAPHIC: The maximum length of the column. SQL_BLOB: The defined length of the column. SQL_CLOB: The defined length of the column. SQL_DBCLOB: The defined length of the column. SQL_DATE: 10 (the number of characters in the format yyyy-mm-dd). SQL_TIME: 8 (the number of characters in the format *hh:mm:ss*). SQL_TIMESTAMP: The number of characters in the format *yyy-mm-dd hh:mm:ss.fff*. If a timestamp does not use seconds or fractional seconds, the precision is 16 (the number of characters in the format *yyyy-mm-dd hh:mm*). If the column is defined as having a character SQL data type, then the returned precision value indicates the maximum number of characters the column can hold. If the column is defined as having a graphic SQL data type, then the returned precision value indicates the maximum number of double-byte characters the column can hold.
SQL_COLUMN_SCALE	32-bit integer	Specifies the scale (number of digits to the right of the decimal point) for the data in the column if the column data type is SQL_DECIMAL, SQL_NUMERIC, or SQL_TIMESTAMP. If the column data type is anything else, this attribute is not applicable.
SQL_COLUMN_SCHEMA_NAME or SQL_COLUMN_OWNER_NAME	Character string	Specifies schema name of the table that contains the column. An empty string will be returned if DB2 CLI cannot determine this information. SQL_COLUMN_OWNER_NAME is defined for compatibility with ODBC. DB2 CLI applications should use SQL_COLUMN_SCHEMA_NAME.
SQL_COLUMN_SEARCHABLE	32-bit integer	Indicates how the column data type is used in a WHERE clause. Valid values for this attribute are: SQL_SEARCHABLE: The column data type can be used with any comparison operators in a WHERE clause. SQL_LIKE_ONLY: The column data type can be used only in a WHERE clause LIKE predicate. SQL_ALL_EXCEPT_LIKE: The column data type can be used with all comparison operators in a WHERE clause except a LIKE predicate. SQL_UNSEARCHABLE: The column data type cannot be used in a WHERE clause.
SQL_COLUMN_TABLE_NAME	Character string	Specifies the name of the table that contains the column. An empty string will be returned if DB2 CLI cannot determine this information.

TABLE 16.2 Column Attributes *(Continued)*

Attribute	Data type	Description
SQL_COLUMN_TYPE	32-bit integer	Identifies the SQL data type of the column. For DB2 CLI, any of the following values are valid: SQL_SMALLINT, SQL_INTEGER, SQL_DECIMAL, SQL_NUMERIC, SQL_REAL, SQL_FLOAT, SQL_DOUBLE, SQL_CHAR, SQL_VARCHAR, SQL_LONGVARCHAR, SQL_BINARY, SQL_VARBINARY, SQL_LONGVARBINARY, SQL_GRAPHIC, SQL_VARGRAPHIC, SQL_LONGVARGRAPHIC, SQL_BLOB, SQL_BLOB_LOCATOR, SQL_CLOB, SQL_CLOB_LOCATOR, SQL_DBCLOB, SQL_DBLOB_LOCATOR, SQL_DATE, SQL_TIME, SQL_TIMESTAMP
SQL_COLUMN_TYPE_NAME	32-bit integer	Identifies the actual data source data type of the column (as entered in an SQL DDL statement). For DB2, any of the following values are valid: SMALLINT, INTEGER, DECIMAL, NUMERIC, REAL, FLOAT, DOUBLE, CHAR, VARCHAR, LONG VARCHAR, CHAR FOR BIT DATA, VARCHAR FOR BIT DATA, LONG VARCHAR FOR BIT DATA, GRAPHIC, VARGRAPHIC, LONG VARGRAPHIC, BLOB, BLOB LOCATOR, CLOB, CLOB LOCATOR, DBCLOB, DBLOB LOCATOR, DATE, TIME, TIMESTAMP LOB locator types are not persistent SQL data types, so columns cannot be defined with a locator type; they are used only to represent a LOB. NUMERIC is a synonym for DECIMAL on DB2 for MVS/ESA, DB2 for VSE and VM, DB2 for Common Servers. REAL is not valid for DB2 for Common Servers.
SQL_COLUMN_UNSIGNED	32-bit integer	Indicates whether or not the column data type is an unsigned type. Valid values for this attribute are TRUE and FALSE. TRUE is returned for all DB2 nonnumeric data types; FALSE is returned for all DB2 numeric data types.
SQL_COLUMN_UPDATABLE	32-bit integer	Indicates whether or not the column data type is an updateable type. Valid values for this attribute are: SQL_ATTR_READWRITE_UNKNOWN It is not known whether or not the column data type is updatable (specified for all DB2 SQL data types). SQL_ATTR_READONLY The column data type is read-only (this value will be returned if the column is obtained from a catalog function call).

Adapted from IBM's Database 2 Call Level Interface Guide and Reference, Table 29 (pages 146 to 148), Table 160 (page 444), Table 159 (page 443), Table 157 (page 441), Table 158 (page 442), and Table 3 (page 26).

If the various attributes about a result data set column (such as the data type and length) are not known, you can call either this or the SQLColAttributes( ) function after a SQL query statement is prepared or executed to determine the attributes of a column before binding it to an application variable.

Specifications DB2 CLI 1.1, ODBC 1.0, X/OPEN CLI, ISO CLI

Note: X/Open and ISO standards define this function as SQLColAttribute( ).

Return Codes SQL_SUCCESS, SQL_SUCCESS_WITH_INFO, SQL_INVALID_HANDLE, SQL_ERROR

SQLSTATEs **01**004, **08**S01, **07**005, **40**003, **58**004, **S1**001, **S1**002, **S1**010, **S1**013, **S1**090, **S1**091, **S1**C00, **S1**T00

Comments

- If the requested attribute information is a string value, it will be returned in the *Description* parameter. If the requested attribute information is a numerical value, it will be returned in the *DescriptionSize* parameter.
- If a specified *DescriptionType* descriptor type does not apply to the connected data source, an empty string will be returned in the *Description* parameter or a 0 will be returned in the *DescriptionSize* parameter, depending on the expected data type (string or numeric) of the attribute information.
- Columns in a result data set can be described in any order.
- Calling the SQLColAttributes( ) function with the *DescriptionType* parameter value set to SQL_COLUMN_COUNT is another way of calling the SQLNum-ResultCols( ) function; either one stores the number of columns found in the result data set.

Prerequisites The SQLPrepare( ) or SQLExecDirect( ) function must be called before this function.

Restrictions There are no restrictions associated with this function call.

See Also SQLBindCol( ), SQLBindFileToParam( ), SQLDescribeCol( ), SQLPrepare( ), SQLExecDirect( ), SQLSetColAttributes( )

Examples The following C program illustrates how to use the SQLColAttributes( ) function to obtain information about how a column in a result data set can be used in a WHERE clause of a SQL query:

```
#include <stdio.h>
#include <stdlib.h>
#include <string.h>
#include <sqlcli1.h>

int main()
{
    /* Declare The Local Memory Variables */
    SQLRETURN     rc = SQL_SUCCESS;
    SQLHENV       EnvHandle;
    SQLHDBC       DSCHandle;
    SQLHSTMT      StmtHandle;
    SQLCHAR       SQLStmt[80];
```

```
SQLSMALLINT  NumCols;
SQLINTEGER   Searchable;

/* Allocate An Environment Handle */
rc = SQLAllocEnv(&EnvHandle);

/* Allocate A Connection Handle */
rc = SQLAllocConnect(EnvHandle, &DSCHandle);

/* Connect To The SAMPLE Database */
rc = SQLConnect(DSCHandle, "SAMPLE", SQL_NTS, "etpdd6z", SQL_NTS,
                "sanders", SQL_NTS);

/* Allocate An SQL Statement Handle */
rc = SQLAllocStmt(DSCHandle, &StmtHandle);

/* Define And Prepare A SELECT SQL Statement */
strcpy(SQLStmt, "SELECT EMPNO FROM USERID.EMP_ACT");
SQLPrepare(StmtHandle, SQLStmt, SQL_NTS);

/* Determine How The First Column In The Result Data Set Can Be */
/* Used In A WHERE Clause                                       */
rc = SQLColAttributes(StmtHandle, 1, SQL_COLUMN_SEARCHABLE, NULL,
                    0, NULL, &Searchable);

if (rc == SQL_SUCCESS)
    {
    printf("The EMPNO column in the USERID.EMP_ACT table ");
    switch (Searchable)
        {
        case SQL_UNSEARCHABLE:
            printf("cannot be used in a WHERE clause.\n");
            break;
        case SQL_LIKE_ONLY:
            printf("can only be used in a LIKE predicate\n");
            printf("of a WHERE clause.\n");
            break;
        case SQL_ALL_EXCEPT_LIKE:
            printf("can not be used in a LIKE predicate\n");
            printf("of a WHERE clause.\n");
            break;
        case SQL_SEARCHABLE:
            printf("can be used in a WHERE clause.\n");
            break;
        }
    }

/* Disconnect From The SAMPLE Database */
SQLDisconnect(DSCHandle);

/* Free The SQL Statement Handle */
if (StmtHandle != NULL)
    SQLFreeStmt(StmtHandle, SQL_DROP);

/* Free The Connection Handle */
if (DSCHandle != NULL)
    SQLFreeConnect(DSCHandle);

/* Free The Environment Handle */
if (EnvHandle != NULL)
    SQLFreeEnv(EnvHandle);
```

```
    /* Return To The Operating System */
    return(rc);
}
```

> Note: The SQLColAttributes( ) function is used in a C++ program in a similar manner.

SQLSetColAttributes

Purpose The SQLSetColAttributes( ) function sets descriptor information (column name, data type, precision, scale, and nullability) for a specified column in a result data set.

Syntax

```
SQLRETURN SQLSetColAttributes (SQLHSTMT      StmtHandle,
                               SQLUSMALLINT  ColNumber,
                               SQLCHAR FAR   *ColName,
                               SQLSMALLINT   ColNameSize,
                               SQLSMALLINT   SQLDataType,
                               SQLUINTEGER   Precision,
                               SQLSMALLINT   Scale,
                               SQLSMALLINT   Nullable);
```

Parameters

StmtHandle The statement handle where the address of the SQL statement buffer is stored.

ColNumber The appropriate column number. Columns are numbered sequentially from left to right, starting with 1, as they appear in the result data set.

ColName A pointer to a location in memory where the column name is stored. If the column is unnamed, this must be a null pointer or a zero length string.

ColNameSize The length of the column name value stored in the *ColName* parameter.

SQLDataType The SQL data type of the column. The following SQL data types are supported:

- SQL_BINARY
- SQL_VARBINARY
- SQL_LONGVARBINARY
- SQL_SMALLINT
- SQL_INTEGER
- SQL_DECIMAL
- SQL_NUMERIC
- SQL_REAL
- SQL_FLOAT
- SQL_DOUBLE
- SQL_CHAR
- SQL_VARCHAR
- SQL_LONGVARCHAR
- SQL_BLOB
- SQL_CLOB

- SQL_DBCLOB
- SQL_DATE
- SQL_TIME
- SQL_TIMESTAMP
- SQL_GRAPHIC
- SQL_VARGRAPHIC
- SQL_LONGVARGRAPHIC

Precision The maximum length, in bytes, for the column.

Scale The number of digits to the right of the decimal point in columns for which the *SQLDataTypes* parameter value is either SQL_DECIMAL, SQL_NUMERIC, or SQL_TIMESTAMP.

Nullable Specifies whether or not the column can contain NULL values. The nullable parameter can contain one of two values:

SQL_NO_NULLS Indicates that the column cannot contain NULL values
SQL_NULLABLE Indicates that the column can contain NULL values.

Includes

```
#include <sqlcli1.h>
```

Description

The SQLSetColAttributes( ) function sets descriptor information (column name, data type, precision, scale, and nullability) for a specified column in a result data set. If an application has advanced knowledge of the characteristics of the descriptor information of a result data set, it can give this information to DB2 CLI so DB2 CLI functions working with the result data set do not have to obtain the descriptor information from the connected data source. This function is designed to help reduce the amount of network traffic when an application is retrieving (fetching) values from result data sets that contain an extremely large number of columns.

Specifications

DB2 CLI 2.1

Return Codes

SQL_SUCCESS, SQL_SUCCESS_WITH_INFO, SQL_INVALID_HANDLE, SQL_ERROR

SQLSTATEs

01004, **08**S01, **24**000, **40**003, **S1**000, **S1**001, **S1**002, **S1**004, **S1**010, **S1**013, **S1**090, **S1**094, **S1**099, **S1**104

Comments

- An application typically calls the SQLSetColAttributes( ) function after the SQL statement is prepared by SQLPrepare( ) and before it is executed by either SQLExecute( ) or SQLExecDirect( ). This function is valid only after the SQL statement option SQL_NODESCRIBE is set to SQL_NO_DESCRIBE_ON for the specified statement handle.
- This function tells DB2 CLI the column name, data type, and length information about a column that will exist in a result data set generated by the subsequent execution of a SQL query. By knowing this information, DB2 CLI can determine whether or not any data conversion will be necessary when the information in the result data set is returned to the application.
- An application should use this function only if it has prior knowledge of the exact nature of the result data set that will be produced when a SQL statement is executed.
- An application must provide descriptor information for every column in the result data set or an error will occur when the subsequent fetch is attempted (SQLSTATE **07**002).
- This function is beneficial only to applications that handle an extremely large number (hundreds) of columns in a result data set; otherwise, the effect is minimal.

Restrictions There are no restrictions associated with this function call.

See Also SQLPrepare( ), SQLExecute( ), SQLExecDirect( ), SQLColAttributes( ), SQLDescribeCol( )

Examples The following C program illustrates how the SQLSetColAttributes( ) function describes the columns in a result data set to DB2 CLI:

```
#include <stdio.h>
#include <stdlib.h>
#include <string.h>
#include <sqlcli1.h>

int main()
{
    /* Declare The Local Memory Variables */
    SQLRETURN      rc = SQL_SUCCESS;
    SQLHENV        EnvHandle;
    SQLHDBC        DSCHandle;
    SQLHSTMT       StmtHandle;
    SQLCHAR        SQLStmt[80];
    SQLSMALLINT    NumCols;
    SQLCHAR        Name[10];
    SQLREAL        Salary;

    /* Allocate An Environment Handle */
    rc = SQLAllocEnv(&EnvHandle);

    /* Allocate A Connection Handle */
    rc = SQLAllocConnect(EnvHandle, &DSCHandle);

    /* Connect To The SAMPLE Database */
    rc = SQLConnect(DSCHandle, "SAMPLE", SQL_NTS, "etpdd6z", SQL_NTS,
                    "sanders", SQL_NTS);

    /* Allocate An SQL Statement Handle */
    rc = SQLAllocStmt(DSCHandle, &StmtHandle);

    /* Tell DB2 CLI Not To Get Column Attribute Information For */
    /* This SQL Statement                                        */
    SQLSetStmtOption(StmtHandle, SQL_NODESCRIBE, SQL_NODESCRIBE_ON);

    /* Define And Prepare A SELECT SQL Statement */
    strcpy(SQLStmt, "SELECT NAME, SALARY FROM USERID.STAFF ");
    strcat(SQLStmt, "WHERE ID <= 100");
    rc = SQLPrepare(StmtHandle, SQLStmt, SQL_NTS);

    /* Describe The Columns In The Result Data Set */
    rc = SQLSetColAttributes(StmtHandle, 1, "NAME", SQL_NTS,
                             SQL_VARCHAR, 9, 0, SQL_NULLABLE);

    rc = SQLSetColAttributes(StmtHandle, 2, "SALARY", SQL_NTS,
                             SQL_DECIMAL, 7, 2, SQL_NULLABLE);

    /* Execute The SQL Statement */
    rc = SQLExecute(StmtHandle);

    if (rc == SQL_SUCCESS)
        {
        /* Bind The Columns In The Result Data Set To Local */
```

```
        /* Storage Variables                                 */
        SQLBindCol(StmtHandle, 1, SQL_C_CHAR, (SQLPOINTER) Name,
                   sizeof(Name), NULL);

        SQLBindCol(StmtHandle, 2, SQL_C_FLOAT, (SQLPOINTER) &Salary,
                   0, NULL);

        /* Retrieve And Display The Results */
        printf("Name         Salary\n");
        printf("-------------------\n");
        while (rc != SQL_NO_DATA_FOUND)
            {

            /* Retrieve A Record From The Result Data Set */
            rc = SQLFetch(StmtHandle);

            /* Print The Information Retrieved */
            if (rc != SQL_NO_DATA_FOUND)
                printf("%-12s $%.2f\n", Name, Salary);
            }
        }

    /* Disconnect From The SAMPLE Database */
    SQLDisconnect(DSCHandle);

    /* Free The SQL Statement Handle */
    if (StmtHandle != NULL)
        SQLFreeStmt(StmtHandle, SQL_DROP);

    /* Free The Connection Handle */
    if (DSCHandle != NULL)
        SQLFreeConnect(DSCHandle);

    /* Free The Environment Handle */
    if (EnvHandle != NULL)
        SQLFreeEnv(EnvHandle);

    /* Return To The Operating System */
    return(rc);
}
```

The following C++ program illustrates how the SQLSetColAttributes( ) function is used by class methods to describe the columns in a result data set to DB2 CLI:

```
#include <iostream.h>
#include <string.h>
#include <sqlcli1.h>

/* Define The CLI Class */
class CLI
{
    /* Declare The Private Attribute Variables */
    private:
       SQLHENV       EnvHandle;
       SQLHDBC       DSCHandle;
       SQLHSTMT      StmtHandle;
       SQLCHAR       SQLStmt[80];
       SQLSMALLINT   NumCols;
       SQLCHAR       Name[10];
       SQLREAL       Salary;
```

```
    /* Declare The Public Attribute Variables */
    public:
       SQLRETURN  rc;

    /* Declare The Member Function Prototypes */
    CLI();                                    // Constructor
    ~CLI();                                   // Destructor
    SQLRETURN Connect();
    SQLRETURN ExecQuery();
    SQLRETURN ShowResults();
    SQLRETURN Disconnect();
} ;

/* Define The Class Constructor */
CLI::CLI()
{
    /* Initialize The Return Code Variable */
    rc = SQL_SUCCESS;

    /* Allocate An Environment Handle */
    rc = SQLAllocEnv(&EnvHandle);

    /* Allocate A Connection Handle */
    rc = SQLAllocConnect(EnvHandle, &DSCHandle);
}

/* Define The Class Destructor */
CLI::~CLI()
{
    /* Free The Connection Handle */
    if (DSCHandle != NULL)
        SQLFreeConnect(DSCHandle);

    /* Free The Environment Handle */
    if (EnvHandle != NULL)
        SQLFreeEnv(EnvHandle);
}

/* Define The Connect() Member Function */
SQLRETURN CLI::Connect()
{
    /* Connect To The SAMPLE Database */
    rc = SQLConnect(DSCHandle, (SQLCHAR *) "SAMPLE", SQL_NTS,
                    (SQLCHAR *) "etpdd6z", SQL_NTS,
                    (SQLCHAR *) "sanders", SQL_NTS);

    /* Allocate An SQL Statement Handle */
    rc = SQLAllocStmt(DSCHandle, &StmtHandle);

    /* Return The CLI Function Return Code */
    return(rc);
}

/* Define The Disconnect() Member Function */
SQLRETURN CLI::Disconnect(void)
{
    /* Disconnect From The Database */
    rc = SQLDisconnect(DSCHandle);

    /* Free The SQL Statement Handle */
    if (StmtHandle != NULL)
        SQLFreeStmt(StmtHandle, SQL_DROP);
```

```
    /* Return The CLI Function Return Code */
    return(rc);
}

/* Define The ExecQuery() Member Function */
SQLRETURN CLI::ExecQuery(void)
{
    /* Tell DB2 CLI Not To Get Column Attribute Information For */
    /* This SQL Statement                                        */
    SQLSetStmtOption(StmtHandle, SQL_NODESCRIBE, SQL_NODESCRIBE_ON);

    /* Define And Prepare A SELECT SQL Statement */
    strcpy((char *) SQLStmt, "SELECT NAME, SALARY FROM USERID.STAFF ");
    strcat((char *) SQLStmt, "WHERE ID <= 100");
    SQLPrepare(StmtHandle, SQLStmt, SQL_NTS);

    /* Describe The Columns In The Result Data Set */
    SQLSetColAttributes(StmtHandle, 1, (SQLCHAR *) "NAME", SQL_NTS,
                        SQL_VARCHAR, 9, 0, SQL_NULLABLE);

    SQLSetColAttributes(StmtHandle, 2, (SQLCHAR *) "SALARY", SQL_NTS,
                        SQL_DECIMAL, 7, 2, SQL_NULLABLE);

    /* Execute The SQL Statement */
    rc = SQLExecute(StmtHandle);

    /* Return The CLI Function Return Code */
    return(rc);
}

/* Define The ShowResults() Member Function */
SQLRETURN CLI::ShowResults(void)
{
    /* Bind The Columns In The Result Data Set To Local */
    /* Storage Variables                                 */
    SQLBindCol(StmtHandle, 1, SQL_C_CHAR, (SQLPOINTER) Name,
               sizeof(Name), NULL);

    SQLBindCol(StmtHandle, 2, SQL_C_FLOAT, (SQLPOINTER) &Salary,
               0, NULL);

    /* Retrieve And Display The Results */
    cout << "Name         Salary" << endl;
    cout << "-------------------" << endl;
    while (rc != SQL_NO_DATA_FOUND)
        {

        /* Retrieve A Record From The Result Data Set */
        rc = SQLFetch(StmtHandle);

        /* Print The Information Retrieved */
        if (rc != SQL_NO_DATA_FOUND)
            {
            cout.setf(ios::left);
            cout.width(13);
            cout << Name << "$";
            cout.setf(ios::showpoint);
            cout.setf(ios::fixed);
            cout.precision(2);
            cout << Salary << endl;
            }
        }
```

```
    /* Return The CLI Function Return Code */
    if (rc == SQL_NO_DATA_FOUND)
        rc = SQL_SUCCESS;
    return(rc);
}

int main()
{
    /* Declare The Local Memory Variables */
    SQLRETURN  rc = SQL_SUCCESS;

    /* Create An Instance Of The CLI Class */
    CLI Sample;

    /* Connect To The SAMPLE Database */
    if ((rc = Sample.Connect()) != SQL_SUCCESS)
        return(rc);

    /* Prepare And Execute An SQL Query */
    rc = Sample.ExecQuery();

    /* If The Query Executed Successfully, Retrieve And Display The */
    /* Results                                                      */
    if (rc == SQL_SUCCESS)
        Sample.ShowResults();

    /* Disconnect From The SAMPLE Database */
    Sample.Disconnect();

    /* Return To The Operating System */
    return(rc);
}
```

SQLBindCol

Purpose The SQLBindCol( ) function associates (binds) a storage buffer and data type to a column in a result set.

Syntax

```
SQLRETURN SQLBindCol (SQLHSTMT          StmtHandle,
                      SQLUSMALLINT      ColNumber,
                      SQLSMALLINT       CDataType,
                      SQLPOINTER        Value,
                      SQLINTEGER        ValueMaxSize,
                      SQLINTEGER FAR   *ValueSize);
```

Parameters

StmtHandle The statement handle where the address of the SQL statement buffer is stored.

ColNumber The appropriate column number. Columns are numbered sequentially from left to right, starting with 1, as they appear in the result data set.

CDataType The C language data type of the column. The following C data types are supported:

- SQL_C_BIT
- SQL_C_BINARY
- SQL_C_TINYINT
- SQL_C_SHORT

- SQL_C_LONG
- SQL_C_FLOAT
- SQL_C_DOUBLE
- SQL_C_CHAR
- SQL_C_DBCHAR
- SQL_C_BLOB_LOCATOR
- SQL_C_CLOB_LOCATOR
- SQL_C_DBCLOB_LOCATOR
- SQL_C_DATE
- SQL_C_TIME
- SQL_C_TIMESTAMP
- SQL_C_DEFAULT

Value A pointer to a location in memory where DB2 CLI is to store the column data (or an array of column data) when it is retrieved from the result data set.

ValueMaxSize The maximum size of the memory storage buffer where this function is to store the retrieved column data.

ValueSize A pointer to a location in memory where DB2 CLI is to store the actual length (or an array of lengths) of the column data stored in the *Value* parameter.

Includes

```
#include <sqlcli1.h>
```

Description

The SQLBindCol( ) function associates (binds) columns in a result data set to either:

- Application variables or arrays of application variables (storage buffers) for all C data types. In this case, data is transferred from the data source to the application when either SQLFetch( ) or SQLExtendedFetch( ) is called. Data conversion might occur as the data is transferred.
- Large object (LOB) locators for LOB columns. In this case, a LOB locator, not the data itself, is transferred from the data source to the application when the SQLFetch( ) statement is called. A LOB locator can represent the entire LOB data value or just a portion of the data. Alternatively, LOB columns can be bound directly to a file with the SQLBindFileToCol( ) function.

The SQLBindCol( ) function is called once for each column in the result data set from which the application needs to retrieve data.

Specifications DB2 CLI 1.1, ODBC 1.0, X/OPEN CLI, ISO CLI

Return Codes SQL_SUCCESS, SQL_INVALID, HANDLE, SQL_ERROR

SQLSTATEs **08**S01, **40**003, **58**004, **S1**001, **S1**002, **S1**003, **S1**010, **S1**013, **S1**090, **S1**C00

Comments

- The SQLBindCol( ) function must be called for each column in the result data set for which data is to be retrieved. You can generate result data sets by calling any of the following functions:
  –SQLPrepare( )
  –SQLExecDirect( )
  –SQLGetTypeInfo( )
  –any other catalog CLI function.

- When the SQLFetch( ) function is called, the data in each bound column is placed into the assigned location (specified by the values in the *Value* and *ValueSize* parameters). If *CDataType* is a LOB locator, a locator value is returned, not the LOB data itself; then the LOB locator can reference the entire data value in the LOB column.
- To retrieve multiple rows from a cursor at one time, call SQLExtendedFetch( ) instead of the SQLFetch( ) function. In this case, the *Value* parameter refers to an array of storage buffers. An application cannot mix SQLFetch( ) function calls with SQLExtendedFetch( ) function calls on the same SQL statement handle.
- Columns are identified by a number, they are numbered sequentially from left to right starting with 1, and they can be described in any order. You can determine the number of columns in a result data by calling either the SQLNumResultCols( ) or SQLColAttributes( ) function with the *DescriptionType* parameter set to SQL_COLUMN_COUNT.
- An application can obtain the attributes (such as data type and length) of a column by calling either the SQLDescribeCol( ) or SQLColAttributes( ) function. As an alternative, an application can specify the attributes of a column by calling the SQLSetColAttributes( ) function when the format of the result data set is known. In either case, you can then use the attribute information to allocate a storage location of the correct data type and length to specify when data conversion should occur or, in the case of LOB data types, to optionally return a LOB locator value.
- An application can choose to bind every column in a result data set in order to bind a few selected columns in the result data set, or it can choose not to bind any columns in a result data set. You can retrieve data in any unbound column of a result data set by calling the SQLGetData( ) function after the bound column values are retrieved (fetched) for the current row.
- Bound columns provide better performance than repetitive calls to the SQLGetData( ) function for columns that contain fixed length data types and small variable-length data types.
- An application can change the binding of previously bound columns or bind previously unbound columns by calling the SQLBindCol( ) function between data retrieval function calls SQLFetch( ) or SQLExtendedFetch( ). The new binding does not apply to data that has already been retrieved. Instead, it will be used on the next call to the SQLFetch( ) or SQLExtendedFetch( ) function.
- To unbind a single previously bound column, including columns bound with the SQLBindFileToCol( ) function, call SQLBindCol( ) with the *Value* parameter set to NULL. To unbind all bound columns, call the SQLFreeStmt( ) function with the *Option* parameter value set to SQL_UNBIND.
- An application must ensure that enough storage is allocated for the data to be retrieved, otherwise data truncation might occur. If the storage buffer is to contain fixed-length data, DB2 CLI assumes that the size of the buffer is the length of the specified C data type. If the storage buffer is to contain variable-length data, you should allocate as much storage as required by the maximum length of the bound column. If data conversion is required, the size of the storage buffer might need to be adjusted.
- If string truncation does occur, the return code SQL_SUCCESS_WITH_INFO will be returned by the SQLFetch( ) or SQLExtendedFetch( ) function and the *ValueSize* parameter will be set to the actual size of the data stored in the *Value* parameter.
- Truncation is also affected by the SQL_MAX_LENGTH statement option. An application can specify that truncation is not to be reported by calling the

SQLSetStmtOption( ) with the SQL_MAX_LENGTH option specified and a value for the maximum length to return for any one column. In this case, the memory buffer where DB2 CLI is to store the column data (*Value*) should be allocated with the same maximum length value (plus 1 for the null terminator) that was specified for the SQL_MAX_LENGTH option. If the retrieved column data is larger than the set maximum length, the return code SQL_SUCCESS will be returned and the maximum length of the data, not the actual length of the data remaining, will be returned in the *ValueSize* parameter.

- If the column to be bound is to contain a SQL_GRAPHIC, SQL_VARGRAPHIC, or SQL_LONGVARGRAPHIC data type, then the *CDataType* parameter can be set to SQL_C_DBCHAR or SQL_C_CHAR. If the *CDataType* is set to SQL_C_CHAR, the data retrieved into the *Value* buffer will not be null-terminated (unless the PATCH1 initialization keyword indicates that it should be). If the *CDataType* is set to SQL_C_DBCHAR, the data retrieved into the *Value* buffer will be null-terminated with a double-byte null terminator. If the *CDataType* is set to SQL_C_CHAR, the data will not be null-terminated. In both cases, the length of the *Value* buffer (in bytes) is stored in the *ValueMaxSize* parameter.
- When binding any column that contains variable-length data, DB2 CLI can provide some performance enhancement if the *Value* buffer is placed consecutively in memory after the *ValueSize* buffer. For example:

```
struct { SQLINTEGER  ValueSize;
         SQLCHAR     Value[MAX_BUFFER];
       } column;
```

- If the SQL data type is a variable-length data type, the *ValueSize* and *Value* buffers are in contiguous memory, the result data set column is NOT NULLABLE, and data (string) truncation occurred, the value SQL_NO_TOTAL will be stored in the *ValueSize* buffer.
- LOB locators can, in general, be treated as any other data type. There are, however, some important differences:
  - –LOB locators are created at the data source when a row is retrieved (fetched), and a LOB locator C data type is specified with the SQLBindCol( ) function or when the SQLGetSubString( ) function is called to define a LOB locator on a portion of another LOB locator value. Only the LOB locator is transferred to the application; the data to which the LOB locator refers remains on the data server.
  - –The value of a LOB locator is valid only within the current transaction. LOB locators cannot be stored for later retrieval (outside the current transaction), even if the cursor that fetches the LOB locator was defined with the WITH HOLD attribute.
  - –You can free a locator before the transaction is was defined in is ended by executing the FREE LOCATOR statement.
  - –Once a LOB locator is returned from the data source, you can use the SQLGetSubString( ) function to either retrieve a portion of the LOB value or generate another LOB locator that represents a portion of the LOB value. You can also use the LOB locator value returned from the data source to replace a parameter marker in a SQL statement, by using it in a SQLBindParameter( ) function call.
  - –A LOB locator does not point to a data source position; rather, it references a snapshot of a LOB value. There is no association between the current position of the cursor position pointer and the row from which the LOB value was extracted. This means that, even after the cursor position pointer has been repo-

sitioned on a different row, the LOB locator (and thus the value it represents) can still be referenced.
–You can use the SQLGetPosition( ) and SQLGetLength( ) functions with the SQLGetSubString( ) to define the substring.
–A given LOB column in the result data set can be bound to a storage buffer (to hold the entire LOB data value), a LOB locator, or a LOB file reference. The most recent bind column function call determines which type of binding is in effect when the SQL statement is executed.

- If the SQL_ERROR return code is returned and the pointer to the environment handle is equal to SQL_NULL_HENV, then the SQLError( ) function cannot be executed since there is no environment handle with which to associate additional diagnostic information.

Prerequisites SQLPrepare( ), SQLExecDirect( ), or one of the schema CLI functions must be called before this function, and either SQLFetch( ) or SQLExtendedFetch( ) should be called after this function. If column attributes are needed before this function can be called, you can obtain them by calling either the SQLDescribeCol( ) or the SQLColAttributes( ) function.

Restrictions LOB data support is available only when you are connected to a server that supports LOB data types. If the application attempts to specify a LOB locator C data type, SQLSTATE **S1**C00 will be returned.

See Also SQLBindFileToCol( ), SQLFetch( ), SQLExtendedFetch( )

Examples The following C program illustrates how to use the SQLBindCol( ) function to bind columns in a result data set to application variables:

```
#include <stdio.h>
#include <stdlib.h>
#include <sqlcli1.h>

int main()
{
    /* Declare The Local Memory Variables */
    SQLRETURN    rc = SQL_SUCCESS;
    SQLHENV      EnvHandle;
    SQLHDBC      DSCHandle;
    SQLHSTMT     StmtHandle;
    SQLCHAR      SQLStmt[80];
    SQLCHAR      Name[10];
    SQLCHAR      Job[6];
    SQLSMALLINT  Years;

    /* Allocate An Environment Handle */
    rc = SQLAllocEnv(&EnvHandle);

    /* Allocate A Connection Handle */
    rc = SQLAllocConnect(EnvHandle, &DSCHandle);

    /* Connect To The SAMPLE Database */
    rc = SQLConnect(DSCHandle, "SAMPLE", SQL_NTS, "etpdd6z", SQL_NTS,
                "sanders", SQL_NTS);

    /* Allocate An SQL Statement Handle */
    rc = SQLAllocStmt(DSCHandle, &StmtHandle);
```

```
    /* Define A SELECT SQL Statement */
    strcpy(SQLStmt, "SELECT NAME, JOB, YEARS FROM USERID.STAFF ");
    strcat(SQLStmt, "WHERE ID >= 100 AND ID <= 200");

    /* Execute The SQL Statement */
    rc = SQLExecDirect(StmtHandle, SQLStmt, SQL_NTS);

    if (rc != SQL_ERROR)
        {
        /* Bind The Columns In The Result Data Set To Local */
        /* Storage Variables                                */
        SQLBindCol(StmtHandle, 1, SQL_C_CHAR, (SQLPOINTER) Name,
                   sizeof(Name), NULL);

        SQLBindCol(StmtHandle, 2, SQL_C_CHAR, (SQLPOINTER) Job,
                   sizeof(Job), NULL);

        SQLBindCol(StmtHandle, 3, SQL_C_SHORT, (SQLPOINTER) &Years,
                   0, NULL);

        /* Retrieve And Display The Results */
        printf("Name          Job      Years Of Service\n");
        printf("---------------------------------------\n");
        while (rc != SQL_NO_DATA_FOUND)
            {

            /* Retrieve A Record From The Result Data Set */
            rc = SQLFetch(StmtHandle);

            /* Print The Information Retrieved */
            if (rc != SQL_NO_DATA_FOUND)
                printf("%-13s %-15s %d\n", Name, Job, Years);
            }
        }

    /* Disconnect From The SAMPLE Database */
    SQLDisconnect(DSCHandle);

    /* Free The SQL Statement Handle */
    if (StmtHandle != NULL)
        SQLFreeStmt(StmtHandle, SQL_DROP);

    /* Free The Connection Handle */
    if (DSCHandle != NULL)
        SQLFreeConnect(DSCHandle);

    /* Free The Environment Handle */
    if (EnvHandle != NULL)
        SQLFreeEnv(EnvHandle);

    /* Return To The Operating System */
    return(rc);
}
```

The following C++ program illustrates how the SQLBindCol( ) function is used by class methods to bind columns in a result data set to application variables:

```
#include <iostream.h>
#include <string.h>
#include <sqlcli1.h>
```

```
/* Define The CLI Class */
class CLI
{
    /* Declare The Private Attribute Variables */
    private:
       SQLHENV      EnvHandle;
       SQLHDBC      DSCHandle;
       SQLCHAR      Name[10];
       SQLCHAR      Job[6];
       SQLSMALLINT  Years;

    /* Declare The Public Attribute Variables */
    public:
       SQLRETURN    rc;
       SQLHSTMT     StmtHandle;

    /* Declare The Member Function Prototypes */
    CLI();                                      // Constructor
    ~CLI();                                     // Destructor
    SQLRETURN Connect();
    SQLRETURN ShowResults();
    SQLRETURN Disconnect();
} ;

/* Define The Class Constructor */
CLI::CLI()
{
    /* Initialize The Return Code Variable */
    rc = SQL_SUCCESS;

    /* Allocate An Environment Handle */
    rc = SQLAllocEnv(&EnvHandle);

    /* Allocate A Connection Handle */
    rc = SQLAllocConnect(EnvHandle, &DSCHandle);
}

/* Define The Class Destructor */
CLI::~CLI()
{
    /* Free The Connection Handle */
    if (DSCHandle != NULL)
        SQLFreeConnect(DSCHandle);

    /* Free The Environment Handle */
    if (EnvHandle != NULL)
        SQLFreeEnv(EnvHandle);
}

/* Define The Connect() Member Function */
SQLRETURN CLI::Connect()
{
    /* Connect To The SAMPLE Database */
    rc = SQLConnect(DSCHandle, (SQLCHAR *) "SAMPLE", SQL_NTS,
                    (SQLCHAR *) "etpdd6z", SQL_NTS,
                    (SQLCHAR *) "sanders", SQL_NTS);

    /* Allocate An SQL Statement Handle */
    rc = SQLAllocStmt(DSCHandle, &StmtHandle);

    /* Return The CLI Function Return Code */
    return(rc);
}
```

```
/* Define The Disconnect() Member Function */
SQLRETURN CLI::Disconnect(void)
{
    /* Disconnect From The Database */
    rc = SQLDisconnect(DSCHandle);

    /* Free The SQL Statement Handle */
    if (StmtHandle != NULL)
        SQLFreeStmt(StmtHandle, SQL_DROP);

    /* Return The CLI Function Return Code */
    return(rc);
}

/* Define The ShowResults() Member Function */
SQLRETURN CLI::ShowResults(void)
{
    /* Bind The Columns In The Result Data Set To Local */
    /* Storage Variables                                */
    SQLBindCol(StmtHandle, 1, SQL_C_CHAR, (SQLPOINTER) Name,
               sizeof(Name), NULL);

    SQLBindCol(StmtHandle, 2, SQL_C_CHAR, (SQLPOINTER) Job,
               sizeof(Job), NULL);

    SQLBindCol(StmtHandle, 3, SQL_C_SHORT, (SQLPOINTER) &Years,
               0, NULL);

    /* Retrieve And Display The Results */
    cout << "Name          Job      Years Of Service" << endl;
    cout << "---------------------------------------" << endl;
    while (rc != SQL_NO_DATA_FOUND)
        {

        /* Retrieve A Record From The Result Data Set */
        rc = SQLFetch(StmtHandle);

        /* Print The Information Retrieved */
        if (rc != SQL_NO_DATA_FOUND)
            {
            cout.setf(ios::left);
            cout.width(14);
            cout << Name;
            cout.setf(ios::left);
            cout.width(16);
            cout << Job << Years << endl;
            }
        }

    /* Return The CLI Function Return Code */
    return(rc);
}

int main()
{
    /* Declare The Local Memory Variables */
    SQLRETURN  rc = SQL_SUCCESS;
    SQLCHAR    SQLStmt[80];

    /* Create An Instance Of The CLI Class */
    CLI Sample;
```

```
    /* Connect To The SAMPLE Database */
    if ((rc = Sample.Connect()) != SQL_SUCCESS)
        return(rc);

    /* Define A SELECT SQL Statement */
    strcpy((char *) SQLStmt, "SELECT NAME, JOB, YEARS FROM ");
    strcat((char *) SQLStmt, "USERID.STAFF WHERE ID >= 100 AND ");
    strcat((char *) SQLStmt, "ID <= 200");

    /* Execute The SQL Statement */
    rc = SQLExecDirect(Sample.StmtHandle, SQLStmt, SQL_NTS);

    /* Display The Results Of The SQL Query */
    if (rc == SQL_SUCCESS)
        Sample.ShowResults();

    /* Disconnect From The SAMPLE Database */
    Sample.Disconnect();

    /* Return To The Operating System */
    return(rc);
}
```

SQLBindFileToCol

Purpose The SQLBindFileToCol( ) function associates (binds) an external file reference to a column in a result set.

Syntax

```
SQLRETURN SQLBindFileToCol (SQLHSTMT          StmtHandle,
                            SQLUSMALLINT      ColNumber,
                            SQLCHAR FAR       *FileName,
                            SQLSMALLINT FAR   *FileNameSize,
                            SQLUINTEGER FAR   *FileOptions,
                            SQLSMALLINT       FileNameMaxSize,
                            SQLINTEGER FAR    *StringLength,
                            SQLINTEGER FAR    *IndicatorValue);
```

Parameters

StmtHandle The statement handle where the address of the SQL statement buffer is stored.

ColNumber The appropriate column number. Columns are numbered sequentially from left to right, starting with 1, as they appear in the result data set.

FileName A pointer to a location in memory where a filename or an array of filenames are stored. Filenames can be specified as complete (with both path names and filenames) or as relative (filename only). This parameter cannot contain a NULL value.

FileNameSize A pointer to a location in memory where the length of the filename or an array of filename lengths referenced by the *FileName* parameter is stored. If this parameter is set to NULL, the length SQL_NTS will be used and the *FileName* value should be a null-terminated string.

FileOptions A pointer to a location in memory where the file option or an array of file options to be used when writing to the file are stored. Any one of the following file options can be specified:

SQL_FILE_CREATE Indicates that a new file is to be created. If a file with the specified name already exists, a SQL_ERROR value will be returned.

SQL_FILE_OVERWRITE	Indicates that a new file is to be created. If a file with the specified name already exists, it will be overwritten.
SQL_FILE_APPEND	Indicates that if a file with the specified name already exists, the data should be appended to it. If a file with the specified name does not already exist, a new file will be created.

FileNameMaxSize The maximum size of the *FileName* memory storage buffer, or the maximum size of each element in the *FileName* array.

StringLength A pointer to a location in memory where this function is to store the size (or an array of sizes) in bytes of any LOB data that is returned. If this pointer is NULL, no LOB information will be returned by the function.

IndicatorValue A pointer to a location in memory where this function is to store an indicator value (or an array of indicator values). For DB2 CLI version 2.1, this indicator value is always 0.

Includes

```
#include <sqlcli1.h>
```

Description

The SQLBindFileToCol( ) function associates (binds) an external file reference or an array of external file references to a column in a result set. This type of binding allows data in a LOB column to be transferred directly to a file as each row of a result data set is retrieved (fetched).

The LOB file reference parameters (*FileName*, *FileNameSize*, and *FileOptions*) refer to a file within the application program's environment (on the client workstation). The application must ensure that these variables contain the name of a file, the length of the filename, and a file option (Create, Overwrite, or Append) before the SQLFetch( ) or the SQLExtendedFetch( ) function is called to retrieve a row from the result data set. The values of these parameters can remain the same or they can be changed between each SQLFetch( ) or SQLExtendedFetch( ) function call.

Specifications DB2 CLI 2.1

Return Codes SQL_SUCCESS, SQL_SUCCESS_WITH_INFO, SQL_INVALID_HANDLE, SQL_ERROR

SQLSTATEs **08**S01, **40**003, **58**004, **S1**001, **S1**002, **S1**009, **S1**010, **S1**013, **S1**090, **S1**C00

Comments

- If relative filename(s) are used, DB2 CLI will attempt to locate the file in the current directory path of the running DB2 CLI application.
- The maximum value that the *FileNameSize* parameter can contain is 255, so filename strings should not exceed 255 characters.
- The SQLBindFileToCol( ) function must be called once for each column in the result data set to be transferred directly to a file when a row is fetched from that data set. LOB data is written directly to the specified file, without any data conversion and without appended null terminators.
- Values must be supplied for the *FileName*, *FileNameSize*, and *FileOptions* parameters before the data is retrieved from the result data set. When the SQLFetch( ) or SQLExtendedFetch( ) function is called, the data for any column bound to a LOB file reference is written to the file or files pointed to by that file reference. Errors associated with the deferred input argument values of the SQLBindFileToCol( ) are reported at fetch time. The LOB file reference and the deferred *StringLength* and *IndicatorValue* output parameters are updated between each fetch operation.

- If the SQLExtendedFetch( ) function retrieves multiple rows of data for a LOB column, the *FileName*, *FileNameSize*, and *FileOptions* parameters must point to arrays of LOB file reference variables, and the *MaxFileNameSize* parameter must point to an array of maximum lengths for each element in the *FileName* array. The *StringLength* and *IndicatorValue* parameters each point to an array whose elements are updated after the SQLExtendedFetch( ) function completes execution. The *MaxFileNameSize* array is used by DB2 CLI to determine the location of each element in the *FileName* array. The contents of the arrays of file reference variables must be valid at the time the SQLExtendedFetch( ) call is made.
- By using the SQLExtendedFetch( ) function, you can write multiple LOB values to multiple files or to the same file, depending on the specified filename(s). If multiple LOB values will be written to the same file, specify the SQL_FILE_APPEND file option (*FileOption* parameter) for each filename entry.
- Only column-wise binding of arrays of file references is supported by the SQLExtendedFetch( ) function.

Restrictions This function is not available when you are connected to DB2 data sources that do not support LOB data types. To determine whether or not this function is supported for the current data source connection, call the SQLGetFunctions( ) function with the *FunctionType* parameter set to SQL_API_SQLBINDFILETOCOL and check the value of the *Exists* output parameter.

See Also SQLBindCol( ), SQLFetch( ), SQLExtendedFetch( ), SQLBindFileToParam( )

Examples The following C program illustrates how to use the SQLBindFileToCol( ) function to bind a LOB column in a result data set to an external data file:

```
#include <stdio.h>
#include <stdlib.h>
#include <string.h>
#include <sqlcli1.h>

int main()
{
    /* Declare The Local Memory Variables */
    SQLRETURN    rc = SQL_SUCCESS;
    SQLHENV      EnvHandle;
    SQLHDBC      DSCHandle;
    SQLHSTMT     StmtHandle;
    SQLCHAR      SQLStmt[100];
    SQLCHAR      FileName[40];
    SQLSMALLINT  FNameSize;
    SQLUINTEGER  FOption;
    SQLINTEGER   FIndicator;

    /* Allocate An Environment Handle */
    rc = SQLAllocEnv(&EnvHandle);

    /* Allocate A Connection Handle */
    rc = SQLAllocConnect(EnvHandle, &DSCHandle);

    /* Connect To The SAMPLE Database */
    rc = SQLConnect(DSCHandle, "SAMPLE", SQL_NTS, "etpdd6z", SQL_NTS,
                    "sanders", SQL_NTS);

    /* Allocate An SQL Statement Handle */
    rc = SQLAllocStmt(DSCHandle, &StmtHandle);
```

```
    /* Define A SELECT SQL Statement */
    strcpy(SQLStmt, "SELECT RESUME FROM USERID.EMP_RESUME ");
    strcat(SQLStmt, "WHERE EMPNO = '000190' AND RESUME_FORMAT = ");
    strcat(SQLStmt, "'ascii'");

    /* Execute The SQL Statement */
    rc = SQLExecDirect(StmtHandle, SQLStmt, SQL_NTS);

    if (rc != SQL_ERROR)
        {
        /* Initialize The SQLBindColToFile() Function's Parameters */
        strcpy(FileName, "RESUME.TXT");
        FNameSize = strlen(FileName);
        FOption = SQL_FILE_OVERWRITE;
        FIndicator = 0;

        /* Bind The Column In The Result Data Set To An External */
        /* File                                                  */
        SQLBindFileToCol(StmtHandle, 1, FileName, &FNameSize,
                         &FOption, sizeof(FileName), NULL,
                         &FIndicator);

        /* Retrieve The Record From The Result Data Set And Write It */
        /* To An External File                                       */
        rc = SQLFetch(StmtHandle);
        if (rc == SQL_SUCCESS)
            printf("Data has been written to the file %s\n",
                   FileName);
        }

    /* Disconnect From The SAMPLE Database */
    SQLDisconnect(DSCHandle);

    /* Free The SQL Statement Handle */
    if (StmtHandle != NULL)
        SQLFreeStmt(StmtHandle, SQL_DROP);

    /* Free The Connection Handle */
    if (DSCHandle != NULL)
        SQLFreeConnect(DSCHandle);

    /* Free The Environment Handle */
    if (EnvHandle != NULL)
        SQLFreeEnv(EnvHandle);

    /* Return To The Operating System */
    return(rc);
}
```

The following C++ program illustrates how the SQLBindFileToCol( ) function is used in class methods to bind a LOB column in a result data set to an external data file:

```
#include <iostream.h>
#include <string.h>
#include <sqlcli1.h>

/* Define The CLI Class */
class CLI
{
```

```
    /* Declare The Private Attribute Variables */
    private:
       SQLHENV       EnvHandle;
       SQLHDBC       DSCHandle;
       SQLSMALLINT   FNameSize;
       SQLUINTEGER   FOption;
       SQLINTEGER    FIndicator;

    /* Declare The Public Attribute Variables */
    public:
       SQLRETURN     rc;
       SQLHSTMT      StmtHandle;

    /* Declare The Member Function Prototypes */
    CLI();                                      // Constructor
    ~CLI();                                     // Destructor
    SQLRETURN Connect();
    SQLRETURN CopyResultsToFile(SQLCHAR *FileName);
    SQLRETURN Disconnect();
} ;

/* Define The Class Constructor */
CLI::CLI()
{
    /* Initialize The Return Code Variable */
    rc = SQL_SUCCESS;

    /* Allocate An Environment Handle */
    rc = SQLAllocEnv(&EnvHandle);

    /* Allocate A Connection Handle */
    rc = SQLAllocConnect(EnvHandle, &DSCHandle);
}

/* Define The Class Destructor */
CLI::~CLI()
{
    /* Free The Connection Handle */
    if (DSCHandle != NULL)
        SQLFreeConnect(DSCHandle);

    /* Free The Environment Handle */
    if (EnvHandle != NULL)
        SQLFreeEnv(EnvHandle);
}

/* Define The Connect() Member Function */
SQLRETURN CLI::Connect()
{
    /* Connect To The SAMPLE Database */
    rc = SQLConnect(DSCHandle, (SQLCHAR *) "SAMPLE", SQL_NTS,
                    (SQLCHAR *) "etpdd6z", SQL_NTS,
                    (SQLCHAR *) "sanders", SQL_NTS);

    /* Allocate An SQL Statement Handle */
    rc = SQLAllocStmt(DSCHandle, &StmtHandle);

    /* Return The CLI Function Return Code */
    return(rc);
}
```

```
/* Define The Disconnect() Member Function */
SQLRETURN CLI::Disconnect(void)
{
    /* Disconnect From The Database */
    rc = SQLDisconnect(DSCHandle);

    /* Free The SQL Statement Handle */
    if (StmtHandle != NULL)
        SQLFreeStmt(StmtHandle, SQL_DROP);

    /* Return The CLI Function Return Code */
    return(rc);
}

/* Define The CopyResultsToFile() Member Function */
SQLRETURN CLI::CopyResultsToFile(SQLCHAR *FileName)
{
    /* Initialize The SQLBindColToFile() Function's Parameters */
    FNameSize = strlen((char *) FileName);
    FOption = SQL_FILE_OVERWRITE;
    FIndicator = 0;

    /* Bind The Column In The Result Data Set To An External File */
    SQLBindFileToCol(StmtHandle, 1, FileName, &FNameSize, &FOption,
                     sizeof(FileName), NULL, &FIndicator);

    /* Retrieve The Record From The Result Data Set And Write It */
    /* To An External File                                        */
    rc = SQLFetch(StmtHandle);
    if (rc == SQL_SUCCESS)
        {
        cout << "Data has been written to the file " << FileName;
        cout << endl;
        }

    /* Return The CLI Function Return Code */
    return(rc);
}

int main()
{
    /* Declare The Local Memory Variables */
    SQLRETURN  rc = SQL_SUCCESS;
    SQLCHAR    SQLStmt[100];
    SQLCHAR    FileName[40];

    /* Create An Instance Of The CLI Class */
    CLI Sample;

    /* Connect To The SAMPLE Database */
    if ((rc = Sample.Connect()) != SQL_SUCCESS)
        return(rc);

    /* Define A SELECT SQL Statement */
    strcpy((char *) SQLStmt, "SELECT RESUME FROM USERID.EMP_RESUME ");
    strcat((char *) SQLStmt, "WHERE EMPNO = '000190' AND ");
    strcat((char *) SQLStmt, "RESUME_FORMAT = 'ascii'");

    /* Execute The SQL Statement */
    rc = SQLExecDirect(Sample.StmtHandle, SQLStmt, SQL_NTS);
```

```
    /* Copy The Results Of The SQL Query To An External File */
    if (rc == SQL_SUCCESS)
        Sample.CopyResultsToFile((SQLCHAR *) "RESUME.TXT");

    /* Disconnect From The SAMPLE Database */
    Sample.Disconnect();

    /* Return To The Operating System */
    return(rc);
}
```

SQLFetch

Purpose The SQLFetch( ) function advances the cursor position pointer of a cursor to the next row of data in a result data set, and retrieves data from any bound columns that exist for that row into their associated application variables.

Syntax

```
SQLRETURN SQLFetch (SQLHSTMT StmtHandle);
```

Parameters *StmtHandle* The statement handle where the address of the SQL statement buffer is stored.

Includes

```
#include <sqlcli1.h>
```

Description The SQLFetch( ) function advances the cursor position pointer of a cursor to the next row of data in a result data set, and retrieved data from any bound columns that exist for that row into their associated application variables. Columns in a result data set can be bound to application storage variables, LOB locator variables, or LOB file references.

When the SQLFetch( ) function is called, the appropriate data transfer is performed, along with any data conversion specified when the columns were bound. You can also retrieve data in unbound columns individually by calling the SQLGetData( ) function after the SQLFetch( ) function executes.

Specifications DB2 CLI 1.1, ODBC 1.0, X/OPEN CLI, ISO CLI

Return Codes SQL_SUCCESS, SQL_SUCCESS_WITH_INFO, SQL_INVALID_HANDLE, SQL_NO_DATA_FOUND, SQL_ERROR

SQLSTATEs **01**004, **07**002, **07**006, **08**S01, **22**002, **22**003, **22**005, **22**007, **22**008, **22**012, **24**000, **40**000, **42**8A1, **54**028, **56**084, **58**004, **S1**001, **S1**010, **S1**013, **S1**C00, **S1**T00

Comments

- Before the first SQLFetch( ) function call is made, the cursor position pointer is positioned before the first row in the result data set.
- The number of application variables bound by the SQLBindCol( ) function must not exceed the number of columns in the result data set; otherwise, the SQLFetch( ) function call will fail.
- If the SQLBindCol( ) function was not used to bind columns to application variables, the SQLFetch( ) function will advance the cursor position pointer to the next row without returning data to the application. In this case, you could call the SQLGetData( ) function to individually obtain data for all columns in the result data set. Data in unbound columns is discarded when the SQLFetch( ) function advances the cursor position pointer to the next row.

- Using bound columns instead of making repetitive calls to the SQLGetData( ) function provides better application performance when retrieving data from columns that contain fixed-length data types and small variable-length data types.
- Columns in a result data set can be bound to:

Application storage variables The SQLBindCol( ) function binds application storage variables to a column. Data is transferred from the data source to the application when the SQLFetch( ) function is called.

LOB locators The SQLBindCol( ) function binds LOB locators to a column. Only the LOB locator (four bytes) is transferred from the data source to the application when the SQLFetch( ) function is called. Once an application receives a LOB locator, it can use it in any of the LOB functions—SQLGetSubString( ), SQLGetPosition( ), or SQLGetLength( )—or as the value of a parameter marker in another SQL statement. All LOB locators remain valid until the transaction in which they were created is terminated (even when the cursor moves to another row), or until you free them by executing the FREE LOCATOR SQL statement.

LOB file references The SQLBindFileToCol( ) function binds a file to a LOB column. Data is transferred from the data source directly to the specified file when the SQLFetch( ) function is called.

- If the data valuc for a column is NULL and the SQLBindCol( ) function bound the column to a local variable, the value SQL_NULL_DATA will be stored in the *Value* buffer specified with the SQLBindCol( ) function call when the data is retrieved from the result data set.
- If the data value for a column is NULL and the SQLBindFileToCol( ) function bound the column to an external file reference, the value SQL_NULL_DATA will be stored in the *IndicatorValue* buffer and 0 will be stored in the *StringLength* parameter specified with the SQLBindFileToCol( ) function call when the data is retrieved from the result data set.
- If LOB values are too large to be retrieved by the SQLFetch( ) function, you can retrieve them in pieces by using either the SQLGetData( ) function (which can be used for any column type), or you can bind a LOB locator to the column and use the SQLGetSubString( ) function.
- If the data retrieved by the SQLFetch( ) function call is greater than or equal to the maximum size of the memory storage buffer bound to the column, truncation will occur. Data truncation is indicated by a return code of SQL_SUCCESS_WITH_INFO coupled with a SQLSTATE that indicates data truncation has occurred. When character data truncation occurs, the *ValueSize* parameter of the SQLBindCol( ) function will contain the actual length of the column data retrieved from the data source. You can compare this value with the maximum size of the buffer (the *ValueMaxSize* parameter of the SQLBindCol( ) function call) to determine which character value columns were truncated.
- Truncation of numeric data types is reported as a warning if the truncation involves digits to the right of the decimal point. If truncation occurs to the left of the decimal point, an error will be returned.
- Truncation of graphic data types is treated the same as character data types, except that the *Value* parameter of the SQLBindCol( ) function contains the nearest multiple of two bytes of data that is less than or equal to the value specified in the *ValueMaxSize* parameter of the SQLBindCol( ) function call. Graphic (DBCS) data transferred between DB2 CLI and an application is not

null-terminated if the specified C data type is SQL_C_CHAR (unless indicated by the PATCH1 initialization keyword). If the specified C data type is SQL_C_DBCHAR, then null-termination of graphic data will occur.

- Truncation is also affected by the SQL_MAX_LENGTH statement option. An application can specify that truncation is not to be reported by calling SQLSet-StmtOption( ) with the SQL_MAX_LENGTH option specified and a value for the maximum length to return for any one column. In this case, the memory buffer where DB2 CLI is to store the column data (*Value*) should be allocated with the same maximum length value (plus 1 for the null terminator) that was specified for the SQL_MAX_LENGTH option. If the column data retrieved is larger than the set maximum length, the return code SQL_SUCCESS will be returned and the maximum length of the data, not the actual length of the data remaining, will be returned in the *ValueSize* parameter.
- To discard data not yet retrieved from a result data set, call the SQLFreeStmt ( ) function to close the cursor. Closing a cursor automatically discards the remaining data rows and all associated resources.
- To retrieve multiple rows from a cursor at one time, call SQLExtendedFetch( ) instead of SQLFetch( ). However, keep in mind that an application cannot mix SQLFetch( ) function calls with SQLExtendedFetch( ) function calls on the same SQL statement handle.
- The SQL_NO_DATA_FOUND return code will be returned if there are no rows to be retrieved from the result data set. This condition can exist if the SQL query did not produce a result data set or the previous SQLFetch( ) function call retrieved the last row of data from the result data set.
- If all rows of data have been retrieved (fetched), the cursor position pointer will be positioned after the last row in the result data set.

Prerequisites This function can be called only after you have generated a result data set for the specified SQL statement handle by executing a SQL query, calling the SQLGet-TypeInfo( ) function, or calling a CLI catalog function.

Restrictions There are no restrictions associated with this function call.

See Also SQLExtendedFetch( ), SQLBindCol( ), SQLBindFileToCol( ), SQLExecute( ), SQLExecDirect( ), SQLGetData( )

Examples See the examples provided for the SQLBindCol( ) function in this chapter.

SQLExtendedFetch

Purpose The SQLExtendedFetch( ) function retrieves a block containing multiple rows of data from a result data set.

Syntax

```
SQLRETURN SQLExtendedFetch (SQLHSTMT           StmtHandle,
                            SQLUSMALLINT       FetchType,
                            SQLINTEGER         RowIndex,
                            SQLUINTEGER FAR    *NumRows,
                            SQLUSMALLINT FAR   *RowStatus);
```

Parameters *StmtHandle* The statement handle where the address of the SQL statement buffer is stored.

FetchType The direction and type of fetch to perform. Only the SQL_FETCH_NEXT cursor direction (forward only) is supported by DB2 CLI.

RowIndex This parameter is not supported by DB2 CLI. Instead, it is treated as a reserved parameter and its value should always be 0.

NumRows A pointer to a location in memory where the number of the rows actually fetched (retrieved) by this function is stored. If an error occurs during processing, *NumRows* will point to the ordinal position of the row (in the cursor data set) that precedes the row where the error occurred.

RowStatus A pointer to a location in memory where an array of status values (one value for each row retrieved) is stored. The following status values are supported:

SQL_ROW_SUCCESS	Indicates that the row was retrieved successfully.
SQL_ROW_NOROW	Indicates that the row was not retrieved.

Includes

```
#include &lt;sqlcli1.h&gt;
```

Description

The SQLExtendedFetch( ) function extends the capabilities of the SQLFetch( ) function by retrieving a block of data containing multiple rows (a rowset), for each bound column in the result data set. You can specify the size of the returned rowset by calling the SQLSetStmtOption( ) function with the SQL_ROWSET_SIZE option specified.

When the SQLExtendedFetch( ) function is called, the appropriate data transfer is performed, along with any data conversion specified when the columns were bound. Refer to the beginning of the chapter for more information on data retrieval and rowsets.

Specifications

DB2 CLI 2.1, ODBC 1.0

Return Codes

SQL_SUCCESS, SQL_SUCCESS_WITH_INFO, SQL_INVALID_HANDLE, SQL_NO_DATA_FOUND, SQL_ERROR

SQLSTATEs

01004, **01**S01, **07**002, **07**006, **08**S01, **22**002, **22**003, **22**005, **22**007, **22**008, **22**012, **24**000, **40**003, **42**8A1, **54**028, **56**084, **58**004, **S1**001, **S1**010, **S1**013, **S1**106, **S1**C00, **S1**T00

Comments

- Before the first SQLFetch( ) function call is made, the cursor position pointer is positioned before the first row in the result data set. After each SQLExtendedFetch( ) function call is executed, the cursor position pointer is positioned on the row in the result data set that corresponds to the last row element in the rowset just retrieved.
- DB2 CLI converts the data for any columns in the result data set bound by either the SQLBindCol( ) or SQLBindFileToCol( ) function as necessary and stores it in the locations bound to the columns. When retrieving data with the SQLExtendedFetch( ) function, you can bind the result data set in either column-wise or row-wise fashion. For column-wise binding of application variables:
  - –You must first call the SQLSetStmtOption( ) function with SQL_BIND_BY_COLUMN specified as the SQL_BIND_TYPE option value. Then you must call the SQLBindCol( ) function to bind each column to an array buffer.
  - –When the application calls the SQLExtendedFetch( ) function, data for the first row is stored at the start of the array buffer. Each subsequent row of data is then stored at an offset of *ValueMaxSize* bytes (SQLBindCol( ) parameter) or, if the associated C data type is a fixed-width type (such as SQL_C_LONG), at an offset corresponding to that fixed length from the data for the previous row.

–For each bound column, the number of bytes available to return for each element is stored in the *Value* array buffer (deferred output parameter for the SQLBindCol( ) function) bound to the column. The number of bytes available to return for the first row of that column is stored at the start of the buffer, and the number of bytes available to return for each subsequent row is stored at an offset of sizeof (SQLINTEGER) bytes from the value for the previous row. If the data in the column is NULL for a particular row, the associated element in the *Value* array buffer will be set to SQL_NULL_DATA.

- For row-wise binding of application variables:
  –You must first call the SQLSetStmtOption( ) function with the SQL_BIND_TYPE option specified and the *Value* parameter set to the size of a structure capable of holding a single row of retrieved data along with the associated data lengths for each column data value.
  –For each bound column, the first row of data is stored at the address stored in the *Value* parameter when the SQLBindCol( ) function was called for the column, and each subsequent row of data is stored at an offset of *ValueSize* bytes (the SQLSetStmtOption( ) parameter) from the data for the previous row.
  –For each bound column, the number of bytes available to return for the first row is stored at the address stored in the *ValueSize* parameter when the SQLBindCol( ) function was called for the column, and the number of bytes available to return for each subsequent row is stored at an offset of *ValueSize* bytes from the address containing the value for the previous row.
- For column-wise binding of LOB file references, the *StringLength* and *IndicatorValue* parameters for the SQLBindFileToCol( ) function are pointers to output arrays. The actual length of the file and the associated indicator value for the first row are stored at the start of the *StringLength* and *IndicatorValue* arrays, respectively. File lengths and indicator values for subsequent rows are written to these arrays at an offset of sizeof (SQLINTEGER) bytes from the previous row. Row-wise binding of LOB file references is not supported by DB2 CLI.
- If an error occurs that applies to the entire rowset, the SQL_ERROR return code will be returned along with the appropriate SQLSTATE. The contents of the rowset buffer are undefined and the cursor position pointer remains unchanged.
- If an error occurs that applies to a single row in the rowset, the corresponding element in the *RowStatus* array for that row will be set to SQL_ROW_ERROR and SQLSTATE **01**S01 will be added to the list of errors that can be obtained by calling the SQLError( ) function when this function has completed. DB2 CLI will continue to fetch the remaining rows in the rowset and the SQL_SUCCESS_WITH_INFO return code value will be returned. Therefore, after the SQLExtendedFetch( ) function has completed, a SQLSTATE of **01**S01 can be retrieved by the SQLError( ) function for each row that encountered an error. Individual errors that apply to specific rows do not affect the cursor position pointer, which continues to advance.
- The number of elements stored in the *RowStatus* array must equal the number of rows in the rowset (as defined by the SQL_ROWSET_SIZE SQL statement option). If the number of rows retrieved (fetched) is less than the number of elements in the status array, the remaining status elements will be set to the value SQL_ROW_NOROW.
- To retrieve (fetch) one row of data at a time from a cursor, call the SQLFetch( ) function instead of SQLExtendedFetch( ).
- An application cannot mix SQLFetch( ) function calls with SQLExtendedFetch ( ) function calls on the same SQL statement handle.
- DB2 CLI cannot detect whether a row has been updated or deleted since the start of the fetch, so the ODBC defined status values SQL_ROW_DELETED and SQL_ROW_UPDATED are not reported.

Restrictions There are no restrictions associated with this function call.

See Also SQLBindCol( ), SQLBindFileToCol( ), SQLExecute( ), SQLExecDirect( ), SQLFetch( )

Examples The following C program illustrates how to use the SQLExtendedFetch( ) function to retrieve multiple rows of data from a result data set using column-wise binding:

```
#include <stdio.h>
#include <stdlib.h>
#include <string.h>
#include <sqlcli1.h>

#define  ROWSET_SIZE      3

int main()
{
    /* Declare The Local Memory Variables */
    SQLRETURN      rc = SQL_SUCCESS;
    int            Index;
    SQLHENV        EnvHandle;
    SQLHDBC        DSCHandle;
    SQLHSTMT       StmtHandle;
    SQLCHAR        SQLStmt[80];
    SQLUINTEGER    NumRows;
    SQLUSMALLINT   RowStatus[ROWSET_SIZE];

    /* Variables For Column-Wise Binding */
    SQLCHAR        ProjNo[ROWSET_SIZE][7];
    SQLINTEGER     ProjNoLen[ROWSET_SIZE];
    SQLCHAR        ProjName[ROWSET_SIZE][25];
    SQLINTEGER     ProjNameLen[ROWSET_SIZE];
    SQLREAL        Staffing[ROWSET_SIZE];

    /* Allocate An Environment Handle */
    rc = SQLAllocEnv(&EnvHandle);

    /* Allocate A Connection Handle */
    rc = SQLAllocConnect(EnvHandle, &DSCHandle);

    /* Connect To The SAMPLE Database */
    rc = SQLConnect(DSCHandle, "SAMPLE", SQL_NTS, "etpdd6z", SQL_NTS,
                "sanders", SQL_NTS);

    /* Allocate An SQL Statement Handle */
    rc = SQLAllocStmt(DSCHandle, &StmtHandle);

    /* Set Maximum Number Of Rows To Retrieve With Each Extended */
    /* Fetch Call To 3                                           */
    SQLSetStmtOption(StmtHandle, SQL_ROWSET_SIZE, ROWSET_SIZE);

    /* Define A SELECT SQL Statement */
    strcpy(SQLStmt, "SELECT PROJNO, PROJNAME, PRSTAFF FROM ");
    strcat(SQLStmt, "USERID.PROJECT WHERE PRSTAFF <= 5");

    /* Execute The SQL Statement */
    rc = SQLExecDirect(StmtHandle, SQLStmt, SQL_NTS);

    if (rc != SQL_ERROR)
        {
```

```
            /* Bind The Columns In The Result Data Set To Local */
            /* Storage Variables (Column-Wise Binding)          */
            SQLBindCol(StmtHandle, 1, SQL_C_CHAR, (SQLPOINTER) ProjNo,
                       7, ProjNoLen);

            SQLBindCol(StmtHandle, 2, SQL_C_CHAR, (SQLPOINTER) ProjName,
                       25, ProjNameLen);

            SQLBindCol(StmtHandle, 3, SQL_C_FLOAT, (SQLPOINTER) Staffing,
                       0, NULL);

            /* Retrieve And Display The Results */
            printf("Project  Project Name            Estimated\n");
            printf("Number                           Mean Staffing\n");
            printf("---------------------------------------------\n");
            do
                {
                /* Retrieve A Group Of Records From The Result Data Set */
                rc = SQLExtendedFetch(StmtHandle, SQL_FETCH_NEXT, 0,
                                      &NumRows, RowStatus);
                if (NumRows < ROWSET_SIZE)
                    break;

                /* Print The Information Retrieved */
                for (Index = 0; Index < NumRows; Index++)
                    printf("%s\t %s\t %.2f\n", ProjNo[Index], ProjName[Index],
                           Staffing[Index]);
                } while (rc == SQL_SUCCESS);
            }

        /* Disconnect From The SAMPLE Database */
        SQLDisconnect(DSCHandle);

        /* Free The SQL Statement Handle */
        if (StmtHandle != NULL)
            SQLFreeStmt(StmtHandle, SQL_DROP);

        /* Free The Connection Handle */
        if (DSCHandle != NULL)
            SQLFreeConnect(DSCHandle);

        /* Free The Environment Handle */
        if (EnvHandle != NULL)
            SQLFreeEnv(EnvHandle);

        /* Return To The Operating System */
        return(rc);
    }
```

The following C program illustrates how to use the SQLExtendedFetch( ) function to retrieve multiple rows of data from a result data set using row-wise binding:

```
#include <stdio.h>
#include <stdlib.h>
#include <string.h>
#include <sqlcli1.h>

#define  ROWSET_SIZE      3

int main()
{
```

```
/* Declare The Local Memory Variables */
SQLRETURN      rc = SQL_SUCCESS;
int            Index;
SQLHENV        EnvHandle;
SQLHDBC        DSCHandle;
SQLHSTMT       StmtHandle;
SQLCHAR        SQLStmt[80];
SQLUINTEGER    NumRows;
SQLUSMALLINT   RowStatus[ROWSET_SIZE];

/* Variable For Row-Wise Binding */
struct RowBind
  {
  SQLINTEGER     ProjNoLen;
  SQLCHAR        ProjNo[7];
  SQLINTEGER     ProjNameLen;
  SQLCHAR        ProjName[25];
  SQLINTEGER     StaffingLen;
  SQLREAL        Staffing;
  }  Row[ROWSET_SIZE];

/* Allocate An Environment Handle */
rc = SQLAllocEnv(&EnvHandle);

/* Allocate A Connection Handle */
rc = SQLAllocConnect(EnvHandle, &DSCHandle);

/* Connect To The SAMPLE Database */
rc = SQLConnect(DSCHandle, "SAMPLE", SQL_NTS, "etpdd6z", SQL_NTS,
                "sanders", SQL_NTS);

/* Allocate An SQL Statement Handle */
rc = SQLAllocStmt(DSCHandle, &StmtHandle);

/* Set Maximum Number Of Rows To Retrieve With Each Extended */
/* Fetch Call To 3                                            */
SQLSetStmtOption(StmtHandle, SQL_ROWSET_SIZE, ROWSET_SIZE);

/* Define A SELECT SQL Statement */
strcpy(SQLStmt, "SELECT PROJNO, PROJNAME, PRSTAFF FROM ");
strcat(SQLStmt, "USERID.PROJECT WHERE PRSTAFF <= 5");

/* Set The Bind Type Statement Option To The Size Of One Row */
SQLSetStmtOption(StmtHandle, SQL_BIND_TYPE,
                 sizeof(struct RowBind));

/* Execute The SQL Statement */
rc = SQLExecDirect(StmtHandle, SQLStmt, SQL_NTS);

if (rc != SQL_ERROR)
    {
    /* Bind The Columns In The Result Data Set To Local */
    /* Storage Variables (Row-Wise Binding)             */
    SQLBindCol(StmtHandle, 1, SQL_C_CHAR,
               (SQLPOINTER) Row[0].ProjNo, 7, &Row[0].ProjNoLen);

    SQLBindCol(StmtHandle, 2, SQL_C_CHAR,
               (SQLPOINTER) Row[0].ProjName, 25,
               &Row[0].ProjNameLen);

    SQLBindCol(StmtHandle, 3, SQL_C_FLOAT,
               (SQLPOINTER) &Row[0].Staffing, 0,
               &Row[0].StaffingLen);
```

```
            /* Retrieve And Display The Results */
            printf("Project  Project Name             Estimated\n");
            printf("Number                            Mean Staffing\n");
            printf("-----------------------------------------------\n");
            do
                {
                /* Retrieve A Group Of Records From The Result Data Set */
                rc = SQLExtendedFetch(StmtHandle, SQL_FETCH_NEXT, 0,
                                      &NumRows, RowStatus);

                if (NumRows < ROWSET_SIZE)
                    break;

                /* Print The Information Retrieved */
                for (Index = 0; Index < NumRows; Index++)
                    printf("%s\t %s\t %.2f\n", Row[Index].ProjNo,
                           Row[Index].ProjName, Row[Index].Staffing);
                }  while (rc == SQL_SUCCESS);
            }

        /* Disconnect From The SAMPLE Database */
        SQLDisconnect(DSCHandle);

        /* Free The SQL Statement Handle */
        if (StmtHandle != NULL)
            SQLFreeStmt(StmtHandle, SQL_DROP);

        /* Free The Connection Handle */
        if (DSCHandle != NULL)
            SQLFreeConnect(DSCHandle);

        /* Free The Environment Handle */
        if (EnvHandle != NULL)
            SQLFreeEnv(EnvHandle);

        /* Return To The Operating System */
        return(rc);
    }
```

Note: The SQLExtendedFetch( ) function is used in a C++ program in a similar manner.

SQLGetData

Purpose The SQLGetData( ) function retrieves data for a single unbound column in the current row of a result data set.

Syntax

```
SQLRETURN SQLGetData (SQLHSTMT         StmtHandle,
                      SQLUSMALLINT     ColNumber,
                      SQLSMALLINT      CDataType,
                      SQLPOINTER       Value,
                      SQLINTEGER       ValueMaxSize,
                      SQLINTEGER FAR   *ValueSize);
```

Parameters *StmtHandle* The statement handle where the address of the SQL statement buffer is stored.

ColNumber The appropriate column number. Columns are numbered sequentially from left to right, starting with 1, as they appear in the result data set.

CDataType The C language data type of the column. The following C data types are supported:

- SQL_C_BIT
- SQL_C_BINARY
- SQL_C_TINYINT
- SQL_C_SHORT
- SQL_C_LONG
- SQL_C_FLOAT
- SQL_C_DOUBLE
- SQL_C_CHAR
- SQL_C_DBCHAR
- SQL_C_BLOB_LOCATOR
- SQL_C_CLOB_LOCATOR
- SQL_C_DBCLOB_LOCATOR
- SQL_C_DATE
- SQL_C_TIME
- SQL_C_TIMESTAMP
- SQL_C_DEFAULT

> Note: The SQL_C_DEFAULT value causes data to be transferred from its default C data type to the specified SQL data type.

Value A pointer to a location in memory where DB2 CLI is to store the column data (or an array of column data) when the data is retrieved from the data source.

ValueMaxSize The maximum size of the memory storage buffer where this function is to store the column data retrieved.

ValueSize A pointer to a location in memory where DB2 CLI is to store the actual length of the column data stored in the *Value* parameter.

Includes

```
#include <sqlcli1.h>
```

Description

The SQLGetData( ) function retrieves data for a single unbound column in the current row of a result data set. This function is an alternative to the SQLBindCol( ) function, and can transfer data directly into application variables or LOB locators on each SQLFetch( ) or SQLExtendedFetch( ) function call. The general steps for data retrieval are:

1. Call the SQLFetch( ) function to advance the cursor position pointer to the first row of data in the result data set, retrieve the first row of data, and transfer the data for all bound columns to the appropriate application storage location.
2. Call the SQLGetData( ) function for each unbound column to transfer the data for the column(s) to the appropriate application storage location. This step can be performed several times, depending on the number of unbound columns in the result data set.

3. Call either the SQLFetch( ) or SQLExtendedFetch( ) function to advance the cursor to next row of data in the result data set, retrieve the first row of data, and transfer the data for all bound columns to the appropriate application storage location.
4. Repeat steps 2 and 3 for each row found in the result data set, or until the result set is no longer needed. You can also use the SQLGetData( ) function to retrieve large data values in pieces.

Specifications DB2 CLI 1.1, ODBC 1.0, X/OPEN CLI, ISO CLI

Return Codes SQL_SUCCESS, SQL_SUCCESS_WITH_INFO, SQL_INVALID_HANDLE, SQL_NO_DATA_FOUND, SQL_ERROR

SQLSTATEs **01**004, **07**006, **08**S01, **22**002, **22**003, **22**005, **22**007, **22**008, **24**000, **40**003, **58**004, **S1**001, **S1**002, **S1**003, **S1**009, **S1**010, **S1**013, **S1**090, **S1**C00, **S1**T00

Comments

- You can use this function to retrieve long columns if the C data type (*CDataType*) SQL_C_CHAR, SQL_C_BINARY, or SQL_C_DBCHAR is specified or if the SQL_C_DEFAULT C data type is specified and the column type denotes a binary or character string.
- If the data retrieved by the SQLGetData( ) function call is greater than or equal to the maximum size of the memory storage buffer where this function is to store the column data (*ValueMaxSize* parameter), truncation will occur. Data truncation is indicated by a return code of SQL_SUCCESS_WITH_INFO coupled with a SQLSTATE that indicates data truncation has occurred. When character data truncation occurs, you can call the SQLGetData( ) function again, with the same *ColNumber* value, to get subsequent data from the same unbound column, starting at the point of data truncation. To obtain all the data in the column, you must repeat this process until the return code SQL_SUCCESS is returned. Once SQL_SUCCESS is returned, another call to the SQLGetData( ) function with the same *ColNumber* value will cause the SQL_NO_DATA_FOUND return code to be generated.
- Truncation of numeric data types is reported as a warning if the truncation involves digits to the right of the decimal point. If truncation occurs to the left of the decimal point, an error will be returned.
- Truncation is also affected by the SQL_MAX_LENGTH statement option. An application can specify that truncation is not to be reported by calling SQLSetStmtOption( ) with the SQL_MAX_LENGTH option specified and a value for the maximum length to return for any one column. In this case, allocate the memory buffer where DB2 CLI is to store the column data (*Value*) using the same maximum length value (plus 1 for the null terminator) that was specified for the SQL_MAX_LENGTH option. If the retrieved column data is larger than the set maximum length, the return code SQL_SUCCESS will be returned and the maximum length of the data, not the actual length of the data remaining, will be returned in the *ValueSize* parameter.
- Although you can use SQLGetData( ) for the sequential retrieval of LOB column data, use the DB2 CLI LOB functions if you need only a portion or a few sections of the LOB column data. The general steps for this type of LOB data retrieval are:
  1. Bind the LOB column to a LOB locator variable.
  2. Fetch the row.
  3. Use the LOB locator in a SQLGetSubString( ) function call to retrieve the data in pieces. The SQLGetLength( ) and SQLGetPosition( ) functions might also be required in order to determine the values of some of the SQLGetSubString( ) function arguments.
  4. Repeat steps 2 and 3.

- To discard column data partway through the retrieval process, call SQLGetData( ) function with the *ColNumber* parameter set to the next column position of interest.
- To discard data not yet retrieved from a result data set, call the SQLFetch( ) function to advance the cursor to the next row, or call the SQLFreeStmt( ) function to close the cursor. Closing a cursor automatically discards the remaining data rows and all associated resources.
- The *CDataType* parameter determines the type of data conversion needed (if any) before the column data is placed into the memory storage buffer pointed to by the *Value* parameter.
- For SQL graphic column data:
  –The length of the *Value* buffer (*ValueMaxSize*) should be a multiple of 2.
  –You can determine the SQL data type of the column by first calling either the SQLDescribeCol( ) or SQLColAttributes( ) function.
  –The pointer to *Value* must not be NULL since DB2 CLI will be storing the number of octets stored for the graphic data in the *Value* buffer.
  –If the graphic data is to be retrieved in piecewise fashion, DB2 CLI will attempt to fill the *Value* buffer to the nearest multiple of two octets that is still less than or equal to the value stored in the *ValueMaxSize* parameter. This means if the value stored in the *ValueMaxSize* parameter is not a multiple of 2, the last byte in that buffer will be untouched since DB2 CLI cannot split a double-byte character.
- The data stored in the *Value* buffer is always null-terminated unless the column data to be retrieved is binary or the SQL data type of the column is graphic (DBCS) and the C data type is SQL_C_CHAR. If an application retrieves the data in multiple chunks, it should make the proper adjustments (strip off the null terminator before concatenating the pieces back together, assuming the null termination environment attribute is in effect).
- Applications that use the SQLExtendedFetch( ) function to retrieve data should call the SQLGetData( ) function only when the rowset size is 1, which is equivalent to calling the SQLFetch( ) function.
- This function can retrieve column data only for the row where the cursor is currently positioned.
- This function can be used along with the SQLBindCol( ) function with the same result data set, as long as the SQLFetch( ) function and not the SQLExtended-Fetch( ) function retrieves the data.
- The SQL_SUCCESS return code is returned whenever a zero-length data string is retrieved by the SQLGetData( ) function. If this occurs, the *ValueSize* parameter will be set to 0 and the *Value* parameter will contain a null terminator.

Prerequisites The SQLFetch( ) function must be called before this function is called. If the SQLFetch( ) call fails, do not call this function.

Restrictions ODBC has defined column 0 in all result data sets for bookmarks, and DB2 CLI does not support bookmarks.

See Also SQLBindCol( ), SQLFetch( ), SQLExtendedFetch( ), SQLGetSubString( )

Examples The following C program illustrates how to use the SQLGetData( ) function to retrieve data from unbound columns in a result data set:

```
#include <stdio.h>
#include <stdlib.h>
#include <string.h>
#include <sqlcli1.h>
```

```
int main()
{
    /* Declare The Local Memory Variables */
    SQLRETURN      rc = SQL_SUCCESS;
    SQLHENV        EnvHandle;
    SQLHDBC        DSCHandle;
    SQLHSTMT       StmtHandle;
    SQLCHAR        SQLStmt[80];
    SQLCHAR        Name[10];
    SQLCHAR        Job[6];
    SQLSMALLINT    Years;

    /* Allocate An Environment Handle */
    rc = SQLAllocEnv(&EnvHandle);

    /* Allocate A Connection Handle */
    rc = SQLAllocConnect(EnvHandle, &DSCHandle);

    /* Connect To The SAMPLE Database */
    rc = SQLConnect(DSCHandle, "SAMPLE", SQL_NTS, "etpdd6z", SQL_NTS,
                "sanders", SQL_NTS);

    /* Allocate An SQL Statement Handle */
    rc = SQLAllocStmt(DSCHandle, &StmtHandle);

    /* Define A SELECT SQL Statement */
    strcpy(SQLStmt, "SELECT NAME, JOB, YEARS FROM USERID.STAFF ");
    strcat(SQLStmt, "WHERE YEARS <= 5");

    /* Execute The SQL Statement */
    rc = SQLExecDirect(StmtHandle, SQLStmt, SQL_NTS);

   if (rc != SQL_ERROR)
        {

        /* Retrieve And Display The Results */
        printf("Name          Job      Years Of Service\n");
        printf("---------------------------------------\n");
        while (rc != SQL_NO_DATA_FOUND)
            {

            /* Retrieve A Record From The Result Data Set */
            rc = SQLFetch(StmtHandle);
            if (rc != SQL_NO_DATA_FOUND)
                {
                SQLGetData(StmtHandle, 1, SQL_C_CHAR,
                           (SQLPOINTER) Name, sizeof(Name), NULL);

                SQLGetData(StmtHandle, 2, SQL_C_CHAR, (SQLPOINTER) Job,
                           sizeof(Job), NULL);

                SQLGetData(StmtHandle, 3, SQL_C_SHORT,
                           (SQLPOINTER) &Years, 0, NULL);

                /* Print The Information Retrieved */
                printf("%-13s %-15s %d\n", Name, Job, Years);
                }
            }
        }

    /* Disconnect From The SAMPLE Database */
    SQLDisconnect(DSCHandle);
```

```
    /* Free The SQL Statement Handle */
    if (StmtHandle != NULL)
        SQLFreeStmt(StmtHandle, SQL_DROP);

    /* Free The Connection Handle */
    if (DSCHandle != NULL)
        SQLFreeConnect(DSCHandle);

    /* Free The Environment Handle */
    if (EnvHandle != NULL)
        SQLFreeEnv(EnvHandle);

    /* Return To The Operating System */
    return(rc);
}
```

The following C++ program illustrates how the SQLGetData( ) function is used in class methods to retrieve data from unbound columns in a result data set:

```
#include <iostream.h>
#include <string.h>
#include <sqlcli1.h>

/* Define The CLI Class */
class CLI
{
    /* Declare The Private Attribute Variables */
    private:
       SQLHENV      EnvHandle;
       SQLHDBC      DSCHandle;
       SQLCHAR      Name[10];
       SQLCHAR      Job[6];
       SQLSMALLINT  Years;

    /* Declare The Public Attribute Variables */
    public:
       SQLRETURN    rc;
       SQLHSTMT     StmtHandle;

    /* Declare The Member Function Prototypes */
    CLI();                                      // Constructor
    ~CLI();                                     // Destructor
    SQLRETURN Connect();
    SQLRETURN ShowResults();
    SQLRETURN Disconnect();
} ;

/* Define The Class Constructor */
CLI::CLI()
{
    /* Initialize The Return Code Variable */
    rc = SQL_SUCCESS;

    /* Allocate An Environment Handle */
    rc = SQLAllocEnv(&EnvHandle);

    /* Allocate A Connection Handle */
    rc = SQLAllocConnect(EnvHandle, &DSCHandle);
}
```

```
/* Define The Class Destructor */
CLI::~CLI()
{
    /* Free The Connection Handle */
    if (DSCHandle != NULL)
        SQLFreeConnect(DSCHandle);

    /* Free The Environment Handle */
    if (EnvHandle != NULL)
        SQLFreeEnv(EnvHandle);
}

/* Define The Connect() Member Function */
SQLRETURN CLI::Connect()
{
    /* Connect To The SAMPLE Database */
    rc = SQLConnect(DSCHandle, (SQLCHAR *) "SAMPLE", SQL_NTS,
                    (SQLCHAR *) "etpdd6z", SQL_NTS,
                    (SQLCHAR *) "sanders", SQL_NTS);

    /* Allocate An SQL Statement Handle */
    rc = SQLAllocStmt(DSCHandle, &StmtHandle);

    /* Return The CLI Function Return Code */
    return(rc);
}

/* Define The Disconnect() Member Function */
SQLRETURN CLI::Disconnect(void)
{
    /* Disconnect From The Database */
    rc = SQLDisconnect(DSCHandle);

    /* Free The SQL Statement Handle */
    if (StmtHandle != NULL)
        SQLFreeStmt(StmtHandle, SQL_DROP);

    /* Return The CLI Function Return Code */
    return(rc);
}

/* Define The ShowResults() Member Function */
SQLRETURN CLI::ShowResults(void)
{
    /* Retrieve And Display The Results */
    cout << "Name          Job      Years Of Service" << endl;
    cout << "---------------------------------------" << endl;
    while (rc != SQL_NO_DATA_FOUND)
        {

        /* Retrieve A Record From The Result Data Set */
        rc = SQLFetch(StmtHandle);
        if (rc != SQL_NO_DATA_FOUND)
            {
            SQLGetData(StmtHandle, 1, SQL_C_CHAR,
                       (SQLPOINTER) Name, sizeof(Name), NULL);

            SQLGetData(StmtHandle, 2, SQL_C_CHAR, (SQLPOINTER) Job,
                       sizeof(Job), NULL);

            SQLGetData(StmtHandle, 3, SQL_C_SHORT,
                       (SQLPOINTER) &Years, 0, NULL);
```

```
                /* Print The Information Retrieved */
                if (rc != SQL_NO_DATA_FOUND)
                    {
                    cout.setf(ios::left);
                    cout.width(14);
                    cout << Name;
                    cout.setf(ios::left);
                    cout.width(16);
                    cout << Job << Years << endl;
                    }
                }
            }

    /* Return The CLI Function Return Code */
    return(rc);
}

int main()
{
    /* Declare The Local Memory Variables */
    SQLRETURN  rc = SQL_SUCCESS;
    SQLCHAR    SQLStmt[80];

    /* Create An Instance Of The CLI Class */
    CLI Sample;

    /* Connect To The SAMPLE Database */
    if ((rc = Sample.Connect()) != SQL_SUCCESS)
        return(rc);

    /* Define A SELECT SQL Statement */
    strcpy((char *) SQLStmt, "SELECT NAME, JOB, YEARS FROM ");
    strcat((char *) SQLStmt, "USERID.STAFF WHERE YEARS <= 5");

    /* Execute The SQL Statement */
    rc = SQLExecDirect(Sample.StmtHandle, SQLStmt, SQL_NTS);

    /* Display The Results Of The SQL Query */
    if (rc == SQL_SUCCESS)
        Sample.ShowResults();

    /* Disconnect From The SAMPLE Database */
    Sample.Disconnect();

    /* Return To The Operating System */
    return(rc);
}
```

SQLMoreResults

Purpose The SQLMoreResults( ) function determines whether or not more information is available for a SQL statement handle that has been associated with an array of input parameters for a query, or a stored procedure that is returning multiple result data sets.

Syntax

```
SQLRETURN SQLMoreResults (SQLHSTMT StmtHandle);
```

Parameters *StmtHandle* The statement handle where the address of the SQL statement buffer is stored.

Includes

```
#include <sqlcli1.h>
```

Description

The SQLMoreResults( ) function identifies multiple result data sets, in a sequential manner, upon the successful execution of:

- A SQL query that was bound to an array of input parameter values specified with the SQLParamOptions( ) and SQLBindParameter( ) functions.
- A stored procedure containing one or more SQL queries, where the cursor(s) are left open so the result data sets remain accessible after the stored procedure has finished execution.

In either case, after the first result data set is processed, you can call this function to determine whether or not another result data set is available. If another result data is available, this function will make it available to the calling application.

Specifications

DB2 CLI 2.1, ODBC 1.0

Return Codes

SQL_SUCCESS, SQL_SUCCESS_WITH_INFO, SQL_INVALID_HANDLE, SQL_NO_DATA_FOUND, SQL_ERROR

> Note: The SQLMoreResults( ) function currently returns SQL_NO_DATA_FOUND unless the following patches are applied to version 2.1.1:
> *OS/2* us8090
> *AIX* u441267, u442530
> These patches can be found on the World Wide Web at:
> http://www.software.ibm.com/data/db2/db2tech/index.html

SQLSTATEs

01504, **01**508, **07**001, **07**006, **08**S01, **21**S01, **21**S02, **22**001, **22**003, **22**005, **22**007, **22**008, **22**012, **23**000, **24**000, **24**504, **34**000, **37***xxx*, **40**000, **40**003, **42***xxx*, **42**8A1, **42**895, **44**000, **56**0084, **58**004, **S0**001, **S0**002, **S0**011, **S0**012, **S0**022, **S1**001, **S1**009, **S1**010, **S1**013, **S1**090, **S1**503, **S1**T00

> Note: *xxx* means that any SQLSTATE subclass value with the class code 37 or 42 can be returned.

Comments

- If this function is called and the current result data set contains unfetched rows, they will be discarded when the SQLMoreResults( ) function closes the current cursor.
- If all the result data sets are processed when the SQLMoreResults( ) function is called, the return code SQL_NO_DATA_FOUND will be returned to the calling application. If another result data set is available when the SQLMoreResults( ) function is called, however, the return code SQL_SUCCESS will be returned to the calling application.
- If the SQLFreeStmt( ) function is called with either the SQL_CLOSE or SQL_DROP option specified, all pending result data sets for this statement handle will be discarded.

Restrictions

The ODBC specification of the SQLMoreResults( ) function also allow counts associated with the execution of parameterized INSERT, UPDATE, and DELETE statements with arrays of input parameter values to be returned. However, DB2 CLI does not support the return of such count information.

See Also SQLParamOptions( )

Examples The following C program illustrates how to use the SQLMoreResults( ) function to advance through each result data set produced when a SELECT SQL statement that produces multiple result data sets is executed:

```
#include <stdio.h>
#include <stdlib.h>
#include <string.h>
#include <sqlcli1.h>

#define NUMSETS      3

int main()
{
    /* Declare The Local Memory Variables */
    SQLRETURN      rc = SQL_SUCCESS;
    int            Index;
    SQLHENV        EnvHandle;
    SQLHDBC        DSCHandle;
    SQLHSTMT       StmtHandle;
    SQLCHAR        SQLStmt[80];
    SQLSMALLINT    ActNums[NUMSETS] = { 110, 130, 140 } ;
    SQLUINTEGER    NumRows = 0;
    SQLCHAR        EmpNo[7];
    SQLCHAR        ProjNo[80];
    SQLSMALLINT    ActNo;

    /* Allocate An Environment Handle */
    rc = SQLAllocEnv(&EnvHandle);

    /* Allocate A Connection Handle */
    rc = SQLAllocConnect(EnvHandle, &DSCHandle);

    /* Connect To The SAMPLE Database */
    rc = SQLConnect(DSCHandle, "SAMPLE", SQL_NTS, "etpdd6z", SQL_NTS,
                    "sanders", SQL_NTS);

    /* Allocate An SQL Statement Handle */
    rc = SQLAllocStmt(DSCHandle, &StmtHandle);

    /* Define An Prepare A SELECT SQL Statement */
    strcpy(SQLStmt, "SELECT EMPNO, PROJNO, ACTNO FROM ");
    strcat(SQLStmt, "USERID.EMP_ACT WHERE ACTNO = ?");
    rc = SQLPrepare(StmtHandle, SQLStmt, SQL_NTS);

    /* Tell CLI That 3 Values Will Be Provided For The Parameter */
    /* Marker In The SQL Statement                               */
    SQLParamOptions(StmtHandle, NUMSETS, &NumRows);

    /* Bind The Parameter Marker To A Local Variable */
    SQLBindParameter(StmtHandle, 1, SQL_PARAM_INPUT, SQL_C_SHORT,
                     SQL_SMALLINT, 0, 0, ActNums, 0, NULL);

    /* Execute The SQL Statement */
    rc = SQLExecute(StmtHandle);

    if (rc != SQL_ERROR)
        {
        /* Bind The Columns In The Result Data Set To Local */
        /* Storage Variables                                */
```

```
        SQLBindCol(StmtHandle, 1, SQL_C_CHAR, (SQLPOINTER) EmpNo,
                   sizeof(EmpNo), NULL);

        SQLBindCol(StmtHandle, 2, SQL_C_CHAR, (SQLPOINTER) ProjNo,
                   sizeof(ProjNo), NULL);

        SQLBindCol(StmtHandle, 3, SQL_C_SHORT, (SQLPOINTER) &ActNo,
                   0, NULL);

        /* Retrieve And Display The Results For Each Result Data */
        /* Set                                                     */
        for (Index = 1; Index <= NUMSETS; Index++)
            {

            /* Print A Header For Each Result Data */
            printf("\n");
            printf("Employee   Project    Account\n");
            printf("Number     Number     Number\n");
            printf("-----------------------------\n");
            while (rc != SQL_NO_DATA_FOUND)
                {

                /* Retrieve A Record From The Result Data Set */
                rc = SQLFetch(StmtHandle);

                /* Print The Information Retrieved */
                if (rc != SQL_NO_DATA_FOUND)
                    printf("%-10s %-10s %d\n", EmpNo, ProjNo, ActNo);
                }

            /* Advance To The Next Result Data Set */
            if (rc == SQL_NO_DATA_FOUND)
                rc = SQL_SUCCESS;
            else
                break;
            SQLMoreResults(StmtHandle);
            }
        }

    /* Disconnect From The SAMPLE Database */
    SQLDisconnect(DSCHandle);

    /* Free The SQL Statement Handle */
    if (StmtHandle != NULL)
        SQLFreeStmt(StmtHandle, SQL_DROP);

    /* Free The Connection Handle */
    if (DSCHandle != NULL)
        SQLFreeConnect(DSCHandle);

    /* Free The Environment Handle */
    if (EnvHandle != NULL)
        SQLFreeEnv(EnvHandle);

    /* Return To The Operating System */
    return(rc);
}
```

Note: The SQLMoreResults( ) function is used in a C++ program in a similar manner.

SQLError

Purpose

The SQLError( ) function retrieves error, warning, and/or status information associated with the most recently executed DB2 CLI function.

Syntax

```
SQLRETURN SQLError (SQLHENV          EnvHandle,
                    SQLHDBC          DSCHandle,
                    SQLHSTMT         StmtHandle,
                    SQLCHAR FAR      *SQLSTATE,
                    SQLINTEGER FAR   *NativeError,
                    SQLCHAR FAR      *ErrorMsg,
                    SQLSMALLINT      ErrorMsgMaxSize,
                    SQLSMALLINT FAR  *ErrorMsgSize);
```

Parameters

EnvHandle The environment handle where the address of the environment buffer is stored.

DSCHandle The data source connection handle where the address of the data source connection information buffer is stored.

StmtHandle The statement handle where the address of the SQL statement buffer is stored.

SQLSTATE A pointer to a location in memory where this function is to store the SQLSTATE as a string of five characters followed by a null terminator character. The first two characters of this string indicate error class, and the last three characters indicate the error subclass.

NativeError A pointer to a location in memory where this function is to store the native error code. For DB2 databases, this memory location contains the SQLCODE value returned by the DBMS. If the error is generated by a DB2 CLI function call instead of the data source, this memory location will contain the value: –99999.

ErrorMsg A pointer to a location in memory where this function is to store the implementation-defined error message text. If the error is detected by DB2 CLI, then the error message will be prefaced by:

```
[IBM] [CLI Driver]
```

to indicate that DB2 CLI detected the error and no data source connection has yet been established. If the error is detected while there is a data source connection, then the error message will be prefaced by:

```
[IBM][CLI Driver][DBMS-Name]
```

where *DBMS-Name* is the name returned when the SQLGetInfo( ) function is called with the SQL_DBMS_NAME value stored in the *InfoType* parameter.

ErrorMsgMaxSize The maximum size of the memory storage buffer where this function is to store the error message text.

ErrorMsgSize A pointer to a location in memory where this function is to store the actual number of bytes written to the error message text memory storage buffer.

Includes

```
#include <sqlcli1.h>
```

Description

The SQLError( ) function retrieves diagnostic (error, warning, and/or status) information associated with the most recently executed DB2 CLI function for a particular statement, connection, or environment handle. This information consists of one or more standardized SQLSTATEs, native error codes, and corresponding text messages. You should always call this function when a return code of SQL_ERROR or SQL_SUCCESS_WITH_INFO is returned by a DB2 CLI function call.

> Note: Some data sources might also provide product-specific diagnostic information whenever a return code of SQL_NO_DATA_FOUND is returned after a SQL statement is executed.

Specifications DB2 CLI 1.1, ODBC 1.0, X/OPEN CLI, ISO CLI

Return Codes SQL_SUCCESS, SQL_INVALID_HANDLE, SQL_NO_DATA_FOUND, SQL_ERROR

SQLSTATEs No SQLSTATE values are returned for this function because it does not generate diagnostic information for itself.

Comments

- To obtain diagnostic information associated with an environment handle, specify a valid environment connection handle in the *EnvHandle* parameter, set the connection handle (*DSCHandle*) parameter to SQL_NULL_HDBC, and set the statement handle (*StmtHandle*) parameter to SQL_NULL_HSTMT.
- To obtain diagnostic information associated with a connection handle, specify a valid data source connection handle in the *DSCHandle* parameter and set the statement handle (*StmtHandle*) parameter to SQL_NULL_HSTMT. The environment handle (*EnvHandle*) will be ignored.
- To obtain diagnostic information associated with a SQL statement handle, specify a valid statement handle in the *StmtHandle* parameter. The environment handle (*EnvHandle*) and connection handle (*DSCHandle)* will be ignored.
- The SQLSTATE values returned by this function correspond directly to the SQLSTATE values defined in the X/Open SQL CAE specification and the ODBC specification, augmented with IBM- and product-specific SQLSTATE values.
- Error messages prefaced by [IBM][CLI Driver][Vendor] indicate that an error was detected while connected to a non-IBM DRDA RDBMS, which is treated by DB2 CLI as a DB2/6000 version 2.1 data source. If the error was generated by the RDBMS (and not DB2 CLI), the IBM-defined SQLSTATE will be appended to the text string.
- If the diagnostic information generated by a DB2 CLI function call is not retrieved by the SQLError( ) function before another CLI function using the same environment, data source connection, or statement handle is called, that information will be lost.
- Multiple diagnostic messages might be generated by a DB2 CLI function call. When this occurs, you can retrieve each diagnostic message, one at a time, by repeatedly calling the SQLError( ) function. Each time a diagnostic message is retrieved, the SQLError( ) function returns the value SQL_SUCCESS and the diagnostic message is removed from the list. When there are no more SQLSTATE values to retrieve, the SQLError( ) function returns the value SQL_NO_DATA_FOUND, the SQLSTATE is set to **00**000, the *NativeError* parameter is set to 0, and both the *ErrorMsgSize* and *ErrorMsg* parameters are undefined.
- If no diagnostic information is available for the specified handle or if all diagnostic messages have been retrieved via multiple calls to the SQLError( ) function, the return code SQL_NO_DATA_FOUND will be returned.
- Diagnostic information stored under a given environment, data source connection, or SQL statement handle is cleared when the SQLError() function or another DB2 CLI function is called with that handle. However, information

associated with a given handle type is not cleared if the SQLError( ) function is called with an associated but different handle type. (For example, if the SQLError( ) function is called with a connection handle, errors associated with statement handles under that connection will not be cleared.)

- The SQL_SUCCESS return code is returned, even if the buffer for the error message text (*ErrorMsg*) is too short, since another SQLError( ) function call will not retrieve the same error message. The actual length of the message text retrieved is returned in the *ErrorMsgSize* parameter. To avoid truncation of error message text, use a buffer that is SQL_MAX_MESSAGE_LENGTH + 1 in length. The message text will never be longer than this.

Restrictions Although ODBC also returns X/Open SQL CAE SQLSTATEs, only DB2 CLI (and the DB2 ODBC driver) can return the additional IBM defined SQLSTATEs. The ODBC driver manager also returns SQLSTATE values with a prefix of "IM." These SQLSTATEs are not defined by X/Open and are not returned by DB2 CLI. For more information on ODBC-specific SQLSTATEs, refer to the *Microsoft ODBC Programmer's Reference*. All branching logic in an application that is dependent on SQLSTATE values, therefore, should rely only on the standard SQLSTATE values. Use the augmented SQLSTATEs only for debugging purposes.

Note: It might be useful to build logic dependencies on SQLSTATE class values (the first two characters of a SQLSTATE value).

See Also SQLGetSQLCA( )

Examples The following C program illustrates how to use the SQLError( ) function to retrieve diagnostic information when a SQL statement fails to execute properly:

```
#include <stdio.h>
#include <stdlib.h>
#include <string.h>
#include <sqlcli1.h>

int main()
{
    /* Declare The Local Memory Variables */
    SQLRETURN    rc = SQL_SUCCESS;
    SQLHENV      EnvHandle;
    SQLHDBC      DSCHandle;
    SQLHSTMT     StmtHandle;
    SQLCHAR      SQLStmt[80];
    SQLCHAR      MsgBuffer[255];
    SQLCHAR      sqlState[255];
    SQLINTEGER   sqlCode;
    SQLSMALLINT  Length;

    /* Allocate An Environment Handle */
    rc = SQLAllocEnv(&EnvHandle);

    /* Allocate A Connection Handle */
    rc = SQLAllocConnect(EnvHandle, &DSCHandle);

    /* Connect To The SAMPLE Database */
    rc = SQLConnect(DSCHandle, "SAMPLE", SQL_NTS, "etpdd6z", SQL_NTS,
                "sanders", SQL_NTS);
```

```
    /* Allocate An SQL Statement Handle */
    rc = SQLAllocStmt(DSCHandle, &StmtHandle);

    /* Define An Invalid SELECT SQL Statement */
    strcpy(SQLStmt, "SELECT NAME, DEPTNAME FROM USERID.ORG ");
    strcat(SQLStmt, "WHERE DEPTNUMB = 10");

    /* Execute The Invalid SQL Statement - An Error Will Be Generated */
    rc = SQLExecDirect(StmtHandle, SQLStmt, SQL_NTS);

    /* Retrieve And Display The Error Message Associated With The */
    /* SQLExecDirect() Function                                     */
    if (rc == SQL_ERROR || rc == SQL_SUCCESS_WITH_INFO)
        {
        SQLError(NULL, NULL, StmtHandle, sqlState, &sqlCode, MsgBuffer,
                 sizeof(MsgBuffer), &Length);

        printf("An Error Has Occurred :\n\n");
        printf("SQLSTATE          = %s\n", sqlState);
        printf("Native Error Code = %ld\n\n", sqlCode);
        printf("%s\n", MsgBuffer);
        }

    /* Disconnect From The SAMPLE Database */
    SQLDisconnect(DSCHandle);

    /* Free The SQL Statement Handle */
    if (StmtHandle != NULL)
        SQLFreeStmt(StmtHandle, SQL_DROP);

    /* Free The Connection Handle */
    if (DSCHandle != NULL)
        SQLFreeConnect(DSCHandle);

    /* Free The Environment Handle */
    if (EnvHandle != NULL)
        SQLFreeEnv(EnvHandle);

    /* Return To The Operating System */
    return(rc);
}
```

The following C++ program illustrates how the SQLError( ) function can be used in a class method to retrieve diagnostic information whenever an error occurs:

```
#include <iostream.h>
#include <string.h>
#include <sqlcli1.h>

/* Define The CLI Class */
class CLI
{
    /* Declare The Private Attribute Variables */
    private:
       SQLHENV      EnvHandle;
       SQLHDBC      DSCHandle;
       SQLCHAR      MsgBuffer[255];
       SQLCHAR      sqlState[255];
       SQLINTEGER   sqlCode;
       SQLSMALLINT  Length;
```

```
    /* Declare The Public Attribute Variables */
    public:
       SQLRETURN     rc;
       SQLHSTMT      StmtHandle;

    /* Declare The Member Function Prototypes */
    CLI();                                   // Constructor
    ~CLI();                                  // Destructor
    SQLRETURN Connect();
    void ShowError();
    SQLRETURN Disconnect();
} ;

/* Define The Class Constructor */
CLI::CLI()
{
    /* Initialize The Return Code Variable */
    rc = SQL_SUCCESS;

    /* Allocate An Environment Handle */
    rc = SQLAllocEnv(&EnvHandle);

    /* Allocate A Connection Handle */
    rc = SQLAllocConnect(EnvHandle, &DSCHandle);
}

/* Define The Class Destructor */
CLI::~CLI()
{
    /* Free The Connection Handle */
    if (DSCHandle != NULL)
        SQLFreeConnect(DSCHandle);

    /* Free The Environment Handle */
    if (EnvHandle != NULL)
        SQLFreeEnv(EnvHandle);
}

/* Define The Connect() Member Function */
SQLRETURN CLI::Connect()
{
    /* Connect To The SAMPLE Database */
    rc = SQLConnect(DSCHandle, (SQLCHAR *) "SAMPLE", SQL_NTS,
                    (SQLCHAR *) "etpdd6z", SQL_NTS,
                    (SQLCHAR *) "sanders", SQL_NTS);

    /* Allocate An SQL Statement Handle */
    rc = SQLAllocStmt(DSCHandle, &StmtHandle);

    /* Return The CLI Function Return Code */
    return(rc);
}

/* Define The Disconnect() Member Function */
SQLRETURN CLI::Disconnect(void)
{
    /* Disconnect From The Database */
    rc = SQLDisconnect(DSCHandle);

    /* Free The SQL Statement Handle */
    if (StmtHandle != NULL)
        SQLFreeStmt(StmtHandle, SQL_DROP);
```

```
    /* Return The CLI Function Return Code */
    return(rc);
}

/* Define The ShowError() Member Function */
void CLI::ShowError(void)
{
    /* Retrieve And Display The Error Information */
    SQLError(EnvHandle, DSCHandle, StmtHandle, sqlState, &sqlCode,
             MsgBuffer, sizeof(MsgBuffer), &Length);

    cout << "An Error Has Occurred :" << endl << endl;
    cout << "SQLSTATE          = " << sqlState << endl;
    cout << "Native Error Code = " << sqlCode << endl << endl;
    cout << MsgBuffer;
}

int main()
{
    /* Declare The Local Memory Variables */
    SQLRETURN  rc = SQL_SUCCESS;
    SQLCHAR    SQLStmt[80];

    /* Create An Instance Of The CLI Class */
    CLI Sample;

    /* Connect To The SAMPLE Database */
    if ((rc = Sample.Connect()) != SQL_SUCCESS)
        return(rc);

    /* Define An Invalid SELECT SQL Statement */
    strcpy((char *) SQLStmt, "SELECT NAME, DEPTNAME FROM USERID.ORG ");
    strcat((char *) SQLStmt, "WHERE DEPTNUMB = 10");

    /* Execute The Invalid SQL Statement - An Error Will Be Generated */
    rc = SQLExecDirect(Sample.StmtHandle, SQLStmt, SQL_NTS);

    /* Display The Results Of The SQL Query */
    if (rc == SQL_ERROR || rc == SQL_SUCCESS_WITH_INFO)
        Sample.ShowError();

    /* Disconnect From The SAMPLE Database */
    Sample.Disconnect();

    /* Return To The Operating System */
    return(rc);
}
```

SQLGetSQLCA

Purpose The SQLGetSQLCA( ) function retrieves the SQLCA data structure value associated with preparing and executing a SQL statement, retrieving data from a cursor (fetching), or closing a cursor.

Syntax

```
SQLRETURN SQLGetSQLCA (SQLHENV          EnvHandle,
                       SQLHDBC          DSCHandle,
                       SQLHSTMT         StmtHandle,
                       struct sqlca FAR *sqlca);
```

Parameters

EnvHandle The environment handle where the address of the environment buffer is stored.

DSCHandle The data source connection handle where the address of the data source connection information buffer is stored.

StmtHandle The SQL statement handle where the address of the SQL statement buffer is stored.

sqlca A pointer to a location in memory where this function is to store a SQL communication area (SQLCA) data structure associated with the *StmtHandle* parameter.

Includes

```
#include <sqlcli1.h>
```

Description

The SQLGetSQLCA( ) function retrieves the SQLCA data structure value associated with preparing and executing a SQL statement, retrieving data from a cursor (fetching), or closing a cursor. In some cases, the SQLCA data structure variable can provide diagnostic information in addition to what can be obtained with the SQLError( ) function.

SQLCA data structure information is not available for CLI functions that are processed strictly on the application side, such as SQLAllocStatement( ). In this case, an empty SQLCA data structure variable is generated and all the field values are set to zero when this function is called. For a detailed description of the SQLCA structure, refer to Appendix A, SQL DATA STRUCTURES.

Specifications

DB2 CLI 2.1

Return Codes

SQL_SUCCESS, SQL_INVALID_HANDLE, SQL_ERROR

SQLSTATEs

No SQLSTATE values exist for this function.

Comments

- To obtain SQLCA diagnostic information associated with an environment handle, specify a valid environment connection handle in the *EnvHandle* parameter, set the connection handle *(DSCHandle)* parameter to SQL_NULL_HDBC, and set the statement handle (*StmtHandle*) parameter to SQL_NULL_HSTMT.
- To obtain SQLCA diagnostic information associated with a connection handle, specify a valid data source connection handle in the *DSCHandle* parameter and set the statement handle (*StmtHandle*) parameter to SQL_NULL_HSTMT. The environment handle (*EnvHandle*) will be ignored.
- To obtain SQLCA diagnostic information associated with a SQL statement handle, specify a valid statement handle in the *StmtHandle* parameter. The environment handle (*EnvHandle*) and connection handle (*DSCHandle*) will be ignored.
- If the diagnostic information generated by a DB2 CLI function call is not retrieved by the either this function or by the SQLError( ) function before another CLI function using the same environment, data source connection, or statement handle is called, that information will be lost.
- Meaningful SQLCA diagnostic information is returned for only the following CLI functions:
  –SQLConnect( )
  –SQLSetConnectOption( ) for SQL_AUTOCOMMIT and SQL_DB2EXPLAIN options
  –SQLDisconnect( )
  –SQLPrepare( )
  –SQLExecute( )
  –SQLExecDirect( )

–SQLFetch( )
–SQLExtendedFetch( )
–SQLMoreResults( )
–SQLGetData( ) if one or more LOB columns are involved
–SQLCancel( )
–SQLTransact( )
–SQLTables( )
–SQLTablePrivileges( )
–SQLColumns( )
–SQLColumnPrivileges( )
–SQLStatistics( )
–SQLPrimaryKeys( )
–SQLForeignKeys( )
–SQLProcedures( )
–SQLProcedureColumns( )

- If the data source connection is to a DB2 for Common Servers, version 2.x data source, two fields in the SQLCA data structure variable might be of particular interest:

The SQLERRD(3) field (sqlca.errd[2]) After a SQL statement is prepared, this field contains an estimate of the number of rows that will be returned to the user when the SQL statement is executed. An application can inform the user of this information to help assess whether or not the appropriate query has been issued. After an INSERT, UPDATE, or DELETE statement is executed, this field contains the actual number of affected rows. After compound SQL processing, this field contains an accumulation of all substatement rows affected by INSERT, UPDATE, or DELETE statements.

The SQLERRD(4) field (sqlca.errd[3]) After a SQL statement is prepared, this field contains a relative cost estimate of the resources required to process the statement. This number is compared to either the DB2ESTIMATE configuration keyword or the SQL_DB2ESTIMATE connection option described in the SQLSetConnectOption( ) function. After compound SQL processing, this field contains an accumulation of all successfully executed SQL substatements.

The accuracy of the information returned in the SQLERRD(3) and SQLERRD(4) fields of a SQLCA data structure variable depends on many factors, such as the use of parameter markers and expressions within the SQL statement. The main factor, which can be easily controlled, is the accuracy of the data source statistics (when the statistical information about the data source was last updated), for example the last time the RUNSTATS command was executed.

Restrictions There are no restrictions associated with this function call.

See Also SQLError( )

Examples The following C program illustrates how to use the SQLGetSQLCA( ) function to obtain statistical information for a SQL statement before it is executed:

```
#include <stdio.h>
#include <stdlib.h>
#include <string.h>
#include <sqlcli1.h>

int main()
{
```

```
    /* Declare The Local Memory Variables */
    SQLRETURN      rc = SQL_SUCCESS;
    SQLHENV        EnvHandle;
    SQLHDBC        DSCHandle;
    SQLHSTMT       StmtHandle;
    SQLCHAR        SQLStmt[80];
    struct sqlca   sqlca;

    /* Allocate An Environment Handle */
    rc = SQLAllocEnv(&EnvHandle);

    /* Allocate A Connection Handle */
    rc = SQLAllocConnect(EnvHandle, &DSCHandle);

    /* Connect To The SAMPLE Database */
    rc = SQLConnect(DSCHandle, "SAMPLE", SQL_NTS, "etpdd6z", SQL_NTS,
                    "sanders", SQL_NTS);

    /* Allocate An SQL Statement Handle */
    rc = SQLAllocStmt(DSCHandle, &StmtHandle);

    /* Define A SELECT SQL Statement */
    strcpy(SQLStmt, "SELECT DEPTNO, DEPTNAME FROM USERID.DEPARTMENT");

    /* Prepare The SQL Statement */
    rc = SQLPrepare(StmtHandle, SQLStmt, SQL_NTS);

    /* Retrieve Statistical Information About The Prepared SQL */
    /* Statement                                               */
    if (rc == SQL_SUCCESS)
        {
        rc = SQLGetSQLCA(EnvHandle, DSCHandle, StmtHandle, &sqlca);
        if (rc == SQL_SUCCESS)
            {
            printf("SQL Statement : %s\n\n", SQLStmt);
            printf("Relative Cost             = %ld\n",
                   sqlca.sqlerrd[3]);
            printf("Estimated Number Of Rows = %ld\n",
                   sqlca.sqlerrd[2]);
            }
        }

    /* Disconnect From The SAMPLE Database */
    SQLDisconnect(DSCHandle);

    /* Free The SQL Statement Handle */
    if (StmtHandle != NULL)
        SQLFreeStmt(StmtHandle, SQL_DROP);

    /* Free The Connection Handle */
    if (DSCHandle != NULL)
        SQLFreeConnect(DSCHandle);

    /* Free The Environment Handle */
    if (EnvHandle != NULL)
        SQLFreeEnv(EnvHandle);

    /* Return To The Operating System */
    return(rc);
}
```

Note: The SQLMoreResults( ) function is used in a C++ program in a similar manner.

SQLGetLength

Purpose

The SQLGetLength( ) function retrieves the length of a large object (LOB) value referenced by a LOB locator value that was retrieved during the current transaction.

Syntax

```
SQLRETURN SQLGetLength (SQLHSTMT        StmtHandle,
                        SQLSMALLINT     LocatorCDataType,
                        SQLINTEGER      Locator,
                        SQLINTEGER FAR *StringLength,
                        SQLINTEGER FAR *IndicatorValue);
```

Parameters

StmtHandle The statement handle where the address of the SQL statement buffer is stored.

LocatorCDataType The C language data type of the LOB locator. The following C data types are supported:

- SQL_C_BLOB_LOCATOR
- SQL_C_CLOB_LOCATOR
- SQL_C_DBCLOB_LOCATOR

Locator The LOB locator.

StringLength A pointer to a location in memory where this function is to store the length (in bytes) of the information referenced by the locator.

IndicatorValue Reserved (always set to zero).

Includes

```
#include <sqlcli1.h>
```

Description

The SQLGetLength( ) function retrieves the length of a LOB value referenced by a LOB locator that was retrieved (as a result of a fetch or SQLGetSubString( ) function call) during the current transaction. Use this function to determine the overall length of the data value referenced by an LOB locator, and thus choose the appropriate strategy for obtaining some or all of the LOB value.

Specifications

DB2 CLI 2.1

Return Codes

SQL_SUCCESS, SQL_SUCCESS_WITH_INFO, SQL_INVALID_HANDLE, SQL_ERROR

SQLSTATEs

07006, **08**S01, **40**003, **58**004, **S1**001, **S1**003, **S1**009, **S1**010, **S1**013, **S1**C00, **S1**F01

Comments

- The size of the information (*StringLength* parameter) referenced by the LOB locator is returned in bytes, even if the LOB locator references DBCLOB data.
- The *Locator* parameter can contain any valid LOB locator that was not explicitly freed by the FREE LOCATOR statement or implicitly freed because the transaction in which the locator was created has terminated.
- The statement handle used by this function must not be associated with any prepared statements or catalog function calls.

Restrictions

This function is not available when you are connected to DB2 data sources that do not support LOB data types. To determine whether or not this function is supported for the current data source connection, call the SQLGetFunctions( ) function with the *FunctionType* parameter set to SQL_API_SQLGETLENGTH and check the value of the *Exists* output parameter.

See Also

SQLBindCol( ), SQLFetch( ), SQLExtendedFetch( ), SQLGetPosition( ), SQL-GetSubString( )

Examples

The following C program illustrates how to use the SQLGetLength( ) function, SQLGetPosition() function, and SQLGetSubString( ) to retrieve a select portion of a LOB data item:

```
#include <stdio.h>
#include <stdlib.h>
#include <string.h>
#include <sqlcli1.h>

int main()
{
    /* Declare The Local Memory Variables */
    SQLRETURN     rc = SQL_SUCCESS;
    SQLHENV       EnvHandle;
    SQLHDBC       DSCHandle;
    SQLHSTMT      StmtHandle[2];
    SQLCHAR       SQLStmt[100];
    SQLINTEGER    clobLocator;
    SQLINTEGER    Length;
    SQLUINTEGER   Position;
    SQLCHAR       *Buffer;
    SQLINTEGER    BuffSize;

    /* Allocate An Environment Handle */
    rc = SQLAllocEnv(&EnvHandle);

    /* Allocate A Connection Handle */
    rc = SQLAllocConnect(EnvHandle, &DSCHandle);

    /* Connect To The SAMPLE Database */
    rc = SQLConnect(DSCHandle, "SAMPLE", SQL_NTS, "etpdd6z", SQL_NTS,
                    "sanders", SQL_NTS);

    /* Allocate An SQL Statement Handle */
    rc = SQLAllocStmt(DSCHandle, &StmtHandle[0]);

    /* Allocate A Second SQL Statement Handle */
    rc = SQLAllocStmt(DSCHandle, &StmtHandle[1]);

    /* Define A SELECT SQL Statement */
    strcpy(SQLStmt, "SELECT RESUME FROM USERID.EMP_RESUME ");
    strcat(SQLStmt, "WHERE EMPNO = '000150' AND RESUME_FORMAT = ");
    strcat(SQLStmt, "'ascii'");

    /* Execute The SQL Statement */
    rc = SQLExecDirect(StmtHandle[0], SQLStmt, SQL_NTS);

    if (rc != SQL_ERROR)
        {
```

```
        /* Bind The Column In The Result Data Set To A Large Object */
        /* Locator                                                   */
        SQLBindCol(StmtHandle[0], 1, SQL_C_CLOB_LOCATOR, &clobLocator,
                   0, NULL);

        /* Retrieve The Record From The Result Data Set */
        rc = SQLFetch(StmtHandle[0]);
        if (rc != SQL_SUCCESS)
            goto EXIT;

        /* Get The Total Length Of The Resume Record */
        SQLGetLength(StmtHandle[1], SQL_C_CLOB_LOCATOR, clobLocator,
                     &Length, NULL);

        /* Get The Starting position Of The "Interests" Section */
        SQLGetPosition(StmtHandle[1], SQL_C_CLOB_LOCATOR, clobLocator,
                       0, "Interests", 9, 1, &Position,
                       NULL);

        /* Allocate A Memory Storage Buffer To Hold The */
        /* "Interests" Section Of The Resume            */
        Buffer = (SQLCHAR *) malloc(Length - Position + 1);

        /* Copy "Interests" Section Of The Resume Into The Buffer */
        SQLGetSubString(StmtHandle[1], SQL_C_CLOB_LOCATOR,
                        clobLocator, Position, Length - Position,
                        SQL_C_CHAR, Buffer, Length - Position + 1,
                        &BuffSize, NULL);

        /* Print Employee Number And The "Interests" Section Of The */
        /* Resume                                                    */
        printf("Employee Number = 000150\n\n");
        printf("%s\n", Buffer);

        /* Free The Allocated Memory Storage Buffer */
        free(Buffer);
        }

    /* Disconnect From The SAMPLE Database */
    SQLDisconnect(DSCHandle);

    /* Free The SQL Statement Handles */
    if (StmtHandle[0] != NULL)
        SQLFreeStmt(StmtHandle[0], SQL_DROP);

    if (StmtHandle[1] != NULL)
        SQLFreeStmt(StmtHandle[1], SQL_DROP);

    /* Free The Connection Handle */
    if (DSCHandle != NULL)
        SQLFreeConnect(DSCHandle);

    /* Free The Environment Handle */
    if (EnvHandle != NULL)
        SQLFreeEnv(EnvHandle);

    /* Return To The Operating System */
    return(rc);
}
```

The following C++ program illustrates how the SQLGetLength( ) function, SQL-GetPosition() function, and SQLGetSubString( ) can be used in a class method to retrieve a select portion of a LOB data item:

```
#include <iostream.h>
#include <string.h>
#include <sqlcli1.h>

/* Define The CLI Class */
class CLI
{
    /* Declare The Private Attribute Variables */
    private:
       SQLHENV        EnvHandle;
       SQLHDBC        DSCHandle;
       SQLINTEGER     clobLocator;
       SQLINTEGER     Length;
       SQLUINTEGER    Position;
       SQLCHAR        *Buffer;
       SQLINTEGER     BuffSize;

    /* Declare The Public Attribute Variables */
    public:
       SQLRETURN      rc;
       SQLHSTMT       StmtHandle[2];

    /* Declare The Member Function Prototypes */
    CLI();                                          // Constructor
    ~CLI();                                         // Destructor
    SQLRETURN Connect();
    SQLRETURN ShowInterests();
    SQLRETURN Disconnect();
} ;

/* Define The Class Constructor */
CLI::CLI()
{
    /* Initialize The Return Code Variable */
    rc = SQL_SUCCESS;

    /* Allocate An Environment Handle */
    rc = SQLAllocEnv(&EnvHandle);

    /* Allocate A Connection Handle */
    rc = SQLAllocConnect(EnvHandle, &DSCHandle);
}

/* Define The Class Destructor */
CLI::~CLI()
{
    /* Free The Connection Handle */
    if (DSCHandle != NULL)
        SQLFreeConnect(DSCHandle);

    /* Free The Environment Handle */
    if (EnvHandle != NULL)
        SQLFreeEnv(EnvHandle);
}
```

```
/* Define The Connect() Member Function */
SQLRETURN CLI::Connect()
{
    /* Connect To The SAMPLE Database */
    rc = SQLConnect(DSCHandle, (SQLCHAR *) "SAMPLE", SQL_NTS,
                    (SQLCHAR *) "etpdd6z", SQL_NTS,
                    (SQLCHAR *) "sanders", SQL_NTS);

    /* Allocate An SQL Statement Handle */
    rc = SQLAllocStmt(DSCHandle, &StmtHandle[0]);

    /* Return The CLI Function Return Code */
    return(rc);
}

/* Define The Disconnect() Member Function */
SQLRETURN CLI::Disconnect(void)
{
    /* Disconnect From The Database */
    rc = SQLDisconnect(DSCHandle);

    /* Free The SQL Statement Handle */
    if (StmtHandle[0] != NULL)
        SQLFreeStmt(StmtHandle[0], SQL_DROP);

    /* Return The CLI Function Return Code */
    return(rc);
}

/* Define The ShowInterests() Member Function */
SQLRETURN CLI::ShowInterests(void)
{
    /* Allocate An SQL Statement Handle */
    rc = SQLAllocStmt(DSCHandle, &StmtHandle[1]);

    /* Bind The Column In The Result Data Set To A Large Object */
    /* Locator                                                  */
    SQLBindCol(StmtHandle[0], 1, SQL_C_CLOB_LOCATOR, &clobLocator,
               0, NULL);

    /* Retrieve The Record From The Result Data Set */
    rc = SQLFetch(StmtHandle[0]);

    /* Get The Total Length Of The Resume Record */
    SQLGetLength(StmtHandle[1], SQL_C_CLOB_LOCATOR, clobLocator,
                 &Length, NULL);

    /* Get The Starting position Of The "Interests" Section */
    SQLGetPosition(StmtHandle[1], SQL_C_CLOB_LOCATOR, clobLocator,
                   0, (SQLCHAR *) "Tnterests", 9, 1, &Position,
                   NULL);

    /* Allocate A Memory Storage Buffer To Hold The "Interests" */
    /* Section Of The Resume                                    */
    Buffer = (SQLCHAR *) new char[Length - Position + 1];

    /* Copy "Interests" Section Of The Resume Into The Buffer */
    SQLGetSubString(StmtHandle[1], SQL_C_CLOB_LOCATOR,
                    clobLocator, Position, Length - Position,
                    SQL_C_CHAR, Buffer, Length - Position + 1,
                    &BuffSize, NULL);
```

```
    /* Print Employee Number And The "Interests" Section Of The */
    /* Resume                                                   */
    cout << "Employee Number = 000150" << endl << endl;
    cout << Buffer << endl;

    /* Free The Allocated Memory Storage Buffer */
    delete[] Buffer;

    /* Free The SQL Statement Handle */
    if (StmtHandle[1] != NULL)
        SQLFreeStmt(StmtHandle[1], SQL_DROP);

    /* Return The CLI Function Return Code */
    return(SQL_SUCCESS);
}

int main()
{
    /* Declare The Local Memory Variables */
    SQLRETURN  rc = SQL_SUCCESS;
    SQLCHAR    SQLStmt[100];

    /* Create An Instance Of The CLI Class */
    CLI Sample;

    /* Connect To The SAMPLE Database */
    if ((rc = Sample.Connect()) != SQL_SUCCESS)
        return(rc);

    /* Define A SELECT SQL Statement */
    strcpy((char *) SQLStmt, "SELECT RESUME FROM USERID.EMP_RESUME ");
    strcat((char *) SQLStmt, "WHERE EMPNO = '000150' AND ");
    strcat((char *) SQLStmt, "RESUME_FORMAT = 'ascii');

    /* Execute The SQL Statement */
    rc = SQLExecDirect(Sample.StmtHandle[0], SQLStmt, SQL_NTS);

    /* Copy The Results Of The SQL Query To An External File */
    if (rc == SQL_SUCCESS)
        Sample.ShowInterests();

    /* Disconnect From The SAMPLE Database */
    Sample.Disconnect();

    /* Return To The Operating System */
    return(rc);
}
```

SQLGetPosition

Purpose The SQLGetPosition( ) function retrieves the starting position of a specified string within a LOB value.

Syntax

```
SQLRETURN SQLGetPosition (SQLHSTMT        StmtHandle,
                          SQLSMALLINT     LocatorCDataType,
                          SQLINTEGER      SourceLocator,
                          SQLINTEGER      SearchLocator,
                          SQLCHAR FAR     *SearchLiteral,
```

```
SQLINTEGER          SearchLiteralSize,
SQLUINTEGER         FromPosition,
SQLUINTEGER FAR     *LocatedAt,
SQLINTEGER FAR      *IndicatorValue);
```

Parameters

StmtHandle The statement handle where the address of the SQL statement buffer is stored.

LocatorCDataType The C language data type of the LOB locator. The following C data types are supported:

- SQL_C_BLOB_LOCATOR
- SQL_C_CLOB_LOCATOR
- SQL_C_DBCLOB_LOCATOR

SourceLocator The LOB locator that references the source LOB data.

SearchLocator The LOB locator that references the search LOB data.

SearchLiteral A pointer to a location in memory where the search string literal is stored.

SearchLiteralSize The length of the search string literal value stored in the *SearchLiteral* parameter.

FromPosition The position (in the source LOB) of the first byte of the source string from which the search is to start.

LocatedAt A pointer to a location in memory where this function is to store the position (in the source LOB) where the string literal was located. If the string literal was not found, this value will be set to 0.

IndicatorValue Reserved (always set to zero).

Includes

```
#include <sqlcli1.h>
```

Description

The SQLGetPosition( ) function retrieves the starting position of a specified string within a LOB value. This function is used in conjunction with the SQLGetSubString( ) function to obtain any portion of a string from a LOB locator value. In order to use the SQLGetSubString( ) function, you must know the starting position of the substring within the overall LOB in advance. In situations where you can determine the starting position of a substring by searching the LOB value for the first word(s) or set of characters of that substring, you can use the SQLGetPosition( ) function to perform the search and return the starting position value.

Specifications

DB2 CLI 2.1

Return Codes

SQL_SUCCESS, SQL_SUCCESS_WITH_INFO, SQL_INVALID_HANDLE, SQL_ERROR

SQLSTATEs

07006, **08**S01, **40**003, **42**818, **58**004, **S1**001, **S1**009, **S1**010, **S1**013, **S1**090, **S1**C00, **S1**F01

Comments

- The specified search string can be either a LOB locator value or a literal string.
- Both the source LOB locator (*SourceLocator*) and the search LOB locator (*SearchLocator*) can be any LOB locator value returned from the data source by a SQLFetch( ), SQLExtendedFetch( ), or SQLGetSubString( ) function call made within the current transaction.
- The *SourceLocator* and *SearchLocator* parameters (if used) can contain any valid LOB locator that was not explicitly freed by the FREE LOCATOR statement or implicitly freed because the transaction in which the locator was created has terminated.

- If a search LOB locator is used, both the *SourceLocator* and the *SearchLocator* parameters must reference the same LOB locator C data type.
- The statement handle used by this function must not be associated with any prepared statements or catalog function calls.

Restrictions This function is not available when you are connected to DB2 data sources that do not support LOB data types. To determine whether or not this function is supported for the current data source connection, call the SQLGetFunctions( ) function with the *FunctionType* parameter set to SQL_API_SQLGETPOSITION and check the value of the *Exists* output parameter.

See Also SQLBindCol( ), SQLFetch( ), SQLExtendedFetch( ), SQLGetLength( ), SQLGetSubString( )

Examples See the examples provided for the SQLGetLength( ) function in this chapter.

SQLGetSubString

Purpose The SQLGetSubString( ) function retrieves a portion of a LOB value referenced by a LOB locator that was retrieved during the current transaction.

Syntax

```
SQLRETURN SQLGetSubString (SQLHSTMT          StmtHandle,
                           SQLSMALLINT       LocatorCDataType,
                           SQLINTEGER        SourceLocator,
                           SQLUINTEGER       FromPosition,
                           SQLUINTEGER       Size,
                           SQLSMALLINT       TargetCDataType,
                           SQLPOINTER        SubString,
                           SQLINTEGER        SubStringMaxSize,
                           SQLINTEGER FAR    *SubStringSize,
                           SQLINTEGER FAR    IndicatorValue);
```

Parameters

StmtHandle The statement handle where the address of the SQL statement buffer is stored.

LocatorCDataType The C language data type of the LOB locator. The following C data types are supported:

- SQL_C_BLOB_LOCATOR
- SQL_C_CLOB_LOCATOR
- SQL_C_DBCLOB_LOCATOR

SourceLocator The LOB locator that references the source LOB.

FromPosition The position (in the LOB) of the first byte to be returned by this function.

Size The length of the string to be returned by this function.

TargetCDataType The C language data type of the string variable or LOB locator that will be used to store the substring value. The following C data types are supported:

- SQL_C_BINARY
- SQL_C_BLOB_LOCATOR
- SQL_C_CHAR

- SQL_C_CLOB_LOCATOR
- SQL_C_DBCHAR
- SQL_C_DBCLOB_LOCATOR

SubString A pointer to a location in memory where this function is to store the retrieved substring value (or LOB locator value).

SubStringMaxSize The maximum size of the memory storage buffer where this function is to store the retrieved substring (or LOB locator).

SubStringSize A pointer to a location in memory where this function is to store the actual number of bytes written to the *SubString* memory storage buffer.

IndicatorValue Reserved (always set to zero).

Includes

```
#include <sqlcli1.h>
```

Description

The SQLGetSubString( ) function retrieves a portion of a LOB value referenced by a LOB locator value that was retrieved (as a result of a fetch or a SQLGetSubString( ) function call) during the current transaction. When any portion of a string represented by a LOB locator is retrieved, the result can be placed in an appropriate C string variable, or you can create a new LOB value on the connected data source and place the result there with another LOB locator.

Specifications

DB2 CLI 2.1

Return Codes

SQL_SUCCESS, SQL_SUCCESS_WITH_INFO, SQL_INVALID_HANDLE, SQL_ERROR

SQLSTATEs

01004, **07**006, **08**S01, **22**011, **40**003, **58**004, **S1**001, **S1**003, **S1**009, **S1**010, **S1**013, **S1**090, **S1**C00, **0F**001

Comments

- You can use SQLGetSubString( ) as an alternative to the SQLGetData( ) function to retrieve data. In this case, a column is bound to a LOB locator, which is then used to by the SQLGetSubString( ) function to fetch the LOB value as a whole or in pieces.
- The *SourceLocator* parameter can contain any valid LOB locator that was not explicitly freed by the FREE LOCATOR statement or implicitly freed because the transaction in which the locator was created has terminated.
- The statement handle used by this function must not be associated with any prepared statements or catalog function calls.

Restrictions

This function is not available when you are connected to DB2 data sources that do not support LOB data types. To determine whether or not the function is supported for the current data source connection, call the SQLGetFunctions( ) function with the *FunctionType* parameter set to SQL_API_SQLGETSUBSTRING and check the value of the *Exists* output parameter.

See Also

SQLBindCol( ), SQLFetch( ), SQLExtendedFetch( ), SQLGetData( ), SQLGetLength( ), SQLGetPosition( )

Examples

See the examples provided for the SQLGetLength( ) function in this chapter.

CHAPTER 17

CLI/ODBC DATA SOURCE SYSTEM CATALOG QUERY FUNCTIONS

The SQL CLI/ODBC data source system catalog query functions are a group of DB2 CLI function calls that can retrieve information from the system catalog of the current connected data source. This group includes:

- CLI functions that retrieve information about tables defined for the data source.
- CLI functions that retrieve information about columns defined for tables in the data source.
- CLI functions that retrieve information about indexes, primary keys, and foreign keys defined for tables in the data source.
- CLI functions that retrieve information about stored procedures that can be executed against the data source.

Table 17.1 lists the SQL CLI/ODBC data source system catalog query functions available with DB2 CLI.

Obtaining System Catalog Information

17

It is often necessary for a CLI application to retrieve information about the data source (database) to which it is connected. Although queries can be issued against the data source system catalog tables themselves, DB2 CLI provides a set of functions, known as the catalog functions, that are specifically designed to interact with the current connected data source's system catalog. By using these generic interface functions, an application can avoid having to rely on one or more catalog queries specific to data source products and product releases.

Calling the catalog functions is conceptually equivalent to using the SQLExecDirect( ) function to execute a SELECT SQL statement against the system catalog tables. The result data set produced when a catalog function executes is returned to the application via a SQL statement handle. After calling one of these functions, the application can retrieve (fetch) individual rows of data from the result data set as it would process column data from any other result data set. The catalog functions operate by returning to the application a result data set through a statement handle.

The columns in the result data set returned by a catalog function are defined in a specified order so, in future releases, other columns can be added to the end of each defined result data set. Therefore, applications that interact with these result data sets should be written so they will not be affected by any future changes to the DB2 CLI catalog functions.

TABLE 17.1 CLI/ODBC Data Source System Catalog Query Functions

Function name	Description
SQLTables( )	Retrieves a list of table names defined for a data source.
SQLTablePrivileges( )	Retrieves a list of table names, along with the authorization information associated with those tables, that are defined for a data source.
SQLColumns( )	Retrieves a list of column names found in a specified table.
SQLColumnPrivileges( )	Retrieves a list of column names, along with the authorization information associated with those columns, that are defined for a specified table.
SQLSpecialColumns( )	Retrieves information about the optimal set of columns that uniquely identify a row of data in a specified table.
SQLStatistics( )	Retrieves statistical information about a specified table along with a list of associated indexes for that table.
SQLPrimaryKeys( )	Retrieves a list of column names that comprise the primary key for a specified table.
SQLForeignKeys( )	Retrieves a list of column names that comprise foreign keys for a specified table.
SQLProcedures( )	Generates a list of stored procedure names stored in and available for a data source.
SQLProcedureColumns( )	Retrieves a list of input and output parameters associated with a specified stored procedure.

Adapted from IBM's Database 2 Call Level Interface Guide and Reference, Table 11, pages 103 to 106.

The execution of some catalog functions can result in the subsequent execution of fairly complex queries. Because of this, call catalog functions only when necessary. If the data produced by the execution of a catalog function will be used several times, an application can improve its overall performance by calling the catalog function once and saving the returned information, rather than making repeated calls to obtain the same information.

Controlling Catalog Function Results with Parameter Values

All the catalog functions have CatalogName and SchemaName (and their associated lengths) in their input parameter list. Other input arguments include TableName, ColumnName, and ProcedureName (and their associated lengths). These input parameters (arguments) either identify or constrain the amount of information that will be returned when the catalog function is executed.

> Note: CatalogName must always be a null pointer (with its length set to 0) since DB2 CLI does not support three-part naming conventions.

Each of these parameters should be treated as either ordinary or pattern-value parameters. Ordinary parameters accept ordinary string values and identify the information the catalog function is to retrieve. Ordinary parameter values are taken literally and the case of the letters in the string is significant. Pattern-value parameters accept both ordinary strings and string patterns containing wildcards, and constrain the size of the result data set returned by acting as though the underlying query were qualified by a WHERE clause (the WHERE clause being the string pattern to match rows against during data retrieval). If a null pointer is provided as pattern-value parameter input, the function will execute as if there are no restrictions on the result data set (as if there is no WHERE clause). If a catalog function has two or more pattern-value parameters, they will be treated as though the WHERE clauses in the underlying query were joined by AND. In this case, a data row will appear in the result data set only if it meets all the conditions of each WHERE clause.

Obtaining Information About Existing Stored Procedures

You saw in Part 3 of this book, STRUCTURED QUERY LANGUAGE (SQL) STATEMENTS, that an application can be designed to run in two parts: one part executing on the client workstation and the other part executing on the server workstation where the database physically resides. A stored procedure is the part that runs at the database within the same transaction as the application. You can invoke stored procedures from a DB2 CLI application by passing the appropriate CALL statement to the data source with either the SQLExecDirect( ) or SQLPrepare( ) function, followed by the SQLExecute( ) function. Although the CALL statement cannot be prepared dynamically by the data source, DB2 CLI will accept the CALL statement as if it can be.

If the data source is DB2 for Common Servers (version 2.1 or later) or DB2 for MVS/ESA (version 4.1 or later), a CLI application can call the SQLProcedures( ) function to obtain a list of stored procedures that are available for execution against the database.

> Note: For DB2 for Common Servers, the SQLProcedures( ) function might not return every available stored procedure. However, DB2 CLI applications can call any valid stored procedure, regardless of whether or not it is returned by an SQLProcedures( ) function call.

If a stored procedure needs information from the calling application, input parameter markers corresponding to the arguments for the stored procedure must be coded in the CALL SQL statement. These parameter markers in the CALL statement are then bound to application variables with the SQLBindParameter( ) function. Although stored procedure arguments can be used both for input and output, an application should specify the parameter type when the SQLBindParameter( ) function is called. This avoids sending unnecessary data between the client and server. If the data source is DB2 for Common Servers (version 2.1 or later) or DB2 for MVS/ESA (version 4.1 or later), the application can call the SQLProcedureColumns( ) function to determine the type of a parameter used in the stored procedure call.

Stored Procedures Catalog Table

With DB2 for Common Servers, a pseudo catalog table (DB2CLI.PROCEDURES) used for stored procedure registration must be created and populated before the SQLProcedures( ) function and the SQLProcedureColumns( ) function can be called; otherwise, these catalog function calls will return empty result data sets. A DB2 command-line processor script that creates this table (STORPROC.DDL) is provided in the misc subdirectory of the **sqllib** directory where DB2 was installed. A second DB2 command-line processor script that populates this table with information about three sample stored procedures (STORPROC.XMP) is also provided in the misc subdirectory of the sqllib directory where DB2 was installed. Refer to the header portions of these files for information on how to use them. You must follow the syntax rules exactly when populating this table; otherwise, the SQLProcedureColumns( ) function call will result in an error.

If the stored procedure resides on a DB2 for MVS/ESA (version 4.1 or later) server, the name of the stored procedure must be defined in the SYSIBM.SYSPROCEDURES catalog table. The pseudo catalog table used by DB2 for Common Servers is a derivation and extension of the DB2 for MVS/ESA SYSIBM.SYSPROCEDURES catalog table. If the stored procedure resides on a DB2 for OS/400 (version 3.1) server, the application must know the actual path and name of the stored procedure ahead of time since there is no real or pseudo catalog table available from which to retrieve information about stored procedures or their argument list.

SQLTables

Purpose

The SQLTables( ) function retrieves a list of table names (and associated information) stored in the system catalog of the current connected data source.

Syntax

```
SQLRETURN SQLTables (SQLHSTMT     StmtHandle,
                     SQLCHAR FAR *CatalogName,
                     SQLSMALLINT CatalogNameSize,
                     SQLCHAR FAR *SchemaName,
                     SQLSMALLINT SchemaNameSize,
                     SQLCHAR FAR *TableName,
                     SQLSMALLINT TableNameSize,
                     SQLCHAR FAR *TableType,
                     SQLSMALLINT TableTypeSize);
```

Parameters

StmtHandle The statement handle where the address of the SQL statement buffer is stored.

CatalogName A pointer to a location in memory where the catalog qualifier of a three-part table name is stored. For DB2, this must be a null pointer or a zero-length string.

CatalogNameSize The length of the catalog qualifier value stored in the *CatalogName* parameter. For DB2, this parameter must be set to 0.

SchemaName A pointer to a location in memory where the schema name of a three-part table name is stored.

SchemaNameSize The length of the schema name value stored in the *SchemaName* parameter.

TableName A pointer to a location in memory where the table name is stored.

TableNameSize The length of the table name value stored in the *TableName* parameter.

TableType A pointer to a location in memory where the table type is stored. Any of the following table types can be specified:

- TABLE
- VIEW
- ALIAS
- SYNONYM
- SYSTEM TABLE

If a null pointer is specified for this parameter, all of these table types will be used.

TableTypeSize The length of the table type value stored in the *TableType* parameter. If 0 is specified for this parameter, all table types listed under the *TableType* parameter will be used.

Includes

```
#include <sqlcli1.h>
```

Description

The SQLTables( ) function retrieves a list of table names (and associated information) stored in the system catalog of the current connected data source (database). The information returned by this function is placed in a SQL result data set and can be processed with the same functions that process a result data set generated by a query. Table 17.2 lists the columns in this result data set.

TABLE 17.2 Result Data Set Returned by SQLTables( )

Column	Column name	Data type	Description
1	TABLE_CAT	VARCHAR(128)	The name of the system catalog table in which the TABLE_SCHEM value is stored. Since DB2 does not support three-part table names, DB2 CLI always sets this column to NULL.
2	TABLE_SCHEM	VARCHAR(128)	The name of the schema that contains the TABLE_NAME value.
3	TABLE_NAME	VARCHAR(128)	The name of the table, view, alias, or synonym.
4	TABLE_TYPE	VARCHAR(128)	Identifies the type of object name provided in the TABLE_NAME column. Valid values for this column are: TABLE, VIEW, INOPERATIVE VIEW, SYSTEM TABLE, ALIAS, and SYNONYM.
5	REMARKS	VARCHAR(254)	Descriptive information about the table.

Adapted from IBM's Database 2 Call Level Interface Guide and Reference, Table 145, page 386.

Note: To determine the type of access permitted on any given table in the result data set produced by this function, call the SQLTablePrivileges( ) function. If you do not use the SQLTablePrivileges( ) function to obtain table authorization information, you must code the application so it can handle situations where users select a table for which they have not been granted SELECT privileges.

Specifications DB2 CLI 2.1, ODBC 1.0, X/OPEN CLI

Return Codes SQL_SUCCESS, SQL_SUCCESS_WITH_INFO, SQL_INVALID_HANDLE, SQL_ERROR

SQLSTATEs **08**S01, **24**000, **40**003, **S1**001, **S1**010, **S1**014, **S1**090, **S1**C00, **S1**T00

Comments

- Since the SQLTables( ) function often maps to a complex and therefore expensive query against the database system catalog tables, use it sparingly. If you need to use the produced result data set more than once, save it rather than regenerating it by invoking the SQLTables( ) function again.
- The *CatalogName*, *SchemaName*, and *TableName* parameters can accept the following search pattern values:

The underscore character (_) Indicates that any single character can be used in place of the underscore character.
The percent character (%) Indicates that any sequence of 0 or more characters can be used in place of the percent character.

If these "wildcard" characters need to be used as themselves (e.g., % = "%"), they must be preceded by an escape character.

- To retrieve a list of valid schema names in the specified data source, store a string containing a single percent character (%) in the *SchemaName* parameter value and set the *CatalogName* and the *TableName* parameter values to empty strings.
- To retrieve a list of valid table types for the specified data source, store a string containing a single percent character in the *TableType* parameter and set the *CatalogName*, *SchemaName*, and the *TableName* parameter values to empty strings. (In this case, all columns in the result data set, except for the TABLE_TYPE column, will contain a NULL value.)
- If the *TableType* parameter does not contain an empty string, it must contain a list of uppercase, comma-separated values that specify the table types for which to retrieve information. Each value in this list can be either enclosed in single quotations or left unquoted. For example, either 'TABLE', 'VIEW' or TABLE, VIEW are valid.
- If the current data source does not support nor recognize a specified table type, no information will be returned for that particular table type.
- This function can be called with null pointers specified for any or all of the following parameters: *SchemaName*, *TableName*, and *TableType*. In this case, no attempt is made to restrict the returned result data set. For data sources that contain a large quantity of tables, views, aliases, etc., this scenario will map to an expensive query (very long retrieval times) against the database system catalog tables, which will produce an extremely large result data set. You can specify three keywords (SCHEMALIST, SYSCHEMA, and TABLETYPE) in the CLI initialization file to help restrict the result data set returned when null pointers are supplied as values for either the *SchemaName* or the *TableType* parameter. If null pointer values are not supplied for either the *SchemaName* or the *TableType* parameter, the associated keyword specification in the CLI initialization file will be ignored.
- The result data set returned by this function is ordered by TABLE_TYPE, TABLE_CAT, TABLE_SCHEM, and TABLE_NAME.
- The VARCHAR columns of the catalog functions result data set have been declared with a maximum length of 128 characters to be consistent with the SQL92 standard limits. Since DB2 names are less than 128 characters, an application can choose to always set aside 128 characters (plus the null terminator) for the output buffer, or alternatively to allocate only the required amount of memory by first calling the SQLGetInfo( ) function with the *InfoType* parameter set to SQL_MAX_CATALOG_NAME_LEN, SQL_MAX_OWNER_SCHEMA_LEN, SQL_MAX_NAME_LEN, and/or SQL_MAX_COLUMN_NAME_LEN to determine (respectively) the actual lengths of the TABLE_CAT, TABLE_SCHEM, TABLE_NAME, and COLUMN_NAME columns supported by the current data source connection.
- Although new columns might be added and the names of the existing columns in the result data set might be changed in future releases of DB2 CLI, the position of the current columns in this data set will not change.

Restrictions There are no restrictions associated with this function call.

See Also SQLTablePrivileges( ), SQLColumns( )

Examples The following C program illustrates how to use the SQLTables( ) function to obtain information about tables that are available in the current connected data source:

```
#include <stdio.h>
#include <stdlib.h>
#include <sqlcli1.h>

int main()
{
    /* Declare The Local Memory Variables */
    SQLRETURN    rc = SQL_SUCCESS;
    SQLHENV      EnvHandle;
    SQLHDBC      DSCHandle;
    SQLHSTMT     StmtHandle;
    SQLCHAR      TableName[129];
    SQLCHAR      TableType[129];

    /* Allocate An Environment Handle */
    rc = SQLAllocEnv(&EnvHandle);

    /* Allocate A Connection Handle */
    rc = SQLAllocConnect(EnvHandle, &DSCHandle);

    /* Connect To The SAMPLE Database */
    rc = SQLConnect(DSCHandle, "SAMPLE", SQL_NTS, "etpdd6z", SQL_NTS,
                    "sanders", SQL_NTS);

    /* Allocate An SQL Statement Handle */
    rc = SQLAllocStmt(DSCHandle, &StmtHandle);

    /* Obtain A List Of Table Names For A Specified Schema */
    rc = SQLTables(StmtHandle, NULL, 0, "USERID", SQL_NTS, NULL,
                   0, NULL, 0);

    if (rc != SQL_ERROR)
        {
        /* Bind The Columns In The Result Data Set To Local */
        /* Storage Variables                                 */
        SQLBindCol(StmtHandle, 3, SQL_C_CHAR, (SQLPOINTER) TableName,
                   sizeof(TableName), NULL);

        SQLBindCol(StmtHandle, 4, SQL_C_CHAR, (SQLPOINTER) TableType,
                   sizeof(TableType), NULL);

        /* Retrieve And Display The Results */
        printf("Table Name      Type\n");
        printf("--------------------\n");
        while (rc != SQL_NO_DATA_FOUND)
            {

            /* Retrieve A Record From The Result Data Set */
            rc = SQLFetch(StmtHandle);

            /* Print The Information Retrieved */
            if (rc != SQL_NO_DATA_FOUND)
                printf("%-15s %s\n", TableName, TableType);
            }
        }

    /* Disconnect From The SAMPLE Database */
    SQLDisconnect(DSCHandle);

    /* Free The SQL Statement Handle */
    if (StmtHandle != NULL)
        SQLFreeStmt(StmtHandle, SQL_DROP);
```

```
    /* Free The Connection Handle */
    if (DSCHandle != NULL)
        SQLFreeConnect(DSCHandle);

    /* Free The Environment Handle */
    if (EnvHandle != NULL)
        SQLFreeEnv(EnvHandle);

    /* Return To The Operating System */
    return(rc);
}
```

The following C++ program illustrates how the SQLTables( ) function is used by class methods to obtain information about tables that are available in the current connected data source:

```
#include <iostream.h>
#include <string.h>
#include <sqlcli1.h>

/* Define The CLI Class */
class CLI
{
    /* Declare The Private Attribute Variables */
    private:
       SQLHENV      EnvHandle;
       SQLHDBC      DSCHandle;
       SQLHSTMT     StmtHandle;
       SQLCHAR      TableName[129];
       SQLCHAR      TableType[129];

    /* Declare The Public Attribute Variables */
    public:
       SQLRETURN  rc;

    /* Declare The Member Function Prototypes */
    CLI();                                  // Constructor
    ~CLI();                                 // Destructor
    SQLRETURN Connect();
    SQLRETURN ShowTables();
    SQLRETURN Disconnect();
} ;

/* Define The Class Constructor */
CLI::CLI()
{
    /* Initialize The Return Code Variable */
    rc = SQL_SUCCESS;

    /* Allocate An Environment Handle */
    rc = SQLAllocEnv(&EnvHandle);

    /* Allocate A Connection Handle */
    rc = SQLAllocConnect(EnvHandle, &DSCHandle);
}

/* Define The Class Destructor */
CLI::~CLI()
{
    /* Free The Connection Handle */
    if (DSCHandle != NULL)
        SQLFreeConnect(DSCHandle);
```

```
    /* Free The Environment Handle */
    if (EnvHandle != NULL)
        SQLFreeEnv(EnvHandle);
}

/* Define The Connect() Member Function */
SQLRETURN CLI::Connect()
{
    /* Connect To The SAMPLE Database */
    rc = SQLConnect(DSCHandle, (SQLCHAR *) "SAMPLE", SQL_NTS,
                    (SQLCHAR *) "etpdd6z", SQL_NTS,
                    (SQLCHAR *) "sanders", SQL_NTS);

    /* Allocate An SQL Statement Handle */
    rc = SQLAllocStmt(DSCHandle, &StmtHandle);

    /* Return The CLI Function Return Code */
    return(rc);
}

/* Define The Disconnect() Member Function */
SQLRETURN CLI::Disconnect(void)
{
    /* Disconnect From The Database */
    rc = SQLDisconnect(DSCHandle);

    /* Free The SQL Statement Handle */
    if (StmtHandle != NULL)
        SQLFreeStmt(StmtHandle, SQL_DROP);

    /* Return The CLI Function Return Code */
    return(rc);
}

/* Define The ShowTables() Member Function */
SQLRETURN CLI::ShowTables(void)
{
    /* Obtain A List Of Table Names For A Specified Schema */
    rc = SQLTables(StmtHandle, NULL, 0, (SQLCHAR *) "USERID",
                   SQL_NTS, NULL, 0, NULL, 0);

    if (rc != SQL_ERROR)
        {
        /* Bind The Columns In The Result Data Set To Local */
        /* Storage Variables                                */
        SQLBindCol(StmtHandle, 3, SQL_C_CHAR, (SQLPOINTER) TableName,
                   sizeof(TableName), NULL);

        SQLBindCol(StmtHandle, 4, SQL_C_CHAR, (SQLPOINTER) TableType,
                   sizeof(TableType), NULL);

        /* Retrieve And Display The Results */
        cout << "Table Name      Type" << endl;
        cout << "---------------------" << endl;
        while (rc != SQL_NO_DATA_FOUND)
            {

            /* Retrieve A Table Name */
            rc = SQLFetch(StmtHandle);

            /* Retrieve A Record From The Result Data Set */
            if (rc != SQL_NO_DATA_FOUND)
                {
```

```
                    cout.setf(ios::left);
                    cout.width(16);
                    cout << TableName << TableType << endl;
                    }
                }
            }

    /* Return The CLI Function Return Code */
    return(rc);
}

int main()
{
    /* Declare The Local Memory Variables */
    SQLRETURN  rc = SQL_SUCCESS;

    /* Create An Instance Of The CLI Class */
    CLI Sample;

    /* Connect To The SAMPLE Database */
    if ((rc = Sample.Connect()) != SQL_SUCCESS)
        return(rc);

    /* Display A List Of All Tables In The USERID Schema */
    Sample.ShowTables();

    /* Disconnect From The SAMPLE Database */
    Sample.Disconnect();

    /* Return To The Operating System */
    return(rc);
}
```

SQLTablePrivileges

Purpose The SQLTablePrivileges( ) function retrieves a list of table names and the privileges associated with them that is stored in the system catalog of the current connected data source (database).

Syntax

```
SQLRETURN SQLTablePrivileges (SQLHSTMT    StmtHandle,
                              SQLCHAR FAR *CatalogName,
                              SQLSMALLINT CatalogNameSize,
                              SQLCHAR FAR *SchemaName,
                              SQLSMALLINT SchemaNameSize,
                              SQLCHAR FAR *TableName,
                              SQLSMALLINT TableNameSize);
```

Parameters

StmtHandle The statement handle where the address of the SQL statement buffer is stored.

CatalogName A pointer to a location in memory where the catalog qualifier of a three-part table name is stored. For DB2, this must be a null pointer or a zero-length string.

CatalogNameSize The length of the catalog qualifier value stored in the *CatalogName* parameter. For DB2, this parameter must be set to 0.

SchemaName A pointer to a location in memory where the schema name of a three-part table name is stored.

SchemaNameSize The length of the schema name value stored in the *SchemaName* parameter.
TableName A pointer to a location in memory where the table name is stored.
TableNameSize The length of the table name value stored in the *TableName* parameter.

Includes

```
#include <sqlcli1.h>
```

Description The SQLTablePrivileges( ) function retrieves a list of table names and the privileges associated with them that is stored in the system catalog of the connected data source (database). The information returned by this function is placed in a SQL result data set, and can be processed with the same functions that process a result data set generated by a query. Table 17.3 lists the columns in this result data set.

TABLE 17.3 Result Data Set Returned by SQLTablePrivileges( )

Column #	Column name	Data type	Description
1	TABLE_CAT	VARCHAR(128)	The name of the system catalog table in which the TABLE_SCHEM value is stored. Since DB2 does not support three-part table names, DB2 CLI will always set this column to NULL.
2	TABLE_SCHEM	VARCHAR(128)	The name of the schema that contains the TABLE_NAME value.
3	TABLE_NAME	VARCHAR(128) NOT NULL	The name of the database table.
4	GRANTOR	VARCHAR(128)	The authorization ID of the user who granted the privilege.
5	GRANTEE	VARCHAR(128)	The authorization ID of the user to whom the privilege is granted.
6	PRIVILEGE	VARCHAR(128)	The table privilege that was granted. Valid values for this column are: ALTER, CONTROL, INDEX, DELETE, INSERT, REFERENCES, SELECT, and UPDATE.
7	IS_GRANTABLE	VARCHAR(3)	Indicates whether or not the grantee is permitted to grant the privilege to other users. Valid values for this column are: YES, NO, and NULL.

Adapted from IBM's Database 2 Call Level Interface Guide and Reference, Table 142, page 381.

Specifications DB2 CLI 2.1, ODBC 1.0

Return Codes SQL_SUCCESS, SQL_SUCCESS_WITH_INFO, SQL_INVALID_HANDLE, SQL_ERROR

SQLSTATEs **08**S01, **24**000, **40**003, **S1**001, **S1**010, **S1**014, **S1**090, **S1**C00, **S1**T00

Comments

- Since the SQLTablePrivileges( ) function often maps to a complex and therefore expensive query against the database system catalog tables, use it sparingly. If you need to use the produced result data set more than once, save it rather than regenerating it by invoking the SQLTablePrivileges( ) function again.

- The *CatalogName*, *SchemaName*, and *TableName* parameters can accept the following search pattern values:

The underscore character (_) Indicates that any single character can be used in place of the underscore character.
The percent character (%) Indicates that any sequence of 0 or more characters can be used in place of the percent character.

If these "wildcard" characters need to be used as themselves (e.g., % = "%"), they must be preceded by an escape character.

- The granularity of each privilege reported by this function might apply at the column level. With some data sources, for example, if a table can be updated, every column in that table can also be updated. For other data sources, you must call the SQLColumnPrivileges( ) function to determine whether or not the individual columns of a table have the same privileges as the table.
- The result data set returned by this function is ordered by TABLE_CAT, TABLE_SCHEM, TABLE_NAME, and PRIVILEGE.
- The VARCHAR columns of the catalog functions result data set have been declared with a maximum length of 128 characters to be consistent with the SQL92 standard limits. Since DB2 names are less than 128 characters, an application can choose to always set aside 128 characters (plus the null terminator) for the output buffer, or alternatively allocate only the required amount of memory by first calling the SQLGetInfo( ) function with the *InfoType* parameter set to SQL_MAX_CATALOG_NAME_LEN, SQL_MAX_OWNER_SCHEMA_LEN, SQL_MAX_NAME_LEN, and/or SQL_MAX_COLUMN_NAME_LEN to determine (respectively) the actual lengths of the TABLE_CAT, TABLE_SCHEM, TABLE_NAME, and COLUMN_NAME columns supported by the current data source connection.
- Although new columns might be added and the names of the existing columns in the result data set might be changed in future releases of DB2 CLI, the position of the current columns in this data set will not change.

Restrictions There are no restrictions associated with this function call.

See Also SQLTables( ), SQLColumnPrivileges( )

Examples The following C program illustrates how to use the SQLTablePrivileges( ) function to obtain authorization information about a specific table in the current connected data source:

```
#include <stdio.h>
#include <stdlib.h>
#include <sqlcli1.h>

int main()
{
    /* Declare The Local Memory Variables */
    SQLRETURN     rc = SQL_SUCCESS;
    SQLHENV       EnvHandle;
    SQLHDBC       DSCHandle;
    SQLHSTMT      StmtHandle;
    SQLCHAR       TableName[129];
    SQLCHAR       Grantee[129];
    SQLCHAR       Privilege[129];
```

```
    /* Allocate An Environment Handle */
    rc = SQLAllocEnv(&EnvHandle);

    /* Allocate A Connection Handle */
    rc = SQLAllocConnect(EnvHandle, &DSCHandle);

    /* Connect To The SAMPLE Database */
    rc = SQLConnect(DSCHandle, "SAMPLE", SQL_NTS, "etpdd6z", SQL_NTS,
                    "sanders", SQL_NTS);

    /* Allocate An SQL Statement Handle */
    rc = SQLAllocStmt(DSCHandle, &StmtHandle);

    /* Obtain A List Of Table Privileges For A Specified Schema */
    rc = SQLTablePrivileges(StmtHandle, NULL, 0, "USERID", SQL_NTS,
                            "EMP_R%", SQL_NTS);

    if (rc != SQL_ERROR)
        {
        /* Bind The Columns In The Result Data Set To Local */
        /* Storage Variables                                */
        SQLBindCol(StmtHandle, 3, SQL_C_CHAR, (SQLPOINTER) TableName,
                   sizeof(TableName), NULL);

        SQLBindCol(StmtHandle, 5, SQL_C_CHAR, (SQLPOINTER) Grantee,
                   sizeof(Grantee), NULL);

        SQLBindCol(StmtHandle, 6, SQL_C_CHAR, (SQLPOINTER) Privilege,
                   sizeof(Privilege), NULL);

        /* Retrieve And Display The Results */
        printf("Table Name      Privilege       Grantee\n");
        printf("---------------------------------------\n");
        while (rc != SQL_NO_DATA_FOUND)
            {

            /* Retrieve A Record From The Result Data Set */
            rc = SQLFetch(StmtHandle);

            /* Print The Information Retrieved */
            if (rc != SQL_NO_DATA_FOUND)
                printf("%-15s %-15s %s\n", TableName, Privilege,
                       Grantee);
            }
        }

    /* Disconnect From The SAMPLE Database */
    SQLDisconnect(DSCHandle);

    /* Free The SQL Statement Handle */
    if (StmtHandle != NULL)
        SQLFreeStmt(StmtHandle, SQL_DROP);

    /* Free The Connection Handle */
    if (DSCHandle != NULL)
        SQLFreeConnect(DSCHandle);

    /* Free The Environment Handle */
    if (EnvHandle != NULL)
        SQLFreeEnv(EnvHandle);

    /* Return To The Operating System */
    return(rc);
}
```

The following C++ program illustrates how the SQLTablePrivileges( ) function is used by class methods to obtain authorization information about a specific table in the current connected data source:

```
#include <iostream.h>
#include <string.h>
#include <sqlcli1.h>

/* Define The CLI Class */
class CLI
{
    /* Declare The Private Attribute Variables */
    private:
       SQLHENV       EnvHandle;
       SQLHDBC       DSCHandle;
       SQLHSTMT      StmtHandle;
       SQLCHAR       TableName[129];
       SQLCHAR       Grantee[129];
       SQLCHAR       Privilege[129];

    /* Declare The Public Attribute Variables */
    public:
       SQLRETURN  rc;

    /* Declare The Member Function Prototypes */
    CLI();                                         // Constructor
    ~CLI();                                        // Destructor
    SQLRETURN Connect();
    SQLRETURN ShowTablePrivileges();
    SQLRETURN Disconnect();
} ;

/* Define The Class Constructor */
CLI::CLI()
{
    /* Initialize The Return Code Variable */
    rc = SQL_SUCCESS;

    /* Allocate An Environment Handle */
    rc = SQLAllocEnv(&EnvHandle);

    /* Allocate A Connection Handle */
    rc = SQLAllocConnect(EnvHandle, &DSCHandle);
}

/* Define The Class Destructor */
CLI::~CLI()
{
    /* Free The Connection Handle */
    if (DSCHandle != NULL)
        SQLFreeConnect(DSCHandle);

    /* Free The Environment Handle */
    if (EnvHandle != NULL)
        SQLFreeEnv(EnvHandle);
}

/* Define The Connect() Member Function */
SQLRETURN CLI::Connect()
{
```

```
    /* Connect To The SAMPLE Database */
    rc = SQLConnect(DSCHandle, (SQLCHAR *) "SAMPLE", SQL_NTS,
                    (SQLCHAR *) "etpdd6z", SQL_NTS,
                    (SQLCHAR *) "sanders", SQL_NTS);

    /* Allocate An SQL Statement Handle */
    rc = SQLAllocStmt(DSCHandle, &StmtHandle);

    /* Return The CLI Function Return Code */
    return(rc);
}

/* Define The Disconnect() Member Function */
SQLRETURN CLI::Disconnect(void)
{
    /* Disconnect From The Database */
    rc = SQLDisconnect(DSCHandle);

    /* Free The SQL Statement Handle */
    if (StmtHandle != NULL)
        SQLFreeStmt(StmtHandle, SQL_DROP);

    /* Return The CLI Function Return Code */
    return(rc);
}

/* Define The ShowTablePrivileges() Member Function */
SQLRETURN CLI::ShowTablePrivileges(void)
{
    /* Obtain A List Of Table Privileges For A Specified Schema */
    rc = SQLTablePrivileges(StmtHandle, NULL, 0, (SQLCHAR *) "USERID",
                            SQL_NTS, (SQLCHAR *) "EMP_R%", SQL_NTS);

    if (rc != SQL_ERROR)
        {
        /* Bind The Columns In The Result Data Set To Local */
        /* Storage Variables                                */
        SQLBindCol(StmtHandle, 3, SQL_C_CHAR, (SQLPOINTER) TableName,
                   sizeof(TableName), NULL);

        SQLBindCol(StmtHandle, 5, SQL_C_CHAR, (SQLPOINTER) Grantee,
                   sizeof(Grantee), NULL);

        SQLBindCol(StmtHandle, 6, SQL_C_CHAR, (SQLPOINTER) Privilege,
                   sizeof(Privilege), NULL);

        /* Retrieve And Display The Results */
        cout << "Table Name      Privilege       Grantee" << endl;
        cout << "---------------------------------------" << endl;
        while (rc != SQL_NO_DATA_FOUND)
            {

            /* Retrieve A Record From The Result Data Set */
            rc = SQLFetch(StmtHandle);

            /* Print The Information Retrieved */
            /* Print The Information Retrieved */
            if (rc != SQL_NO_DATA_FOUND)
                {
                cout.setf(ios::left);
```

```
                    cout.width(16);
                    cout << TableName;
                    cout.setf(ios::left);
                    cout.width(16);
                    cout << Privilege << Grantee << endl;
                    }
                }
            }

        /* Return The CLI Function Return Code */
        return(rc);
}

int main()
{
        /* Declare The Local Memory Variables */
        SQLRETURN  rc = SQL_SUCCESS;

        /* Create An Instance Of The CLI Class */
        CLI Sample;

        /* Connect To The SAMPLE Database */
        if ((rc = Sample.Connect()) != SQL_SUCCESS)
            return(rc);

        /* Display A List Of Selected Table Privileges */
        Sample.ShowTablePrivileges();

        /* Disconnect From The SAMPLE Database */
        Sample.Disconnect();

        /* Return To The Operating System */
        return(rc);
}
```

SQLColumns

Purpose The SQLColumns( ) function retrieves a list of columns associated with a specified table.

Syntax

```
SQLRETURN SQLColumns (SQLHSTMT     StmtHandle,
                      SQLCHAR FAR *CatalogName,
                      SQLSMALLINT CatalogNameSize,
                      SQLCHAR FAR *SchemaName,
                      SQLSMALLINT SchemaNameSize,
                      SQLCHAR FAR *TableName,
                      SQLSMALLINT TableNameSize,
                      SQLCHAR FAR *ColumnName,
                      SQLSMALLINT ColumnNameSize);
```

Parameters

StmtHandle The statement handle where the address of the SQL statement buffer is stored.

CatalogName A pointer to a location in memory where the catalog qualifier of a three-part table name is stored. For DB2, this must be a null pointer or a zero-length string.

CatalogNameSize The length of the catalog qualifier value stored in the *CatalogName* parameter. For DB2, this parameter must be set to 0.

SchemaName A pointer to a location in memory where the schema name of a three-part table name is stored.

SchemaNameSize The length of the schema name value stored in the *SchemaName* parameter.

TableName A pointer to a location in memory where the table name is stored.

TableNameSize The length of the table name value stored in the *TableName* parameter.

ColumnName A pointer to a location in memory where the column name is stored.

ColumnNameSize The length of the column name value stored in the *ColumnName* parameter.

Includes

```
#include <sqlcli1.h>
```

Description The SQLColumns( ) function retrieves a list of columns for a specified table. The information returned by this function is placed in a SQL result data set, and can be processed with the same functions used to process a result data set generated by a query. Table 17.4 lists the columns in this result data set.

TABLE 17.4 Result Data Set Returned by SQLColumns( )

Column	Column name	Data type	Description
1	TABLE_CAT	VARCHAR(128)	The name of the system catalog table that the TABLE_SCHEM value is stored in. Since DB2 does not support three part table neames, this column will always be set to NULL by DB2 CLI.
2	TABLE_SCHEM	VARCHAR(128)	The name of the schema that contains the TABLE-NAME value.
3	TABLE_NAME	VARCHAR(128) NOT NULL	The name of the table, view, alias, or synonym.
4	COLUMN_NAME	VARCHAR(128) NOT NULL	The name of the column of the specified table, view, alias, or synonym.
5	DATA_TYPE	SMALLINT NOT NULL	The SQL data type of the column identified by COLUMN_NAME. For DB2 CLI, any of the following values are valid: SQL_SMALLINT SQL_INTEGER SQL_DECIMAL SQL_NUMERIC SQL_REAL SQL_FLOAT SQL_DOUBLE SQL_CHAR SQL_VARCHAR SQL_LONGVARCHAR SQL_BINARY SQL_VARBINARY SQL_LONGVARBINARY SQL_GRAPHIC SQL_VARGRAPHIC SQL_LONGVARGRAPHIC SQL_BLOB SQL_BLOB_LOCATOR SQL_CLOB SQL_CLOB_LOCATOR SQL_DBCLOB SQL_DBLOB_LOCATOR SQL_DATE SQL_TIME SQL_TIMESTAMP
	TYPE_NAME	VARCHAR(128) NOT NULL	The DBMS character representation of the SQL data type name associated with the DATA_TYPE column value. For DB2, any of the following values are valid: SMALLINT INTEGER GRAPHIC VARGRAPHIC

TABLE 17.4 Result Data Set Returned by SQLColumns( ) *(Continued)*

Column	Column name	Data type	Description
			DECIMAL LONG
VARGRAPHIC			
			NUMERIC REAL FLOAT DOUBLE CHAR VARCHAR LONG VARCHAR CHAR FOR BIT DATA VARCHAR FOR BIT DATA LONG VARCHAR FOR BIT DATA BLOB BLOB LOCATOR CLOB CLOB LOCATOR DBCLOB DBLOB LOCATOR DATE TIME TIMESTAMP
7	COLUMN_SIZE	INTEGER	The maximum number of bytes needed to display the column data in character form. For numeric data types, this is either the total number of digits or the total number of bits allowed in the column, depending on the value in the NUM_PREC_RADIX column. For character or binary string data types, this is the size of the string (string length) in bytes. For date, time, and timestamp data types, this is the total number of characters required to display the value when it is converted to a character string. For graphic (DBCS) data types, this is the size of the graphic string (string length) in double-byte characters.
8	BUFFER_LENGTH	INTEGER	The maximum number of bytes needed for the associated C application buffer to store data from this column if the value SQL_C _DEFAULT was specified for the *CDataType* parameter for the SQLBindCol( ), SQLGetData( ), or SQLBind Parameter( ) function call. This length does not include the null terminator for null-terminated strings. The following list shows the default length used for each DB2 SQL data type: SQL_SMALLINT: Two bytes. SQL_INTEGER: Four bytes. SQL_DECIMAL: The maximum number of digits plus 2 (a sign, digits, a decimal point, and digits). SQL_NUMERIC: The maximum number of digits plus 2 (a sign, digits, a decimal point, and digits). SQL_REAL: Four bytes. SQL_FLOAT: Eight bytes. SQL_DOUBLE: Eight bytes. SQL_CHAR: The defined length of the column. SQL_VARCHAR: The defined length of the column. SQL_LONGVARCHAR: The maximum length of the column. SQL_BINARY: The defined length of the column.

TABLE 17.4 Result Data Set Returned by SQLColumns( ) *(Continued)*

Column	Column name	Data type	Description
			SQL_VARBINARY: The defined length of the column. SQL_LONGVARBINARY: The maximum length of the column. SQL_GRAPHIC: The defined length of the column times 2. SQL_VARGRAPHIC: The defined length of the column times 2. SQL_LONGVARGRAPHIC: The maximum length of the column times 2. SQL_BLOB: The defined length of the column. SQL_DBCLOB: The defined length of the column times 2. SQL_CLOB: The defined length of the column. SQL_DATE: 6 (the size of the DATE _STRUCT structure). SQL_TIME: 6 (the size of the TIME _STRUCT structure). SQL_TIMESTAMP: 16 (the size of the TIMESTAMP_STRUCT structure).
9	DECIMAL_DIGITS	SMALLINT	The scale (number of digits to the right of the decimal point) of the column if TYPE_NAME is any of the following: SQL_DECIMAL, SQL_NUMERIC, or SQL_TIMESTAMP. If TYPE_NAME is anything else, this column will be set to NULL.
10	NUM_PREC_RADIX	SMALLINT	The radix value of the column. If DATA_TYPE is an approximate numeric data type, this column contains the value 2 and the COLUMN_SIZE column contains the number of bits allowed in the column. If DATA_TYPE is an exact numeric data type, this column contains the value 10 and the COLUMN_SIZE column contains the number of decimal digits allowed for the column. For numeric data types, this column can contain either 10 or 2. For data types where radix is not applicable, this column is set to NULL.
11	NULLABLE	SMALLINT NOT NULL	Indicates whether or not the column accepts a NULL value. Valid values for this column are: SQL_NO_NULLS (the column does not accept NULL values) SQL_NULLABLE (the column accepts NULL values).
12	REMARKS	VARCHAR(254)	Descriptive information about the column (if any exists).
13	COLUMN_DEF	VARCHAR(254)	The column's default value. If the default value is a numeric literal, this column contains the character representation of the numeric literal with no enclosing single quotes.

TABLE 17.4 Result Data Set Returned by SQLColumns( ) *(Continued)*

Column	Column name	Data type	Description
			If the default value is a character string, this column contains that string enclosed in single quotes. If the default value is a pseudo-literal (as is the case for DATE, TIME, and TIMESTAMP columns), this column contains the keyword of the pseudo-literal (for example, CURRENT DATE) with no enclosing single quotes. If the default value is NULL or if no default value is specified, this column contains the word NULL with no enclosing single quotes. If the default value cannot be represented without truncation, this column contains the word TRUNCATED with no enclosing single quotes.
14	DATETIME_CODE	INTEGER	Reserved. This column is currently set to NULL.
15	CHAR_OCTET_LENGTH	INTEGER	Contains the maximum length, in octets, for a character data type column. For single-byte character sets, this column contains the same value as the COLUMN_SIZE column. For all other data types, this column is set to NULL.
16	ORDINAL_POSITION	SMALLINT NOT NULL	The column sequence number in the table. The first column in the table is number 1, the second column is number 2, and so on.
17	IS_NULLABLE	VARCHAR(254)	Indicates whether or not the column is known to be nullable. Valid values for this column are: NO (the column is known to be not nullable). YES (the column is known to be nullable).

Adapted from IBM's Database 2 Call Level Interface Guide and Reference, Table 35, pages 157 to 159.

Specifications DB2 CLI 2.1, ODBC 1.0, X/OPEN CLI

Return Codes SQL_SUCCESS, SQL_SUCCESS_WITH_INFO, SQL_INVALID_HANDLE, SQL_ERROR

SQLSTATEs **08**S01, **24**000, **40**003, **S1**001, **S1**010, **S1**014, **S1**090, **S1**C00, **S1**T00

Comments

- Since the SQLColumns( ) function often maps to a complex and therefore expensive query against the database system catalog tables, use it sparingly. If the produced result data set needs to be used more than once, save it rather than regenerating it by invoking the SQLColumns( ) function again.
- This function returns only information about columns in base tables, so it should not be used to return information on columns in an existing result data set. Use either the SQLDescribeCol( ) or the SQLColAttributes( ) function to retrieve information about these types of columns.
- Character string values returned in the TABLE_SCHEMA and TABLE_NAME columns of the SQLTables( ) function result data set can be provided as input to this function.
- The result data set returned by this function is ordered by TABLE_CAT, TABLE_SCHEM, TABLE_NAME, and ORDINAL_POSITION.
- The *CatalogName*, *SchemaName*, *TableName*, and *ColumnName* parameters can accept the following search pattern values:

The underscore character (_) Indicates that any single character can be used in place of the underscore character.

The percent character (%) Indicates that any sequence of 0 or more characters can be used in place of the percent character.

If these "wildcard" characters need to be used as themselves (e.g., % = "%"), they must be preceded by an escape character.

- If you set the SQL_LONGDATA_COMPAT option to SQL_LD_COMPAT_YES (either by calling the SQLSetConnectOption( ) or by setting the LONGDATA-COMPAT option in the DB2 CLI initialization file), large object (LOB) data types will be reported as SQL_LONGVARCHAR, SQL_LONGVARBINARY, or SQL_LONGVARGRAPHIC.
- The VARCHAR columns of the catalog functions result data set have been declared with a maximum length of 128 characters to be consistent with the SQL92 standard limits. Since DB2 names are less than 128 characters, an application can always set aside 128 characters (plus the null terminator) for the output buffer, or alternatively allocate only the required amount of memory by first calling the SQLGetInfo( ) function with the *InfoType* parameter set to SQL_MAX_CATALOG _NAME_LEN, SQL_MAX_OWNER_SCHEMA_LEN, SQL_MAX_NAME _LEN, and/or SQL_MAX_COLUMN_NAME_LEN to determine (respectively) the actual lengths of the TABLE_CAT, TABLE_SCHEM, TABLE_NAME, and COLUMN_NAME columns supported by the current data source connection.
- Although new columns might be added and the names of the existing columns in the result data set might be changed in future releases of DB2 CLI, the position of the current columns in this data set will not change.

Restrictions There are no restrictions associated with this function call.

See Also SQLTables( ), SQLColumnPrivileges( ), SQLSpecialColumns( )

Examples The following C program illustrates how to use the SQLColumns( ) function to obtain information about the columns in a specific data source table:

```
#include <stdio.h>
#include <stdlib.h>
#include <sqlcli1.h>

int main()
{
    /* Declare The Local Memory Variables */
    SQLRETURN     rc = SQL_SUCCESS;
    SQLHENV       EnvHandle;
    SQLHDBC       DSCHandle;
    SQLHSTMT      StmtHandle;
    SQLCHAR       ColumnName[129];
    SQLSMALLINT   ColumnSize;

    /* Allocate An Environment Handle */
    rc = SQLAllocEnv(&EnvHandle);

    /* Allocate A Connection Handle */
    rc = SQLAllocConnect(EnvHandle, &DSCHandle);

    /* Connect To The SAMPLE Database */
    rc = SQLConnect(DSCHandle, "SAMPLE", SQL_NTS, "etpdd6z", SQL_NTS,
                    "sanders", SQL_NTS);

    /* Allocate An SQL Statement Handle */
    rc = SQLAllocStmt(DSCHandle, &StmtHandle);
```

```
    /* Obtain A List Of Column Names For A Specified Table And */
    /* Schema                                                  */
    rc = SQLColumns(StmtHandle, NULL, 0, "USERID", SQL_NTS, "PROJECT",
                    SQL_NTS, NULL, 0);

    if (rc != SQL_ERROR)
        {
        /* Bind The Columns In The Result Data Set To Local */
        /* Storage Variables                                */
        SQLBindCol(StmtHandle, 4, SQL_C_CHAR, (SQLPOINTER) ColumnName,
                   sizeof(ColumnName), NULL);

        SQLBindCol(StmtHandle, 7, SQL_C_SHORT, (SQLPOINTER)
                  &ColumnSize,0, NULL);

        /* Retrieve And Display The Results */
        printf("Table Name : USERID.PROJECTS\n");
        printf("Column Name     Size\n");
        printf("--------------------\n");
        while (rc != SQL_NO_DATA_FOUND)
            {

            /* Retrieve A Record From The Result Data Set */
            rc = SQLFetch(StmtHandle);

            /* Print The Information Retrieved */
            if (rc != SQL_NO_DATA_FOUND)
                printf("%-15s %d\n", ColumnName, ColumnSize);
            }
        }

    /* Disconnect From The SAMPLE Database */
    SQLDisconnect(DSCHandle);

    /* Free The SQL Statement Handle */
    if (StmtHandle != NULL)
        SQLFreeStmt(StmtHandle, SQL_DROP);

    /* Free The Connection Handle */
    if (DSCHandle != NULL)
        SQLFreeConnect(DSCHandle);

    /* Free The Environment Handle */
    if (EnvHandle != NULL)
        SQLFreeEnv(EnvHandle);

    /* Return To The Operating System */
    return(rc);
}
```

The following C++ program illustrates how to use the SQLColumns( ) function to obtain information about the column in a specific data source table:

```
#include <iostream.h>
#include <string.h>
#include <sqlcli1.h>

/* Define The CLI Class */
class CLI
```

```
{
    /* Declare The Private Attribute Variables */
    private:
       SQLHENV      EnvHandle;
       SQLHDBC      DSCHandle;
       SQLHSTMT     StmtHandle;
       SQLCHAR      ColumnName[129];
       SQLSMALLINT  ColumnSize;

    /* Declare The Public Attribute Variables */
    public:
       SQLRETURN  rc;

    /* Declare The Member Function Prototypes */
    CLI();                                  // Constructor
    ~CLI();                                 // Destructor
    SQLRETURN Connect();
    SQLRETURN ShowColumns();
    SQLRETURN Disconnect();
} ;

/* Define The Class Constructor */
CLI::CLI()
{
    /* Initialize The Return Code Variable */
    rc - SQL_SUCCESS;

    /* Allocate An Environment Handle */
    rc = SQLAllocEnv(&EnvHandle);

    /* Allocate A Connection Handle */
    rc = SQLAllocConnect(EnvHandle, &DSCHandle);
}

/* Define The Class Destructor */
CLI::~CLI()
{
    /* Free The Connection Handle */
    if (DSCHandle != NULL)
        SQLFreeConnect(DSCHandle);

    /* Free The Environment Handle */
    if (EnvHandle != NULL)
        SQLFreeEnv(EnvHandle);
}

/* Define The Connect() Member Function */
SQLRETURN CLI::Connect()
{
    /* Connect To The SAMPLE Database */
    rc = SQLConnect(DSCHandle, (SQLCHAR *) "SAMPLE", SQL_NTS,
                    (SQLCHAR *) "etpdd6z", SQL_NTS,
                    (SQLCHAR *) "sanders", SQL_NTS);

    /* Allocate An SQL Statement Handle */
    rc = SQLAllocStmt(DSCHandle, &StmtHandle);

    /* Return The CLI Function Return Code */
    return(rc);
}
```

```
/* Define The Disconnect() Member Function */
SQLRETURN CLI::Disconnect(void)
{
    /* Disconnect From The Database */
    rc = SQLDisconnect(DSCHandle);

    /* Free The SQL Statement Handle */
    if (StmtHandle != NULL)
        SQLFreeStmt(StmtHandle, SQL_DROP);

    /* Return The CLI Function Return Code */
    return(rc);
}

/* Define The ShowColumns() Member Function */
SQLRETURN CLI::ShowColumns(void)
{
    /* Obtain A List Of Column Names For A Specified Table And */
    /* Schema                                                  */
    rc = SQLColumns(StmtHandle, NULL, 0, (SQLCHAR *) "USERID",
                    SQL_NTS, (SQLCHAR *) "PROJECT", SQL_NTS, NULL, 0);

    if (rc != SQL_ERROR)
        {
        /* Bind The Columns In The Result Data Set To Local */
        /* Storage Variables                                */
        SQLBindCol(StmtHandle, 4, SQL_C_CHAR, (SQLPOINTER) ColumnName,
                   sizeof(ColumnName), NULL);

        SQLBindCol(StmtHandle, 7, SQL_C_SHORT, (SQLPOINTER) &ColumnSize,
                   0, NULL);

        /* Retrieve And Display The Results */
        cout << "Table Name : USERID.PROJECTS" << endl;
        cout << "Column Name     Size" << endl;
        cout << "--------------------" << endl;
        while (rc != SQL_NO_DATA_FOUND)
            {

            /* Retrieve A Record From The Result Data Set */
            rc = SQLFetch(StmtHandle);

            /* Print The Information Retrieved */
            if (rc != SQL_NO_DATA_FOUND)
                {
                cout.setf(ios::left);
                cout.width(16);
                cout << ColumnName << ColumnSize << endl;
                }
            }
        }

    /* Return The CLI Function Return Code */
    return(rc);
}

int main()
{
    /* Declare The Local Memory Variables */
    SQLRETURN  rc = SQL_SUCCESS;
```

```
    /* Create An Instance Of The CLI Class */
    CLI Sample;

    /* Connect To The SAMPLE Database */
    if ((rc = Sample.Connect()) != SQL_SUCCESS)
        return(rc);

    /* Display A List Of Columns For The PROJECTS Table In The */
    /* USERID Schema                                           */
    /* In The PROJECTS Table                                  */
    Sample.ShowColumns();

    /* Disconnect From The SAMPLE Database */
    Sample.Disconnect();

    /* Return To The Operating System */
    return(rc);
}
```

SQLColumnPrivileges

Purpose The SQLColumnPrivileges( ) function retrieves a list of column names and the privileges associated with them for a specified table.

Syntax

```
SQLRETURN SQLTablePrivileges (SQLHSTMT     StmtHandle,
                              SQLCHAR FAR  *CatalogName,
                              SQLSMALLINT  CatalogNameSize,
                              SQLCHAR FAR  *SchemaName,
                              SQLSMALLINT  SchemaNameSize,
                              SQLCHAR FAR  *TableName,
                              SQLSMALLINT  TableNameSize,
                              SQLCHAR FAR  *ColumnName,
                              SQLSMALLINT  ColumnNameSize);
```

Parameters

StmtHandle The statement handle where the address of the SQL statement buffer is stored.

CatalogName A pointer to a location in memory where the catalog qualifier of a three-part table name is stored. For DB2, this must be a null pointer or a zero-length string.

CatalogNameSize The length of the catalog qualifier value stored in the *CatalogName* parameter. For DB2, this parameter must be set to 0.

SchemaName A pointer to a location in memory where the schema name of a three-part table name is stored.

SchemaNameSize The length of the schema name value stored in the *SchemaName* parameter.

TableName A pointer to a location in memory where the table name is stored.

TableNameSize The length of the table name value stored in the *TableName* parameter.

ColumnName A pointer to a location in memory where the column name is stored.

ColumnNameSize The length of the column name value stored in the *ColumnName* parameter.

Includes

```
#include <sqlcli1.h>
```

Description The SQLColumnPrivileges( ) function retrieves a list of column names and the privileges associated with them for a specified table. The information returned by this function is placed in a SQL result data set, and can be processed with the same functions that process a result data set generated by a query. Table 17.5 lists the columns in this result data set.

TABLE 17.5 Result Data Set Returned by SQLColumnPrivileges( )

Column	Column name	Data type	Description
1	TABLE_CAT	VARCHAR(128)	The name of the system catalog table in which the TABLE_SCHEM value is stored. Since DB2 does not support three-part table names, DB2 CLI will always set this column to NULL.
2	TABLE_SCHEM	VARCHAR(128)	The name of the schema that contains the TABLE_NAME value.
3	TABLE_NAME	VARCHAR(128) NOT NULL	The name of the database table or view.
4	COLUMN_NAME	VARCHAR(128) NOT NULL	The name of the column of the specified table or view.
5	GRANTOR	VARCHAR(128)	The authorization ID of the user who granted the privilege.
6	GRANTEE	VARCHAR(128)	The authorization ID of the user to whom the privilege is granted.
7	PRIVILEGE	VARCHAR(128)	The table privilege that was granted. Valid values for this column are: INSERT, REFERENCES, SELECT, and UPDATE.
8	IS_GRANTABLE	VARCHAR(3)	Indicates whether or not the grantee is permitted to grant the privilege to other users. Valid values for this column are: YES and NO.

Adapted from IBM's Database 2 Call Level Interface Guide and Reference, Table 32, page 152 to 153.

Specifications DB2 CLI 2.1, ODBC 1.0

Return Codes SQL_SUCCESS, SQL_SUCCESS_WITH_INFO, SQL_INVALID_HANDLE, SQL_ERROR

SQLSTATEs **08**S01, **24**000, **40**003, **S1**001, **S1**009, **S1**014, **S1**090, **S1**C00, **S1**T00

Comments

- Since the SQLColumnPrivileges( ) function often maps to a complex and therefore expensive query against the database system catalog tables, use it sparingly. If you need to use the produced result data set more than once, saved it rather than regenerating it by invoking the SQLColumnPrivileges( ) function again.
- The *ColumnName* parameter can accept the following search pattern values:

The underscore character (_) Indicates that any single character can be used in place of the underscore character.

The percent character (%) Indicates that any sequence of 0 or more characters can be used in place of the percent character.

If these "wildcard" characters need to be used as themselves (e.g., % = "%"), they must be preceded by an escape character.

- Character string values returned in the TABLE_SCHEM, TABLE_NAME, and COLUMN_NAME columns of the SQLColumns( ) function result data set can be provided as input to this function.
- The result data set returned by this function is ordered by TABLE_CAT, TABLE_SCHEM, TABLE_NAME, COLUMN_NAME, and PRIVILEGE.
- The VARCHAR columns of the catalog functions result data set have been declared with a maximum length of 128 characters to be consistent with the SQL92 standard limits. Since DB2 names are less than 128 characters, an application can choose to always set aside 128 characters (plus the null terminator) for the output buffer, or alternatively to allocate only the required amount of memory by first calling the SQLGetInfo( ) function with the *InfoType* parameter set to SQL_MAX_CATALOG_NAME_LEN, SQL_MAX_OWNER_SCHEMA_LEN, SQL_MAX_NAME_LEN, and/or SQL_MAX_COLUMN_NAME_LEN to determine (respectively) the actual lengths of the TABLE_CAT, TABLE_SCHEM, TABLE_NAME, and COLUMN_NAME columns supported by the current data source connection.
- Although new columns might be added and the names of the existing columns in the result data set might be changed in future releases of DB2 CLI, the position of the current columns in this data set will not change.

Restrictions There are no restrictions associated with this function call.

See Also SQLColumns( ), SQLTables( )

Examples The following C program illustrates how to use the SQLColumnPrivileges( ) function to obtain authorization information for a column in a specific table:

```
#include <stdio.h>
#include <stdlib.h>
#include <sqlcli1.h>

int main()
{
    /* Declare The Local Memory Variables */
    SQLRETURN    rc = SQL_SUCCESS;
    SQLHENV      EnvHandle;
    SQLHDBC      DSCHandle;
    SQLHSTMT     StmtHandle;
    SQLCHAR      ColumnName[129];
    SQLCHAR      Grantee[129];
    SQLCHAR      Privilege[129];

    /* Allocate An Environment Handle */
    rc = SQLAllocEnv(&EnvHandle);

    /* Allocate A Connection Handle */
    rc = SQLAllocConnect(EnvHandle, &DSCHandle);

    /* Connect To The SAMPLE Database */
    rc = SQLConnect(DSCHandle, "SAMPLE", SQL_NTS, "etpdd6z", SQL_NTS,
                "sanders", SQL_NTS);

    /* Allocate An SQL Statement Handle */
    rc = SQLAllocStmt(DSCHandle, &StmtHandle);
```

```
    /* Obtain A List Of Column Privileges For A Specified Table And */
    /* Schema                                                       */
    rc = SQLColumnPrivileges(StmtHandle, NULL, 0, "USERID", SQL_NTS,
                             "EMPLOYEE", SQL_NTS, "L%", 2);

    if (rc != SQL_ERROR)
        {
        /* Bind The Columns In The Result Data Set To Local */
        /* Storage Variables                                */
        SQLBindCol(StmtHandle, 4, SQL_C_CHAR, (SQLPOINTER) ColumnName,
                   sizeof(ColumnName), NULL);

        SQLBindCol(StmtHandle, 6, SQL_C_CHAR, (SQLPOINTER) Grantee,
                   sizeof(Grantee), NULL);

        SQLBindCol(StmtHandle, 7, SQL_C_CHAR, (SQLPOINTER) Privilege,
                   sizeof(Privilege), NULL);

        /* Retrieve And Display The Results */
        printf("Table Name : EMPLOYEE\n");
        printf("Column Name     Privilege       Grantee\n");
        printf("----------------------------------------\n");
        while (rc != SQL_NO_DATA_FOUND)
            {

            /* Retrieve A Record From The Result Data Set */
            rc = SQLFetch(StmtHandle);

            /* Print The Information Retrieved */
            if (rc != SQL_NO_DATA_FOUND)
                printf("%-15s %-15s %s\n", ColumnName, Privilege,
                       Grantee);
            }
        }

    /* Disconnect From The SAMPLE Database */
    SQLDisconnect(DSCHandle);

    /* Free The SQL Statement Handle */
    if (StmtHandle != NULL)
        SQLFreeStmt(StmtHandle, SQL_DROP);

    /* Free The Connection Handle */
    if (DSCHandle != NULL)
        SQLFreeConnect(DSCHandle);

    /* Free The Environment Handle */
    if (EnvHandle != NULL)
        SQLFreeEnv(EnvHandle);

    /* Return To The Operating System */
    return(rc);
}
```

The following C++ program illustrates how the SQLColumnPrivileges( ) function is used by class methods to obtain authorization information for a column in a specific table:

```
#include <iostream.h>
#include <string.h>
#include <sqlcli1.h>
```

```
/* Define The CLI Class */
class CLI
{
    /* Declare The Private Attribute Variables */
    private:
       SQLHENV       EnvHandle;
       SQLHDBC       DSCHandle;
       SQLHSTMT      StmtHandle;
       SQLCHAR       ColumnName[129];
       SQLCHAR       Grantee[129];
       SQLCHAR       Privilege[129];

    /* Declare The Public Attribute Variables */
    public:
       SQLRETURN  rc;

    /* Declare The Member Function Prototypes */
    CLI();                                      // Constructor
    ~CLI();                                     // Destructor
    SQLRETURN Connect();
    SQLRETURN ShowColPrivileges();
    SQLRETURN Disconnect();
} ;

/* Define The Class Constructor */
CLI::CLI()
{
    /* Initialize The Return Code Variable */
    rc = SQL_SUCCESS;

    /* Allocate An Environment Handle */
    rc = SQLAllocEnv(&EnvHandle);

    /* Allocate A Connection Handle */
    rc = SQLAllocConnect(EnvHandle, &DSCHandle);
}

/* Define The Class Destructor */
CLI::~CLI()
{
    /* Free The Connection Handle */
    if (DSCHandle != NULL)
        SQLFreeConnect(DSCHandle);

    /* Free The Environment Handle */
    if (EnvHandle != NULL)
        SQLFreeEnv(EnvHandle);
}

/* Define The Connect() Member Function */
SQLRETURN CLI::Connect()
{
    /* Connect To The SAMPLE Database */
    rc = SQLConnect(DSCHandle, (SQLCHAR *) "SAMPLE", SQL_NTS,
                    (SQLCHAR *) "etpdd6z", SQL_NTS,
                    (SQLCHAR *) "sanders", SQL_NTS);

    /* Allocate An SQL Statement Handle */
    rc = SQLAllocStmt(DSCHandle, &StmtHandle);
```

```
    /* Return The CLI Function Return Code */
    return(rc);
}

/* Define The Disconnect() Member Function */
SQLRETURN CLI::Disconnect(void)
{
    /* Disconnect From The Database */
    rc = SQLDisconnect(DSCHandle);

    /* Free The SQL Statement Handle */
    if (StmtHandle != NULL)
        SQLFreeStmt(StmtHandle, SQL_DROP);

    /* Return The CLI Function Return Code */
    return(rc);
}

/* Define The ShowColPrivileges() Member Function */
SQLRETURN CLI::ShowColPrivileges(void)
{
    /* Obtain A List Of Column Privileges For A Specified Table And */
    /* Schema                                                       */
    rc = SQLColumnPrivileges(StmtHandle, NULL, 0,
                             (SQLCHAR *) "USERID", SQL_NTS,
                             (SQLCHAR *) "EMPLOYEE", SQL_NTS,
                             (SQLCHAR *) "L%", 2);

    if (rc != SQL_ERROR)
        {
        /* Bind The Columns In The Result Data Set To Local */
        /* Storage Variables                                */
        SQLBindCol(StmtHandle, 4, SQL_C_CHAR, (SQLPOINTER) ColumnName,
                   sizeof(ColumnName), NULL);

        SQLBindCol(StmtHandle, 6, SQL_C_CHAR, (SQLPOINTER) Grantee,
                   sizeof(Grantee), NULL);

        SQLBindCol(StmtHandle, 7, SQL_C_CHAR, (SQLPOINTER) Privilege,
                   sizeof(Privilege), NULL);

        /* Retrieve And Display The Results */
        cout << "Table Name : EMPLOYEE" << endl;
        cout << "Column Name     Privilege       Grantee" << endl;
        cout << "---------------------------------------" << endl;
        while (rc != SQL_NO_DATA_FOUND)

        while (rc != SQL_NO_DATA_FOUND)
            {

            /* Retrieve A Record From The Result Data Set */
            rc = SQLFetch(StmtHandle);

            /* Print The Information Retrieved */
            if (rc != SQL_NO_DATA_FOUND)
                {
                cout.setf(ios::left);
                cout.width(16);
                cout << ColumnName;
                cout.setf(ios::left);
                cout.width(16);
```

```
                    cout << Privilege << Grantee << endl;
                    }
                }
            }

    /* Return The CLI Function Return Code */
    return(rc);
}

int main()
{
    /* Declare The Local Memory Variables */
    SQLRETURN  rc = SQL_SUCCESS;

    /* Create An Instance Of The CLI Class */
    CLI Sample;

    /* Connect To The SAMPLE Database */
    if ((rc = Sample.Connect()) != SQL_SUCCESS)
        return(rc);

    /* Display A List Of Column Privileges For The EMPLOYEE Table    */
    /* In The USERID Schema                                          */
    Sample.ShowColPrivileges();

    /* Disconnect From The SAMPLE Database */
    Sample.Disconnect();

    /* Return To The Operating System */
    return(rc);
}
```

SQLSpecialColumns

Purpose The SQLSpecialColumns( ) function retrieves unique row identifier information (e.g., primary key or unique index information) for a specified table.

Syntax

```
SQLRETURN SQLSpecialColumns (SQLHSTMT      StmtHandle,
                             SQLUSMALLINT RowIdentifier,
                             SQLCHAR FAR  *CatalogName,
                             SQLSMALLINT  CatalogNameSize,
                             SQLCHAR FAR  *SchemaName,
                             SQLSMALLINT  SchemaNameSize,
                             SQLCHAR FAR  *TableName,
                             SQLSMALLINT  TableNameSize,
                             SQLUSMALLINT Scope,
                             SQLUSMALLINT Nullable);
```

Parameters

StmtHandle The statement handle where the address of the SQL statement buffer is stored.

RowIdentifier Specifies the type of column information to return. The row identifier parameter can contain either of the following values:

SQL_BEST_ROWID Indicates that the optimal set of columns that can uniquely identify any row in the specified table is to be returned.

SQL_ROWVER Provided only for compatibility with ODBC applications. This value is not supported by DB2 CLI and, if used, an empty result data set will be returned by the function.

CatalogName A pointer to a location in memory where the catalog qualifier of a three-part table name is stored. For DB2, this must be a null pointer or a zero-length string.

CatalogNameSize The length of the catalog qualifier value stored in the *CatalogName* parameter. For DB2, this parameter must be set to 0.

SchemaName A pointer to a location in memory where the schema name of a three-part table name is stored.

SchemaNameSize The length of the schema name value stored in the *SchemaName* parameter.

TableName A pointer to a location in memory where the table name is stored.

TableNameSize The length of the table name value stored in the *TableName* parameter.

Scope Specifies the minimum duration for which the unique row identifier will be valid. The scope parameter can contain any of the following values:

SQL_SCOPE_CURROW Indicates that the unique row identifier is guaranteed to be valid only while positioned on that row.

SQL_SCOPE_TRANSACTION Indicates that the unique row identifier is guaranteed to be valid for the duration of the current transaction.

SQL_SCOPE_SESSION Indicates that the unique row identifier is guaranteed to be valid for the duration of the current connection.

Nullable Specifies whether or not special columns that can contain NULL values are to be returned by this function. The nullable parameter can contain either of the following values:

SQL_NO_NULLS Indicates that special columns that can contain NULL values should be excluded from the set of columns that can uniquely identify any row in the specified table.

SQL_NULLABLE Indicates that special columns that can contain NULL values should be included in the set of columns that can uniquely identify any row in the specified table.

Includes

```
#include <sqlcli1.h>
```

Description The SQLSpecialColumns( ) function retrieves unique row identifier information (e.g., primary key or unique index information) for a specified table. The information returned by this function is placed in a SQL result data set, and can be processed with the same functions used to process a result data set generated by a query. Table 17.6 lists the columns in this result data set.

TABLE 17.6 Result Data Set Returned by SQLSpecialColumns( )

Column	Column name	Data type	Description
1	SCOPE	SMALLINT	The duration for which the name in COLUMN_NAME is guaranteed to point to the same row. Valid values for this column are: SQL_SCOPE_CURROW: Indicates that the unique row identifier is guaranteed to be valid only while positioned on that row. SQL_SCOPE_TRANSACTION: Indicates that the unique row identifier is guaranteed to be valid for the duration of the current transaction.

TABLE 17.6 Result Data Set Returned by SQLSpecialColumns( ) *(Continued)*

Column	Column name	Data type	Description
			SQL_SCOPE_SESSION: Indicates that the unique row identifier is guaranteed to be valid for the duration of the current connection.
2	COLUMN_NAME	VARCHAR(128) NOT NULL	The name of the column that is either the table's primary key or part of the table's primary key.
3	DATA_TYPE	SMALLINT NOT NULL	The SQL data type of the column identified by COLUMN_NAME. For DB2 CLI, any of the following values are valid: SQL_SMALLINT SQL_GRAPHIC SQL_INTEGER SQL_VARGRAPHIC SQL_DECIMAL SQL_LONGVARGRAPHIC SQL_NUMERIC SQL_BLOB SQL_REAL SQL_BLOB_LOCATOR SQL_FLOAT SQL_CLOB SQL_DOUBLE SQL_CLOB_LOCATOR SQL_CHAR SQL_DBCLOB SQL_VARCHAR SQL_DBLOB_LOCATOR SQL_LONGVARCHAR SQL_DATE SQL_BINARY SQL_TIME SQL_VARBINARY SQL_TIMESTAMP SQL_LONGVARBINARY
4	TYPE_NAME	VARCHAR(128) NOT NULL	The DBMS character representation of the SQL data type name associated with the DATA_TYPE column value. For DB2, any of the following values are valid: SMALLINT GRAPHIC INTEGER VARGRAPHIC DECIMAL LONG VARGRAPHIC NUMERIC BLOB REAL BLOB LOCATOR FLOAT CLOB DOUBLE CLOB LOCATOR CHAR DBCLOB VARCHAR DBLOB LOCATOR LONG VARCHAR DATE CHAR FOR BIT DATA TIME VARCHAR FOR BIT DATA TIMESTAMP LONG VARCHAR FOR BIT DATA
5	COLUMN_SIZE	INTEGER	The maximum number of bytes needed to display the column data in character form. For numeric data types, this is either the total number of digits or the total number of bits allowed in the column, depending on the value in the NUM_PREC_RADIX column in the result data set. For character or binary string data types, this is the size of the string (string length) in bytes. For date, time, and timestamp data types, this is the total number of characters required to display the value when it is converted to a character string. For graphic (DBCS) data types, this is the size of the graphic string (string length) in double byte characters.
6	BUFFER_LENGTH	INTEGER	The maximum number of bytes needed for the associated C application buffer to store data from this column if the value SQL_C_DEFAULT was specified for the *CDataType* parameter for the SQLBindCol( ),

TABLE 17.6 Result Data Set Returned by SQLSpecialColumns( ) *(Continued)*

Column	Column name	Data type	Description
			SQLGetData( ), or SQLBindParameter( ) function call. This length does not include the null terminator for null-terminated strings. The following list shows the default length used for each DB2 SQL data type: SQL_SMALLINT — Two bytes. SQL_INTEGER — Four bytes. SQL_DECIMAL — The maximum number of digits plus 2 (a sign, digits, a decimal point, and digits). SQL_NUMERIC — The maximum number of digits plus 2 (a sign, digits, a decimal point, and digits). SQL_REAL — Four bytes. SQL_FLOAT — Eight bytes. SQL_DOUBLE — Eight bytes. SQL_CHAR — The defined length of the column. SQL_VARCHAR — The defined length of the column. SQL_LONGVARCHAR — The maximum length of the column. SQL_BINARY — The defined length of the column. SQL_VARBINARY — The defined length of the column. SQL_LONGVARBINARY — The maximum length of the column. SQL_GRAPHIC — The defined length of the column times 2. SQL_VARGRAPHIC — The defined length of the column times 2. SQL_LONGVARGRAPHIC — The maximum length of the column times 2. SQL_BLOB — The defined length of the column. SQL_DBCLOB — The defined length of the column times 2. SQL_CLOB — The defined length of the column. SQL_DATE — 6 (the size of the DATE_STRUCT structure). SQL_TIME — 6 (the size of the TIME_STRUCT structure). SQL_TIMESTAMP — 16 (the size of the TIMESTAMP _STRUCT structure).
7	DECIMAL_DIGITS	SMALLINT	The scale (number of digits to the right of the decimal point) of the column if TYPE_NAME is any of the following: SQL_DECIMAL, SQL_NUMERIC, or SQL_TIMESTAMP.

TABLE 17.6 Result Data Set Returned by SQLSpecialColumns( ) *(Continued)*

Column	Column name	Data type	Description
			If TYPE_NAME is anything else, this column will be set to NULL.
8	PSEUDO_COLUMN	SMALLINT	Indicates whether or not the column is a pseudo-column. Because DB2 RDBMS databases do not support pseudo-columns, DB2 CLI will return only SQL_PC _NOT_PSEUDO. ODBC applications can also return QL_PC_UNKNOWN and SQL_PC_PSEUDO from other non-IBM RDBMS databases.

Adapted from IBM's Database 2 Call Level Interface Guide and Reference, Table 136, pages 370 to 371.

If there are multiple ways to uniquely identify any row in the specified table (for example, if there are multiple unique indexes defined for the specified table), this function will retrieve the best set of row identifier column data, based on DB2 CLI's internal selection criteria.

Specifications DB2 CLI 2.1, ODBC 1.0, X/OPEN CLI

Return Codes SQL_SUCCESS, SQL_SUCCESS_WITH_INFO, SQL_INVALID_HANDLE, SQL_ERROR

SQLSTATEs **08**S01, **24**000, **40**003, **S1**001, **S1**010, **S1**014, **S1**090, **S1**097, **S1**098, **S1**099, **S1**C00, **S1**T00

Comments

- Since the SQLSpecialColumns( ) function often maps to a complex and therefore expensive query against the database system catalog tables, use it sparingly. If the produced result data set needs to be used more than once, save it rather than regenerating it by invoking the SQLSpecialColumns( ) function again.
- If no unique row identifier information exists for the specified table (if no primary key or unique index has been defined), this function will return an empty result data set.
- The result data set returned by this function is ordered by SCOPE.
- The duration for which a unique row identifier value is guaranteed to be valid depends on the isolation level being used by the current transaction. Refer to Chapter 2 for more information about transaction isolation levels.
- The VARCHAR columns of the catalog functions result data set have been declared with a maximum length of 128 characters to be consistent with the SQL92 standard limits. Since DB2 names are less than 128 characters, an application can always set aside 128 characters (plus the null terminator) for the output buffer, or alternatively allocate only the required amount of memory by first calling the SQLGetInfo( ) function with the *InfoType* parameter set to SQL_MAX_CATALOG_NAME _LEN, SQL_MAX_OWNER_SCHEMA_LEN, SQL_MAX_NAME_LEN, and/ or SQL_MAX_COLUMN_NAME_LEN to determine (respectively) the actual lengths of the TABLE_CAT, TABLE_SCHEM, TABLE_NAME, and COLUMN_NAME columns supported by the current data source connection.
- Although new columns might be added and the names of the existing columns in the result data set might be changed in future releases of DB2 CLI, the position of the current columns in this data set will not change.

Restrictions There are no restrictions associated with this function call.

See Also SQLColumns( ), SQLTables( ), SQLStatistics( )

Examples The following C program illustrates how to use the SQLSpecialColumns( ) function to obtain information about the unique row identifier columns in a specific table:

```
#include <stdio.h>
#include <stdlib.h>
#include <sqlcli1.h>
int main()
{
    /* Declare The Local Memory Variables */
    SQLRETURN    rc = SQL_SUCCESS;
    SQLHENV      EnvHandle;
    SQLHDBC      DSCHandle;
    SQLHSTMT     StmtHandle;
    SQLCHAR      ColumnName[129];
    SQLSMALLINT  ColumnSize;

    /* Allocate An Environment Handle */
    rc = SQLAllocEnv(&EnvHandle);

    /* Allocate A Connection Handle */
    rc = SQLAllocConnect(EnvHandle, &DSCHandle);

    /* Connect To The SAMPLE Database */
    rc = SQLConnect(DSCHandle, "SAMPLE", SQL_NTS, "etpdd6z", SQL_NTS,
                    "sanders", SQL_NTS);

    /* Allocate An SQL Statement Handle */
    rc = SQLAllocStmt(DSCHandle, &StmtHandle);

    /* Obtain A List Of Special Column Names For A Specified Table */
    /* And Schema                                                  */
    rc = SQLSpecialColumns(StmtHandle, SQL_BEST_ROWID, NULL, 0,
                           "USERID", SQL_NTS, "EMP_PHOTO", SQL_NTS,
                           SQL_SCOPE_CURROW, SQL_NULLABLE);

    if (rc != SQL_ERROR)
        {
        /* Bind The Columns In The Result Data Set To Local */
        /* Storage Variables                                */
        SQLBindCol(StmtHandle, 2, SQL_C_CHAR, (SQLPOINTER) ColumnName,
                   sizeof(ColumnName), NULL);

        SQLBindCol(StmtHandle, 5, SQL_C_SHORT, (SQLPOINTER)
                   &ColumnSize, 0, NULL);

        /* Retrieve And Display The Results */
        printf("Table Name : USERID.EMP_PHOTO\n");
        printf("Column Name        Size\n");
        printf("-----------------------\n");
        while (rc != SQL_NO_DATA_FOUND)
            {

            /* Retrieve A Record From The Result Data Set */
            rc = SQLFetch(StmtHandle);

            /* Print The Information Retrieved */
            if (rc != SQL_NO_DATA_FOUND)
                printf("%-18s %d\n", ColumnName, ColumnSize);
            }
        }

    /* Disconnect From The SAMPLE Database */
```

```
    SQLDisconnect(DSCHandle);

    /* Free The SQL Statement Handle */
    if (StmtHandle != NULL)
        SQLFreeStmt(StmtHandle, SQL_DROP);
    /* Free The Connection Handle */
    if (DSCHandle != NULL)
        SQLFreeConnect(DSCHandle);

    /* Free The Environment Handle */
    if (EnvHandle != NULL)
        SQLFreeEnv(EnvHandle);

    /* Return To The Operating System */
    return(rc);
}
```

The following C++ program illustrates how the SQLSpecialColumns( ) function is used by class methods to obtain information about unique row identifier columns in a specific table:

```
#include <iostream.h>
#include <string.h>
#include <sqlcli1.h>

/* Define Thc CLI Class */
class CLI
{
    /* Declare The Private Attribute Variables */
    private:
       SQLHENV      EnvHandle;
       SQLHDBC      DSCHandle;
       SQLHSTMT     StmtHandle;
       SQLCHAR      ColumnName[129];
       SQLSMALLINT  ColumnSize;

    /* Declare The Public Attribute Variables */
    public:
       SQLRETURN  rc;

    /* Declare The Member Function Prototypes */
    CLI();                                      // Constructor
    ~CLI();                                     // Destructor
    SQLRETURN Connect();
    SQLRETURN ShowSpecialCols();
    SQLRETURN Disconnect();
} ;

/* Define The Class Constructor */
CLI::CLI()
{
    /* Initialize The Return Code Variable */
    rc = SQL_SUCCESS;

    /* Allocate An Environment Handle */
    rc = SQLAllocEnv(&EnvHandle);

    /* Allocate A Connection Handle */
    rc = SQLAllocConnect(EnvHandle, &DSCHandle);
}

/* Define The Class Destructor */
CLI::~CLI()
{
```

```
    /* Free The Connection Handle */
    if (DSCHandle != NULL)
        SQLFreeConnect(DSCHandle);
    /* Free The Environment Handle */
    if (EnvHandle != NULL)
        SQLFreeEnv(EnvHandle);
}

/* Define The Connect() Member Function */
SQLRETURN CLI::Connect()
{
    /* Connect To The SAMPLE Database */
    rc = SQLConnect(DSCHandle, (SQLCHAR *) "SAMPLE", SQL_NTS,
                    (SQLCHAR *) "etpdd6z", SQL_NTS,
                    (SQLCHAR *) "sanders", SQL_NTS);

    /* Allocate An SQL Statement Handle */
    rc = SQLAllocStmt(DSCHandle, &StmtHandle);

    /* Return The CLI Function Return Code */
    return(rc);
}

/* Define The Disconnect() Member Function */
SQLRETURN CLI::Disconnect(void)
{
    /* Disconnect From The Database */
    rc = SQLDisconnect(DSCHandle);

    /* Free The SQL Statement Handle */
    if (StmtHandle != NULL)
        SQLFreeStmt(StmtHandle, SQL_DROP);

    /* Return The CLI Function Return Code */
    return(rc);
}

/* Define The ShowSpecialCols() Member Function */
SQLRETURN CLI::ShowSpecialCols(void)
{
    /* Obtain A List Of Special Column Names For A Specified Table */
    /* And Schema                                                  */
    rc = SQLSpecialColumns(StmtHandle, SQL_BEST_ROWID, NULL, 0,
                           (SQLCHAR *) "USERID", SQL_NTS,
                           (SQLCHAR *) "EMP_PHOTO", SQL_NTS,
                           SQL_SCOPE_CURROW, SQL_NULLABLE);

    if (rc != SQL_ERROR)
        {
        /* Bind The Columns In The Result Data Set To Local */
        /* Storage Variables                                */
        SQLBindCol(StmtHandle, 2, SQL_C_CHAR, (SQLPOINTER) ColumnName,
                   sizeof(ColumnName), NULL);

        SQLBindCol(StmtHandle, 5, SQL_C_SHORT, (SQLPOINTER) &ColumnSize,
                   0, NULL);

        /* Retrieve And Display The Results */
        cout << "Table Name : USERID.EMP_PHOTO" << endl;
        cout << "Column Name        Size" << endl;
        cout << "-----------------------" << endl;
        while (rc != SQL_NO_DATA_FOUND)
```

```
            {

            /* Retrieve A Record From The Result Data Set */
            rc = SQLFetch(StmtHandle);

            /* Print The Information Retrieved */
            if (rc != SQL_NO_DATA_FOUND)
                {
                cout.setf(ios::left);
                cout.width(19);
                cout << ColumnName << ColumnSize << endl;
                }
            }
        }

    /* Return The CLI Function Return Code */
    return(rc);
}

int main()
{
    /* Declare The Local Memory Variables */
    SQLRETURN  rc = SQL_SUCCESS;

    /* Create An Instance Of The CLI Class */
    CLI Sample;

    /* Connect To The SAMPLE Database */
    if ((rc = Sample.Connect()) != SQL_SUCCESS)
        return(rc);

    /* Display A List Of The Special Columns For The EMP_PHOTO */
    /* Table In The USERID Schema                               */
    Sample.ShowSpecialCols();

    /* Disconnect From The SAMPLE Database */
    Sample.Disconnect();

    /* Return To The Operating System */
    return(rc);
}
```

SQLStatistics

Purpose The SQLStatistics( ) function retrieves a list of statistics about a specified table and its associated indexes.

Syntax

```
SQLRETURN SQLStatistics (SQLHSTMT      StmtHandle,
                         SQLCHAR FAR   *CatalogName,
                         SQLSMALLINT   CatalogNameSize,
                         SQLCHAR FAR   *SchemaName,
                         SQLSMALLINT   SchemaNameSize,
                         SQLCHAR FAR   *TableName,
                         SQLSMALLINT   TableNameSize,
                         SQLUSMALLINT  IndexType,
                         SQLUSMALLINT  Accuracy);
```

Parameters *StmtHandle* The statement handle where the address of the SQL statement buffer is stored.

CatalogName A pointer to a location in memory where the catalog qualifier of a three-part table name is stored. For DB2, this must be a null pointer or a zero-length string.

CatalogNameSize The length of the catalog qualifier value stored in the *CatalogName* parameter. For DB2, this parameter must be set to 0.

SchemaName A pointer to a location in memory where the schema name of a three-part table name is stored.

SchemaNameSize The length of the schema name value stored in the *SchemaName* parameter.

TableName A pointer to a location in memory where the table name is stored.

TableNameSize The length of the table name value stored in the *TableName* parameter.

IndexType Specifies the type of index information to be returned by this function. The index type value can be either of the following:

SQL_INDEX_UNIQUE Indicates that only information pertaining to unique indexes is to be retrieved.

SQL_INDEX_ALL Indicates that information about all indexes is to be retrieved.

Accuracy Specifies whether or not the CARDINALITY and PAGES columns in the result data set are to contain the most current information. The accuracy value can be one of the following:

SQL_QUICK Indicates that only information that is readily available at the database server is to be retrieved.

SQL_ENSURE Indicates that the most up-to-date available information is to be retrieved. This value is reserved for future use and should not be used at this time.

Includes

```
#include <sqlcli1.h>
```

Description

The SQLStatistics( ) function retrieves information about a specified table. When invoked, this function returns two types of information about the specified table:

- Statistical information about the table itself (if it is available), such as the number of rows in the table and the number of pages used to store the table.
- Statistical information about each index defined for the specified table, such as the number of unique values in an index and the number of pages used to store the table's indexes.

The information returned by this function is placed in a SQL result data set, and can be processed with the same functions that process a result data set generated by a query. Table 17.7 lists the columns in this result data set.

TABLE 17.7 Result Data Set Returned by SQLStatistics( )

Column	Column name	Data type	Description
1	TABLE_CAT	VARCHAR(128)	The name of the system catalog table in which the TABLE_SCHEM value is stored. Since DB2 does not support three-part table names, DB2 CLI will always set this column to NULL.
2	TABLE_SCHEM	VARCHAR(128)	The name of the schema that contains the TABLE _NAME value.
3	TABLE_NAME	VARCHAR(128) NOT NULL	The name of the table.
4	NON_UNIQUE	SMALLINT	Indicates whether or not the index prohibits duplicate values. Valid values for this column are:

TABLE 17.7 Result Data Set Returned by SQLStatistics( ) *(Continued)*

Column	Column name	Data type	Description
			SQL_TRUE: The index allows duplicate values. SQL_FALSE: The index values must be unique. NULL: The TYPE column indicates that this row is a SQL_TABLE_STAT row (it contains statistics information on the table itself).
5	INDEX_QUALIFIER	VARCHAR(128)	The character string for qualifying the index name in a DROP INDEX SQL statement. Append a period (.) followed by the INDEX_NAME value to this character string to produce the full specification name of the index.
6	INDEX_NAME	VARCHAR(128)	The name of the index. If the TYPE column contains the value SQL_TABLE_STAT, this column will be set to NULL.
7	TYPE	SMALLINT NOT NULL	Identifies the type of information contained in the current row of the result data set. Valid values for this column are: SQL_TABLE_STAT: Indicates that the current row contains statistics information on the table itself. SQL_INDEX_CLUSTERED: Indicates that the current row contains information on an index, and the index type is a clustered index. SQL_INDEX_HASHED: Indicates that the current row contains information on an index and the index type is a hashed index. SQL_INDEX_OTHER: Indicates that this row contains information on an index and the index type is other than clustered or hashed.
8	ORDINAL_POSITION	SMALLINT	The column sequence number in the index whose name is stored in the INDEX_NAME. The first column in the index is number 1, the second column is number 2, and so on. If the TYPE column contains the value SQL_TABLE_STAT, this column will be set to NULL.
9	COLUMN_NAME	VARCHAR(128)	The name of the column in the index. If the TYPE column contains the value SQL _TABLE_STAT, this column will be set to NULL.
10	ASC_OR_DESC	CHAR(1)	The sort sequence to be used for the column. Valid values for this column are: A: The column is sorted in ascending order. D: The column is sorted in descending order. NULL: This is returned if the value in the TYPE column is SQL_TABLE_STAT.
11	CARDINALITY	INTEGER	The number of unique values in the index. If the TYPE column contains the value SQL_TABLE_STAT, this column will contain the number of rows in the table. If the TYPE column does not contain the value SQL_TABLE_STAT, this column will contain the number of unique values in the index.

TABLE 17.7 Result Data Set Returned by SQLStatistics( ) *(Continued)*

Column	Column name	Data type	Description
			If this information is not available from the data source, this column will be set to NULL.
12	PAGES	INTEGER	The number of pages needed to store the table or index. If the TYPE column contains the value SQL_TABLE_STAT, this column will contain the number of pages used to store the table. If the TYPE column contains the value SQL_TABLE_STAT, this column will contain the number of pages used to store the indexes. If this information is not available from the data source, this column will be set to NULL.
13	FILTER_CONDITION	VARCHAR(128)	Identifies the filter condition used if the index is a filtered index. Since DB2 database servers do not support filtered indexes, this column will always be set to NULL. This column will be also be set to NULL if the TYPE column contains the value SQL_TABLE_STAT.

Adapted from IBM's Database 2 Call Level Interface Guide and Reference, Table 139, pages 376 to 377.

Specifications DB2 CLI 2.1, ODBC 1.0, X/OPEN CLI

Return Codes SQL_SUCCESS, SQL_SUCCESS_WITH_INFO, SQL_INVALID_HANDLE, SQL_ERROR

SQLSTATEs **08**S01, **24**000, **40**003, **S1**001, **S1**010, **S1**014, **S1**090, **S1**100, **S1**101, **S1**C00, **S1**T00

Comments

- Since the SQLStatistics( ) function often maps to a complex and therefore expensive query against the database system catalog tables, use it sparingly. If the produced result data set needs to be used more than once, save it rather than regenerating it by invoking the SQLStatistics( ) function again.
- The result data set returned by this function is ordered by NON_UNIQUE, TYPE, INDEX_QUALIFIER, INDEX_NAME, and ORDINAL_POSITION.
- The VARCHAR columns of the catalog functions result data set have been declared with a maximum length of 128 characters to be consistent with the SQL92 standard limits. Since DB2 names are less than 128 characters, an application can choose to always set aside 128 characters (plus the null terminator) for the output buffer, or alternatively to allocate only the required amount of memory by first calling the SQLGetInfo( ) function with the *InfoType* parameter set to SQL_MAX_CATALOG_NAME_LEN, SQL_MAX_OWNER_SCHEMA_LEN, SQL_MAX_NAME_LEN, and/or SQL_MAX_COLUMN_NAME_LEN to determine respectively the actual lengths of the TABLE_CAT, TABLE_SCHEM, TABLE_NAME, and COLUMN_NAME columns supported by the current data source connection.
- Although new columns might be added and the names of the existing columns in the result data set might be changed in future releases of DB2 CLI, the position of the current columns in this data set will not change.

- For rows in the result data set that contain table statistics (e.g., TYPE is set to SQL_TABLE_STAT), the column values of NON_UNIQUE, INDEX_QUALIFIER, INDEX_NAME, ORDINAL_POSITION, COLUMN_NAME, and ASC_OR_DESC are set to NULL. If you cannot determine CARDINALITY or PAGES information, these columns will also be set to NULL.

Note: The accuracy of the information returned by the SQLStatistics( ) function depends on many factors. The main factor, which can be controlled, is the accuracy of the database statistics at the time the SQL statement is executed. Database statistics are updated for DB2 for OS/2 and DB2 for AIX databases each time the RUNSTATS utility is run.

Restrictions There are no restrictions associated with this function call.

See Also SQLColumns( ), SQLSpecialColumns( )

Examples The following C program illustrates how to use the SQLStatistics( ) function to obtain information about the indexes that have been defined for a specific table in the current connected data source:

```
#include <stdio.h>
#include <stdlib.h>
#include <sqlcli1.h>

int main()
{
    /* Declare The Local Memory Variables */
    SQLRETURN    rc = SQL_SUCCESS;
    SQLHENV      EnvHandle;
    SQLHDBC      DSCHandle;
    SQLHSTMT     StmtHandle;
    SQLCHAR      IndexName[129];
    SQLCHAR      ColumnName[129];

    /* Allocate An Environment Handle */
    rc = SQLAllocEnv(&EnvHandle);

    /* Allocate A Connection Handle */
    rc = SQLAllocConnect(EnvHandle, &DSCHandle);

    /* Connect To The SAMPLE Database */
    rc = SQLConnect(DSCHandle, "SAMPLE", SQL_NTS, "etpdd6z", SQL_NTS,
                    "sanders", SQL_NTS);

    /* Allocate An SQL Statement Handle */
    rc = SQLAllocStmt(DSCHandle, &StmtHandle);

    /* Obtain A List Of Index Names For A Specified Table And Schema */
    rc = SQLStatistics(StmtHandle, NULL, 0, "USERID", SQL_NTS,
                       "EMP_RESUME", SQL_NTS, SQL_INDEX_ALL,
                       SQL_QUICK);

    if (rc != SQL_ERROR)
        {
        /* Bind The Columns In The Result Data Set To Local */
        /* Storage Variables                                */
        SQLBindCol(StmtHandle, 6, SQL_C_CHAR, (SQLPOINTER) IndexName,
                   sizeof(IndexName), NULL);
```

```
        SQLBindCol(StmtHandle, 9, SQL_C_CHAR, (SQLPOINTER) ColumnName,
                sizeof(ColumnName), NULL);
        /* Retrieve And Display The Results */
        printf("Table Name : USERID.EMP_RESUME\n");
        printf("Index Name          Column Name\n");
        printf("--------------------------------\n");
        while (rc != SQL_NO_DATA_FOUND)
            {

            /* Retrieve A Record From The Result Data Set */
            rc = SQLFetch(StmtHandle);

            /* Print The Information Retrieved */
            if (rc != SQL_NO_DATA_FOUND)
                printf("%-20s %s\n", IndexName, ColumnName);
            }
        }

    /* Disconnect From The SAMPLE Database */
    SQLDisconnect(DSCHandle);

    /* Free The SQL Statement Handle */
    if (StmtHandle != NULL)
        SQLFreeStmt(StmtHandle, SQL_DROP);

    /* Free The Connection Handle */
    if (DSCHandle != NULL)
        SQLFreeConnect(DSCHandle);

    /* Free The Environment Handle */
    if (EnvHandle != NULL)
        SQLFreeEnv(EnvHandle);

    /* Return To The Operating System */
    return(rc);
}
```

The following C++ program illustrates how the SQLStatistics( ) function is used by class methods to obtain information about the indexes that have been defined for a specific table in the current connected data source:

```
#include <iostream.h>
#include <string.h>
#include <sqlcli1.h>

/* Define The CLI Class */
class CLI
{
    /* Declare The Private Attribute Variables */
    private:
       SQLHENV       EnvHandle;
       SQLHDBC       DSCHandle;
       SQLHSTMT      StmtHandle;
       SQLCHAR       IndexName[129];
       SQLCHAR       ColumnName[129];

    /* Declare The Public Attribute Variables */
    public:
       SQLRETURN  rc;

    /* Declare The Member Function Prototypes */
```

```
    CLI();                                  // Constructor
    ~CLI();                                 // Destructor
    SQLRETURN Connect();
    SQLRETURN ShowIndexes();
    SQLRETURN Disconnect();
} ;

/* Define The Class Constructor */
CLI::CLI()
{
    /* Initialize The Return Code Variable */
    rc = SQL_SUCCESS;

    /* Allocate An Environment Handle */
    rc = SQLAllocEnv(&EnvHandle);

    /* Allocate A Connection Handle */
    rc = SQLAllocConnect(EnvHandle, &DSCHandle);
}

/* Define The Class Destructor */
CLI::~CLI()
{
    /* Free The Connection Handle */
    if (DSCHandle != NULL)
        SQLFreeConnect(DSCHandle);

    /* Free The Environment Handle */
    if (EnvHandle != NULL)
        SQLFreeEnv(EnvHandle);
}

/* Define The Connect() Member Function */
SQLRETURN CLI::Connect()
{
    /* Connect To The SAMPLE Database */
    rc = SQLConnect(DSCHandle, (SQLCHAR *) "SAMPLE", SQL_NTS,
                    (SQLCHAR *) "etpdd6z", SQL_NTS,
                    (SQLCHAR *) "sanders", SQL_NTS);

    /* Allocate An SQL Statement Handle */
    rc = SQLAllocStmt(DSCHandle, &StmtHandle);

    /* Return The CLI Function Return Code */
    return(rc);
}

/* Define The Disconnect() Member Function */
SQLRETURN CLI::Disconnect(void)
{
    /* Disconnect From The Database */
    rc = SQLDisconnect(DSCHandle);

    /* Free The SQL Statement Handle */
    if (StmtHandle != NULL)
        SQLFreeStmt(StmtHandle, SQL_DROP);

    /* Return The CLI Function Return Code */
    return(rc);
}
```

```
/* Define The ShowIndexes() Member Function */
SQLRETURN CLI::ShowIndexes(void)
{
    /* Obtain A List Of Index Names For A Specified Table And */
    /* Schema                                                 */
    rc = SQLStatistics(StmtHandle, NULL, 0, (SQLCHAR *) "USERID",
                       SQL_NTS, (SQLCHAR *) "EMP_RESUME", SQL_NTS,
                       SQL_INDEX_ALL, SQL_QUICK);

    if (rc != SQL_ERROR)
        {
        /* Bind The Columns In The Result Data Set To Local */
        /* Storage Variables                                */
        SQLBindCol(StmtHandle, 6, SQL_C_CHAR, (SQLPOINTER) IndexName,
                   sizeof(IndexName), NULL);

        SQLBindCol(StmtHandle, 9, SQL_C_CHAR, (SQLPOINTER) ColumnName,
                   sizeof(ColumnName), NULL);

        /* Retrieve And Display The Results */
        cout << "Table Name : USERID.EMP_RESUME" << endl;
        cout << "Index Name           Column Name" << endl;
        cout << "--------------------------------" << endl;
        while (rc != SQL_NO_DATA_FOUND)
            {

            /* Retrieve A Record From The Result Data Set */
            rc = SQLFetch(StmtHandle);

            /* Print The Information Retrieved */
            if (rc != SQL_NO_DATA_FOUND)
                {
                cout.setf(ios::left);
                cout.width(21);
                cout << IndexName << ColumnName << endl;
                }
            }
        }

    /* Return The CLI Function Return Code */
    return(rc);
}

int main()
{
    /* Declare The Local Memory Variables */
    SQLRETURN  rc = SQL_SUCCESS;

    /* Create An Instance Of The CLI Class */
    CLI Sample;

    /* Connect To The SAMPLE Database */
    if ((rc = Sample.Connect()) != SQL_SUCCESS)
        return(rc);

    /* Display A List Of All Indexes Defined For The EMP_RESUME */
    /* Table In The USERID Schema                               */
    Sample.ShowIndexes();

    /* Disconnect From The SAMPLE Database */
    Sample.Disconnect();
```

```
    /* Return To The Operating System */
    return(rc);
}
```

SQLPrimaryKeys

Purpose The SQLPrimaryKeys( ) function retrieves the list of column names that comprise the primary key for the specified table.

Syntax

```
SQLRETURN SQLPrimaryKeys (SQLHSTMT     StmtHandle,
                          SQLCHAR FAR  *CatalogName,
                          SQLSMALLINT  CatalogNameSize,
                          SQLCHAR FAR  *SchemaName,
                          SQLSMALLINT  SchemaNameSize,
                          SQLCHAR FAR  *TableName,
                          SQLSMALLINT  TableNameSize);
```

Parameters

StmtHandle The statement handle where the address of the SQL statement buffer is stored.

CatalogName A pointer to a location in memory where the catalog qualifier of a three-part table name is stored. For DB2, this must be a null pointer or a zero-length string.

CatalogNameSize The length of the catalog qualifier value stored in the *CatalogName* parameter. For DB2, this parameter must be set to 0.

SchemaName A pointer to a location in memory where the schema name of a three-part table name is stored.

SchemaNameSize The length of the schema name value stored in the *Schema Name* parameter.

TableName A pointer to a location in memory where the table name is stored.

TableNameSize The length of the table name value stored in the *TableName* parameter.

Includes

```
#include <sqlcli1.h>
```

Description The SQLPrimaryKeys( ) function retrieves a list of column names that comprise the primary key for the specified table. The information returned by this function is placed in a SQL result data set, and can be processed with the same functions used to process a result data set generated by a query. Table 17.8 lists the columns in this result data set.

TABLE 17.8 Result Data Set Returned by SQLPrimaryKeys( )

Column	Column name	Data type	Description
1	TABLE_CAT	VARCHAR(128)	The name of the system catalog table in which the TABLE_SCHEM value is stored. Since DB2 does not support three-part table names, DB2 CLI will always set this column to NULL.
2	TABLE_SCHEM	VARCHAR(128)	The name of the schema that contains the TABLE_NAME value.
3	TABLE_NAME	VARCHAR(128) NOT NULL	The name of the specified table.
4	COLUMN_NAME	VARCHAR(128) NOT NULL	The name of the primary key column.

TABLE 17.8 Result Data Set Returned by SQLPrimaryKeys( ) *(Continued)*

Column	Column name	Data type	Description
5	ORDINAL_POSITION	SMALLINT NOT NULL	The column sequence number in the primary key. The first column in the primary key is number 1, the second column is number 2, and so on.
6	PK_NAME	VARCHAR(128)	The primary key name (identifier). This column will be set to NULL if a primary key name is not applicable for data source.

Adapted from IBM's Database 2 Call Level Interface Guide and Reference, Table 106, page 309.

Specifications DB2 CLI 2.1, ODBC 1.0

Return Codes SQL_SUCCESS, SQL_SUCCESS_WITH_INFO, SQL_INVALID_HANDLE, SQL_ERROR

SQLSTATEs **08**S01, **24**000, **40**003, **S1**001, **S1**010, **S1**014, **S1**090, **S1**C00, **S1**T00

Comments

- Since the SQLPrimaryKeys( ) function often maps to a complex and therefore expensive query against the database system catalog tables, use it sparingly. If the produced result data set needs to be used more than once, save it rather than regenerating it by invoking the SQLPrimaryKeys( ) function again.
- The result data set returned by this function is ordered by TABLE_CAT, TABLE_SCHEM, TABLE_NAME, and ORDINAL_POSITION.
- The VARCHAR columns of the catalog functions result data set have been declared with a maximum length of 128 characters to be consistent with the SQL92 standard limits. Since DB2 names are less than 128 characters, an application can choose to always set aside 128 characters (plus the null terminator) for the output buffer, or alternatively to allocate only the required amount of memory by first calling the SQLGetInfo( ) function with the *InfoType* parameter set to SQL_MAX_CATALOG_NAME_LEN, SQL_MAX_OWNER_SCHEMA_LEN, SQL_MAX_NAME_LEN, and/or SQL_MAX_COLUMN_NAME_LEN to determine respectively the actual lengths of the TABLE_CAT, TABLE_SCHEM, TABLE_NAME, and COLUMN_NAME columns supported by the current data source connection.
- Although new columns might be added and the names of the existing columns in the result data set might change in future releases of DB2 CLI, the position of the current columns in this data set will not change.

Restrictions There are no restrictions associated with this function call.

See Also SQLForeignKeys( ), SQLStatistics( )

Examples The following C program illustrates how to use the SQLPrimaryKeys( ) function to obtain information about the columns used in a primary key of a specific table:

```
#include <stdio.h>
#include <stdlib.h>
#include <sqlcli1.h>

int main()
{
    /* Declare The Local Memory Variables */
```

```
SQLRETURN     rc = SQL_SUCCESS;
SQLHENV       EnvHandle;
SQLHDBC       DSCHandle;
SQLHSTMT      StmtHandle;
SQLCHAR       TableName[129];
SQLCHAR       ColumnName[129];
SQLSMALLINT   Position;

/* Allocate An Environment Handle */
rc = SQLAllocEnv(&EnvHandle);

/* Allocate A Connection Handle */
rc = SQLAllocConnect(EnvHandle, &DSCHandle);

/* Connect To The SAMPLE Database */
rc = SQLConnect(DSCHandle, "SAMPLE", SQL_NTS, "etpdd6z", SQL_NTS,
                "sanders", SQL_NTS);

/* Allocate An SQL Statement Handle */
rc = SQLAllocStmt(DSCHandle, &StmtHandle);

/* Obtain A List Of Primary Keys For A Specified Table And Schema */
rc = SQLPrimaryKeys(StmtHandle, NULL, 0, "USERID", SQL_NTS,
                    "EMP_PHOTO", SQL_NTS);

if (rc != SQL_ERROR)
    {
    /* Bind The Columns In The Result Data Set To Local */
    /* Storage Variables                                 */
    SQLBindCol(StmtHandle, 3, SQL_C_CHAR, (SQLPOINTER) TableName,
               sizeof(TableName), NULL);

    SQLBindCol(StmtHandle, 4, SQL_C_CHAR, (SQLPOINTER) ColumnName,
               sizeof(ColumnName), NULL);

    SQLBindCol(StmtHandle, 5, SQL_C_SHORT, (SQLPOINTER) &Position,
               0, NULL);

    /* Retrieve And Display The Results */
    printf("Table Name      Column Name     Position\n");
    printf("----------------------------------------\n");
    while (rc != SQL_NO_DATA_FOUND)
        {

        /* Retrieve A Record From The Result Data Set */
        rc = SQLFetch(StmtHandle);

        /* Print The Information Retrieved */
        if (rc != SQL_NO_DATA_FOUND)
            printf("%-15s %-15s %d\n", TableName, ColumnName,
                   Position);
        }
    }

/* Disconnect From The SAMPLE Database */
SQLDisconnect(DSCHandle);

/* Free The SQL Statement Handle */
if (StmtHandle != NULL)
    SQLFreeStmt(StmtHandle, SQL_DROP);

/* Free The Connection Handle */
```

```
    if (DSCHandle != NULL)
        SQLFreeConnect(DSCHandle);

    /* Free The Environment Handle */
    if (EnvHandle != NULL)
        SQLFreeEnv(EnvHandle);

    /* Return To The Operating System */
    return(rc);
}
```

The following C++ program illustrates how the SQLPrimaryKeys( ) function is used by class methods to obtain information about the columns used in a primary key of a specific table:

```
#include <iostream.h>
#include <string.h>
#include <sqlcli1.h>

/* Define The CLI Class */
class CLI
{
    /* Declare The Private Attribute Variables */
    private:
       SQLHENV      EnvHandle;
       SQLHDBC      DSCHandle;
       SQLHSTMT     StmtHandle;
       SQLCHAR      TableName[129];
       SQLCHAR      ColumnName[129];
       SQLSMALLINT  Position;

    /* Declare The Public Attribute Variables */
    public:
       SQLRETURN  rc;
    /* Declare The Member Function Prototypes */
    CLI();                                    // Constructor
    ~CLI();                                   // Destructor
    SQLRETURN Connect();
    SQLRETURN ShowPrimaryKeys();
    SQLRETURN Disconnect();
} ;

/* Define The Class Constructor */
CLI::CLI()
{
    /* Initialize The Return Code Variable */
    rc = SQL_SUCCESS;

    /* Allocate An Environment Handle */
    rc = SQLAllocEnv(&EnvHandle);

    /* Allocate A Connection Handle */
    rc = SQLAllocConnect(EnvHandle, &DSCHandle);
}

/* Define The Class Destructor */
CLI::~CLI()
{
    /* Free The Connection Handle */
    if (DSCHandle != NULL)
        SQLFreeConnect(DSCHandle);
```

```
    /* Free The Environment Handle */
    if (EnvHandle != NULL)
        SQLFreeEnv(EnvHandle);
}

/* Define The Connect() Member Function */
SQLRETURN CLI::Connect()
{
    /* Connect To The SAMPLE Database */
    rc = SQLConnect(DSCHandle, (SQLCHAR *) "SAMPLE", SQL_NTS,
                    (SQLCHAR *) "etpdd6z", SQL_NTS,
                    (SQLCHAR *) "sanders", SQL_NTS);

    /* Allocate An SQL Statement Handle */
    rc = SQLAllocStmt(DSCHandle, &StmtHandle);

    /* Return The CLI Function Return Code */
    return(rc);
}

/* Define The Disconnect() Member Function */
SQLRETURN CLI::Disconnect(void)
{
    /* Disconnect From The Database */
    rc = SQLDisconnect(DSCHandle);

    /* Free The SQL Statement Handle */
    if (StmtHandle != NULL)
        SQLFreeStmt(StmtHandle, SQL_DROP);

    /* Return The CLI Function Return Code */
    return(rc);
}

/* Define The ShowPrimaryKeys() Member Function */
SQLRETURN CLI::ShowPrimaryKeys(void)
{
    /* Obtain A List Of Primary Keys For A Specified Table And Schema */
    rc = SQLPrimaryKeys(StmtHandle, NULL, 0, (SQLCHAR *) "USERID",
                        SQL_NTS, (SQLCHAR *) "EMP_PHOTO", SQL_NTS);

    if (rc != SQL_ERROR)
        {
        /* Bind The Columns In The Result Data Set To Local */
        /* Storage Variables                                */
        SQLBindCol(StmtHandle, 3, SQL_C_CHAR, (SQLPOINTER) TableName,
                   sizeof(TableName), NULL);

        SQLBindCol(StmtHandle, 4, SQL_C_CHAR, (SQLPOINTER) ColumnName,
                   sizeof(ColumnName), NULL);

        SQLBindCol(StmtHandle, 5, SQL_C_SHORT, (SQLPOINTER) &Position,
                   0, NULL);

        /* Retrieve And Display The Results */
        cout << "Table Name      Column Name     Position" << endl;
        cout << "----------------------------------------" << endl;
        while (rc != SQL_NO_DATA_FOUND)
            {

            /* Retrieve A Record From The Result Data Set */
            rc = SQLFetch(StmtHandle);
```

```
                /* Print The Information Retrieved */
                if (rc != SQL_NO_DATA_FOUND)
                    {
                    cout.setf(ios::left);
                    cout.width(16);
                    cout << TableName;
                    cout.setf(ios::left);
                    cout.width(16);
                    cout << ColumnName << Position << endl;
                    }
                }
            }

    /* Return The CLI Function Return Code */
    return(rc);
}

int main()
{
    /* Declare The Local Memory Variables */
    SQLRETURN  rc = SQL_SUCCESS;

    /* Create An Instance Of The CLI Class */
    CLI Sample;

    /* Connect To The SAMPLE Database */
    if ((rc = Sample.Connect()) != SQL_SUCCESS)
        return(rc);

    /* Display A List Of All Primary Keys For The EMP_PHOTO Table */
    /* In The USERID Schema                                       */
    Sample.ShowPrimaryKeys();

    /* Disconnect From The SAMPLE Database */
    Sample.Disconnect();

    /* Return To The Operating System */
    return(rc);
}
```

SQLForeignKeys

Purpose The SQLForeignKeys( ) function retrieves information about the foreign keys that are defined for a specified table.

Syntax

```
SQLRETURN SQLForeignKeys (SQLHSTMT     StmtHandle,
                          SQLCHAR FAR *PKCatalogName,
                          SQLSMALLINT PKCatalogNameSize,
                          SQLCHAR FAR *PKSchemaName,
                          SQLSMALLINT PKSchemaNameSize,
                          SQLCHAR FAR *PKTableName,
                          SQLSMALLINT PKTableNameSize,
                          SQLCHAR FAR *FKCatalogName,
                          SQLSMALLINT FKCatalogNameSize,
                          SQLCHAR FAR *FKSchemaName,
                          SQLSMALLINT FKSchemaNameSize,
                          SQLCHAR FAR *FKTableName,
                          SQLSMALLINT FKTableNameSize);
```

Parameters

StmtHandle The statement handle where the address of the SQL statement buffer is stored.

PKCatalogName A pointer to a location in memory where the catalog qualifier of a three-part table name of the table containing the primary key is stored. For DB2, this must be a null pointer or a zero-length string.

PKCatalogNameSize The length of the catalog qualifier value stored in the *PKCatalogName* parameter. For DB2, this parameter must be set to 0.

PKSchemaName A pointer to a location in memory where the schema name of a three-part table name of the table containing the primary key is stored.

PKSchemaNameSize The length of the schema name value stored in the *PKSchemaName* parameter.

PKTableName A pointer to a location in memory where the table name of the table containing the primary key is stored.

PKTableNameSize The length of the table name value stored in the *PKTableName* parameter.

FKCatalogName A pointer to a location in memory where the catalog qualifier of a three-part table name of the table containing the foreign key is stored. For DB2, this must be a null pointer or a zero-length string.

FKCatalogNameSize The length of the catalog qualifier value stored in the *FKCatalogName* parameter. For DB2, this parameter must be set to 0.

FKSchemaName A pointer to a location in memory where the schema name of a three-part table name of the table containing the foreign key is stored.

FKSchemaNameSize The length of the schema name value stored in the *FKSchemaName* parameter.

FKTableName A pointer to a location in memory where the table name of the table containing the foreign key is stored.

FKTableNameSize The length of the table name value stored in the *FKTableName* parameter.

Includes

```
#include <sqlcli1.h>
```

Description

The SQLForeignKeys( ) function retrieves information about the foreign keys defined for a specified table. The information returned by this function is placed in a SQL result data set, and can be processed with the same functions used to process a result data set generated by a query. Table 17.9 lists the columns in this result data set.

TABLE 17.9 Result Data Set Returned by SQLForeignKeys( )

Column	Column name	Data type	Description
1	PKTABLE_CAT	VARCHAR(128)	The name of the system catalog table in which the PKTABLE_SCHEM value is stored. Since DB2 does not support three-part table names, DB2 CLI will always set this column to NULL.
2	PKTABLE_SCHEM	VARCHAR(128)	The name of the schema that contains the PKTABLE_NAME value.
3	PKTABLE_NAME	VARCHAR(128) NOT NULL	The name of the table that contains the primary key.
4	PKCOLUMN_NAME	VARCHAR(128) NOT NULL	The name of the primary key column.
5	FKTABLE_CAT	VARCHAR(128)	The name of the system catalog table in which the FKTABLE_SCHEM value is stored. Since DB2 does not support three part table names, DB2 CLI will always set this column to NULL.

TABLE 17.9 Result Data Set Returned by SQLForeignKeys( ) *(Continued)*

Column	Column name	Data type	Description
6	FKTABLE_SCHEM	VARCHAR(128)	The name of the schema that contains the FKTABLE_NAME value.
7	FKTABLE_NAME	VARCHAR(128) NOT NULL	The name of the table that contains the foreign key.
8	FKCOLUMN_NAME	VARCHAR(128) NOT NULL	The name of the foreign key column.
9	ORDINAL_POSITION	SMALLINT NOT NULL	The column sequence number in the key. The first column in the key is number 1, the second column is number 2, and so on.
10	UPDATE_RULE	SMALLINT	Identifies the action to be applied to the foreign key when the SQL operation is UPDATE. Valid values for this column are SQL_NO_ACTION and SQL_RESTRICT. The update rule for IBM DB2 databases is always either SQL_NO_ACTION or SQL_RESTRICT. ODBC applications can also return SQL_CASCADE and SQL_SET_NULL from other non-IBM RDBMS databases.
11	DELETE_RULE	SMALLINT	Identifies the action to be applied to the foreign key when the SQL operation is DELETE. Valid values for this column are: SQL_NO_ACTION, SQL _CASCADE, SQL_RESTRICT, SQL_SET _DEFAULT, and SQL_SET_NULL.
12	FK_NAME	VARCHAR(128)	The foreign key name (identifier). This column is set to NULL if a foreign key name is not applicable for data source.
13	PK_NAME	VARCHAR(128)	The primary key name (identifier). This column is set to NULL if a primary key name is not applicable for data source.

Adapted from IBM's Database 2 Call Level Interface Guide and Reference, Table 57, pages 218 to 219.

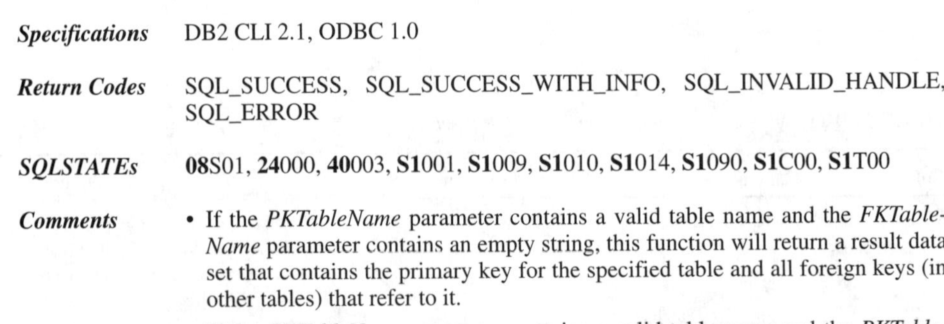

Specifications DB2 CLI 2.1, ODBC 1.0

Return Codes SQL_SUCCESS, SQL_SUCCESS_WITH_INFO, SQL_INVALID_HANDLE, SQL_ERROR

SQLSTATEs **08**S01, **24**000, **40**003, **S1**001, **S1**009, **S1**010, **S1**014, **S1**090, **S1**C00, **S1**T00

Comments

- If the *PKTableName* parameter contains a valid table name and the *FKTableName* parameter contains an empty string, this function will return a result data set that contains the primary key for the specified table and all foreign keys (in other tables) that refer to it.
- If the *FKTableName* parameter contains a valid table name and the *PKTableName* parameter contains an empty string, this function will return a result set that contains all of the foreign keys for the specified table and all primary keys (in other tables) to which they refer.
- If both the *PKTableName* and *FKTableName* parameters contain valid table names, this function will return the foreign keys in the table specified in the *FKTableName* parameter that refer to the primary key of the table specified in the *PKTableName* parameter. This result data set should contain, at the most, one key.

- If the schema name (qualifier) associated with a table name is not specified, the schema name will default to the one currently in effect for the current data source connection.
- If the foreign keys associated with a primary key are requested, the result data set returned by this function is ordered by FKTABLE_CAT, FKTABLE _SCHEM, FKTABLE_NAME, and ORDINAL_POSITION. If the primary keys associated with a foreign key are requested, the result set returned by this function will be ordered by PKTABLE_CAT, PKTABLE_SCHEM, PKTABLE_NAME, and ORDINAL_POSITION.
- The VARCHAR columns of the catalog functions result data set have been declared with a maximum length of 128 characters to be consistent with the SQL92 standard limits. Since DB2 names are less than 128 characters, an application can choose to always set aside 128 characters (plus the null terminator) for the output buffer, or alternatively to allocate only the required amount of memory by first calling the SQLGetInfo( ) function with the *InfoType* parameter set to SQL_MAX_CATALOG_NAME_LEN, SQL_MAX_OWNER_SCHEMA_LEN, SQL_MAX_NAME_LEN, and/or SQL_MAX_COLUMN_NAME_LEN to determine respectively the actual lengths of the TABLE_CAT, TABLE_SCHEM, TABLE_NAME, and COLUMN_NAME columns supported by the current data source connection.
- Although new columns might be added and the names of the existing columns in the result data set might be changed in future releases of DB2 CLI, the position of the current columns in this data set will not change.

Restrictions There are no restrictions associated with this function call.

See Also SQLPrimaryKeys( ), SQLStatistics( )

Examples The following C program illustrates how to use the SQLForeignKeys( ) function to obtain information about the columns used in a foreign key for a specific table:

```
#include <stdio.h>
#include <stdlib.h>
#include <sqlcli1.h>

int main()
{
    /* Declare The Local Memory Variables */
    SQLRETURN    rc = SQL_SUCCESS;
    SQLHENV      EnvHandle;
    SQLHDBC      DSCHandle;
    SQLHSTMT     StmtHandle;
    SQLCHAR      TableName[129];
    SQLCHAR      ColumnName[129];
    SQLSMALLINT  Position;

    /* Allocate An Environment Handle */
    rc = SQLAllocEnv(&EnvHandle);

    /* Allocate A Connection Handle */
    rc = SQLAllocConnect(EnvHandle, &DSCHandle);

    /* Connect To The SAMPLE Database */
    rc = SQLConnect(DSCHandle, "SAMPLE", SQL_NTS, "etpdd6z", SQL_NTS,
                    "sanders", SQL_NTS);

    /* Allocate An SQL Statement Handle */
    rc = SQLAllocStmt(DSCHandle, &StmtHandle);
```

```
    /* Obtain A List Of Foreign Keys For A Specified Table And Schema */
    rc = SQLForeignKeys(StmtHandle, NULL, 0, "ETPDD6Z", SQL_NTS,
                        "EXPLAIN_INSTANCE", SQL_NTS, NULL, 0, NULL,
                        SQL_NTS, NULL, SQL_NTS);

    if (rc != SQL_ERROR)
        {
        /* Bind The Columns In The Result Data Set To Local */
        /* Storage Variables                                */
        SQLBindCol(StmtHandle, 3, SQL_C_CHAR, (SQLPOINTER) TableName,
                   sizeof(TableName), NULL);

        SQLBindCol(StmtHandle, 8, SQL_C_CHAR, (SQLPOINTER) ColumnName,
                   sizeof(ColumnName), NULL);

        SQLBindCol(StmtHandle, 9, SQL_C_SHORT, (SQLPOINTER) &Position,
                   0, NULL);

        /* Retrieve And Display The Results */
        printf("Table Name : ETPDD6Z:EXPLAIN_INSTANCE\n");
        printf("Primary Key Table   Foreign Key Column   Position\n");
        printf("-----------------------------------------------\n");
        while (rc != SQL_NO_DATA_FOUND)
            {

            /* Retrieve A Record From The Result Data Set */
            rc = SQLFetch(StmtHandle);

            /* Print The Information Retrieved */
            if (rc != SQL_NO_DATA_FOUND)
                printf("%-19s %-20s %d\n", TableName, ColumnName,
                       Position);
            }
        }

    /* Disconnect From The SAMPLE Database */
    SQLDisconnect(DSCHandle);

    /* Free The SQL Statement Handle */
    if (StmtHandle != NULL)
        SQLFreeStmt(StmtHandle, SQL_DROP);

    /* Free The Connection Handle */
    if (DSCHandle != NULL)
        SQLFreeConnect(DSCHandle);

    /* Free The Environment Handle */
    if (EnvHandle != NULL)
        SQLFreeEnv(EnvHandle);

    /* Return To The Operating System */
    return(rc);
}
```

The following C++ program illustrates how the SQLForeignKeys( ) function is used by class methods to obtain information about the columns used in a foreign key for a specific table:

```
#include <iostream.h>
#include <string.h>
#include <sqlcli1.h>
```

```
/* Define The CLI Class */
class CLI
{
    /* Declare The Private Attribute Variables */
    private:
       SQLHENV      EnvHandle;
       SQLHDBC      DSCHandle;
       SQLHSTMT     StmtHandle;
       SQLCHAR      TableName[129];
       SQLCHAR      ColumnName[129];
       SQLSMALLINT  Position;

    /* Declare The Public Attribute Variables */
    public:
       SQLRETURN  rc;

    /* Declare The Member Function Prototypes */
    CLI();                                       // Constructor
    ~CLI();                                      // Destructor
    SQLRETURN Connect();
    SQLRETURN ShowForeignKeys();
    SQLRETURN Disconnect();
} ;

/* Define The Class Constructor */
CLI::CLI()
{
    /* Initialize The Return Code Variable */
    rc = SQL_SUCCESS;

    /* Allocate An Environment Handle */
    rc = SQLAllocEnv(&EnvHandle);

    /* Allocate A Connection Handle */
    rc = SQLAllocConnect(EnvHandle, &DSCHandle);
}

/* Define The Class Destructor */
CLI::~CLI()
{
    /* Free The Connection Handle */
    if (DSCHandle != NULL)
        SQLFreeConnect(DSCHandle);

    /* Free The Environment Handle */
    if (EnvHandle != NULL)
        SQLFreeEnv(EnvHandle);
}

/* Define The Connect() Member Function */
SQLRETURN CLI::Connect()
{
    /* Connect To The SAMPLE Database */
    rc = SQLConnect(DSCHandle, (SQLCHAR *) "SAMPLE", SQL_NTS,
                    (SQLCHAR *) "etpdd6z", SQL_NTS,
                    (SQLCHAR *) "sanders", SQL_NTS);

    /* Allocate An SQL Statement Handle */
    rc = SQLAllocStmt(DSCHandle, &StmtHandle);

    /* Return The CLI Function Return Code */
    return(rc);
}
```

```
/* Define The Disconnect() Member Function */
SQLRETURN CLI::Disconnect(void)
{
    /* Disconnect From The Database */
    rc = SQLDisconnect(DSCHandle);

    /* Free The SQL Statement Handle */
    if (StmtHandle != NULL)
        SQLFreeStmt(StmtHandle, SQL_DROP);

    /* Return The CLI Function Return Code */
    return(rc);
}

/* Define The ShowForeignKeys() Member Function */
SQLRETURN CLI::ShowForeignKeys(void)
{
    /* Obtain A List Of Foreign Keys For A Specified Table And Schema */
    rc = SQLForeignKeys(StmtHandle, NULL, 0, (SQLCHAR *) "ETPDD6Z",
                        SQL_NTS, (SQLCHAR *) "EXPLAIN_INSTANCE",
                        SQL_NTS, NULL, 0, NULL, SQL_NTS, NULL,
                        SQL_NTS);

    if (rc != SQL_ERROR)
        {
        /* Bind The Columns In The Result Data Set To Local */
        /* Storage Variables                                */
        SQLBindCol(StmtHandle, 3, SQL_C_CHAR, (SQLPOINTER) TableName,
                   sizeof(TableName), NULL);

        SQLBindCol(StmtHandle, 8, SQL_C_CHAR, (SQLPOINTER) ColumnName,
                   sizeof(ColumnName), NULL);

        SQLBindCol(StmtHandle, 9, SQL_C_SHORT, (SQLPOINTER) &Position,
                   0, NULL);

        /* Retrieve And Display The Results */
        cout << "Table Name : ETPDD6Z:EXPLAIN_INSTANCE" << endl;
        cout << "Primary Key Table   Foreign Key Column   Position";
        cout << endl;
        cout << "-------------------------------------------------";
        cout << endl;
        while (rc != SQL_NO_DATA_FOUND)
            {

            /* Retrieve A Record From The Result Data Set */
            rc = SQLFetch(StmtHandle);

            /* Print The Information Retrieved */
            if (rc != SQL_NO_DATA_FOUND)
                {
                cout.setf(ios::left);
                cout.width(20);
                cout << TableName;
                cout.setf(ios::left);
                cout.width(21);
                cout << ColumnName << Position << endl;
                }
            }
        }
```

```
    /* Return The CLI Function Return Code */
    return(rc);
}

int main()
{
    /* Declare The Local Memory Variables */
    SQLRETURN  rc = SQL_SUCCESS;

    /* Create An Instance Of The CLI Class */
    CLI Sample;

    /* Connect To The SAMPLE Database */
    if ((rc = Sample.Connect()) != SQL_SUCCESS)
        return(rc);

    /* Display A List Of All Foreign Keys For The EXPLAIN_INSTANCE */
    /* Table In The ETPDD6Z Schema                                 */
    Sample.ShowForeignKeys();

    /* Disconnect From The SAMPLE Database */
    Sample.Disconnect();

    /* Return To The Operating System */
    return(rc);
}
```

SQLProcedures

Purpose The SQLProcedures( ) function retrieves a list of procedure names registered at the specified data source that match the specified search pattern.

Syntax

```
SQLRETURN SQLProcedures (SQLHSTMT     StmtHandle,
                         SQLCHAR FAR  *ProcCatalog,
                         SQLSMALLINT  ProcCatalogSize,
                         SQLCHAR FAR  *ProcSchema,
                         SQLSMALLINT  ProcSchemaSize,
                         SQLCHAR FAR  *ProcName,
                         SQLSMALLINT  ProcNameSize);
```

Parameters

StmtHandle The statement handle where the address of the SQL statement buffer is stored.

ProcCatalog A pointer to a location in memory where the catalog qualifier of a three-part procedure name is stored. For DB2, this must be a null pointer or a zero-length string.

ProcCatalogSize The length of the catalog qualifier value stored in the *ProcCatalog* parameter. For DB2, this parameter must be set to 0.

ProcSchema A pointer to a location in memory where the schema name of a three-part procedure name is stored.

ProcSchemaSize The length of the schema name value stored in the *ProcSchema* parameter.

ProcName A pointer to a location in memory where the procedure name is stored.

ProcNameSize The length of the procedure name value stored in the *ProcName* parameter.

Includes `#include <sqlcli1.h>`

Description The SQLProcedures( ) function retrieves a list of procedure names registered at the specified data source that match the specified search pattern. The information returned by this function is placed in a SQL result data set, and can be processed with the same functions that process a result data set generated by a query. Table 17.10 lists the columns in this result data set.

TABLE 17.10 Result Data Set Returned by SQLProcedures( )

Column	Column name	Data type	Description
1	PROCEDURE_CAT	VARCHAR(128)	The name of the system catalog table in which the PROCEDURE_SCHEM value is stored. Since DB2 does not support three-part procedure names, DB2 CLI will always set this column to NULL.
2	PROCEDURE_SCHEM	VARCHAR(128)	The name of the schema that contains the PROCEDURE_NAME value.
3	PROCEDURE_NAME	VARCHAR(128) NOT NULL	The name of the stored procedure.
4	NUM_INPUT_PARAMS	INTEGER NOT NULL	The number of input parameters defined for the stored procedure.
5	NUM_OUTPUT_PARAMS	INTEGER NOT NULL	The number of output parameters defined for the stored procedure.
6	NUM_RESULT_SETS	INTEGER NOT NULL	The number of result data sets that will be returned when the stored procedure is executed.
7	REMARKS	VARCHAR(254)	Descriptive information about the stored procedure (if any exists).
8	PROCEDURE_TYPE	SMALLINT	Defines the stored procedure type. Valid values for this column are: SQL_PT_UNKNOWN (it cannot be determined whether the stored procedure returns a value or not), SQL_PT_PROCEDURE (the returned object is a stored procedure; it does not return a value), and SQL_PT_FUNCTION (the returned object is a function; it returns a value). DB2 CLI always returns the value SQL_PT_PROCEDURE for this column.

Adapted from IBM's Database 2 Call Level Interface Guide and Reference, Table 112, pages 318 to 319.

Specifications DB2 CLI 2.1, ODBC 1.0

Return Codes SQL_SUCCESS, SQL_SUCCESS_WITH_INFO, SQL_INVALID_HANDLE, SQL_ERROR

SQLSTATEs **08**S01, **24**000, **40**003, **S1**001, **S1**010, **S1**014, **S1**090, **S1**C00, **S1**T00

Comments

- In order for the SQLProcedures( ) function to return a list of stored procedures when the application is connected to DB2 for Common Servers (version 2.1), the pseudo catalog table for stored procedure registration (the table named PROCEDURES in the DB2 CLI schema) must have already been created and populated. Refer to the beginning of the chapter for more information about this pseudo catalog table. It is imperative to follow the exact rules outlined at the beginning of the chapter when populating this table, or the SQLProcedures( ) call will result in an error.

- If this function is to return a list of stored procedures at a DB2 for MVS/ESA (version 4.1 or later) server, the names of the stored procedures must be registered in the server's SYSIBM.SYSPROCEDURES catalog table.
- Since the SQLProcedures( ) function often maps to a complex and therefore expensive query against the database system catalog tables, use it sparingly. If the produced result data set needs to be used more than once, save it rather than regenerating it by invoking the SQLProcedures( ) function again.
- The *SchemaName* and *ProcName* parameters can accept the following search pattern values:

The underscore character (_) Indicates that any single character can be used in place of the underscore character.

The percent character (%) Indicates that any sequence of 0 or more characters can be used in place of the percent character.

If these "wildcard" characters need to be used as themselves (e.g., % = "%"), they must be preceded by an escape character.

- The result data set returned by this function is ordered by PROCEDURE_CAT, PROCEDURE_SCHEMA, and PROCEDURE_NAME.
- If you set the SQL_LONGDATA_COMPAT option to SQL_LD_COMPAT_YES, either by calling the SQLSetConnectOption( ) or by setting the LONGDATACOMPAT option in the DB2 CLI initialization file, large object (LOB) data types will be reported as SQL_LONGVARCHAR, SQL_LONGVARBINARY, or SQL_LONGVARGRAPHIC.
- The VARCHAR columns of the catalog functions result data set have been declared with a maximum length of 128 characters to be consistent with the SQL92 standard limits. Since DB2 names are less than 128 characters, an application can choose to always set aside 128 characters (plus the null terminator) for the output buffer, or alternatively to allocate only the required amount of memory by first calling the SQLGetInfo( ) function with the *InfoType* parameter set to SQL_MAX_CATALOG_NAME_LEN, SQL_MAX_OWNER_SCHEMA_LEN, SQL_MAX_NAME_LEN, and/or SQL_MAX_COLUMN_NAME_LEN to determine respectively the actual lengths of the TABLE_CAT, TABLE_SCHEM, TABLE_NAME, and COLUMN_NAME columns supported by the current data source connection.
- Although new columns might be added and the names of the existing columns in the result data set might be changed in future releases of DB2 CLI, the position of the current columns in this data set will not change.

Restrictions If this function attempts to return a list of stored procedures from a DB2 server that does not provide facilities to support a stored procedure catalog, or from a DB2 server that does not provide support for stored procedures, an empty result data set will be returned.

See Also SQLProcedureColumns( )

Examples The following C program illustrates how to use the SQLProcedures( ) function to obtain information about the stored procedures that are available in the current connected data source:

```
#include <stdio.h>
#include <stdlib.h>
#include <sqlcli1.h>
```

```
int main()
{
    /* Declare The Local Memory Variables */
    SQLRETURN    rc = SQL_SUCCESS;
    SQLHENV      EnvHandle;
    SQLHDBC      DSCHandle;
    SQLHSTMT     StmtHandle;
    SQLCHAR      ProcName[129];
    SQLSMALLINT  NumIParams;

    /* Allocate An Environment Handle */
    rc = SQLAllocEnv(&EnvHandle);

    /* Allocate A Connection Handle */
    rc = SQLAllocConnect(EnvHandle, &DSCHandle);

    /* Connect To The SAMPLE Database */
    rc = SQLConnect(DSCHandle, "SAMPLE", SQL_NTS, "etpdd6z", SQL_NTS,
                    "sanders", SQL_NTS);

    /* Allocate An SQL Statement Handle */
    rc = SQLAllocStmt(DSCHandle, &StmtHandle);

    /* Obtain A List Of Available Stored Procedures */
    rc = SQLProcedures(StmtHandle, NULL, 0, "ExampleSchema", SQL_NTS,
                       "Comp%", SQL_NTS);

    if (rc != SQL_ERROR)
        {
        /* Bind The Columns In The Result Data Set To Local */
        /* Storage Variables                                */
        SQLBindCol(StmtHandle, 3, SQL_C_CHAR, (SQLPOINTER) ProcName,
                   sizeof(ProcName), NULL);

        SQLBindCol(StmtHandle, 4, SQL_C_SHORT, (SQLPOINTER) &NumIParams,
                   0, NULL);

        /* Retrieve And Display The Results */
        printf("Procedure Name          Number Of Input\n");
        printf("                        Parameters\n");
        printf("---------------------------------------\n");
        while (rc != SQL_NO_DATA_FOUND)
            {

            /* Retrieve A Record From The Result Data Set */
            rc = SQLFetch(StmtHandle);

            /* Print The Information Retrieved */
            if (rc != SQL_NO_DATA_FOUND)
                printf("%-22s %d\n", ProcName, NumIParams);
            }
        }

    /* Disconnect From The SAMPLE Database */
    SQLDisconnect(DSCHandle);

    /* Free The SQL Statement Handle */
    if (StmtHandle != NULL)
        SQLFreeStmt(StmtHandle, SQL_DROP);
```

```
    /* Free The Connection Handle */
    if (DSCHandle != NULL)
        SQLFreeConnect(DSCHandle);

    /* Free The Environment Handle */
    if (EnvHandle != NULL)
        SQLFreeEnv(EnvHandle);

    /* Return To The Operating System */
    return(rc);
}
```

The following C++ program illustrates how the SQLProcedures( ) function is used by class methods to obtain information about the stored procedures that are available in the current connected data source:

```
#include <iostream.h>
#include <string.h>
#include <sqlcli1.h>

/* Define The CLI Class */
class CLI
{
    /* Declare The Private Attribute Variables */
    private:
       SQLHENV      EnvHandle;
       SQLHDBC      DSCHandle;
       SQLHSTMT     StmtHandle;
       SQLCHAR      ProcName[129];
       SQLSMALLINT  NumIParams;

    /* Declare The Public Attribute Variables */
    public:
       SQLRETURN  rc;

    /* Declare The Member Function Prototypes */
    CLI();                                      // Constructor
    ~CLI();                                     // Destructor
    SQLRETURN Connect();
    SQLRETURN ShowProcedures();
    SQLRETURN Disconnect();
} ;

/* Define The Class Constructor */
CLI::CLI()
{
    /* Initialize The Return Code Variable */
    rc = SQL_SUCCESS;

    /* Allocate An Environment Handle */
    rc = SQLAllocEnv(&EnvHandle);

    /* Allocate A Connection Handle */
    rc = SQLAllocConnect(EnvHandle, &DSCHandle);
}

/* Define The Class Destructor */
CLI::~CLI()
{
```

```
    /* Free The Connection Handle */
    if (DSCHandle != NULL)
        SQLFreeConnect(DSCHandle);

    /* Free The Environment Handle */
    if (EnvHandle != NULL)
        SQLFreeEnv(EnvHandle);
}

/* Define The Connect() Member Function */
SQLRETURN CLI::Connect()
{
    /* Connect To The SAMPLE Database */
    rc = SQLConnect(DSCHandle, (SQLCHAR *) "SAMPLE", SQL_NTS,
                    (SQLCHAR *) "etpdd6z", SQL_NTS,
                    (SQLCHAR *) "sanders", SQL_NTS);

    /* Allocate An SQL Statement Handle */
    rc = SQLAllocStmt(DSCHandle, &StmtHandle);

    /* Return The CLI Function Return Code */
    return(rc);
}

/* Define The Disconnect() Member Function */
SQLRETURN CLI::Disconnect(void)
{
    /* Disconnect From The Database */
    rc = SQLDisconnect(DSCHandle);

    /* Free The SQL Statement Handle */
    if (StmtHandle != NULL)
        SQLFreeStmt(StmtHandle, SQL_DROP);

    /* Return The CLI Function Return Code */
    return(rc);
}

/* Define The ShowProcedures() Member Function */
SQLRETURN CLI::ShowProcedures(void)
{
    /* Obtain A List Of Available Stored Procedures */
    rc = SQLProcedures(StmtHandle, NULL, 0,
                       (SQLCHAR *) "ExampleSchema", SQL_NTS,
                       (SQLCHAR *) "Comp%", SQL_NTS);

    if (rc != SQL_ERROR)
        {
        /* Bind The Columns In The Result Data Set To Local */
        /* Storage Variables                                */
        SQLBindCol(StmtHandle, 3, SQL_C_CHAR, (SQLPOINTER) ProcName,
                   sizeof(ProcName), NULL);

        SQLBindCol(StmtHandle, 4, SQL_C_SHORT, (SQLPOINTER)
                   &NumIParams, 0, NULL);

        /* Retrieve And Display The Results */
        cout << "Procedure Name         Number Of Input" << endl;
        cout << "                       Parameters" << endl;
        cout << "--------------------------------------" << endl;
```

```
        while (rc != SQL_NO_DATA_FOUND)
            {

            /* Retrieve A Record From The Result Data Set */
            rc = SQLFetch(StmtHandle);

            /* Print The Information Retrieved */
            if (rc != SQL_NO_DATA_FOUND)
                {
                cout.setf(ios::left);
                cout.width(23);
                cout << ProcName << NumIParams << endl;
                }
            }
        }

    /* Return The CLI Function Return Code */
    return(rc);
}

int main()
{
    /* Declare The Local Memory Variables */
    SQLRETURN  rc = SQL_SUCCESS;

    /* Create An Instance Of The CLI Class */
    CLI Sample;

    /* Connect To The SAMPLE Database */
    if ((rc = Sample.Connect()) != SQL_SUCCESS)
        return(rc);

    /* Display A List Of Available Stored Procedures */
    Sample.ShowProcedures();

    /* Disconnect From The SAMPLE Database */
    Sample.Disconnect();

    /* Return To The Operating System */
    return(rc);
}
```

SQLProcedureColumns

Purpose The SQLProcedureColumns( ) function retrieves a list of input and output parameters for a specified procedure, as well as a list of the columns that make up the result data set.

Syntax

```
SQLRETURN SQLProcedureColumns (SQLHSTMT     StmtHandle,
                               SQLCHAR FAR *ProcCatalog,
                               SQLSMALLINT ProcCatalogSize,
                               SQLCHAR FAR *ProcSchema,
                               SQLSMALLINT ProcSchemaSize,
                               SQLCHAR FAR *ProcName,
                               SQLSMALLINT ProcNameSize,
                               SQLCHAR FAR *ColumnName,
                               SQLSMALLINT ColumnNameSize);
```

Parameters

StmtHandle The statement handle where the address of the SQL statement buffer is stored.

ProcCatalog A pointer to a location in memory where the catalog qualifier of a three-part procedure name is stored. For DB2, this must be a null pointer or a zero-length string.

ProcCatalogSize The length of the catalog qualifier value stored in the *ProcCatalog* parameter. For DB2, this parameter must be set to 0.

ProcSchema A pointer to a location in memory where the schema name of a three-part procedure name is stored.

ProcSchemaSize The length of the schema name value stored in the *ProcSchema* parameter.

ProcName A pointer to a location in memory where the procedure name is stored.

ProcNameSize The length of the procedure name value stored in the *ProcName* parameter.

ColumnName A pointer to a location in memory where the column name is stored.

ColumnNameSize The length of the column name value stored in the *ColumnName* parameter.

Includes

```
#include <sqlcli1.h>
```

Description

The SQLProcedureColumns( ) function retrieves the list of input and output parameters for a specified procedure, as well as a list of the columns that make up the result data set. The information returned by this function is placed in a SQL result data set, and can be processed with the same functions that process a result data set generated by a query. Table 17.11 lists the columns in this result data set.

TABLE 17.11 Result Data Set Returned by SQLProcedureColumns( )

Column	Column name	Data type	Description
1	PROCEDURE_CAT	VARCHAR(128)	The name of the system catalog table in which the PROCEDURE_SCHEM value is stored. Since DB2 does not support three-part procedure names, DB2 CLI will always set this column to NULL.
2	PROCEDURE_SCHEM	VARCHAR(128)	The name of the schema that contains the PROCEDURE_NAME value.
3	PROCEDURE_NAME	VARCHAR(128)	The name of the stored procedure.
4	COLUMN_NAME	VARCHAR(128)	The name of the parameter.
5	COLUMN_TYPE	SMALLINT NOT NULL	The parameter type. Valid values for this column are: SQL_PARAM_TYPE_UNKNOWN: The parameter type is unknown (DB2 CLI does not return this value). SQL_PARAM_INPUT: This parameter is an input parameter. SQL_PARAM_OUTPUT: This parameter is an output parameter. SQL_PARAM_INPUT_OUTPUT: This parameter is both an input and an output parameter. SQL_RETURN_VALUE: The parameter column is actually the return value of the stored procedure (DB2 CLI does not return this value).

TABLE 17.11 Result Data Set Returned by SQLProcedureColumns( ) *(Continued)*

Column	Column name	Data type	Description
			SQL_RESULT_COL: This parameter is actually a column in the result set (DB2 CLI does not return this value).
6	DATA_TYPE	SMALLINT NOT NULL	The SQL data type of the parameter identified by COLUMN_NAME. For DB2 CLI, any of the following values are valid: SQL_SMALLINT SQL_GRAPHIC SQL_INTEGER SQL_VARGRAPHIC SQL_DECIMAL SQL_LONGVARGRAPHIC SQL_NUMERIC SQL_BLOB SQL_REAL SQL_BLOB_LOCATOR SQL_FLOAT SQL_CLOB SQL_DOUBLE SQL_CLOB_LOCATOR SQL_CHAR SQL_DBCLOB SQL_VARCHAR SQL_DBLOB_LOCATOR SQL_LONGVARCHAR SQL_DATE SQL_BINARY SQL_TIME SQL_VARBINARY SQL_TIMESTAMP SQL_LONGVARBINARY
7	TYPE_NAME	VARCHAR(128) NOT NULL	The DBMS character representation of the SQL data type name associated with the DATA_TYPE column value. For DB2, any of the following values are valid: SMALLINT GRAPHIC INTEGER VARGRAPHIC DECIMAL LONG VARGRAPHIC NUMERIC BLOB REAL BLOB LOCATOR FLOAT CLOB DOUBLE CLOB LOCATOR CHAR DBCLOB VARCHAR DBLOB LOCATOR LONG VARCHAR DATE CHAR FOR BIT DATA TIME VARCHAR FOR BIT DATA TIMESTAMP LONG VARCHAR FOR BIT DATA
8	COLUMN_SIZE	INTEGER	The maximum number of bytes needed to display the column data in character form. For numeric data types, this is either the total number of digits or the total number of bits allowed in the column, depending on the value in the NUM_PREC_RADIX column. For character or binary string data types, this is the size of the string (string length) in bytes. For date, time, and timestamp data types, this is the total number of characters required to display the value when it is converted to a character string. For graphic (DBCS) data types, this is the size of the graphic string (string length) in double-byte characters.
9	BUFFER_LENGTH	INTEGER	The maximum number of bytes needed for the associated C application buffer to store data from this parameter if the value SQL_C_DEFAULT was

TABLE 17.11 Result Data Set Returned by SQLProcedureColumns( ) *(Continued)*

Column	Column name	Data type	Description	
			specified for the *CDataType* parameter for the SQL BindCol( ), SQLGetData( ), or SQLBindParameter ( ) function call. This length does not include the null terminator for null-terminated strings. The following list shows the default length used for each DB2 SQL data type:	
			SQL_SMALLINT	Two bytes.
			SQL_INTEGER	Four bytes.
			SQL_DECIMAL	The maximum number of digits plus 3 (a sign, digits, a decimal point, and digits).
			SQL_NUMERIC	The maximum number of digits plus 3 (a sign, digits, a decimal point, and digits).
			SQL_REAL	Four bytes.
			SQL_FLOAT	Eight bytes.
			SQL_DOUBLE	Eight bytes.
			SQL_CHAR	The defined length of the column.
			SQL_VARCHAR	The defined length of the column.
			SQL_LONGVARCHAR	The maximum length of the column.
			SQL_BINARY	The defined length of the column.
			SQL_VARBINARY	The defined length of the column.
			SQL_LONGVARBINARY	The maximum length of the column.
			SQL_GRAPHIC	The defined length of the column times 2.
			SQL_VARGRAPHIC	The defined length of the column times 2.
			SQL_LONGVARGRAPHIC	The maximum length of the column times 2.
			SQL_BLOB	The defined length of the column.
			SQL_DBCLOB	The defined length of the column times 2.
			SQL_CLOB	The defined length of the column.
			SQL_DATE	6 (the size of the DATE_STRUCT structure).
			SQL_TIME	6 (the size of the TIME_STRUCT structure).
			SQL_TIMESTAMP	16 (the size of the TIMESTAMP_ STRUCT structure).

TABLE 17.11 Result Data Set Returned by SQLProcedureColumns( ) *(Continued)*

Column	Column name	Data type	Description
10	DECIMAL_DIGITS	SMALLINT	The scale (number of digits to the right of the decimal point) of the parameter if TYPE_NAME is SQL _DECIMAL, SQL_NUMERIC, or SQL _TIMESTAMP. If TYPE_NAME is anything else, this column will be set to NULL.
11	NUM_PREC_RADIX	SMALLINT	The radix value of the identified column. If DATA_TYPE is an approximate numeric data type, this column will contain the value 2 and the COLUMN_SIZE column will contain the number of bits allowed in the column. If DATA_TYPE is an exact numeric data type, this column will contain the value 10 and the COLUMN_SIZE column will contain the number of decimal digits allowed for the column. For numeric data types, this column can contain either 10 or 2. For data types where radix is not applicable, this column is set to NULL.
12	NULLABLE	SMALLINT NOT NULL	Indicates whether or not the parameter accepts a NULL value. Valid values for this column are: SQL_NO_NULLS (the parameter does not accept NULL values) and SQL_NULLABLE (the parameter accepts NULL values).
13	REMARKS	VARCHAR(254)	Descriptive information about the parameter (if any exists).

Adapted from IBM's Database 2 Call Level Interface Guide and Reference, Table 109, pages 313 to 314.

This function can return information on either the input or output parameters or both the input and the output parameters associated with a stored procedure, but it cannot return information about the descriptor information for any result data sets returned.

Specifications DB2 CLI 2.1, ODBC 1.0

Return Codes SQL_SUCCESS, SQL_SUCCESS_WITH_INFO, SQL_INVALID_HANDLE, SQL_ERROR

SQLSTATEs **08**S01, **24**000, **40**003, **42**601, **S1**001, **S1**010, **S1**014, **S1**090, **S1**C00, **S1**T00

Comments

- In order for the SQLProcedureColumns( ) function to return a list of input and output parameters associated with stored procedures when the application is connected to DB2 for Common Servers (version 2.1), the pseudo catalog table for stored procedure registration (the table named PROCEDURES in the DB2 CLI schema) must have already been created and populated. Refer to the beginning of the chapter for more information about this pseudo catalog table. It is imperative to follow the exact rules when populating this table, or the SQL-Procedures( ) call will result in an error.
- If this function is to return a list of input and output parameters associated with stored procedures at a DB2 for MVS/ESA (version 4.1 or later) server, the names of the stored procedures must be registered in the server's SYSIBM .SYSPROCEDURES catalog table.

- Since the SQLProcedureColumns( ) function often maps to a complex and therefore expensive query against the database system catalog tables, use it sparingly. If you need to use the produced result data set more than once, save it rather than regenerating it by invoking the SQLProcedureColumns( ) function again.
- The *SchemaName*, *ProcName*, and *ColumnName* parameters can accept the following search pattern values:

The underscore character (_) Indicates that any single character can be used in place of the underscore character.
The percent character (%) Indicates that any sequence of 0 or more characters can be used in place of the percent character.

If these "wildcard" characters need to be used as themselves (e.g., % = "%"), they must be preceded by an escape character.

- The result data set returned by this function is ordered by PROCEDURE_CAT, PROCEDURE_SCHEMA, PROCEDURE_NAME, and COLUMN_TYPE.
- If the SQL_LONGDATA_COMPAT option is set to SQL_LD_COMPAT_YES, either by calling the SQLSetConnectOption( ) or by setting the LONGDATA-COMPAT option in the DB2 CLI initialization file), large object (LOB) data types will be reported as SQL_LONGVARCHAR, SQL_LONGVARBINARY, or SQL_LONGVARGRAPHIC.
- The VARCHAR columns of the catalog functions result data set have been declared with a maximum length of 128 characters to be consistent with the SQL92 standard limits. Since DB2 names are less than 128 characters, an application can choose to always set aside 128 characters (plus the null terminator) for the output buffer, or alternatively to allocate only the required amount of memory by first calling the SQLGetInfo( ) function with the *InfoType* parameter set to SQL_MAX_CATALOG_NAME_LEN, SQL_MAX_OWNER_SCHEMA_LEN, SQL_MAX_NAME_LEN, and/or SQL_MAX_COLUMN_NAME_LEN to determine respectively the actual lengths of the TABLE_CAT, TABLE_SCHEM, TABLE_NAME, and COLUMN_NAME columns supported by the current data source connection.
- Although new columns might be added and the names of the existing columns in the result data set might be changed in future releases of DB2 CLI, the position of the current columns in this data set will not change.

Restrictions This function does not return information about the attributes of result sets that might be produced when a stored procedure executes. If this function attempts to return a list of input and/or output parameters associated with stored procedures from a DB2 server that does not provide facilities to support a stored procedure catalog or from a DB2 server that does not provide support for stored procedures, an empty result data set will be returned.

See Also SQLProcedures( )

Examples The following C program illustrates how to use the SQLProcedureColumns( ) function to obtain information about a stored procedure's input and output parameters:

```
#include <stdio.h>
#include <stdlib.h>
#include <sqlcli1.h>

int main()
{
    /* Declare The Local Memory Variables */
    SQLRETURN    rc = SQL_SUCCESS;
```

```
SQLHENV      EnvHandle;
SQLHDBC      DSCHandle;
SQLHSTMT     StmtHandle;
SQLCHAR      ColName[129];
SQLCHAR      DTypeName[129];
SQLSMALLINT  Nullable;
/* Allocate An Environment Handle */
rc = SQLAllocEnv(&EnvHandle);

/* Allocate A Connection Handle */
rc = SQLAllocConnect(EnvHandle, &DSCHandle);

/* Connect To The SAMPLE Database */
rc = SQLConnect(DSCHandle, "SAMPLE", SQL_NTS, "etpdd6z", SQL_NTS,
                "sanders", SQL_NTS);

/* Allocate An SQL Statement Handle */
rc = SQLAllocStmt(DSCHandle, &StmtHandle);

/* Obtain Information About A Stored Procedure's Parameters */
rc = SQLProcedureColumns(StmtHandle, NULL, 0, "%", SQL_NTS,
                         "ComputeSales", SQL_NTS, "%",
                         SQL_NTS);

if (rc != SQL_ERROR)
    {
    /* Bind The Columns In The Result Data Set To Local */
    /* Storage Variables                                */
    SQLBindCol(StmtHandle, 4, SQL_C_CHAR, (SQLPOINTER) ColName,
               sizeof(ColName), NULL);

    SQLBindCol(StmtHandle, 7, SQL_C_CHAR, (SQLPOINTER) DTypeName,
               sizeof(DTypeName), NULL);

    SQLBindCol(StmtHandle, 12, SQL_C_SHORT, (SQLPOINTER) &Nullable,
               0, NULL);

    /* Retrieve And Display The Results */
    printf("Parameter Name   Data Type     Nullable\n");
    printf("---------------------------------------\n");
    while (rc != SQL_NO_DATA_FOUND)
        {

        /* Retrieve A Record From The Result Data Set */
        rc = SQLFetch(StmtHandle);

        /* Print The Information Retrieved */
        if (rc != SQL_NO_DATA_FOUND)
            {
            printf("%-16s %-14s\n", ColName, DTypeName);
            if (Nullable == TRUE)
                printf("Yes\n");
            else
                printf("No\n");
            }
        }
    }

/* Disconnect From The SAMPLE Database */
SQLDisconnect(DSCHandle);

/* Free The SQL Statement Handle */
if (StmtHandle != NULL)
```

```
        SQLFreeStmt(StmtHandle, SQL_DROP);

    /* Free The Connection Handle */
    if (DSCHandle != NULL)
        SQLFreeConnect(DSCHandle);
    /* Free The Environment Handle */
    if (EnvHandle != NULL)
        SQLFreeEnv(EnvHandle);

    /* Return To The Operating System */
    return(rc);
}
```

The following C++ program illustrates how the SQLProcedureColumns( ) function is used by class methods to obtain information about a stored procedure's input and output parameters:

```
#include <iostream.h>
#include <string.h>
#include <sqlcli1.h>

/* Define The CLI Class */
class CLI
{
    /* Declare The Private Attribute Variables */
    private:
       SQLHENV      EnvHandle;
       SQLHDBC      DSCHandle;
       SQLHSTMT     StmtHandle;
       SQLCHAR      ColName[129];
       SQLCHAR      DTypeName[129];
       SQLSMALLINT  Nullable;

    /* Declare The Public Attribute Variables */
    public:
       SQLRETURN  rc;

    /* Declare The Member Function Prototypes */
    CLI();                                    // Constructor
    ~CLI();                                   // Destructor
    SQLRETURN Connect();
    SQLRETURN ShowProcParams();
    SQLRETURN Disconnect();
} ;

/* Define The Class Constructor */
CLI::CLI()
{
    /* Initialize The Return Code Variable */
    rc = SQL_SUCCESS;

    /* Allocate An Environment Handle */
    rc = SQLAllocEnv(&EnvHandle);

    /* Allocate A Connection Handle */
    rc = SQLAllocConnect(EnvHandle, &DSCHandle);
}

/* Define The Class Destructor */
CLI::~CLI()
{
```

```
    /* Free The Connection Handle */
    if (DSCHandle != NULL)
        SQLFreeConnect(DSCHandle);

    /* Free The Environment Handle */
    if (EnvHandle != NULL)
        SQLFreeEnv(EnvHandle);
}

/* Define The Connect() Member Function */
SQLRETURN CLI::Connect()
{
    /* Connect To The SAMPLE Database */
    rc = SQLConnect(DSCHandle, (SQLCHAR *) "SAMPLE", SQL_NTS,
                    (SQLCHAR *) "etpdd6z", SQL_NTS,
                    (SQLCHAR *) "sanders", SQL_NTS);

    /* Allocate An SQL Statement Handle */
    rc = SQLAllocStmt(DSCHandle, &StmtHandle);

    /* Return The CLI Function Return Code */
    return(rc);
}

/* Define The Disconnect() Member Function */
SQLRETURN CLI::Disconnect(void)
{
    /* Disconnect From The Database */
    rc = SQLDisconnect(DSCHandle);

    /* Free The SQL Statement Handle */
    if (StmtHandle != NULL)
        SQLFreeStmt(StmtHandle, SQL_DROP);

    /* Return The CLI Function Return Code */
    return(rc);
}

/* Define The ShowProcParams() Member Function */
SQLRETURN CLI::ShowProcParams(void)
{
    /* Obtain Information About A Stored Procedure's Parameters */
    rc = SQLProcedureColumns(StmtHandle, NULL, 0, (SQLCHAR *) "%",
                             SQL_NTS, (SQLCHAR *) "ComputeSales",
                             SQL_NTS, (SQLCHAR *) "%", SQL_NTS);

    if (rc != SQL_ERROR)
        {
        /* Bind The Columns In The Result Data Set To Local */
        /* Storage Variables                                */
        SQLBindCol(StmtHandle, 4, SQL_C_CHAR, (SQLPOINTER) ColName,
                   sizeof(ColName), NULL);

        SQLBindCol(StmtHandle, 7, SQL_C_CHAR, (SQLPOINTER) DTypeName,
                   sizeof(DTypeName), NULL);

        SQLBindCol(StmtHandle, 12, SQL_C_SHORT, (SQLPOINTER) &Nullable,
                   0, NULL);

        /* Retrieve And Display The Results */
        cout << "Parameter Name   Data Type     Nullable" << endl;
        cout << "----------------------------------------" << endl;
```

```
        while (rc != SQL_NO_DATA_FOUND)
            {

            /* Retrieve A Record From The Result Data Set */
            rc = SQLFetch(StmtHandle);

            /* Print The Information Retrieved */
            if (rc != SQL_NO_DATA_FOUND)
                {
                cout.setf(ios::left);
                cout.width(17);
                cout << ColName;
                cout.setf(ios::left);
                cout.width(15);
                cout << DTypeName;
                if (Nullable == TRUE)
                    cout << "Yes" << endl;
                else
                    cout << "No" << endl;
                }
            }
        }

    /* Return The CLI Function Return Code */
    return(rc);
}

int main()
{
    /* Declare The Local Memory Variables */
    SQLRETURN  rc = SQL_SUCCESS;

    /* Create An Instance Of The CLI Class */
    CLI Sample;

    /* Connect To The SAMPLE Database */
    if ((rc = Sample.Connect()) != SQL_SUCCESS)
        return(rc);

    /* Display A List Of The CalculateSales Stored Procedure's */
    /* Input Parameters                                        */
    Sample.ShowProcParams();

    /* Disconnect From The SAMPLE Database */
    Sample.Disconnect();

    /* Return To The Operating System */
    return(rc);
}
```

Part 5

APPLICATION PROGRAMMING INTERFACE (API) FUNCTIONS

This section describes the application programming interface (API) functions for developing utility and maintenance applications for DB2 or supplementing embedded SQL applications written for DB2. It is designed as a reference that provides information about the syntax and semantics of each API function supported by DB2. It is also designed to show, by example, how each API function is coded in a C application program.

> *Note: Because these APIs are used in a similar manner in C++ application programs and because there is little, if any, overhead required for the API functions, I have not provided C++ examples in this section.*

Each function is presented as a main section, and the subsections under each function contain the following information:

Purpose	*Short description telling what the API function does.*
Syntax	*Full API function syntax.*
Parameters	*Detailed description of all API function parameters.*
Includes	*Header files that must be included by the application calling the API function.*
Description	*Detailed information about the API function.*
Comments	*Special notes or instructions about the API function.*
Required Connection	*The type of connection that must exist before the API function can be executed.*
Authorizations	*Authorization requirements for using the API function.*
See Also	*Related API functions.*
Examples	*C example demonstrating how the API function is used in a source-code file.*

HOW THE EXAMPLES WERE DEVELOPED

All the sample programs shown in this section were compiled and executed on the OS/2 Warp operating system, and most were compiled and executed on the AIX 4.0 operating system. They were compiled with IBM VisualAge C++ for OS/2 Warp and IBM C Set++ for AIX, version 3.0 for AIX.

The following command file (C_COMP.CMD) was used to compile the C sample programs that did not require a database connection on the OS/2 Warp operating system:

```
REM *** BUILD API EXAMPLES COMMAND FILE                     ***
echo off
```

```
REM *** COMPILE THE SOURCE CODE FILE                   ***
icc /W3 /Ti+ /G4 /Gs+ /Ss+ /DLINT_ARGS /c %1.c > ERROR.DAT
REM *** LINK THE PROGRAM                               ***
ilink /NOFREE /NOI /DEBUG /ST:128000 %1.obj,,,OS2386 DB2API
   SQL_DYN,DB2_DEF.DEF > ERROR.DAT

REM *** CLEAN UP                                       ***
del %1.obj
```

The following command file (SQC_COMP.CMD) was used to compile the C sample programs that required a database connection on the OS/2 Warp operating system:

```
REM *** BUILD EMBEDDED SQL-API EXAMPLES COMMAND FILE ***
echo off

REM *** CONNECT TO THE SAMPLE DATABASE                 ***
db2 connect to sample user etpdd6z using sanders

REM *** PRECOMPILE THE EMBEDDED SQL-API SOURCE CODE FILE ***
db2 prep %1.sqc bindfile using %1.bnd > ERROR.DAT

REM *** COMPILE THE SOURCE CODE FILE                   ***
icc /W3 /Ti+ /G4 /Gs+ /Ss+ /DLINT_ARGS /c %1.c > ERROR.DAT

REM *** LINK THE PROGRAM                               ***
ilink /NOFREE /NOI /DEBUG /ST:32000 %1.obj,,,OS2386 DB2API SQL_DYN,DB2_DEF.DEF
   > ERROR.DAT

REM *** BIND THE APPLICATION TO THE SAMPLE DATABASE  ***
db2 bind %1.bnd > ERROR.DAT

REM *** DISCONNECT FROM THE SAMPLE DATABASE          ***
db2 connect reset

REM *** CLEAN UP                                       ***
del %1.c
del %1.obj
```

The following command file (C_COMP) was used to compile the C sample programs that did not require a database connection on the AIX 4.0 operating system:

```
# BUILD API EXAMPLES COMMAND FILE
#! /bin/ksh
#
# COMPILE THE SOURCE CODE FILE
compstr='xlC -I/usr/lpp/db2_02_01/include -qcpluscmt -c '${1} .c
echo $compstr
$compstr
#
# LINK THE PROGRAM
linkstr='xlC -o '${1} ' '${1} '.o -ldb2 -L/usr/lpp/db2_02_01/lib'
echo $linkstr
$linkstr
```

The following command file (SQC_COMP) was used to compile the C sample programs that required a database connection on the AIX 4.0 operating system:

```
# BUILD EMBEDDED SQL-API EXAMPLES COMMAND FILE
#! /bin/ksh
#
# CONNECT TO THE SAMPLE DATABASE
db2 connect to sample user etpdd6z using sanders
#
# PRECOMPILE THE EMBEDDED SQL SOURCE CODE FILE
db2 prep ${1} .sqc bindfile
#
# COMPILE THE SOURCE CODE FILE
compstr='xlC -I/usr/lpp/db2_02_01/include -qcpluscmt -c '${1} .c
echo $compstr
$compstr
#
# LINK THE PROGRAM
linkstr='xlC -o '${1} ' '${1} '.o -ldb2 -L/usr/lpp/db2_02_01/lib'
echo $linkstr
$linkstr
#
# BIND THE APPLICATION TO THE SAMPLE DATABASE
db2 bind ${1} .bnd
#
# DISCONNECT FROM THE SAMPLE DATABASE
db2 connect reset
```

You must start the DB2 database manager by issuing either the startdbm command (OS/2) or the db2 start database manager command (AIX) at the command prompt before executing API applications that require a connection to a DB2 database manager instance. Also, keep in mind that the default qualifier USERID is valid only for OS/2. When DB2 is installed on AIX, the default qualifier for the SAMPLE database is determined by the authorization ID of the user installing the DB2 product.

SPECIAL CASES

DB2 is designed to automatically resolve indoubt transactions whenever they are detected. Because of this, it is difficult to create indoubt transactions for a small testing environment. I created the transaction processing API examples in Chapter 25 with the help of Mr. Peter Shum and Mr. Al Sabawi of IBM's facility at Toronto, Canada.

CHAPTER 18

PROGRAM PREPARATION AND GENERAL APPLICATION PROGRAMMING API'S

The program preparation and general application programming APIs are a group of DB2 API function calls that allow you to use other API functions within a high-level language source-code file. This group includes:

- API functions that precompile, bind, and rebind embedded SQL applications.
- API functions that facilitate interrupt signal handler processing.
- API functions that perform memory manipulations for high-level programming languages that do not provide pointer support.
- API functions that generate descriptive text strings for SQL and API return codes and SQLSTATE values.

Table 18.1 lists the program preparation and general application programming API functions available with DB2.

Embedded SQL Application Preparation

18

As discussed in Chapter 4, embedded SQL source-code files must always be precompilied. The precompile process converts a source-code file with embedded SQL statements into a high-level language source-code file made up entirely of high-level language statements. This is important because the high-level language compiler cannot interpret SQL statements, so it cannot create the appropriate object code files used by the linker to produce an executable program. The precompile process also creates a corresponding package that contains, among other things, one or more data access plans. Data access plans contain information on how the SQL statements in the source-code file are processed by DB2 at application runtime.

Normally, the SQL precompiler is invoked from either the DB2 command-line processor or from a batch or make utility file. There might be times, however, when the SQL precompiler needs to be invoked from an application program (for example, when an embedded SQL source-code file is provided for a portable application and the application's installation program needs to precompile it in order to produce the corresponding execution package). In these cases, you can use the PRECOMPILE PROGRAM function to invoke the SQL precompiler.

TABLE 18.1 Program Preparation and General Application Programming APIs

Function name	Description
PRECOMPILE PROGRAM	Preprocesses a source-code file that contains embedded SQL statements.
BIND	Prepares the SQL statements stored in a bind file and generates a corresponding package stored in the database.
REBIND	Recreates a package stored in a database without using an external bind file.
GET INSTANCE	Retrieves the current value of the DB2INSTANCE environment variable.
INSTALL SIGNAL HANDLER	Installs the default interrupt signal handler in a DB2 database application program.
INTERRUPT	Safely stops execution of the current database request.
GET ADDRESS	Stores the address of one variable in another variable.
COPY MEMORY	Copies data from one memory storage area to another.
DEREFERENCE ADDRESS	Copies data from a buffer defined by a pointer to a variable that is directly accessible by an application.
GET ERROR MESSAGE	Retrieves the message text associated with an SQLCA error code from a special DB2 error message file.
GET SQLSTATE MESSAGE	Retrieves the message text associated with a SQLSTATE value.
GET AUTHORIZATIONS	Retrieves the authorizations granted to the current user.

When an embedded SQL source-code file is precompiled, the corresponding execution package that is produced can either be automatically stored in a database or written to an external bind file and bound to the database later (the process of storing this package in the appropriate database is known as binding). By default, packages are automatically bound to the database used for precompiling during the precompile process. By specifying the appropriate precompiler options, however, you can elect to store this package in a separate file and perform the binding process at a later time. Just as the SQL precompiler is normally invoked from either the DB2 command-line processor or from a batch or make utility file, the DB2 bind utility is normally invoked in the same manner. There might be times, however, when you need to invoke the bind utility from an application program (for example, when a bind file is provided for a portable application and the application's installation program needs to bind it to the database against which the application will run). You can use the BIND function to invoke the DB2 bind utility for cases such as these.

When producing execution packages for embedded SQL applications, the SQL precompiler determines the best access plan to use by evaluating the data objects available at package creation time. As more data objects, such as indexes, are added to the database, older packages need to be rebound so they can take advantage of the new data objects (and possibly produce more efficient data access plans). If the bind files associated with an application are available, you can rebind older packages by invoking the DB2 bind utility. If the bind files are no longer available, you can still rebind existing packages by using the REBIND API function. When the REBIND function is invoked, the specified package is recreated from the SQL statements stored in the SYSCAT.STATEMENTS system catalog table when the package was first created.

Exception, Signal, and Interrupt Handlers

A DB2 database application program must be able to shut down gracefully whenever an exception, signal, or interrupt occurs. This is usually done through an exception, signal, or interrupt handler routine. The INSTALL SIGNAL HANDLER function can install a default exception, signal, or interrupt handler routine in all DB2 applications. If this function is called before any other API calls or SQL statements, any DB2 operations currently in progress will be ended gracefully whenever an exception, signal, or interrupt occurs (normally a ROLLBACK SQL statement is executed, in order to avoid the risk of inconsistent data).

The default exception, signal, or interrupt handler is adequate for most simple, single-task applications. If your application program is a multithread or multiprocess application, however, you might want to provide a customized exception, signal, or interrupt handler. In this case, call the INTERRUPT function from custom exception, signal, or interrupt handler routines to ensure that all DB2 operations currently in progress are ended gracefully. This API call notifies DB2 that a termination has been requested. DB2 then examines what, if any, database operation is in progress and takes appropriate action to cleanly terminate that operation. Some database operations, such as the COMMIT and the ROLLBACK SQL statement, cannot be terminated and are allowed to complete, since their completion is necessary to maintain consistent data.

> Note: SQL statements other than COMMIT and ROLLBACK SQL should never be placed in customized exception, signal, and interrupt handler routines.

Pointer Manipulation and Memory Copy Functions

Because many DB2 API functions use pointers for either input or output parameters, some type of pointer manipulation is often required when API functions are included in application programs. Some host languages, such as C and C++, support pointer manipulation and provide memory copy functions. Other host languages, such as FORTRAN and COBOL, do not. The GET ADDRESS, COPY MEMORY, and DEREFERENCE ADDRESS functions are designed to provide pointer manipulation and memory copy functions for applications written in host languages that do not inherently provide this functionality.

Evaluating SQLCA Return Codes and SQLSTATE Values

Most API functions require a pointer to a SQLCA data structure variable as an output parameter. When an API function or an embedded SQL statement completes execution, this variable contains error, warning, or status information. To save on space, this information is stored in the form of a coded number. If the GET ERROR MESSAGE function is executed with the SQLCA data structure variable returned from another API function, the coded number will be translated into a more meaningful error message description. Standardized error code values are also stored in the SQLCA data structure variable. Like the SQLCA return code value, the SQLSTATE information is stored in the form of a coded number. You can use the GET SQLSTATE API to translate this coded number into a more meaningful error message description. By including either (or both) of these API functions in your DB2 database applications, you can return meaningful error and warning information to the end user whenever error and/or warning conditions occur.

PRECOMPILE PROGRAM

Purpose The PRECOMPILE PROGRAM function preprocesses an application program source-code file that contains embedded SQL statements.

Syntax

```
SQL_API_RC SQL_API_FN sqlaprep (char          *ProgramName,
                                char          *MsgFileName,
                                struct sqlopt *PrepOptions,
                                struct sqlca  *SQLCA);
```

Parameters

ProgramName A pointer to a location in memory where the name of the source-code file to be precompiled is stored.

MsgFileName A pointer to a location in memory where the name of the file or the device to which all error, warning, and informational messages are to be written is stored.

PrepOptions A pointer to a *sqlopt* structure that contains the precompiler options (if any) that should be used when precompiling the source-code file.

SQLCA A pointer to a location in memory where a SQL communication area (SQLCA) data structure variable is stored. This variable sends either status information (if the function executed successfully) or error information (if the function failed) back to the calling application.

Includes

```
#include <sql.h>
```

Description

The PRECOMPILE PROGRAM function preprocesses an application program source-code file that contains embedded SQL statements. When a source-code file containing embedded SQL statements is precompiled, a modified source file containing host language function calls for each SQL statement is produced and, by default, a package for the SQL statements coded in the file is created and bound to the database to which a connection has been established. The name of the package to be created is, by default, the same as the first eight characters of the source-code file name (minus the file extension and converted to uppercase) from which the package was generated. However, you can overwrite bind file names and package names by using the SQL_BIND_OPT and the SQL_PKG_OPT options with the PRECOMPILE PROGRAM function call.

A special structure (*sqlopt*) passes different precompile options to the SQL precompiler when this function is called. The *sqlopt* structure is defined in *sql.h* as follows:

```
struct sqlopt
{
   struct sqloptheader header;    /* A Precompile/Bind options header */
   struct sqloptions   option[1]; /* An Array of Precompile/Bind      */
                                  /* options                          */
};
```

This structure is composed of two or more additional structures: one *sqloptheader* and one or more *sqloptions*. The *sqloptheader* structure is defined in *sql.h* as follows:

```
struct sqloptheader
{
unsigned long  allocated;   /* Number of sqloptions structures     */
                            /* allocated (the number of elements   */
                            /* in the option array of the          */
                            /* sqlopt structure)                   */
unsigned long  used;        /* The actual number of sqloptions     */
                            /* structures used (the actual         */
                            /* number of type and val option       */
                            /* pairs supplied)                     */
};
```

The *sqloptions* structure is defined in *sql.h* as follows:

```
struct sqloptions
{
unsigned long  type;  /* Precompile/Bind option type  */
unsigned long  val;   /* Precompile/Bind option value */
};
```

Table 18.2 lists the values that can be used for the *type* and *val* fields of the *sqloptions* structure, as well as a description about what each type/val option combination causes the SQL precompiler (or the DB2 bind utility) to do.

TABLE 18.2 Precompile/Bind Options and Values

Precompile/bind option	Value	Currently supported	Description
SQL_ACTION_OPT	SQL_ACTION_ADD	No	Specifies that the package does not already exist and is to be created.
	SQL_ACTION_REPLACE	No	Specifies that the package exists and is to be replaced. This is the default value for SQL_ACTION_OPT option.
SQL_BIND_OPT	Null	Yes	Indicates that no bind file is to be generated by the precompiler. This option can only be used with the SQL precompiler.
	sqlchar structure	Yes	Indicates that a bind file with the specified name is to be generated by the precompiler. This option can only be used with the SQL precompiler.
SQL_BLOCK_OPT	SQL_BL_ALL	Yes	Specifies that row blocking should be performed for read-only cursors, cursors not specified as FOR UPDATE OF, and cursors for which no static DELETE WHERE CURRENT OF statements are executed. In this case, ambiguous cursors are treated as read-only cursors.
	SQL_BL_NO	Yes	Specifies that row blocking is not to be performed for cursors. In this case, ambiguous cursors are treated as updatable cursors.
	SQL_BL_UNAMBIG	Yes	Specifies that row blocking should be performed for read-only cursors, cursors not specified as FOR UPDATE OF, cursors for which no static DELETE WHERE CURRENT OF statements are executed, and cursors that do not have dynamic statements associated with them. In this case, ambiguous cursors are treated as updateable cursors.
SQL_CCSIDG_OPT	Integer value	No	Specifies the coded character set identifier that is to be used for double-byte characters in character column definitions specified in CREATE TABLE and ALTER TABLE SQL statements.

TABLE 18.2 Precompile/Bind Options and Values *(Continued)*

Precompile/bind option	Value	Currently supported	Description
SQL_CCSIDM_OPT	Integer value	No	Specifies the coded character set identifier that is to be used for mixed-byte characters in character column definitions specified in CREATE TABLE and ALTER TABLE SQL statements.
SQL_CCSIDS_OPT	Integer value	No	Specifies the coded character set identifier that is to be used for single-byte characters in character column definitions specified in CREATE TABLE and ALTER TABLE SQL statements.
SQL_CHARSUB_OPT	SQL_CHARSUB_BIT	No	Specifies that the FOR BIT DATA SQL character subtype is to be used in all new character column definitions specified in CREATE TABLE and ALTER TABLE SQL statements (unless otherwise explicitly specified).
	SQL_CHARSUB_MIXED	No	Specifies that the FOR MIXED DATA SQL character subtype is to be used in all new character column definitions specified in CREATE TABLE and ALTER TABLE SQL statements (unless otherwise explicitly specified).
	SQL_CHARSUB_SBCS	No	Specifies that the FOR SBCS DATA SQL character subtype is to be used in all new character column definitions specified in CREATE TABLE and ALTER TABLE SQL statements (unless otherwise explicitly specified).
	SQL_CHARSUB_DEFAULT	No	Specifies that the target system defined default character subtype is to be used in all new character column definitions specified in CREATE TABLE and ALTER TABLE SQL statements (unless otherwise explicitly specified). This is the default value for SQL_CHARSUB_OPT.
SQL_COLLECTION_OPT	*sqlchar* structure	Yes	Specifies an eight-character collection identifier that is to be used for the package being created. If no collection identifier is specified, the authorization ID of the user executing the PRECOMPILE PROGRAM function or the BIND function will be used.
SQL_DATETIME_OPT	SQL DATETIME_DEF	Yes	Specifies that a date and time format associated with the country code of the database is to be used for date and time values.

TABLE 18.2 Precompile/Bind Options and Values (Continued)

Precompile/bind option	Value	Currently supported	Description
	SQL DATETIME_EUR	Yes	Specifies that the IBM standard for Europe date and time format is to be used for date and time values.
	SQL_DATETIME_ISO	Yes	Specifies that the International Standards Organization date and time format is to be used for date and time values.
	SQL_DATETIME_JIS	Yes	Specifies that the Japanese Industrial Standard date and time format is to be used for date and time values.
	SQL_DATETIME_LOC	Yes	Specifies that the local date and time format associated with the country code of the database is to be used for date and time values.
	SQL_DATETIME_USA	Yes	Specifies that the IBM standard for United States of America date and time format is to be used for date and time values.
SQL_DECDEL_OPT	SQL_DECDEL_COMMA	No	Specifies that a comma will be used as a decimal point indicator in decimal and floating point literals.
	SQL_DECDEL_PERIOD	No	Specifies that a period will be used as a decimal point indicator in decimal and floating point literals.
SQL_DEC_OPT	SQL_DEC_15	No	Specifies that 15-digit precision is to be used in decimal arithmetic operations.
	SQL_DEC_31	No	Specifies that 31-digit precision is to be used in decimal arithmetic operations.
SQL_DEGREE_OPT	SQL_DEGREE_ANY	No	Specifies that queries are to be executed using I/O parallel processing.
	Integer between 2 and 32767	No	Specifies the degree of parallel I/O processing that is to be used when executing queries.
	SQL_DEGREE_1	No	Specifies that I/O parallel processing cannot be used to execute SQL queries. This is the default value for the SQL_DEGREE_OPT option.
SQL_DYNAMICRULES_OPT	SQL_DYNAMICRULES_BIND	No	Specifies that the authorization identifier used for the execution of dynamic SQL statements is the package owner.
	SQL_DYNAMICRULES_RUN	No	Specifies that the authorization identifier used for the execution of dynamic SQL statements is the authorization ID of the user executing the package.
SQL_EXPLAIN_OPT	SQL_EXPLAIN_NO	No	Specifies that Explain information about the access plans chosen for each SQL statement in the package will not be stored in the Explain tables.

TABLE 18.2 Precompile/Bind Options and Values *(Continued)*

Precompile/bind option	Value	Currently supported	Description
	SQL_EXPLAIN_YES	No	Specifies that Explain tables are to be populated with information about the access plans chosen for each SQL statement in the package.
SQL_EXPLSNAP_OPT	SQL_EXPLSNAP_NO	No	Specifies that an Explain snapshot will not be written to the Explain tables for each eligible static SQL statement in the package.
	SQL_EXPLSNAP_YES	No	Specifies that an Explain snapshot is to be written to the Explain tables for each eligible static SQL statement in the package.
	SQL_EXPLSNAP_ALL	No	Specifies that an Explain snapshot is to be written to the Explain tables for each eligible static SQL statement in the package and that Explain snapshot information is also to be gathered for eligible dynamic SQL statements at application runtime, even if the CURRENT EXPLAIN SNAPSHOT register is set to NO.
SQL_FUNCTION_PATH	*sqlchar* structure	No	Specifies the function path to be used when resolving user-defined distinct data types and functions referenced in static SQL statements.
SQL_GRANT_OPT	*sqlchar* structure	Yes	Specifies that the EXECUTE and BIND authorizations are to be granted to a specified user ID or group ID (the group ID specified can be PUBLIC). This option can be used only with the DB2 bind utility.
SQL_INSERT_OPT	SQL_INSERT_BUF	Yes	Specifies that insert operations performed by an application should be buffered.
	SQL_INSERT_DEF	Yes	Specifies that insert operations performed by an application should not be buffered.
SQL_ISQLATION_OPT	SQL_ISQLATION_RS	Yes	Specifies that the Read Stability isolation level should be used to isolate the effects of other executing applications from the application using this package.
	SQL_ISQLATION_NC	No	Specifies that commitment control is not to be used by this package.
	SQL_ISQLATION_CS	Yes	Specifies that the Cursor Stability isolation level should be used to isolate the effects of other executing applications from the application using this package.

TABLE 18.2 Precompile/Bind Options and Values *(Continued)*

Precompile/bind option	Value	Currently supported	Description
	SQL_ISQLATION_RR	Yes	Specifies that the Repeatable Read isolation level should be used to isolate the effects of other executing applications from the application using this package.
	SQL_ISQLATION_UR	Yes	Specifies that the Uncommitted Read isolation level should be used to isolate the effects of other executing applications from the application using this package.
SQL_LEVEL_OPT	*sqlchar* structure	No	Specifies the level for a module using the consistency token stored in a package. This token verifies that the requesting application and the database package are synchronized. This option can only be used with the SQL precompiler.
SQL_OWNER_OPT	*sqlchar* structure	No	Specifies an eight-character authorization ID that identifies the package owner. By default, the authorization ID of the user performing the precompile or bind process is used to identify the package owner.
SQL_PKG_OPT	NULL	Yes	Specifies that a package is not to be created. This option can only be used with the SQL precompiler.
	sqlchar structure	Yes	Specifies the name of the package that is to be created. If a package name is not specified, the package name is the uppercase name of the source-code file being precompiled (truncated to eight characters and minus the extension). This option can only be used with the SQL precompiler.
SQL_QUALIFIER_OPT	*sqlchar* structure	No	Specifies an implicit qualifier name to use for all unqualified table names, views, indexes, and aliases contained in the package. By default, the authorization ID of the user performing the precompile or bind process is the implicit qualifier.
SQL_QUERYOPT_OPT	*sqlchar* structure	No	Specifies the level of optimization to use when precompiling the static SQL statements contained in the package. The default optimization level is 5.
SQL_RELEASE_OPT	SQL_RELEASE_COMMIT	No	Specifies that resources acquired for dynamic SQL statements are to be released at each COMMIT point. This is the default value for the SQL_RELEASE_OPT option.

TABLE 18.2 Precompile/Bind Options and Values *(Continued)*

Precompile/bind option	Value	Currently supported	Description
	SQL_RELEASE_DEALLOCATE	No	Specifies that resources acquired for dynamic SQL statements are to be released when the application terminates.
SQL_REPLVER_OPT	*sqlchar* structure	No	Identifies a specific version of a package to replace when the SQL_ACTION_REPLACE value is specified for the SQL_ACTION_OPT option. This option can only be used with the DB2 bind utility.
SQL_RETAIN_OPT	SQL_RETAIN_NO	No	Specifies that EXECUTE authorizations are not to be preserved when a package is replaced. This option can only be used with the DB2 bind utility.
	SQL_RETAIN_YES	No	Specifies that EXECUTE authorizations are to be preserved when a package is replaced. This option can only be used with the DB2 bind utility. This is the default value for SQL_RETAIN_OPT.
SQL_SQLERROR_OPT	SQL_SQLERROR_CHECK	Yes	Specifies that the target system performs all syntax and semantic checks on the SQL statements being bound to the database. If an error is encountered, a package will not be created.
	SQL_SQLERROR_CONTINUE	No	Specifies that the target system performs all syntax and semantic checks on the SQL statements being bound to the database. If an error is encountered, a package will still be created.
	SQL_SQLERROR_NOPACKAGE	No	Specifies that the precompiler performs all syntax and semantic checks on the SQL statements being precompiled. If an error is encountered, a package or a bind file will not be created. This is the default value for SQL_SQLERROR_OPT.
SQL_SQLWARN OPT	SQL_SQLWARN_NO	No	Specifies that warning messages will not be returned from the SQL precompiler.
	SQL_SQLWARN_YES	No	Specifies that warning messages will be returned from the SQL precompiler. This is the default value for SQL_SQLWARN_OPT option.
SQL_STRDEL_OPT	SQL_STRDEL_APOSTROPHE	No	Specifies that an apostrophe will be used as the string delimiter within SQL statements.
	SQL_STRDEL_QUOTE	No	Specifies that double quotation marks will be used as the string delimiter within SQL statements.

TABLE 18.2 Precompile/Bind Options and Values *(Continued)*

Precompile/bind option	Value	Currently supported	Description
SQL_TEXT_OPT	*sqlchar* structure	No	Specifies a description that is to be assigned to the package. The description can be up to 255 characters long.
SQL_VALIDATE_OPT	SQL_VALIDATE_BIND	No	Specifies that authorization validation is to be performed by the DB2 database manager at precompile/bind time.
	SQL_VALIDATE_RUN	No	Specifies that authorization validation is performed by the DB2 database manager at bind time. This is the default value for SQL_VALIDATE_OPT.
SQL_VERSION_OPT	*sqlchar* structure	No	Specifies the Version identifier for a package. This option can only be used with the SQL precompiler.

Notes: When *sqlchar* structure option values are specified, the *sqlopt.sqloptions.val* field must contain a pointer to a valid *sqlchar* structure. This structure contains a character string that specifies the option value to be set, along with the length of the character string. In most cases, if an unsupported option is specified, the option will be ignored and a warning will be returned by the SQL precompiler or the DB2 bind utility.

Adapted from IBM's *DATABASE 2 API Reference*, Table 2, pages 9 to 11 and Table 3, pages 20 to 22, and the PRECOMPILE PROGRAM and BIND commands documentation in IBM's *Database 2 Command Reference*, pages 41 to 48 and 181 to 193.

The PRECOMPILE PROGRAM function executes under the transaction that was started by a connection to a database. Upon completion, this function automatically issues either a COMMIT or a ROLLBACK SQL statement to terminate the current transaction.

Comments

- The *MsgFileName* parameter can contain the path and name of an operating system file or a standard device (such as standard error or standard out).
- If the *MsgFileName* parameter contains the path and name of an operating system file that already exists, the existing file will be overwritten when the function is executed. If the path and name of an operating system file that does not exist is specified, a new file will be created.
- The SQL precompiler expects the following high-level language source-code file extensions:

  .sqc C applications
  .sqx C++ applications (OS/2)
  .sqC C++ applications (AIX)

- The precompile process stops whenever a fatal error occurs or whenever more than 100 general errors occur. If the precompile process stops, the PRECOMPILE PROGRAM function will attempt to close all opened files and the corresponding package will be discarded.
- For more detailed information about precompiling and binding embedded SQL application programs to DB2 databases, refer to Chapter 4, WRITING EMBEDDED SQL APPLICATIONS.

Required Connection This function can be called only if a connection to a database exists.

Authorization Only users with system administrator (SYSADM) authority, database administrator (DBADM) authority, BINDADD authority (if the package that will be generated does not exist), or BIND authority (if the package that will be generated already exists) are allowed to execute this function call.

The user also needs all authorizations that are required to compile any static SQL statements coded in the specified source-code file. Authorization privileges granted to groups and PUBLIC are not used when authorization checking is performed for static SQL statements.

> Note: If a user has SYSADM authority but not explicit authority to complete the bind process, the DB2 database manager will automatically give the user explicit DBADM authority.

See Also BIND

Example The following C program illustrates how to use the PRECOMPILE PROGRAM function to precompile an embedded SQL source-code file:

```
#include <stdio.h>
#include <stdlib.h>
#include <string.h>
#include <sqlutil.h>
#include <sql.h>

int main()
{
    /* Include The SQLCA Data Structure Variable */
    EXEC SQL INCLUDE SQLCA;

    /* Set Up A Simple SQL Error Handler */
    EXEC SQL WHENEVER SQLERROR GOTO EXIT;

    /* Declare The Local Memory Variables */
    int                    rc = EXIT_SUCCESS;
    struct sqlopt          *PrepOptions;
    struct sqloptheader    Header;
    struct sqloptions      *OptionsPtr;

    struct sqlchar         *BindFile;
    char                   szString[14];
    int                    iBuffSize;

    /* Store The Bind File Name In A SQLCHAR Structure */
    strcpy(szString, "CH18EX9A.BND");
    BindFile = (struct sqlchar *) malloc (strlen(szString) +
                                   sizeof(struct sqlchar));
    BindFile->length = strlen(szString);
    strncpy(BindFile->data, szString, strlen(szString));

    /* Allocate And Initialize The Precompiler Options Structure */
    iBuffSize = sizeof(struct sqlopt) + sizeof(struct sqloptheader) +
                (2 * sizeof(struct sqloptions));
    PrepOptions = (struct sqlopt *) malloc(iBuffSize);
    PrepOptions->header.allocated = 2;
    PrepOptions->header.used = 1;
    OptionsPtr = (struct sqloptions *) PrepOptions->option;
```

```
        OptionsPtr->type = SQL_BIND_OPT;
        OptionsPtr->val = (unsigned long) BindFile;

        /* Connect To The SAMPLE Database */
        EXEC SQL CONNECT TO SAMPLE USER etpdd6z USING sanders;

        /* Precompile The Specified Source Code File */
        sqlaprep("CH18EX9A.SQC", "PREPINFO.DAT", PrepOptions, &sqlca);

        /* Display A Success Message */
        printf("CH18EX9A.SQC has been precompiled. Check the file ");
        printf("PREPINFO.DAT for\ninformation.\n");

    EXIT:
        /* If An Error Has Occurred, Display The SQL Return Code */
        if (sqlca.sqlcode != SQL_RC_OK)
            {
            printf("ERROR : %ld\n", sqlca.sqlcode);
            rc = EXIT_FAILURE;
            }

        /* Issue A Rollback To Free All Locks */
        EXEC SQL ROLLBACK;

        /* Turn Off The SQL Error Handler */
        EXEC SQL WHENEVER SQLERROR CONTINUE;

        /* Disconnect From The SAMPLE Database */
        EXEC SQL DISCONNECT CURRENT;

        /* Free All Allocated Memory */
        if (BindFile != NULL)
            free(BindFile);

        if (PrepOptions != NULL)
            free(PrepOptions);

        /* Return To The Operating System */
        return(rc);
    }
```

BIND

Purpose The BIND function invokes the bind utility, which prepares the SQL statements stored in a bind file that was generated by the SQL precompiler, and creates a corresponding package that is stored in the database.

Syntax

```
SQL_API_RC SQL_API_FN sqlabndx (char            *BindFileName,
                                 char            *MsgFileName,
                                 struct sqlopt   *BindOptions,
                                 struct sqlca    *SQLCA);
```

Parameters

BindFileName A pointer to a location in memory where the path and name of the bind file (or the name of a file containing a list of bind files) to be bound is stored.

MsgFileName A pointer to a location in memory where the name of the file or the device that all error, warning, and informational messages are to be written to is stored.

BindOptions A pointer to a *sqlopt* structure that contains the bind options (if any) that should be used when the specified bind file(s) are bound to the current database.

SQLCA A pointer to a location in memory where a SQL communication area (SQLCA) data structure variable is stored. This variable sends either status information (if the function executed successfully) or error information (if the function failed) back to the calling application.

Includes

```
#include <sql.h>
```

Description

The BIND function invokes the bind utility, which prepares the SQL statements stored in a bind file that was generated by the SQL precompiler and creates a corresponding package that is stored in the database. Binding can be performed as part of the precompile process for an application program source-code file, or as a separate process at a later time. This function is used when binding is performed as a separate process.

A special structure (*sqlopt*) passes different bind options to the bind utility when this function is called. Refer to the PRECOMPILE PROGRAM function for more information about the elements in the *sqlopt* structure and for more information about the available bind options.

The BIND function executes under the transaction that was started by a connection to a database. Upon completion, this function automatically issues either a COMMIT or a ROLLBACK SQL statement to terminate the current transaction.

Comments

- The bind utility expects all bind files to have the extension **.bnd**.
- The *BindFileName* parameter can contain the name of a specific bind file or the name of a file that contains a list of bind file names. If the name of a file containing a list of bind filenames is specified, it must be preceded with the at symbol (@) and the file itself must have the extension **.lst**. For example, a fully qualified bind list file name under OS/2 might be **C:all.lst**.
- Path specifications can be supplied with the bind file names in a bind list file. If the bind list file contains two or more bind file names, all but the last bind file name should be followed by a plus sign (+). The bind file paths and names can be placed on one or more lines in the bind list file. For example, an OS/2 bind list file might contain the following list:

```
mybind1.bnd+mybind2.bnd+
C:mybind3.bnd+
mybind4.bnd
```

- The name of the package to be created is stored in the bind file. By default, this name is the same as the first eight characters of the source-code file name (minus the file extension and converted to uppercase) from which the bind file was generated. However, you can overwrite bind filenames and package names by using the SQL_BIND_OPT and SQL_PKG_OPT options with the PRECOMPILE PROGRAM function.
- The bind process stops whenever a fatal error occurs or whenever more than 100 general errors occur. If the bind process stops, the BIND function will attempt to close all opened files and discard the corresponding package.
- For more detailed information about precompiling and binding embedded SQL application programs to DB2 databases, refer to Chapter 4.

Required Connection This function can be called only if a connection to a database exists.

Authorization Only users with system administrator (SYSADM) authority, database administrator (DBADM) authority, BINDADD authority (if the package that will be generated does not exist), or BIND authority (if the package that will be generated already exists) are allowed to execute this function call.

The user also needs all authorizations required to compile any static SQL statements coded in the specified source-code file. Authorization privileges granted to groups and PUBLIC are not used when authorization checking is performed for static SQL statements.

> Note: If a user has SYSADM authority but not explicit authority to complete the bind process, the DB2 database manager will automatically give the user explicit DBADM authority.

See Also PRECOMPILE PROGRAM

Example The following C program illustrates how to use the BIND function to bind the contents of an external bind file to the current connected database:

```
#include <stdio.h>
#include <stdlib.h>
#include <string.h>
#include <sqlutil.h>
#include <sql.h>

int main()
{
    /* Include The SQLCA Data Structure Variable */
    EXEC SQL INCLUDE SQLCA;

    /* Set Up A Simple SQL Error Handler */
    EXEC SQL WHENEVER SQLERROR GOTO EXIT;

    /* Declare The Local Memory Variables */
    int                   rc = EXIT_SUCCESS;
    struct sqlopt         *BindOptions;
    struct sqloptheader   Header;
    struct sqloptions     *OptionsPtr;

    struct sqlchar        *Collection;
    char                  szString[10];
    int                   iBuffSize;

    /* Store The Collection Name In A SQLCHAR Structure */
    strcpy(szString, "ETPDD6Z");
    Collection = (struct sqlchar *) malloc (strlen(szString) +
                                       sizeof(struct sqlchar));
    Collection->length = strlen(szString);
    strncpy(Collection->data, szString, strlen(szString));

    /* Allocate And Initialize The Bind Options Structure */
    iBuffSize = sizeof(struct sqlopt) + sizeof(struct sqloptheader) +
                (2 * sizeof(struct sqloptions));
    BindOptions = (struct sqlopt *) malloc(iBuffSize);
    BindOptions->header.allocated = 2;
```

```
    BindOptions->header.used = 1;
    OptionsPtr = (struct sqloptions *) BindOptions->option;

    OptionsPtr->type = SQL_COLLECTION_OPT;
    OptionsPtr->val = (unsigned long) Collection;

    /* Connect To The SAMPLE Database */
    EXEC SQL CONNECT TO SAMPLE USER etpdd6z USING sanders;

    /* Bind The Specified Bind File To The SAMPLE Database */
    sqlabndx("CH18EX9A.BND", "BINDINFO.DAT", BindOptions, &sqlca);

    /* Display A Success Message */
    printf("CH18EX9A.BND has been bound to the SAMPLE database. ");
    printf("Check the file\nBINDINFO.DAT for additional ");
    printf("information.\n");

EXIT:
    /* If An Error Has Occurred, Display The SQL Return Code */
    if (sqlca.sqlcode != SQL_RC_OK)
        {
        printf("ERROR : %ld\n", sqlca.sqlcode);
        rc = EXIT_FAILURE;
        }

    /* Issue A Rollback To Free All Locks */
    EXEC SQL ROLLBACK;

    /* Turn Off The SQL Error Handler */
    EXEC SQL WHENEVER SQLERROR CONTINUE;

    /* Disconnect From The SAMPLE Database */
    EXEC SQL DISCONNECT CURRENT;

    /* Free All Allocated Memory */
    if (Collection != NULL)
        free(Collection);

    if (BindOptions != NULL)
        free(BindOptions);

    /* Return To The Operating System */
    return(rc);
}
```

REBIND

Purpose The REBIND function re-creates a package stored in the database without using a corresponding bind file.

Syntax

```
SQL_API_RC SQL_API_FN sqlarbnd (char          *PackageName,
                                struct sqlca *SQLCA,
                                void          *Reserved);
```

Parameters

PackageName A pointer to a location in memory where the name (qualified or unqualified) of the package to be rebound is stored.

SQLCA A pointer to a location in memory where a SQL communication area (SQLCA) data structure variable is stored. This variable sends either status information (if the function executed successfully) or error information (if the function failed) back to the calling application.

Reserved A pointer currently reserved for later use. For now, this parameter must always be set to NULL.

Includes

```
#include <sql.h>
```

Description

The REBIND function re-creates a package stored in the database without using a corresponding bind file. When this function is executed, the DB2 database manager re-creates the package from the SQL statements stored in the SYSCAT.STATEMENTS system catalog table. The REBIND function provides a user or application with:

- A quick way to re-create a package when the original bind file is not available, which enables a user to take advantage of changes in the system. For example, if an index is created for a table, you can use the REBIND function to re-create the package so SQL statements in the application can take advantage of the new index. Likewise, you can use this function to re-create packages after the RUN STATISTICS function is executed, so all access plans generated for the packages can take advantage of the new statistical information.
- The ability to re-create inoperative packages. A package is marked inoperative (the VALID column of the SYSCAT.PACKAGES system catalog table is set to "X") when a function instance on which the package depends is dropped. Inoperative packages must be explicitly rebound to a database with either the bind or rebind utility before they can be used by any application that references them.
- Control over the process of rebinding of invalid packages. Invalid packages are automatically (or implicitly) rebound by the DB2 database manager when they are executed. This can result in a noticeable delay in the execution of the first SQL request for an invalid package. It might be more desirable to explicitly rebind invalid packages rather than allow DB2 to implicitly rebind them, in order to eliminate this initial delay and to trap and process unexpected SQL error messages, which might be returned if the implicit rebind fails. For example, when an earlier version of DB2 database is migrated, all packages stored in that database are invalidated by the DB2 version 2.1 migration process. This might affect a large number of packages, so you might want to explicitly rebind all the invalid packages at one time.

Comments

- If the package name specified in the *PackageName* parameter is unqualified, it is implicitly qualified by the current authorization ID. Note that this default qualifier might be different from the authorization ID used when the package was originally bound to the database.
- The same bind options specified when the package was originally created and bound to the database are used when the package is rebound.
- This function does not automatically commit or roll back the transaction after the rebind has occurred. Instead, the user must explicitly commit or roll back the transaction. This allows the user to update different table statistics and then rebind the package to see what, if anything, changes. This also allows a single transaction to perform multiple rebind operations.
- During the rebind process, an exclusive lock is acquired and held on a package's record in the SYSCAT.PACKAGES system catalog table.

Therefore, if the rebind utility attempts to rebind a package that is in use by another application, it must wait until the transaction that is using the package ends (so it can acquire the appropriate exclusive lock).

- The rebind process will stop if a fatal or general error occurs. If the rebind process stops before the specified package is re-created, the REBIND function will attempt to close all opened files, and the corresponding package will be left in its original state.
- The rebind utility will reexplain packages that were created with the SQL_EXPLSNAP_OPT precompile/bind option set to SQL_EXPLAIN_YES or SQL_EXPLAIN_ALL (as indicated by the EXPLAIN_SNAPSHOT column in the SYSCAT.PACKAGES catalog table entry for the package). However, the Explain facility will use the explain tables of the user requesting the REBIND operation, not the user who performed the original bind operation.
- The REBIND function is supported by distributed database connectivity services (DDCS).
- Explicit rebinding can be done with the BIND function, the REBIND function, or the db2rbind tool (refer to the IBM Database 2 Command Reference for more information about the db2rbind tool). Since both the BIND and REBIND functions can explicitly rebind a package to a database, the choice of which function to use depends on the circumstances. Since the performance of the REBIND function is significantly better than that of the BIND function, use the REBIND function whenever the situation does not specifically require the use of the BIND function. The BIND function (and not the REBIND function) must be used to explicitly rebind a package when:
  - –The embedded SQL application program has been modified (when SQL statements have been added or deleted, or when the package does not match the executable program image).
  - –The user wants to modify any of the bind options as part of the rebind process. The REBIND function does not allow the user to specify bind options.
  - –The package does not currently exist in the database.
  - –You want to detect all general bind errors. The REBIND function returns only the first error it detects (and then ends), whereas the BIND function returns the first 100 errors it encounters during the binding process.

Required Connection This function can be called only if a connection to a database exists.

Authorization Only users with system administrator (SYSADM) authority, database administrator (DBADM) authority, or BIND authority for the package can execute this function call.

The authorization ID stored in the BOUNDBY column of the SYSCAT.PACKAGES system catalog table, which is the authorization ID of the most recent binder of the package, is used as the binder authorization ID for the rebind operation and the default schema for all table references in the package.

See Also BIND, RUN STATISTICS

Example The following C program illustrates how to use the REBIND function to rebind a package that already exists in the current connected database:

```
#include <stdio.h>
#include <stdlib.h>
#include <sqlutil.h>
#include <sql.h>

int main()
{
    /* Include The SQLCA Data Structure Variable */
    EXEC SQL INCLUDE SQLCA;

    /* Set Up A Simple SQL Error Handler */
    EXEC SQL WHENEVER SQLERROR GOTO EXIT;

    /* Declare The Local Memory Variables */
    int  rc = EXIT_SUCCESS;

    /* Declare The SQL Host Memory Variables */
    EXEC SQL BEGIN DECLARE SECTION;
        char     szPackageName[9];
        char     szBindTime[30];
    EXEC SQL END DECLARE SECTION;

    /* Connect To The SAMPLE Database */
    EXEC SQL CONNECT TO SAMPLE USER etpdd6z USING sanders;

    /* Retrieve A Record From The SYSCAT.PACKAGES Table */
    EXEC SQL SELECT PKGNAME,
                    CHAR(LAST_BIND_TIME)
        INTO :szPackageName,
             :szBindTime
        FROM SYSCAT.PACKAGES
        WHERE PKGNAME = 'CH8EX1A' AND BOUNDBY = 'ETPDD6Z';

    /* Print The Information Retrieved - This Will Show The */
    /* Timestamp For The Package Before It Is Rebound       */
    printf("Package Name : %8s\tLast Bound : %s\n",
           szPackageName, szBindTime);

    /* Rebind The Package Associated With The One Of The Embedded */
    /* SQL Example Programs (Created In Chapter 8)               */
    sqlarbnd("CH8EX1A", &sqlca, NULL);

    /* Retrieve The Record From The SYSCAT.PACKAGES Table Again */
    EXEC SQL SELECT PKGNAME,
                    CHAR(LAST_BIND_TIME)
        INTO :szPackageName,
             :szBindTime
        FROM SYSCAT.PACKAGES
        WHERE PKGNAME = 'CH8EX1A' AND BOUNDBY = 'ETPDD6Z';

    /* Print The Information Retrieved - This Will Show The */
    /* Timestamp For The Package After It Has Been Rebound  */
    printf("Package Name : %8s\tRebound     : %s\n",
           szPackageName, szBindTime);

EXIT:
    /* If An Error Has Occurred, Display The SQL Return Code */
    if (sqlca.sqlcode != SQL_RC_OK)
        {
```

```
            printf("ERROR : %ld\n", sqlca.sqlcode);
            rc = EXIT_FAILURE;
            }

        /* Issue A Rollback To Free All Locks */
        EXEC SQL ROLLBACK;

        /* Turn Off The SQL Error Handler */
        EXEC SQL WHENEVER SQLERROR CONTINUE;

        /* Disconnect From The SAMPLE Database */
        EXEC SQL DISCONNECT CURRENT;

        /* Return To The Operating System */
        return(rc);
    }
```

GET INSTANCE

Purpose

The GET INSTANCE function retrieves the current value of the DB2INSTANCE environment variable.

Syntax

```
SQL_API_RC SQL_API_FN sqlegins (char          *Instance,
                                struct sqlca *SQLCA);
```

Parameters

Instance A pointer to a location in memory where this function is to store the current DB2 database manager instance name (the current value of the DB2INSTANCE environment variable).

SQLCA A pointer to a location in memory where a SQL communication area (SQLCA) data structure variable is stored. This variable sends either status information (if the function executed successfully) or error information (if the function failed) back to the calling application.

Includes

```
#include <sqlenv.h>
```

Description

The GET INSTANCE function retrieves the current value of the DB2INSTANCE environment variable. This value usually identifies the instance-level node to which the application is currently attached.

Comments

- The buffer in which this function is to store the DB2 database manager instance name (the *Instance* parameter) must be at least eight bytes long.
- The value in the DB2INSTANCE environment variable is not necessarily the DB2 database manager instance to which the application is currently attached. To identify the DB2 database manager instance to which an application is currently attached, call the ATTACH function with all parameters except *SQLCA* set to NULL.

Required Connection

This function can be called at any time; a connection to a DB2 database manager instance or to a DB2 database does not have to be established first.

Authorization

No authorization is required to execute this function call.

Example The following C program illustrates how to use the GET INSTANCE function to obtain the current value of the DB2INSTANCE environment variable:

```
#include <stdio.h>
#include <stdlib.h>
#include <sqlenv.h>
#include <sqlca.h>

int main()
{
    /* Declare The Local Memory Variables */
    int           rc = EXIT_SUCCESS;
    char          szInstance[9];
    struct sqlca  sqlca;

    /* Obtain The Current Value Of The DB2INSTANCE Environment */
    /* Variable                                                */
    sqlegins(szInstance, &sqlca);

    /* Display The Current Value Of The DB2INSTANCE Environment Variable */
    printf("Current value of the DB2INSTANCE environment ");
    printf("variable : %s\n", szInstance);

    /* Return To The Operating System */
    return(rc);
}
```

INSTALL SIGNAL HANDLER

Purpose The INSTALL SIGNAL HANDLER function installs the default interrupt signal handler provided with DB2.

Syntax

```
SQL_API_RC SQL_API_FN sqleisig (struct sqlca *SQLCA);
```

Parameters

SQLCA A pointer to a location in memory where a SQL communication area (SQLCA) data structure variable is stored. This variable sends either status information (if the function executed successfully) or error information (if the function failed) back to the calling application.

Includes

```
#include <sqlenv.h>
```

Description The INSTALL SIGNAL HANDLER function installs the default interrupt signal handler that is provided with the DB2 software development kit (SDK). When the default interrupt signal handler detects an interrupt signal (usually Ctrl-C and/or Ctrl-Break), it resets the signal and calls the INTERRUPT function to gracefully stop the processing of the current database request.

Comments

- If an application has not installed an interrupt signal handler and an interrupt signal is received, the application will be terminated. This function provides simple interrupt signal handling, and should always be used if an application does not have extensive interrupt handling requirements.

- If an application requires a more elaborate interrupt handling scheme, you can develop a signal handling routine that resets the signal, calls the INTERRUPT function, and then performs additional tasks.
- You must call this API function before the default interrupt signal handler will function property.
- This function cannot be used in applications run on the Windows or Windows NT operating system.

Required Connection This function can be called at any time; a connection to a DB2 database manager instance or to a DB2 database does not have to be established first.

Authorization No authorization is required to execute this function call.

See Also INTERRUPT

Example The following C program illustrates how the INSTALL SIGNAL HANDLER function installs the default interrupt signal handling routine in an embedded SQL application:

```
#include <stdio.h>
#include <stdlib.h>
#include <sqlenv.h>
#include <sql.h>

int main()
{
    /* Include The SQLCA Data Structure Variable */
    EXEC SQL INCLUDE SQLCA;

    /* Declare The Local Memory Variables */
    int  rc = EXIT_SUCCESS;

    /* Declare The SQL Host Memory Variables */
    EXEC SQL BEGIN DECLARE SECTION;
        long   lTotalComm;
    EXEC SQL END DECLARE SECTION;

    /* Install DB2's Default Interrupt Signal Handler */
    sqleisig(&sqlca);

    /* Set Up A Simple SQL Error Handler */
    EXEC SQL WHENEVER SQLERROR GOTO EXIT;

    /* Display A Message Telling The User To Generate An Interrupt */
    /* Signal By Pressing Ctrl-Break                               */
    printf("Press Ctrl-Break to terminate this program.\n");

    /* Connect To The SAMPLE Database */
    EXEC SQL CONNECT TO SAMPLE USER etpdd6z USING sanders;

    /* Retrieve The Total Amount Of Commissions Paid From The */
    /* EMPLOYEE Table                                         */
    EXEC SQL SELECT SUM(COMM)
        INTO :lTotalComm
        FROM USERID.EMPLOYEE;

    /* Print The Information Retrieved */
    printf("The company paid $ %.2ld.00 in commissions.\n",
```

```
            lTotalComm);

EXIT:
    /* If The Process Was Terminated By A Signal Interrupt, Display */
    /* An Error Message Saying So                                   */
    if (sqlca.sqlcode == -952)
        {
        printf("Processing was terminated due to an interrupt.\n");
        rc = EXIT_FAILURE;
        }

    /* Otherwise, If An Error Has Occurred, Display The SQL Return */
    /* Code                                                        */
    else if (sqlca.sqlcode != SQL_RC_OK)
        {
        printf("ERROR : %ld\n", sqlca.sqlcode);
        rc = EXIT_FAILURE;
        }

    /* Issue A Rollback To Free All Locks */
    EXEC SQL ROLLBACK;

    /* Turn Off The SQL Error Handler */
    EXEC SQL WHENEVER SQLERROR CONTINUE;

    /* Disconnect From The SAMPLE Database */
    EXEC SQL DISCONNECT CURRENT;

    /* Return To The Operating System */
    return(rc);
}
```

INTERRUPT

Purpose

The INTERRUPT function stops the processing of the current database request.

Syntax

```
SQL_API_RC SQL_API_INTR sqleintr( );
```

Includes

```
#include <sqlenv.h>
```

Description

The INTERRUPT function stops the processing of the current database request. This is normally the first function called in an interrupt signal handler routine. An application's interrupt signal handler can be the default signal handler installed by the INSTALL SIGNAL HANDLER function or a more elaborate interrupt handler routine supplied by the application developer and installed with the appropriate operating system call. In either case, when an interrupt handler detects an interrupt signal (usually Ctrl-C and/or Ctrl-Break), it takes control and performs one or more actions to ensure that all active processing is terminated gracefully.

When the INTERRUPT function is called while other API functions are executing, the executing API functions are either interrupted or allowed to complete execution, depending on the work they are performing. Table 18.3 lists the effects the INTERRUPT function has on other API functions.

TABLE 18.3 Interrupt Effects on SQL and API Actions

Database activity	Action
IMPORT	The import process is canceled and all database updates are rolled back.
EXPORT	The export process is canceled and all database updates are rolled back.
RUNSTATS	The Run Statistics process is canceled and all database updates are rolled back.
REORGANIZE TABLE	The reorganize table process is canceled and the table is left in its previous state.
BACKUP	The backup process is canceled and the backup data stored on the specified media might be incomplete.
RESTORE	The restore process is canceled and the database being restored is deleted (DROP DATABASE is performed). Not applicable to table space level restore operations.
LOAD	The load process is canceled and the data stored in table might be incomplete.
PREP (PRECOMPILE PROGRAM)	The precompile process is canceled and package creation is rolled back.
BIND	The bind process is canceled and package creation is rolled back.
COMMIT	The COMMIT process runs to completion.
FORCE APPLICATION	The FORCE APPLICATION process runs to completion.
ROLLBACK	The ROLLBACK process runs to completion.
CREATE DATABASE	After a certain point, the CREATE DATABASE process cannot be terminated. If the interrupt signal is received before this point, the database is not created and the database creation process is canceled. If the interrupt is received after this point, the CREATE DATABASE process runs to completion and the database is created.
DROP DATABASE	The DROP DATABASE process runs to completion.
Directory Services	The specified directory is left in a consistent state. Utility functions might be performed.
SQL Data Definition Statements	Database transactions are set to the state they were in before the SQL statement was executed.
Other SQL statements	Database transactions are set to the state they were in before the SQL statement was executed.

Adapted from IBM's *DATABASE 2 API Reference*, Table 4, page 164.

Comments

- No DB2 function other than INTERRUPT should be called from a user-defined interrupt handler.
- When creating an interrupt handling routine, follow all operating system programming techniques and practices to ensure that all previously installed signal handlers continue to work properly.
- Any transaction in the process of being committed or rolled back cannot be interrupted.
- When an API function is interrupted, it places a return code that indicates it was interrupted in the appropriate SQLCA data structure variable.

Required Connection This function can be called at any time; a connection to a DB2 database manager instance or to a DB2 database does not have to be established first.

Authorization No authorization is required to execute this function call.

See Also INSTALL SIGNAL HANDLER

Example

The following C program illustrates how the INTERRUPT function is used in a user-defined interrupt signal handling routine (OS/2):

```
#define INCL_DOSEXCEPTIONS          // DOS Exception Values
#define INCL_ERRORS                 // DOS Error Values
#include <os2.h>
#include <stdio.h>
#include <stdlib.h>
#include <sqlenv.h>
#include <sql.h>

/* Declare The Interrupt Signal Handler Routine Function Prototype */
ULONG _System MyIntHandler(PEXCEPTIONREPORTRECORD   Report,
                           PEXCEPTIONREGISTRATIONRECORD Registration,
                           PCONTEXTRECORD           Context,
                           PVOID                    VoidPtr);

int main()
{
    /* Include The SQLCA Data Structure Variable */
    EXEC SQL INCLUDE SQLCA;

    /* Declare The Local Memory Variables */
    int                          rc = EXIT_SUCCESS;
    APIRET                       APIrc = NO_ERROR;
    EXCEPTIONREGISTRATIONRECORD  RegRec = {0} ;  // Exception
                                                 // Registration
                                                 // Record

    /* Declare The SQL Host Memory Variables */
    EXEC SQL BEGIN DECLARE SECTION;
        long   lTotalComm;
    EXEC SQL END DECLARE SECTION;

    /* Install The User-Defined Interrupt Signal Handler */
    RegRec.ExceptionHandler = (ERR) MyIntHandler;
    APIrc = DosSetExceptionHandler(&RegRec);

    /* Set Up A Simple SQL Error Handler */
    EXEC SQL WHENEVER SQLERROR GOTO EXIT;

    /* Display A Message Telling The User To Generate An Interrupt */
    /* Signal By Pressing Ctrl-Break                                */
    printf("Press Ctrl-Break to terminate this program.\n");

    /* Connect To The SAMPLE Database */
    EXEC SQL CONNECT TO SAMPLE USER etpdd6z USING sanders;

    /* Retrieve The Total Amount Of Commissions Paid From The */
    /* EMPLOYEE Table                                         */
    EXEC SQL SELECT SUM(COMM)
        INTO :lTotalComm
        FROM USERID.EMPLOYEE;

    /* Print The Information Retrieved */
    printf("The company paid $ %.2ld.00 in commissions.\n",
           lTotalComm);
```

```
EXIT:
    /* If An Error Has Occured, Display The SQL Return Code */
    if (sqlca.sqlcode != SQL_RC_OK)
        {
        printf("ERROR : %ld\n", sqlca.sqlcode);
        rc = EXIT_FAILURE;
        }

    /* Issue A Rollback To Free All Locks */
    EXEC SQL ROLLBACK;

    /* Turn Off The SQL Error Handler */
    EXEC SQL WHENEVER SQLERROR CONTINUE;

    /* Disconnect From The SAMPLE Database */
    EXEC SQL DISCONNECT CURRENT;

    /* Remove The User-Defined Interrupt Signal Handler */
    APIrc = DosUnsetExceptionHandler(&RegRec);

    /* If The User-Defined Interrupt Signal Handler Could Not Be */
    /* Removed, Display An Error Message                         */
    if (APIrc != NO_ERROR)
        {
        printf("ERROR : Unable to remove user-defined interrupt ");
        printf("signal handler\n\n[Return Code = %u\n", APIrc);
        }

    /* Return To The Operating System */
    return(rc);
}

/* Define The User-Defined Interrupt Signal Handler Routine (OS/2) */
ULONG _System MyIntHandler(PEXCEPTIONREPORTRECORD    Report,
                           PEXCEPTIONREGISTRATIONRECORD Registration,
                           PCONTEXTRECORD            Context,
                           PVOID                     VoidPtr)
{
    /* Declare The Local Memory Variables */
    int   rc = EXIT_SUCCESS;

    /* Terminate All DB2 Database Requests That Are In Progress */
    sqleintr();

    /* Process The Interrupt Signal Appropriately */
    switch(Report->ExceptionNum)
        {
        case XCPT_SIGNAL:
            {
            switch(Report->ExceptionInfo[0])
                {
                case XCPT_SIGNAL_INTR:
                case XCPT_SIGNAL_KILLPROC:
                case XCPT_SIGNAL_BREAK:
                    printf("Processing was terminated due to an ");
                    printf("interrupt signal.\n\n");

                    /* Remove The User-Defined Interrupt Signal */
                    /* Handler                                  */
                    DosUnsetExceptionHandler(Registration);
```

```
                    /* If The User-Defined Interrupt Signal Handler */
                    /* Could Not Be Removed, Display An Error       */
                    /* Message                                      */
                    if (rc != NO_ERROR)
                        {
                        printf("ERROR : Unable to remove user-");
                        printf("defined interrupt signal handler.\n");
                        }

                    /* Stop Recursive Entry To This Handler */
                    rc = DosUnwindException(0, (PVOID) 0, 0);

                    break;
                }
            }

        case XCPT_PROCESS_TERMINATE:
            printf("Process Terminate Signal Received.\n");
            break;
        case XCPT_ASYNC_PROCESS_TERMINATE:
            printf("Async Process Terminate Signal Received.\n");
            break;
        case XCPT_UNWIND:
            printf("XCPT_UNWIND Signal Received.\n");
            break;
        default:
            break;
        }

    return XCPT_CONTINUE_SEARCH;        // Exception Unresolved
}
```

GET ADDRESS

Purpose

The GET ADDRESS function stores the address of one variable into another variable in applications written in host languages that do not support pointer manipulation.

Syntax

```
SQL_API_RC SQL_API_FN sqlgaddr (char *Variable,
                                char *OutputAddress);
```

Parameters

Variable A pointer to a location in memory where the address of the specified variable is stored.

OutputAddress The address of a pointer to a location in memory where this function is to store the address retrieved for the variable specified in the *Variable* parameter.

Includes

```
#include <sqlutil.h>
```

Description

The GET ADDRESS function stores the address of one variable into another variable in applications written in host languages that do not support pointer manipulation. This function should be used only in applications written in either COBOL or FORTRAN. Applications written in host languages that support pointer manipulation (such as C and C++) should use the language-specific pointer manipulation elements provided.

Comments The buffer in which this function is to store the retrieved address (the *OutputAddress* parameter) must be four bytes long.

Required Connection This function can be called at any time; a connection to a DB2 database manager instance or to a DB2 database does not have to be established first.

Authorization No authorization is required to execute this function call.

See Also DEREFERENCE ADDRESS, COPY MEMORY

Example Since this function should be used only in applications written in either the COBOL or the FORTRAN programming language, an example program is not provided. Refer to the *IBM Database 2 API Reference* for examples of how this function is used in COBOL and FORTRAN applications.

COPY MEMORY

Purpose The COPY MEMORY function copies data from one memory storage area to another in applications written in host languages that do not provide memory block copy functions.

Syntax

```
SQL_API_RC SQL_API_FN sqlgmcpy (void           *Target,
                                const void     *Source,
                                unsigned long  NumBytes);
```

Parameters

Target A pointer to a location in memory where this function is to copy data to.

Source A pointer to a location in memory where this function is to copy data from.

NumBytes The number of bytes of data that is to be copied from the *Source* memory storage area to the *Target* memory storage area.

Includes

```
#include <sqlutil.h>
```

Description The COPY MEMORY function copies data from one memory storage area to another in applications written in host languages that do not provide memory block copy functions. This function should be used only in applications written in either COBOL or FORTRAN. Applications written in host languages that provide memory copy functions (such as C and C++) should use the language memory copy functions provided.

Comments The host programming language variable that contains the number of bytes of data to be copied (the *NumBytes* parameter) must be four bytes long.

Required Connection This function can be called at any time; a connection to a DB2 database manager instance or to a DB2 database does not have to be established first.

Authorization No authorization is required to execute this function call.

See Also GET ADDRESS, DEREFERENCE ADDRESS

Example Since this function should be used only in applications written in either the COBOL or the FORTRAN programming language, an example program is not provided. Refer to the *IBM Database 2 API Reference* for examples of how this function is used in COBOL and FORTRAN applications.

DEREFERENCE ADDRESS

Purpose The DEREFERENCE ADDRESS function copies data from a buffer defined by a pointer to a local data storage variable in applications written in host languages that do not support pointer manipulation.

Syntax

```
SQL_API_RC SQL_API_FN sqlgdref (unsigned int NumBytes,
                                char         *TargetVariable,
                                char         *SourceBuffer);
```

Parameters

NumBytes The number of bytes of data to be copied from the *SourceBuffer* memory storage area to the *TargetVariable* variable.

TargetVariable A pointer to a local storage variable where this function is to copy data to.

SourceBuffer The address of a pointer to a location in memory where this function is to copy data from.

Includes

```
#include <sqlutil.h>
```

Description The DEREFERENCE ADDRESS function copies data from a buffer defined by a pointer to a local data storage variable in applications written in host languages that do not support pointer manipulation. This function should be used only in applications written in either COBOL or FORTRAN. Applications written in host languages that support pointer manipulation (such as C and C++) should use the language-specific pointer manipulation elements provided.

You can use this function to obtain results from other API functions that return pointers to data storage areas that contain the data values retrieved, such as GET NEXT NODE DIRECTORY ENTRY.

Comments The host programming language variable that contains the number of bytes of data to be copied (the *NumBytes* parameter) must be four bytes long.

Required Connection This function can be called at any time; a connection to a DB2 database manager instance or to a DB2 database does not have to be established first.

Authorization No authorization is required to execute this function call.

See Also GET ADDRESS, COPY MEMORY

Example Since this function should be used only in applications written in either COBOL or FORTRAN, an example program is not provided. Refer to the *IBM Database 2 API Reference* for examples of how this function is used in COBOL and FORTRAN applications.

GET ERROR MESSAGE

Purpose

The GET ERROR MESSAGE function retrieves the message text associated with an error or warning condition (specified by the value of the *sqlcode* field of a *sqlca* data structure variable) from a special DB2 error message file.

Syntax

```
SQL_API_RC SQL_API_FN sqlaintp (char          *Buffer,
                                short         BufferSize,
                                short         MaxLineSize,
                                struct sqlca  *SQLCA);
```

Parameters

Buffer A pointer to a location in memory where this function is to store the retrieved message text.

BufferSize The size, in bytes, of the memory buffer that is to hold the retrieved message text.

MaxLineSize The maximum number of characters that one line of message text should contain before a line break is inserted. A value of zero indicates that the message text is to be returned without line breaks.

SQLCA A pointer to a location in memory where a SQL communication area (SQLCA) data structure variable is stored. The value in the *sqlcode* field of this variable locates and returns the corresponding error message.

Includes

```
#include <sql.h>
```

Description

The GET ERROR MESSAGE function retrieves the message text associated with an error or warning condition from a special DB2 error message file. The DB2 error message file (**db2sql.mo**, located in the **misc** subdirectory of the **sqllib** directory where DB2 was installed) contains error message text corresponding to each error code value that can be generated by DB2. Each time this function is called, the value in the *sqlcode* field of a *sqlca* data structure variable is used to locate and retrieve the corresponding error message text from this file. One error message is returned per GET ERROR MESSAGE function call.

Return Codes

When this function has completed execution, it returns one of the following values:

+i A positive integer value indicating the number of bytes contained in the formatted message. If this value is greater than the value specified in the *BufferSize* parameter, the message text will be truncated. If the message must be truncated to fit in the buffer, the truncation will include room for the string NULL terminator.

–1 Insufficient memory is available for the message formatting services to work properly. The requested message text is not returned.

–2 The specified SQLCA data structure variable did not contain an error code (SQLCODE = 0).

–3 The message text file is inaccessible or incorrect.

–4 The value specified in the *MaxLineSize* parameter is less than zero.

–5 An invalid SQLCA data structure variable, bad buffer address, or bad buffer length (size) was specified.

If the return code is –1 or –3, the message buffer will contain additional information about the problem.

Comments

- A new line (line feed or carriage return/line feed) sequence is automatically placed at the end of each retrieved message text string.
- If a positive value is specified for the *MaxLineSize* parameter, new line sequences will be inserted between words so the lines of the message text string do not exceed the specified line length. If the last word in a line will cause that line to be longer than the specified line width, the line is filled with as many characters of the word that will fit, a new line sequence is inserted, and the remaining characters of the word are placed on the next line.

Required Connection

This function can be called at any time; a connection to a DB2 database manager instance or to a DB2 database does not have to be established first.

Authorization

No authorization is required to execute this function call.

See Also

GET SQLSTATE MESSAGE

Example

The following C program illustrates how to use the GET ERROR MESSAGE function to retrieve the error message text associated with the error code stored in a SQLCA data structure variable after another API function failed:

```
#include <stdio.h>
#include <stdlib.h>
#include <sqlenv.h>
#include <sqlca.h>

int main()
{
    /* Declare The Local Memory Variables */
    int            rc = EXIT_SUCCESS;
    char           szErrorMsg[1024];
    struct sqlca   sqlca;

    /* Attempt To Change The Comment Associated With An Invalid */
    /* Database - This Should Generate An Error                 */
    sqledcgd("INVALID", "", "Invalid Database", &sqlca);

    /* If The "Change Comment" Function Failed, Retrieve The */
    /* Error Message Text For The Error Code Returned        */
    if (sqlca.sqlcode != SQL_RC_OK)
        {

        /* Retrieve The Error Message Text For The Error Code */
        rc = sqlaintp(szErrorMsg, sizeof(szErrorMsg), 70, &sqlca);
        switch (rc)
            {
            case -1:
                printf("ERROR : Insufficient memory.\n");
                break;
            case -3:
                printf("ERROR : Message file is inaccessible.\n");
                break;
            case -5:
                printf("ERROR : Invalid sqlca, bad buffer, ");
                printf("or bad buffer length specified.\n");
                break;
```

```
                default:
                    printf("%s\n", szErrorMsg);
                    break;
                }
            }

    /* Return To The Operating System */
    return(rc);
}
```

GET SQLSTATE MESSAGE

Purpose

The GET SQLSTATE MESSAGE function retrieves the message text associated with a SQLSTATE value (specified by the value of the *sqlstate* field of a *sqlca* data structure variable).

Syntax

```
SQL_API_RC SQL_API_FN sqlogstt (char  *Buffer,
                                short BufferSize,
                                short MaxLineSize,
                                char  *SQLSTATE);
```

Parameters

Buffer A pointer to a location in memory where this function is to store the retrieved message text.

BufferSize The size, in bytes, of the memory buffer to hold the retrieved message text.

MaxLineSize The maximum number of characters that one line of message text should contain before a line break is inserted. A value of zero indicates that the message text is to be returned without line breaks.

SQLSTATE A pointer to a location in memory where the SQLSTATE for which this function is to retrieve message text is stored.

Includes

```
#include <sql.h>
```

Description

The GET SQLSTATE MESSAGE function retrieves the message text associated with a SQLSTATE value. Each time this function is called, the value in the *sqstate* field of a *sqlca* data structure variable locates and retrieves the corresponding error message text. One message is returned per GET SQLSTATE MESSAGE function call.

Return Codes

When this function has completed execution, it returns one of the following values:

+i A positive integer value indicating the number of bytes contained in the formatted message. If this value is greater than the value specified in the *BufferSize* parameter, the message text will be truncated. If the message must be truncated to fit in the buffer, the truncation will include room for the string NULL terminator.

–1 Insufficient memory is available for the message formatting services to work properly. The requested message text is not returned.

–2 The specified SQLSTATE value is in the wrong format. This value must be alphanumeric and either two or five digits in length (and NULL-terminated if two digits long).

–3 The message text is inaccessible or incorrect.

–4 The value specified in the *MaxLineSize* parameter is less than zero.

–5 An invalid *SQLSTATE* value, bad buffer address, or bad buffer length (size) was specified.

If the return code is –1 or –3, the message buffer will contain additional information about the problem.

Comments

- A new line (line feed or carriage return/line feed) sequence is automatically placed at the end of each retrieved message text string.
- If a positive value is specified for the *MaxLineSize* parameter, new line sequences will be inserted between words so the lines of the message text string do not exceed the specified line length. If the last word in a line will cause that line to be longer than the specified line width, the line is filled with as many characters of the word that will fit, a new line sequence is inserted, and the remaining characters of the word are placed on the next line.
- The value specified in the *SQLSTATE* parameter must be either a five-digit specific SQLSTATE value or a two-digit SQLSTATE class value (the first two digits of a SQLSTATE value). If the value provided for this parameter is a two-digit SQLSTATE class value, it must be NULL-terminated.
- This function cannot be used in applications that run from the Windows or Windows NT operating system.

Required Connection

This function can be called at any time; a connection to a DB2 database manager instance or to a DB2 database does not have to be established first.

Authorization

No authorization is required to execute this function call.

See Also

GET ERROR MESSAGE

Example

The following C program illustrates how the GET SQLSTATE MESSAGE function retrieves the error message text associated with the SQLSTATE value stored in a SQLCA data structure variable after another API function failed:

```
#include <stdio.h>
#include <stdlib.h>
#include <sqlenv.h>
#include <sqlca.h>
#include <sql.h>

int main()
{
    /* Declare The Local Memory Variables */
    int             rc = EXIT_SUCCESS;
    char            szErrorMsg[1024];
    struct sqlca    sqlca;

    /* Attempt To Change The Comment Associated With An Invalid */
    /* Database - This Should Generate An Error                 */
    sqledcgd("INVALID", "", "Invalid Database", &sqlca);

    /* If The "Change Comment" Function Failed, Retrieve The */
    /* SQLSTATE Message Text For The SQLSTATE Code Returned  */
    if (sqlca.sqlcode != SQL_RC_OK)
        {

        /* Retrieve The SQLSTATE Message Text For The SQLSTATE Code */
        rc = sqlogstt(szErrorMsg, sizeof(szErrorMsg), 70,
                      (unsigned char *) &sqlca.sqlstate);
```

```
            switch (rc)
                {
                case -1:
                    printf("ERROR : Insufficient memory.\n");
                    break;
                case -2:
                    printf("ERROR : SQLSTATE is in the wrong format.\n");
                    break;
                case -3:
                    printf("ERROR : Message file is inaccessible.\n");
                    break;
                case -5:
                    printf("ERROR : Invalid sqlca, bad buffer, ");
                    printf("or bad buffer length specified.\n");
                    break;
                default:
                    printf("%s\n", szErrorMsg);
                    break;
                }
            }

        /* Return To The Operating System */
        return(rc);
    }
```

GET AUTHORIZATIONS

Purpose

The GET AUTHORIZATIONS function retrieves the authorizations of the current user from both the database configuration file and the authorization system catalog view (SYSCAT.DBAUTH).

Syntax

```
SQL_API_RC SQL_API_FN sqluadau (struct sql_authorizations *Authorizations,
                                struct sqlca              *SQLCA);
```

Parameters

Authorizations A pointer to a *sql_authorizations* structure where this function is to store the retrieved authorization information.

SQLCA A pointer to a location in memory where a SQL communication area (SQLCA) data structure variable is stored. This variable sends either status information (if the function executed successfully) or error information (if the function failed) back to the calling application.

Includes

```
#include <sqlutil.h>
```

Description

The GET AUTHORIZATIONS function retrieves the authorizations of the current user from both the database configuration file and the authorization system catalog view (SYSCAT.DBAUTH). The retrieved authorization information is stored in a *sql_authorizations* structure that contains short integer elements indicating which authorizations the current user does and does not hold. The *sql_authorizations* structure is defined in *sqlutil.h* as follows:

```
struct sql_authorizations
{
short sql_authorizations_len;   /* The Size of the              */
                                /* sql_authorizations_len structure.*/
```

```
short sql_sysadm_auth;          /* The user has SYSADM authority  */
short sql_dbadm_auth;           /* The user has DBADM authority */
short sql_createtab_auth;       /* The user has CREATETAB authority  */
short sql_bindadd_auth;         /* The user has BINDADD authority */
short sql_connect_auth;         /* The user has CONNECT authority */
short sql_sysadm_grp_auth;      /* The user belongs to a group that  */
                                /* has SYSADM authority            */
short sql_dbadm_grp_auth;       /* The user belongs to a group that  */
                                /* has DBADM authority             */
short sql_createtab_grp_auth;   /* The user belongs to a group that  */
                                /* has CREATETAB authority         */
short sql_bindadd_grp_auth;     /* The user belongs to a group that  */
                                /* has BINDADD authority           */
short sql_connect_grp_auth;     /* The user belongs to a group that  */
                                /* has CONNECT authority           */
short sql_sysctrl_auth;         /* The user has SYSCTRL authority  */
short sql_sysctrl_grp_auth;     /* The user belongs to a group that  */
                                /* has SYSCTRL authority           */
short sql_sysmaint_auth;        /* The user has SYSMAINT           */
                                /* authority                       */
short sql_sysmaint_grp_auth;    /* The user belongs to a group that  */
                                /* has SYSMAINT authority          */
short sql_create_not_fenc_auth; /* The user has CREATE NOT         */
                                /* FENCED authority                */
short sql_create_not_fenc_grp_auth; /* The user belongs to a group that  */
                                /* has CREATE NOT FENCED           */
                                /* authority                       */
};
```

The first element in this structure, *sql_authorizations_len*, must be initialized to the size of the structure itself before the GET AUTHORIZATIONS function is called.

Comments

- Explicit SQL commands can grant direct authorities to a specific user. SYSADM, SYSMAINT, and SYSCTRL are indirect authorities and therefore cannot be granted directly to a user. Instead, they are available only through the groups to which a user belongs. PUBLIC is a special group to which all users belong.
- If this function executes without error, each field of the *sql_authorizations* structure variable will contain either a **0** or a **1**. A value of **1** indicates that the current user holds the corresponding authorization, while a value of **0** indicates that the user does not.

Required Connection This function can be called only if a connection to a database exists.

Authorization No authorization is required to execute this function call.

Example The following C program illustrates how to use the GET AUTHORIZATIONS function to determine whether or not the current user has been granted the authorizations needed to execute most of the DB2 API functions:

```
#include <stdio.h>
#include <stdlib.h>
#include <sqlutil.h>
#include <sql.h>
int main()
{
```

```
    /* Include The SQLCA Data Structure Variable */
    EXEC SQL INCLUDE SQLCA;

    /* Declare The Local Memory Variables */
    int                         rc = EXIT_SUCCESS;
    struct sql_authorizations   AuthInfo;

    /* Set Up A Simple SQL Error Handler */
    EXEC SQL WHENEVER SQLERROR GOTO EXIT;

    /* Connect To The SAMPLE Database */
    EXEC SQL CONNECT TO SAMPLE USER etpdd6z USING sanders;

    /* Initialize The First Element Of The AuthInfo Structure */
    /* And Retrieve The Current User's Authorizations         */
    AuthInfo.sql_authorizations_len = sizeof(struct sql_authorizations);
    sqluadau(&AuthInfo, &sqlca);

    /* Display A Message Stating Whether Or Not The User Has The */
    /* Necessary Authorizations To Execute Most Of The DB2 APIs  */
    if (AuthInfo.sql_sysadm_auth    == 1 ||
        AuthInfo.sql_sysmaint_auth == 1 ||
        AuthInfo.sql_sysctrl_auth  == 1 ||
        AuthInfo.sql_dbadm_auth    == 1)
        {
        printf("The current user has the authorizations needed ");
        printf("to execute most of\nthe DB2 APIs.\n");
        }

    else
        {
        printf("The current user does not have the authorizations ");
        printf("that are needed to execute many of\nthe DB2 APIs.\n");
        }

EXIT:
    /* If An Error Has Occurred, Display The SQL Return Code */
    if (sqlca.sqlcode != SQL_RC_OK)
        {
        printf("ERROR : %ld\n", sqlca.sqlcode);
        rc = EXIT_FAILURE;
        }

    /* Issue A Rollback To Free All Locks */
    EXEC SQL ROLLBACK;

    /* Turn Off The SQL Error Handler */
    EXEC SQL WHENEVER SQLERROR CONTINUE;

    /* Disconnect From The SAMPLE Database */
    EXEC SQL DISCONNECT CURRENT;

    /* Return To The Operating System */
    return(rc);
}
```

CHAPTER 19

DB2 DATABASE MANAGER CONTROL AND DATABASE CONTROL API'S

The DB2 database manager control and database control APIs are a group of DB2 API function calls that control the DB2 database manager server processes, along with connections to databases and DB2 database manager instances. This group includes:

- API functions that start and stop the DB2 database manager server processes.
- API functions that create, restart, and delete DB2 databases.
- API functions that attach to and detach from DB2 database manager instances.
- API functions that control connection account strings and setting values for an application.
- An API function that terminates all connections to a database.

Table 19.1 lists the DB2 database manager control and database control API functions available with DB2.

The DB2 Database Manager Server Processes

Before a database connection or DB2 database manager instance connection can be established by an embedded SQL or DB2 API application, the DB2 database manager server processes must first be started. DB2 database manager server processes are usually started when you execute the program **startdbm** from an OS/2 window or issue the START DATABASE MANAGER command from the DB2 command-line processor (OS/2 or AIX). On DB2 server workstations, the DB2 database manager server processes are often started as part of the workstation boot-up sequence. You can also start the DB2 database manager server processes from within an application program by calling the START DATABASE MANAGER function.

Once started, these processes run in the background until they are explicitly stopped (when an application terminates, the DB2 database manager server processes continue running in the background). You can stop the DB2 database manager server processes by executing the program **stopbm** from an OS/2 window or by issuing the STOP DATABASE MANAGER command from the DB2 command-line processor (OS/2 or AIX). You can also stop the DB2 database manager server processes from within an application program by calling the STOP DATABASE MANAGER function.

TABLE 19.1 DB2 Database Manager Control and Database Control APIs

Function name	Description
START DATABASE MANAGER	Starts the DB2 database manager server processes.
STOP DATABASE MANAGER	Stops the DB2 database manager server processes.
CREATE DATABASE	Creates a new database and its associated support files.
RESTART DATABASE	Restarts a database that was abnormally terminated and left in an inconsistent state.
DROP DATABASE	Deletes an existing database and all its associated support files.
ATTACH	Specifies the node at which DB2 database manager instance-level functions are to be executed.
DETACH	Removes a logical DB2 database manager instance attachment.
SET ACCOUNTING STRING	Specifies accounting information that is to be sent to Distributed Relational Database Architecture (DRDA) servers along with connect requests.
QUERY CLIENT	Retrieves the current connection setting values for an application.
SET CLIENT	Specifies connection setting values for a DB2 application.
FORCE APPLICATION	Forces all local and remote users and applications off a database connection instance.

Creating, Deleting, and Restarting DB2 Databases

A database is simply a set of all DB2-related objects. When you create a DB2 database, you are establishing an administrative entity that provides an underlying structure for an eventual collection of tables, views, associated indexes, etc., as well as the table spaces in which they reside.

You can create all the objects in a database through various embedded SQL statements. You must create the database itself, however, by some other means, and it must exist before any of its objects can be created. You can create DB2 databases by issuing the CREATE DATABASE command from the DB2 command-line processor (OS/2 or AIX). In many cases, however, it is desirable to create one or more databases from an application program. This is especially true in applications designed for installing database applications on new workstations and ensuring that the necessary databases exist. Fortunately, you can create databases from an application program by calling the CREATE DATABASE function.

When a database is no longer needed, you can delete it by issuing the DROP DATABASE command from the DB2 command-line processor (OS/2 or AIX). You can also delete databases from within an application program by calling the DROP DATABASE function. If, for some reason, an application needs to use a temporary database, it can create a database when it starts execution and drop it when it is no longer needed.

Whenever a transaction using a database is terminated abnormally (for example, due to power failure), the database is left in an inconsistent state. As long as a database is in an inconsistent state, applications and users are unable to connect to it. This condition is normally discovered when an application attempts to execute a CONNECT SQL statement and the appropriate return code value is generated. When a database has been left in an inconsistent state, it must be restarted before a user or an application can connect to it again. An application can restart a database by calling the RESTART DATABASE function. Although it is good programming practice to conditionally call this function in a CONNECT error-handling routine, keep in mind that the routine can cause a substantial delay in application processing. For this reason, always provide proper user feedback when invoking this function.

Specifying Connection Accounting Strings

DB2 database applications designed to run in a distributed environment might need to connect to and retrieve data from a distributed relational database architecture (DRDA) application server (such as

DB2 for MVS). DRDA servers often use a process known as chargeback accounting to charge customers for their use of system resources. By calling the SET ACCOUNTING STRING function, applications running on a common server workstation can pass chargeback accounting information directly to a DRDA server when a connection is established. Accounting strings typically contain 56 bytes of system-generated data and up to 199 bytes of user-supplied data (suffix). Table 19.2 shows the fields and format of a typical accounting string. The following is an example of an accounting string:

```
X'3C'SQL02010OS/2    CH19EX6A    ETPDD6Z x'05'DEPT1
```

TABLE 19.2 DB2 Database Manager Control and Database Control APIs

Field name	Size (in bytes)	Description
acct_str_len	1	A hexadecimal value representing the overall length of the accounting string minus 1. For example, this value would be 0x3C for a string containing 61 characters.
client_prdid	8	The product ID of the client's DB2 Client Application Enabler software. For example, the product ID for the DB2 Client Application Enabler, Version 2.1 is SQL02010.
client_platform	18	The platform (or operating system) on which the client application runs, for example OS/2, AIX, DOS, or Windows.
client_appl_name	20	The first 20 characters of the application name, for example CH19EX6A.
client_authid	8	The authorization ID used to precompile and bind the application, for example ETPDD6Z.
suffix_len	1	A hexadecimal value representing the overall length of the user-supplied suffix string. This field should be set to 0x00 if no user-supplied suffix string is provided.
suffix	<= 199	The user-supplied suffix string. This string can be a value specified by an application, the value of the DB2ACCOUNT environment variable, the value of the DFT_ACCOUNT_STR DB2 database manager configuration parameter, or a null string.

Adapted from IBM's *Distributed Database Connection Services Users Guide*, Figure 10, page 52.

The SET ACCOUNTING STRING function combines system-generated data with a suffix, which is provided as one of its input parameters, to produce the accounting string sent to the specified server at the next connect request. Therefore, an application should call this function before attempting to connect to a DRDA application server. An application can also call this function any time it needs to change the accounting string (for example, to send a different string when a connection is made to a different database). If the SET ACCOUNTING STRING function is not called before a connection to a DRDA application server is made, the value stored in the DB2ACCOUNT environment variable will be used as the default. If no value exists for the DB2ACCOUNT environment variable, the value of the DFT_ACCOUNT_STR DB2 database manager configuration parameter will be used.

Retrieving and Setting Other Connection Setting Values

The type of connection an application makes to one or more databases is often determined by the precompiler options that were specified when the application was precompiled. An application can retrieve these values by calling the QUERY CLIENT function any time during its processing. You can leave these settings as they are or modify them by calling the SET CLIENT function before a connection to a database is established. This method of specifying connection options is particularly helpful when used by applications that contain no static embedded SQL statements and therefore do not need to be precompiled.

Controlling DB2 Database Manager Connection Instances

As long as an application executes against a local database, one or more connections to the background DB2 database manager server processes is sufficient for most processing needs. When an application is designed to execute against one or more remote databases, you must first establish a connection to the DB2 database manager server process instance that is controlling the remote database. The ATTACH function establishes a logical instance attachment to the DB2 database manager server processes running at a remote workstation. When an application attaches to the remote DB2 database manager server processes, it starts a physical communications connection to the workstation if one does not already exist. When all remote processing is complete, you can call the DETACH function to close the physical communications connection to the workstation and detach from the remote DB2 database manager server processes.

START DATABASE MANAGER

Purpose

The START DATABASE MANAGER function starts the DB2 database manager server processes.

Syntax

```
SQL_API_RC SQL_API_FN sqlestar ( );
```

Includes

```
#include <sqlenv.h>
```

Description

The START DATABASE MANAGER function starts the DB2 database manager server processes. These processes must be started before any database connections or instance attachments to the DB2 database manager can be made. Once started, the DB2 database manager server processes run in the background until the STOP DATABASE MANAGER function or command is executed.

Comments

- You do not need to call this function on a client workstation if the applications running on that workstation will access only databases on a server workstation (i.e., if no local databases stored on the client workstation are to be accessed).
- The DB2 database manager instance to be started is determined by the value in the DB2INSTANCE environment variable. You can determine the current value of this environment variable by calling the GET INSTANCE function.
- If the DB2 database manager server processes are successfully started, a successful completion message will be sent to the standard output device. If the DB2 database manager server processes are not successfully started, processing will stop and an error message will be sent to the standard output device. The standard output device is normally the display monitor, unless it has otherwise been redirected.
- If this function is called while the DB2 database manager server processes are already running, an error will be generated. If this occurs, the application can ignore the error and continue execution (because the server processes are already running).
- This function cannot be used in applications that run on Windows or Windows NT.

Required Connection

This function can be called at any time; a connection to a DB2 database manager instance or to a DB2 database does not have to be established first.

Authorization

Only users with either system control (SYSCTRL) authority, system administrator (SYSADM) authority, or system maintenance (SYSMAINT) authority can execute this function call.

See Also

STOP DATABASE MANAGER

Example

The following C program illustrates how to use the START DATABASE MANAGER function to start the DB2 database manager server processes:

```
#include <stdio.h>
#include <stdlib.h>
#include <sqlenv.h>
#include <sqlca.h>

int main()
{
    /* Declare The Local Memory Variables */
    int           rc = EXIT_SUCCESS;
    struct sqlca  sqlca;

    /* Start The DB2 Database Manager Server Processes */
    rc = sqlestar();

    /* Display A Success Message */
    printf("The DB2 database manager has been started.\n");

    /* Return To The Operating System */
    return(rc);
}
```

STOP DATABASE MANAGER

Purpose

The STOP DATABASE MANAGER function stops all DB2 database manager server processes running in the background, and frees all system resources held by the DB2 database manager.

Syntax

```
SQL_API_RC SQL_API_FN sqlestop (struct sqlca *SQLCA);
```

Parameters

SQLCA A pointer to a location in memory where a SQL communication area (SQLCA) data structure variable is stored. This variable sends either status information (if the function executed successfully) or error information (if the function failed) back to the calling application.

Includes

```
#include <sqlenv.h>
```

Description

The STOP DATABASE MANAGER function stops all DB2 database manager server processes running in the background and frees all system resources held by the DB2 database manager. Unless explicitly stopped, the DB2 database manager server processes will continue running in the background, even after all application programs using the processes have ended.

Comments

- This function does not need to be called on a client workstation if the applications running on that workstation access only databases on a server workstation (if no local databases stored on the client workstation are to be accessed).
- The DB2 database manager instance to be stopped is determined by the value in the DB2INSTANCE environment variable. You can determine the current value of this environment variable by calling the GET INSTANCE function.
- If the DB2 database manager server processes are successfully stopped, a successful completion message will be sent to the standard output device. If the DB2 database manager server processes are not successfully stopped, processing will stop and an error message will be sent to the standard output device. The standard output device is normally the display monitor, unless it has otherwise been redirected.
- The database manager server processes cannot be stopped if any DB2 application programs are currently connected to the DB2 database manager instance. You can call the FORCE APPLICATION function to disconnect all applications connected to a DB2 database manager instance.
- If this function is called when the database manager server processes are not running, an error will be generated.
- This function cannot be used in applications run on the Windows or Windows NT operating systems.

Required Connection

This function can be called at any time; a connection to a DB2 database manager instance or to a DB2 database does not have to be established first.

Authorization

Only users with system control (SYSCTRL) authority, system administrator (SYSADM) authority, or system maintenance (SYSMAINT) authority can execute this function call.

See Also

START DATABASE MANAGER

Example

The following C program illustrates how to use the STOP DATABASE MANAGER function to stop the DB2 database manager server processes:

```
#include <stdio.h>
#include <stdlib.h>
#include <sqlenv.h>
#include <sqlca.h>

int main()
{
    /* Declare The Local Memory Variables */
    struct sqlca  sqlca;

    /* Stop The DB2 Database Manager Server Processes */
    sqlestop(&sqlca);

    /* Display A Success Message */
    printf("The DB2 database manager has been stopped.\n");
```

```
    /* Return To The Operating System */
    return(EXIT_SUCCESS);
}
```

CREATE DATABASE

Purpose

The CREATE DATABASE function creates a new database (with an optional user-defined collating sequence), its three initial table spaces, its system tables, and its recovery log file.

Syntax

```
SQL_API_RC SQL_API_FN sqlecrea (char                       *DBName,
                                char                       *LocalDBAlias,
                                char                       *Path,
                                struct sqledbdesc          *DBDescriptor,
                                struct sqledbcountryinfo   *CountryInfo,
                                char                       Reserved1,
                                void                       *Reserved2,
                                struct sqlca               *SQLCA);
```

Parameters

DBName A pointer to a location in memory where the name of the database to be created is stored.

LocalDBAlias A pointer to a location in memory where the local alias of the database to be created is stored. This parameter can contain a NULL value.

Path A pointer to a location in memory where the path name (AIX) or the disk drive ID (OS/2) that specifies where the database to be created is stored. This parameter can contain a NULL value.

DBDescriptor A pointer to a *sqledbdesc* structure that contains database description information to be used when the database is created.

CountryInfo A pointer to a *sqledbcountryinfo* structure that contains the locale and code set to be used when the database is created.

Reserved1 A character value that, at this time, is reserved for later use. For now, this parameter must always be set to '\0'.

Reserved2 A pointer that, at this time, is reserved for later use. For now, this parameter must always be set to NULL.

SQLCA A pointer to a location in memory where a SQLCA data structure variable is stored. This variable will send either status information (if the function executed successfully) or error information (if the function failed) back to the calling application.

Includes

```
#include <sqlenv.h>
```

Description

The CREATE DATABASE function creates a new database (with an optional user-defined collating sequence), its three initial table spaces, its system tables, and its recovery log file. When this function is executed, it performs the following actions:

1. Creates a database on a specified path (AIX) or drive (OS/2).
2. Creates the system catalog tables and recovery log for the new database.
3. Creates an entry in the server's local database directory on the path indicated by the value specified in the *Path* parameter (or on the default path if no path is specified).

4. Creates an entry in the server's system database directory and sets the database alias equal to the database name if no other alias was specified (*LocalDBAlias* parameter).
5. Creates a second entry in the server's system database directory if a local alias was specified and if the function was issued locally; otherwise, creates an entry in the client's system database directory (if the API was called from a remote client).
6. Creates a system or local database directory if neither exists. If a description is specified in the *DBDescriptor* parameter, the description (comment) will be placed in both directories.
7. Assigns the code set and territory specified in the *CountryInfo* parameter to the database.
8. Assigns the collating sequence specified in the *DBDescriptor* parameter to the database. A flag is set in the database configuration file if the collating sequence consists of unique weights or an identity sequence.
9. Binds the previously defined database manager bind files to the database.
10. Performs a special system catalog step that creates extra views.
11. Grants the following database authorizations:
    –Database administrator (DBADM) authority with CONNECT, CREATETAB, and BINDADD privileges to the database creator.
    –SELECT privilege on each system catalog to PUBLIC.
    –BIND privilege to PUBLIC for each successfully bound utility.

Once the database is successfully created in the database server's system database directory, it is automatically cataloged in the system database directory with a database alias set to the database name. Two special structures (*sqledbdesc* and *sqledbcountryinfo*) pass characteristics about a database to the DB2 database manager when this function is called. The first structure, *sqledbdesc*, is defined in *sqlenv.h*, as follows:

```
struct sqledbdesc
{
char             sqldbdid[8];     /* A structure identifier and          */
                                  /* eye-catcher for storage dumps. It   */
                                  /* is a string of eight bytes that must */
                                  /* be initialized with the value       */
                                  /* "SQLDBD02". The contents of         */
                                  /* this field are validated for version */
                                  /* control.                            */
long             sqldbccp;        /* Code page value used for the        */
                                  /* database comment                    */
long             sqldbcss;        /* Source of database collating        */
                                  /* sequence                            */
unsigned char    sqldbudc[256];   /* User-defined collating sequence     */
                                  /* The nth byte of this field contains */
                                  /* the sort weight of the code point   */
                                  /* whose underlying decimal            */
                                  /* representation is n in the code     */
                                  /* page of the database. If this field */
                                  /* is not set to SQL_CS_USER, it is    */
                                  /* ignored.                            */
char             sqldbcmt[31];    /* Optional database comment           */
char             pad[1];          /* Reserved                            */
unsigned long    sqldbsgp;        /* Reserved; no longer used            */
short            sqldbnsg;        /* The number of file segments to be   */
```

```
                                  /* created in the database. The          */
                                  /* minimum value for this field is 1     */
                                  /* and the maximum value is 256. If      */
                                  /* the value -1 is specified, this field */
                                  /* will default to 1. If the value 0 is  */
                                  /* specified, a value for version 1      */
                                  /* compatibility is provided.            */
 char           pad2[2];          /* Reserved                              */
 long           sqltsext;         /* The default extent size, in 4KB       */
                                  /* pages, for each table space in the    */
                                  /* database. The minimum value for       */
                                  /* this field is 2 and the maximum       */
                                  /* value is 256. If the value -1 is      */
                                  /* specified, this field will be set     */
                                  /* to 32 by default.                     */
 struct SQLETSDESC *sqlcatts;     /* A pointer to a table space            */
                                  /* description control block that        */
                                  /* defines the catalog table space.      */
                                  /* If NULL is specified, a catalog       */
                                  /* table space based on the values       */
                                  /* in sqltstext and sqldbnsg will be     */
                                  /* created.                              */
 struct SQLETSDESC *sqlusrts;     /* A pointer to a table space            */
                                  /* description control block that        */
                                  /* defines a user table space. If        */
                                  /* NULL is specified, a user table       */
                                  /* space based on the values in          */
                                  /* sqltstext and sqldbnsg will be        */
                                  /* created.                              */
 struct SQLETSDESC *sqltmpts;     /* A pointer to a table space            */
                                  /* description control block that        */
                                  /* defines a temporary table space.      */
                                  /* If NULL is specified, a temporary     */
                                  /* table space based on the values       */
                                  /* in sqltstext and sqldbnsg will be     */
                                  /* created.                              */
 };
```

This structure contains three pointers to an additional structure, SQLETS-DESC, which holds various table space description information. The SQLETSDESC structure is defined in *sqlenv.h* as follows:

```
struct SQLETSDESC
{
char            sqltsdid[8]; /* A structure identifier and          */
                             /* eye-catcher for storage dumps. It   */
                             /* is a string of eight bytes that must */
                             /* be initialized with the value       */
                             /* "SQLTS001". The contents of         */
                             /* this field are validated for version */
                             /* control.                            */
long            sqlextnt;    /* The table space extent size, in     */
                             /* 4KB pages. If the value -1 is       */
                             /* specified, this field will be set   */
                             /* to the current value of the         */
                             /* dft_extent_sz database              */
                             /* configuration parameter by default. */
long            sqlprftc;    /* The table space prefetch size, in   */
                             /* 4KB pages. If the value -1 is       */
                             /* specified, this field will be set   */
```

```
                                       /* be set to the current value of the     */
                                       /* dft_prefetch_sz database               */
                                       /* configuration parameter by default.    */
double              sqlpovhd;          /* The table space I/O overhead, in       */
                                       /* milliseconds. If the value -1 is       */
                                       /* specified, this field will default to */
                                       /* 24.1 ms (this value could change       */
                                       /* in future releases of DB2).            */
double              sqltrfrt;          /* The table space I/O transfer rate,     */
                                       /* in milliseconds. If the value -1 is   */
                                       /* specified, this field will default to */
                                       /* 0.9 ms (this value could change in    */
                                       /* future releases of DB2.                */
char                sqltstyp;          /* Indicates whether the table space      */
                                       /* is system-managed (SQL_TBS_TYP_SMS)    */
                                       /* or database-managed (SQL_TBS_TYP_DMS).*/
char                pad1;              /* Reserved                               */
short               sqlccnt;           /* The number of containers assigned      */
                                       /* to the table space (the number of      */
                                       /* elements in the containr array).       */
struct SQLETSCDESC containr[1];        /* An array of SQLETSCDESC                */
                                       /* structures that define table space     */
                                       /* containers to be assigned to the       */
                                       /* tablespace.                            */
};
```

This structure contains an array of SQLETSCDESC structures that store table space container information. The SQLETSCDESC structure is defined in *sqlenv.h* as follows:

```
struct SQLETSCDESC
{
char    sqlctype;                      /* Indicates whether the table space      */
                                       /* container is a device                  */
                                       /* (SQL_TBSC_TYP_DEV), a file             */
                                       /* (SQL_TBSC_TYP_FILE), or a              */
                                       /* directory path                         */
                                       /* (SQL_TBSC_TYP_PATH). Note: The value   */
                                       /* specified in this field cannot be      */
                                       /* SQL_TBSC_TYP_PATH if the               */
                                       /* sqltstyp field of the                  */
                                       /* SQLETSDESC structure is set to         */
                                       /* SQL_TBS_TYP_DMS.                       */
char    pad1[3];                       /* Reserved                               */
long    sqlcsize;                      /* The size of the container, specified   */
                                       /* in 4KB pages. The value in this        */
                                       /* field is valid only when the sqltstyp */
                                       /* field of the SQLETSDESC structure      */
                                       /* is set to  SQL_TBS_TYP_DMS.            */
short   sqlclen;                       /* The length of the container name       */
char    sqlcontr[256];                 /* The container name                     */
char    pad2[2];                       /* Reserved; 2 bytes of padding           */
                                       /* between container descriptions.        */
};
```

If the database description block structure (*sqledbdesc*) is not set correctly when this function is called, an error message will be returned and the database will not be created. The second special structure used by this function, *sqledbcountryinfo*, is defined in *sqlenv.h* as follows:

```
struct sqledbcountryinfo
{
char  sqldbcodeset[10];          /* The code set that will be used by */
                                 /* the database                      */
char  sqldblocale[6];            /* The database territory            */
};
```

If this structure is not set correctly or, if no code set or territory values are specified, the locale of the application making the CREATE DATABASE function call will determine the default code set and territory values to use. For a list of valid locale and code set values, refer to either the *Database 2 for AIX Installation and Operation Guide* or the *Database 2 for OS/2 Installation and Operation Guide*.

Comments

- The directory that contains the database is always placed in the root directory of the specified drive on OS/2.
- If one or more of the previously defined database manager bind files are not successfully bound to the new database, this function will return a warning in the *sqlca* data structure variable along with information about the binds that failed. If a bind fails, you can take corrective action by manually binding the bind file that failed to the new database when it is created. The failure of one or more predefined bind files does not prevent the database from being created.
- When users have database administrator (DBADM) authority for a database, they can grant authorizations to (and revoke authorizations from) other users or the PUBLIC group. Another user with either system administrator (SYSADM) authority or database administrator (DBADM) authority cannot revoke DBADM authority from the database creator.
- This function will fail if the application calling the CREATE DATABASE function is connected to a database.
- After a database is created, all character comparisons performed in that database use the specified collating sequence. This sequence affects the structure of indexes as well as the results of queries. The following sample of user-defined collating sequences are available in the C and C++ language include files:

sqle819a If the code page of the database is 819 (ISO Latin/1), this sequence will perform sorting according to the host CCSID 500 (EBCDIC International).

sqle819b If the code page of the database is 819 (ISO Latin/1), this sequence will perform sorting according to the host CCSID 037 (EBCDIC U.S. English).

sqle850a If the code page of the database is 850 (ASCII Latin/1), this sequence will sort according to the host CCSID 500 (EBCDIC International).

sqle850b If the code page of the database is 850 (ASCII Latin/1), this sequence will sort according to the host CCSID 037 (EBCDIC U.S. English).

sqle932a If the code page of the database is 932 (ASCII Japanese), this sequence will sort according to the host CCSID 5035 (EBCDIC Japanese).

sqle932b If the code page of the database is 932 (ASCII Japanese), this sequence will sort according to the host CCSID 5026 (EBCDIC Japanese).

- You must specify the collating sequence when calling the CREATE DATABASE function; it cannot be changed once the database is created.

Required Connection This function can be called only if no connection to a database exists. In order to create a database at another node, you must first attach to that node; if necessary, a temporary database connection is established by this function while it executes.

Authorization Only users with either system control (SYSCTRL) authority or system administrator (SYSADM) authority can execute this function call.

See Also BIND, CATALOG DATABASE, DROP DATABASE

Example The following C program illustrates how the CREATE DATABASE function creates a new database:

```
#include <stdio.h>
#include <stdlib.h>
#include <string.h>
#include <sqlenv.h>
#include <sqlca.h>

int main()
{
    /* Declare The Local Memory Variables */
    int                 rc = EXIT_SUCCESS;
    char                szDBName[40];
    char                szDBAlias[40];
    struct sqledbdesc   DBDescriptor;
    struct sqlca        sqlca;

    /* Initialize The Local Memory Variables */
    strcpy(szDBName, "TEST_DB");
    strcpy(szDBAlias, "TEST_DB");

    /* Initialize The Database Descriptor Variable */
    strcpy(DBDescriptor.sqldbdid, "SQLDBD02");
    strcpy(DBDescriptor.sqldbcmt, "Test Database");
    DBDescriptor.sqldbnsg = -1;
    DBDescriptor.sqltsext = -1;
    DBDescriptor.sqlcatts = NULL;
    DBDescriptor.sqlusrts = NULL;
    DBDescriptor.sqltmpts = NULL;

    /* Create A New Database */
    sqlecrea(szDBName, szDBAlias, NULL, &DBDescriptor, NULL, '\0',
             NULL, &sqlca);

    /* Display A Success Message */
    printf("The database %s has been created.\n", szDBName);

    /* Drop The Specified Database */
    sqledrpd(szDBAlias, &sqlca);

    /* Display A Success Message */
    printf("The database %s has been deleted.\n", szDBAlias);

    /* Return To The Operating System */
    return(rc);
}
```

RESTART DATABASE

Purpose

The RESTART DATABASE function restarts a database that has been abnormally terminated and left in an inconsistent state.

Syntax

```
SQL_API_RC SQL_API_FN sqlerstd (char          *DBAlias,
                                char          *UserID,
                                char          *Password,
                                struct sqlca  *SQLCA);
```

Parameters

DBAlias A pointer to a location in memory where the alias of the database to be restarted is stored.

UserID A pointer to a location in memory where the authorization name (user identifier) of the user is stored. This is the name under which the attachment is authenticated. This parameter can contain a NULL value.

Password A pointer to a location in memory where the password for the specified authorization name is stored. This parameter can contain a NULL value.

SQLCA A pointer to a location in memory where a SQLCA data structure variable is stored. This variable sends either status information (if the function executed successfully) or error information (if the function failed) back to the calling application.

Includes

```
#include <sqlenv.h>
```

Description

The RESTART DATABASE function restarts a database that was abnormally terminated and left in an inconsistent state. Execute this function whenever an attempt to connect to a database produces an error message indicating that the database must be restarted. This error message is generated only if the previous session with the specified database was terminated abnormally, for example, because of a power failure.

Comments

- Upon the successful completion of this function, a shared connection to the specified database is maintained if the user who called the function has CONNECT authorization.
- Whenever a database is restarted, a SQL warning is generated if one or more indoubt transactions exist. In this case, the database is usable; if the indoubt transactions are not resolved before the last connection to the database is terminated, however, another RESTART DATABASE function call must be issued before the database can be used again. The transaction APIs discussed in Chapter 25 can be used to generate a list of and correctly process indoubt transactions.

Required Connection

When this function is called, it establishes a connection to the specified database.

Authorization

No authorization is required to execute this function call.

See Also

CONNECT (SQL statement)

Example

The following C program illustrates how the RESTART DATABASE function restarts a database left in an inconsistent state:

```
#include <stdio.h>
#include <stdlib.h>
```

```
#include <string.h>
#include <sqlenv.h>
#include <sql.h>

int main()
{
    /* Include The SQLCA Data Structure Variable */
    EXEC SQL INCLUDE SQLCA;

    /* Declare The Local Memory Variables */
    int  rc = EXIT_SUCCESS;

    /* Declare The SQL Host Memory Variables */
    EXEC SQL BEGIN DECLARE SECTION;
        long   lAvgSalary;
        char   szDBAlias[40];
        char   szUserID[40];
        char   szPassword[40];
    EXEC SQL END DECLARE SECTION;

    /* Initialize The Local Memory Variables */
    strcpy(szDBAlias, "SAMPLE");
    strcpy(szUserID, "etpdd6z");
    strcpy(szPassword, "sanders");

    /* Connect To The SAMPLE Database */
    EXEC SQL CONNECT TO :szDBAlias USER :szUserID USING :szPassword;

    /* If Necessary, Restart The Specified Database */
    if (sqlca.sqlcode == -1015)
        {
        printf("Restarting the database. Please wait.\n");
        sqlerstd(szDBAlias, szUserID, szPassword, &sqlca);
        }

    /* Set Up A Simple SQL Error Handler */
    EXEC SQL WHENEVER SQLERROR GOTO EXIT;

    /* Retrieve The Average Salary From The EMPLOYEE Table */
    EXEC SQL SELECT AVG(SALARY)
        INTO :lAvgSalary
        FROM USERID.EMPLOYEE;

    /* Print The Information Retrieved */
    printf("The average salary is $ %.2ld.00.\n",
           lAvgSalary);

EXIT:
    /* If An Error Has Occurred, Display The SQL Return Code */
    if (sqlca.sqlcode != SQL_RC_OK)
        {
        printf("ERROR : %ld\n", sqlca.sqlcode);
        rc = EXIT_FAILURE;
        }

    /* Issue A Rollback To Free All Locks */
    EXEC SQL ROLLBACK;

    /* Turn Off The SQL Error Handler */
    EXEC SQL WHENEVER SQLERROR CONTINUE;
```

```
    /* Disconnect From The SAMPLE Database */
    EXEC SQL DISCONNECT CURRENT;

    /* Return To The Operating System */
    return(rc);
}
```

DROP DATABASE

Purpose

The DROP DATABASE function uncatalogs and delete the contents of a database, along with all log files associated with the database and the database subdirectory.

Syntax

```
SQL_API_RC SQL_API_FN sqledrpd (char         *DBAlias,
                                struct sqlca *SQLCA);
```

Parameters

DBAlias A pointer to a location in memory where the alias of the database to be dropped is stored.

SQLCA A pointer to a location in memory where a SQLCA data structure variable is stored. This variable sends either status information (if the function executed successfully) or error information (if the function failed) back to the calling application.

Includes

```
#include <sqlenv.h>
```

Description

The DROP DATABASE function uncatalogs and deletes the contents of a database, along with all log files associated with the database and the database subdirectory. A database must be cataloged in the system database directory before it can be dropped. When the database is dropped, only the specified database alias is removed from the system database directory. If other aliases with the same database name exist, their entries are not affected. If the database being dropped is the last entry in the local database directory, the local database directory is automatically deleted.

Comments

- Since this function deletes all user data and database log files, if you need the log files for a roll-forward recovery (after a database restore operation), save them before calling this function.
- The specified database must not be in use (i.e., no application can be connected to the database) if it is to be dropped. You can call the FORCE APPLICATION function to disconnect all applications connected to the DB2 database manager instance that is controlling access to the specified database.
- If the DROP DATABASE function call is issued from a remote client (or from a different instance on the same workstation), the specified alias will be removed from the client's system database directory, and the corresponding database name will be removed from the server's system database directory.

Required Connection

This function cannot be called unless a connection to a DB2 database manager instance exists. It is not necessary to call the ATTACH function before dropping a remote database, however; if the database is cataloged as remote, an instance attachment to the DB2 database manager instance at the remote node will automatically be established for the duration of the function call.

Authorization Only users with either system control (SYSCTRL) authority or system administrator (SYSADM) authority are allowed to execute this function call.

See Also CREATE DATABASE, CATALOG DATABASE, UNCATALOG DATABASE

Example See the example provided for the CREATE DATABASE function in this chapter.

ATTACH

Purpose The ATTACH function specifies the node at which instance-level functions (for example, CREATE DATABASE and FORCE APPLICATION) are to be executed.

Syntax

```
SQL_API_RC SQL_API_FN sqleatin (char          *NodeName,
                                char          *UserID,
                                char          *Password,
                                struct sqlca *SQLCA);
```

Parameters

NodeName A pointer to a location in memory where the name or alias name of the DB2 database manager instance to which the application is to attach is stored. This parameter can contain a NULL value.

UserID A pointer to a location in memory where the authorization name (user identifier) of the user is stored. This is the name under which the attachment is to be authenticated. This parameter can contain a NULL value.

Password A pointer to a location in memory where the password for the specified authorization name is stored. This parameter can contain a NULL value.

SQLCA A pointer to a location in memory where a SQLCA data structure variable is stored. This variable sends either status information (if the function executed successfully) or error information (if the function failed) back to the calling application.

Includes

```
#include <sqlenv.h>
```

Description The ATTACH function specifies the node at which instance-level API functions (for example, CREATE DATABASE and FORCE APPLICATION) are to be executed. This node might be the current DB2 database manager instance (as defined by the value of the DB2INSTANCE environment variable), another DB2 database manager instance on the same workstation, or a DB2 database manager instance on a remote workstation. This function establishes a logical instance attachment to the specified node, and starts a physical communications connection to the node if one does not already exist.

Comments

- If an attach request succeeds, the *sqlerrmc* field of the *SQLCA* data structure variable will contain eight tokens separated by the hexadecimal value 0xFF (similar to the tokens returned when a CONNECT SQL statement is successful). These tokens will contain the following information:

Token 1 The country code of the application server.
Token 2 The code page of the application server.
Token 3 The authorization ID.
Token 4 The node name, as specified with the ATTACH function.
Token 5 The identity and the platform type of the database server.
Token 6 The agent ID of the agent started at the database server.
Token 7 The agent index.
Token 8 The node number of the server (always zero).

- If the node name specified in the *NodeName* parameter is a zero-length string or the NULL value, information about the current state of attachment will be returned in the *sqlerrmc* field of the *SQLCA* data structure variable (as previously outlined). If no attachment exists, an error will be returned.
- The alias name specified in the *NodeName* parameter must have a matching entry in the local node directory. The only exception to this is the local DB2 database manager instance (as specified by the DB2INSTANCE environment variable), which can be specified as the object of an ATTACH function call, but cannot be used as a node name in the node directory. A node name in the node directory can be regarded as an alias for a DB2 database manager instance.
- If this function is never executed, all instance-level API functions are executed against the current DB2 database manager instance, which is specified by the DB2INSTANCE environment variable.
- Certain functions (for example, START DATABASE MANAGER, STOP DATABASE MANAGER, and all directory services functions) are never executed remotely.
- If an attachment already exists when this function is issued with a node name, the current attachment will be dropped and an attempt to attach to the new node will be made. If the attempt to attach to a new node fails, the application will be left in an unattached state.
- Where the *User ID/Password* pair is authenticated depends on the value of the authentication parameter in the database manager configuration file, which is located on the node to which the application attempts to attach. If this configuration parameter contains the value CLIENT, the *User ID/Password* pair will be authenticated at the client machine from which the ATTACH function call is issued. If this configuration parameter contains the value SERVER, the *User ID/Password* pair will be authenticated at the node to which the application attempts to attach. If a *User ID/Password* pair is not provided, the user ID associated with the current application process will be used for authentication.

Required Connection This function establishes a DB2 database manager instance attachment (and possibly a physical database connection) when it is executed.

Authorization No authorization is required to execute this function call.

See Also DETACH

Example The following C program illustrates how to use the ATTACH function to obtain information about the current DB2 database manager instance attachment:

```
#include <stdio.h>
#include <stdlib.h>
#include <string.h>
#include <sqlenv.h>
#include <sqlca.h>

int main()
{
   /* Declare The Local Memory Variables */
   int            chSeparator = 0xFF;
   int            iCounter;
   int            iLength;
   char           szInfoString[71];
   char           *pszBuffer;
   char           szResults[9][71];
   struct sqlca   sqlca;

   /* Attach To The Default DB2 Database Manager Instance */
   sqleatin("DB2", "etpdd6z", "sanders", &sqlca);

   /* Obtain Information About The Current State Of Attachment */
   sqleatin(NULL, "etpdd6z", "sanders", &sqlca);

   /* If Information About The Current Attachment Was */
   /* Obtained, Parse It                               */
   strncpy(szInfoString, sqlca.sqlerrmc, 70);
   iLength = strlen(szInfoString);
   for (iCounter = 8; iCounter >= 0; iCounter—)
      {
      pszBuffer = strrchr(szInfoString, chSeparator);
      if (pszBuffer != NULL)
         {
         strcpy(szResults[iCounter], pszBuffer + 1);
         szInfoString[iLength - strlen(pszBuffer)] = '\O';
         }
      else
         strcpy(szResults[iCounter], szInfoString);
      iLength = strlen(szInfoString);
      }

   /* Display The Parsed Information */
   printf("Current Attachment Settings :\n\n ");
   printf("Country Code       : %s\n", szResults[0]);
   printf("Server Code Page : %s\n", szResults[1]);
   printf("Authorization ID : %s\n", szResults[2]);
   printf("Node Name          : %s\n", szResults[3]);
   printf("Server Platform   : %s\n", szResults[4]);
   printf("Agent ID            : %s\n", szResults[5]);
   printf("Agent Index        : %s\n", szResults[6]);
   printf("Node Number       : %s\n", szResults[7]);

   /* Detach From The Default DB2 Database Manager Instance */
   sqledtin(&sqlca);

   /* Return To The Operating System */
   return(EXIT_SUCCESS);
}
```

DETACH

Purpose

The DETACH function removes a logical DB2 database manager instance attachment, and terminates the physical communication connection if there are no other logical connections using the instance attachment being removed.

Syntax

```
SQL_API_RC SQL_API_FN sqledtin (struct sqlca *SQLCA);
```

Parameters

SQLCA A pointer to a location in memory where a SQLCA data structure variable is stored. This variable sends either status information (if the function executed successfully) or error information (if the function failed) back to the calling application.

Includes

```
#include <sqlenv.h>
```

Description

The DETACH function removes a logical DB2 database manager instance attachment. If there are no other logical connections using the DB2 database manager instance attachment when the logical instance is removed, the physical communication connection will be terminated.

Required Connection

This function can be called at any time; a connection to a DB2 database manager instance or to a DB2 database does not have to be established first. When this function executes, an existing DB2 database manager instance attachment (and possibly a physical communications connection) will be removed.

Authorization

No authorization is required to execute this function call.

See Also

ATTACH

Example

See the example provided for the ATTACH function in this chapter.

SET ACCOUNTING STRING

Purpose

The SET ACCOUNTING STRING function specifies accounting information to be sent to a distributed relational database architecture (DRDA) server with the application's next connect request.

Syntax

```
SQL_API_RC SQL_API_FN sqlesact (char          *AccountingString,
                                struct sqlca *SQLCA);
```

Parameters

AccountingString A pointer to a location in memory where the accounting information string is stored.

SQLCA A pointer to a location in memory where a SQLCA data structure variable is stored. This variable sends either status information (if the function executed successfully) or error information (if the function failed) back to the calling application.

Includes

```
#include <sqlenv.h>
```

Description

The SET ACCOUNTING STRING function specifies accounting information to be sent to a DRDA server with the application's next connect request. An application should call this API function before attempting to connect to a DRDA database (DB2 for MVS, DB2 for OS/400, or SQL/DS). If an application contains multiple CONNECT SQL statements, you can use this function to change the accounting string before attempting to connect to each database. Refer to the beginning of the chapter for more information about the format and usage of accounting string information.

Comments

- Once accounting string information has been set, it remains in effect until the application terminates.
- The specified accounting string cannot exceed 199 bytes in length (this value is defined as SQL_ACCOUNT_STR_SZ in the file *sqlenv.h*); longer accounting strings will automatically be truncated.
- To ensure that the accounting string is converted correctly when being transmitted to the DRDA server, use only the characters A to Z, 0 to 9, and the underscore (_).

Required Connection

This function can be called at any time; a connection to a DB2 database manager instance or to a DB2 database does not have to be established first.

Authorization

No authorization is required to execute this function call.

See Also

Refer to the *IBM Distributed Database Connection Services User's Guide* for more information about accounting strings and the DRDA servers that support them.

Example

The following C program illustrates how to use the SET ACCOUNTING STRING function to set accounting string information before a connection to a database is established:

```
#include <stdio.h>
#include <stdlib.h>
#include <string.h>
#include <sqlenv.h>
#include <sql.h>

int main()
{
    /* Include The SQLCA Data Structure Variable */
    EXEC SQL INCLUDE SQLCA;

    /* Declare The Local Memory Variables */
    char  szAccountingString[199];

    /* Define The Accounting String */
    strcpy(szAccountingString, "DB2_EXAMPLES");

    /* Set The Accounting String */
    sqlesact(szAccountingString, &sqlca);

    /* Display A Success Message */
    printf("The specified accounting string has been set.\n");

    /* Connect To The SAMPLE Database Using The Specified     */
    /* Accounting String - In This Case The Accounting String */
```

```
    /* Will Be Ignored                                                    */
    EXEC SQL CONNECT TO SAMPLE USER etpdd6z USING sanders;

    /* Disconnect From The SAMPLE Database */
    EXEC SQL DISCONNECT CURRENT;

    /* Return To The Operating System */
    return(EXIT_SUCCESS);
}
```

QUERY CLIENT

Purpose

The QUERY CLIENT function retrieves the current connection setting values for an application process.

Syntax

```
SQL_API_RC SQL_API_FN sqleqryc (struct sqle_conn_setting *ConnectionSettings
                                unsigned short          NumSettings,
                                struct sqlca            *SQLCA);
```

Parameters

ConnectionSettings A pointer to a *sqle_conn_setting* structure or an array of *sqle_conn_setting* structures where this function is to store the retrieved connection setting information.

NumSettings An integer value that specifies the number of connection option values to retrieve. The value for this parameter can be any number between 0 and 5.

SQLCA A pointer to a location in memory where a SQLCA data structure variable is stored. This variable sends either status information (if the function executed successfully) or error information (if the function failed) back to the calling application.

Includes

```
#include <sqlenv.h>
```

Description

The QUERY CLIENT function retrieves the current connection setting values for an application process. This information is stored in a *sqle_conn_setting* structure or an array of *sqle_conn_setting* structures that contain one or more connection options and their corresponding values. The *sqle_conn_setting* structure is defined in *sqlenv.h* as follows:

```
struct sqle_conn_setting
{
unsigned short  type;             /* Connection setting type  */
unsigned short  value;            /* Connection setting value */
};
```

Table 19.3 lists each value that can be specified for the *type* field of the *sqle_conn_setting* structure, along with a description of each value that can be specified for the corresponding *value* field of this structure.

Before this function can be executed, an array of *sqle_conn_setting* connection setting structures must be allocated and the *type* field of each structure in this array must be set to one of the five possible connection setting options listed in Table 19.3. After this function has executed, the *value* field of each connection setting structure in the array will contain the current value (setting) of the option specified.

TABLE 19.3 Connection Settings

Connection setting type	Connection setting value	Description
SQL_CONNECT_TYPE	SQL_CONNECT_1	Type 1 CONNECTs are supported. This enforces the single database per transaction semantics of older releases. Type 1 CONNECTs are also known as rules for remote unit of work (RUOW) connects.
	SQL_CONNECT_2	Type-2 CONNECTs (multiple databases per transaction semantics of DUOW) are supported.
SQL_RULES	SQL_RULES_DB2	Allows the CONNECT SQL statement to switch from the current connection to an established (dormant) connection.
	SQL_RULES_STD	Allows the CONNECT SQL statement to only establish a new connection. The SET CONNECTION SQL statement must be used to switch from the current connection to an established (dormant) connection.
SQL_DISCONNECT	SQL_DISCONNECT_EXPL	Terminates all connections explicitly marked for release by the RELEASE SQL statement when the COMMIT SQL statement is executed.
	SQL_DISCONNECT_COND	Terminates all connections explicitly marked for release by the RELEASE SQL statement and all connections with no WITH HOLD cursors when the COMMIT SQL statement is executed.
	SQL_DISCONNECT_AUTO	Terminates all connections when the COMMIT SQL statement is executed.
SQL_SYNCPOINT	SQL_SYNC_TWOPHASE	Uses two-phase commits to commit the work done by each database in multiple-database transactions. This setting requires a transaction manager (TM) to coordinate two-phase commits among databases that support this protocol.
	SQL_SYNC_ONEPHASE	Uses one-phase commits to commit the work done by each database in multiple-database transactions. Enforces single-updater, multiple-read behavior.
	SQL_SYNC_NONE	Uses one-phase commits to commit the work done by each database in multiple-database transactions, but does not enforce single-updater, multiple-read behavior.
SQL_MAX_NETBIOS_CONNECTIONS	Any number between 1 and 254	Specifies the maximum number of concurrent connections that can be made in an application running on a workstation that is using the NETBIOS protocol.

Adapted from IBM's *Database 2 API Reference*, Table 22, page 446.

Comments

- The connection settings for an application can be queried at any time while the application is executing.
- If this function is executed before the SET CLIENT function is called, the *sqle_conn_setting* structure will contain the values of the precompile

options used if a SQL statement has already been processed; otherwise, it will contain the default values for the precompile options.

Required Connection This function can be called at any time; a connection to a DB2 database manager instance or to a DB2 database does not have to be established first.

Authorization No authorization is required to execute this function call.

See Also SET CLIENT

Example The following C program illustrates how to use the QUERY CLIENT function to obtain the current values of an application's connection settings:

```
#include <stdio.h>
#include <stdlib.h>
#include <sqlenv.h>
#include <sqlca.h>

int main()
{
    /* Declare The Local Memory Variables */
    struct sqle_conn_setting  ConnInfo[3];
    struct sqlca              sqlca;

    /* Initialize The Array Of Connection Information Structures */
    ConnInfo[0].type = SQL_CONNECT_TYPE;
    ConnInfo[1].type = SQL_RULES;
    ConnInfo[2].type = SQL_DISCONNECT;

    /* Obtain Information About The Current Connection */
    sqleqryc(&ConnInfo[0], 3, &sqlca);

    /* Display The Connection Information Retrieved */
    printf("Current Connection Settings:\n");

    printf("Connection Type  : ");
    if (ConnInfo[0].value == SQL_CONNECT_1)
        printf("Type 1\n");
    else
        printf("Type 2\n");

    printf("SQL Rules        : ");
    if (ConnInfo[1].value == SQL_RULES_DB2)
        printf("DB2 Rules\n");
    else
        printf("Standard Rules\n");

    printf("Disconnect Type  : ");
    if (ConnInfo[2].value == SQL_DISCONNECT_EXPL)
        printf("Explicit\n");
    else if (ConnInfo[2].value == SQL_DISCONNECT_COND)
        printf("Conditional\n");
    else
        printf("Automatic\n");

    /* Return To The Operating System */
    return(EXIT_SUCCESS);
}
```

SET CLIENT

Purpose

The SET CLIENT function specifies connection setting values for a DB2 application.

Syntax

```
SQL_API_RC SQL_API_FN sqlesetc (struct sqle_conn_setting *ConnectionSettings,
                                unsigned short       NumSettings,
                                struct sqlca         *SQLCA);
```

Parameters

ConnectionSettings A pointer to a *sqle_conn_setting* structure or an array of *sqle_conn_setting* structures that contain connection setting options and their corresponding values.

NumSettings An integer value that specifies the number of connection option values to set. The value for this parameter can be any number between 0 and 5.

SQLCA A pointer to a location in memory where a SQLCA data structure variable is stored. This variable sends either status information (if the function executed successfully) or error information (if the function failed) back to the calling application.

Includes

```
#include <sqlenv.h>
```

Description

The SET CLIENT function specifies connection setting values for a DB2 application. Before this function can be executed, an array of special structures (*sqle_conn_setting* structures) must first be allocated. Refer to the QUERY CLIENT function for a detailed description of this structure and for more information about the available connection options. Once this array of *sqle_conn_setting* structures is allocated, the *type* field of each structure in this array must be set to one of the five possible connection setting options and the corresponding *value* field must be set to the value desired for the specified connection option.

Comments

- If this function is unsuccessful, the connection setting values for an application will remain unchanged.
- The connection setting values for an application can be changed only when there are no active database connections associated with the application (before any connection is established or after a RELEASE ALL SQL statement, followed by a COMMIT SQL statement, is executed).
- Once the SET CLIENT function has executed successfully, the connection settings are fixed and the corresponding precompiler options used to precompile the application's source code modules are overridden. All connections made by subsequent transactions will use the new connection settings. You can change these new connection settings only by re-executing the SET CLIENT function.

Required Connection

This function can be called only when no database connection exists.

Authorization

No authorization is required to execute this function call.

See Also

QUERY CLIENT

Example

The following C program illustrates how to use the SET CLIENT function to change the type of connections an application makes to a database, from Type 1 to Type 2:

```
#include <stdio.h>
#include <stdlib.h>
#include <sqlenv.h>
#include <sqlca.h>

int main()
{
    /* Declare The Local Memory Variables */
    int                      rc = EXIT_SUCCESS;
    struct sqle_conn_setting ConnInfo;
    struct sqlca             sqlca;

    /* Initialize The Connection Information Structure */
    ConnInfo.type = SQL_CONNECT_TYPE;

    /* Obtain Information About The Current Connection's */
    /* Connection Type                                   */
    sqleqryc(&ConnInfo, 1, &sqlca);

    /* Display The Connection Type Information Retrieved */
    printf("Original Connection Type : ");
    if (ConnInfo.value == SQL_CONNECT_1)
        printf("Type 1\n");
    else
        printf("Typc 2\n");

    /* Set The Current Connection Type To Type 2 */
    ConnInfo.value = SQL_CONNECT_2;
    sqlesetc(&ConnInfo, 1, &sqlca);

    /* Retrieve The Connection Type Information Again To Verify */
    /* That It Has Been Changed                                 */
    sqleqryc(&ConnInfo, 1, &sqlca);

    /* Display The Connection Type Information Retrieved */
    printf("New Connection Type      : ");
    if (ConnInfo.value == SQL_CONNECT_1)
        printf("Type 1\n");
    else
        printf("Type 2\n");

    /* Return To The Operating System */
    return(rc);
}
```

FORCE APPLICATION

Purpose The FORCE APPLICATION function forces both local and remote users and/or applications off a DB2 database manager instance.

Syntax

```
SQL_API_RC SQL_API_FN sqlefrce (long           NumAgentIDs,
                                unsigned long  *AgentIDs,
                                unsigned short ForceMode,
                                struct sqlca   *SQLCA);
```

Parameters

NumAgentIDs The number of agent connections that are to be terminated. This value should be the same as the number of elements specified in the array of *AgentIDs*.

AgentIDs A pointer to a location in memory where an array of unsigned long integers that contain the agent IDs of database users and/or applications is stored.

ForceMode The operating mode in which the FORCE APPLICATION function is to execute. Only the asynchronous operating mode is currently supported, so this parameter must always be set to SQL_ASYNCH.

SQLCA A pointer to a location in memory where a SQLCA data structure variable is stored. This variable sends either status information (if the function executed successfully) or error information (if the function failed) back to the calling application.

Includes

```
#include <sqlenv.h>
```

Description

The FORCE APPLICATION function forces both local and remote users and/or applications off a DB2 database manager instance. Forcing a user or an application off a DB2 database manager instance will result in the loss of that user's or application's connections to all databases. To preserve database integrity, only users and applications that are either idle or executing interruptible database operations can be forced off a DB2 database manager instance.

Comments

- When the value of the *ForceMode* parameter is SQL_ASYNCH (the only value permitted at this time), the FORCE APPLICATION function does not wait until all specified users and applications are terminated before returning. Instead, it returns as soon as the function has completed or as soon as an error occurs. As a result, there might be a short interval between the time FORCE APPLICATION completes and the specified connections are terminated.
- The STOP DATABASE MANAGER function cannot be executed by another application during a FORCE APPLICATION process. Instead, the DB2 database manager server remains active so subsequent database manager operations can be handled without a START DATABASE MANAGER function call.
- Users and/or applications in the process of creating a database cannot be forced off a DB2 database manager instance.
- After a FORCE APPLICATION function call is issued, the DB2 database manager will still accept database connect requests. Therefore, additional FORCE APPLICATION function calls may be required to completely force all users off a DB2 database manager instance.
- You can use the GET SNAPSHOT function to obtain a list of the agent IDs of all active applications currently connected to a database, and then use other database system monitor functions to gather additional information about the users and/or applications attached to the database.
- Minimal validation is performed on the array of agent IDs specified in the *AgentIDs* parameter. The application using this function must ensure that the value specified in the *AgentIDs* parameter points to an array that contains the same number of elements specified in the *NumAgentIDs* parameter.
- If the value specified in the *NumAgentIDs* parameter is SQL_ALL_USERS, all users and applications will be forced off the DB2 database manager instance and any values specified in the *AgentIDs* parameter will be ignored. If the value specified in the *NumAgentIDs* parameter is 0, an error will be returned.

- All users and applications that can be forced off a database connection instance will be. If one or more specified agent IDs cannot be found, an error will occur. (An agent ID might not be found, for instance, if the agent signs off between the time the agent ID information is collected and the time the FORCE APPLICATION function call is issued.)
- The application that issues the FORCE APPLICATION function call is never forced off the DB2 database manager instance.
- When a user and/or application is terminated by the FORCE APPLICATION function, a ROLLBACK is performed to ensure database consistency.
- Agent IDs are recycled, so when one user signs off another user might sign on and acquire the same agent ID. Because of this, if there is a large period of time between the time agent IDs are collected and the time the FORCE APPLICATION function is executed, the wrong user might be forced off the DB2 database manager instance.
- If an operation that cannot be interrupted (such as BACKUP DATABASE or RESTORE DATABASE) is terminated because the application performing the operation was terminated by the FORCE APPLICATION function, the operation must be successfully reexecuted before the specified database will become available again.

Required Connection This function cannot be called unless a connection to a DB2 database manager instance exists. To force users and/or applications off a remote database server, it is necessary to first attach to that server. If no attachment exists, the FORCE APPLICATION function is executed locally.

Authorization Only users with either system control (SYSCTRL) authority or system administrator (SYSADM) authority are allowed to execute this function call.

See Also ATTACH, DETACH

Example The following C program illustrates how to use the FORCE APPLICATION function to force all users and applications off a DB2 database manager instance:

```
#include <stdio.h>
#include <stdlib.h>
#include <sqlenv.h>
#include <sqlca.h>

int main()
{
    /* Declare The Local Memory Variables */
    int             rc = EXIT_SUCCESS;
    unsigned long   ulAgentID;
    struct sqlca    sqlca;

    /* Start The DB2 Database Manager Server Processes */
    rc = sqlestar();

    /* Display A Success Message */
    printf("The DB2 database manager has been started.");

    /* Force All Applications Off The DB2 Database Manager Instance */
    sqlefrce(SQL_ALL_USERS, &ulAgentID, SQL_ASYNCH, &sqlca);
```

```
    /* Display A Success Message */
    printf("All users have been forced off the current DB2 ");
    printf("database manager instance.\n");

    /* Stop The DB2 Database Manager Server Processes */
    sqlestop(&sqlca);

    /* Display A Success Message */
    printf("The DB2 database manager has been stopped.\n");

    /* Return To The Operating System */
    return(rc);
}
```

CHAPTER 20

DB2 DATABASE MANAGER AND DATABASE CONFIGURATION API'S

The DB2 database manager and database configuration APIs are a group of DB2 API function calls that allow an application to retrieve, update, and reset the values of DB2 database manager and database configuration file parameters. This group includes:

- API functions that retrieve the current values of DB2 database manager and DB2 database configuration parameters.
- API functions that modify the values of DB2 database manager and DB2 database configuration parameters.
- API functions that reset DB2 database manager and DB2 database configuration files.

Table 20.1 lists the DB2 database manager and database configuration API functions available with DB2.

Configuring DB2

DB2 is designed around an extensive array of configuration parameters. These parameters are used to fine-tune the performance of the DB2 database manager or specific DB2 databases. The DB2 database manager uses the values stored in two sets of configuration parameters to determine how to allocate system resources (disk space and memory) for itself and for each open database. In many cases, the default values provided for the configuration parameters are sufficient to meet an application's needs. However, since the default values provided are oriented towards workstations that both have relatively small amounts of memory and are dedicated database servers, you can improve overall system and application performance by changing one or more configuration parameter values.

DB2 database applications can range from simple data entry systems that contain one or two simple insert SQL statements to large data collection and management systems that contain hundreds of complex SQL queries for accessing dozens of tables within a single transaction. Different types of applications (and users) have different response time requirements and expectations. Additionally, each application's transaction processing environment contains one or more unique aspect within it. These differences can have a profound impact on the performance of the DB2 database manager, especially when the default configuration parameter values are used.

TABLE 20.1 DB2 Database Manager and Database Configuration APIs

Function name	Description
GET DATABASE MANAGER CONFIGURATION	Retrieves the current values of one or more DB2 database manager configuration file parameters.
GET DATABASE MANAGER CONFIGURATION DEFAULTS	Retrieves the system default values of one or more DB2 database manager configuration file parameters.
UPDATE DATABASE MANAGER CONFIGURATION	Changes the values of one or more DB2 database manager configuration file parameters.
RESET DATABASE MANAGER CONFIGURATION	Resets all DB2 database manager configuration file parameters to their system default values.
GET DATABASE CONFIGURATION	Retrieves the current values of one or more database configuration file parameters.
GET DATABASE CONFIGURATION DEFAULTS	Retrieves the system default values of one or more database configuration file parameters.
UPDATE DATABASE CONFIGURATION	Changes the values of one or more database configuration file parameters.
RESET DATABASE CONFIGURATION	Resets all database configuration file parameters to their system default values.

For this reason, it is strongly recommended that you fine-tune the DB2 configuration files to obtain the maximum performance from your particular operating environment. Configuration parameter values should always be modified if your database environment contains one or more of the following elements:

- Large databases
- Databases that normally service a large number of concurrent connections
- One or more special applications that have high-performance requirements
- A special hardware configuration
- Unique query and/or transaction loads
- Unique query and/or transaction types

DB2 Database Manager Configuration Parameters

DB2 database manager configuration parameter values are stored in the file **db2systm**, which is located in the **sqllib** directory where DB2 was installed. This file is created along with the DB2 database manager during the DB2 product installation process. Most of the parameter values in this file control the amount of system resources allocated to a single instance of the DB2 database manager. Other parameter values in this file contain informative information about the DB2 database manager itself, and cannot be changed.

You can use any of the following methods to view, change, or reset the value of one or more DB2 database manager configuration parameters from an application program:

- The DB2 database director
- The GET DATABASE MANAGER CONFIGURATION command

- The GET DATABASE MANAGER CONFIGURATION function
- The UPDATE DATABASE MANAGER CONFIGURATION command
- The UPDATE DATABASE MANAGER CONFIGURATION function
- The RESET DATABASE MANAGER CONFIGURATION command
- The RESET DATABASE MANAGER CONFIGURATION function
- The GET DATABASE MANAGER CONFIGURATION DEFAULTS function

DB2 Database Configuration Parameters

Configuration parameter values for an individual database are stored in the file **SQLDBCON**, which is located in the **SQL***xxxxx* directory that was created when the database was created (*xxxxx* represents the number assigned by DB2 during the database creation process). This file is created along with the directory and other database control files whenever a new database is created. Most of the parameter values in this file control the amount of system resources allocated to the specified database. Other parameter values in this file contain informative information about the DB2 database itself, and cannot be changed.

You can use any of the following methods can be used to view, change, or reset the value of one or more DB2 database configuration parameters from an application program:

- The DB2 database director
- The GET DATABASE CONFIGURATION command
- The GET DATABASE CONFIGURATION function
- The UPDATE DATABASE CONFIGURATION command
- The UPDATE DATABASE CONFIGURATION function
- The RESET DATABASE CONFIGURATION command
- The RESET DATABASE CONFIGURATION function
- The GET DATABASE CONFIGURATION DEFAULTS function

GET DATABASE MANAGER CONFIGURATION

Purpose

The GET DATABASE MANAGER CONFIGURATION function retrieves the current values of one or more configuration parameters (entries) in a DB2 database manager configuration file.

Syntax

```
SQL_API_RC SQL_API_FN sqlfxsys (unsigned short NumItems,
                                struct sqlfupd *ItemList,
                                struct sqlca   *SQLCA);
```

Parameters

NumItems An integer value that specifies the number of DB2 database manager configuration parameter values to retrieve. This value identifies the number of elements contained in the array of *sqlfupd* structures specified in the *ItemList* parameter.

ItemList A pointer to an array of *sqlfupd* structures that specify which DB2 database manager configuration parameters value are to be retrieved.

SQLCA A pointer to a location in memory where an SQL communication area (SQLCA) data structure variable is stored. This variable sends either status information (if the function executed successfully) or error information (if the function failed) back to the calling application.

Includes

```
#include <sqlutil.h>
```

Description

The GET DATABASE MANAGER CONFIGURATION function retrieves the current values of one or more configuration parameters (entries) in a DB2 database manager configuration file. DB2 database manager configuration parameter values are stored in the file **db2systm**, which is located in the **sqllib** directory where DB2 was installed. This file is created along with the DB2 database manager when the DB2 product is installed. Most of the parameter values in this file control the amount of system resources allocated to a single instance of the DB2 database manager, and can be modified to increase DB2's overall performance. Other parameter values in this file contain static information about the DB2 database manager itself, and cannot be changed.

This function uses an array of *sqlfupd* structures to retrieve the current value of one or more DB2 database manager configuration parameters. The *sqlfupd* structure is defined in *sqlutil.h* as follows:

```
struct sqlfupd
{
unsigned short  token;       /* A token that identifies the      */
                             /* configuration parameter whose    */
                             /* value is to be retrieved         */
char            *ptrvalue;   /* A pointer to a location in       */
                             /* memory where the configuration   */
                             /* parameter value is to be stored */
};
```

Table 20.2 lists each DB2 database manager configuration parameter token that can be specified for the *token* field of a *sqlfupd* structure, a description of each corresponding DB2 database manager configuration parameter, and information about the C (and C++) data type of the retrieved value.

TABLE 20.2 DB2 Database Manager Configuration Parameters

Parameter name	Description	Token	C data type
agent_stack_sz	Specifies the amount of memory allocated and committed by the operating system for each agent. This parameter specifies the number of pages for each agent stack on an OS/2 server.	SQLF_KTN_AGENT_STACK_SZ	unsigned int
agentpri	Specifies the execution priority assigned to DB2 database manager processes and threads on a particular workstation.	SQLF_KTN_AGENTPRI	int
aslheapsz	Specifies the size (in pages) of the memory shared between a local client application and a DB2 database manager agent.	SQLF_KTN_ASLHEAPSZ	unsigned long
authentication	Specifies how and where authentication of a user takes place. A value of CLIENT indicates that all authentication takes place at the client workstation. A value of SERVER indicates that the user ID and password are sent from the client workstation to the server workstation so authentication can take place at the server.	SQLF_KTN_AUTHENTICATION	unsigned int

TABLE 20.2 DB2 Database Manager Configuration Parameters *(Continued)*

Parameter name	Description	Token	C data type
backbufsz	Specifies the size (in pages) of the buffer that backs up a database. This value is used only if the buffer size is not specified when the backup utility is called.	SQLF_KTN_BACKBUFSZ	unsigned long
cpuspeed	Specifies the CPU speed (in milliseconds per instruction) used by the SQL optimizer to estimate the cost of performing certain operations. The value of this parameter is set automatically when the DB2 product is installed, but it can be modified to model a production environment on a test system or to assess the impact of upgrading hardware.	SQLF_KTN_CPUSPEED	float
dft_account_str	Specifies the default accounting string used when connecting to DRDA servers.	SQLF_KTN_DFT_ACCOUNT_STR	char[25]
dft_client_comm	Specifies the communication protocols that all client applications on attached to a specific DB2 database manager instance can use for establishing remote connections.	SQLF_KTN_DFT_CLIENT_COMM	char[31]
dft_monswitches	Specifies all default values for the snapshot monitor in a single value. You can manipulate the bits of this unsigned integer value or you can use the individual tokens that make up this value (see the footnote for more information).	SQLF_KTN_DFT_MONSWITCHES	unsigned int
dft_mon_bufpool	Specifies the default value of the snapshot monitor's buffer pool switch.	SQLF_KTN_DFT_MON_BUFPOOL	unsigned int
dft_mon_lock	Specifies the default value of the snapshot monitor's lock switch.	SQLF_KTN_DFT_MON_LOCK	unsigned int
dft_mon_sort	Specifies the default value of the snapshot monitor's sort switch.	SQLF_KTN_DFT_MON_SORT	unsigned int
dft_mon_stmt	Specifies the default value of the snapshot monitor's statement switch.	SQLF_KTN_DFT_MON_STMT	unsigned int
dft_mon_table	Specifies the default value of the snapshot monitor's table switch.	SQLF_KTN_DFT_MON_TABLE	unsigned int
dft_mon_uow	Specifies the default value of the snapshot monitor's unit of work (UOW) switch.	SQLF_KTN_DFT_MON_UOW	unsigned int
dftdbpath	Specifies the default drive (OS/2) or directory path (AIX) to use to store databases. If no path is specified when a database is created, the database is created in the location specified by this parameter.	SQLF_KTN_DFTDBPATH	char[215]
diaglevel	Specifies the diagnostic error capture level that is used to determine the severity of diagnostic errors that get recorded in the error log file (db2diag.log).	SQLF_KTN_DIAGLEVEL	unsigned int
diagpath	Specifies the fully qualified path for DB2 diagnostic information.	SQLF_KTN_DIAGPATH	char[215]

TABLE 20.2 DB2 Database Manager Configuration Parameters *(Continued)*

Parameter name	Description	Token	C data type
dir_cache	Specifies whether or not directory cache support is enabled. If this parameter is set to YES, database, node, and DCS directory files are cached in memory. This reduces connect overhead by eliminating directory file I/O and minimizing the directory searches required to retrieve directory information.	SQLF_KTN_DIR_CACHE	unsigned int
dir_obj_name	Specifies the object name that represents a DB2 database manager instance (or a database) in the DCE directory name space. The concatenation of this value and the *dir_path_name* value yields a global name that uniquely identifies the DB2 database manager instance or database in the name space governed by the directory services specified in the *dir_type* parameter.	SQLF_KTN_DIR_OBJ_NAME	char[255]
dir_path_name	Specifies the directory path name in the DCE name space. The unique name of the DB2 database manager instance in the global name space is made up of this value and the value in the *dir_obj_name* parameter.	SQLF_KTN_DIR_PATH_NAME	char[255]
dir_type	Specifies the type of directory services used (indicates whether or not the DB2 database manager instance uses the DCE global directory services).	SQLF_KTN_DIR_TYPE	unsigned int
dos_rqrioblk	Specifies the DOS requester I/O block size. This parameter is applicable only on DOS clients, including DOS clients running under OS/2. This parameter controls the size of the I/O blocks allocated on both the client and the server workstations.	SQLF_KTN_DOS_RQRIOBLK	unsigned int
drda_heap_sz	Specifies the size, in pages, of the DRDA heap. This heap is used by the DRDA AS clause.	SQLF_KTN_DRDA_HEAP_SZ	unsigned int
fileserver	Specifies the IPX/SPX file server name (the name of the Novell NetWare file server) where the internetwork address of the DB2 database manager is registered. Note: The following characters are not valid: / \ : ; * ?	SQLF_KTN_FILESERVER	char[48]
indexrec	Specifies when invalid database *indexes* should be recreated. This parameter is used if the database configuration parameter *indexrec* is set to SYSTEM. Possible output values for this parameter are ACCESS and RESTART.	SQLF_KTN_INDEXREC	unsigned int
ipx_socket	Specifies a well-known IPX/SPX socket number and represents the connection end point in a DB2 server's NetWare internetwork address.	SQLF_KTN_IPX_SQCKET	char[4]
keepdari	Specifies whether or not to keep a Database Application Remote Interface (DARI) process after each DARI call. If this parameter is set to	SQLF_KTN_KEEPDARI	unsigned int

TABLE 20.2 DB2 Database Manager Configuration Parameters *(Continued)*

Parameter name	Description	Token	C data type
	NO, a new DARI process will be created and terminated for each DARI invocation. If this parameter is set to YES, a DARI process will be reused for subsequent DARI calls and be terminated only when the associated user application exits.		
max_idleagents	Specifies the maximum number of idle agents allowed. Idle agents exist, but are not assigned to any client.	SQLF_KTN_MAX_IDLEAGENTS	unsigned int
maxagents	Specifies the maximum number of DB2 database manager agents that can exist simultaneously, regardless of which database is being used.	SQLF_KTN_MAXAGENTS	unsigned long
maxcagents	Specifies the maximum number of DB2 database manager agents that can be concurrently executing a database manager transaction. This parameter can be set to the same value as the *maxagents* parameter.	SQLF_KTN_MAXCAGENTS	long
maxdari	Specifies the maximum number of DARI processes that can reside at the database server. The value of this parameter cannot exceed the value of the *maxagents* parameter.	SQLF_KTN_MAXDARI	long
maxtotfilop	Specifies the maximum number of files that can be open per OS/2 application. The value specified in this parameter defines the total database and application file handles that can be used by a specific process connected to a database (OS/2 only).	SQLF_KTN_MAXTOTFILOP	unsigned int
min_pri_mem	Specifies the number of pages that the database server process will reserve as private virtual memory when a DB2 database manager instance is started (OS/2 only).	SQLF_KTN_MIN_PRIV_MEM	unsigned long
mon_heap_sz	Specifies the amount (in 4KB pages) of memory to allocate for database system monitor data (database system monitor heap size).	SQLF_KTN_MON_HEAP_SZ	unsigned int
nname	Specifies the name of the node or workstation. Database clients use this value to access database server workstations using NetBIOS. If the database server workstation changes the name specified in *nname*, all clients that access the database server workstation must catalog it again and specify the new name.	SQLF_KTN_NNAME	char[8]
nodetype	Specifies whether the node is configured as a server with local and remote clients, a client, or a server with local clients. This parameter is not updatable.	SQLF_KTN_NODETYPE	unsigned int
numdb	Specifies the maximum number of local databases that can be concurrently active (that have applications connected to them).	SQLF_KTN_NUMDB	unsigned int
objectname	Specifies the IPX/SPX database manager object name of the database manager instance in a Novell NetWare network.	SQLF_KTN_OBJECTNAME	char[48]

TABLE 20.2 DB2 Database Manager Configuration Parameters *(Continued)*

Parameter name	Description	Token	C data type
	Note: The following characters are not valid: / : ; , * ?		
priv_mem_thresh	Specifies a threshold below which a server will not release the memory associated with a client when that client's connection is terminated.	SQLF_KTN_PRIV_MEM_THRESH	long
query_heap_sz	Specifies the maximum amount of memory (in 4 KB pages) that can be allocated for the query heap A query heap stores each query in the agent's private memory.	SQLF_KTN_QUERY_HEAP_SZ	long
release	Specifies the release level of the DB2 database manager configuration file. This parameter is not updatable.	SQLF_KTN_RELEASE	unsigned int
restbufsz	Specifies the size (in 4 KB pages) of the buffer that restores a database. This value is used only if the buffer size is not specified when the restore utility is called.	SQLF_KTN_RESTBUFSZ	unsigned long
resync_interval	Specifies the time interval (in seconds) after which a Transaction Manager (TM) or Resource Manager (RM) retries the recovery of any outstanding indoubt transactions found in the TM or the RM. This parameter value is used only when transactions are running in a distributed unit of work (DUOW) environment.	SQLF_KTN_RESYNC_INTERVAL	unsigned int
route_obj_name	Specifies the name of the default routing information object entry used by all client applications attempting to access a DRDA server.	SQLF_KTN_ROUTE_OBJ_NAME	char[255]
rqrioblk	Specifies the size (in bytes) of the communication buffer by remote applications and their database agents on the database server.	SQLF_KTN_RQRIOBLK	unsigned int
sheapthres	Specifies the limit on the total amount of memory (in 4 KB pages) available for sorting across the entire DB2 database manager instance.	SQLF_KTN_SHEAPTHRES	unsigned long
sqlstmtsz	Specifies the maximum amount of dynamic SQL statement text (in bytes) returned by the database system monitor.	SQLF_KTN_SQLSTMTSZ	unsigned long
svcename	Specifies a service name that represents the DB2 database manager instance in a TCP/IP network.	SQLF_KTN_SVCENAME	char[14]
sysadm_group	Specifies the group name that has system administration (SYSADM) authority for the DB2 database manager instance. This is the highest level of authority within the database manager, and controls all database objects.	SQLF_KTN_SYSADM_GROUP	char[16]
sysctrl_group	Specifies the group name that has system control (SYSCTRL) authority for the DB2 database manager instance. This level allows operations that affect system resources, but does not allow direct access to data.	SQLF_KTN_SYSCTRL_GROUP	char[l6]
sysmaint_group	Specifies the group name that has system maintenance (SYSMAINT) authority for the	SQLF_KTN_SYSMAINT_GROUP	char[l6]

TABLE 20.2 DB2 Database Manager Configuration Parameters *(Continued)*

Parameter name	Description	Token	C data type
	DB2 database manager instance. This level allows maintenance operations on all databases associated with an instance, but does not allow direct access to data.		
tm_database	Specifies the name of the transaction manager (TM) database for each DB2 instance.	SQLF_KTN_TM_DATABASE	char[8]
tp_mon_name	Specifies the name of the transaction processing (TP) monitor product being used.	SQLF_KTN_TP_MON_NAME	char[19]
tpname	Specifies the name of the remote transaction program that the database client must use when it issues an allocate request to the DB2 database manager instance using the APPC communication protocol.	SQLF_KTN_TPNAME	char[64]
udf_mem_sz	For a fenced user-defined function (UDF), this parameter specifies the default allocation for memory to be shared between the database process and the UDF. For an unfenced process, this parameter specifies the size of the private memory set. In both cases, this memory passes data to a UDF and back to a database.	SQLF_KTN_UDF_MEM_SZ	unsigned int

Note: The bits of the SQLF_KTN_DFT_MONSWITCHES parameter value indicate the default monitor switch settings. The individual bits making up this composite parameter value are:

Bit 1 (xxxx xxxl): dft_mon_uow
Bit 2 (xxxx xxlx): dft_mon_stmt
Bit 3 (xxxx xlxx): dft_mon_table
Bit 4 (xxxx lxxx): dft_mon_buffpool
Bit 5 (xxxl xxxx): dft_mon_lock
Bit 6 (xxlx xxxx): dft_mon_sort

Adapted from IBM's *Database 2 API Reference*, Table 40, pages 471 to 472, and the sqlfxys Get -Database Manager Configuration API, pages 251 to 256.

Before this function can be executed, an array of *sqlfupd* structures must be allocated, the token field of each structure in this array must be set to one of the DB2 database manager configuration parameter tokens listed in Table 20.2, and the *ptrvalue* field of each structure must contain a pointer to a valid location in memory where the retrieved configuration parameter value is to be stored. When this function is executed, the current value (setting) of each specified DB2 database manager configuration parameter is placed in the memory storage areas (local variables) referred to by the *ptrvalue* field of each *sqlfupd* structure in the array.

Comments

- If an application is attached to a remote DB2 database manager instance (or to a different local DB2 database manager instance), the current values of the DB2 database manager configuration file parameters for the attached server will be returned; otherwise, the current values of the local DB2 database manager configuration file parameters will be returned.
- The application that calls this function is responsible for allocating sufficient memory for each retrieved data value.
- If an error occurs while this function is executing, the returned DB2 database manager configuration information will be invalid. If an error oc-

curs because the DB2 database manager configuration file has been corrupted, an error message will be returned and you must reinstall the DB2 product to correct the problem.

- For detailed information about each DB2 database manager configuration file parameter, refer to the *IBM Database 2 Administration Guide*.

Required Connection

You can call this function at any time to retrieve DB2 database manager configuration file parameter values from the current DB2 database manager instance (as defined by the value of the DB2INSTANCE environment variable); a connection to the current DB2 database manager instance does not have to be established first.

In order to retrieve DB2 database manager configuration file parameter values for a DB2 database manager instance located at a remote node, you must first attach to that node before calling this function.

Authorization

No authorization is required to execute this function call.

See Also

GET DATABASE MANAGER CONFIGURATION DEFAULTS, RESET DATABASE MANAGER CONFIGURATION, UPDATE DATABASE MANAGER CONFIGURATION

Example

The following C program illustrates how to use the GET DATABASE MANAGER CONFIGURATION function to retrieve DB2 database manager configuration file parameter values:

```
#include <stdio.h>
#include <stdlib.h>
#include <sqlutil.h>
#include <sqlca.h>

int main()
{
    /* Declare The Local Memory Variables */
    struct sqlfupd  DBManagerInfo[3];
    float           fCPUSpeed;
    char            szDBPath[216];
    unsigned int    uiNumDB = 0;
    struct sqlca    sqlca;

    /* Initialize The Array Of DB2 Database Manager Configuration */
    /* Parameter Structures                                       */
    DBManagerInfo[0].token = SQLF_KTN_CPUSPEED;
    DBManagerInfo[0].ptrvalue = (unsigned char *) &fCPUSpeed;
    DBManagerInfo[1].token = SQLF_KTN_DFTDBPATH;
    DBManagerInfo[1].ptrvalue = szDBPath;
    DBManagerInfo[2].token = SQLF_KTN_NUMDB;
    DBManagerInfo[2].ptrvalue = (unsigned char *) &uiNumDB;

    /* Obtain The Current Values Of The Specified DB2 Database */
    /* Manager Configuration Parameters                        */
    sqlfxsys(3, &DBManagerInfo[0], &sqlca);

    /* Display The Current Values Of The Specified Configuration */
    /* Parameters                                                */
    printf("CPU speed used by the SQL optimizer              : %f\n",
           fCPUSpeed);
    printf("Max. number of local databases that can be active : %d\n",
           uiNumDB);
```

```
    printf("Disk drive used to store all databases          : %s\n",
           szDBPath);

    /* Return To The Operating System */
    return(EXIT_SUCCESS);
}
```

GET DATABASE MANAGER CONFIGURATION DEFAULTS

Purpose

The GET DATABASE MANAGER CONFIGURATION DEFAULTS function retrieves the system default values for one or more parameters (entries) in a DB2 database manager configuration file.

Syntax

```
SQL_API_RC SQL_API_FN sqlfdsys (unsigned short NumItems,
                                struct sqlfupd *ItemList,
                                struct sqlca   *SQLCA);
```

Parameters

NumItems An integer value that specifies the number of DB2 database manager configuration parameter values to retrieve. This value identifies the number of elements contained in the array of *sqlfupd* structures specified in the *ItemList* parameter.

ItemList A pointer to an array of *sqlfupd* structures that specifies which DB2 database manager configuration parameters system default values are to be retrieved.

SQLCA A pointer to a location in memory where a SQLCA data structure variable is stored. This variable sends either status information (if the function executed successfully) or error information (if the function failed) back to the calling application.

Includes

```
#include <sqlutil.h>
```

Description

The GET DATABASE MANAGER CONFIGURATION DEFAULTS function retrieves the system default values for one or more parameters (entries) in a DB2 database manager configuration file. This function uses an array of *sqlfupd* structures to retrieve the system default values for one or more DB2 database manager configuration parameters. Refer to the GET DATABASE MANAGER CONFIGURATION function for a detailed description of this structure and for more information about available DB2 database manager configuration parameters.

Before this function can be executed, an array of *sqlfupd* structures must be allocated, the *token* field of each structure in this array must be set to one of the DB2 database manager configuration parameter tokens listed in Table 20.2 (refer to the GET DATABASE MANAGER CONFIGURATION function), and the *ptrvalue* field of each structure must contain a pointer to a valid location in memory where the retrieved configuration parameter value is to be stored. When this function is executed, the system default value for each specified DB2 database manager configuration parameter is placed in the memory storage areas (local variables) referred to by the *ptrvalue* field of each *sqlfupd* structure in the array.

Comments

- If an application is attached to a remote DB2 database manager instance (or to a different local DB2 database manager instance), the current values of the DB2 database manager configuration file parameters for the attached server will be returned; otherwise, the current values of the local DB2 database manager configuration file parameters will be returned.

- The application that calls this function is responsible for allocating sufficient memory for each retrieved data value.
- The current value of a nonupdatable configuration parameter is returned as that configuration parameter's system default value.
- If an error occurs while this function is executing, the returned DB2 database manager configuration information will be invalid. If an error occurs because the DB2 database manager configuration file has been corrupted, an error message will be returned and you must reinstall the DB2 product to correct the problem.
- For a brief description about each DB2 database manager configuration file parameter, refer to the GET DATABASE MANAGER CONFIGURATION function. For detailed information about each DB2 database manager configuration file parameter, refer to the *IBM Database 2 Administration Guide.*

Required Connection You can call this function at any time to retrieve default DB2 database manager configuration file parameter values for the current DB2 database manager instance (as defined by the value of the DB2INSTANCE environment variable); a connection to the current DB2 database manager instance does not have to be established first.

In order to retrieve default DB2 database manager configuration file parameter values for a DB2 database manager instance located at a remote node, you must first attach to that node before calling this function.

Authorization No authorization is required to execute this function call.

See Also GET DATABASE MANAGER CONFIGURATION, RESET DATABASE MANAGER CONFIGURATION, UPDATE DATABASE MANAGER CONFIGURATION

Example The following C program illustrates how to use the GET DATABASE MANAGER CONFIGURATION DEFAULTS function to retrieve DB2 database manager configuration file parameter system default values:

```
#include <stdio.h>
#include <stdlib.h>
#include <sqlutil.h>
#include <sqlca.h>

int main()
{
    /* Declare The Local Memory Variables */
    struct sqlfupd  DBManagerInfo[3];
    float           fCPUSpeed;
    char            szDBPath[216];
    unsigned int    uiNumDB = 0;
    struct sqlca    sqlca;

    /* Initialize The Array Of DB2 Database Manager Configuration */
    /* Parameter Structures                                       */
    DBManagerInfo[0].token = SQLF_KTN_CPUSPEED;
    DBManagerInfo[0].ptrvalue = (unsigned char *) &fCPUSpeed;
    DBManagerInfo[1].token = SQLF_KTN_DFTDBPATH;
```

```
    DBManagerInfo[1].ptrvalue = szDBPath;
    DBManagerInfo[2].token = SQLF_KTN_NUMDB;
    DBManagerInfo[2].ptrvalue = (unsigned char *) &uiNumDB;

    /* Obtain The System Default Values Of The Specified DB2 */
    /* Database Manager Configuration Parameters             */
    sqlfdsys(3, &DBManagerInfo[0], &sqlca);

    /* Display The System Default Values Of The Specified */
    /* Configuration Parameters                           */
    printf("CPU speed used by the SQL optimizer               : %f\n",
           fCPUSpeed);
    printf("Max. number of local databases that can be active : %d\n",
           uiNumDB);
    printf("Disk drive used to store all databases            : %s\n",
           szDBPath);

    /* Return To The Operating System */
    return(EXIT_SUCCESS);
}
```

UPDATE DATABASE MANAGER CONFIGURATION

Purpose

The UPDATE DATABASE MANAGER CONFIGURATION function changes the value of one or more configuration parameters (entries) in a DB2 database manager configuration file.

Syntax

```
SQL_API_RC SQL_API_FN sqlfusys (unsigned short NumItems,
                                struct sqlfupd *ItemList,
                                struct sqlca   *SQLCA);
```

Parameters

NumItems An integer value that specifies the number of DB2 database manager configuration parameters values to update. This value identifies the number of elements contained in the array of *sqlfupd* structures specified in the *ItemList* parameter.

ItemList A pointer to an array of *sqlfupd* structures that specifies which DB2 database manager configuration parameters are to be updated, along with their corresponding values.

SQLCA A pointer to a location in memory where a SQLCA data structure variable is stored. This variable sends either status information (if the function executed successfully) or error information (if the function failed) back to the calling application.

Includes

```
#include <sqlutil.h>
```

Description

The UPDATE DATABASE MANAGER CONFIGURATION function changes the value of one or more configuration parameters (entries) in a DB2 database manager configuration file. This function uses an array of *sqlfupd* structures to update the value of one or more DB2 database manager configuration parameters. The *sqlfupd* structure is defined in *sqlutil.h* as follows:

```
struct sqlfupd
{
unsigned short token;      /* A token that identifies the      */
```

```
                                  /* configuration parameter whose    */
                                  /* value is to be updated           */
char               *ptrvalue;     /* A pointer to a location in       */
                                  /* memory where the new             */
                                  /* configuration parameter value is */
                                  /* stored                           */
};
```

Before this function can be executed, an array of *sqlfupd* structures must be allocated, the *token* field of each structure in this array must be set to one of the DB2 database manager configuration parameter tokens listed in Table 20.2 (refer to the GET DATABASE MANAGER CONFIGURATION function), and the *ptrvalue* field of each structure must contain a pointer to a valid location in memory where the new configuration parameter value is stored. When this function is executed, the new DB2 database manager configuration parameter values are copied from the memory storage areas (local variables) referred to by the *ptrvalue* field of each *sqlfupd* structure in the array to the appropriate location in the DB2 database manager configuration file. Some DB2 database manager configuration file parameters cannot be updated.

Note: If a user attempts to edit a DB2 database manager configuration file using a method other than those provided by DB2, the database management system can become unusable. A DB2 database manager configuration file should be updated only with one of the following methods:

–The DB2 database director
–The DB2 command-line processor (UPDATE DATABASE MANAGER CONFIGURATION and RESET DATABASE MANAGER CONFIGURATION commands)
–The appropriate DB2 API function calls (UPDATE DATABASE MANAGER CONFIGURATION and RESET DATABASE MANAGER CONFIGURATION)

Comments

- If an application is attached to a remote DB2 database manager instance (or to a different local DB2 database manager instance), the current values of the DB2 database manager configuration file parameters for the attached server will be updated; otherwise, the current values of the local DB2 database manager configuration file parameters will be updated.
- Changes to DB2 database manager configuration file parameters become effective only when the modified configuration file is loaded into memory. For database server workstations, the DB2 database manager must be stopped and restarted before the new values take effect (refer to the STOP DATABASE MANAGER function and the START DATABASE MANAGER function). For client workstations, the new values will take effect the next time a client application connects to a server workstation. Even though new configuration parameter values do not take effect immediately, when configuration parameter values are retrieved, the most recent update values are always returned.
- If an error occurs while this function is executing, the DB2 database manager configuration file will remain unchanged.
- A DB2 database manager configuration file cannot be updated if its checksum is invalid. Checksums can become invalid if a DB2 database

manager configuration file is changed by something other than the methods provided with the DB2 product. If a DB2 database manager configuration file cannot be updated, an error message will be returned and you must reinstall the DB2 product to correct the problem.

- The values used for each database configuration parameter differ for each type of configured database node (server, client, or server with remote clients). For detailed information about the ranges and values that can be set for each node type, refer to the *IBM Database 2 Administration Guide*.
- Use the GET DATABASE MANAGER CONFIGURATION function to retrieve the current value of one or more DB2 database manager configuration file parameters.
- Use the GET DATABASE MANAGER CONFIGURATION DEFAULTS function to retrieve the system default value of one or more DB2 database manager configuration file parameters.
- Use the RESET DATABASE MANAGER CONFIGURATION function to set the values of all DB2 database manager configuration file parameters to the values used when the DB2 database manager configuration file was created initially.
- For a brief description about each DB2 database manager configuration file parameter, refer to the GET DATABASE MANAGER CONFIGURATION function. For detailed information about each DB2 database manager configuration file parameter, refer to the *IBM Database 2 Administration Guide.*

Required Connection

You can call this function at any time to update DB2 database manager configuration file parameter values for the current DB2 database manager instance (as defined by the value of the DB2INSTANCE environment variable); a connection to the current DB2 database manager instance does not have to be established first.

In order to update DB2 database manager configuration file parameter values for a DB2 database manager instance that is located at a remote node, it is necessary to first attach to that node before calling this function.

Authorization

Only users with system administrator (SYSADM) authority are allowed to execute this function call.

See Also

GET DATABASE MANAGER CONFIGURATION DEFAULTS, GET DATABASE MANAGER CONFIGURATION, RESET DATABASE MANAGER CONFIGURATION

Example

The following C program illustrates how to use the UPDATE DATABASE MANAGER CONFIGURATION function to change the values of DB2 database manager configuration file parameters:

```
#include <stdio.h>
#include <stdlib.h>
#include <sqlutil.h>
#include <sqlca.h>

int main()
{
    /* Declare The Local Memory Variables */
    int             rc = EXIT_SUCCESS;
```

```
    struct sqlfupd  DBManagerInfo[2];
    unsigned int    uiNumDB = 0;
    int             iQueryHeapSize = 0;
    struct sqlca    sqlca;

    /* Initialize The Array Of DB2 Database Manager Configuration */
    /* Parameter Structures                                        */
    DBManagerInfo[0].token = SQLF_KTN_NUMDB;
    DBManagerInfo[0].ptrvalue = (unsigned char *) &uiNumDB;
    DBManagerInfo[1].token = SQLF_KTN_QUERY_HEAP_SZ;
    DBManagerInfo[1].ptrvalue = (unsigned char *) &iQueryHeapSize;

    /* Obtain The Current Values Of The Specified DB2 Database */
    /* Manager Configuration Parameters                         */
    sqlfxsys(2, &DBManagerInfo[0], &sqlca);

    /* Display The Current Values Of The Specified Configuration */
    /* Parameters                                                 */
    printf("Before Update :\n");
    printf("Max. number of local databases that can be active ");
    printf("at one time   : %d\n", uiNumDB);
    printf("Max. amount of memory that can be allocated for the ");
    printf("query heap : %d\n", iQueryHeapSize);

    /* Modify The Values Of The Specified DB2 Database Manager */
    /* Configuration Parameters                                 */
    uiNumDB = 4;
    iQueryHeapSize = 1024;
    sqlfusys(2, &DBManagerInfo[0], &sqlca);

    /* Obtain The Current Value Of The Specified DB2 Database  */
    /* Manager Configuration Parameters - Verify That The      */
    /* Values Have Been Changed                                 */
    sqlfxsys(2, &DBManagerInfo[0], &sqlca);

    /* Display The Current Values Of The Specified Configuration */
    /* Parameters                                                 */
    printf("\nAfter Update :\n");
    printf("Max. number of local databases that can be active ");
    printf("at one time   : %d\n", uiNumDB);
    printf("Max. amount of memory that can be allocated for the ");
    printf("query heap : %d\n", iQueryHeapSize);

    /* Return To The Operating System */
    return(rc);
}
```

RESET DATABASE MANAGER CONFIGURATION

Purpose

The RESET DATABASE MANAGER CONFIGURATION function resets the values of all updatable configuration parameters (entries) in a DB2 database manager configuration file to their system defaults.

Syntax

```
SQL_API_RC SQL_API_FN sqlfrsys (struct sqlca *SQLCA);
```

Parameters

SQLCA A pointer to a location in memory where a SQLCA data structure variable is stored. This variable sends either status information (if the

function executed successfully) or error information (if the function failed) back to the calling application.

Includes

```
#include <sqlutil.h>
```

Description

The RESET DATABASE MANAGER CONFIGURATION function resets the values of all updatable configuration parameters (entries) in a DB2 database manager configuration file to their system defaults. When this function is executed, all non-updatable parameters in the configuration file remain unchanged.

Comments

- If an application is attached to a remote DB2 database manager instance (or a different local DB2 database manager instance), the values of the DB2 database manager configuration file parameters for the attached server will be reset; otherwise, the values of the local DB2 database manager configuration file parameters will be reset.
- Changes to DB2 database manager configuration file parameters become effective only when the modified configuration file is loaded into memory. For database server workstations, the DB2 database manager must be stopped and restarted before the new values take effect (refer to the STOP DATABASE MANAGER and START DATABASE MANAGER functions). For client workstations, the new values will take effect the next time a client application connects to a server workstation. Even though new configuration parameter values do not take effect immediately, when configuration parameter values are retrieved, the most recent update values are always returned.
- If an error occurs while this function is executing, the DB2 database manager configuration file will remain unchanged.
- A DB2 database manager configuration file cannot be updated if its checksum is invalid. Checksums can become invalid if a DB2 database manager configuration file is changed by something other than the methods provided with the DB2 product. If a DB2 database manager configuration file cannot be updated, an error message will be returned and you must reinstall the DB2 product before correcting the problem.
- Use the GET DATABASE MANAGER CONFIGURATION function to retrieve the current value of one or more DB2 database manager configuration file parameters.
- Use the GET DATABASE MANAGER CONFIGURATION DEFAULTS function to retrieve the system default value of one or more DB2 database manager configuration file parameters.
- Use the UPDATE DATABASE MANAGER CONFIGURATION function to change the value of one or more DB2 database manager configuration file parameters.
- For a brief description about each DB2 database manager configuration file parameter, refer to the GET DATABASE MANAGER CONFIGURATION function. For detailed information about each DB2 database manager configuration file parameter, refer to the *IBM Database 2 Administration Guide*.

Required Connection

You can call this function at any time to reset DB2 database manager configuration file parameter values for the current DB2 database manager instance (as defined by the value of the DB2INSTANCE environment variable); a connection to the current DB2 database manager instance does not have to be established first.

In order to reset DB2 database manager configuration file parameter values for a DB2 database manager instance that is located at a remote node, it is necessary to first attach to that node before calling this function.

Authorization

Only users with system administrator (SYSADM) authority are allowed to execute this function call.

See Also

GET DATABASE MANAGER CONFIGURATION DEFAULTS, GET DATABASE MANAGER CONFIGURATION, UPDATE DATABASE MANAGER CONFIGURATION

Example

The following C program illustrates how the RESET DATABASE MANAGER CONFIGURATION function resets DB2 database manager configuration file parameters to their system default values:

```
#include <stdio.h>
#include <stdlib.h>
#include <sqlutil.h>
#include <sqlca.h>

int main()
{
    /* Declare The Local Memory Variables */
    int             rc = EXIT_SUCCESS;
    struct sqlfupd  DBManagerInfo[2];
    unsigned int    uiNumDB = 0;
    int             iQueryHeapSize = 0;
    struct sqlca    sqlca;

    /* Initialize The Array Of DB2 Database Manager Configuration */
    /* Parameter Structures                                        */
    DBManagerInfo[0].token = SQLF_KTN_NUMDB;
    DBManagerInfo[0].ptrvalue = (unsigned char *) &uiNumDB;
    DBManagerInfo[1].token = SQLF_KTN_QUERY_HEAP_SZ;
    DBManagerInfo[1].ptrvalue = (unsigned char *) &iQueryHeapSize;

    /* Obtain The Current Values Of The Specified DB2 Database */
    /* Manager Configuration Parameters                        */
    sqlfxsys(2, &DBManagerInfo[0], &sqlca);

    /* Display The Current Values Of The Specified Configuration */
    /* Parameters                                                */
    printf("Before Reset :\n");
    printf("Max. number of local databases that can be active ");
    printf("at one time  : %d\n", uiNumDB);
    printf("Max. amount of memory that can be allocated for the ");
    printf("query heap : %d\n", iQueryHeapSize);

    /* Reset The Values Of The Specified DB2 Database Manager  */
    /* Configuration Parameters To Their System Default Values */
    sqlfrsys(&sqlca);

    /* Obtain The Current Value Of The Specified DB2 Database */
    /* Manager Configuration Parameters - Verify That The     */
    /* Values Have Been Changed                               */
    sqlfxsys(2, &DBManagerInfo[0], &sqlca);
```

```
    /* Display The Current Values Of The Specified Configuration */
    /* Parameters                                                 */
    printf("\nAfter Reset :\n");
    printf("Max. number of local databases that can be active ");
    printf("at one time  : %d\n", uiNumDB);
    printf("Max. amount of memory that can be allocated for the ");
    printf("query heap : %d\n", iQueryHeapSize);

    /* Return To The Operating System */
    return(rc);
}
```

GET DATABASE CONFIGURATION

Purpose

The GET DATABASE CONFIGURATION function retrieves the current values of one or more configuration parameters (entries) in a specific database configuration file.

Syntax

```
SQL_API_RC SQL_API_FN sqlfxdb (char           *DBAlias,
                               unsigned short NumItems,
                               struct sqlfupd *ItemList,
                               struct sqlca   *SQLCA);
```

Parameters

DBAlias A pointer to a location in memory where the alias name of the database is stored.

NumItems An integer value that specifies the number of database configuration parameter values to retrieve. This value identifies the number of elements contained in the array of *sqlfupd* structures specified in the *ItemList* parameter.

ItemList A pointer to an array of *sqlfupd* structures that specify which database configuration parameters value are to be retrieved.

SQLCA A pointer to a location in memory where a SQLCA data structure variable is stored. This variable sends either status information (if the function executed successfully) or error information (if the function failed) back to the calling application.

Includes

```
#include <sqlutil.h>
```

Description

The GET DATABASE CONFIGURATION function retrieves the current values of one or more configuration parameters (entries) in a specific database configuration file. Configuration parameter values for an individual database are stored in the file **SQLDBCON**, which is located in the **SQL***xxxxx* directory that was created when the database was created (*xxxxx* represents the number assigned by DB2 during the database creation process). This file is created along with the directory and other database control files whenever a new database is created. Most of the parameter values in this file control the amount of system resources allocated to the corresponding database, and can be modified to increase the database's overall performance. Other parameter values in this file contain static information about the database itself, and cannot be changed.

This function uses an array of *sqlfupd* structures to retrieve the current value of one or more database configuration parameters. The *sqlfupd* structure is defined in *sqlutil.h* as follows:

```
struct sqlfupd
{
unsigned short token;      /* A token that identifies the       */
                           /* configuration parameter whose     */
                           /* value is to be retrieved          */
char           *ptrvalue;  /* A pointer to a location in        */
                           /* memory where the configuration    */
                           /* parameter value is to be stored */
};
```

Table 20.3 lists each database configuration parameter token that can be specified for the *token* field of a *sqlfupd* structure, a description of each corresponding database configuration parameter, and information about the C (and C++) data type of the retrieved value.

TABLE 20.3 DB2 Database Configuration Parameters

Parameter name	Description	Token	C data type
applheapsz	Specifies the size, in pages, of the application heap available for each individual agent. Memory to be used for caching packages (specified by the *pckcachesz*) is allocated from the application heap.	SQLF_DBTN_APPLHEAPSZ	unsigned int
autorestart	Specifies whether or not the DB2 database manager can automatically issue a RESTART DATABASE command when a connection is attempted, if the last database connection was disrupted, or if the database was not terminated normally during the previous session. This parameter can be set to ON (specifies that a database is restarted automatically) or OFF (specifies that a database must be restarted manually).	SQLF_DBTN_AUTO_RESTART	unsigned int
avg_appls	Specifies the average number of active applications that will access the database. This parameter is used by the SQL optimizer to help estimate how much buffer pool memory will be available for the chosen access plan at application runtime.	SQLF_DBTN_AVG_APPLS	unsigned int
backup_pending	Specifies whether or not a database needs to be backed up. This parameter can be set to NO (specifies that the database is in a usable state) or YES (specifies that an OFFLINE backup must be performed before the database can be used). This parameter is not updatable.	SQLF_DBTN_BACKUP_PENDING	unsigned int
buff_page	Specifies the size, in pages, of the buffer pool that stores and manipulate data read in from the database.	SQLF_DBTN_BUFF_PAGE	unsigned long
catalogcache_sz	Specifies the size, in pages, of the internal catalog cache (allocated from the *dbheap*) used by the SQL precompiler to hold the packed descriptors for commonly referenced objects such as tables and constraints.	SQLF_DBTN_CATALOGCACHE_SZ	long

TABLE 20.3 DB2 Database Configuration Parameters *(Continued)*

Parameter name	Description	Token	C data type
chngpgs_thresh	Specifies the level (percentage) of pages that must be changed before the asynchronous page cleaners will be started, if they are not already active.	SQLF_DBTN_CHNGPGS_THRESH	unsigned int
codepage	Specifies the code page of the database. This parameter is not updatable.	SQLF_DBTN_CODEPAGE	unsigned int
codeset	Specifies the code set of the database. This parameter is not updatable.	SQLF_DBTN_CODESET	char[9]
collate_info	Specifies the collate sequence that is used by the database when making character comparisons. This parameter is not updatable.	SQLF_DBTN_COLLATE_INFO	char[260]
none	Specifies all database attributes in a single value. You can manipulate the bits of this unsigned integer value or use the individual tokens making up this value (see the footnote for more information).	SQLF_DBTN_DETS	unsigned int
copyprotect	Enables or disables the database copy-protect attribute (OS/2 only).	SQLF_DBTN_COPY_PROTECT	unsigned int
country	Specifies the country code of the database. This parameter is not updatable.	SQLF_DBTN_COUNTRY	unsigned int
database_consistent	Specifies whether or not the database is in a consistent state. This parameter can be set to YES (specifies that all transactions have been committed or rolled back and that the data in the database is consistent) or NO (specifies that a transaction or some other task is pending on the database and that the data in the database is not consistent at this point). This parameter is not updatable.	SQLF_DBTN_CONSISTENT	unsigned int
database_level	Specifies the release level of the DB2 database managers that can use the database. This parameter is not updatable.	SQLF_DBTN_DATABASE_LEVEL	unsigned int
dbheap	Specifies the size, in pages, of the database heap that holds control information on all open cursors accessing the database. Both log buffers and catalog cache buffers are allocated from the database heap.	SQLF_DBTN_DBHEAP	unsigned int
dft_extent_sz	Specifies the default extent size (in pages) of all table spaces.	SQLF_DBTN_DFT_EXTENT_SZ	unsigned long
dft_loadrec_ses	Specifies the default number of load recovery sessions used during the recovery of a table load operation. This parameter is applicable only if roll-forward recovery is enabled.	SQLF_DBTN_DFT_LOADREC_SES	int
dft_prefetch_sz	Specifies the default prefetch size (in pages) of all table spaces.	SQLF_DBTN_DFT_PREFETCH_SZ	int
dir_obj_name	Specifies the object name in the DCE name space that represents a DB2 database	SQLF_DBTN_DIR_OBJ_NAME	char[255]

TABLE 20.3 DB2 Database Configuration Parameters *(Continued)*

Parameter name	Description	Token	C data type
	manager instance (or database) in the directory.		
dlchktime	Specifies the time interval frequency (in milliseconds) at which the DB2 database manager is to check for deadlocks among all the applications connected to a database.	SQLF_DBTN_DLCHKTIME	unsigned long
indexrec	Specifies when invalid indexes are recreated. This parameter can be set to SYSTEM (ACCESS), SYSTEM(RESTART), ACCESS, or RESTART. The default setting is SYSTEM, which specifies that the value of the DB2 database manager configuration parameter *indexrec* is to be used.	SQLF_DBTN_INDEXREC	unsigned int
indexsort	Specifies whether or not index key sorting is to occur during index creation.	SQLF_DBTN_INDEXSQRT	unsigned int
locklist	Specifies the maximum storage (in pages) allocated to the lock list.	SQLF_DBTN_LOCKLIST	unsigned int
locktimeout	Specifies the number of seconds an application will wait to obtain a lock before timing out.	SQLF_DBTN_LOCKTIMEOUT	int
logbufsz	Specifies the number of pages used to buffer log records before they are written to disk. This buffer is allocated from the database heap.	SQLF_DBTN_LOGBUFSZ	unsigned int
logfilsiz	Specifies the amount of disk storage space (in pages) allocated to log files that are used for data recovery. This parameter defines the size of each primary and secondary log file.	SQLF_DBTN_LOGFILSIZ	unsigned int
loghead	Specifies the name of the log file that contains the head of the active log. The next log record written will start at the head of the active log file. This parameter is not updatable.	SQLF_DBTN_LOGHEAD	char[12]
logpath	Specifies the current path used to access log files. This parameter is not updatable.	SQLF_DBTN_LOGPATH	char[242]
logprimary	Specifies the number of primary log files that can be used for database recovery.	SQLF_DBTN_LOGPRIMARY	unsigned int
logretain	Specifies whether or not active log files are to be retained as archived log files for use in roll-forward recovery (also known as log retention logging).	SQLF_DBTN_LOG_RETAIN	unsigned int
log_retain_status	Specifies whether or not log files are retained for use in roll-forward recovery. This parameter is not updatable.	SQLF_DBTN_LOG_RETAIN_STATUS	unsigned int
logsecond	Specifies the number of secondary log files that can be used for database recovery.	SQLF_DBTN_LOGSECOND	unsigned int
maxappls	Specifies the maximum number of application programs (both local and remote) that can connect to the database at one time.	SQLF_DBTN_MAXAPPLS	unsigned int

TABLE 20.3 DB2 Database Configuration Parameters *(Continued)*

Parameter name	Description	Token	C data type
maxfilop	Specifies the maximum number of database files an application program can have open at one time.	SQLF_DBTN_MAXFILOP	unsigned int
maxlocks	Specifies the maximum percentage of the lock list that any one application program can use.	SQLF_DBTN_MAXLOCKS	unsigned int
mincommit	Specifies the number of SQL commits that can be grouped for the database. You can achieve better control of I/O and log activity by grouping SQL commits.	SQLF_DBTN_MINCOMMIT	unsigned int
newlogpath	Specifies an alternate path to use when searching for recovery log files. Since this parameter accepts only fully qualified directories, you must specify the absolute path.	SQLF_DBTN_NEWLOGPATH	char[242]
nextactive	Specifies the name of the next recovery log file to be used for logging. This parameter is not updatable.	SQLF_DBTN_NEXTACTIVE	char[12]
num_freqvalues	Specifies the number of most-frequent values that will be collected when the WITH DISTRIBUTION option is specified in the RUN STATISTICS function (or command).	SQLF_DBTN_NUM_FREQVALUES	unsigned int
num_iocleaners	Specifies the number of asynchronous page cleaners for a database.	SQLF_DBTN_NUM_IOCLEANERS	unsigned int
num_ioservers	Specifies the number of I/O servers for a database. I/O servers are used on behalf of database agents to perform prefetch and asynchronous I/O needed by utilities such as BACKUP and RESTORE.	SQLF_DBTN_NUM_IOSERVERS	unsigned int
num_quantiles	Specifies the number of quantiles (values in a column that satisfy a RANGE predicate) that will be collected when the WITH DISTRIBUTION option is specified in the RUN STATISTICS function or command.	SQLF_DBTN_NUM_QUANTILES	unsigned int
numsegs	Specifies the number of containers created within the default SMS table spaces. This parameter is not updatable.	SQLF_DBTN_NUMSEGS	unsigned int
pckcachesz	Specifies the amount of application heap memory used for caching packages.	SQLF_DBTN_PCKCACHESZ	unsigned int
rec_his_retentn	Specifies the number of days that historical information on backups is retained.	SQLF_DBTN_REC_HIS_RETENTN	int
release	Specifies the release level of the database configuration file. This parameter is not updatable.	SQLF_DBTN_RELEASE	unsigned int
rollfwd_pending	Specifies whether or not a roll-forward recovery procedure needs to be performed before the database can be used. This parameter can be set to NO (neither the database nor any of its table space is in roll-	SQLF_DBTN_ROLLFWD_PENDING	unsigned int

TABLE 20.3 DB2 Database Configuration Parameters *(Continued)*

Parameter name	Description	Token	C data type
	forward pending state), DATABASE (the database needs to be rolled forward before it can be used), or TABLESPACES (one or more table spaces in the database needs to be rolled forward). This parameter is not updatable.		
seqdetect	Specifies whether or not sequential detection for the database is enabled or disabled.	SQLF_DBTN_SEQDETECT	unsigned int
softmax	Specifies the maximum percentage of log file space to be consumed before a soft checkpoint is taken.	SQLF_DBTN_SOFTMAX	unsigned int
sortheap	Specifies the number of private memory pages available for each sort operation in an application program.	SQLF_DBTN_SORT_HEAP	unsigned long
stat_heap_sz	Specifies the maximum size of the heap space (in pages) for creating and collecting all table statistics when distribution statistics are being gathered.	SQLF_DBTN_STAT_HEAP_SZ	unsigned long
stmtheap	Specifies the heap size (in pages) used to compile SQL statements.	SQLF_DBTN_STMTHEAP	unsigned int
territory	Specifies the territory of the database. This parameter is not updatable.	SQLF_DBTN_TERRITORY	char[8]
userexit	Specifies whether or not a user exit function for archiving or retrieving log files can be called the next time the database is opened. This parameter can be set to OFF (specifies that a user exit function cannot be called) or ON (specifies that a user exit function can be called).	SQLF_DBTN_USER_EXIT	unsigned int
user_exit_status	Specifies whether or not a user exit function can be called to store archive log files. This parameter can be set to OFF (specifies that a user exit function cannot be called to store archive log files) or ON (specifies that a user exit function can be called to store archive log files). This parameter is not updatable.	SQLF_DBTN_USER_EXIT_STATUS	unsigned int
util_heap_sz	Specifies the maximum amount of shared memory that can be used simultaneously by the backup, restore, and load utilities.	SQLF_DBTN_UTIL_HEAP_SZ	unsigned long
none	Specifies the database status in a single value. You may examine the bits of this unsigned integer value, or you can use the individual tokens that make up this value (see footnote for more information).	SQLF_DBTN_INTFLAGS	unsigned int

The bits of the SQLF_DBTN_DETS parameter value indicate the database attribute settings. The individual bits making up this composite parameter value are:

Bit 1 (xxxx xxxl): copyprotect
Bit 2 (xxxx xxlx): logretain

TABLE 20.3 DB2 Database Configuration Parameters *(Continued)*

Bit 3 (xxxx xlxx): userexit
Bit 4 (xxxx lxxx): autorestart

The bits of the SQLF_DBTN_INTFLAGS parameter value indicate database status. The individual bits making up this composite parameter value are:

Bit 1 (xxxx xxxl): database_consistent
Bit 3 (xxxx xlxx): backup_pending
Bit 4 (xxxx 1xxx): rollfwd_pending
Bit 5 (xxx1 xxxx): log_retain_status
Bit 6 (xx1x xxxx): user_exit_status
Bit 7 (x1xx xxxx): tablespace roll-forward pending

The combination of bits 4 and 7 make up the rollfwd_pending parameter. If the rollfwd_pending bit (4) is on, the database needs to be rolled forward (rollfwd_pending = DATABASE). If the rollfwd_pending bit (4) is off and bit 7 is on, one or more table spaces need to be rolled forward (rollfwd_pending = TABLESPACES). If both bits are off, neither the database nor any of its table spaces need to be rolled forward (rollfwd_pending = NO).

Adapted from IBM's *Database 2 API Reference*, Table 39, pages 468 to 470 and the sqlfxdb- Get Database Configuration API, pages 245 to 249.

Before this function can be executed, an array of *sqlfupd* structures must be allocated, the *token* field of each structure in this array must be set to one of the database configuration parameter tokens listed in Table 20.3, and the *ptrvalue* field of each structure must contain a pointer to a valid location in memory where the retrieved configuration parameter value is to be stored. When this function is executed, the current value (setting) of each specified database configuration parameter is placed in the memory storage areas (local variables) referred to by the *ptrvalue* field of each *sqlfupd* structure in the array.

Comments

- Entries in the database configuration file that do not have a corresponding token value listed in Table 20.3 are not accessible to an application.
- The application that calls this function is responsible for allocating sufficient memory for each retrieved data value.
- If an error occurs while this function is executing, the returned database configuration information will be invalid. If an error occurs because the database configuration file has been corrupted, an error message will be returned and you must restore the database from a good backup image before correcting the problem.
- For detailed information about each database configuration file parameter, refer to the *IBM Database 2 Administration Guide*.

Required Connection

This function can be called only if a connection to a DB2 database manager instance exists. In order to retrieve database configuration file parameter values for a DB2 database located at a remote node, you must first attach to that node; if necessary, a temporary connection is established by this function during its execution.

Authorization

No authorization is required to execute this function call.

See Also

GET DATABASE CONFIGURATION DEFAULTS, RESET DATABASE CONFIGURATION, UPDATE DATABASE CONFIGURATION

Example

The following C program illustrates how to use the GET DATABASE CONFIGURATION function to retrieve database configuration file parameter values for the SAMPLE database:

```
#include <stdio.h>
#include <stdlib.h>
#include <sqlutil.h>
#include <sqlca.h>

int main()
{
    /* Declare The Local Memory Variables */
    int             rc = EXIT_SUCCESS;
    struct sqlfupd  DBaseInfo[4];
    unsigned int    uiAutoRestart = 0;
    unsigned int    uiAvgApplications = 0;
    unsigned int    uiDeadlockChkTime = 0;
    unsigned int    uiLockTimeout = 0;
    struct sqlca    sqlca;

    /* Initialize The Array Of SAMPLE Database Configuration */
    /* Parameter Structures                                  */
    DBaseInfo[0].token = SQLF_DBTN_AUTO_RESTART;
    DBaseInfo[0].ptrvalue = (unsigned char *) &uiAutoRestart;
    DBaseInfo[1].token = SQLF_DBTN_AVG_APPLS;
    DBaseInfo[1].ptrvalue = (unsigned char *) &uiAvgApplications;
    DBaseInfo[2].token = SQLF_DBTN_DLCHKTIME;
    DBaseInfo[2].ptrvalue = (unsigned char *) &uiDeadlockChkTime;
    DBaseInfo[3].token = SQLF_DBTN_LOCKTIMEOUT;
    DBaseInfo[3].ptrvalue = (unsigned char *) &uiLockTimeout;

    /* Obtain The Current Values Of The Specified SAMPLE Database */
    /* Configuration Parameters                                   */
    sqlfxdb("SAMPLE", 4, &DBaseInfo[0], &sqlca);

    /* Display The Current Values Of The Specified */
    /* Configuration Parameters                                  */
    printf("Automatically restart the database if necessary : ");
    if (uiAutoRestart == 0)
        printf("No\n");
    else
        printf("Yes\n");
    printf("Avg. number of active applications allowed      : %d\n",
           uiAvgApplications);
    printf("Time interval between deadlock checks           : ");
    printf("%d milliseconds\n", uiDeadlockChkTime);
    printf("Lock timeout                                    : ");
    printf("%d seconds\n", uiLockTimeout);

    /* Return To The Operating System */
    return(EXIT_SUCCESS);
}
```

GET DATABASE CONFIGURATION DEFAULTS

Purpose

The GET DATABASE CONFIGURATION DEFAULTS function retrieves the system default values for one or more configuration parameters (entries) in a database configuration file.

Syntax

```
SQL_API_RC SQL_API_FN sqlfddb (char           *DBAlias,
                               unsigned short NumItems,
                               struct sqlfupd *ItemList,
                               struct sqlca   *SQLCA);
```

Parameters

DBAlias A pointer to a location in memory where the alias name of the database is stored.

NumItems An integer value that specifies the number of database configuration parameter default values to retrieve. This value identifies the number of elements contained in the array of *sqlfupd* structures specified in the *ItemList* parameter.

ItemList A pointer to an array of *sqlfupd* structures that specify which database configuration parameters system default values are to be retrieved.

SQLCA A pointer to a location in memory where a SQLCA data structure variable is stored. This variable sends either status information (if the function executed successfully) or error information (if the function failed) back to the calling application.

Includes

```
#include <sqlutil.h>
```

Description

The GET DATABASE CONFIGURATION DEFAULTS function retrieves the system default values of one or more configuration parameters (entries) in a database configuration file. This function uses an array of *sqlfupd* structures to retrieve the system default values for one or more database configuration parameters. Refer to the GET DATABASE CONFIGURATION function for a detailed description of this structure and for more information about the database configuration parameters available.

Before this function can be executed, an array of *sqlfupd* structures must be allocated, the *token* field of each structure in this array must be set to one of the database configuration parameter tokens listed in Table 20.3 (refer to the GET DATABASE CONFIGURATION function), and the *ptrvalue* field of each structure must contain a pointer to a valid location in memory where the retrieved configuration parameter value is to be stored. When this function is executed, the system default value for each specified database configuration parameter is placed in the memory storage areas (local variables) referred to by the *ptrvalue* field of each *sqlfupd* structure in the array.

Comments

- The application that calls this function is responsible for allocating sufficient memory for each retrieved data value.
- The current value of a nonupdatable configuration parameter is returned as that configuration parameter's system default value.
- If an error occurs while this function is executing, the returned database configuration information will be invalid. If an error occurs because the database configuration file has been corrupted, an error message will be returned and you must restore the database from a good backup image before correcting the problem.
- For a brief description about each database configuration file parameter, refer to the GET DATABASE CONFIGURATION function. For detailed information about each database configuration file parameter, refer to the *IBM Database 2 Administration Guide*.

Required Connection

This function can be called only if a connection to a DB2 database manager instance exists. In order to retrieve default database configuration file parameter values for a DB2 database located at a remote node, you must first attach to that node; if necessary, a temporary connection is established by this function while it executes.

Authorization No authorization is required to execute this function call.

See Also RESET DATABASE CONFIGURATION, UPDATE DATABASE CONFIGURATION, GET DATABASE CONFIGURATION

Example The following C program illustrates how to use the GET DATABASE CONFIGURATION DEFAULTS function to retrieve default database configuration file parameter values:

```
#include <stdio.h>
#include <stdlib.h>
#include <sqlutil.h>
#include <sqlca.h>

int main()
{
    /* Declare The Local Memory Variables */
    struct sqlfupd  DBaseInfo[4];
    unsigned int    uiAutoRestart = 0;
    unsigned int    uiAvgApplications = 0;
    unsigned int    uiDeadlockChkTime = 0;
    unsigned int    uiLockTimeout = 0;
    struct sqlca    sqlca;

    /* Initialize The Array Of SAMPLE Database Configuration */
    /* Parameter Structures                                  */
    DBaseInfo[0].token = SQLF_DBTN_AUTO_RESTART;
    DBaseInfo[0].ptrvalue = (unsigned char *) &uiAutoRestart;
    DBaseInfo[1].token = SQLF_DBTN_AVG_APPLS;
    DBaseInfo[1].ptrvalue = (unsigned char *) &uiAvgApplications;
    DBaseInfo[2].token = SQLF_DBTN_DLCHKTIME;
    DBaseInfo[2].ptrvalue = (unsigned char *) &uiDeadlockChkTime;
    DBaseInfo[3].token = SQLF_DBTN_LOCKTIMEOUT;
    DBaseInfo[3].ptrvalue = (unsigned char *) &uiLockTimeout;

    /* Obtain The System Default Values Of The Specified SAMPLE */
    /* Database Configuration Parameters                        */
    sqlfddb("SAMPLE", 4, &DBaseInfo[0], &sqlca);

    /* Display The System Default Values Of The Specified Configuration */
    /* Parameters                                                       */
    printf("Automatically restart the database if necessary : ");
    if (uiAutoRestart == 0)
        printf("No\n");
    else
        printf("Yes\n");
    printf("Avg. number of active applications allowed      : %d\n",
           uiAvgApplications);
    printf("Time interval between deadlock checks           : ");
    printf("%d milliseconds\n", uiDeadlockChkTime);
    printf("Lock timeout                                    : ");
    printf("%d seconds\n", uiLockTimeout);

    /* Return To The Operating System */
    return(EXIT_SUCCESS);
}
```

UPDATE DATABASE CONFIGURATION

Purpose

The UPDATE DATABASE CONFIGURATION function changes the value of one or more configuration parameters (entries) in a specific database configuration file.

Syntax

```
SQL_API_RC SQL_API_FN sqlfudb (char           *DBAlias,
                                unsigned short NumItems,
                                struct sqlfupd *ItemList,
                                struct sqlca   *SQLCA)
```

Parameters

DBAlias A pointer to a location in memory where the alias name of the database is stored.

NumItems An integer value that specifies the number of database configuration parameters values to update. This value identifies the number of elements contained in the array of *sqlfupd* structures specified in the *ItemList* parameter.

ItemList A pointer to an array of *sqlfupd* structures that specify which database configuration parameter values are to be updated, along with their corresponding values.

SQLCA A pointer to a location in memory where a SQLCA data structure variable is stored. This variable sends either status information (if the function executed successfully) or error information (if the function failed) back to the calling application.

Includes

```
#include <sqlutil.h>
```

Description

The UPDATE DATABASE CONFIGURATION function changes the value of one or more configuration parameters (entries) in a specific database configuration file. This function uses an array of *sqlfupd* structures to update the value of one or more database configuration parameters. The *sqlfupd* structure is defined in *sqlutil.h* as follows:

```
struct sqlfupd
{
unsigned short token;      /* A token that identifies the      */
                           /* configuration parameter whose    */
                           /* value is to be updated           */
char           *ptrvalue;  /* A pointer to a location in       */
                           /* memory where the new             */
                           /* configuration parameter value is */
                           /* stored                           */
};
```

Before this function can be executed, an array of *sqlfupd* structures must be allocated, the *token* field of each structure in this array must be set to one of the database configuration parameter tokens listed in Table 20.3 (refer to the GET DATABASE CONFIGURATION function), and the *ptrvalue* field of each structure must contain a pointer to a valid location in memory where the new configuration parameter value is stored. When this function is executed, the new database configuration parameter values are copied from the memory storage areas (local variables) referred to by the *ptrvalue* field of each *sqlfupd* structure in the array to the appropriate location in the database configuration file. Some database configuration file parameters cannot be updated.

Note: If a user attempts to edit a database configuration file using a method other than those provided by DB2, the database can become unusable. A database configuration file should be updated only with one of the following methods:
- The DB2 database director
- The DB2 command-line processor (UPDATE DATABASE CONFIGURATION and RESET DATABASE CONFIGURATION commands)
- The appropriate DB2 API function calls (UPDATE DATABASE CONFIGURATION and RESET DATABASE CONFIGURATION function calls)

Comments

- Changes to database configuration file parameters become effective only when the modified configuration file is loaded into memory. This will not occur until all applications are disconnected from the database and a new connect attempt is made (when the first new connection to the database is established, the new values will take effect). Even though new configuration parameter values do not take effect immediately, when configuration parameter values are retrieved, the most recent update values are always returned.
- If an error occurs while this function is executing, the database configuration file will remain unchanged.
- A database configuration file cannot be updated if its checksum is invalid. Checksums can become invalid if a database configuration file is changed by something other than the methods provided with the DB2 product. If a database configuration file cannot be updated, an error message is returned and you must restore the database from a good backup image before the problem can be corrected.
- The values used for each database configuration parameter differ for each type of configured database node (server, client, or server with remote clients). For detailed information about the ranges and values that can be set for each node type, refer to the *IBM Database 2 Administration Guide.*
- When some database configuration parameter values are changed, they can affect the access plans chosen by the SQL precompiler. After changing any of the following database configuration parameters, consider rebinding all packages stored in the database to ensure that the best access plan is used to process your application's SQL statements:
  - buffpage
  - sortheap
  - locklist
  - maxlocks
  - seqdetect
  - avg_appls
- Use the GET DATABASE CONFIGURATION function to retrieve the current value of one or more database configuration file parameters.
- Use the GET DATABASE CONFIGURATION DEFAULTS function to retrieve the system default value of one or more database configuration file parameters.
- Use the RESET DATABASE CONFIGURATION function to set the values of all database configuration file parameters to the values used when the database configuration file was initially created.

- For a brief description about each database configuration file parameter, refer to the GET DATABASE CONFIGURATION function. For detailed information about each database configuration file parameter, refer to the *IBM Database 2 Administration Guide*.

Required Connection This function can be called only if a connection to a DB2 database manager instance exists. In order to update database configuration file parameter values for a DB2 database located at a remote node, it is necessary to first attach to that node; if necessary, a temporary connection is established by this function while it executes.

Authorization Only users with system control (SYSCTRL) authority, system administrator (SYSADM) authority, or system maintenance (SYSMAINT) authority can execute this function call.

Restrictions There are no restrictions associated with this function call.

See Also GET DATABASE CONFIGURATION DEFAULTS, GET DATABASE CONFIGURATION, RESET DATABASE CONFIGURATION

Example The following C program illustrates how the UPDATE DATABASE CONFIGURATION function changes the values of database configuration file parameters:

```
#include <stdio.h>
#include <stdlib.h>
#include <sqlutil.h>
#include <sqlca.h>

int main()
{
    /* Declare The Local Memory Variables */
    int             rc = EXIT_SUCCESS;
    struct sqlfupd  DBaseInfo[2];
    unsigned int    uiAutoRestart = 0;
    unsigned int    uiDeadlockChkTime = 0;
    struct sqlca    sqlca;

    /* Initialize The Array Of SAMPLE Database Configuration */
    /* Parameter Structures                                  */
    DBaseInfo[0].token = SQLF_DBTN_AUTO_RESTART;
    DBaseInfo[0].ptrvalue = (unsigned char *) &uiAutoRestart;
    DBaseInfo[1].token = SQLF_DBTN_DLCHKTIME;
    DBaseInfo[1].ptrvalue = (unsigned char *) &uiDeadlockChkTime;

    /* Obtain The Current Values Of The Specified SAMPLE Database */
    /* Configuration Parameters                                   */
    sqlfxdb("SAMPLE", 2, &DBaseInfo[0], &sqlca);

    /* Display The Current Values Of The Specified Configuration */
    /* Parameters                                                */
    printf("Before Update :\n");
    printf("Automatically restart the database if necessary : ");
    if (uiAutoRestart == 0)
        printf("No\n");
    else
        printf("Yes\n");
    printf("Time interval between deadlock checks           : ");
    printf("%d milliseconds\n", uiDeadlockChkTime);
```

```
    /* Modify The Values Of The Specified SAMPLE Database */
    /* Configuration Parameters                           */
    uiAutoRestart = 0;
    uiDeadlockChkTime = 8000;
    sqlfudb("SAMPLE", 2, &DBaseInfo[0], &sqlca);

    /* Obtain The Current Value Of The Specified SAMPLE Database */
    /* Configuration Parameters - Verify That The Values Have    */
    /* Been Changed                                              */
    sqlfxdb("SAMPLE", 2, &DBaseInfo[0], &sqlca);

    /* Display The Current Values Of The Specified Configuration */
    /* Parameters                                                */
    printf("\nAfter Update :\n");
    printf("Automatically restart the database if necessary : ");
    if (uiAutoRestart == 0)
        printf("No\n");
    else
        printf("Yes\n");
    printf("Time interval between deadlock checks           : ");
    printf("%d milliseconds\n", uiDeadlockChkTime);

    /* Return To The Operating System */
    return(rc);
}
```

RESET DATABASE CONFIGURATION

Purpose

The RESET DATABASE CONFIGURATION function resets the values of all updatable configuration parameters (entries) in a database configuration file to their system defaults.

Syntax

```
SQL_API_RC SQL_API_FN sqlfrdb (char          *DBAlias,
                               struct sqlca *SQLCA);
```

Parameters

DBAlias A pointer to a location in memory where the alias name of the database is stored.

SQLCA A pointer to a location in memory where a SQLCA data structure variable is stored. This variable sends either status information (if the function executed successfully) or error information (if the function failed) back to the calling application.

Includes

```
#include <sqlutil.h>
```

Description

The RESET DATABASE CONFIGURATION function resets the values of all updatable configuration parameters (entries) in a database configuration file to their system defaults. When this function is executed, all nonupdatable parameters in the configuration file remain unchanged.

Comments

- Changes to database configuration file parameters become effective only when the modified configuration file is loaded into memory. This will not occur until all applications have disconnected from the database and a new connect attempt is made (when the first new connection to the database is established, the new values will take effect). Even though new configuration parameter values do not take effect immediately, when configuration parameter values are retrieved, the most recent update values are always returned.

- If an error occurs while this function is executing, the database configuration file will remain unchanged.
- A database configuration file cannot be updated if its checksum is invalid. Checksums can become invalid if a database configuration file is changed by something other than the methods provided with the DB2 product. If a database configuration file cannot be updated, an error message is returned and you must restore the database from a good backup image before correcting the problem.
- When some database configuration parameter values are changed, they can affect the access plans chosen by the SQL precompiler. After changing any of the following database configuration parameters, consider rebinding all packages stored in the database to ensure that the best access plan is used to process your application's SQL statements:
  –buffpage
  –sortheap
  –locklist
  –maxlocks
  –seqdetect
  –avg_appls
- Use the GET DATABASE CONFIGURATION function to retrieve the current value of one or more database configuration file parameters.
- Use the GET DATABASE CONFIGURATION DEFAULTS function to retrieve the system default value of one or more database configuration file parameters.
- Use the UPDATE DATABASE CONFIGURATION function to change the value of one or more database configuration parameters.
- For a brief description about each database configuration file parameter, refer to the GET DATABASE CONFIGURATION function. For detailed information about each database configuration file parameter, refer to the *IBM Database 2 Administration Guide*.

Required Connection

This function can be called only if a connection to a DB2 database manager instance exists. In order to reset database configuration file parameter values for a DB2 database located at a remote node, you must first attach to that node; if necessary, a temporary connection is established by this function while it executes.

Authorization

Only users with system control (SYSCTRL) authority, system administrator (SYSADM) authority, or system maintenance (SYSMAINT) authority can execute this function call.

See Also

GET DATABASE CONFIGURATION DEFAULTS, GET DATABASE CONFIGURATION, UPDATE DATABASE CONFIGURATION, RESTORE DATABASE

Example

The following C program illustrates how the RESET DATABASE CONFIGURATION function resets the SAMPLE database's database configuration file parameters to their system default values:

```
#include <stdio.h>
#include <stdlib.h>
```

```
#include <sqlutil.h>
#include <sqlca.h>

int main()
{
    /* Declare The Local Memory Variables */
    int             rc = EXIT_SUCCESS;
    struct sqlfupd  DBaseInfo[2];
    unsigned int    uiAutoRestart = 0;
    unsigned int    uiDeadlockChkTime = 0;
    struct sqlca    sqlca;

    /* Initialize The Array Of SAMPLE Database Configuration */
    /* Parameter Structures                                  */
    DBaseInfo[0].token = SQLF_DBTN_AUTO_RESTART;
    DBaseInfo[0].ptrvalue = (unsigned char *) &uiAutoRestart;
    DBaseInfo[1].token = SQLF_DBTN_DLCHKTIME;
    DBaseInfo[1].ptrvalue = (unsigned char *) &uiDeadlockChkTime;

    /* Obtain The Current Values Of The Specified SAMPLE Database */
    /* Configuration Parameters                                   */
    sqlfxdb("SAMPLE", 2, &DBaseInfo[0], &sqlca);

    /* Display The Current Values Of The Specified Configuration */
    /* Parameters                                                */
    printf("Before Reset :\n");
    printf("Automatically restart the database if necessary : ");
    if (uiAutoRestart == 0)
        printf("No\n");
    else
        printf("Yes\n");
    printf("Time interval between deadlock checks           : ");
    printf("%d milliseconds\n", uiDeadlockChkTime);

    /* Reset The Values Of The Specified SAMPLE Database       */
    /* Configuration Parameters To Their System Default Values */
    sqlfrdb("SAMPLE", &sqlca);

    /* Obtain The Current Value Of The Specified SAMPLE Database */
    /* Configuration Parameters - Verify That The Values Have    */
    /* Been Changed                                              */
    sqlfxdb("SAMPLE", 2, &DBaseInfo[0], &sqlca);

    /* Display The Current Values Of The Specified Configuration */
    /* Parameters                                                */
    printf("\nAfter Reset :\n");
    printf("Automatically restart the database if necessary : ");
    if (uiAutoRestart == 0)
        printf("No\n");
    else
        printf("Yes\n");
    printf("Time interval between deadlock checks           : ");
    printf("%d milliseconds\n", uiDeadlockChkTime);

    /* Return To The Operating System */
    return(rc);
}
```

CHAPTER 21

DATABASE, NODE, AND DCS DIRECTORY MANAGEMENT API'S

The database, node, and DCS directory management APIs are a group of DB2 API function calls that allow an application to add entries to, delete entries from, and retrieve a list of entries stored in the various DB2 directories. This group includes:

- API functions that catalog databases, workstation nodes, and DCS databases.
- API functions that uncatalog databases, workstation nodes, and DCS databases.
- API functions that retrieve the contents of the system and local database directories.
- API functions that retrieve the contents of the workstation node directory.
- API functions that retrieve the contents of the DCS directory.
- API functions that register and deregister a DB2 database server workstation with a Novell NetWare file server.

Table 21.1 lists the database, node, and DCS directory management API functions available with DB2.

DB2 Directories

DB2 uses the following set of directories to access both local and other remote workstations and databases:

- A system database directory
- One or more volume (local) directories
- A workstation (node) directory
- A database connection services (DCS) directory

TABLE 21.1 Database, Node, and DCS Directory Management APIs

Function name	Description
CATALOG DATABASE	Stores information about a database in the system database directory.
UNCATALOG DATABASE	Removes information about a database from the system database directory.
CHANGE DATABASE COMMENT	Adds or changes the comment (description) associated with a database that is cataloged in either the system or the local database directory.
OPEN DATABASE DIRECTORY SCAN	Stores a snapshot copy of the system or local database directory in memory.
GET NEXT DATABASE DIRECTORY ENTRY	Retrieves an entry from the copy of the database directory that was placed in memory by the OPEN DATABASE DIRECTORY SCAN function.
CLOSE DATABASE DIRECTORY SCAN	Frees system resources allocated by the OPEN DATABASE DIRECTORY SCAN function.
CATALOG NODE	Stores information about a remote workstation in the node directory.
UNCATALOG NODE	Removes information about a remote workstation from the node directory.
OPEN NODE DIRECTORY SCAN	Stores a snapshot copy of the node directory in memory.
GET NEXT NODE DIRECTORY ENTRY	Retrieves an entry from the copy of the node directory that was placed in memory by the OPEN NODE DIRECTORY SCAN function.
CLOSE NODE DIRECTORY SCAN	Frees system resources allocated by the OPEN NODE DIRECTORY SCAN function.
CATALOG DCS DATABASE	Stores information about a DRDA database in the DCS directory.
UNCATALOG DCS DATABASE	Removes information about a DRDA database from the DCS directory.
OPEN DCS DIRECTORY SCAN	Returns the number of entries found in the DCS directory.
GET DCS DIRECTORY ENTRIES	Copies entries in the DCS directory to a user-allocated memory storage area.
GET DCS DIRECTORY ENTRY FOR DATABASE	Retrieves an entry from the copy of the DCS directory that was placed in memory by the GET DCS DIRECTORY ENTRIES function.
CLOSE DCS DIRECTORY SCAN	Frees system resources allocated by the OPEN DCS DIRECTORY SCAN function.
REGISTER	Registers a DB2 database server at a Novell NetWare file server registry.
DEREGISTER	Removes a DB2 database server from a Novell NetWare file server registry.

The System Database Directory

Whenever a database is cataloged, an entry containing information that DB2 needs to establish a connection to the database is stored in the system database directory. Think of this directory as the master directory for a DB2 workstation because it contains one entry for each local and remote cataloged database that can be accessed by that workstation.

Databases are implicitly cataloged in this directory when the CREATE DATABASE function or command is executed. You can explicitly catalog new databases and aliases for existing databases in this directory by calling the CATALOG DATABASE function in an application or by issuing the CATALOG DATABASE command from the DB2 command-line processor. You can remove (uncatalog) entries from this directory when they are no longer valid (or needed) by calling the UNCATALOG DATABASE function in an application or by issuing the UNCATALOG DATABASE command from the DB2 command-line processor. You can retrieve entries in this directory by calling the OPEN DATABASE DIRECTORY SCAN, GET NEXT DATABASE DIRECTORY ENTRY, and CLOSE DATABASE DIRECTORY SCAN functions from within an application program.

Volume Directories

In addition to the system database directory, a volume directory exists on every logical disk drive available on a workstation that contains one or more DB2 databases. The number of volume database directories that exist on a workstation is determined by the number of logical disk drives on that workstation that contain one or more DB2 databases. A volume directory contains one entry for each database physically stored on the logical disk drive.

Volume directories are automatically created the first time a database is created on a logical disk drive, and DB2 updates their contents (with implicit CATALOG and UNCATALOG commands) each time a database creation or deletion event occurs. You can explicitly catalog or uncatalog new databases and aliases for existing databases in a volume directory the same way you would explicitly catalog and uncatalog them in the system directory. Likewise, you can retrieve entries stored in a volume directory the same way you would entries in the system directory. However, the actual volume database directory where entries are to be added, deleted, or retrieved must be specified in the CATALOG DATABASE, UNCATALOG DATABASE, and OPEN DATABASE DIRECTORY function calls.

The Workstation (Node) Directory

The workstation or node directory contains one entry for each remote database server workstation that can be accessed. Entries in the workstation directory are used in conjunction with entries in the system directory for making connections to remote DB2 for Common Servers database servers. Entries in the workstation directory are also used in conjunction with entries in the database connection services directory for making connections to host (MVS, AS/400, etc.) database servers. You can explicitly catalog new workstation nodes in this directory by calling the CATALOG NODE function in an application or by issuing the CATALOG NODE command from the DB2 command-line processor. You can uncatalog node directory entries when they are no longer valid (or needed) by calling the UNCATALOG NODE function in an application or by issuing the UNCATALOG NODE command from the DB2 command-line processor. You can retrieve entries in this directory by calling the OPEN NODE DIRECTORY SCAN, GET NEXT NODE DIRECTORY ENTRY, and CLOSE NODE DIRECTORY SCAN functions from within an application program.

The Database Connection Services (DCS) Directory

A database connection services (DCS) directory exists only if the distributed database connection services (DDCS) product is installed on the workstation. This directory contains one entry for each host (MVS, AS/400, etc.) database that DB2 can access via the DDCS distributed database relational architecture (DRDA) services. You can explicitly catalog new DCS databases in this directory by calling the CATALOG DCS DATABASE function in an application or by issuing the CATALOG DCS DATABASE command from the DB2 command-line processor. You can remove entries from this directory when they are no longer valid (or needed) by calling the UNCATALOG DCS DATABASE function in an application or by issuing the UNCATALOG DCS DATABASE command from the DB2 command-line processor. You can retrieve an entry in this database directory by calling the OPEN DCS DIRECTORY SCAN, GET DCS DIRECTORY ENTRIES, the GET DCS DIRECTORY ENTRY FOR DATABASE, and CLOSE DCS DIRECTORY SCAN functions from within an application program.

Registering/Deregistering DB2 Database Servers with NetWare

As long as DB2 database servers are serving clients in an environment that uses the communications manager to handle network processing, server workstations are always visible to their clients. If Novell NetWare handles the network processing, a DB2 server must be made visible to the network registry before clients can access it. You can add DB2 servers to a Novell NetWare registry by calling the REGISTER function in an application or by issuing the REGISTER command from the DB2 command-line processor. You can remove DB2 servers from a NetWare registry by calling the DEREGISTER function in an application or by issuing the DEREGISTER command from the DB2 command-line processor.

CATALOG DATABASE

Purpose

The CATALOG DATABASE function stores information about a database in the system database directory.

Syntax

```
SQL_API_RC SQL_API_FN sqlectdd (char            *DBName,
                                char            *DBAlias,
                                unsigned char   Type,
                                char            *NodeName,
                                char            *Path,
                                char            *Comment,
                                unsigned short  Authentication,
                                struct sqlca    *SQLCA);
```

Parameters

DBName A pointer to a location in memory where the name of the database is stored.

DBAlias A pointer to a location in memory where the alias name of the database is stored.

Type A single character that designates whether the database is local (indirect), remote, or accessed via the distributed computing environment (DCE). This parameter can be set to any of the following values:

- SQL_INDIRECT Specifies that the database is local (i.e., that it resides at the same location as the DB2 database manager instance).
- SQL_REMOTE Specifies that the database resides at another instance.
- SQL_DCE Specifies that the database is accessed via DCE.

NodeName A pointer to the location in memory that contains the name of the node where the database physically resides (if the database being cataloged is not a local database).

Path A pointer to a location in memory where the letter of the drive (OS/2) or the name of the path (AIX) on which the database being cataloged resides (if the database being cataloged is a local database).

Comment A pointer to a location in memory where a description of the database is stored. If this parameter contains a NULL value, no comment will be stored in the database directory for the database.

Authentication Specifies where user authentication is to occur. Authentication is the process by which DB2 verifies that database users are who they claim to be. This parameter can be set to any of the following values:

SQL_AUTHENTICATION_SERVER	Specifies that user authentication is to take place on the node containing the database.
SQL_AUTHENTICATION_CLIENT	Specifies that user authentication is to takes place on the node where applications that access the cataloged database are invoked.
SQL_AUTHENTICATION_DCS	Specifies that user authentication is to take place on the node containing the database, except when DDCS is used (when the DRDA AS option specifies that authentication is to takes place at the DRDA server).
SQL_AUTHENTICATION_NOT_SPEC	The location on which user authentication is to take place is not specified.

SQLCA A pointer to a location in memory where a SQL communication area (SQLCA) data structure variable is stored. This variable sends either status information (if the function executed successfully) or error information (if the function failed) back to the calling application.

Includes

```
#include <sqlenv.h>
```

Description

The CATALOG DATABASE function stores information about a database in the system database directory. This function can catalog databases that are physically located on either the same physical workstation as the DB2 database manager instance or on a different remote workstation node. It can also recatalog databases that, for some reason, have been uncataloged. This function can also catalog multiple aliases for a database regardless of its physical location.

DB2 automatically catalogs an entry in the local (volume) database directory and another entry in the system database directory whenever a new database is created. If a database is created from a remote client workstation (or from a client application executing from a different DB2 database manager instance on the same machine), an entry for the database will also be made in the system database directory stored at the client instance.

Comments

- The value specified for the *Path* parameter cannot exceed 215 characters in length. If a NULL value is specified for this parameter, the database path will default to the current value specified in the *dftdbpath* database manager configuration file parameter.
- The value specified for the *Comment* parameter cannot exceed 30 characters in length.
- You can call the CATALOG DATABASE function to recatalog a database that has been removed (uncataloged) from the system database directory, as long as the database has not been deleted (dropped).
- Access to all database objects depends on user authentication. The *Authentication* parameter should always be set to SQL_AUTHENTICA-

TION_NOT_SPEC, except when you are cataloging a database that resides on a DB2/2, version 1.x or a DB2/6000, version 1.x server.

- If a NULL pointer is specified for the both the *Path* and the *NodeName* parameters, DB2 will assume that the database is local and the location of the database is in the default path specified in the DB2 database manager configuration file.
- If a database is cataloged with the *Type* parameter set to SQL_INDIRECT, the value of the provided *Authentication* parameter will be ignored and the authentication value in the system database directory will be set to SQL_AUTHENTICATION_NOT_SPEC.
- Databases created at the current DB2 database manager instance (as defined by the value of the DB21NSTANCE environment variable) are cataloged as indirect (local). Databases created at other DB2 database manager instances are cataloged as remote (even if they physically reside on the same machine).
- The CATALOG DATABASE function will automatically create a system database directory if one does not already exist. On OS/2 and DOS, the system database directory is stored on the disk drive that contains the DB2 database manager instance currently being used. On AIX, the system database directory is stored in the directory where the DB2 product was installed.
- The system database directory is maintained outside of the database. Each entry in this directory contains the following information:
  –Database name
  –Database alias
  –Database comment (description)
  –Database entry type
  –Local database directory (if the database is a local database)
  –Node name (if the database is a remote database)
  –Authentication type
  –DB2 release (version) information
- You can use the OPEN DATABASE DIRECTORY SCAN, GET NEXT DATABASE DIRECTORY ENTRY, and CLOSE DATABASE DIRECTORY SCAN functions to list the contents of the system database directory. Together, these three function calls work like a SQL cursor because they use the OPEN/FETCH/CLOSE paradigm.
- If directory caching is enabled, database, node, and DCS directory files are cached in memory. An application's directory cache is created during the first directory lookup. Since the cache is refreshed only when an application modifies one of the directory files, directory changes made by other applications might not be effective until the application is restarted. To refresh DB2's shared cache (server only), an application should stop and then restart the database. To refresh an application's directory cache, the user should stop and then restart that application. For more information about directory caching, refer to the GET DATABASE MANAGER CONFIGURATION function.

Required Connection This function can be called at any time; a connection to a DB2 database manager instance or to a DB2 database does not have to be established first.

Authorization Only users with either system control (SYSCTRL) or system administrator (SYSADM) authority are allowed to execute this function call.

See Also

UNCATALOG DATABASE, OPEN DATABASE DIRECTORY SCAN, GET NEXT DATABASE DIRECTORY ENTRY, CLOSE DATABASE DIRECTORY SCAN

Example

The following C program illustrates how to use the CATALOG DATABASE function to catalog an alias for the SAMPLE database:

```
#include <stdio.h>
#include <stdlib.h>
#include <string.h>
#include <sqlenv.h>
#include <sqlca.h>

int main()
{
    /* Declare The Local Memory Variables */
    char          szDBName[9];
    char          szDBAlias[9];
    char          szComment[31];
    struct sqlca  sqlca;

    /* Initialize The Local Memory Variables */
    strcpy(szDBName, "SAMPLE");
    strcpy(szDBAlias, "SAMPLEDB");
    strcpy(szComment, "IBM Sample Database");

    /* Catalog A New Alias For The SAMPLE Database */
    sqlectdd(szDBName, szDBAlias, SQL_INDIRECT, NULL, NULL,
             szComment, SQL_AUTHENTICATION_NOT_SPEC, &sqlca);

    /* Display A Success Message */
    printf("The alias %s has been cataloged for the %s database.\n",
           szDBAlias, szDBName);

    /* Return To The Operating System */
    return(EXIT_SUCCESS);
}
```

UNCATALOG DATABASE

Purpose

The UNCATALOG DATABASE function deletes an entry from the system database directory.

Syntax

```
SQL_API_RC SQL_API_FN sqleuncd (char          *DBAlias,
                                struct sqlca *SQLCA);
```

Parameters

DBAlias A pointer to a location in memory where the alias name of the database to be uncataloged is stored.

SQLCA A pointer to a location in memory where a SQLCA data structure variable is stored. This variable sends either status information (if the function executed successfully) or error information (if the function failed) back to the calling application.

Includes

```
#include <sqlenv.h>
```

Description

The UNCATALOG DATABASE function deletes an entry from the system database directory. This function can delete only entries in the system database directory. Entries in the local (volume) database directory can be deleted only with the DROP DATABASE function.

Comments

- You can change the authentication type of a database, used for communicating with a down-level server, by first uncataloging the database and then cataloging it again with a different authentication type. Refer to the CATALOG DATABASE function for more information about authorization types.
- You can use the OPEN DATABASE DIRECTORY SCAN, GET NEXT DATABASE DIRECTORY ENTRY, and CLOSE DATABASE DIRECTORY SCAN functions to list the contents of the system database directory. Together, these three function calls work like a SQL cursor because they use the OPEN/FETCH/CLOSE paradigm.
- If directory caching is enabled, database, node, and DCS directory files are cached in memory. An application's directory cache is created during the first directory lookup. Since the cache is refreshed only when an application modifies one of the directory files, directory changes made by other applications might not be effective until the application has been restarted. To refresh DB2's shared cache (server only), an application should stop and then restart the database. To refresh an application's directory cache, the user should stop and then restart that application. For more information about directory caching, refer to the GET DATABASE MANAGER CONFIGURATION function.

Required Connection

This function can be called at any time; a connection to a DB2 database manager instance or to a DB2 database does not have to be established first.

Authorization

Only users with either system control (SYSCTRL) authority or system administrator (SYSADM) authority can execute this function call.

See Also

CATALOG DATABASE, OPEN DATABASE DIRECTORY SCAN, GET NEXT DATABASE DIRECTORY ENTRY, CLOSE DATABASE DIRECTORY SCAN

Example

The following C program illustrates how the UNCATALOG DATABASE function removes an alias for the SAMPLE database from the system database directory:

```
#include <stdio.h>
#include <stdlib.h>
#include <string.h>
#include <sqlenv.h>
#include <sqlca.h>

int main()
{
    /* Declare The Local Memory Variables */
    char          szDBAlias[9];
    struct sqlca  sqlca;

    /* Initialize The Local Memory Variables */
    strcpy(szDBAlias, "SAMPLEDB");

    /* Uncatalog An Alias For The SAMPLE Database */
    sqleuncd(szDBAlias, &sqlca);
```

```
    /* Display A Success Message */
    printf("The alias %s has been uncataloged.\n", szDBAlias);

    /* Return To The Operating System */
    return(EXIT_SUCCESS);
}
```

CHANGE DATABASE COMMENT

Purpose

The CHANGE DATABASE COMMENT function adds or changes the comment (description) associated with a database that is cataloged in either the system database directory or the local (volume) database directory.

Syntax

```
SQL_API_RC SQL_API_FN sqledcgd (char          *DBAlias,
                                char          *Path,
                                char          *Comment,
                                struct sqlca *SQLCA);
```

Parameters

DBAlias A pointer to the location in memory that contains the alias name of the database whose comment is to be updated.

Path A pointer to a location in memory where the path on which the local database directory resides is stored. If the value specified for this parameter is NULL, the system database directory will be used.

Comment A pointer to a location in memory where descriptive information for the database is stored. This parameter can contain a NULL value.

SQLCA A pointer to a location in memory where a SQLCA data structure variable is stored. This variable sends either status information (if the function executed successfully) or error information (if the function failed) back to the calling application.

Includes

```
#include <sqlenv.h>
```

Description

The CHANGE DATABASE COMMENT function adds or changes the comment (description) associated with a database that was cataloged in either the system database directory or the local database directory. Only the comment associated with the database alias specified is modified by this function. Other entries in the system database directory or the local database directory that have the same database name but different aliases are not affected.

Comments

- The value specified for the *DBAlias* parameter cannot exceed eight characters in length.
- If a path name is specified in the *Path* parameter, the database alias specified in the *DBAlias* parameter must be cataloged in the local database directory. If no path name is specified, the database alias must be cataloged in the system database directory.
- The value specified for the *Comment* parameter cannot exceed 30 characters in length. If the *Comment* parameter is set to NULL, the database comment will be unchanged.
- If the *Comment* parameter contains comment text, the new comment text will replace any existing comment text when this function is executed. To modify an existing database comment, an application should perform the following steps:

1. Call the OPEN DATABASE DIRECTORY SCAN function.
2. Call the GET NEXT DATABASE DIRECTORY ENTRY function to retrieve the existing database comment.
3. Modify the retrieved comment.
4. Call the CLOSE DATABASE DIRECTORY SCAN function.
5. Call this function with the modified comment.

Required Connection This function can be called at any time; a connection to a DB2 database manager instance or to a DB2 database does not have to be established first.

Authorization Only users with either system control (SYSCTRL) authority or system administrator (SYSADM) authority are allowed to execute this function call.

See Also CREATE DATABASE, CATALOG DATABASE

Example The following C program illustrates how to use the CHANGE DATABASE COMMENT function to change the description (comment) associated with the SAMPLE database:

```
#include <stdio.h>
#include <stdlib.h>
#include <string.h>
#include <sqlenv.h>
#include <sqlca.h>

int main()
{
    /* Declare The Local Memory Variables */
    char          szDBAlias[9];
    char          szComment[31];
    struct sqlca  sqlca;

    /* Initialize The Local Memory Variables */
    strcpy(szDBAlias, "SAMPLE");
    strcpy(szComment, "DB2 V2.1.1 Sample Database");

    /* Change The Comment Associated With The SAMPLE Database */
    /* Alias                                                  */
    sqledcgd(szDBAlias, "", szComment, &sqlca);

    /* Display A Success Message */
    printf("The comment associated with the %s database alias has ",
           szDBAlias);
    printf("been changed.\n");

    /* Return To The Operating System */
    return(EXIT_SUCCESS);
}
```

OPEN DATABASE DIRECTORY SCAN

Purpose The OPEN DATABASE DIRECTORY SCAN function stores a copy of the system database directory or the local database directory in memory, and returns the number of entries found in the specified directory to the calling application.

Syntax

```
SQL_API_RC SQL_API_FN sqledosd (char           *Path,
                                unsigned short *Handle,
                                unsigned short *NumEntries,
                                struct sqlca   *SQLCA);
```

Parameters

Path A pointer to the location in memory that contains the path on which the local database directory resides. If the value specified for this parameter is NULL, the system database directory will be used.

Handle A pointer to a location in memory where this function stores a directory scan buffer identifier that will be used in subsequent GET NEXT DATABASE DIRECTORY ENTRY and CLOSE DATABASE DIRECTORY SCAN function calls.

NumEntries A pointer to a location in memory where this function stores the number of entries found in the specified database directory.

SQLCA A pointer to a location in memory where a SQLCA data structure variable is stored. This variable sends either status information (if the function executed successfully) or error information (if the function failed) back to the calling application.

Includes

```
#include <sqlenv.h>
```

Description

The OPEN DATABASE DIRECTORY SCAN function stores a copy of the system database directory or the local database directory in memory, and returns the number of entries found in the specified directory to the calling application. The copy of the database directory that is placed in memory represents a snapshot of the directory when the directory scan is opened. This copy is never updated, even if the directory itself changes.

This function is normally followed by one or more GET NEXT DATABASE DIRECTORY ENTRY functions calls and one CLOSE DATABASE DIRECTORY SCAN function call. Together, these three function calls work like an SQL cursor because they use the OPEN/FETCH/CLOSE paradigm. The memory buffer that stores the database directory data obtained by the directory scan is automatically allocated by this function. A pointer to that buffer (the buffer identifier) is stored in the *Handle* parameter. This identifier is then used by subsequent GET NEXT DATABASE DIRECTORY ENTRY and CLOSE DATABASE DIRECTORY SCAN function calls to access the memory buffer area.

Comments

- Multiple OPEN DATABASE DIRECTORY SCAN function calls can be issued against the same database directory. However, because the directory can change between each call, the directory entries copied into memory by each call might vary.
- An application can have up to eight database directory scans open at one time.

Required Connection

This function can be called at any time; a connection to a DB2 database manager instance or to a DB2 database does not have to be established first.

Authorization

No authorization is required to execute this function call.

See Also

CLOSE DATABASE DIRECTORY SCAN, GET NEXT DATABASE DIRECTORY ENTRY

Example

The following C program illustrates how to use the OPEN DATABASE DIRECTORY SCAN, GET NEXT DATABASE DIRECTORY ENTRY, and CLOSE DATABASE DIRECTORY SCAN functions to retrieve the entries in the system database directory:

```
#include <stdio.h>
#include <stdlib.h>
#include <string.h>
#include <sqlenv.h>
#include <sqlca.h>

int main()
{
    /* Declare The Local Memory Variables */
    int                rc = EXIT_SUCCESS;
    unsigned short     usHandle;
    unsigned short     usDBCount;
    struct sqledinfo   *DB_DirInfo = NULL;
    struct sqlca       sqlca;

    /* Open The Database Directory Scan */
    sqledops('0', &usHandle, &usDBCount, &sqlca);

    /* Scan The Database Directory Buffer And Retrieve All   */
    /* Database Names And Descriptions Stored There          */
    printf("Alias          Description\n");
    printf("---------------------------------------\n");
    for (;usDBCount != 0; usDBCount--)
        {

        /* Retrieve The Next Database Directory Entry */
        sqledgne(usHandle, &DB_DirInfo, &sqlca);

        /* Display The Retrieved Entry */
        printf("%.8s\t", DB_DirInfo->alias);
        printf("%.30s\n", DB_DirInfo->comment);
        }

    /* Close The Database Directory Scan And Free All Resources */
    /* Obtained By The Open Database Directory Scan API         */
    sqledcls(usHandle, &sqlca);

    /* Return To The Operating System */
    return(rc);
}
```

GET NEXT DATABASE DIRECTORY ENTRY

Purpose

The GET NEXT DATABASE DIRECTORY ENTRY function retrieves the next entry from the copy of the system database directory or the local database directory that was placed in memory by the OPEN DATABASE DIRECTORY SCAN function.

Syntax

```
SQL_API_RC SQL_API_FN sqledgne (unsigned short   Handle,
                                struct sqledinfo **DBDirEntry,
                                struct sqlca     *SQLCA);
```

Parameters

Handle The directory scan buffer identifier returned from the associated OPEN DATABASE DIRECTORY SCAN function.

DBDirEntry A pointer to the address of an *sqledinfo* structure where this function stores the database directory entry information retrieved.

SQLCA A pointer to a location in memory where a SQLCA data structure variable is stored. This variable sends either status information (if the function executed successfully) or error information (if the function failed) back to the calling application.

Includes

```
#include <sqlenv.h>
```

Description

The GET NEXT DATABASE DIRECTORY ENTRY function retrieves the next entry from the copy of the system database directory or the local database directory placed in memory by the OPEN DATABASE DIRECTORY SCAN function. The retrieved information is stored in a special structure, *sqledinfo*, that is defined in *sqlenv.h* as follows:

```
struct sqledinfo
{
char            alias[8];       /* The database alias (alternate) name     */
char            dbname[8];      /* The database name                       */
char            drive[215];     /* The path name (AIX) or the disk drive ID */
                                /* (OS/2) that specifies where the database */
                                /* resides. A value is returned for this    */
                                /* field only if the system database        */
                                /* directory was opened for scanning.       */
char            intname[8];     /* The subdirectory name where the database */
                                /* resides. A value is returned for this    */
                                /* field only if the local database         */
                                /* directory was opened for scanning.       */
char            nodename[8];    /* The name of the node where the database  */
                                /* is located. A value is returned for this */
                                /* field only if the database is a remote   */
                                /* database.                                */
char            dbtype[20];     /* DB2 database manager release             */
                                /* information                              */
char            comment[30];    /* The comment (description) that is        */
                                /* associated with the database             */
short           com_codepage;   /* The code page of comment. This field is  */
                                /* no longer used.                          */
char            type;           /* Indicates whether the database was       */
                                /* was created by the current instance      */
                                /* (SQL_INDIRECT), resides at a different   */
                                /* instance (SQL_REMOTE), resides on        */
                                /* this volume (SQL_HOME), or resides in    */
                                /* a DCE directory (SQL_DCE).               */
unsigned short  authentication; /* Indicates whether user ID and password   */
                                /* authentication occurs at the database    */
                                /* server workstation                       */
                                /* (SQL_AUTHENTICATION_SERVER),             */
                                /* at the client workstation                */
                                /* (SQL_AUTHENTICATION_CLIENT),             */
                                /* or at the DCS server                     */
                                /* (SQL_AUTHENTICATION_DCS)                 */
char            glbdbname[255]; /* The global name of the target database   */
                                /* in the DCE directory if the type field   */
                                /* of this structure is set to SQL_DCE      */
};
```

Comments

- All character fields in the database directory entry information buffer are right-padded with blanks.

- When this function is executed, the value in the *DBDirEntry* parameter points to the next database directory entry in the copy of the database directory that resides in memory. Each subsequent GET NEXT DATABASE DIRECTORY ENTRY function call obtains the database directory entry immediately following the current directory entry, unless there are no more directory entries to retrieve (in which case an error is returned).
- You can use the value stored in the *NumEntries* parameter after the OPEN DATABASE DIRECTORY SCAN function is executed to set up a loop that scans through the entire database directory by issuing GET NEXT DATABASE DIRECTORY ENTRY function calls, one at a time, until the number of calls issued equals the number of entries found in the directory.

Prerequisites The OPEN DATABASE DIRECTORY SCAN function must be executed before this function is called.

Required Connection This function can be called at any time; a connection to a DB2 database manager instance or to a DB2 database does not have to be established first.

Authorization No authorization is required to execute this function call.

See Also OPEN DATABASE DIRECTORY SCAN, CLOSE DATABASE DIRECTORY SCAN

Example See the example provided for the OPEN DATABASE DIRECTORY SCAN function in this chapter.

CLOSE DATABASE DIRECTORY SCAN

Purpose The CLOSE DATABASE DIRECTORY SCAN function frees system resources that were allocated by the OPEN DATABASE DIRECTORY SCAN function.

Syntax

```
SQL_API_RC SQL_API_FN sqledcls (unsigned short Handle,
                                struct sqlca   *SQLCA);
```

Parameters

Handle The directory scan buffer identifier returned from the associated OPEN DATABASE DIRECTORY SCAN function.

SQLCA A pointer to a location in memory where a SQLCA data structure variable is stored. This variable sends either status information (if the function executed successfully) or error information (if the function failed) back to the calling application.

Includes

```
#include <sqlenv.h>
```

Description The CLOSE DATABASE DIRECTORY SCAN function frees system resources that were allocated by the OPEN DATABASE DIRECTORY SCAN function.

Required Connection This function can be called at any time; a connection to a DB2 database manager instance or to a DB2 database does not have to be established first.

Authorization No authorization is required to execute this function call.

See Also OPEN DATABASE DIRECTORY SCAN, GET NEXT DATABASE DIRECTORY ENTRY

Example See the example provided for the OPEN DATABASE DIRECTORY SCAN function in this chapter.

CATALOG NODE

Purpose The CATALOG NODE function stores information about the location of another DB2 database manager instance and the associated communications protocol used to access that instance in the workstation node directory.

Syntax

```
SQL_API_RC SQL_API_FN sqlectnd (struct sqle_node_struct *NodeInfo,
                                void                    *ProtocolInfo,
                                struct sqlca            *SQLCA);
```

Parameters

NodeInfo A pointer to a *sqle_node_struct* structure that contains information about the node to be cataloged.

ProtocolInfo A pointer to the appropriate protocol information structure containing information about the communications protocol that will be used to access the specified node.

SQLCA A pointer to a location in memory where a SQLCA data structure variable is stored. This variable sends either status information (if the function executed successfully) or error information (if the function failed) back to the calling application.

Includes

```
#include <sqlenv.h>
```

Description The CATALOG NODE function stores information about the location of another DB2 database manger instance and the associated communications protocol used to access that instance in the workstation node directory. This information must be stored in the node directory before an application residing on one workstation can connect to a database residing on another workstation. This information is also necessary for attaching an application to another DB2 database manager instance.

Two special structures (*sqle_node_struct* and an appropriate protocol information structure) pass characteristics about a node to the DB2 database manager when this function is called. The first of these structures, *sqle_node_struct*, is defined in *sqlenv.h* as follows:

```
struct sqle_node_struct
{
unsigned short  struct_id;       /* A unique structure identifier value.   */
                                 /* This field must always be set to       */
                                 /* SQL_NODE_STR_ID.                       */
unsigned short  codepage;        /* Code page value used for the node      */
                                 /* comment                                */
char            comment[31];     /* Optional node comment                  */
char            nodename[9];     /* Node name                              */
unsigned char   protocol;        /* Indicates whether the protocol that    */
                                 /* communicates with the node is          */
                                 /* APPC (SQL_PROTOCOL_APPC),              */
```

```
                                          /* NetBIOS (SQL_PROTOCOL_NETB),              */
                                          /* APPN (SQL_PROTOCOL_APPN),                */
                                          /* TCP/IP (SQL_PROTOCOL_TCPIP),             */
                                          /* CPIC (SQL_PROTOCOL_CPIC),                */
                                          /* IPX/SPX (SQL_PROTOCOL_IPXSPX),           */
                                          /* LOCAL protocol for an instance on the    */
                                          /* same workstation (SQL_PROTOCOL_LOCAL),   */
                                          /* or a named pipe (SQL_PROTOCOL_NPIPE)     */
};
```

The second special structure used by this function, the protocol information structure, is determined by the type of communications protocol that is used to communicate with the cataloged node. This structure can be any of the following DB2-defined structures:

sqle_node_appc Advanced program-to-program communications (APPC) protocol
sqle_node_netb Network basic input/output system (NetBIOS) protocol
sqle_node_appc Advanced peer-to-peer networking (APPN) protocol
sqle_node_tcpip Transmission control protocol/internet protocol (TCP/IP) protocol
sqle_node_cpic Common programming interface communications (CPIC) protocol
sqle_node_ipxspx Internetwork packet exchange/sequenced packet exchange (IPX/SPX) protocol
sqle_node_local LOCAL protocol

The *sqle_node_appc* structure is defined in *sqlenv.h* as follows:

```
struct sqle_node_appc
{
char  local_lu[9];               /* The logical unit (SNA port) name used   */
                                 /* to establish the connection.            */
char  partner_lu[9];             /* The logical unit (SNA port) name at the */
                                 /* remote DB2 instance.                    */
char  mode[9];                   /* The name of the transmission mode to    */
                                 /* use. This field is usually set to       */
                                 /* SQLL0001.                               */
};
```

The *sqle_node_netb* structure is defined in *sqlenv.h* as follows:

```
struct sqle_node_netb
{
unsigned short  adapter;          /* The LAN adapter number. This parameter */
                                  /* can be set to any of the following     */
                                  /* values:                                */
                                  /* SQL_ADAPTER_0 (adapter number 0),      */
                                  /* SQL_ADAPTER_1 (adapter number 1),      */
                                  /* SQL_ADAPTER_MIN (the minimum           */
                                  /* adapter number), or                    */
                                  /* SQL_ADAPTER_MAX (the maximum           */
                                  /* adapter number.                        */
char            remote_nname[9];  /* The workstation name that is stored    */
                                  /* in the nname parameter of the          */
                                  /* database manager configuration file    */
                                  /* on the remote workstation.             */
                                  /* Note: This field must be either        */
                                  /* null-terminated or blank filled        */
                                  /* up to 9 characters.                    */
};
```

The *sqle_node_appn* structure is defined in *sqlenv.h* as follows:

```
struct sqle_node_appn
{
char   networkid[9];               /* The network ID                    */
char   remote_lu[9];               /* The logical unit (SNA port) name  */
                                   /* at the remote DB2 instance        */
char   local_lu[9];                /* The logical unit (SNA port) name  */
                                   /* used to establish the connection  */
char   mode[9];                    /* The name of the transmission mode */
                                   /* to use. This field is usually set */
                                   /* to SQLL0001.                      */
};
```

The *sqle_node_tcpip* structure is defined in *sqlenv.h* as follows:

```
struct sqle_node_tcpip
{
char   hostname[256];              /* The TCP/IP host name at the DB2 */
                                   /* instance (server)               */
char   service_name[15];           /* The TCP/IP service name of the  */
                                   /* DB2 instance (server)           */
};
```

The *sqle_node_cpic* structure is defined in *sqlenv.h* as follows:

```
struct sqle_node_cpic
{
char              sym_dest_name[9];   /* The symbolic destination name of   */
                                      /* the remote partner                 */
unsigned short    security_type;      /* The security type used. This field */
                                      /* can be set to                      */
                                      /* SQL_CPIC_SECURITY_NONE,            */
                                      /* SQL_CPIC_SECURITY_PROGRAM,         */
                                      /* or SQL_CPIC_SECURITY_SAME.         */
};
```

The *sqle_node_ipxspx* structure is defined in *sqlenv.h* as follows:

```
struct sqle_node_ipxspx
{
char   fileserver[49];             /* The NetWare file server name where */
                                   /* the DB2 server instance is         */
char   objectname[49];             /* registered The name of a particular */
                                   /* DB2 server instance that is stored */
                                   /* in the NetWare file server bindery */
};
```

The *sqle_node_local structure* is defined in *sqlenv.h* as follows:

```
struct sqle_node_local
{
char   instance_name[9];           /* The name of a DB2 database manager */
                                   /* instance                           */
};
```

Comments

- The CATALOG NODE function will automatically create a node directory if one does not already exist. On OS/2 and DOS, the node directory is stored on the disk drive that contains the DB2 database manager instance currently being used. On AIX, the node directory is stored in the directory where the DB2 product was installed.

- You can use the OPEN NODE DIRECTORY SCAN, GET NEXT NODE DIRECTORY ENTRY, and CLOSE NODE DIRECTORY SCAN functions to list the contents of the node directory. Together, these three function calls work like a SQL cursor because they use the OPEN/FETCH/CLOSE paradigm.
- If directory caching is enabled, database, node, and DCS directory files are cached in memory. An application's directory cache is created during the first directory lookup. Since the cache is refreshed only when an application modifies one of the directory files, directory changes made by other applications might not be effective until the application is restarted. To refresh DB2's shared cache (server only), an application should stop and then restart the database. To refresh an application's directory cache, the user should stop and then restart that application. For more information about directory caching, refer to the GET DATABASE MANAGER CONFIGURATION function.

Required Connection

This function can be called at any time; a connection to a DB2 database manager instance or to a DB2 database does not have to be established first.

Authorization

Only users with either system control (SYSCTRL) authority or system administrator (SYSADM) authority can execute this function call.

See Also

UNCATALOG NODE, OPEN NODE DIRECTORY SCAN, GET NEXT NODE DIRECTORY ENTRY, CLOSE NODE DIRECTORY SCAN

Example

The following C program illustrates how to use the CATALOG NODE function to catalog a remote workstation node:

```
#include <stdio.h>
#include <stdlib.h>
#include <string.h>
#include <sqlenv.h>
#include <sqlca.h>

int main()
{
    /* Declare The Local Memory Variables */
    struct sqle_node_struct  NodeInfo;
    struct sqle_node_netb    Protocol;
    struct sqlca             sqlca;

    /* Initialize The Node Information Data Structure */
    NodeInfo.struct_id = SQL_NODE_STR_ID;
    strcpy(NodeInfo.comment, "Test Database Server");
    strcpy(NodeInfo.nodename, "TESTSVR");
    NodeInfo.protocol = SQL_PROTOCOL_NETB;

    /* Initialize The NetBIOS Protocol Data Structure */
    Protocol.adapter = SQL_ADAPTER_0;
    strcpy(Protocol.remote_nname, "TESTSVR");

    /* Catalog A New Workstation Node */
    sqlectnd(&NodeInfo, (void *) &Protocol, &sqlca);
```

```
    /* Display A Success Message */
    printf("The node %s has been cataloged.\n", NodeInfo.nodename);

    /* Return To The Operating System */
    return(EXIT_SUCCESS);
}
```

UNCATALOG NODE

Purpose The UNCATALOG NODE function deletes an entry from the node directory.

Syntax

```
SQL_API_RC SQL_API_FN sqleuncn (char          *NodeName,
                                 struct sqlca *SQLCA);
```

Parameters

NodeName A pointer to a location in memory where the name of the node to be uncataloged is stored.

SQLCA A pointer to a location in memory where a SQLCA data structure variable is stored. This variable sends either status information (if the function executed successfully) or error information (if the function failed) back to the calling application.

Includes

```
#include <sqlenv.h>
```

Description The UNCATALOG NODE function deletes an entry from the node directory.

Comments

- You can call CATALOG NODE to recatalog a node that was removed (uncataloged) from the node directory.
- You can use the OPEN NODE DIRECTORY SCAN, GET NEXT NODE DIRECTORY ENTRY, and CLOSE NODE DIRECTORY SCAN functions to list the contents of the node directory. Together, these three function calls work like a SQL cursor because they use the OPEN/FETCH/CLOSE paradigm.
- If directory caching is enabled, database, node, and DCS directory files are cached in memory. An application's directory cache is created during the first directory lookup. Since the cache is refreshed only when an application modifies one of the directory files, directory changes made by other applications might not take effect until the application is restarted. To refresh DB2's shared cache (server only), an application should stop and then restart the database. To refresh an application's directory cache, the user should stop and then restart that application. For more information about directory caching, refer to the GET DATABASE MANAGER CONFIGURATION function.

Required Connection This function can be called at any time; a connection to a DB2 database manager instance or to a DB2 database does not have to be established first.

Authorization Only users with either system control (SYSCTRL) authority or system administrator (SYSADM) authority are allowed to execute this function call.

See Also CATALOG NODE, OPEN NODE DIRECTORY SCAN, GET NEXT NODE DIRECTORY ENTRY, CLOSE NODE DIRECTORY SCAN

Example

The following C program illustrates how to use the UNCATALOG NODE function to uncatalog a remote workstation node:

```
#include <stdio.h>
#include <stdlib.h>
#include <string.h>
#include <sqlenv.h>
#include <sqlca.h>

int main()
{
    /* Declare The Local Memory Variables */
    char            szNodeName[9];
    struct sqlca    sqlca;

    /* Initialize The Local Memory Variables */
    strcpy(szNodeName, "TESTSVR");

    /* Uncatalog The Specified Node Name */
    sqleuncn(szNodeName, &sqlca);

    /* Display A Success Message */
    printf("The node %s has been uncataloged.\n", szNodeName);

    /* Return To The Operating System */
    return(EXIT_SUCCESS);
}
```

OPEN NODE DIRECTORY SCAN

Purpose

The OPEN NODE DIRECTORY SCAN function stores a copy of the node directory in memory and returns the number of entries found in the node directory to the calling application.

Syntax

```
SQL_API_RC SQL_API_FN sqlenops (unsigned short *Handle,
                                unsigned short *NumEntries,
                                struct sqlca   *SQLCA);
```

Parameters

Handle A pointer to a location in memory where this function stores a directory scan buffer identifier that will be used in subsequent GET NEXT NODE DIRECTORY ENTRY and CLOSE NODE DIRECTORY SCAN function calls.

NumEntries A pointer to a location in memory where this function stores the number of entries found in the node directory.

SQLCA A pointer to a location in memory where a SQLCA data structure variable is stored. This variable sends either status information (if the function executed successfully) or error information (if the function failed) back to the calling application.

Includes

```
#include <sqlenv.h>
```

Description

The OPEN NODE DIRECTORY SCAN function stores a copy of the node directory in memory and returns the number of entries found in the node directory to the calling application. The copy of the node directory placed in memory represents a snapshot of the directory when the directory is opened. This copy is never updated, even if the directory itself changes.

This function is normally followed by one or more GET NEXT NODE DIRECTORY ENTRY functions calls and one CLOSE NODE DIRECTORY SCAN function call. Together, these three function calls work like a SQL cursor because they use the OPEN/FETCH/CLOSE paradigm. The memory buffer that stores the database directory data obtained by the directory scan is automatically allocated by this function. A pointer to that buffer (the buffer identifier) is stored in the *Handle* parameter. This identifier is then used by subsequent GET NEXT NODE DIRECTORY ENTRY and CLOSE NODE DIRECTORY SCAN function calls to access the memory buffer area.

Comments

- Multiple OPEN NODE DIRECTORY SCAN function calls can be issued against the same node directory. However, because the directory can change between each call, the directory entries copied into memory by each call might vary.
- An application can have up to eight node directory scans open at one time.

Required Connection

This function can be called at any time; a connection to a DB2 database manager instance or to a DB2 database does not have to be established first.

Authorization

No authorization is required to execute this function call.

See Also

GET NEXT NODE DIRECTORY ENTRY, CLOSE NODE DIRECTORY SCAN

Example

The following C program illustrates how to use the OPEN NODE DIRECTORY SCAN, GET NEXT NODE DIRECTORY ENTRY, and CLOSE NODE DIRECTORY SCAN functions to retrieve the entries in the node directory:

```
#include <stdio.h>
#include <stdlib.h>
#include <string.h>
#include <sqlenv.h>
#include <sqlca.h>

int main()
{
    /* Declare The Local Memory Variables */
    int                  rc = EXIT_SUCCESS;
    unsigned short       usHandle;
    unsigned short       usNodeCount;
    struct sqleninfo     *Node_DirInfo = NULL;
    struct sqlca         sqlca;

    /* Open The Node Directory Scan */
    sqlenops(&usHandle, &usNodeCount, &sqlca);

    /* Scan The Node Directory Buffer And Retrieve All Node */
    /* Names And Descriptions Stored There                  */
    printf("Node Name        Description\n");
    printf("-----------------------------------\n");
    for (;usNodeCount != 0; usNodeCount--)
        {
```

```
            /* Retrieve The Next Node Directory Entry */
            sqlengne(usHandle, &Node_DirInfo, &sqlca);

            /* Display The Retrieved Entry */
            printf("%.8s\t", Node_DirInfo->nodename);
            printf("%.30s\n", Node_DirInfo->comment);
            }

        /* Close The Node Directory Scan And Free All Resources */
        /* Obtained By The Open Node Directory Scan API         */
        sqlencls(usHandle, &sqlca);

        /* Return To The Operating System */
        return(rc);
    }
```

GET NEXT NODE DIRECTORY ENTRY

Purpose

The GET NEXT NODE DIRECTORY ENTRY function retrieves the next entry from the copy of the node directory that was placed in memory by the OPEN NODE DIRECTORY SCAN function.

Syntax

```
SQL_API_RC SQL_API_FN sqlengne (unsigned short   Handle,
                                struct sqleninfo **NodeDirEntry,
                                struct sqlca      *SQLCA);
```

Parameters

Handle The directory scan buffer identifier returned from the associated OPEN NODE DIRECTORY SCAN function.

NodeDirEntry A pointer to the address of an *sqleninfo* structure where this function stores the node directory entry information retrieved.

SQLCA A pointer to a location in memory where a SQLCA data structure variable is stored. This variable sends either status information (if the function executed successfully) or error information (if the function failed) back to the calling application.

Includes

```
#include <sqlenv.h>
```

Description

The GET NEXT NODE DIRECTORY ENTRY function retrieves the next entry from the copy of the node directory that was placed in memory by the OPEN NODE DIRECTORY SCAN function. The retrieved information is stored in a special structure, *sqleninfo*, that is defined in *sqlenv.h* as follows:

```
struct sqleninfo
{
char            nodename[8];      /* Node name                               */
char            local_lu[8];      /* The logical unit (SNA port)             */
                                  /* name used to establish the connection   */
char            partner_lu[8];    /* The logical unit (SNA port) name at     */
                                  /* the remote DB2 database manager         */
                                  /* instance                                */
char            mode[8];          /* The name of the transmission service    */
                                  /* mode used                               */
char            comment[30];      /* Optional node comment                   */
unsigned short  com_codepage;     /* Code page value used for the node       */
                                  /* comment                                 */
unsigned short  adapter;          /* The NetBIOS LAN adapter number          */
```

```
char            networkid[8];       /* The APPN network ID                   */
char            protocol;           /* Identifies the protocol that is used  */
                                    /* to communicate with the node. This    */
                                    /* field can be set to                   */
                                    /* SQL_PROTOCOL_APPC, SQL_PROTOCOL_NETB, */
                                    /* SQL_PROTOCOL_APPN, SQL_PROTOCOL_TCPIP, */
                                    /* SQL_PROTOCOL_CPIC,                    */
                                    /* SQL_PROTOCOL_IPXSPX,                  */
                                    /* SQL_PROTOCOL_LOCAL, or                */
                                    /* SQL_PROTOCOL_NPIPE.                   */
char            sym_dest_name[8];   /* The CPIC symbolic destination name of */
                                    /* the remote partner                    */
unsigned short  security_type;      /* The CPIC security type. This field    */
                                    /* can be set to                         */
                                    /* SQL_CPIC_SECURITY_NONE,               */
                                    /* SQL_CPIC_SECURITY_PROGRAM,            */
                                    /* or SQL_CPIC_SECURITY_SAME.            */
char            hostname[255];      /* The TCP/IP host name at the DB2       */
                                    /* database manager instance (server)    */
char            service_name[14];   /* The TCP/IP service name of the DB2    */
                                    /* database manager instance (server)    */
char            fileserver[48];     /* The NetWare file server name where    */
                                    /* the DB2 server instance is            */
                                    /* registered                            */
char            objectnamc[48];     /* The name of a particular DB2 database */
                                    /* manager instance (server) that is     */
                                    /* stored in the Novell NetWare file     */
                                    /* server bindery                        */
char            instance_name[8];   /* The LOCAL name of a DB2 database      */
                                    /* manager instance                      */
};
```

Comments

- All character fields in the node directory entry information buffer are right-padded with blanks.
- When this function is executed, the value in the *NodeDirEntry* parameter points to the next node directory entry in the copy of the node directory that resides in memory. Each subsequent GET NEXT NODE DIRECTORY ENTRY function call obtains the node directory entry immediately following the current directory entry, unless there are no more directory entries to retrieve (in which case an error is returned).
- You can use the value stored in the *NumEntries* parameter after the OPEN NODE DIRECTORY SCAN function is executed to set up a loop that scans through the entire node directory by issuing GET NEXT NODE DIRECTORY ENTRY function calls, one at a time, until the number of calls issued equals the number of entries found in the directory.

Prerequisites

The OPEN NODE DIRECTORY SCAN function must be executed before this function is called.

Required Connection

This function can be called at any time; a connection to a DB2 database manager instance or to a DB2 database does not have to be established first.

Authorization

No authorization is required to execute this function call.

See Also

OPEN NODE DIRECTORY SCAN, CLOSE NODE DIRECTORY SCAN

Example See the example provided for the OPEN NODE DIRECTORY SCAN function in this chapter.

CLOSE NODE DIRECTORY SCAN

Purpose The CLOSE NODE DIRECTORY SCAN function frees resources that were allocated by the OPEN NODE DIRECTORY SCAN function.

Syntax

```
SQL_API_RC SQL_API_FN sqlencls (unsigned short Handle,
                                struct sqlca   *SQLCA);
```

Parameters

Handle The directory scan buffer identifier returned from the associated OPEN NODE DIRECTORY SCAN function.

SQLCA A pointer to a location in memory where a SQLCA data structure variable is stored. This variable sends either status information (if the function executed successfully) or error information (if the function failed) back to the calling application.

Includes

```
#include <sqlenv.h>
```

Description The CLOSE NODE DIRECTORY SCAN function frees resources that were allocated by the OPEN NODE DIRECTORY SCAN function.

Required Connection This function can be called at any time; a connection to a DB2 database manager instance or to a DB2 database does not have to be established first.

Authorization No authorization is required to execute this function call.

See Also OPEN NODE DIRECTORY SCAN, GET NEXT NODE DIRECTORY ENTRY

Example See the example provided for the OPEN NODE DIRECTORY SCAN function in this chapter.

CATALOG DCS DATABASE

Purpose The CATALOG DCS DATABASE function stores information about a distributed relational database architecture (DRDA) database in the database connection services (DCS) directory.

Syntax

```
SQL_API_RC SQL_API_FN sqlegdad (struct sql_dir_entry *DCSDirEntry,
                                struct sqlca         *SQLCA);
```

Parameters

DCSDirEntry A pointer to a *sql_dir_entry* structure that contains information about the DCS database to be cataloged.

SQLCA A pointer to a location in memory where a SQLCA data structure variable is stored. This variable sends either status information (if the function executed successfully) or error information (if the function failed) back to the calling application.

Includes

```
#include <sqlenv.h>
```

Description

The CATALOG DCS DATABASE function stores information about a DRDA database in the DCS directory. These databases are accessed through an application requester, such as IBM's distributed database connection services (DDCS) product. When a DCS directory entry with a database name that matches a database name in the system database directory exists, the application requester associated with the DCS database forwards all SQL requests made against the database to the remote server where the database physically resides.

A special structure, *sql_dir_entry*, passes characteristics about a DCS database to the DB2 database manager when this function is called. The *sql_dir_entry* structure is defined in *sqlenv.h* as follows:

```
struct sql_dir_entry
{
unsigned short  struct_id;    /* The structure identifier. This field must */
                              /* always be set to SQL_DCS_STR_ID.          */
unsigned short  release;      /* Release level of the DCS database entry   */
unsigned short  codepage;     /* Code page value used for the DCS          */
                              /* database comment                          */
char            comment[31];  /* Optional DCS database comment             */
char            ldb[9];       /* Local database name                       */
char            tdb[19];      /* Actual host database name                 */
char            ar[9];        /* Application client library name           */
char            parm[513];    /* Transaction program prefix, transaction   */
                              /* program name, SQLCODE mapping file        */
                              /* name, disconnect option, and security     */
                              /* option                                    */
};
```

Note: Each character field in this structure must be either null-terminated or blank filled up to the specified length of the field.

Comments

- The CATALOG DCS DATABASE function will automatically create a DCS directory if one does not already exist. On OS/2 and DOS, the DCS directory is stored on the disk drive that contains the DB2 database manager instance currently being used. On AIX, the DCS directory is stored in the directory where the DB2 product was installed.
- The DCS directory is maintained outside of the database.
- If a database is cataloged in the DCS directory, it must also be cataloged as a remote database in the system database directory.
- You can use the OPEN DCS DIRECTORY SCAN, GET DCS DIRECTORY ENTRIES, GET DCS DIRECTORY ENTRY FOR DATABASE, and CLOSE DCS DIRECTORY SCAN functions to obtain information about entry in the DCS directory.
- If directory caching is enabled, database, node, and DCS directory files are cached in memory. An application's directory cache is created during the first directory lookup. Since the cache is refreshed only when an application modifies one of the directory files, directory changes made by other applications might not take effect until the application is restarted. To refresh DB2's shared cache (server only), an application should stop

and then restart the database. To refresh an application's directory cache, the user should stop and then restart that application. For more information about directory caching, refer to the GET DATABASE MANAGER CONFIGURATION function.

- IBM's DDCS product provides connections to DRDA application servers such as:
  –Database 2 (DB2) for MVS on System/370 and System/390 architecture host computers.
  –Structured query language/data system (SQL/DS) on System/370 and System/390 architecture host computers.
  –OS/400 on Application System/400 (AS/400) host computers.

Required Connection This function can be called at any time; a connection to a DB2 database manager instance or to a DB2 database does not have to be established first.

Authorization Only users with either system control (SYSCTRL) authority or system administrator (SYSADM) authority are allowed to execute this function call.

See Also UNCATALOG DCS DATABASE

Example The following C program illustrates how the CATALOG DCS DATABASE function catalogs an alias for a DCS database:

```
#include <stdio.h>
#include <stdlib.h>
#include <string.h>
#include <sqlenv.h>
#include <sqlca.h>

int main()
{
    /* Declare The Local Memory Variables */
    struct sql_dir_entry  DCSInfo;
    struct sqlca          sqlca;

    /* Initialize The DCS Information Data Structure */
    DCSInfo.struct_id = SQL_DCS_STR_ID;
    strcpy(DCSInfo.comment, "DB2 For MVS Database");
    strcpy(DCSInfo.ldb, "SAMPLEDB");
    strcpy(DCSInfo.tdb, "SAMPLE");

    /* Catalog A DCS Database */
    sqlegdad(&DCSInfo, &sqlca);

    /* Display A Success Message */
    printf("The DCS database %s has been cataloged.\n", DCSInfo.ldb);

    /* Return To The Operating System */
    return(EXIT_SUCCESS);
}
```

UNCATALOG DCS DATABASE

Purpose The UNCATALOG DCS DATABASE function deletes an entry from the DCS directory.

Syntax

```
SQL_API_RC SQL_API_FN sqlegdel (struct sql_dir_entry *DCSDirEntry,
                                struct sqlca         *SQLCA);
```

Parameters

DCSDirEntry A pointer to a *sql_dir_entry* structure that contains information about the DCS database to be uncataloged.

SQLCA A pointer to a location in memory where a SQLCA data structure variable is stored. This variable sends either status information (if the function executed successfully) or error information (if the function failed) back to the calling application.

Includes

```
#include <sqlenv.h>
```

Description

The UNCATALOG DCS DATABASE function deletes an entry from the DCS directory. Before this function can be executed, a special structure (*sql_dir_entry*) must contain information about the DCS database to be uncataloged. Refer to the CATALOG DCS DATABASE function for a detailed description of this structure. Only two fields of this structure are used by the UNCATALOG DCS DATABASE function: *struct_id* and *ldb*. The database name stored in the *ldb* field of this structure specifies the local name of the DRDA database to be uncataloged.

Comments

- A DCS database should always be cataloged in the system database directory as a remote database. When a DCS database is uncataloged, its corresponding entry in the system database directory should be uncataloged (with the UNCATALOG DATABASE function).
- You can use the OPEN DCS DIRECTORY SCAN, GET DCS DIRECTORY ENTRIES, GET DCS DIRECTORY ENTRY FOR DATABASE, and CLOSE DCS DIRECTORY SCAN functions to obtain information about an entry in the DCS directory.
- If directory caching is enabled, database, node, and DCS directory files are cached in memory. An application's directory cache is created during the first directory lookup. Since the cache is refreshed only when an application modifies one of the directory files, directory changes made by other applications might not be effective until the application is restarted. To refresh DB2's shared cache (server only), an application should stop and then restart the database. To refresh an application's directory cache, the user should stop and then restart that application. For more information about directory caching, refer to the GET DATABASE MANAGER CONFIGURATION function.

Required Connection

This function can be called at any time; a connection to a DB2 database manager instance or to a DB2 database does not have to be established first.

Authorization

Only users with either system control (SYSCTRL) authority or system administrator (SYSADM) authority can execute this function call.

See Also

CATALOG DCS DATABASE, OPEN DCS DIRECTORY SCAN, GET DCS DIRECTORY ENTRIES, GET DCS DIRECTORY ENTRY FOR DATABASE, CLOSE DCS DIRECTORY SCAN, UNCATALOG DATABASE

Example

The following C program illustrates how the UNCATALOG DCS DATABASE function uncatalogs an alias for a DCS database:

```
#include <stdio.h>
#include <stdlib.h>
#include <string.h>
#include <sqlenv.h>
#include <sqlca.h>

int main()
{
    /* Declare The Local Memory Variables */
    struct sql_dir_entry  DCSInfo;
    struct sqlca          sqlca;

    /* Initialize The DCS Information Data Structure */
    DCSInfo.struct_id = SQL_DCS_STR_ID;
    strcpy(DCSInfo.ldb, "SAMPLEDB");

    /* Uncatalog The Specified DCS Database */
    sqlegdel(&DCSInfo, &sqlca);

    /* Display A Success Message */
    printf("The DCS database %s has been uncataloged.\n",
           DCSInfo.ldb);

    /* Return To The Operating System */
    return(EXIT_SUCCESS);
}
```

OPEN DCS DIRECTORY SCAN

Purpose The OPEN DCS DIRECTORY SCAN function returns the number of entries found in the DCS directory to the calling application.

Syntax

```
SQL_API_RC SQL_API_FN sqlegdsc (short         *NumEntries,
                                struct sqlca *SQLCA);
```

Parameters

NumEntries A pointer to a location in memory where this function is to store the number of entries found in the DCS directory.

SQLCA A pointer to a location in memory where a SQLCA data structure variable is stored. This variable sends either status information (if the function executed successfully) or error information (if the function failed) back to the calling application.

Includes

```
#include <sqlenv.h>
```

Description The OPEN DCS DIRECTORY SCAN function returns the number of entries found in the DCS directory to the calling application. An application should use this number to determine the amount of memory it needs to allocate in order to retrieve information about each DCS directory entry. Once the correct amount of memory is allocated, you can use the GET DCS DIRECTORY ENTRIES function along with GET DCS DIRECTORY ENTRY FOR DATABASE to retrieve information about each entry stored in the DCS directory.

Required Connection This function can be called at any time; a connection to a DB2 database manager instance or to a DB2 database does not have to be established first.

Authorization

No authorization is required to execute this function call.

See Also

CLOSE DCS DIRECTORY SCAN, GET DCS DIRECTORY ENTRIES, GET DCS DIRECTORY ENTRY FOR DATABASE

Example

The following C program illustrates how to use the OPEN DCS DIRECTORY SCAN, GET DCS DIRECTORY ENTRIES, GET DCS DIRECTORY ENTRY FOR DATABASE, and CLOSE DCS DIRECTORY SCAN functions to retrieve the DCS directory entry for a specified database:

```
#include <stdio.h>
#include <stdlib.h>
#include <string.h>
#include <sqlenv.h>
#include <sqlca.h>

int main()
{
    /* Declare The Local Memory Variables */
    int                    rc = EXIT_SUCCESS;
    short                  sDCSCount;
    struct sql_dir_entry   *DCS_DirInfo = NULL;
    struct sqlca           sqlca;

    /* Open The DCS Directory Scan */
    sqlegdsc(&sDCSCount, &sqlca);

    /* Copy The DCS Directory Entries Into A User-Allocated Memory */
    /* Storage Buffer                                              */
    DCS_DirInfo = (struct sql_dir_entry *)
                  malloc(sDCSCount * sizeof(struct sql_dir_entry));
    sqlegdgt(&sDCSCount, DCS_DirInfo, &sqlca);

    /* Initialize The DCS Information Data Structure */
    DCS_DirInfo->struct_id = SQL_DCS_STR_ID;
    strcpy(DCS_DirInfo->ldb, "SAMPLEDB");

    /* Retrieve The DCS Directory Entry For The Specified DCS */
    /* Database From The Memory Storage Buffer                */
    sqlegdge(DCS_DirInfo, &sqlca);

    /* Display The Retrieved DCS Directory Entry */
    printf("DCS Database Name   Database Name   Description\n");
    printf("------------------------------------------------");
    printf("--------\n");
    printf("%.8s            ", DCS_DirInfo->ldb);
    printf("%.8s           ", DCS_DirInfo->tdb);
    printf("%.30s\n", DCS_DirInfo->comment);

    /* Close The DCS Directory Scan And Free The User-Allocated */
    /* Memory Storage Buffer                                     */
    sqlegdcl(&sqlca);
    free(DCS_DirInfo);

    /* Return To The Operating System */
    return(rc);
}
```

GET DCS DIRECTORY ENTRIES

Purpose

The GET DCS DIRECTORY ENTRIES function transfers a copy of the DCS directory entries to a user-allocated memory buffer supplied by the calling application.

Syntax

```
SQL_API_RC SQL_API_FN sqlegdgt (short                   *NumEntries,
                                struct sql_dir_entry *DCSDirEntries,
                                struct sqlca          *SQLCA);
```

Parameters

NumEntries A pointer to a location in memory where the number of *sql_dir_entry* structures in the user-allocated memory buffer is stored. When this function is executed, the number of entries actually copied from the DCS directory to the user-allocated memory buffer is stored in the location referred to by this parameter.

DCSDirEntries A pointer to an array of *sql_dir_entry* structures where this function is to copy the collected DCS directory entry information.

SQLCA A pointer to a location in memory where a SQLCA data structure variable is stored. This variable sends either status information (if the function executed successfully) or error information (if the function failed) back to the calling application.

Includes

```
#include <sqlenv.h>
```

Description

The GET DCS DIRECTORY ENTRIES function transfers a copy of the DCS directory entries to a user-allocated memory buffer. Before this function is executed, a memory storage buffer containing an array of a *sql_dir_entry* structures must first be allocated. Refer to the CATALOG DCS DATABASE function for a detailed description of this structure. You can determine the size of this memory storage buffer by multiplying the number of entries found in the DCS directory by the OPEN DCS DIRECTORY SCAN function by the size of a *sql_dir_entry* structure.

Once the memory buffer is allocated, the number of DCS directory entries that the buffer can hold (the number of elements in the array of *sql_dir_entry* structures) must be stored in the *NumEntries* parameter. When this function is executed, the number of DCS directory entries actually copied to the memory storage buffer is returned in the NumEntries parameter. By comparing the "before" function call and "after" function call values of this parameter, an application can determine whether or not all DCS directory entries were copied to the storage buffer area.

Comments

- If this function is executed when a copy of the DCS directory entries is already in memory, the previous copy will be released and a new copy of DCS directory entries will be collected.
- If all DCS directory entries are copied to the user-allocated memory storage area, the DCS directory scan will automatically be closed and all resources allocated by the OPEN DCS DIRECTORY SCAN function will be released.
- If one or more DCS directory entries were not copied to the user-allocated memory storage area, you can make subsequent calls to this function to copy them.
- If the DCS directory entries not copied to the user-allocated memory storage area are not needed, you can call the CLOSE DCS DIRECTORY SCAN function to free system resources that were allocated by the OPEN DCS DIRECTORY SCAN function.

Prerequisites The OPEN DCS DIRECTORY SCAN function should be executed before this function is called so the calling application can allocate a memory storage buffer that is large enough to hold the entries stored in the DCS directory.

Required Connection This function can be called at any time; a connection to a DB2 database manager instance or to a DB2 database does not have to be established first.

Authorization No authorization is required to execute this function call.

See Also OPEN DCS DIRECTORY SCAN, GET DCS DIRECTORY ENTRY FOR DATABASE, CLOSE DCS DIRECTORY SCAN

Example See the example provided for the OPEN DCS DIRECTORY SCAN function in this chapter.

GET DCS DIRECTORY ENTRY FOR DATABASE

Purpose The GET DCS DIRECTORY ENTRY FOR DATABASE function retrieves an entry for a specified database from the copy of the DCS directory that was placed in memory by the GET DCS DIRECTORY ENTRIES function.

Syntax

```
SQL_API_RC SQL_API_FN sqlegdge (struct sql_dir_entry *DCSDirEntry,
                                struct sqlca         *SQLCA);
```

Parameters

DCSDirEntry A pointer to a *sql_dir_entry* structure where this function is to store the retrieved DCS directory entry information.

SQLCA A pointer to a location in memory where a SQLCA data structure variable is stored. This variable sends either status information (if the function executed successfully) or error information (if the function failed) back to the calling application.

Includes

```
#include <sqlenv.h>
```

Description The GET DCS DIRECTORY ENTRY FOR DATABASE function retrieves an entry for a specified database from the copy of the DCS directory that was placed in memory by the GET DCS DIRECTORY ENTRIES function. The retrieved information is stored in a special structure, *sql_dir_entry*, that is defined in *sqlenv.h*. Refer to the CATALOG DCS DATABASE function for a detailed description of this structure.

Before this function is executed, the local name of the database whose DCS directory entry is to be retrieved must be placed in the *ldb* field of the *sql_dir_entry* structure. The remaining fields of this structure are filled in when this function executes.

Required Connection This function can be called at any time; a connection to a DB2 database manager instance or to a DB2 database does not have to be established first.

Authorization No authorization is required to execute this function call.

See Also CATALOG DCS DATABASE, UNCATALOG DCS DATABASE, OPEN DCS DIRECTORY SCAN, GET DCS DIRECTORY ENTRIES, CLOSE DCS DIRECTORY SCAN

Example See the example provided for the OPEN DCS DIRECTORY SCAN function in this chapter.

CLOSE DCS DIRECTORY SCAN

Purpose The CLOSE DCS DIRECTORY SCAN function frees resources that were allocated by the OPEN DCS DIRECTORY SCAN function.

Syntax

```
SQL_API_RC SQL_API_FN sqlegdcl (struct sqlca *SQLCA);
```

Parameters

SQLCA A pointer to a location in memory where a SQLCA data structure variable is stored. This variable sends either status information (if the function executed successfully) or error information (if the function failed) back to the calling application.

Includes

```
#include <sqlenv.h>
```

Description The CLOSE DCS DIRECTORY SCAN function frees resources that were allocated by the OPEN DCS DIRECTORY SCAN function. This function should be called only if one or more DCS directory entries were not copied to the user-allocated memory storage area by the GET DCS DIRECTORY ENTRIES function.

Required Connection This function can be called at any time; a connection to a DB2 database manager instance or to a DB2 database does not have to be established first.

Authorization No authorization is required to execute this function call.

See Also OPEN DCS DIRECTORY SCAN, GET DCS DIRECTORY ENTRIES, GET DCS DIRECTORY ENTRY FOR DATABASE

Example See the example provided for the OPEN DCS DIRECTORY SCAN function in this chapter.

REGISTER

Purpose The REGISTER function registers a DB2 database server at a Novell NetWare file server.

Syntax

```
SQL_API_RC SQL_API_FN sqleregs (unsigned short Registry,
                                void           *RegisterInfo,
                                struct sqlca   *SQLCA);
```

Parameters

Registry Indicates where on the network server to register the DB2 database server. For now, this parameter must be set to SQL_NWBINDERY.

RegisterInfo A pointer to a *sqle_reg_nwbindery* structure that contains a NetWare user name and password for accessing the network server.

SQLCA A pointer to a location in memory where a SQLCA data structure variable is stored. This variable sends either status information (if the

function executed successfully) or error information (if the function failed) back to the calling application.

Includes

```
#include <sqlenv.h>
```

Description

The REGISTER function registers a DB2 database server at a Novell NetWare file server. When this function is executed, the DB2 database server's network address is stored in a specified registry on the file server, where it can be retrieved by any client application that uses the IPX/SPX communication protocol. Before this function can be called, valid user ID and password information for accessing the Novell network server must be stored in a special structure, *sql_reg_nwbindery*, that is defined in *sqlenv.h* as follows:

```
struct sqle_reg_nwbindery
{
char            uid[49];         /* The user ID that is to be used to */
                                 /* log into the Novell NetWare file  */
                                 /* server                            */
unsigned short  reserved_len_1;  /* Reserved                          */
char            pswd[130];       /* The password that is to be used   */
                                 /* to validate the user ID           */
unsigned short  reserved_len_2;  /* Reserved                          */
};
```

When the value specified in the *Registry* parameter is SQL _NWBINDERY (this is the only value currently supported), the NetWare user name and password supplied in the *sql_reg_nwbindery* structure logs onto the network server specified in the *fileserver* parameter of the DB2 database manager configuration file. This function determines the IPX/SPX address of the workstation to register (the workstation from which it was invoked) and then creates an object in the specified *fileserver* bindery using the DB2 database manager object name specified in the *objectname* parameter of the DB2 database manager configuration file. The IPX/SPX address of the server is stored as an attribute in that object. In order for a client to connect or attach using this information, it must first catalog an IPX/SPX node (using the same *fileserver* and *objectname* values) in its node directory.

Comments

- The Novell NetWare user name and password specified in the *sqle_reg _nwbindery* structure must have supervisory or equivalent authority.
- This function can be issued only locally from a DB2 database server workstation. Remote execution of this function is not supported.
- After DB2 version 2.1 IPX/SPX support software is installed and configured, the DB2 database server should be registered on the network server (unless IPX/SPX clients will be using only *direct addressing* to connect to this DB2 server).
- Once a DB2 database server is registered on the network server, if you need to reconfigure the IPX/SPX fields or change the DB2 server's network address, deregister the DB2 server from the network server (with the DEREGISTER function) and then register it again after making your changes.
- This function cannot be used in applications that run on the Windows or the Windows NT operating system.

Required Connection This function can be called at any time; a connection to a DB2 database manager instance or to a DB2 database does not have to be established first.

Authorization No authorization is required to execute this function call.

See Also DEREGISTER

Example The following C program illustrates how to use the REGISTER function to register the current DB2 database server at a NetWare file server:

```
#include <stdio.h>
#include <stdlib.h>
#include <string.h>
#include <sqlenv.h>
#include <sqlutil.h>
#include <sqlca.h>

int main()
{
    /* Declare The Local Memory Variables */
    struct sqle_reg_nwbindery  NWInfo;
    struct sqlca               sqlca;
    struct sqlfupd             DBManagerInfo;
    char                       szFileServer[10];

    /* Initialize The DB2 Database Manager Configuration */
    /* Parameter Structure                               */
    strcpy(szFileServer, "PCHOST");
    DBManagerInfo.token = SQLF_KTN_FILESERVER;
    DBManagerInfo.ptrvalue = (unsigned char *) szFileServer;

    /* Store The Novell NetWare File Server Name In The DB2 */
    /* Database Manager Configuration File                  */
    sqlfusys(1, &DBManagerInfo, &sqlca);

    /* Stop The DB2 Database Manager Server Processes */
    sqlestop(&sqlca);

    /* Re-Start The DB2 Database Manager Server Processes (This */
    /* Will Make DB2 See The Changes Made To The Configuration  */
    /* File)                                                    */
    sqlestar();

    /* Initialize The NetWare Registry Information Data Structure */
    strcpy(NWInfo.uid, "sasrys");
    strcpy(NWInfo.pswd, "");

    /* Register The Current DB2 Server On A NetWare File Server */
    sqleregs(SQL_NWBINDERY, &NWInfo, &sqlca);

    /* Display A Success Message */
    printf("The current DB2 Server has been registered at the ");
    printf("NetWare file server.\n");

    /* Return To The Operating System */
    return(EXIT_SUCCESS);
}
```

DEREGISTER

Purpose

The DEREGISTER function deregisters a DB2 server (removes a DB2 server's network address) from a specific registry at a Novell NetWare file server.

Syntax

```
SQL_API_RC SQL_API_FN sqledreg (unsigned short Registry,
                                void           *RegisterInfo,
                                struct sqlca   *SQLCA);
```

Parameters

Registry Indicates where on the network server to register the DB2 database server. For now, this parameter must be set to SQL_NWBINDERY.

RegisterInfo A pointer to a *sqle_reg_nwbindery* structure that contains a NetWare user name and password for accessing the network server.

SQLCA A pointer to a location in memory where a SQLCA data structure variable is stored. This variable sends either status information (if the function executed successfully) or error information (if the function failed) back to the calling application.

Includes

```
#include <sqlenv.h>
```

Description

The DEREGISTER function deregisters a DB2 server (removes a DB2 server's network address) from a specific registry at a Novell NetWare file server. Before calling this function, you must store valid user ID and password information for accessing the network server in a special structure (*sql_reg_nwbindery*) defined in *sqlenv.h*. Refer to the REGISTER function for a detailed description of this structure.

Comments

- The Novell NetWare user name and password specified in the *sqle_reg_nwbindery* structure must have supervisory or equivalent authority.
- This function can be issued only locally from a DB2 database server workstation. Remote execution of this function is not supported.
- Once a DB2 database server is registered on the network server, if you want to reconfigure the IPX/SPX fields or change the DB2 server's network address, deregister the DB2 server from the network server and then register it again (with the REGISTER function) after the changes are made.
- This function cannot be used in applications that run on the Windows or the Windows NT operating system.

Required Connection

This function can be called at any time; a connection to a DB2 database manager instance or to a DB2 database does not have to be established first.

Authorization

No authorization is required to execute this function call.

See Also

REGISTER

Example

The following C program illustrates how the DEREGISTER function deregisters the current DB2 database server from a NetWare file server:

```
#include <stdio.h>
#include <stdlib.h>
```

```
#include <string.h>
#include <sqlenv.h>
#include <sqlutil.h>
#include <sqlca.h>

int main()
{
    /* Declare The Local Memory Variables */
    struct sqle_reg_nwbindery  NWInfo;
    struct sqlca               sqlca;
    struct sqlfupd             DBManagerInfo;
    char                       szFileServer[10];

    /* Initialize The DB2 Database Manager Configuration */
    /* Parameter Structure                               */
    strcpy(szFileServer, "PCHOST");
    DBManagerInfo.token = SQLF_KTN_FILESERVER;
    DBManagerInfo.ptrvalue = (unsigned char *) szFileServer;

    /* Store The Novell NetWare File Server Name In The DB2 */
    /* Database Manager Configuration File                  */
    sqlfusys(1, &DBManagerInfo, &sqlca);

    /* Stop The DB2 Database Manager Server Processes */
    sqlestop(&sqlca);

    /* Re-Start The DB2 Database Manager Server Processes (This */
    /* Will Make DB2 See The Changes Made To The Configuration  */
    /* File                                                     */
    sqlestar();

    /* Initialize The NetWare Registry Information Data Structure */
    strcpy(NWInfo.uid, "sasrys");
    strcpy(NWInfo.pswd, "");

    /* Deregister The Current DB2 Server From A NetWare File Server */
    sqledreg(SQL_NWBINDERY, &NWInfo, &sqlca);

    /* Display A Success Message */
    printf("The current DB2 Server has been deregistered from the ");
    printf("NetWare file server.\n");

    /* Return To The Operating System */
    return(EXIT_SUCCESS);
}
```

CHAPTER 22

TABLE AND TABLE SPACE MANAGEMENT API'S

The table and table space management APIs are a group of DB2 API function calls that allow an application to obtain information about table spaces and table space containers that were created for a database, and to reorganize data in and update statistics for a database table. This group includes:

- API functions that retrieve information about one or more table spaces that were defined for a database.
- API functions that retrieve information about one or more table space containers that were defined for a table space.
- An API function that reorganizes (orders) all data in a database table.
- An API function that updates the statistical information stored for a database table.

Table 22.1 lists the table and table space management API functions available with DB2.

Table Spaces and Table Space Containers

Table spaces logically group (or partition) data objects such as tables, views, and indexes. They are designed to provide a level of indirection between user tables and the database in which they reside. There are two basic types of table spaces: database-managed space (DMS) table spaces, which supports raw devices and files, and system-managed space (SMS) table spaces, which supports directories. SMS table spaces are primarily used for compatibility with existing DB2/2 and DB2/6000 version 1.x databases.

You can retrieve information about all table spaces defined for a specified database by calling the TABLESPACE QUERY function. This function retrieves information about all table spaces defined for a single database and copies it into a large memory storage buffer. If many table spaces are defined for a database, you might want to retrieve the information in smaller pieces by calling the OPEN TABLESPACE QUERY, FETCH TABLESPACE QUERY, and CLOSE TABLESPACE QUERY functions.

A single table space can consist of one or more containers; for example, a DMS table space can reference many different drives and/or directories. You can retrieve information about all containers defined for a specified table space by calling the TABLESPACE CONTAINER QUERY function. This function retrieves information about all table space containers defined for a single table space and copies it into a large memory storage buffer. If a table space consists of many table space containers, you might want to retrieve the information in smaller pieces. You can retrieve information

TABLE 22.1 Table and Table Space Management APIs

Function name	Description
OPEN TABLESPACE QUERY	Returns the number of table spaces defined for the current connected database.
FETCH TABLESPACE QUERY	Retrieves and copies a specified number of rows of table space information to a user-defined memory buffer.
CLOSE TABLESPACE QUERY	Ends a table space query request and frees all system resources allocated by the OPEN TABLESPACE QUERY function.
TABLESPACE QUERY	Stores a copy of all table space data for the current connected database in a large memory storage buffer.
SINGLE TABLESPACE QUERY	Retrieves information about a single, currently defined table space.
OPEN TABLESPACE CONTAINER QUERY	Returns the number of table space containers defined for either a specified table space or for the current connected database.
FETCH TABLESPACE CONTAINER QUERY	Retrieves and copies a specified number of rows of table space container information to a user-defined memory buffer.
CLOSE TABLESPACE CONTAINER QUERY	Ends a table space container query request and frees all system resources allocated by the OPEN TABLESPACE CONTAINER QUERY function.
TABLESPACE CONTAINER QUERY	Stores a copy of all table space container data for a specified table space or for the current connected database in a large memory storage buffer.
FREE MEMORY	Frees memory allocated by either the TABLESPACE QUERY or the TABLESPACE CONTAINER QUERY function.
REORGANIZE TABLE	Reorganizes a table by eliminating fragmented data and compacting information.
RUN STATISTICS	Updates statistical information about a table and any or all of its associated indexes.

about table space containers in smaller pieces by calling the OPEN TABLESPACE CONTAINER QUERY, FETCH TABLESPACE CONTAINER QUERY, and CLOSE TABLESPACE CONTAINER QUERY functions. These three functions work in a manner similar to their OPEN/FETCH/CLOSE TABLESPACE QUERY counterparts.

Reorganizing Table Data

Database tables that undergo many updates and deletes will, in time, become fragmented (i.e., the table and its indexes will contain empty space). As a table becomes fragmented, its performance drops. DB2 provides a utility that can reorganize the data in a table in order to reclaim this lost space. You can invoke this utility from within an application by calling the REORGANIZE TABLE function.

Table reorganization exports data (in some particular order) to an external file, deletes all entries in the table, and then imports the data back. This can be a very time-consuming operation and can require a large amount of disk space as tables grow in size. While a table is being reorganized, no other applications and/or users can access it. This restriction makes table reorganization a difficult task to add to the normal flow of an application. Therefore, applications that call the REORGANIZE TABLE function should be executed only when they will not significantly affect other users and applications. You can specify how the data in a table is physically ordered when invoking the REORGANIZE function. To achieve optimum table performance, always order tables based on the most frequently used index.

Updating Table Statistics

The system catalog tables that are created for a database contain, among other things, statistics on all tables and indexes. Database statistics include items such as the number of rows in a table, information about indexes that are created for a table, and the overall size of a table. These statistics are important because they are used by the SQL optimizer to build the most optimal access plans for embedded SQL statements in an application. This influences the choice of using either an index scan or table scan to work with specified rows in a table.

Unfortunately, these statistics are not automatically kept up to date. This means that if you develop an application that accesses a particular database table and later create an index for that table, the static SQL statements in your application will not be able to take advantage of the new index. An application can update statistics for a specified table by calling the RUN STATISTICS function. Once a table's statistic information is updated, you need to rebind all packages that access the table so they can take full advantage of the updated statistical information.

OPEN TABLESPACE QUERY

Purpose

The OPEN TABLESPACE QUERY function returns the number of table spaces defined for the current connected database to the calling application.

Syntax

```
SQL_API_RC SQL_API_FN sqlbotsq (struct sqlca *SQLCA,
                                unsigned long  TableSpaceQueryOptions,
                                unsigned long *NumTableSpaces);
```

Parameters

SQLCA A pointer to a location in memory where a SQL communication area (SQLCA) data structure variable is stored. This variable sends either status information (if the function executed successfully) or error information (if the function failed) back to the calling application.

TableSpaceQueryOptions An integer value that specifies the type of table space information to be retrieved. This parameter can be set to any of the following values:

SQLB_OPEN_TBS_ALL	Retrieve information about all table spaces defined for the current database.
SQLB_OPEN_TBS_RESTORE	Retrieve only information about table spaces being restored by the user's agent.

NumTableSpaces A pointer to a location in memory where this function is to store the actual number of table spaces found in the current connected database that meet the specified *TableSpaceQueryOptions* value.

Includes

```
#include <sqlutil.h>
```

Description

The OPEN TABLESPACE QUERY function returns the number of table spaces defined for the current connected database to the calling application.

This function is normally followed by one or more FETCH TABLESPACE QUERY functions calls and one CLOSE TABLESPACE QUERY function call. These three functions can be used by an application to scan a list of table spaces and search for specific information.

Comments

- Only one table space query can be active at one time.

Required Connection

This function can be called only if a connection to a database exists.

Authorization

Only users with system control (SYSCTRL) authority, system administrator (SYSADM) authority, system maintenance (SYSMAINT) authority, or database administrator (DBADM) authority can execute this function call.

See Also

FETCH TABLESPACE QUERY, CLOSE TABLESPACE QUERY, TABLESPACE QUERY, SINGLE TABLESPACE QUERY

Example

The following C program illustrates how to use the OPEN TABLESPACE QUERY, FETCH TABLESPACE QUERY, and CLOSE TABLESPACE QUERY functions to retrieve information about the table spaces defined for a database:

```
#include <stdio.h>
#include <stdlib.h>
#include <sqlutil.h>
#include <sql.h>

int main()
{
    /* Include The SQLCA Data Structure Variable */
    EXEC SQL INCLUDE SQLCA;

    /* Declare The Local Memory Variables */
    int                       rc = EXIT_SUCCESS;
    unsigned long             ulTSCount;
    struct SQLB_TBSQRY_DATA   *TableSpaceData = NULL;
    struct SQLB_TBSQRY_DATA   *TSDataPtr = NULL;
    unsigned long             ulNumRows;

    /* Set Up A Simple SQL Error Handler */
    EXEC SQL WHENEVER SQLERROR GOTO EXIT;

    /* Connect To The SAMPLE Database */
    EXEC SQL CONNECT TO SAMPLE USER etpdd6z USING sanders;

    /* Open The Table Space Query */
    sqlbotsq(&sqlca, SQLB_OPEN_TBS_ALL, &ulTSCount);

    /* Allocate A Memory Storage Buffer */
    TableSpaceData = (struct SQLB_TBSQRY_DATA *)
```

```
                  malloc(ulTSCount * sizeof(struct SQLB_TBSQRY_DATA));
     TSDataPtr = TableSpaceData;

     /* Copy The Table Space Data Into The Memory Storage Buffer */
     sqlbftsq(&sqlca, ulTSCount, TableSpaceData, &ulNumRows);

     /* Display The Table Space Data */
     printf("Table Spaces Defined For The SAMPLE Database\n");
     printf("ID   Name         Type\n");
     printf("-------------------------------------\n");
     for (; ulTSCount != 0; ulTSCount--)
         {
         printf("%-4d ", TSDataPtr->id);
         printf("%-12s ", TSDataPtr->name);
         switch (TSDataPtr->flags)
             {
             case SQLB_TBS_SMS:
                 printf("System Managed Space\n");
                 break;
             case SQLB_TBS_DMS:
                 printf("Database Managed Space\n");
                 break;
             case SQLB_TBS_ANY:
                 printf("Regular Contents\n");
                 break;
             case SQLB_TBS_LONG:
                 printf("Long Field Data\n");
                 break;
             case SQLB_TBS_TMP:
                 printf("Temporary Data\n");
                 break;
             default:
                 printf("\n");
             }
         TSDataPtr++;
         }

     /* Close The Table Space Query And Free All Resources Obtained */
     sqlbctsq(&sqlca);
     free(TableSpaceData);

EXIT:
     /* If An Error Has Occurred, Display The SQL Return Code */
     if (sqlca.sqlcode != SQL_RC_OK)
         {
         printf("ERROR : %ld\n", sqlca.sqlcode);
         rc = EXIT_FAILURE;
         }
     /* Issue A Rollback To Free All Locks */
     EXEC SQL ROLLBACK;
     /* Turn Off The SQL Error Handler */
     EXEC SQL WHENEVER SQLERROR CONTINUE;

     /* Disconnect From The SAMPLE Database */
     EXEC SQL DISCONNECT CURRENT;

     /* Return To The Operating System */
     return(rc);
}
```

FETCH TABLESPACE QUERY

Purpose The FETCH TABLESPACE QUERY function retrieves (fetches), and copies a specified number of rows of table space information to a user-allocated memory buffer supplied by the calling application.

Syntax

```
SQL_API_RC SQL_API_FN sqlbftsq (struct sqlca          *SQLCA,
                                unsigned long          MaxTableSpaces,
                                struct SQLB_TBSQRY_DATA *TableSpaceData,
                                unsigned long          *NumTableSpaces);
```

Parameters

SQLCA A pointer to a location in memory where a SQLCA data structure variable is stored. This variable sends either status information (if the function executed successfully) or error information (if the function failed) back to the calling application.

MaxTableSpaces The maximum number of rows of table space data that the user-allocated memory storage buffer can hold.

TableSpaceData A pointer to a user-allocated memory storage buffer (defined as an array of *SQLB_TBSQRY_DATA* structures) where this function is to store the retrieved table space data.

NumTableSpaces A pointer to a location in memory where this function is to store the actual number of rows of table space information retrieved.

Includes

```
#include <sqlutil.h>
```

Description The FETCH TABLESPACE QUERY function retrieves (fetches), and copies a specified number of rows of table space information to a user-allocated memory buffer supplied by the calling application. Before this function is executed, a memory storage buffer containing an array of *SQLB_TBSQRY_DATA* structures must first be allocated and the *MaxTableSpaces* parameter must indicate the number of elements in this array. The *SQLB_TBSQRY_DATA* structure is defined in *sqlutil.h* as follows:

```
struct SQLB_TBSQRY_DATA
{
unsigned long  id;            /* The internal ID for the table space         */
unsigned long  nameLen;       /* The length of the table space name (for     */
                              /* languages other than C and C++)             */
char           name[128];     /* The table space name (null-terminated)      */
unsigned long  totalPages;    /* Total number of pages occupied by the       */
                              /* table space (DMS table spaces only)         */
unsigned long  usablePages;   /* Total number of 4KB pages occupied by the */
                              /* table space overhead (DMS table spaces      */
                              /* only)                                       */
unsigned long  flags;         /* Bit attributes for the table space.         */
unsigned long  pageSize;      /* The size (in bytes) of one page of          */
                              /* memory. This value is currently set (in     */
                              /* bytes) at 4KB.                              */
unsigned long  extSize;       /* The extent size (in pages) of the table     */
                              /* space                                       */
unsigned long  prefetchSize;  /* The table space prefetch buffer size        */
unsigned long  nContainers;   /* The number of containers in the table       */
                              /* space                                       */
unsigned long  tbsState;      /* The table space states                      */
char           lifeLSN[6];    /* The date and time that the table space      */
```

```
                                 /* was created                              */
char            pad[2];          /* Reserved; used for alignment             */
};
```

The copy of table space data placed in memory represents a snapshot of the current table space information at the time this function is executed. Since no locking is performed, the information in memory might not reflect more recent changes made by other applications.

Comments

- The *flags* field of the *SQLB_TBSQRY_DATA* structure can contain one of the following values:
  –*SQLB_TBS_SMS* System-managed space (SMS) table space.
  –*SQLB_TBS_DMS* Database-managed space (DMS) table space.
  –*SQLB_TBS_ANY* Regular data.
  –*SQLB_TBS_LONG* Long field data.
  –*SQLB_TBS_TMP* Temporary data.
- The *tbsState* field of the *SQLB_TBSQRY_DATA* structure can contain one of the following values:
  –*SQLB_NORMAL* Normal.
  –*SQLB_QUIESCED_SHARE* Quiesced: SHARE.
  –*SQLB_QUIESCED_UPDATE* Quiesced: UPDATE.
  –*SQLB_QUIESCED_EXCLUSIVE* Quiesced: EXCLUSIVE.
  –*SQLB_LOAD_PENDING* Load pending.
  –*SQLB_DELETE_PENDING* Delete pending.
  –*SQLB_BACKUP_PENDING* ackup pending.
  –*SQLB_ROLLFORWARD_IN_PROGRESS* Roll-forward recovery in progress.
  –*SQLB_ROLLFORWARD_PENDING* Roll-forward recovery pending.
  –*SQLB_RESTORE_PENDING* Restore pending.
  –*SQLB_DISABLE_PENDING* Disable pending.
  –*SQLB_REORG_IN_PROGRESS* Table reorganization in progress.
  –*SQLB_BACKUP_IN_PROGRESS* Backup in progress.
  –*SQLB_STORDEF_PENDING* Storage must be defined.
  –*SQLB_RESTORE_IN_PROGRESS* Restore in progress.
  –*SQLB_STORDEF_ALLOWED* Storage can be defined.
  –*SQLB_STORDEF_FINAL_VERSION* Storage definition in final state.
  –*SQLB_STORDEF_CHANGED* Storage definition changed prior to roll-forward recovery.
  –*SQLB_REBAL_IN_PROGRESS* DMS rebalancer active.
  –*SQLB_PSTAT_DELETION* Table space deletion in progress.
  –*SQLB_PSTAT_CREATION* Table space creation in progress.
- When the memory storage buffer containing the array of *SQLB_TBSQRY_DATA* structures allocated for this function is no longer needed, it must be freed by the application that allocated it.
- If the FETCH TABLE SPACE QUERY function is executed when a snapshot of table space information is already in memory, the previous snapshot will be replaced with refreshed table space information.
- There is one snapshot buffer storage area for table space queries and another snapshot buffer storage area for table space container queries. These buffers are independent of one another.

Prerequisites

The OPEN TABLESPACE QUERY function must be executed before this function is called.

Required Connection This function can be called only if a connection to a database exists.

Authorization Only users with system control (SYSCTRL) authority, system administrator (SYSADM) authority, system maintenance (SYSMAINT) authority, or database administrator (DBADM) authority can execute this function call.

See Also OPEN TABLESPACE QUERY, CLOSE TABLESPACE QUERY, TABLE SPACE QUERY, SINGLE TABLESPACE QUERY, GET TABLESPACE STATISTICS

Example See the example provided for the OPEN TABLESPACE QUERY function in this chapter.

CLOSE TABLESPACE QUERY

Purpose The CLOSE TABLESPACE QUERY function ends a table space query request made by the OPEN TABLESPACE QUERY function.

Syntax

```
SQL_API_RC SQL_API_FN sqlbctsq (struct SQLCA *SQLCA);
```

Parameters

SQLCA A pointer to a location in memory where a SQLCA data structure variable is stored. This variable sends either status information (if the function executed successfully) or error information (if the function failed) back to the calling application.

Includes

```
#include <sqlutil.h>
```

Description The CLOSE TABLESPACE QUERY function ends a table space query request made by the OPEN TABLESPACE QUERY function.

Required Connection This function can be called only if a connection to a database exists.

Authorization Only users with system control (SYSCTRL) authority, system administrator (SYSADM) authority, system maintenance (SYSMAINT) authority, or database administrator (DBADM) authority are allowed to execute this function call.

See Also OPEN TABLESPACE QUERY, FETCH TABLESPACE QUERY, TABLESPACE QUERY, SINGLE TABLESPACE QUERY, GET TABLESPACE STATISTICS

Example See the example provided for the OPEN TABLESPACE QUERY function in this chapter.

TABLESPACE QUERY

Purpose The TABLESPACE QUERY function stores a copy of the table space data for the current connected database in a large DB2-allocated memory storage buffer, and returns the number of table spaces defined for the current connected database to the calling application.

Syntax

```
SQL_API_RC SQL_API_FN sqlbtsq (struct sqlca          *SQLCA,
                               unsigned long         *NumTableSpaces,
                               struct SQLB_TBSQRY_DATA **TableSpaceData);
```

Parameters

SQLCA A pointer to a location in memory where a SQLCA data structure variable is stored. This variable sends either status information (if the function executed successfully) or error information (if the function failed) back to the calling application.

NumTableSpaces A pointer to a location in memory where this function stores the actual number of table spaces found in the current connected database.

TableSpaceData A pointer to the address of an array of *SQLB_TBSQRY_DATA* structures where this function stores the retrieved table space data.

Includes

```
#include <sqlutil.h>
```

Description

The TABLESPACE QUERY function stores a copy of the table space data for the current connected database in a large DB2-allocated memory storage buffer, and returns the number of table spaces defined for the current connected database to the calling application. This function provides a one-call interface to the OPEN TABLESPACE QUERY, FETCH TABLESPACE QUERY, and CLOSE TABLESPACE QUERY functions that can be used to retrieve all the table space data for a connected database at one time.

When this function is executed, a memory buffer that stores the complete set of retrieved table space information is automatically allocated, a pointer to that buffer is stored in the *TableSpaceData* parameter, and the number of table spaces found in the current connected database is stored in the *NumTableSpaces* parameter. The memory storage buffer that holds the table space information is actually an array of *SQLB_TBSQRY_DATA* structures and the *NumTableSpaces* parameter specifies the number of elements in the array. Refer to the FETCH TABLESPACE QUERY function for a detailed description of the *SQLB_TBSQRY_DATA* structure.

Comments

- When this function is executed, if a sufficient amount of free memory is available, a memory storage buffer will automatically be allocated. You can free this memory storage buffer only by calling the FREE MEMORY function. It is the application's responsibility to ensure that all memory allocated by this function is freed when it is no longer needed. If sufficient memory is not available, this function simply returns the number of table spaces found in the connected database and no memory is allocated.
- If there is not enough free memory available to retrieve the complete set of table space data at one time, you can use the OPEN TABLESPACE QUERY, FETCH TABLESPACE QUERY and CLOSE TABLESPACE QUERY functions to retrieve the table space data in smaller pieces.

Required Connection

This function can be called only if a connection to a database exists.

Authorization

Only users with system control (SYSCTRL) authority, system administrator (SYSADM) authority, system maintenance (SYSMAINT) authority, or database administrator (DBADM) authority are allowed to execute this function call.

See Also

OPEN TABLESPACE QUERY, FETCH TABLESPACE QUERY, CLOSE TABLESPACE QUERY, SINGLE TABLESPACE QUERY, GET TABLESPACE STATISTICS, FREE MEMORY

Example

The following C program illustrates how to use the TABLESPACE QUERY function to retrieve information about the table spaces defined for a database:

```
#include <stdio.h>
#include <stdlib.h>
#include <sqlenv.h>
#include <sqlutil.h>
#include <sql.h>

int main()
{
    /* Include The SQLCA Data Structure Variable */
    EXEC SQL INCLUDE SQLCA;

    /* Declare The Local Memory Variables */
    int                          rc = EXIT_SUCCESS;
    unsigned long                ulTSCount;
    struct SQLB_TBSQRY_DATA      *TableSpaceData = NULL;
    struct SQLB_TBSQRY_DATA      *TSDataPtr = NULL;
    unsigned long                ulNumRows;

    /* Set Up A Simple SQL Error Handler */
    EXEC SQL WHENEVER SQLERROR GOTO EXIT;

    /* Connect To The SAMPLE Database */
    EXEC SQL CONNECT TO SAMPLE USER etpdd6z USING sanders;

    /* Retrieve The Table Space Data */
    sqlbtsq(&sqlca, &ulTSCount, &TableSpaceData);

    /* Display The Table Space Data */
    printf("ID   Name          Type\n");
    printf("-------------------------------------\n");
    TSDataPtr = TableSpaceData;
    for (; ulTSCount != 0; ulTSCount--)
        {
        printf("%-4d ", TSDataPtr->id);
        printf("%-12s ", TSDataPtr->name);
        switch (TSDataPtr->flags)
            {
            case SQLB_TBS_SMS:
                printf("System Managed Space\n");
                break;
            case SQLB_TBS_DMS:
                printf("Database Managed Space\n");
                break;
            case SQLB_TBS_ANY:
                printf("Regular Contents\n");
                break;
            case SQLB_TBS_LONG:
                printf("Long Field Data\n");
                break;
            case SQLB_TBS_TMP:
                printf("Temporary Data\n");
                break;
            default:
```

```
                    printf("\n");
                }
            TSDataPtr++;
            }

        /* Free All Resources Associated With The Table Space Query */
        sqlefmem(&sqlca, TableSpaceData);

EXIT:
        /* If An Error Has Occurred, Display The SQL Return Code */
        if (sqlca.sqlcode != SQL_RC_OK)
            {
            printf("ERROR : %ld\n", sqlca.sqlcode);
            rc = EXIT_FAILURE;
            }

        /* Issue A Rollback To Free All Locks */
        EXEC SQL ROLLBACK;

        /* Turn Off The SQL Error Handler */
        EXEC SQL WHENEVER SQLERROR CONTINUE;

        /* Disconnect From The SAMPLE Database */
        EXEC SQL DISCONNECT CURRENT;

        /* Return To The Operating System */
        return(rc);
}
```

SINGLE TABLESPACE QUERY

Purpose

The SINGLE TABLESPACE QUERY function retrieves information about a single, currently defined table space.

Syntax

```
SQL_API_RC SQL_API_FN sqlbstsq (struct sqlca          *SQLCA,
                                unsigned long          TableSpaceID,
                                struct SQLB_TBSQRY_DATA *TableSpaceData);
```

Parameters

SQLCA A pointer to a location in memory where a SQLCA data structure variable is stored. This variable sends either status information (if the function executed successfully) or error information (if the function failed) back to the calling application.

TableSpaceID The ID of the table space for which information is to be retrieved.

TableSpaceData A pointer to a *SQLB_TBSQRY_DATA* structure where this function is to store the retrieved table space data.

Includes

```
#include <sqlutil.h>
```

Description

The SINGLE TABLESPACE QUERY function retrieves information about a single, currently defined table space. The retrieved information is stored in a special structure, *SQLB_TBSQRY_DATA*, that is defined in *sqlutil.h*. Refer to the FETCH TABLESPACE QUERY function for a detailed description of this structure.

The SINGLE TABLESPACE QUERY function provides an alternative to the more expensive combination of OPEN TABLESPACE QUERY,

FETCH TABLESPACE QUERY, and CLOSE TABLESPACE QUERY function calls when the table space identifier of a table space is already known.

Comments

- Table space IDs for table spaces can be found in the SYSCAT.TABLESPACES system catalog table.
- No agent snapshot is taken when this function is executed; since there is only one table space entry to return, it is returned directly.
- When the table space identifier is not known in advance, you must use the OPEN TABLESPACE QUERY, FETCH TABLESPACE QUERY, and CLOSE TABLESPACE QUERY functions to retrieve information about the desired table space.

Required Connection

This function can be called only if a connection to a database exists.

Authorization

Only users with system control (SYSCTRL) authority, system administrator (SYSADM), system maintenance (SYSMAINT) authority, or database administrator (DBADM) authority are allowed to execute this function call.

See Also

OPEN TABLESPACE QUERY, FETCH TABLESPACE QUERY, CLOSE TABLESPACE QUERY, TABLESPACE QUERY, GET TABLESPACE STATISTICS

Example

The following C program illustrates how to use the SINGLE TABLESPACE function to retrieve information about a table space whose ID is already known:

```
#include <stdio.h>
#include <stdlib.h>
#include <sqlutil.h>
#include <sql.h>

int main()
{
    /* Include The SQLCA Data Structure Variable */
    EXEC SQL INCLUDE SQLCA;

    /* Declare The Local Memory Variables */
    int                        rc = EXIT_SUCCESS;
    unsigned long              ulTSCount;
    struct SQLB_TBSQRY_DATA    TableSpaceData;
    unsigned long              ulNumRows;

    /* Set Up A Simple SQL Error Handler */
    EXEC SQL WHENEVER SQLERROR GOTO EXIT;

    /* Connect To The SAMPLE Database */
    EXEC SQL CONNECT TO SAMPLE USER etpdd6z USING sanders;

    /* Retrieve The Table Space Data Into A Local Variable */
    sqlbstsq(&sqlca, 2, &TableSpaceData);

    /* Display The Table Space Data */
    printf("ID   Name          Type\n");
    printf("-------------------------------------\n");
    printf("%-4d ", TableSpaceData.id);
    printf("%-12s ", TableSpaceData.name);
    switch (TableSpaceData.flags)
```

```
        {
        case SQLB_TBS_SMS:
            printf("System Managed Space\n");
            break;
        case SQLB_TBS_DMS:
            printf("Database Managed Space\n");
            break;
        case SQLB_TBS_ANY:
            printf("Regular Contents\n");
            break;
        case SQLB_TBS_LONG:
            printf("Long Field Data\n");
            break;
        case SQLB_TBS_TMP:
            printf("Temporary Data\n");
            break;
        default:
            printf("\n");
        }

EXIT:
    /* If An Error Has Occurred, Display The SQL Return Code */
    if (sqlca.sqlcode != SQL_RC_OK)
        {
        printf("ERROR : %ld\n", sqlca.sqlcode);
        rc = EXIT_FAILURE;
        }

    /* Issue A Rollback To Free All Locks */
    EXEC SQL ROLLBACK;

    /* Turn Off The SQL Error Handler */
    EXEC SQL WHENEVER SQLERROR CONTINUE;

    /* Disconnect From The SAMPLE Database */
    EXEC SQL DISCONNECT CURRENT;

    /* Return To The Operating System */
    return(rc);
}
```

GET TABLESPACE STATISTICS

Purpose

The GET TABLESPACE STATISTICS function retrieves information about the space usage of a table space.

Syntax

```
SQL_API_RC SQL_API_FN sqlbgtss (struct sqlca           *SQLCA,
                                unsigned long          TableSpaceID,
                                struct SQLB_TBS_STATS  *TableSpaceStats);
```

Parameters

SQLCA A pointer to a location in memory where a SQLCA data structure variable is stored. This variable sends either status information (if the function executed successfully) or error information (if the function failed) back to the calling application.

TableSpaceID The ID of the table space for which space usage information is to be retrieved.

TableSpaceStats A pointer to a *SQLB_TBS_STATS* structure where this function is to store the retrieved table space usage information.

Includes

```
#include <sqlutil.h>
```

Description

The GET TABLESPACE STATISTICS function retrieves information about the space usage of a table space. The retrieved information is stored in a special structure, *SQLB_TBS_STATS*, that is defined in *sqlutil.h* as follows:

```
struct SQLB_TBS_STATS
{
unsigned long  totalPages;     /* The total amount of operating         */
                               /* system space (in 4KB pages)           */
                               /* needed by the table space. For        */
                               /* DMS table spaces, this is the sum     */
                               /* of the table space container sizes    */
                               /* (including overhead). For SMS         */
                               /* table spaces, this is the sum of all  */
                               /* file space used for the tables        */
                               /* stored in this table space.           */
unsigned long  usablePages;    /* The total amount of operating         */
                               /* system space (in 4KB pages)           */
                               /* needed by the table space minus       */
                               /* overhead (for DMS table spaces).      */
                               /* For SMS table spaces, this value is   */
                               /* equal to the totalPages value.        */
unsigned long  usedPages;      /* The total number of 4KB pages         */
                               /* currently being used by the table     */
                               /* space (for DMS table spaces).         */
                               /* For SMS table spaces, this value is   */
                               /* equal to the totalPages value.        */
unsigned long  freePages;      /* The total number of 4KB pages         */
                               /* that are available for a DMS table    */
                               /* space (usablePages value minus        */
                               /* usedPages value). This field is not   */
                               /* applicable for SMS table spaces.      */
unsigned long  highWaterMark;  /* The current "end" of the DMS          */
                               /* table space address space, in other   */
                               /* words, the page number of the         */
                               /* first free 4KB page following the     */
                               /* last allocated extent of the table    */
                               /* space. This field is not applicable   */
                               /* for SMS table spaces. Note: this is   */
                               /* not really a "high-water mark" but    */
                               /* rather a "current-water mark"         */
                               /* since the value can increase or       */
                               /* decrease.                             */
};
```

Required Connection This function can be called only if a connection to a database exists.

Authorization Only users with system control (SYSCTRL) authority, system administrator (SYSADM) authority, system maintenance (SYSMAINT) authority, or database administrator (DBADM) authority can execute this function call.

See Also OPEN TABLESPACE QUERY, FETCH TABLESPACE QUERY, CLOSE TABLESPACE QUERY, TABLESPACE QUERY, SINGLE TABLESPACE QUERY

Example

The following C program illustrates how to use the GET TABLESPACE STATISTICS function to retrieve space usage information for the SYSCATSPACE table space:

```
#include <stdio.h>
#include <stdlib.h>
#include <sqlutil.h>
#include <sql.h>

int main()
{
    /* Include The SQLCA Data Structure Variable */
    EXEC SQL INCLUDE SQLCA;

    /* Declare The Local Memory Variables */
    int                     rc = EXIT_SUCCESS;
    unsigned long           ulTSCount;
    struct SQLB_TBS_STATS   TableSpaceStats;
    unsigned long           ulNumRows;

    /* Set Up A Simple SQL Error Handler */
    EXEC SQL WHENEVER SQLERROR GOTO EXIT;

    /* Connect To The SAMPLE Database */
    EXEC SQL CONNECT TO SAMPLE USER etpdd6z USING sanders;

    /* Retrieve The Table Space Statistics */
    sqlbgtss(&sqlca, 0, &TableSpaceStats);

    /* Display The Table Space Statistical Data */
    printf("Statistics for SYSCATSPACE Table Space :\n\n");
    printf("Total Number Of Pages          : %ld\n",
           TableSpaceStats.totalPages);
    printf("Total Number Of Usable Pages   : %ld\n",
           TableSpaceStats.usablePages);
    printf("Total Number Of Used Pages     : %ld\n",
           TableSpaceStats.usedPages);
    printf("Total Number Of Free Pages     : %ld\n",
           TableSpaceStats.freePages);
    printf("Current End Of Address Space   : %ld\n",
           TableSpaceStats.highWaterMark);

EXIT:
    /* If An Error Has Occurred, Display The SQL Return Code */
    if (sqlca.sqlcode != SQL_RC_OK)
        {
        printf("ERROR : %ld\n", sqlca.sqlcode);
        rc = EXIT_FAILURE;
        }

    /* Issue A Rollback To Free All Locks */
    EXEC SQL ROLLBACK;

    /* Turn Off The SQL Error Handler */
    EXEC SQL WHENEVER SQLERROR CONTINUE;

    /* Disconnect From The SAMPLE Database */
    EXEC SQL DISCONNECT CURRENT;

    /* Return To The Operating System */
    return(rc);
}
```

OPEN TABLESPACE CONTAINER QUERY

Purpose

The OPEN TABLESPACE CONTAINER QUERY function returns the number of table space containers defined for either a specified table space or for the current connected database to the calling application.

Syntax

```
SQL_API_RC SQL_API_FN sqlbotcq (struct sqlca  *SQLCA,
                                unsigned long TableSpaceID,
                                unsigned long *NumContainers);
```

Parameters

SQLCA A pointer to a location in memory where a SQLCA data structure variable is stored. This variable sends either status information (if the function executed successfully) or error information (if the function failed) back to the calling application.

TableSpaceID The ID of the table space for which container information is to be retrieved. If the value specified for this parameter is SQLB _ALL_TABLESPACES, a composite list of table space containers for the entire database will be returned.

NumContainers A pointer to a location in memory where this function is to store the actual number of containers found in the specified table space (or database).

Includes

```
#include <sqlutil.h>
```

Description

The OPEN TABLESPACE CONTAINER QUERY function returns the number of table space containers defined for either a specified table space or for the current connected database to the calling application.

This function is normally followed by one or more FETCH TABLESPACE CONTAINER QUERY functions calls and one CLOSE TABLESPACE CONTAINER QUERY function call. An application can use these three functions to scan a list of table containers spaces and search for specific information.

Comments

- Only one table space container query can be active at one time.

Required Connection

This function can be called only if a connection to a database exists.

Authorization

Only users with system control (SYSCTRL) authority, system administrator (SYSADM) authority, system maintenance (SYSMAINT) authority, or database administrator (DBADM) authority can execute this function call.

See Also

FETCH TABLESPACE CONTAINER QUERY, CLOSE TABLESPACE CONTAINER QUERY, TABLESPACE CONTAINER QUERY

Example

The following C program illustrates how to use the OPEN TABLESPACE CONTAINER QUERY, FETCH TABLESPACE CONTAINER QUERY, and CLOSE TABLESPACE CONTAINER QUERY functions to retrieve a list of containers for a specified table space:

```
#include <stdio.h>
#include <stdlib.h>
#include <sqlutil.h>
#include <sql.h>

int main()
```

```
{
    /* Include The SQLCA Data Structure Variable */
    EXEC SQL INCLUDE SQLCA;

    /* Declare The Local Memory Variables */
    int                             rc = EXIT_SUCCESS;
    unsigned long                   ulTSCCount;
    struct SQLB_TBSCONTQRY_DATA     *TSContainerData = NULL;
    struct SQLB_TBSCONTQRY_DATA     *TSCDataPtr = NULL;
    unsigned long                   ulNumRows;

    /* Set Up A Simple SQL Error Handler */
    EXEC SQL WHENEVER SQLERROR GOTO EXIT;

    /* Connect To The SAMPLE Database */
    EXEC SQL CONNECT TO SAMPLE USER etpdd6z USING sanders;

    /* Open The Table Space Container Query */
    sqlbotcq(&sqlca, 0, &ulTSCCount);

    /* Allocate A Memory Storage Buffer */
    TSContainerData = (struct SQLB_TBSCONTQRY_DATA *)
            malloc(ulTSCCount * sizeof(struct SQLB_TBSCONTQRY_DATA));
    TSCDataPtr = TSContainerData;

    /* Copy The Table Space Container Data Into The Memory */
    /* Storage Buffer                                       */
    sqlbftcq(&sqlca, ulTSCCount, TSContainerData, &ulNumRows);

    /* Display The Table Space Container Data */
    printf("Containers Defined For The SYSCATSPACE Table Space\n");
    printf("ID   Name\n");
    printf("---------------------------\n");
    for (; ulTSCCount != 0; ulTSCCount--)
        {
        printf("%-4d ", TSCDataPtr->id);
        printf("%-12s\n", TSCDataPtr->name);
        TSCDataPtr++;
        }

    /* Close The Table Space Container Query And Free All Resources */
    /* Obtained                                                      */
    sqlbctcq(&sqlca);
    free(TSContainerData);

EXIT:
    /* If An Error Has Occurred, Display The SQL Return Code */
    if (sqlca.sqlcode != SQL_RC_OK)
        {
        printf("ERROR : %ld\n", sqlca.sqlcode);
        rc = EXIT_FAILURE;
        }

    /* Issue A Rollback To Free All Locks */
    EXEC SQL ROLLBACK;

    /* Turn Off The SQL Error Handler */
    EXEC SQL WHENEVER SQLERROR CONTINUE;

    /* Disconnect From The SAMPLE Database */
```

```
    EXEC SQL DISCONNECT CURRENT;

    /* Return To The Operating System */
    return(rc);
}
```

FETCH TABLESPACE CONTAINER QUERY

Purpose

The FETCH TABLESPACE CONTAINER QUERY function retrieves (fetches) and transfers a specified number of rows of table space container information to a user-allocated memory buffer supplied by the calling application.

Syntax

```
SQL_API_RC SQL_API_FN sqlbftcq (struct sqlca               *SQLCA,
                                unsigned long               MaxContainers,
                                struct SQLB_TBSCONTQRY_DATA *ContainerData
                                unsigned long               *NumContainers);
```

Parameters

SQLCA A pointer to a location in memory where a SQLCA data structure variable is stored. This variable sends either status information (if the function executed successfully) or error information (if the function failed) back to the calling application.

MaxContainers The maximum number of rows of table space container data that the user-allocated memory storage buffer can hold.

ContainerData A pointer to a user-allocated memory storage buffer (defined as an array of *SQLB_TBSCONTQRY_DATA* structures) where this function is to store the retrieved table space container data.

NumContainers A pointer to a location in memory where this function is to store the actual number of rows of table space container information retrieved.

Includes

```
#include <sqlutil.h>
```

Description

The FETCH TABLESPACE CONTAINER QUERY function retrieves (fetches) and transfers a specified number of rows of table space container information to a user-allocated memory buffer supplied by the calling application. Before this function is executed, a memory storage buffer containing an array of *SQLB_TBSCONTQRY_DATA* structures must first be allocated and the *MaxContainers* parameter must indicate the number of elements in this array. The *SQLB_TBSCONTQRY_DATA* structure is defined in *sqlutil.h* as follows:

```
struct SQLB_TBSCONTQRY_DATA
{
unsigned long  id;          /* The container identifier                   */
unsigned long  nTbs;        /* The number of table spaces sharing this    */
                            /* container. The value for this parameter    */
                            /* is always 1 (DMS table spaces can have     */
                            /* only 1 container space at this time).      */
unsigned long  tbsID;       /* The table space identifier                 */
unsigned long  nameLen;     /* The length of the container name (for      */
                            /* languages other than C and C++)            */
char           name[256];   /* The container name (null-terminated)       */
unsigned long  underDBDir;  /* Indicates whether the table space          */
                            /* container is under the database            */
                            /* directory (1) or not (0).                  */
```

```
unsigned long  contType;     /* Indicates whether the table space        */
                             /* container specifies a directory path     */
                             /* (SQLB_CONT_PATH), a raw device           */
                             /* (SQLB_CONT_DISK), or a file              */
                             /* (SQLB_CONT_FILE). Note: the value        */
                             /* SQLB_CONT_PATH is valid only for         */
                             /* SMS table spaces.                        */
unsigned long  totalPages;   /* Total number of 4KB pages occupied by    */
                             /* the table space container (DMS table     */
                             /* spaces only)                             */
unsigned long  usablePages;  /* Total number of 4KB pages occupied by the */
                             /* table space container overhead (DMS      */
                             /* table spaces only)                       */
unsigned long  ok;           /* Indicates whether the table space        */
                             /* container is accessible (1) or           */
                             /* inaccessible (0). A value of 0 indicates */
                             /* an abnormal situation that might require */
                             /* the database administrator's attention.  */
};
```

The copy of table space container data that is placed in memory represents a snapshot of the current table space container information when the function executes. Since no locking is performed, the information in memory might not reflect more recent changes made by other applications.

Comments

- When the memory storage buffer containing the array of *SQLB_TBSCONTQRY_DATA* structures allocated for this function is no longer needed, it must be freed by the application that allocated it.
- If the FETCH TABLE SPACE CONTAINER QUERY function is executed when a snapshot of table space container information is already in memory, the previous snapshot will be replaced with refreshed table space container information.
- There is one snapshot buffer storage area for table space queries and another snapshot buffer storage area for table space container queries. These buffers are independent of one another.

Prerequisites

The OPEN TABLESPACE CONTAINER QUERY function must be executed before this function is called.

Required Connection

This function can be called only if a connection to a database exists.

Authorization

Only users with system control (SYSCTRL) authority, system administrator (SYSADM) authority, system maintenance (SYSMAINT) authority, or database administrator (DBADM) authority can execute this function call.

See Also

OPEN TABLESPACE CONTAINER QUERY, CLOSE TABLESPACE CONTAINER QUERY, TABLESPACE CONTAINER QUERY

Example

See the example provided for the OPEN TABLESPACE CONTAINER QUERY function in this chapter.

CLOSE TABLESPACE CONTAINER QUERY

Purpose

The CLOSE TABLESPACE CONTAINER QUERY function ends a table space container query request made by the OPEN TABLESPACE CONTAINER QUERY function.

Syntax

```
SQL_API_RC SQL_API_FN sqlbctcq (struct sqlca *SQLCA);
```

Parameters

SQLCA A pointer to a location in memory where a SQLCA data structure variable is stored. This variable sends either status information (if the function executed successfully) or error information (if the function failed) back to the calling application.

Includes

```
#include <sqlutil.h>
```

Description

The CLOSE TABLESPACE CONTAINER QUERY function ends a table space container query request made by the OPEN TABLESPACE CONTAINER QUERY function.

Required Connection

This function can be called only if a connection to a database exists.

Authorization

Only users with system control (SYSCTRL) authority, system administrator (SYSADM) authority, system maintenance (SYSMAINT) authority, or database administrator (DBADM) authority can execute this function call.

See Also

OPEN TABLESPACE CONTAINER QUERY, FETCH TABLESPACE CONTAINER QUERY, TABLESPACE CONTAINER QUERY

Example

See the example provided for the OPEN TABLESPACE CONTAINER QUERY function in this chapter.

TABLESPACE CONTAINER QUERY

Purpose

The TABLESPACE CONTAINER QUERY function stores a copy of the table space container data for a table space (or for all table spaces in the current connected database) in a large DB2-allocated memory storage buffer, and returns the number of table space containers defined for a specified table space (or for all table spaces in the current connected database) to the calling application.

Syntax

```
SQL_API_RC SQL_API_FN sqlbtcq (struct sqlca            *SQLCA,
                              unsigned long            TableSpaceID,
                              unsigned long            *NumContainers,
                              struct SQLB_TBSCONTQRY_DATA **ContainerData);
```

Parameters

SQLCA A pointer to a location in memory where a SQLCA data structure variable is stored. This variable sends either status information (if the function executed successfully) or error information (if the function failed) back to the calling application.

TableSpaceID The ID of the table space for which container information is to be retrieved. If the value specified for this parameter is SQLB _ALL_TABLESPACES, a composite list of table space containers for all table spaces in the entire database will be returned.

NumContainers A pointer to a location in memory where this function is to store the actual number of rows of table space container information retrieved.

ContainerData A pointer to the address of an array of *SQLB_TBSCONTQRY_DATA* structures where this function is to store the retrieved table space container data.

Includes

```
#include <sqlutil.h>
```

Description

The TABLESPACE CONTAINER QUERY function stores a copy of the table space container data for a table space (or for all table spaces in the current connected database) in a large DB2-allocated memory storage buffer, and returns the number of table space containers defined for a specified table space (or for all table spaces in the current connected database) to the calling application. This function provides a one-call interface to the OPEN TABLESPACE CONTAINER QUERY, FETCH TABLESPACE CONTAINER QUERY, and CLOSE TABLESPACE CONTAINER QUERY functions, which can retrieve all the table space container data for one or more table spaces.

When this function is executed, a memory buffer that stores the complete set of table space container information retrieved is automatically allocated, a pointer to that buffer is stored in the *ContainerData* parameter, and the number of table space containers found in either the specified table space or the current connected database is stored in the *NumContainers* parameter. The memory storage buffer that holds the table space container information is actually an array of *SQLB_TBSCONTQRY_DATA* structures and the *NumContainers* parameter specifies the number of elements in the array. Refer to the *FETCH TABLESPACE CONTAINER QUERY* function for a detailed description of the *SQLB_TBSCONTQRY_DATA* structure.

Comments

- When this function is executed, if a sufficient amount of free memory is available, a memory storage buffer will automatically be allocated. You can free this memory storage buffer only by calling the FREE MEMORY function. It is the application's responsibility to ensure that all memory allocated by this function is freed when it is no longer needed. If sufficient memory is not available, this function will simply return the number of table space containers found and no memory will be allocated.
- If there is not enough free memory available to retrieve the complete set of table space container data at one time, you can use the OPEN TABLESPACE CONTAINER QUERY, FETCH TABLESPACE CONTAINER QUERY, and CLOSE TABLESPACE CONTAINER QUERY functions to retrieve the table space container data in smaller pieces.

Required Connection

This function can be called only if a connection to a database exists.

Authorization

Only users with system control (SYSCTRL) authority, system administrator (SYSADM) authority, system maintenance (SYSMAINT) authority, or database administrator (DBADM) authority are allowed to execute this function call.

See Also

OPEN TABLESPACE CONTAINER QUERY, FETCH TABLESPACE CONTAINER QUERY, CLOSE TABLESPACE CONTAINER QUERY

Example

The following C program illustrates how to use the TABLESPACE CONTAINER QUERY function to retrieve information about the table space containers defined for the SYSCATSPACE table space:

```
#include <stdio.h>
#include <stdlib.h>
#include <sqlenv.h>
#include <sqlutil.h>
#include <sql.h>

int main()
{
    /* Include The SQLCA Data Structure Variable */
```

```
    EXEC SQL INCLUDE SQLCA;
    /* Declare The Local Memory Variables */
    int                            rc = EXIT_SUCCESS;
    unsigned long                  ulTSCCount;
    struct SQLB_TBSCONTQRY_DATA    *TSContainerData = NULL;
    struct SQLB_TBSCONTQRY_DATA    *TSCDataPtr = NULL;
    unsigned long                  ulNumRows;

    /* Set Up A Simple SQL Error Handler */
    EXEC SQL WHENEVER SQLERROR GOTO EXIT;

    /* Connect To The SAMPLE Database */
    EXEC SQL CONNECT TO SAMPLE USER etpdd6z USING sanders;

    /* Retrieve The Table Space Container Data */
    sqlbtcq(&sqlca, 0, &ulTSCCount, &TSContainerData);

    /* Display The Table Space Container Data */
    printf("Containers Defined For The SYSCATSPACE Table Space\n");
    printf("ID   Name\n");
    printf("--------------------------\n");
    TSCDataPtr = TSContainerData;
    for (; ulTSCCount != 0; ulTSCCount--)
        {
        printf("%-4d ", TSCDataPtr->id);
        printf("%-12s\n", TSCDataPtr->name);
        TSCDataPtr++;
        }

    /* Free All Resources Associated With The Table Space Container */
    /* Query                                                         */
    sqlefmem(&sqlca, TSContainerData);

EXIT:
    /* If An Error Has Occurred, Display The SQL Return Code */
    if (sqlca.sqlcode != SQL_RC_OK)
        {
        printf("ERROR : %ld\n", sqlca.sqlcode);
        rc = EXIT_FAILURE;
        }

    /* Issue A Rollback To Free All Locks */
    EXEC SQL ROLLBACK;

    /* Turn Off The SQL Error Handler */
    EXEC SQL WHENEVER SQLERROR CONTINUE;

    /* Disconnect From The SAMPLE Database */
    EXEC SQL DISCONNECT CURRENT;

    /* Return To The Operating System */
    return(rc);
}
```

FREE MEMORY

Purpose The FREE MEMORY function frees memory allocated by either the TABLESPACE QUERY or the TABLESPACE CONTAINER QUERY function call.

Syntax

```
SQL_API_RC SQL_API_FN sqlefmem (struct sqlca *SQLCA,
                                void          *Buffer);
```

Parameters

SQLCA A pointer to a location in memory where a SQLCA data structure variable is stored. This variable sends either status information (if the function executed successfully) or error information (if the function failed) back to the calling application.

Buffer A pointer to a location in memory that contains the starting address of the memory buffer this function is to free.

Includes

```
#include <sqenv.h>
```

Description

The FREE MEMORY function frees memory allocated by either the TABLESPACE QUERY or TABLESPACE CONTAINER QUERY function call.

Comments

- Because the TABLESPACE CONTAINER QUERY and TABLESPACE QUERY functions do not release the memory they allocate, make sure to call the FREE MEMORY function when using either of these two functions.

Required Connection

This function can be called at any time; a connection to a DB2 database manager instance or to a DB2 database does not have to be established first.

Authorization

No authorization is required to execute this function call.

Example

See the examples provided for the TABLESPACE QUERY and TABLESPACE CONTAINER QUERY functions in this chapter.

REORGANIZE TABLE

Purpose

The REORGANIZE TABLE function reorganizes a table by reconstructing the rows in the table so fragmented data is eliminated and information is compacted.

Syntax

```
SQL_API_RC SQL_API_FN sqlureot_api (char         *TableName,
                                    char         *IndexName,
                                    char         *TableSpace,
                                    struct sqlca *SQLCA);
```

Parameters

TableName A pointer to a location in memory where the name of the table to be reorganized is stored. The specified table name can be an alias, except in the case of down-level servers, in which case a fully qualified table name must be used.

IndexName A pointer to a location in memory that contains the fully qualified name of the index to use when reorganizing the table. If this parameter is set to NULL, the data will be reorganized in no specific order.

TableSpace A pointer to a location in memory where the name of a temporary table space is stored (if a secondary work area is to be used). This parameter can contain a NULL value.

SQLCA A pointer to a location in memory where a SQLCA data structure variable is stored. This variable sends either status information (if the function executed successfully) or error information (if the function failed) back to the calling application.

Includes

```
#include <sqlutil.h>
```

Description

The REORGANIZE TABLE function reorganizes a table by reconstructing the rows in the table so fragmented data is eliminated and information is compacted. Tables that are frequently modified often contain fragmented data, which noticeably slows down access performance. These are excellent candidates for reorganization. You must complete all database operation and release all acquired locks (by issuing either COMMIT or ROLLBACK SQL statements from all active transactions) before this function can be called.

After a table is reorganized, execute the RUN STATISTICS function to update the table's statistics and rebind packages that reference the table (with either the BIND or the REBIND function or command) so new and possibly more efficient access plans will be generated.

Comments

- You can use the REORGCHK command to determine whether or not a table needs to be reorganized.
- If the name of an index name is specified in the *IndexName* parameter, the DB2 database manager will reorganize the data according to the order in the index. To maximize DB2 and application performance, specify indexes that are used often in SQL queries.
- This function cannot be used to reorganize views.
- This function cannot be used on a DMS table while an online backup of the table space in which the table resides is being performed.
- To complete a table space roll-forward recovery following a table reorganization, all DATA and LONG table spaces used must be enabled for roll-forward.
- If a table contains LOB columns that do not use the COMPACT option, the LOB DATA storage object can be significantly larger following table reorganization. This increase in size can result from the order in which the rows were reorganized and the types of table spaces used (SMS or DMS).
- DB2 for Common Servers, version 2.x servers do not support down-level client requests to reorganize a table. Since servers before version 2 do not support table spaces, the *TableSpace* parameter is treated as the version-1 *Path* parameter when version-2 clients are used with a down-level server. If a version-2 client requests to reorganize a table on a version-2 server and that request specifics a path instead of a temporary table space name in the *TableSpace* parameter, The REORGANIZE TABLE function will choose a temporary table space in which to place the work files on behalf of the user.
- A valid temporary table space name containing a path separator character (/ or \) should not be specified; it will be interpreted as a temporary path (a request before version 2) and the REORGANIZE TABLE function will choose a temporary table space on behalf of the user.
- If the specified table is not successfully reorganized when this function is executed, do not delete any temporary files that are created. The DB2 database manager will need these files in order to recover the database.

Required Connection This function can be called only if a connection to a database exists.

Authorization Only users with system control (SYSCTRL) authority, system administrator (SYSADM) authority, system maintenance (SYSMAINT) authority, or database administrator (DBADM) authority (or CONTROL authority for the specified table) are allowed to execute this function call.

See Also RUN STATISTICS, REBIND

Example The following C program illustrates how to use the REORGANIZE TABLE function to reorganize the EMPLOYEE table in the SAMPLE database:

```
#include <stdio.h>
#include <stdlib.h>
#include <sqlutil.h>
#include <sql.h>

int main()
{
    /* Include The SQLCA Data Structure Variable */
    EXEC SQL INCLUDE SQLCA;

    /* Declare The Local Memory Variables */
    int            rc = EXIT_SUCCESS;
    unsigned long  ulTSCCount;

    /* Set Up A Simple SQL Error Handler */
    EXEC SQL WHENEVER SQLERROR GOTO EXIT;

    /* Connect To The SAMPLE Database */
    EXEC SQL CONNECT TO SAMPLE USER etpdd6z USING sanders;

    /* Create An Index On The EMPLOYEE Table */
    EXEC SQL CREATE INDEX EMP_NUM ON USERID.EMPLOYEE(EMPNO);
    printf("Index EMP_NUM has been created for the EMPLOYEE table.\n");

    /* Reorganize The EMPLOYEE Table, Using The EMP_NUM Index */
    sqlureot("USERID.EMPLOYEE", "ETPDD6Z.EMP_NUM", NULL, &sqlca);
    if (sqlca.sqlcode == SQL_RC_OK)
        {
        printf("The EMPLOYEE table has been organized by Employee ");
        printf("Number.\n");
        }

    /* Delete The Index On The EMPLOYEE Table */
    EXEC SQL DROP INDEX EMP_NUM;
    printf("Index EMP_NUM has been deleted.\n");

    /* Commit The Changes */
    EXEC SQL COMMIT;

EXIT:
    /* If An Error Has Occurred, Display The SQL Return Code */
    if (sqlca.sqlcode != SQL_RC_OK)
        {
        printf("SQL ERROR : %ld\n", sqlca.sqlcode);
        rc = EXIT_FAILURE;
        }
```

```
    /* Turn Off The SQL Error Handler */
    EXEC SQL WHENEVER SQLERROR CONTINUE;

    /* Disconnect From The SAMPLE Database */
    EXEC SQL DISCONNECT CURRENT;

    /* Return To The Operating System */
    return(rc);
}
```

RUN STATISTICS

Purpose

The RUN STATISTICS function updates statistical information about the characteristics of a table and any or all of its associated indexes.

Syntax

```
SQL_API_RC SQL_API_FN sqlustat (char           *TableName,
                                unsigned short NumIndexes,
                                char           **IndexList,
                                unsigned char  StatsOption,
                                unsigned char  ShareLevel,
                                struct sqlca   *SQLCA);
```

Parameters

TableName A pointer to a location in memory where the name of the table for which statistics are to be updated is stored. The specified table name can be an alias, except for down-level servers, in which case a fully qualified table name must be used.

NumIndexes An integer value that specifies the number of indexes for which statistics are to be updated. If this parameter is set to 0, statistics will be calculated for all indexes defined for the table.

IndexList A pointer to a location in memory where an array of fully qualified index names is stored.

StatsOption A character value that specifies which statistical calculations are to be updated. This parameter can be set to any of the following values:

SQL_STATS_TABLE	Update basic table statistics only.
SQL_STATS_EXTTABLE_ONLY	Update basic table statistics with extended (distribution) statistics.
SQL_STATS_BOTH	Update both basic table statistics and basic statistics for indexes.
SQL_STATS_EXTTTABLE_INDEX	Update both basic table statistics (with distribution statistics) and basic statistics for indexes.
SQL_STATS_INDEX	Update basic statistics for indexes only.
SQL_STATS_EXTINDEX_ONLY	Update extended statistics for indexes only.
SQL_STATS_EXTINDEX_TABLE	Update extended statistics for indexes and basic table statistics.
SQL_STATS_ALL	Update extended statistics for indexes and basic table statistics with distribution statistics.

ShareLevel A character value that specifies how the statistics are to be gathered with respect to other users. This parameter can be set to any of the following values:

SQL_STATS_REF	Allows other users to have read-only access while the statistics are being gathered.
SQL_STATS_CHG	Allows other users to have both read and write access while the statistics are being gathered.

SQLCA A pointer to a location in memory where a SQLCA data structure variable is stored. This variable sends either status information (if the function executed successfully) or error information (if the function failed) back to the calling application.

Includes

```
#include <sqlutil.h>
```

Description

The RUN STATISTICS function updates statistical information about the characteristics of a table and any or all of its associated indexes. This information includes, among other things, the number of records in the table, the number of pages used to store the table, and the average record length. The SQL optimizer uses these statistics to determine the best access path to use when preparing SQL statements. Call this function whenever:

- A table has have been modified many times (for example, if a large number of updates have been made or if a significant amount of data has been inserted or deleted).
- A table has been reorganized.
- One or more new indexes have been created.

After a table's statistics are updated, rebind packages that reference the table (with either the BIND or the REBIND function or command) so new and possibly more efficient access plans will be generated.

Comments

- Each string in the index list array should contain a fully qualified index name. The value stored in the *NumIndexes* parameter should be equivalent to the number of index names stored in this index list (unless the *NumIndexes* parameter is set to 0).
- If the *StatsOption* parameter is to be set to SQL_STATS_TABLE or SQL_STATS_EXTTTABLE, collect statistics before creating any indexes. This guarantees that statistics gathered during index creation will not be overlaid by estimates gathered during the calculation of the table statistics.
- If index statistics are requested and statistics have never been run on the table containing the index, statistics for both the table and the indexes will be collected.
- After calling this function, an application should issue a COMMIT SQL statement to release all locks acquired.

Required Connection

This function can be called only if a connection to a database exists.

Authorization

Only users with system control (SYSCTRL) authority, system administrator (SYSADM) authority, system maintenance (SYSMAINT) authority, or database administrator (DBADM) authority (or CONTROL authority for the specified table) are allowed to execute this function call.

See Also

GET DATABASE CONFIGURATION, REORGANIZE TABLE, BIND, REBIND

Example

The following C program illustrates how to use the RUN STATISTICS function to update the statistics for the EMPLOYEE table in the SAMPLE database after a new index is created:

```
#include <stdio.h>
#include <stdlib.h>
#include <sqlutil.h>
#include <sql.h>

int main()
{
    /* Include The SQLCA Data Structure Variable */
    EXEC SQL INCLUDE SQLCA;

    /* Declare The Local Memory Variables */
    int            rc = EXIT_SUCCESS;
    unsigned long  ulTSCCount;
    char           *IndexArray = "ETPDD6Z.EMP_NUM";

    /* Set Up A Simple SQL Error Handler */
    EXEC SQL WHENEVER SQLERROR GOTO EXIT;

    /* Connect To The SAMPLE Database */
    EXEC SQL CONNECT TO SAMPLE USER etpdd6z USING sanders;

    /* Create An Index On The EMPLOYEE Table */
    EXEC SQL CREATE INDEX EMP_NUM ON USERID.EMPLOYEE(EMPNO);
    printf("Index EMP_NUM has been created for the EMPLOYEE table.\n");

    /* Update The Statistics For The EMPLOYEE Table, So That The */
    /* EMP_NUM Index Will Be Used When Creating Access Plans   */
    sqlustat("USERID.EMPLOYEE", 1, &IndexArray, SQL_STATS_ALL,
             SQL_STATS_REF, &sqlca);
    if (sqlca.sqlcode == SQL_RC_OK)
        {
        printf("The statistical information for the EMPLOYEE table ");
        printf("has been updated.\n");
        }

    /* Commit The Changes */
    EXEC SQL COMMIT;

EXIT:

    /* If An Error Has Occurred, Display The SQL Return Code */
    if (sqlca.sqlcode != SQL_RC_OK)
        {
        printf("ERROR : %ld\n", sqlca.sqlcode);
        rc = EXIT_FAILURE;
        }
    /* Turn Off The SQL Error Handler */
    EXEC SQL WHENEVER SQLERROR CONTINUE;

    /* Disconnect From The SAMPLE Database */
    EXEC SQL DISCONNECT CURRENT;

    /* Return To The Operating System */
    return(rc);
}
```

CHAPTER 23

DATABASE MIGRATION AND RECOVERY API'S

The database migration and recovery APIs are a group of DB2 API function calls that allow an application to migrate and perform data recovery operations on DB2 databases. This group includes:

- An API function that converts databases created with earlier versions of DB2 to DB2 for Common Servers, version 2.1.
- An API function that creates a backup image of a DB2 database.
- An API function that restores a database from a backup image.
- An API function that performs roll-forward recovery operations on a restored database.
- API functions that list the contents of a database's recovery history file.
- API functions that modify (and delete) entries in a database recovery history file.

Table 23.1 lists the database migration and recovery API functions available with DB2.

Database Migration

DB2 for Common Servers, version 2.1 is the fifth form of the Database 2 software product to be released for microcomputers. Each form of DB2 has its own unique internal format for creating and storing database information. Because of significant differences between each internal format, databases created under one form of the DB2 product cannot be directly accessed by another form of DB2. However, databases created under one form of DB2 can be converted to a more recent form. The MIGRATE DATABASE function can be used by an application to convert databases created under DB2/2 or DB2/6000, version 1.x to DB2 for Common Servers, version 2.1. Unfortunately, the database conversion process performs upward compatibility conversions only; you cannot convert DB2 databases to an earlier DB2 format.

Creating Backup Images

Problems can and sometimes do occur when you work with DB2 databases. Typically, database problems are caused by some type of media or storage problem, power interruption, and application failure. Fortunately, DB2 provides a way for an application to both create a backup image of a database or individual table spaces and rebuild them if they become damaged or corrupted. You can create a 23

TABLE 23.1 Database Migration and Recovery APIs

Function name	Description
MIGRATE DATABASE	Converts databases created under previous versions of DB2/2 and DB2/6000 to DB2 for Common Servers, version 2.1.
BACKUP DATABASE	Creates a backup image of a database or of one or more table spaces.
RESTORE DATABASE	Rebuilds a database (or one or more table spaces) by restoring them from a backup image.
SET TABLESPACE CONTAINERS	Allows a database to be restored into a different set of table space storage containers.
ROLLFORWARD DATABASE	Restores a database (or one or more table spaces) by applying transactions recorded in the database log files to it after it has been restored from a backup image.
OPEN RECOVERY HISTORY FILE SCAN	Stores a copy of selected records retrieved from a database recovery history file in memory.
GET NEXT RECOVERY HISTORY FILE ENTRY	Retrieves a record from the copy of recovery history file records that was placed in memory by the OPEN RECOVERY HISTORY FILE SCAN function.
CLOSE RECOVERY HISTORY FILE SCAN	Frees system resources allocated by the OPEN RECOVERY HISTORY FILE SCAN function.
UPDATE RECOVERY HISTORY FILE	Changes the location, device type, or comment associated with a record in a recovery history file.
PRUNE RECOVERY HISTORY FILE	Removes one or more records from a recovery history file.

backup image by using the BACKUP DATABASE function or command. The database's recovery history file is automatically updated with summary information whenever a backup image is created. This file is then used as a tracking mechanism for any recovery (restore) operations performed for the database.

Multiple backup images can be created and stored on the same media when backup operations are directed to disks. In order to uniquely identify each backup image, a special naming convention is used by the backup utility. A backup filename consists of the concatenation of the following units of information, separated by periods:

Database alias The database alias name that was specified when the backup utility was invoked (one to eight characters).

Backup type The type of backup image made (0 for full database or 3 for table space level backup).

Instance name The name of the current DB2 database manager instance (one to eight characters; the current value of the DB2INSTANCE environment variable).

Node Reserved for future use (The value 0 is currently used).

Time stamp The date and time the back image was created. The timestamp is in the format *yyyymmddhhnnss*, where:

- *yyyy* is the year (1995 to 1999)
- *mm* is the month (01 to 12)
- *dd* is the day of the month (01 to 31)
- *hh* is the hour (00 to 23)
- *nn* is the minutes (00 to 59)
- *ss* is the seconds (00 to 59)

Sequence number A file extension consisting of a three-digit sequence number. On OS/2, in order to satisfy the requirements of both FAT and HPFS file systems, the backup image filename complies with the 8.3 naming restriction. For tape-directed output, filenames are not created, but the same information is stored in the backup image header so it can be used later for verification purposes.

Restoring from Backup Images

Whenever a database or one of its table spaces becomes damaged or corrupt, you can restore it to the state it was in when the last backup image was made by using the RESTORE DATABASE function or command. You can use the backup image to restore the same database from which the backup image was created, or create a new database that is an exact duplicate of the database that the backup image was created from.

A backup image contains a list of all table space containers being used by the database or table space at the time the backup image is made. During a restore operation, all table space containers listed in the backup image are checked to see if they currently exist and are accessible. If one or more table space containers no longer exist or are inaccessible, the restore operation will fail. In order to allow a backup image to be used in such a situation, you can add, change, or remove table space containers during a restore operation. This type of restore operation is referred to as a redirected restore. The SET TABLESPACE CONTAINERS function allows an application to perform a redirected restore operation.

Roll-forward Recovery

When a database is restored from a backup image, all changes made to the database since the backup image was created are discarded. Fortunately, all databases have transaction log files that contain a record of all database changes made. Roll-forward recovery uses these logs to rebuild a database to a specified point in time by reapplying the changes recorded in the log files to the database after a restore operation. The roll-forward recovery utility can also use these log files to reapply previous changes to a database. A roll-forward recovery operation can follow the completion of a full database restore operation, or it can be performed on any table space that is in a roll-forward pending state. In either case, before the roll-forward utility can be used, a database must be configured so that roll-forward recovery is enabled. Figure 23.1 illustrates how roll-forward recovery is used in conjunction with the backup and restore utilities to return a database to the state it was in at a specified point in time.

If a roll-forward recovery operation is to perform a redirected restore, you might not want to reapply table space container changes found in the log files (for example, if the specified table spaces no longer exist). When an application calls the SET TABLESPACE CONTAINERS function, it can specify whether or not table space container operations found in a transaction log file are reapplied or ignored.

Recovery History Files

A recovery history file is created when a database is created, and is automatically updated whenever:

- The database or one of its table spaces is backed up.
- The database or one of its table spaces is restored.
- One of the database's tables is loaded.

The recovery history file contains a summary of backup information that is used in case all or part of the database must be recovered to a specific point in time. The information stored in this file includes:

- The tables and table spaces of the database that were backed up, restored, or loaded.
- How the backup, restore, or load operation was performed.
- The time the backup image was made (if a backup operation was performed).

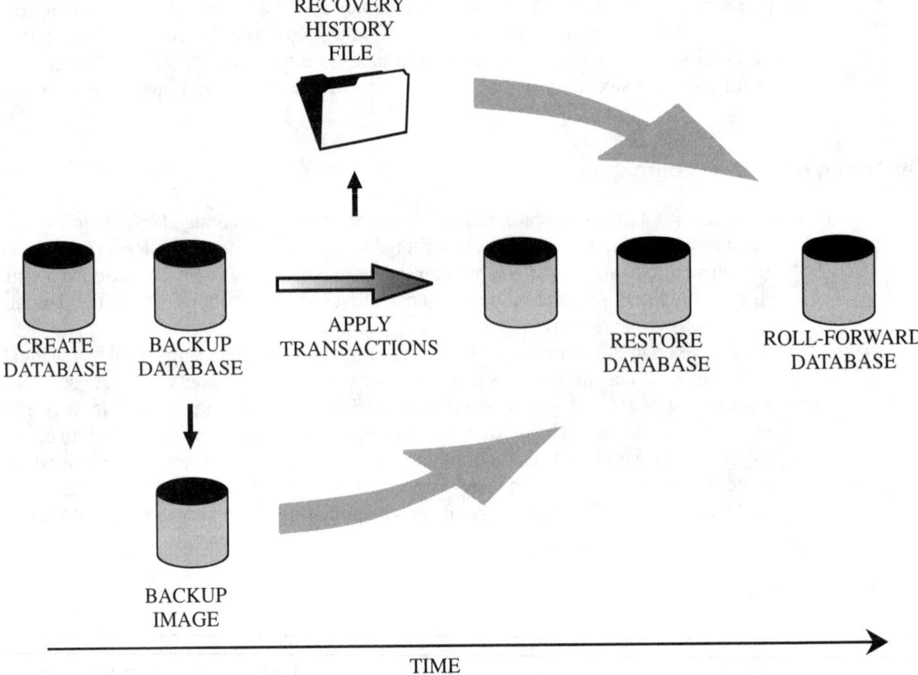

FIGURE 23-1 How the backup, restore, and roll-forward recovery utilities work.
From left to right: 1. A database is created. 2. The database is backed up (a backup image is created). 3. As transactions are applied to the database they are also written to the recovery history file. 4. When the database is restored from the backup image; all changes made to the database since the backup image was created are lost. 5. Roll-forward recovery is applied to the database, using the recovery history file. This leaves the database in the same state it was in before the restore opeation began.

- The location of the backup or copy image that was created (stating both the device information and the logical way to access the image).
- The last time a restore operation was performed.

Each backup image contains a copy of the database's recovery history file. When a backup image is restored to a database that already has a recovery history file, the existing recovery history file is not overwritten. However, if a backup image is restored to a new database, the recovery history file stored in the backup image becomes the recovery history file for that database. If the current database is unstable or unavailable and if its recovery history file is damaged or has been deleted, just the recovery history file itself can be restored from a backup image.

An application can retrieve records (entries) stored in a database recovery history file by performing the following steps:

1. Call the OPEN RECOVERY HISTORY FILE SCAN function to copy select recovery history file records to a function allocated memory storage buffer.
2. Allocate an *sqluhinfo* structure with space for *x* number of table spaces, where *x* is the value returned in the *NumEntries* parameter after the OPEN RECOVERY HISTORY FILE SCAN function is called. This number is normally the number of table spaces that have been defined for the specified database. You can use the macro SQLUHINFOSIZE(n), defined in *sqlutil.h*, to determine how much memory is required for a *sqluhinfo* structure with *x* table space fields.
3. Set the *sqln* field of the allocated *sqluhinfo* structure to *x*.
4. In a loop, perform the following steps:
   a. Call the GET NEXT RECOVERY FILE HISTORY ENTRY function to retrieve records from the history file.

b. Check the *sqlca.sqlcode* value returned by the GET NEXT RECOVERY FILE HISTORY ENTRY function call. If the *sqlca.sqlcode* value is SQL_RC_OK, use the *sqld* field of the *sqluhinfo* structure to determine the number of table space entries returned. If the *sqlca.sqlcode* value is SQLUH_SQLUHINFO_VARS_WARNING (meaning not enough space is allocated for all the table spaces that DB2 is trying to return), free and reallocate the *sqluhinfo* structure with enough space for *sqld* table space entries, and set *sqln* to *sqld*. If the *sqlca.sqlcode* value is SQLE_RC_NOMORE, all records have been retrieved.
c. Display or process the retrieved information.

5. When all recovery history file records are retrieved, call the CLOSE RECOVERY HISTORY FILE SCAN function to free the resources allocated by the OPEN RECOVERY HISTORY FILE SCAN function.

You can change entries in a database recovery history file by calling the UPDATE RECOVERY HISTORY FILE function, and remove entries in a recovery history file that are no longer valid (or needed) by calling the PRUNE RECOVERY HISTORY FILE function.

MIGRATE DATABASE

Purpose

The MIGRATE DATABASE function converts databases created under previous versions of DB2/2 and DB2/6000 to DB2 for Common Servers, version 2.1.

Syntax

```
SQL_API_RC SQL_API_FN sqlemgdb (char          *DBAlias,
                                char          *UserID,
                                char          *Password,
                                struct sqlca  *SQLCA);
```

Parameters

DBAlias A pointer to a location in memory where the alias of a database that was created with an earlier version of DB2 is stored.

UserID A pointer to a location in memory where the authorization name (user identifier) of the user is stored. This is the name under which the attachment is authenticated. This parameter can contain a NULL value.

Password A pointer to a location in memory where the password for the specified authorization name is stored. This parameter can contain a NULL value.

SQLCA A pointer to a location in memory where a SQL communication area (SQLCA) data structure variable is stored. This variable sends either status information (if the function executed successfully) or error information (if the function failed) back to the calling application.

Includes

```
#include <sqlenv.h>
```

Description

The MIGRATE DATABASE function converts databases created under previous versions of DB2/2 and DB2/6000 to DB2 for Common Servers, version 2.1. Once a database is converted to DB2 for Common Servers, version 2.1, it can not be converted back to its original format. Because of this, it is a good idea to create a backup image of a database before it is migrated.

Comments

- Only Extended Services 1.0 databases, DB2/2 version 1.x databases, and DB2/6000 version 1.x databases can be migrated.
- A database must be cataloged in the system database directory before it can be migrated.

- You can use the *db2ckmig* tool to determine whether or not a DB2 database can be migrated (refer to the *IBM Database 2 for AIX Installation and Operation Guide* or the *IBM Database 2 for OS/2 Installation and Operation Guide* for more information about this tool).
- This function cannot be used in applications that run on the Windows or Windows NT operating system.

Required Connection This function can be called at any time; a connection to a DB2 database manager instance or DB2 database does not have to be established first. When this function is called, it establishes a connection to the specified database.

Authorization Only users with system administrator (SYSADM) authority can execute this function call.

See Also BACKUP DATABASE

Example The following C program illustrates how to use the MIGRATE DATABASE function to convert a DB2/2 version 1.0 database to the DB2 for Common Servers, version 2.1 format:

```
#include <stdio.h>
#include <stdlib.h>
#include <string.h>
#include <sqlenv.h>
#include <sqlca.h>

int main()
{
    /* Declare The Local Memory Variables */
    struct sqlca  sqlca;

    /* Migrate A DB2 Version 1.1 Database To DB2 Version 2.1 */
    sqlemgdb ("BOOKSAMP", "etpdd6z", "sanders", &sqlca);

    /* Display A Success Message */
    printf("Database BOOKSAMP has been migrated to DB2 Version 2.1.\n");

    /* Return To The Operating System */
    return(EXIT_SUCCESS);
}
```

BACKUP DATABASE

Purpose The BACKUP DATABASE function creates a backup copy of a database or of one or more table spaces.

Syntax

```
SQL_API_RC SQL_API_FN
   sqlubkup (char                              *DBAlias,
             unsigned long                     BufferSize,
             unsigned long                     BackupMode,
             unsigned long                     BackupType,
             unsigned long                     CallerAction,
```

```
char                                *ApplicationID,
char                                *TimeStamp,
unsigned long                       NumBuffers,
struct sqlu_tablespace_bkrst_list   *TableSpaceList,
struct sqlu_media_list              *MediaTargetList,
char                                *UserName,
char                                *Password,
void                                *Reserved1,
unsigned long                       *VendorOptionsSize,
void                                *VendorOptions,
void                                *Reserved2,
struct sqlca                        *SQLCA);
```

Parameters

DBAlias A pointer to a location in memory where the alias name of the database to back up is stored.

BufferSize The size, in 4KB units, that all temporary buffers created and used during the backup operation should be. Temporary backup buffers must be at least sixteen 4KB pages in size.

BackupMode Specifies how the backup utility is to be run. This parameter can be set to any of the following values:

SQLUB_OFFLINE Specifies that the backup utility is to be run offline (i.e., no other applications can connect to the database while the backup operation is in progress).

SQLUB_ONLINE Specifies that the backup utility is to be run online (i.e., other applications can connect to and access the database while the backup operation occurs).

BackupType Specifies the type of backup image to create. This parameter can be set to any of the following values:

SQLUB_FULL Specifies that a full database backup image is to be created.

SQLUB_TABLESPACE Specifies that a backup image containing one or more table spaces is to be created. If this value is specified, a list of the appropriate table spaces must be provided in the *TableSpaceList* parameter.

CallerAction Specifies the action this function is to take when it is executed. This parameter can be set to any of the following values:

SQLUB_BACKUP Specifies that the backup operation is to be started.

SQLUB_NOINTERRUPT Specifies that the backup operation is to be started and that it is to run unattended. When this option is specified, scenarios that normally require user intervention will be attempted without returning to the calling application or they will generate an error.

SQLUB_CONTINUE Specifies that the backup operation is to be continued after the user performs some action requested by the backup utility (inserting a diskette, mounting a new tape, etc.).

SQLUB_TERMINATE	Specifies that the backup operation is to be terminated after the user fails to perform some action requested by the backup utility.
SQLUB_DEVICE_TERMINATE	Specifies that a particular device be removed from the list of devices used by backup utility. When a particular medium is full, the backup utility returns a warning to the caller (while continuing to process using the remaining devices). By calling the BACKUP function again with this caller action specified, you can remove the device that generated the warning condition from the list of devices being used.
SQLUB_PARAM_CHECK	Specifies that the parameter values specified for the BACKUP function call are to be checked for validity. This caller action does not invoke the backup utility.

ApplicationID A pointer to a location in memory where this function is to store a string that identifies the agent servicing the application. You can use the application ID string to obtain information about the progress of the backup operation (using the database monitor).

TimeStamp A pointer to a location in memory where this function is to store the time stamp (in ISO format) that identifies when the backup image was created. This value is also stored in the backup image.

NumBuffers The number of temporary buffers to be created and used by the backup utility.

TableSpaceList A pointer to a *sqlu_tablespace_bkrst_list* structure that contains a list of table space names to be used when creating a table space backup image. If a database backup is being performed, this parameter will be ignored.

MediaTargetList A pointer to a *sqlu_media_list* structure that contains a list of destination devices to be used for storing the backup image.

UserName A pointer to a location in memory where the authorization name (user identifier) to be used to connect to the database is stored.

Password A pointer to a location in memory where the password for the specified authorization name is stored. This parameter can contain a NULL value.

Reserved1 A pointer that is reserved for later use. For now, this parameter must always be set to NULL.

VendorOptionsSize The size, in bytes, of the data stored in the structure referenced by the *VendorOptions* parameter.

VendorOptions A pointer to a *sqlu_vendor* structure that contains vendor specific information to be passed from the application calling the backup utility to one or more vendor-supplied functions.

Reserved2 A pointer that is reserved for later use. For now, this parameter must always be set to NULL.

SQLCA A pointer to a location in memory where a SQLCA data structure variable is stored. This variable sends either status information (if the function executed successfully) or error information (if the function failed) back to the calling application.

Includes

```
#include <sqlutil.h>
```

Description

The BACKUP DATABASE function creates a backup copy of a database or of one or more table spaces. All databases should be backed up on a regular basis. If you have an available database backup image and the database becomes damaged or corrupted, it can be returned to the state it was in the last time it was backed up. Furthermore, if the database is enabled for roll-forward recovery, it can be restored to the state it was in just before the damage occurred. Table space level backup images can also be made for a database. You can use these backup images to recover from problems that affect only specific table spaces.

Two special structures (*sqlu_tablespace_bkrst_list* and *sqlu_media_list*) pass table space names and backup device information to the DB2 backup utility when this function is called. The first of these structures, *sqlu_tablespace_bkrst_list*, is defined in *sqlutil.h* as follows:

```
typedef struct sqlu_tablespace_bkrst_list
{
long                              num_entry;       /* The number of entries      */
                                                   /* in the list of table space */
                                                   /* names that is stored in the */
                                                   /* the tablespace field       */
struct sqlu_tablespace_entry      *tablespace;     /* A pointer to an array of   */
                                                   /* sqlu_tablespace_entry      */
                                                   /* structures that contains a */
                                                   /* list of table space names  */
} sqlu_tablespace_bkrst_list;
```

This structure contains a pointer to an array of additional *sqlu_tablespace_entry* structures that are used to hold table space names. The *sqlu_tablespace_entry* structure is defined in *sqlutil.h* as follows:

```
typedef struct sqlu_tablespace_entry
{
unsigned long  reserve_len;                        /* The length of the table    */
                                                   /* space name stored in the   */
                                                   /* tablespace_entry field.    */
                                                   /* This field is used only if */
                                                   /* the table space name is not */
                                                   /* null-terminated.           */
char           tablespace_entry[19];               /* The table space name       */
char           filler[1];                          /* Reserved                   */
} sqlu_tablespace_entry;
```

The second special structure used by the BACKUP DATABASE function is *sqlu_media_list*. This structure describes the type(s) of media to which the backup image is to be written. The *sqlu_media_list* structure is defined in *sqlutil.h* as follows:

```
typedef struct sqlu_media_list
{
char                          media_type; /* Indicates that the media type is one */
                                          /* or more local devices                */
                                          /* (SQLU_LOCAL_MEDIA),                  */
                                          /* a DB2 ASDM shared library            */
                                          /* (SQLU_ASDM_MEDIA),                   */
                                          /* a vendor product shared library      */
                                          /* (SQLU_OTHER_MEDIA),                  */
```

```
                                        /* or a user exit routine          */
                                        /* (SQLU_USER_EXIT). Local         */
                                        /* devices can be any combination of */
                                        /* tapes (AIX only), disks, or     */
                                        /* diskettes.                      */
char                     filler[3];     /* Reserved.                       */
long                     sessions;      /* The number of entries in the list of */
                                        /* devices that is stored in the target */
                                        /* field.                          */
union sqlu_media_list_targets  target;  /* A pointer to an array of one of */
                                        /* two types of structures that    */
                                        /* contains additional device      */
                                        /* information. The type of structure */
                                        /* to use is determined by the value */
                                        /* specified in the media_type field. */
} sqlu_media_list;
```

This structure contains a pointer to an array of structures that provide additional information about the specific media devices to be used. This array can contain either of the following DB2-defined structures:
sqlu_media_entry Local media information (SQLU_LOCAL_MEDIA)
sqlu_vendor Other media information (SQLU_OTHER_MEDIA)
The *sqlu_media_entry* structure is defined in *sqlutil.h* as follows:

```
typedef struct sqlu_media_entry
{
unsigned long  reserve_len;             /* The length of the path name     */
                                        /* stored in the media_entry field. */
                                        /* This field is used only if the path */
                                        /* name is not null-terminated.    */
char           media_entry[216];        /* A valid path name               */
} sqlu_media_entry;
```

The *sqlu_vendor* structure is defined in *sqlutil.h* as follows:

```
typedef struct sqlu_vendor
{
unsigned long  reserve_len1;            /* The length of the shared library */
                                        /* name stored in the shr_lib field. */
                                        /* This field is used only if the shared */
                                        /* library name is not null-terminated. */
char           shr_lib[256];            /* The name of a vendor-supplied   */
                                        /* shared library that is used for */
                                        /* storing and retrieving data     */
unsigned long  reserve_len2;            /* The length of the load input    */
                                        /* source-file name stored in the  */
                                        /* filename field. This field is used */
                                        /* only if the source-file name is not */
                                        /* null-terminated.                */
char           filename[256];           /* The name of an input source file */
                                        /* that is to be used for providing */
                                        /* information to a shared library */
} sqlu_vendor;
```

The type of structure that provides additional information about specific devices is determined by the value specified in the *media_type* field of the *sqlu_media_list* structure, as follows:
SQLU_LOCAL_MEDIA One or more *sqlu_media_entry* structures.

SQLU_ADSM_MEDIA No structure is needed if the ADSTAR distributed storage manager (ADSM) shared library provided with DB2 is used. If a different version of an ADSM shared library is used, use the SQLU_OTHER_MEDIA value.

SQLU_OTHER_MEDIA One or more *sqlu_vendor* structures.

SQLU_USER_EXIT No structure is needed. (This value can be specified only under OS/2.)

Refer to the *IBM Database 2 Administration Guide* for a general discussion of the backup and restore utilities.

Comments

- If the *BackupType* parameter is set to SQLUB_TABLESPACE, the *TableSpaceList* parameter must contain a valid list of table space names.
- The *CallerAction* parameter must be set to SQLUB_BACKUP, SQLUB_NOINTERRUPT, or SQLUB_PARM_CHECK the first time this function is called.
- The *CallerAction* parameter should be set to SQLUB_NOINTERRUPT whenever all the media needed for the backup operation are available and utility prompts are not needed.
- The application ID string returned by this function can be up to 33 characters long (including the null-terminator character).
- The time stamp string returned by this function can be up to 15 characters long (including the null-terminator character).
- The *sqlu_vendor* structure that the *VendorOptions* parameter references must be flat (it must not contain any level of indirection). Byte reversal is not performed on this structure and code page values are not compared.
- Online backups are permitted only if roll-forward recovery is enabled. An online backup can be performed while the database is being accessed and modified by other applications.
- In order to perform an offline backup, the backup utility must be able to connect to the specified database in exclusive mode. The BACKUP DATABASE function will therefore fail if any application, including the application calling the BACKUP DATABASE function, is connected to the specified database. If the backup utility can connect to the specified database in exclusive mode, it will lock out other applications until the backup operation is complete. Since the time required to create a database backup image can be significant (especially for large databases), perform offline backups only when the database will not be needed by other applications.
- An offline backup operation will fail if the specified database or table space(s) are not in a consistent state. If the specified database is not in a consistent state, you must restart it with the RESTART DATABASE function (to bring it back to a consistent state through crash recovery) before you can execute the BACKUP DATABASE function.
- Backup images can be directed to fixed disks, diskettes, tapes, ADSM, or other vendor products that are enabled for DB2. Since there is no native tape support on OS/2, each type of tape device requires a unique device driver, and backups to tape must be performed through user exits.
- Although you can use the BACKUP DATABASE function to back up databases located at remote sites, the backup image itself must be directed to devices that are local to the machine on which the database

resides (unless ADSM or another DB2-enabled vendor product is used). With ADSM and other DB2-enabled vendor products, the interface for the backup is local, but the location of the storage media to which the backup image is to be written can be remote.

- If a database that is enabled for roll-forward recovery is backed up, it can be returned to the state it was in prior to the damage (refer to the RESTORE DATABASE and ROLLFORWARD DATABASE functions for more information).
- If the database is left in a partially restored state because of a system failure during restoration, the restore operation must be successfully rerun before the BACKUP DATABASE function can be executed. If the database is placed in the *rollforward_pending* state after a successful restoration, the database must also be rolled forward to a consistent state before the BACKUP DATABASE function can be executed.
- If a database is changed from the roll-forward disabled to the roll-forward enabled state, either the *logretain* or *userexit* database configuration parameter must be set appropriately before the BACKUP DATABASE function can be executed (refer to Chapter 20 for more information about retrieving and setting database configuration parameters).
- A table space level backup can contain one or more table spaces for a database.
- While one table space is being restored, all other table spaces are available for processing.
- To ensure that restored table spaces are synchronized with the rest of the database, they must be rolled forward to the end of the recovery history log file (or to the point where the table spaces were last used). Because of this, table space level backup images can be made only if roll-forward recovery is enabled.
- A user might choose to store data, indexes, long field (LONG) data, and large object (LOB) data in different table spaces. If LONG and LOB data do not reside in the same table space, a table space backup cannot be performed.
- You can back up and restore each component of a table by independently backing up and restoring each table space in which the table components reside.
- Temporary table spaces cannot be backed up. If a list of table spaces to be backed up contains one or more temporary table space names, the BACKUP DATABASE function will fail.
- Table space level backups and restores cannot be run concurrently.

Note: Currently (as of the writing of this book), the BACKUP DATABASE function will not work correctly in OS/2 if a diskette drive is specified as the backup target device, unless the us8110 patch has been applied to version 2.1.1. This problem does not exist in version 2.1.1, but it does exist in version 2.1 and in the us8090 patch. This patch can be found on the World Wide Web at: http://www.software.ibm.com/data/db2/db2tech/index.html.

Required Connection This function can be called at any time; a connection to a DB2 database manager instance or a DB2 database does not have to be established first. When this function is called, it establishes a connection to the specified database.

Authorization

Only users with system control (SYSCTRL) authority, system administrator (SYSADM) authority, or system maintenance (SYSMAINT) authority can execute this function call.

See Also

RESTORE DATABASE, ROLLFORWARD DATABASE, MIGRATE DATABASE

Example

The following C program illustrates how to use the BACKUP DATABASE function to back up the SAMPLE database to diskettes on the A: drive:

```
#include <stdio.h>
#include <stdlib.h>
#include <string.h>
#include <sqlutil.h>
#include <sqlca.h>

int main()
{
    /* Declare The Local Memory Variables */
    struct sqlu_media_list   Media_List;
    struct sqlu_media_entry  Media_Entry;
    char                     szApplicationID[33];
    char                     szTimeStamp[27];
    int                      iDiskCounter = 1;
    char                     cKeyPress;
    struct sqlca             sqlca;

    /* Initialize The Media List Information Data Structure */
    Media_List.media_type = SQLU_LOCAL_MEDIA;
    Media_List.sessions = 1;
    strcpy(Media_Entry.media_entry, "A:");
    Media_List.target.media = &Media_Entry;

    /* Prompt The User To Insert The First Diskette In The Drive */
    printf("Insert Disk %d in Drive A:\n", iDiskCounter);
    printf("Press Enter to continue.\n");
    cKeyPress = getchar();
    iDiskCounter++;

    /* Start Backing Up The SAMPLE Database To Diskettes */
    sqlubkup("SAMPLE", 16, SQLUB_OFFLINE, SQLUB_FULL,
             SQLUB_BACKUP, szApplicationID, szTimeStamp, 4, NULL,
             &Media_List, "etpdd6z", "sanders", NULL, 0, NULL,
             NULL, &sqlca);

    /* As Long As The Backup Database Function Indicates That A */
    /* New Diskette Is Needed, Prompt The User To Insert One    */
    while (sqlca.sqlcode == SQLU_DEVICE_FULL_WARNING)
        {

        /* Prompt The User For A New Diskette */
        printf("Insert Disk %d in Drive A:\n", iDiskCounter);
        printf("Press Enter to continue.\n");
        cKeyPress = getchar();
        iDiskCounter++;

        /* If A Diskette Was Inserted In The Drive, Continue The */
        /* Backup Process                                        */
        sqlubkup ("SAMPLE", 16, SQLUB_OFFLINE, SQLUB_FULL,
                  SQLUB_CONTINUE, szApplicationID, szTimeStamp, 4,
```

```
                    NULL, &Media_List, "etpdd6z", "sanders", NULL, 0,
                    NULL, NULL, &sqlca);
        }

    /* If The Database Could Not Be Backed Up, Display An Error */
    /* Message And Terminate The Backup Process                 */
    if (sqlca.sqlcode != SQL_RC_OK)
        {
        printf("ERROR : %ld\n", sqlca.sqlcode);

        sqlubkup ("SAMPLE", 16, SQLUB_OFFLINE, SQLUB_FULL,
                  SQLUB_TERMINATE, szApplicationID, szTimeStamp, 4,
                  NULL, &Media_List, "etpdd6z", "sanders", NULL, 0,
                  NULL, NULL, &sqlca);

        return(EXIT_FAILURE);
        }

    /* Display A Success Message */
    printf("The SAMPLE database has been successfully backed up.\n");

    /* Return To The Operating System */
    return(EXIT_SUCCESS);
}
```

RESTORE DATABASE

Purpose The RESTORE DATABASE function rebuilds a damaged or corrupted database (or one or more damaged or corrupted table spaces) by restoring it from a backup image created with the BACKUP DATABASE function.

Syntax

```
SQL_API_RC SQL_API_FN
  sqlursto (char                                  *SourceDBAlias,
  char                                            *TargetDBAlias,
  unsigned long                                   BufferSize,
  unsigned long                                   RollForwardMode,
  unsigned long                                   RestoreType,
  unsigned long                                   CallerAction,
  char                                            *ApplicationID,
  char                                            *TimeStamp,
  char                                            *TargetPath,
  unsigned long                                   NumBuffers,
  struct sqlu_tablespace_bkrst_list               *TableSpaceList,
  struct sqlu_media_list                          *MediaSourceList,
  char                                            *UserName,
  char                                            *Password,
  void                                            *Reserved1,
  unsigned long                                   VendorOptionsSize,
  void                                            *VendorOptions,
  void                                            *Reserved2,
  struct sqlca                                    *SQLCA);
```

Parameters

SourceDBAlias A pointer to a location in memory where the alias name of the source database that was used to create the backup image is stored.

TargetDBAlias A pointer to a location in memory that contains the alias name of the target database to which the backup image is to be restored.

If this parameter is set to NULL, the database is restored to the alias specified in the *SourceDBAlias* parameter.

BufferSize The size, in 4KB units, that all temporary buffers created and used during the restore operation should be. Temporary restore buffers must be at least sixteen 4KB pages in size.

RollForwardMode Specifies whether or not the database should be placed in the roll-forward pending state after the database is restored. This parameter can be set to any of the following values:

SQLUD_ROLLFWD	Specifies that the database is to be placed in roll-forward pending state after it is successfully restored.
SQLUD_NOROLLFWD	Specifies that the database is not to be placed in roll-forward pending state after it is successfully restored.

RestoreType Specifies the type of restore operation to perform. This parameter can be set to any of the following values:

SQLUD_FULL	Specifies that everything found in the backup image is to be restored. If this value is specified, the restore utility will be ran offline.
SQLUD_ONLINE_TABLESPACE	Specifies that only table space level information found in the backup image is to be restored. If this value is specified, the restore utility will be ran online.
SQLUD_HISTORY	Specifies that only the recovery history file is to be restored.

CallerAction Specifies the action this function is to take when it is executed. This parameter can be set to any of the following values:

SQLUD_RESTORE	Specifies that the restore operation is to be started.
SQLUD_NOINTERRUPT	Specifies that the restore operation is to be started and that it is to run unattended. When this option is specified, scenarios that normally require user intervention will be attempted without returning to the calling application or they will generate an error.
SQLUD_CONTINUE	Specifies that the restore operation is to be continued after the user performs some action requested by the restore utility (for example, inserting a diskette or mounting a new tape).
SQLUD_TERMINATE	Specifies that the restore operation is to be terminated after the user fails to perform some action requested by the restore utility.
SQLUD_DEVICE_TERMINATE	Specifies that a particular device is removed from the list of devices used by the restore utility. When a particular device has exhausted its input, the restore utility returns a

warning to the caller (while continuing to process using the remaining devices). By calling the RESTORE function again with this caller action specified, you can remove the device that generated the warning condition from the list of devices being used.

SQLUD_PARAM_CHECK Specifies that the parameter values specified for the RESTORE function call are to be checked for validity. This caller action does not invoke the restore utility.

SQLUD_RESTORE_STORDEF Specifies that one or more table space redefinitions are to be performed during the restore operation.

ApplicationID A pointer to a location in memory where this function is to store a string that identifies the agent servicing the application. You can use this application ID string to obtain information about the progress of the restore operation (using the database monitor).

TimeStamp A pointer to a location in memory that contains the time stamp that identifies when the backup image was created. This value is not needed if there is only one backup image on the specified backup image source media.

TargetPath A pointer to a location in memory where the relative or fully qualified name of the target database is stored. This parameter is used only if a new database is to be created from the backup image being restored.

NumBuffers The number of temporary buffers to be created and used by the restore utility.

TableSpaceList A pointer to a *sqlu_tablespace_bkrst_list* structure that is currently reserved for later use. For now, this parameter must always be set to NULL.

MediaSourceList A pointer to a *sqlu_media_list* structure that contains a list of devices to be used when restoring the database or one or more table spaces from a backup image created by the backup utility.

UserName A pointer to a location in memory where the authorization name (user identifier) for connecting to the database is stored.

Password A pointer to a location in memory where the password for the specified authorization name is stored. This parameter can contain a NULL value.

Reserved1 A pointer that is currently reserved for later use. For now, this parameter must always be set to NULL.

VendorOptionsSize The size, in bytes, of the data stored in the structure referenced by the *VendorOptions* parameter.

VendorOptions A pointer to a *sqlu_vendor* structure that contains vendor-specific information to be passed from the application calling the restore utility to one or more vendor-supplied functions.

Reserved2 A pointer that is currently reserved for later use. For now, this parameter must always be set to NULL.

SQLCA A pointer to a location in memory where a SQLCA data structure variable is stored. This variable sends either status information (if the function executed successfully) or error information (if the function failed) back to the calling application.

Includes

```
#include <sqlutil.h>
```

Description

The RESTORE DATABASE function rebuilds a damaged or corrupted database (or one or more damaged or corrupted table spaces) by restoring it from a backup image that was created with the BACKUP DATABASE function. When a database is restored, it is placed in the same state it was in when the backup copy image was made. If the database was enabled for roll-forward recovery when the backup image was made, you can return it to the state it was in just before the damage occurred by executing the ROLLFORWARD DATABASE function after the RESTORE DATABASE function is successfully executed.

Note: Database log files must be copied to a separate directory before a database is restored if they are to be used to roll a database forward (otherwise, they will be replaced with the log files stored in the backup image during the restore operation). These log files must then be copied to the appropriate log file path (as specified in the database configuration file) after the restore operation executes and before the ROLLFORWARD DATABASE function is called. Or the directory they are stored in must be specified in the *OverflowLogPath* parameter of the ROLLFORWARD DATABASE function. If these log files cannot be accessed by the roll-forward recovery utility, the roll-forward recovery operation will fail (refer to the ROLLFORWARD DATABASE function for more information).

Also note: Backup images of databases or table spaces must have been created with the BACKUP DATABASE function in order to be used by the RESTORE DATABASE function.

A database backup image can be restored as a new database if the original database from which the backup image was made no longer exists (the new database will have the same name). Also, since a database backup image can be restored to a database with a different name, the RESTORE DATABASE function essentially provides a method for copying entire databases. You can also use the RESTORE DATABASE function to restore one or more table spaces from a table space level backup image created with the BACKUP DATABASE function. Table space backup images can be used to recover from problems that affect only specific table spaces.

Two special structures (*sqlu_tablespace_bkrst_list* and *sqlu_media_list*) pass table space names and restore device information to the DB2 restore utility when this function is called. Refer to the BACKUP DATABASE function for a detailed description of these structures and for more information about how they are initialized.

Comments

- After a database is successfully restored, if it is placed in the roll-forward pending state, the ROLLFORWARD DATABASE function must be executed to bring the database up to the current point in time before it can be used by other applications.
- The *CallerAction* parameter must be set to SQLUD_RESTORE, SQLUD_NOINTERRUPT, SQLUD_RESTORE_STORDEF, or SQLUD_PARM_CHECK the first time this function is called.
- The *CallerAction* parameter should be set to SQLUD_NOINTERRUPT whenever all the media needed for the backup operation is available and utility prompts are not needed.

- The *CallerAction* parameter should be set to SQLUD_DEVICE_TERMINATE to close a device when it is no longer needed. For example, if a user is restoring a database from a backup image stored on three tape volumes using two tape devices, and all the data on one of the tapes has been restored, the application calling the RESTORE function will receive control from the function, along with an *sqlca.sqlcode,* which indicating that the end of the tape was reached. The application can then prompt the user to mount another tape, and if the user indicates that there are no more tapes, the application can call the RESTORE function again with the *CallerAction* parameter set to SQLUD_DEVICE_TERMINATE to signal the end of the media. The device driver will be terminated, but the rest of the devices involved in the restore operation will continue to have their input processed until all segments of the backup image are restored (the number of segments in the backup image is placed on the last media device during the backup process).
- The application ID string returned by this function can be up to 33 characters long (including the null terminator).
- The time stamp string specified in the *TimeStamp* parameter can be up to 15 characters long (including the null terminator).
- The *sqlu_vendor* structure referenced by the *VendorOptions* parameter must be flat (it must not contain any level of indirection). Byte reversal is not performed on this structure and code page values are not compared.
- In order to perform an offline restore, the restore utility must be able to connect to the specified database in exclusive mode. The RESTORE DATABASE function will therefore fail if any application, including the application calling the RESTORE DATABASE function, is connected to the specified database. If the restore utility can connect to the specified database in exclusive mode, it will lock out other applications until the restore operation is complete. Since the time required to restore a database from a backup image can be significant (especially for large databases), perform offline restores only when the database will not be needed by other applications.
- The current database configuration file will not be replaced when the database is restored unless it is has been corrupted. If the database configuration file is replaced with the database configuration file stored in the backup image, a warning will be returned in the SQLCA data structure variable.
- When restoring an existing database, if a system failure occurs during a crucial stage of the restore operation, the database will be left in a partially restored state and the restore operation must be successfully rerun before any users and/or applications can connect to it. This condition will not be detected until an application or user attempts to connect to the partially restored database.
- When restoring to a nonexistent or new database, if a system failure occurs during a crucial stage of the restore operation, the restored database will be deleted (dropped).
- If a database was not configured for roll-forward recovery when its backup image was made and if the current database configuration file has roll-forward recovery enabled, the user is required to either make a new backup of the database or disable the *logretain* and *userexit* database configuration file parameters immediately after the restore operation is

completed. No user or application can connect to the database until one of these actions is performed.

- If the *RestoreType* parameter is set to SQLUD_HISTORY, the recovery history file stored in the backup image will be restored over the existing recovery history file for the database, effectively erasing any changes made to the recovery history file after the backup image was created. If this action is undesirable, restore the recovery history file to a new or test database so you can view its contents without destroying any updates that have taken place since the backup image was made. Refer to the OPEN RECOVERY HISTORY FILE SCAN, GET NEXT RECOVERY HISTORY FILE ENTRY, and CLOSE RECOVERY HISTORY FILE SCAN functions for information on viewing the contents of a recovery history file.
- If roll-forward recovery is disabled for a database after a table space level backup image was made, you cannot restore the table space(s) from the backup table space image and then roll the table space(s) forward to the current point in time. Instead, all table space level backup images made prior to the time roll-forward recovery was disabled can no longer be used by the RESTORE DATABASE function (the RESTORE function will fail if the user attempts to restore from such a backup image). In cases where you cannot determine whether or a backup image is invalid, the restore operation might appear to be successful; the invalid restore set will be detected only during the roll-forward recovery operation.
- In order to perform a redirected restore (a restore operation in which a database is restored and a different set of operating system storage containers are desired or required), the *CallerAction* parameter must be set to SQLUD_RESTORE_STORDEF and the SET TABLESPACE CONTAINERS function must identify the new system storage locations. Refer to the SET TABLESPACE CONTAINERS function for more information.

Required Connection

The connection requirements for this function depend on the type of restore operation being performed:

- When restoring a backup image to an existing database, this function can be called at any time; a connection to a DB2 database manager instance or to a DB2 database does not have to be established first. When this function is called, it establishes a connection to the specified database.
- When restoring a backup image to a new database, this function cannot be called unless a connection to a DB2 database manager instance and a DB2 database exists (an instance attachment is required to create the new database).
- When restoring a backup image to a new database at a remote DB2 database manager instance, an instance attachment must exist (the ATTACH function must be called) before this function is called.

Authorization

Only users with system control (SYSCTRL) authority, system administrator (SYSADM) authority, or system maintenance (SYSMAINT) authority can execute this function call to restore a backup image to an existing database. Only users with either SYSCTRL or SYSADM authority can execute this function call to restore a backup image to a new database.

See Also

BACKUP DATABASE, ROLLFORWARD DATABASE, MIGRATE DATABASE, SET TABLESPACE CONTAINERS, GET DATABASE CONFIGURATION

Example

The following C program illustrates how to use the RESTORE DATABASE function to restore the SAMPLE database from a backup image stored on diskettes on the A: drive:

```
#include <stdio.h>
#include <stdlib.h>
#include <string.h>
#include <sqlutil.h>
#include <sqlca.h>

int main()
{
    /* Declare The Local Memory Variables */
    struct sqlu_media_list    Media_List;
    struct sqlu_media_entry   Media_Entry;
    char                      szApplicationID[33];
    int                       iDiskCounter = 1;
    char                      cKeyPress;
    struct sqlca              sqlca;

    /* Initialize The Media List Information Data Structure */
    Media_List.media_type = SQLU_LOCAL_MEDIA;
    Media_List.sessions = 1;
    strcpy(Media_Entry.media_entry, "A:");
    Media_List.target.media = &Media_Entry;

    /* Prompt The User To Insert The First Diskette In The Drive */
    printf("Insert Disk %d in Drive A:\n", iDiskCounter);
    printf("Press Enter to continue.\n");
    cKeyPress = getchar();
    iDiskCounter++;

    /* Start Restoring The SAMPLE Database From Diskettes */
    sqlursto("SAMPLE", "SAMPLE", 16, SQLUD_NOROLLFWD, SQLUD_FULL,
             SQLUD_RESTORE, szApplicationID, 0, "F:",
             4, NULL, &Media_List, "etpdd6z", "sanders", NULL, 0,
             NULL, NULL, &sqlca);

    /* Ignore The Warning Message Stating That The Existing */
    /* Database Will Be Overwritten                          */
    if (sqlca.sqlcode == 2529 || sqlca.sqlcode == 2539)
        {
        sqlursto ("SAMPLE", "SAMPLE", 16, SQLUD_NOROLLFWD, SQLUD_FULL,
               SQLUD_CONTINUE, szApplicationID, 0, "F:",
               4, NULL, &Media_List, "etpdd6z", "sanders", NULL, 0,
               NULL, NULL, &sqlca);
        }

    /* As Long As The Restore Database Function Indicates That */
    /* Another Backup Diskette Is Needed, Prompt The User To   */
    /* Insert One                                              */
    while (sqlca.sqlcode == SQLU_END_OF_MEDIA_WARNING)
        {

        /* Prompt The User For A New Diskette */
        printf("Insert Disk %d in Drive A:\n", iDiskCounter);
        printf("Press Enter to continue.\n");
        cKeyPress = getchar();
        iDiskCounter++;
```

```
        /* If A Diskette Was Inserted In The Drive, Continue The */
        /* Restore Process                                         */
        sqlursto ("SAMPLE", "SAMPLE", 16, SQLUD_NOROLLFWD, SQLUD_FULL,
              SQLUD_CONTINUE, szApplicationID, 0, "F:",
              4, NULL, &Media_List, "etpdd6z", "sanders", NULL, 0,
              NULL, NULL, &sqlca);
        }

    /* If The Database Could Not Be Restored, Display An Error */
    /* Message And Terminate The Restore Process               */
    if (sqlca.sqlcode != SQL_RC_OK)
        {
        printf("ERROR : %ld\n", sqlca.sqlcode);

        sqlursto ("SAMPLE", "SAMPLE", 16, SQLUD_NOROLLFWD, SQLUD_FULL,
              SQLUD_TERMINATE, szApplicationID, 0, "F:",
              4, NULL, &Media_List, "etpdd6z", "sanders", NULL, 0,
              NULL, NULL, &sqlca);

        return(EXIT_FAILURE);
        }

    /* Display A Success Message */
    printf("The SAMPLE database has been successfully restored.\n");

    /* Return To The Operating System */
    return(EXIT_SUCCESS);
}
```

SET TABLESPACE CONTAINERS

Purpose

The SET TABLESPACE CONTAINERS function supports a redirected restore operation (a restore operation in which a database is restored and a different set of table space storage containers are desired or required).

Syntax

```
SQL_API_RC SQL_API_FN
    sqlbstsc (struct sqlca                *SQLCA,
              unsigned long               RollForwardRecoveryOption,
              unsigned long               TableSpaceID,
              unsigned long               NumContainers,
              struct SQLB_TBSCONTQRY_DATA *ContainerData);
```

Parameters

SQLCA A pointer to a location in memory where a SQLCA data structure variable is stored. This variable sends either status information (if the function executed successfully) or error information (if the function failed) back to the calling application.

RollForwardRecoveryOption A long integer that specifies how ALTER TABLESPACE operations that exist in a recovery log file are to be handled when a roll-forward database recovery operation is performed. This parameter can be set to any of the following values:

SQLB_SET_CONT_INIT_STATE Redo ALTER TABLESPACE operations that exist in the recovery log file(s) when performing a roll-forward recovery operation.

SQLB_SET_CONT_FINAL_STATE	Ignore ALTER TABLESPACE operations that exist in the recovery log file(s) when performing a roll-forward recovery operation.

TableSpaceID The ID of the table space for which one or more storage containers are to be redefined.

NumContainers The number of table space container definitions (elements) that are stored in the array of *SQLB_TBSCONTQRY_DATA* structures referenced by the *ContainerData* parameter.

ContainerData A pointer to an array of *SQLB_TBSCONTQRY_DATA* structures that contain one or more table space container definitions.

Includes

```
#include <sqlutil.h>
```

Description

The SET TABLESPACE CONTAINERS function supports a *redirected* restore operation (a restore operation in which a database is restored and a different set of table space storage containers are desired or required). Before this function is executed, an array of special structures (*SQLB_TBSCONTQRY_DATA* structures) must first be allocated and initialized with table space container definitions. Refer to the FETCH TABLESPACE CONTAINER QUERY function for a detailed description of this structure. Although an array of *SQLB_TBSCONTQRY_DATA* structures must be provided, only the *contType, totalPages, name*, and *nameLen* fields of each structure must be initialized (for languages other than C and C++); all other fields in this structure are ignored.

This function is used in conjunction with the RESTORE DATABASE function to restore a database or one or more table spaces that were backed up with the BACKUP DATABASE command or function. A backup image of a database, or of one or more table spaces, contains information about all table space containers defined for the database or table space(s) when the backup operation took place. During a restore operation, all containers identified in the backup image are checked to see if they currently exist and are accessible. If one or more of these containers no longer exists or, for some reason, has become inaccessible, the restore operation will fail. You can use the SET TABLESPACE CONTAINERS function to add, change, or remove table space containers during a restore operation, thereby getting around this type of situation and allowing a backup image to be successfully restored.

The following steps illustrate how to use this function in a redirected restore operation:

1. Call the RESTORE DATABASE function with the *CallerAction* parameter set to SQLUD_RESTORE.
2. Wait for the RESTORE DATABASE function to return a *sqlca.sqlcode* that indicates that one or more of the table space containers are inaccessible.
3. Call the SET TABLESPACE CONTAINER function with the appropriate table space container definitions, and the *RollForwardRecoveryOption* parameter set to the appropriate state (SQLB_SET_CONT_FINAL_STATE is the recommended state to use).
4. Call the RESTORE DATABASE function again, this time with the *CallerAction* parameter set to SQLUD_RESTORE_STORDEF.

This sequence will allow the restore operation to use the new table space container definitions; any table space container referenced in recovery log file(s) will be ignored when the ROLLFORWARD DATABASE function is called (if the SQLB_SET_CONT_FINAL_STATE state was specified).

Comments

- Use this function only when a table space is in a *storage definition pending* or a *storage definition allowed* state. These states occur during a restore operation, immediately prior to the restoration of database or table space pages.
- When creating the container list, keep in mind that there must be sufficient disk space to allow for the restore and roll-forward operations to place all the original data into these new containers. If there is not enough available disk space, one or more table spaces will be left in the *recovery pending* state until sufficient disk space is made available. It is a good idea to keep records of disk usage on a regular basis. Then, when a restore and roll-forward operation needs to be performed, you can determine how much disk space is required.
- When new containers are defined for an existing table space, they will replace any containers that exist for the table space when the redirected restore operation is performed. When new containers replace existing containers, the existing containers are not automatically removed from the storage media where they are stored. Therefore, it is the user's responsibility to remove unused containers after a redirected restore operation is performed.

Required Connection

This function can be called only if a connection to a database exists.

Authorization

Only users with either system control (SYSCTRL) authority or system administrator (SYSADM) authority are allowed to execute this function call.

See Also

BACKUP DATABASE, RESTORE DATABASE, ROLLFORWARD DATABASE

Example

The following C program illustrates how to use the SET TABLESPACE CONTAINERS function to redefine table space containers during a restore operation:

```
#include <stdio.h>
#include <stdlib.h>
#include <string.h>
#include <sqlutil.h>
#include <sqlca.h>

/* Declare The Function Prototypes */
int BackupDatabase(void);
int RestoreDatabase(void);

int main()
{
    /* Include The SQLCA Data Structure Variable */
    EXEC SQL INCLUDE SQLCA;

    /* Set Up A Simple SQL Error Handler */
    EXEC SQL WHENEVER SQLERROR GOTO EXIT;

    /* Declare The Local Memory Variables */
    int   rc = EXIT_SUCCESS;
    char  szDefinerID[9];
```

```
    /* Declare The SQL Host Memory Variables */
    EXEC SQL BEGIN DECLARE SECTION;
        char        szTBSpace[18];
        char        szDefiner[8];
    EXEC SQL END DECLARE SECTION;

    /* Connect To The SAMPLE Database */
    EXEC SQL CONNECT TO SAMPLE USER etpdd6z USING sanders;

    /* Create A Temporary SMS Table Space */
    EXEC SQL CREATE TEMPORARY TABLESPACE MY_SPACE
        MANAGED BY SYSTEM
        USING ('G:.TSP', 'G:.TSP')
        EXTENTSIZE 256;

    /* Print A Message Telling That The Table Space Was Created */
    printf("\nSMS Table Space MY_SPACE has been created.\n");

    /* Commit The Transaction */
    EXEC SQL COMMIT;

    /* Disconnect From The SAMPLE Database */
    EXEC SQL DISCONNECT CURRENT;

    /* Backup The SAMPLE Database */
    printf("Starting the database back up process.\n\n");
    rc = BackupDatabase();
    if (rc != EXIT_SUCCESS)
        goto EXIT;

    /* Connect To The SAMPLE Database */
    EXEC SQL CONNECT TO SAMPLE USER etpdd6z USING sanders;

    /* Delete The Table Space */
    EXEC SQL DROP TABLESPACE MY_SPACE;

    /* Commit The Transaction */
    EXEC SQL COMMIT;

    /* Re-Create The Temporary SMS Table Space (Minus 1 Container) */
    EXEC SQL CREATE TEMPORARY TABLESPACE MY_SPACE
        MANAGED BY SYSTEM
        USING ('G:.TSP')
        EXTENTSIZE 256;

    /* Print A Message Telling That The Table Space Was Modified */
    printf("The SMS Table Space MY_SPACE has been modified.\n");

    /* Commit The Transaction */
    EXEC SQL COMMIT;

    /* Disconnect From The SAMPLE Database */
    EXEC SQL DISCONNECT CURRENT;

    /* Restore The SAMPLE Database */
    printf("Starting the database restore process.\n");
    rc = RestoreDatabase();

EXIT:
    /* If An Error Has Occurred, Display The SQL Return Code */
    if (sqlca.sqlcode != SQL_RC_OK)
```

```
        {
        printf("ERROR : %ld\n", sqlca.sqlcode);
        rc = EXIT_FAILURE;
        }

    /* Turn Off The SQL Error Handler */
    EXEC SQL WHENEVER SQLERROR CONTINUE;

    /* Return To The Operating System */
    return(rc);
}

/* Define The Backup Database Function */
int BackupDatabase()
{

    /* Declare The Local Memory Variables */
    struct sqlu_media_list   Media_List;
    struct sqlu_media_entry  Media_Entry;
    char                     szApplicationID[33];
    char                     szTimeStamp[27];
    int                      iDiskCounter = 1;
    char                     cKeyPress;
    struct sqlca             sqlca;

    /* Initialize The Media List Information Data Structure */
    Media_List.media_type = SQLU_LOCAL_MEDIA;
    Media_List.sessions = 1;
    strcpy(Media_Entry.media_entry, "A:");
    Media_List.target.media = &Media_Entry;

    /* Prompt The User To Insert The First Diskette In The Drive */
    printf("Insert Disk %d in Drive A:\n", iDiskCounter);
    printf("Press Enter to continue.\n");
    cKeyPress = getchar();
    iDiskCounter++;

    /* Start Backing Up The SAMPLE Database To Diskettes */
    sqlubkup("SAMPLE", 16, SQLUB_OFFLINE, SQLUB_FULL,
             SQLUB_BACKUP, szApplicationID, szTimeStamp, 4, NULL,
             &Media_List, "etpdd6z", "sanders", NULL, 0, NULL,
             NULL, &sqlca);

    /* As Long As The Backup Database Function Indicates That A */
    /* New Diskette Is Needed, Prompt The User To Insert One   */
    while (sqlca.sqlcode == SQLU_DEVICE_FULL_WARNING)
        {

        /* Prompt The User For A New Diskette */
        printf("Insert Disk %d in Drive A:\n", iDiskCounter);
        printf("Press Enter to continue.\n");
        cKeyPress = getchar();
        iDiskCounter++;

        /* If A Diskette Was Inserted In The Drive, Continue The */
        /* Backup Process                                         */
        sqlubkup ("SAMPLE", 16, SQLUB_OFFLINE, SQLUB_FULL,
                  SQLUB_CONTINUE, szApplicationID, szTimeStamp, 4,
                  NULL, &Media_List, "etpdd6z", "sanders", NULL, 0,
                  NULL, NULL, &sqlca);
        }
```

```
    /* If The Database Could Not Be Backed Up, Display An Error */
    /* Message And Terminate The Backup Process                 */
    if (sqlca.sqlcode != SQL_RC_OK)
       {
       printf("ERROR : %ld\n", sqlca.sqlcode);

       sqlubkup ("SAMPLE", 16, SQLUB_OFFLINE, SQLUB_FULL,
                 SQLUB_TERMINATE, szApplicationID, szTimeStamp, 4,
                 NULL, &Media_List, "etpdd6z", "sanders", NULL, 0,
                 NULL, NULL, &sqlca);

       return(EXIT_FAILURE);
       }

    /* Display A Success Message */
    printf("The SAMPLE database has been successfully backed up.\n\n");

    /* Return To The Calling Function */
    return(EXIT_SUCCESS);
}

/* Define The Restore Database Function */
int RestoreDatabase()
{

    /* Declare The Local Memory Variables */
    int                          rc = 0;
    int                          FirstPass = 0;
    struct sqlu_media_list       Media_List;
    struct sqlu_media_entry      Media_Entry;
    char                         szApplicationID[33];
    struct SQLB_TBSCONTQRY_DATA  TSContainers[3];
    int                          iDiskCounter = 1;
    char                         cKeyPress;
    struct sqlca                 sqlca;

    /* Initialize The Media List Information Data Structure */
    Media_List.media_type = SQLU_LOCAL_MEDIA;
    Media_List.sessions = 1;
    strcpy(Media_Entry.media_entry, "A:");
    Media_List.target.media = &Media_Entry;

    /* Prompt The User To Insert The First Diskette In The Drive */
    printf("Insert Disk %d in Drive A:\n", iDiskCounter);
    printf("Press Enter to continue.\n");
    cKeyPress = getchar();
    iDiskCounter++;

    /* Start Restoring The SAMPLE Database From Diskettes */
    sqlursto("SAMPLE", "SAMPLE", 16, SQLUD_NOROLLFWD, SQLUD_FULL,
             SQLUD_RESTORE_STORDEF, szApplicationID, 0, "F:",
             4, NULL, &Media_List, "etpdd6z", "sanders", NULL, 0,
             NULL, NULL, &sqlca);

    /* Ignore The Warning Message Stating That The Existing */
    /* Database Will Be Overwritten - Exit If Any Other     */
    /* Error Occurs                                         */
    if (sqlca.sqlcode != 2539)
       {
       printf("ERROR : %ld\n", sqlca.sqlcode);
```

```
    sqlursto ("SAMPLE", "SAMPLE", 16, SQLUD_NOROLLFWD, SQLUD_FULL,
        SQLUD_TERMINATE, szApplicationID, 0, "F:", 4, NULL,
        &Media_List, "etpdd6z", "sanders", NULL, 0, NULL, NULL,
        &sqlca);

    return(EXIT_FAILURE);
    }

/* Continue Restoring The SAMPLE Database From Diskettes */
sqlursto ("SAMPLE", "SAMPLE", 16, SQLUD_NOROLLFWD, SQLUD_FULL,
          SQLUD_CONTINUE, szApplicationID, 0, "F:",
          4, NULL, &Media_List, "etpdd6z", "sanders", NULL, 0,
          NULL, NULL, &sqlca);

/* If The Error Message Stating That A Table Space Container */
/* No Longer Exists Is Generated, Define New Table Space     */
/* Containers                                                */
if (sqlca.sqlcode == 1277)
    {

    /* Set A New List Of Table Space Containers */
    TSContainers[0].contType = SQLB_CONT_PATH;
    sprintf(TSContainers[0].name, "G:\NEW_TSP1.1");
    TSContainers[1].contType = SQLB_CONT_PATH;
    sprintf(TSContainers[1].name, "G:\NEW_TSP1.2");

    rc = sqlbstsc(&sqlca, SQLB_SET_CONT_INIT_STATE, 3, 2,
              (struct SQLB_TBSCONTQRY_DATA *) &TSContainers[0]);

    /* If The New List Of Table Space Containers Could Not Be */
    /* Set, Display An Error Message                          */
    if (sqlca.sqlcode != SQL_RC_OK)
        {
        printf("ERROR : %ld\n", sqlca.sqlcode);
        return(EXIT_FAILURE);
        }

    /* If New Table Space Containers Have Been Created, */
    /* Display A Message Saying So                      */
    printf("New Table Space Containers Have Been Defined.\n\n");

    }

/* As Long As The Restore Database Function Indicates That */
/* Another Backup Diskette Is Needed, Prompt The User To   */
/* Insert One                                              */
sqlca.sqlcode = SQLU_END_OF_MEDIA_WARNING;
FirstPass = 1;
while (sqlca.sqlcode == SQLU_END_OF_MEDIA_WARNING)
    {

    /* Prompt The User For A New Diskette */
    if (FirstPass != 1)
        {
        printf("Insert Disk %d in Drive A:\n", iDiskCounter);
        printf("Press Enter to continue.\n");
        cKeyPress = getchar();
        iDiskCounter++;
        }
    else
        FirstPass = 0;
```

```
        /* If A Diskette Was Inserted In The Drive, Continue The */
        /* Restore Process                                       */
        sqlursto ("SAMPLE", "SAMPLE", 16, SQLUD_NOROLLFWD,
              SQLUD_FULL, SQLUD_CONTINUE, szApplicationID, 0, "F:",
              4, NULL, &Media_List, "etpdd6z", "sanders", NULL, 0,
              NULL, NULL, &sqlca);
        }

    /* If The Database Could Not Be Restored, Display An Error */
    /* Message And Terminate The Restore Process               */
    if (sqlca.sqlcode != SQL_RC_OK)
        {
        printf("ERROR : %ld\n", sqlca.sqlcode);

        sqlursto ("SAMPLE", "SAMPLE", 16, SQLUD_NOROLLFWD, SQLUD_FULL,
              SQLUD_TERMINATE, szApplicationID, 0, "F:",
              4, NULL, &Media_List, "etpdd6z", "sanders", NULL, 0,
              NULL, NULL, &sqlca);

        return(EXIT_FAILURE);
        }

    /* Display A Success Message */
    printf("The SAMPLE database has been successfully restored.\n\n");

    /* Return To The Calling Function */
    return(EXIT_SUCCESS);
}
```

ROLLFORWARD DATABASE

Purpose

The ROLLFORWARD DATABASE function restores a damaged or corrupted database (or one or more damaged or corrupted table spaces) to the state it was in just before the damage occurred by applying transactions recorded in the database log files to it after a successful restore operation has occurred.

Syntax

```
SQL_API_RC SQL_API_FN sqlurllf (char           *DBAlias,
                                unsigned short CallerAction,
                                char           *ApplicationID,
                                char           *StopTime,
                                char           *NextArcFileName,
                                char           *FirstDelArcFileName,
                                char           *LastDelArcFileName,
                                char           *LastCommitTime,
                                char           *UserID,
                                char           *Password,
                                char           *OverflowLogPath,
                                unsigned short ConnectMode,
                                void           *Reserved,
                                struct sqlca   *SQLCA);
```

Parameters

DBAlias A pointer to a location in memory where the alias name of the database cataloged in the system directory is stored.

CallerAction Specifies the action this function takes when it is executed. This parameter can be set to any of the following values:

SQLUM_ROLLFWD	Specifies that the database is to be rolled forward to the point in time specified by the value stored in the *PointInTime* parameter. If this caller action is specified, the database will be placed in *rollforward_pending* state.
SQLUM_STOP	Specifies that the roll-forward operation is to be terminated. If this caller action is specified, the database will be taken out of the *rollforward_pending* state, no new log records will be processed, and all uncommitted transactions will be backed out.
SQLUM_ROLLFWD_STOP	Specifies that the database is to be rolled forward to the point in time specified by the value stored in the *PointInTime* parameter, and that the roll-forward operation is to be terminated. If this caller action is specified, the database will be taken out of the *rollforward_pending* state when the roll-forward operation terminates.
SQLUM_QUERY	Specifies that values for the *NextArcFileName, FirstDelArcFileName, Last DelArcFileName*, and *LastCommitTime* parameters are to be obtained from the recovery log files. This caller action does not invoke the roll-forward utility.
SQLUM_PARAM_CHECK	Specifies that the parameter values specified for the ROLLFORWARD DATABASE function call are to be checked for validity. This caller action does not invoke the roll-forward utility.
SQLUM_LOADREC _CONTINUE	Specifies that the roll-forward opera tion is to be continued after the user has performed some action requested by the roll-forward utility (for example, mounting a new tape).
SQLUM_LOADREC _DEVICE_TERMINATE	Specifies that a particular device is re moved from the list of devices used by the roll-forward utility. When a particular device has exhausted its input, the roll-forward utility returns a warning to the caller (while continuing to process using the remaining devices). By calling the ROLLFORWARD DATABASE function again with this caller action specified, you can remove the device that generated the warning condition from the list of devices being used.
SQLUD_LOADREC _TERMINATE	Specifies that all devices being used by roll-forward recovery are to be terminated.

ApplicationID A pointer to a location in memory where this function is to store a string that identifies the agent servicing the application. You can use this application ID string to obtain information about the progress of the roll-forward operation (using the database monitor). This parameter can contain a NULL value.

StopTime A pointer to a location in memory that contains a character string containing a time stamp (in ISO format) for determining when to terminate roll-forward recovery. Database roll-forward recovery will stop when this time stamp is exceeded. The parameter can contain a NULL value.

NextArcFileName A pointer to a location in memory where this function is to store the name of the next required recovery archive log file.

FirstDelArcFileName A pointer to a location in memory where this function is to store the name of the first recovery archive log file used (which is no longer needed for roll-forward recovery).

LastDelArcFileName A pointer to a location in memory where this function is to store the name of the last recovery archive log file used (which is no longer needed for roll-forward recovery).

LastCommitTime A pointer to a location in memory where this function is to store the time stamp, in ISO format, of the last transaction committed when roll-forward recovery terminates.

UserID A pointer to a location in memory where the authorization name (user identifier) for connecting to the database is stored.

Password A pointer to a location in memory where the password for the specified authorization name is stored. This parameter can contain a NULL value.

OverflowLogPath A pointer to a location in memory where an alternate log file path to be used when searching for active and archived log files is stored. This parameter can contain a NULL value.

ConnectMode Specifies how the roll-forward utility runs. This parameter can be set to any of the following values:

SQLUM_OFFLINE Specifies that the roll-forward utility is to be run offline (no other applications can connect to the database while the roll-forward operation is in progress). This value must be specified for database roll-forward recovery.

SQLUM_ONLINE Specifies that the roll-forward utility is to be run online (other applications can connect to and access the database while the roll-forward operation occurs). This value can be used only with table space roll-forward recovery.

Reserved A pointer that is currently reserved for later use. For now, this parameter must always be set to NULL.

SQLCA A pointer to a location in memory where a SQLCA data structure variable is stored. This variable sends either status information (if the function executed successfully) or error information (if the function failed) back to the calling application.

Includes

```
#include <sqlutil.h>
```

Description

The ROLLFORWARD DATABASE function restores a damaged or corrupted database (or one or more damaged or corrupted table spaces) to the state it was in just before the damage occurred by applying transactions recorded in the database log files to it after a successful restore operation. When this function is called, the DB2 database manager uses information stored in both archived and active log files to reconstruct the transactions performed on the database since its last backup image was made.

The ROLLFORWARD DATABASE function is normally called after a database or table space backup image is used to restore a database or one or more table spaces, or when one or more table spaces are taken offline by the database due to a media error. A database must be enabled for roll-forward recovery (that is, either the *logretain* parameter and/or the *userexit* parameter in the database configuration file must be set appropriately) before it can be recovered with the roll-forward recovery utility.

> Note: Log files must be copied to a separate directory before a database is restored if they are to be used to roll a database forward (otherwise, they will be replaced with the log files stored in the backup image during the restore operation). These log files must then be copied to the appropriate log file path (as specified in the database configuration file) after the restore operation executes and before the ROLLFORWARD DATABASE function is called or the directory in which they are stored must be specified in the *OverflowLogPath* parameter. If these log files cannot be accessed by the roll-forward recovery utility, the roll-forward recovery operation will fail.

Once roll-forward recovery is started, it will not stop until one of the following events occurs:

- No more recovery log files are found in the specified directories.
- A time stamp in the current recovery log file being used exceeds the completion time stamp specified in the *StopTime* parameter.
- An error occurs during the reading of a recovery log file.

Comments

- The *CallerAction* parameter must be set to SQLUM_ROLLFWD, SQLUM_QUERY, or SQLUM_PARM_CHECK the first time this function is called.
- The application ID string returned by this function can be up to 33 characters long (including the null terminator).
- If the *StopTime* parameter contains the value SQLUM_INFINITY _TIMESTAMP, the database will be rolled forward as far as possible. If the *CallerAction* parameter is set to anything other than SQLUM _ROLLFWD, SQLUM_STOP, or SQLUM_ROLLFWD_STOP, the *StopTime* parameter can be set to NULL.
- For table space roll-forward recovery, the *StopTime* parameter must always be set to SQLUM_INFINITY_TIMESTAMP.
- If the *CallerAction* parameter is set to anything other than SQLUM _QUERY and a filename is returned in the *NextArcFileName* parameter, an error occurred while attempting to access that file. Possible causes of this type of error are:
  - –The file was not found in the database log directory nor in the path specified in the *OverflowLogPath* parameter.
  - –The user exit program failed to return the archived recovery log file.
- The filename returned in the *NextArcFileName* parameter can be up to 13 characters long (including the null terminator).
- The filename returned in the *FirstDelArcFileName* parameter can be up to 13 characters long (including the null terminator). This file and all files

up to and including the filename returned in the *LastDelArcFileName* parameter can be removed from the storage media to make room for other files. For example, if the recovery log filename returned in the *First DelArcFileName* parameter is S0000001.LOG and the recovery log filename returned in the *LastDelArcFileName* parameter is S0000005.LOG, the following recovery log files can be deleted: S0000001.LOG, S0000002.LOG, S0000003.LOG, S0000004.LOG, and S0000005.LOG.

- The filename returned in the *LastDelArcFileName* parameter can be up to 13 characters long (including the null terminator).
- The time stamp returned in the *LastCommitTime* parameter is 27 characters long (including the null terminator).
- During roll-forward recovery, all recovery log files are searched for, first in the directory specified in the *logpath* parameter of the database configuration file and then in the overflow log path. If no overflow log path is specified, both active log files and archived log files need to be located in the *logpath* directory. This means that the user might have to physically move one or more archived log files from one location to another before they can be used by the roll-forward utility. This can cause problems if there is not sufficient space in the *logpath* directory. If you store the location of archived recovery log files in the *OverflowLogPath* parameter, recovery log files do not have to be moved and potential problems can be avoided. The overflow log path specified must be a valid, fully qualified path.
- For table space roll-forward recovery operations, the SQLM_ROLLFWD, SQLM_STOP, and SQLM_ROLLFWD_STOP caller actions have the same effect, which is rolling forward all table spaces in the roll-forward pending (SQLB_ROLLFORWARD_PENDING) or roll-forward in progress (SQLB_ROLLFORWARD_IN_PROGRESS) states.
- The action performed when this function is executed depends on the current value of the database's *rollforward_pending* flag (you can determine the value of this flag by executing the GET DATABASE CONFIGURATION function). If the database is in the roll-forward pending state (SQLB_ROLLFORWARD_PENDING), this flag will be set to **DATABASE**. If one or more table spaces are in the roll-forward pending state (SQLB_ROLLFORWARD_PENDING) or roll-forward-in-progress state (SQLB_ROLLFORWARD_IN_PROGRESS), this flag will be set to **TABLESPACE**. If neither the database nor any of its table spaces needs to be rolled forward, this flag will be set to **NO**.
- If the database is in the roll-forward pending state (the *rollforward_pending* flag is set to DATABASE) when this function is called, the entire database (and all of its table spaces that are not in an abnormal state) will be rolled forward. If one or more table spaces are in the *roll-forward* pending state (the *rollforward_pending* flag is set to TABLESPACE), only the table spaces in the roll-forward pending state will be rolled forward. If a table space roll-forward operation terminates abnormally, table spaces that were being rolled forward will be put in the roll-forward-in-progress state (the *rollforward_pending* flag is set to TABLESPACE) and, the next time the ROLLFORWARD DATABASE function is executed, only the table spaces in the roll-forward-in-progress state will be processed.
- If the specified database is not in the roll-forward pending state, no action will be taken when this function is called.
- More information must be stored in recovery log files for LOB data and LONG VARCHAR fields in databases if roll-forward recovery is en-

abled (less information has to be retained if the database is not enabled for roll-forward recovery).

- The ROLLFORWARD DATABASE function reads recovery log files, starting with the log file that is matched with the backup image. You can determine the name of the log file by calling this function with the *CallerAction* parameter set to SQLUM_QUERY before the roll-forward recovery operation is started.
- All transactions contained in recovery log files are reapplied to the database as they are read. Recovery log files are processed as far forward in time as information is available, unless an earlier time is specified. If an earlier time is specified, the *LastCommitTime* parameter will contain the time stamp of the last committed transaction that was applied to the database.
- If a database recovery was necessary because of application or human error, a time stamp value can be specified in the *StopTime* parameter so roll-forward recovery processing will end before the application or human error occurred. Also, if a time stamp value is specified for the *StopTime* parameter, you can stop the roll-forward recovery process before a recovery log file read error occurs (if this type of error occurred during an earlier roll-forward recovery attempt). This applies only to full database roll-forward recovery operations.
- When the *rollforward_pending* flag is set to DATABASE, the specified database is not available for use by other applications until the roll-forward recovery process terminates. You can terminate the process by calling this function with the *CallerAction* parameter set to SQLUM_STOP or SQLUM_ROLLFORWARD_STOP; either of these values will bring the database out of roll-forward pending state. If the *rollforward_pending* flag is set to TABLESPACE, the database is available for use by other applications during the roll-forward recovery process, but table spaces in the roll-forward pending and roll-forward-in-progress states will not be available until this function is called to perform the necessary table space roll-forward recovery.
- Rolling databases forward might involve prerequisites and restrictions that are beyond the scope of this reference. Refer to the *IBM Database 2 Administration Guide* for more information about roll-forward recovery.

Required Connection This function can be called at any time; a connection to a DB2 database manager instance or to a DB2 database does not have to be established first. When this function is called, it establishes a connection to the specified database.

Authorization Only users with system control (SYSCTRL) authority, system administrator (SYSADM) authority, or system maintenance (SYSMAINT) authority can execute this function call.

See Also BACKUP DATABASE, RESTORE DATABASE, LOAD

Example The following C program illustrates how to use the ROLLFORWARD DATABASE function to bring the SAMPLE database to the state it was in just before a crucial error occurred:

```
#define INCL_DOSFILEMGR
#define INCL_DOSERRORS
```

```
#include <os2.h>
#include <stdio.h>
#include <stdlib.h>
#include <string.h>
#include <sqlenv.h>
#include <sqlutil.h>
#include <sqlca.h>

/* Declare The Function Prototypes */
int BackupDatabase(void);
int RestoreDatabase(void);

int main()
{
    /* Include The SQLCA Data Structure Variable */
    EXEC SQL INCLUDE SQLCA;

    /* Set Up A Simple SQL Error Handler */
    EXEC SQL WHENEVER SQLERROR GOTO EXIT;

    /* Declare The Local Memory Variables */
    APIRET          APIrc  = NO_ERROR;
    int             rc = EXIT_SUCCESS;
    struct sqlfupd  DBaseInfo[2];
    unsigned int    uiLogRetain = 1;
    unsigned int    uiUserExit = 1;
    char            szApplicationID[33];
    char            szTimeStamp[27];
    char            szNextArcFile[13];
    char            szFirstDelArcFile[13];
    char            szLastDelArcFile[13];

    /* Declare The SQL Host Memory Variable */
    EXEC SQL BEGIN DECLARE SECTION;
        char    szInsertString[180];
    EXEC SQL END DECLARE SECTION;

    /* Turn On Roll-Forward Recovery For The SAMPLE Database */
    DBaseInfo[0].token = SQLF_DBTN_LOG_RETAIN;
    DBaseInfo[0].ptrvalue = (unsigned char *) &uiLogRetain;
    DBaseInfo[1].token = SQLF_DBTN_USER_EXIT;
    DBaseInfo[1].ptrvalue = (unsigned char *) &uiUserExit;
    sqlfudb("SAMPLE", 2, &DBaseInfo[0], &sqlca);

    /* Backup The SAMPLE Database */
    printf("Starting the database back up process.\n\n");
    rc = BackupDatabase();
    if (rc != EXIT_SUCCESS)
        goto EXIT;

    /* Connect To The SAMPLE Database */
    EXEC SQL CONNECT TO SAMPLE USER etpdd6z USING sanders;

    /* Build An Insert SQL Statement String */
    strcpy(szInsertString, "INSERT INTO USERID.EMPLOYEE VALUES ( ");
    strcat(szInsertString, "'000500', 'Roger', 'E', 'Sanders', ");
    strcat(szInsertString, "'A00', '9396', '1993-03-15', 'WRITER', ");
    strcat(szInsertString, "16, 'M', '1961-11-18', 52500, 1000, ");
    strcat(szInsertString, "2609)");
```

```
    /* Prepare The Insert SQL Statement */
    EXEC SQL PREPARE SQL_STMNT FROM :szInsertString;

    /* Execute The Insert Statement */
    EXEC SQL EXECUTE SQL_STMNT;

    /* Commit The Transaction */
    EXEC SQL COMMIT;
    printf("New data has been added to the SAMPLE database.\n\n");

    /* Disconnect From The SAMPLE Database */
    EXEC SQL DISCONNECT CURRENT;

    /* Create A Temporary Directory And Copy The SAMPLE Database's */
    /* Transaction Log Files To It                                 */
    APIrc = DosCreateDir("G:\LOGDIR", NULL);
    if (APIrc == NO_ERROR)
        {
        APIrc = DosCopy("F:\SQL00001\SQLOGDIR", "G:\LOGDIR",
                        DCPY_EXISTING);

        if (APIrc != NO_ERROR)
            goto EXIT;
        }

    /* Restore The SAMPLE Database - This Will Overwrite The */
    /* Existing Log Files (Which Is Why They Were Copied To  */
    /* A New Location Before The Restore Is Started)         */
    printf("Starting the database restore process.\n\n");
    rc = RestoreDatabase();
    if (rc != EXIT_SUCCESS)
        goto EXIT;

    /* Perform Roll-Forward Recovery For The SAMPLE Database -  */
    /* Specify The Temporary Directory As An Alternate Log File */
    /* Path                                                     */
    printf("Starting the database roll-forward recovery process.\n\n");
    sqlurllf ("SAMPLE", SQLUM_ROLLFWD_STOP, szApplicationID,
              SQLUM_INFINITY_TIMESTAMP, szNextArcFile,
              szFirstDelArcFile, szLastDelArcFile,
              szTimeStamp, "etpdd6z", "sanders", "G:\\LOGDIR",
              SQLUM_OFFLINE, NULL, &sqlca);

    /* Display A Success Message */
    printf("The SAMPLE database has been successfully rolled ");
    printf("forward.\n");

EXIT:
    /* If An Error Has Occurred, Display The SQL Return Code */
    if (sqlca.sqlcode != SQL_RC_OK)
        {
        printf("ERROR : %ld\n", sqlca.sqlcode);
        rc = EXIT_FAILURE;
        }

    /* Turn Off The SQL Error Handler */
    EXEC SQL WHENEVER SQLERROR CONTINUE;

    /* Return To The Operating System */
    return(rc);
}
```

```
/* Define The Backup Database Function */
int BackupDatabase()
{

    /* Declare The Local Memory Variables */
    struct sqlu_media_list    Media_List;
    struct sqlu_media_entry   Media_Entry;
    char                      szApplicationID[33];
    char                      szTimeStamp[27];
    int                       iDiskCounter = 1;
    char                      cKeyPress;
    struct sqlca              sqlca;

    /* Initialize The Media List Information Data Structure */
    Media_List.media_type = SQLU_LOCAL_MEDIA;
    Media_List.sessions = 1;
    strcpy(Media_Entry.media_entry, "D:");
    Media_List.target.media = &Media_Entry;

    /* Start Backing Up The SAMPLE Database To Diskettes */
    sqlubkup("SAMPLE", 16, SQLUB_OFFLINE, SQLUB_FULL,
             SQLUB_BACKUP, szApplicationID, szTimeStamp, 4, NULL,
             &Media_List, "etpdd6z", "sanders", NULL, 0, NULL,
             NULL, &sqlca);

    /* If The Database Could Not Be Backed Up, Display An Error */
    /* Message And Terminate The Backup Process                 */
    if (sqlca.sqlcode != SQL_RC_OK)
        {
        printf("ERROR : %ld\n", sqlca.sqlcode);

        sqlubkup ("SAMPLE", 16, SQLUB_OFFLINE, SQLUB_FULL,
                  SQLUB_TERMINATE, szApplicationID, szTimeStamp, 4,
                  NULL, &Media_List, "etpdd6z", "sanders", NULL, 0,
                  NULL, NULL, &sqlca);

        return(EXIT_FAILURE);
        }

    /* Display A Success Message */
    printf("The SAMPLE database has been successfully backed up.\n\n");

    /* Return To The Calling Function */
    return(EXIT_SUCCESS);
}

/* Define The Restore Database Function */
int RestoreDatabase()
{

    /* Declare The Local Memory Variables */
    struct sqlu_media_list    Media_List;
    struct sqlu_media_entry   Media_Entry;
    char                      szApplicationID[33];
    int                       iDiskCounter = 1;
    char                      cKeyPress;
    struct sqlca              sqlca;

    /* Initialize The Media List Information Data Structure */
    Media_List.media_type = SQLU_LOCAL_MEDIA;
    Media_List.sessions = 1;
```

```
    strcpy(Media_Entry.media_entry, "D:");
    Media_List.target.media = &Media_Entry;

    /* Start Restoring The SAMPLE Database */
    sqlursto("SAMPLE", "SAMPLE", 16, SQLUD_ROLLFWD, SQLUD_FULL,
            SQLUD_RESTORE, szApplicationID, 0, "F:",
            4, NULL, &Media_List, "etpdd6z", "sanders", NULL, 0,
            NULL, NULL, &sqlca);

    /* Ignore The Warning Message Stating That The Existing */
    /* Database Will Be Overwritten                         */
    if (sqlca.sqlcode == 2529 || sqlca.sqlcode == 2539)
        {
        sqlursto ("SAMPLE", "SAMPLE", 16, SQLUD_ROLLFWD, SQLUD_FULL,
              SQLUD_CONTINUE, szApplicationID, 0, "F:",
              4, NULL, &Media_List, "etpdd6z", "sanders", NULL, 0,
              NULL, NULL, &sqlca);
        }

    /* If The Database Could Not Be Restored, Display An Error */
    /* Message And Terminate The Restore Process               */
    if (sqlca.sqlcode != SQL_RC_OK)
        {
        printf("ERROR : %ld\n", sqlca.sqlcode);

        sqlursto ("SAMPLE", "SAMPLE", 16, SQLUD_ROLLFWD, SQLUD_FULL,
              SQLUD_TERMINATE, szApplicationID, 0, "F:",
              4, NULL, &Media_List, "etpdd6z", "sanders", NULL, 0,
              NULL, NULL, &sqlca);

        return(EXIT_FAILURE);
        }

    /* Display A Success Message */
    printf("The SAMPLE database has been successfully restored.\n\n");

    /* Return To The Calling Function */
    return(EXIT_SUCCESS);
}
```

OPEN RECOVERY HISTORY FILE SCAN

Purpose The OPEN RECOVERY HISTORY FILE SCAN function stores a copy of selected records retrieved from a database recovery history file in memory, and returns the number of records found in the recovery history file that meet specified selection criteria to the calling application.

Syntax

```
SQL_API_RC SQL_API_FN sqluhops (char           *DBAlias,
                                char           *TimeStamp,
                                char           *ObjectName,
                                unsigned short *NumEntries,
                                unsigned short *Handle,
                                unsigned short CallerAction,
                                void           *Reserved,
                                struct sqlca   *SQLCA);
```

Parameters

DBAlias A pointer to a location in memory where the alias name of the database is stored.

TimeStamp A pointer to a location in memory where a string specifying a time stamp for selecting recovery history file records is stored. Records whose time stamp value is equal to or greater than the time stamp value specified are retrieved. This parameter can contain a NULL value.

ObjectName A pointer to a location in memory where the table name or table space name for selecting recovery history file records is stored. This parameter can contain a NULL value.

NumEntries A pointer to a location in memory where this function stores the number of records found in the recovery history file that match the specified selection criteria.

Handle A pointer to a location in memory where this function stores a recovery history file scan buffer identifier to be used in subsequent GET NEXT RECOVERY HISTORY FILE ENTRY and CLOSE RECOVERY HISTORY FILE SCAN function calls.

CallerAction Specifies which records in the recovery history that meet the selection criteria are to be retrieved. This parameter can be set to any of the following values:

SQLUH_LIST_HISTORY	Specifies that all records in the recovery history file that meet the selection criteria are to be retrieved.
SQLUH_LIST_BACKUP	Specifies that only backup and restore records in the recovery history file that meet the selection criteria are to be retrieved.

Reserved A pointer that is currently reserved for later use. For now, this parameter must always be set to NULL.

SQLCA A pointer to a location in memory where a SQLCA data structure variable is stored. This variable sends either status information (if the function executed successfully) or error information (if the function failed) back to the calling application.

Includes

```
#include <sqlutil.h>
```

Description

The OPEN RECOVERY HISTORY FILE SCAN function stores a copy of selected records retrieved from a database recovery history file in memory, and returns the number of records found in the recovery history file that meet specified selection criteria to the calling application. The copy of the recovery history file records placed in memory represents a snapshot of the recovery history file at the time the recovery history file scan is opened. This copy is never updated, even if the recovery history file itself changes.

This function is normally followed by one or more GET NEXT RECOVERY HISTORY FILE ENTRY functions calls and one CLOSE RECOVERY HISTORY FILE SCAN function call. Together, these three function calls work like a SQL cursor because they use the OPEN/FETCH/CLOSE paradigm. The memory buffer that stores the recovery history file records obtained by the recovery history file scan is automatically allocated by DB2. A pointer to that buffer (the buffer identifier) is stored in the *Handle* parameter. This identifier is then used by subsequent GET NEXT RECOVERY HISTORY FILE ENTRY and CLOSE RECOVERY HISTORY FILE SCAN function calls to access the memory buffer area.

Comments

- The values specified in the *TimeStamp*, *ObjectName*, and *CallerAction* parameters are combined to define the selection criteria that filters the records in the recovery history file. Only records that meet the specified selection criteria are copied to the memory storage buffer.

- If the *TimeStamp* parameter is set to NULL (or to the address of a local variable that contains the value 0), time stamp information will not be a part of the recovery history file record (entry) selection criteria.
- If the *ObjectName* parameter is set to NULL (or to the address of a local variable that contains the value 0), the object name will not be a part of the recovery history file record (entry) selection criteria.
- The filtering effect of the *ObjectName* parameter depends on the type of object name specified:
  –If a table name is specified, only records for loads can be retrieved, since this is the only information kept for tables in the recovery history file.
  –If a table space name is specified, records for backups, restores, and loads can be retrieved.
- If the *ObjectName* parameter refers to a database table name, the fully qualified table name must be specified.
- If both the *TimeStamp* parameter and the *ObjectName* parameter are set to NULL and the *CallerAction* parameter is set to SQLU_LIST_HISTORY, every record found in the recovery history file will be copied to the memory storage buffer.
- An application can have up to eight recovery history file scans open at one time.

Required Connection

This function cannot be called unless a connection to a DB2 database manager instance exists. In order to create a database at another node, you must first attach to that node; if necessary, the function can establish a temporary DB2 database manager instance attachment while it is executing.

Authorization

No authorization is required to execute this function call.

See Also

GET NEXT RECOVERY HISTORY FILE ENTRY, CLOSE RECOVERY HISTORY FILE SCAN, UPDATE RECOVERY HISTORY FILE, PRUNE RECOVERY HISTORY FILE

Example

The following C program illustrates how to use the OPEN RECOVERY HISTORY FILE SCAN, GET NEXT RECOVERY HISTORY FILE ENTRY, and CLOSE RECOVERY HISTORY FILE SCAN functions to retrieve records from the SAMPLE database's recovery history file:

```
#include <stdio.h>
#include <stdlib.h>
#include <string.h>
#include <sqlutil.h>
#include <sqlca.h>

int main()
{
    /* Declare The Local Memory Variables */
    int                 rc = EXIT_SUCCESS;
    short               Size;
    unsigned short      usHandle;
    unsigned short      usNumRows;
    struct sqluhinfo    *HistoryInfo;
    struct sqlca        sqlca;
```

```
    /* Open The Recovery History File Scan */
    sqluhops("SAMPLE", NULL, NULL, &usNumRows, &usHandle,
             SQLUH_LIST_HISTORY, NULL, &sqlca);

    /* Allocate Memory For A Recovery History File Record Using */
    /* The Three Default Table Spaces                           */
    HistoryInfo = (struct sqluhinfo *) malloc (SQLUHINFOSIZE(3));
    HistoryInfo->sqln = 3;

    /* Scan The Recovery History File Buffer And Retrieve The */
    /* Information Stored There                               */
    printf("Object                First Log File  Last Log File\n");
    printf("--------------------------------------------------\n");
    for (;usNumRows != 0; usNumRows--)
        {

        /* Retrieve The Next Recovery History File Entry */
        sqluhgne(usHandle, NULL, HistoryInfo, &sqlca);

        /* If The Memory Allocated For A Recovery History File */
        /* Record Was Too Small, Reallocate It                 */
        if (sqlca.sqlcode == SQLUH_SQLUHINFO_VARS_WARNING)
            {
            Size = HistoryInfo->sqld;
            free(HistoryInfo);
            HistoryInfo = (struct sqluhinfo *)
                          malloc (SQLUHINFOSIZE(Size));
            HistoryInfo->sqln = Size;
            sqluhgne(usHandle, NULL, HistoryInfo, &sqlca);
            }

        /* Display The Retrieved Recovery History File Entry */
        /* Information                                       */
        printf("%.18s\t", HistoryInfo->object_part);
        printf("%.14s\t", HistoryInfo->first_log);
        printf("%.14s\n", HistoryInfo->last_log);
        }

    /* Close The Recovery History File Scan And Free All Resources */
    /* Obtained By The Open Recovery History File Scan API         */
    sqluhcls(usHandle, NULL, &sqlca);
    free(HistoryInfo);

EXIT:
    /* Return To The Operating System */
    return(rc);
}
```

GET NEXT RECOVERY HISTORY FILE ENTRY

Purpose

The GET NEXT RECOVERY HISTORY FILE ENTRY function retrieves the next record from the copy of recovery history file records that was placed in memory by the OPEN RECOVERY HISTORY FILE SCAN function.

Syntax

```
SQL_API_RC SQL_API_FN sqluhgne (unsigned short   Handle,
                                void             *Reserved,
                                struct sqluhinfo *HistoryInfo,
                                struct sqlca     *SQLCA);
```

Parameters

Handle The recovery history file scan buffer identifier returned from the associated OPEN RECOVERY HISTORY FILE SCAN function.

Reserved A pointer that is currently reserved for later use. For now, this parameter must always be set to NULL.

HistoryInfo A pointer to a *sqluhinfo* structure where this function is to store the retrieved recovery history file record information.

SQLCA A pointer to a location in memory where a SQLCA data structure variable is stored. This variable sends either status information (if the function executed successfully) or error information (if the function failed) back to the calling application.

Includes

```
#include <sqlutil.h>
```

Description

The GET NEXT RECOVERY HISTORY FILE ENTRY function retrieves the next record from the copy of recovery history file records that was placed in memory by the OPEN RECOVERY HISTORY FILE SCAN function. The information retrieved is stored in a special structure (*sqluhinfo*) that is defined in *sqlutil.h* as follows:

```
struct sqluhinfo
{
char     sqluhinfoid[8];              /* A structure identifier and          */
                                      /* eye-catcher for storage dumps. It   */
                                      /* is a string of eight bytes that must */
                                      /* be initialized with the value       */
                                      /* SQLUHINF.                           */
long     sqluhinfobc;                 /* The size of the sqluhinfo structure */
short    sqln;                        /* The total number of table space     */
                                      /* elements referenced                 */
short    sqld;                        /* The total number of table space     */
                                      /* elements used                       */
char     operation[2];                /* Indicates whether the recovery      */
                                      /* operation is a backup operation     */
                                      /* (B), a restore operation (R), a     */
                                      /* load operation (L), or an unload    */
                                      /* unload operation (U).               */
char     object[2];                   /* Indicates whether the recovery      */
                                      /* operation is a full operation (D),  */
                                      /* a table space operation (P), or a   */
                                      /* table operation (T). This field     */
                                      /* specifies the granularity used in the */
                                      /* recovery operation.                 */
char     object_part[18];             /* The recovery history file record    */
                                      /* identifier. The first 14 characters */
                                      /* of this identifier are a time stamp */
                                      /* value (with the format              */
                                      /* yyyymmddhhnnss) that indicates      */
                                      /* when the operation was performed.   */
                                      /* The last three characters of this   */
                                      /* identifier are a unique operation   */
                                      /* sequence number.                    */
char     optype[2];                   /* Specifies additional qualification  */
                                      /* information about the operation.    */
                                      /* If the operation was a full level   */
                                      /* database or table space backup,     */
                                      /* F indicates offline backup and      */
                                      /* N indicates online backup. If       */
                                      /* the operation was a load            */
                                      /* operation, R indicates replace, A   */
```

```
                                          /* indicates append, and C indicates      */
                                          /* copy. For all other operations, this   */
                                          /* field is left blank.                   */
    char    device_type[2];               /* Indicates how information in the       */
                                          /* location field is to be interpreted.   */
                                          /* Information in this field can be       */
                                          /* interpreted to mean a disk (D), a      */
                                          /* diskette (K), a tape (T), an           */
                                          /* ADSTAR distributed storage             */
                                          /* manager (A), a user exit routine       */
                                          /* (U), or something else (O).            */
    char    first_log[13];                /* The most recent log file ID used       */
                                          /* Values for this field range from       */
                                          /* S0000000 to S9999999.                  */
    char    last_log[13];                 /* The latest log file ID used. Values    */
                                          /* for this field range from S0000000     */
                                          /* to S9999999.                           */
    char    backup_id[15];                /* A time stamp value with the            */
                                          /* format yyyymmddhhnnss that             */
                                          /* refers to one or more file entries     */
                                          /* that represent backup operations.      */
                                          /* For a full database restore, the       */
                                          /* value stored in this field refers to   */
                                          /* the full database backup image         */
                                          /* that was restored. For a table         */
                                          /* space restore, the value in this       */
                                          /* field refers to the table space        */
                                          /* backup image or the full               */
                                          /* database backup image that was         */
                                          /* used to restore the specified table    */
                                          /* spaces. For any other operation,       */
                                          /* this field is left blank.              */
    char    table_creator[9]              /* The authorization ID of the user       */
                                          /* who created the table. This field is   */
                                          /* filled in only for load operations.    */
    char    table_name[19];               /* The name of the table. This field is   */
                                          /* filled in only for load operations.    */
    char    num_of_tablespaces[6];        /* The number of table spaces             */
                                          /* involved in a backup or restore        */
                                          /* operation                              */
    char    location[256];                /* For backups and copies for             */
                                          /* loads, this field indicates where the  */
                                          /* data has been saved. For backup        */
                                          /* operations that have multiple          */
                                          /* entries in the file, this field        */
                                          /* contains the sequence number           */
                                          /* that identifies which part             */
                                          /* of the backup is found in the          */
                                          /* specified location. For restore and    */
                                          /* load operations, the field identifies  */
                                          /* where the first part of the data       */
                                          /* restored or loaded (sequence           */
                                          /* number 001) has been saved.            */
                                          /* Otherwise, the value stored in this    */
                                          /* field contains different information,  */
                                          /* depending on the value stored in       */
                                          /* the device_type field. For disk or     */
                                          /* diskette (D or K) values, this field   */
                                          /* contains a fully qualified filename;   */
                                          /* for tape (T) values, this field        */
                                          /* contains a volume label; for           */
```

```
                                        /* ADSM (A) values, this field        */
                                        /* contains the server name; and      */
                                        /* for user exit or other (U or O)    */
                                        /* values, this field contains free-  */
                                        /* form text.                         */
char            comment[31];            /* A free-form comment that           */
                                        /* describes the recovery history file */
                                        /* record (entry).                    */
char            filler;                 /* Reserved; used to define the size  */
                                        /* of this structure.                 */
struct sqluhtsp tablespace[1];          /* An array of sqluhtsp structures    */
                                        /* that contain the table space names */
                                        /* that are associated with the       */
                                        /* recovery operation.                */
};
```

This structure contains an array of *sqluhtsp* structures that are used to store table space name information. The sqluhtsp structure is defined in *sqlutil.h* as follows:

```
struct sqluhtsp
{
char    tablespace_name[19];            /* The name of a table space          */
char    filler;                         /* Reserved; used to define the size of */
                                        /* this structure.                    */
};
```

Comments

- The recovery history file records that reside in memory are selected from a recovery history file based on the selection criteria specified when the OPEN RECOVERY HISTORY FILE SCAN function was executed.
- When this function is executed, the value in the *HistoryInfo* parameter points to the next recovery history file record in the copy of recovery history file records that reside in memory. Each subsequent GET NEXT RECOVERY HISTORY FILE ENTRY function call obtains the recovery history file record immediately following the current recovery history file record, unless there are no more records to retrieve (in which case an error is returned).
- You can use the value stored in the *NumEntries* parameter after the OPEN RECOVERY HISTORY FILE SCAN function is executed to set up a loop that scans through all of the recovery history file records by issuing GET NEXT RECOVERY HISTORY FILE ENTRY function calls, one at a time, until the number of calls issued equals the number of records copied from the recovery history file.
- Since each backup operation can produce multiple records in a recovery history file (when the backup image is saved in multiple files or on multiple tapes). The sequence number used in the recovery history file record identifier (returned in the *object_part* field of the *sqluhinfo* structure) allows you to specify multiple locations during a backup operation. Since restore and load operations produce only one record in a recovery history file, the sequence number 001 is always used for these types of operations.
- The value stored in the *first_log* field of the *sqluhinfo* structure is:
  –Required to apply roll-forward recovery for an online backup.
  –Required to apply roll-forward recovery for an offline backup.

–Applied after restoring a full database or table space level backup that was current when the load operation started.

- The value stored in the *last_log* field of the *sqluhinfo* structure is:
  –Required to apply roll-forward recovery for an online backup.
  –Required to apply roll-forward recovery to the current point in time for an offline backup.
  –Applied after restoring a full database or table space level backup that was current when the load finished (this value will be the same as the *first_log* value if roll-forward recovery is not applied).
- Each table space backup image can contain one or more table spaces, and each table space restore operation replaces one or more table spaces. If the *num_of_tablespaces* field of the *sqluhinfo* structure is not zero (indicating a table space level backup or restore operation), subsequent records in the recovery history file will contain the name(s) of the table space(s) backed up or restored, represented by an 18-character string. One record is written to the recovery history file for each table space contained in the backup image.

Prerequisites The OPEN RECOVERY HISTORY FILE SCAN function must be executed before this function is called.

Required Connection This function cannot be called unless a connection to a DB2 database manager instance exists. In order to create a database at another node, you must first attach to that node; if necessary, the function will establish a temporary DB2 database manager instance while it is executing.

Authorization No authorization is required to execute this function call.

See Also OPEN RECOVERY HISTORY FILE SCAN , CLOSE RECOVERY HISTORY FILE SCAN, UPDATE RECOVERY HISTORY FILE, PRUNE RECOVERY HISTORY FILE

Example See the example provided for the OPEN RECOVERY HISTORY FILE SCAN function in this chapter.

CLOSE RECOVERY HISTORY FILE SCAN

Purpose The CLOSE RECOVERY HISTORY FILE SCAN function frees system resources that were allocated by the OPEN RECOVERY HISTORY FILE SCAN function.

Syntax

```
SQL_API_RC SQL_API_FN sqluhcls (unsigned short Handle,
                                void           *Reserved,
                                struct sqlca   *SQLCA);
```

Parameters

Handle The recovery history file scan buffer identifier returned from the associated OPEN RECOVERY HISTORY FILE SCAN function.

Reserved A pointer that is currently reserved for later use. For now, this parameter must always be set to NULL.

SQLCA A pointer to a location in memory where a SQLCA data structure variable is stored. This variable sends either status information (if the function executed successfully) or error information (if the function failed) back to the calling application.

Includes

```
#include <sqlutil.h>
```

Description

The CLOSE RECOVERY HISTORY FILE SCAN function frees system resources that were allocated by the OPEN RECOVERY HISTORY FILE SCAN function.

Required Connection

This function cannot be called unless a database connection instance exists. It is not necessary to call the ATTACH function before executing this function against a remote database, however; if the database is cataloged as remote, an instance attachment to the remote node is established for the duration of the function call.

Authorization

No authorization is required to execute this function call.

See Also

OPEN RECOVERY HISTORY FILE SCAN, GET NEXT RECOVERY HISTORY FILE ENTRY, UPDATE RECOVERY HISTORY FILE, PRUNE RECOVERY HISTORY FILE

Example

See the example provided for the OPEN RECOVERY HISTORY FILE SCAN function in this chapter.

UPDATE RECOVERY HISTORY FILE

Purpose

The UPDATE RECOVERY HISTORY FILE function changes the location, device type, or comment associated with a record in a recovery history file.

Syntax

```
SQL_API_RC SQL_API_FN sqluhupd (char          *RHFEntryID,
                                char          *NewLocation,
                                char          *NewDeviceType,
                                char          *NewComment,
                                void          *Reserved,
                                struct sqlca  *SQLCA);
```

Parameters

RHFEntryID A pointer to a location in memory where the identifier for the backup, restore, or load copy recovery history file record to update is stored. This identifier has the form of a time stamp followed by a sequence number, ranging from 001 to 999.

NewLocation A pointer to a location in memory where the new location for the backup, restore, or load copy image associated with a specific recovery history file record is stored. This parameter can contain a NULL value.

NewDeviceType A pointer to a location in memory where a new device type for storing the backup, restore, or load copy image associated with a specific recovery history file record is stored. This parameter can contain a NULL value.

NewComment A pointer to a location in memory where a new comment describing a specific recovery history file record is stored. This parameter can contain a NULL value.

Reserved A pointer that is currently reserved for later use. For now, this parameter must always be set to NULL.

SQLCA A pointer to a location in memory where a SQLCA data structure variable is stored. This variable sends either status information (if the

function executed successfully) or error information (if the function failed) back to the calling application.

Includes

```
#include <sqlutil.h>
```

Description

The UPDATE RECOVERY HISTORY FILE function changes the location, device type, or comment associated with a record in a recovery history file. When a record in a recovery history file is updated, all information associated with the record that existed prior to the update operation is replaced with the new information. Unfortunately, all original information is lost since changes made to the recovery history file are not written to the transaction log.

The recovery history file is used for activity recording purposes only, and is not used directly by the RESTORE DATABASE or the ROLL FORWARD DATABASE functions. During a restore operation, you can specify the location of the backup image of a database and use the recovery history file to keep track of this location. You can then provide this location information to additional BACKUP DATABASE function calls so other backup images are stored in the same location.

Comments

- If the *NewLocation* parameter is set to NULL (or to the address of a local variable that contains the value 0), the location information for the recovery history file record will remain unchanged.
- If the *NewDeviceType* parameter is set to NULL (or to the address of a local variable that contains the value 0), the device type information for the recovery history file record will remain unchanged.
- If the *NewComment* parameter is set to NULL (or to the address of a local variable that contains the value 0), the comment that describes the recovery history file record will remain unchanged.
- If the location of a load copy image is moved, the roll-forward recovery operation must be informed of the new location and its type of storage media.

Required Connection

This function cannot be called unless a database connection exists. In order to update records in the recovery history file for a database other than the default database, an application must first establish a connection to the other database before this function is called.

Authorization

Only users with system control (SYSCTRL) authority, system administrator (SYSADM), system maintenance (SYSMAINT) authority, or database administrator (DBADM) authority can execute this function call.

See Also

OPEN RECOVERY HISTORY FILE SCAN, GET NEXT RECOVERY HISTORY FILE ENTRY, CLOSE RECOVERY HISTORY FILE SCAN, PRUNE RECOVERY HISTORY FILE

Example

The following C program illustrates how to use the UPDATE RECOVERY HISTORY FILE function to change the comment associated with a record stored in the SAMPLE database's recovery history file:

```
#include <stdio.h>
#include <stdlib.h>
#include <string.h>
#include <sqlutil.h>
#include <sqlca.h>
```

```
/* Declare The Function Prototype */
int DisplayRecords(void);

int main()
{
    /* Include The SQLCA Data Structure Variable */
    EXEC SQL INCLUDE SQLCA;

    /* Declare The Local Memory Variables */
    int                 rc = EXIT_SUCCESS;
    short               Size;
    unsigned short      usHandle;
    unsigned short      usNumRows;
    struct sqluhinfo    *HistoryInfo;

    /* Set Up A Simple SQL Error Handler */
    EXEC SQL WHENEVER SQLERROR GOTO EXIT;

    /* Connect To The SAMPLE Database */
    EXEC SQL CONNECT TO SAMPLE USER etpdd6z USING sanders;

    /* Display The Contents Of The Recovery History File */
    rc = DisplayRecords();
    if (rc != EXIT_SUCCESS)
        goto EXIT;

    /* Change The Comment Associated With The Recovery History */
    /* File Entry For The Last Backup Operation                */
    sqluhupd("19960721225726001", NULL, NULL, "Last Backup",
             NULL, &sqlca);

    /* Display The Contents Of The Recovery History File Again */
    /* The Record Should Be Updated                            */
    printf("\n");
    rc = DisplayRecords();
    if (rc != EXIT_SUCCESS)
        goto EXIT;

EXIT:
    /* If An Error Has Occurred, Display The SQL Return Code */
    if (sqlca.sqlcode != SQL_RC_OK)
        {
        printf("ERROR : %ld\n", sqlca.sqlcode);
        rc = EXIT_FAILURE;
        }

    /* Issue A Rollback To Free All Locks */
    EXEC SQL ROLLBACK;

    /* Turn Off The SQL Error Handler */
    EXEC SQL WHENEVER SQLERROR CONTINUE;

    /* Disconnect From The SAMPLE Database */
    EXEC SQL DISCONNECT CURRENT;

    /* Return To The Operating System */
    return(rc);
}

int DisplayRecords()
{
```

```
    /* Declare The Local Memory Variables */
    int                 rc = EXIT_SUCCESS;
    short               Size;
    unsigned short      usHandle;
    unsigned short      usNumRows;
    struct sqluhinfo    *HistoryInfo;
    struct sqlca        sqlca;

    /* Open The Recovery History File Scan */
    sqluhops("SAMPLE", "19960721", NULL, &usNumRows, &usHandle,
             SQLUH_LIST_HISTORY, NULL, &sqlca);

    /* Allocate Memory For A Recovery History File Record Using */
    /* The Three Default Table Spaces                           */
    HistoryInfo = (struct sqluhinfo *) malloc (SQLUHINFOSIZE(3));
    HistoryInfo->sqln = 3;

    /* Scan The Recovery History File Buffer And Retrieve The */
    /* Information Stored There                               */
    printf("Backup ID       Comment\n");
    printf("---------------------------------------------\n");
    for (;usNumRows != 0; usNumRows--)
        {

        /* Retrieve The Next Recovery History File Entry */
        sqluhgne(usHandle, NULL, HistoryInfo, &sqlca);

        /* If The Memory Allocated For A Recovery History File */
        /* Record Was To Small, Reallocate It                  */
        if (sqlca.sqlcode == SQLUH_SQLUHINFO_VARS_WARNING)
            {
            Size = HistoryInfo->sqld;
            free(HistoryInfo);
            HistoryInfo = (struct sqluhinfo *)
                          malloc (SQLUHINFOSIZE(Size));
            HistoryInfo->sqln = Size;
            sqluhgne(usHandle, NULL, HistoryInfo, &sqlca);
            }

        /* Display The Retrieved Recovery History File Entry */
        printf("%.18s\t", HistoryInfo->backup_id);
        printf("%.30s\n", HistoryInfo->comment);
        }

    /* Close The Recovery History File Scan And Free All Resources */
    /* Obtained By The Open Recovery History File Scan API        */
    sqluhcls(usHandle, NULL, &sqlca);
    free(HistoryInfo);

    /* Return To The Calling Function */
    return(EXIT_SUCCESS);
}
```

PRUNE RECOVERY HISTORY FILE

Purpose The PRUNE RECOVERY HISTORY FILE function removes one or more records from a recovery history file.

Syntax

```
SQL_API_RC SQL_API_FN sqluhprn (char           *TimeStamp,
                                unsigned short ForceOption,
                                void           *Reserved,
                                struct sqlca   *SQLCA);
```

Parameters

TimeStamp A pointer to a location in memory that contains a string specifying a time stamp for selecting recovery history file records to be deleted. Records whose time stamp value is equal to or greater than the specified time stamp value are deleted. This parameter can contain a NULL value.

ForceOption Specifies whether or not history file records for the most recent full backup and its corresponding restore set should be kept. A restore set includes all table space backups and load copies taken since the last (most recent) full database backup operation was performed. This parameter can be set to any of the following values:

SQLUH_NO_FORCE Specifies that all recent restore set records are to be kept, even if the time stamp is less than or equal to the time stamp specified.

SQLUH_FORCE Specifies that the recovery history file are pruned according to the time stamp specified; recent restore set records with time stamps less than or equal to the time stamp specified are deleted from the file.

Reserved A pointer that is currently reserved for later use. For now, this parameter must always be set to NULL.

SQLCA A pointer to a location in memory where a SQLCA data structure variable is stored. This variable sends either status information (if the function executed successfully) or error information (if the function failed) back to the calling application.

Includes

```
#include <sqlutil.h>
```

Description

The PRUNE RECOVERY HISTORY FILE function removes one or more records from a recovery history file. When records in a recovery history file are deleted, the actual backup images and load copy files to which the records refer remain untouched. The application that calls this function must manually delete these files to free up the disk storage space they consume.

Comments

- If the latest full database backup records need to be pruned from a recovery history file (and the corresponding files deleted from the media (disk storage) where they are stored), the user must ensure that all table spaces, including the system catalog table space and all user table spaces on which the database resides, are backed up first. Failure to back up these table spaces might result in a database that cannot be recovered or the loss of some portion of user data in the database.

Required Connection

This function cannot be called unless a database connection exists. In order to delete records in the recovery history file for a database other than the default database, an application must first establish a connection to that database before calling this function.

Authorization

Only users with system control (SYSCTRL) authority, system administrator (SYSADM) authority, system maintenance (SYSMAINT) authority, or database administrator (DBADM) authority are allowed to execute this function call.

See Also

OPEN RECOVERY HISTORY FILE SCAN, GET NEXT RECOVERY HISTORY FILE ENTRY, CLOSE RECOVERY HISTORY FILE SCAN, UPDATE RECOVERY HISTORY FILE

Example

The following C program illustrates how to use the PRUNE RECOVERY HISTORY FILE function to remove records from the SAMPLE database's recovery history file:

```
#include <stdio.h>
#include <stdlib.h>
#include <string.h>
#include <sqlutil.h>
#include <sqlca.h>

/* Declare The Function Prototype */
int DisplayRecords(void);

int main()
{
    /* Include The SQLCA Data Structure Variable */
    EXEC SQL INCLUDE SQLCA;

    /* Declare The Local Memory Variables */
    int                 rc = EXIT_SUCCESS;
    short               Size;
    unsigned short      usHandle;
    unsigned short      usNumRows;
    struct sqluhinfo    *HistoryInfo;

    /* Set Up A Simple SQL Error Handler */
    EXEC SQL WHENEVER SQLERROR GOTO EXIT;

    /* Connect To The SAMPLE Database */
    EXEC SQL CONNECT TO SAMPLE USER etpdd6z USING sanders;

    /* Display The Contents Of The Recovery History File */
    rc = DisplayRecords();
    if (rc != EXIT_SUCCESS)
        goto EXIT;

    /* Delete All Entries In The Recovery History File That Were */
    /* Added Before 12:30 AM, July 21, 1996 - Keep All Records   */
    /* Associated With The Last Restore Operation                */
    sqluhprn("19960721225111", SQLUH_NO_FORCE, NULL, &sqlca);

    /* Display The Contents Of The Recovery History File Again */
    /* The Records Should Be Deleted                           */
    printf("\n");
    rc = DisplayRecords();
    if (rc != EXIT_SUCCESS)
        goto EXIT;

EXIT:
    /* If An Error Has Occurred, Display The SQL Return Code */
    if (sqlca.sqlcode != SQL_RC_OK)
        {
        printf("ERROR : %ld\n", sqlca.sqlcode);
        rc = EXIT_FAILURE;
        }
```

```
    /* Issue A Rollback To Free All Locks */
    EXEC SQL ROLLBACK;

    /* Turn Off The SQL Error Handler */
    EXEC SQL WHENEVER SQLERROR CONTINUE;

    /* Disconnect From The SAMPLE Database */
    EXEC SQL DISCONNECT CURRENT;

    /* Return To The Operating System */
    return(rc);
}

int DisplayRecords()
{

    /* Declare The Local Memory Variables */
    int                 rc = EXIT_SUCCESS;
    short               Size;
    unsigned short      usHandle;
    unsigned short      usNumRows;
    struct sqluhinfo    *HistoryInfo;
    struct sqlca        sqlca;

    /* Open The Recovery History File Scan */
    sqluhops("SAMPLE", "19960721", NULL, &usNumRows, &usHandle,
             SQLUH_LIST_HISTORY, NULL, &sqlca);

    /* Allocate Memory For A Recovery History File Record Using */
    /* The Three Default Table Spaces                           */
    HistoryInfo = (struct sqluhinfo *) malloc (SQLUHINFOSIZE(3));
    HistoryInfo->sqln = 3;

    /* Scan The Recovery History File Buffer And Retrieve The */
    /* Information Stored There                               */
    printf("Backup ID       Comment\n");
    printf("----------------------------------------------\n");
    for (;usNumRows != 0; usNumRows--)
        {

        /* Retrieve The Next Recovery History File Entry */
        sqluhgne(usHandle, NULL, HistoryInfo, &sqlca);

        /* If The Memory Allocated For A Recovery History File */
        /* Record Was To Small, Reallocate It                  */
        if (sqlca.sqlcode == SQLUH_SQLUHINFO_VARS_WARNING)
            {
            Size = HistoryInfo->sqld;
            free(HistoryInfo);
            HistoryInfo = (struct sqluhinfo *)
                          malloc (SQLUHINFOSIZE(Size));
            HistoryInfo->sqln = Size;
            sqluhgne(usHandle, NULL, HistoryInfo, &sqlca);
            }

        /* Display The Retrieved Recovery History File Entry */
        printf("%.18s\t", HistoryInfo->backup_id);
        printf("%.30s\n", HistoryInfo->comment);
        }
```

```
    /* Close The Recovery History File Scan And Free All Resources */
    /* Obtained By The Open Recovery History File Scan API     */
    sqluhcls(usHandle, NULL, &sqlca);
    free(HistoryInfo);

    /* Return To The Calling Function */
    return(EXIT_SUCCESS);
}
```

CHAPTER 24

DATA HANDLING API'S

The data handling APIs are a group of DB2 API function calls that allow an application to copy data between DB2 databases and external data files. This group includes:

- An API function that copies specific data in a database to an external data file.
- An API function that inserts data stored in an external data file into a database table.
- An API function that loads data stored in external files, tapes, and named pipes into a database table.
- An API function that determines the current status of a load operation.
- An API function that restricts table space access during a load operation.

Table 24.1 lists the data handling API functions available with DB2.

TABLE 24.1 Data Handling APIs

Function name	Description
EXPORT	Copies data from a DB2 database to an external file.
IMPORT	Copies data from an external file to a DB2 database table.
LOAD	Loads data from files, tapes, or named pipes into a DB2 database table.
LOAD QUERY	Queries the DB2 database server for the current status of a load operation.
QUIESCE TABLESPACES FOR TABLE	Places all table spaces associated with a particular database table in a quiesced (restricted access) state.

Exporting Data

Although a database is normally a self-contained entity, there are times when you need to make some or all of a database's data available to "the outside world." When these occasions arise, an application can make select portions of database data available to other applications by calling the EXPORT function (which, in turn, invokes the export facility). The EXPORT function can:

- Copy the contents of a table, along with its indexes, to an external file (using a format that other DB2 products can access).
- Make a backup copy of a database table.
- Copy select data to an external file and put it in a format that other applications can use.

A SELECT SQL statement specifies the data to export. When large object (LOB) columns are included in this SELECT statement, the first 32KB of data are written to the file by default. By specifying different values in one of the EXPORT function's input parameters, you can store LOB data, in its entirety, in different external files.

Importing Data

Just as there are times to export data to an external file, you will also need to occasionally make data stored in external files available to a DB2 database. An application can make data in an external file available to a database by calling the IMPORT function (which invokes the import facility) or by calling the LOAD function (which invokes the load facility). The IMPORT function can:

- Create a table, along with its indexes, from an external file (provided the file is stored in a format that DB2 products can access).
- Restore a database table from a backup copy made by the export facility.
- Copy data from an external file produced by another application to a database table.

When data is imported, if the table or updateable view receiving the data already contains data, the new data can either replace or be appended to the existing data as long as the base table receiving the data does not contain a primary key that is referenced by a foreign key of another table. (If the base table contains a primary key that is referenced by a foreign key, imported data can only be appended to the existing table.) LOB data can reside either in the file being imported or in a separate external file referenced by the imported file. If LOB data resides in external files, there will be a separate file for each LOB data value.

The import facility can also create new tables from the external file being imported, provided the file was created by another DB2 product using the DB2 product standard file format.

Loading Data

The load facility works similar to the import facility, but some functional differences do exist. These differences are outlined in Table 24.2.

The load facility is intended to be used for an initial load (or append) of a base table when large amounts of data need to be moved. The load facility is significantly faster than the import facility because it writes formatted data pages directly to the database, where the import facility writes data by executing multiple INSERT SQL statements. The load facility also eliminates almost all transaction logging associated with the loading of data; instead of logging transactions, the load facility optionally stores a copy of the data loaded in an external file. The load process consists of three separate phases:

Load Data is written to the table.
Build Indexes are created for the table.
Delete Data that caused a unique key violation is removed from the table.

During the load phase, data is loaded into the specified database table, then index key and table statistics information is collected. Save points (also known as points of consistency) are established when the load process is started and a specified number of rows are committed each time they are loaded. If a failure occurs during the load phase, you can skip the number of rows successfully committed at the last save point when the load process is restarted.

During the build phase, indexes are created based on the index key information collected during the load phase. Index keys are automatically sorted during the load phase and index statistics are col-

TABLE 24.2 Differences Between IMPORT and LOAD

IMPORT	LOAD
Significantly slower than LOAD on large amounts of data.	Significantly faster than IMPORT on large amounts of data.
Tables and indexes can be created from IXF format files.	Tables and indexes must exist before data can be loaded into them.
Files formatted in work sheet format (WSF) are supported.	Files formatted in work sheet format (WSF) are not supported.
Data can be imported into tables and views (aliases are supported).	Data can be loaded only into tables (aliases are supported).
Table spaces in which the table and its indexes reside remain online during an import operation.	Table spaces in which the table and its indexes reside are taken offline during a load operation.
All row transactions are written to the log file.	Minimal logging is performed.
Triggers can be fired during the import process.	Triggers are not supported.
If an import operation is interrupted and a commit frequency value is specified, the table will remain usable and contain all rows that were inserted up to the last commit operation. The user can restart the import operation or leave the table as it is.	If a load operation is interrupted and a consistency point (commit frequency) value is specified, the table remains in a load pending state and cannot be used until either the load process is restarted in order to continue the load operation or the table space in which the table resides is restored from a backup image created before the load operation was started.
The amount of free disk space needed to import data is approximately the size of the largest index being imported plus about 10 percent. This space is allocated from the temporary table spaces defined for the database.	The amount of free disk space needed to load data is approximately as large as the sum of all indexes for the database. This space is temporarily allocated outside the database.
All constraint checking is performed during an import operation.	Only uniqueness checking is performed during a load operation. All other constraint checking must be performed after the load operation has completed (with the SET CONSTRAINTS SQL statement).
The keys of each row are inserted into the appropriate index during an import operation.	All keys are sorted during a load operation and the indexes are rebuilt when the load operation is complete.
The RUN STATISTICS function or command must be executed after an import operation so the statistics for the affected table are up to date.	Statistics are collected and updated during a load operation.
Data can be imported into a host database through DDCS.	Data cannot be loaded into a host database.
Data files to be imported must reside on the same workstation from which the import facility is invoked.	Data files and named pipes to be loaded must reside on the same workstation on which the database receiving the data resides.
A backup image is not created during an import operation.	A backup image can be created during a load operation.

Adapted from IBM's *Database 2 Administration Guide*, page 102.

lected. If a failure occurs during the build phase, it is restarted from the beginning when the load operation is restarted. Rows containing values that cause unique key violations to occur are placed in an exception table (if one is specified) and messages about the rows are written to a message file so they can be manually corrected after the load process has completed.

During the delete phase, all rows containing values that caused unique key violations to occur are removed from the table. Information about these rows is stored in a temporary file. If a failure occurs during the delete phase, it must be manually restarted. When a load operation is restarted, beginning at the delete phase, violating rows are removed from the table based on information stored in the temporary file. If no temporary files exist, the load operation should be restarted at the beginning of the build phase. You must not modify temporary files in any way and you must call the LOAD function with the same parameter values used when the load facility was originally started, or the restart of the delete phase will fail.

It is always a good idea to restrict access to the table spaces associated with the table receiving the loaded data. You can restrict table space access by calling the QUIESCE TABLESPACES FOR TABLE function before the load operation is started, and you can call the function again to restore the table spaces to their original state after the load process has completed.

Supported Export, Import, and Load File Formats

Four types of file formats are supported by the import facility, and three types of formats are supported by the export and load facilities. File formats determine how data is physically stored in a file. The supported file formats are:

Delimited ASCII This format consists of data values (variable in length) that are separated by a delimiting (field separator) character. Because commas are typically used as the field separator character, this format is sometimes referred to as comma-separated variable (CSV) format. This format is used for exchanging data with a wide variety of application products, especially other database products.

Nondelimited ASCII This format consists of data values (common length) that are column-aligned. This format is also used for exchanging data with a wide variety of application products, especially spreadsheet products.

Worksheet format This format is specifically intended to define data stored in a file format that is compatible with Lotus Development Corporation's Lotus 1-2-3 and Lotus Symphony products. The load utility does not support this file format.

PC integrated exchange format This format defines data stored in a file format that is compatible with DB2 products. When this format is used, tables in the database do not have to exist before data can be imported into them.

Refer to the *IBM Database 2 Administration Guide* for more information about the export, import, and load facilities, and for more information about their supported file formats.

EXPORT

Purpose The EXPORT function exports data from a database to one of several external file formats.

Syntax

```
SQL_API_RC SQL_API_FN sqluexpr (char                 *DataFileName,
                                sqlu_media_list      *LOBPathList,
                                sqlu_media_list      *LOBFileList,
                                struct sqldcol       *DataDescriptor,
                                struct sqlchar       *SelectStatement,
                                char                 *FileType,
                                struct sqlchar       *FileTypeMod,
                                char                 *MsgFileName,
                                short                CallerAction,
                                struct sqluexpt_out  *NumRows,
                                void                 *Reserved,
                                struct sqlca         *SQLCA);
```

Parameters *DataFileName* A pointer to a location in memory that contains the path and name of the external file into which data is to be exported.

LOBPathList A pointer to a *sqlu_media_list* structure that contains a list of local paths on the client workstation that identify where LOB data files are to be stored.

LOBFileList A pointer to a *sqlu_media_list* structure that contains a list of base LOB filenames to be generated.

DataDescriptor A pointer to a *sqldcol* structure that specifies the column names for the output data file.

SelectStatement A pointer to a *sqlchar* structure that contains a valid dynamic SQL SELECT statement that specifies which data is to be extracted from the database and written to the external file.

FileType A pointer to a location in memory that contains a string that specifies the format to use when writing data to the external file. This parameter can be set to any of the following values:

DEL (or SQL_DEL)	Specifies that data is to be written to the external file using delimited ASCII format.
WSF (or SQL_WSF)	Specifies that data is to be written to the external file using a worksheet (Lotus Symphony and Lotus 1-2-3) format.
IXF (or SQL_IXF)	Specifies that data is to be written to the external file using the PC/integrated exchange format.

FileTypeMod A pointer to a *sqlchar* structure that contains additional information unique to the format being used to write data to the external file.

MsgFileName A pointer to a location in memory that contains the name of the file where all EXPORT error, warning, and informational messages are to be stored.

CallerAction Specifies the action this function is to take when it executes. This parameter can be set to any of the following values:

SQLU_INITIAL	Specifies that the export operation is to be started.
SQLU_CONTINUE	Specifies that the export operation is to be continued after the user has performed some action requested by the export utility (for example, inserting a diskette or mounting a new tape).
SQLU_TERMINATE	Specifies that the export operation is to be terminated after the user fails to perform some action requested by the export utility.

NumRows A pointer to a *sqluexpt_out* structure where this function is to store the number of rows exported (written) to the external file.

Reserved A pointer that is currently reserved for later use. For now, this parameter must always be set to NULL.

SQLCA A pointer to a location in memory where a SQL communication area (SQLCA) data structure variable is stored. This variable sends either status information (if the function executed successfully) or error information (if the function failed) back to the calling application.

Includes

```
#include <sqlutil.h>
```

Description

The EXPORT function copies data from a database to an external file. The data to be copied is specified by a SELECT SQL statement. Data can be written to an external file in one of three internal formats:

- Delimited ASCII
- Lotus worksheet
- PC integrated exchange format (IXF)

Note: IXF is the preferred format to use when exporting data from a table. Files created in this format can later be imported or loaded into the same table or into another database table.

Three special structures (*sqldcol, sqlu_media_list*, and *sqlchar*) pass general information to the DB2 export utility when this function is called. An additional structure, *sqluexpt_out*, obtains the number of records copied to the external file by the export utility. The first of these structures, *sqldcol*, is defined in *sqlutil.h* as follows:

```
struct sqldcol
{
short            dcolmeth;          /* A value indicating the method to   */
                                    /* use to select and name columns     */
                                    /* within the data file               */
short            dcolnum;           /* The number of columns specified    */
                                    /* in the dcolname array.             */
struct sqldcoln  dcolname[1];       /* A pointer to an array of sqldcoln  */
                                    /* structures that contains a list of */
                                    /* column names                       */
};
```

This structure contains a pointer to an array of *sqldcoln* structures that holds a list of column names to be written to the external file during the export process. The *sqldcoln* structure is defined in *sqlutil.h* as follows:

```
struct sqldcoln
{
short  dcolnlen;                    /* The size of the data element pointed to    */
                                    /* by the dcolnptr field                      */
char   *dcolnptr;                   /* A pointer to a location in memory where    */
                                    /* the data element specified by the dcolmeth */
                                    /* field of the sqldcol structure is stored   */
};
```

The second special structure used by this function, *sqluexpt_out*, obtains information about the number of records that were written to the external file after the export operation is completed. The *sqluexpt_out* structure is defined in *sqlutil.h* as follows:

```
struct sqluexpt_out
{
unsigned long  sizeOfStruct;        /* The size of the sqluexpt_out     */
                                    /* structure                        */
unsigned long  rowsExported;        /* The number of records copied     */
                                    /* from the database to the target */
                                    /* file                             */
};
```

Another structure, the *sqlu_media_list* structure is used to describe the type of media that the external file is to be written to. Refer to the BACKUP DATABASE function for a detailed description of the *sqlu_media_list* structure and for more information about how it is initialized.

Comments

- If a list of local paths that identify where LOB data files are to be stored is specified in the *LOBPathList* parameter, LOB data will be written to the first path in this list until file space is exhausted, then to the second path, and so on.

- When LOB data files are created during an export operation, DB2 constructs the filenames by combining the current base name in the list of base LOB file names specified in the *LOBFileList* parameter with the current path (obtained from the list of paths provided in the *LOBFilePath* parameter), and then appending a three-digit sequence number to it. For example, if the current LOB path is the directory **/usr/local/LOB/emp-data** and the current base LOB filename is **resume**, then the LOB files will be named **/usr/local/LOB/empdata/resume.001**, **/usr/local/LOB /emp-data/resume.002**, and so on.
- The *dcolmeth* field of the *sqldcol* structure specified in the *DataDescriptor* parameter defines how column names are to be provided for the exported data file. This parameter can be set to either of the following values:

  SQL_METH_N Specifies that column names in the external file are provided via the *sqldcol* structure.

  SQL_METH_D Specifies that column names in the external file are derived from processing the SELECT statement specified in *SelectStatement* parameter (the column names specified in the SELECT statement become the names of the columns in the external file).
- If the *DataDescriptor* parameter is set to NULL or if the *dcolmeth* field of the *sqldcol* structure is set to SQL_METH_D, the *dcolnum* and *dcolname* fields of the *sqldcol* structure are ignored.
- A warning message is issued whenever the number of columns specified in the external column name array (*DataDescriptor* parameter) is not equal to the number of columns generated by the SELECT SQL statement that retrieves the data from the database. When these numbers do not match, the number of columns written to the external file is the lesser of the two numbers; excess database columns or external file column names are not used to generate the output file.
- The *sqlca* structure specified in the *SelectStatement* parameter must contain a valid dynamic SELECT SQL statement. The SELECT statement specifies how data is to be extracted from the database and written to the external file. The columns for the external file (specified in the *DataDescriptor* parameter) and the database columns returned from the SELECT statement are matched according to their respective list/structure positions. When the EXPORT function executes, the SELECT statement is passed to the database for processing, and the first column of data retrieved from the database is placed in the first column of the external file, the second column retrieved is placed in the second column, and so on.
- A warning message is issued whenever a character column with a length greater than 254 is selected for export to a delimited ASCII (DEL) file.
- If the *MsgFileName* parameter contains the path and the name of an operating system file that already exists, the existing file will be overwritten when this function is executed. If the path and the name of an operating system file that does not exist is specified, a new file will be created.
- Messages placed in the external message file include information returned from the message retrieval service. Each message begins on a new line.
- The *CallerAction* parameter must be set to SQLUB_INITIAL the first time this function is called.
- All table operations need to be completed and all locks must be released before this function is called. You can accomplish this by issuing either a

COMMIT SQL statement after closing all cursors opened with the WITH HOLD option or a ROLLBACK SQL statement. One or more COMMIT SQL statements are automatically issued during the export process.

- You can use delimited ASCII format files to exchange data with the IBM personal decision series programs, as well as many other database manager and file manager programs.
- If character data containing row separators is exported to a delimited ASCII (DEL) file and processed by a text transfer program, fields that contain row separators will either shrink or expand in size.
- Use the PC/IXF file format when exporting data to files that will be imported into other databases. This is because PC/IXF file format specifications permit the migration of data between DB2 for Common Servers products. You can perform data migration by executing the following steps:
  1. Export the data from one database to a file.
  2. Binary copy the files between operating systems. This step is not necessary if the source and target databases are both accessible from the same workstation.
  3. Import the data from the file into the other database.
- You can use DDCS to export tables from DRDA servers such as DB2 for MVS, SQL/DS, and OS/400. In this case, only the PC/IXF file format is supported.
- Index definitions for a table are included in PC/IXF format files when the contents of a single database table are exported with a *SelectStatement* beginning with SELECT * FROM <tablename> and the *DataDescriptor* parameter is set so default column names are specified. Indexes are not saved if the SELECT statement specified in the *SelectStatement* parameter contains a join or if the SELECT statement references views. WHERE, GROUP BY, and HAVING clauses do not affect the saving of indexes.
- NOT NULL WITH DEFAULT attributes for a table are included in PC/IXF format files when the contents of a single database table are exported with a *SelectStatement* beginning with SELECT * FROM <tablename>.
- The EXPORT utility cannot create multiple-part PC/IXF format files when it is executed on an AIX system.
- The *data* field of the *sqlchar* structure specified in the *FileTypeMod* parameter must contain one of the following values:
  –lobsinfile
  –coldel
  –chardel
  –decpt
  –decplusblank
  –datesiso
  –1
  –2
  –3
  –L
  –S

  These values provide additional information about the chosen file format. Only a portion of these values are used with a particular file format. If the *FileTypeMod* parameter is set to NULL or if the *length* field of the *sqlchar* structure is set to 0, default information is provided for the file format specified.

- If data is being exported to either a delimited ASCII (DEL) or PC/IXF format file, the *FileTypeMod* parameter can specify where LOB data is stored. If this parameter is set to *lobsinfile*, LOB data will be stored in separate files; otherwise, all LOB data will be truncated to 32KB and stored in the exported file. When *lobsinfile* is specified for PC/IXF files, the original length of the LOB data is lost and the LOB file length is stored in the exported file. If the IMPORT function is later used to import the file and if the CREATE option is specified, the created LOB value will be 267 bytes in size.
- If data is exported to a delimited ASCII (DEL) format file, you can use the *FileTypeMod* parameter to specify characters to override the following options:

  Column delimiters By default, columns are delimited with commas. Specifying *coldel*, followed by a character, will cause the specified character to be used in place of a comma to signal the end of a column.

  Character string delimiters By default, character strings are delimited with double quotation marks. Specifying *chardel*, followed by a character, will cause the specified character to be used in place of double quotation marks to enclose a character string.

  Decimal point characters By default, decimal points are specified with periods. Specifying *decpt*, followed by a character, will cause the specified character to be used in place of a period as a decimal point character.

  Plus sign character By default, positive decimal values are prefixed with a plus sign. Specifying *decplusblank* will cause positive decimal values to be prefixed with a blank space instead of a plus sign.

  Date format Specifying *datesiso* will cause all date data values to be exported in International Organization for Standardization (ISO) format

If two or more delimiters are specified, they must be separated by blank spaces. Blank spaces cannot be used as delimiters.

- Each specified delimiter character must be different from all other delimiter characters already being used so it can be uniquely identified. Table 24.3 lists the characters that can be used as delimiter overrides.
- If data is being exported to a worksheet (WSF) format file, the *FileTypeMod* parameter can specify which release (version) of Lotus 1-2-3 or Lotus Symphony the WSF file is compatible with (only one product designator can be specified for a WSF format file):

  –Specifying *1* causes a WSF format file that is compatible with Lotus 1-2-3 release 1 or Lotus 1-2-3 release la to be created. This is the default version.

  –Specifying *2* causes a WSF format file that is compatible with Lotus Symphony release 1.0 to be created.

  –Specifying *3* causes a WSF format file that is compatible with Lotus 1-2-3 version 2 or Lotus Symphony release 1.1 to be created.

  –Specifying *L* causes a WSF format file that is compatible with Lotus 1-2-3 version 2 to be created.

  –Specifying *S* causes a WSF format file that is compatible with Lotus Symphony release 1.1 to be created.
- The EXPORT function will not issue a warning if you attempt to use unsupported file types with the MODIFIED BY option. Instead, the EXPORT function will fail and an error code will be returned.
- If any bind files (particularly **db2uexpm.bnd**) shipped with DB2 have to be manually bound to a database, do not use the format option during the bind process; if you do, the EXPORT function will not work correctly.

TABLE 24.3 Delimiter Characters for Use with Delimited ASCII Files

Character	Decimal value	Hex value	Description
"	34	0x22	Double quotation marks
%	37	0x25	Percent sign
&	38	0x26	Ampersand
'	39	0x27	Apostrophe
(	40	0x28	Left parenthesis
)	41	0x29	Right parenthesis
*	42	0x2A	Asterisk
,	44	0x2C	Comma
.	46	0x2E	Period (not valid as a character string delimiter)
/	47	0x2F	Slash or forward slash
:	58	0x3A	Colon
;	59	0x3B	Semicolon
<	60	0x3C	Less-than sign
=	61	0x3D	Equal
>	62	0x3E	Greater-than sign
?	63	0x3F	Question mark
_	95	0x5F	Underscore (valid only in single-byte character systems)
|	124	0x7C	Vertical bar

These characters are the same for all code page values.
Adapted from IBM's Database 2 API Reference, Table 5, pages 317 and 318.

Required Connection This function can be called only if a connection to a database exists.

Authorization Only users with system administrator (SYSADM) authority, or database administrator (DBADM) authority, or CONTROL or SELECT authority for each specified table and/or view can execute this function call.

See Also IMPORT, LOAD

Example The following C program illustrates how to use the EXPORT function to copy data from the DEPARTMENT table in the SAMPLE database to a PC/IXF formatted external file:

```
#include <stdio.h>
#include <stdlib.h>
#include <string.h>
#include <sqlutil.h>
#include <sql.h>

int main()
{
    /* Include The SQLCA Data Structure Variable */
    EXEC SQL INCLUDE SQLCA;

    /* Declare The Local Memory Variables */
    int                 rc = EXIT_SUCCESS;
    char                String[100];
    char                DataFileName[80];
    char                MsgFileName[80];
```

```
    struct sqlchar       *SelectString;
    struct sqldcol       DataDescriptor;
    struct sqluexpt_out  OutputInfo;

    /* Set Up A Simple SQL Error Handler */
    EXEC SQL WHENEVER SQLERROR GOTO EXIT;

    /* Connect To The SAMPLE Database */
    EXEC SQL CONNECT TO SAMPLE USER etpdd6z USING sanders;

    /* Initialize The Local Variables */
    strcpy(DataFileName, "DEPT.IXF");
    strcpy(MsgFileName, "EXP_MSG.DAT");
    OutputInfo.sizeOfStruct = SQLUEXPT_OUT_SIZE;

    /* Define The SELECT Statement That Will Be Used To Select The */
    /* Data To Be Exported                                         */
    strcpy(String, "SELECT * FROM USERID.DEPARTMENT");
    SelectString = (struct sqlchar *)
        malloc (strlen(String) + sizeof(struct sqlchar));
    SelectString->length = strlen(String);
    strncpy(SelectString->data, String, strlen(String));

    /* Export The Data To An IXF Format File */
    sqluexpr(DataFileName, NULL, NULL, NULL, SelectString,
             SQL_IXF, NULL, MsgFileName, SQLU_INITIAL, &OutputInfo,
             NULL, &sqlca);

    /* Display A Success Message */
    printf("Data in the USERID.DEPARTMENT table has been exported ");
    printf("to the\nfile DEPT.IXF.\n");

EXIT:
    /* If An Error Has Occurred, Display The SQL Return Code */
    if (sqlca.sqlcode != SQL_RC_OK)
        {
        printf("SQL ERROR : %ld\n", sqlca.sqlcode);
        rc = EXIT_FAILURE;
        }

    /* Issue A Rollback To Free All Locks */
    EXEC SQL ROLLBACK;

    /* Turn Off The SQL Error Handler */
    EXEC SQL WHENEVER SQLERROR CONTINUE;
    /* Disconnect From The SAMPLE Database */
    EXEC SQL DISCONNECT CURRENT;

    /* Free All Allocated Memory */
    if (SelectString != NULL)
        free(SelectString);

    /* Return To The Operating System */
    return(rc);
}
```

IMPORT

Purpose

The IMPORT function inserts data stored in an external file (written in a supported file format) into a database table or view.

Syntax

```
SQL_API_RC SQL_API_FN sqluimpr (char                  *FileName,
                                sqlu_media_list       *LOBPathList,
                                struct sqldcol        *DataDescriptor,
                                struct sqlchar        *ActionString,
                                char                  *FileType,
                                struct sqlchar        *FileTypeMod,
                                char                  *MsgFileName,
                                short                 CallerAction,
                                struct sqluimpt_in    *ImportInfoIn,
                                struct sqluimpt_out   *ImportInfoOut,
                                long                  *NullIndicators,
                                void                  *Reserved,
                                struct sqlca          *SQLCA);
```

Parameters

FileName A pointer to a location in memory that contains the path and name of the external file from which data is to be imported.

LOBPathList A pointer to a *sqlu_media_list* structure that contains a list of local paths that identify where, on the client workstation, LOB data files are to be imported from.

DataDescriptor A pointer to a *sqldcol* structure that contains information about the columns in the external data file that are being selected for import. The value of the *dcolmeth* field of this structure determines how columns are selected from the external file.

ActionString A pointer to a *sqlchar* structure that contains a valid dynamic SQL statement, followed by an array of characters that identifies the action to be taken when importing data into tables that already contain data.

FileType A pointer to a location in memory where a string that specifies the format of the external data file is stored. This parameter can be set to any of the following values:

DEL (or SQL_DEL)	Specifies that the data in the external file is stored in delimited ASCII format.
ASC (or SQL_ASC)	Specifies that the data in the external file is stored in nondelimited ASCII format.
WSF (or SQL_WSF)	Specifies that the data in the external file is stored in worksheet (Lotus Symphony and Lotus 1-2-3) format.
IXF (or SQL_IXF)	Specifies that the data in the external file is stored in PC integrated exchange format.

FileTypeMod A pointer to a *sqlchar* structure that contains additional information that is unique to the format used in the external file.

MsgFileName A pointer to a location in memory that contains the name of the file where all IMPORT error, warning, and informational messages are stored.

CallerAction Specifies the action this function is to take when it executes. This parameter can be set to any of the following values:

SQLU_INITIAL	Specifies that the import operation is to be started.
SQLU_CONTINUE	Specifies that the import operation is to be continued after the user has performed some action requested by the import utility (for example, inserting a diskette or mounting a new tape).
SQLU_TERMINATE	Specifies that the import operation is to be terminated after the user fails to perform some action requested by the import utility.

ImportInfoIn A pointer to a *sqluimpt_in* structure that contains information about the number of records to skip and the number of records to retrieve before committing them to the database.

ImportInfoOut A pointer to a *sqluimpt_out* structure where this function is to store summary information about the import operation.

NullIndicators A pointer to an array of integers that indicates whether or not each retrieved column of data can contain NULL values. This parameter is used only if the *FileType* parameter is set to DEL (SQL_DEL).

Reserved A pointer that is currently reserved for later use. For now, this parameter must always be set to NULL.

SQLCA A pointer to a location in memory where a SQLCA data structure variable is stored. This variable sends either status information (if the function executed successfully) or error information (if the function failed) back to the calling application.

Includes

```
#include <sqlutil.h>
```

Description

The IMPORT function inserts data stored in an external file (written with a supported file format) into a database table or view. Data can be imported from any file that contains one of the following internal file formats:

- Delimited ASCII
- Nondelimited ASCII
- Lotus worksheet
- PC integrated exchange format (IXF)

Note: IXF is the preferred format to use when exporting data from and importing data to a DB2 database table.

Three special structures (*sqldcol*, *sqlu_media_list*, and *sqlchar*) pass general information to the DB2 import utility when this function is called. Refer to the EXPORT function for a detailed description of the *sqldcol* structure and refer to the BACKUP DATABASE function for a detailed description of the *sqlu_media_list* structure.

A special structure (the *sqlloctab* structure) can be used by the *sqldcol* structure when this function is executed. The *sqlloctab* structure is defined in *sqlutil.h* as follows:

```
struct sqlloctab

{
       struct sqllocpair  locpair[1];  /* A pointer to an array of sqllocpair   */
                                       /* structures that contains a list of    */
                                       /* column starting and ending            */
                                       /* positions                             */

};
```

This structure contains a pointer to an array of *sqllocpair* structures that are used to hold a list of starting and ending column positions that identify how data is stored in an external file. The *sqllocpair* structure is defined in *sqlutil.h* as follows:

```
struct sqllocpair

{
       short  begin_loc;      /* The starting position of the      */
                              /* column data in the external file  */
       short  end_loc;        /* The ending position of the column */
                              /* data in the external file         */
};
```

Two additional structures, *sqluimpt_in* and *sqluimpt_out*, pass import-specific information to and from the DB2 import facility when this function is called. The first of these structures, *sqluimpt_in*, passes information about when data is to be committed to the database to the import facility and is defined in *sqlutil.h* as follows:

```
struct sqluimpt_in
{
unsigned long  sizeOfStruct; /* The size of the sqluimpt_in structure       */
unsigned long  commitcnt;    /* The number of records to import before      */
                             /* a COMMIT SQL statement is executed.         */
                             /* A COMMIT statement is executed each         */
                             /* time this number of records are imported    */
                             /* to make the additions permanent.            */
unsigned long  restartcnt;   /* The number of records to skip in the file   */
                             /* before starting the import process. This    */
                             /* field can be used if a previous attempt to  */
                             /* import records failed after n number of     */
                             /* rows of data were already committed         */
                             /* to the database.                            */
};
```

The second of these structures, *sqluimpt_out*, obtains statistical information about the import operation after all data has been imported into the table. The *sqluimpt_out* structure is defined in *sqlutil.h* as follows:

```
struct sqluimpt_out
{
unsigned long  sizeOfStruct;    /* The size of the sqluimpt_out       */
                                /* structure                          */
unsigned long  rowsRead;        /* The number of records read from    */
                                /* the external file                  */
unsigned long  rowsSkipped;     /* The number of records skipped      */
                                /* before the import process was      */
                                /* started                            */
unsigned long  rowsInserted;    /* The number of rows inserted into   */
                                /* the specified database table       */
unsigned long  rowsUpdated;     /* The number of rows updated in      */
                                /* the specified table. Indicates the */
                                /* number of records in the file that */
                                /* have matching primary key values   */
                                /* in the table.                      */
unsigned long  rowsRejected;    /* The number of records in the file  */
                                /* that, for some reason, could not   */
                                /* be imported                        */
unsigned long  rowsCommitted;   /* The number of rows successfully    */
                                /* imported and committed             */
};
```

Note: Data that has minor incompatibility problems will be accepted by the import facility (for example, you can import character data by using padding or truncation, and numeric data by using a different numeric data type). Data that has major incompatibility problems will be rejected.

Comments

- The *dcolmeth field* of the *sqldcol* structure specified in the *DataDescriptor* parameter defines how columns are to be selected for import from the external data file. This parameter can be set to any of the following values:
  - *SQL_METH_N* Specifies that column names provided in the *sqldcol* structure identify the data to be imported from the external file. This method cannot be used if the external file does not contain column names (if the file is in delimited ASCII format).
  - *SQL_METH_P* Specifies that starting column positions provided in the *sqldcol* structure identify the data to be imported from the external file. This method cannot be used if the external file is in delimited ASCII format.
  - *SQL_METH_L* Specifies that starting and ending column positions provided in the *sqldcol* structure identify the data to be imported from the external file. This is the only method to use if the external file is in delimited ASCII format.
  - *SQL_METH_D* Specifies that the first column in the external file is to be imported into the first column of the table, the second column in the external file into the second column of the table, and so on.
- If the *DataDescriptor* parameter is set to NULL or if the *dcolmeth* field of the *sqldcol* structure is set to SQL_METH_D, the *dcolnum* and *dcolname* fields of the *sqldcol* structure are ignored.
- If the *dcolmeth* field of the *sqldcol* structure in the *DataDescriptor* parameter is set to SQL_METH_N, the *dcolnptr* pointer of each element of the *dcolname* array must point to a string, *dcolnlen* characters in length, that contains the name of a valid column in the external file to be imported.
- If the *dcolmeth* field of the *sqldcol* structure in the *DataDescriptor* parameter is set to SQL_METH_P, the *dcolnptr* pointer of each element of the *dcolname* array is ignored and the *dcolnlen* field of each element of the *dcolname* array must contain a valid column position in the external file to be imported. The lowest column (byte) position value that can be specified is 1 (indicating the first column or byte), and the largest column (byte) position value that can be specified is determined by the number of columns (bytes) contained in one row of data in the external file.
- If the *dcolmeth* field of the *sqldcol* structure in the *DataDescriptor* parameter is set to SQL_METH_L, the *dcolnptr* pointer of the first element of the *dcolname* array points to a *sqlloctab* structure that consists of an array of *sqllocpair* structures. The number of elements in this array must be stored in the *dcolnum* field of the *sqldcol* structure. Each element in this array contains a pair of integer values that indicates the position in the file where a column begins and ends. The first integer value is the byte position (in a row) in the file where the column begins, and the second integer value is the byte position (in the same row) where the column ends. The first byte position value that can be specified is 1 (indicating the first byte in a row of data), and the largest byte position value that can be specified is determined by the number of bytes contained in a row in the external file. Columns defined by starting and ending byte positions can overlap.
- If the *dcolmeth* field of the *sqldcol* structure in the *DataDescriptor* parameter is set to SQL_METH_L, the DB2 database manager will reject an IMPORT call if a location pair is invalid because of any of the following conditions:
  - –Either the beginning or the ending location is not in the range from 1 to the largest signed two-byte integer.
  - –The ending location value is smaller than the beginning location value.

–The input column width defined by the beginning/end location pair is not compatible with the data type and length of the target database table column.

- A location pair with both location values set to 0 indicates that a nullable column is to be filled with NULL values.
- If the *DataDescriptor* parameter is set to NULL or if the *dcolmeth* field of the *sqldcol* structure in the *DataDescriptor* parameter is set to SQL_METH_D, the first *n* columns (where *n* is the number of database columns into which the data is to be imported) of data found in the external file will be imported in their natural order.
- Columns in external files can be specified more than once, but anything that is not a valid specification of an external column (i.e., a name, position, location, or default) will cause an error. Every column found in an external file does not have to be imported.
- The character string specified in the *ActionString* parameter must be in the following format:

```
[Action] INTO [TableName <(ColumnName,...)>
```

where:

Action Specifies how the data is to be imported into the database table. The action can be any of the following values:

INSERT — Specifies that imported data rows are to be added to a table that already exists in the database, and that any data previously stored in the table should not be changed.

INSERT_UPDATE — Specifies that imported data rows are to be added to a table if their primary keys do not match existing table data, and that they are to be used to update data in a table if matching primary keys are found. This option is valid only when the target table has a primary key and when the specified (or implied) list of target columns being imported includes all columns for the primary key. This option cannot be applied to views.

REPLACE — Specifies that all previously entered data in a table is to be deleted before data is imported. When existing data is deleted, table and index definitions remain undisturbed unless otherwise specified (indexes are deleted and replaced if the *FileTypeMod* parameter is set to *indexixf* and the *FileType* parameter is set to SQL_IXF). If the table is not already defined, an error will be returned. If an error occurs after existing data is deleted, that data will be lost and can be recovered only if the database was backed up before the IMPORT function was called.

CREATE — Specifies that if the table does not already exist, it will be created using the table definition stored in the specified PC/IXF format data file. If the PC/IXF file was exported from a DB2 database, indexes will also be created. If the specified table name is already defined, an error will be returned. This option is valid only for PC/IXF format files.

REPLACE_CREATE Specifies that if the table already exists, any data previously stored in it will be replaced with the data imported from the PC/IXF format file. If the table does not already exist, it will be created using the table definition stored in the specified PC/IXF format data file. If the PC/IXF file was exported from a DB2 database, indexes will also be created when the table is created. This option is valid only for PC/IXF format files. If an error occurs after existing data is deleted from the table, that data will be lost and can be recovered only if the database was backed up before the IMPORT function was called.

TableName Specifies the name of the table or updatable view into which the data is to be inserted. A alias name can be used if the REPLACE, INSERT_UPDATE, or INSERT option is specified, except in the case of a down-level server. In this case, a table name (either qualified or unqualified) should always be used.

ColumnName Specifies one or more column names within the table or view into which data from the external file is to be inserted. Commas must separate each column name in this list. If no column names are specified, the column names defined for the table will be used.

- The *TableName* and the *ColumnName* list parameters correspond to the *TableName* and *ColName* list parameters of the INSERT SQL statement that are used to import the data, and have the same restrictions.
- The columns in the *ColumnName* list and the columns (either specified or implied) in the external file are matched according to their position in the list or in the *sqldcol* structure (data from the first column specified in the *sqldcol* structure is inserted into the table or view field corresponding to the first element of the *ColumnName* list). If unequal numbers of columns are specified, the number of columns actually processed is the lesser of the two numbers. This could cause an error message (because there are no values to place in some NOT NULL table columns) or an informational message (because some external file columns are ignored) to be generated.
- If the *MsgFileName* parameter contains the path and the name of an operating system file that already exists, the existing file will be overwritten when this function is executed. If the path and the name of an operating system file that does not exist is specified, a new file will be created.
- Messages placed in the message file include information returned from the message retrieval service. Each message begins on a new line.
- The *CallerAction* parameter must be set to SQLU_INITIAL the first time this function is called.
- The caller action repeat call facility provides support for multiple PC/IXF format files created on platforms that support diskettes.
- The number of elements in the *NullIndicators* array must match the number of columns in the input file (the number of elements must equal the *dcolnum* field of the *sqldcol* structure in the *DataDescriptor* parameter).

There is a one-to-one ordered correspondence between the elements of this array and the columns being imported from the data file. Each element of this array must either contain a number identifying a column in the data file to be used as a null indicator field, or a 0 to indicate that the table column is not nullable. If the element contains a number identifying a column in the data file, the column identified must contain either a Y or an N (a Y value indicates that the table column data is null, and a N value indicates that the table column data is not null).

- All table operations need to be completed and all locks must be released before this function is called. You can accomplish this by issuing either a COMMIT SQL statement after closing all cursors opened with the WITH HOLD option or a ROLLBACK SQL statement. One or more COMMIT SQL statements are automatically issued during the import process.
- Whenever a COMMIT is performed, two messages are written to the message file; one indicates the number of records to be committed, and the other is written after a COMMIT SQL statement is successfully executed. When restarting the import after a system failure has occurred, specify the number of records to skip, as determined from the last messages generated form the successful COMMIT.
- When importing PC/IXF format files to a remote database, the performance can be greatly improved if the external PC/IXF file resides on a hard drive rather than on diskettes.
- Specifying non-default column values in the *DataDescriptor* parameter or an explicit list of table columns in the *ActionString* parameter makes importing to a remote database slower.
- When importing to a remote database, make sure there is enough disk space on the server workstation for a copy of the input data file, the output message file, and the potential growth in the size of the database.
- If IMPORT is run against a remote database and the output message file is very large (more than 60KB in size), the message file returned to the user on the client workstation might be missing messages from the middle of the import process. This is because the first and last 30KB of message information is always retained.
- After old rows of data are deleted during a REPLACE or REPLACE _CREATE import, a COMMIT SQL statement is automatically issued. Consequently, if a system failure occurs or if an application interrupts the DB2 database manager after the records are deleted, part or all of the original data will be lost. Ensure that the original data is no longer needed before using either of these options.
- When the recovery log becomes full during a CREATE, REPLACE, or REPLACE_CREATE import, a COMMIT SQL statement is automatically issued to commit all inserted records. If a system failure occurs or if the application interrupts the DB2 database manager after the COMMIT statement executes, a table that is partially filled with data will remain in the database. If this occurs, perform a REPLACE or a REPLACE_CREATE import to import the whole file again, or perform an INSERT import with the *restartcount* field of the *sqluimpt_in* structure set to the number of rows already imported.
- By default, automatic commits are not performed if the INSERT or INSERT_UPDATE option is specified. However, they are performed if the *commitcnt* field of the *sqluimpt_in* structure contains anything other than 0.

- If the recovery log file becomes full during an INSERT or INSERT_UPDATE import, all changes will be removed (rolled back).
- The import utility adds rows to the target database table using the INSERT SQL statement. This utility issues one INSERT statement for each row of data in the input file. If an INSERT statement fails, one of two actions will result:

  –If it is likely that subsequent INSERT statements can be successful, a warning message will be written to the message file and processing will continue.

  –If it is likely that subsequent INSERT statements will fail and there is potential for database damage, an error message will be written to the message file and processing will stop.
- Data from external files cannot be imported to system catalog tables.
- Views cannot be created with a CREATE import.
- REPLACE and REPLACE_CREATE imports cannot be performed on object tables that have other dependents (other than themselves) or on object views whose base tables have other dependents (including themselves). To replace such a table or a view, perform the following steps:
  1. Drop all foreign keys in which the table is a parent.
  2. Execute the IMPORT function.
  3. Alter the table to recreate the foreign keys. If an error occurs while recreating the foreign keys, modify the data so it maintains referential integrity.
- Referential constraints and key definitions are not preserved when tables are created (CREATE option) from PC/IXF format files.
- You can use the IMPORT function to recover a previously exported table if the PC/IXF format was used. When the IMPORT function is executed, the table returns to the state it was in when it was exported. This operation is similar to but distinct from the backup and restore utility.
- The *data* field of the *sqlchar* structure specified in the *FileTypeMod* parameter must contain one of the following values:

  –lobsinfile
  –compound=x
  –noeofchar
  –padwithzero
  –reclen=xxxx
  –coldel
  –T
  –chardel
  –decpt
  –forcein
  –indexixf
  –indexschema=schema

  These values provide additional information about the chosen file format. Only a portion of these values are used with a particular file format. If the *FileTypeMod* parameter is set to NULL or if the *length* field of the *sqlchar* structure is set to 0, default information is provided for the file format specified.
- You can use the value stored in the *FileTypeMod* parameter to specify where LOB data is stored. If this parameter is set to *lobsinfle,* LOB data is stored in separate files; otherwise, all LOB data is truncated to 32KB and stored in a single file.

- If the *FileTypeMod* parameter is set to *lobsinfile* and the CREATE option is used, the original LOB length is lost and the LOB value stored in the file is truncated to 32KB.
- If the *FileTypeMod* parameter is set to *compound=x* (where *x* is any number between 1 and 100 or 7 on DOS/Windows platforms), nonatomic compound SQL is used to insert the imported data (*x* number of statements will be processed as a single compound SQL statement).
- If data is being imported from a delimited ASCII (DEL) format file, the *FileTypeMod* parameter can be set to *noeofchar* to specify that the optional end-of-file character (0x1A) is not to be recognized as the end-of-file character. If this option is set, the end-of-file character (0x1A) is treated as a normal character (OS/2 only).
- If data is being imported from a delimited ASCII (DEL) format file, the *FileTypeMod* parameter can be set to *T* to specify that trailing blanks after the last nonblank character are to be removed (truncated) when the data is imported. If this option is not set, trailing blanks are kept. If this option is used in conjunction with the *padwithzero* option, 0x00 characters are truncated instead of blank characters.
- If data is being imported from a delimited ASCII (DEL) format file, the *FileTypeMod* parameter can be set to *reclen=xxxx* (where *xxxx* is a number no larger than 32767) to specify that *xxxx* characters are to be read in for each row. In this case, a new-line character does not indicate the end of a row.
- If data is being imported from a delimited ASCII (DEL) format file, you can use the *FileTypeMod* parameter to specify characters to override the following options:

Column delimiters By default, columns are delimited with commas. Specifying *coldel*, followed by a character, will cause the specified character to be used in place of a comma to signal the end of a column.

Character string delimiters By default, character strings are delimited with double quotation marks. Specifying *chardel*, followed by a character, will cause the specified character to be used in place of double quotation marks to enclose a character string.

Decimal point characters By default, decimal points are specified with periods. Specifying *decpt*, followed by a character, will cause the specified character to be used in place of a period as a decimal point character. If two or more delimiters are specified, they must be separated by blank spaces. Blank spaces cannot be used as delimiters. Each delimiter character specified must be different from the delimiter characters already being used so all delimiters can be uniquely identified. Table 24.3 (refer to the EXPORT function) lists the characters that can be used as delimiter overrides.

- If data is being imported from a worksheet (WSF) format file, the *FileTypeMod* parameter is ignored.
- If data is being imported from a PC/IXF (IXF) format file, set the *FileTypeMod* parameter to *forcein* to tell the import utility to accept data in spite of code page mismatches and to suppress all translations between code pages.
- If data is being imported from a PC/IXF (IXF) format file, set the *FileTypeMod* parameter to *indexixf* to tell the import utility to drop all indexes currently defined on the existing table and create new ones from

the index definitions found in the PC/IXF format file being imported. This option can be used only when the contents of a table are being replaced. This option cannot be used with a view.

- If data is being imported from a PC/IXF (IXF) format file, set the *FileTypeMod* parameter to *indexschema=schema* to indicate that the specified schema is to be used for the index name whenever indexes are created. If no *schema* is specified, the authorization ID used to establish the current database connection will be used as the default schema.
- The IMPORT function will not issue a warning if you attempt to use unsupported file types with the MODIFIED BY option. Instead, the IMPORT function will fail and an error code will be returned.
- The LOAD function is a faster alternative to the IMPORT function.

Required Connection

This function can be called only if a connection to a database exists.

Authorization

Only users with system administrator (SYSADM) authority or database (DBADM) authority, or CONTROL, INSERT, or SELECT authority for the specified table or view can execute this function call with the INSERT option (*ActionString* parameter) specified. Only users with SYSADM or DBADM authority, or CONTROL authority for the specified table or view can execute this function call with the INSERT_UPDATE, REPLACE, or REPLACE_CREATE (*ActionString* parameter) option specified. Only users with SYSADM or DBADM authority, or CREATETAB authority for the specified table or view can execute this function call with the CREATE or the REPLACE_CREATE (*ActionString* parameter) option specified.

See Also

EXPORT, LOAD

Example

The following C program illustrates how to use the IMPORT function to insert data from an external file into the DEPARTMENT table of the SAMPLE database:

```
#include <stdio.h>
#include <stdlib.h>
#include <string.h>
#include <sqlutil.h>
#include <sql.h>

int main()
{
    /* Include The SQLCA Data Structure Variable */
    EXEC SQL INCLUDE SQLCA;

    /* Declare The Local Memory Variables */
    int                     rc = EXIT_SUCCESS;
    char                    String[100];
    char                    DataFileName[80];
    char                    MsgFileName[80];
    struct sqlchar          *ActionString;
    struct sqluimpt_in      ImportInfoIn;
    struct sqluimpt_out     ImportInfoOut;

    /* Set Up A Simple SQL Error Handler */
    EXEC SQL WHENEVER SQLERROR GOTO EXIT;

    /* Connect To The SAMPLE Database */
    EXEC SQL CONNECT TO SAMPLE USER etpdd6z USING sanders;
```

```
    /* Initialize The Local Variables */
    strcpy(DataFileName, "DEPT.IXF");
    strcpy(MsgFileName, "IMP_MSG.DAT");

    /* Initialize The Import Input Structure */
    ImportInfoIn.sizeOfStruct = SQLUIMPT_IN_SIZE;
    ImportInfoIn.commitcnt = 20;

    /* Initialize The Import Output Structure */
    ImportInfoOut.sizeOfStruct = SQLUIMPT_OUT_SIZE;

    /* Define The Action String That Will Be Used To Control How */
    /* Data Is Imported                                          */
    strcpy(String, "REPLACE INTO USERID.DEPARTMENT");
    ActionString = (struct sqlchar *)
        malloc (strlen(String) + sizeof(struct sqlchar));
    ActionString->length = strlen(String);
    strncpy(ActionString->data, String, strlen(String));

    /* Import Data Into The USERID.DEPARTMENT Table From An IXF  */
    /* Format File (This File Was Created By The EXPORT Example) */
    sqluimpr(DataFileName, NULL, NULL, ActionString, SQL_IXF, NULL,
             MsgFileName, SQLU_INITIAL, &ImportInfoIn, &ImportInfoOut,
             NULL, NULL, &sqlca);

    /* Display A Success Message */
    printf("Data in the the file DEPT.IXF has been imported into ");
    printf("the\ntable USERID.DEPARTMENT.\n");

EXIT:
    /* If An Error Has Occurred, Display The SQL Return Code */
    if (sqlca.sqlcode != SQL_RC_OK)
        {
        printf("SQL ERROR : %ld\n", sqlca.sqlcode);
        rc = EXIT_FAILURE;
        }

    /* Issue A Rollback To Free All Locks */
    EXEC SQL ROLLBACK;

    /* Turn Off The SQL Error Handler */
    EXEC SQL WHENEVER SQLERROR CONTINUE;

    /* Disconnect From The SAMPLE Database */
    EXEC SQL DISCONNECT CURRENT;

    /* Free All Allocated Memory */
    if (ActionString != NULL)
        free(ActionString);

    /* Return To The Operating System */
    return(rc);
}
```

LOAD

Purpose

The LOAD function loads data from external files, tapes, or named pipes into DB2 database tables.

Syntax

```
SQL_API_RC SQL_API_FN sqluload (sqlu_media_list      *DataFileList,
                                sqlu_media_list      *LOBPathList,
                                struct sqldcol       *DataDescriptor,
                                struct sqlchar       *ActionString,
                                char                 *FileType,
                                struct sqlchar       *FileTypeMod,
                                char                 *LocalMsgFileName,
                                char                 *RemoteMsgFileName,
                                short                CallerAction,
                                struct sqluload_in   *LoadInfoIn,
                                struct sqluload_out  *LoadInfoOut,
                                sqlu_media_list      *WorkDirectoryList,
                                sqlu_media_list      *CopyTargetList,
                                long                 *NullIndicators,
                                void                 *Reserved,
                                struct sqlca         *SQLCA);
```

Parameters

DataFileList A pointer to a *sqlu_media_list* structure that contains a list of external data files, devices, vendors, or named pipes that identify where data is to be loaded from.

LOBPathList A pointer to a *sqlu_media_list* structure that contains a list of local paths that identify where, on the client workstation, LOB data files are to be loaded from.

DataDescriptor A pointer to a *sqldcol* structure that contains information about the columns in the external data file being selected for loading. The value of the *dcolmeth* field of this structure determines how columns are selected from the external file.

ActionString A pointer to a *sqlchar* structure that contains a valid dynamic SQL statement, followed by an array of characters that identifies the action to be taken when importing data into tables that already contain data.

FileType A pointer to a location in memory where a string that specifies the format of the external data file is stored. This parameter can be set to any of the following values:

DEL (or SQL_DEL)	Specifies that the data in the external file is stored in delimited ASCII format.
ASC (or SQL_ASC)	Specifies that the data in the external file is stored in nondelimited ASCII format.
IXF (or SQL_IXF)	Specifies that the data in the external file is stored in PC integrated exchange format.

FileTypeMod A pointer to a *sqlchar* structure that contains additional information that is unique to the format used in the external file.

LocalMsgFileName A pointer to a location in memory that contains the name of the file where all LOAD error, warning, and informational messages are to be written.

RemoteMsgFileName A pointer to a location in memory where the base name used for naming temporary files created by the load operation currently in progress is stored.

CallerAction Specifies the action this function is to take when it executes. This parameter can be set to any of the following values:

SQLU_INITIAL	Specifies that the load operation is to be started.
SQLU_CONTINUE	Specifies that the load operation is to be continued after the user has performed some action requested by the load utility (for example,

inserting a diskette or mounting a new tape).

SQLU_TERMINATE	Specifies that the load operation is to be terminated after the user fails to perform some action requested by the load utility.
SQLU_NOINTERRUPT	Specifies that the load operation cannot suspend processing.
SQLU_ABORT	Specifies that the load operation is to be terminated.
SQLU_RESTART	Specifies that the load operation is to be restarted.
SQLU_DEVICE_TERMINATE	Specifies that a particular device should be removed from the list of devices used by the load utility. When a particular device has exhausted its input, the load utility returns a warning to the caller (while continuing to process using the remaining devices). By calling the LOAD function again with this caller action specified, you can remove the device that generated the warning condition from the list of devices being used.

LoadInfoIn A pointer to a *sqluload_in* structure that contains information about the number of records to skip, number of records to load, sizes of internal buffer, and load fail conditions.

LoadInfoOut A pointer to a *sqluload_out* structure where this function is to store summary information about the load operation.

WorkDirectoryList A pointer to a *sqlu_media_list* structure that contains a list of optional work directories for sorting index keys during the load operation. This parameter can be set to NULL.

CopyTargetList A pointer to a *sqlu_media_list* structure that contains a list of external data files, devices, or shared libraries where copy images (if created) are to be written.

NullIndicators A pointer to an array of integers that indicates whether or not each retrieved column of data can contain NULL values. This parameter is used only if the *FileType* parameter is set to DEL (SQL_DEL).

Reserved A pointer that is currently reserved for later use. For now, this parameter must always be set to NULL.

SQLCA A pointer to a location in memory where a SQLCA data structure variable is stored. This variable sends either status information (if the function executed successfully) or error information (if the function failed) back to the calling application.

Includes

```
#include <sqlutil.h>
```

Description

The LOAD function loads data from external files, tapes, or named pipes into DB2 database tables. Data can be loaded from any file that contains one of the following internal file formats:

- Delimited ASCII
- Nondelimited ASCII
- PC integrated exchange format (IXF)

Three special structures (*sqldcol, sqlu_media_list,* and *sqlchar*) pass general information to the DB2 load utility when this function is called. Refer to the EXPORT function for a detailed description of the *sqldcol* structure and the BACKUP DATABASE function for a detailed description of the *sqlu_media_list* structure. A special structure (the *sqlloctab* structure) can also be used by the *sqldcol* structure when this function is executed. Refer to the IMPORT function for a detailed description of this structure.

Two additional structures, *sqluload_in* and *sqluload_out*, pass load specific information to and from the DB2 load facility when this function is called. The first of these structures, *sqluload_in*, passes information such as when data is to be committed and the number of records to skip before starting the load to the database to the load facility and is defined in *sqlutil.h* as follows:

```
struct sqluload_in
{
unsigned long  sizeOfStruct;      /* The size of the sqluload_in structure      */
unsigned long  savecnt;           /* The number of records to load before       */
                                  /* a COMMIT SQL statement is executed         */
                                  /* A COMMIT statement is executed each        */
                                  /* time this number of records are loaded     */
                                  /* to make the additions permanent            */
unsigned long  restartcnt;        /* The number of records to skip in the file  */
                                  /* before starting the load process. This     */
                                  /* field can be used if a previous attempt to */
                                  /* load records failed after n number of      */
                                  /* rows of data had already been committed    */
                                  /* to the database.                           */
unsigned long  rowcnt;            /* The number of rows of data to load         */
unsigned long  warningcnt;        /* The number of warning conditions to        */
                                  /* ignore before failing                      */
unsigned long  data_buffer_size;  /* The size, in 4KB pages, of the buffer to   */
                                  /* be used when loading data                  */
unsigned long  sort_buffer_size;  /* The size, in 4KB pages, of the buffer to   */
                                  /* be used when sorting data                  */
unsigned short hold_quiesce;      /* A flag indicating whether or not the table */
                                  /* spaces for the table being loaded are      */
                                  /* in a quiesced state                        */
char           restartphase;      /* Indicates that an interrupted load         */
                                  /* operation is to be restarted at the load   */
                                  /* phase (SQLU_LOAD_PHASE), at the            */
                                  /* build phase (SQLU_BUILD_PHASE),            */
                                  /* or at the delete phase                     */
                                  /* (SQLU_DELETE_PHASE)                        */
char           statsopt;          /* Specifies the granularity to use when      */
                                  /* collecting statistical information during  */
                                  /* the load operation. This field can contain */
                                  /* any of the following values:               */
                                  /* SQL_STATS_TABLE,                           */
                                  /* SQL_STATS_EXTTABLE_ONLY,                   */
                                  /* SQL_STATS_BOTH,                            */
                                  /* SQL_STATS_EXTTTABLE_INDEX,                 */
                                  /* SQL_STATS_INDEX,                           */
                                  /* SQL_STATS_EXTINDEX_ONLY,                   */
                                  /* SQL_STATS_EXTINDEX_TABLE,                  */
                                  /* SQL_STATS_ALL. Refer to the RUN            */
                                  /* STATISTICS function for more               */
                                  /* information about statistic granularity.   */
} ;
```

The second of these structures, *sqluload_out*, obtains statistical information about the load operation after all data is loaded into the table. The *sqluload_out* structure is defined in *sqlutil.h* as follows:

```
struct sqluload_out
{
unsigned long  sizeOfStruct;        /* The size of the sqluload_out       */
                                    /* structure                          */
unsigned long  rowsRead;            /* The number of records read from    */
                                    /* the external file                  */
unsigned long  rowsSkipped;         /* The number of records skipped      */
                                    /* before the load process was        */
                                    /* started                            */
unsigned long  rowsLoaded;          /* The number of rows inserted into   */
                                    /* the specified database table       */
unsigned long  rowsRejected;        /* The number of records in the file  */
                                    /* that, for some reason, could not   */
                                    /* be loaded                          */
unsigned long  rowsDeleted;         /* The number of duplicate rows that  */
                                    /* were deleted.                      */
unsigned long  rowsCommitted;       /* The number of rows successfully    */
                                    /* loaded and committed               */
};
```

Note: Data that has minor incompatibility problems will be accepted by the load facility (for example, you can load character data by using padding or truncation, and numeric data by using a different numeric data type). Data with major incompatibility problems will be rejected.

Comments

- The type of structure that provides information about external data files, devices, vendors, or named pipes identifying where data is to be loaded from is determined by the value specified in the *media_type* field of the *sqlu_media_list* structure stored in the *DataFileList* parameter, as follows:

SQLU_SERVER_LOCATION One or more *sqlu_location_entry* structures. The *sessions* field of the *sqlu_media_list* structure should indicate the number of *sqlu_location_entry* structures used.

SQLU_ADSM_MEDIA One *sqlu_vendor* structure. The *filename* field of the *sqlu_vendor* structure should contain a unique identifier for the data source to be loaded. The load utility will start each session with a different sequence number, but with the same data specified in the *sqlu_vendor* structure.

SQLU_OTHER_MEDIA One *sqlu_vendor* structure. The *shr_lib* field of the *sqlu_vendor* structure should contain a valid shared library name, and the *filename* field of the *sqlu_vendor* structure should contain a unique identifier for the data source to be loaded. The load utility will start each session with a different sequence number, but with the same data specified in the *sqlu_vendor* structure.

- Data files that were created with the EXPORT function or command will have LOB data filenames stored in them (if the specified data set contained LOB data and if the *lobsinfile* option was specified). These names are appended to the paths specified in the *sqlu_media_list* structure during the load process to provide a reference to LOB data.

- The type of structure that provides information about external LOB data file paths is determined by the value specified in the *media_type* field of the *sqlu_media_list* structure stored in the *LOBPathList* parameter, as follows:

SQLU_LOCAL_MEDIA One or more *sqlu_media_entry* structures. The sessions field of the *sqlu_media_list* structure should indicate the number of *sqlu_media_entry* structures used.

SQLU_ADSM_MEDIA One *sqlu_vendor* structure. The *filename* field of the *sqlu_vendor* structure should contain a unique identifier for the data source to be loaded. The load utility will start each session with a different sequence number, but with the same data specified in the *sqlu_vendor* structure.

SQLU_OTHER_MEDIA One *sqlu_vendor* structure. The *shr_lib* field of the *sqlu_vendor* structure should contain a valid shared library name, and the *filename* field of the *sqlu_vendor* structure should contain a unique identifier for the data source to be loaded. The load utility will start each session with a different sequence number, but with the same data specified in the *sqlu_vendor* structure.

- The *dcolmeth* field of the *sqldcol* structure specified in the *DataDescriptor* parameter defines how columns are selected for loading from the external data file. This parameter can be set to any of the following values:

SQL_METH_N Specifies that column names provided in the *sqldcol* structure identify the data to be loaded from the external file. This method cannot be used if the external file does not contain column names (if the file is in delimited ASCII format).

SQL_METH_P Specifies that starting column positions provided in the *sqldcol* structure identify the data to be loaded from the external file. This method cannot be used if the external file is in delimited ASCII format.

SQL_METH_L Specifies that starting and ending column positions provided in the *sqldcol* structure identify the data to be loaded from the external file. This is the only method to use if the external file is in delimited ASCII format.

SQL_METH_D Specifies that the first column in the external file is to be loaded into the first column of the table, the second column in the external file is to be loaded into the second column of the table, and so on.

- If the *DataDescriptor* parameter is set to NULL or if the *dcolmeth* field of the *sqldcol* structure is set to SQL_METH_D, the *dcolnum* field and the *dcolname* field of the sqldcol structure are ignored.
- If the *dcolmeth* field of the *sqldcol* structure in the *DataDescriptor* parameter is set to SQL_METH_N, the *dcolnptr* pointer of each element of the *dcolname* array must point to a string, *dcolnlen* characters in length, that contains the name of a valid column in the external file to be loaded.
- If the *dcolmeth* field of the *sqldcol* structure in the *DataDescriptor* parameter is set to SQL_METH_P, the *dcolnptr* pointer of each element of the *dcolname* array is ignored and the *dcolnlen* field of each element of the *dcolname* array must contain a valid column position in the external file to be loaded. The lowest column (byte) position value that can be specified is 1 (indicating the first column or byte) and the largest column (byte) position value that can be specified is determined by the number of columns (bytes) contained in one row of data in the external file.

- If the *dcolmeth* field of the *sqldcol* structure in the *DataDescriptor* parameter is set to SQL_METH_L, the *dcolnptr* pointer of the first element of the *dcolname* array points to a *sqlloctab* structure that consists of an array of *sqllocpair* structures. The number of elements in this array must be stored in the *dcolnum* field of the *sqldcol* structure. Each element in this array contains a pair of integer values that indicate the position in the file where a column begins and ends. The first integer value is the byte position (in a row) in the file where the column begins, and the second integer value is the byte position (in the same row) where the column ends. The first byte position value that can be specified is 1 (indicating the first byte in a row of data) and the largest byte position value that can be specified is determined by the number of bytes contained in a row in the external file. Columns defined by starting and ending byte positions can overlap.
- If the *dcolmeth* field of the *sqldcol* structure in the *DataDescriptor* parameter is set to SQL_METH_L, the DB2 database manager will reject a LOAD call if a location pair is invalid because of any of the following conditions:
  - –Either the beginning or the ending location is not in the range from 1 to the largest signed two-byte integer.
  - –The ending location value is smaller than the beginning location value.
  - –The input column width defined by the beginning/end location pair is not compatible with the data type and length of the target database table column.
- A location pair with both location values set to 0 indicates that a nullable column is to be filled with NULL values.
- If the *DataDescriptor* parameter is set to NULL or if the *dcolmeth* field of the *sqldcol* structure in the *DataDescriptor* parameter is set to SQL_METH_D, the first *n* columns (where *n* is the number of database columns into which the data is to be loaded) of data found in the external file will be loaded in their natural order.
- Columns in external files can be specified more than once, but anything that is not a valid specification of an external column (a name, position, location, or default) will cause an error. Every column found in an external file does not have to be loaded.
- The character string specified in the *ActionString* parameter must be in the following format:

```
[Action] INTO [TableName <(ColumnName,...)> <FOR EXCEPTION ETableName>
```

where:

Action Specifies how the data is to be loaded into the database table. The action can be any of the following values:

INSERT Specifies that loaded data rows are to be added to a table that already exists in the database, and that any data previously stored in the table should not be changed.

REPLACE Specifies that all previously entered data in a table is to be deleted before data is loaded. When existing data is deleted, table and index definitions remain undisturbed unless otherwise specified (indexes are deleted and replaced if the *FileTypeMod* parameter is set to *indexixf* and the *FileType* parameter is set to SQL_IXF). If the table is not already defined, an error is returned. If an error occurs after existing data is deleted, that data is lost and can be recovered only if the database was backed up before the LOAD function was called.

RESTART — Specifies that a load operation that was started and later interrupted, is to be restarted. The last commit point of the interrupted load must be provided in the LOAD call that specifies the RESTART action. The LOAD QUERY function can be used to obtain this value.

TERMINATE — Specifies that a previously interrupted load operation is to be terminated. When this action is specified, all table spaces in which the table being loaded resides are changed from load pending to recovery pending state and they cannot be used until they are restored and rolled forward. This option is not recommended for general use and should be used only if an unrecoverable error has occurred. Attempt to restart an interrupted load whenever possible.

TableName Specifies the name of the table in which the data is to be loaded. A alias name or a fully qualified or unqualified name can be specified. If an unqualified name is specified, the authorization ID of the current user will be used as the default qualifier.

ColumnName Specifies one or more column names within the table into which data from the external file is to be loaded. Commas must separate each column name in this list. If no column names are specified, the column names defined for the table are used.

ETableName Specifies the name of the exception table to which the data causing an error during the load operation is to be copied. All data that violates a unique index or a primary key index defined for the specified table is stored here.

- The *TableName* and the *ColumnName* list parameters correspond to the *TableName* and *ColName* list parameters of the INSERT SQL statement that will load the data, and have the same restrictions.
- The columns in the *ColumnName* list and the columns (either specified or implied) in the external file are matched according to their position in the list or the *sqldcol* structure (data from the first column specified in the *sqldcol* structure is inserted into the table or view field corresponding to the first element of the *ColumnName* list). If unequal numbers of columns are specified, the number of columns actually processed is the lesser of the two numbers. This could cause an error message (because there are no values to place in some NOT NULL table columns) or an informational message (because some external file columns are ignored) to be generated.
- The load utility builds indexes based on existing definitions. The exception tables handle duplicates on unique keys. The load utility does not perform referential integrity or constraint checking. If referential integrity and constraint checks are included in the table definition, the tables are placed in check pending state and the user must either force the check flag or execute the SET CONSTRAINTS SQL statement.
- If the *LocalMsgFileName* parameter contains the path and name of an operating system file that already exists, the existing file will be overwritten when this function is executed. If the path and the name of an op-

erating system file that does not exist is specified, a new file will be created.

- Messages placed in the message file include information returned from the message retrieval service. Each message begins on a new line.
- The *CallerAction* parameter must be set to SQLU_INITIAL the first time this function is called.
- If a list of work directories to use for sorting index keys during the load operation is not specified in the *WorkDirectoryList* parameter, the **tmp** subdirectory of the **sqllib** directory will be used.
- The type of structure used to provide information about paths, devices, or shared libraries where copy images of loaded data are to be stored is determined by the value specified in the *media_type* field of the *sqlu_media_list* structure stored in the *CopyTargetList* parameter, as follows:

SQLU_LOCAL_MEDIA One or more *sqlu_media_entry* structures. The sessions field of the *sqlu_media_list* structure should indicate the number of *sqlu_media_entry* structures used.

SQLU_ADSM_MEDIA No other structure is needed.

SQLU_OTHER_MEDIA One *sqlu_vendor* structure. The *shr_lib* field of the *sqlu_vendor* structure should contain the shared library name of the vendor product being used. The load utility will start each session with a different sequence number, but with the same data specified in the *sqlu_vendor* structure.

- The number of elements in the *NullIndicators* array must match the number of columns in the input file (i.e., the number of elements must equal the *dcolnum* field of the *sqldcol* structure in the *DataDescriptor* parameter). There is a one-to-one ordered correspondence between the elements of this array and the columns being loaded from the data file. Each element of this array must contain either a number identifying a column in the data file that is to be used as a null indicator field, or a 0 to indicate that the table column is not nullable. If the element contains a number identifying a column in the data file, the identified column must contain either a Y or an N (a Y value indicates that the table column data is null, and a N value indicates that the table column data is not null).
- The *data* field of the *sqlchar* structure specified in the *FileTypeMod* parameter must contain one of the following values:

  –lobsinfile
  –pagefreespace=x
  –norowwarnings
  –totalfreespace
  –noeofchar
  –T
  –padwithzero
  –reclen=xxxx
  –coldel
  –chardel
  –decpt
  –forcein

  These values provide additional information about the chosen file format. Only a portion of these values is used with a particular file format. If the *FileTypeMod* parameter is set to NULL or if the *length* field of the *sqlchar* structure is set to 0, default information is provided for the specified file format.

- You can use the value stored in the *FileTypeMod* parameter to specify where LOB data is stored. If this parameter is set to *lobsinfile*, LOB data is stored in separate files; otherwise, all LOB data is truncated to 32KB and stored in a single file.
- If the *FileTypeMod* parameter is set to *norowwarnings*, all warnings generated because rows of data were rejected are ignored.
- If the *FileTypeMod* parameter is set to *pagefreespace=x* (where *x* is an integer between 0 and 100), the value specified for *x* is interpreted as the percentage of each data page to be left as free storage space.
- If the *FileTypeMod* parameter is set to *totalpagefreespace=x* (where *x* is an integer between 0 and 100), the value specified for *x* is interpreted as the percentage of the total number of pages in the table to be appended to the end of the table as free storage space. For example, if *x* is 20 and the table contains 100 data pages, 20 additional empty pages will be appended to the table. If a value of 100 is specified for *x*, each row of data will be placed on a separate page.
- If data is being loaded from a delimited ASCII (DEL) format file, the *FileTypeMod* parameter can be set to *noeofchar* to specify that the optional end-of-file character (0x1A) is not to be recognized as the end-of-file character. If this option is set, the end-of-file character (0x1A) is treated as a normal character (OS/2 only).
- If data is being loaded from a delimited ASCII (DEL) format file, the *FileTypeMod* parameter can be set to *T* to specify that trailing blanks after the last non-blank character are to be removed (truncated) when the data is loaded. If this option is not set, trailing blanks will be kept. If this option is used in conjunction with the *padwithzero* option, 0x00 characters are truncated instead of blank characters.
- If data is being loaded from a delimited ASCII (DEL) format file, the *FileTypeMod* parameter can be set to *reclen=xxxx* (where *xxxx* is an number no larger than 32767) to specify that *xxxx* characters are to be read in for each row. In this case, a new-line character does not indicate the end of a row.
- If data is being loaded from a delimited ASCII (DEL) format file, you can use the *FileTypeMod* parameter to specify characters to override the following options:

Column delimiters By default, columns are delimited with commas. Specifying *coldel*, followed by a character, causes the specified character to be used in place of a comma to signal the end of a column.

Character string delimiters By default, character strings are delimited with double quotation marks. Specifying *chardel*, followed by a character, causes the specified character to be used in place of double quotation marks to enclose a character string.

Decimal point characters By default, decimal points are specified with periods. Specifying *decpt*, followed by a character, causes the specified character to be used in place of a period as a decimal point character.

- If two or more delimiters are specified, they must be separated by blank spaces. Blank spaces cannot be used as delimiters. Each delimiter character specified must be different from the delimiter characters already being used so all delimiters can be uniquely identified. Table 24.3 (refer to the EXPORT function), lists the characters that can be used as delimiter overrides.

- If data is being loaded from a PC/IXF (IXF) format file, the *FileTypeMod* parameter can be set to *forcein* to tell the load utility to accept data in spite of code page mismatches and to suppress all translations between code pages.
- Data cannot be loaded to system catalog tables.
- Data is loaded in the same sequence (order) it is stored in. If you want a particular data sequence, make sure the data is sorted before it is loaded.
- The LOAD function does not issue a warning if you attempt to use unsupported file types with the MODIFIED BY option. Instead, the LOAD function will fail and an error code will be returned.

Authorization

Only users with either system administrator (SYSADM) authority or database administrator (DBADM) authority can execute this function call.

See Also

IMPORT, EXPORT, LOAD QUERY, QUIESCE TABLESPACES FOR TABLE

Example

The following C program illustrates how to use the LOAD function to load data into the DEPARTMENT table of the SAMPLE database:

```
#include <stdio.h>
#include <stdlib.h>
#include <string.h>
#include <sqlenv.h>
#include <sqlutil.h>
#include <sql.h>

int main()
{
    /* Include The SQLCA Data Structure Variable */
    EXEC SQL INCLUDE SQLCA;

    /* Declare The Local Memory Variables */
    int                            rc = EXIT_SUCCESS;
    char                           String[100];
    char                           MsgFileName[80];
    char                           TempFileName[80];
    struct sqlu_media_list         DataFiles;
    struct sqlu_location_entry     Location_Entry;
    struct sqlchar                 *ActionString;
    struct sqldcol                 DataDescriptor;
    struct sqluload_in             InputInfo;
    struct sqluload_out            OutputInfo;

    /* Set Up A Simple SQL Error Handler */
    EXEC SQL WHENEVER SQLERROR GOTO EXIT;

    /* Connect To The SAMPLE Database */
    EXEC SQL CONNECT TO SAMPLE USER etpdd6z USING sanders;

    /* Initialize The Local Variables */
    strcpy(MsgFileName, "LOAD_MSG.DAT");
    strcpy(TempFileName, "TEMP");
    DataDescriptor.dcolmeth = SQL_METH_D;

    /* Initialize The Load Input Structure */
    InputInfo.sizeOfStruct = SQLULOAD_IN_SIZE;
    InputInfo.restartphase = SQLU_LOAD_PHASE;
```

```
    InputInfo.statsopt = SQL_STATS_ALL;
    /* Initialize The Load Output Structure */
    OutputInfo.sizeOfStruct = SQLULOAD_OUT_SIZE;

    /* Define The Action String That Will Be Used To Control How */
    /* Data Is Loaded                                            */
    strcpy(String, "REPLACE INTO USERID.DEPARTMENT");
    ActionString = (struct sqlchar *)
        malloc (strlen(String) + sizeof(struct sqlchar));
    ActionString->length = strlen(String);
    strncpy(ActionString->data, String, strlen(String));

    /* Initialize The Media List Information Data Structure */
    DataFiles.media_type = SQLU_SERVER_LOCATION;
    DataFiles.sessions = 1;
    strcpy(Location_Entry.location_entry, "DEPT.IXF");
    DataFiles.target.location = &Location_Entry;

    /* Restrict Access To The Table Spaces That Are Associated With */
    /* The USERID.DEPARTMENT Table (Quiesce The Table Spaces)       */
    sqluvqdp("USERID.DEPARTMENT", SQLU_QUIESCEMODE_EXCLUSIVE, NULL,
             &sqlca);

    /* Load Data Into The USERID.DEPARTMENT Table From An IXF    */
    /* Format File (This File Was Created By The EXPORT Example) */
    sqluload(&DataFiles, NULL, &DataDescriptor, ActionString, SQL_IXF,
             NULL, MsgFileName, TempFileName, SQLU_INITIAL, &InputInfo,
             &OutputInfo, NULL, NULL, NULL, NULL, &sqlca);

    /* Display A Success Message */
    printf("Data in the the file DEPT.IXF has been loaded into ");
    printf("the\ntable USERID.DEPARTMENT.\n");

    /* Remove The Access Restriction Placed On The Table Spaces That */
    /* Are Associated With The USERID.DEPARTMENT Table               */
    sqluvqdp("USERID.DEPARTMENT", SQLU_QUIESCEMODE_RESET, NULL,
             &sqlca);

EXIT:
    /* If An Error Has Occurred, Display The SQL Return Code */
    if (sqlca.sqlcode != SQL_RC_OK)
        {
        printf("SQL ERROR : %ld\n", sqlca.sqlcode);
        rc = EXIT_FAILURE;
        }

    /* Issue A Rollback To Free All Locks */
    EXEC SQL ROLLBACK;

    /* Turn Off The SQL Error Handler */
    EXEC SQL WHENEVER SQLERROR CONTINUE;

    /* Disconnect From The SAMPLE Database */
    EXEC SQL DISCONNECT CURRENT;

    /* Free All Allocated Memory */
    if (ActionString != NULL)
        free(ActionString);

    /* Return To The Operating System */
    return(rc);
}
```

LOAD QUERY

Purpose

The LOAD QUERY function queries a DB2 database manager instance for the current status of a load operation.

Syntax

```
SQL_API_RC SQL_API_FN sqluqry (char           *LocalMsgFileName,
                               char           *RemoteMsgFileName,
                               struct sqlca *SQLCA);
```

Parameters

LocalMsgFileName A pointer to a location in memory where the name of the local file to which all load status messages are to be written is stored.

RemoteMsgFileName A pointer to a location in memory that contains the name of the remote message file where all load error, warning, and informational messages are written.

SQLCA A pointer to a location in memory where a SQLCA data structure variable is stored. This variable sends either status information (if the function executed successfully) or error information (if the function failed) back to the calling application.

Includes

```
#include <sqlutil.h>
```

Description

The LOAD QUERY function queries a DB2 database manager instance for the current status of a load operation. This function retrieves the status of a load operation from the remote message file that is created and used by the load operation in progress, and places the results in the file specified by the *LocalMsgFileName* parameter.

Comments

- The specified remote filename must be the same as the filename specified in the *RemoteMsgFileName* parameter of the LOAD function call.

Required Connection

This function can be called only if a connection to a DB2 database manager instance exists.

Authorization

No authorization is required to execute this function call.

See Also

LOAD

Example

The following C program illustrates how the LOAD QUERY function is used:

```
#include <stdio.h>
#include <stdlib.h>
#include <string.h>
#include <sqlenv.h>
#include <sqlutil.h>
#include <sql.h>

int main()
{
    /* Include The SQLCA Data Structure Variable */
    EXEC SQL INCLUDE SQLCA;

    /* Declare The Local Memory Variables */
    int     rc = EXIT_SUCCESS;
    char    MsgFileName[80];
    char    StatsFileName[80];
```

```
    /* Set Up A Simple SQL Error Handler */
    EXEC SQL WHENEVER SQLERROR GOTO EXIT;

    /* Connect To The SAMPLE Database */
    EXEC SQL CONNECT TO SAMPLE USER etpdd6z USING sanders;

    /* Initialize The Local Variables */
    strcpy(MsgFileName, "TEMP");
    strcpy(StatsFileName, "LSTATS.DAT");

    /* Query The Status Of The Current Load Process */
    sqluqry(StatsFileName, MsgFileName, &sqlca);

    /* Display A Success Message */
    printf("The status of the current load process has been ");
    printf("collected and placed in\nthe file LSTATS.DAT.\n");

EXIT:
    /* If An Error Has Occurred, Display The SQL Return Code */
    if (sqlca.sqlcode != SQL_RC_OK)
        {
        printf("SQL ERROR : %ld\n", sqlca.sqlcode);
        rc = EXIT_FAILURE;
        }

    /* Issue A Rollback To Free All Locks */
    EXEC SQL ROLLBACK;

    /* Turn Off The SQL Error Handler */
    EXEC SQL WHENEVER SQLERROR CONTINUE;

    /* Disconnect From The SAMPLE Database */
    EXEC SQL DISCONNECT CURRENT;

    /* Return To The Operating System */
    return(rc);}
```

QUIESCE TABLESPACES FOR TABLE

Purpose

The QUIESCE TABLESPACES FOR TABLE function places all table spaces associated with a particular database table in a quiesced (restricted access) state.

Syntax

```
SQL_API_RC SQL_API_FN sqluvqdp (char          *TableName,
                                long          QuiesceMode,
                                void          *Reserved,
                                struct sqlca  *SQLCA);
```

Parameters

TableName A pointer to a location in memory where the name of the table, as used in the system catalog, is stored.

QuiesceMode Specifies the quiesce mode to be used. This parameter can be set to any of the following values:

SQLU_QUIESCEMODE_SHARE — Specifies that the table space(s) are to be placed in QUIESCED SHARE state.

SQLU_QUIESCEMODE_INTENT_UPDATE	Specifies that the table space(s) are to be placed in QUIESCE INTENT TO UPDATE state.
SQLU_QUIESCEMODE_EXCLUSIVE	Specifies that the table space(s) are to be placed in QUIESCE EXCLUSIVE state.
SQLU_QUIESCEMODE_RESET	Specifies that the table space(s) are to be returned to their normal state.

Reserved A pointer that is currently reserved for later use. For now, this parameter must always be set to NULL.

SQLCA A pointer to a location in memory where a SQLCA data structure variable is stored. This variable sends either status information (if the function executed successfully) or error information (if the function failed) back to the calling application.

Includes

```
#include <sqlutil.h>
```

Description

The QUIESCE TABLESPACES FOR TABLE function places all table spaces associated with a particular database table in a quiesced (restricted access) state. When this function is executed, only transactions that are holding the table space in a quiesced state are granted access to the table space. All other transactions are "locked out" of the table space until it is returned to its normal state. Table spaces can be placed one of the following quiesce states:

- QUIESCED SHARE
- QUIESCED UPDATE
- QUIESCED EXCLUSIVE

These states determine how other transactions that currently hold a quiesce state on the table space or that attempt to set a quiesce state for the table space can access it.

Comments

- The table name specified in the *TableName* parameter can be a two-part name with the *schema* and table name separated by a period. If the *schema* is not provided, the authorization ID that was used to establish the database connection will be used. The specified table name cannot be a system catalog table.
- When the SQLU_QUIESCEMODE_SHARE value is specified in the *QuiesceMode* parameter, the transaction requests a share lock for the specified table and intent share locks for all associated table spaces. When the transaction obtains the locks, the state of the table spaces is changed to QUIESCED SHARE. This state is granted to the application that quiesced the table space (the quiescer) only if there is no conflicting state held by other applications. The state of the table spaces is recorded in the table space table, along with the authorization ID and the database agent ID of the quiescer, so the state is persistent. The specified table cannot be changed while the table spaces for that table are in the QUIESCED SHARE state. However, other share mode requests to the table

and table spaces are allowed. When the transaction is committed or rolled back, the locks are released but the table spaces for the table remain in QUIESCED SHARE state until the state is explicitly reset.

- When the SQLU_QUIESCEMODE_EXCLUSIVE value is specified in the *QuiesceMode* parameter, the transaction requests a super-exclusive lock for the specified table and super-exclusive locks for all associated table spaces. When the transaction obtains the locks, the state of the table spaces changes to QUIESCED EXCLUSIVE and the state of the table spaces, along with the authorization ID and the database agent ID of the quiescer, are recorded in the table space table. Since the table spaces are held in super-exclusive mode, no other access to the table spaces is allowed. The transaction that invokes the QUIESCE TABLESPACES FOR TABLE function, however, has exclusive access to the table and the table spaces.
- When the SQLU_QUIESCEMODE_INTENT_UPDATE value is specified in the *QuiesceMode* parameter, the transaction requests an update lock for the specified table and intent exclusive locks for all associated table spaces. When the transaction obtains the locks, the state of the table spaces changes to QUIESCED UPDATE and the state of the table spaces, along with the authorization ID and the database agent ID of the quiescer, are recorded in the table space table. Since the table spaces are held in exclusive mode, no other access to the table spaces is allowed. The transaction that invokes the QUIESCE TABLESPACES FOR TABLE function, however, has exclusive access to the table and the table spaces.
- There is a limit of five quiescers on a table space at any given time. Since the QUIESCED EXCLUSIVE state is incompatible with any other state and a QUIESCED UPDATE state is incompatible with another QUIESCED UPDATE state, the five-quiescer limit, if reached, must consist of at least four QUIESCED SHARE states and, at most, one QUIESCED UPDATE or one QUIESCED EXCLUSIVE state.
- A quiescer can upgrade the state of a table space from a less restrictive state to a more restrictive one (for example, SHARE to UPDATE or UPDATE to EXCLUSIVE). If a user requests a state lower than one that is already held, the original state will be returned. Quiesce states cannot be downgraded.
- You must explicitly reset the quiesced state of a table space by executing this function with the SQLU_QUIESCEMODE_RESET value specified in the *QuiesceMode* parameter.

Required Connection This function can be called only if a connection to a database exists.

Authorization Only users with system control (SYSCTRL) authority, system administrator (SYSADM) authority, system maintenance (SYSMAINT) authority, or database administrator (DBADM) authority can execute this function call.

See Also LOAD

Example See the example provided for the LOAD function in this chapter.

CHAPTER 25

DATABASE MONITOR AND INDOUBT TRANSACTION PROCESSING API'S

The database monitor and indoubt transaction processing APIs are a group of DB2 API function calls that allow an application to obtain information about database activity at a specific point in time and to process any indoubt transactions that exist. This group includes:

- An API function that obtains the current value and/or sets of snapshot monitor group switches.
- An API function that resets all snapshot monitor counters.
- An API function that collects snapshot monitor information.
- An API function that obtains a listing of all indoubt transactions that exist for a database.
- API functions that roll back or commit an indoubt transaction.
- An API function that tells the resource manager to erase knowledge of an indoubt transaction.

Table 25.1 lists the database monitor and indoubt transaction processing API functions available with DB2.

The DB2 Snapshot Monitor

The DB2 snapshot monitor is a facility that can collect information about select database activity at a specific point in time. Snapshot monitors can collect the following types of information:

- Status information at the DB2 database manager (instance), database, table, and table space levels. Status information contains counters, status indicators, and other data that is specific to each level.
- Application-level information. This information includes transaction status, lock status, numerous counters, and information about the current SQL statement being processed.
- Locking details, such as lock waits and deadlocks.
- Status information on distributed database connection services (DDCS) applications (if an application is using a DDCS gateway to access a DRDA database server).

A snapshot can also contain SQL statement information. When this type of information is collected, information for the SQL statement being processed when the snapshot was taken is returned. If no SQL statement is being processed at the time the snapshot is taken, information for the last SQL statement processed is returned. You can specify what information a snapshot monitor collects and access collected snapshot monitor information by using the commands provided with the DB2 command-line processor interface or by including the database system monitor APIs in an application program.

TABLE 25.1 Database Monitor and Indoubt Transaction Processing APIs

Function name	Description
GET/UPDATE MONITOR SWITCHES	Turns various database monitor switches on or off and queries the DB2 database monitor for a group monitoring switch's current state.
RESET MONITOR	Resets the internal data monitor switches of a specified database (or of all active databases) to zero.
ESTIMATE DATABASE SYSTEM MONITOR BUFFER SIZE	Estimates the size of the buffer needed to hold the information collected by the GET SNAPSHOT function.
GET SNAPSHOT	Retrieves specific DB2 database manager status information and copies it to a user-allocated data storage buffer.
LIST INDOUBT TRANSACTIONS	Retrieves a list of all indoubt transactions for the current connected database.
COMMIT AN INDOUBT TRANSACTION	Commits an indoubt transaction.
ROLLBACK AN INDOUBT TRANSACTION	Rolls back an indoubt transaction.
FORGET TRANSACTION STATUS	Tells the resource manager to erase knowledge of an indoubt transaction that was heuristically committed or rolled back.

Snapshot Monitor Switches The information collected by a snapshot monitor is divided into six (6) separate groups, to simplify data collection and interpretation. Table 25.2 lists these six groups along with a description of some of the information collected for each group.

TABLE 25.2 Database Monitor Groups

Monitor group	Information collected
Sorts	Number of heaps used, overflows, and number of sorts performed.
Locks	Number of locks held and number of deadlocks detected.
Tables	Amount of activity (number of rows read and written).
Buffer pools	Number of reads and writes, and the time taken for each read and write operation.
Units of work (transactions)	Transaction start times, transaction end times, and transaction completion status.
SQL statements	Start time, stop time, and statement identification.

Adapted from IBM's *Database 2 Database System Monitor Guide and Reference*, page 14

You can determine whether or not information is being collected for any of the monitor groups listed in Table 25.2 by calling the GET/UPDATE MONITOR SWITCHES function from an application program. Information about when the monitoring of these different groups was started (that is, when the group switch was turned on), along with the current state of each monitor group switch is returned when this function executes. The GET/UPDATE MONITOR SWITCHES function can also be used to turn one or more monitor group switches ON or OFF (which, in turn, starts or stops data collection for the specified monitor groups). If the SQL statement monitor switch is turned on while an SQL statement is being processed, the database system monitor will start collecting information when the next SQL statement is executed. As a result, the snapshot monitor will not return information about SQL statements that the DB2 database manager is in the process of executing when the SQL statement monitor group switch is turned on. The same applies to unit of work (transaction) information and the unit of work (transaction) switch. When a monitor group switch is turned OFF, the counter elements related to that group are automatically reset to zero and all of its data elements will contain either zero or blank values, depending on their data types.

You can set default values for each snapshot monitor using the appropriate DB2 database manager configuration file parameters (refer to Chapter 20 for more information about setting DB2 database manager configuration file parameters). If a snapshot monitor group switch is turned on in the configuration file and an application takes a snapshot without updating or resetting that monitor group switch, the returned data will reflect the database activity since the DB2 database manager was started. Every application that connects to a database automatically inherits these default switch settings.

> Note: The snapshot monitor always collects some basic snapshot information, even if all monitor group switches are turned off. Obtaining detailed information from some monitor groups can significantly affect application performance. Take this into consideration whenever you turn on a monitor group switch.

When Counting Starts A snapshot contains, among other things, cumulative information that covers all database activity from the time database monitoring was started to the time the snapshot is taken. This cumulative information is collected by various activity counters. When you use counters to monitor activity, the counting begins at the following times:

- When an application connects to the database (at the application level, when the application establishes a connection; at the database level, when the first application establishes a connection; at the table level, when the table is first accessed; and at the table space level, when the table space is first accessed.
- When counters are reset.
- When a monitor group switch is turned on.

In many cases, you will want to collect counter information for a specific period of time. This means that you might need to reset counters while an application is running. (For example, if you are running iterative tests and obtaining snapshot information for each iteration, you might want to reset the counters between iterations.) You can reset counters for one or all databases controlled by the DB2 database manager by calling the RESET MONITOR function. When counters are reset, their current values are set to zero. If the counters for all active databases are reset, some DB2 database manager information will also be reset to maintain consistency.

You cannot selectively reset specific data items of monitor groups with the RESET MONITOR function; when this function is called, all resettable data items for the specified database or for all active databases are set to zero. You can, however, reset all the data items related to a specific monitor group by turning that monitor group switch off and then on again.

Retrieving Snapshot Monitor Data Before an application program can collect snapshot monitor data, it must first allocate a memory storage buffer large enough to hold the retrieved snapshot information. The amount of memory required for this buffer depends on the number of monitoring applications (snapshot and event), the types of monitor information being collected, and the level of database activity.

> Note: Stopping certain applications allows you to focus on a single application or on a group of applications, which might make it easier for you to interpret the database system monitor output. Subsequently, as the number of applications running decreases, the amount of memory required to hold snapshot monitor data also decreases.

An application can accurately estimate the appropriate size of this buffer by calling the ESTIMATE DATABASE SYSTEM MONITOR BUFFER SIZE function. After the buffer has been allocated, you can collect a snapshot of the specified monitor data by calling the GET SNAPSHOT function. When this function is executed, the snapshot data is collected and copied directly to the allocated memory storage buffer (provided a large enough buffer is allocated). Portions of this buffer must then be type-cast to specially defined data structures so the application can retrieve the collected snapshot data.

If all applications disconnect from a database, that database's snapshot monitor data will no longer be available. Alternatively, you can maintain one permanent connection to the database that will not disconnect until your final snapshot is taken. Keep in mind that if you are maintaining a permanent connection to a database, there is some amount of resource overhead associated with that connection.

Working with Multiple Databases

When data is stored in multiple databases, an application may need to read and update several databases in a single transaction. In DRDA terminology, these types of transactions are known as distributed units of work (DUOW). The type of environment needed to support multiple database transactions is a little more complex than the type of environment needed to support single database transactions. The DB2 database manager contains a component, known as the transaction manager (or transaction coordinator), that is used to coordinate updates made to several databases within a single transaction. The transaction manager does not belong to a particular database. Instead, it uses a special database, known as the Transaction Manager database, to register each transaction (unit of work) and to track the completion status of that transaction across all databases that it involves. The database to be used as a Transaction Manager database is determined by the value stored in the *tm_database* parameter of the DB2 database manager configuration file. The Transaction Manager database can be any database that an application can connect to; however, for operational and administration reasons, it must reside on a robust machine that is up and running most of the time. All connections to the Transaction Manager database should be made by the transaction manager; an application program should never attempt to connect directly to the Transaction Manager database.

Understanding the Two-Phase Commit Process

Applications that execute in a distributed unit of work environment utilize a process known as two-phase commit to roll back or commit changes made by a transaction. The two-phase commit process is designed to maintain data consistency across multiple databases while transactions are executing. The following list describes the steps used in the two-phase commit process:

1. When the application program starts a transaction, it will automatically connect to the Transaction Manager database.
2. Just before the first SQL statement in the transaction is executed, the transaction manager sends a Transaction Register (XREG) request to the Transaction Manager database in order to register the new transaction.
3. The Transaction Manager database responds to the application program by providing a unique global transaction ID for the new transaction (since the XREG request was sent without a predefined ID).
4. After receiving the transaction ID, the application program registers the new transaction (using the transaction ID) with the database containing the required user data. A response is sent back to the application program when the transaction has been successfully registered.
5. SQL statements issued against the database containing the user data are handled in the normal manner, with the return code for each SQL statement processed being returned in the SQLCA data structure.
6. Steps 2 and 5 are repeated for each database that is accessed by the transaction. All other databases accessed in the transaction receive the global transaction ID just before the first SQL statement is executed against it. The SET CONNECTION SQL statement is used to switch between database connections.

7. When the application program requests that the current transaction be committed, a "PREPARE" message is sent to all databases that have been accessed by the transaction. Each database that receives this message writes a "PREPARED" record to their log files and sends a response back to the application program.
8. When the application program receives a positive response from all databases that the "PREPARE" message was sent to, it sends a message to the Transaction Manager database to inform it that the transaction has been PREPARED and is now ready to be committed. This completes the first phase of the two-phase commit process.
9. The Transaction Manager database writes a "PREPARED" record to its log file and sends a message back to the application program informing it that the second phase of the commit process can be now be started.
10. When the application program receives the message to begin the second phase of the commit process, it sends a "COMMIT" message to all databases that the "PREPARE" message was sent to (telling them to commit all changes made by the transaction). Each database that receives this message writes a "COMMITTED" record to its log file and releases all locks that were held by this transaction. When each database has completed committing its changes, it sends a reply back to the application program.
11. After the application program receives a positive response from all databases that the "COMMIT" message was sent to, it sends a request to the Transaction Manager database to inform it that the transaction has been completed. The Transaction Manager database then writes a "COMMITTED" record to its log file, to indicate that the transaction is complete and sends a message to the application program to indicate that it has finished processing.

Two-Phase Commit Error Recovery When databases are distributed over several remote servers, the potential for errors resulting from network or communication failures is greatly increased. To ensure data integrity while using two-phase commits, the DB2 database manager handles two-phase commit errors as follows:

First-phase errors If a database responds that it failed to PREPARE a transaction, the transaction will be rolled back during the second phase of the commit process. In this case, a PREPARE message is not sent to the transaction manager database. During the second phase of the commit, the application program sends a roll-back message to all participating databases that successfully prepared the transaction during the first phase of the commit. Each database that receives this message writes an ABORT record to its log file and releases all locks held by the transaction.

Second-phase errors Error handling at the second stage of a commit depends on whether the second phase is committing or rolling back the transaction. The second phase will roll back the transaction only if the first phase encountered an error. If one of the participating databases fails to commit the transaction (possibly due to a communications failure), the transaction manager will continue trying to commit the transaction to the database that failed. The value stored in the *resync_interval* parameter of the DB2 database manager configuration file determines how long the transaction manager will wait between attempts to commit a transaction.

Transaction manager database errors If for some reason the transaction manager database fails, the transaction manager will resynchronize the transaction when the transaction manager database is restarted. This resynchronization process attempts to complete all indoubt transactions (all transactions that completed the first but not the second phase of the two-phase commit process). The DB2 database manager instance where the transaction manager database resides will perform the resynchronization by:

1. Connecting to databases that replied that they were PREPARED to commit during the first phase of the commit process.
2. Attempting to commit the indoubt transactions at that database. (If no indoubt transactions are found, the DB2 database manager will assume that the database successfully committed the transaction during the second phase of the commit process.)
3. Committing the indoubt transactions in the transaction manager database after all indoubt transactions are committed in the participating databases.

Other database errors If one of the databases accessed in the transaction fails and is restarted, the DB2 database manager for that database will check the log files of the transaction manager database to determine whether the transaction should be rolled back or committed. If the transaction is not found in the transaction manager database log files, the DB2 database manager will assume the transaction was rolled back, and the indoubt transactions for this database will be rolled back. Otherwise, the database will wait for a commit request from the transaction manager.

Manual Recovery of Indoubt Transactions If, for some reason, you cannot wait for the transaction manager to automatically resolve an indoubt transaction, you can manually resolve it. This manual process is sometimes referred to as "making a heuristic decision." Before an indoubt transaction can be manually resolved, its global transaction ID must first be acquired. You can use the LIST INDOUBT TRANSACTIONS function or command to obtain the global transaction ID for all indoubt transactions that exist for a specified database. Once you have obtained an indoubt transaction's global transaction ID, you can use the COMMIT AN INDOUBT TRANSACTION function to commit it and the ROLLBACK AN INDOUBT TRANSACTION function to roll it back. An application can then tell the transaction manager to "forget" transactions that were heuristically committed or rolled back by calling the FORGET TRANSACTION STATUS function (which removes the log records that refer to the transactions and releases their log space).

Use the indoubt transaction processing functions with **EXTREME CAUTION** and only as a last resort. The best way to resolve indoubt transactions is to wait for the transaction manager to drive the resynchronization process. Otherwise, you could cause data integrity problems (for example, if you manually commit or roll back a transaction in one database and perform the opposite action for another database). Recovering from data integrity problems requires that you understand the application logic and the data that was changed or rolled back, and that you either perform a point-in-time recovery of the database or manually undo/redo the database changes.

If the transaction manager is not available for an extended period of time (while it initiates the resynchronization process) and if an indoubt transaction is tying up resources that are urgently needed (e.g., locks on tables and indexes, log space, or storage space), manually resolving the indoubt transaction might be necessary. There are no foolproof ways to manually recover indoubt transactions, but you can use the following steps as a guideline:

1. Connect to the database for which you require all transactions to be complete.

2. Use the LIST INDOUBT TRANSACTIONS function or command or display the indoubt transactions. The returned transaction ID represents the global transaction ID and is identical in all other databases accessed by a transaction, including the transaction manager database.

3. For each indoubt transaction you find, use your knowledge about the application and the *tm_database* parameter of the DB2 database manager configuration file to determine the names of the transaction manager database and other databases accessed by the transaction.

4a. Connect to the transaction manager database and use the LIST INDOUBT TRANSACTIONS function or command to display the indoubt transactions recorded in the transaction manager database:
–If there is an indoubt transaction with the same global transaction ID as that found in step 2 with type TM, you can connect to each database participating in the transaction and heuristically commit the transaction using the COMMIT AN INDOUBT TRANSACTION function or the LIST INDOUBT TRANSACTIONS command.
–If there is not an indoubt transaction with the same global transaction ID as that found in step 2 with type TM, you can connect to the each database participating in the transaction and heuristically roll back the transaction using the ROLLBACK AN INDOUBT TRANSACTION function or the LIST INDOUBT TRANSACTIONS command.

4b. If you are unable to connect to the transaction manager database, you will have to use the status of the transaction in other participating databases to determine what action you should take:
–If at least one of the other databases has committed the transaction, then you should heuristically commit the transaction in all the participating databases using the COMMIT AN INDOUBT TRANSACTION function or the LIST INDOUBT TRANSACTIONS command.
–If at least one of the other databases has rolled back the transaction, then you should heuristically roll back the transaction in all the participating databases using the ROLLBACK AN INDOUBT TRANSACTION function or the LIST INDOUBT TRANSACTIONS command.
–If the transaction is in a PREPARED (indoubt) state in all of the participating databases, then you should heuristically roll back the transaction in all the participating databases using the

ROLLBACK AN INDOUBT TRANSACTION function or the LIST INDOUBT TRANSACTIONS command.

–If you are unable to connect to one or more of the other participating databases, then you should heuristically roll back the transaction in all the participating databases using the ROLLBACK AN INDOUBT TRANSACTION function or the LIST INDOUBT TRANSACTIONS command.

If you heuristically commit or roll back an indoubt transaction, you do not have to "forget" it immediately afterward. Instead, it is a good idea to wait until the Transaction Manager database is accessible so that your decisions can be verified. That way, if a transaction was committed or rolled back incorrectly, the Transaction Manager database can detect it. When errors of this type are found, the Transaction Manager will write a message to the *db2diag.log* file indicating "heuristic damage" to a particular database occurred when the Transaction Manager attempted to synchronize.

GET/UPDATE MONITOR SWITCHES

Purpose

The GET/UPDATE MONITOR SWITCHES function selectively turns various database monitor switches (information groups to be monitored) on or off, and queries the database monitor for a group monitoring switch's current state.

Syntax

```
int SQL_API_FN sqlmon (unsigned long          Version,
                       char                   *Reserved,
                       sqlm_recording_group   GroupStates[ ],
                       struct sqlca           *SQLCA);
```

Parameters

Version The version number of the database monitor being used. This parameter can be set to any of the following values:

SQLM_DBMON_VERSION2 Specifies that the DB2 version 2.1 database monitor is being used.

SQLM_DBMON_VERSION1 Specifies that a database monitor other than DB2 version 2.1 is being used.

Reserved A pointer that is currently reserved for later use. For now, this parameter must always be set to NULL.

GroupStates A pointer to a location in memory that contains the address of an array of six *sqlm_recording_group* structures containing state information about available group monitor switches.

SQLCA A pointer to a location in memory where a SQL communication area (SQLCA) data structure variable is stored. This variable sends either status information (if the function executed successfully) or error information (if the function failed) back to the calling application.

Includes

```
#include <sqlmon.h>
```

Description

The GET/UPDATE MONITOR SWITCHES function selectively turns various database monitor switches (information groups to be monitored) on or off, and queries the database monitor for a group monitoring switch's current state. This function uses one or more *sqlm_recording_group* structures to retrieve and update database monitor switch values. The *sqlm_recording_group* structure is defined in *sqlmon.h* as follows:

```
struct sqlm_recording_group
{
unsigned long   input_state;  /* Indicates whether the specified    */
                              /* information group monitoring       */
                              /* switch should be turned on         */
```

```
                                /* (SQLM_ON), turned off          */
                                /* (SQLM_OFF), or left in its     */
                                /* current state (SQLM_HOLD).     */
unsigned long   output_state;  /* The current state of the specified */
                                /* group monitoring switch. Indicates */
                                /* whether the specified information */
                                /* group monitoring switch is     */
                                /* currently turned on (SQLM_ON)  */
                                /* or turned off (SQLM_OFF).      */
sqlm_timestamp  start_time;    /* The date and time that the     */
                                /* specified group monitoring switch */
                                /* was turned on. If the specified */
                                /* group monitoring switch is turned */
                                /* off, this field's value is set  */
                                /* to 0.                          */
};
```

This structure contains a reference to an additional structure, *sqlm_timestamp*, that stores timestamp information about when a group monitoring switch was turned on. The *sqlm_timestamp* structure (type defined as *sqlm_timestamp*) is defined in *sqlmon.h* as follows:

```
typedef struct sqlm_timestamp
{
unsigned long  seconds;        /* The date and time, expressed as */
                                /* the number of seconds since     */
                                /* January 1, 1970 (GMT).          */
unsigned long  microsec;       /* The number of elapsed           */
                                /* microseconds, ranging from 0 to */
                                /* 999999, in the current second.  */
} sqlm_timestamp;
```

An array of six *sqlm_recording_group* structures must be defined or allocated before this function is called. If this function sets the values of group monitor switches, each structure in the array must also be initialized before this function is invoked. After this function executes, the array will contain state information about each group monitor switch. You can obtain information about a specific group monitor switch by indexing the array with one of the following symbolic values:

SQLM_UOW_SW References unit of work (transaction) group monitor switch information.

SQLM_STATEMENT_SW References SQL statement group monitor switch information.

SQLM_TABLE_SW References table group monitor switch information.

SQLM_BUFFER_POOL_SW References buffer pool group monitor switch information.

SQLM_LOCK_SW References lock group monitor switch information.

SQLM_SORT_SW References sort group monitor switch information.

Refer to the beginning of the chapter for more information about the database system monitor elements associated with each of these monitoring groups.

Comments

- If database monitor data is to be collected for earlier versions of the DB2 database monitor (i.e., if the *Version* parameter is set to SQLM_DBMON_VERSION1), this function cannot be executed remotely.
- You can use this function to query the current state of different information groups without modifying them, by specifying SQLM_HOLD for all switches.
- For detailed information on using the database system monitor, refer to the *IBM Database 2 Database System Monitor Guide and Reference*.

Required Connection This function cannot be called unless a connection to a DB2 database manager instance exists. In order to obtain or set the database monitor switch settings for a remote instance (or for a different local instance), an application must first attach to that instance.

Authorization Only users with system control (SYSCTRL), system administrator (SYSADM), or system maintenance (SYSMAINT) authority can execute this function call.

See Also ESTIMATE DATABASE SYSTEM MONITOR BUFFER SIZE, GET SNAPSHOT, RESET MONITOR

Example The following C program illustrates how to use the GET/UPDATE MONITOR SWITCHES function to change and retrieve the current values of the database monitor group switches:

```
#include <stdio.h>
#include <stdlib.h>
#include <sqlmon.h>
#include <sqlca.h>

int main()
{
    /* Declare The Local Memory Variables */
    struct sqlm_recording_group  GroupStates[6];
    struct sqlca                 sqlca;

    /* Initialize The Database Monitor Group States Array      */
    /* (Turn The Table Switch On, The Unit Of Work Switch Off, */
    /* And Query The Settings Of The Other Switches)           */
    GroupStates[SQLM_UOW_SW].input_state         = SQLM_OFF;
    GroupStates[SQLM_STATEMENT_SW].input_state   = SQLM_HOLD;
    GroupStates[SQLM_TABLE_SW].input_state       = SQLM_ON;
    GroupStates[SQLM_BUFFER_POOL_SW].input_state = SQLM_HOLD;
    GroupStates[SQLM_LOCK_SW].input_state        = SQLM_HOLD;
    GroupStates[SQLM_SORT_SW].input_state        = SQLM_HOLD;

    /* Set/Query The Database Monitor Switches */
    sqlmon(SQLM_DBMON_VERSION2, NULL, GroupStates, &sqlca);

    /* Display The Current Values Of The Database Monitor Switches */
    printf("Current values of the Database Monitor Switches :\n\n");
    printf("Unit Of Work Switch   : ");
    if (GroupStates[SQLM_UOW_SW].input_state == SQLM_ON)
        printf("ON\n");
    else
        printf("OFF\n");
    printf("SQL Statements Switch : ");
    if (GroupStates[SQLM_STATEMENT_SW].input_state == SQLM_ON)
        printf("ON\n");
    else
        printf("OFF\n");
    printf("Table Switch          : ");
    if (GroupStates[SQLM_TABLE_SW].input_state == SQLM_ON)
        printf("ON\n");
    else
        printf("OFF\n");
    printf("Buffer Pool Switch    : ");
    if (GroupStates[SQLM_BUFFER_POOL_SW].input_state == SQLM_ON)
```

```
        printf("ON\n");
    else
        printf("OFF\n");
    printf("Lock Switch           : ");
    if (GroupStates[SQLM_LOCK_SW].input_state == SQLM_ON)
        printf("ON\n");
    else
        printf("OFF\n");
    printf("Sort Switch           : ");
    if (GroupStates[SQLM_SORT_SW].input_state == SQLM_ON)
        printf("ON\n");
    else
        printf("OFF\n");

    /* Return To The Operating System */
    return(EXIT_SUCCESS);
}
```

RESET MONITOR

Purpose

The RESET MONITOR function resets the internal database system monitor data monitor switches of a specified database (or of all active databases) to zero.

Syntax

```
int SQL_API_FN sqlmrset (unsigned long  Version,
                         char           *Reserved,
                         unsigned long  ResetAllIndicator,
                         char           *DBAlias,
                         struct sqlca   *SQLCA);
```

Parameters

Version The version number of the database monitor being used. This parameter can be set to any of the following values:

- SQLM_DBMON_VERSION2 Specifies that the DB2 version 2.1 database monitor is used.
- SQLM_DBMON_VERSION1 Specifies that a database monitor other than the DB2 version 2.1 database monitor is used.

Reserved A pointer currently reserved for later use. For now, this parameter must always be set to NULL.

ResetAllIndicator Specifies whether to reset data monitor switches for a specific database or for all active databases. This parameter can be set to any of the following values:

- SQLM_OFF Resets the data monitor switches and areas for a specific database.
- SQLM_ON Resets the data monitor switches and areas for all active databases.

DBAlias A pointer to a location in memory where the alias of the database whose data monitor switches are to be reset is stored.

SQLCA A pointer to a location in memory where a SQLCA data structure variable is stored. This variable sends either status information (if the function executed successfully) or error information (if the function failed) back to the calling application.

Includes

```
#include <sqlmon.h>
```

Description

The RESET MONITOR function resets the internal database system monitor data monitor switches of a specified database (or of all active databases) to zero. When the data monitor switches of a database are set to zero, the database's internal system monitor data areas are automatically cleared. These data areas include the data areas used both by each application connected to the database and by the database itself.

Each application attached to a database has its own private view of database system monitor data. If an application resets or turns off a database system monitor switch, other applications are not affected.

Comments

- If database monitor data is to be collected for earlier versions of the DB2 database monitor (i.e., if the *Version* parameter is set to SQLM_DBMON_VERSION1), this function cannot be executed remotely.
- If the *ResetAllIndicator* parameter is set to SQLM_ON, the value in the *DBAlias* parameter is ignored and the data monitor switches for all active databases are reset.
- To make global changes to a database system monitor switch, modify the settings of the monitor switch configuration parameters in the database manager configuration file. Refer to the UPDATE DATABASE MANAGER CONFIGURATION function for more information.

Required Connection

This function cannot be called unless a connection to a DB2 database manager instance exists. In order to obtain or set the database monitor switch settings for a remote instance (or for a different local instance), an application must first attach to that instance.

Authorization

Only users with system control (SYSCTR) authority, system administrator (SYSADM) authority, or system maintenance (SYSMAINT) authority can execute this function call.

See Also

GET/UPDATE MONITOR SWITCHES, ESTIMATE DATABASE SYSTEM MONITOR BUFFER SIZE, GET SNAPSHOT

Example

The following C program illustrates how to use the RESET MONITOR function to reset the database monitor group switches for the SAMPLE database:

```
#include <stdio.h>
#include <stdlib.h>
#include <sqlmon.h>

int main()
{
    /* Include The SQLCA Data Structure Variable */
    EXEC SQL INCLUDE SQLCA;

    /* Declare The Local Memory Variables */
    int  rc = EXIT_SUCCESS;

    /* Set Up A Simple SQL Error Handler */
    EXEC SQL WHENEVER SQLERROR GOTO EXIT;

    /* Connect To The SAMPLE Database */
    EXEC SQL CONNECT TO SAMPLE USER etpdd6z USING sanders;

    /* Reset The Database System Monitor Data Areas For The SAMPLE */
    /* Database                                                    */
    sqlmrset(SQLM_DBMON_VERSION2, NULL, SQLM_OFF, "SAMPLE", &sqlca);
```

```
    /* Display A Success Message */
    printf("The Database System Monitor Data Areas for the SAMPLE ");
    printf("database have\nbeen reset.\n");

EXIT:
    /* If An Error Has Occurred, Display The SQL Return Code */
    if (sqlca.sqlcode != SQL_RC_OK)
        {
        printf("SQL ERROR : %ld\n", sqlca.sqlcode);
        rc = EXIT_FAILURE;
        }

    /* Issue A Rollback To Free All Locks */
    EXEC SQL ROLLBACK;

    /* Turn Off The SQL Error Handler */
    EXEC SQL WHENEVER SQLERROR CONTINUE;

    /* Disconnect From The SAMPLE Database */
    EXEC SQL DISCONNECT CURRENT;

    /* Return To The Operating System */
    return(rc);
}
```

ESTIMATE DATABASE SYSTEM MONITOR BUFFER SIZE

Purpose

The ESTIMATE DATABASE SYSTEM MONITOR BUFFER SIZE function estimates the size of the buffer needed by the GET SNAPSHOT function.

Syntax

```
int SQL_API_FN sqlmonsz (unsigned long Version,
                         char          *Reserved,
                         sqlma         *SQLMA,
                         unsigned long *BufferSize,
                         struct sqlca  *SQLCA);
```

Parameters

Version The version number of the database monitor being used. This parameter can be set to any of the following values:

SQLM_DBMON_VERSION2 Specifies that the DB2 version 2.1 database monitor is used.

SQLM_DBMON_VERSION1 Specifies that a database monitor other than the DB2 version 2.1 database monitor is used.

Reserved A pointer currently reserved for later use. For now, this parameter must always be set to NULL.

SQLMA A pointer to a *sqlma* structure that contains a list of objects to collect monitor data for.

BufferSize A pointer to a location in memory where this function is to store the estimated size of the buffer needed by the GET SNAPSHOT function.

SQLCA A pointer to a location in memory where a SQLCA data structure variable is stored. This variable sends either status information (if the function executed successfully) or error information (if the function failed) back to the calling application.

Includes

```
#include <sqlmon.h>
```

Description

The ESTIMATE DATABASE SYSTEM MONITOR BUFFER SIZE function estimates the size of the buffer needed by the GET SNAPSHOT function. You can manually calculate the size of the buffer needed by the GET SNAPSHOT function by adding the sizes of the structures returned for each object to be monitored, but you should use this function instead since the GET SNAPSHOT function can return an unknown number of data structures (if, for example, a snapshot of all active databases is requested).

A special structure, *sqlma*, passes information about the list of objects to be monitored to the DB2 database system monitor when this function is called. The *sqlma* structure (type defined as *sqlma*) is defined in *sqlmon.h* as follows:

```
typedef struct sqlma
{
unsigned long    obj_num;          /* The number of objects to be          */
                                   /* monitored                            */
sqlm_obj_struct  obj_var[1];       /* An array of sqlm_obj_struct          */
                                   /* structures that contain descriptions */
                                   /* about the objects to be monitored    */
} sqlma;
```

This structure contains an array of one or more additional *sqlm_object_struct* structures that store characteristics about each object to be monitored. The *sqlm_object_struct* structure (type defined as *sqlm_obj_struct*) is defined in *sqlmon.h* as follows:

```
typedef struct sqlm_obj_struct
{
unsigned long  agent_id;         /* The ID of the agent to be monitored    */
unsigned long  obj_type;         /* The type of object to be monitored     */
char           object[36];       /* The name of the object to be monitored */
} sqlm_obj_struct;
```

Comments

- The *obj_type* field of the *sqlm_obj_struct* structure (an element in the *sqlma* structure) must contain one of the following values:
  SQLMA_DB2 DB2-related information is to be monitored.
  SQLMA_DBASE Database-related information is to be monitored.
  SQLMA_APPL Application information, organized by the application ID, is to be monitored.
  SQLMA_AGENT_ID Application information, organized by the agent ID, information is to be monitored.
  SQLMA_DBASE_TABLES Table information for a database is to be monitored.
  SQLMA_DBASE_APPLS Application information for a database is to be monitored.
  SQLMA_DBASE_APPLINFO Summary application information for a database is to be monitored.
  SQLMA_DBASE_LOCKS Locking information for a database is to be monitored.
  SQLMA_DBASE_ALL Database information for all active databases in the database manager instance is to be monitored.
  SQLMA_APPL_ALL Application information for all active applications in the database manager instance is to be monitored.
  SQLMA_APPLINFO_ALL Summary application information for all active applications in the database manager instance is to be monitored.

SQLMA_DCS_APPLINFO_ALL Summary database connection services (DCS) application information for all active applications in the database manager instance is to be monitored.

- If database monitor data is to be collected for earlier versions of the DB2 database monitor (i.e., if the *Version* parameter is set to SQLM_DBMON_VERSION1), this function cannot be executed remotely.

Required Connection This function cannot be called unless a connection to a DB2 database manager instance exists. In order to obtain or set the database monitor switch settings for a remote instance (or for a different local instance), an application must first attach to that instance.

Authorization Only users with system control (SYSCTRL) authority, system administrator (SYSADM) authority, or system maintenance (SYSMAINT) authority can execute this function call.

See Also GET SNAPSHOT, GET/UPDATE MONITOR SWITCHES, RESET MONITOR

Example See the example provided for the GET SNAPSHOT function in this chapter.

GET SNAPSHOT

Purpose The GET SNAPSHOT function retrieves specific DB2 database manager status information and copies it to a user-allocated data storage buffer.

Syntax

```
int SQL_API_FN sqlmonss (unsigned long  Version,
                         char           *Reserved,
                         sqlma          *SQLMA,
                         unsigned long  BufferSize,
                         void           *Buffer,
                         sqlm_collected *Collected,
                         struct sqlca   *SQLCA);
```

Parameters

Version The version number of the database monitor being used. This parameter can be set to any of the following values:

SQLM_DBMON_VERSION2 Specifies that the DB2 version 2.1 database monitor is used.

SQLM_DBMON_VERSION1 Specifies that a database monitor other than the DB2 version 2.1 database monitor is used.

Reserved A pointer currently reserved for later use. For now, this parameter must always be set to NULL.

SQLMA A pointer to a *sqlma* structure that contains a list of objects to collect snapshot data for.

BufferSize The size, in bytes, of the memory buffer that holds the retrieved snapshot information.

Buffer A pointer to a location in memory where this function stores the retrieved snapshot information.

Collected A pointer to the address of a *sqlm_collected* structure where this function stores summary information about each type of data structure written to the buffer storage area.

SQLCA A pointer to a location in memory where a SQLCA data structure variable is stored. This variable sends either status information (if the

function executed successfully) or error information (if the function failed) back to the calling application.

Includes

```
#include <sqlmon.h>
```

Description

The GET SNAPSHOT function retrieves specific DB2 database manager status information and copies it to a user-allocated data storage buffer. The returned DB2 database manager status information represents a snapshot of the database manager's operational status at the time this function was executed. You can update this information, therefore, only by reexecuting the GET SNAPSHOT function call.

A special structure, *sqlma*, passes information about the list of objects to be monitored to the DB2 database system monitor when this function is called. Refer to the ESTIMATE DATABASE SYSTEM MONITOR BUFFER SIZE function for a detailed description of this structure. After the function has executed, summary statistics about the collected snapshot information is stored in a special structure, *sqlm_collected* (type defined as *sqlm_collected*), that is defined in *sqlmon.h* as follows:

```
typedef struct sqlm_collected
{
unsigned long   size;                      /* The size of the sqlm_collected      */
                                           /* structure                           */
unsigned long   db2;                       /* Indicates whether DB2 database      */
                                           /* manager instance information        */
                                           /* was collected in the snapshot (1),  */
                                           /* or not (0)                          */
unsigned long   databases;                 /* The number of databases for         */
                                           /* which snapshot information was      */
                                           /* collected                           */
unsigned long   table_databases;           /* The number of databases for which   */
                                           /* table snapshot information was      */
                                           /* collected                           */
unsigned long   lock_databases;            /* The number of databases for which   */
                                           /* locking snapshot information was    */
                                           /* collected                           */
unsigned long   applications;              /* The number of applications for      */
                                           /* which snapshot information was      */
                                           /* collected                           */
unsigned long   applinfos;                 /* The number of applications for      */
                                           /* which summary information was       */
                                           /* collected                           */
unsigned long   dcs_applinfos;             /* The number of applications for      */
                                           /* which Database Connection Services  */
                                           /* (DCS) summary information was       */
                                           /* collected                           */
unsigned long   server_db2_type;           /* The DB2 database manager            */
                                           /* server type                         */
sqlm_timestamp  time_stamp;                /* The date and time the snapshot      */
                                           /* was taken                           */
sqlm_recording_group  group_states[6];     /* The current state of the            */
                                           /* information group monitoring        */
                                           /* switches                            */
char            server_prdid[20];          /* The product name and version        */
                                           /* number of the database manager      */
                                           /* on the server workstation           */
char            server_nname[20];          /* The workstation name stored in      */
```

```
                                                /* the nname parameter of the        */
                                                /* database manager configuration    */
                                                /* file on the server workstation    */
char            server_instance_name[20];       /* The instance name of the          */
                                                /* DB2 database manager              */
char            reserved[32];                   /* Reserved for future use           */
unsigned long   tablespace_databases;           /* The number of databases for which */
                                                /* table space snapshot information  */
                                                /* was collected                     */
unsigned long   server_version;                 /* The version number of the server  */
                                                /* returning the snapshot data       */
} sqlm_collected;
```

This structure contains a reference to two additional structures, *sqlm_recording_group* and *sqlm_timestamp*, that store information about specific group monitoring switches and timestamp information about when a group monitoring switch was turned on. Refer to the GET MONITOR SWITCHES function for a detailed description of these two structures.

When snapshot information is collected, it is stored in a user-allocated buffer (specified by the *Buffer* parameter). Portions of this buffer must be typecast with special structures before the collected information can be extracted from it. For more information about these structures, refer to the *IBM Database 2 Database System Monitor Guide and Reference*.

Comments

- The *obj_type* field of the *sqlm_obj_struct* structure (an element in the *sqlma* structure) must contain one of the following values:
  SQLMA_DB2 DB2-related information is to be monitored.
  SQLMA_DBASE Database-related information is to be monitored.
  SQLMA_APPL Application information, organized by the application ID, is to be monitored.
  SQLMA_AGENT_ID Application information, organized by the agent ID, information is to be monitored.
  SQLMA_DBASE_TABLES Table information for a database is to be monitored.
  SQLMA_DBASE_APPLS Application information for a database is to be monitored.
  SQLMA_DBASE_APPLINFO Summary application information for a database is to be monitored.
  SQLMA_DBASE_LOCKS Locking information for a database is to be monitored.
  SQLMA_DBASE_ALL Database information for all active databases in the database manager instance is to be monitored.
  SQLMA_APPL_ALL Application information for all active applications in the database manager instance is to be monitored.
  SQLMA_APPLINFO_ALL Summary application information for all active applications in the database manager instance is to be monitored.
  SQLMA_DCS_APPLINFO_ALL Summary DCS application information for all active applications in the database manager instance is to be monitored.
- If database monitor data is to be collected for earlier versions of the DB2 database monitor (i.e., if the *Version* parameter is set to SQLM_DBMON_VERSION1) this function cannot be executed remotely.
- You can determine the amount of memory needed to store the snapshot information returned by this function by calling the ESTIMATE DATABASE SYSTEM MONITOR BUFFER SIZE function. If one specific

object is being monitored, only the amount of memory needed to store the returned structure for that object needs to be allocated. If the buffer storage area is not large enough to hold all the information returned by this function, a warning will be returned and the returned information will be truncated to fit in the assigned buffer area. When this happens, you might need to resize the memory storage buffer and issue the GET SNAPSHOT function call again.

- If the alias for a database residing at a different instance is specified, an error message will be returned.
- No snapshot data will be returned from a request for table information if any of the following conditions exist:
  –The TABLE recording switch is turned off.
  –No tables have been accessed since the TABLE recording switch was turned on.
  –No tables have been accessed since the last RESET MONITOR function call.

Required Connection This function cannot be called unless a connection to a DB2 database manager instance exists. In order to obtain or set the database monitor switch settings for a remote instance (or for a different local instance), an application must first attach to that instance.

Authorization Only users with system control (SYSCTRL) authority, system administrator (SYSADM) authority, or system maintenance (SYSMAINT) authority are allowed to execute this function call.

See Also GET/UPDATE MONITOR SWITCHES, ESTIMATE DATABASE SYSTEM MONITOR BUFFER SIZE, RESET MONITOR

Example The following C program illustrates how to use the GET SNAPSHOT function to collect snapshot information for the SAMPLE database and the DB2 database manager:

```
#include <stdio.h>
#include <stdlib.h>
#include <string.h>
#include <time.h>
#include <sqlmon.h>
#include <sqlca.h>

/* Declare The Function Prototypes */
void Process_DB2(struct sqlm_db2  *db2_ptr);
void Process_DBase(struct sqlm_dbase *dbase_ptr);

int main()
{
    /* Declare The Local Memory Variables */
    int                     rc = EXIT_SUCCESS;
    char                    *pchBuffer;
    char                    *pchBufferIndex;
    unsigned long           ulBuffSize;
    unsigned int            uiNumStructs = 0;
    struct sqlma            *sqlma;
    struct sqlm_collected   Collected;
    struct sqlca            sqlca;
    struct sqlm_db2         *DB2_Ptr;
    struct sqlm_dbase       *DBase_Ptr;
```

```
/* Specify The Data Monitors To Collect Information For */
sqlma = (struct sqlma *) malloc(SQLMASIZE(2));
sqlma->obj_num = 2;
sqlma->obj_var[0].obj_type = SQLMA_DB2;
strcpy(sqlma->obj_var[0].object, "SAMPLE");
sqlma->obj_var[1].obj_type = SQLMA_DBASE;
strcpy(sqlma->obj_var[1].object, "SAMPLE");

/* Estimate The Database Monitor Buffer Size */
sqlmonsz(SQLM_DBMON_VERSION2, NULL, sqlma, &ulBuffSize, &sqlca);

/* Allocate The Database Monitor Buffer */
pchBuffer = (char *) malloc(ulBuffSize);

/* Collect Monitor Snapshot Information */
sqlmonss(SQLM_DBMON_VERSION2, NULL, sqlma, ulBuffSize, pchBuffer,
         &Collected, &sqlca);

/* If Snapshot Information Could Not Be Obtained, Display An */
/* Error Message And Exit
if (sqlca.sqlcode != SQL_RC_OK)
    {
    printf("ERROR : %ld\n", sqlca.sqlcode);
    return(EXIT_FAILURE);
    goto EXIT;
    }

/* Add Up All Structures Returned In The Buffer */
   uiNumStructs = Collected.db2 +
                  Collected.databases +
                  Collected.table_databases +
                  Collected.lock_databases +
                  Collected.applications +
                  Collected.applinfos +
                  Collected.dcs_applinfos +
                  Collected.tablespace_databases;

/* Loop Until All Data Structures Have Been Processed */
for (pchBufferIndex = pchBuffer; uiNumStructs > 0; uiNumStructs—)
    {

    /* Determine The Structure Type */
    switch ((unsigned char) *(pchBufferIndex + 4))
        {

        /* Display Select DB2 Information Collected */
        case SQLM_DB2_SS:
            DB2_Ptr = (struct sqlm_db2 *) pchBufferIndex;
            Process_DB2(DB2_Ptr);
            pchBufferIndex += DB2_Ptr->size;
            break;

        /* Display Select Database Information Collected */
        case SQLM_DBASE_SS:
            DBase_Ptr = (struct sqlm_dbase *) pchBufferIndex;
            Process_DBase(DBase_Ptr);
            pchBufferIndex += DBase_Ptr->size;
            break;

        /* Exit If Anything Else Was Collected */
        default:
```

```
                    goto EXIT;
                }
            }

    EXIT:
        /* Free Allocated Memory */
        if (sqlma != NULL)
            free(sqlma);

        if (pchBuffer != NULL)
            free(pchBuffer);

        /* Return To The Operating System */
        return(EXIT_SUCCESS);
    }

    /* Declare The Process_DB2 Function */
    void Process_DB2(struct sqlm_db2  *DB2_Ptr)
    {

        /* Declare The Local Memory Variables */
        long    ltime;

        /* Display The DB2 Status Information */
        printf("DB2 DATABASE MANAGER STATUS INFORMATION\n");
        printf("--------------------------------------------------");
        printf("-----------\n");
        printf("DB2 Database Manager Status              : ");
        switch (DB2_Ptr->db2_status)
            {
            case SQLM_DB2_ACTIVE:
                printf("Active\n");
                break;
            case SQLM_DB2_QUIESCE_PEND:
                printf("Quiesce Pending\n");
                break;
            case SQLM_DB2_QUIESCED:
                printf("Quiesced\n");
                break;
            }

        /* Display Time Started Information */
        ltime = DB2_Ptr->db2start_time.seconds;
        printf("Time DB2 Database Manager Was Started  : %24.24s\n\n",
               ctime(&ltime));

        /* Display Select DB2 Connection Information */
        printf("DB2 DATABASE MANAGER CONNECTION INFORMATION\n");
        printf("--------------------------------------------------");
        printf("-----------\n");
        printf("Remote Connections To The DB2 Instance : %lu\n",
               DB2_Ptr->rem_cons_in);
        printf("Local Connections To The DB2 Instance  : %lu\n",
               DB2_Ptr->local_cons);
        printf("Local Active Databases                 : %lu\n",
               DB2_Ptr->con_local_dbases);

        /* Return To The Calling Function */
        return;
    }
```

```
/* Declare The Process_DBase Function */
void Process_DBase(struct sqlm_dbase  *DBase_Ptr)
{

    /* Declare The Local Memory Variables */
    long    ltime;

    /* Display The Database Identification Information */
    printf("DATABASE INFORMATION\n");
    printf("---------------------------------------------");
    printf("-----------\n");
    printf("Database Alias                              : %0.*s\n",
           SQLM_IDENT_SZ, DBase_Ptr->input_db_alias);
    printf("Database Name                               : %0.*s\n",
           SQLM_IDENT_SZ, DBase_Ptr->db_name);
    printf("Database Path (Truncated)                   : %0.20s\n",
           DBase_Ptr->db_path);

    /* Display The DB2 Status Information */
    printf("Current Database Status                     : ");
    switch (DBase_Ptr->db_status)
        {
        case SQLM_DB_ACTIVE:
            printf("Active\n\n");
            break;
        case SQLM_DB_QUIESCE_PEND:
            printf("Quiesce Pending\n\n");
            break;
        case SQLM_DB_QUIESCED:
            printf("Quiesced\n\n");
            break;
        }

    /* Return To The Calling Function */
    return;
}
```

LIST INDOUBT TRANSACTIONS

Purpose

The LIST INDOUBT TRANSACTIONS function retrieves a list of all in-doubt transactions for the current connected database.

Syntax

```
int SQL_API_FN sqlxhqry (SQLXA_RECOVER **InDoubtData,
                         long          *NumInDoubts,
                         struct sqlca  *SQLCA);
```

Parameters

InDoubtData A pointer to a location in memory where this function stores the address of a *sqlxa_recover_t* structure that contains a list of indoubt transactions.

NumInDoubts A pointer to a location in memory where this function stores the number of indoubt transactions found.

SQLCA A pointer to a location in memory where a SQLCA data structure variable is stored. This variable sends either status information (if the function executed successfully) or error information (if the function failed) back to the calling application.

Includes

```
#include <sqlxa.h>
```

Description

The LIST INDOUBT TRANSACTIONS function retrieves a list of all indoubt transactions that exist for the currently connected database. Information about an indoubt transaction is stored in a *sqlxa_recover_t* structure (type defined as SQLXA_RECOVER), which is defined in *sqlxa.h* as follows:

```
typedef struct sqlxa_recover_t
{
unsigned long        timestamp;       /* The date and time when the            */
                                      /* transaction entered the indoubt       */
                                      /* state.                                */
struct sqlxa_xid_t   xid;             /* The XA identifier assigned by the     */
                                      /* transaction manager that uniquely     */
                                      /* identifies the global transaction.    */
char                 dbalias[8];      /* The alias of the database where       */
                                      /* the indoubt transaction is found.     */
char                 applid[32];      /* The application identifier assigned   */
                                      /* to this transaction by the DB2        */
                                      /* database manager.                     */
char                 sequence_no[4];  /* The sequence number assigned as       */
                                      /* an extension to the application       */
                                      /* identifier by the DB2 database        */
                                      /* manager.                              */
char                 auth_id[8];      /* The authorization ID of the user      */
                                      /* who initiated this transaction.       */
char                 log_full;        /* Indicates whether or not this         */
                                      /* transaction caused a LOG FULL         */
                                      /* condition to occur.                   */
char                 connected;       /* Indicates whether or not the          */
                                      /* application that initiated the        */
                                      /* transaction is still connected to     */
                                      /* the database.                         */
char                 indoubt_status;  /* Specifies the current status of the   */
                                      /* indoubt transaction.                  */
char                 reserved[9];     /* The first byte of this field          */
                                      /* indicates the indoubt transaction     */
                                      /* type; the rest of this field is set   */
                                      /* to zeros.                             */
} SQLXA_RECOVER;
```

This structure contains a reference to an additional structure, *sqlxa_xid_t*, that retrieves the unique XA identifier assigned to all transactions by the transaction manager. The *sqlxa_xid_t* structure is defined in *sqlxa.h* as follows:

```
struct sqlxa_xid_t
{
long   formatID;                      /* XA format identifier                  */
long   gtrid_length;                  /* The length of the global              */
                                      /* transaction identifier                */
long   bqual_length;                  /* The length of the branch identifier   */
char   data[128];                     /* The global transaction identifier,    */
                                      /* followed by the branch identifier,    */
                                      /* followed by trailing blanks for a     */
                                      /* total of 128 characters (bytes)       */
};
```

When this function is executed, it allocates sufficient space to hold the list of indoubt transactions and returns a pointer to this space in the *Indoubt-Data* parameter.

Comments

- The space allocated to hold the list of indoubt transactions is released automatically when the application that called this function terminates. Do not use the FREE MEMORY function to free this memory since it contains pointers to other dynamically allocated structures that will not be freed by the FREE MEMORY function call.
- Possible values for the *log_full* field of the *SQLXA_RECOVER* structure are:
  SQLXA_TRUE The transaction caused a LOG FULL condition to occur.
  SQLXA_FALSE The transaction did not cause a LOG FULL condition to occur.
- Possible values for the *connected* field of the *SQLXA_RECOVER* structure are:
  SQLXA_TRUE The transaction is undergoing normal syncpoint processing and is waiting for the second phase of a two-phase commit.
  SQLXA_FALSE The transaction was left indoubt by an earlier failure and is now waiting for a resync from a transaction manager.
- Possible values for the *indoubt_status* field of the *SQLXA_RECOVER* structure are:
  SQLXA_TS_PREP The transaction has been prepared.
  SQLXA_TS_HCOM The transaction has been heuristically committed with the COMMIT AN INDOUBT TRANSACTION function.
  SQLXA_TS_HROL The transaction has been heuristically rolled back with the ROLLBACK AN INDOUBT TRANSACTION function.
  SQLXA_TS_END The transaction is idle.
- The maximum value that can be specified for both the *gtrid_length* and *bqual_length* fields of the *sqlxa_xid_t* structure is 64.
- For detailed information on using two-phase commits and indoubt transaction recovery, refer to the *IBM Database 2 Administration Guide.*

Required Connection

This function can be called only if a connection to a database exists.

Authorization

Only users with either system administrator (SYSADM) authority or database administrator (DBADM) authority can execute this function call.

See Also

COMMIT AN INDOUBT TRANSACTION, ROLLBACK AN INDOUBT TRANSACTION, FORGET TRANSACTION STATUS

Example

The following C program illustrates how the LIST INDOUBT TRANSACTIONS function retrieves a list of all indoubt transactions that exist for the MYDB1 database (this example was created and tested on the AIX operating system):

```
#include <stdio.h>
#include <stdlib.h>
#include <string.h>
#include <sqlenv.h>
#include <sqlxa.h>
#include <sql.h>
```

```
int main()
{
    /* Include The SQLCA Data Structure Variable */
    EXEC SQL INCLUDE SQLCA;

    /* Declare The Local Memory Variables */
    int            rc = EXIT_SUCCESS;
    SQLXA_RECOVER  *IndoubtTrans = NULL;
    long           lNumITrans;

    /* Restart The MYDB1 Database */
    printf("Restarting the database. Please wait.\n\n");
    sqlerstd("MYDB1", "etpdd6z", "sanders", &sqlca);

    /* Set Up A Simple SQL Error Handler */
    EXEC SQL WHENEVER SQLERROR GOTO EXIT;

    /* Retrieve All Indoubt Transactions */
    sqlxhqry(&IndoubtTrans, &lNumITrans, &sqlca);

    /* Display The Information Obtained For All Indoubt Transactions */
    /* Found                                                          */
    for (; lNumITrans > 0; lNumITrans--)
        {
        printf("Transaction ID :\n");
        printf("  Format ID      : %ld\n",
               IndoubtTrans->xid.formatID);
        printf("  GTRID Length   : %ld\n",
               IndoubtTrans->xid.gtrid_length);
        printf("  BQUAL Length   : %ld\n",
               IndoubtTrans->xid.bqual_length);
        printf("  Data           : %s\n\n",
               IndoubtTrans->xid.data);

        printf("Database         : %s\n", IndoubtTrans->dbalias);
        printf("Application ID   : %s\n", IndoubtTrans->applid);
        printf("Timestamp        : %ld\n", IndoubtTrans->timestamp);
        printf("Sequence No.     : %s\n", IndoubtTrans->sequence_no);
        printf("Authorization ID : %s\n", IndoubtTrans->auth_id);
        printf("Log Full         : ");
        if (IndoubtTrans->log_full == SQLXA_TRUE)
            printf("Yes\n");
        else
            printf("No\n");
        printf("Connected        : ");
        if (IndoubtTrans->connected == SQLXA_TRUE)
            printf("Yes\n");
        else
            printf("No\n");
        printf("Status           : %c\n\n",
               IndoubtTrans->indoubt_status);
        IndoubtTrans++;
        }

EXIT:
    /* If An Error Has Occurred, Display The SQL Return Code */
    if (sqlca.sqlcode != SQL_RC_OK)
        {
        printf("SQL ERROR : %ld\n", sqlca.sqlcode);
        rc = EXIT_FAILURE;
        }
```

```
    /* Issue A Rollback To Free All Locks */
    EXEC SQL ROLLBACK;

    /* Turn Off The SQL Error Handler */
    EXEC SQL WHENEVER SQLERROR CONTINUE;

    /* Disconnect From The MYDB1 Database */
    EXEC SQL DISCONNECT CURRENT;

    /* Return To The Operating System */
    return(rc);
}
```

COMMIT AN INDOUBT TRANSACTION

Purpose

The COMMIT AN INDOUBT TRANSACTION function heuristically commits an indoubt transaction.

Syntax

```
int SQL_API_FN sqlxhcom (sqlxa_xid_t  *TransactionID,
                         struct sqlca *SQLCA);
```

Parameters

TransactionID A pointer to a location in memory where the XA identifier of the indoubt transaction to be committed is stored.

SQLCA A pointer to a location in memory where a SQLCA data structure variable is stored. This variable sends either status information (if the function executed successfully) or error information (if the function failed) back to the calling application.

Includes

```
#include <sqlxa.h>
```

Description

The COMMIT AN INDOUBT TRANSACTION function commits an indoubt transaction. If this function is successfully executed, the specified transaction's state becomes *heuristically committed.*

When a transaction is initiated, it is assigned a unique XA identifier by the transaction manager, which is then used to globally identify it. This unique XA identifier is used to specify which indoubt transaction this function is to commit. Refer to the LIST INDOUBT TRANSACTIONS function for a detailed description of the XA identifier structure.

Comments

- The maximum value that can be specified for both the *gtrid_length* and the *bqual_length* fields of the *sqlxa_xid_t* structure is 64.
- You can obtain all *sqlxa_xid_t* structure information for a particular transaction by calling the LIST INDOUBT TRANSACTIONS function.
- Only transactions with a status of PREPARED or IDLE can be placed in the *heuristically committed* state.
- The database manager remembers the state of an indoubt transaction until the FORGET TRANSACTION STATUS function is executed.

Required Connection

This function can be called only if a connection to a database exists.

Authorization

Only users with either system administrator (SYSADM) or database administrator (DBADM) authority are allowed to execute this function call.

See Also

LIST INDOUBT TRANSACTIONS, ROLLBACK AN INDOUBT TRANSACTION, FORGET TRANSACTION STATUS

Example

The following C program illustrates how to use the COMMIT AN INDOUBT TRANSACTION function to heuristically commit an indoubt transaction (this example was created and tested on the AIX operating system):

```
#include <stdio.h>
#include <stdlib.h>
#include <string.h>
#include <sqlenv.h>
#include <sqlxa.h>
#include <sql.h>

int main()
{
    /* Include The SQLCA Data Structure Variable */
    EXEC SQL INCLUDE SQLCA;

    /* Declare The Local Memory Variables */
    int             rc = EXIT_SUCCESS;
    SQLXA_RECOVER   *IndoubtTrans = NULL;
    SQLXA_XID       ITransID;
    long            lNumITrans;

    /* Restart The MYDB1 Database */
    printf("Restarting the database. Please wait.\n\n");
    sqlerstd("MYDB1", "etpdd6z", "sanders", &sqlca);

    /* Set Up A Simple SQL Error Handler */
    EXEC SQL WHENEVER SQLERROR GOTO EXIT;

    /* Retrieve All Indoubt Transactions */
    sqlxhqry(&IndoubtTrans, &lNumITrans, &sqlca);

    /* If An Indoubt Transaction Was Found, Display Its Information */
    printf("Transaction ID :\n");
    printf("  Format ID     : %ld\n", IndoubtTrans->xid.formatID);
    printf("   GTRID Length : %ld\n", IndoubtTrans->xid.gtrid_length);
    printf("   BQUAL Length : %ld\n", IndoubtTrans->xid.bqual_length);
    printf("  Data           : %s\n\n", IndoubtTrans->xid.data);

    /* Heurstically Commit The First Indoubt Transaction Found */
    sqlxhcom(&IndoubtTrans->xid, &sqlca);

    /* Display A Success Message */
    printf("Transaction has been heuristically committed.\n");

    /* Forget The Heurstically Committed Indoubt Transaction */
    sqlxhfrg(&IndoubtTrans->xid, &sqlca);

    /* Display A Success Message */
    printf("Transaction has been forgotten.\n");

EXIT:
    /* If An Error Has Occurred, Display The SQL Return Code */
    if (sqlca.sqlcode != SQL_RC_OK)
        {
        printf("SQL ERROR : %ld\n", sqlca.sqlcode);
```

```
        rc = EXIT_FAILURE;
        }

    /* Issue A Rollback To Free All Locks */
    EXEC SQL ROLLBACK;

    /* Turn Off The SQL Error Handler */
    EXEC SQL WHENEVER SQLERROR CONTINUE;

    /* Disconnect From The MYDB1 Database */
    EXEC SQL DISCONNECT CURRENT;

    /* Return To The Operating System */
    return(rc);
}
```

ROLLBACK AN INDOUBT TRANSACTION

Purpose

The ROLLBACK AN INDOUBT TRANSACTION function heuristically rolls back an indoubt transaction.

Syntax

```
int SQL_API_FN sqlxhrol (sqlxa_xid_t   *TransactionID,
                         struct sqlca *SQLCA);
```

Parameters

TransactionID A pointer to a location in memory where the XA identifier of the indoubt transaction to be rolled back is stored.

SQLCA A pointer to a location in memory where a SQLCA data structure variable is stored. This variable sends either status information (if the function executed successfully) or error information (if the function failed) back to the calling application.

Includes

```
#include <sqlxa.h>
```

Description

The ROLLBACK AN INDOUBT TRANSACTION function rolls back an indoubt transaction. If this function is successfully executed, the specified transaction's state becomes *heuristically rolled back.*

When a transaction is initiated, it is assigned a unique XA identifier by the transaction manager, which is then used to globally identify it. This unique XA identifier is used to specify which indoubt transaction this function is to roll back. Refer to the LIST INDOUBT TRANSACTIONS function for a detailed description of the XA identifier structure.

Comments

- Only transactions with a status of PREPARED or IDLE can be placed in the *heuristically rolled-back* state.
- The database manager remembers the state of an indoubt transaction until the FORGET TRANSACTION STATUS function is executed.

Required Connection

This function can be called only if a connection to a database exists.

Authorization

Only users with either system administrator (SYSADM) authority or database administrator (DBADM) authority are allowed to execute this function call.

See Also

COMMIT AN INDOUBT TRANSACTION, LIST INDOUBT TRANSACTIONS, FORGET TRANSACTION STATUS

Example

The following C program illustrates how to use the ROLLBACK AN INDOUBT TRANSACTION function to heuristically roll back an indoubt transaction (this example was created and tested on the AIX operating system):

```
#include <stdio.h>
#include <stdlib.h>
#include <string.h>
#include <sqlenv.h>
#include <sqlxa.h>
#include <sql.h>

int main()
{
    /* Include The SQLCA Data Structure Variable */
    EXEC SQL INCLUDE SQLCA;

    /* Declare The Local Memory Variables */
    int              rc = EXIT_SUCCESS;
    SQLXA_RECOVER    *IndoubtTrans = NULL;
    SQLXA_XID        ITransID;
    long             lNumITrans;

    /* Restart The MYDB1 Database */
    printf("Restarting the database. Please wait.\n\n");
    sqlerstd("MYDB1", "etpdd6z", "sanders", &sqlca);

    /* Set Up A Simple SQL Error Handler */
    EXEC SQL WHENEVER SQLERROR GOTO EXIT;

    /* Retrieve All Indoubt Transactions */
    sqlxhqry(&IndoubtTrans, &lNumITrans, &sqlca);

    /* If An Indoubt Transaction Was Found, Display Its Information */
    printf("Transaction ID :\n");
    printf(" Format ID      : %ld\n", IndoubtTrans->xid.formatID);
    printf(" GTRID Length   : %ld\n", IndoubtTrans->xid.gtrid_length);
    printf(" BQUAL Length   : %ld\n", IndoubtTrans->xid.bqual_length);
    printf(" Data           : %s\n\n", IndoubtTrans->xid.data);

    /* Heurstically Roll Back The First Indoubt Transaction Found */
    sqlxhrol(&IndoubtTrans->xid, &sqlca);

    /* Display A Success Message */
    printf("Transaction has been heuristically rolled back.\n");

    /* Forget The Heurstically Rolled Back Indoubt Transaction */
    sqlxhfrg(&IndoubtTrans->xid, &sqlca);

    /* Display A Success Message */
    printf("Transaction has been forgotten.\n");

EXIT:
    /* If An Error Has Occurred, Display The SQL Return Code */
    if (sqlca.sqlcode != SQL_RC_OK)
        {
        printf("SQL ERROR : %ld\n", sqlca.sqlcode);
        rc = EXIT_FAILURE;
        }
```

```
    /* Issue A Rollback To Free All Locks */
    EXEC SQL ROLLBACK;

    /* Turn Off The SQL Error Handler */
    EXEC SQL WHENEVER SQLERROR CONTINUE;

    /* Disconnect From The MYDB1 Database */
    EXEC SQL DISCONNECT CURRENT;

    /* Return To The Operating System */
    return(rc);
}
```

FORGET TRANSACTION STATUS

Purpose

The FORGET TRANSACTION STATUS function allows the transaction manager (or resource manager) to erase knowledge of a completed transaction that was heuristically committed with the COMMIT AN INDOUBT TRANSACTION function or heuristically rolled back with the ROLLBACK AN INDOUBT TRANSACTION function.

Syntax

```
int SQL_API_FN sqlxhfrg (sqlxa_xid_t  *TransactionID,
                         struct sqlca *SQLCA);
```

Parameters

TransactionID A pointer to a location in memory where the XA identifier of the indoubt transaction to be erased is stored.

SQLCA A pointer to a location in memory where a SQLCA data structure variable is stored. This variable sends either status information (if the function executed successfully) or error information (if the function failed) back to the calling application.

Includes

```
#include <sqlxa.h>
```

Description

The FORGET TRANSACTION STATUS function allows the transaction manager (or resource manager) to erase knowledge of a completed transaction that was placed in either the *heuristically committed* or *heuristically rolled-back* state. Indoubt transactions can be placed in either of these states when the COMMIT AN INDOUBT TRANSACTION function or the ROLLBACK AN INDOUBT TRANSACTION function is executed.

When a transaction is initiated, it is assigned a unique XA identifier by the transaction manager, which is then used to globally identify it. This unique XA identifier is used to specify which indoubt transaction this function is to erase. Refer to the LIST INDOUBT TRANSACTIONS function for a detailed description of the XA identifier structure.

Comments

- Only transactions with a status of *heuristically committed* or *heuristically rolled back* can be processed by the FORGET TRANSACTION STATUS function.

Required Connection

This function can be called only if a connection to a database exists.

Authorization

Only users with either system administrator (SYSADM) authority or database administrator (DBADM) authority can execute this function call.

See Also

LIST INDOUBT TRANSACTIONS, COMMIT AN INDOUBT TRANSACTION, ROLLBACK AN INDOUBT TRANSACTION

Example

See the examples provided for the COMMIT AN INDOUBT TRANSACTION and ROLLBACK AN INDOUBT TRANSACTION functions in this chapter.

APPENDIX A

SQL DATA STRUCTURES

THE SQL COMMUNICATIONS AREA (SQLCA) STRUCTURE

The SQL communications area (SQLCA) structure is a collection of variables that are updated at the end of the execution of every SQL statement and DB2 API function call. Application programs that contain embedded SQL statements (other than embedded DECLARE, INCLUDE, and WHENEVER statements) or API function calls must define at least one SQLCA data structure variable (you can also place one SQLCA data structure variable in each thread of a multithreaded application). You can use the SQL INCLUDE statement to provide the declaration of the SQLCA data structure in embedded SQL applications written in C and C++. The *sqlca* structure is defined in *sqlca.h* as follows:

```
struct sqlca
{
char  sqlcaid[8];    /* An "eye catcher" for storage dumps. This field      */
                     /* contains the value "SQLCA".                          */
long  sqlcabc;       /* The size of the SQLCA structure (136 bytes)         */
long  sqlcode;       /* The SQL return code value. A value of 0 means       */
                     /* "successful execution," a positive value means      */
                     /* "successful execution with warnings," and a         */
                     /* negative value means "error." Refer to the IBM      */
                     /* DB2 Messages Reference for specific meanings        */
                     /* of SQL return code values.                           */
short  sqlerrml;     /* The size, in bytes, of the data stored in the       */
                     /* sqlerrmc field of this structure. This value can be */
                     /* any number between 0 and 70. A value of 0           */
                     /* indicates that no data is stored in the sqlerrmc    */
                     /* field.                                               */
char  sqlerrmc[70];  /* One or more error message tokens, separated by      */
                     /* 0xFF, that are substituted for variables in the     */
                     /* descriptions of error conditions. This field is also */
                     /* used when a successful connection is established.   */
                     /* Refer to the IBM DB2 Messages Reference for specific */
                     /* meanings of SQL return code values.                  */
char  sqlerrp[8];    /* A diagnostic value that begins with a three-letter  */
                     /* code identifying the product and is followed by     */
                     /* five digits that identify the version, release, and */
                     /* modification level of the product. For example,     */
                     /* "SQL02010" means DB2 for Common Servers,            */
                     /* version 2, release 1, modification level 0. If      */
```

```
                               /* the sqlcode field contains a negative value, this    */
                               /* field identifies the module that returned an error.  */
    long   sqlerrd[6];         /* An array of six integer values that provide          */
                               /* additional diagnostic information                    */
    char   sqlwarn[11];        /* An array of warning indicators, each containing      */
                               /* a blank or the letter 'W'. If compound SQL was       */
                               /* invoked, this field will contain an accumulation of  */
                               /* the warning indicators set for all substatements     */
    char   sqlstate[5];        /* The SQLSTATE value that indicates the outcome of     */
                               /* the most recently executed SQL statement             */
};
```

Table A.1 describes the types of diagnostic information that can be returned in the *sqlerrd* array, and Table A.2 describes the types of warning information that can be returned in the *sqlwarn* array.

TABLE A.1 Elements of the *sqlca.sqlerrd* Array

Array element	Diagnostic information
SQLERRD(1)	Reserved for internal return code.
SQLERRD(2)	Reserved for internal return code. If the SQLCA data reflects a *not atomic* compound SQL statement that encountered one or more errors, this element will contain the number of SQL statements that failed.
SQLERRD(3)	If the SQLCA data reflects an PREPARE operation, this element will contain an estimate of the number of rows returned when the SQL statement is executed. If the SQLCA data reflects an INSERT, UPDATE, or DELETE operation, this element will contain the actual number of rows affected. If the SQLCA data reflects a compound SQL statement, this element will contain an accumulation of all substatement rows. If the SQLCA data reflects a CONNECT operation, this element will contain a **1** if the database is updatable and a **2** if the database is read-only.
SQLERRD(4)	If the SQLCA data reflects a PREPARE operation, this element will contain a relative cost estimate of the resources required to process the statement. If the SQLCA data reflects a compound SQL statement, this element will contain a count of the number of successfully executed substatements. If the SQLCA data reflects a CONNECT operation, this element will contain a **0** if a one-phase commit from a down-level client was executed; a **1** if a one-phase commit was executed; a **2** if a one-phase, read-only commit was executed; and a **3** if a two-phase commit was executed.
SQLERRD(5)	This element contains the total number of rows deleted, inserted, or updated as a result of the enforcement of constraints after a successful DELETE operation and the processing of triggered SQL statements from activated triggers. If the SQLCA data reflects a compound SQL statement, this element will contain an accumulation of the number of such rows for all substatements.
SQLERRD(6)	Reserved for future use.

TABLE A.2 Elements of the *sqlca.sqlwarn* Array

Array element	Warning information
SQLWARN0	This element is blank if all other indicators are blank; it contains a **'W'** if at least one other indicator is not blank.
SQLWARN1	This element contains a **'W'** if the value of a string column was truncated when assigned to a host variable. It contains a **'N'** if the null terminator was truncated.
SQLWARN2	This element contains a **'W'** if NULL values were eliminated from the argument of a function.
SQLWARN3	This element contains a **'W'** if the number of columns is not equal to the number of host variables provided.

TABLE A.2 Elements of the *sqlca.sqlwarn* Array *(Continued)*

Array element	Warning information
SQLWARN4	This element contains a '**W**' if a prepared UPDATE or DELETE statement does not include a WHERE clause.
SQLWARN5	Reserved for future use.
SOLWARN6	This element contains a '**W**' if the result of a date calculation was adjusted to avoid an invalid date.
SQLWARN7	Reserved for future use.
SQLWARN8	Reserved for future use.
SQLWARN9	Reserved for future use.
SQLWARNA	This element contains a '**W**' if there was a conversion error while converting a character data value in one of the fields in the SQLCA data structure.

THE SQL DESCRIPTOR AREA (SQLDA) STRUCTURE

The SQL descriptor area (SQLDA) structure is a collection of variables that are required to execute the DESCRIBE SQL statement. The SQLDA data structure variables can also provide options to the PREPARE, OPEN, FETCH, EXECUTE, and CALL SQL statements. Because a SQLDA data structure communicates with dynamic SQL, it can be used in a DESCRIBE statement, modified with the addresses of host variables, and then reused in a FETCH statement. The *sqlda* structure is defined in *sqlda.h* as follows:

```
struct sqlda
{
char           sqldaid[8]; /* An "eye catcher" for storage dumps. This     */
                           /* field contains the value "SQLDA"             */
long           sqldabc;    /* The size, in bytes, of the SQLDA structure.  */
                           /* The size of an SQLDA data structure is       */
                           /* determined with the following formula:       */
                           /* sqldabc = 16 + (44 * sqln).                  */
short          sqln;       /* The total number of elements in the sqlvar   */
                           /* array                                        */
short          sqld;       /* The number of columns in the result data     */
                           /* set returned for DESCRIBE and PREPARE SQL    */
                           /* statements or the number of host variables   */
                           /* described by the elements in the sqlvar      */
                           /* array for FETCH, OPEN, EXECUTE, and          */
                           /* CALL SQL statements                          */
struct sqlvar sqlvar[1];   /* An array of sqlvar data structures that      */
                           /* contain information about host variables     */
                           /* or result data set columns                   */
};
```

Note: The *sqlvar* field will be followed by an array of *sqlvar2* structures if a secondary SQLVAR is needed.

Along with basic structure information, a SQLDA structure variable contains an arbitrary number of occurrences of *sqlvar* or *sqlvar2* structures (referred to as SQLVAR variables). The information stored in the SQLVAR variables depends on where the SQLDA data structure variable is used. When a SQLDA data structure variable is used in PREPARE and DESCRIBE SQL statements, the SQLVAR variables provide information about the prepared statement to the application program. The information provided usually describes the columns in a result data set. If any of the columns being described are defined with a LOB data type or a distinct data type, the number of SQLVAR variables used will be doubled. When a SQLDA data structure variable is used in OPEN, EXECUTE, FETCH, and CALL SQL statements, the SQLVAR variables describe application host variables to the DB2 database manager. Again, if any of the host variables being described are defined with a LOB data type or a distinct data type, the number of SQLVAR entries for the SQLDA data structure variable will be doubled. Two types of SQLVAR variable entries are used:

Base SQLVARs These entries contain base information (such as data type code, length attribute, column name, host variable address, and indicator variable address) for result data set columns or host variables.

Secondary SQLVARs These entries are present only if the number of SQLVAR entries is doubled because LOB or distinct data types are used. For distinct data types, these SQLVARs contain the distinct data type name. For LOB data types, these SQLVARs contain the length attribute of the column or host variable and a pointer to the buffer that contains the actual length. If locators or file reference variables represent LOBS data types, secondary SQLVAR entries are not used.

Base SQLVARs are stored in one or more *sqlvar* structures. The *sqlvar* structure is defined in *sqlda.h* as follows:

```
struct sqlvar
{
short           sqltype;        /* The data type of the column in the result data */
                                /* set or the data type of the host variable      */
short           sqllen;         /* The size (length) of the column in the result  */
                                /* data set or the length of the host variable    */
char            *sqldata;       /* A pointer to a location in memory where the    */
                                /* data for the column or host variable is        */
                                /* (or is to be) stored                           */
short           *sqlind;        /* A pointer to a location in memory where the    */
                                /* data for the null indicator associated with    */
                                /* the column or host variable is (or is to be)   */
                                /* stored                                         */
struct sqlname sqlname;         /* The unqualified name of the column or the host */
                                /* variable name                                  */
};
```

This structure uses an additional structure, *sqlname*, to store column and host variable names. The *sqlname* structure is defined in *sqlda.h* as follows:

```
struct sqlname
{
short            length;     /* The length of the column or host variable name  */
char             data[30];   /* The column or host variable name                */
};
```

Secondary SQLVARs are stored in one or more *sqlvar2* structures. The *sqlvar2* structure is defined in *sqlda.h* as follows:

```
struct sqlvar2
{
union sql8bytelen          len;                /* The length attribute of a LOB      */
                                               /* column or host variable.           */
char                       *sqldatalen;        /* A pointer to a four-byte buffer    */
                                               /* that can hold the length of the    */
                                               /* host variables that have LOB data */
                                               /* types.                             */
```

```
struct sqldistinct_type  sqldatatype_name;  /* The fully qualified distinct type */
                                            /* name. This is used only for       */
                                            /* columns or host variables that    */
                                            /* have distinct data types.         */
};
```

This structure uses a special union structure, *sql8bytelen*, to store eight-byte length attribute values (only four-byte integers are currently supported). The *sql8bytelen* union is defined in *sqlda.h* as follows:

```
union sql8bytelen
{
long  reserve1[2];          /* Reserved for future eight-byte lengths.     */
long  sqllonglen;           /* The length attribute of a LOB column or host */
                            /* variable.                                    */
};
```

The *sqlvar* structure uses a second structure, *sqldistinct_type*, to store information about distinct data types. The *sqldistinct_type* structure is defined in *sqlda.h* as follows:

```
struct sqldistinct_type
{
short  length;          /* The length of the distinct data type name.         */
char   data[27];        /* The fully qualified name of the distinct data type. */
char   reserved1[3];    /* Reserved for later use.                            */
};
```

In SQLDA data structure variables that contain both base and secondary SQLVAR entries, the base SQLVARs are placed in a block before the block of secondary SQLVARs. In each block, the number of entries provided is equal to the value of the *sqld* field in the SQLDA data structure (even though many of the secondary SQLVAR entries might be unused).

Table A.3 describes the data stored in the header portion of the SQLDA data structure variable when it is used with a PREPARE, DESCRIBE, OPEN, EXECUTE, FETCH, and/or CALL SQL statement. Table A.4 describes the data stored in a base SQLVAR variable when a SQLDA data structure is used with a PREPARE, DESCRIBE, OPEN, EXECUTE, FETCH, and/or CALL SQL statement. Table A.5 describes the type of data stored in a secondary SQLVAR variable when a SQLDA data structure is used with a PREPARE, DESCRIBE, OPEN, EXECUTE, FETCH, and/or CALL SQL statement.

TABLE A.3 Data Stored in the Header Portion of a SQLDA Data Structure Variable

SQLDA structure field	Usage in DESCRIBE and PREPARE SQL statement (set by the DB2 database manager—except for *sqln*)	Usage in FETCH, OPEN, EXECUTE, and CALL SQL statement (set by the application prior to executing the statement)
sqldaid	The seventh byte of this field is a flag byte named SQLDOUBLED. The DB2 database manager will set SQLDOUBLED to 2 if two SQLVAR entries were created for each column; otherwise it will be set to a blank (0x20 in ASCII, 0x40 in EBCDIC).	The seventh byte of this field is used when the number of SQLVARs is doubled. It is named SQLDOUBLED. If any of the host variables being described is a BLOB, CLOB, or DBCLOB, the seventh byte must be set to 2; otherwise it can be set to any character, but it is advisable to use a blank. When used with the CALL statement and one or more SQLVARs to define a data field as FOR BIT DATA, the sixth byte must be set to the + character; otherwise it can be set to any character, but it is advisable to use a blank.
sqldabc	The length of the SQLDA data structure variable.	The length of the SQLDA data structure variable.

TABLE A.3 Data Stored in the Header Portion of a SQLDA Data Structure Variable *(Continued)*

SQLDA structure field	Usage in DESCRIBE and PREPARE SQL statement (set by the DB2 database manager—except for *sqln*)	Usage in FETCH, OPEN, EXECUTE, and CALL SQL statement (set by the application prior to executing the statement)
sqln	Unchanged by the DB2 database manager. Must be set to a value greater than or equal to zero before the DESCRIBE statement is executed. Indicates the total number of occurrences of SQLVAR.	The total number of SQLVARs provided in the SQLDA. The *sqln* field must be set to a value greater than or equal to zero.
sqld	Set by the DB2 database manager to the number of columns in the result data set (or to zero if the statement being described is not a SELECT statement).	The number of host variables described by SQLVARs.

Adapted from IBM's *Database 2 SQL Reference*, Table 22, pages 494 to 495.

TABLE A.4 Data Stored in a Base SQLVAR Variable

SQLVAR structure field	Usage in DESCRIBE and PREPARE SQL statements	Usage in FETCH, OPEN, EXECUTE, and CALL SQL (set by the application prior to executing the statement)
sqltype	Indicates the data type of the column and whether or not it can contain nulls. For a distinct type, the data type of the base type is placed into this field. There is no indication in the base SQLVAR that it is part of the description of a distinct type.	Indicates the data type of the host variable and whether or not it can contain nulls. Host variables for datetime values must be character string variables. For FETCH SQL statements, a datetime type code means a fixed-length character string.
sqllen	The length attribute of the column. For datetime columns, this is the length of the string representation of the values. The value is set to 0 for large object strings (even for those whose length attribute is small enough to fit into a two-byte integer).	The length attribute of the host variable. This value is ignored by the DB2 database manager for CLOB, DBCLOB, and BLOB columns, The *len.sqllonglen* field in the secondary SQLVAR is used instead.
sqldata	For character-string columns, this field contains 0 if the column is defined with the FOR BIT DATA attribute. If the column was not defined with the FOR BIT DATA attribute, the value in this field depends on the database type: for SBCS databases, *sqldata* contains the database code page; for DBCS databases, this field contains the DBCS code page associated with the (composite) database code page; for all other column types, *sqldata* is undefined.	Contains the address of the host variable (where the fetched data will be stored).
sqlind	For character-string columns, this field contains 0 if the column is defined with the FOR BIT DATA attribute. If the column does not have the FOR BIT DATA attribute, the value depends on the database type: for SBCS databases, the field contains 0; for DBCS databases, the field contains the DBCS code page	Contains the address of an associated indicator variable if there is one; otherwise, this field is not used.

TABLE A.4 Data Stored in a Base SQLVAR Variable *(Continued)*

SQLVAR structure field	Usage in DESCRIBE and PREPARE SQL statements	Usage in FETCH, OPEN, EXECUTE, and CALL SQL (set by the application prior to executing the statement)
	associated with the (composite) database code page; for all other column types, the field is undefined.	
sqlname	Contains the unqualified name of the column. For columns that have a system-generated name (the result column was not directly derived from a single column and did not specify a name using the AS clause), the 30th byte is set to 0xFF. In all other cases, this byte is set to 0x00.	When used with the CALL SQL statement, this field can be set to indicate a FOR BIT DATA string as follows: the length of *sqlname* is 8; the first four bytes of *sqlname* are 0x00000000; the remaining four bytes of *sqlname* are reserved (and are currently ignored); the *sqltype* field must indicate a CHAR, VARCHAR, or LONG VARCHAR; and the sixth byte of the *sqidaid* field is set to the + character. You can also use this technique with OPEN and EXECUTE when using DDCS to access the server.

Adapted from IBM's *Database 2 SQL Reference*, Table 23, pages 495 to 496.

TABLE A.5 Data Stored in a Secondary SQLVAR Variable

SQLDA structure field	Usage in DESCRIBE and PREPARE SQL statements	Usage in FETCH, OPEN, EXECUTE, and CALL SQL statements (set by the application prior to executing the statement).
len.sqllonglen	The length attribute of a BLOB, CLOB, or DBCLOB column.	The length attribute of a BLOB, CLOB, or DBCLOB host variable. The DB2 database manager ignores the *sqllen* field in the base SQLVAR for these data types. The length attribute stores the number of bytes for a BLOB or CLOB, and the number of characters for a DBCLOB.
sqldatalen	Not used.	Used for BLOB, CLOB, and DBCLOB host variables only. If this field is NULL, then the length should be stored in the four bytes immediately before the start of the data, and the *sqldata* field of the matching base SQLVAR should point to the first byte of the field length. If this field is not NULL, it contains a pointer to a four-byte buffer that contains the actual length, in bytes (even for DBCLOB), of the data in the buffer pointed to by the *sqldata* field of the matching base SQLVAR. Whether or not this field is used, the *len.sqllognlen* field must be set.
sqldatatype_name	For a distinct type column, the DB2 database manager sets this field to the fully qualified distinct type name. The first eight bytes contain the schema name of the distinct type (right-padded with spaces, if necessary), byte 9 contains a period, and bytes 10 to 27 contain the low-order portion of the distinct type name, which is not right-padded with spaces. Although the prime purpose of this field is to store the names of distinct data types, it is also set for IBM predefined data	Not used.

TABLE A.5 Data Stored in a Secondary SQLVAR Variable

SQLDA structure field	Usage in DESCRIBE and PREPARE SQL statements	Usage in FETCH, OPEN, EXECUTE, and CALL SQL statements (set by the application prior to executing the statement).
	types. In this case, the schema name is always SYSIBM and the low-order portion of the name is the name stored in the TYPENAME column of the SYSCAT.DATATYPES system catalog view.	
reserved	Not used.	Not used.

Adapted from IBM's *Database 2 SQL Reference*, Table 24, page 497.

THE SQLCHAR STRUCTURE

The SQLCHAR structure is a combination of a character string and a string length value. This structure works with VARCHAR data types. The *sqlchar* structure is defined in *sql.h* as follows:

```
struct sqlchar
{
short           length;                    /* The length of the character string */
                                           /* stored in the data filed of this   */
                                           /* structure.                         */
char            data[1];                   /* A character string.                */
};
```

APPENDIX B

SQL FUNCTIONS

An SQL function is an operation that is denoted by a function name followed by a pair of parentheses enclosing specified arguments. SQL functions are classified as either column or scalar. The argument of a column function is a collection of values. The argument of a scalar function is a single value. If multiple arguments are allowed, each argument is treated as a single value. Many of the SQL functions include variations of the input parameters allowing either different data types or different numbers of arguments. Because each SQL function returns a value, SQL functions can be specified in a SQL statement wherever an *expression* can be used.

Table B.1 describes all the functions provided by DB2. The Input column of this table identifies the data type(s) expected for each argument during function invocation. The Output column identifies the data type returned after each function call is executed. There are some distinctions you should understand about these data types; in some cases the specified data type is a specific built-in data type and in other cases it is a general data type (such as a *numeric type*). When a specific data type is listed, this means that an exact match must occur with the specified data type. When a general data type is listed, each of the data types associated with that general data type will result in an exact match.

TABLE B.1 SQL Functions

Function/Syntax	Description	Input	Output
ABS([*argument*])	Returns the absolute value of *argument*. ABSVAL is a synonym for ABS.	SMALLINT INTEGER DOUBLE	SMALLINT INTEGER DOUBLE
ACOS([*argument*])	Returns the arccosine of *argument* as an angle, expressed in radians.	DOUBLE	DOUBLE
ASCII([*argument*])	Returns the ASCII code value of the leftmost character of argument as an integer.	CHAR VARCHAR CLOB(1 M)	INTEGER INTEGER INTEGER
ASIN([*argument*])	Returns the arcsine of *argument* as an angle, expressed in radians.	DOUBLE	DOUBLE
ATAN([*argument*])	Returns the arctangent of *argument* as an angle, expressed in radians.	DOUBLE	DOUBLE

TABLE B.1 SQL Functions *(Continued)*

Function/Syntax	Description	Input	Output
ATAN2([*argument1*],[*argument2*])	Returns the arctangent of *x* and *y* coordinates, specified by *argument1* and *argument2*, respectively, as an angle expressed in radians.	DOUBLE, DOUBLE	DOUBLE
AVG <ALL/DISTINCT> ([*numeric-expression*])	Returns the average of a set of numbers (column function).	numeric type	numeric type
BLOB([*string-expression*]<,*length*>)	Casts from source type to BLOB, with optional length.	string type, INTEGER	BLOB
CEIL([*argument*])	Returns the smallest integer greater than or equal to *argument*. CEILING is a synonym for CEIL.	SMALLINT INTEGER DOUBLE	SMALLINT INTEGER DOUBLE
CHR([*argument*])	Returns the character that has the ASCII code value specified by *argument*. The value of *argument* should be between 0 and 255; otherwise the return value is NULL.	INTEGER	CHAR(1)
CHAR([*character-expression*] <,*length*>)	Returns a character string representation of a character or character string.	character type, INTEGER	CHAR (integer)
CHAR([*integer-expression*])	Returns a character string representation of an integer.	SMALLINT INTEGER	CHAR(6) CHAR(11)
CHAR([*decimal-expression*] <,*decimal-character*>)	Returns a character string representation of a decimal number.	DECIMAL, VARCHAR	CHAR(2 + precision)
CHAR([*datetime-expression*]<,ISO>)	Returns a character string representation of a date, time, or timestamp in ISO format.	CHAR	CHAR
CHAR([*datetime-expression*]<,USA>)	Returns a character string representation of a date, time, or timestamp in IBM USA standard (USA) format).	CHAR	CHAR
CHAR([*datetime-expression*]<,EUR>)	Returns a character string representation of a date, time, or timestamp in IBM European standard (EUR) format.	CHAR	CHAR
CHAR([*datetime-expression*]<,JIS>)	Returns a character string representation of a date, time, or timestamp in Japanese industrial standard (JIS) format.	CHAR	CHAR
CHAR([*datetime-expression*] <,LOCAL>)	Returns a character string representation of a date, time, or timestamp in site-defined (LOCAL) format.	CHAR	CHAR
CLOB([*character-expression*] <,*length*>)	Casts from source type to CLOB, with optional length.	character type, INTEGER	CLOB
COALESCE([*argument1*] <,*argument2*...>)	Returns the first non-null argument in the set of arguments. VALUE is a synonym for COALESCE.	any type	any type

TABLE B.1 SQL Functions *(Continued)*

<table>
<tr><th>Function/Syntax</th><th>Description</th><th>Input</th><th>Output</th></tr>
<tr><td>CONCAT([argument1],[argument2])</td><td>Returns the concatenation of two string arguments. || is a synonym for CONCAT.</td><td>string type, compatible string type</td><td>string type</td></tr>
<tr><td>COS([argument])</td><td>Returns the cosine of argument, where argument is an angle expressed in radians.</td><td>DOUBLE</td><td>DOUBLE</td></tr>
<tr><td>COT([argument])</td><td>Returns the cotangent of argument, where argument is an angle expressed in radians.</td><td>DOUBLE</td><td>DOUBLE</td></tr>
<tr><td>COUNT([*]|[<ALL|DISTINCT> argument])</td><td>Returns the count of the number of rows in a set of rows or values (column function).</td><td>any built-in type</td><td>any built-in type</td></tr>
<tr><td>DATE([argument])</td><td>Returns a date from argument.</td><td>DATE
TIMESTAMP
DOUBLE
VARCHAR</td><td>DATE
DATE
DATE
DATE</td></tr>
<tr><td>DAY([argument])</td><td>Returns the day part of argument.</td><td>DATE
TIMESTAMP
DECIMAL
VARCHAR</td><td>INTEGER
INTEGER
INTEGER
INTEGER</td></tr>
<tr><td>DAYNAME([argument])</td><td>Returns a mixed-case character string containing the name of day (e.g., Friday) for the day portion of argument based on what the locale was when the START DATABASE MANAGER command or function call was issued.</td><td>DATE
TIMESTAMP
VARCHAR(26)</td><td>VARCHAR(100)
VARCHAR(100)
VARCHAR(100)</td></tr>
<tr><td>DAYOFWEEK([argument])</td><td>Returns the day of the week in argument as an integer value in the range 1 to 7, where 1 represents Sunday.</td><td>DATE
TIMESTAMP
VARCHAR(26)</td><td>INTEGER
INTEGER
VARCHAR(26)</td></tr>
<tr><td>DAYOFYEAR([argument])</td><td>Returns the day of the year in argument as an integer value in the range 1 to 366.</td><td>DATE
TIMESTAMP
VARCHAR(26)</td><td>INTEGER
INTEGER
INTEGER</td></tr>
<tr><td>DAYS([argument])</td><td>Returns an integer representation of a date.</td><td>DATE
TIMESTAMP
VARCHAR</td><td>INTEGER
INTEGER
INTEGER</td></tr>
<tr><td>DBCLOB([<i>graphic-expression</i>] <,<i>length</i>>)</td><td>Casts from source type to DBCLOB, with optional length.</td><td>graphic type, INTEGER</td><td>DBCLOB</td></tr>
<tr><td>DECIMAL([<i>numeric-expression</i>] <,<i>precision</i>><,<i>scale</i>>)</td><td>Returns a decimal representation of a number, with optional precision and scale. DEC is a synonym for DECIMAL.</td><td>numeric type, INTEGER, INTEGER</td><td>DECIMAL</td></tr>
<tr><td>DECIMAL([<i>varchar-expression</i>] <,<i>precision</i>><,<i>scale</i>> <,<i>decimal-character</i>>)</td><td>Returns a decimal representation of a character string, with optional precision, scale, and decimal character.</td><td>VARCHAR, INTEGER, INTEGER, VARCHAR</td><td>DECIMAL</td></tr>
<tr><td>DEGREES([argument])</td><td>Returns the number of degrees converted from argument, expressed in radians.</td><td>DOUBLE</td><td>DOUBLE</td></tr>
</table>

TABLE B.1 SQL Functions *(Continued)*

Function/Syntax	Description	Input	Output
DIFFERENCE([*argument1*], [*argument2*])	Returns the difference between the sounds of the words in the two argument strings, as determined with the SOUNDEX function. A value of 0 indicates that the strings sound the same.	VARCHAR(4), VARCHAR(4)	INTEGER
DIGITS([*argument*])	Returns the character string representation of *argument*.	DECIMAL	CHAR
DOUBLE([*argument*])	Returns the floating-point representation of *argument*. DOUBLE_PRECISION, or FLOAT are synonyms of DOUBLE	numeric type	DOUBLE
EVENT_MON_STATE ([*monitor-switch*])	Returns the operational state of a particular event monitor.	VARCHAR	INTEGER
EXP([*argument*])	Returns the exponential function of *argument*.	DOUBLE	DOUBLE
FLOOR([*argument*])	Returns the largest integer less than or equal to *argument*.	SMALLINT INTEGER DOUBLE	SMALLINT INTEGER DOUBLE
GRAPHIC([*graphic-expression*] <,*length*>)	Casts from source type to GRAPHIC, with optional length.	graphic type, INTEGER	GRAPHIC
HEX([*argument*])	Returns the hexadecimal representation of *argument*.	any built-in type	VARCHAR
HOUR([*argument*])	Returns the hour part of *argument*.	TIME TIMESTAMP DECIMAL VARCHAR	INTEGER INTEGER INTEGER INTEGER
INSERT([*argument1*],[*position*], [*size*],[*argument2*])	Returns a string where *size* bytes are deleted from *argument1* beginning at *position*, and where *argument2* is inserted into *argument1* beginning at *position*.	VARCHAR, INTEGER INTEGER, VARCHAR CLOB(1M), INTEGER INTEGER,CLOB(1M) BLOB(1M), INTEGER INTEGER, BLOB(1M)	VARCHAR CLOB(1M) BLOB(1M)
INTEGER([*argument*])	Returns the integer representation of *argument*. INT is a synonym of INTEGER	numeric type VARCHAR	INTEGER INTEGER
LCASE([*argument*])	Returns the string in which all the characters are converted to lowercase. LCASE will handle only characters in the invariant set. Therefore, LCASE(UCASE (*argument*)) will not necessarily return the same result as LCASE (*argument*).	VARCHAR CLOB(1M) BLOB(1M)	VARCHAR CLOB(1M) BLOB(1M)
LEFT([*argument*],[*length*])	Returns a string consisting of the leftmost *length* bytes in *argument*.	VARCHAR, INTEGER CLOB(1M), INTEGER BLOB(1M), INTEGER	VARCHAR CLOB(1M) BLOB(1M)
LENGTH([*argument*])	Returns the length of *argument* in bytes (if *argument* is a double-byte character string).	any built-in type	INTEGER

TABLE B.1 SQL Functions *(Continued)*

Function/Syntax	Description	Input	Output
LN([argument])	Returns the natural logarithm of *argument* (same as LOG).	DOUBLE	DOUBLE
LOCATE([*argument*1],[*argument*2] <,*position*>)	Returns the starting position of the first occurrence of *argument1* within *argument2*. If a *position* is specified, it indicates the character position in *argument2* where the search is to begin. If *argument*1 is not found within *argument2*, value 0 is returned.	VARCHAR, VARCHAR, INTEGER CLOB(1M), CLOB(1M), INTEGER BLOB(1M), BLOB(1M), INTEGER	INTEGER INTEGER INTEGER
LOG([*argument*])	Returns the natural logarithm of *argument* (same as LN).	DOUBLE	DOUBLE
LOG10([*argument*])	Returns the base-10 logarithm of *argument*.	DOUBLE	DOUBLE
LONG_VARCHAR ([*character-expression*]<,*length*>)	Casts from source type to LONG VARCHAR, with optional length.	character type	LONG VARCHAR
LONG_VARGRAPHIC ([*graphic-expression*]<,length>)	Casts from source type to LONG VARGRAPHIC, with optional length.	graphic type	LONGVARGRAPHIC
LTRIM([*argument*])	Returns the characters of *argument* with leading blanks removed.	VARCHAR CLOB(1M)	VARCHAR CLOB(1M)
MAX(<ALL|DISTINCT>[*argument*])	Returns the maximum value in a set of values (column function).	any built-in type	same as input type
MICROSECOND([*argument*])	Returns the microsecond (time unit) part of *argument*.	VARCHAR TIMESTAMP DECIMAL	INTEGER INTEGER INTEGER
MIN(<ALL|DISTINCT>[*argument*])	Returns the minimum value in a set of values (column function).	any built-in type	same as input type
MINUTE([*argument*])	Returns the minute part of *argument*.	TIME TIMESTAMP VARCHAR DECIMAL	INTEGER INTEGER INTEGER INTEGER
MOD([*argument1*],[*argument2*])	Returns the remainder (modulus) of *argument1* divided by *argument2*. The result is negative only if *argument1* is negative.	SMALLINT, SMALLINT INTEGER, INTEGER	SMALLINT INTEGER
MONTH([*argument*])	Returns the month part of *argument*.	DATE TIMESTAMP DECIMAL VARCHAR	INTEGER INTEGER INTEGER INTEGER
MONTHNAME([*argument*])	Returns a mixed-case character string containing the name of a month (e.g., January) for the month portion of *argument* that is date or timestamp, based on what the locale was when the database was started.	DATE TIMESTAMP VARCHAR(26)	VARCHAR(100) VARCHAR(100) VARCHAR(100)
NULLIF([*argument1*],[*argument2*])	Returns NULL if *argument1* and *argument2* are equal; otherwise it returns *argument1*.	any type, any comparable type	any type

TABLE B.1 SQL Functions *(Continued)*

Function/Syntax	Description	Input	Output
POSSTR([*argument1*],[*argument2*])	Returns the position at which one string is contained in another.	string type, compatible string type	INTEGER
POWER([*argument1*],[*argument2*])	Returns the value of *argument1* to the power of *argument2*.	INTEGER, INTEGER DOUBLE, INTEGER DOUBLE, DOUBLE	INTEGER DOUBLE DOUBLE
QUARTER([*argument*])	Returns an integer value in the range 1 to 4, representing the quarter of the year for the date specified in *argument*.	DATE TIMESTAMP VARCHAR(26)	INTEGER INTEGER INTEGER
RADIANS([*argument*])	Returns the number of radians converted from *argument*, expressed in degrees.	DOUBLE	DOUBLE
RAISE_ERROR ([*SQLSTATE*],[*error-msg*])	Raises an error in the SQLCA. The SQLSTATE returned is indicated by *SQLSTATE*. The second argument contains any text to be returned.	VARCHAR, VARCHAR	any type
RAND(<*argument*>)	Returns a random floating-point value between 0 and 1 using *argument* as the optional seed value.	INTEGER	DOUBLE
REPEAT([*argument*],[*num-times*])	Returns a character string composed of *argument1* repeated *num-times* times.	VARCHAR, INTEGER CLOB(1M), INTEGER BLOB(1M), INTEGER	VARCHAR CLOB(1M) BLOB(1M)
REPLACE([*argument1*], [*argument2*],[*argument3*])	Replaces all occurrences of *argument2* in *argument1* with *argument3*.	VARCHAR, VARCHAR, VARCHAR CLOB(1M), CLOB(1M), CLOB(1M) BLOB(1M), BLOB(1M), BLOB(1M)	VARCHAR CLOB(1M) BLOB(1M)
RIGHT([*argument*],[*length*])	Returns a string consisting of the rightmost *length* bytes in *argument*.	VARCHAR, INTEGER CLOB(1M), INTEGER BLOB(1M), INTEGER	VARCHAR CLOB(1M) BLOB(1M)
ROUND([*argument1*],[*argument2*])	Returns *argument1* rounded to *argument2* places right of the decimal point. If *argument2* is negative, *argument1* is rounded to the absolute value of *argument2* places to the left of the decimal.	INTEGER, INTEGER DOUBLE, INTEGER	INTEGER DOUBLE
RTRIM([*argument*])	Returns the characters of *argument* with trailing blanks removed.	VARCHAR CLOB(1M)	VARCHAR CLOB(1M)
SECOND([*argument*])	Returns the second (time unit) part of *argument*.	TIME TIMESTAMP DECIMAL VARCHAR	INTEGER INTEGER INTEGER INTEGER
SIGN([*argument*])	Returns an indicator of the sign of *argument*. If *argument* is less than 0, –1 is returned. If *argument* equals 0, 0 is returned. If *argument* is greater than 0, 1 is returned.	SMALLINT INTEGER DOUBLE	SMALLINT INTEGER DOUBLE

TABLE B.1 SQL Functions *(Continued)*

Function/Syntax	Description	Input	Output
SIN([*argument*])	Returns the sine of *argument*, where the *argument* is an angle expressed in radians.	DOUBLE	DOUBLE
SMALLINT([*numeric-expression*])	Casts from source type to SMALLINT.	numeric type VARCHAR	SMALLINT SMALLINT
SOUNDEX([*argument*])	Returns a four-character code representing the sound of the words in *argument*. You can use the result to compare the sounds of strings.	VARCHAR	CHAR(4)
SPACE([*argument*])	Returns a character string consisting of *argument* blanks.	INTEGER	VARCHAR
SQRT([*argument*])	Returns the square root of *argument*.	DOUBLE	DOUBLE
SUBSTR([*argument1*], [*argument2*]<,*length*>)	Returns a substring of *argument1* starting at *argument2*, *length* characters in length. If *length* is not specified, the remainder of the string is returned.	string type, INTEGER, INTEGER	string type
SUM(<ALL|DISTINCT>[*argument*])	Returns the sum of a set of numbers (column function).	numeric type	max numeric type
TABLE_NAME ([*argument*]<,*schema*>)	Returns an unqualified name of a table or view based on the object name specified in *argument* and the optional schema name specified in *schema*. It is used to resolve aliases.	VARCHAR, VARCHAR	VARCHAR
TABLE_SCHEMA ([*argument*]<,*schema*>)	Returns the schema name portion portion of the two part table or view name given by the object name in *argument* and the optional schema name specified in *schema*. It is used to resolve aliases.	VARCHAR, VARCHAR	CHAR(8)
TAN([*argument*])	Returns the tangent of *argument*, where *argument* is an angle expressed in radians.	DOUBLE	DOUBLE
TIME([*argument*])	Returns a time from *argument*.	TIME TIMESTAMP VARCHAR	TIME TIME TIME
TIMESTAMP ([*argument1*],<*argument2*>)	Returns a timestamp from a value or a pair of values.	TIMESTAMP VARCHAR, VARCHAR VARCHAR, TIME DATE, VARCHAR DATE, TIME	TIMESTAMP TIMESTAMP TIMESTAMP TIMESTAMP TIMESTAMP
TIMESTAMP_ISO([*argument*])	Returns a timestamp in the ISO format (*yyyy-mm-dd hh:mm:ss. nnnnnn*) converted from the IBM format(*yyyy-mm-dd-hh.mm.ss. nnnnnn*). If the *argument* is a date, it inserts zero for all the time elements. If the *argument* is a time,	DATE TIME TIMESTAMP VARCHAR(26)	TIMESTAMP TIMESTAMP TIMESTAMP TIMESTAMP

TABLE B.1 SQL Functions *(Continued)*

Function/Syntax	Description	Input	Output
	it inserts the value of CURRENT DATE for the date elements and zero for the fractional time element.		
TIMESTAMPDIFF ([*interval*],[*argument*])	Returns an estimated number of intervals of type *interval* based on the difference between two timestamps. The value specified for *argument* is the result of subtracting two timestamps and converting the result to CHAR. Valid values for *interval* are: 1 (fractions of a second), 2 (seconds), 4 (minutes), 8 (hours), 16 (days), 32 (weeks), 64 (months), 128 (quarters), and 256 (years).	INTEGER, CHAR(22)	INTEGER
TRUNCATE ([*argument*],[*num-decimals*])	Returns *argument* truncated to *num-decimals* places right of the decimal point. If *num-decimals* is negative, *argument* is truncated to the absolute value of *num-decimals* places to the left of the decimal point. TRUNC is a synonym of TRUNCATE	INTEGER, INTEGER DOUBLE, INTEGER	INTEGER DOUBLE
TRANSLATE ([*argument*]<,*to-argument*> <,*from-argument*><,*padding*>)	Returns a string in which one or more characters might have been translated into other characters.	CHAR	CHAR
		VARCHAR	VARCHAR
		CHAR, VARCHAR, VARCHAR	CHAR
		VARCHAR, VARCHAR, VARCHAR	VARCHAR
		CHAR, VARCHAR, VARCHAR, VARCHAR	CHAR
		VARCHAR, VARCHAR, VARCHAR, VARCHAR	VARCHAR
		GRAPHIC, VARGRAPHIC, VARGRAPHIC	GRAPHIC
		VARGRAPHIC, VARGRAPHIC, VARGRAPHIC	VARGRAPHIC
		GRAPHIC, VARGRAPHIC, VARGRAPHIC, VARGRAPHIC	GRAPHIC
		VARGRAPHIC, VARGRAPHIC, VARGRAPHIC, VARGRAPHIC	VARGRAPHIC
UCASE([*argument*])	Returns a string in which all the characters have been converted to uppercase.	VARCHAR	VARCHAR
VARCHAR ([*character-expression*]<,*length*>)	Casts from source type to VARCHAR, with optional length.	character type, INTEGER datetime type	VARCHAR VARCHAR

TABLE B.1 SQL Functions *(Continued)*

Function/Syntax	Description	Input	Output
VARGRAPHIC ([*graphic-expression*]<,*length*>)	Casts from source type to VARGRAPHIC, with optional length.	graphic type, INTEGER VARCHAR	VARGRAPHIC VARGRAPHIC
WEEK([*argument*])	Returns the week of the year in *argument* as an integer value in the range 1 to 53.	DATE TIMESTAMP VARCHAR (26)	INTEGER INTEGER INTEGER
YEAR([*argument*])	Returns the year part of *argument*.	DATE TIMESTAMP DECIMAL VARCHAR	INTEGER INTEGER INTEGER INTEGER
+: *argument1+argument2*	Adds two operands.	numeric type, numeric type DATE, DECIMAL(8,0) TIME, DECIMAL(6,0) TIMESTAMP, DECIMAL(20,6) DECIMAL(8,0), DATE DECIMAL(6,0), TIME DECIMAL(20,6), TIMESTAMP datetime type, DOUBLE, labeled duration code	numeric type DATE TIME TIMESTAMP DATE TIME TIMESTAMP datetime type
–: *argument1 – argument2*	Subtracts two operands.	numeric type DATE, DATE TIME, TIME TIMESTAMP, TIMESTAMP DATE, VARCHAR TIME, VARCHAR TIMESTAMP, VARCHAR VARCHAR, DATE VARCHAR, TIME VARCHAR, TIMESTAMP DATE, DECIMAL(8,0) TIME, DECIMAL(6,0) TIMESTAMP, DECIMAL(20,6) datetime type, DOUBLE, labeled duration code	numeric type DECIMAL(8,0) DECIMAL(6,0) DECIMAL(20,6) DECIMAL(8,0) DECIMAL(6,0) DECIMAL(20,6) DECIMAL(8,0) DECIMAL(6,0) DECIMAL(20,6) DATE TIME TIMESTAMP datetime type
*:*argument1*argument2*	Multiplies two operands.	numeric type	numeric type
/:*argument1/argument2*	Divides two operands.	numeric type	numeric type

Adapted from the *IBM Database 2 SQL Reference*, Table 10, pages 137–149.

Additional functions can also be available since user-defined functions can be created (refer to the CREATE FUNCTION SQL statement for more information).

APPENDIX C

SQLSTATE CROSS-REFERENCE

Table C.1 contains a cross-reference of all SQLSTATE values that can be returned by the call-level interface (CLI) functions. DB2 CLI can also return SQLSTATEs that are generated by the connected data source but are not listed in this table. Refer to the documentation for the data source being used for information about additional SQLSTATE values that might be returned.

TABLE C.1 SQLSTATE Cross-Reference

SQLSTATE	Description	CLI function(s)
01000	Warning: an internal COMMIT has been issued on behalf of the application as part of the DB2 CLI function processing.	SQLSetConnectOption( )
01002	An error occurred while attempting to disconnect from a connected data source. The CLI operation was successful; SQL_SUCCESS_WITH_INFO was returned.	SQLDisconnect( )
01004	The data returned in one or more DB2 CLI function parameters or for one or more columns was longer than the buffer or column size specified. Because of this, data was truncated.	SQLColAttributes( ) SQLDataSources( ) SQLDescribeCol( ) SQLDriverConnect( ) SQLExtendedFetch( ) SQLFetch( ) SQLGetCursorName( ) SQLGetData( ) SQLGetInfo( ) SQLGetSubString( ) SQLNativeSql( ) SQLPutData( ) SQLSetColAttributes( )
01504	An UPDATE or DELETE SQL statement that did not contain a valid WHERE clause was specified. The CLI operation was successful; SQL_SUCCESS_WITH _INFO or SQL_NO_DATA_FOUND was returned.	SQLExecDirect( ) SQLExecute( ) SQLParamData( ) SQLPrepare( )
01508	The specified SQL statement was disqualified for blocking for reasons other than storage needs.	SQLExecDirect( ) SQLExecute( ) SQLParamData( ) SQLPrepare( )

TABLE C.1 SQLSTATE Cross-Reference *(Continued)*

SQLSTATE	Description	CLI function(s)
01S00	An invalid keyword or attribute value was specified in the connection string. The connection was successful anyway because one of the following occurred: the unrecognized keyword was ignored, the invalid attribute value was ignored and the default value was used, or the CLI operation was successful and SQL_SUCCESS _WITH_INFO was returned.	SQLDriverConnect( )
01S01	An error occurred while retrieving (fetching) one or more rows from a result data set. The CLI operation was successful and SQL_SUCCESS_WITH_INFO was returned.	SQLExtendedFetch( )
01S02	A recognized concurrency value was specified for the SQL_CONCURRENCY option, but the value is not supported by DB2 CLI	SQLSetStmtOption( )
07001	The number of parameters bound to application variables was less than the number of parameter markers coded in the specified SQL statement.	SQLExecDirect( ) SQLExecute( ) SQLParamData( )
07002	A column number specified while binding columns to application variables was greater than the number of columns found in the result data set, or the application used SQLSetColAttributes( ) to provide DB2 CLI with descriptor information for a result data set, but information was not provided for every column in the result data set.	SQLExtendedFetch( ) SQLFetch( )
07005	The SQL statement specified did not produce a result data set.	SQLColAttributes( ) SQLDescribeCol( )
07006	The data value could not be converted in a meaningful manner to the specified data type; an incompatible data conversion is not allowed	SQLBindParameter( ) SQLExecDirect( ) SQLExecute( ) SQLParamData( ) SQLExtendedFetch( ) SQLFetch( ) SQLGetData( ) SQLGetLength( ) SQLGetPosition( ) SQLGetSubString( ) SQLSetParam( )
08001	DB2 CLI was unable to establish a connection with the specified data source. The connection request might have been rejected because a connection to the data source via embedded SQL already exists.	SQLConnect( ) SQLDriverConnect( )
08002	The specified connection handle was already used to establish a connection to a data source and that connection is still open.	SQLConnect( ) SQLDriverConnect( )
08003	The connection specified by the connection handle parameter is not open. A connection must be established successfully (and the connection must be open) before the DB2 CLI function can be executed.	SQLAllocStmt( ) SQLDisconnect( ) SQLGetConnectOption( ) SQLGetInfo( ) SQLNativeSql( ) SQLSetConnection( ) SQLSetConnectOption( ) SQLTransact( )
08004	The application server (data source) rejected the attempt to establish a connection.	SQLConnect( ) SQLDriverConnect( )
08007	The connection to the data source failed while the DB2 CLI function was executing. Whether the requested COMMIT or ROLLBACK operation occurred before or after the connection failure occurred cannot be determined.	SQLTransact( )
08S01	The communication link between the application and the data source failed before the DB2 CLI function completed.	SQLAllocStmt( ) SQLBindCol( )

TABLE C.1 SQLSTATE Cross-Reference *(Continued)*

SQLSTATE	Description	CLI function(s)
		SQLBindFileToCol( ) SQLBindFileToParam( ) SQLBindParameter( ) SQLCancel( ) SQLColumns( ) SQLColumnPrivileges( ) SQLColAttributes( ) SQLDescribeCol( ) SQLExecDirect( ) SQLExecute( ) SQLParamData( ) SQLExtendedFetch( ) SQLFetch( ) SQLForeignKeys( ) SQLFreeStmt( ) SQLGetConnectOption( ) SQLGetCursorName( ) SQLGetData( ) SQLGetFunctions( ) SQLGetInfo( ) SQLGetLength( ) SQLGetPosition( ) SQLGetStmtOption( ) SQLGetSubString( ) SQLGetTypeInfo( ) SQLMoreResults( ) SQLNumParams( ) SQLNumResultCols( ) SQLParamData( ) SQLParamOptions( ) SQLPrepare( ) SQLPrimaryKeys( ) SQLProcedures( ) SQLProcedureColumns( ) SQLPutData( ) SQLRowCount( ) SQLSetColAttributes( ) SQLSetConnectOption( ) SQLSetCursorName( ) SQLSetParam( ) SQLSetStmtOption( ) SQLSpecialColumns( ) SQLStatistics( ) SQLTables( ) SQLTablePrivileges( )
21S01	An INSERT SQL statement was specified and the number of values specified in the insert value list did not match the number of columns specified in the table column list.	SQLExecDirect( ) SQLExecute( ) SQLParamData( ) SQLPrepare( )
21S02	A CREATE VIEW SQL statement was specified and the number of names specified in the table column list is not the same as the derived table defined by the query specification.	SQLExecDirect( ) SQLExecute( ) SQLParamData( ) SQLPrepare( )

TABLE C.1 SQLSTATE Cross-Reference *(Continued)*

SQLSTATE	Description	CLI function(s)
22001	A character string assigned to a character data type column exceeded the column's maximum length and was truncated. The CLI operation was successful and SQL_SUCCESS_WITH_INFO was returned.	SQLExecDirect( ) SQLExecute( ) SQLParamData( ) SQLPutData( )
22002	A specified pointer value was a NULL pointer and the value of the corresponding column or LOB column is NULL. There is no method for reporting SQL_NULL_DATA.	SQLExtendedFetch( ) SQLFetch( ) SQLGetData( )
22003	A numeric value assigned to a numeric data type column caused truncation of the whole part of the number, either at the time of assignment or in computing an inter mediate result, or the SQL statement specified contained an arithmetic expression that caused a division by zero error to occur. As a result, the cursor state is undefined for DB2 for Common Servers (the cursor will remain open for other RDBMSs).	SQLExecDirect( ) SQLExecute( ) SQLParamData( ) SQLExtendedFetch( ) SQLFetch( ) SQLGetData( ) SQLPutData( )
22005	A value or literal was incompatible with the data type associated with the parameter, or a specified data type was a graphic data type but the length was an odd value (length values must be even for graphic data types).	SQLExecDirect( ) SQLExecute( ) SQLParamData( ) SQLExtendedFetch() SQLFetch( ) SQLGetData( ) SQLPutData( )
22007	A datetime value (or the string representation of a datetime value) represented an invalid date.	SQLExecDirect( ) SQLExecute( ) SQLParamData( ) SQLExtendedFetch( ) SQLFetch( ) SQLGetData( ) SQLPutData( )
22008	An arithmetic operation on a date or timestamp produced a result that is not within the valid range of dates or timestamps, or a datetime value cannot be assigned to a bound variable because it is too small.	SQLExecDirect( ) SQLExecute( ) SQLParamData( ) SQLExtendedFetch( ) SQLFetch( ) SQLGetData( )
22011	The starting position specified is greater than the length of the string from which the substring is to be extracted.	SQLGetSubString( )
22012	An arithmetic expression caused a division by zero to occur.	SQLExecDirect( ) SQLExecute( ) SQLParamData( ) SQLExtendedFetch( ) SQLFetch( )
23000	The execution of the specified SQL statement is not permitted because its execution would cause an integrity constraint violation in the DBMS.	SQLExecDirect( ) SQLExecute( ) SQLParamData( )
24000	A cursor has already been opened for the specified SQL statement handle, or the cursor associated with the specified SQL statement handle is not positioned on a row in the result data set.	SQLColumns( ) SQLColumnPrivileges( ) SQLExecDirect( ) SQLExecute( ) SQLParamData( ) SQLExtendedFetch( ) SQLFetch( )

TABLE C.1 SQLSTATE Cross-Reference *(Continued)*

SQLSTATE	Description	CLI function(s)
		SQLForeignKeys( ) SQLGetData( ) SQLGetStmtOption( ) SQLGetTypeInfo( ) SQLPrepare( ) SQLPrimaryKeys( ) SQLProcedures( ) SQLProcedureColumns( ) SQLSetColAttributes( ) SQLSetStmtOption SQLSpecialColumns( ) SQLStatistics( ) SQLTables( ) SQLTablePrivileges( )
24504	The cursor identified in an UPDATE, DELETE, SET, or GET SQL statement is not positioned on a row in the result data set. This is because results from a previous query are pending on the specified SQL statement handle or because the cursor associated with the specified SQL statement handle has not been closed.	SQLExecDirect( ) SQLExecute( ) SQLParamData( )
25000	A transaction is in progress at the specified data source connection. As long as this transaction remains active, the connection cannot be terminated.	SQLDisconnect( )
25501	A transaction is in progress at the specified data source connection. As long as this transaction remains active, the connection cannot be terminated.	SQLDisconnect( )
28000	The user ID and/or password specified violated the restrictions defined by the data source.	SQLConnect( ) SQLDriverConnect( )
34000	The specified cursor name is invalid or already exists, or the SQL statement specified contains a positioned DELETE or UPDATE and the cursor referenced by the statement is not open.	SQLExecDirect( ) SQLExecute( ) SQLParamData( ) SQLPrepare( ) SQLSetCursorName( )
37000	The specified SQL statement contains one or more syntax errors.	SQLNativeSql( )
37*xxx*	The specified SQL statement contains one or more of the following: a COMMIT SQL statement, a ROLLBACK SQL statement, or an SQL statement that the connected data source could not prepare.	SQLExecDirect( ) SQLExecute( ) SQLParamData( ) SQLPrepare( )
40000	The current transaction to which the SQL statement belonged was rolled back because of a deadlock or timeout situation.	SQLExecDirect( ) SQLExecute( ) SQLParamData( ) SQLPrepare( )
40003	The communication link between the application and the data source failed before the DB2 CLI function completed.	SQLAllocStmt( ) SQLBindCol( ) SQLBindFileToCol( ) SQLBindFileToParam( ) SQLBindParameter( ) SQLCancel( ) SQLColumns( ) SQLColumnPrivileges( ) SQLColAttributes( ) SQLDescribeCol( ) SQLExecDirect( ) SQLExecute( ) SQLParamData( )

SQLSTATE	Description	Functions
		SQLExtendedFetch( ) SQLFetch( ) SQLForeignKeys( ) SQLFreeStmt( ) SQLGetConnectOption( ) SQLGetCursorName( ) SQLGetData( ) SQLGetFunctions( ) SQLGetInfo( ) SQLGetLength( ) SQLGetPosition( ) SQLGetStmtOption( ) SQLGetSubString( ) SQLGetTypeInfo( ) SQLMoreResults( ) SQLNumParams( ) SQLNumResultCols( ) SQLParamData( ) SQLParamOptions( ) SQLPrepare( ) SQLPrimaryKeys( ) SQLProcedures( ) SQLProcedureColumns( ) SQLPutData( ) SQLRowCount( ) SQLSetColAttributes( ) SQLSetConnectOption( ) SQLSetCursorName( ) SQLSetParam( ) SQLSetStmtOption( ) SQLSpecialColumns( ) SQLStatistics( ) SQLTables( ) SQLTablePrivileges( )
42*xxx*	There are one or more syntax or access problems with the specified SQL statement.	SQLExecDirect( ) SQLExecute( ) SQLParamData( ) SQLPrepare( )
425*xx*	The user does not have the authorizations necessary to execute the specified SQL statement.	SQLExecDirect( ) SQLExecute( ) SQLParamData( ) SQLPrepare( )
42601	The PARMLIST value in the stored procedures catalog table contains a syntax error.	SQLProcedureColumns( )
428A1	Unable to access a file that is referenced by a host file variable. This error can be raised for any number of reasons. The following associated reason codes can be used to identify the particular error: 01 (The filename length specified is invalid or the filename and/or the path has an invalid format); 02 (The file option specified is invalid). It must have one of the following values: SQL_FILE_READ: Read from an existing file. SQL_FILE_CREATE: Create a new file for write. SQL_FILE_OVERWRITE: Overwrite an existing file. If the file does not exist, create it. SQL_FILE_APPEND: Append to an existing file. If the file does not exist, create it. 03 (The file cannot be found); 04 (The SQL_FILE_CREATE option was specified for a file with the same names as an existing file);	SQLExecDirect( ) SQLExecute( ) SQLParamData( ) SQLExtendedFetch( ) SQLFetch( )

TABLE C.1 SQLSTATE Cross-Reference *(Continued)*

SQLSTATE	Description	CLI function(s)
	05 (Access to the file was denied. The user does not have permission to open the file); 06 (Access to the file was denied. The file is in use with incompatible modes. Files to be written to are opened in exclusive mode); 07 (Disk full was encountered while writing to the file); 08 (Unexpected end of file encountered while reading from the file); and 09 (A media error was encountered while accessing the file).	
42818	The operands of an operator or function are not compatible because the length of the pattern specified exceeds 4000 bytes.	SQLGetPosition( )
42895	The value of a host variable in an EXECUTE or OPEN SQL statement cannot be used because of its data type, or a LOB locator type specified for a bound parameter does not match the LOB data type of the parameter marker, or a LOB locator type was specified but the corresponding parameter marker is not an LOB data type.	SQLExecDirect( ) SQLExecute( ) SQLParamData( )
44000	The SQL statement contained a parameter or literal NULL value for a column defined as NOT NULL in the associated table column, or the SQL statement contained a duplicate value for a column constrained to contain only unique values (or some other integrity constraint was violated).	SQLExecDirect( ) SQLExecute( ) SQLParamData( )
54028	The maximum number of concurrent LOB locator handles has been reached. A new LOB locator cannot be assigned until some other LOB locator is explicitly freed.	SQLExtendedFetch( ) SQLFetch( )
56084	LOB columns cannot be selected or updated when connected to a DRDA server (using DDCS).	SQLExecDirect( ) SQLExecute( ) SQLParamData( ) SQLExtendedFetch( ) SQLFetch( )
58004	An unexpected system error has occurred. A possible cause is the code page of the environment in which the application is running is not supported by DB2 CLI.	SQLAllocEnv( ) SQLAllocStmt( ) SQLBindCol( ) SQLBindFileToCol( ) SQLBindFileToParam( ) SQLBindParameter( ) SQLColAttributes( ) SQLConnect( ) SQLDriverConnect( ) SQLDataSources( ) SQLDescribeCol( ) SQLDisconnect( ) SQLExecDirect( ) SQLExecute( ) SQLParamData( ) SQLExtendedFetch( ) SQLFetch( ) SQLFreeConnect( ) SQLFreeEnv( ) SQLFreeStmt( ) SQLGetCursorName( ) SQLGetData( ) SQLGetFunctions( ) SQLGetInfo( ) SQLGetLength( ) SQLGetPosition( ) SQLGetSubString( ) SQLMoreResults( )

TABLE C.1 SQLSTATE Cross-Reference *(Continued)*

SQLSTATE	Description	CLI function(s)
		SQLNumResultCols( ) SQLPrepare( ) SQLRowCount( ) SQLSetCursorName( ) SQLSetParam( ) SQLTransact( )
0F001	The specified LOB token variable does not currently represent a LOB value.	SQLGetLength( ) SQLGetPosition( )
S0001	A CREATE TABLE or a CREATE VIEW SQL statement was specified and the corresponding table name or view name specified already exists.	SQLExecDirect( ) SQLExecute( ) SQLParamData( ) SQLPrepare( )
S0002	The specified SQL statement referenced a table name or view name that does not exist.	SQLExecDirect( ) SQLExecute( ) SQLParamData( ) SQLPrepare( )
S0011	A CREATE INDEX SQL statement was specified and the corresponding index name specified already exists.	SQLExecDirect( ) SQLExecute( ) SQLParamData( ) SQLPrepare( )
S0012	A DROP INDEX SQL statement was specified and the corresponding index name specified does not exist.	SQLExecDirect( ) SQLExecute( ) SQLParamData( ) SQLPrepare( )
S0021	An ALTER TABLE SQL statement was specified and the one or more column names specified in the ADD clause already exist in the base table.	SQLExecDirect( ) SQLExecute( ) SQLParamData( ) SQLPrepare( )
S0022	The specified SQL statement referenced a column name in a table that does not exist.	SQLExecDirect( ) SQLExecute( ) SQLParamData( ) SQLPrepare( )
S1C00	DB2 CLI recognizes but does not support the data type specified, or a LOB locator type was specified but the connected server does not support LOB data types, or the data type is not recognized by DB2 CLI.	SQLBindCol( ) SQLBindFileToCol( ) SQLBindFileToParam( ) SQLBindParameter( ) SQLColumns( ) SQLColumnPrivileges( ) SQLColAttributes( ) SQLDescribeCol( ) SQLExtendedFetch( ) SQLFetch( ) SQLForeignKeys( ) SQLGetConnectOption( ) SQLGetData( ) SQLGetInfo( ) SQLGetLength( ) SQLGetPosition( ) SQLGetStmtOption( ) SQLGetSubString( ) SQLPrimaryKeys( ) SQLProcedures( )

TABLE C.1 SQLSTATE Cross-Reference *(Continued)*

SQLSTATE	Description	CLI function(s)
		SQLProcedureColumns( ) SQLSetConnectOption( ) SQLSetEnvAttr( ) SQLSetParam( ) SQLSetStmtOption( ) SQLSpecialColumns( ) SQLStatistics( ) SQLTables( ) SQLTablePrivileges( )
S1T00	The timeout period expired before the data source finished processing the SQL statement or before the data source returned the result data set.	SQLColumns( ) SQLColumnPrivileges( ) SQLColAttributes( ) SQLDescribeCol( ) SQLExecDirect( ) SQLExecute( ) SQLParamData( ) SQLExtendedFetch( ) SQLFetch( ) SQLForeignKeys( ) SQLGetData( ) SQLGetTypeInfo( ) SQLMoreResults( ) SQLNumParams( ) SQLNumResultCols( ) SQLParamData( ) SQLPrepare( ) SQLPrimaryKeys( ) SQLProcedures( ) SQLProcedureColumns( ) SQLPutData( ) SQLSpecialColumns( ) SQLStatistics( ) SQLTables( ) SQLTablePrivileges( )
S1000	A general error occurred for which there is no specific SQLSTATE and for which no specific SQLSTATE has been defined. The SQLError( ) function can describe the error and its cause. If the SQLDriverConnect( ) function returns this error, the information specified in the connection string was insufficient for making a connect request, and an attempt to display the connect dialog failed.	SQLDataSources( ) SQLDriverConnect( ) SQLSetColAttributes( ) SQLSetConnection( ) SQLSetStmtOption( )
S1001	DB2 CLI is unable to allocate the memory needed to support the execution or completion of the function.	All functions.
S1002	The column number specified was less than one or greater than the maximum number of columns supported by the data source.	SQLBindCol( ) SQLBindFileToCol( ) SQLColAttributes( ) SQLDescribeCol( ) SQLGetData( ) SQLSetColAttributes( )
S1003	The specified C data type is not a valid C data type for this DB2 CLI function.	SQLBindCol( ) SQLBindParameter( ) SQLGetData( ) SQLGetLength( ) SQLGetSubString( ) SQLSetParam( )

TABLE C.1 SQLSTATE Cross-Reference *(Continued)*

SQLSTATE	Description	CLI function(s)
S1004	The specified SQL data type is not a valid SQL data type for this DB2 CLI function.	SQLBindFileToParam( ) SQLBindParameter( ) SQLGetTypeInfo( ) SQLSetColAttributes( ) SQLSetParam( )
S1009	The specified one or more parameter values contain a NULL pointer or an invalid value.	SQLAllocConnect( ) SQLAllocStmt( ) SQLBindFileToCol( ) SQLBindFileToParam( ) SQLBindParameter( ) SQLColumnPrivileges( ) SQLConnect( ) SQLDriverConnect( ) SQLExecDirect( ) SQLForeignKeys( ) SQLGetConnectOption( ) SQLGetData( ) SQLGetFunctions( ) SQLGetInfo( ) SQLGetLength( ) SQLGetPosition( ) SQLGetStmtOption( ) SQLGetSubString( ) SQLNativeSql( ) SQLNumParams( ) SQLNumResultCols( ) SQLPrepare( ) SQLPutData( ) SQLSetConnectOption( ) SQLSetCursorName( ) SQLSetEnvAttr( ) SQLSetParam( ) SQLSetStmtOption( )
S1010	The DB2 CLI function was called while in a data-at-execute sequence or a BEGIN COMPOUND/END COMPOUND SQL operation, or the function was called before the SQLPrepare( ) or SQLExecDirect( ) function was called (for the same SQL statement handle).	SQLBindCol( ) SQLBindFileToCol( ) SQLBindFileToParam( ) SQLBindParameter( ) SQLColumns( ) SQLColAttributes( ) SQLDescribeCol( ) SQLDisconnect( ) SQLExecute( ) SQLExtendedFetch( ) SQLFetch( ) SQLForeignKeys( ) SQLFreeConnect( ) SQLFreeEnv( ) SQLFreeStmt( ) SQLGetCursorName( ) SQLGetData( ) SQLGetFunctions( ) SQLGetLength( ) SQLGetPosition( )

TABLE C.1 SQLSTATE Cross-Reference *(Continued)*

SQLSTATE	Description	CLI function(s)
		SQLGetStmtOption( ) SQLGetSubString( ) SQLGetTypeInfo( ) SQLMoreResults( ) SQLNumParams( ) SQLNumResultCols( ) SQLParamData( ) SQLParamOptions( ) SQLPrepare( ) SQLPrimaryKeys( ) SQLProcedures( ) SQLProcedureColumns( ) SQLPutData( ) SQLRowCount( ) SQLSetColAttributes( ) SQLSetConnectOption( ) SQLSetCursorName( ) SQLSetParam( ) SQLSetStmtOption( ) SQLSpecialColumns( ) SQLStatistics( ) SQLTables( ) SQLTablePrivileges( )
S1011	The environment attribute, connection option, or SQL statement option cannot be set at this time.	SQLSetConnectOption( ) SQLSetEnvAttr( ) SQLSetStmtOption( )
S1012	The value specified for the Action parameter was neither SQL_ROLLBACK nor SQL_COMMIT.	SQLTransact( )
S1013	DB2 CLI is unable to access the memory needed to support the execution or completion of the function.	SQLAllocConnect( ) SQLAllocStmt( ) SQLBindCol( ) SQLBindFileToCol( ) SQLBindFileToParam( ) SQLBindParameter( ) SQLCancel( ) SQLColAttributes( ) SQLConnect( ) SQLDriverConnect( ) SQLDataSources( ) SQLDescribeCol( ) SQLDisconnect( ) SQLExecDirect( ) SQLExecute( ) SQLParamData( ) SQLExtendedFetch( ) SQLFetch( ) SQLFreeConnect( ) SQLFreeEnv( ) SQLGetCursorName( ) SQLGetData( ) SQLGetFunctions( ) SQLGetLength( ) SQLGetPosition( )

TABLE C.1 SQLSTATE Cross-Reference *(Continued)*

SQLSTATE	Description	CLI function(s)
		SQLGetSubString( ) SQLMoreResults( ) SQLNumParams( ) SQLNumResultCols( ) SQLPrepare( ) SQLRowCount( ) SQLSetColAttributes( ) SQLSetCursorName( ) SQLSetParam( ) SQLTransact( )
S1014	DB2 CLI is unable to allocate an environment, connection, or SQL statement handle. Check the value of the SQL_MAXCONN attribute.	SQLAllocConnect( ) SQLAllocStmt( ) SQLColumns( ) SQLColumnPrivileges( ) SQLForeignKeys( ) SQLPrimaryKeys( ) SQLProcedures( ) SQLProcedureColumns( ) SQLSpecialColumns( ) SQLStatistics( ) SQLTables( ) SQLTablePrivileges( )
S1090	The value specified for a string or buffer parameter's size is less than one and not equal to SQL_NTS	SQLBindCol( ) SQLBindFileToCol( ) SQLBindFileToParam( ) SQLBindParameter( ) SQLColumns( ) SQLColumnPrivileges( ) SQLColAttributes( ) SQLConnect( ) SQLDriverConnect( ) SQLDataSources( ) SQLDescribeCol( ) SQLDriverConnect( ) SQLExecDirect( ) SQLExecute( ) SQLParamData( ) SQLForeignKeys( ) SQLGetCursorName( ) SQLGetData( ) SQLGetInfo( ) SQLGetPosition( ) SQLGetSubString( ) SQLNativeSql( ) SQLPrepare( ) SQLPrimaryKeys( ) SQLProcedures( ) SQLProcedureColumns( ) SQLPutData( ) SQLSetColAttributes( ) SQLSetCursorName( ) SQLSpecialColumns( ) SQLStatistics( )

TABLE C.1 SQLSTATE Cross-Reference *(Continued)*

SQLSTATE	Description	CLI function(s)
		SQLTables( ) SQLTablePrivileges( )
S1091	The value specified for the descriptor type is invalid.	SQLColAttributes( )
S1092	An invalid option was specified.	SQLFreeStmt( ) SQLGetConnectOption( ) SQLGetEnvAttr( ) SQLGetStmtOption( ) SQLSetConnectOption( ) SQLSetEnvAttr( ) SQLSetStmtOption( )
S1093	The value specified for a function parameter was either less than one or greater than the maximum number of supported parameters.	SQLBindFileToParam( ) SQLBindParameter( ) SQLSetParam( )
S1094	The scale value specified was less than zero or greater than the specified precision value.	SQLBindParameter( ) SQLSetColAttributes( ) SQLSetParam( )
S1096	An invalid information type was specified.	SQLGetInfo( )
S1097	An invalid column type was specified.	SQLSpecialColumns( )
S1098	An invalid scope was specified.	SQLSpecialColumns( )
S1099	An invalid nullable type was specified.	SQLSetColAttributes( ) SQLSpecialColumns( )
S1100	An invalid uniqueness value was specified.	SQLStatistics( )
S1101	An invalid accuracy value was specified.	SQLStatistics( )
S1103	An invalid direction option was specified.	SQLDataSources( ) SQLGetInfo( )
S1104	The precision value specified was less than one.	SQLBindParameter( ) SQLSetColAttributes( ) SQLSetParam( )
S1105	The specified parameter type was not SQL_PARAM_INPUT, SQL_PARAM_OUTPUT, or SQL_PARAM_INPUT_OUTPUT.	SQLBindParameter( )
S1106	The value specified for the fetch type was invalid.	SQLExtendedFetch( )
S1107	The specified row value was less than one.	SQLParamOptions( )
S1110	The specified driver completion value was invalid.	SQLDriverConnect( )
S1501	An invalid data source name was specified.	SQLConnect( ) SQLDriverConnect( )
S1503	The specified filename length was less than zero, but not equal to SQL_NTS.	SQLExecDirect( ) SQLExecute( ) SQLParamData( )
S1506	An error occurred while attempting to close the temporary file generated by DB2 CLI during a data-at-execution sequence.	SQLCancel( ) SQLFreeStmt( ) SQLParamData( )
S1509	An error occurred while attempting to delete the temporary file generated by DB2 CLI during a data-at-execution sequence.	SQLParamData( )

xxx and *xx* refer to any SQLSTATE within the specified class code. For example, 37*xxx* refers to any SQLSTATE in the 37 class.

Adapted from IBM's *Database 2 Call Level Interface Guide and Reference*, Table 156, pages 425 to 437.

BIBLIOGRAPHY

Baker, David C., William L. Banning, and William Myre. *Creating Applications with the IBM OS/2 Extended Edition Database Manager*. Reading, MA: Addison-Wesley Publishing Company, Inc. 1989.

Mullins, Craig S. *DB2 Developer's Guide*, 2nd ed. Indianapolis, IN: SAMS Publishing. 1994.

Orfali, Robert, and Dan Harkey. *Client/Server Programming with OS/2 2.1.*, 3rd ed. New York, NY: Van Nostrand Reinhold. 1993.

Ranade, Jay, and Angelo Bobak. *Ranade's OS/2 Extended Edition: Database Manager*. New York, NY: Bantam Books. 1989.

IBM C Set++ for AIX User's Guide: Version 3 Release 1, SCO9-1968. North York, Ontario, Canada: International Business Machines Corporation. 1993, 1995.

IBM C Set++ User's Guide: Version 3.0. North York, Ontario, Canada: International Business Machines Corporation. 1992, 1995.

Database 2 Administration Guide: for Common Servers Version 2, S2OH-4580. North York, Ontario, Canada: International Business Machines Corporation. 1994, 1995.

Database 2 API Reference: for Common Servers Version 2, S2OH-4984. North York, Ontario, Canada: International Business Machines Corporation. 1994, 1995.

Database 2 Application Programming Guide: for Common Servers Version 2, S2OH-4643. North York, Ontario, Canada: International Business Machines Corporation. 1994, 1995.

Database 2 Call Level Interface Guide and Reference: for Common Servers Version 2, S2OH-4644. North York, Ontario, Canada: International Business Machines Corporation. 1994, 1995.

Database 2 Command Reference: for Common Servers Version 2, S2OH-4645. North York, Ontario, Canada: International Business Machines Corporation. 1994, 1995.

Database 2 Database System Monitor Guide and Reference: for Common Servers Version 2, S2OH-4871. North York, Ontario, Canada: International Business Machines Corporation. 1994, 1995.

Database 2 Information and Concepts Guide: for Common Servers Version 2, S2OH-4664. North York, Ontario, Canada: International Business Machines Corporation. 1994, 1995.

Database 2 Messages Reference: for Common Servers Version 2, S2OH-4808. North York, Ontario, Canada: International Business Machines Corporation. 1994, 1995.

Database 2 SQL Reference: for Common Servers Version 2, S2OH-4665. North York, Ontario, Canada: International Business Machines Corporation. 1994, 1995.

IBM Distributed Database Connection Services User's Guide: for Common Servers Version 2.3, S2OH-4665. North York, Ontario, Canada: International Business Machines Corporation. 1993, 1995.

Microsoft ODBC 2.0 Programmer's Reference and SDK Guide. Redmond, WA: Microsoft Press. 1992, 1993, 1994.

INDEX

E

F

G

U

V

W

X

Y

ABOUT THE AUTHOR

Roger E. Sanders is an Associate Systems Developer with the Database Interfaces development group at SAS Institute, Inc. He has been designing and programming software in the IBM environment for more than 10 years, and specializes in system programming in C, C++, and 80x86 Assembly Language. His background in database application development is extensive, and includes experience with dBASE, DB2, INGRES and other popular database software.